THE INTE
Ftutnn i iun.

World of Tennis

1992

The year of 1991 will be remembered for the historic and emotional French success in the *Davis Cup*, 49 years after their last victory, and for a first *Federation Cup* victory for the ladies of Spain. Elsewhere the men's season had been dominated by the seesaw battle for the world's No. 1 ranking between Stefan Edberg, the quiet Swede, and the man who twice dethroned him, the powerful folk hero of German tennis, Boris Becker. As in 1991, all four of the major titles ended in different hands to underline the growing strength-in-depth of the modern men's game. It was Becker in Melbourne, Courier in Paris, Stich at Wimbledon and Edberg in New York, while America's David Wheaton won the year's biggest prize, $2 million, at the *Compaq Grand Slam Cup*. Among the women, the remarkable Yugoslav teenager, Monica Seles, imposed her formidable double-barrelled game and her strong personality on affairs by winning three of the four Grand Slam Championships as well as the Virginia Slims Championships. Monica also caused a furore by disappearing from sight after her late withdrawal from Wimbledon. She then fanned the flames of controversy by disqualifying herself from this year's Olympic Games through her refusal to compete for her country in the *Federation Cup* competition. All these events and more are reflected within the pages of this twenty-fourth edition of *World of Tennis*, the International Tennis Federation's official yearbook. There are two special features – one gives us a privileged insight into the career of that great Australian of the 1930s, Jack Crawford, through the eyes of his nephew, the other unveils the personalities of Arantxa, Emilio and Javier Sanchez, the Royal Family of Spanish tennis. As always, there are tournament and team results, articles on the world of junior and veteran tennis, world rankings and prize money, as well as detailed biographies of more than 200 of the leading men and women and every one of the great past champions. Also, for the first time this year, there are comprehensive lists of all the men and women who competed in the principal tournaments, together with their nationalities and dates of birth.

THE INTERNATIONAL TENNIS FEDERATION

World of Tennis

1992

Edited by John Barrett
Compiled by Marijke Volger
Biographies by Christine Forrest

CollinsWillow
An Imprint of HarperCollins*Publishers*

Abbreviations used in this book

ARG	Argentina	**FIN**	Finland	**PAK**	Pakistan
AUS	Australia	**FRA**	France	**PAR**	Paraguay
AUT	Austria	**GBR**	Great Britain	**PER**	Peru
BAH	Bahamas	**GER**	Germany	**PHI**	Philippines
BEL	Belgium	**GRE**	Greece	**POL**	Poland
BER	Bermuda	**HAI**	Haiti	**POR**	Portugal
BOL	Bolivia	**HKG**	Hong Kong	**PUR**	Puerto Rico
BRA	Brazil	**HOL**	Netherlands	**ROM**	Rumania
BUL	Bulgaria	**HUN**	Hungary	**RSA**	South Africa
CAN	Canada	**INA**	Indonesia	**SEN**	Senegal
CHI	Chile	**IND**	India	**SUI**	Switzerland
CHN	People's Republic of China	**IRL**	Ireland	**SWE**	Sweden
		IRN	Iran	**TCH**	Czechoslovakia
CIS	Commonwealth of Independent States	**ISR**	Israel	**THA**	Thailand
		ITA	Italy	**TUR**	Turkey
CIV	Côte d'Ivoire	**JPN**	Japan	**UKR**	Ukraine
COL	Colombia	**KEN**	Kenya	**URS**	USSR
CRO	Croatia	**KOR**	Korea	**URU**	Uruguay
CUB	Cuba	**LUX**	Luxembourg	**USA**	United States of America
DEN	Denmark	**MAR**	Morocco		
ECU	Ecuador	**MEX**	Mexico	**VEN**	Venezuela
EGY	Arab Republic of Egypt	**NGR**	Nigeria	**YUG**	Yugoslavia
		NOR	Norway	**ZIM**	Zimbabwe
ESP	Spain	**NZL**	New Zealand		

Cover photograph: Davis Cup Final – Guy Forget and Henri Leconte (T. Hindley)

First published in 1992 by
Collins Willow
an imprint of HarperCollins Publishers
London

© **John Barrett 1992**

A CIP catalogue record for this book
is available from the British Library

ISBN: 0 00 218430 3

Set in Univers by Phoenix Photosetting, Chatham, Kent
Printed and bound in Great Britain by
Mackays of Chatham PLC, Chatham, Kent

CONTENTS

PREFACE

At a time of violent political change in Europe and deepening economic recession through-out the world, it was both a relief and a surprise to find that the game was still in good health in 1991. Thanks to the injection of $2 million from the *Compaq Grand Slam Cup*, the activities of the ITF Development Department introduced a further 100,000 youngsters to the joys of tennis, while the men's and women's professional circuits survived unharmed – prospered even.

As the year unfolded, however, we began to see evidence of the new political realities. The appearance of mysterious new initials, like CRO and CIS, after a player's name, was a reminder that certain of them had lost their homelands and were competing under new national affiliations. Change is often painful.

As the Rules Committee of the ITF discovered, change is also difficult to introduce – even when everyone has recognized the need for it. As we went to press, the problem of excessive power in the men's game was at last being addressed at meetings in Miami where, the following week, the ATP Tour had organized a Forum to debate those same issues. The outcome of these deliberations and the new rules that should result will have a decisive effect on the future of our sport. We have been slow to recognize the need for legislation to preserve those very qualities of competition which are most enjoyed by spectators and players alike – namely the cut and thrust of rally play between players who employ racket skills as well as power. Yet we are all in the entertainment business. The moment we cease to entertain (and there is evidence to suggest that the men's game is already at that point on fast surfaces), tennis will lose its attraction for sponsors, for the media and for the general public.

To entertain and inform has always been the purpose of this publication during the 24 years we have been charting the convoluted progress of the worldwide game. There have been many changes in our content and format during that time and this year's volume contains one which we hope will make it both more interesting and more useful. For the first time we include, in two alphabetical lists, the names, nationalities and birthdays of all the men and women who have competed in the four Grand Slam Championships, the tournaments of the ATP Tour and the Kraft General Foods Tour, as well as the *Davis Cup*. This will make it easier to trace a player whose name may be unfamiliar.

As always, I am indebted to those colleagues among the tennis writers who have lent their expertise to this year's edition to bring alive the events of another crowded year. Equally important are the lively pictures submitted by that cheerful band of peripatetic packhorses, the tennis photographers, whose artistic contributions are very much appreci-ated. Their uncanny ability to arrive at courtside at the critical moment in a match never fails to amaze me.

The continuing enthusiasm of Christine Forrest for the minutiae of performance has once again made our player biographies an invaluable source of reference. Long may she continue to enjoy her indispensable role.

No less enthusiastic are the indefatigable staff at the ITF headquarters in London where Ian Barnes has been a tower of strength and John Trelevan has increasingly become a mine of statistical information. Thanks are due twice over to Marijke Volger who was inexcusably forgotten last year. Now that I have consumed my somewhat indigestible slice of humble pie, I hope I am forgiven! This year Marijka's erstwhile assistant, Karina Hardingham, has performed prodigies of work at the keyboard, all with a willing cheerful-ness that was much appreciated.

Another indispensable member of the Grand Slam information team is that energetic and peripatetic American lady, Barbara Travers, whose omniscient computer seems to have a mind almost as active as her own. Whatever would we all do without her meticulously researched men's profiles? Not much, is the answer!

Our fellow sufferers at the Florida offices of the ATP Tour and the Women's Tennis Association deserve special mention. Apart from supplying basic information about their respective organisations, my good friends Greg Sharko and Gene Beckwith have once again been unfailingly helpful in solving those last-minute problems that always seem to occur in a project of this sort. To them both, my thanks.

In welcoming Peter Alfano, who has come in to replace Jay Beck as chief of ATP Communications, we must also salute Jay and the European Director Richard Evans, for continually improving the quality of the information we all receive. On the road, the increasing complexities of the two Tours mean that the front line troops are always under fire from impatient media men and women, each one of whom believes that theirs is the only query that matters. For the likes of the ever-willing George Rubenstein and Craig the 'Angel' Gabriel, and the rather prettier Meg Donovan, Anna Legnani, Patricia Jolly and Lauren Goldenberg, life on the ATP Tour is one long battle to stay ahead of the facts. They do a fine job.

The same is true of Ana Leaird's WTA team – Giselle Marrou, Susan Vosburgh, Robin Reynolds, Tracey Robinson and Ann Fahey. How these good ladies retain their equilibrium in the media madhouse is a mystery. To see them at the end of another busy week still smiling, still patient, still willing to search out that last obstinate fact, is to know that they love their work. For that, we love them all.

For the first time this year we have taken the electronic route. The vast majority of the material within these pages was supplied to our friends at Phoenix Photosetting on disk. This has imposed a greater-than-usual strain on our publishers and here I must pay tribute to the efforts of Barbara Dixon at HarperCollins who has undertaken the monumental task of proofing the entire book almost single-handed. She has achieved the impossible with barely a frown.

Once again it has been a privilege to work with so many talented people. To them all, my thanks. I hope we have succeeded in providing another interesting commentary on the game's affairs. Of that you must be the judge.

JOHN BARRETT
London, March 1992

FOREWORD

If the strength of international sport is in the diversity of its champions then tennis can look back on 1991 and forward to the beginning of the next century with great satisfaction and high hopes. Our game is flourishing as never before.

The base of the pyramid is becoming ever broader and, so long as we remain on our guard against the complacency that comes from overconfidence or over ambition, the prospects for further progress remain good.

Our two great team competitions continue to provide wonderful entertainment and excitement and the major championships all reported increased public awareness, both at home and, through the medium of television, in many parts of the world.

The *Davis Cup by NEC* provided one of its most thrilling and emotional finishes for many years as France recaptured the trophy from the Americans after a 59-year gap. And who can forget the sheer joy of the young Spanish girls who triumphed for the first time in the *Federation Cup by NEC* in Nottingham!

Both events were wonderful advertisements for the game and it is no surprise that record numbers of our member nations have entered for the 1992 competitions.

This growth could not, of course, have been so spectacular without the support of our title sponsors, NEC, and we were particularly pleased during the year that they pledged their continued support.

In individual championships we also saw encouraging signs of growth and diversity with four different men winning the singles titles at the Grand Slam events for the second year in succession and Monica Seles consolidating her position as our World Champion by overcoming the challenges of such players as Steffi Graf, Arantxa Sanchez-Vicario, Jennifer Capriati, Gabriela Sabatini and Martina Navratilova.

There are two areas of great satisfaction in this. The first is that the work we have undertaken to develop the game and broaden its base is now paying the dividends we hoped for, namely champions from an increasing number of different countries. The second is that these champions encourage young players in their particular countries and provide role-models for the next generation of title winners.

We at the ITF have the duty to encourage our member nations to provide their young players with opportunities for coaching and competition which will enable them to reach their full potential and fulfil their ambitions. The many changes in the political map which we saw during 1991 and further developments, which appear likely to continue for some time to come, will provide a further challenge for international sport. It will be up to the ITF and our stronger and more successful member nations to lead the way forward and show, by example, what can be achieved.

Since assuming the mantle of President at the 1991 Annual General Meeting in Hamburg, I have been impressed by the professional approach so many national federations now have. This will surely rub off on those countries which have the ambition to achieve success both in the numbers who play tennis and in producing the champions of future generations. In this, the 24th edition of *World of Tennis*, we have attempted once again to provide the definitive work of reference in the game and a book which will serve as an inspiration to young players through its recording of the achievements of past and present champions. Everything is arranged in easy-to-follow fashion and we again have expert comment from some of the game's leading writers and a variety of pictures from the world's top sports photographers.

They bring the year to life. Enjoy their work.

BRIAN TOBIN
President, International Tennis Federation

Jimmy Connors celebrated his 39th birthday by fighting through to the semi-finals of the US Open for the 14th time with pulsating comeback victories over Patrick McEnroe, Aaron Krickstein and Paul Haarhuis amid unprecedented scenes of hysteria at Flushing Meadow. *(T. Hindley)*

THE YEAR IN REVIEW

Ronald Atkin

A tennis year which was ushered in by the Gulf War and which closed with the collapse of the Soviet Union should be placed firmly in perspective. Even so there were, in context, moments of high drama and political import, reputations made or restored, goodbyes said and, as ever in any sport, bright new stars to be hailed.

As far as France, and a great majority of those in tennis were concerned, the best of the year came in the final month. In Lyon's Stade Gerland the holders of the *Davis Cup by NEC*, the United States, were overthrown by Yannick Noah's inspired squad. As well as the highlight of the year, it was without doubt the upset of the year. What a scene to savour for those fortunate enough to have been present as Guy Forget fell flat on his back after steering away the volley which landed the trophy back in French hands for the first time in 59 years, the era of the Four Musketeers. And how appropriate that one of those legends, the 93-year-old Jean Borotra, should be at courtside as one of the delighted witnesses of France's biggest sporting moment for many years.

Noah's choice of Henri Leconte, just recovered from his third back operation, for the second singles spot on the French team, was not, the team captain insisted, a gamble. With benefit of hindsight perhaps not (though few would have been prepared to put many francs on Leconte to beat Pete Sampras) but the frenzied occasion certainly allowed Leconte to present bold credentials for Comeback of the Year. In a normal 12-month period the extravagantly gifted but deeply inconsistent Leconte would have walked away with the accolade but in 1991 there was an even brighter contender for the crown – the old alleycat himself, Jimmy Connors. If France's was the team achievement of the year, then Connors, at 39, collared the plaudits for his sensational wild card run through the US Open and into the semi-finals before he was halted.

Like Leconte, Connors had spent long months of recuperation wondering whether he would ever play tennis meaningfully again. In the American's case, the doubts concerned the recuperation from an operation on the wrist of his racket hand in October 1990. All doubts were gloriously swept aside, first in the French Open, then at Wimbledon and finally in the tournament he has won five times and where he has annually captivated the citizens of New York. His rantings at umpires apart, it was a marvellous performance guaranteed to strike just the right chord in a Peter Pan nation like America.

Another 1991 development of inestimable political importance was the gradual return of South Africa to the family of nations. Inevitably, that nation's ostracized sportsmen and women benefitted from the warmth of the changes ushered in by their political leaders. Swiftly, South Africa found itself back in the draw for the 1992 *Davis Cup*, the ATP Tour World Doubles Championship was staged in Johannesburg and two ATP Tour tournaments will be played in the country this year. Truly, South Africa is back in tennis.

It was a year which also brought the provisional readmission of the Baltic states, Estonia, Latvia and Lithuania, by the ITF to international tennis. This positive news came on the heels of the draw for the 1992 *Davis Cup by NEC* which featured a record total of 93 nations, including South Africa for the first time since 1978.

The sad side of this most popular of tennis team competitions proved to be the fragmentation of a fine Yugoslavian squad because of the civil strife within that country. With their best players, Goran Ivanisevic and Goran Prpic (both Croats), refusing to represent what they claimed was a Serbian-dominated Federation, a desperately weakened team was overwhelmed by France in the 1991 World Group semi-finals. Already Croatia has made a bid to enter the *Davis Cup* as an independent nation and chosen a captain

(Bruno Oresar) before, realistically, it actually has a recognised team.

Yugoslavia's agony can in no way be seen to provide any form of mixed blessings, but the political chaos has put to one side, at least for the time being, the dilemma of whether Monica Seles should represent the country of her birth or the nation of her adoption when she plays international events. Seles teamed with Prpic for Yugoslavia in the *Hopman Cup* at the very start of the year but her ambitions to appear in the Barcelona Olympics were frustrated by dispute with the ITF over whether she should have played for that country in the *Federation Cup* in Nottingham. Her Olympic ban which followed failure to turn up in Nottingham, together with the mystery leg injury which kept her away from Wimbledon, were the only dark moments in an otherwise brilliant year for the girl who did not turn 18 until December. She swept all three Grand Slams for which she entered, taking the French for the second year and the Australian and US Opens for the first time. She reached the final in all 16 events she entered, winning ten of them and ending 1991 with a 74–6 playing record which included the Virginia Slims Championship in New York as well as the hat-trick of Grand Slams. Her prize money of $2,457,758 set a new women's record. There could, then, be no doubt about her right to be the ITF's World Champion for 1991.

Stefan Edberg was named as men's World Champion. He ended the year ranked number one, having swapped that honour a couple of times with Boris Becker over the 12 months. He won his first US Open and was a semi-finalist at both Wimbledon and the Australian Open. Having been rather surprisingly overlooked in favour of Ivan Lendl for the honour in 1990, there was no question Edberg merited the recognition.

The Connors pyrotechnics at Flushing Meadows tended to overshadow the quiet excellence of Edberg's tennis, which was entirely to the Swede's liking. 'I kind of sneak up behind people,' was his way of describing a steady advance to the final, culminating in a straight-sets success against Jim Courier. The US Open launched Edberg on a run of 21 successive singles victories which also brought him autumn titles in Sydney and Tokyo before the gallop was halted by Becker in the final of Stockholm's Open.

The close of what had already become the best season of Edberg's career was marred when the problems associated with a knee injury which had been bothering him since midsummer flared up anew. In order to be fit for the 1992 Australian Open he was forced to rest and missed the big end-of-year occasions, the ATP Tour Championship in Frankfurt (brilliantly won by Pete Sampras) and the *Compaq Grand Slam Cup* in Munich.

Becker also missed the *Grand Slam Cup* because of flu, the latest in a series of debilitating illnesses or injuries which seem to have plagued his progress. The sickness meant a muted end to a year which had begun so brightly with victory in the Australian Open, followed by accession to the number one ranking. Becker was a semi-finalist at the French Open (where he lost to his current nemesis, Andre Agassi) and went out in the third round of the US Open, complaining of injury.

Becker's year, of course, stands or falls by what he achieves at Wimbledon and in 1991 he fell at the last fence. That fence was built around the booming serve and incredibly confident net play of Becker's compatriot, Michael Stich, who found irresistible form at just the right moment for the world's premier tournament.

Stich went on to prove Wimbledon had been no fluke by winning events on all four surfaces on which the professional game is played. Having started the year ranked 42nd, he ended it as number four. This rocket rise was, astonishingly, matched by Courier, the red-headed American from Florida, who marched into 1991 ranked 25th and closed out his playing year as the world's number two, having collected the French Open along the way, as well as back-to-back titles in Indian Wells and Key Biscayne during the spring.

Not since the emergence of the computer rankings in 1973 had two players leapt into the world's leading quartet from outside the top 20 in the same year. If Paris provided Courier and the United States with a triumph on clay, it was Germany all the way on Wimbledon's grass. In 1989 Becker and Steffi Graf had produced joy for Germany on Centre Court; in 1991 it was Stich who shared the top titles with Steffi.

That Championship, by the narrowest of margins in the tightest of finishes with Gabriela Sabatini, redeemed an otherwise patchy and fraught time for Graf, who suffered some setbacks as the leading elements among the opposition 'rumbled' her game and took belated revenge. She fell to Jana Novotna in the semi-finals of the Australian Open, suffered her worst-ever humiliation in the semi-finals of the French Open, collecting only two games from Arantxa Sanchez-Vicario, and also had a semi-final loss at the US Open, this time to Martina Navratilova. There were the familiar snuffles from Graf's allergies, but no complaints about the results. However, she did concede after a further early, disappointing exit at the Virginia Slims Championships that she needed to rethink her game and how it was played. Accordingly, her coach of five years, Pavel Slozil, was jettisoned and she entered the new year with a new mentor, Switzerland's Heinz Gunthardt.

At a time when belts were being tightened and jobs lost in many countries, Wimbledon announced a profit bordering on £12 million, more than £2 million up on the previous year and a boon for the fortunate recipients, the Lawn Tennis Association of Great Britain. On the subject of huge amounts of money, the *Grand Slam Cup* again offered its participants $6 million in prizes, plus $2 million for the fund which will push the development of tennis in less affluent nations around the world. The gross amount on offer in Munich brought fewer media complaints – perhaps one becomes inured to astronomical amounts in all sports, never mind just tennis – and the prime pickings were shared for the second year in succession by Americans. In the *Grand Slam Cup*'s inaugural year the finalists had been Pete Sampras and Brad Gilbert. This time, neither of these even having qualified for the 16-man field, the top dollar (or top $2 million) went to David Wheaton, who prepared meticulously for his favourite tournament, played impeccably and purposefully and was a thoroughly deserving winner over Michael Chang. In Chang's defence, however, he had played five tough sets against Ivan Lendl in the semi-finals, repeating his feat of the 1989 French Open in coming back from a two-set deficit to overcome Lendl.

There was more talk in Munich of making the event truly representative of the Grand Slam competitions and including the leading women. For now, despite a willingness bordering on anxiety by the ITF to bring in the ladies, talks are stalled on – you guessed it – money. Except that, to borrow an old saying, it's not the money, it's the principle.

The principle of the Women's Tennis Association is that not only are they entitled to level earnings at the *Grand Slam Cup* but parity at all four Grand Slams too. While these two issues remain linked, chances of significant progress are slight. Unlike the Australian and US Opens, Wimbledon and the French Open do not pay equal prize money and are unlikely to concede on this contentious issue. Notwithstanding, it would be wonderful – both for the event and for the public – to see the women playing in Munich this year.

In what was without doubt the political shaker of the year, the WTA's Executive Director, Gerard Smith, produced an 18-page document proposing a restructuring of the women's circuit along the lines of the route down which the ATP Tour marched in 1990. In many respects the timing was, to say the least, unfortunate coming, as it did, on the eve of the Virginia Slims Championships when all participants in women's tennis, especially the sponsors, gathered in New York to buss cheeks and pronounce solidarity.

Before making their move, the ATP Tour had waited until all sponsor and management contracts had expired. The WTA's talk of 'restructuring' and 'renegotiating' came while the contract with their main sponsor, Kraft General Foods, still had three years to run. As Eugene Scott pointed out in *Tennis Week*, 'Not only has [Smith] threatened the tranquillity of the sponsor but he has also spooked the ITF, the nerve centre of the official game.' There was other condemnation. Donald Dell, head of ProServ, suggested Smith 'may have misjudged his timing', while Mark McCormack of IMG was a good deal more blunt: 'To unilaterally go off and do this without consulting the parties on the specifics reminds me of Disney World.'

The backpedalling was not long coming. That great panacea, a Working Group, was hastily announced, while the Women's International Professional Tennis Council, through its new Managing Director, Anne Person, confirmed support of the Kraft sponsorship and emphasised the 'continuing spirit of co-operation' in women's tennis. This was crisis (hastily) averted.

If that aborted move constituted the 'fizzle' of the year in tennis politics, the biggest disappointment on the playing side was the comeback at 34 of Bjorn Borg. After virtually an eight-year absence, Borg trained hard for his return but chose to undertake it with an outdated wooden racket. His first match at the Monte Carlo Open brought embarrassing defeat by the journeyman Spaniard, Jordi Arrese, rapidly followed by news of the attempted suicide of Borg's wife, Loredana Berte. Now, it is reported, Borg intends to join the Seniors' Tour.

Despite the Connors miracle, that would seem eminently more sensible for Borg after so many years out of the game. However, Martina Navratilova, only a year younger than Borg, played so well in 1991 that she drew level with Chris Evert's career record of 157 tournament titles and seems certain soon to hold the title alone.

Meanwhile, Evert (aka Mrs Andy Mill), emerged triumphant from her toughest-ever contest, a 20-hour labour to produce her first child, Alexander James, who weighed in at 8lb 6oz.

The Federation Cup by NEC, the women's world team event which Evert had been instrumental in winning for the United States a record 14 times, headed off in a different direction during a summer when she was happily contemplating motherhood. Spain marked up their first-ever success in the competition, after a highly successful week at the new Nottingham Tennis Centre, by defeating the Americans 2–1.

The memorable opening ceremony in Nottingham was one of the first official functions of the new President of the ITF, Brian Tobin, who succeeded Philippe Chatrier at the ITF's Annual General Meeting in Hamburg. After 14 years in the post, Chatrier stepped down to conclude an historic term of office marked by exhilarating progress and profound change in the world of tennis. Hamburg was the city where Chatrier had first been elected ITF President in 1977, and the 1991 AGM turned into a thinly disguised farewell occasion for Philippe, who received a seven-minute ovation at the end of an emotional goodbye speech.

Sadly, the closing months of 1991 saw the deaths of two outstanding pre-war Australians, Jack Crawford (83) and Adrian Quist (79) and one post-war *Davis Cup* man, Ian Ayre. Crawford and Quist had been long-time friends and rivals. Crawford won Wimbledon in 1933 and that year was only prevented from becoming the first to achieve the Grand Slam when he was beaten by Fred Perry in the final of the fourth event, the US Open.

PLAYERS OF THE YEAR

John Barrett

STEFAN EDBERG

There were two major disappointments in Stefan Edberg's year. First there was a traumatic loss to Ivan Lendl in the semi-finals of the Australian Open, when he double-faulted on one of his two match points. That defeat alone would have been bad enough, for it had allowed Boris Becker to displace the 25-year-old Swede as the world's No.1 for three short weeks. But then, in July, came the frustrating semi-final loss at Wimbledon to an 'unknown' German, Michael Stich. Although Stefan never once lost his serve that day, he still lost his title – and again Becker overtook him at the top of the rankings.

A lesser man would never have recovered from those cruel blows to pride and confidence. But, as we have come to discover these past few years, there is a basic soundness about the character of the quiet Swede that enables him, with the help and shrewd advice of his British coach Tony Pickard, to shrug off life's disappointments. Stefan simply got on with the job of proving that he is unquestionably still the finest tennis player in the world. He confirmed the fact majestically at the US Open where, in a spectacular final full of irresistible power and delicate finesse, he swept aside French Open champion Jim Courier to win the title for the first time. This was the prelude to a late season surge of 21 winning matches that brought Edberg two more titles in Sydney and Tokyo and took him to the final in Stockholm. It was sad for the game that injury prevented him from competing in either the IBM/ATP Tour World Championships or the *Compaq Grand Slam Cup*. Nevertheless, there was no doubt about who was THE Player of the Year for 1991. It was Sweden's super athlete Stefan Edberg.

BORIS BECKER

For Boris Becker the moment of fulfilment came early in 1991. All his young life, he told us, he had dreamt of becoming the finest tennis player in the world, the first among equals. With an extraordinary performance of highs and lows against Ivan Lendl in the final of the Australian Open the 24-year-old German achieved his ambition. Then, for a while, it seemed that ambition had died. Boris, struggling to find motivation, unsure whether he really wanted to compete or whether he should consider a university career, was no longer the dominant champion. Three weeks later he was back at No.2 and the top of the mountain was shrouded in cloud.

A career-first clay court title eluded him in the Monte Carlo final but at his beloved Wimbledon Boris, playing in his fourth consecutive final, believed he might regain the summit. Indeed he did – but only because his *Davis Cup* colleague Michael Stich had disposed of his old rival Edberg in the semi-finals. Boris' No.1 position felt rather hollow when Stich, with an extraordinary display of serving power and backhand control, beat him in straight sets.

The season's switchback took an upward curve when in the Stockholm final Boris beat Edberg to retain his title and break a nine-month winning drought. It sped downhill again in Paris the following week when, for the first time in his life, Boris was forced to withdraw in mid-tournament with influenza. This was a bleak moment for it meant that Courier would now overtake him in the No.2 ranking spot. Nor was there any joy in Frankfurt where, to intense national disappointment, Boris narrowly failed to reach the semi-finals of the IBM/ATP Tour World Championships. So the year ended as it had begun with Becker still gazing towards his mountain top.

Above (left): *A first Australian Open win was the highlight of an otherwise disappointing year for Boris Becker. (T. Hindley)* **(right):** *A career-best year for Jim Courier who challenged strongly for the No. 1 world ranking. (M. Cole)* **Below (left):** *After a sensational first win at Wimbledon Michael Stich consolidated his position among the world's top ten. (T. Hindley)* **(right):** *Man-of-the-year Stefan Edberg reached perfection at the US Open and remained the No. 1 player in the world. (M. Cole)*

JIM COURIER

It was a year of firsts for the likeable 20-year-old from Dade county in Florida. In the spring this accomplished baseline slugger produced his first back-to-back victories in Indian Wells and Key Biscayne which lifted his ranking to No.9. This was a first appearance in the exclusive top ten club and promised much for the remainder of the year. Gentleman Jim did not disappoint. Thanks to the help and advice of his Spanish coach, Jose Higueras, there was another magnificent first in June when Jim blasted his way to the French Open title to score his first Grand Slam success. This was only the second time an American had succeeded in Paris since 1955. Now he was at No.4 in the world for the first time, a position he would improve to No.3 when he reached his first US Open final in September soon after his 21st birthday. Then it was up once more to the No.2 spot for the first time when Becker was forced to withdraw during the Paris Indoor. The season ended with yet another milestone as Jim battled through to the final of the IBM/ATP Tour World Championships for the first time. At this rate you wonder how long it will be before Jim Courier, the lion-hearted scrapper with a soaring ambition, will claim the ultimate first, the No.1 world ranking.

MICHAEL STICH

It was one of those poignant moments in sport when an heroic performance transforms a good performer into a great one. As 22-year-old Michael Stich sank to his knees on the Centre Court and raised his arms heavenwards at the end of his stunning straight sets defeat of three-time champion and fellow German, Boris Becker, we all recognized that a budding talent had suddenly and magnificently come to full flower. This improbable first Grand Slam success came almost from nowhere and had included the defeat of defending champion and world No.1 Stefan Edberg in the semi-final. Ironically, in modern times only Becker and Edberg themselves had previously beaten the Nos.1 and 2 players in the world to win a Grand Slam title.

Until that moment the only professional tournament Michael had ever won had been Memphis 1990, thanks to the partnership he had forged with his coach, Mark Lewis. Yet it had been apparent as long ago as Queen's Club 1989, where he had taken a set from Ivan Lendl, that the tall German had the right credentials to succeed on grass courts. His was a tremendous serve, especially the fast second delivery, and his volleys were instinctive and full of a true artist's touch. There was a penetrating quality about his backhand, too, which always seemed to be so sweetly timed. After such an unexpected and dramatic success, it was almost more impressive that Michael should have won three more titles in 1991 – in Stuttgart, Schenectady and Vienna. This run gave him titles on all four surfaces, a feat last accomplished by Miloslav Mecir in 1987. After completing more singles and doubles matches than anyone else in 1991 – over 150 of them – Michael ended the year with the most improved year-end ranking of anyone, leaping from No.38 to No.4. Yes, Michael Stich was very much a Player of the Year in 1991.

MONICA SELES

In 1991 it was a case of Monica Seles first, the rest nowhere. With victory in all three of the Grand Slam Championships she contested, the only sorrow is that Monica allowed her non-appearance at Wimbledon to be surrounded with such mystery and suspicion. Her record elsewhere was formidable indeed. She reached the final of all 16 tour events she entered and won 10 of them. Only Steffi Graf in 1987 (13 events, 11 titles) and 1989 (16 events, 14 titles) has done better.

The manner of Monica's whirlwind successes has been breathtaking. Was there ever a more aggressive woman on a tennis court than this grunting Yugoslav 17-year-old? If there has been, I have not had the privilege of watching her. The way the ball is struck fiercely and fearlessly with two hands for the lines on both sides, each blow accompanied by an explosive grunt, is itself remarkable. That the ball, savagely attacked on the rise

It was Monica Seles first, the rest nowhere, in 1991. *(M. Cole)*

practically as a half-volley, almost never flies beyond the confines of the court, is another miracle – a miracle of timing and of confidence.

As a match-player on the important occasions Monica has no peer. In Melbourne against Fernandez, who had a winning chance, she was staunchly defiant; in Paris against Ceccini, who had made the fatal mistake of winning the first set, she was ruthless; at the US Open against Jennifer Capriati, with everything to lose, she was magnificently confident, going for the lines with laser-like precision. Yes, as Monica Seles celebrated her 18th birthday last December, she could congratulate herself on being THE Player of the Year, a worthy successor to Graf, Navratilova and Evert. One cannot heap praise more highly than that.

STEFFI GRAF

By any normal standards Steffi Graf had a fabulous year. The 22-year-old German regained her Wimbledon title, became the youngest player to accumulate 500 wins and stretched her reign atop the women's rankings to a record 186 weeks before she was overtaken by Seles at Key Biscayne in March.

But then how can you judge the golden Grand Slam Champion of 1988 by normal standards? After that fabulous performance we all expected her to win every match in every tournament she played. And for a year she almost did. In 1989 there were only two defeats, the one in Paris costing her another Grand Slam. It was hardly surprising that a reaction set in as she spent most of 1990 in the wilderness, beset by physical problems and the emotional turmoil surrounding her father's private life. It was crucial, therefore, that she should reinstate herself in her own eyes. At Wimbledon she did, despite the agonizing pressures of a determined challenge in the final from her old rival Gabriela Sabatini who twice served for the match.

For Steffi, 1991 will be remembered as the year when she returned to normality, when she came to terms with her fame and its pressures and when she parted company tearfully with her Czech coach Pavel Slozil after a partnership of 5½ years that had brought her 10 Grand Slam titles. Steffi Graf may not have been the outstanding player of the year in 1991, but with the fires of ambition re-ignited and a more balanced outlook on life, there is every reason to believe that she might well be again in 1992.

The recapture of her Wimbledon title was the high point of Steffi Graf's year.   *(M. Cole)*

FRENCH *DAVIS CUP* TEAM

It would not be right to let 1991 pass without acknowledging the outstanding achievement of Yannick Noah and his team in bringing back the *Davis Cup* to France for the first time since 1932. The 3–1 win in Lyon over the holders, the United States, represented by Andre Agassi and Pete Sampras in singles, Ken Flach and Robert Seguso in doubles, was a performance of heroic proportions that certainly made Guy Forget and Henri Leconte Players of the Year, and Noah himself Captain of the Year.

The unbeaten Leconte was an inspiration to the whole team. It was astonishing that he could play so well against Sampras on the opening day and again in the doubles on the second with Forget to beat Flach and Seguso after only a handful of matches since undergoing surgery on his back for the third time in July. But then, as Noah said when he made the somewhat controversial selection, 'On his day Henri can beat anyone, anywhere, anytime!' How right he was! To his credit Forget, having lost a nervy opening rubber to Agassi, played with magnificent flair and panache to score the winning point against the wretched Sampras on the third day.

The scenes of unparalleled national emotion in Lyon that day are graphically described elsewhere in these pages. However, due credit for this historic win must be paid to Philippe Chatrier, appointed as President of the French Tennis Federation in 1973, and his entire team who have worked tirelessly for the past 18 years to restructure and rebuild the game in France. The success of their efforts, which has made the sport second only in national popularity to football, is obvious. Well done France – the entire tennis world salutes you!

Joy unconfined in Lyons. *(M. Cole)*

THE ITF YEAR

THE ITF YEAR
DAVIS CUP
FEDERATION CUP

The remarkable American fifteen-year-old, Jennifer Capriati played one of the year's great matches to beat Navratilova at Wimbledon where she became the youngest-ever ladies' semi-finalist. *(M. Cole)*

A year of declining fortunes for Ivan Lendl, who lost his Australian Open title to a rampant Becker and saw his ranking slip to No. 5. *(R. Adams)*

THE ITF YEAR

Ian Barnes

If 1989 and 1990 were years of trauma and drama for the International Tennis Federation, 1991 will be recalled as a year of confidence and consolidation. It was the year when the ITF demonstrated that it had become a thoroughly professional organisation with an up-to-date approach to the many facets of a game which had evolved into a massive, international business.

This change in the public perception of the ITF was almost certainly due to the foresight of former President Philippe Chatrier, whose idea it was to strengthen the chain of command by the appointment of a full-time executive president to succeed him when, at the Annual General Meeting, in Hamburg, in July, he retired after 14 years as leader.

Brian Tobin, the former President of Tennis Australia, had been groomed for the post as the first Executive Vice President based at the London headquarters, a position he assumed towards the end of 1990. By the time he subsequently took over from Mr Chatrier as President – by a unanimous vote of the member nations – he had created an enthusiasm within the ITF team not only to get things done but to be seen doing it.

Within hours of his appointment Mr Tobin announced that he would lead a delegation from the ITF to South Africa to help that country's efforts to return to the international sporting fold. With Committee of Management members, Heinz Grimm of Switzerland and Jean-Claude Delafosse of Cote D'Ivoire, Mr Tobin met with the leaders of the three tennis groups in South Africa and with Prime Minister F.W. De Klerk.

Their talks laid the foundations for agreements, and promises of future investment in development, which enabled South Africa to be readmitted to the Federation and to stage two international tournaments before the end of the year. Such diplomacy will undoubtedly be called upon again during 1992 as the map of Eastern Europe and parts of Asia is re-drawn and more and more nations claim a place in the international sporting family.

On the playing front, 1991 will be seen in retrospect as a year when many promises were delivered, when new names were etched on some historic trophies, not only on individual ones but international ones as well.

Spain emerged as a nation to be reckoned with by winning the *Federation Cup by NEC* in Nottingham, where Arantxa Sanchez-Vicario and Conchita Martinez upset the United States in a thrilling final, and by taking the World Youth Cup for boys in Barcelona.

Germany proved there will be life after Boris Becker and Steffi Graf when Michael Stich became Wimbledon champion, 16-year-old Anke Huber and 18-year-old Barbara Rittner reached the semi-finals of the *Federation Cup* after Steffi had withdrawn from the competition with an injury, and the German girls' team triumphed again in the World Youth Cup.

And who could forget the emotion and excitement as France re-emerged as a force in the game by winning the *Davis Cup by NEC* after an interval of 59 years? Certainly not the title sponsors, NEC, who decided during the year to extend their support until 1995 for a competition which is now recognised as the biggest annual international team event in sport. The Japanese computer and communications company will by then have been involved for 15 years, one of the longest running sponsorships in sport. Their title sponsorship of the *Federation Cup* began in 1980, and will complete 15 years association with that competition in 1994.

In addition, NEC have supported the World Youth Cup and, during 1991, agreed to a grant from its Social Contribution Programmes Department to the International

Wheelchair Tennis Federation to fund an expansion of its activities and competitions all over the world.

The popularity of the French *Davis Cup* victory was matched only by the enduring magic which the game's oldest team competition provides and the demand for participation. Increasing numbers of member nations enter year after year and 1991 set another record with 87 countries involved. The Gulf War reduced this to 86 when Iraq were ruled out, and caused some postponements to ties in the areas most closely involved in the conflict.

Internal political problems also affected Yugoslavia who, having reached the semi-finals with victories over Sweden and Czechoslovakia in which Croatians Goran Ivanisevic and Goran Prpic played a significant part, had to face France with Slobodan Zivojinovic and the untried Srdan Muskatirovic and were defeated 5–0.

The *Davis Cup* year ended, however, on the highest possible note with full houses in Lyon to witness the historic French triumph.

The four Grand Slam events again produced four different champions on the men's side, Boris Becker in Australia, Jim Courier in France, Michael Stich at Wimbledon and Stefan Edberg at the US Open, while the women's championships were dominated by Monica Seles. She won in Australia, successfully defended the French championship, and defeated Martina Navratilova in New York. Unfortunately, she missed Wimbledon for reasons which continued to mystify most observers for the rest of the year.

Monica's late withdrawal from the Yugoslav team at the *Federation Cup by NEC* in Nottingham two weeks after Wimbledon was also not explained to the ITF's satisfaction and she was subsequently ruled out of eligibility for nomination for a place in the Olympic Games in Barcelona.

Nevertheless, Miss Seles finished the year on a high note by claiming the title at the Virginia Slims Championships. She reached the finals of all 16 tournaments she entered during the year and won 10 of them. This consistency earned her top place in the Kraft General Foods points standings, which decides the ITF World Champion on the women's side of the game.

Deciding who should be the men's World Champion again gave the panel of former champions, Fred Perry, Frank Sedgman and Tony Trabert, plenty to ponder. They eventually gave the award to Stefan Edberg, not only for his outstanding display in the US Open final but for his five other title triumphs during a year in which he won more matches, 76, than any other player. He demonstrated his all-round flair by winning on indoor carpet, outdoor hard courts and grass.

For the ITF's Development Department, 1991 was a landmark year – the first in which the $2 million donation from the *Compaq Grand Slam Cup* was available to the Grand Slam Development Fund to be invested in programmes for the benefit of the game world-wide.

More young players of promise were provided with opportunities to travel and compete outside their immediate geographic areas; more Satellite events for men and Futures Circuits for women players were established, grants were made to help the ITF officiating programme, and the fast-growing veterans' side of the game also benefited from the Fund.

Plans were made, following the pioneering work of Angus Macaulay in East Africa, for the appointment of more Development Officers, in the Caribbean countries and in the South Pacific, and it was decided to extend the World Class Team idea, in which groups of young players were provided with the services of a coach but were expected to cover their own expenses by on-court success.

The first World Class Team, of players from African countries, achieved considerable success, with Byron Black of Zimbabwe moving impressively up the men's ranking list by the year's end. The demonstration of the benefits to be gained for the game as a whole from the *Compaq Grand Slam Cup* was instrumental in winning over many of those who had been critical of its concept and prize money only 12 months earlier.

The second staging of the event, in Munich in December, had full support from the German authorities, the players and especially the public. There were 58,000 spectators during the week, despite the late withdrawal through injury of Stefan Edberg and the even later pull-out, on the eve of the tournament, of Boris Becker who was ill.

ITF WORLD CHAMPIONS

The ITF Men's World Champion is decided by the men's world champions panel. The ITF Women's World Champion title is awarded to the player who heads the Kraft General Foods points table for the year.

MEN				**WOMEN**			
1978	Bjorn Borg	1985	Ivan Lendl	1978	Chris Evert	1985	Martina Navratilova
1979	Bjorn Borg	1986	Ivan Lendl	1979	Martina Navratilova	1986	Martina Navratilova
1980	Bjorn Borg	1987	Ivan Lendl	1980	Chris Evert Lloyd	1987	Steffi Graf
1981	John McEnroe	1988	Mats Wilander	1981	Chris Evert Lloyd	1988	Steffi Graf
1982	Jimmy Connors	1989	Boris Becker	1982	Martina Navratilova	1989	Steffi Graf
1983	John McEnroe	1990	Ivan Lendl	1983	Martina Navratilova	1990	Steffi Graf
1984	John McEnroe	1991	Stefan Edberg	1984	Martina Navratilova	1991	Monica Seles

Former ITF World Champion Mats Wilander sank to No. 157 in the rankings at the end of a year which included knee surgery. *(T. Hindley)*

The successful French team (above, l to r: Leconte, Delaitre, Santoro, Noah [Capt.], Forget, Boetsch) which brought the Davis Cup back to France for the first time since the famous Musketeers had won in 1932. The 3–1 victory in Lyon over the Americans (below, l to r: Seguso, Flach, Agassi, Sampras, Gorman [Capt.]) was accompanied by unprecedented scenes of patriotic delight. (T. Hindley)

THE *DAVIS CUP by NEC*

Ian Barnes

Dreams really do come true. Ask Yannick Noah, Henri Leconte or Guy Forget. All three admitted to a feeling of unreality as they celebrated – and how they celebrated – France's amazing triumph over the United States in the 1991 final of the *Davis Cup by NEC* at the Palais des Sports in Lyon.

Magic moments in sport are few and far between. But this was one of them. Noah, in his first year as captain, had his hands on the most famous trophy in tennis; the first French leader to do that since the days of the legendary Four Musketeers, Jean Borotra, Rene Lacoste, Henri Cochet and Jacques Brugnon, who had won the Cup six years in succession between 1927 and 1932.

Borotra was there to witness the amazing scenes as his successors ambushed the Americans and relieved them of the old silver punchbowl they had confidently expected to be taking back with them across the Atlantic. It was, he said, a sublime moment.

It was also incredibly noisy, wildly chaotic, amazingly emotional. As Guy Forget's backhand volley clinched the final point that gave him a 7–6, 3–6, 6–3, 6–4 victory over Pete Sampras, and France the winning third point in the tie, nobody would have been surprised to see the high-domed roof of the stadium lift off.

Forget fell on his back as captain Noah leapt in the air. They, and a tearful Leconte were then buried in a mass of bodies as team-mates, French officials and anybody who could get near joined in the frenzied celebrations.

The Americans watched in open-mouthed amazement as the realisation sank in that they had totally underestimated just what winning the Cup after a break of 59 years would mean to the French players and, equally, to the 8,300 of their supporters who had managed to get tickets. If ever there had been proof that pride and passion count for more in *Davis Cup* competition than rankings and reputations, this was it.

Captain Noah knew that Henri Leconte, despite only five competitive matches during the previous four months following a third operation on his troublesome spine, had what it takes to succeed in the unique atmosphere of a *Davis Cup* final.

What appeared a gamble to many commentators proved a winning hand as Leconte rose magnificently to the challenge. He kept French hopes alive on the opening day by destroying Sampras 6–4, 7–5, 6–4 with a magnificent display of determination and concentration after Andre Agassi had given the holders a winning start by outsmarting a clearly nervous Forget 6–7, 6–2, 6–1, 6–2.

More vitally, Leconte repaid Noah's faith in the crucial doubles by assuming total responsibility and encouraging Forget to outwit Ken Flach and Robert Seguso 6–1, 6–4, 4–6, 6–2. Here the left-hander was at his exuberant best, twisting and turning, his racket flashing in the lights as he made dazzling returns and amazing interceptions. Noah had said that recalling Henri to action was like bringing him back from the dead. He certainly played like an angel while Flach and Seguso looked as if they had seen a ghost.

Sampras, hinting that, at 20, perhaps he has a long *Davis Cup* career ahead of him, played superbly against Forget on the final day without ever quite coming to terms with the crowd's participation in the match. He demonstrated, however, that he had learned from the experience of his debut of fire against Leconte and made Forget take risks he admitted he would not have attempted had the circumstances been more normal. But then, when is a *Davis Cup* final 'normal'? Certainly not when it ends a 59-year drought.

Looking back, Lyon was probably an appropriate last chapter to a year in which Thomas Hallberg, the Director of the *Davis Cup* competition, and his colleagues had faced all sorts of abnormalities caused by wars both declared and unofficial.

France had been handed an easy passage through the semi-finals when internal conflict in Yugoslavia prevented Goran Ivanisevic and Goran Prpic, both from Croatia, from taking part in international competition. The inexperienced Srdan Muskatirovic, who was given the task of supporting veteran Slobodan Zivojinovic, was clearly out of his depth and failed to win a set in his three matches.

The Americans, in contrast, had been taken all the way to the final rubber in their encounter with Germany (who were without the injured Boris Becker) on an indoor clay court in Kansas City. Their place in the final was clinched only by Agassi's devastating display against Carl-Uwe Steeb.

The dates for the opening rounds had been drastically chopped and changed as a result of the Gulf War in the early part of the year. The hostilities not only caused postponement of ties involving the Gulf States and their opponents in the Asia/Oceania Zone and some African Zone matches but also affected ties in the World Group involving France and Israel as well as Mexico's tie with the United States.

Both these encounters were played over the weekend set aside for second round matches, and additionally involved the French in a change of venue from Marseilles to Rennes.

Noah's men then played again in early May, defeating Australia in Nimes, while the United States followed their victory in Mexico by taking their second round tie to the grass courts of the International Tennis Hall of Fame at Newport, Rhode Island, where Brad Gilbert and John McEnroe comfortably disposed of Spain in mid-June.

The Qualifying Round to decide the composition of the World Group in 1992 produced some of the most closely contested matches of the year. Belgium, who defeated Israel 4–1 in Brussels, and Canada, who defeated Cuba 3–2 in Havana, retained their places among the elite 16 for a second year while Great Britain, the Netherlands, Switzerland and Brazil returned at the expense of Austria, Mexico, New Zealand and India respectively.

Sweden, first round losers for the second successive year, easily defeated the Philippines 5–0 while Italy dismissed Denmark 4–1 in Bari.

Norway, Chile, Chinese Taipei and Kenya earned promotion to their respective Zonal Group One competitions in 1992 when, with a record entry of 93 nations, a Zonal Group Three competition will be played for the first time.

An inspired choice by captain Noah and inspired performances in singles and doubles from Henri Leconte (left) were the foundations of an unexpected French victory. (T. Hindley)

THE *DAVIS CUP BY NEC*, 1991
WORLD GROUP

FIRST ROUND – **USA d. Mexico 3–2, Mexico City:** J. Courier lost to L. Herrera 4–6 6–2 5–7 4–6; B. Gilbert d. L. Lavalle 6–3 6–2 6–7(4) 6–3; R. Leach/J. Pugh d. Lavalle/J. Lozano 6–4 4–6 7–6(2) 6–7(3) 6–4; Gilbert d. Herrera 4–6 6–3 7–5 3–6 6–3; Courier lost to Lavalle 4–6 7–6(2) 5–7. **Spain d. Canada 4–1, Cartagena:** S. Bruguera d. A. Sznajder 6–4 6–2 1–6 6–1; E. Sanchez d. M. Wostenholme 6–3 3–6 6–1 6–4; S. Casal/Sanchez d. G. Connell/G. Michibata 7–6(3) 6–2 6–1; Sanchez lost to Sznajder 5–7 7–5 3–6; Bruguera d. Wostenholme 6–1 7–6(5). **Argentina d. New Zealand 4–1, Christchurch:** M. Jaite d. B. Steven 7–5 6–2 6–2; J. Frana d. K. Evernden 7–6(4) 3–6 6–8; Frana/C. Miniussi d. Evernden/D. Lewis 6–4 3–6 7–6(4) 7–5; Miniussi lost to Evernden 7–6(4) 3–6 6–8; Frana d. Steven 6–3 6–3. **Germany d. Italy 3–2, Dortmund:** B. Becker d. P. Cane 3–6 6–1 6–4 6–4; M. Stich lost to O. Camporese 6–7(2) 1–6 3–6; Becker/E. Jelen lost to Camporese/D. Nargiso 6–4 4–6 6–7(6) 6–4 3–6; Becker d. Camporese 3–6 4–6 6–3 6–4 6–3; Stich d. Cane 7–6(4) 6–7(1) 7–5 6–1. **Yugoslavia d. Sweden 4–1, Zagreb:** G. Ivanisevic d. J.B. Svensson 6–2 4–6 6–3 6–4; G. Prpic d. S. Edberg 6–4 6–3 6–2; Ivanisevic/Prpic d. Edberg/P. Lundgren 6–4 6–4 6–4; Ivanisevic d. Edberg 6–4 6–2; Prpic lost to M. Gustafsson 2–6 3–6. **Czechoslovakia d. Austria 4–1, Prague:** P. Korda d. H. Skoff 6–3 3–6 6–7(9) 6–1 6–3; K. Novacek d. A. Antonitsch 7–6(5) 6–4 1–6 1–6 6–3; Korda/M. Srejber d. Antonitsch/Skoff 6–4 7–6(4) 0–6 6–4; Novacek lost to T. Buchmayer 6–7(7) 5–7; Srejber d. Antonitsch 7–6(5) 7–6(3). **France d. Israel 5–0, Rennes:** H. Leconte d. A. Mansdorf 6–3 7–6(3) 3–6 7–6(4); G. Forget d. G. Bloom 6–4 6–7(5) 6–2 6–4; Forget/Leconte d. Bloom/Mansdorf 7–5 6–4 6–3; Forget d. Mansdorf 6–4 6–2; Leconte d. Bloom 6–3 7–5. **Australia d. Belgium 5–0, Perth:** R. Fromberg d. F. De Wulf 6–4 6–3 1–6 6–4; W. Masur d. E. Masso 6–3 6–3 6–1; D. Cahill/T. Woodbridge d. Masso/L. Pimek 6–3 6–3 6–3; Fromberg d. Masso 6–3 1–6 6–3; Masur d. De Wulf 6–1 6–2. **QUARTER-FINALS** – **USA d. Spain 4–1, Newport, Rhode Island:** B. Gilbert d E. Sanchez 6–4 6–4 6–2; J. McEnroe d. T. Carbonell 6–3 6–2 6–1; R. Leach/J. Pugh d. S. Casal Sanchez 7–6(6) 6–3 7–6(3); McEnroe d. Sanchez 6–4 3–6 6–3; Leach lost to Carbonell 6–7(1) 7–5 4–6. **Germany d. Argentina 5–0, Berlin:** M. Stich d. M. Jaite 7–5 6–3 6–4; B. Becker d. J. Frana 6–4 6–4; E. Jelen/Stich d. Frana/C. Miniussi 7–5 6–7(3) 7–6(7) 6–7(7) 6–4; Becker d. Jaite 6–1 7–6(6); Stich d. Frana 6–7(10) 6–1 6–1. **Yugoslavia d. Czechoslovakia 4–1, Prague:** G. Ivanisevic d. P. Korda 6–1 7–6(3) 4–6 6–1; S. Zivojinovic lost to K. Novacek 1–6 6–4 4–6 5–7; Ivanisevic/Zivojinovic d. Korda/M. Srejber 7–6(5) 6–4 6–4; Ivanisevic d. Novacek 6–3 3–6 7–6(4) 3–6 6–4; Zivojinovic d. Korda 7–6(6) 2–6 8–6. **France d. Australia 3–2, Nimes:** G. Forget d. W. Masur 6–3 6–3 6–4; F. Santoro lost to R. Fromberg 3–6 4–6 6–7(4); Forget/H. Leconte d. M. Kratzmann/T. Woodbridge 6–7(2) 7–5 5–7 7–6(2) 6–4; Forget lost to Fromberg 7–6(2) 6–7(8) 3–6 3–6; Santoro d. Masur 6–3 6–4 4–6 6–1. **SEMI-FINALS** – **USA d. Germany 3–2, Kansas City:** A. Agassi d. M. Stich 6–3 6–1 6–4; J. Courier d. C/U Steeb 4–6 6–1 6–3 6–4; S. Davis/D. Pate lost to E. Jelen/Stich 4–3 6–4 6; Courier lost to Stich 4–6 5–7 4–6; Agassi d. Steeb 6–2 6–2 6–3. **France d. Yugoslavia 5–0, Pau:** G. Forget d. S. Muskatirovic 6–2 6–1 6–4; F. Santoro d. S. Zivojinovic 4–6 7–5 7–6(0) 3–6 6–3; A. Boetsch/Forget d. Muskatirovic/Zivojinovic 6–4 6–3 6–2; Forget d. Zivojinovic 6–1 3–6 6–2; Santoro d. Muskatirovic 6–7(1) 6–3 7–5. **FINAL** – **France d. USA 3–1, Lyon:** (French names first) G. Forget lost to A. Agassi 7–6 2–6 1–6 2–6; H. Leconte d. P. Sampras 6–4 7–5 6–4; Forget/Leconte d. K. Flach/R. Seguso 6–1 6–4 4–6 6–2; Forget d. Sampras 7–6 3–6 6–3 6–4; Leconte v. Agassi not played. Captains: France – Yannick Noah; USA – Tom Gorman. Non-playing team members: France – Olivier Delaitre, Arnaud Boetsch.

QUALIFYING ROUND FOR WORLD GROUP 1992

Great Britain d. Austria 3–1 (1 unfinished), Manchester: J. Bates d. T. Buchmayer 6–2 4–6 6–3 7–5; M. Petchey d. T. Muster 6–2 3–6 7–6(5) 6–2; Bates/N. Brown d. G. Mandl Muster 6–7(1) 6–3 6–0 7–5; Bates lost to Mandl 5–7 6–4 8–10; Buchmayer v. Petchey 6–6(6–5) unfinished. **Belgium d. Israel 4–1, Brussels:** E. Masso d. A. Mansdorf 3–6 7–6(3) 6–4 6–1; B. Wuyts d. G. Bloom 7–6(4) 6–1 5–7 6–2; F. De Wulf/T. Van Houdt lost to Bloom/S. Perkiss 6–7(4) 5–7 6–4 5–7; Wuyts d. Mansdorf 2 5–7 7–6(3) 6–1; Masso d. Bloom 7–6(6) 6–3. **Italy d. Denmark 4–1, Bari:** O. Camporese lost to F. Fetterlein 6–3 3–6 2–6 4–6; C. Pistolesi d. M. Tauson 6–1 6–2 7–6(4); Camporese/D. Nargiso d. Fetterlein/Tauson 3–6 3–6 6–4; Camporese d. Tauson 7–6(5) 6–1 6–2; Pistolesi d. Fetterlein 7–6(3) 6–3. **Brazil d. India 4–1, Sao Paulo:** J. Oncins d. R. Krishnan 6–2 6–2 6–3; L. Mattar d. L. Paes 6–4 6–3 6–2; N. Aerts/F. Roese lost to Krishnan/Paes 6–7(1) 7–6(5) 6–3 3–6 4–6; Mattar d. Krishnan 5–7 6–3 6–3 6–4; Oncins d. Paes 6–4 6–1. **Netherlands d. Mexico 5–0, Mexico City:** M. Koevermans d. L. Herrera 6–3 6–4 6–4; P. Haarhuis d. L. Lavalle 4–6 7–6(3) 7–6 6–3; R. Krajicek/J. Siemerink d. Lavalle/J. Lozano 6–2 6–3 6–4; Haarhuis d. Herrera 6–3 6–3; Koevermans d. Lavalle 6–2 6–4. **Switzerland d. New Zealand 5–0, Baden:** M. Rosset d. B. Steven 7–5 6–4 6–4; J. Hlasek d. K. Evernden 7–6(2) 6–4 6–3; Hlasek/Rosset d. Evernden/Steven 4–6 7–6(4) 6–4; Hlasek d. Steven 7–5 6–4; Rosset d. Evernden 7–6(3) 3–6 6–3. **Sweden d. Philippines 5–0, Manila:** N. Kulti d. F. Barrientos 6–3 6–1 6–4; C. Bergstrom d. R. So 6–1 7–5 6–1; R. Bergh/Bergstrom d. Barrientos/S. Palahang 6–4 6–2 6–2; Bergstrom d. Barrientos 6–0 6–4; Kulti d. So 6–2 7–6(3). **Canada d. Cuba 3–2, Havana:** A. Sznajder lost to M. Tabares 3–6 6–2 6–3 3–6

6–8; G. Connell d. J. Pino 7–6(2) 6–3 6–2; Connell/S. La Reau d. Pino/Tabares 6–4 7–6(4) 4–6 4–6 6–3; Connell d. Tabares 6–1 6–3 6–4; Sznajder lost to Pino 3–6 1–6.

ZONAL COMPETITION

GROUP I

EURO/AFRICAN ZONE – ZONE A

FIRST ROUND – Portugal d. Ireland 5–0, Porto: J. Cunha/Silva d. O. Casey 5–7 6–1 6–2 6–3; N. Marques d. P. Wright 6–3 7–5 6–2; Cunha/Silva-Marques d. Casey/Wright 6–1 6–4 6–1; Marques d. Casey 7–5 6–4; B. Mota d. S. Doyle 6–1 6–1. *Poland d. Romania 5–0, Poznan:* W. Kowalski d. A. Marcu 3–6 6–3 6–7(1) 7–6(3) 7–5; D. Nowicki d. D. Pescariu 6–3 6–3 5–7 7–6(5); T. Iwanski/Kowalski d. G. Cosac/F.Segarceanu 6–2 7–6(4) 7–6(5); Iwanski d. Pescariu 7–6(4) 1–6 6–2; Nowicki d. Marcu 6–7(1) 6–4 11–9.
SECOND ROUND – Netherlands d. Portugal 4–1, Lisbon: P. Haarhuis d. J. Cunha/Silva 4–6 6–0 6–4 6–1; M. Koevermans d. N. Marques 6–3 2–6 7–5 6–0; Haarhuis/Koevermans d. Cunha/Silva-Marques 4–6 7–5 7–6(5) 6–3; Koevermans d. Cunha/Silva 3–6 6–4 6–2; Haarhuis lost to Marques 6–4 4–6 4–6. *Great Britain d. Poland 4–1, Warsaw:* D. Sapsford d. W. Kowalski 7–6(3) 6–2 6–7(2) 6–1; J. Bates d. T. Iwanski 6–4 6–0 6–4; Bates/N. Brown d. Iwanski/Kowalski 6–2 7–5 3–6 6–7(3) 6–4; Bates lost to Kowalski 2–6 6–3 3–6; C. Wilkinson d. B. Dabrowski 7–6(7) 6–3.
RELEGATION PLAY-OFF – Romania d. Ireland 5–0, Bucharest: A. Pavel d. O. Casey 6–4 6–1 6–1; A. Marcu d. E. Collins 6–4 6–2 6–3; G. Cosac/F. Segarceanu d. Collins/P. Wright 4–6 6–4 6–2 7–6(4) 6–0; Pavel d. Wright 7–6(2) 6–3; Marcu d. S. Doyle 6–2 6–2.

ZONE B

FIRST ROUND – Finland bye. Denmark d. Morocco 5–0, Rungsted: F. Fetterlein d. K. Alami 6–4 6–3 6–1; M. Tauson d. Y. El Aynaoui 6–1 6–3 6–3; M. Christensen/Tauson d. Alami/M. Ridaoui 6–2 6–2 6–2; Tauson d. Alami 6–3 6–4; Fetterlein d. El Aynaoui 6–3 6–1. *USSR d. Hungary 4–1, Budapest:* A. Cherkasov d. A. Lanyi 6–3 6–3 6–3; A. Volkov d. L. Markovits 6–3 6–4 6–4; A. Chesnokov/D. Poliakov lost to Lanyi/Markovits 3–6 7–6(6) 4–6 4–6; Cherkasov d. Markovits 7–6(2) 7–5 6–3; Volkov d. S. Noszaly 6–3 6–3; *Switzerland bye.*
SECOND ROUND – Denmark d. Finland 3–2, Helsinki: M. Tauson lost to O. Rahnasto 7–6(2) 6–7(8) 6–3 6–7(3) 1–6; F. Fetterlein d. A. Rahunen 6–4 6–0 6–3; M.Christensen/Fetterlein d. Rahnasto/P. Virtanen 4–6 6–0 6–4 6–4; Christensen lost to Rahunen 4–6 4–6 1–6; Fetterlein d. Rahnasto 6–1 6–2 6–1. *Switzerland d. USSR 3–2, Davos:* M. Rosset d. A. Chesnokov 7–6(5) 5–7 3–6 6–4 11–9; J. Hlasek d. A. Cherkasov 7–5 7–5 6–3; Hlasek/C. Mezzadri d. Cherkasov/D. Poliakov 6–3 7–6(4) 6–3; Hlasek lost to Chesnokov 3–6 4–6; Rosset lost to Cherkasov 4–6 4–6.
RELEGATION PLAY-OFF – Hungary d. Morocco 5–0, Budapest: S. Noszaly d. A. Chekrouni 6–1 6–4 6–3; L. Markovits d. K. Alami 6–3 6–2 7–6(4); A. Lanyi/Markovits d. Alami/Chekrouni 6–3 6–4 4–6 3–6 6–3; Noszaly d. Alami 6–2 1–6 7–5; V. Nagy d. Chekrouni 6–4 6–1.

AMERICAN ZONE

FIRST ROUND – Brazil d. Peru 3–1 (1 not played), Sao Paulo: L. Mattar d. C. Di Laura 6–7(3) 6–3 6–2 6–1; J. Oncins d. J. Noriega 6–3 6–2 6–2; M. Menezes/F. Roese lost to Di Laura/Noriega 5–7 7–6(6) 6–7(4) 7–5 13–15; Mattar d. Noriega 6–2 6–1 7–5; Oncins v. Di Laura not played. *SECOND ROUND – Brazil d. Uruguay 4–1, Brasilia:* J. Oncins d. M. Filippini 6–4 6–4 6–7(2) 6–3; L. Mattar lost to D. Perez 6–2 5–7 4–6 4–6; N. Aerts/F. Roese d. Filippini/Perez 6–3 7–6(7) 6–3; Mattar d. Filippini 7–6(2) 6–4 6–3; Oncins d. Perez 6–4 6–3. *Cuba d. Paraguay 5–0, Havana:* J. Pino d. R. Alvarenga 6–1 6–1 5–7 4–6 6–1; M. Tabares d. R. Mena 6–2 6–0 4–6 6–2; Pino/Tabares d. Alvarenga/O. de la Sobera 6–2 7–5 6–4; Tabares d. Alvarenga 6–2 6–1; Pino d. Mena 6–4 4–6 6–3.

ASIA/OCEANIA ZONE

PRELIMINARY ROUND – India d. Thailand 5–0, Bangkok: L. Paes d. W. Thongkhamchu 6–3 6–1 6–4; S. Vasudevan d. N. Srichaphan 6–3 6–7(5) 4–6 6–2 6–3; Z. Ali/Paes d. W. Samrej/T. Srichaphan 1–6 7–6(4) 6–2 6–4; Vasudevan d. Thongkhamchu 6–3 6–2; Paes d. N. Srichaphan 6–4 6–4.
FIRST ROUND – India d. Indonesia 4–1, Jaipur: R. Krishnan d. B. Wiryawan 6–2 6–2 6–4; L. Paes d. D. Heryanto 6–4 6–3 6–2; Krishnan/Paes d. Heryanto/Wiryawan 6–2 6–3 6–3; Z. Ali lost to Heryanto 2–6 6–2 10–12; Paes d. B. Wijaya 6–2 6–4. *Philippines d. Japan 4–1, Kagoshima:* R. So d. S. Matsuoka 7–5 6–2 6–2; F. Barrientos d. D. Furusho 6–3 6–4 6–4; Barrientos/So lost to Matsuoka/T. Sato 6–7(9) 6–7(7) 3–6; Barrientos d. Matsuoka 6–3 6–4 6–2; So d. Sato 6–2 6–1.
SECOND ROUND – India d. Korea Rep. 3–2, New Delhi: R. Krishnan d. S-H. Ji 4–6 6–2 6–0 6–3; L. Paes lost to E-J. Chang 4–6 7–5 4–6 6–7(4); Krishnan/Paes d. Chang/Ji 7–6(5) 6–4 7–5; Krishnan lost to Chang 6–4 4–6 6–1 3–6 4–6; Paes d. Ji 7–6(5) 6–3 6–2. *Philippines d. China P.R. 4–1, Manila:* R. So

lost to J-P. Xia 7–5 7–6(3) 2–6 2–6 3–6; F. Barrientos d. B. Pan 6–3 6–3 6–2; Barrientos/S. Palahang d. Q-H. Meng/Xia 7–5 7–6(2) 7–5; Barrientos d. Xia 6–3 6–2 6–1; So d. Pan 6–1 6–2.

GROUP II

EUROPEAN ZONE

FIRST ROUND – Norway d. Bulgaria 5–0, Oslo: A. Haaseth d. O. Stanoichev 3–6 6–1 6–2 6–4; C. Ruud d. K. Lazarov 6–3 7–6(5) 7–6(1); A. Raabe/A. Rolfsen d. Lazarov/S. Tzvetkov 6–3 6–2 6–2; Haaseth d. Lazarov 6–2 4–6 8–6; Ruud d. Stanoichev 6–2 6–3. **Greece d. Cyprus 5–0, Nicosia:** A. Fikas d. A. Papamichael 6–4 6–4 6–2; T. Bavelas d. Y. Hadjigeorgiou 6–2 6–1 6–4; Bavelas/J. Rigas d. S. Charalambous/S. Constantinou 6–1 6–0 6–1; Bavelas d. Papamichael 6–1 6–2; Fikas d. Hadjigeorgiou 7–6(0) 6–3. **Luxembourg d. Monaco 5–0, Luxembourg:** J. Goudenbour d. B. Balleret 6–1 6–0 6–1; J. Radoux d. J. Seguin 6–4 6–4 6–3; S. Brueck/Goudenbour d. O. Peyret/Seguin 6–3 6–4 6–3; Goudenbour d. Seguin 6–1 6–3; Radoux d. C. Collange 6–2 6–1. **Turkey d. Malta 3–2, Marsa:** A. Karagoz d. G. Asciak 6–2 4–6 6–3 3–6 6–2; Y. Erkangil lost to C. Gatt 6–7(3) 2–6 6–4 0–6; M. Azkara/Karagoz lost to Asciak/Gatt 2–6 6–7(5) 2–6; Karagoz d. Gatt 4–6 6–1 3–6 7–6(3) 9–7; Erkangil d. Asciak 2–6 6–1 7–6(4) 4–6 6–4.

SEMI-FINALS – Norway d. Greece 4–1, Oslo: C. Ruud d. T. Bavelas 6–3 6–2 6–4; B. Pedersen d. G. Kalovelonis 6–4 6–3 2–6 3–6 8–6; Pedersen/A. Rolfsen d. Bavelas/Kalovelonis 6–2 6–1 6–4; Pedersen lost to Bavelas 6–1 5–7 8–10; Ruud d. Kalovelonis 6–3 3–6 6–2. **Luxembourg d. Turkey 5–0, Luxembourg:** J. Goudenbour d. Y. Erkangil 6–4 6–0 6–4; J. Radoux d. A. Karagoz 6–2 6–1 6–1; S. Bruck/Goudenbour d. M. Azkara/M. Ertunga 6–1 6–2 3–6 6–2; Goudenbour d. Karagoz 6–2 6–3; Radoux d. Erkangil 6–0 6–1.

FINAL – Norway d. Luxembourg 4–1, Oslo: A. Haaseth d. J. Goudenbour 7–6(5) 3–6 6–3 6–2; C. Ruud d. A. Paris 6–3 6–3 6–1; B. Pedersen/A. Rolfsen d. S. Brueck/Paris 7–5 6–3 7–5; Pedersen d. Goudenbour 6–2 6–1; Haaseth lost to J. Radoux 6–7(3) 6–7(0).

AFRICAN ZONE

FIRST ROUND – Zambia d. Cameroon 3–2, Ndola: F. Kangwa d L. Kemajou 2–6 6–3 6–2 6–2; S. Kangwa d. L. Ondobo 6–2 2–6 6–0 6–3; F. Kangwa/N. Simunyola lost to Kemajou/A. Mvogo 6–4 1–6 4–6 6–3 10–12; S. Kangwa lost to Kemajou 2–6 4–6 6–2 1–6; F. Kangwa d. Ondobo 6–4 6–4 4–6 6–1. **Kenya d. Congo 5–0, Nairobi:** E. Polo d. C. Ossombi 6–1 6–2 6–0; K. Bhardwaj d. C. Bemba 6–0 6–2 6–4; N. Odour/Polo d. Bemba/Ossombi 6–2 6–1 6–0; Odour d. Bemba 6–4 6–4; Bhardwaj d. Ossombi 6–1 6–2. **Cote d'Ivoire d. Algeria 3–2, Algiers:** C. N'Goran d. M. Benyebka 6–3 7–5 6–4; J. Nabi lost to A. Hameurlane 7–5 6–7(4) 2–1 6–1; C. N'Goran/E. N'Goran d. Benyebka/S. Tounsi 6–2 1–2 6 6–4 7–6(9); C. N'Goran d. Hameurlaine 6–1 6–3 7–6(3); Nabi lost to Benyebka 3–6 1–6. **Egypt d. Senegal 3–2, Cairo:** H. El Aroussy d. A. Berthe 6–3 6–2 7–6(4); T. El Sawy d. F. Berthe 5–7 6–1 6–1 6–2; El Sawy/H. Nasser lost to A. Berthe/F. Berthe 7–5 6–7(4) 2–6 7–6(4) 4–6; El Sawy d. A. Berthe 6–0 6–2 6–0; El Aroussy lost to F. Berthe 6–1 3–6 6–3 2–6 3–6.

SECOND ROUND – Nigeria d. Zambia 3–2, Ndola: K. Nwokedi lost to F. Kangwa 5–7 6–7(3) 6–3 6–7(3); N. Odizor d. S. Kangwa 2–4 ret.; Nwokedi/Odizor d. F. Kangwa/D. Sweeney 6–3 7–6(3) 6–7(4) 6–4; Odizor d. F. Kangwa 6–4 6–2 6–2; Nwokedi lost to Sweeney 6–7(4) 2–6. **Kenya d. Zimbabwe 4–1, Harare:** E. Polo d. G. Rodger 4–6 6–3 6–4 7–6(4); P. Wekesa d. G. Thomson 6–0 6–0 6–1; Polo/Wekesa d. M. Birch/Rodger 6–4 6–4 6–2; Wekesa d. Rodger 6–2 6–4; Polo lost to Thomson 6–3 6–7(8) 3–6. **Cote d'Ivoire d. Togo 5–0, Abidjan:** J. Nabi d. K. Agnamba 6–0 6–0 6–3; E. N'Goran d. K. Apeti 6–2 6–1 6–0; L. Ilou/N'Goran d. Agnamba/Apeti 6–2 6–2 6–7(4) 6–1; Nabi d. Apeti 3–6 6–1 7–5; Ilou d. M. Gbeboume 6–0 6–2. **Egypt d. Ghana 5–0, Cairo:** T. El Sawy d. M. Amoah 6–1 6–0 6–2; H. El Aroussy d. F. Ofori 6–7(5) 7–6(5) 2–0 ret.; El Aroussy/El Sawy d. K. Atiso/K. Dowuona 6–4 6–2 6–2; A. Ghonem d. Atiso 7–6(4) 7–5; El Aroussy d. Amoah 6–7(5) 7–6(4) 8–6.

SEMI-FINALS – Kenya d. Nigeria 3–2, Nairobi: E. Polo lost to N. Odizor 6–4 1–6 2–6 6–1 4–6; P. Wekesa d. Y. Sulieman 6–2 6–4 7–5; Polo/Wekesa d. Odizor/Sulieman 6–7(6) 7–6(5) 7–5 6–3; Wekesa d. Odizor 7–5 6–4 6–1; Polo lost to Sulieman 3–6 6–4 3–6. **Cote d'Ivoire d. Egypt 4–1, Abidjan:** C. N'Goran d. H. El Aroussy 6–2 6–0 6–2; E. N'Goran lost to T. El. Sawy 2–6 6–3 3–6 3–6; C. N'Goran/E. N'Goran d. El Aroussy/El Sawy 6–0 6–1 6–3; C. N'Goran d. El Sawy 6–2 6–4 6–1; E. N'Goran d. El Aroussy 6–2 6–0.

FINAL – Kenya d. Cote d'Ivoire 4–1, Nairobi: P. Wekesa d. J. Nabi 6–1 6–1 7–6(0); E. Polo lost to C. N'Goran 3–6 3–6 4–6; Polo/Wekesa d. C. N'Goran/E. N'Goran 4–6 7–6(8) 6–4 6–4; Wekesa d. C. N'Goran 7–5 6–0 6–2; Polo d. Nabi 6–3 7–6(5).

AMERICAN ZONE

FIRST ROUND – Dominican Rep. d. El Salvador 4–1, San Salvador: R. Moreno d. M. Tejada 4–6 5–7 6–4 6–4 6–4; G. De Leon lost to M. Merz 7–6(5) 3–6 6–7(5) 6–1 3–6; De Leon/Moreno d. Merz/J. Pineda 6–1 6–4 6–4; De Leon d. Tejada 6–4 6–3 3–6 6–1; Moreno d. Merz 6–4 7–5. **Ecuador d. Trinidad & Tobago 5–0, Port of Spain:** L. Morejon d. O. Adams 6–2 6–2 6–1; P. Campana d. M. Webster 6–2 6–2

6–2; Campana/Morejon d. Adams/C. Mark 3–6 5–7 7–6(2) 6–2 6–4; Campana d. Adams 6–4 7–6(7); Morejon d. Webster 6–4 6–2. *Venezuela d. Haiti 4–1, Port-au-Prince:* M. Ruah d. B. Lacombe 6–2 4–6 6–3 6–1; B. Colvee lost to B. Madsen 2–6 6–1 3–6 7–6(0) 3–6; H. Castillo/A. Mora d. Lacombe/R. Lamothe 3–6 7–5 6–3 6–2; Ruah d. Madsen 4–6 6–4 7–6(8) 6–3; Colvee d. Lacombe 7–6(4) 6–3. *Bahamas d. Costa Rica 4–1, Nassau:* J. Farrington lost to R. Brenes 7–6(4) 4–6 6–3 5–7 5–7; R. Smith d. C. Paez 6–0 6–2 6–2; Farrington/Smith d. Brenes/M. Delgado 6–1 6–2 6–1; Smith d. Delgado 6–0 6–4 6–1; Farrington d. Paez 6–4 6–4. *Barbados d. Bolivia 3–2, Cochabamba:* R. Ashby d. J. Medrano 4–6 7–6(4) 6–3 5–7 20–18; L. Eli lost to R. Navarro 6–7(1) 4–6 7–6(1) 6–3 3–6; Ashby/B. Frost d. R. Aguirre/Navarro 6–4 7–5 6–4; Ashby d. Navarro 7–6(4) 6–3 6–4; Eli lost to Medrano 5–7 7–6(4) 6–8. *Eastern Caribbean d. Guatemala 3–2, St. John's Antigua:* V. Lewis d. D. Chavez 6–1 6–7(1) 6–3 7–6(5); J. Maginley d. C. Chavez 4–6 3–6 7–5 6–4 9–7; Lewis/Maginley lost to D. Chavez/F. Sical 2–6 4–6 6–7(3); Lewis d. Sical 6–1 6–3 6–0; Maginley lost to D. Chavez 6–4 1–6 4–6. *Colombia d. Jamaica 3–2, Kingston:* M. Rincon lost to D. Burke 7–5 6–7(2) 3–6 2–6; A. Jordan d. N. Rutherford 5–7 7–6(6) 7–5 6–2; M. Hadad/Jordan lost to Burke/K. Hale 6–7(4) 6–7(7) 6–3 3–6; Rincon d. Rutherford 6–4 6–7(7) 7–5 4–6 6–1; Jordan d. Burke 6–3 6–2 6–4.

SECOND ROUND – Chile d. Dominican Rep. 5–0, Santiago: J-A. Fernandez d. G. De Leon 6–1 6–2 6–4; P. Rebolledo d. R. Moreno 6–2 6–1 6–1; H. Gildemeister/F. Rivera d. De Leon/Moreno 6–4 6–4 7–5; Rebolledo d. De Leon 6–3 6–1; Fernandez d. Moreno 6–4 6–3. *Venezuela d. Ecuador 3–2, Caracas:* B. Colvee lost to H. Nunez 6–7(6) 6–0 6–7(5) 5–7; M. Ruah d. L. Morejon 5–7 6–2 6–4 6–2; J. Bianchi/A. Mora lost to P. Campana/Nunez 6–4 3–6 6–7(5) 4–6; Ruah d. Nunez 6–4 6–4 6–3; Colvee d. Morejon 7–6(1) 3–6 7–5 6–3. *Bahamas d. Barbados 3–2, Nassau:* R. Smith d. L. Eli 6–1 6–3 6–1; J. Farrington lost to R. Ashby 6–7(5) 6–3 4–6 6–7(5); Farrington/Smith lost to Ashby/B. Frost 6–3 4–6 6–3 6–7(5) 12–14; Smith d. Ashby 7–5 7–5 5–7 6–4; Farrington d. Eli 6–2 5–7 6–7(4) 6–4 6–4. *Colombia d. Eastern Caribbean 5–0, St. John's Antigua:* J. Cortes d. V. Lewis 6–4 6–1 6–7(4) 6–4; A. Jordan d. J. Maginley 6–7(5) 6–0 7–5 6–2; M. Hadad/Jordan d. R. Hughes/J. Williams 6–2 3–6 7–5 6–3; Jordan d. Lewis 6–2 6–4; Cortes d. Williams 6–3 6–2.

SEMI-FINALS – Chile d. Venezuela 3–2, Santiago: J-A. Fernandez d. M. Ruah 3–6 6–2 3–6 6–1 6–3; P. Rebolledo d. N. Pereira 6–3 6–1 2–6 6–4; H. Gildemeister/G. Vacarezza lost to A. Mora/Pereira 4–6 6–1 6–7(5) 3–6; Rebolledo d. Ruah 5–7 6–3 6–2 6–4; Fernandez lost to Pereira 6–4 0–6 3–6. *Colombia d. Bahamas 4–1, Cali:* M. Hadad d. R. Smith 6–4 4–6 6–3 6–1; A. Jordan d. J. Farrington 6–2 6–2 6–2; J. Cortes/M. Rincon lost to Farrington/Smith 3–6 5–7 4–6; Jordan d. Smith 6–3 6–7(5) 6–7(4) 6–0 6–3; Hadad d. Farrington 6–4 6–2.

FINAL – Chile d. Colombia 3–1 (1 unfinished), Medellin: P. Rebolledo d. J. Cortes 6–3 6–0 6–1; J-A. Fernandez d. A. Jordan 6–4 7–5 6–3; H. Gildemeister/G. Vacarezza d. M. Hadad/Jordan 4–6 6–4 7–6(4) 6–3; Rebolledo lost to Jordan 6–2 3–6 5–7; Fernandez v Cortes 6–1 5–7 3–2, unfinished.

ASIA/OCEANIA ZONE

FIRST ROUND – Malaysia d. Saudi Arabia 4–1, Kuala Lumpur: V. Selvam d. K-H. Fitiani 6–0 6–2 6–3; N. Ramachandran lost to B-M. Al Mokial 4–6 6–7(7) 7–5 3–2, ret.; Selvam/W-R. Yousef d. Al Mokial/T-A. Ibrahim 6–1 6–2 6–1; Selvam d. Al Mokial 6–4 6–3 6–1; Ramachandran d. Ibrahim 6–3 6–3. *Bangladesh d. Bahrain 3–2, Manama:* S. Iftekhar lost to E-J. Abdul Aal 2–6 3–6 2–6; S. Jamaly d. S-R. Shehab 6–1 6–1 6–4; Iftekhar/Jamaly d. Abdul Aal/Shehab 6–2 6–2 6–3; Jamaly lost to Abdul Aal 6–2 6–4 6–7(5) 6–1 13–15; Iftekhar d. Shehab 6–3 3–6 6–1 7–5. *Sri Lanka d. Syria 5–0, Colombo:* U. Wallooppillai d. S. Mourad 6–1 6–0 6–0; A. Fernando d. J. Sheet 6–1 6–0 6–1; Fernando/J. Wijesekera d. A. Hafeez/Mourad 6–1 6–1 6–1; Fernando d. Mourad 6–0 6–0; Wallooppillai d. Sheet 6–0 6–0. *Singapore d. Kuwait 5–0, Singapore:* T-Y. Kho d. A. Al Ashwak 6–2 6–3 6–7(3) 6–2; W-Y. Liu d. K-H. Rashed 7–5 6–4 6–3; F. Ho/Liu d. Al Ashwak/Rashed 6–7(2) 4–6 7–6(4) 7–5 6–0; Liu d. Al Ashwak 6–2 6–4; Kho d. Rashed 1–6 6–3 6–2. *Hong Kong bye.*

SECOND ROUND – Pakistan d. Jordan 5–0, Amman: H. Ul-Haq d. H. Al-Ali 6–4 6–2 3–6 6–2; R. Malik d. E. Abou/Hamdeh 6–2 6–2 6–4; Malik/Ul-Haq d. Abou-Hamdeh/A. Abou Jaber 6–0 6–1 6–4; O. Rashid d. S. Bushnaq 6–3 6–2; Ul-Haq d. Abou-Hamdeh 7–6(2) 6–0. *Chinese Taipei d. Malaysia 3–2, Kuala Lumpur:* Y-H. Lien d. V. Selvam 5–7 6–3 6–4 6–4; C-H. Liu lost to A. Malik 3–6 4–6 2–6; Lien/Liu d. Malik/Selvam 7–5 4–6 6–7(5) 7–6(1) 6–1; Lien lost to Malik 3–6 4–6 6–7(4); Liu d. Selvam 7–6 6–4 6–7(5) 7–6(6) 6–3. *Sri Lanka d. Bangladesh 5–0, Dhaka:* A. Fernando d. S. Iftekhar 6–0 6–1 6–1; R. De Silva d. S. Jamaly 6–4 6–2 7–5; De Silva/Fernando d. Iftekhar/Jamaly 6–4 6–4 6–3; Fernando d. Jamaly 6–4 6–3; De Silva d. Iftekhar 7–5 5–7 6–2. *Hong Kong d. Singapore 5–0, Singapore:* C. Grant d. W-Y. Liu 6–0 6–0 6–0; M. Walker d. F. Ho 6–1 6–0 6–1; M. Bailey/Walker d. Ho/Liu 6–1 7–5 6–1; Walker d. T-Y. Kho 6–1 6–0 6–3; L. Pang d. Ho 6–2 6–2 6–2.

SEMI-FINALS – Chinese Taipei d. Pakistan 5–0, Taipei: Y-H. Lien d. H. Ul-Haq 6–3 6–3 6–3; C-H. Liu d. R. Malik 7–6(3) 6–3 6–0; Lien/Liu d. Malik/Ul-Haq 6–1 6–4 6–1; C-J. Chen d. O. Rashid 6–3 6–4; Liu d. Ul-Haq 6–2 3–6 6–3. *Hong Kong d. Sri Lanka 3–2, Causeway Bay, Hong Kong:* M. Bailey d. A. Fernando 7–6(7) 1–6 4–6 6–3 6–2; M. Walker lost to U. Wallooppillai 5–7 6–4 5–7 2–6; Bailey/Walker d. R. De Silva/Fernando 7–6(9) 5–7 5–7 6–3 6–1; Walker d. Fernando 6–2 6–3 6–0; Bailey lost to Wallooppillai 1–6 2–6.

FINAL – Chinese Taipei d. Hong Kong 3–2, Taipei: Y-H. Lien d. C. Grant 6–2 6–2 6–3; C-J. Chen lost to M. Walker 4–6 3–6 3–6; Lien/C-H. Liu d. M. Bailey/Walker 7–6(6) 6–4 6–2; Lien lost to Walker 6–7(6) 4–6 4–6; Chen d. Grant 7–5 6–3 6–3.

DAVIS CUP **PRIZE MONEY** (provided by NEC)

WORLD GROUP COMPETITION: Champion Nation $316,000. Runner-up $158,000. Semi-finalists $119,000. Quarter-finalists $71,000. First-round winners $26,000. Qualifying-round winners $20,000. Qualifying-round losers $14,000.
ZONAL COMPETITION: Group 1: $4,500 per tie. *Bonuses:* Second-round winners $3,000. First-round winners $2,000. Play-off/preliminary round winners $1,000. *Group II:* $3,000 per tie. *Bonuses:* Winners $3,500. Semi-finalists $2,000. Quarter-finalists $1,000. First-round winners $1,000.

Qualifying Round

Zonal Winners and World Group First Round Losers	Promoted to World Group 1992
AUSTRIA	Great Britain
Great Britain	3–1
Israel	Belgium
Belgium	4–1
ITALY	ITALY
Denmark	4–1
Brazil	Brazil
India	4–1
NETHERLANDS	NETHERLANDS
Mexico	5–0
New Zealand	Switzerland
Switzerland	5–0
SWEDEN	SWEDEN
Philippines	5–0
Cuba	Canada
Canada	3–2

DAVIS CUP by NEC 1991
World Group

FIRST ROUND	SECOND ROUND	SEMI-FINALS	FINAL	WINNERS
USA	USA			
Mexico	3–2	USA		
SPAIN	SPAIN	4–1		
Canada	4–1		USA	
ARGENTINA	ARGENTINA		3–2	
New Zealand	4–1	GERMANY		
GERMANY	GERMANY	5–0		
Italy	3–2			FRANCE
Yugoslavia	Yugoslavia			3–1
SWEDEN	4–1	Yugoslavia		
Czechoslovakia	Czechoslovakia	4–1		
AUSTRIA	4–1		FRANCE	
Israel	FRANCE		5–0	
FRANCE	5–0	FRANCE		
Belgium	AUSTRALIA	3–2		
AUSTRALIA	5–0			

Capital letters denote seeded nations.

Zonal Competition
ZONE A

FIRST ROUND	SECOND ROUND	WINNERS
NETHERLANDS Bye Portugal Ireland Poland Romania Bye GREAT BRITAIN	NETHERLANDS Portugal 5–0 Poland 5–0 GREAT BRITAIN	NETHERLANDS 4–1 GREAT BRITAIN 4–1

ZONE B

FIRST ROUND	SECOND ROUND	WINNERS
FINLAND Bye Morocco Denmark USSR Hungary Bye SWITZERLAND	FINLAND Denmark 5–0 USSR 4–1 SWITZERLAND	Denmark 3–2 SWITZERLAND 3–2

AMERICAN ZONE GROUP I

FIRST ROUND	SECOND ROUND	WINNERS
URAGUAY Bye Brazil Peru Cuba Bye Bye PARAGUAY	URAGUAY Brazil 3–1 Cuba PARAGUAY	Brazil 4–1 Cuba 5–0

ASIA/OCEANIA ZONE GROUP I

PRELIMINARY ROUND	FIRST ROUND	SECOND ROUND	WINNERS
India Thailand	KOREA Bye India 5–0 Indonesia Philippines Japan Bye CHINA	KOREA India 4–1 Philippines 4–1 CHINA	India 3–2 Philippines 4–1

EUROPEAN ZONE GROUP II

FIRST ROUND	SEMI-FINALS	FINAL	WINNERS
NORWAY Bulgaria Greece Cyprus Luxembourg Monaco Malta TURKEY	NORWAY 5–0 Greece 5–0 Luxembourg 5–0 TURKEY 3–2	NORWAY 4–1 Luxembourg 5–0	NORWAY 4–1 (Promoted to Euro/African Zone Group I 1992)

AFRICAN ZONE GROUP II

FIRST ROUND	SECOND ROUND	SEMI FINALS	FINAL	WINNERS
NIGERIA				
Bye	NIGERIA	NIGERIA		
Zambia	Zambia	3–2		
Cameroon	3–2		Kenya	
ZIMBABWE	ZIMBABWE		3–2	
Bye		Kenya		Kenya
Kenya	Kenya	4–1		4–1
Congo	5–0			(Promoted to
Algeria	Côte d'Ivoire			Euro/African
Côte d'Ivoire	3–2	Côte d'Ivoire		Zone Group I
Bye		5–0		1992)
TOGO	TOGO		Côte d'Ivoire	
Senegal	Egypt		4–1	
Egypt	3–2	Egypt		
Bye		5–0		
GHANA	GHANA			

AMERICAN ZONE GROUP II

FIRST ROUND	SECOND ROUND	SEMI-FINALS	FINAL	WINNERS
CHILE				
Bye	CHILE	CHILE		
Dom. Repub.	Dom. Repub.	5–0		
El Salvador	4–1		CHILE	
ECUADOR	ECUADOR		3–2	
Trin. & Tob.	5–0	Venezuela		CHILE
Haiti	Venezuela	3–2		3–1
Venezuela	4–1			(Promoted to
Bahamas	Bahamas			American Zone
Costa Rica	4–1	Bahamas		Group I 1992)
Bolivia	BARBADOS	3–2		
BARBADOS	3–2		COLOMBIA	
East Carib.	E. Carib.		4–1	
Guatemala	3–2	COLOMBIA		
Jamaica	COLOMBIA	5–0		
COLOMBIA	3–2			

ASIA/OCEANIA ZONE

FIRST ROUND	SECOND ROUND	SEMI-FINALS	FINAL	WINNERS
PAKISTAN				
Bye	PAKISTAN	PAKISTAN		
Iraq	Jordan	5–0		
Jordan	w/o		CH TAIPEI	
CH TAIPEI	CH TAIPEI		5–0	
Bye		CH TAIPEI		CH TAIPEI
Saudi Arabia	Malaysia	3–2		3–2
Malaysia	4–1			(Promoted to
Bangladeshi	Bangladesh			Asia/Oceania
Bahrain	3–2	SRI LANKA		Zone Group I
Syria	SRI LANKA	5–0		1992)
SRI LANKA	5–0		HONG KONG	
Singapore	Singapore		3–2	
Kuwait	5–0	HONG KONG		
Bye	HONG KONG	5–0		
HONG KONG				

Capital letters denote seeded nations.

THE *FEDERATION CUP by NEC*

Henry Wancke

For many years the *Federation Cup by NEC* has been described as a 'festival of women's tennis'. The 29th staging of this competition for national teams at Nottingham reflected this description most aptly for the organisers delivered a festival in the truest sense of the word. It was opened by HRH The Princess of Wales.

The focal point remained the competition, which attracted 56 nations to make it the largest entry ever in *Federation Cup* history. But the other activities, centred on a purpose-built tennis court for coaching and displays, surrounded by marquees and various exhibits plus public facilities – including a large exhibition area for tennis goods and accessories – created the very special festival atmosphere which will long be associated with Nottingham 1991. The purpose behind all this extra activity was to use the *Federation Cup* to promote tennis, not just for the surrounding area, but within the UK as a whole. And it succeeded, for some 77,000 attended the full week – another record – both to participate in what was offered off-court, and to watch the best players in the world compete for their respective nations.

Nottingham will also be remembered as the last occasion when an open entry was employed for, at future venues, preliminary rounds for places in the 32 strong Main Draw would be discontinued. From 1992, separate qualifying competitions will be played for the last four places. The 1991 competition also marked the last year of the Consolation Event. To replace it there will be Play-Offs between the first round losers to establish which nations retain a place in the following year's draw, with 4 nations eventually dropping into the aforementioned Qualifying competitions.

The favourites were the defending champions, the USA, despite being seeded 2, for no one could ignore their record in *Federation Cup* competition over the years. Led by Zina Garrison, they were going for a fifteenth title and fielded a strong team which included Jennifer Capriati and Gigi Fernandez with Mary Joe Fernandez making her debut. Monica Seles was expected to make her own debut with the Yugoslav team, but controversially failed to make an appearance which resulted in her nation being fined and eventually being relegated into the 1992 zonal Qualifying competitions.

Spain, the top seeds, were the second favourites. They relied on stalwarts Arantxa Sanchez-Vicario and Conchita Martinez, whilst Germany, seeded third and playing for the first time as a united nation, called on the services of Steffi Graf and the up-and-coming Anke Huber to lead their bid for a second title. Czechoslovakia, playing without Helena Sukova who had helped them to four of their five overall wins, relied on Jana Novotna and Radka Zrubakova, both with excellent records in the competition.

Rain disrupted some of the proceedings during the week but not enough to prevent the competition reaching its eventual conclusion on time, though a number of ties were restricted to 2–0 winning leads.

All the top four seeded nations progressed to the semi-finals with Spain the only team reaching that stage without dropping a rubber. The Germans, however, suddenly found that their challenge was weakened when Steffi Graf withdrew with a shoulder injury. This had flared up during her match against Patricia Hy. However, she refused to give in and eventually kept her undefeated *Federation Cup* singles record intact by beating the Canadian 6–3 3–6 6–2. That proved to be her last match in the competition as she flew to Germany for medical attention. Anke Huber was promoted to the No. 1 singles slot and kept the German momentum going into the semis where Spain beat them 3–0.

Meanwhile the USA had endured a bad moment in the quarter-finals when Jennifer

A first Federation Cup *victory for the popular Spaniards in Nottingham where, in a thrilling final, they beat the Americans 2–1.* *(T. Hindley)*

Capriati suffered her first loss. Judith Wiesner (Austria), playing solidly and volleying securely, saved two match points before she claimed the opening rubber 6–2 0–6 8–6 to record the American's first ever loss in *Federation Cup* play. Mary Joe Fernandez then had the task of levelling the score to give their doubles pair a chance to keep them in the competition. Happily for the Americans she did – and so did the doubles players. The US then went on to beat the Czechs 3–0 and took on Spain for the 1991 title.

The Championship match was one which did more than justice to the competition. To a packed house basking in glorious sunshine, Conchita Martinez faced Jennifer Capriati in the first rubber and played entirely from the baseline to keep the American on the defensive. Martinez refused to be hurried and successfully disorientated her opponent to claim the first set 6–4. Leading 6–5 in the second, she was poised to claim the first rubber for Spain and came within two points of her objective. But Capriati suddenly found her rhythm and fought back to turn the tables. The 15-year-old American levelled the match and eventually went on to win 4–6 7–6(7-3) 6–1 after 133 minutes of play.

From the start of the second rubber Arantxa Sanchez-Vicario attacked Mary Joe Fernandez with great determination. She harried her opponent and despite a few momentary lapses in the second set, claimed the match with a positive 6–3 6–4 victory to put Spain back in contention.

As things stood, the Americans should have won the doubles comfortably on the basis of the experience their pair, Zina Garrison and Gigi Fernandez, could call on. Furthermore, the Spaniards sent their singles players back on, so the Americans were also fresher than their opponents. It was no surprise when they swept into a 4–0 lead. But then, ominously, Gigi Fernandez was broken; despite that, the Americans secured the first set 6–3. In the second set the Spaniards jumped into a 5–0 lead and drew level two games later. Using every psychological tactic that they could muster they never allowed the American pair back into the match and claimed their first ever *Federation Cup* title with that 3–6 6–1 6–1 doubles victory.

'We lost our rhythm,' Marty Riessen, the US Team Captain commented. 'We were happy to be at 1-all and felt we had a chance in the doubles,' he stated wryly.

The success of Nottingham as a *Federation Cup* venue immediately put them into contention for staging the 1993 event. However, the ITF decided later in the year that Frankfurt would stage the competition for two years starting in 1992.

PRELIMINARY EVENT
QUALIFYING ROUND – *Israel d.* **Venezuela 3–0** (I. Berger d. N. Marra 6–4 6–1; Y. Segal d. M. Mazzota 6–4 6–4; I. Berger/L. Zaltz d. M. Francesa/M. Mazzota 7–6 (7–4) 6–3); **Romania d. Cuba 3–0** (R. Dragomir d. B. Rodriguez 6–1 6–4; I. Spirlea d. R. Pichardo 6–3 4–6 6–3; L. Bujor/I. Spirlea d. B. Rodriguez/I. Concepcion 6–2 6–4); **Poland d. Uruguay 3–0** (M. Mroz d. L. Olave 7–6 (7–3) 6–1; K. Nowak d. P. Miller 6–0 6–0; M. Mroz/K. Toodorowioz d. P. Millor/C. Brauco 6 3 6 2); **China P.R. d. Luxembourg 2–1** (L. Yang lost to A. Kremer 5–7 5–7; T. Min d. C. Goy 1–6 6–4 6–3; T. Min/L. Fang d. C. Goy/R. Moyen 6–3 6–2); **Denmark d. Mexico 3–0** (K. Ptaszek d. I. Petrov 5–7 6–2 6–3; S. Albinus d. L. Novelo 6–2 6–3; K. Ptaszek/S. Albinus d. L. Novelo/A. Gallardo 7–6 (8–6) 6–3); **Paraguay d. Chile 2–1** (L. Schaerer d. P. Cabezas 6–1 7–5; R. De Los Rios d. M. Miranda 6–2 6–3; L. Schaerer/R. De Los Rios lost to P. Cabezas/M. Miranda 3–6 3–6); **Greece d. Malta 2–1** (C. Papadaki d. H. Asciak 6–4 6–2; A. Kanellopoulou d. C. Curmi 6–2 6–4; L. Soulti/C. Papadaki lost to C. Curmi/H. Asciak 6–0 4–6 2–6); **Portugal d. Chinese Taipei 2–1** (T. Couto d. Y. Lin 6–0 6–1; S. Prazeres lost to S. Wang 4–6 3–6; T. Couto/S. Prazeres d. S. Lai/S. Wang 6–4 3–6 6–4).

MAIN DRAW
FIRST ROUND – *Australia d.* **Japan 2–1** (N. Provis d. A. Kijimuta 6–0 6–1; R. McQuillan lost to N. Sawamatsu 4–6 3–6; N. Provis/E. Smylie d. K. Date/M. Kidowaki 6–3 6–3); **Poland d. France 2–1** (M. Mroz lost to M. Pierce 4–6 2–6; K. Nowak d. N. Tauziat 4–6 6–4 6–4; M. Mroz/K. Teodorowicz d. N. Tauziat/M. Pierce 6–4 6–4); **Canada d. Denmark 2–1** (R. Altur lost to K. Ptaszek 2–6 6–2 4–6; P. Hy d. S. Albinus 7–5 6–1; J. Hetherington/P. Hy d. K. Ptaszek/S. Albinus 6–3 6–4); **China P.R. d. Brazil 3–0** (T. Min d. C. Chabalgoity 7–5 4–6 6–0; L. Fang d. L. Corsato 6–0 6–2; L. Yang/J. Yi d. L. Corsato/S. Giusto 6 2 6–3); **Finland d. Romania 3–0** (N. Dahlman d. R. Dragomir 6–0 6–4; P. Thoren d. I. Spirlea 6–2 6–2; A. Aallonen/N. Dahlman d. R. Dragomir/I. Spirlea 4–6 6–2 6–2); **Bulgaria d. Hungary 3–0** (M. Maleeva d. P. Schmitt 6–1 6–2; K. Maleeva d. V. Csurgo 6–0 6–2; M. Maleeva/K. Maleeva d. V. Csurgo/A. Muzamel 6–1 6–2); **USSR d. Paraguay 3–0** (E. Brioukhovets d. L. Schaerer 6–4 7–5; N. Zvereva d. R. De Los Rios 6–2 6–2; N. Medvedeva/L. Savchenko d. R. De Los Rios/L. Schaerer 6–3 6–2); **Indonesia d. Yugoslavia 3–0** (S. Wibowo d. L. Pavlov 6–3 6–3; Y. Basuki d. N. Ercegovic 6–4 7–5; Y. Basuki/S. Wibowo d. N. Ercegovic/L. Pavlov 6–2 6–2); **Spain d. Belgium 2–0** (C. Martinez d. D. Monami 6–3 6–1; A. Sanchez d. S. Appelmans 7–6 (7–5) 6–3; doubles not played due to lateness and weather); **Germany d. Greece 3–0** (A. Huber d. C. Papadaki 3–6 6–3 6–3; S. Graf d. A. Kanellopoulou 6–1 6–2; B. Rittner/S. Graf d. A. Kanellopoulou/C. Papadaki 6–3 6–0); **Great Britain d. New Zealand 2–0** (C. Wood d. C. Toleafoa 6–3 6–2; M. Javer d. B. Cordwell 6–3 6–1; doubles not played due to lateness and weather); **Switzerland d. Argentina 2–0** (E. Zardo d. F. Labat 2–6 6–2 8–6; M. Maleeva-Fragnière d. M. Paz 6–0 7–6 (7–5); doubles not played due to lateness and weather); **Czechoslovakia d. Sweden 2–0** (R. Zrubakova d. M. Strandlund 6–0 6–1; J. Novotna d. C. Dahlman 7–6 (7–5) 6–2; doubles not played due to lateness and weather); **Austria d. Portugal 3–0** (J. Wiesner d. T. Couto 6–2 6–2; B. Paulus d. S. Prazeres 7–5 6–0; P. Ritter/M. Maruska d. T. Couto/S. Prazeres 6–1 6–1); **USA d. Netherlands 2–0** (Z. Garrison d. N. Jagerman 7–5 6–4; J. Capriati d. M. Bollegraf 6–2 6–3; doubles not played due to lateness and weather); **Italy d. Israel 2–1** (L. Ferrando lost to I. Berger 2–6 4–3 3–6; R. Reggi d. Y. Segal 0–6 6–4 6–4; A. Cecchini/L. Ferrando d. I. Berger/L. Zaltz 6–3 6–7 (7–1) 6–3).
SECOND ROUND – *Germany d.* **Canada 2–1** (A. Huber d. R. Simpson-Altur 6–4 6–3; S. Graf d. P. Hy 6–3 3–6 6–2; A. Huber/B. Rittner lost to J. Hetherington/P. Hy 7–5 1–6 2–6); **Italy d. Great Britain 2–0** (R. Reggi d. M. Javer 2–6 7–6 (7–4) 9–7; S. Cecchini d. J. Durie 7–5 6–4; doubles not played due to lateness); **Austria d. Finland 2–1** (J. Wiesner d. N. Dahlman 7–5 6–1; B. Paulus lost to P. Thoren 0–6 3–6; J. Wiesner/P. Ritter d. P. Thoren/A. Aallonen 6–3 7–6 (10–8)); **Indonesia d. Poland 2–1** (S. Wibowo lost to M. Mroz 2–6 1–6; Y. Basuki d. K. Nowak 6–1 6–1; S. Wibowo/Y. Basuki d. M. Mroz/K. Teodorowicz 6–1 6–1); **Switzerland d. China P.R. 2–1** (E. Zardo d. T. Min 6–2 5–7 6–1; M. Maleeva-Fragnière d. L. Fang 6–7 (7–5) 7–5 6–2; M. Maleeva-Fragnière/C. Caverzasio lost to J. Yi/L. Fang 1–3, retired due to injury); **Czechoslovakia d. USSR 2–1** (R. Zrubakova d. E. Brioukhovets 6–3 3–6 6–2; J. Novotna d. N. Zvereva 6–4 6–1; E. Sviglerova/R. Zrubakova lost to L. Savchenko/N. Zvereva 1–6 4–6); **Spain d. Australia 3–0** (C. Martinez d. N. Provis 6–0 2–6 7–5; A. Sanchez d. R. McQuillan 6–1 3–6 6–2; C. Martinez/A. Sanchez d. E. Smylie/K. Godridge 6–3 6–4); **USA d. Bulgaria 3–0** (J. Capriati d. M. Maleeva 7–5 6–2; M. Fernandez d. K. Maleeva 6–2 6–3; C. Fernandez/Z. Garrison d. M. Maleeva 6–2 6–1).
QUARTER-FINALS – *Czechoslovakia d.* **Switzerland 2–1** (R. Zrubakova d. E. Zardo 6–1 5–7 6–4; J. Novotna d. M. Maleeva-Fragnière 6–4 6–4; R. Rajchrtova/J. Novotna lost to M. Maleeva-Fragnière/C. Caverzasio 4–6 1–2, retired ill); **USA d. Austria 2–1** (J. Capriati lost to J. Wiesner 2–6 6–0 6–8; M. Fernandez d. B. Paulus 6–1 6–1; Z. Garrison/G. Fernandez d. P. Ritter/J. Wiesner 6–4 6–1); **Germany d. Italy 2–1** (B. Rittner d. R. Reggi 6–3 1–6 6–3; A. Huber d. A. Cecchini 6–2 6–3; B. Rittner/A. Huber lost to L. Ferrando/F. Bonsignori 0–1, Rittner retired ill); **Spain d. Indonesia 2–0** (C. Martinez d. S. Wibowo 6–2 6–0; A. Sanchez d. Y. Basuki 4–6 7–5 6–4; doubles not played due to injury of C. Martinez and A. Sanchez).
SEMI-FINALS – *Spain d.* **Germany 3–0** (C. Martinez d. B. Rittner 6–4 6–1; A. Sanchez d. A. Huber 6–1 2–6 6–2; C. Martinez/A. Sanchez d. B. Rittner/A. Huber 6–1 6–1); **USA d. Czechoslovakia 3–0** (J. Capriati d. R. Zrubakova 6–3 6–4; M. Fernandez d. J. Novotna 6–4 0–6 9–7; G. Fernandez/Z. Garrison d. E. Sviglerova/R. Rajchrtova 6–2 6–3).
FINAL – *Spain d.* **USA 2–1** (C. Martinez lost to J. Capriati 6–4 6–7 (3) 1–6; A. Sanchez d. M. Fernandez 6–3 6–4; C. Martinez/A. Sanchez d. G. Fernandez/Z. Garrison 3–6 6–1 6–1).

NEC WORLD YOUTH CUP

Spain met with contrasting fortune in the NEC World Youth Cup Finals played on clay courts at the Real Club de Polo, Barcelona, Spain from 11–15 September 1991.

After impressive results in their European Qualifying Zone and in individual tournaments throughout the year, the Spanish boys were seeded No. 1 and the girls team at No. 2. However, the Spanish girls were one of the two seeded nations to fall in the first round of the girls event, comprehensively beaten 3–0 by their rivals, Italy. The Argentine girls, on their favourite surface, got off to a good start with Paola Suarez defeating Maaike Koutstaal of the Netherlands, only for the Dutch No. 1, Lara Bitter, to level the tie at 1–1 by defeating Valeria Strappa in straight sets. The deciding doubles seemed to be going the way of the seeded team when Argentina took the first set 6–3 but the Dutch girls fought back to take the next two sets and the tie.

In the boys' first round, the only African representatives, Cote d'Ivoire, could not have had a tougher start when they found themselves up against the favourites, Spain. Despite losing the two singles rubbers they did not let Spain have everything their own way, taking the doubles rubber in a close fought match 6–4 3–6 6–3.

A total of 5 of the 8 first round matches in the boys' event went to the deciding doubles, with only Switzerland recording a 3–0 victory over their opponents, Brazil.

Seeded two, Czechoslovakia had a hard match with New Zealand on the show court. After the Czechs had won the opening rubber between the second singles players, James Greenhalgh levelled the tie for New Zealand with an impressive victory over the Czechoslovakian No. 1 Filip Kascak. However, the seeded team proved superior in the deciding doubles and posted a relatively comfortable 6–0 7–5 win to take the tie.

Probably the most exciting tie of the day took place between the Canadian boys and unseeded Indonesia. Bobby Mahal had a terrific struggle against Andrian Raturandang who saved two match points before beating the No.2 Canadian 2–6 7–6 9–7. The Canadian No. 1, Russell Stuart, also had a struggle against Champy Halim but managed to emerge as victor 7–5 2–6 6–3, to level matters. The deciding doubles was a topsy-turvy match with Canada taking the first set 6–3 only for Indonesia to fire themselves up and fight back to take the next two sets 6–4 6–2.

The girls' quarter-finals were not good for the higher seeded nations. The second favourites, Czechoslovakia, who included the current No.1 18-and-Under Junior World Ranking leader, Zdenka Malkova, were well beaten by the German team. Japan and USA both lost in their deciding doubles matches to the Netherlands and Paraguay respectively, and Italy came down to earth in the doubles against the USSR.

In the boys' event Spain continued their good run at the expense of Switzerland, and Indonesia found the United States in good form. Germany just managed to win their singles matches against France when Christian Vinck defeated Nicolas Escude 7–6 6–7 6–3 and Lars Rehmann edged past Sebastien Corbelli 6–3 4–6 6–3 – both crucial victories as France looked very impressive in the remaining doubles rubber.

Czechoslovakia were not having the easiest time in their attempt to justify their second seeding and Israel almost proved too difficult a hurdle. David Skoch defeated Israeli Lior Mor only for Noam Behr to level the tie with victory over Filip Kascak. The doubles was a very exciting match with Israel cheered on by all the other nations who had qualified from their regional zone. Czechoslovakia simply could not clinch the match, despite taking the first set 6–2. They lost the 2nd set on a tie-break and in the third set whenever they broke Israel's serve, they promptly followed by losing their own. Israel held match point at 6–5 but a dispute over his first serve caused Danny Erez to lose his concentration, and his double fault proved to be very costly as Czechoslovakia went on to take the final set 8–6.

The eventual finalists in the girls' competition had a relatively easy passage through the semi-finals when Germany defeated the Netherlands 3–0 and Paraguay defeated the USSR by the same score. In the boys' event Spain continued to look good with a 3–0 victory over USA while Czechoslovakia also took both singles rubbers in a 2–1 win over Germany. Importantly for the winners, Filip Kascak posted his first singles win at No. 1 singles, beginning to look more at home on the slow clay courts.

For Finals days the two main show courts were made into one court and both the boys' and girls' finals were televised and watched live by reasonable crowds at the Royal Polo Club.

The girls' final, held on Saturday, was watched by special guest Juan-Antonio Samaranch, President of the International Olympic Committee, together with Brian Tobin, President of the International Tennis Federation. Germany have a fine record in the World Youth Cup competition with their girls winning the event in 1989 and finishing in 3rd position in 1990. Paraguay, however, have had disappointing results over the last few years but had now made up for this by reaching the finals, which generated enormous interest at home. Paraguayan television, radio and officials of their National Association were ringing constantly throughout the matches for up-dates on the score. Larissa Schaerer did nothing to dampen enthusiasm when she defeated the Germany No. 2 Heike Rusch 7–6 6–3. The impressive German No.1, Marketa Kochta, had not dropped a singles set all week, however, and she soon levelled the tie with a 6–3 6–1 victory over Rossana de los Rios. When de los Rios and Schaerer took the first set of the deciding doubles against Kirstin Freye and Kochta, Paraguayan radio could contain themselves no longer and took a live commentary, broadcast by telephone for the remainder of the match. The tense battle finally ended with victory for the German girls, with Kochta adding a gold medal to the bronze she had won the previous year.

The closeness of the girls' final had greatly contributed to the atmosphere but there was even more enthusiasm the following day when Spain contested the boys final against Czechoslovakia. The personality of the competition, Gonzalo Corrales, got the host nation off to a perfect start with a 7–5 7–5 victory over David Skoch. Filip Kascak, however, found his best form of the week to level matters at 1–1 with 6–4 7–5 victory over Spanish No. 1 Albert Costa. Singles players for both nations then combined for the final doubles match with Czechoslovakia looking to be on top holding a 4–2 lead in the first set. Corrales, we later learnt, had told his partner to relax and although Costa had replied 'you relax at 4–2 down, first set' it did the trick as the Spanish boys took that set and the next for a 6–4 6–2 victory, much to the delight of the spectators. It was a wonderful reward for the organisers following their hard work leading up to and during the competition.

Placement ties were held throughout the week and were as competitively fought as the main draw matches. In the match for 3rd place, the Dutch girls defeated the USSR in the deciding doubles and German boys responded to the achievement of their girls' team by taking both singles rubbers and the tie against USA.

The week in Spain was rounded-off with a sightseeing day for the players and captains, organised by the Spanish Tennis Federation. The day began with a visit to a most attractive beach on the Costa Brava for some relaxation, followed by a tour to the impressive Olympic facilities of the Barcelona '92 Olympic Games.

NEC WORLD YOUTH CUP 1991

Boys' and Girls' 16 & Under International Team Championships
58 nations competed, 54 taking part in the boys' event and 49 in the girls' event. Final stages took place in Barcelona, Spain 11–15 September.

FINAL POSITIONS – BOYS: Champion nation – Spain; runners-up – Czechoslovakia; 3rd – Germany; 4th – USA; 5th – Switzerland; 6th – France; 7th – Israel; 8th – Indonesia; 9th – Netherlands; 10th – Argentina; 11th – Brazil; 12th – Chile; 13th – New Zealand; 14th – Cote d'Ivoire; 15th – Canada; 16th – India. *GIRLS:* Champion nation – Germany; runners-up – Paraguay; 3rd – Netherlands; 4th – USSR; 5th – USA; 6th – Japan; 7th – Czechoslovakia; 8th – Italy; 9th – Argentina; 10th – Spain; 11th – Korea, Rep of; 12th – Colombia; 13th – Canada; 14th – China, P.R; 15th – India; 16th – Zimbabwe.

BOYS' CHAMPIONSHIP – Semi-finals: Spain d. USA 3–0 (G.Corrales d. E.Taino 7–5 7–5; A.Costa d. J.Jackson 6–3 6–2; Corrales/Costa d. Jackson/J.Appel 6–4 6–0). *Czechoslovakia d. Germany 2–1* (D.Skoch d. L.Rehmann 6–1 6–1; F.Kascak d. C.Tambue 6–4 4–6 6–4; Kascak/Skoch lost to Rehmann/ C.Vinck 6–4 4–6 4–6). *3rd place play-off: Germany d. USA 2–1* (C.Vinck d. E. Taino 6–3 6–4; L.Rehmann d. J.Jackson 6–4 3–6 6–4; Rehmann/C.Tambue lost to Jackson/J.Appel 0–6 6–4 1–6). *Final: Spain d. Czechoslovakia 2–1* (G.Corrales d. D.Skoch 7–5 7–5; A.Costa lost to F.Kasck 4–6 5–7: Corrales/Costa d. Kascak/Skoch 6–4 6–2).

GIRLS' CHAMPIONSHIP – Semi-finals: Germany d. Netherlands 3–0 (H.Rusch d. M.Koutstaal 2–6 6–2 6–3; M.Kochta d. L.Bitter 6–0 6–3; K.Freye/Kochta d. Bitter/Koutstaal 6–7 6–4 6–0). *Paraguay d. USSR 3–0* (L.Schaerer d. V.Zvereva 4–6 6–3 6–3; R.de los Rios d. J.Lutrova 3–6 7–5 6–3; M.Benitez/ Schaerer d. E.Likhovtseva/Zvereva 6–2 7–5). *3rd place play-off: Netherlands d. USSR 2–1* (M.Koutstaal lost to V.Zvereva 6–7 3–6; L.Bitter d. J.Lutrova 6–3 6–0; Bitter/Koutstaal d. E. Likhovtseva/Lutrova 6–2 6–4). *Final: Germany d. Paraguay 2–1* (H.Rusch lost to L.Schaerer 6–7 3–6; M.Kochta d. R.de los Rios 6–3 6–1; K.Freye/Kochta d. de los Rios/Schaerer 5–7 6–3 6–3).

Magdalena Maleeva, 16, the youngest of the three Bulgarian sisters and already a Federation Cup *player, set high standards for juniors everywhere.* (R. Adams)

NTT WORLD JUNIOR TENNIS 1991

The first NTT World Junior Tennis event, the ITF Team Championships for boys and girls of 14 and under, was successfully completed in Yamanakako, Japan, on 9 August.

This event, sponsored by Nippon Telephone and Telegraph Corporation, was organised by the Japan Tennis Association, in co-operation with the ITF, and was held at the lovely Yamanakako Tennis Club at the foot of Mount Fuji.

Unfortunately Mount Fuji was a spectacle denied to most except the very early risers, as bad weather disrupted the first few days of play and forced the competition indoors. The seeded nations all received a bye in the first round, but the first day of play saw several hard-fought and entertaining matches.

In the boys' event, Daniel de Melo (Brazil) set his country on the way to victory over Australia with a 6–4 5–7 6–4 win against Scott Graham. The honours for the longest matches, if not tie, however, belong to Japan and Morocco. After a comparatively short opening match, Takeshi Yoshino (Japan) defeated Kasim Azdad (Morocco) 6–4 7–6, but Morocco fought back through Mohamed El Mehdi Tahiri, who defeated the Japanese No. 1, Yaoki Ishii, 7–6 4–6 5–7. All the singles players combined to contest the deciding doubles which caused a great deal of excitement amongst the local supporters. To their delight the Japanese pairing finally triumphed 6–3 6–7 7–5, on their 5th match point.

In the girls' event, the host nation, Japan, were victorious over Brazil, but the hardest fought tie of the day was between Argentina and Yugoslavia. Katarina Djuric (Yugoslavia) had travelled to Japan at only a few hours notice, when two first choice team members had been forced to withdraw at the last minute. Despite this, she pushed her opponent Marina Maina to the limit, before just losing out 3–6 7–5 6–7. Her compatriot, Tatjana Jecmenica, newly promoted to first singles player, was to remain unbeaten all week, and she duly dispatched Valentina Solari 6–3 6–3 to level the tie at 1–1. The deciding doubles was a straight sets win for Argentines Maina and Solari over Djuric and Jecmenica, but the 6–4 6–4 scoreline does not really indicate what a tense match it was for all involved.

Day two saw the seeded nations in action. It was a tough day for the seeds as they had been unable to practise due to bad weather, and they were all playing opponents who had already completed a match. However, despite a scare for Israel and Spain, who each dropped their opening match in the boys' event, and Madagascar, who did the same in the girls' event, all seeds came safely through with just one exception. Canada, the No. 3/4 seeds, got away to a good start with Michelle Smith recording a 6–2 6–4 win over Maria-Rosa Calio. However, Francesca Lubiani proved too strong for Eva Januskova and levelled the tie at 1–1 for Italy before teaming with Maria Zavagli to defeat Januskova and Alison Nash 6–2 6–3, to clinch the tie.

The semi-finals saw the top four seeded nations face each other in the boys' event and these ties proved to be the highlights of the week. Israel, the No. 3/4 seeds, managed to split the singles rubbers with top seeded Spain when their No. 1 Eyal Erlich defeated Juan-Antonio Saiz 7–5 7–5. The Spanish, however, had an outstanding doubles player in their team, Jose-Maria Vicente, who teamed with Alberto Martin to defeat Erlich and Avi Carmi 4–6 6–3 6–1.

In the other boys' semi-final Italy (2), faced Argentina (3/4) and again, after the two singles matches, the tie was level at 1–1. The Italians, captained by the experienced ex-*Davis Cup* player Paolo Bertolucci, finally came through with a comfortable win, Claudio Zoppi and Paolo Tabini defeating Gustavo Cavallaro and Gaston Tedesco 6–2 6–4.

The girls' semi-finals saw the No. 1 seeds Czechoslovakia against unseeded Italy, and the No. 2 seeds Australia against the No. 3/4 seeds Madagascar. Lenka Cenkova (Czechoslovakia) started with a strong performance against Maria-Rosa Calio, winning 6–2 6–2, only for Lubiani to reply with a great performance for Italy against the Czech No. 1 Alena Havrlikova, defeating her 6–1 7–6. Cenkova and Havrlikova, however, proved too strong in the deciding doubles, defeating Lubiani and Zavagli, 6–0 6–3.

Australia's Captain, Jan Blackshaw, certainly won't mind us pointing out that she was almost more excited than her players in their semi-final against Madagascar. Annabel Ellwood got Australia off to a good start taking her match against Natacha Randriantefy 6–1 6–2, only for Natacha's sister, Dally, to level matters with a 6–4 6–4 victory over Aarthi Venkatesan. For the deciding match the Australians brought in Esther Knox to partner Ellwood against the Randriantefy partnership. In a tense, close match the Australians finally emerged as winners, 7–5 6–4.

On finals day, which saw the best weather of the competition, members of the Japanese Royal Family, Prince and Princess Takamado, were present, as well as the President of the ITF, Brian Tobin. The victors in each event proved dominant in the singles rubbers with both the Spanish boys and the Czechoslovak girls taking winning 2–0 leads.

The Czech girls went on to complete a 3–0 victory, although the Australians fought hard to the very end. The final match of the day was the boys' doubles between Spain and Italy. Although the tie was by this stage already over, neither side was prepared to give any ground, much to the delight of the spectators. The match was a fitting tribute to the event, with the Italian team of Andrea Ciceroni and Paolo Tabini finally emerging as victors. Their 5–7 6–4 8–6 win over Alberto Martin and Jose-Maria Vicente was as sporting as it was entertaining.

The week's activity was not confined to the main events. Ties for defeated teams had been organised to decide overall placings and these were as hotly contested as the main draw matches.

NTT WORLD JUNIOR TENNIS 1991
ITF Team Championships for 14 & Under
FINAL POSITIONS – BOYS: Champion nation – Spain; runners-up – Italy; 3rd – Israel; 4th – Argentina; 5th – USSR; 6th – Mexico; 7th – Brazil; 8th – Japan; 9th – Sweden; 10th – Morocco; 11th – Australia; 12th – Canada. **GIRLS:** Champion nation – Czechoslovakia; runners-up – Australia; 3rd – Madagascar; 4th – Italy; 5th – Japan; 6th – Germany; 7th – Argentina; 8th – Canada; 9th – Yugoslavia; 10th – Korea, Rep. of; 11th – Mexico; 12th – Brazil.
BOYS' CHAMPIONSHIP – Semi-finals: Spain d. Israel 2–1 (J-A. Saiz lost to E. Erlich 5–7 5–7; A. Martin d. A. Carmi 7–5 6–0; Martin/J-M. Vincente d. Carmi/Erlich 4–6 6–3 6–1). **Italy d. Argentina 2–1** (P. Tabini d. R. Cerdera 7–5 6–4; C. Zoppi lost to G. Cavallaro 2–6 6–2 2–6; Tabini/Zoppi d. Cavallaro/G. Tedesco 6–2 6–4). **3rd place play-off: Israel d. Argentina 3–0** (E. Erlich d. R. Cerdera 6–4 6–3; S. Baranes d. G. Tedesco 6–2 6–1; Baranes/Erlich d. G. Cavallaro/Cerdera 6–1 6–4). **Final: Spain d. Italy 2–1** (J-A. Saiz d. P. Tabini 6–2 6–1; A. Martin d. C. Zoppi 6–2 7–6; Martin/J-M. Vincente lost to A. Ciceroni/Tabini 7–5 4–6 6–8).
GIRLS' CHAMPIONSHIP – Semi-finals: Czechoslovakia d. Italy 2–1 (A. Havrlikova lost to F. Lubiani 1–6 6–7; L. Cenkova d. M-R. Calio 6–2 6–2; Cenkova/Havrikova d. Lubiani/M. Zavagli 6–0 6–3). **Australia d. Madagascar 2–1** (A. Venkatesan lost to D. Randriantefy 4–6 4–6; A. Ellwood d. N. Randriantefy 6–1 6–2; Ellwood/E. Knox d. Randriantefy/Randriantefy 7–5 6–4). **3rd place play-off: Madagascar d. Italy 3–0** (D. Randriantefy d. F. Lubiani 6–2 6–2; N. Randriantefy d. M-R. Calio 6–0 6–4; H. Rabeson/N. Randriantefy d. Lubiani/M. Zavagli 6–2 6–3). **Final: Czechoslovakia d. Australia 3–0** (A. Havrlikova d. A.Venkatesan 6–1 6–2; L. Cenkova d. A. Ellwood 7–5 6–2; Cenkova/Havrlikova d. Ellwood/E. Knox 6–2 7–6).

*The elegant Australian, Jack Crawford, whose graceful style set new standards in his
country where he was a national hero in the 1930s.* *(Hulton Picture Library)*

GENTLEMAN JACK

Allan Kendall

I was all of four-and-a-half when I first saw my uncle Jack play tennis. One point was all I saw, but it made a vivid impression on me. This is how it happened.

My mother's hairdressing salon was right next door to the cinema in the country town of Orange, New South Wales, where we lived. One day an usherette came dashing in, positively shrieking for my mother to come quickly. Jack Crawford, it seemed, was on the screen in a newsreel clip describing the Wimbledon final. My mother fled next door with a pair of scissors still in her hand and with me in tow, just in time to see her brother complete his famous 1933 victory against Ellsworth Vines.

Of course, I had no idea how mighty a moment that was for the family and for Australia, but I certainly remember the excitement. The cinema audience clapped and cheered and the usherette picked me up and gave me a hug and a kiss.

In those childhood days I don't remember thinking it odd that everyone seemed to know my uncle Jack. After all he came to Orange to play in our tournaments. Then when we moved country towns to Albury, there he was again, playing exhibition matches.

At school the two sportsmen all the kids idolised were Jack Crawford and Don Bradman. Their photos were the ones we saw in shop windows advertising the Nestlés Pictorial Collection of Sporting Heroes. It was great when you got a Crawford or a Bradman in your chocolate bar. They were always worth two of any other hero in a swap.

As a schoolboy, I took all that for granted. Although Jack was famous, he was still my uncle and when I was in Sydney on holiday I would think nothing of asking him to give me a hit at White City. And he did, as any uncle should. We got on famously.

It was only later that I began to realise he was not just any uncle and that he was, in fact, a unique figure in the tennis world. Yet when I eventually came to try and assess his prodigious achievements and gauge their significance, I found Jack himself very little help. He was self-effacing to a degree and always understated his own record, largely because the records themselves interested him little. It was the game and its people he loved.

And how they loved him, his legion of fans across the world. To them he was, quite simply, the most beautiful tennis player who had ever lived. The Crawford style – easy, flowing, graceful – was what people always wanted to talk about . . . and wanted to emulate. In my countless conversations with enthusiasts who had seen him play there would come this moment, as though someone had just pressed a pleasure button, when they would say '. . . oh, Jack! He would just . . .', then the words fail, the face takes on a blissful look, the eyes gaze vacantly into the distance of hallowed memory and the arm rises in slow motion to demonstrate a perfect backhand swing. Oh, the graceful arc of that sweeping sliced backhand!

Who cared who was the greatest or who had won the most Slams? As it happens Jack and the French Musketeer, Jean Borotra, each won 17 of the major titles. This was more than any of the other great stars of the 1930s – Cochet (16), Budge (14), Perry (14), Lacoste (11) and Vines (6) – but that was hardly the point. For those admirers Jack was the **only** tennis player and the joy he gave was unique. Crawford could not be reduced merely to a catalogue of wins.

More, perhaps, than any player in history, Jack Crawford was watched for his style alone. In awarding him the Blue Riband for style over his main rival, Germany's Baron Gottfried von Cramm, author Paul Metzler wrote '. . . Crawford was the supreme racquet-handler, making beautiful strokes from almost every ball he received.'

In his own day Crawford was often compared with Henri Cochet. Today there is no parallel. There have been glimpses, perhaps, in McEnroe, Nastase, Goolagong, Mecir – all graceful, easy stylists in an age of jerk and grunt – but even they did not play as effortlessly as Crawford. It was sometimes said that he hypnotised audiences or cast a spell. 'He brought more joy to tennis galleries around the world than possibly anyone in the history of tennis', wrote tennis journalist Ron McLean: and from Al Laney, the leading American sportswriter of the time, 'I do not think any tennis player has given me more genuine pleasure than Jack Crawford.'

Stanley Doust, himself an Australian *Davis Cup* player who settled in England and became dean of tennis writers on Fleet Street, named Crawford the most popular Wimbledon winner in history. A press report from the 1937 Championships noted, in passing, that 'as usual' the Jack Crawford picture postcards had sold out before the others.

Queen Mary made no bones about her views. Crawford was her favourite player and she said so. Only for Crawford did she leave her Royal Box seat on Centre Court to stand with the crowd on an outside court just to watch him play. The photograph of her standing with the King on the steps alongside No.3 court is one of my most cherished possessions. And a moment from the presentation ceremony at Wimbledon in 1933 which made the world smile:

'How old are you Crawford?,' asked the King.

'He was 25 on 22nd of March,' said the Queen!

In his own country Jack Crawford was a Pied Piper throughout a magnificent career spanning thirty years. Even when he gave up competitive play, people would drain from Centre Court matches in Sydney to watch him play a social game on an outside court.

So where did he come from, this sporting phenomenon? Who was the gifted coach who masterminded such a brilliant career? The simple and astonishing truth is that he came from nowhere and never had a lesson in his life.

Young Jack grew up on an isolated farm at Urangeline in the bush, learning to play as best he could. There had been Crawfords living in the Riverina district of Southern New South Wales since the first Crawford had migrated from Argyleshire in the mid-1800s. It was 'Craw's' father, my grandfather Jack, who built the first tennis court in the area and the local farmers used to visit for a social game on Sundays. They were all modest players. Jack senior did not play much. My grandmother did, but she whacked the ball with two hands – a lady ahead of her time, and certainly no model for the graceful Jack junior. Anyway, young Jack was not considered old enough to play with the adults. The older children were away at school so Jack simply played against a brother he could beat easily – or against the side of the house. That was it! There was no competitive play at that time. He did not even see a good player until he came to the city at the age of 13. Yet by then he was already a match-winner with a beautiful, natural style!

Although he cannot have realised it at the time, young Jack was lucky in having to learn against a wall. Where he hit against the side of the house (which he did incessantly) there was very little runback. Accordingly he had to play rising balls or low volleys all the time. Blessed with natural timing, he developed a flair for taking the ball early; without prompting he used the Continental grip, so suitable for quick play when there was no time to readjust the hand on the racquet handle. Everyone else used Eastern or Western grips.

However, none of this explains the 'effortless grace'. That remains a mystery. My mother simply says, 'Oh, he always played like that!!.' No help at all. One can easily accept that a John Bromwich, with that weird but effective style, was self-taught. But a Jack Crawford?

There are other clues. He had to hit up accurately to avoid breaking windows. And he seems to have practised hitting objects placed on the court – shades of Suzanne Lenglen, but in Jack's case it apparently was his own idea. Then there was the mental side. Although his shrewd old father had never seen top class tennis played, he seemed to have an instinctive feel for the game. He and Jack would talk tactics together for hours on end.

Jack was uncommonly perceptive, too, which might help to explain his uncanny anticipation. I remember once playing a club doubles with him and being astonished when, all of 60 seconds into the warm-up, he said 'My chap's no good wide on the forehand and he can't hit his backhand down the line if he's moving.'

He was also blessed with an equable temperament. My mother cannot remember a single incident when Jack, even as a very young child, lost his temper. A hint perhaps of the cool match-winner who was later to impress Norman Brookes.

Thus equipped he arrived in Sydney at the age of 13 and at once started winning mixed doubles at the local church club with weak, older ladies against seasoned senior pairs. He simply banished his poor partner to the side fence. She would serve or return, then flee, leaving the 13-year-old maestro to play singles!

Jack languished in the church mixed for a couple of years and then came a series of giant leaps for which there are no satisfactory explanations. He was invited to the elite grass-court club, White City, to try for the junior inter-State team. In his first match on grass he beat the best junior in the State. Then, quite suddenly, he was the best junior in the land. Suddenly again he won his first open tournament – the State doubles with Harry Hopman (the first of ten). Then, astonishingly, he had beaten the reigning champion of Australia, J.B.Hawkes. The tennis establishment was incredulous. In three years, with compara-tively little experience of tournament play, he had jumped right to the top. When he beat the great Jean Borotra in the first international match against France in 1928, Australia knew it had a world-beater. The rest is history.

He had attracted crowds from the beginning. In the mid-1920s they came to see the freak kid who made tennis look so easy and was already beating the senior champions. Then, when he began to beat visiting overseas stars who were invited out to play him, attendances leapt dramatically. After Borotra he faced Satoh and Harada from Japan and Allison, Gledhill and the reigning world champion, Ellsworth Vines, from America. All of them fell to Crawford.

In 1933, when he again beat Vines to win Wimbledon, Australians everywhere shared in the excitement through the first 'live' radio broadcast from Wimbledon to Down Under. More than any champion before him he entered into the lives of ordinary Australians. For them he was already Mr Tennis, a legend in his own lifetime with the characteristic long white flannels, the cricket shirt buttoned at the wrist, and the unmistakable flat-topped racket. He was universally admired as 'Gentleman Jack', a great champion who, in the words of a recent obituary, '. . . was loved for his beautiful artistry, his unfailing graciousness and his instinctive sportsmanship.' Ironically, Jack himself disliked the 'Gentleman' tag; he thought it was unfair on the other gents in the game.

Then came a terrible hiccup. Fred Perry! In 1934 the Englishman dethroned Crawford in Australia, and later at Wimbledon. When Perry returned to Australia at the end of the year, however, Crawford met him in the New South Wales final at the White City and, saving a match-point, beat him in five wonderful sets before a record crowd of nearly 11,000 ecstatic fans. For five minutes they cheered hysterically and did so again in Melbourne weeks later when Crawford again beat Perry to win his fourth Australian title. 'The King is on his throne again', blazoned the headlines.

It was a new pinnacle for Australian tennis. Crawford's victories and his extraordinary popularity had done more than boost national pride. He had put Australia on the map and lifted the status of the Australian title from that of a minor, local event to that of a great international Championship where the world's best competed. But, more, he had engen-dered a fascination with the game of tennis among his fellow citizens. Attendances had doubled and what had been a minor sport was now a major one. He had laid down the tracks for future generations to follow.

Everyone wanted to play like Jack Crawford. There was that something about him that set racket arms a-twitching. Before Crawford hardly anyone in Australia had played his elegant, low-wristed, free-flowing, Continental-grip style of tennis. After Crawford, almost everyone did – or tried to. The Crawford style became the Australian style. Some, like Adrian Quist, copied him directly. Others, like Hoad, modelled themselves on someone who had copied Crawford, or were coached by someone who had. Either way, the styles of Quist, Sedgman, Hoad, Rosewall, Cooper, Emerson, Laver, Anderson, Roche, Stolle, Newcombe – all are in the Crawford mould. They attacked from the net more than he did, but they all hit the ball in the Crawford way. That is a matter of style.

Don Budge thought that the obsession with Crawford's style obscured the fact that he was in fact a great tennis player. So, just how good was Crawford? According to Australian journalist George McGann . . . 'Budge rates Crawford as the greatest Australian he ever met and places him far above Bromwich, Quist, Pails, and Sedgman.' Budge had reason to respect Crawford. In their epic *Davis Cup* match of 1936, played in Philadelphia, Crawford held match point against him and lost it on a foot-fault call – the only one of the match Budge went on to win a titanic struggle 13–11 in the fifth set. Quist said it was one of the greatest matches he ever saw.

Ellsworth Vines also rates Crawford highly. He thought there was little to choose between Budge, Perry, Crawford and himself. 'We were about on a par,' he told me.

Press reports of the time – I have read hundreds at my grandparents' house in Bondi – often talked of the curious Vines-Perry-Crawford triangle. 'Vines beats Perry, Perry beats Crawford, Crawford beats Vines.' There is no doubt, however, who was top dog in 1933. That was Crawford's greatest year and one of the greatest in tennis. When he won Wimbledon that year it was his thirteenth consecutive tournament win. There has been no parallel in men's tennis since. In winning the Australian, French and Wimbledon titles he became the first player in history to win three of the four major titles in one year.

The Wimbledon final against Vines was described by A. Wallis Myers, the doyen of English tennis writers, as '. . . one of the finest matches in the history of the Championships.' Al Laney named it 'The best final I ever saw at Wimbledon.'

Suzanne Lenglen, in a note to Crawford after the match, wrote: 'You played the most marvellous and perfect tennis I have ever seen.' That note is now in the Wimbledon Lawn Tennis Museum.

When Crawford reached the final at Forest Hills, the press buzzed with excitement. Crawford, it seemed, was about to rewrite the history books. John Kieran, the sports columnist of the *New York Times*, wrote: 'If Crawford wins, that would mean something like scoring a Grand Slam on the courts, doubled and vulnerable.' That was the first time that anyone had used the term Grand Slam in association with tennis.

Crawford led by two sets to one in that final against Perry but lost in five. He thus failed by a single set to become the first winner of the Grand Slam and the concept, conceived in 1933, lay dormant until 1938 when Allison Danzig revived it in celebration of Budge's wonderful feat.

Jack had been suffering from insomnia for three weeks in New York and couldn't relax. Before the final Sidney Wood had said to him, 'You'll never beat Perry in that state. Leave it to me. I'll put a tonic in your pot of tea' – the pot Jack always had at courtside. Only afterwards did he discover that Sidney had administered some Kentucky Bourbon! This became quite a talking point at the time but Jack himself refused to offer it as an excuse. To the press he simply said, 'Did anyone notice that Fred played rather well?'

In terms of today's prize money, how much I wonder would Crawford have won in 1933? He would have been a multi-millionaire, certainly. By the year's end he had won 16 tournaments from 19 finals. In 1991 Monica Seles amassed over $2.4 million for 10 wins from 16 finals.

For Australian tennis, Jack Crawford had created, single-handed, a golden age. In 1933–34, he reached seven consecutive Grand Slam finals – all four in 1933 and the Australian, French and Wimbledon in 1934 – a feat unequalled in men's tennis, before or since. (For the record, Budge and Laver both reached six.)

In 1935, Crawford was also clearly the number one doubles player. With three different partners (Quist, McGrath and Hopman) he won the Australian, French and Wimbledon titles, the Championships of Italy and Germany, plus all the major State titles in Australia.

Many fans preferred to watch Crawford in doubles because it was there they saw more of his artistry on the volley, especially the low volley – 'superb,' said McGann, 'with his great racket control, nothing was beyond him.'

He was no slouch in mixed, either, winning three consecutive Australian titles with his wife Marjorie, the French with Peggy Scriven and Wimbledon with the great Elizabeth Ryan. In all he won 17 singles, doubles and mixed events from some 32 Grand Slam finals.

Throughout his life Jack Crawford suffered badly from asthma. As a child he nearly died from it, my mother tells me. In later years it was aggravated by sea travel and he was not always at his best abroad. It is at home that his record is really startling.

Between 1926 and 1949, over a span of 23 years, his tally of major State and National titles in Australia was a phenomenal 69. In a land of champions, that record has never been approached. Pat Cash, for example, has won 6.

Long after he had peaked in the mid-1930s, the great Crawford would still appear from time to time. In 1940 he played a glorious match to beat *Davis Cup* hero John Bromwich in the National semi-finals before losing to Quist. Several weeks later he beat both of them in a State title in Dubbo – Quist in the morning and Bromwich in the afternoon!

From his twilight years after the war I still hold some fond memories. 'Craw', as he was universally known within the game, touching 40, beating the 20-year-old Frank Sedgman; 'Craw' tottering to victory in five sets over Billy Sidwell and nearly beating Dinny Pails the next day in the fifth; and then, at 43, 'Craw' dashing out from his office one lunch time to beat a startled young champion of 16 years called Lew Hoad in a city exhibition match. The skill was there to the last.

Looking at old film clips of this stately gentleman strolling around the baseline, young pro's of today must find it very difficult to believe that old 'Craw' was any good. His contemporaries had the same problem! Bunny Austin described Crawford as looking like someone who had just popped into the Vicar's for a Sunday knock. At your end of the court, Bunny said, it did not feel like that at all. (Austin lost 5 out of 6 matches to Crawford).

I played uncle Jack every Sunday for years. He was well past his best, but still a shock to the system. He attacked from the baseline; there was none of this standing back near the netting and swapping high bounces. He took everything on the rise and gave you no time. He treated your best length with contempt and played it with absolute certainty and piercing accuracy – an accuracy matched only by Bobby Riggs, according to Julius D. Heldman of *World Tennis*.

My grandfather loved to describe one freak rally he saw Jack play at White City where he raised the chalk on the baseline twelve times in a row. He played chessboard tennis with great subtlety, using every inch of your court – drops, angles you didn't even know existed, perfect length drives that shot through '. . . like a ton of lead', to quote Vines. And everything took you by surprise because, as Norman Brookes said '. . . the concealment of his shots was extraordinary.'

It was the snap of the racquet head around the outside of the ball that did the damage. He could get that 'weight' into the shot from any position and he would vary it with the wrist. The 'flow' always looked the same but it was infinitely varied. The body language of Eastern and Western grip players give more clues. Crawford gave you nothing. He was totally unreadable either for pace or direction. So, he simply ran you ragged; then he hit a winner! To the spectators it all looked ridiculously easy. As you were left running the wrong way they would chuckle as if deciding that they really must hit a few winners like that themselves next Sunday!

In my lifetime two strokes have given me goose-pimples. One is Budge's backhand, the other is Crawford's forehand. 'One of the greatest shots in tennis,' said Harry Hopman. 'He could thread the eye of a needle with it and he had unbelievable control of the cross-court angles.'

Cannonballs? He would step in on those as if he had all the time in the world – even against Vines whose cannonball serves left skid marks 18 inches long on the turf at Wimbledon. 'It took me a year to learn how,' he once told me apologetically, as though he had been a slow learner!

Perry thought it unwise to go to the net on serve against Crawford because his returns were too good. Even when you got there, the passing shots were a problem. Cochet described them as 'miraculous' after losing the 1933 French final to Crawford 8–6 6–1 6–3.

Meanwhile, as you are engaged in your enforced cross-country at your end, what is Crawford doing? Standing still! The occasional potter to keep the circulation going. Quite eerie. 'He was always there,' said Vines. Or, if you prefer Quist: 'His anticipation was simply phenomenal.' When you consider that the seamless and smoother ball of the early 1930s was, as Vines says, much faster through the air than the ball used today, Crawford's ability to cover the court so effortlessly was all the more remarkable. They once filmed Crawford's feet for a whole match just to see how he did it. He moved. . . well. . . sort of invisibly.

Jack Crawford would never have been selected for a modern Institute of Sport. He did not look like an athlete. He did not care to run. A casual stroll, perhaps. He had skinny legs. He was badly asthmatic. He had smoked from the age of ten. He wasn't good at other sports. He made a duck the only time he played cricket.

In later years he joked about that and would speak of the all-round sporting ability of Don Bradman and Fred Perry. 'Don and Fred would have been champions at anything they played,' he would say, 'But me? I was only good for hitting a tennis ball over the net.'

But how he hit it! Yes, for all his lack of normal athletic prowess, on a tennis court Jack Crawford was, unquestionably, a genius.

Crawford during his memorable 1933 Wimbledon victory over Ellsworth Vines, the greatest men's final ever, in the opinion of those who witnessed it.

(Hulton Picture Library)

GRAND SLAM CHAMPIONSHIPS

AUSTRALIAN OPEN CHAMPIONSHIPS
FRENCH OPEN CHAMPIONSHIPS
WIMBLEDON CHAMPIONSHIPS
US OPEN CHAMPIONSHIPS

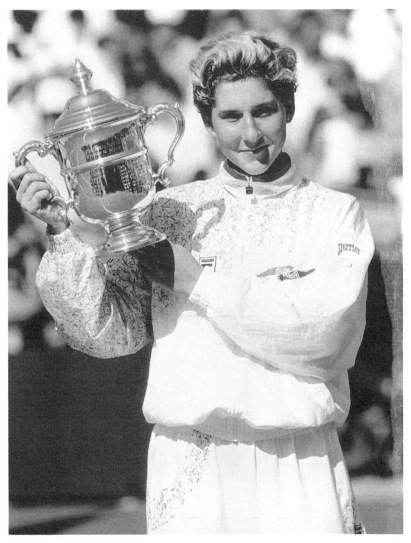

With her three Grand Slam victories in Melbourne, Paris and New York, and success in the Virginia Slims Championships, Monica Seles set the seal on a triumphant year in which she reached the final of all 16 tournaments she contested, winning 10 of them.   *(T. Hindley)*

A first victory in Melbourne also brought Boris Becker to the top of the men's rankings for the first time. He lost that position to Edberg, regained it at Wimbledon and lost it again soon afterwards to end the year ranked No. 3. *(T. Hindley)*

AUSTRALIAN OPEN CHAMPIONSHIPS

Alan Trengove

In the first few days at Flinders Park the fans had half their minds on the Gulf War, while in the dressing rooms and press room the centre of attention was often the live telecasts from Baghdad, Jerusalem and Riyadh rather than the Centre Court action.

Nevertheless, as the tournament progressed it created a great deal of interest, climaxing, as it did, in two very good singles finals and victories of historic significance. In the men's singles, Boris Becker became the first German to win the Australian title. In doing so he seized the world's number one ranking (albeit for only three weeks) from Stefan Edberg. The women's singles was won for the first time by a Yugoslav, Monica Seles, who, at 17 years and almost two months, became the youngest player ever to hold the title – Margaret Smith having been 17 years and six months when in 1960 she had won the first of her 11 Australian Championships. Jeremy Bates and Jo Durie added to the number of 'firsts' by becoming the first British pair to win the Australian mixed doubles crown; and the pattern continued when for the first time the men's doubles final was an all-American affair, with Scott Davis and David Pate emerging triumphant.

Perhaps the most remarkable precedent of all was set by Becker when, immediately after beating Ivan Lendl in the men's final, he disappeared from the stadium, leaving the crowd of 15,000 and organisers of the presentation ceremony completely bewildered. Most of us assumed he was answering a call of nature or that he would quickly surface in the stands, perhaps to embrace his Australian coach, Bob Brett. Instead, as we discovered later, Becker had run 200 metres along an underground passage and out of the stadium into a public park where, to the amazement of a few passers-by, he skipped ecstatically around the trees until an official coaxed him back onto Centre Court. He was, it seems, still so charged with energy and so consumed by emotion that he could not resist an urge to break away from the tumultuous scene of his triumph to reflect alone on his achievement.

Becker's sudden elevation to the number one ranking was probably what excited him most. This had been his goal throughout the previous year; a goal for which he had sacrificed his participation in the *Davis Cup*, and which, at the end of 1990, had eluded him only narrowly. But simply winning in Melbourne meant a lot psychologically, too.

In five previous sorties he had never advanced beyond the quarter-finals of the Open. Strange things always seemed to happen to him. Possibly, he mused, it was the heat or something in the air. Or could it be some evil spirit – some Ned Kelly of the nether world of tennis – that waited to ambush him. The suspicious, brooding part of Boris's Teutonic imagination was ever active in Melbourne.

Once, he was tipped out of the Open by Michiel Schapers. Another time, he was ousted by Wally Masur, behaving so erratically that he was heavily fined. This had led to a split with his old coach, Gunther Bosch. In 1989, Jonas Svensson had routed him in straight sets; and in 1990 Mats Wilander, who could hardly beat anyone else, had done the same.

This time, Becker arrived at Melbourne almost four weeks before the Open to acclimatise and make his peace with those Antipodean demons. In his first outing, however, he lost in the first round at Adelaide to Magnus Larsson and thought to himself – 'What the hell am I doing here? I am here already three weeks and I am playing bad.'

It was then that his luck started to change. Because of an arm injury, Thomas Muster had to pull out of the rich Adelaide exhibition event, The Rio Challenge, and Becker replaced him, gaining valuable match practice on the *Rebound Ace* court surface. More luck followed. The brilliant Pete Sampras played the Rio, but recurring shin splints forced him to withdraw from the Open. He was the fourth seed and would have been in Becker's half of the draw. As the tournament unfolded, fortune continued to favour the burly young man from Leimen. It was unseasonably cool, and on no day did we have the scorching heat that Becker feared. He was not only in the easier half of the draw, with Edberg, Lendl, Ivanisevic, Gilbert, Cash, Krickstein and Courier packed into the other half, but it became oasier all tho timo ao firot tho oixth oood, Emilio Sanohoz, wao oliminatod by Mark Woodforde and next the eighth, Jonas Svensson, was removed by Todd Woodbridge.

One unexpected obstacle in the third round was Omar Camporese, the free-hitting Italian who didn't know when he was beaten. Becker laboured to win the first two sets from him in tiebreakers, only to drop the next two sets 6–0 6–4. In the fifth set, as he teetered close to defeat, Court 1 rang out with German cries of rage and frustration. Towards the end, with darkness approaching, Camporese was broken twice, but each time hit back gallantly as Becker vainly served for victory. Finally, Becker served and held. The score was 14–12; the match had lasted 5 hours and 22 minutes, the longest ever singles in the tournament's history; and some would swear that Camporese, who now sported a beard, didn't have one when it had all begun.

That escape, like his celebrated cliff-hanger against Derrick Rostagno at the 1989 US Open, was possibly a portent for Becker. In reaching the semi-finals he had to overcome only one seeded player, Guy Forget (10), whom he had beaten in their last five matches.

His semi-final opponent was, to everyone's surprise, Patrick McEnroe, ranked 114, playing in only his second Grand Slam, and only once before a semi-finalist in any singles event. Right-handed Patrick lacks the genius of his left-handed brother, John; he has the same quick racquet dexterity, the same quick mind, but not the same speedy legs or stiletto-like penetration. Most conspicuously, he has not the same volatile, explosive temperament of the older McEnroe, which had led to his disqualification at the 1990 Open.

John did not come to Melbourne because of a shoulder injury, but Patrick did the McEnroe clan proud. After coming from two sets down to beat Thomas Hogstedt in the first round, he beat Johan Anderson, 12th seed Jay Berger, Woodforde and another battler in Italy's Cristiano Caratti. Then he confronted Becker. Boris must have thought those Centre Court demons were rather benign fairies after all as he won 6–7 6–4 6–1 6–4.

By then, his destiny was clearly beckoning him. For, earlier that day, Lendl had recovered from a two sets to one deficit and fought off two match points to beat a wavering top seed, Edberg, 6–4 5–7 3–6 7–6 6–4 in the first semi-final. Victory in the final would now mean that the number one ranking would be Becker's.

The Edberg-Lendl match almost certainly would have been won by the Swede but for a decline in his serving. He served 11 double-faults in all, several of them on critical points.

The final was memorable for some spectacular rallies between two of the game's hardest hitters, and above all for Becker's willpower and opportunism. It was the 19th match Becker had played against Lendl and their head-to-head record was nicely balanced with nine wins apiece. The first set did not augur well for Boris. He made many unforced errors and Lendl was altogether sharper. Stiffness and a slight muscle spasm in his back troubled the German and during three changeovers in the second set he was treated by trainer Todd Snyder.

Gradually he picked up his serve and, with it, his game and his confidence. Leading 5–4 30-all in the second set, he seized his chance with a startling forehand winner off Lendl's second serve, and then an angled forehand drop volley that ended a fierce baseline rally.

In the first game of the third set, Becker saved two break points with diving volleys. In all, Lendl was to hold a total of nine break points over the last three sets, but failed to convert more than one, possibly because he could not lift his game or wasn't quite as desperate.

Becker had come through his rough patch with his mind intact and it was Lendl who blew up over what he considered bad line-calls in the second game of the third set. After he lost that game the match became increasingly Becker's. Though it took him six set points to clinch the set, he was irresistible. In the fourth Lendl kept fighting, as he always does, but Becker simply wouldn't allow him back. With another display of ruthless opportunism he brilliantly sealed victory, burying his Australian bogey at last.

The minor heroes of the men's draw were Goran Prpic, the amiable Yugoslav who plays with his surgery-scarred right leg encased in a brace, the gentlemanly Patrick McEnroe, up till now regarded more as a doubles player, and the ever-popular Mats Wilander. Prpic gave his sometimes devastating but temperamentally flawed compatriot, Goran Ivanisevic, a lesson in courtcraft before losing to Lendl in the quarters. McEnroe's resourcefulness won him as many Aussie fans as his mercurial brother. And Wilander, a three-time Australian champion, was almost the Mats of yore as he eliminated the seventh seed, Gilbert.

That the women's tournament was just as engrossing as the men's was largely due to the spellbinding Seles, making her first trip Down Under, and some splendid tennis by the rapidly improving Jana Novotna and Mary Joe Fernandez. Novotna ousted Steffi Graf in a dramatic three-set quarter-final, thus ending the defending champion's three-year reign. Not since the 1984 semi-final, in which Helena Sukova had ended Martina Navratilova's 74-match winning streak, had there been such an upset. As for Fernandez, the runner-up of 1990, she held a match point against Seles in a semi-final that was just as gripping.

Although Novotna had won the New South Wales Open a couple of weeks earlier, Graf seemed to be in good enough form to hold the 10th seed at bay. After all, she had conceded only one set to her in their previous nine meetings and had cruised through the early rounds. But there were ominous signs of her fallibility in the first set, which she barely won 7–5 after leading 4–1. Errors came from her celebrated forehand as well as her backhand, and she was unconvincing when venturing to the net.

Novotna won the second set 6–4 after leading 4–0, and she always held the edge in the decider, winning it 8–6. Overall, it was a very controlled performance by a young woman who hitherto had never quite done justice to her enormous talent. She gave most of the credit to her new coach, Hana Mandlikova, who, she said, had helped raise her physical fitness, and taught her to choose the right shot at the right time.

There was also plenty of other drama in the quarter-finals, what with Arantxa Sanchez-Vicario dismissing Gabriela Sabatini 6–1 6–3, and 16-year-old Anke Huber of West Germany leading Seles 3–0. Like Graf, Sabatini had not played any lead-up tournaments in Australia, whereas players such as Novotna and Sanchez were perfectly tuned to the *Rebound Ace* courts and match-sharp. The Argentine was merely a shadow of the player who had won the US Open a few months before, and was no match for the stocky Spaniard, who manoeuvred and probed like a relentless matador facing a sluggish Ferdinand.

Huber's success against Seles was short-lived, but she did enough to impress her opponent, who thought the robust German hit as hard as Graf and Jennifer Capriati.

The two giant killers, Novotna and Sanchez-Vicario, met for the right to play in their first Australian Open final. This time Arantxa's consistency fell away and she lost rather easily 6–2 6–4. It was left to Fernandez, who had comfortably beaten Katerina Maleeva in the quarter-finals, to provide the fireworks. For much of her 2 hour 38 minute match with Seles she seemed to have her opponent's measure. Seles did not hit with her usual depth or accuracy and could not win a game in the second set against a player whose all-round strengths are developing. But Monica was as tenacious as ever, and after surviving her crisis in the third set it was her determination that saw her through 6–3 0–6 9–7.

For a while in the final Novotna who, at 22, could almost be said in this age of teenage prodigies to be a late bloomer, had a real chance of causing a further sensation. Her fine all-court game gave her the first set 7–5 and Monica was clearly unsettled. However, Novotna was slightly hampered by a hamstring strain, and this, along with her opponent's growing resistance, induced her to rush a few shots. She wanted to avoid long rallies in which she would have to run from side to side, but increasing errors marked her downfall.

As for Seles, she responded to the challenge like a true champion. 'I pretty much got a little bit mad and said, "You can't play like this against her",' she recalled. 'You have to go for your shots.' And indeed she did, slamming her feared double-handers with tremendous authority, and bringing off some breathtaking crosscourt passes. She won the last two sets 6–3 6–1 and then, with precocious charm and aplomb, entertained the crowd with a speech as long and chatty as Becker's was to be tongue-tied and brief.

Seles thoroughly enjoyed herself even on the doubles court. She and Anne Smith, pairing for the first time, got through to the semi-finals, where they lost to the eventual champions, Patty Fendick and Mary Joe Fernandez. It was a memorable women's event, and perhaps marked a watershed – and a new order – in the women's game.

MEN'S SINGLES

Holder: I. Lendl (TCH)

Champion's final score: 1-6 6-4 6-4 6-4

FIRST ROUND

1 S. EDBERG (SWE) (1)
2 D. Poliakov (URS) (Q)
3 B. Pearce (USA)
4 E. Masso (BEL)
5 K. Novacek (TCH)
6 P. Cash (AUS)
7 C. Van Rensburg (RSA)
8 M. Katzman (AUS)
9 N. Marques (POR)
10 J. Cunha-Silva (POR)
11 J. Arbanas (AUS) (Q)
12 J. Oncins (BRA)
13 D. Perez (URU) (LL)
14 D. Bloom (ISR)
15 J. Gunnarsson (SWE)
16 J. COURIER (USA) (16)
17 A. CHESNOKOV (URS) (9)
18 J. Arias (USA)
19 B. Wuyts (BEL) (Q)
20 D. Johnson (SWE)
21 J. Yzaga (PER)
22 D. Vacek (TCH) (Q)
23 M. Schapers (HOL) (LL)
24 M. Sinner (GER) (Q)
25 C. Saceanu (GER)
26 J. Tarango (USA)
27 M. Wilander (SWE)
28 H. Denman (AUS) (WC)
29 P. Doohan (AUS) (WC)
30 R. Fromberg (AUS)
31 D. Wheaton (USA)
32 B. GILBERT (USA) (7)
33 I. LENDL (TCH) (3)
34 T. Benhabiles (FRA)
35 T. Davis (USA)
36 A. Antonitsch (AUT)
37 J. Morgan (AUS) (WC)
38 M. Gustafsson (SWE)
39 S. Stolle (AUS) (WC)
40 W. Masur (AUS)
41 P. Kuhnen (GER)
42 T. Raoux (FRA)
43 G. Frana (ARG) (Q)
44 C. Dosedel (TCH) (Q)
45 A. Sznajder (CAN)
46 A. Mansdorf (ISR)
47 S. Youl (AUS) (WC)
48 J. HLASEK (SUI) (11)
49 A. KRICKSTEIN (USA) (13)
50 J. Stoltenberg (AUS)
51 M. Koevermans (HOL)
52 D. Pate (USA)
53 J. Siemerink (HOL) (Q)
54 D. Altur (ESP)
55 C. Steeb (GER)
56 C. Pistolesi (ITA)
57 J. Pugh (USA)
58 J. Prpic (YUG)
59 L. Mattar (BRA)
60 N. Kulti (SWE)
61 R. Krishnan (IND)
62 E. Jelen (GER)
63 S. Bruguera (ESP)
64 G. IVANISEVIC (YUG) (5)

SECOND ROUND

EDBERG (1) 6-1 7-6 6-2
Masso 6-7 6-1 6-3 8-6
Cash 6-2 6-4 6-1
Van Rensburg 6-3 6-1 7-5
Marques 4-6 6-4 1-6 6-3 6-4
Oncins 6-3 6-3 7-5
Bloom 7-5 6-2 6-3
COURIER (16) 6-3 6-4 6-2
Arias 6-0 6-3 4-6 2-6 6-4
Wuyts 5-7 6-7 4-7 6-3 9-7
Yzaga 6-4 6-2 6-2
Schapers 6-3 6-2 3-6 2-6 6-6
Saceanu 3-6 3-6 2-3 6-7 5
Wilander 7-6 3-6 4
Fromberg 7-6 7-5
GILBERT (7) 4-6 6-3 7-6
LENDL (3) 6-1 6-3
Davis 3-6 6-2 6-4 6-3
Gustafsson 6-1 6-0 6-3
Masur 6-1 6-2 6-2
Kuhnen 6-2 6-4 7-6
Dosedel 7-5 6-4 6-3 6-3
Mansdorf 6-0 6-3 6-3
KRICKSTEIN (13) 6-4 6-4 6-2
Stoltenberg 0-6 6-4 7-5 6-4
Koevermans 6-4 6-2 3-6 2-6 6-0
Siemerink 6-3 6-3
Steeb 6-2 6-2 6-3
Prpic 6-3 6-2 3-6 6-2
Krishnan 7-6 ret'd
IVANISEVIC (5) 6-4 0-6 6-1 6-4

THIRD ROUND

EDBERG (1) 6-1 6-2 6-3
Cash 7-6 4-6 6-4
Oncins 6-3 6-0 6-2
COURIER (16) 6-2 6-3 6-2
Arias 6-3 6-1 6-2
Yzaga 7-6 6-4 6-2
Wilander 7-6 4-3 6-4 6-6 6-4
GILBERT (7) 4-6 4-6 4-4 6-6 6-0
LENDL (3) 7-6 6-3 6-2
Gustafsson
Kuhnen 6-2 6-4 6-4
KRICKSTEIN (13) 7-5 3-7 6-2
Koevermans 6-3 6-3 6-2
Siemerink 6-2 5-7 4-6 6-4 6-1
Prpic 6-3 6-1 6-1
IVANISEVIC (5) 6-4 3-6 4-6 6-1 6-2

FOURTH ROUND

EDBERG (1) 7-6 7-5 6-2
COURIER (16) 6-3 6-1 6-1
Yzaga 3-6 7-6 6-1 6-3
Wilander 7-6 6-1 6-4
LENDL (3) 4-6 6-2 6-3 6-2
KRICKSTEIN (13) 6-4 6-4 6-1
Siemerink 4-6 6-2 6-4 3-6 6-1
Prpic 6-3 6-4 6-3

QUARTER-FINALS

EDBERG (1) 4-6 6-0 6-4 5-7 6-2
Yzaga 7-5 2-6 6-1 3-6 6-1
LENDL (3) 6-2 6-2 6-1
Prpic 7-6 6-7 6-0 7-6

SEMI-FINALS

EDBERG (1) 6-2 6-3 6-2
LENDL (3) 6-0 7-6 7-6

FINAL

LENDL (3) 6-4 5-7 3-6 6-4

B. BECKER (GER) (2)

First round

	Player	R1 winner / score
65	E. SANCHEZ (ESP) (6)	Woodforde
66	M. Woodforde (AUS)	0-6 7-5 7-6 6-2
67	P. Cane (ITA)	Shelton
68	G. Shelton (USA)	7-6 4-6 6-3 6-4
69	B. Muller (RSA)	Jarryd
70	A. Jarryd (SWE)	6-4 6-3 6-1
71	N. Kroon (SWE)	Connell
72	G. Connell (CAN)	6-1 6-4 6-2
73	P. McEnroe (USA)	McEnroe
74	T. Hogstedt (SWE)	4-6 4-6 6-3 6-1 6-3
75	J. Anderson (AUS) (WC)	Anderson
76	A. Rahunen (FIN)	6-2 6-4 6-3
77	J. Jones (USA) (Q)	Witsken
78	T. Witsken (USA)	6-0 6-1 6-0
79	M. Larsson (SWE)	BERGER (12)
80	J. BERGER (USA) (12)	6-3 6-4 6-0
81	A. CHERKASOV (URS) (14)	A. CHERKASOV (URS) (14)
82	D. Rostagno (USA)	3-6 6-4 6-1 4-6 10-8
83	D. Cahill (AUS)	Cahill
84	J. Canter (USA) (Q)	6-1 6-4 6-3
85	A. Volkov (URS)	Korda
86	P. Korda (TCH)	6-1 1-6 6-4 7-5
87	K. Krajicek (HOL)	Krajicek
88	F. Santoro (FRA)	2-6 6-1 6-2 6-3
89	C. Caratti (ITA)	Caratti
90	B. Dyke (AUS) (WC)	6-3 2-6 6-4 6-3
91	P. Engel (SWE)	Engel
92	K. Evernden (NZL)	6-3 2-6 6-1 6-0
93	U. Riglewski (GER)	Layendecker
94	G. Layendecker (USA) (LL)	6-3 6-3 4-6 6-7 6-2
95	J. Lundgren (SWE)	Lundgren
96	J. Lavalle (MEX) (Q)	7-6 6-7 7-6 6-1
97	J. SVENSSON (SWE) (8)	SVENSSON (8)
98	T. Champion (FRA)	6-3 6-4 6-1
99	A. Castle (GBR) (Q)	Clavet
100	F. Clavet (ESP)	6-7 6-2 6-1 6-2
101	M. Kaplan (RSA) (Q)	Woodbridge
102	T. Woodbridge (AUS)	1-6 6-3 6-1
103	C. Poline (FRA)	Bergstrom
104	D. Bergstrom (SWE)	6-4 6-2 1-6 7-6
105	L. Herrera (MEX)	Jaite
106	M. Jaite (ARG)	6-3 6-1 3-6 6-7 6-4
107	M. Stich (GER)	Stich
108	M. Washington (USA)	4-6 5-7 7-6 6-1 6-4
109	J. Fitzgerald (AUS) (WC)	Mronz
110	A. Mronz (GER)	6-4 6-4
111	R. Skoff (AUT)	FORGET (10)
112	G. FORGET (FRA) (10)	7-6 2-6 6-4
113	M. ROSSET (SUI) (15)	Wahlgren
114	L. Wahlgren (SWE) (Q)	4-6 2-6 7-6 6-3 9-7
115	F. Luna (ESP)	Ferreira
116	W. Ferreira (RSA) (Q)	6-1 6-3 6-2
117	R. Weiss (USA)	Eltingh
118	J. Eltingh (HOL)	3-6 6-2 6-3 7-5
119	J. Fleurian (FRA)	Fleurian
120	R. Furlan (ITA)	6-1 6-0 6-0
121	O. Camporese (ITA)	Camporese
122	M. Zoecke (GER) (Q)	3-6 6-2 7-6 6-4
123	P. Haarhuis (HOL)	Haarhuis
124	J. Sanchez (ESP)	6-1 6-2 7-6
125	M. Vajda (TCH)	Vajda
126	R. Garrow (USA)	2-6 6-4 7-5 6-3
127	J. Bates (GBR)	BECKER (2)
128	B. BECKER (GER) (2)	6-4 6-2 6-3

Second round

- Woodforde 7-6 3-6 6-3
- Connell 6-1 7-5 6-2
- McEnroe 6-3 6-3 5-7 6-1
- BERGER (12) 6-1 6-3 6-0
- Cahill 4-6 2-6 6-3 7-5 7-5
- Krajicek 4-6 7-6 6-3 6-4
- Caratti 3-6 6-2 6-3 6-4
- Layendecker 3-6 1-6 7-5 6-3 6-4
- SVENSSON (8) 6-2 7-5 3-6 6-1
- Woodbridge 7-5 6-2 6-1
- Stich 6-3 7-6 7-6
- FORGET (10) 7-6 7-6 4-6 6-3
- Ferreira 6-2 6-4 7-6
- Eltingh 6-1 3-6 7-6 3-6 6-1
- Camporese 7-5 7-5 3-6 6-3
- BECKER (2) 7-6 7-6 0-6 4-6 14-12

Third round

- Woodforde 6-4 3-6 7-5 6-3
- McEnroe 6-1 7-5 7-5
- Krajicek 6-4 6-4 6-3
- Caratti 6-4 6-4 5-7 4-6 7-5
- Woodbridge 7-5 6-2 6-1
- FORGET (10) 6-3 7-6 7-6
- Ferreira 6-2 6-4 7-6
- BECKER (2) 7-6 7-6 6-3

Fourth round

- McEnroe 6-2 6-4 6-1
- Caratti 6-3 6-4 6-7 3-6 6-4
- FORGET (10) 6-4 3-6 6-3 6-4
- BECKER (2) 6-4 7-6 6-4

Quarter-finals

- McEnroe 7-6 6-3 4-6 4-6 6-2
- BECKER (2) 6-2 7-6 6-3

Semi-final

- BECKER (2) 6-7 6-4 6-1 6-4

Capital letters denote seeded players. Number following player's name gives seeding order. (Q) – Qualifier. (WC) – Wild Card. (LL) – Lucky Loser.

Holder: S. Graf (GER)

5–7 6–3 6–1

WOMEN'S SINGLES

FIRST ROUND	SECOND ROUND	THIRD ROUND	FOURTH ROUND	QUARTER-FINALS	SEMI-FINALS	FINAL
1 S. GRAF (GER) (1)	GRAF (1)	GRAF (1) 6–1 6–0	GRAF (1) 6–4 6–2	GRAF (1) 6–0 6–1	NOVOTNA (10) 5–7 6–4 8–6	NOVOTNA (10) 6–2 6–4
2 J. Santrock (USA)	6–3 6–0					
3 M. Kidowaki (JPN)	Kidowaki 6–1 6–4					
4 K. Sharpe (AUS)						
5 N. Herreman (FRA)	Date	Provis 4–6 6–0 6–4				
6 K. Date (JPN)	6–2 6–1					
7 E. Reinach (RSA)	Provis 6–2 6–0					
8 N. Provis (AUS)						
9 C. Tessi (ARG)	Habsudova 6–2 7–6	Habsudova 7–6 6–2	Habsudova 6–0 3–6 8–6			
10 K. Habsudova (TCH)						
11 A. Smith (USA)	Smith 6–3 6–4					
12 E. Sviglerova (TCH)						
13 C. Kohde-Kilsch (GER)	Smylie	Smylie 6–3 2–6 9–7				
14 P. Smylie (AUS)	2–6 6–4 6–4					
15 P. Vasquez (PER)	GILDEMEISTER (15) 6–1 6–1					
16 L. GILDEMEISTER (PER) (15)						
17 H. NOVOTNA (TCH) (10)	NOVOTNA (10) 7–6 6–2	NOVOTNA (10) 6–2 6–2	NOVOTNA (10) 6–7 6–1 8–6	NOVOTNA (10) 7–6 6–4		
18 A. Minter (AUS)						
19 L. Grossman (USA)	Quentrec					
20 K. Quentrec (FRA)						
21 M. Bollegraf (HOL)	Stafford 7–5	Stafford 5–7 6–2 6–2				
22 S. Stafford (USA)	Stafford 6–4 6–4					
23 G. Magers (USA)	Magers 6–4 6–2					
24 E. Zardo (SUI)						
25 A. Coordige (AUS)	Dechaume 6–3 7–5	Dechaume 6–2 6–3				
26 A. Dechaume (FRA)						
27 A. Kijimuta (JPN)	Martinek 6–3 6–1					
28 V. Martinek (GER)						
29 N. Miyagi (JPN)	Miyagi 7–5 1–6 8–6	GARRISON (8) 2–6 6–0 6–2	GARRISON (8) 6–2 6–4			
30 A. Gavaldon (USA)						
31 R. Stubbs (USA) (WC)	GARRISON (8) 6–2 6–0					
32 Z. GARRISON (USA) (8)						
33 G. SABATINI (ARG) (4)	SABATINI (4) 6–3 6–1	SABATINI (4) 6–1 6–1	SABATINI (4) 6–1 6–1	SABATINI (4) 6–3 6–1	SANCHEZ-VICARIO (6) 6–1 6–3	
34 L. Harvey-Wild (USA)						
35 J. Pospisilova (TCH)	Ekstrand					
36 M. Ekstrand (SWE) (Q)						
37 M. Wassermann (BEL)	Strnadova 7–6 6–4	Strnadova 6–3 6–2				
38 A. Strnadova (TCH)						
39 T. Morton (AUS) (WC)	Dune 6–1 3–6 7–5	Schefflin 6–2 6–4	McQuillan 6–4 6–0			
40 J. Durie (GBR)						
41 E. Fendick (USA)	Takagi 3–6 6–3					
42 N. Takagi (JPN)						
43 M. Oremans (HOL) (LL)	Schefflin 7–5 6–4					
44 S. Schefflin (USA) (Q)						
45 R. McQuillan (AUS)	McQuillan	McQuillan 6–4 6–7 6–4				
46 E. Brioukhovets (URS)						
47 U. Thoren (FIN)	PAULUS (12) 2–6 6–4 6–1					
48 B. PAULUS (AUT) (12)						
49 A. FRAZIER (USA) (13)	FRAZIER (13) 6–3 6–4	FRAZIER (13) 6–3 6–0	FRAZIER (13) 3–6 6–2 6–2	SANCHEZ-VICARIO (6) 6–3 6–2		
50 K. McDonald (AUS) (WC)						
51 A. Leand (USA)	Leand					
52 I. Driehuis (HOL) (Q)						
53 C. MacGregor (USA)	Lindqvist 7–5 4–6 6–3	Cunningham 6–1 6–0				
54 C. Lindqvist (SWE)						
55 C. Cunningham (USA)	Cunningham 6–1 6–0					
56 N. Pratt (AUS) (WC)						
57 L. McNeil (USA)	McNeil 7–6 6–1	McNeil 6–3 4–6 6–3	SANCHEZ-VICARIO (6) 6–4 3–6 6–0			
58 K. Rinaldi (USA)						
59 L. Savchenko (URS)	Savchenko 6–2 6–2					
60 D. Jones (AUS) (WC)						
61 A. Keller (GER)	Javer	SANCHEZ-VICARIO (6) 4–6 6–4 6–2				
62 M. Javer (GBR)						
63 N. Medvedeva (URS)	SANCHEZ-VICARIO (6) 6–0 6–2					
64 A. SANCHEZ-VICARIO (ESP) (6)						

M. SELES (YUG) (2)

Winner: SELES (2) 6-3 0-6 9-7

First round — Second round — Third round — Fourth round — Quarter-finals — Semi-finals:

Seed/No.	First Round	R2	R3	R4	QF	SF	Final
65 K. MALEEVA (BUL) (5)	K. MALEEVA (5) 6-1 6-3	K. MALEEVA (5) 6-1 6-3	K. MALEEVA (5) 6-2 6-0	K. MALEEVA (5) 6-3 6-2			
66 B. Schultz (HOL)							
67 C. Barclay (AUS) (WC)	Martin 6-1 6-1						
68 S. Martin (USA)							
69 A. Henricksson (USA)	Probst 4-6 7-6 6-4	Faber 6-2 6-0					
70 W. Probst (GER)							
71 D. Faber (USA)	Faber 5-7 6-3 6-2						
72 E. de Lone (USA)							
73 C. Toleafoa (NZL)	Toleafoa 7-5 6-0	M. Maleeva 6-0 6-3	M. Maleeva 6-0 6-3				
74 S. Richter (HOL)							
75 M. Maleeva (BUL)	M. Maleeva 6-4 5-7 6-4						
76 M. Jaggard (AUS)							
77 M. Reggi (ITA)	Whitlinger 6-2 6-2	FAIRBANK-NIDEFFER (14) 6-4 6-1					
78 T. Whitlinger (USA)							
79 G. Fernandez (USA)	FAIRBANK-NIDEFFER (14) 6-3 6-2						
80 R. FAIRBANK-NIDEFFER (USA) (14)							
81 S. APPELMANS (BEL) (16)	APPELMANS (16) 6-0 6-1	APPELMANS (16) 7-5 6-1	APPELMANS (16) 6-4 6-3	FERNANDEZ (3) 6-3 6-3			
82 M. Paz (ARG)							
83 P. Tarabini (ARG)	Tarabini (ARG) 6-4 6-0						
84 M. Strandlund (SWE)							
85 D. Szabova (TCH)	Halard 6-2 6-3	Kamstra 6-3 6-4					
86 J. Halard (FRA)							
87 P. Kamstra (HOL) (Q)	Kamstra 6-4 6-2						
88 R. White (USA)							
89 B. Rittner (GER)	Rittner 4-6 6-3 6-1	Sawamatsu 6-3 6-3	FERNANDEZ (3) 6-1 6-1				
90 S. Loosemore (GBR)							
91 N. Sawamatsu (JPN)	Sawamatsu 6-4 6-3						
92 E. Burgin (USA)							
93 M. Zvec-Skulj (GER) (Q)	Romano 7-5 6-2	FERNANDEZ (3) 6-1 6-2					
94 S. Romano (ITA)							
95 S. Gomer (GBR)	FERNANDEZ (3) 6-1 6-0						
96 M. J. FERNANDEZ (USA) (3)						FERNANDEZ (3) 6-3 6-2	
97 M. MALEEVA-FRAGNIERE (SUI) (7)	MALEEVA-FRAGNIERE (7) 6-2 6-0	Huber 6-4 6-4	Huber 6-3 7-5	Huber 6-3 6-4			
98 J. Faull (AUS) (WC)							
99 J. Richardson (NZL)	Huber 6-4 6-1						
100 A. Huber (GER)							
101 E. Pfaff (GER)	Pfaff 7-6 3-6 6-3	Shriver 6-3 7-6					
102 L. Field (AUS)							
103 P. Shriver (USA)	Shriver 6-3 6-1						
104 N. Van Lottum (FRA)							
105 N. Guerree (FRA)	Barton 6-3 6-2	Wood 3-6 6-3 6-0	ZVEREVA (11) 6-1 6-3				
106 C. Barton (SUI)							
107 C. Wood (GBR)	Wood 3-6 7-6 6-0						
108 S. Collins (USA) (Q)							
109 M. Kochta (GER) (Q)	Porwik 6-3 6-3	ZVEREVA (11) 6-1 6-3					
110 C. Porwik (GER)							
111 G. Helgeson (USA) (Q)	ZVEREVA (11) 6-3 6-4						
112 N. ZVEREVA (URS) (11)							
113 H. SUKOVA (TCH) (9)	SUKOVA (9) 6-2 6-1	SUKOVA (9) 6-2 7-5	Tanvier 4-6 6-1 6-4	SELES (2) 6-2 6-1			
114 B. Cordwell (NZL)							
115 P. Ritter (AUT)	Cueto 6-4 2-6 7-5						
116 I. Cueto (GER)							
117 C. Tanvier (FRA)	Tanvier 6-4 6-1	Tanvier 6-7 7-5 6-1					
118 R. Baranski (POL)							
119 P. Hy (CAN)	Hy 6-4 6-3						
120 B. Bowes (USA)							
121 K. Kschwendt (LUX)	Kschwendt 2-6 6-2	Kschwendt 6-1 6-1	SELES (2) 6-3 6-1			SELES (2) 6-3 6-1	
122 P. Langrova (TCH)							
123 L. Stacey (AUS) (WC)	Raichrtova 4-6 7-5 8-6						
124 R. Raichrtova (TCH)							
125 S. Meier (GER)	Caverzasio 6-3 3-6 6-3	SELES (2) 6-1 6-0					
126 C. Caverzasio (ITA)							
127 L. Hack (GER)	SELES (2) 6-0 6-0						
128 M. SELES (YUG) (2)					SELES (2) 6-2 6-1		

Capital letters denote seeded players. Number following player's name gives seeding order: (Q) – Qualifier; (WC) – Wild Card; (LL) – Lucky Loser.

MEN'S DOUBLES

Holders: P. Aldrich (RSA)/D. Visser (RSA)

S. DAVIS (USA)/D. PATE (USA) (3) 6–7 7–6 6–3 7–5

FIRST ROUND	SECOND ROUND	THIRD ROUND	QUARTER-FINALS	SEMI-FINALS	FINAL
1 ALDRICH/VISSER (1)	Haarhuis/Koevermans 7–6 7–6	Haarhuis/Koevermans 3–6 6–4 6–3			
2 Haarhuis/Koevermans					
3 Evernden/Pereira	Evernden/Pereira 6–3 6–4			BATES/JONES (16) 6–3 6–4	
4 Anderson/Wahlgren (WC)			BATES/JONES (16) 6–4 6–2		
5 Doohan/Warder	Doohan/Warder 6–3 6–4	BATES/JONES (16) 6–2 7–6			
6 Cunha-Silva/Masso					
7 Mora/Page	BATES/JONES (16) 6–6 6–2				
8 BATES/JONES (16)					
9 KORDA/IVANISEVIC (10)	N. Brown/Oosting 6–1 5–7 6–3	N. Brown/Oosting 6–3 2–6 8–6			
10 N. Brown/Oosting			N. Brown/Oosting 6–7 7–6 6–3		
11 Kinnear/Shelton	Kinnear/Shelton 6–3 7–6				S. DAVIS/PATE (3) 6–1 4–6 4–5–7 9–7
12 Cherkasov/Zvojinovic					
13 Doyle/Eagle (WC)	Doyle/Eagle 7–6 6–4	BROAD/MULLER (8) 6–3 6–1			
14 Jaite/Perez					
15 Kruger/Van Rensburg	BROAD/MULLER (8) 6–1 7–6			S. DAVIS/PATE (3) 4–6 4–6 6–3 6–3 8–6	
16 BROAD/MULLER (8)			S. DAVIS/PATE (3) 7–5 6–3		
17 S. DAVIS/PATE (3)	S. DAVIS/PATE (3) 7–6 7–5	S. DAVIS/PATE (3) 6–2 7–5			
18 Henricsson/Utgren					
19 Devries/MacPherson	Devries/MacPherson 7–6 6–3				
20 Borwick/Lewis					
21 Beckman/Cannon	Beckman/Cannon 6–3 6–2	J. Brown/Salumaa 5–7 7–6 6–4			
22 Odizor/Wilkison					
23 J. Brown/Salumaa	J. Brown/Salumaa 6–2 7–6 6–3				
24 CAMPORESE/J. SANCHEZ (14)					
25 DYKE/LUNDGREN (12)	DYKE/LUNDGREN (12) 2–6 7–6 6–3	Becker/Kuhnen 4–6 6–3 7–5			
26 Carratti/Mordegan			Garrow/Pearce 6–3 4–6 8–6		
27 Becker/Kuhnen	Becker/Kuhnen 6–3 6–0				
28 Flegl/Vacek					
29 Canter/Derlin	Garrow/Pearce 7–6 6–2	Garrow/Pearce 6–1 6–4			
30 Garrow/Pearce					
31 Pozzi/Rostagno	Pozzi/Rostagno 7–5 2–6 6–4				
32 CASAL/E. SANCHEZ (6)					
33 CONNELL/MICHIBATA (5)	CONNELL/MICHIBATA (5) 6–3 6–2	CONNELL/MICHIBATA (5) 6–1 7–6			
34 Van Emburgh/Youl					
35 Luza/Rosset	Luza/Rosset 6–4 6–1			RIGLEWSKI/STICH (11) 5–7 6–3 7–5	
36 Castle/R. Smith			RIGLEWSKI/STICH (11) 5–7 6–3 7–5		
37 Arthurs/Limberger (WC)	Novacek/Pimek 6–4 6–4	RIGLEWSKI/STICH (11) 6–1 6–4			
38 Novacek/Pimek					
39 Schapers/Siemerink	RIGLEWSKI/STICH (11) 6–2 6–4				
40 RIGLEWSKI/STICH (11)					P. McENROE/WHEATON ‖3) 7–5 6–4 6–1
41 P. McENROE/WHEATON (13)	P. McENROE/WHEATON (13) 6–2 6–4	P. McENROE/WHEATON (13) 6–4 6–4			
42 Engel/Siner					
43 Arias/Layendecker	Arias/Layendecker 7–6 6–3			P. McENROE/WHEATON (13) 7–6 6–3 6–3	
44 Edberg/Guy			P. McENROE/WHEATON (13) 6–4 3–6 6–2		
45 Fromberg/Stolle (WC)	Fromberg/Stolle 6–2 7–6	Fitzgerald/Jarryd 7–6 3–6 6–3			
46 M. Brown/A. Kratzmann (WC)					
47 Fitzgerald/Jarryd	Fitzgerald/Jarryd 6–3 6–3				
48 FORGET/HLASEK (4)					
49 CAHILL/M. KRATZMANN (7)	CAHILL/M. KRATZMANN (7) 6–4 6–3	CAHILL/M. KRATZMANN (7) 6–3 5–7 6–2			
50 Garnett/Partridge			Woodbridge/Woodforde 7–6 6–4		
51 Herrera/Lavalle	Bloom/Clavet 6–3 6–3				
52 Bloom/F. Clavet					
53 Annacone/Nijssen	Woodbridge/Woodforde 6–3 6–3	Woodbridge/Woodforde 6–3 2–6 6–3		Woodbridge/Woodforde 7–6 3–6 6–3 6–1	
54 Woodbridge/Woodforde					
55 Eltingh/Ferreira	GALBRAITH/WITSKEN (9) 6–4 6–4				
56 GALBRAITH/WITSKEN (9)					
57 MASUR/STOLTENBERG (15)	MASUR/STOLTENBERG (15) 7–6 6–4	MASUR/STOLTENBERG (15) 7–6 1–6 8–6			
58 Fleurian/Van't Hof			MASUR/STOLTENBERG (15) 6–3 4–6 6–4		
59 M. Davis/Drewett	Frana/Miniussi 6–4 6–3				
60 Frana/Miniussi					
61 Gunnarsson/Mronz	Krajicek/Suk 6–1 6–4	LEACH/PUGH (2) 7–6 6–4			
62 Krajicek/Suk					
63 Cane/Prpic	LEACH/PUGH (2) 6–3 6–4				
64 LEACH/PUGH (2)					

Capital letters denote seeded pairings. Number following players' names gives seeding order. (Q) – Qualifier; (WC) – Wild Card; (LL) – Lucky Loser.

WOMEN'S DOUBLES

Holders: J. Novotna (TCH)/H. Sukova (TCH)

Winner: P. FENDICK (USA)/M. J. FERNANDEZ (USA) (4) 7–6 6–1

FIRST ROUND

1 G. FERNANDEZ/NOVOTNA (1)
2 Langrova/Pospisilova
3 McQuillan/Tanvier
4 Garrison/Shriver
5 Dechaume/Herreman
6 Kidowaki/Scott
7 Harvey-Wild/Tarabini
8 FAULL/JAGGARD (14)
9 K. MALEEVA/M. MALEEVA (16)
10 Appelmans/Reggi
11 Devries/Drehuis
12 Hy/Toleafoa
13 Lindstrom/Ludloff
14 Guse/Hodder
15 McDonald/Pierning
16 PAZ/SABATINI (8)
17 SAVCHENKO/ZVEREVA (3)
18 Pfaff/Stubbs
19 Meier/Szabova
20 Strnadova/Sviglerova
21 Frazier/Grossman
22 Godridge/Sharpe
23 Hack/Nishiya
24 BRIOUKHOVETS/MEDVEDEVA (12)
25 PROVIS/REINACH (9)
26 Van Lottum/Wood
27 Keller/Mawdsley (WC)
28 Caverzasio/Wasserman
29 Basuki/Wibowo
30 Hetherington/Rinaldi
31 Limmer/Woolcock (WC)
32 MAGERS/WHITE (6)
33 BOLLEGRAF/GREGORY (7)
34 Huber/Rittner (WC)
35 Hakami/Vasquez
36 Minter/Morton
37 Jones/Thompson
38 Borneo/Salmon
39 Bowes/Stafford
40 BURGIN/FAIRBANK-NIDEFFER (11)
41 KOHDE-KILSCH/SCHULTZ (13)
42 Maleeva-Fragniere/McNeil
43 Leand/Loosemore
44 Stacey/Taylor (WC)
45 Korvowic/Probst
46 Cordwell/Richardson
47 Barclay/Pratt
48 FENDICK/M. J. FERNANDEZ (4)
49 JORDAN/SMYLIE (5)
50 Rajchrtova/Mlvidskaia
51 Faber/Thoren
52 Dahlman/Ekstrand
53 Antonoplis/Javer
54 Collins/Whitinger
55 Henricksson/MacGregor
56 DIE/FIELD (15)
57 SELES/SMITH (10)
58 Gildemeister/Lindqvist
59 Radford/Smoller
60 Arnach/Strandlund
61 Baranski/Seeman
62 Kschwendt/Rajchrtova
63 May/Miyagi
64 SANCHEZ-VICARIO/SUKOVA (2)

SECOND ROUND

G. FERNANDEZ/NOVOTNA (1) 6–3 6–2
Garrison/Shriver 6–2 3–6 6–3
Kidowaki/Scott 6–4 6–3
FAULL/JAGGARD (14) 6–3 6–2
Appelmans/Reggi 6–4 6–2
Devries/Drehuis 7–5 7–6
Lindstrom/Ludloff 6–0 5–7 6–2
PAZ/SABATINI (8) 6–1 6–1
SAVCHENKO/ZVEREVA (3) 3–6 6–3
Strnadova/Sviglerova 6–3 7–5
Godridge/Sharpe 6–4 6–3
Hack/Nishiya 2–6 6–2 8–6
Van Lottum/Wood 6–7 7–6 6–2
Caverzasio/Wasserman 6–3 7–6
Hetherington/Rinaldi 7–6 7–5
MAGERS/WHITE (6) 6–0 6–3
BOLLEGRAF/GREGORY (7) 6–1 6–4
Minter/Morton 7–6 7–6
Borneo/Salmon 5–7 6–2 6–4
BURGIN/FAIRBANK-NIDEFFER (11) 7–5 6–2
Maleeva-Fragniere/McNeil 6–4 6–4
Stacey/Taylor 6–2 6–1
Cordwell/Richardson 6–0 6–3
FENDICK/M. J. FERNANDEZ (4) 6–1 6–2
JORDAN/SMYLIE (5) 6–1 6–2
Faber/Thoren 6–3 6–7 7–5
Collins/Whitinger 6–4 6–1
Henricksson/MacGregor 7–5 6–2
SELES/SMITH (10) 6–1 6–1
Radford/Smoller 7–5 6–2
Baranski/Seeman 6–4 7–6
SANCHEZ-VICARIO/SUKOVA (2) 6–1 6–1

THIRD ROUND

G. FERNANDEZ/NOVOTNA (1) 6–3 3–6 6–1
FAULL/JAGGARD (14) 3–6 6–3 6–3
Appelmans/Reggi 6–3 6–3
PAZ/SABATINI (8) 7–5 6–1
SAVCHENKO/ZVEREVA (3) 6–2 4–6 6–2
Godridge/Sharpe
Cwaverzasio/Wasserman 6–1 2–6 6–2
Hetherington/Rinaldi 6–3 6–3
BOLLEGRAF/GREGORY (7) 6–2 6–4
BURGIN/FAIRBANK-NIDEFFER (11) 6–1 6–1
Maleeva-Fragniere/McNeil w/o
FENDICK/M. J. FERNANDEZ (4) 6–0 6–0
JORDAN/SMYLIE (5) 6–2 6–1
Henricksson/MacGregor 6–3 7–6
SELES/SMITH (10) 6–1 6–1
SANCHEZ-VICARIO/SUKOVA (2) 6–0 6–0

QUARTER-FINALS

G. FERNANDEZ/NOVOTNA (1) 6–4 6–2
PAZ/SABATINI (8) 7–5 6–1
Appelmans/Reggi 6–4 2–6 6–2
SAVCHENKO/ZVEREVA (3) 6–1 6–2
Hetherington/Rinaldi 6–0 2–6 6–3
BOLLEGRAF/GREGORY (7) 5–7 6–4 11–9
FENDICK/M. J. FERNANDEZ (4) 6–2 6–2
JORDAN/SMYLIE (5) 6–2 6–3
SELES/SMITH (10) 7–5 3–6 6–2

SEMI-FINALS

G. FERNANDEZ/NOVOTNA (1) 6–4 6–2
SAVCHENKO/ZVEREVA (3) 6–1 6–2
Hetherington/Rinaldi 2–6 6–3 6–4
FENDICK/M. J. FERNANDEZ (4) 6–4 6–4
SELES/SMITH (10) 4–6 6–0 10–8

FINAL

G. FERNANDEZ/NOVOTNA (1) 6–3 6–7 6–3
FENDICK/M. J. FERNANDEZ (4) 6–1 3–6 6–2

G. FERNANDEZ/NOVOTNA (1) 6–0 3–6 6

Capital letters denote seeded pairings. Number following players' names gives seeding order. (Q) – Qualifier. (WC) – Wild Card. (LL) – Lucky Loser.

MIXED DOUBLES

Holders: J. Pugh (USA)/N. Zvereva (URS)

J. BATES (GBR)/J. DURIE (GBR) 2–6 6–4 6–4

FIRST ROUND	SECOND ROUND	QUARTER-FINALS	SEMI-FINALS	FINAL
1 **PUGH/ZVEREVA** (1)	PUGH/ZVEREVA (1) 7–5 7–6	PUGH/ZVEREVA (1) 6–3 6–2		
2 Warder/Burgin				
3 Suk/Sukova	Woodforde/Graf 7–6 6–3			
4 Woodforde/Graf (WC)			Kratzmann/Shriver 7–6 6–4	
5 Pimek/Savchenko	Kratzmann/Shriver 2–6 6–4 8–6	Kratzmann/Shriver 6–4 6–4		
6 Kratzmann/Shriver (WC)				
7 Devries/Cordwell	WOODBRIDGE/PROVIS (8) 6–3 6–4			Bates/Durie 7–5 6–4
8 **WOODBRIDGE/PROVIS** (8)				
9 **GALBRAITH/FENDICK** (4)	GALBRAITH/FENDICK (4) 6–4 7–6	Miniussi/Paz 6–4 6–7 6–2		
10 Kinnear/Magers				
11 Van Emburgh/Smith	Miniussi/Paz 6–3 6–2			
12 Miniussi/Paz			Bates/Durie 6–3 7–6	
13 Bates/Durie	Bates/Durie 6–7 7–5 8–6	Bates/Durie 6–4 7–5		
14 Smith/Fairbank-Nideffer				
15 Frana/Tarabini	MICHIBATA/HETHERINGTON (6) 6–3 6–2			
16 **MICHIBATA/HETHERINGTON** (6)				
17 **BROAD/REINACH** (5)	Van't Hof/MacGregor 1–6 6–3 6–4	Van't Hof/MacGregor 7–5 6–2		
18 Van't Hof/MacGregor				
19 Shelton/Jordan	Shelton/Jordan 6–4 7–5			
20 Odizor/McNeil			DAVIS/WHITE (3) 6–4 6–4	
21 MacPherson/Richardson	Witsken/Collins 7–6 6–3	DAVIS/WHITE (3) 4–6 7–6 6–4		
22 Witsken/Collins				
23 Castle/Reggi	DAVIS/WHITE (3) 6–2 6–4			DAVIS/WHITE (3) 6–4 5–7 8–6
24 **DAVIS/WHITE** (3)				
25 **JONES/MEDVEDEVA** (7)	Dyke/Jaggard 6–4 4–6 6–4	Evernden/McQuillan 6–4 3–6 6–1		
26 Dyke/Jaggard				
27 Evernden/McQuillan	Evernden/McQuillan 6–4 6–7 6–3			
28 Salumaa/Pfaff			Fitzgerald/Smylie 6–4 6–2	
29 Fitzgerald/Smylie	Fitzgerald/Smylie 6–3 7–5	Fitzgerald/Smylie 6–1 7–5		
30 Nijssen/Bollegraf				
31 Kruger/Gregory	Kruger/Gregory 7–5 6–2			
32 **LEACH/GARRISON** (2)				

Capital letters denote seeded pairings. Number following players' names gives seeding order. (Q) – Qualifier; (WC) – Wild Card; (LL) – Lucky Loser.

JUNIOR EVENTS

BOYS' SINGLES – Final: Thomas Enqvist (SWE) (1) d. Stephen Gleeson (AUS) (4) 7–6 6–7 6–1.
GIRLS' SINGLES – Final: Nicole Pratt (AUS) (4) d. Kristen Godridge (AUS) (3) 6–4 6–3.
BOY'S DOUBLES – Final: Grant Doyle (AUS)/Joshua Eagle (AUS) (1) d. Jamie Holmes(AUS)/Paul Kilderry (AUS) (2) 7–6 6–4.
GIRLS' DOUBLES – Final: Karina Habsudova (TCH)/Barbara Rittner (GER) (1) d. Joanne Limmer (AUS)/Angie Woolcock (AUS) (2) 6–2 6–0.

AUSTRALIAN OPEN CHAMPIONSHIPS PRIZE MONEY – AUS $4,647,000

MEN'S SINGLES – Winner $320,000. Runner-up $160,000. Semi-finalists $80,000. Quarter-finalists $40,000. Fourth-round losers $21,000. Third-round losers $12,000. Second-round losers $7,500. First-round losers $4,600.
Total: $1,694,400.
WOMEN'S SINGLES – Winner $320,000. Runner-up $160,000. Semi-finalists $80,000. Quarter-finalists $40,000. Fourth-round losers $21,000. Third-round losers $12,000. Second-round losers $7,500. First-round losers $4,600.
Total: $1,694,400.
MEN'S DOUBLES (per team) – Winners $125,000. Runners-up $62,500. Semi-finalists $32,000. Quarter-finalists $16,000. Third-round losers $9,000. Second-round losers $4,800. First-round losers $2,900.
Total $557,100.
WOMEN'S DOUBLES (per team) – Winners $125,000. Runners-up $65,000. Semi-finalists $32,000. Quarter-finalists $16,000. Third-round losers $9,000. Second-round losers $4,800. First-round losers $2,900.
Total $557,100.
MIXED DOUBLES (per team) – Winners $40,000. Runners-up $20,000. Semi-finalists $10,000. Quarter-finalists $5,200. Second-round losers $2,600. First-round losers $1,400.
Total $144,000.

The rugged American, Jim Courier, confirmed his advance by winning a first Grand Slam crown in Paris where his victim in the title round was compatriot Andre Agassi, who had been a finalist in 1990. *(T. Hindley)*

FRENCH OPEN CHAMPIONSHIPS

David Irvine

It would have been quite a coup. Coach to both the men's and women's title winners in the tournament's centenary year. Instead Nick Bollettieri, who chose to stake everything on Andre Agassi, had once again to endure his protégé's last fence fall in Paris as Jim Courier and Monica Seles – two former pupils who he allowed to get away – took the premier prizes at the French Open.

Time alone will show us if Bolletttieri made the correct decision. Agassi has an enormous talent – up to the final he was the tournament's outstanding player – and it was well worth remembering that even Ivan (Lendl, that is) suffered four losses in major finals before he made his decisive breakthrough in 1984.

Yet Agassi's second Paris setback only 12 months after that damaging four-sets defeat at the hands of the Ecuadorian veteran Andres Gomez was an intense disappointment. And a defeat, moreover, which quite clearly influenced the rest of his year. 'Who knows how many shots you'll get?' he wondered aloud. 'For sure, it's not going to get any easier.'

Courier's victory, following his hard court successes at Indian Wells and Key Biscayne, was certainly a surprise as he had had a fairly modest career on clay, achieving nothing to suggest that this 20-year-old from Dade City in Florida might win the biggest clay court event of them all.

For years the only thing that could be said with any degree of certainty about the French Championships, arguably the toughest of the Grand Slams, was that it would not go to an American. Arthur Ashe, Stan Smith, Jimmy Connors, John McEnroe – all had visited Paris repeatedly and failed, finding the unforgiving red clay as barren as the Arizona desert.

It had taken the little-known, inexperienced, yet mature 17-year-old Michael Chang in 1989 to breach what had become, by then, as much a psychological barrier as a physical one, though Courier's remark that it was just another tournament was a rather tactless over-simplification.

It was, however, the first all-American men's final seen at Roland Garros since Tony Trabert beat Art Larsen in 1954. On that occasion Trabert had won in straight sets; this one went the full distance, Courier defeating a rival with whom he had once shared a room at Bollettieri's Academy in Bradenton, 3–6 6–4 2–6 6–1 6–4. It was a stunning defeat for a man who by his play and personality had rightly won the crowd's support but another to add to a liturgy of similar losses – notably those from match point against Alberto Mancini in the 1989 Italian final and from two sets clear against Boris Becker in the *Davis Cup* competition.

Courier felt he had been a trifle fortunate because a rain break, when he was a set and 1–3 behind, gave his coach, Jose Higueras, the chance to offer some advice; especially to stand further back on the Agassi serve and return with greater depth. 'That, I believe, was the turning point for me,' he said. 'Without Jose, I wouldn't be the champion.' It was a generous tribute but Courier still had to implement his changed game-plan. And in the end it was the pressure he applied which finally undermined Agassi – above all with his forehand.

There was a time, of course, when it was argued that experience was the only key to winning in Paris. Yet in the last 10 years the men's title has been won by a succession of teenagers: Mats Wilander, at his first attempt in 1982, Chang at his second in 1989 and now Courier at his third. Maybe, after all, ignorance really is what brings bliss!

Unlike Seles, who as defending champion and No.1 seed was a focus of attention from the start, Courier slid quietly and unobtrusively into the quarter-finals, his way being cleared by the early exit of Goran Ivanisevic while, at the same time, his game was being sharpened by a testing five-setter against the Swede, Magnus Larsson.

Courier's big advantage, in a sense, was a lop-sided draw that did not work out as had been anticipated. Stefan Edberg, Lendl, Pete Sampras, McEnroe, Ivanisevic, Michael Stich, Wilander and the unseeded but awkward Soviet Andrei Chesnokov were all bracketed with him in the top half. The bottom half, by comparison, despite the presence of Chang, was tailor-made for producing – as in the event it did – an Agassi versus Becker semi-final.

However, Lendl's withdrawal less than 24 hours before the Championships began, because of a build up of callouses on his racket-hand that required surgery, put a different complexion on things. A first round defeat for McEnroe was followed by the second round dismissal not only of Ivanisevic but also of Sampras and Wilander. The road was open – especially, it seemed, for Edberg.

Though his Grand Slam record as the No.1 seed was disastrous, including as it did those first round defeats at both Paris and Flushing Meadow in 1990, the Swede had shown the necessary patience, skill and confidence to reach the last eight at a cost of only one set, beating the talented Soviet pair Chesnokov and Andrei Cherkasov en route.

Courier did not seem an insurmountable barrier but, on the day, the Swede's serve-and-volley game was well below par and the American's pounding back-court assault saw him through in under three hours, leaving the tournament without a Swedish semi-finalist for the first time in 14 years.

Meanwhile Stich, who had also benefited from the early carnage by avoiding any seeded player until the last eight, met and duly routed the hapless Argentine Franco Davin with a performance that offered a clear hint that on grass he could be an even greater menace. A violent striker of the ball, the tall Stich had the 5'8" Davin ducking and diving to avoid being decapitated. In his last 12 service games the German never dropped more than a single point; moreover his telescopic reach made it almost impossible for Davin to get the ball past him.

In the lower half the advances of Agassi and Becker, though impressive, were for the first week almost totally overshadowed by the progress of a certain Jimmy Connors. The American left-hander, nearing his 39th birthday proved himself to be still a formidable competitor, as Todd Witsken, Ronald Agenor and Chang would testify.

Out of the game, injured, for more than a year and only back in Paris thanks to a wild card and a successful operation on a wrist (his original intention was solely to work for TV), Jimbo – ranked 324 and unseeded in a Grand Slam for the first time since 1972 – left his indelible print on the tournament and earned the sort of acclaim normally reserved for champions.

The greatest moment for Connors, strangely, came in defeat. Though the crowd had revelled in his straight-sets win over Witsken and marvelled at his five-sets victory over Agenor, his battle with Chang could be summed-up in one word – *incroyable!* Connors, required to play two marathons within 48 hours, quite literally played until he dropped. Even Chang admitted he was not sure that, had it lasted through a fifth set, he would have won. In the end Connors, a single point ahead in the fifth, conceded. 'It's impossible; I just can't play any more,' he admitted.

It was Becker, his concentration firmed after being taken to five sets by Australia's Todd Woodbridge, whose greater power finally saw off Chang, while Agassi, with almost perfect tennis, clinched their projected semi-final clash by overwhelming the Swiss No.1, Jakob Hlasek, at the cost of only five games.

As so often, though, the semi-finals were a disappointment. America achieved a clean sweep over Germany as Agassi defeated Becker 7–5 6–3 3–6 6–1 and Courier beat Stich 6–2 6–7 6–2 6–4 to set up the first one-nation final since Rod Laver beat Ken Rosewall in 1969.

Apart from the first round defeat of Zina Garrison, who had appeared only out of a sense of duty ('I just can't play on this stuff'), it was the seventh day of the tournament before any of the other top seven seeds in the women's singles dropped a set – a fact that did little to enhance their campaign for equal prize money.

It was Seles who faltered, though only momentarily, against Sandra Cecchini, and although it was Jana Novotna who, twice at match point against Gabriela Sabatini in the quarters, should have sprung the first real surprise, that was left to Arantxa Sanchez-Vicario in the semis.

Shock, perhaps, would be a better word than surprise to describe the tiny Spaniard's 6–0 6–2 annihilation of the No.2 seed Steffi Graf. As the record showed, the great German world champion had never been beaten so badly. To compound her misery, Graf, who had no explanation for her failure, then had to endure a grilling following an incident in the competitor's stand in which her father was alleged to have struck a fellow spectator.

Despite the irritating distraction of two rain breaks, Seles had no real difficulty in withstanding Sabatini's timid challenge. The Argentine's serve proved a serious weakness in a match that failed to live up to expectations raised by Sabatini's victory four weeks earlier in Rome.

As expected, the final was a relentless baseline duel and closer than the 6–3 6–4 score suggests. Unfortunately for Sanchez-Vicario, whenever she tried to take the initiative she pressed too hard and made errors. Seles succeeded because her concentration was total throughout and she always had the ability to raise the tempo without sacrificing authority.

New champions emerged in all three of the doubles events, though both Anders Jarryd and John Fitzgerald, who won the men's, had triumphed previously with other partners. Helena Sukova and Cyril Suk, winners of the mixed, became the first sister-brother to win a Grand Slam title since Tracy and John Austin at Wimbledon in 1980.

A semi-finalist in 1989, the 19-year-old American, Mary Joe Fernandez, was beaten this time one round earlier by the eventual finalist, Arantxa Sanchez-Vicario. *(R. Adams)*

MEN'S SINGLES

Holder: A. Gomez (ECU)

Final score: 3–6 6–4 2–6 6–1 6–4

	FIRST ROUND	SECOND ROUND	THIRD ROUND	FOURTH ROUND	QUARTER-FINALS	SEMI-FINALS	FINAL
1	S. EDBERG (SWE) (1)	EDBERG (1) 6-2 6-3	EDBERG (1) 6-4 5-7 7-6 6-3	EDBERG (1) 6-1 6-4 6-3	EDBERG (1) 7-6 6-4 6-3		
2	B. Wuyts (BEL) (LL)						
3	D. Wheaton (USA)	Skoff 6-2 6-7 3-6 6-2 6-4					
4	H. Skoff (AUT)						
5	G. Raoux (FRA)	Kuhnen 4-6 6-2 6-4	Chesnokov 4-6-3 3-6 6-3 8-6				
6	P. Kuhnen (GER)						
7	A. Chesnokov (URS)	Chesnokov 4-6 6-3 3-6 6-3 8-6					
8	M. Koevermans (HOL)						
9		Pescariu 5-7 7-5 6-2 6-3	Yzaga 6-2 2-6 6-0	Cherkasov 7-5 3-6 6-3 6-3			
10	F. Rivera (CHI) (Q)						
11	T. Tulasne (FRA) (WC)	Yzaga 6-1 1-4-6 6-4 6-2					
12	J. Yzaga (PER)						
13	P. Cash (AUS)	Cash 6-4 7-6 6-3	Cherkasov 6-7 6-1 6-3 3-6 7-5				
14	S. Noszay (HUN) (Q)						
15	A. Cherkasov (URS)	Cherkasov 2-6 6-4 7-5 7-6					
16	J. McENROE (USA) (15)						
17	J. COURIER (USA) (9)	COURIER (9) 2-6 6-4 7-5 7-6	COURIER (9) 6-2 6-3 6-4	COURIER (9) 6-3 4-6-4 6-7 5-6 2	COURIER (9) 6-2 6-3 6-3	COURIER (9) 6-4 2-6-3 6-4	COURIER (9) 6-2 6-7 6-2 6-4
18	D. Rostagno (USA)						
19	W. Ferreira (RSA)	Ferreira 6-4 6-1 6-4					
20	C. Steeb (GER)						
21	E. Furlan (ITA)	Dosedel 6-3 6-0 6-2	Larsson 7-5 6-2 6-4	Martin 6-2 4-6-6-3 6-4			
22	C. Dosedel (TCH) (Q)						
23	N. Marques (POR)	Larsson 6-1 6-3 6-2					
24	M. Larsson (SWE)						
25	T. Martin (USA) (Q)	Martin 6-3 6-7 6-4 6-4	Martin 6-1 6-2 6-4				
26	L. Herrera (MEX)						
27	G. Muller (USA)	Muller 6-4 4-6 6-4 6-7 6-0	Haarhuis 6-1 6-1				
28	G. Connell (CAN)						
29	P. Haarhuis (HOL)	Haarhuis 6-3 6-1					
30	R. Reneberg (USA)						
31	F. Fontang (FRA) (WC)	IVANISEVIC (8) 6-3 6-1	Davin 6-4 6-3 6-2	Davin 6-2 2-6-6-4-3 6-6-4	Davin 7-6 4-6 6-3 6-1		
32	G. IVANISEVIC (YUG) (8)						
33	M. Ingaramo (ARG) (LL)	Davin 6-3 4-6-1					
34	M. Jaite (ARG)						
35	C. Bergstrom (SWE)	Leconte 6-3 6-4 6-1	Vajda 3-6 6-4 7-6 6-4				
36	R. Davin (ARG)						
37	F. Rdbert (FRA)	Vajda 6-2 6-1					
38	H. Leconte (FRA)						
39	M. Vajda (TCH)	Vajda 3-6 6-3 1-6 3					
40	N. Kroon (SWE) (Q)						
41	N. Kulti (SWE)	Kulti 6-4 3-6 6-4 6-2	Boetsch 6-3 6-3	Boetsch 5-7 7-6 3-6 2	STICH (12) 6-3 6-1 6-2	STICH (12) 6-4 6-4 6-4	STICH (12) 6-4 6-4 6-4
42	P. Baur (GER)						
43	L. Mattar (BRA)	Boetsch 6-4 6-3 6-1					
44	A. Boetsch (FRA) (WC)						
45	M. Woodforde (AUS)	Perez 6-1 6-7 6-1 6-3	Markus 2-6 6-2 6-4 6-4 6-3				
46	D. Perez (URU) (Q)						
47	P. Markus (ARG) (Q)	Markus 7-5 6-4					
48	A. Snabel (CAN) (LL)						
49	M. STICH (GER) (12)	STICH (12) 6-3 6-3 7-5	STICH (12) 6-7 7-6 6-3 6-2	STICH (12) 3-6 7-5 7-6 6-2			
50	B. Pearce (USA)						
51	R. Krajicek (HOL)	Krajicek 6-0 6-4 6-1					
52	J. Aitur (ESP) (LL)						
53	J. Eltingh (HOL)	Costa 6-2 6-3 6-3	Costa 7-5 6-1 6-2				
54	C. Costa (ESP) (Q)						
55	J. Grabb (USA)	Benhabiles 4-6 4-6 6-4 6-2 6-3					
56	T. Benhabiles (FRA) (WC)						
57	F. Santoro (FRA)	Santoro 6-4 6-3 6-1	Santoro 6-2 6-3 6-2	Santoro 6-2 6-0 6-4			
58	A. Mronz (GER)						
59	L. Lavalle (MEX) (Q)	Wilander 6-4 6-3 6-2					
60	T. Wilander (SWE)						
61	A. Rahunen (FIN)	Champion 7-6 7-5 1-6 6-1	Champion 6-3 6-1 6-1				
62	T. Champion (FRA)						
63	T. Muster (AUT)	SAMPRAS (6)					
64	P. SAMPRAS (USA) (6)						

J. COURIER (USA) (9)

First round

65 S. **BRUGUERA** (ESP) (5)
66 S. Davis (USA)
67 U. Riglewski (GER)
68 O. Camporese (ITA)
69 J. Baguena (ESP) (Q)
70 C. Miniussi (ARG) (Q)
71 M. Filippini (URU)
72 R. Fromberg (AUS)
73 M. Caratti (ITA)
74 G. Lopez (ESP) (Q)
75 T. Carbonell (ESP)
76 J. Gunnarsson (SWE)
77 J. Hlasek (SUI)
78 D. Pate (USA)
79 A. Jarryd (SWE)
80 E. **SANCHEZ** (ESP) (11)
81 K. **NOVACEK** (TCH) (14)
82 M. Gustafsson (SWE)
83 E. Masso (BEL)
84 A. Krickstein (USA)
85 G. Prpic (YUG)
86 M. Robertson (RSA) (Q)
87 A. Mancini (ARG) (WC)
88 E. Jelen (GER)
89 P. McEnroe (USA)
90 G. Bloom (ISR)
91 O. Soules (FRA) (WC)
92 J. Stoltenberg (AUS)
93 P. Korda (TCH)
94 J. Fleurian (FRA)
95 M. Rosset (SUI)
96 A. **AGASSI** (USA) (4)
97 G. **FORGET** (FRA) (7)
98 M. Washington (USA)
99 J. Arias (USA)
100 J. Rebolledo (CHI)
101 J. Tarango (USA)
102 V. Paloheimo (FIN)
103 M. Ondruska (RSA) (Q)
104 J. Aguilera (ESP)
105 R. Matsuoka (JPN)
106 R. Agenor (HAI)
107 T. Witsken (USA)
108 J. Connors (USA) (WC)
109 H. De La Pena (ARG)
110 J. Jonsson (SWE)
111 J. Siemerink (HOL)
112 M. **CHANG** (USA) (10)
113 B. **GILBERT** (USA) (16)
114 C. Pioline (FRA) (WC)
115 F. Clavet (ESP)
116 K. Evernden (N.Z.)
117 G. Perez-Roldan (ARG)
118 O. Delaitre (FRA) (Q)
119 P. Lundgren (SWE)
120 A. Volkov (URS)
121 J. Cunha-Silva (POR)
122 W. Masur (AUS)
123 E. Sanchez (ESP)
124 J. Oncins (BRA)
125 C. Saceanu (GER)
126 T. Woodbridge (AUS)
127 J. Arrese (ESP)
128 B. **BECKER** (GER) (2)

Second round (first-round winners)

- **BRUGUERA** (5) — 6-2 6-2 6-1
- Camporese — 6-4 6-2 6-2
- Miniussi — 6-4 3-6 2-6 6-3 6-3
- Filippini — 6-4 3-6 6-1 6-2
- Caratti — 2-6 6-2 6-3 6-4
- Carbonell — 5-7 6-2 6-3 6-1
- Hlasek — 6-4 6-1 7-5
- E. **SANCHEZ** (11) — 6-2 6-3 6-2
- Gustafsson — 6-2 3-6 5-1 ret'd
- Krickstein — 6-7 6-4 2-6 6-4 7-5
- Prpic — 7-6 6-3 6-3
- Mancini — 7-5 6-4 7-6
- P. McEnroe — 7-5 6-4 6-2
- Stoltenberg — 6-3 6-7 6-4
- Korda — 4-6 6-4 6-2 6-4
- **AGASSI** (4) — 6-1 6-2 6-4
- **FORGET** (7) — 7-5 2-6 7-5 1-6 7-5
- Arias — 6-0 3-6 6-0 6-2
- Paloheimo — 6-2 6-2 6-1
- Ondruska — 3-6 6-1 6-1 2-6 6-0
- Agenor — 3-6 7-5 6-3 6-4
- Connors — 6-4 2-6 3-6 0-6 6-4
- Jonsson — 6-3 6-3 7-5
- **CHANG** (10) — 6-3 6-1 6-1
- Pioline — 6-4 2-6 6-1 6-4
- Clavet — 6-2 6-3 7-6
- Delaitre — 6-2 6-7 6-4 6-2
- Lundgren — 6-3 6-1
- Masur — 6-1 7-6 7-5
- Oncins — 5-7 6-4 6-4 6-3
- Woodbridge — 6-4 7-6 5-6 4-6
- **BECKER** (2) — 6-2 7-5 6-2

Third round (second-round winners)

- Camporese — 1-6 2-6 6-4 1-0 ret'c
- Miniussi — 1-6 6-2 4-4 ret'd
- Carbonell — 6-1 7-5 3-6 6-1
- Hlasek — 6-3 4-6 6-2 7-6
- Gustafsson — 6-1 4-6 6-4 6-2
- Mancini — 1-6 7-5 6-4 1-6 6-2
- P. McEnroe — 7-5 6-4 7-6
- **AGASSI** (4) — 6-1 6-2 6-2
- **FORGET** (7) — 6-3 6-2 5-7 7-6
- Ondruska — 3-6 6-1 6-1 2-6 6-0
- Connors — 6-4 2-3 6-0 6-4
- **CHANG** (10) — 7-6 6-4 4-3 6-3
- Clavet — 6-2 6-3 7-6
- Delaitre — 6-2 6-7 6-4 6-2
- Masur — 6-1 7-6 7-5
- **BECKER** (2) — 5-7 6-4 6-4 6-4

Fourth round (third-round winners)

- Miniussi — 2-6 6-3 6-1 6-3
- Hlasek — 7-6 4-6 6-4 6-3
- Mancini — 6-3 3-6 6-2 6-3
- **AGASSI** (4) — 6-2 6-2 6-0
- **FORGET** (7) — 6-1 6-4 3-6 6-3
- **CHANG** (10) — 4-6 7-5 2-4 6-? ret'd
- Clavet — 4-6 6-2 6-3 6-4
- **BECKER** (2) — 6-3 6-3 6-2

Fourth round winners

- Hlasek — 4-6 6-3 5-7 7-5 6-2
- **AGASSI** (4) — 6-3 6-3 5-7 6-1
- **CHANG** (10) — 6-1 6-1 4-6 6-3
- **BECKER** (2) — 7-6 6-4 6-3

Quarter-finals

- **AGASSI** (4) — 6-3 6-1 6-1
- **BECKER** (2) — 6-4 6-4 6-2

Semi-final

- **AGASSI** (4) — 7-5 6-3 3-6 6-1

WOMEN'S SINGLES

Holder: M. Seles (YUG)

FIRST ROUND	SECOND ROUND	THIRD ROUND	FOURTH ROUND	QUARTER-FINALS	SEMI-FINALS	FINAL
1 **M. SELES (YUG) (1)**	**SELES (1)** 6–3 6–0	**SELES (1)** 6–0 6–2	**SELES (1)** 6–1 6–2	**SELES (1)** 3–6 6–3 6–0	**SELES (1)** 6–0 7–5	**SELES (1)** 6–4 6–1
2 R. Zrubakova (TCH)						
3 M. De Swardt (RSA)	De Swardt 6–7 7–6 6–1					
4 A. Fusai (FRA) (WC)		Quentrec 6–1 4–6 6–3				
5 A. Kanellopoulou (GRE)	Fendick 6–4 6–2					
6 P. Fendick (USA)						
7 K. Quentrec (FRA)	Quentrec 7–6 7–6					
8 G. Helgeson (USA)						
9 I. Cueto (GER)	Cecchini 6–3 3–6 7–5	Cecchini 6–2 6–2	Cecchini 6–3 6–4			
10 S. Cecchini (ITA)						
11 C. Suire (FRA) (WC)	Suire 6–2 6–3					
12 F. Paradis (FRA)						
13 F. Bonsignori (ITA)	Bonsignori 6–3 6–4	HUBER (16) 6–0 6–2				
14 N. Herreman (FRA)						
15 L. Garrone (ITA)	**HUBER (16)** 6–2 6–3					
16 **A. HUBER (GER) (16)**						
17 **J. CAPRIATI (USA) (10)**	**CAPRIATI (10)** 6–2 7–5	CAPRIATI (10) 6–2 6–1	CAPRIATI (10) 6–3 6–0	MARTINEZ (7) 6–3 6–3		
18 K. Piccolini (ITA)						
19 N. Miyagi (JPN)	Temesvari 6–1 6–3					
20 A. Temesvari (HUN)						
21 E. Pampoulova (BUL)	Van Lottum 6–4 2–6 6–3	Kidowaki 6–3 5–7 8–6				
22 N. Van Lottum (FRA) (WC)						
23 B. Schultz (HOL)	Kidowaki 6–4 6–4					
24 M. Kidowaki (JPN)						
25 C. Cunningham (USA)	Cunningham 6–2 6–2	Cunningham 6–2 7–5	MARTINEZ (7) 6–1 6–4			
26 S. Martin (USA)						
27 K. Habsudova (TCH)	Halard 6–4 7–5					
28 J. Halard (FRA)						
29 S. Rehe (USA)	Rehe 7–5 6–3	**MARTINEZ (7)** 6–1 7–6				
30 Y. Basuki (INA)						
31 J. Wiesner (AUT)	**MARTINEZ (7)** 6–4 6–3					
32 **C. MARTINEZ (ESP) (7)**						
33 **G. SABATINI (ARG) (3)**	**SABATINI (3)** 6–1	SABATINI (3) 6–1 6–1	SABATINI (3) 6–2 6–1	SABATINI (3) 6–3 6–0	SABATINI (3) 5–7 7–6 6–0	
34 M. Verdel (USA)						
35 E. Zardo (SUI)	Zardo 6–3 6–2					
36 M. Paz (ARG)						
37 V. Martinek (GER)	Martinek 6–1 6–0	Pierce 6–3 6–0				
38 K. Porwik (GER)						
39 M. Pierce (FRA)	Pierce 7–6 6–0					
40 C. Dahlman (SWE)						
41 T. Takagi (JPN)	G. Fernandez 7–6 6–2	McQuillan 6–2 6–2	McQuillan 6–4 2–6 6–4			
42 G. Fernandez (USA)						
43 C. Bartos (SUI)	McQuillan 6–3 7–5					
44 R. McQuillan (AUS)						
45 H. Kelesi (CAN)	Kelesi 6–0 6–2	Kelesi 4–6 7–5 6–0				
46 J. Rittner (GER)						
47 E. Sviglerova (TCH)	**SUKOVA (12)** 6–0 6–1					
48 **H. SUKOVA (TCH) (12)**						
49 **L. MESKHI (URS) (14)**	**MESKHI (14)** 6–2 6–2	**MESKHI (14)** 7–5 6–1	MESKHI (14) 6–3 6–1	NOVOTNA (6) 6–0 7–6		
50 S. Dopfer (AUT) (LL)						
51 P. Paradis (FRA) (LL)	Kohde-Kilsch 6–1 6–3					
52 S. Loosemore (GBR)						
53 L. Harvey-Wild (USA)	Harvey-Wild 6–4 7–5	Harvey-Wild 7–6 6–7 11–9				
54 N. Baudone (ITA) (Q)						
55 P. Gildemeister (PER)	Gildemeister 6–3 2–6 6–1					
56 J. Smith (GBR)						
57 A. Keller (USA)	Caverzasio 6–4 6–3	Brioukhovets	NOVOTNA (6) 7–6 6–2			
58 C. Caverzasio (SUI)						
59 A. Dechaume (FRA)	Brioukhovets 1–6 6–2 7–5					
60 E. Brioukhovets (URS)						
61 E. Mothes (FRA)	Hy 6–2 6–2	**NOVOTNA (6)** 6–2 6–1				
62 R. Hy (CAN)						
63 S. Farina (ITA) (LL)	**NOVOTNA (6)** 7–5 6–2					
64 **J. NOVOTNA (TCH) (6)**						

M. SELES (YUG) (1)

First round entrants (65–128)

65 A. SANCHEZ-VICARIO (ESP) (5)
66 K. McNeil (USA)
67 K. Godridge (AUS)
68 M. McGrath (USA)
69 B. Fulco (ARG) (Q)
70 E. Smylie (AUS)
71 C. Tessi (ARG)
72 C. Wood (GBR)
73 K. Rinaldi (USA)
74 L. Laskova (TCH) (Q)
75 T. Whitlinger (USA)
76 E. De Lone (USA)
77 A. Grossman (USA)
78 L. Golarsa (ITA)
79 D. Faber (USA)
80 N. ZVEREVA (URS) (15)
81 K. MALEEVA (BUL) (11)
82 M. Jaggard (AUS) (Q)
83 A. Kijimuta (JPN)
84 M. Strandlund (SWE)
85 M. Bollegraf (HOL)
86 E. Reinach (RSA)
87 H. Cioffi (USA)
88 L. Ferrando (ITA)
89 M. Javer (GBR)
90 P. Thoren (FIN) (Q)
91 N. Housset (FRA) (WC)
92 L. Savchenko (URS)
93 J. Durie (GBR)
94 S. Hack (GER)
95 R. Romano (ITA)
96 M. J. FERNANDEZ (USA) (4)
97 Z. GARRISON (USA) (8)
98 M. Sawamatsu (JPN)
99 M. Laval (FRA) (WC)
100 R. Baranski (USA)
101 S. Niox-Chateau (FRA) (WC)
102 K. Lemonnier (FRA)
103 P. Reinstadler (AUT)
104 D. Graham (USA)
105 N. Jagerman (HOL)
106 A. Strnadova (TCH)
107 R. Hiraki (JPN)
108 R. Provis (AUS)
109 N. Guerree (FRA) (WC)
110 N. Gomer (GBR)
111 F. Etchemendy (FRA) (WC)
112 N. TAUZIAT (FRA) (13)
113 M. MALEEVA-FRAGNIERE (SUI) (9)
114 N. Dahlman (FIN) (Q)
115 W. Probst (GER)
116 R. Rajchtrova (TCH)
117 A. Coetzer (RSA)
118 K. Minter (AUS)
119 S. Appelmans (BEL)
120 R. Bowes (USA) (Q)
121 C. Tanvier (FRA)
122 S. Stafford (USA)
123 F. Labat (ARG)
124 S. Rottier (HOL) (Q)
125 S. Testud (FRA)
126 P. Langrova (TCH)
127 M. Maleeva (BUL)
128 S. GRAF (GER) (2)

Round 1 (→ 32)

SANCHEZ-VICARIO (5) 6-2 6-2
Godridge 6-4 4-6 6-3
Fulco 6-4 6-0
Tessi 6-4 6-1
Rinaldi 6-2 6-3
Whitlinger 6-1 7-6
Grossman 7-5 6-0
ZVEREVA (15) 6-0 6-0
K. MALEEVA (11) 6-3 6-4
Kijimuta 6-0 6-4
Reinach 6-0 6-2
Cioffi 7-5 4-6 6-0
Thoren 6-2 6-2
Savchenko 6-1 6-4
Hack 6-4 7-5
M.J. FERNANDEZ (4) 6-4 6-0
Sawamatsu 6-4 6-0
Baranski 3-6 6-4 6-3
Niox-Chateau 6-4 6-4
Graham 6-1 7-5
Jagerman 6-2 6-4
Provis 4-6 7-6 6-2
Guerree 6-3 7-6
TAUZIAT (13) 6-3 6-1
MALEEVA-FRAGNIERE (9) 6-2 6-2
Rajchtrova 6-4 6-3
Coetzer 5-7 7-5 6-3
Appelmans 6-1 3-6 7-5
Stafford 6-2 6-1
Labat 7-5 6-1
Langrova 6-2 0-6 9-7
GRAF (2) 6-3 7-6

Round 2 (→ 16)

SANCHEZ-VICARIO (5) 6-1 6-2
Fulco 6-2 6-2
Whitlinger 6-4 6-0
Grossman 4-6 6-1 6-4
K. MALEEVA (11) 6-2 6-3
Reinach 6-0 6-2
Thoren 6-3 3-6 7-5
M.J. FERNANDEZ (4) 6-4 6-0
Sawamatsu 6-0 7-6
Graham 6-4 6-0
Jagerman 6-4 5-7 6-3
TAUZIAT (13) 6-2 6-1
Rajchtrova 6-4 6-0
Appelmans 6-3 5-7 6-1
Stafford 6-3 7-5
GRAF (2) 6-0 6-1

Round 3 (→ 8)

SANCHEZ-VICARIO (5) 6-1 6-1
Whitlinger 7-6 6-4
Reinach 6-4 6-4
M.J. FERNANDEZ (4) 6-4 6-3
Sawamatsu 5-7 6-2 6-4
TAUZIAT (13) 6-4 6-0
Appelmans 6-2 6-0
GRAF (2) 6-2 6-0

Round 4 (→ 4)

SANCHEZ-VICARIO (5) 6-2 6-1
M.J. FERNANDEZ (4) 6-4 7-6
TAUZIAT (13) 7-5 2-6 12-10
GRAF (2) 6-2 6-2

Quarterfinals (→ 2)

SANCHEZ-VICARIO (5) 6-3 6-2
GRAF (2) 6-3 6-2

Semifinal (→ 1)

SANCHEZ-VICARIO (5) 6-0 6-2

Capital letters denote seeded players. Number following player's name gives seeding order. (Q) – Qualifier. (WC) – Wild Card. (LL) – Lucky Loser.

MEN'S DOUBLES

Holders: S. Casal (ESP)/E. Sanchez (ESP)

Winner: FITZGERALD (AUS)/JARRYD (SWE) (9) 6-0 7-6

FIRST ROUND

1 S. DAVIS/PATE (1)
2 Lozano/Minussi
3 Clavet/Costa
4 T. Brown/Rostagno
5 Rauo/Santoro (WC)
6 Beckman/Melville
7 Bahrami/Winogradsky
8 JENSEN/WARDER (15)
9 FITZGERALD/JARRYD (9)
10 Mattar/Perez
11 Engel/Jonsson
12 Benhabiles/Pioline (WC)
13 Eltingh/Pimek
14 Garnett/Van Emburgh
15 Davids/Siemerink
16 B&P McENROE (8)
17 GALBRAITH/WITSKEN (4)
18 Devries/MacPherson
19 Flach/Nargiso
20 Carbonell/De La Pena
21 Kuhl/Larsson
22 Kinnear/Salumaa
23 Reneberg/Wheaton
24 HAARHUIS/KOEVERMANS (13)
25 WOODBRIDGE/WOODFORDE (12)
26 Henricsson/Utgren
27 Apsin/Solves
28 Luza/Motta
29 Damm/Oncins
30 Bloom/Wekesa
31 Kruger/Norval
32 CONNELL/MICHIBATA (6)
33 FORGET/HLASEK (5)
34 Gunnarsson/Mortensen
35 Oosting/Vacek
36 Patridge/Thorne
37 Cannon/Smith
38 Nijssen/Suk
39 Dykt/Lundgren
40 CAHILL/KRATZMANN (11)
41 IVANISEVIC/KORDA (14)
42 Fleuran/Rosset (WC)
43 Evernden/Rive
44 Krajicek/Schapers
45 Pearce/Talbot
46 Bates/N. Brown
47 Gorriz/Olhovskiy
48 LEACH/PUGH (3)
49 Muller/Visser
50 Delaitre/Gilbert
51 Stankovic/Vogel
52 Borwick/Youl
53 Boetsch/Champion
54 Annacone/Pereira
55 J. Sanchez/Zivojinovic
56 RIGLEWSKI/STICH (10)
57 FLACH/SEGUSO (16)
58 Albano/Mora
59 Frana/Lavalle
60 Bağuena/Svantesson
61 Flegl/Prpic
62 Masur/Stoltenberg
63 Bathman/Bergh
64 CASAL/E. SANCHEZ (2)

SECOND ROUND

Lozano/Minussi 6-7 6-3 6-2
Clavet/Costa 6-4 7-6
Beckman/Melville
JENSEN/WARDER (15) 3-6 6-3 6-4
FITZGERALD/JARRYD (9) 7-5 6-2
Engel/Jonsson 6-4 7-6
Eltingh/Pimek
Davids/Siemerink 6-3 6-4
Devries/MacPherson 6-3 6-4
Carbonell/De La Pena 6-2 2-6 7-6 3
Reneberg/Wheaton
HAARHUIS/KOEVERMANS (13) 6-3 6-2
WOODBRIDGE/WOODFORDE (12) 6-3 6-2
Luza/Motta 6-2 4-6 6-1
Bloom/Wekesa 7-6 6-3
CONNELL/MICHIBATA (6) 6-7 6-1 6-0
FORGET/HLASEK (5) 4-6 7-6 7-5
Oosting/Vacek 5-7 7-6 6-3
Nijssen/Suk 7-6 7-5
CAHILL/KRATZMANN (11) 6-4 7-5
IVANISEVIC/KORDA (14) 7-6 6-7 6-4
Krajicek/Schapers 6-4 7-6
Bates/N. Brown 7-5 4-6 6-2
LEACH/PUGH (3) 6-4 2-6 6-2
Muller/Visser 7-6 6-4
Borwick/Youl 6-4 7-6
Boetsch/Champion 6-2 7-6
RIGLEWSKI/STICH (10) 6-2 7-6 3
FLACH/SEGUSO (16) 6-1 6-4
Frana/Lavalle 7-6 6-4
Flegl/Prpic 7-6 6-4
CASAL/E. SANCHEZ (2) 6-3 6-4

THIRD ROUND

Lozano/Minussi 6-3 6-4
JENSEN/WARDER (15) 2-6 6-3 9-7
FITZGERALD/JARRYD (9) 7-5 6-3
Eltingh/Pimek 6-2 6-1
Devries/MacPherson 4-6 6-4 6-3
HAARHUIS/KOEVERMANS (13) 7-5 4-6 6-3
WOODBRIDGE/WOODFORDE (12) 6-1 6-4
CONNELL/MICHIBATA (6) 6-4 6-4
FORGET/HLASEK (5) 6-2 6-2
Nijssen/Suk 6-4 6-4
Krajicek/Schapers 4-6 7-5 6-2
LEACH/PUGH (3) 6-7 7-5 6-3
Muller/Visser 7-6 6-3
RIGLEWSKI/STICH (10) 6-4 6-4
Frana/Lavalle 5-7 6-3 7-5
CASAL/E. SANCHEZ (2) 6-4 6-7 6-3

QUARTER-FINALS

JENSEN/WARDER (15) 5-7 6-4 6-3
FITZGERALD/JARRYD (9) 6-3 6-4
HAARHUIS/KOEVERMANS (13) 6-2 6-2
CONNELL/MICHIBATA (6) 7-6 3
Nijssen/Suk 6-2 6-1
LEACH/PUGH (3) 1-6 6-3 9-7
Muller/Visser 7-6 7-5
Frana/Lavalle 6-4 6-4

SEMI-FINALS

FITZGERALD/JARRYD (9) 7-6 5-7 9-7
CONNELL/MICHIBATA (6) 6-2 7-5
LEACH/PUGH (3) 6-4 1-6 6-4
Frana/Lavalle 6-4 6-4

FINAL

FITZGERALD/JARRYD (9) 6-0 6-4
LEACH/PUGH (3) 6-3 7-5

WOMEN'S DOUBLES

Holders: J. Novotna (TCH)/H. Sukova (TCH)

G. FERNANDEZ (USA)/J. NOVOTNA (TCH) (1) 6–4 6–0

FIRST ROUND

1. G. FERNANDEZ/NOVOTNA (1)
2. Bakkum/Jagerman
3. Demongeot/Kowalski
4. Coorengel/Van Buuren
5. Pospisilova/Scott
6. Harvey-Wild/Stafford
7. Halard/Huber (WC)
8. KELESI/RINALDI (10)
9. KOHDE-KILSCH/MESKHI (13)
10. Amiach/Quentrec (WC)
11. Langrova/Zrubakova
12. Suire/Testud
13. Cunningham/Temesvari
14. Novelo/Somerville
15. Fauli/Jagard
16. BURGIN/FENDICK (7)
17. SANCHEZ-VICARIO/SUKOVA (3)
18. Baranski/Fulco
19. Housset/Niox-Chateau (WC)
20. Laskova/Nohakova
21. Chabalgoity/Smith
22. Pampoulova/Sviglerova
23. Helgeson/Probst
24. SCHULTZ/VIS (15)
25. FAIRBANK-NIDEFFER/REINACH (11)
26. Field/Strandlund
27. Pfaff/Stubbs
28. Collins/Pierce
29. Gregory/Mager
30. Morton/Wood
31. Rajchtmova/Smadova
32. PROVIS/SMYLIE (6)
33. PAZ/SABATINI (8)
34. Whittinger/Whittington
35. Dechaume/Labat
36. Budarova/Meier
37. Basuki/Fuchs
38. Grossman/Kijimuta
39. K. Maleeva/M. Maleeva
40. ADAMS/BOLLEGRAF (9)
41. McQUILLAN/TANVIER (14)
42. Fusai/Gravereaux (WC)
43. Ferrando/Golarsa
44. Benjamin/Coetzer
45. Blumberga/Schneider
46. Fendick/Scheuer-Larsen
47. Alter/Frei Rei
48. M. J. FERNANDEZ/GARRISON (4)
49. JORDAN/McGRATH (5)
50. McNeil/Rehe
51. Maleeva-Fragniere/Strebel
52. Cecchini/Herreman
53. Garrone/Kschwendt
54. Nagelsen/Smoller
55. Milvidskaia/Sabas
56. TAUZIAT/WIESNER (12)
57. APPELMANS/CECCHINI (16)
58. Brioukhovets/Manokova
59. Devries/Wasserman
60. Jankovska/Melicharova
61. Hack/Sprung
62. Farina/Godridge
63. Magdalinkova/Witbow
64. SAVCHENKO/ZVEREVA (2)

SECOND ROUND

- G. FERNANDEZ/NOVOTNA (1) 6–3 6–3
- Coorengel/Van Buuren 4-6 4 6-2
- Harvey-Wild/Stafford 6-1 6-3
- Halard/Huber 6-1 6-1
- KOHDE-KILSCH/MESKHI 6-0 6-3
- Langrova/Zrubakova 6-3 6-1
- Novelo/Somerville 1-6 6-3 6-4
- BURGIN/FENDICK (7) 6-4 6-4
- SANCHEZ-VICARIO/SUKOVA (3) 6-1 6-2
- Housset/Niox-Chateau 6-3 7-6
- Pampoulova/Sviglerova 6-2 6-4
- Helgeson/Probst 6-1 6-1
- FAIRBANK-NIDEFFER/REINACH (11) 6-2 6-2
- Collins/Pierce 4-6 6-1 6-4
- PROVIS/SMYLIE (6) 5-7 6-3 6-4
- PAZ/SABATINI (8) 6-0 6-1
- Dechaume/Labat 6-1 6-1
- ADAMS/BOLLEGRAF (9) 6-0 3-6 6-2
- McQUILLAN/TANVIER (14) 6-2 7-5
- Ferrando/Golarsa 6-2 6-2
- M. J. FERNANDEZ/GARRISON (4) 6-4 6-1
- Blumberga/Schneider 6-4 6-1
- JORDAN/McGRATH (5) 4-6 6-4 6-3
- Maleeva-Fragniere/Strebel
- Garrone/Kschwendt 6-4 6-4
- TAUZIAT/WIESNER (12) 7-5 7-6
- Brioukhovets/Manokova
- Jankovska/Melicharova 6-3 '-6 6-4
- Farina/Godridge 6-2 7-6
- SAVCHENKO/ZVEREVA (2) 5-7 6-1 7-5

THIRD ROUND

- G. FERNANDEZ/NOVOTNA (1) 6-2 6-2
- Halard/Huber 6-1 6-2
- KOHDE-KILSCH/MESKHI (13) 6-2 6-3
- BURG.N/FENDICK (7) 6-2 3-6 6-4
- SANCHEZ-VICARIO/SUKOVA (3) 6-0 5-0
- Helgeson/Probst 6-3 6-2
- Collins/Pierce 6-3 6-2
- Morton/Wood 6-3 7-5
- PAZ/SABATINI (8) 6-2 6-3
- ADAMS/BOLLEGRAF (9) 6-4 6-2
- McQUILLAN/TANVIER (14) 6-1 7-5
- M. J. FERNANDEZ/GARRISON (4) 6-1 6-2
- JORDAN/McGRATH (5) 6-1 6-3
- TAUZIAT/WIESNER (12) 6-2 6-3
- Jankovska/Melicharova 6-3 '-6 6-4
- SAVCHENKO/ZVEREVA (2) 6-2 6-3

QUARTER-FINALS

- G. FERNANDEZ/NOVOTNA (1) 6-4 7-6
- BURGIN/FENDICK (7) 6-4 6-3
- SANCHEZ-VICARIO/SUKOVA (3) 6-2 6-3
- Collins-Pierce 6-2 6-4
- PAZ/SABATINI (8) 6-2 6-2
- M. J. FERNANDEZ/GARRISON (4) 6-2 ret'd
- JORDAN/McGRATH (5) 4-6 6-2 8-6
- SAVCHENKO/ZVEREVA (2) 6-2 6-4

SEMI-FINALS

- G. FERNANDEZ/NOVOTNA (1) 6-3 6-4
- SANCHEZ-VICARIO/SUKOVA (3) 6-3 6-2
- PAZ/SABATINI (8) 6-1 6-2
- SAVCHENKO/ZVEREVA (2) 6-3 5-7 9-7

FINAL

- G. FERNANDEZ/NOVOTNA (1) 7-5 5-7 6-4
- SAVCHENKO/ZVEREVA (2) 6-3 5-7 9-7

Capital letters denote seeded pairings. Number following pairings' names gives seeding order. (Q) – Qualifier. (WC) – Wild Card. (LL) – Lucky Loser.

MIXED DOUBLES

Holders: J. Lozano (MEX)/A. Sanchez-Vicario (ESP)

Winner: C. SUK (TCH)/H. SUKOVA (TCH) (12) 3–6 6–4 6–1

FIRST ROUND

1 GALBRAITH/FENDICK (1)
2 bye
3 Luza/Temesvari
4 Motta/Chabalgoity
5 Bloom/McQuillan
6 J. Brown/Stafford
7 bye
8 CANNON/ADAMS (15)
9 SEGUSO/BURGIN (11)
10 bye
11 Grabb/Graham (WC)
12 Gilbert/Housset (WC)
13 Stoltenberg/Stubbs
14 Annacone/Rehe
15 bye
16 VISSER/FAIRBANK-NIDEFFER (7)
17 Rive/Collins
18 bye
19 Frana/Paz
20 MacPherson/Morton
21 Norval/Demongeot
22 Nijssen/Bollegraf
23 bye
24 KRUGER/GREGORY (9)
25 HAARHUIS/VIS (14)
26 bye
27 Bergh/Strandlund
28 Borwick/Field
29 Winogradsky/Suire
30 Bahrami/Tanvier
31 bye
32 Garnett/Bakkum
33 WOODFORDE/JORDAN (8)
34 bye
35 Talbot/Reinach
36 Smith/McNeil
37 Soule/Van Lottum (WC)
38 Pereira/Pfaff
39 bye
40 KOEVERMANS/SCHULTZ (10)
41 SUK/SUKOVA (12)
42 bye
43 Salumaa/Schneider
44 Patridge/Labat
45 Kinnear/Benjamin
46 Svantesson/Whitlinger
47 bye
48 LEACH/GARRISON (3)
49 LOZANO/SANCHEZ-VICARIO (6)
50 bye
51 Warder/Wood
52 N. Brown/Mager
53 Perez/Kschwendt
54 Dyke/Jaggard
55 bye
56 FLACH/PIERCE (16)
57 PIMEK/SAVCHENKO (13)
58 bye
59 Benhabiles/Herreman (WC)
60 Schapers/Golarsa
61 Michibata/Helgeson
62 Vacek/Strnadova
63 bye
64 WOODBRIDGE/McGRATH (2)

SECOND ROUND

GALBRAITH/FENDICK (1)
Luza/Temesvari 6–3 6–3
J. Brown/Stafford 7–6 7–6
CANNON/ADAMS (15)
SEGUSO/BURGIN (11)
Gilbert/Housset 6–4 7–5
Annacone/Rehe 1–6 6–3 9–7
VISSER/FAIRBANK-NIDEFFER (7)
Rive/Collins
MacPherson/Morton 6–3 7–5
Norval/Demongeot 6–4 6–2
KRUGER/GREGORY (9)
HAARHUIS/VIS (14)
Bergh/Strandlund 7–5 4–6 6–4
Bahrami/Tanvier 6–7 6–3 6–4
Garnett/Bakkum
WOODFORDE/JORDAN (8)
Talbot/Reinach 7–6 6–2
Pereira/Pfaff 6–2 6–4
KOEVERMANS/SCHULTZ (10)
SUK/SUKOVA (12)
Salumaa/Schneider 6–2 6–3
Kinnear/Benjamin 5–7 6–4 6–3
LEACH/GARRISON (3)
LOZANO/SANCHEZ-VICARIO (6)
N. Brown/Mager 6–3 6–1
Dyke/Jaggard 6–4 4–6 6–3
FLACH/PIERCE (16)
PIMEK/SAVCHENKO (13)
Benhabiles/Herreman 7–6 2–6 6–3
Michibata/Helgeson 6–3 6–0
WOODBRIDGE/McGRATH (2)

THIRD ROUND

Luza/Temesvari 6–2 7–5
CANNON/ADAMS (15) 6–2 6–2
Gilbert/Housset 6–3 6–4
VISSER/FAIRBANK-NIDEFFER (7) 2–6 6–2 6–4
MacPherson/Morton 4–6 6–4 7–5
Norval/Demongeot 6–1 6–2
HAARHUIS/VIS (14) 7–6 6–4
WOODFORDE/JORDAN (8) 6–1 6–4
KOEVERMANS/SCHULTZ (10) 6–1 7–6
SUK/SUKOVA (12) 6–3 6–3
LEACH/GARRISON (3) 4–6 7–6 6–4
LOZANO/SANCHEZ-VICARIO (6) 6–2 6–3
FLACH/PIERCE (16) 7–5 4–6 7–5
PIMEK/SAVCHENKO (13) 6–4 6–4
WOODBRIDGE/McGRATH (2) 5–7 7–6 6–2

QUARTER-FINALS

Luza/Temesvari 7–5 6–7 6–1
Gilbert/Housset 6–4 6–3
MacPherson/Morton 7–6 6–4
HAARHUIS/VIS (14) 6–3 6–3
WOODFORDE/JORDAN (8) 6–2 6–3
SUK/SUKOVA (12) 7–5 6–2
LOZANO/SANCHEZ-VICARIO (6) 6–4 6–3
PIMEK/SAVCHENKO (13) 7–5 7–5

SEMI-FINALS

Luza/Temesvari 6–4 5–7 6–1
HAARHUIS/VIS (14) 6–4 6–4
SUK/SUKOVA (12) 4–6 6–4 6–3
LOZANO/SANCHEZ-VICARIO (6) 7–5 6–3

FINAL

HAARHUIS/VIS (14) 2–6 7–6 6–...
SUK/SUKOVA (12) 1–6 6–2 9–...

JUNIOR EVENTS

BOYS' SINGLES – Final: Andrei Medvedev (URS) d. Thomas Enqvist (SWE) 6–4 7–6.
GIRLS' SINGLES – Final: Anna Smashnova (ISR) d. Ines Gorrochategui (ARG) 2–6 7–5 6–1.
BOYS' DOUBLES – Final: Thomas Enqvist (SWE)/Magnus Martinelle (SWE) d. Julian Knowle (AUT)/Johannes Unterberger (AUT) 6–1 6–3.
GIRLS' DOUBLES – Final: Eva Bes (ESP)/Ines Gorrochategui (ARG) d. Zdenka Malkova (TCH)/Eva Martincova (TCH) 6–1 6–3.

FRENCH OPEN CHAMPIONSHIPS PRIZE MONEY – 37,370,000FF

MEN – Total: 17,870,000 plus Per Diem allowances 1,000,000
MEN'S SINGLES – Winner 2,448,000. Runner-up 1,224,000. Semi-finalists 612,000. Quarter-finalists 317,680. Fourth-round losers 172,150. Third-round losers 99,330. Second-round losers 61,050. First-round losers 36,300.
Total: 13,410,000.
MEN'S DOUBLES (per team) – Winners 1,000,000. Runners-up 500,000. Semi-finalists 2499,920. Quarter-finalists 127,800. Third-round losers 72,900. Second-round losers 36,300. First-round losers 24,530.
Total: 4,460,000.
WOMEN – Total: 14,900,000 plus Per Diem allowance 1,000,000
WOMEN'S SINGLES – Winner 2,237,000. Runner-up 1,118,500. Semi-finalists 560,850. Quarter-finalists 280,750. Fourth-round losers 147,250. Third-round losers 81,600. Second-round losers 48,100. First-round losers 30,500.
Total: 11,575,000.
WOMEN'S DOUBLES (per team) – Winners 786,500. Runners-up 393,000. Semi-finalists 196,450. Quarter-finalists 99,850. Third-round losers 51,150. Second-round losers 27,300. First-round losers 15,850.
Total: 3,325,000.
MIXED DOUBLES (per team) – Winners 220,00. Runners-up 132,000. Semi-finalists 79,000. Quarter-finalists 48,400. Second-round losers 26,350. First-round losers 11,600.
Total 1,100,000.
QUALIFYING – MEN (each): 16 × Third-round losers 20,200. 32 × Second-round losers 10,100. 64 × First-round losers 5,525.
Total: 1,000,000.
QUALIFYING – WOMEN (each): 8 × Third-round losers 20,200. 16 × Second-round losers 10,100. 32 × First-round losers 5,525.
Total: 500,000.

For the second time in three years there was a German double at The Championships when Michael Stich scored a remarkable first victory by beating Becker, and Steffi Graf a memorable third by outlasting Sabatini. *(T. Hindley)*

THE CHAMPIONSHIPS – WIMBLEDON
John Barrett

The 1991 Championships, which saw two German singles winners for the second time in three years through Michael Stich's first success and Steffi Graf's third, became an historic meeting when, for the first time in the tournament's 114-year history, play was scheduled on the middle Sunday. The reason for this necessary innovation was rain – days of it, gallons of it, almost oceans of it.

It was Wimbledon's worst-ever start. There was no play at all on the opening day, which became the 26th blank day since 1877. On the Tuesday only 28 matches were completed, among them Martina Navratilova's 100th Wimbledon victory. This was a nervy affair against Elna Reinach of South Africa who, leading 4–3 and 0–30 on Martina's serve in the final set, very nearly upset a defending women's champion in the first round for the first time at The Championships. 'I thought I might lose throughout the whole match – that was one of the problems . . . I don't think I've ever come back from being a break down three times in the final set . . . in the end I just won on emotion.' The effort left all of us as drained as she was.

For most of the gloomy first week players, officials and hardy spectators just sat there and hoped. On Wednesday, with play brought forward to 11.00am on the outside courts and to 1.00pm on the Centre and No.1 Courts, only 18 matches were completed and another 6 on Thursday included the survival of top-seeded Stefan Edberg who had first walked out to defend his title against the Swiss giant, Marc Rosset, four days earlier. 'This is the longest match I've ever played!,' said a relieved champion, smiling.

This was also the day when the charismatic young American, Andre Agassi, made his return after a three-year absence. There had been great speculation about what this colourful character would wear for his match against the left-handed Canadian Grant Connell. He had kept us guessing, but at last he stripped off his shining white tracksuit to reveal a pristine white outfit that would not have disgraced a choir boy. From that moment there developed a love affair between Agassi and his adoring young fans that was to contribute greatly to the eventual success of the meeting. But that first day, Agassi's progress was interrupted at one set all, one game all, as the rains returned.

When, by Thursday night, only 52 of the scheduled 240 matches had been completed (55 fewer than had been played in 1987, the previous wettest first week), the Referee, Alan Mills, called for an 11.00am start on the Friday and Saturday – even on the two main show courts – and started to make preparations behind the scenes to schedule play on Sunday. By now the men's doubles had been reduced to the best of three sets up to the quarter-finals and rest days for the singles players were forgotten as the Referee strove to catch up with the programme.

This was partly achieved over the next two days. Seventy-two matches were completed on Friday and in one of them Agassi eventually survived, but not before Connell, leading two sets to one, had held a point to go 6–5 ahead in the fourth. It was denied him by a dead net-cord. 'That one shot was the reason I'm still in the tournament,' admitted the American afterwards.

Two of the seeded men were beaten – Michael Chang (9) by fellow American Tim Mayotte and Emilio Sanchez (11) by Patrick McEnroe. Mayotte smiled a lot on court No1. He had good reason. Chang had led by two sets to love and had held four match points in the fourth before Mayotte had triumphed 6–2 in the decider. Sanchez, yearning for some Spanish sun on his back, did not have much to smile about as he departed in straight sets.

Three of the British wild cards survived – Jeremy Bates predictably against another drowning Spaniard, Jose Altur; Nick Brown commendably against Mark Keil, the American who had beaten Sampras at Queen's Club two weeks earlier; and Mark Petchey bravely at 8–6 in the fifth set against another wild card, Jim Pugh, the US *Davis Cup* doubles expert.

Another 87 matches on a rain-free Saturday eased the frown on the Referee's face which became wreathed in smiles when the news was brought to him of a dramatic British success out on court thirteen. The fact that Nick Brown, ranked 591 in the world and the recipient of a wild card, had eliminated one of his seeds, Goran Ivanisevic (10), tempered his enthusiasm but there was no doubt about the reaction of the great British public. Starved of home success for so long, they cheered Brown from the court after his four sets win. He was the first Briton to beat a seed since John Lloyd's defeat of Eliot Teltscher in 1985. Overnight the 29-year-old from Cheshire became a national hero. Fortunately for the Yugoslav's self esteem, Ivanisevic did manage to salvage something from the wreckage of the day by teaming with John McEnroe to eliminate the holders of the men's doubles, Rick Leach and Jim Pugh.

Another two men's seeds plus a former champion were lost that day, too. Pete Sampras (8) allowed fellow American Derrick Rostagno to dominate from the net, as the Californian had done the previous year to eliminate John McEnroe, and Jakob Hlasek (13) fell to the young Australian Todd Woodbridge in four sets. That was a feather in Australia's cap but the loss of their 1987 winner, Pat Cash, looking strangely disinterested as he allowed the Frenchman Thierry Champion to escape from two match points and eventually to beat him 12–10 in the final set, was a real Antipodean setback.

While the sun shone on the spectators there was little cheer for two of the women's seeds who lost unexpectedly. The Australian Open finalist Jana Novotna (6) could not contain the service power of the big Dutch girl Brenda Schultz, and Natalia Zvereva (12) was outrallied by the American newcomer, Linda Harvey-Wild.

Alive to the danger that crowds of up to 50,000 might throng to the ground and cause dangerous congestion, the announcement about Sunday play was not made until late on Saturday afternoon. The public heard that 11,000 Centre Court tickets and 7,000 for No.1 Court, all unreserved, would be available at a cost of £10 per head on a first come, first served basis and ground passes would be sold at £5 each. Following dire warnings about likely traffic congestion, the overnight queues – mostly eager young people who had never been to Wimbledon before – were of manageable size and easily marshalled by the local police and Wimbledon Stewards.

The day itself, with play on all courts starting at noon, was an outstanding success, a day of unforgettable scenes of spontaneous enthusiasm – never over the top – which produced an atmosphere of warmth and good-natured fun that no-one who experienced it will ever forget. Gabriela Sabatini and Andrea Strnadova were greeted with happy chants and the first of many 'Mexican waves' that were to set a precedent for the smiling Centre Court which, like an energetic old lady performing the cancan, seemed to revel in a new-found freedom.

It was the same all day long. They joyously applauded victories by defending champion Stefan Edberg and the ebullient Spaniard, Arantxa Sanchez-Vicario. The fact that an old favourite, Jimmy Connors, was beaten in straight sets by Rostagno did not seem to matter. They still chanted, waved and cheered the 33-year-old American's every winner. 'I wish it had been like that for the last twenty years,' he said. 'It really was a great atmosphere.'

Martina admitted to disappointment at being asked to play on court No.2. Once or twice in between matches she popped into the Royal Box, filled for the day with past champions and their families, to enjoy all the fun. Nor did it seem to matter (except to the player himself) that Brown, reacting to his famous win, went down to Frenchman Thierry Champion out on Court 13. The day itself had become bigger than any individual result.

On the second Monday things were returning to normal. All eight of the women's fourth round singles matches were completed and all the third round encounters in the lower half of the men's draw were played to complete the symmetry in that event. By the day's end there had been a major casualty. Ivan Lendl (3), having survived heroically the previous day by recovering to beat Malivai Washington 7–5 in the fifth set after trailing by 2 sets to love –

his 200th Grand Slam singles win – went down disappointingly in four sets to the superior volleying of David Wheaton. By comparison, the loss of Brad Gilbert (15) to Sweden's Christian Bergstrom, a quarter-finalist in 1990, was almost irrelevant.

So fierce had been the competition during seven congested days that half of the 16 favoured men had fallen. Manuela Maleeva (8) was the only women's seed not to take her appointed place in the last eight. She was beaten in the fourth round by Laura Gildemeister of Peru.

Only two of the women's quarter-finals were completed on the second Tuesday. Steffi Graf (1) took revenge against Zina Garrison (7) for the beating she had sustained in the 1990 semi-final and Mary Joe Fernandez (5) beat Miss Sanchez-Vicario (4) for the first time in four meetings. Miss Navratilova (3) was probably glad of the rain. When play ceased in mid-afternoon she had lost the first set to the youngest competitor, Jennifer Capriati (9), and had struggled to break for a 3–2 lead in the second. Miss Sabatini (2), too, was left in mid-air, leading by a set and 1–0 against Miss Gildemeister.

Of the eight men's fourth round clashes only four were completed. Edberg (1) ended the hopes of former champion John McEnroe whose verbal abuse of a linesman, later confirmed by a television news recording, cost him a fine of $10,000. Wheaton beat Jan Gunnarsson of Sweden, while Jim Courier (4) and Stich (6) emerged to do battle in the quarters at the expense of Karel Novacek (14) and Alexander Volkov respectively. This last was a desperately close-run thing with the Russian left-hander leading 3–1 and 30–40 in the fifth set only to see a Stich ace flash past. Serving at 5–4 Volkov was just two points from victory. At 30–15 a German backhand pass hit the line. On the next point a forehand, going wide, clipped the top of the net and was deflected for a winner. Stich went on to break back. 'That was the most important point I have ever played,' he said afterwards. And, for the unfortunate Volkov, the unluckiest.

Wednesday completed the round with Champion coming through at the expense of Rostagno to challenge Edberg (1), and Agassi (5) beating unseeded Dutchman Jacco Eltingh to face Wheaton. In the last quarter Forget (7) beat Mayotte to face Becker who ranted and raved at his own shortcomings (and was warned for racket abuse) in beating Bergstrom without ever looking convincing.

It was also on Wednesday that Miss Capriati celebrated the greatest win of her young life. After remaining commendably cool in completing her 6–4 7–5 defeat of the nine times former champion (achieved with some deadly serves and a barrage of piercing service returns and passes) she became, at 15 years and 96 days, Wimbledon's youngest-ever semi-finalist. Thus, for the first time since 1981, Navratilova would not be in the final. 'I guess she's had her day,' said Capriati without any disrespect for the lady she often refers to as 'The Lege'. 'A lot of good young players are coming up now and there's a new generation beginning to take over.'

Jennifer's part in the takeover ended the following day when Miss Sabatini brought her down to earth 6–4 6–4. It was a magnificent battle in which the winner needed five match points to clinch her sixth successive victory against her young opponent. Miss Capriati was less consistent than the previous day. 'I was still so excited last night I hardly slept,' she said. Everyone could understand that.

Miss Graf had lost no sets and only 17 games in reaching her fifth consecutive Wimbledon semi-final. Fernandez, in her first, could make no impression. Graf's 6–2 6–4 win was as one-sided as the score suggests, as easy as any of her five previous straight sets wins against the Floridian.

The four men's quarter-finals were also played on the Thursday. In two one-sided encounters Edberg accounted for the unseeded Champion and Stich ended the run of the French Open winner, Jim Courier, who had beaten him in the semi-finals in Paris. Courier fought bravely but vainly on a surface alien to his heavy topspin game. The other two were thrillers. It took Becker 3hrs and 47mins to achieve his 6–7 7–6 6–2 7–6 victory over Forget, whose left-handed serve was skidding low and wide off the No.1 Court surface to produce in Becker another of those self-recriminatory performances that left one questioning his sanity.

Agassi, on the Centre Court, appeared to injure his right thigh early in the first set against

Wheaton and received treatment at courtside several times. The injury did not seem to impair his speedy court coverage as he raced into a 2–6 6–0 6–3 lead with some glorious flashing forehands that brought gasps from the crowd.

Agassi led 4–2 in the fourth set and, as Wheaton delivered his 11th double fault to go 0–40, the match seemed as good as over. But Wheaton replied with his 7th and 8th aces (of the 15 he served altogether) and escaped. There seemed no escape, though, when Agassi broke again and served for the match at 6–5. But from 30–15 belief died. As on so many other important occasions, Agassi slumped to defeat from a winning position. The tie-break was lost 3–7 and the fifth set 2–6.

The men's semi-finals provided an impressive array of firepower as first Stich dethroned the reigning champion Edberg 4–6 7–6 7–6 7–6 and then Becker overcame Wheaton 6–4 7–6 7–5 to displace Edberg again as the No.1 ranked player, a position he had held for a month after winning the Australian Open in January. Edberg felt frustrated that in losing his title he did not ever lose his serve. 'I hope it never happens again – I felt I lost it . . . three or four points cost me the match . . . I blew the chances I had.' It was a curious coincidence that, the previous day, the inventor of the tie-break, Jimmy Van Allen, had fallen from a terrace at his Newport, Rhode Island home and died.

For sheer excitement the women's final was the most enjoyable in years with the outcome in doubt until, after 127 agonising minutes, a last nerve-jangling forehand service return was too fast for the lunging Sabatini who went down 6–4 3–6 8–6. It gave Miss Graf her third Wimbledon crown and the first prize of £216,000. This 10th Grand Slam singles title, her first since the 1990 Australian Open, was psychologically vital for Steffi who had endured a traumatic year. A skiing accident, a sinus operartion, a thumping 6–0 6–2 loss to Sanchez in the French semi-finals amid a brawl between an American spectator and her father who was still surrounded by his personal scandal – all these problems had contributed to her unsettled mental state.

Technically it was not a great match, there were too many unforced errors for that. But the tension and suspense made it compulsive viewing, as the Princess of Wales and young Prince William demonstrated by bouncing up and down with excitement in the Royal Box. Although Steffi held a 20–9 advantage in career meetings against Sabatini she had lost six of their eight matches since the 1990 loss in New York that had given Sabatini her only Grand Slam crown – and every one of the last five. Thus, when Sabatini broke to lead 5–4 in the final set as Graf delivered her 6th double fault, that run seemed likely to continue. But Sabatini's serve by now was a thing of frailty and she lost the 10th game to 15. Amazingly, she broke again as Graf sprayed the ball wide but, once more, failed on her own delivery. It was virtually the end.

When Graf had last won in 1989 Becker had followed with a victory the next day and most people expected him to repeat that feat. But Stich had other ideas as this first all-German men's final unfolded. Certainly the 7th ranked player in the world was now a much better player than the man whom Becker had beaten 6–1 6–2 at the 1990 Paris Indoor tournament, their only previous meeting. When Stich broke the three-time champion's serve in the opening game with two blazing backhand returns and a forehand pass after Becker had led 40–30, and then held his own from 30–40, the danger was clear. Becker, instead of leading 2–0 was 0–2. He was never allowed to escape the stranglehold as Stich's backhand and serve became shots of wonderment. His 15 aces gave him a total of 97 for the tournament – just three less than Pete Sampras had served in winning the 1990 US Open title.

In 151 minutes it was all over. Playing in his first Grand Slam final, Stich had handed a decisive 6–4 7–6 6–4 beating to his country's national hero. The fact that he was playing a fellow German had made it all the harder for the tortured Becker to relax. At times it appeared as if he might be taken from the court by men in white coats but he did manage a brave smile at the end as Stich went forward to receive, from the Duke and Duchess of Kent, his cheque for £240,000 and the famous Gold Cup that Boris knew so well. One could only guess at Becker's thoughts as he sat there on the court where previously he had been beaten only twice – both times by Stefan Edberg – since his momentous first win as a 17-year-old in 1985.

John Fitzgerald and Anders Jarryd, the French titleholders, were worthy winners of the men's doubles where matches had been reduced to the best of three sets prior to the quarter-finals. They beat Argentina's Javier Frana and Leo Lavalle of Mexico, left-handers both, 6–3 6–4 6–7 6–1.

The 6–4 3–6 6–4 victory by Larissa Savchenko and Natalia Zvereva (finalists in 1988 and 1989) over Gigi Fernandez and Jana Novotna in the women's doubles final meant that the Soviet Union were winning a first title at Wimbledon, a significant happening in a year of tumultuous change in that great country. They were denied a second when Fitzgerald and fellow Australian, Liz Smylie, beat the top seeds Zvereva and her American partner Jim Pugh 7–6 6–2.

So a Championship that had begun in rain-soaked gloom ended happily in sunshine. Altogether 378,411 spectators attended the meeting – a figure boosted by the 24,894 who had thronged to the ground on the joyous Middle Sunday. This was still well below the record of 400,288 set in 1989 before the voluntary restriction in numbers came into effect.

A finalist in 1990, America's Zina Garrison was halted in the quarter-finals by the eventual champion, Steffi Graf.

(R. Adams)

MEN'S SINGLES

Holder: S. Edberg (SWE)

Final: 6–4 7–6 6–4

FIRST ROUND	SECOND ROUND	THIRD ROUND	FOURTH ROUND	QUARTER-FINALS	SEMI-FINALS	FINAL
1 S. EDBERG (SWE) (1)	EDBERG (1) 6–4 6–4	EDBERG (1) 6–2 6–2 6–3	EDBERG (1) 6–1 6–3 6–2	EDBERG (1) 7–6 6–1 6–4	EDBERG (1) 6–3 6–2 7–5	STICH (6) 4–6 7–6 7–6
2 M. Rosset (SUI)						
3 P. Baur (GER)	Pate 4–6 6–7 6–4 6–2 6–3					
4 D. Pate (USA)						
5 W. Ferreira (RSA)	Ferreira 6–4 6–3 6–3	Van Rensburg 7–6 6–2				
6 J. Aguilera (ESP)						
7 C. Van Rensburg (RSA)	Van Rensburg 7–6 4–6 6–4					
8 C. Wittsken (USA)						
9 S. Raoux (FRA)	Skoff 6–4 6–4 6–3	Fleurian 6–2 6–0 6–3	J. McENROE (16) 6–2 7–6 6–1			
10 H. Skoff (AUT)						
11 A. Mronz (GER)	Fleurian 6–4 6–0 6–3					
12 J. Fleurian (FRA)						
13 M. Kratzmann (AUS) (Q)	Stolle 6–3 6–7 7–6 6–4	J. McENROE (16) 7–6 5–7 6–0 7–6				
14 S. Stolle (AUS) (Q)						
15 J. Oncins (BRA)	J. McENROE (16) 6–1 6–2 6–4					
16 J. McENROE (USA) (16)						
17 G. IVANISEVIC (YUG) (10)	IVANISEVIC (10) 7–6 7–6 6–2	Brown 4–6 6–3 7–6 6–3	Champion 7–6 1–6 7–5 6–3	Champion 6–7 6–2 6–1 3–6 6–3		
18 A. Castle (GBR) (WC)						
19 N. Brown (GBR) (WC)	Cash 6–4 7–5 6–1					
20 M. Keil (USA) (Q)						
21 J. Tarango (USA)	Champion 6–2 6–3 6–3	Champion 7–5 6–7 4–6 6–1 12–10				
22 P. Cash (AUS)						
23 T. Champion (FRA)	Connors 6–2 6–0 7–5					
24 C. Wilkinson (GBR) (WC)						
25 J. S. Connors (USA) (WC)	Krickstein 6–1 6–3 6–7 7–5	Connors 6–3 6–2 6–3	Rostagno 7–6 6–1 6–4			
26 V. Palcheimo (FIN)						
27 A. Krickstein (USA)	Rostagno 6–0 6–3 6–4					
28 S. Pescosolido (ITA)						
29 D. Rostagno (USA)	SAMPRAS (8) 6–1 6–2 6–2	Rostagno 6–4 3–6 7–6 6–4				
30 E. Furlan (ITA)						
31 D. Marcelino (BRA) (Q)	COURIER (4) 6–4 6–2 7–6					
32 P. SAMPRAS (USA) (8)						
33 J. COURIER (USA) (4)	COURIER (4) 6–4 6–2 7–6	COURIER (4) 6–4 7–6 2–6 4–6 6–3	COURIER (4) 6–2 6–2 6–0	COURIER (4) 6–3 6–4 6–2	STICH (6) 6–3 7–6 6–2	
34 R. Gilbert (FRA)						
35 N. Marques (POR)	Gabb 7–5 6–7 6–4 6–1					
36 J. Grabb (USA)						
37 G. Pozzi (ITA) (Q)	Pozzi 4–6 6–3 6–2 6–2	Boetsch 4–6 7–6 6–4				
38 B. Pearce (USA)						
39 B. Dyke (AUS) (Q)	Boetsch 6–3 7–6 6–3					
40 A. Boetsch (FRA) (Q)						
41 E. Herrera (MEX)	Frana 3–6 2–6 6–3 6–3 6–3	Frana 7–6 6–2 6–2	NOVACEK (14) 6–4 6–4 5–7 6–4			
42 J. Frana (ARG) (Q)						
43 F. Roese (BRA) (Q)	Curren 6–3 6–3 6–1					
44 K. Curren (USA)						
45 J. Sanchez (ESP)	J. Sanchez 6–4 6–4 6–7 6–3	NOVACEK (14) 6–0 6–1 7–6				
46 J. Krek (USA) (Q)						
47 U. Riglewski (GER)	NOVACEK (14) 7–6 6–3 6–4					
48 K. NOVACEK (TCH) (14)						
49 A. CHERKASOV (URS) (12)	Reneberg 6–4 6–3 6–4	Laurendeau 3–6 6–4 6–7 6–4 6–2	Volkov 6–1 6–2 6–1	STICH (6) 4–6 3–6 7–5 1–6 7–5		
50 R. A. Reneberg (USA)						
51 D. E. Sapsford (GBR) (WC)	Laurendeau 6–3 7–6 6–3					
52 M. Laurendeau (CAN) (LL)						
53 B. Wuyts (BEL)	Volkov 6–1 6–2 6–2	Volkov 6–2 3–6 6–4 3–6 8–6				
54 A. Volkov (URS)						
55 M. Jarryd (SWE)	Jarryd 6–3 6–4 3–6 6–3					
56 N. Kroon (SWE) (LL)						
57 D. Pistolesi (ITA)	Camporese 6–1 6–3 2–6 6–3	Camporese 7–5 6–2 6–1	STICH (6) 7–5 6–2 6–7 6–4			
58 G. Camporese (ITA)						
59 G. Michibata (CAN) (Q)	Michibata 5–7 6–4 3–6 7–6 6–4					
60 P. J. Stoltenberg (AUS)						
61 D. Nargiso (ITA) (LL)	Nargiso 6–4 7–6	STICH (6) 6–3 6–4 6–7 6–2				
62 M. Woodforde (AUS)						
63 M. Goellner (GER)	STICH (6) 6–4 6–1 6–2					
64 M. STICH (GER) (6)						

M. STICH (GER) (6)

Final

BECKER (2)
6-4 7-6 7-5

Semi-finals

Wheaton
6-2 0-6 3-6 7-6 6-2

BECKER (2)
6-7 7-6 6-2 7-6

Quarter-finals

AGASSI (5)
6-3 3-6 6-3 6-4

Wheaton
6-4 6-3 6-1

FORGET (7)
6-7 7-5 6-2 6-4

BECKER (2)
6-4 6-7 6-1 7-6

Fourth round

Eltingh
6-3 4-6 6-4 7-5

Gunnarsson
7-6 4-6 6-3 6-4

Wheaton
6-3 3-6 7-6 6-3

LENDL (3)
4-6 2-6 6-4 6-4 7-5

FORGET (7)
3-6 4-6 6-1 4-1 ret'd

Mayotte
3-6 6-2 7-6 6-4

Bergstrom
6-3 6-2 3-6 6-3

BECKER (2)
6-1 6-4 3-6 6-3

Third round

AGASSI (5)
7-6 3-6 6-4 6-2

Saceanu
7-6 4-3 6-7 6-3

Eltingh
7-6 6-1 6-6 6-4 12-10

Woodbridge
6-3 1-6 7-5 6-3

Gunnarsson
6-2 6-3 2-6 7-6

Wheaton
6-4 6-3 6-4 7-6

LENDL (3)
6-2 7-5 7-6-1

FORGET (7)
6-4 6-3 6-4

Leconte
6-4 6-2 6-3

Kuhnen
6-2 6-4 6-3

Mayotte
6-3 6-6 6-4 7-6

GILBERT (15)
7-5 2-6 6-3 5-7 6-4

Bergstrom
6-3 6-2 3-6 6-3

Olhovskiy
2-6 7-6 6-4 4-6-3

BECKER (2)
7-6 7-5 7-5

Second round

AGASSI (5)
7-5 3-6 6-4 6-2

Krajicek
6-3 6-4 6-3

Saceanu
7-6 4-3 6-7 6-3

Eltingh
7-6 6-1 6-6 6-4 12-10

Woodbridge
6-3 1-6 7-5 6-3

Jonsson
7-5 6-3 7-5

Gunnarsson
6-2 6-3 2-6 7-6

Wheaton
4-6 6-3 6-4 7-6

LENDL (3)
6-2 7-5 7-6-1

FORGET (7)
6-4 6-3 6-4

Leconte
6-3 6-1 7-6

Kuhnen
6-2 6-4 6-3

Mayotte
6-3 6-6 6-4 7-6

GILBERT (15)
7-5 2-6 6-3 5-7 6-4

Bergstrom
7-5 6-0 6-4

Olhovskiy
2-6 7-6 6-4 4-6-3

BECKER (2)
7-6 7-5 7-5

First round

No.	Player	Result
65	**A. AGASSI** (USA) (5)	4-6 6-1 6-7 7-5 6-3
66	G. Connell (CAN)	
67	G. Prpic (YUG)	6-3 6-3 6-3 10-8
68	V. Siemerink (HOL)	
69	M. Larsson (SWE)	6-4 1-6 6-3 6-1
70	P. Haarhuis (HOL)	
71	M. Ruah (VEN) (LL)	5-7 6-1 3-6 6-3 6-4
72	R. Krajicek (HOL)	
73	G. Muller (RSA)	6-2 6-3 6-3
74	J. Arrese (ESP)	
75	S. E. Davis (USA)	6-4 7-6 6-4
76	C. Saceanu (GER)	
77	R. Vogel (TCH) (Q)	7-6 6-7 7-6 6-3
78	J. Eltingh (HOL)	
79	P. McEnroe (USA)	6-3 7-6 6-1
80	**E. SANCHEZ** (ESP) (11)	
81	**J. HLASEK** (SUI) (13)	6-2 3-6 6-3 6-2
82	S. Zivojinovic (YUG) (Q)	
83	F. Araya (PER)	2-6 6-2 6-3 6-1
84	T. A. Woodbridge (AUS)	
85	M. Vajda (TCH)	7-5 6-3 7-5
86	L. Jonsson (SWE)	
87	J. Gunnarsson (SWE)	6-1 7-5 6-2
88	C. Rebolledo (CHI)	
89	E. Poline (FRA)	4-6 6-3 6-4 7-6
90	G. Layendecker (USA) (Q)	
91	D. Wheaton (USA)	7-6 6-7 6-4 6-2
92	T. Korda (TCH)	
93	M. Koevermans (HOL)	6-3 6-2 6-1
94	M. Washington (USA)	
95	K. Evernden (NZL)	6-2 7-5 7-6-1
96	**I. LENDL** (TCH) (3)	
97	**G. FORGET** (FRA) (7)	6-2 6-7 5-7 6-4
98	G. Bloom (ISR)	
99	M. Gustafsson (SWE)	7-6 6-3 6-3
100	F. Clavet (ESP)	
101	H. Leconte (FRA)	6-3 6-1 7-6
102	T. Carbonell (ESP)	
103	N. Kulti (SWE)	6-2 7-5 5-7 6-1
104	J. Yzaga (PER)	
105	M. R. J. Petchey (GBR) (WC)	4-6 6-3 6-3 8-6
106	J. Pugh (USA) (WC)	
107	P. Kuhnen (GER)	6-4 6-3 6-4
108	A. Rahunen (FIN)	
109	M. J. Bates (GBR) (WC)	6-4 6-4 6-2
110	J. F. Altur (ESP)	
111	S. Mayotte (USA)	6-7 4-6 6-1 7-6 6-2
112	**M. CHANG** (USA) (9)	
113	**B. GILBERT** (USA) (15)	6-7 5-1 6-2
114	D. Orsanic (ARG) (Q)	
115	W. Masur (AUS)	7-5 6-1 6-2
116	A. Mansdorf (ISR)	
117	H. Holm (SWE)	7-6 6-3 6-4
118	C. Caratti (ITA)	
119	E. Masso (BEL)	6-1 7-5 6-3
120	T. Bergstrom (SWE)	
121	S. Matsuoka (JPN)	6-4 6-7 5-7 7-5
122	L. Mattar (BRA)	
123	A. Olhovskiy (URS) (LL)	3-6 6-3 6-3 7-6
124	E. Jelen (GER)	
125	R. Fromberg (AUS)	6-4 7-6 6-2
126	P. Lundgren (SWE)	
127	C. Steeb (GER)	6-4 6-2 6-4
128	**B. BECKER** (GER) (2)	

Capital letters denote seeded players. Number following player's name gives seeding order. (Q) – Qualifier. (WC) – Wild Card. (LL) – Lucky Loser.

WOMEN'S SINGLES

Holder: M. Navratilova (USA)

FIRST ROUND	SECOND ROUND	THIRD ROUND	FOURTH ROUND	QUARTER-FINALS	SEMI-FINALS	FINAL
1 **S. GRAF** (GER) (1)	GRAF (1) 6–2 6–2	GRAF (1) 6–0 6–1	GRAF (1) 6–2 6–3	GRAF (1) 6–2 6–1	GRAF (1) 6–1 6–3	GRAF (1) 6–2 6–4
2 C. Appelmans (BEL)						
3 C. Porwik (GER)	Harper 6–4 6–1					
4 T. A. Harper (USA)						
5 K. S. Rinaldi (USA)	Herreman 7–5 6–2	Basuki 6–4 6–4				
6 N. Herreman (FRA)						
7 A. B. Henricksson (USA)	Basuki 6–4 7–6					
8 V. Basuki (INA)						
9 J. Halard (FRA)	Halard 6–1 2–6 6–3	Werdel 6–2 6–4	FRAZIER (14) 6–2 6–1			
10 C. N. Toleafoa (NZL) (LL)						
11 D. A. Graham (USA)	Werdel 6–3 6–2					
12 M. Werdel (USA)						
13 F. Bonsignori (ITA)	White 6–1 6–1	FRAZIER (14) 7–5 6–4				
14 R. M. White (USA)						
15 K. Kschwendt (LUX)	FRAZIER (14) 7–6 6–4					
16 **A. FRAZIER** (USA) (14)						
17 **A. HUBER** (GER) (13)	HUBER (13) 6–1 6–2	HUBER (13) 6–2 6–1	HUBER (13) 6–3 6–7 6–0	GARRISON (7) 4–6 6–3 6–0		
18 C. Martinek (GER)						
19 T. S. Whitlinger (USA)	Whitlinger 6–1 6–3					
20 M. Maleeva (BUL)						
21 M. M. Bollegraf (HOL)	Bollegraf 6–4 6–4	Bollegraf 6–3 5–7 6–3				
22 V. S. Humphreys-Davies (GBR) (WC)						
23 J. M. Durie (GBR)	Durie 6–3 6–2					
24 H. Kelesi (CAN)						
25 N. Miyagi (JPN)	Zardo 6–0 6–3	Strandlund 6–4 6–4	GARRISON (7) 6–3 6–3			
26 E. Zardo (SUI)						
27 M. Strandlund (SWE)	Strandlund 6–2 7–6					
28 R. Hiraki (JPN)						
29 R. Pampoulova (BUL)	Pampoulova 2–6 6–3 6–4	GARRISON (7) 6–3 6–1				
30 B. A. Borneo (GBR) (WC)						
31 L. Gomer (GBR)	GARRISON (7) 6–3 6–3					
32 **Z. L. GARRISON** (USA) (7)						
33 **A. SANCHEZ-VICARIO** (ESP) (4)	SANCHEZ-VICARIO (4) 6–1 6–2	SANCHEZ-VICARIO (4) 6–4 6–1	SANCHEZ-VICARIO (4) 6–2 6–4	SANCHEZ-VICARIO (4) 7–5 3–6 6–1	M. J. FERNANDEZ (5) 6–2 7–5	
34 B. Rittner (GER)						
35 P. Romano (ITA)	Coetzer 7–6 6–2					
36 A. J. Coetzer (RSA)						
37 P. Langrova (TCH)	McNeil 6–4 7–5	McNeil 3–6 6–2 6–2				
38 L. M. McNeil (USA)						
39 N. Sawamatsu (JPN)	Sawamatsu 6–2 6–2					
40 C. Bartos (SUI)						
41 J. A. Faull (AUS) (LL)	Faull 6–0 6–2	Minter 6–3 6–2	Minter 6–3 6–3			
42 K. Godridge (AUS)						
43 A. L. Minter (AUS)	Minter 6–4 6–0					
44 S. Martin (USA)						
45 D. L. Faber (USA)	Faber 3–6 7–6 6–2	G. Fernandez 7–5 7–5				
46 C. Caverzasio (SUI)						
47 G. Fernandez (USA)	G. Fernandez 4–6 6–1 6–4					
48 **H. SUKOVA** (TCH) (10)						
49 **H. WIESNER** (AUT) (16)	WIESNER (16) 6–1 6–2	WIESNER (16) 6–3 6–0	WIESNER (16) 3–6 7–5 6–1	M. J. FERNANDEZ (5) 6–0 7–5		
50 H. Cioffi (USA)						
51 E. Sanchez (URS)	Sanchez 6–2 6–7 8–6					
52 A. Temesvari (HUN)						
53 B. Griffiths (GBR) (WC)	Kohde-Kilsch 6–1 6–3	Kohde-Kilsch 7–6 6–2				
54 C. Kohde-Kilsch (GER)						
55 N. A. M. Jagerman (HOL) (Q)	Jagerman 7–5 6–4					
56 M. Oremans (HOL) (Q)						
57 P. H. Shriver (USA)	Shriver 6–0 7–5	Shriver 6–0 6–3	M. J. FERNANDEZ (5) 6–3 7–5			
58 A. C. Leand (USA)						
59 E. De Lone (USA)	Fulco 3–6 6–2 6–4					
60 B. Fulco (ARG)						
61 A. A. Keller (USA)	Keller 7–5 6–2	M. J. FERNANDEZ (5) 7–6 6–1				
62 F. Golarsa (ITA)						
63 P. Kamstra (HOL) (Q)	M. J. FERNANDEZ (5) 6–2 6–4					
64 **M. J. FERNANDEZ** (USA) (5)						

6–4 3–6 8–6

S. GRAF (GER) (1)

Semi-final winner (this half): SABATINI (2) 6-4 6-4

No.	Entry	Round 1	Round 2	Round 3	Round 4	Quarter-final
65	J. NOVOTNA (BUL) (6)	NOVOTNA (6) 6-3 6-0	Schultz 4-6 7-6 6-4	Schultz 5-7 6-4 7-5	CAPRIATI (9) 3-6 6-1 6-1	CAPRIATI (9) 6-4 7-5
66	N. Pratt (AUS) (LL)					
67	B. Schultz (HOL)	Schultz 6-3 6-0				
68	B. Reinstadler (AUT)					
69	B. Nagelsen (USA)	Brioukhovets 6-2 6-1	Brioukhovets 7-6 6-4			
70	E. Brioukhovets (URS)					
71	S. L. Smith (GBR)	Provs 3-6 6-4 6-2				
72	N. Provis (AUS)					
73	W. Probst (GER)	Probst 7-6 7-5	Probst 7-6 6-3	CAPRIATI (9) 6-3 1-6 6-3		
74	E. Callens (BEL) (Q)					
75	K. Van Lottum (FRA)	Callens 7-6 2-6 7-5				
76	N. Zrubakova (TCH)					
77	R. McQuillan (AUS)	Zrubakova 7-6 6-2	CAPRIATI (9) 6-2 6-3			
78	S. C. Stafford (USA)					
79	C. Stafford (USA)	CAPRIATI (9) 6-0 7-5				
80	J. CAPRIATI (USA) (9)					
81	A. M. CECCHINI (ITA) (15)	Smylie 6-3 3-6 6-1	Smylie 6-3 6-4	Lindqvist 6-1 7-6	NAVRATILOVA (3) 6-1 6-3	
82	P. D. Smylie (AUS)					
83	P. Sloane (USA)	Suire 6-2 6-2				
84	C. Suire (FRA)					
85	I. Demongeot (FRA) (Q)	Lindqvist 6-1 6-0	Lindqvist 6-3 6-2			
86	C. Lindqvist (SWE)					
87	K. Habsudova (TCH)	Habsudova 6-3 6-2				
88	E. Dahlman (SWE)					
89	S. L. Bentley (GBR) (WC)	Kidowaki 1-6 7-5 6-1	Garrone 6-4 6-3	Garrone 6-4 6-3		
90	M. Kidowaki (JPN)					
91	L. Garrone (ITA)	Garrone 6-4 7-6				
92	S. W. Magers (USA)					
93	A. Debaume (FRA)	Grunfeld 6-4 6-4	NAVRATILOVA (3) 6-3 6-1	NAVRATILOVA (3) 6-2 6-2		
94	A. Grunfeld (GBR) (WC)					
95	E. Reinach (RSA)	NAVRATILOVA (3) 4-6 6-2 6-4				
96	M. NAVRATILOVA (USA) (3)					
97	K. MALEEVA (BUL) (8)	K. MALEEVA (8) 6-4 6-4	K. MALEEVA (8) 6-4 6-4	K. MALEEVA (8) 6-3 6-4	Gildemeister 3-6 6-2 6-3	SABATINI (2) 6-2 6-1
98	J. A. Salmon (GBR) (WC)					
99	K. Hand (GBR) (WC)	Hy 6-2 3-6 6-0	Hy 4-6 6-4 6-2			
100	A. Grossman (USA)					
101	R. D. Fairbank-Nideffer (USA)	Paradis-Mangon 6-3 6-2				
102	P. Hy (CAN)					
103	P. Paradis-Mangon (FRA)	De Swardt 6-3 3-6 6-4	Gildemeister 6-4 6-1	Gildemeister 2-2 retd		
104	K. Radford (AUS) (Q)					
105	K. Rehe (USA)	Gildemeister 6-4 6-4				
106	M. De Swardt (RSA)					
107	C. J. Wood (GBR)	Harvey-Wild 6-4 6-1	Harvey-Wild 6-4 6-1			
108	L. Gildemeister (PER)					
109	J. M. Harvey-Wild (USA)	ZVEREVA (12) 6-4 6-2				
110	L. Kreiss (USA)					
111	C. Tessi (ARG)	TAUZIAT (11) 7-6 6-4	TAUZIAT (11) 3-6 6-2 6-2	TAUZIAT (11) 6-1 6-1	SABATINI (2) 7-6 6-3	
112	N. ZVEREVA (URS) (12)					
113	N. TAUZIAT (FRA) (11)	Kimura 6-4 7-5				
114	R. Rajchrtova (TCH)					
115	A. Minter (AUS)	Fendick 7-6 4-6 6-1	Ferrando 4-6 6-1 7-5			
116	A. Paz (ARG)					
117	J. M. Hetherington (CAN) (LL)	Ferrando 6-4 3-6 6-2				
118	P. A. Fendick (USA)					
119	L. Ferrando (ITA)	Cunningham 7-6 6-4	Strnadova 6-1 6-3	SABATINI (2) 6-1 6-3		
120	K. Date (JPN) (LL)					
121	G. Helgeson (USA)	Strnadova 7-6 6-4				
122	C. E. Cunningham (USA)					
123	A. Strnadova (TCH)	Quentrec 6-4 7-5	SABATINI (2) 6-4 6-2			
124	S. J. Loosemore (GBR) (WC)					
125	R. P. Stubbs (AUS) (Q)	SABATINI (2) 6-4 6-0				
126	Z. Quentrec (FRA)					
127	M. Javer (GBR)					
128	G. SABATINI (ARG) (2)					

MEN'S DOUBLES

Holders: R. Leach (USA)/J. Pugh (USA)

Winner: J. B. FITZGERALD (AUS)/A. JARRYD (SWE) (2) 6-3 6-4 6-7 6-1

FIRST ROUND

1 S. DAVIS/PATE (1)
2 Mora/Svantesson
3 Flegl/Prpic
4 Holm/Nyborg (Q)
5 Botfield/Turner (WC)
6 Davids/Siemerink
7 Oosting/Meiesa
8 FERREIRA/NORVAL (15)
9 RIGLEWSKI/STICH (9)
10 Devries/MacPherson
11 Haygarth/Talbot (Q)
12 Mattar/Oncins
13 Patridge/Rive
14 Ison/Petchey (WC)
15 Mordegan/Vogel
16 WOODBRIDGE/WOODFORDE (8)
17 LEACH/PUGH (3)
18 Ivanisevic/J. McEnroe (WC)
19 Courier/D. Flach
20 Olhovskiy/Pimek
21 Annacone/Evernden
22 Novacek/Smid
23 Black/Middleton (Q)
24 GRABB/P. McENROE (13)
25 HAARHUIS/KOEVERMANS (12)
26 Schapers/Smith
27 Layendecker/Reneberg
28 Nelson/Shelton
29 Grom/Pillot
30 Frana/Lavalle
31 Aerts/Van't Hof
32 MULLER/VISSER (5)
33 Adams/Dzelde (LL)
34 J. Erreat/Salumaa
35 J. Brown/Garnett
36 Boscatto/Pessosolido
37 Albano/Cannon
38 Nargso/Sanchez
39 Bates/N. Brown
40 K. JONES/LOZANO (11)
41 BROAD/CURREN (14)
42 Krajicek/Vacek
43 K. Flach/Seguso
44 Bathman/Bergh
45 Carbonell/Korda
46 Melville/Van Emburgh
47 Castle/Van Emburgh
48 CONNELL/MICHIBATA (4)
49 GALBRAITH/WITSKEN (7)
50 Bahrami/Gilbert
51 Kratpp/Van Rensburg
52 Garrow/Pearce
53 Nijssen/Suk
54 Laurendeau/Roese (Q)
55 Bloom/Doohan
56 JENSEN/WARDER (10)
57 DYKE/LUNDGREN (16)
58 Fulwood/Sapsford (WC)
59 Hand/Wilkinson (WC)
60 M. Kratzmann/Youl
61 Borwick/A. Kratzmann (Q)
62 Luza/Motta
63 Masur/Stoltenberg
64 FITZGERALD/JARRYD (2)

SECOND ROUND

S. DAVIS/PATE (1)
Holm/Nyborg — 6-2 6-3
Botfield/Turner — 7-6 7-6
FERREIRA/NORVAL (15) — 7-5 6-3
Haygarth/Talbot — 7-6 6-3
Devries/MacPherson — 6-3 7-5
Patridge/Rive — 6-3 6-4
WOODBRIDGE/WOODFORDE (8) — 6-4 6-3
LEACH/PUGH (3) — 6-3 6-4
Ivanisevic/J. McEnroe — 6-3 6-4
Courier/D. Flach — 6-3 6-3
Annacone/Evernden — 6-7 7-6 6-3
Black/Middleton — 6-4 6-3
HAARHUIS/KOEVERMANS (12) — 6-1 7-6
Layendecker/Reneberg — 6-2 5-7 6-2
Frana/Lavalle — 6-2 6-2
MULLER/VISSER (5) — 6-3 6-4
Adams/Dzelde — 6-3 6-4
J. Brown/Garnett — 6-3 6-4
Albano/Cannon — 3-6 6-3 6-4
K. JONES/LOZANO (11) — 6-3 7-5
Krajicek/Vacek — 7-6 6-4
K. Flach/Seguso — 7-6 6-4
CONNELL/MICHIBATA (4) — 6-4 6-2
GALBRAITH/WITSKEN (7) — 7-5 6-3
Garrow/Pearce — 6-3 6-3
Nijssen/Suk — 6-4 6-4
JENSEN/WARDER (10) — 6-4 6-3
Fulwood/Sapsford — 6-4 6-4
M. Kratzmann/Youl — 7-6 6-3
Luza/Motta — 6-1 6-3
FITZGERALD/JARRYD (2) — 6-3 6-4

THIRD ROUND

S. DAVIS/PATE (1) — 6-3 7-6
FERREIRA/NORVAL (15) — 7-5 6-3
Haygarth/Talbot — 6-4 6-4
WOODBRIDGE/WOODFORDE (8) — 6-4 6-4
Courier/D. Flach — 3-6 7-6 6-4
Annacone/Evernden — 6-3 7-5
Frana/Lavalle — 7-6 6-3
HAARHUIS/KOEVERMANS (12) — 7-6 6-3
J. Brown/Garnett — 7-6 6-4
Albano/Cannon — 6-3 6-4
K. Flach/Seguso — 7-6 6-3
CONNELL/MICHIBATA (4) — 6-4 7-5
GALBRAITH/WITSKEN (7) — 6-7 6-4 6-3
Nijssen/Suk — 7-5 3-6 7-5
M. Kratzmann/Youl — 6-3 6-4
FITZGERALD/JARRYD (2) — 6-4 7-6

QUARTER-FINALS

FERREIRA/NORVAL (15) — 7-6 5-7 9-7
WOODBRIDGE/WOODFORDE (8) — 6-2 6-3
Annacone/Evernden — 6-2 7-6
Frana/Lavalle — 6-3 6-4
Albano/Cannon — 7-6 6-3
CONNELL/MICHIBATA (4) — 6-4 7-6
GALBRAITH/WITSKEN (7) — 6-4 4-6 13-11
FITZGERALD/JARRYD (2) — 7-6 6-4

SEMI-FINALS

FERREIRA/NORVAL (15) — 7-6 6-4 6-4
Frana/Lavalle — 6-4 6-4 7-5
CONNELL/MICHIBATA (4) — 5-7 2-6 7-6 7-6 10-8
FITZGERALD/JARRYD (2) — 6-4 6-0 6-4

FINAL

Frana/Lavalle — 6-2 6-4 7-6
FITZGERALD/JARRYD (2) — 6-2 6-7 7-6 6-4

Capital letters denote seeded pairings. Number following players' names gives seeding order. (Q) – Qualifier; (WC) – Wild Card; (LL) – Lucky Loser.

WOMEN'S DOUBLES

Holders: J. Novotna (TCH)/H. Sukova (TCH)

Winner: L. SAVCHENKO (URS)/N. ZVEREVA (URS) (2) 6–4 3–6 6–4

FIRST ROUND

1. G. FERNANDEZ/NOVOTNA (1)
2. Langrova/Zrubakova
3. Rehe/Temesvari
4. K. Maleeva/M. Maleeva
5. Gunnoldt/Loosemore (WC)
6. Griffiths/J. Wood (Q)
7. Jankovska/Melicharova
8. HETHERINGTON/RINALDI (12)
9. BURGIN/FENDICK (9)
10. Stafford/T. S. Whitinger
11. Borneo/C. J. Wood
12. Bakkum/Jaederman
13. Pfaff/Stubbs
14. Basuki/Wibowo
15. Demongeot/Durie
16. MAGERS/WHITE (7)
17. M. J. FERNANDEZ/GARRISON (4)
18. Laskova/Maniokova
19. Novelo/Somerville (LL)
20. Coorengel/Van Buuren
21. Hiranki/Nishiya (Q)
22. Jagaard/Suire
23. Kelesi/Smoller
24. KOHDE-KILSCH/REINACH (13)
25. GREGORY/MAY (16)
26. Kijimuta/Mugi
27. Benjamin/Whitington (Q)
28. Rajchrtova/Strnadova
29. Paradis-Mangon/Scott
30. Ferrando/Golarsa
31. Dechaume/Probst
32. JORDAN/McNEIL (5)
33. NAVRATILOVA/SHRIVER (8)
34. Hand/Salmon (WC)
35. Gomer/Lake (WC)
36. Harper/Kidowaki
37. Fauli/McQuillan
38. Garrone/Kschwendt
39. Collins/Radford
40. FAIRBANK-NIDEFFER/SCHULTZ (15)
41. CAPRIATI/PAZ (11)
42. Pospisilova/Sviglerova
43. Bernard/Henricksson
44. Appelmans/Vis
45. Graf/Porwik
46. Cioffi/Frazier
47. Hábel/Huber (Q)
48. SANCHEZ-VICARIO/SUKOVA (3)
49. PROVIS/SMYLIE (6)
50. Baranski/Morton
51. Cordwell/Lindqvist
52. Budarova/Nohacova
53. MacGregor/Mager
54. Date/Iida
55. Field/Strandlund
56. ADAMS/BOLLEGRAF (10)
57. TAUZIAT/WIESNER (14)
58. Godridge/Helgeson
59. Gildemeister/Scheuer-Larsen
60. Spadea/Ter Riet
61. Limmer/Woolcock (LL)
62. Javer/Smith (WC)
63. Caverzasio/Herreman
64. SAVCHENKO/ZVEREVA (2)

SECOND ROUND

- G. FERNANDEZ/NOVOTNA (1) 6-1 6-1
- Rehe/Temesvari 7-6 7-6
- Griffiths/J. Wood 6-4 6-4
- HETHERINGTON/RINALDI (12) 6-3 6-2
- Stafford/T. S. Whitinger 2-6 6-2 6-4
- Borneo/C. J. Wood 6-3 7-5
- Pfaff/Stubbs 6-4 4-6 6-3
- MAGERS/WHITE (7) 6-5 7-5
- M. J. FERNANDEZ/GARRISON (4) 6-2 6-3
- Coorengel/Van Buuren 6-4 6-4
- Jagaard/Suire 7-6
- KOHDE-KILSCH/REINACH (13) 6-3 6-3
- GREGORY/MAY (16) 6-4 6-1
- Rajchrtova/Strnadova 6-7 7-6 3-7
- Paradis-Mangon/Scott 7-5 6-2
- JORDAN/McNEIL (5) 6-1 6-0
- NAVRATILOVA/SHRIVER (8) 6-1 6-0
- Harper/Kidowaki 4-6 7-6 6-4
- Fauli/McQuillan 7-5 4-6 6-1
- FAIRBANK-NIDEFFER/SCHULTZ (15) 6-2 1-6 6-4
- CAPRIATI/PAZ (11) 6-1 6-4
- Appelmans/Vis 6-4 7-6
- Cioffi/Frazier 7-6 1-6 6-4
- SANCHEZ-VICARIO/SUKOVA (3) 6-2 6-3
- PROVIS/SMYLIE (6) 6-3 6-1
- Budarova/Nohacova 6-3 6-1
- Date/Iida 7-6 7-5
- ADAMS/BOLLEGRAF (10) 6-2 7-6
- TAUZIAT/WIESNER (14) 6-3 6-1
- Gildemeister/Scheuer-Larsen 6-4 6-2
- Javer/Smith 7-6 6-3
- SAVCHENKO/ZVEREVA (2) 6-2 6-2

THIRD ROUND

- G. FERNANDEZ/NOVOTNA (1) 6-7 6-4 6-2
- HETHERINGTON/RINALDI (12) 6-4 6-2
- Stafford/T. S. Whitinger 6-2 6-2
- MAGERS/WHITE (7) 6-4 6-2
- M. J. FERNANDEZ/GARRISON (4) 6-1 6-3
- KOHDE-KILSCH/REINACH (13) 6-4 6-4
- Rajchrtova/Strnadova 6-0 7-5
- JORDAN/McNEIL (5) 6-1 6-1
- NAVRATILOVA/SHRIVER (8) 6-4 6-0
- Fauli/McQuillan 6-2 1-6 6-4
- CAPRIATI/PAZ (11) 6-2 6-3
- SANCHEZ-VICARIO/SUKOVA (3) 4-6 6-1
- PROVIS/SMYLIE (6) 6-4 6-2
- ADAMS/BOLLEGRAF (10) 7-6 6-3
- TAUZIAT/WIESNER (14) 7-6 6-3
- SAVCHENKO/ZVEREVA (2) 6-3 6-3

QUARTER-FINALS

- G. FERNANDEZ/NOVOTNA (1) 6-2 7-6
- MAGERS/WHITE (7) 6-2 6-2
- M. J. FERNANDEZ/GARRISON (4) 6-3 6-1
- JORDAN/McNEIL (5) 6-2 7-6
- NAVRATILOVA/SHRIVER (8) 6-7 6-2 6-2
- SANCHEZ-VICARIO/SUKOVA (3) 6-2 6-7 6-1
- ADAMS/BOLLEGRAF (10) 6-2 7-6
- SAVCHENKO/ZVEREVA (2) 6-1 6-0

SEMI-FINALS

- G. FERNANDEZ/NOVOTNA (1) 6-3 6-3
- M. J. FERNANDEZ/GARRISON (4) 4-6 7-6 6-2
- NAVRATILOVA/SHRIVER (8) 6-3 7-6
- SAVCHENKO/ZVEREVA (2) 6-4 6-2

FINAL

- G. FERNANDEZ/NOVOTNA (1) 7-5 6-2
- SAVCHENKO/ZVEREVA (2) 2-6 6-2 6-4

Winner: L. SAVCHENKO (URS)/N. ZVEREVA (URS) (2) 6-4 3-6 6-4

Capital letters denote seeded pairings. Number following players' names gives seeding order. (Q) – Qualifier; (WC) – Wild Card; (LL) – Lucky Loser.

MIXED DOUBLES

Holders: J. Leach (USA)/Z. Garrison (USA)

Winner: J. B. FITZGERALD (AUS)/P. D. SMYLIE (AUS) (2) 7–6 6–2

FIRST ROUND

1. PUGH/ZVEREVA (1)
2. Brown/Wood
3. Evernden/McQuillan
4. Stolle/Van Lottum (Q)
5. Bates/Durie
6. Broad/Pfaff
7. Morgan/Jones (LL)
8. LOZANO/SANCHEZ-VICARIO (12)
9. FERREIRA/GREGORY (15)
10. Kinnear/Benjamin
11. Beckman/Harper
12. Leconte/Graf
13. Norval/Bielegraf
14. Petchey/Loosemore (WC)
15. Amend/Ludioff (Q)
16. MICHIBATA/HETHERINGTON (6)
17. DAVIS/WHITE (3)
18. Canter/May
19. Koevermans/Ter Riet
20. MacPherson/Godridge
21. Talbot/Cordwell
22. Melville/Somerville
23. Dyke/Jaggard
24. GRABB/BURGIN (14)
25. WOODBRIDGE/PROVIS (9)
26. Nelson/Magers
27. Fulwood/Gomer (WC)
28. Smith/Suire
29. Seguso/Bassett-Seguso (WC)
30. Colombini/Golarsa
31. Thorne/Wibowo
32. CONNELL/RINALDI (8)
33. GALBRAITH/FENDICK (5)
34. Woodforde/Frazier (LL)
35. Brown/Stafford
36. Van Rensburg/Reinach (WC)
37. Borwick/Scott
38. Siemerink/Vis
39. Youll/Field
40. M. KRATZMANN/SHRIVER (16)
41. FLACH/JORDAN (11)
42. Cannon/Adams
43. Van 't Hof/MacGregor
44. Salumaa/Kschwendt
45. Schapers/Schultz
46. Nijssen/Ternesvari
47. Kruger/Strnadova
48. LEACH/GARRISON (4)
49. Bale/Van Buuren (LL)
50. Devries/Miyagi
51. Rive/Collins
52. Warder/Faull
53. Stoltenberg/Stubbs
54. Mayotte/G. Fernandez (WC)
55. A. Kratzmann/Guse (Q)
56. VISSER/FAIRBANK-NIDEFFER (10)
57. SUK/SUKOVA (13)
58. Shelton/McNeil
59. Garnett/Bakkum
60. Svartensson/T. S. Whitlinger
61. Pimek/Savchenko
62. Van Emburgh/Mager
63. Annacone/Rehe
64. FITZGERALD/SMYLIE (2)

SECOND ROUND

- PUGH/ZVEREVA (1) 6–3 6–4
- Evernden/McQuillan 3–6 6–3 6–4
- Bates/Durie 6–3 6–2
- LOZANO/SANCHEZ-VICARIO (12) 7–6 6–3
- Kinnear/Benjamin 2–6 6–4 14–12
- Leconte/Graf 6–3 7–6
- Norval/Bielegraf 4–6 6–1
- MICHIBATA/HETHERINGTON (6) 6–4 6–7 9–7
- Canter/May 6–3 6–4
- Koevermans/Ter Riet 4–6 6–3 6–4
- Talbot/Cordwell 7–6 6–1
- Dyke/Jaggard 6–3 6–2
- WOODBRIDGE/PROVIS (9) 6–2 6–2
- Smith/Suire 7–5 7–5
- Colombini/Golarsa 6–4 6–2
- CONNELL/RINALDI (8) 6–4 6–3
- Woodforde/Frazier 6–1 6–4
- Van Rensburg/Reinach 6–2 2–6 6–3
- Siemerink/Vis 4–6 6–3 12–10
- M. KRATZMANN/SHRIVER (16) 6–3
- FLACH/JORDAN (11) 7–6 6–4
- Salumaa/Kschwendt 4–6 1–1 9
- Schapers/Schultz 6–3 5–7 29–27
- LEACH/GARRISON (4) 3–6 6–1 6–2
- Devries/Miyagi 6–7 7–6
- Rive/Collins 6–7 6–4 6–2
- Stoltenberg/Stubbs 4–6 6–2 6–2
- VISSER/FAIRBANK-NIDEFFER (10) 6–2 6–2
- SUK/SUKOVA (13) 7–6 7–6 2
- Garnett/Bakkum 6–4 6–2
- Pimek/Savchenko 6–4 6–3
- FITZGERALD/SMYLIE (2) 6–3 6–2

THIRD ROUND

- PUGH/ZVEREVA (1) 2–6 6–3 6–4
- Leconte/Graf 6–2 7–5
- MICHIBATA/HETHERINGTON (6) 7–6 7–6
- Koevermans/Ter Riet 7–5 6–7 6–4
- Dyke/Jaggard 6–4 6–7 6–3
- WOODBRIDGE/PROVIS (9) 7–5 6–3
- CONNELL/RINALDI (8) 5–7 6–1 6–4
- Van Rensburg/Reinach 6–4 6–1
- Siemerink/Vis 7–6 3–6 10–8
- Salumaa/Kschwendt 6–4 6–3
- Schapers/Schultz 3–6 6–3 13–11
- Devries/Miyagi 4–6 6–3 6–4
- Stoltenberg/Stubbs 6–3 3–6 6–3
- SUK/SUKOVA (13) 7–6 7–6
- FITZGERALD/SMYLIE (2) 6–3 6–2

QUARTER-FINALS

- PUGH/ZVEREVA (1) 7–5 6–4
- MICHIBATA/HETHERINGTON (6) 6–4 7–6
- Dyke/Jaggard 6–2 6–3
- CONNELL/RINALDI (8) 5–7 7–6 6–4
- Van Rensburg/Reinach 6–2 6–4
- Schapers/Schultz 3–6 6–2 6–1
- Stoltenberg/Stubbs 7–6 6–3
- FITZGERALD/SMYLIE (2) 6–3 6–4

SEMI-FINALS

- PUGH/ZVEREVA (1) 6–4 6–3
- CONNELL/RINALDI (8) 6–4 6–4
- Van Rensburg/Reinach 7–6 7–6
- FITZGERALD/SMYLIE (2) 6–4 6–2

FINAL

- PUGH/ZVEREVA (1) 7–5 6–2
- FITZGERALD/SMYLIE (2) 7–5 3–6 7–5

Capital letters denote seeded pairings. Number following players' names gives seeding order (Q) – Qualifier. (WC) – Wild Card. (LL) – Lucky Loser.

JUNIOR EVENTS

BOYS' SINGLES – **Final:** Thomas Enqvist (SWE) (2) d. Michael Joyce (USA) 6 4 6–3.
GIRLS' SINGLES – **Final:** Barbara Rittner (GER) (1) d. Elena Makarova (URS) 6–7 6–2 6–3.
BOYS' DOUBLES – **Final:** Karim Alami (MAR)/Greg Rusedski (CAN) (4) d. John DeJager (RSA)/Andrei Medvedev (URS) (3) 1–6 7–6 6–4.
GIRLS' DOUBLES – **Final:** Catherine Barclay (AUS)/Limor Zaltz (ISR) (4) d. Joanne Limmer (AUS)/Angie Woolcock (AUS) (2) 6–4 6–4.

OVER-35 INVITATION EVENTS

MEN'S SINGLES – **Final:** Tim Gullikson (USA) (2) d. John Lloyd (GBR) (3) 7–6 3–6 6–2.
MEN'S DOUBLES – **Final:** Peter Fleming (USA)/Stan Smith (USA) d. Peter McNamara (AUS)/Paul McNamee (AUS) (1) 7–6 7–6.
WOMEN'S DOUBLES – **Final:** Wendy Turnbull (AUS)/Virginia Wade (GBR) (1) d. Rosie Casals (USA)/Mrs. Sharon Pete (USA) (2) 6–3 6–4.

WIMBLEDON CHAMPIONSHIPS PRIZE MONEY – £4,010,970

MEN'S SINGLES – Winner £240,000. Runner-up £120,000. Semi-finalists £60,000. Quarter-finalists £31,200. Fourth-round losers £16,800. Third-round losers £9,715. Second-round losers £5,880. First-round losers £3,600.
Total: £1,313,200.
WOMEN'S SINGLES – Winner £216,000. Runner-up £108,000. Semi-finalists £52,500. Quarter-finalists £26,520. Fourth-round losers £13,440. Third-round losers £7,530. Second-round losers £4,560. First-round losers £2,790.
Total: £1,087,560.
MEN'S DOUBLES (per pair) – Winners £98,330. Runners-up £49,160. Semi-finalists £25,230. Quarter-finalists £13,100. Third-round losers £6,980. Second-round losers £3,790. First-round losers £2,220.
Total: £437,870.
WOMEN'S DOUBLES (per pair) – Winners £85,060. Runners-up £42,520. Semi-finalists £20,190. Quarter-finalists £10,480. Third-round losers £5,230. Second-round losers £2,840. First-round losers £1,610.
Total: £348,680.
MIXED DOUBLES (per pair) – Winners £41,720. Runners-up £20,860. Semi-finalists £10,430. Quarter-finalists £4,800. Third-round losers £2,400. Second-round losers £1,200. First-round losers £540.
Total: £158,320.
35 AND OVER MEN'S INVITATION SINGLES – Winner £15,000. Runner-up £12,000. Semi-finalists £7,500. Quarter-finalists £3,000. First-round losers £2,000.
Total: £62,000,
35 AND OVER MEN'S INVITATION DOUBLES (per pair) – Winners £12,000. Runners-up £9,000. Semi-finalists £6,000. Quarter-finalists £4,500. First-round losers £3,000.
Total: £75,000.
35 AND OVER WOMEN'S INVITATION DOUBLES (per pair) – Winners £9,600. Runners-up £7,200. Semi-finalists £4,800. First-round losers £2,400.
Total: £36,000.
QUALIFYING – MEN (each): 16 × Third-round losers £2,400. 32 × Second-round losers £1,200. 64 × First-round losers £600.
Total £115,200.
QUALIFYING – WOMEN (each): 8 × Third-round losers £1,860. 16 × Second-round losers £930. 32 × First-round losers £465.
Total: £44,640.

Per Diem allowances (estimated): £332,500

The sweetest of Stefan Edberg's six tournament victories in 1991 came at the US Open where, at the ninth attempt, he joined Mats Wilander as the only Swede to win the world's second oldest Grand Slam title.

(T. Hindley)

Doubles team of the year, Anders Jarryd of Sweden and his Australian partner, John Fitzgerald, who won the French, Wimbledon and US titles – the first pair since Newcombe and Roche in 1967 to win three of the major crowns in one year. *(T. Hindley)*

US OPEN CHAMPIONSHIPS
Bud Collins

Long in the tooth, but with sharklike molars intact, they'd been around the block – and the world – a few times, these two named Navratilova and Connors. Still, considerable years and countless miles of exertion weren't evident at Flushing Meadow.

Seventeen years before, Jimmy Connors had been half of the triumphant 'Lovebird Double' at Wimbledon, sharing it with his sweetheart of the time, Chris Evert. Thirteen years before, Martina Navratilova had won her first major there, beating the said Evert.

But in 1991 – his 20th US Open, her 19th – they became linked as the spectacular Golden Oldie Double, and almost made it. What stratospheric odds would have been quoted on victories by 39-year-old Connors and 34-year-old Navratilova if bookmaking were legal in New York? Or even on their survival into the Open's penultimate day?

His onetime manager, Bill Riordan, used to refer to the Brash Basher from Belleville, Illinois – James Scott Connors – as the 'one and only'. Though mellowed off the court, and seemingly pastured as a TV analyst, Connors astoundingly reappeared at The Meadow (a wrist injury had kept him away in 1990) bigger than a life already decorated by two decades of success. Eureka! Bash and brashness were fully restored. It was clear that 174th ranked Connors, in on a freebie, a wild card, had been truly rehabilitated by surgery as hinted at by flashes-of-the-past at the French and Wimbledon.

How could a 39-year-old play so well and effectively? Jimmy remembered one: Ken Rosewall, whom he had beaten in two finals in 1974 to win both at Wimbledon and the US Open. 'Never imagined it could happen to me,' Connors chuckled.

But after a couple of escapes worthy of Houdini, Jimmy evolved as truly the one and only to millions who audited, in person or via the tube. And Martina wasn't far behind in affection for these Golden Oldies who thrilled so many on their unlikely runs for the titles. Each seemed to be merely 'an entry', as they say at the race track. If Jimmy wore 1, Martina flaunted 1A at the world's longest continuously operating tournament, this 111th edition of the US Championships.

The fact that their quests ultimately failed at the wire – hers for a fifth time in the final, his for a sixth in the semis – could not negate the broad and joyous feeling that the Open was theirs; emotionally, anyway, if not in the trophy case. In reality, though almost incidentally, the titles belonged elsewhere, an oh-by-the-way sort of thing. As in, oh-by-the-way Monica Seles and Stefan Edberg won Martina's and Jimmy's Open.

This is not to denigrate the superbness of the 17-year-old triple-crown-wearing Seles. Unbeaten in the two Grand Slams she had played (the unsolved mystery of her non-appearance at Wimbledon was the season's most intriguing riddle), the feisty Yugoslav was too deadly a markswoman in pulling away from Navratilova 7–6 6–1 to add the US Open to her Australian and French crowns.

Nor should it disparage the quality of the 25-year-old Swede, who finally broke loose from Borg Syndrome and ravaged French Open king, Jim Courier, 6–2 6–4 6–0. Mats Wilander, on his seventh try in 1988, had been the lone Swedish victor at the US Open. Bjorn Borg holds their country's record for New York futility: 10 flops. Edberg had come in with eight. But throughout two sweltering weeks Stefan had never looked anything less than the champ, despite some early shaking down when Americans Bryan Shelton and Jim Grabb snatched the only two sets he would lose. The Swede was magnificent in fighting off, in three stiff sets, the dangerous Michael Chang who had evicted ex-champ and 1990 semi-finalist John McEnroe in a post-midnight 5-set third round screamer.

In the opening round Edberg, with momentary visions of his unexpected 1990 defeat dancing in his head like triphammers, did have to serve-and-swerve out of three set points (4–5, 0–40) in taking the pivotal third stanza from high-velocity Shelton. But that, really, was his only dire moment during a devastating fortnight. Edberg, going from worst to first, accelerated in every round. A 1990 starting gate loss to Alexander Volkov was followed 12 months later by a derby-winning run, a recovery last seen in this Championship 34 years ago. Aussie Mal Anderson had rebounded from first round disappointment in 1956 to triumph a year later.

Wary but determined in dodging Chang (his nemesis in the 1989 French final), 2nd seeded Edberg simply soared, a hawk among roosters, in ripping off nine straight sets against the 14th, 5th and 4th seeds – Emilio Sanchez, Ivan Lendl and Jim Courier – only once losing as many as four games.

After a 122-minute strafing of Courier in the title match (avenging a quarter-final defeat in Paris), Edberg modestly conceded he'd 'played like a dream'. A nightmare in the view of Courier, who might logically have been regarded as the year's No.1 if he'd won. But it was no 'what-if' afternoon for the overrun Courier, the forehand-blasting Floridian who had ended the 361-day reign of Pete Sampras in the quarters, 6–2 7–6 (7–4) 7–6 (7–5). Only two break points were extended him by the sword-edged Swede – swiftly removed with bloody-minded serves.

Sure, the Meadow's pavement gives a fair-and-square chance to baseliners as well as deal-and-charge types. But when somebody is serving-and-volleying as powerfully as Edberg (has anyone done it so thoroughly at Flushing?) then the game is over. For anyone.

The Jimmy Connors Revival was simply the most riveting piece of drama in a rousing US Open as hot as the temperature and humidity that brought heat prostration to several.

If the Juvenile Jolter, 15-year-old Jennifer Capriati, had not surely come of age at Wimbledon by riddling Navratilova, she accomplished the same for her countrymen's delectation in dethroning one champion, Gabriela Sabatini, and coming within two points of preventing the ascension of another, Seles, in perhaps the most gripping struggle of the entire tournament.

Almost before anyone had settled into the stadium or had time to don sunglasses to ward off wardrobe glare from Andre Agassi, the zippy 1990 finalist was gone. The manner of Aaron Krickstein's flattening of a flat Agassi served notice that no big-wig was safe.

Serve-booming Dutch kid, Richard Krajicek, seconded that opening round thought a day later against three-time champion, eight-time finalist, Ivan Lendl. But Krajicek, dehydrating, couldn't quite close a double match-point trap (6–5, 40–15) in the fourth set. Conditioning, pride, grit and resourceful returns got Lendl his service break. He was out of that and into a tie-breaker, eventually gaining victory 6–0 in the fifth. Another Netherlander, Jan Siemerink, had better luck in the second round, squashing 7th seeded Guy Forget.

Having made himself instantly known in Flushing two years earlier by shocking John McEnroe, one more Dutchman, tenacious Paul Haarhuis, enhanced his Open rep by making the redbearded leading seed, Boris Becker, look black and blue – as well as desultory – in a straight sets third rounder.

All the while the Connors' odyssey was building to a roaring crescendo. It had to flame out, and did on the second Saturday as Courier broke the hearts of Jimmy's snowballing claque by just saying 'No!', 6–3 6–3 6–2. However, all that came before would be legend. It began at graveside as a two-day job stretched from the first Tuesday night until 1.35am the next morning, 4 hrs and 18 mins. Connors had so often battled McEnroe in this precinct, and now here was the other McEnroe, kid-brother Patrick, taking over where John left off. Almost. As Patrick built a 2-set, 3–0 lead, Connors ducked into a phone booth – and emerged SuperJim, coming away with a dramatic victory 4–6 6–7 (4–7) 6–4 6–2 6–4. 'I would have cheered for him too,' shrugged Patrick, alone in a Connors' cauldron.

It was only the lift-off. Next came Michiel Schapers and a bedazzled 10th seed, Karel Novacek. Then the 39th birthday epic, another tomb-buster, over Krickstein. Five times champion, Jimmy has usually rapped and wrapped his own birthday present on Sept 2nd. However, he'd never found a way to melodramatize himself like this one. Happy-birthday-to-me was a theme he played for a roaring full house throng of 20,000, rising from 2–5 down in the fifth set. Twice Jimmy was two points from defeat as Krickstein served at 5–3. Nevertheless, he came out of it charging in the clutch, daring Krickstein to pass him. It was 3–6 7–6 (10–8) 1–6 6–3 7–6 (7–4), even though Kricker had two set points in the second.

Quarter-final time found Connors mired again, a set behind, and Haarhuis serving for the second at 5–4. Time for the point-of-the-fortnight – won, naturally, by Connors (and his elderly leg). A break point. Jimmy patched it together with four lobbed saves of smashes and brought it to a close with a winning backhand.

Connors was in the semis for a 14th time. Wimbledon champ and fourth seed, Michael Stich, and everybody else (except Lendl), thought he would be there for a first. Rain stopped Stich in the third set, but next day the spidery, free-flowing German had that set for a 2–1 lead over Lendl. He looked a potential champion because his serve had carried him through rough passages (five sets with Washington, four with Rostagno), and was doing fine as he won the first three points of the fourth set tiebreaker. There Lendl firmed while Stich faltered, losing it 7–5. Soon Lendl, not Stich, was in the semis – his ninth.

Radka Zrubakova's 6–1 6–2 victory over a listless Mary Joe Fernandez, a 1990 semi-finalist, was just about the only female surprise prior to the quarters. That opened a spot for the lone non-seeded Gigi Fernandez (no relation). Gigi erased the diminutive Czechoslovak after slithering past 13th seed Leila Meskhi in a record-tying triple breaker match, 7–6 6–7 7–6. Steffi Graf had beaten Pam Shriver in the other 39-game max-match in 1986.

The heating-up began in the fourth round with Navratilova springing into an enthralling offensive of three successive three-set victories carrying her into the final. It felt good to bump her victimizer of the previous year, Manuela Maleeva-Fragnière, and even better to overcome the dynamic Spaniard, Arantxa Sanchez-Vicario 6–7 (6–8) 7–6 (7–5) 6–2. At 4–4 in the second set 'breaker Sanchez-Vicario was three points from victory, and on serve. But Martina's attacking tactics pulled her through – just as they did in the nervous 7–6 (7–2) 6–7 (6–8) 6–4 semi win over 1st-seeded 1988-89 champion, Graf.

When Martina failed to serve it out at 5–4 in the second, and Steffi finished strongly in the 8–6 tie-breaker, after squandering three set points, it appeared the German had taken control. Nothing of the sort! Martina second-winded her way to 3–0 and somehow held on in an excruciatingly uneven stretch. Leading 4–1, Martina lost her serve to 4–2; Steffi barely held to 3–4 and Martina got to 5–3 and deuce from 0–30. Hanging on grimly to win through two break points, she had her first victory over Graf since the 1987 final.

Gabriela Sabatini, unimpressive in her defence – perhaps still haunted by such a near miss against Graf in the Wimbledon final – was gone after a 360-day reign. Banging away with abandon, Capriati scored a clear knock-out in the quarters 6–3 7–6 (7–1).

Mystery girl Seles, back from her Wimbledon vanishing act, disappeared again, momentarily, in the third round – for one set – in beating the anonymous Swiss, Emanuela Zardo 6–0 4–6 6–0. Otherwise it was smooth, two-fisted flailing sailing except for the cannon-ading semi-final with the unblinking Capriati 6–3 3–6 7–6 (7–3).

The concussive kids pounded each other breathtakingly for two hours as their fortunes soared and sank. Seles led by a set and 3–1. Capriati recovered to go 3–1 up in the third, a compelling passage littered with eight service breaks. At 6–5 Jenny served for it and crept within two points of victory (30–15, 30–all), but was curbed by the power of Seles' forehand. In the high pressure tie-breaker, the first seven points went against the serve to leave Seles 4–3 ahead. Suddenly, the deathgrip brawl was over as Capriati missed a return and Seles nailed two winners.

The Aussie-Swedish coalition, John Fitzgerald and Anders Jarryd, beat Americans David Pate and Scott Davis 6–3 3–6 6–3 6–3 to complete a perfect season in the majors. After missing the Australian they had also won the French and Wimbledon titles – the first pair to take three biggies in one year since John Newcombe and Tony Roche in 1967.

Pam Shriver recorded a 5th US title, this time alongside Soviet Natalia Zvereva – 6–4 4–6 7–6 (7–5), winners over Jana Novotna and Zvereva's countrywoman and Wimbledon-winning accomplice, Larissa Savchenko.

In the mixed, an unseeded Dutch treat, Manon Bollegraf and Tom Nijssen, beat the Sanchez family, Arantxa and Emilio 6–2 7–6 (7–2).

But the mix that will be remembered is that aged blend of Navratilova and Connors.

Holder: P. Sampras (USA)

6-2 6-4 6-0

MEN'S SINGLES

FIRST ROUND	SECOND ROUND	THIRD ROUND	FOURTH ROUND	QUARTER-FINALS	SEMI-FINALS	FINAL
1 **B. BECKER** (GER) (1)	BECKER (1) 7-6 6-4 6-4	BECKER (1) 6-0 7-6 6-1	Haarhuis 6-3 6-4 6-2	Haarhuis 6-2 6-3 6-4	Connors 4-6 7-6 6-4 6-2	COURIER (4) 6-3 6-2
2 M. Jaite (ARG)	Volkov					
3 L. Herrera (MEX)	Haarhuis 2-6 6-2 6-1 3-6 6-2	Haarhuis 6-1 4-6 6-2 7-6				
4 A. Volkov (URS)	Chesnokov 6-2 6-2 6-3					
5 E. Jelen (GER)	Stafford 6-3 7-6 3-6 6-3	Steeb 6-0 7-6 6-1	Steeb 3-6 6-3 6-4 6-4			
6 P. Haarhuis (HOL)	Steeb 6-2 7-5 6-3					
7 M. Pernfors (SWE)	Bergstrom 6-7 4-6 6-3 6-0 6-3	Boetsch 6-2 6-3 2-1 ret'd				
8 A. Chesnokov (URS)	Boetsch 6-3 3-6 6-2					
9 J. Pugh (USA) (WC)	NOVACEK (10) 6-3 5-7 6-1 6-3	NOVACEK (10) 6-7 7-6 4-3 6-6 3	Connors 6-1 6-4 6-3	Connors 3-6 7-6 1-6 6-3 7-6		
10 G. Stafford (RSA) (Q)	Marques 6-3 6-4 7-6					
11 C. Adams (USA) (WC)	Connors 6-3 6-4 6-2	Connors 6-2 6-3 6-2				
12 C. Steeb (GER)	Schapers 4-6 7-6 4-6 2-6 4					
13 F. Montana (USA) (Q)	Raoux 5-7 6-3 4-6 6-3	Clavet 6-1 6-1 6-4	Krickstein 6-4 6-4 6-7 7-6			
14 C. Bergstrom (SWE)	Clavet 7-6 7-6 4-6 2					
15 J. Bergstrom (SWE)	Yzaga 7-5 7-5 7-5	Krickstein 6-1 3-6 6-1 3-2 ret'd				
16 **K. KORDA** (TCH) (15)	Krickstein 7-5 4-6 6-2					
17 **K. NOVACEK** (TCH) (10)	COURIER (4) 6-3 6-4 6-4	COURIER (4) 6-3 6-2 6-0	COURIER (4) 6-3 6-2 6-2	COURIER (4) 6-4 6-4 6-3	COURIER (4) 6-2 7-6 7-6	
18 S. Davis (USA)	Arias 7-5 7-5 3-6 6-3					
19 G. Michibata (CAN) (Q)	Champion 3-6 6-3 6-2 6-2	Jarryd 7-5 6-2 1-1 ret'd				
20 N. Marques (POR)	Jarryd 6-1 6-3 6-3					
21 J. Connors (USA) (WC)	Masur 4-6 6-3 6-2	Masur 6-4 6-3 3-6 6-3	E. SANCHEZ (14) 6-4 7-6 7-6			
22 P. McEnroe (USA)	Joyce 7-6 7-6 6-4					
23 M. Schapers (HOL) (Q)	Castle 0-6 7-5 6-4 7-5	E. SANCHEZ (14) 6-3 6-2				
24 J. Altur (ESP)	E. SANCHEZ (14) 6-3 4-6 6-3					
25 M. Rosset (SUI)	WHEATON (11) 6-0 4-6 7-6 6-3	WHEATON (11) 6-1 6-2 6-2	WHEATON (11) 7-6 4-6 6-3 6-4	SAMPRAS (6) 3-6 6-2 6-2 6-4		
26 F. Roux (FRA)	Skoff 4-6 7-6 6-4 6-2					
27 R. Reneberg (USA)	Martin 6-3 7-6 6-2	Martin 6-2 6-3 3-6 4-6 6-2				
28 F. Clavet (ESP)	Sapsford 6-3 7-5 6-1					
29 J. Yzaga (PER)	Simian 6-1 6-7 3-6 6-4 6-2	Simian 6-3 6-7 7-6 6-4	SAMPRAS (6) 7-6 6-4 6-7 6-3			
30 T. Mayotte (USA)	Curren 3-6 2-6 6-3 6-3 6-3					
31 A. Krickstein (USA)	Ferreira 7-6 4-6 6-2 2-6 6-3	SAMPRAS (6) 6-1 6-2 2-2 ret'd				
32 **J. AGASSI** (USA) (8)	SAMPRAS (6) 6-0 6-3 6-2					
33 **J. COURIER** (USA) (4)						
34 N. Kulti (SWE)						
35 J. Arias (USA)						
36 P. Lundgren (SWE)						
37 C. Pistolesi (ITA)						
38 T. Champion (FRA)						
39 A. Jarryd (SWE)						
40 J. Arraya (PER)						
41 W. Masur (AUS)						
42 P. Williamson (USA) (Q)						
43 M. Joyce (USA) (WC)						
44 P. Crow (USA) (Q)						
45 A. Castle (GBR) (Q)						
46 B. Wuyts (BEL)						
47 D. Witt (USA) (WC)						
48 **E. SANCHEZ** (ESP) (14)						
49 **D. WHEATON** (USA) (11)						
50 P. Fromberg (AUS)						
51 K. Evernden (NZL)						
52 H. Skoff (AUT)						
53 T. Martin (USA) (WC)						
54 G. Muller (RSA)						
55 D. Sapsford (GBR) (Q)						
56 A. Olhovskiy (URS)						
57 J.-P. Fleurian (FRA)						
58 S. Simian (FRA) (Q)						
59 K. Curren (USA)						
60 F. Santoro (FRA)						
61 C. Pioline (FRA)						
62 W. Ferreira (RSA)						
63 C. Van Rensburg (RSA)						
64 **P. SAMPRAS** (USA) (6)						

S. EDBERG (SWE) (2)

Winner: EDBERG (2) 6-3 6-3 6-4

Draw (players 65–128)

No.	Player	First round
65	I. LENDL (TCH) (5)	LENDL (5) 3-6 2-6 6-4 7-6 6-0
66	R. Krajicek (HOL)	
67	S. Youl (AUS) (Q)	Kuhnen 7-6 7-6 4-6 2
68	C. Kuhnen (GER)	
69	C. Saceanu (GER)	Saceanu 2-6 7-6 6-4 6-4
70	M. Vajda (TCH)	
71	T. Woodbridge (AUS)	Woodbridge 6-2 6-0 6-2
72	B. Madsen (HAI) (Q)	
73	G. Bloom (ISR)	Caratti 4-6 3-6 6-2 6-2 6-4
74	C. Caratti (ITA)	
75	L. Mattar (BRA)	Mattar 6-3 3-6 7-6 6-2
76	R. Leach (USA) (WC)	
77	G. Prpic (YUG)	Prpic 2-6 6-4 6-2 1-6 6-4
78	J. Gilbert (USA)	
79	H. Holm (SWE)	IVANISEVIC (12) 6-7 6-3 6-3 7-6
80	G. IVANISEVIC (YUG) (12)	
81	A. CHERKASOV (URS) (13)	Svensson 7-6 6-2 6-2
82	J. Svensson (SWE)	
83	A. Azar (ARG)	Hlasek 6-3 7-5 6-3
84	M. Hlasek (SUI)	
85	P. Baur (GER)	Rostagno 6-0 6-2 6-3
86	D. Rostagno (USA)	
87	R. Gilbert (FRA)	R. Gilbert 6-1 6-2 5-7 1-6 7-6
88	J. Palmer (USA) (WC)	
89	C. Camporese (ITA)	Camporese 5-7 6-4 7-5 3-6 6-3
90	A. Mansdorf (ISR)	
91	M. Washington (USA)	Washington 6-2 6-2 6-1
92	J. Oncins (BRA)	
93	A. Mancini (ARG)	Brown 6-2 6-4 3-6 6-7 6-2
94	J. Brown (USA) (Q)	
95	J. Frana (ARG)	STICH (3) 7-6 6-1 6-0
96	M. STICH (GER) (3)	
97	G. FORGET (FRA) (7)	FORGET (7) 7-5 6-3 6-1
98	M. Ondruska (RSA) (Q)	
99	J. Siemerink (HOL)	Siemerink 5-7 7-5 3-6 6-4 6-4
100	D. Poliakov (URS)	
101	D. Markus (ARG)	Markus 7-6 7-6 7-6
102	D. Nargiso (ITA)	
103	P. Pescosolido (ITA)	Pescosolido 7-6 6-7 2-6 6-2 6-3
104	D. Pate (USA)	
105	M. Larsson (SWE)	Larsson 4-6 3-6 7-6 2-6 6-1
106	A. Gomez (ECU)	
107	D. Engel (SWE) (Q)	Frana 6-3 6-4 6-4
108	J. Frana (ARG)	
109	J. Sanchez (ESP)	J. Sanchez 6-2 6-3 3-1 ret'd
110	A. Mronz (GER)	
111	J. Carbonell (ESP)	BRUGUERA (9) 3-6 6-4 6-3 7-6 6-3
112	S. BRUGUERA (ESP) (9)	
113	J. McENROE (USA) (16)	J. McENROE (16) 6-4 6-3 6-3
114	G. Lavendecker (USA) (Q)	
115	M. Laurendeau (CAN) (Q)	Laurendeau 7-5 7-6 3-6 7-5
116	A. Agenor (HAT)	
117	V. Paloheimo (FIN)	Witsken 6-3 5-7 6-4 6-1
118	T. Witsken (USA)	
119	M. Chang (USA)	Chang 6-3 6-0 6-2
120	M. Woodforde (AUS)	
121	M. Koevermans (HOL)	Grabb 6-4 7-6 6-2
122	J. Grabb (USA)	
123	J. Stoltenberg (AUS)	Stoltenberg 6-4 7-6 6-2
124	G. Connell (CAN)	
125	R. Krishnan (IND)	Tarango 6-2 6-1 6-7 5-7 6-3
126	J. Tarango (USA)	
127	B. Shelton (USA)	EDBERG (2) 6-4 2-6 7-6 6-1
128	S. EDBERG (SWE) (2)	

Second round (last 32)

- LENDL (5) 6-3 6-2 6-4
- Woodbridge 6-2 6-3 6-3
- Mattar 3-6 3-6 6-0 7-6
- IVANISEVIC (12) 6-1 6-3 6-4
- Hlasek 6-4 7-5 6-7 6-3
- Rostagno 7-6 7-6 7-6
- Washington 4-6 6-1 6-1 6-4
- STICH (3) W/O
- Siemerink 4-6 6-3 6-2 7-6
- Markus 6-2 1-6 4-6 7-6 6-2
- Larsson 4-6 4-6 6-4 6-4
- J. Sanchez 7-6 7-6 6-0
- J. McENROE (16) 6-3 6-4 6-2
- Chang 6-3 6-0 6-2
- Grabb 7-5 6-4 4-6 7-5
- EDBERG (2) 6-3 7-5 6-0

Third round (last 16)

- LENDL (5) 3-6 6-3 6-4 6-3
- Mattar 3-6 3-6 6-0 7-6
- IVANISEVIC (12) 6-3 6-2
- Rostagno 6-7 7-6 7-6
- STICH (3) 5-7 7-5 6-2 4-6 6-3
- Markus 6-4 6-4 1-6 6-7 7-6
- J. Sanchez 6-4 6-2 6-3
- Chang 6-4 4-6 7-6 2-6 6-3
- EDBERG (2) 7-6 7-5 6-3

Fourth round (last 8)

- LENDL (5) 7-5 6-7 6-4 6-2
- IVANISEVIC (12) 6-3 6-2
- STICH (3) 6-2 3-6 6-1 7-6
- J. Sanchez 6-4 6-2 6-3
- EDBERG (2) 6-3 6-2 6-3

Quarter-finals

- LENDL (5) 6-3 3-6 4-6 7-6 6-1
- EDBERG (2) 7-6 7-5 6-3

Semi-final

- EDBERG (2) 6-3 6-3 6-4

Capital letters denote seeded players. Number following player's name gives seeding order. (Q) – Qualifier. (WC) – Wild Card. (LL) – Lucky Loser.

WOMEN'S SINGLES

Holder: G. Sabatini (ARG)

Winner: NAVRATILOVA (6) — 7-6 6-1

FIRST ROUND	SECOND ROUND	THIRD ROUND	FOURTH ROUND	QUARTER-FINALS	SEMI-FINALS	FINAL
1 S. GRAF (GER) (1)	GRAF (1) 6-1 6-2	GRAF (1) 6-0 6-0	GRAF (1) 6-4 7-5	GRAF (1) 7-5 6-4	GRAF (1) 6-1 6-3	NAVRATILOVA (6) 7-6 6-7 6-4
2 A. Temesvari (HUN)						
3 M. Maruska (AUT)	Mothes 6-3 6-4					
4 C. Mothes (FRA)						
5 C. Lindqvist (SWE)	Lindqvist 6-3 6-3	Sviglerova 6-2 6-2				
6 R. Alter (CAN) (Q)						
7 E. Sviglerova (TCH)	Sviglerova 6-4 6-1					
8 C. Caverzasio (SUI)						
9 J. Wiesner (AUT)	Wiesner 4-6 6-3 6-3	Wiesner 3-6 6-1 6-4	Wiesner 6-4 7-5			
10 A. Dechaume (FRA)						
11 S. Stafford (USA)	Stafford 6-3 6-3					
12 C. Tessi (ARG)						
13 A. Frazier (USA)	Frazier 6-3 7-6	Labat 2-6 7-5 6-2				
14 C. Wood (GBR)						
15 C. Labat (ARG)	Labat 6-4					
16 N. TAUZIAT (FRA) (14)						
17 Z. GARRISON (USA) (12)	GARRISON (12) 7-5 6-4	GARRISON (12) 6-1 6-1	GARRISON (12) 6-2 3-6 6-4	MARTINEZ (8) 6-4 6-4		
18 S. Appelmans (BEL)						
19 S. Cecchini (ITA)	Cecchini 7-6 6-1					
20 M. Javer (USA)						
21 S. Sloane (USA)	Rittner 6-4 6-1	Rittner 6-2 6-0				
22 B. Rittner (GER)						
23 A. Coetzer (RSA)	Halard 7-5 6-1					
24 J. Halard (FRA)						
25 M. Kidowaki (JPN)	Habsudova 6-1 6-4	Fendick 6-2 6-3	MARTINEZ (8) 7-5 6-3			
26 K. Habsudova (TCH)						
27 P. Thoren (FIN)	Fendick 6-1 6-4					
28 P. Fendick (USA)						
29 A. Keller (USA)	Basuki 6-4 6-2	MARTINEZ (8) 6-3 6-4				
30 Y. Basuki (IND)						
31 C. Dahlman (SWE)	MARTINEZ (8) 6-1					
32 C. MARTINEZ (ESP) (8)						
33 A. SANCHEZ-VICARIO (ESP) (4)	SANCHEZ-VICARIO (4) 6-0 6-1	SANCHEZ-VICARIO (4) 6-1 6-1	SANCHEZ-VICARIO (4) 6-2 6-2	SANCHEZ-VICARIO (4) 6-3 7-6	NAVRATILOVA (6) 6-7 7-6 6-2	
34 K. Piccolini (ITA)						
35 E. Smylie (AUS)	Godridge 6-3 6-4					
36 K. Godridge (AUS)						
37 E. Brioukhovets (URS)	Brioukhovets 6-3 6-0	Herreman 3-6 7-6 7-6				
38 L. Bonder-Kreiss (USA)						
39 N. Herreman (FRA) (LL)	Herreman 4-6 6-4 6-3					
40 E. Kohde-Kilsch (GER)						
41 E. Burgin (USA) (WC)	Po 6-4 6-4	Po 6-2 6-4	Zvereva 6-1 3-6 6-2			
42 K. Po (USA) (WC)						
43 A. Langrova (TCH)	Smith 6-4 7-5					
44 A. Smith (USA) (WC)						
45 W. Probst (GER)	Zvereva 6-1 7-6	Zvereva 6-2 6-4				
46 N. Zvereva (URS)						
47 A. Minter (AUS)	HUBER (16) 6-3 6-1					
48 A. HUBER (GER) (16)						
49 M. MALEEVA-FRAGNIERE (SUI) (10)	MALEEVA-FRAGNIERE (10) 6-3 6-1	MALEEVA-FRAGNIERE (10) 7-5 6-2	MALEEVA-FRAGNIERE (10) 4-6 6-1 5-1 ret'd	NAVRATILOVA (6) 7-6 1-6 6-2		
50 S. Birch (USA) (WC)						
51 C. Porwik (GER)	Strnadova 6-3 6-2					
52 A. Strnadova (TCH)						
53 L. Garrone (ITA)	Pierce 4-6 6-0 7-6	Pierce 6-3 3-6 7-6				
54 J. Pierce (FRA)						
55 L. McNeil (USA)	McNeil 6-2 6-3					
56 R. White (USA)						
57 M. Maleeva (BUL)	M. Maleeva 7-6 4-6 6-4	Shriver 6-7 6-1 6-2	NAVRATILOVA (6) 7-5 6-1			
58 K. Kschwendt (LUX)						
59 N. Hiraki (JPN)	Shriver 6-1 6-1					
60 P. Shriver (USA)						
61 L. Davenport (USA) (WC)	Graham 6-3 6-2	NAVRATILOVA (6) 6-1 6-4				
62 D. Graham (USA)						
63 P. Tarabini (ARG)	NAVRATILOVA (6) 6-2 6-2					
64 M. NAVRATILOVA (USA) (6)						

M. SELES (YUG) (2)

#	Player	1st round	2nd round	3rd round	4th round	Quarterfinal	Semifinal
65	J. CAPRIATI (USA) (7)	CAPRIATI (7) 6-1 6-0	CAPRIATI (7) 6-3 6-0	CAPRIATI (7) 6-1 6-4	CAPRIATI (7) 6-1 6-2	CAPRIATI (7) 6-3 7-6	SELES (2) 6-3 3-6 7-6
66	E. Pfaff (GER) (Q)						
67	E. Fairbank-Nideffer (RSA)	Ritter 6-4 7-6					
68	P. Ritter (AUT)						
69	R. McQuillan (AUS)	McQuillan 6-4 3-6 6-0	Hy 6-1 6-2				
70	S. Niox-Chateau (FRA) (Q)						
71	P. Hy (CAN)	Hy 6-3 6-0					
72	M. Strandlund (SWE)						
73	E. Reinach (RSA)	Fulco 6-2 4-6 7-6	Durie 6-4 6-0	Durie 6-4 2-6 6-1			
74	B. Fulco (ARG)						
75	J. Durie (GBR)	Durie 6-4 6-2					
76	C. Cunningham (USA)						
77	E. De Lone (USA)	De Lone 6-2 6-7 6-3	SUKOVA (15) 6-1 6-3				
78	H. Cioffi (USA)						
79	J. Emmons (USA) (WC)	SUKOVA (15) 6-4 6-2					
80	H. SUKOVA (TCH) (15)						
81	J. NOVOTNA (TCH) (9)	NOVOTNA (9) 6-3 4-6 6-1	NOVOTNA (9) 6-2 6-3	NOVOTNA (9) 6-2 6-3	SABATINI (3) 6-4 7-6		
82	A. Grossman (USA)						
83	M. Werdel (USA)	Harper 6-4 5-7 6-4					
84	P. Harper (USA)						
85	F. Romano (ITA)	Monami 6-1 6-4	Monami 6-4 6-3				
86	D. Monami (BEL) (Q)						
87	C. Rubin (USA) (WC)	Rubin 6-4 6-3					
88	S. Farina (ITA)						
89	G. Helgeson (USA)	Faber 6-4 6-4	Magers 6-3 6-3	SABATINI (3) 6-3 6-4			
90	A. Faber (USA)						
91	G. Magers (USA)	Magers 5-7 6-4 6-3					
92	E. Maniokova (URS) (Q)						
93	S. Hack (GER)	Paulus 6-7 6-4 6-4	SABATINI (3) 6-3 4-6 5-1 ret'd				
94	B. Paulus (AUT)						
95	L. Provis (AUS)	SABATINI (3) 7-6 6-3					
96	G. SABATINI (ARG) (3)						
97	M. J. FERNANDEZ (USA) (5)	M. J. FERNANDEZ (5) 6-3 6-3	M. J. FERNANDEZ (5) 7-6 6-3	Zrubakova 6-1 6-2	G. Fernandez 6-2 6-2	SELES (2) 6-1 6-2	
98	L. Savchenko (URS)						
99	A. Kijimuta (JPN)	Schultz 3-6 6-3 6-2					
100	R. Schultz (HOL)						
101	R. Baranski (USA) (Q)	Zrubakova 6-2 7-6	Zrubakova 6-1 6-2				
102	R. Zrubakova (TCH)						
103	K. Date (JPN)	Date 7-6 6-4					
104	Tami Whitlinger (USA)						
105	G. Fernandez (USA)	G. Fernandez 6-0 6-4	G. Fernandez 6-4 6-1	G. Fernandez 7-6 6-7 7-6			
106	S. Frankl (GER)						
107	K. Rinaldi (USA)	Rinaldi 6-7 6-4 6-1					
108	M. Paz (ARG)						
109	M. Jaggerman (HOL)	Gildemeister 7-6 6-4	MESKHI (13) 6-4 3-6 6-0	MESKHI (13) 7-6 6-4			
110	L. Gildemeister (PER)						
111	L. Paradis-Mangon (FRA)	MESKHI (13) 6-3 6-2					
112	L. MESKHI (URS) (13)						
113	K. MALEEVA (BUL) (11)	K. MALEEVA (11) 6-3 6-4	K. MALEEVA (11) 6-3 6-4	SELES (2) 6-1 6-4	SELES (2) 6-1 6-2		
114	M. Bollegraf (HOL)						
115	C. Suire (FRA)	De Swardt 6-1 6-7 6-3					
116	M. De Swardt (RSA)						
117	R. Rajchrtova (TCH)	Rajchrtova 6-1 6-3	Rajchrtova 2-6 6-3 6-3				
118	C. Bartos (SUI)						
119	J. Ferrando (ITA)	Sawamatsu 6-4 6-2					
120	N. Sawamatsu (JPN)						
121	N. Van Lottum (FRA)	Kelesi 6-3 7-5	Gomer 6-2 2-6 6-3				
122	H. Kelesi (CAN)						
123	S. Rottier (HOL) (Q)	Gomer 6-3 6-1					
124	S. Gomer (GBR)						
125	K. Nowak (POL) (Q)	Zardo 7-5 6-1	SELES (2) 6-0 4-6 6-0				
126	E. Zardo (SUI)						
127	N. Arendt (USA) (WC)	SELES (2) 6-2 6-0					
128	M. SELES (YUG) (2)						

MEN'S DOUBLES

Holders: P. Aldrich (RSA)/D. Visser (RSA)

Winner: J. FITZGERALD (AUS)/A. JARRYD (SWE) (1) 6–3 3–6 6–3 6–3

FIRST ROUND

1 FITZGERALD/JARRYD (1)
2 Engel/Marcelino
3 Cannon/Smith
4 Annacone/Jones
5 Mattar/Oncins
6 Bruguera/Carbonell
7 Beckman/Salumaa
8 GRABB/KRATZMANN (15)
9 R. LEACH/PUGH (10)
10 Broom/Flach
11 Korda/Novacek
12 Fromberg/J. Sanchez
13 Lucena/Pedersen
14 Nijssen/Suk
15 Evernden/Oosting
16 JENSEN/WARDER (8)
17 CONNELL/MICHIBATA (3)
18 J. Brown/Melville
19 DeVries/MacPherson
20 Kulti/Montana
21 N. Brown/Castle
22 Kinnear/Thorne
23 Bates/Curren
24 FRANA/LAVALLE (14)
25 FERREIRA/NORVAL (12)
26 Garrow/Pearce
27 Patridge/Talbot
28 Davids/Eltingh
29 Nelson/Washington
30 Jonsson/Mora
31 Leendertse/Rieneberg
32 WOODBRIDGE/WOODFORDE (6)
33 K. FLACH/SEGUSO (5)
34 Arraya/Poliakov
35 Aerts/Roese
36 Hlasek/Smid
37 Broad/Kruger
38 Gómez/E. Sanchez
39 Dyke/Lundgren
40 HAARHUIS/KOEVERMANS (11)
41 CAMPORESE/IVANISEVIC (13)
42 Alegi/Vacek
43 Adoff/W.Menezes
44 J. McEnroe/P. McEnroe
45 Svantesson/Van Emburgh
46 Bathman/Bergh
47 Clavet/Nargiso
48 GALBRAITH/WITSKEN (4)
49 MÜLLER/VISSER (7)
50 Schapers/Svensson
51 Palmer/Stark
52 Lozano/Rive
53 Bowcock/Shelton
54 Borwick/Youl
55 Garnett/Van't Hof
56 RIGLEWSKI/STICH (9)
57 MASUR/STOLTENBERG (16)
58 Pimek/Wekesa
59 Bahrami/Gilbert
60 Siemerink/Van Rensburg
61 Ho/Martin
62 Leach/Witt
63 Adams/Olhovskiy
64 S. DAVIS/PATE (2)

SECOND ROUND

FITZGERALD/JARRYD (1) 6-4 6-1
Annacone/Jones 6-3 7-6
Mattar/Oncins 6-2 6-4
Beckman/Salumaa 6-3 6-4
R. LEACH/PUGH (10) 6-7 6-2
Korda/Novacek 6-4 6-4
Lucena/Pedersen 6-4 6-1
JENSEN/WARDER (8) 6-2 6-1
CONNELL/MICHIBATA (3) 7-6 7-6
DeVries/MacPherson 6-4 6-1
N. Brown/Castle 3-6 6-2 7-6
FRANA/LAVALLE (14) 6-3 6-2
FERREIRA/NORVAL (12) 6-4 6-3 6-2
Davids/Eltingh 6-4 6-2
Nelson/Washington 6-4 6-4
WOODBRIDGE/WOODFORDE (6) 5-7 6-3 6-2
K. FLACH/SEGUSO (5) 6-1 7-5
Aerts/Roese 6-2 6-4
Gómez/E. Sanchez 6-4 7-6
HAARHUIS/KOEVERMANS (11) 6-4 6-2
CAMPORESE/IVANISEVIC (13) 6-3 6-2
J. McEnroe/P. McEnroe 6-3 6-2
Bathman/Bergh 6-3 2-6 6-4
GALBRAITH/WITSKEN (4) 3-6 6-3 6-2
Schapers/Svensson 6-7 6-3 7-5
Palmer/Stark 6-4 6-1
Bowcock/Youl 6-7 6-3 7-6
RIGLEWSKI/STICH (9) 6-4 6-2
Pimek/Wekesa 6-4 6-2
Siemerink/Van Rensburg 7-5 6-2
Ho/Martin 7-6 6-3
S. DAVIS/PATE (2) 6-4 6-4

THIRD ROUND

FITZGERALD/JARRYD (1) 6-7 7-5 6-3
Beckman/Salumaa 4-6 6-3 6-4
Korda/Novacek 6-3 7-6
Lucena/Pedersen 7-5 6-3
DeVries/MacPherson 7-5 7-6
FRANA/LAVALLE (14) 6-4 6-4
Davids/Eltingh w/o
WOODBRIDGE/WOODFORDE (6) 6-3 6-2
K. FLACH/SEGUSO (5) 7-5 6-4
Gómez/E. Sanchez 7-6 3-6 7-6
J. McEnroe/P. McEnroe 7-6 6-4
Bathman/Bergh 6-1 7-6
Palmer/Stark 6-3 3-6 6-4
RIGLEWSKI/STICH (9) 7-6 6-2
Pimek/Wekesa 6-4 6-4
S. DAVIS/PATE (2) 6-4 6-2

QUARTER-FINALS

FITZGERALD/JARRYD (1) 6-3 3-6 6-4
Lucena/Pedersen 6-3 6-2
DeVries/MacPherson 6-7 7-6 6-3
WOODBRIDGE/WOODFORDE (6) 6-4 6-2
K. FLACH/SEGUSO (5) 6-0 6-3
Bathman/Bergh 7-5 1-6 6-3
RIGLEWSKI/STICH (9) 6-1 6-2
S. DAVIS/PATE (2) 6-3 6-4

SEMI-FINALS

FITZGERALD/JARRYD (1) 5-7 7-6 6-2 6-4
WOODBRIDGE/WOODFORDE (6) 6-2 6-4 6-1
K. FLACH/SEGUSO (5) 6-2 6-3 7-6
S. DAVIS/PATE (2) 6-4 3-6 7-6 3-6 6-3

FINAL

FITZGERALD/JARRYD (1) 6-2 6-7 6-4 6-3
S. DAVIS/PATE (2) 7-5 6-4 6-4

P. SHRIVER (USA)/N. ZVEREVA (URS) (6) 6–4 4–6 7–6

FIRST ROUND

1 NOVOTNA/SAVCHENKO (1)
2 Fuoco/Jagerman
3 Stafford/Werdel
4 Dechaume/Labat
5 Halard/Huber
6 Graham/McCarthy
7 Franati/Garrone
8 DANIELS/GREGORY (12)
9 COLLINS/McQUILLAN (16)
10 Cordwell/Lindqvist
11 Ferrando/Probst
12 Lindstrom/Sure
13 Tarri Whitlinger/Teri Whitlinger
14 Alter/Helgeson
15 Burgin/Temesvari
16 MAGERS/WHITE (5)
17 M. J. FERNANDEZ/GARRISON (4)
18 Miyagi/Somerville
19 Langrova/Zrubakova
20 Godridge/Radford
21 Harper/May
22 Faull/Jaggard
23 Appelmans/Benjamin
24 Herreman/Rinaldi (9)
25 FAIRBANK-NID/KOHDE-KILSCH (14)
26 Brioukhovets/K. Maleeva
27 Pierce/Spadea
28 Morton/Wood
29 Frazier/Kidowaki
30 MacGregor/Mager
31 Maniokova/Thoren
32 REINACH/SMITH (8)
33 PROVIS/SMYLIE (7)
34 Baranski/Borneo
35 Goconcelli/Buuren
36 Basuki/Dune
37 M. Maleeva/Maleeva-Fragniere
38 Guse/Nishiya
39 DeVries/Wasserman
40 TAUZIAT/WIESNER (15)
41 MESKHI/PAZ (13)
42 Cunningham/Glidemeister
43 Field/Strandlund
44 Keles/Vis
45 Demongeot/Martinez
46 Grossman/Stubbs
47 Date/Kijimuta
48 SANCHEZ-VICARIO/SUKOVA (3)
49 SHRIVER/ZVEREVA (6)
50 Hennicksson/Smoller
51 Kschwendt/Schultz
52 Cecchni/Tarabini
53 Arendt/Alexander
54 Caverzasio/Herreman
55 Gooden/Hiraki
56 FENDICK/McNEIL (11)
57 ADAMS/BOLLEGRAF (10)
58 Jankovski/Melicharova
59 Paradis/Testud
60 Nohacova/Sviglerova
61 Pfaff/Porwik
62 Davenport/London
63 Reichtrova/Strnadova
64 G. FERNANDEZ/NAVRATILOVA (2)

SECOND ROUND

NOVOTNA/SAVCHENKO (1) 6–4 7–6
Stafford/Werdel 6–1 6–3
Graham/McCarthy 7–6 6–2
DANIELS/GREGORY (12) 6–3 6–1
COLLINS/McQUILLAN (16) 6–4 6–3
Ferrando/Probst 6–1 6–2
Whitlinger/Whitlinger 6–2 7–5
M. J. FERNANDEZ/GARRISON (4)
Godridge/Radford 7–6 6–2
Faull/Jaggard 6–2 7–5
Appelmans/Benjamin 6–2 7–5
FAIRBANK-NID/KOHDE-KILSCH (14) 7–5 6–3
Morton/Wood 6–4 6–1
Frazier/Kidowaki 6–4 6–1
REINACH/SMITH (8) 5–7 6–4 7–5
PROVIS/SMYLIE (7) 6–3 6–1
Basuki/Dune 6–2 6–1
Guse/Nishiya 2–6–1
TAUZIAT/WIESNER (15) 7–5 6–4
MESKHI/PAZ (13) 6–4 3–6 6–4
Keles/Vis 1–6 6–1 6–2
Demongeot/Martinez 6–2 6–2
SANCHEZ-VICARIO/SUKOVA (3) 6–2 6–2
SHRIVER/ZVEREVA (6) 6–2 6–2
Kschwendt/Schultz 6–2 6–2
Caverzasio/Herreman 6–2 6–7 7–6
FENDICK/McNEIL (11) 6–1 6–2
ADAMS/BOLLEGRAF (10) 6–1 6–2
Paradis/Testud 6–4 6–2
Pfaff/Porwik 6–4 6–2
G. FERNANDEZ/NAVRATILOVA (2) 6–2 6–4

THIRD ROUND

NOVOTNA/SAVCHENKO (1) 6–4 6–1
DANIELS/GREGORY (12) 6–2 6–3
COLLINS/McQUILLAN (16) 6–2 7–5
Whitlinger/Whitlinger 6–3 4–6 6–3
M. J. FERNANDEZ/GARRISON (4) 6–3 6–0
Appelmans/Benjamin 6–4 6–2
FAIRBANK-NID/KOHDE-KILSCH (14) 6–4 6–2
REINACH/SMITH (8) 6–4 6–3
Basuki/Dune 6–3 6–3
TAUZIAT/WIESNER (15) 6–1 6–3
MESKHI/PAZ (13) 6–1 7–6
SANCHEZ-VICARIO/SUKOVA (3) 6–1 6–1
SHRIVER/ZVEREVA (6) 4–6 6–2 7–6
FENDICK/McNEIL (11) 6–2 6–3
ADAMS/BOLLEGRAF (10) 6–3 6–3
G. FERNANDEZ/NAVRATILOVA (2) 6– 6–4

QUARTER-FINALS

NOVOTNA/SAVCHENKO (1) 6–4 6–2
COLLINS/McQUILLAN (16) 6–1 3–6 6–0
M. J. FERNANDEZ/GARRISON (4) 4–9 7–5 6–4
REINACH/SMITH (8) 6–4 7–6
Basuki/Dune 6–2 3–6 6–1
MESKHI/PAZ (13) 7–6 6–4
SHRIVER/ZVEREVA (6) 6–4 7–5
ADAMS/BOLLEGRAF (10) 7–6 6–1

SEMI-FINALS

NOVOTNA/SAVCHENKO (1) 3–6 2–6 6–4
M. J. FERNANDEZ/GARRISON (4) 7–5 4–6 6–3
MESKHI/PAZ (13) 6–3 6–4
SHRIVER/ZVEREVA (6) 6–4 6–3

FINAL

NOVOTNA/SAVCHENKO (1) 6–4 6–2
SHRIVER/ZVEREVA (6) 6–1 6–0

Capital letters denote seeded pairings. Number following players' names gives seeding order. (Q) – Qualifier. (WC) – Wild Card. (LL) – Lucky Loser.

MIXED DOUBLES

Holders: T. Woodbridge (AUS)/E. Smylie (AUS)

Winner: T. NIJSSEN (HOL)/M. Bollegraf (HOL) 6-2 7-6

FIRST ROUND	SECOND ROUND	QUARTER-FINALS	SEMI-FINALS	FINAL
1 FITZGERALD/SMYLIE (1)	FITZGERALD/SMYLIE (1) 6-4 7-6	Van Rensburg/Reinach 2-6 6-2 7-5	Van Rensburg/Reinach 3-6 6-3 6-3	Nijssen/Bollegraf 4-6 7-6 6-4
2 Leach/Garrison				
3 Galbraith/May	Van Rensburg/Reinach 6-3 5-7 6-2			
4 Van Rensburg/Reinach				
5 Cannon/Adams	Cannon/Adams 7-6 4-6 7-6	Cannon/Adams 7-6 2-6 6-3		
6 Shelton/McNeil				
7 Jensen/Jensen	WOODFORDE/FENDICK (6) 6-3 6-4			
8 WOODFORDE/FENDICK (6)				
9 PUGH/ZVEREVA (4)	Suk/Sukova 6-1 6-4	Nijssen/Bollegraf 7-6 4-6 6-3	Nijssen/Bollegraf 7-6 6-3	
10 Suk/Sukova				
11 Kinnear/Gregory	Nijssen/Bollegraf 6-4 6-2			
12 Nijssen/Bollegraf				
13 Pimek/Daniels	Salumaa/Savchenko 7-5 5-7 6-3	WOODBRIDGE/PROVIS (8) 6-4 6-3		
14 Salumaa/Savchenko				
15 Kratzmann/Shriver	WOODBRIDGE/PROVIS (8) 3-6 6-2 6-3			
16 WOODBRIDGE/PROVIS (8)				
17 WITSKEN/MAGERS (7)	WITSKEN/MAGERS (7) 6-3 6-4	Warder/Durie 6-2 6-0	Warder/Durie 7-6 7-6	SANCHEZ/SANCHEZ-VICARIO (2) 6-2 6-2
18 Norval/Faull				
19 K. Jones/A. Smith	Warder/Durie 6-3 7-6			
20 Warder/Durie				
21 Melville/Fairbank-Nideffer	Melville/Fairbank-Nideffer 6-3 6-3	MICHIBATA/HETHERINGTON (3) 6-4 6-4		
22 Palmer/Graham				
23 R. Smith/Frazier	MICHIBATA/HETHERINGTON (3) 6-7 6-1 7-5			
24 MICHIBATA/HETHERINGTON (3)				
25 VISSER/WHITE (5)	VISSER/WHITE (5) 6-7 6-3 6-4	VISSER/WHITE (5) 4-6 7-6 6-4	SANCHEZ/SANCHEZ-VICARIO (2) 6-4 7-5	
26 Bergh/Burgin				
27 Schapers/Schultz	Lavalle/Paz 6-3 6-4			
28 Lavalle/Paz				
29 N. Brown/Pfaff	N. Brown/Pfaff 6-0 6-4	SANCHEZ/SANCHEZ-VICARIO (2) 6-0 7-5		
30 Lozano/Pierce				
31 MacPherson/McQuillan	SANCHEZ/SANCHEZ-VICARIO (2) 6-4 7-6			
32 SANCHEZ/SANCHEZ-VICARIO (2)				

Capital letters denote seeded pairings. Number following players' names gives seeding order. (Q) – Qualifier; (WC) – Wild Card; (LL) – Lucky Loser.

JUNIOR EVENTS

BOYS' SINGLES – Final: Leander Paes (IND) (2) d. Karim Alami (MAR) (4) 6–4 6–4.
GIRLS' SINGLES – Final: Karina Habsudova (TCH) (2) d. Anne Mall (USA) 6–1 6–3.
BOYS' DOUBLES – Final: Karim Alami (MAR)/John DeJager (RSA) (1) d. Michael Joyce (USA)/Vincent Spadea (USA) (6) 6–4 6–7 6–1.
GIRLS' DOUBLES – Final: Kristin Godridge (AUS)/Nicole Pratt (AUS) (1) d. Asa Carlsson (SWE)/Catalina Cristea (ROM) 7–6 7–5.

SENIOR EVENTS

MEN'S INVITATIONAL SINGLES – Final: Hank Pfister (USA) (4) d. Tom Gullikson (USA) (2) 1–6 7–6 6–4.
MEN'S INVITATIONAL DOUBLES – Final: Peter Fleming (USA/Hank Pfister (USA) (3) d. Mark Edmondson (AUS)/Sherwood Stewart (USA) (4) 4–6 7–6 7–5.
WOMEN'S INVITATIONAL DOUBLES – Final: Rosie Casals (USA)/Billie Jean King (USA) (1) d. Wendy Turnbull (AUS)/Virginia Wade (GBR) (2) 7–5 6–4.
MIXED INVITATIONAL DOUBLES – Final: Bob Hewitt (RSA)/Wendy Turnbull (AUS) (3) d. Gene Mayer (USA)/Maria Bueno (BRA) (4) 6–4 7–5.

U.S. OPEN CHAMPIONSHIPS PRIZE MONEY – $7,250,000

MEN'S SINGLES – Winner $400,000. Runner-up $200,000. Semi-finalists $100,000. Quarter-finalists $51,900. Fourth-round losers $28,100. Third-round losers $16,200. Second-round losers $10,000. First-round losers $6,000.
Total: $2,195,600.
WOMEN'S SINGLES – Winner $400,000. Runner-up $200,000. Semi-finalists $100,000. Quarter-finalists $51,900. Fourth-round losers $28,100. Third-round losers $16,200. Second-round losers $10,000. First-round losers $6,000.
Total: $2,195,600.
MEN'S DOUBLES (per pair) – Winners $163,500. Runners-up $81,650. Semi-finalists $40,875. Quarter-finalists $21,000. Third-round losers $12,000. Second-round losers $6,000. First-round losers $4,050.
Total $ 732,500.
WOMEN'S DOUBLES (per pair) – Winners $163,500. Runners-up $81,650. Semi-finalists $40,875. Quarter-finalists $21,000. Third-round losers $12,000. Second-round losers $6,000. First-round losers $4,050.
Total $ 732,500.
MIXED DOUBLES (per pair) – Winners $46,500. Runners-up $22,000. Semi-finalists $11,000. Quarter-finalists $6,200. Second-round losers $3,500. First-round losers $1,400.
Total: $165,700.
QUALIFYING COMPETITIONS – $256,800
MEN (each): 16 × Third-round losers $3,000. 32 × Second-round losers $1,650. 64 × First-round losers $1,100.
Total: $171,200.
WOMEN (each): 32 × Third-round losers $3,000. 16 × Second-round losers $1,650. 32 × First-round losers $1,100.
Total $85,500.
Total for senior events – $385,900.
Total for per diem allowances and other fees – $585,400.

The richest prize of 1991, a cool $2 million, fell to the enterprising American David Wheaton who had planned all year for a determined attack on the Compaq Grand Slam Cup *in which he had been a semi-finalist in 1990.* (T. Hindley)

COMPAQ GRAND SLAM CUP

John Barrett

It was fitting that the two men who had laid long-term plans should have fought out the final of the season's richest tournament. When David Wheaton beat fellow American Michael Chang 7–5 6–2 6–4 in 3 hrs and 4 mins of devastating attacking tennis to win the second $6 million *Compaq Grand Slam Cup*, he said that this title and the $2 million reward for the winner had been a major objective for him throughout 1991. Similarly Chang who, like Wheaton, had been a semi-finalist at the inaugural event in 1990, had realised after a disappointing first half of the year that here in the cavernous Munich Olympiahalle was the chance to make amends – both financially and in terms of prestige.

How well these two young men took their chances! Wheaton, seeded No.7 and drawn in the top quarter of the 16-man draw, had the easier time of it. David had benefited from the enforced withdrawal of the ailing Boris Becker whose mystery virus refused to respond to treatment in time. The absence of the tournament's biggest draw card, announced by his manager Ion Tiriac during the first day of play, might have been expected to deal the event a mortal blow – especially as the world No.1 Stefan Edberg had also withdrawn on the eve of the tournament with the same leg injury that had prevented him from competing in the ATP Tour Championship. But the presence of the local hero, Wimbledon champion Michael Stich, plus a vigorous promotional campaign and a revised ticket policy which allowed the public to purchase tickets for individual days instead of being offered only season tickets as in 1990, brought the fans out in large numbers. Almost 59,000 people attended the 6 days of play, an increase of some 10,000 on the previous year.

Once Wheaton had recovered from the shock of losing the first set 1–6 in his opening match against Paul Haarhuis of Holland, the 6'4" native of Lake Minnetonka, Minnesota settled into a relentless rhythm of serve-and-volley tennis on the fast *Supreme* carpet with the fast English-made *Slazenger Wimbledon* balls that was to prove irresistible. He would lose no more sets as he swept past Todd Woodbridge and Stich on his way to the final.

Young Woodbridge, the son of a retired policeman from Woolaware, N.S.W., wore a wide grin from day one. The 20-year-old Australian had started the week happy enough as an alternate, with a guarantee of $50,000. When Becker withdrew he came in to face Edberg's replacement, the American Aaron Krickstein, and was thereby assured of at least $100,000. Not content merely to play double your money he promptly beat Krickstein before giving Wheaton a good run for his money. Then it was time for Todd to run with his money – a whopping $300,000 was the sum he took home for Christmas. No wonder he was grinning!

Wheaton's semi-final against Stich was a dramatic affair with the huge crowd desperately urging on the man who had left Hamburg, the city of his birth, to make his home among them. Mark Lewis, his coach from the Iphitos Club, for whom Stich had returned from his Wimbledon triumph to play in the Bundesleague, was there to support him; so were many of the members. The crowd's encouragement had been an important element in Stich's 7–6 6–4 defeat of Guy Forget in the previous round, a match in which the serving of both men had been outstanding with Stich delivering 17 aces and Forget 11. The left-handed Frenchman had won their three previous meetings, two of them in 1991 and he held a set point in the opening set this time. But he never looked confident and now understood what a difference the venue makes. He also realised how Pete Sampras must have felt when, two weeks earlier in Lyon, the French crowd had erupted as he had beaten the American in the decisive fourth rubber of the 1991 *Davis Cup* final.

In the lower, stronger half Chang had seized the initiative against a lacklustre Jim Courier to beat the French Open champion 6–4 6–2 on the opening day. It was a poor performance by the man who had impressed everyone during the year with his never-say-die attitude. Worse were his comments after his loss. Courier freely admitted he had come to Munich purely to collect the record prize money and said he felt it impossible to interrupt his pre-ordained practice period (which he was in the middle of) to prepare for what he described as an exhibition event. This immature attitude to an event that most players believe will become the biggest tournament outside the four Grand Slams, casts serious doubt upon Courier's ability to retain his high place in the world rankings.

After dealing severely with Patrick McEnroe, the unseeded Chang came face to face with the No.2 seed Lendl in the semi-finals. Although Lendl had not dropped a set either to Cristiano Caratti of Italy or the Swiss No.1 Jakob Hlasek (who had dealt summarily with a carefree Jimmy Connors in his first match, after losing the first six games), the 31-year-old nevertheless had looked less than usually decisive. He was a fraction slower than of old and was missing the odd ball from mid-court – an unusual failing.

The match against Chang, which built up slowly from quiet beginnings, became a classic. When Lendl won the first two sets 6–2 6–4 and held a 40–0 lead on Chang's serve in the opening game of the third set with a magnificent exhibition of bludgeoning power from the back of the court, there were few in the Olympiahalle who would have placed any money on Chang. But perhaps they had forgotten that the little battler from California had been born in Hoboken, New Jersey, the birthplace of one, Francis Sinatra, whose 'My Way' had made even the weakest of mortals realise that heart and belief can overcome even the most daunting of odds. Chang's way was to step in and meet the ball earlier than he has ever met it before. The effect was dramatic as the little man projected a series of blazing winners, half-volleys many of them, beyond the reach of the startled Lendl.

With Chang now striding towards his chair at the change of ends, all steely purpose, Lendl began to wilt. When Chang moved to 4–1 Lendl made a major effort to re-establish himself. He almost succeeded. Level at 4–4 as Chang served his first double fault it seemed that power would overcome finesse after all. But, leading now 5–4, Chang pressed unexpectedly towards the net on his second set point and Lendl's trusty forehand pass found the net.

The match had lasted 2 hrs 18 mins and no-one could have known that it had not yet reached the half-way mark. As both men held a succession of serves in the fourth set, it was Chang who twice had to save break points. In the tie-break he led 3–1, trailed 3–4, led again 6–5 and on his second set point forced another error from Lendl's racket. After 3 hrs 20 mins, two sets all!

Memories of Paris 1989 came flooding back. Surely, though, on a fast indoor carpet Chang could not repeat that win from 2 sets down that had launched his successful bid to become the youngest-ever French Champion. However, the records suggested he might. In 12 previous five-set matches Chang had come back to win from two sets down on five occasions. (In losing 18 of his 51 five-set career matches Lendl had three times allowed an opponent to escape after winning the first two sets.) Once Lendl, tiring now, had lost the 3–1 lead he had built in the fifth set a Chang win seemed possible. Even when Lendl held a match point in the 12th game it surprised no-one that Chang's backhand pass found its mark. The only surprise was that Lendl should have attempted a volleying coup at such a juncture. Three games later Lendl, visibly slower, surrendered his serve and was powerless to prevent Chang from holding to 30 for an improbable victory against the odds that had spanned 4 hrs and 42 mins of compelling tennis. It had been a victory of willpower and belief over flailing power and both men had added something to the event.

The weakness of the scheduling, with no rest day between semi-finals and final, meant that Chang simply had insufficient time to recover. Although Wheaton's match against Stich had not ended until 1.00am, at least it had lasted 'only' 3 hrs and 20 mins and had not been as punishing physically. Accordingly, the final was one-sided. Throughout Wheaton's concentration was superb. So was his game plan, honed after beating Chang in two of their three previous meetings, the latest of them on the grass at Queen's Club in June. He served and volleyed with rare precision; he played up and down the middle of the court to deny Chang any angles to create his openings; he chipped and charged against any short serves, or blasted away for first-time winners. Altogether he showed just how to overpower a smaller opponent on a fast court with fast balls.

Chang was philosophical about his defeat – as anyone might be who had just won $1 million for losing! Despite the huge prizes at stake the deportment of both men was faultless – chivalrous even as they applauded one another's wining shots.

Clearly in two short years the event had begun to create it's own momentum. Apart from the huge daily crowds of up to 11,500 on site there was an estimated potential TV audience of more than a billion viewers from programmes beamed to over 80 countries throughout the week. Contractual obligations make it unlikely that this culmination of the Grand Slam year will combine with the ATP Tour's season-ending Championship in the near future – even if either party thought that this would be a good idea. In fact it would be a good idea for the *Compaq Grand Slam Cup* to take place earlier – say in October. Whether this will ever happen will depend upon the attitudes of the Grand Slam Chairmen and the ATP Tour Board.

However, it does seem likely that the women will become part of the event – perhaps even in 1992 if disagreements about prize money distribution can be resolved. Their presence would add to the occasion and mirror the formula that already exists at the four Grand Slam Championships themselves. Eight men playing matches over the best of five sets every other day and women playing three set matches on the days between – perhaps even with a five-set women's final – would certainly produce a winning formula.

MUNICH, 10–15 DECEMBER
1st round: Todd Woodbridge d. Aaron Krickstein 6–3 6–3; David Wheaton (7) d. Paul Haarhuis; Michael Stich (3) d. Goran Prpic 6–4 6–3; Guy Forget (5) d. Jaime Yzaga 6–3 6–3; Jakob Hlasek d. Jimmy Connors (6) 0–6 6–4 6–4; Ivan Lendl (4) d. Cristiano Caratti 6–4 6–1; Patrick McEnroe (8) d. Thierry Champion 4–6 6–1 6–4; Michael Chang d. Jim Courier (2) 6–4 6–2.
Quarter-finals: Wheaton (7) d. Woodbridge 6–4 7–6; Stich (3) d. Forget (5); Lendl (4) d. Hlasek 7–6 6–3; Chang d. McEnroe (8).
Semi-finals: Wheaton (7) d. Stich (3) 7–6 7–6 7–6; Chang d. Lendl (4) 2–6 4–6 6–4 7–6 9–7.
Final: Wheaton (7) d. Chang 7–5 6–2 6–4.
Prize Money: Winner $2m; Finalist $1m; Semi-finalists $450,000; Quarter-finalists $300,000; First round $100,000; Alternates $50,000.

THE GRAND SLAM DEVELOPMENT FUND

The first donation of $2 million from the 1990 *Compaq Grand Slam Cup* to the Grand Slam Development Fund had a tremendous impact on the International Tennis Federation's ability to press forward with its world-wide development plans.

The Fund, which is administered by the ITF, was able not only to help grass roots tennis but also to provide grants to support satellite circuits and other events for men and the Women's Futures circuit, as well as officiating programmes, educational projects and veterans' tennis. Travel grants to enable youngsters to compete with their peers on an international basis were also increased substantially.

The Equipment Distribution Programme helped numerous junior projects under the direction of National Associations. Wilson and Prince were the most enthusiastic supporters of the programme for which the help provided by Lufthansa was invaluable. The major effort was again in Africa, but the South Pacific, South America and the Caribbean area all enjoyed improvements in facilities and competition.

As a region, Central America provides a good example of the value of the Fund with substantial progress over the last three years. El Salvador, Guatemala and Costa Rica have all become full members of the ITF and are now fielding *Davis Cup* teams. This in turn has created a boom in tennis interest. The three countries each hosted a leg of the first Central American Men's Satellite Circuit, of which the Masters was held in Mexico. Television and press coverage, good crowds, enthusiastic organisation and a positive Supervisor's report all indicated that the investment in that area is a good one.

The first ITF World Class team was launched in April. While player development in countries like Australia, the United States, Canada, Israel and numerous European nations becomes more sophisticated, the gap widens between them and the less developed countries. This is particularly true for Africa so this year, after spending a large portion of our time and resources in that Continent, and seeing a number of promising young players emerge, it was decided to give them the chance to test themselves in the mainstream of international tennis.

The first team consisted of Karim Alami (Morocco), Paul Wekesa (Kenya), Clement N'Goran (Cote D'Ivoire) and Byron Black (Zimbabwe) with Jai DiLouie, an American who is a former international tour player, as coach. The players, as professionals, are responsible for covering their own expenses with the ITF providing the full-time coach. Early response has been encouraging and the idea is likely, eventually, to be extended to other regions when players have made sufficient progress.

Angus Macaulay completed his first twelve months as the ITF East African Development officer based in Nairobi and it has been decided, in view of the success so far, to extend the project for another year. Provision has also been made to extend the idea in 1992 with the appointment of three additional development officers to cover the English-speaking Caribbean countries, the Spanish-speaking Caribbean and Central America and the South Pacific.

THE SANCHEZ DYNASTY

Barry Wood

They are the Royal Family of Spanish tennis. Emilio, Javier and Arantxa Sanchez are respected the world over, not only as superb players but as pleasant, courteous, unassuming people with bubbly personalities. Largely because of their well-publicised successes these last eight years, which have built up the interest originally created by Andres Gimeno, Manuel Santana and Manolo Orantes, tennis is enjoying an unprecedented boom in Spain where it is now second only in popularity to soccer.

The Sanchez parents – Emilio, an engineer and Marisa, a schoolteacher – are a proud couple as they accompany their brood around the world. It is a sign of their peripatetic lifestyle that the three best known children were all born in different cities – Emilio in Madrid, Javier in Pamplona and Arantxa in Barcelona.

There are other members of the family, too. Marisa is the eldest sibling; she is now married and no longer plays tennis, although she was once one of Spain's best young players. William 'Pato' Alvarez, who started coaching Emilio when he was just 14, is an unofficial member of the family and is always to be seen waddling, ducklike, between courts to keep an eye on the boys' matches. Then there is Roland, a Yorkshire Terrier bought in celebration of Arantxa's 1989 French Open victory. He is a familiar sight at tournaments, with his head poking out of a bag carried everywhere by Arantxa's mother.

Arantxa lives with her parents in a house in Barcelona, while Emilio and Javier have an apartment nearby. Marisa's home is a short distance outside Barcelona, but she gets together with the others quite frequently.

The family became involved in tennis purely by chance. The parents were not really very interested in the game when they were young. They loved skiing and one day Emilio was out walking and saw a sign announcing a new club where they were planning to build an artificial ski slope. He and Marisa decided to become members, but the ski surface never materialised so they took up tennis instead. The rest is history.

The way the parents met is equally amusing. One bright summer's day Marisa was in a little village and went with some friends to the river. She was sitting quietly on the bank reading a book, when Emilio came by. He engaged Marisa in conversation and while they were talking he noticed that she was reading the book upside down! It was love at first sight.

In due course they were married and the first daughter was born. As she grew up Marisa became quite a successful player, at one time ranked No.4 in Spain, but she decided to pursue a more academic path. The story of her invitation to study in America amuses the rest of the family. Apparently Marisa was alone at home one day when the telephone rang. The call was from someone in California wanting to speak to brother Emilio about a scholarship at Pepperdine University. Marisa explained that Emilio wasn't home, but said that she was quite a good player too. Rather to her surprise they offered her a place instead. She accepted and spent four very happy years there. She is now back in Spain working for Spanish television as a sports reporter. Arantxa remembers Marisa's decision to go to University. 'At first I was a little surprised that she gave up playing professionally, because she was a good player and was ranked about 150 in the world, and I thought she was going to continue and try to reach the top 50. But she had the opportunity to go to Pepperdine and wanted to take it. She played number one on their team and studied business administration, and when she came back she decided she didn't want to play as a professional anymore. She's not too disappointed, but maybe in her mind she sometimes wishes to be where we are. But she has a great career and is very happy.'

The family are delightfully modest about their successes, seemingly unaware of their

Arantxa and Emilio Sanchez, finalists in the mixed doubles at the US Open, who, with their brother Javier, have precipitated a tennis boom in Spain that will reach its climax this year with the Olympic Games. *(M. Cole)*

unique position in the world game. To have three of the four playing professionally at the same time is unusual enough but to have them competing at such a high level is astonishing. Emilio, 27, is a speedy clay-court specialist who excelled as a junior, has been as high as No.7 in the world rankings and won his 15th career singles title last January on hard courts in Sydney. It was typical of this popular and chivalrous competitor that he should have been equally concerned about trying to add a 39th career doubles title as well that afternoon, in partnership with his regular *Davis Cup* team-mate and long-time friend, Sergio Casal. To the delight of their many fans, the Spaniards did just that!

Javier, three years younger, was the No.1 junior in the world at the age of 17 and turned professional in 1986, two years after Emilio. Though not yet as prominent as his brother, Javier has won two singles and 14 doubles titles in a career that is still blossoming.

Arantxa, the baby of the family, is 20 now and the darling of crowds wherever she plays. Her effervescent personality and ready smile make it clear that she enjoys playing tennis and her enthusiasm is infectious. All the family were there that special day in Paris in 1989 when, aged 17 years 6 months, Arantxa beat the world No.1 Steffi Graf to become the youngest-ever winner of the French Open Championships. The following year she rose to No.3 in the rankings and has been in the top five ever since. With her natural speed and consistency she is one of the most reliable of competitors and last year reached at least the semi-finals of the first nine tournament she entered. Her best result was in Paris where she allowed Graf only two games as she went through to her second French Open final.

Arantxa is fully aware of the benefits of coming from a tennis family. 'In my case it's a big advantage because I am the youngest, and the others have been able to help me and teach me the right way to do things. I can listen and learn from my brothers, and I think it's great,' said Arantxa. 'I enjoy watching them in matches, but sometimes I get more nervous watching my brothers play than if I was out there myself.' Then her eyes smile as she adds '. . . but when they get on top I can relax.'

Emilio finds it an advantage too, because they can all understand exactly what the others are going through. 'If I have problems and need advice they can really help me. They may have already passed through the problems I have, so it's a very great advantage to be from a professional tennis family,' he considered.

With their lives so completely involved with tennis, it is inevitable that the sport dominates their conversation at home. Or does it? It depends on who you talk to.

'We don't talk much about tennis,' claims Arantxa. 'Sometimes if I need some help I talk with my brothers, but we try not to talk tennis because on the tour is enough. So we talk about other things, not tennis.'

But Emilio qualifies that. 'We try to forget about the tennis and try to talk about other things,' he agrees, 'but the conversation always comes around to tennis, even if we don't want it to, because it's our life.'

The 1992 Olympic Games in Spain have special significance for the Sanchez family. 'The Olympics are very important,' Emilio asserts, 'I think more so because they are in Barcelona. They are in our country and everyone feels really involved. I shall give everything I can to do well there. It will be great for me, for the city and for the country.'

Arantxa is extremely proud to represent her country, and places Spain's 1991 victory in the *Federation Cup* even above winning the French Open two years before. 'The first favourite memory of my career was the French Open, because I was very young and it was my first Grand Slam. It was like a dream come to reality. I'm not going to forget it. Nobody's going to forget it!,' she stressed. 'But also winning the *Federation Cup*, not losing a match in singles and doubles and winning victory for Spain was a great moment for me, a great feeling. Now the Olympics is very important and very special to me because it's in my town and my country. You can only play it every four years, and I want to try and win a gold medal for my country. It's a great event I think.'

With the Sanchez family enjoying so much international success, it was natural that they should have inspired others to play. 'I hope we have, and that many kids will play and keep playing,' said Emilio. 'Sometimes I do clinics, or my club asks me to hit with the guys, but I can only do that once or twice a year. I think it's good for the kids if they see you playing anywhere, Europe or America, and see you winning.'

Of course, they are all major celebrities in their homeland, acclaimed wherever they go. 'We are a very popular family and everybody looks at us, and the people are always looking for my results when I'm in other countries, and that makes me feel more confident and helps me to play better,' Arantxa says. 'I know that I'm one of the most popular people in my country, and to be so young yet be so famous is great. People call out to me in the street or restaurants, and want to take my picture. Everybody wants to be my friend.'

The family have mixed feelings about the amount of travelling they must do, for it certainly interrupts their close relationship. 'Sometimes it's tough because you're away for a long time and you can't have a normal life,' Emilio admits. 'But at other times it's good, because you know many people and many countries. Some people don't like to look around, but if you want to you can find time to see things. I like what I do – I like to play tennis, I like the competition, so I don't mind the travelling so much. The only difficult thing is when you're disappointed and have problems, and your family or someone you love is not with you. Then it's tough mentally to play tennis. But if you're happy with yourself then it's not too tough.'

Javier says the travel was a novelty at first, but it has now become routine. 'When I finished with the juniors and started to play the pro circuit I liked travelling very much,' he says. 'But now I've been doing it for 4 or 5 years I know all the places and all the people who work at the tournaments, and it's not the same. But I still like it. It's my job and my life.'

Arantxa, though, still finds the lifestyle stimulating. 'Yes, I think maybe because I travel with my family. That gives me more motivation. I really enjoy it,' she says. But there are things that upset her, and her brothers, things they are sensitive about. 'What I don't like is people with two faces', says Arantxa. 'People who say something to you and something else behind your back. I hate those people. And I don't like jealous people.'

Emilio is disturbed by the manner in which some people form an opinion of him without really knowing what he is like. 'It bothers me that, because we are tennis players and are popular, people have an image of us, and it's very superficial. They are never going to know a person from an interview or whatever. Then when I go around and meet people they say that I'm much different to what they thought. I don't like that, because people make images of us, and in reality we are not like that. Whether it's good or bad things, they cannot know us from an interview or the way we play or whatever.'

Nor can outsiders truly understand the difficulties and pressures of being a top player. 'It's tough to handle it, always to be nice to the people, and they don't understand,' Emilio continues. 'They come to us for an autograph, and we may already have signed 99, and the next guy may not know we've signed 99 and when we say no he's upset. So sometimes it's difficult. But it's hard for me to understand when some very famous people complain about that. They are there because they want it. If they don't like it they should stop and do something else. They say they lose their privacy, but I don't think so. You can live your life and do whatever you want. It's just that sometimes it is difficult.'

I wondered who they would most like to spend an evening with, given a limitless choice. Their replies all demonstrated their warmth and caring natures. 'I would like to spend the time with a guy I really like, and he loves me and I love him,' said Arantxa.

Emilio has similar views. 'There are so many interesting people, but I suppose being with the person I'm in love with is the best.'

It is the same with Javier. 'It would definitely be with a girlfriend. That's the best.'

Finally, if they could have one wish, what would it be?

'My greatest wish would be to win a Grand Slam tournament,' said Javier. 'When I started playing tennis it was on clay, so I'd like to win Roland Garros. To me that's the best tournament, but if I won another one instead I wouldn't care!'

Emilio's wish is simple, but important. 'I would like to be healthy enough to keep playing for a while.'

And Arantxa? She would love to win a medal at the Olympics. 'That would make me very happy and very proud,' she says.

With or without medals, the whole nation can be exceedingly proud of their second Royal Family for wherever they go they make new friends for Spain. That is how they would like to be remembered.

IBM/ATP TOUR

TOUR REVIEW
POINTS EXPLANATION
IBM/ATP TOUR TOURNAMENTS
ATP TOUR WORLD CHAMPIONSHIP

With six tournament successes in 1991 the French left-hander, Guy Forget, equalled the performance of Stefan Edberg and raised his year-end ranking to a career high of No. 7. *(Professional Sport)*

Despite tournament wins in Orlando and Washington during 1991, and two victories over Becker, the colourful American, Andre Agassi, slipped to No. 10 in the rankings, his lowest showing for four years. *(T. Hindley)*

IBM/ATP TOUR REVIEW

John Parsons

The IBM/ATP Tour ended, as it had begun, with Stefan Edberg on top of the world rankings. He had been overtaken for two short periods by Boris Becker – first when the German emotionally achieved his inaugural success at the Australian Open in January, and again when Becker reached the Wimbledon final as Edberg lost frustratingly to Michael Stich in the semi-finals without ever losing his serve. But few would deny that the London-based Swede's tennis, like his temperament, maintained a steady, affable consistency throughout the year.

Of course there were occasional hiccups and disappointments, yet Edberg's overall match record for the year was 76–17, better than his 70–14 a year earlier. He won six tournaments, chief among them the US Open – a title which Mats Wilander alone of his countrymen had won (not even the mighty Bjorn Borg ever solved the riddles of Flushing Meadow). These performances accurately reflected Edberg's general supremacy which earned him respect from the public and fellow players alike.

It was all the more impressive when one considers that from mid-summer onwards, even at Flushing Meadow, he was feverishly nursing and trying to conceal the full impact of increasing tendonitis in the left knee. It was only after a particularly frustrating defeat by Becker in the Stockholm final where, naturally enough, the crowd most wanted to see him win, and then his painful loss to Michael Chang in Bercy, that he eventually listened to those voices within and without which had been telling him to stop.

Edberg was forced to miss both the Tour finals in Frankfurt and the *Compaq Grand Slam Cup* in Munich but could still reflect proudly on a year when he had produced some of his most consistently positive and fluent tennis. To underline his improving versatility, he could boast of wins on three different surfaces – hard courts, indoors and grass, this last a maiden success in the *Stella Artois* at Queen's Club.

Although Guy Forget, who was to become one of France's *Davis Cup* winning heroes, equalled Edberg's total of six tournaments, his victories were achieved on only two different surfaces, indoor carpet and hard courts. The most impressively versatile tournament winner of the year was Stich, whose four titles, headed spectacularly by Wimbledon, were won on all four Tour surfaces – grass, hard, indoor carpet and clay. The last man to achieve that was Miloslav Mecir in 1987. Stich, who had joined the Tour relatively late at the age of 19 three years earlier, had started the year with a world ranking of 42 and ended it in fifth place, the biggest improvement by any member of the top ten. The German also played more singles and doubles matches (146) than anyone else. His singles record in Tour and *Davis Cup* fixtures was 71-25 and for doubles was 29-24.

Perhaps the most extraordinary feature of the year once more was that the 79 tournaments in Championship and World Series events produced 44 different winners, only three fewer than the record figure in 1990. On the other hand the number of countries they represented, which perhaps is an even more significant guide to the worldwide health of men's tennis, fell yet again, to 17, which is four fewer than in 1989.

Variety, they say, is the spice of life. On the surface therefore, the sizeable number of different champions is obviously no bad thing. Even so, that fact still has to be weighed against the number of top flight players beaten, sometimes for apparently no good reason, in early rounds.

Edberg could hardly be accused of failure in this respect. His opening round loss against fellow Swede Magnus Larsson in Monte Carlo, in his first match of the year on European clay, was the only instant dismissal he suffered. Boris Becker also was beaten only once in his opening match. Others were not so reliable. Andre Agassi lost five times in his opening match in a tour event. So, too, did Forget and Stich although the overall number of first or second round losses for the top eight players dropped from 40 to 29.

Of the 151 events in which they competed, the original eight qualifiers for Frankfurt produced 29 winners, slightly down on the previous year, although the number of matches they played, at 575, represented an encouraging increase of eight per cent.

Although the number of matches in which the top eight played against each other in 1991 also showed an increase on the previous year, in keeping with one of the most strongly expressed original aims of the Tour, the figure was in some ways misleading. For of the total of 44 clashes between players who were in the top eight at the time, no less than 19 of these were in the four Grand Slam tournaments or *Davis Cup* ties, so that the true figure on the Tour itself was a meagre 27, considerably lower than on the last year of the Grand Prix.

Indeed if you exclude ITF events, Agassi did not once compete against another top ten player before Frankfurt, and Becker's defeat of Edberg in Stockholm was the only time these principal rivals for the number one spot met all year.

It is worrying to note that the first or second seed was beaten in no less than 31 of the World Series tournaments in which appearance money is now legally paid. This is a statistic that needs to be watched closely in future years. Even the hint that there were some players who were prepared to 'take the money and run', would soon destroy the game's credibility.

With so many different tournament winners, there was no outstanding example of consistency, although Edberg fittingly enough also produced the best winning steak of 21 matches between August and October. Next best was the near-veteran Ivan Lendl who won 14 consecutive matches between February and March while Michael Stich extended his seven games winning stretch at Wimbledon by another six on his way to the US Open and Pete Sampras banished a dreadful first half of the year by finishing stronger than anyone else once the American hardcourts season began. Three tournament successes contributed to his 32 wins from 37 matches going into Frankfurt.

No fewer than 17 players won tour titles for the first time, two of them in Championship Series events – Petr Korda at New Haven, where a magnificent new stadium in keeping with the game's modern image was also being used for the first time, and Omar Camporese in Rotterdam. First time winners in World Series tournaments were Nicklas Kulti (Adelaide), Alexander Volkov (Milan), Patrick Baur (Guaruja), Sergi Bruguera (Estoril), Richard Krajicek (Hong Kong), Jan Siemerink (Singapore), Richey Renenberg (Tampa), Magnus Gustafsson (Munich), Dmitri Poliakov (Umag), Bryan Shelton (Newport), Gianluca Pozzi (Brisbane), Frederic Fontang (Palermo), Leonardo Lavalle (Tel Aviv), Javier Frana (Guaruja) and Christian Miniussi (Sao Paulo).

Miniussi was a lucky loser, having been beaten in the final round of qualifying in Sao Paulo, only the fifth man in the history of the Tour to achieve such a feat. Lavalle and Poliakov were both first time winners as qualifiers, while the richly talented but erratic Goran Ivanisevic, understandably tormented by the civil strife in his native Yugoslavia during the year, also collected his only title of the year as a qualifier, ranked eleven at the time but not an original entry, on the grass in Manchester.

The decline of American supremacy in terms of providing tournament winners and the corresponding rise of the European influence – further underlined by the French *Davis Cup* triumph – continued in 1991. Although the United States remained top of the list, with seven of their players winning 13 tournaments between them, this was four titles fewer than in 1990. However, they would no doubt point out that they were also represented in 19 other finals. The European total climbed to a record 59 titles from 108 finals.

Among the Europeans, Sweden, thanks principally to Edberg's six victories, were once more the leaders, with 11 titles. Spain, second in the list a year earlier, slipped into fourth place behind Germany who had 10, and Czechoslovakia with 9.

Of the players who had begun the year in the top ten, five were still there 12 months later, one more than between 1989 and 1990. Agassi survived only by a whisker; he was the third American among the select group. There were also three Czechs including Lendl who, legally at least, they can still lay claim to. If Agassi had not been awarded the points from the previous year's Tour play-offs which all eight received (a controversial decision this), then Czechoslovakia would have been out on their own and Agassi himself would have been out of this year's play-offs.

The number of countries with players in the top ten dropped from eight to five, although nine could point to players in the top 50. The United States led the way with 13, unchanged from the previous year, followed by Sweden and Spain (5), France (4) plus five countries with three each – Germany, Czechoslovakia, USSR, Argentina and, most spectacular of all, Holland.

In addition to Wimbledon champion, Stich, and Forget, others who broke into the top ten for the first time were the indefatigable Czech Karel Novacek, who won three tournaments on clay and one on hard, his fellow countryman Petr Korda, and most triumphantly of all, Jim Courier.

Courier, revelling in his description as 'the cool Dude from Dade City', soared from 25th to 2nd place. His considerable competitive spirit, which he combined so effectively with fine serving and power off the ground, was well reflected in the three titles he won, at the French Open, Indian Wells and Key Biscayne. In all of them, especially at Roland Garros where he lost the first and third sets to Agassi, he came from behind to win.

At the level where it is most difficult to make significant progress, Courier's ranking improvement was arguably the most impressive of the year. There were some notable other claimants, not least the redoubtable Jimmy Connors who, in the year he celebrated both his full return to the circuit after surgery on his left wrist and also his 39th birthday, climbed from 906 to 48th.

Alberto Mancini also resurrected his career, which had slumped in 1990, by climbing back from 127 to 22, while among newcomers or late developers the most noteworthy improvements were achieved by Dutchman Jan Siemerink (from 135 to 26), Patrick McEnroe (120 to 36), Olivier Delaitre (152 to 41), Wayne Ferreira (176 to 50), Arnaud Boetsch (176 to 54) and Frederic Fontang (215 to 58).

The youngest title winner of the year was Chang, 19 years 8 months, at Birmingham, the oldest was John McEnroe, 32, in Chicago, while the lowest ranked winner was Paolo Cane, at No.224 when he won in Bologna. There were six players who won singles and doubles titles at the same event – Courier (with Javier Sanchez in Indian Wells), Edberg (with Todd Woodbridge at the Japan Open), Goran Ivanisevic (with Camporese in Manchester), Forget (with Boetsch in Bordeaux), Jakob Hlasek (with Patrick McEnroe in Basel) and Korda, who managed it twice (with Wally Masur at New Haven and Novacek in Berlin).

After last year's retrenchment in prize money, stemming entirely from the abolition of the old Grand Prix bonus pool, figures noticeably increased again during 1991. Edberg finished with $2,363,575, nearly $20,000 more than the previous record established by Ivan Lendl two years earlier.

With the exception of last year, there has generally been a steady upward curve in the prize money charts ever since the advent of Open tennis in 1968, not just at the highest levels but well down the scale. That tradition was certainly maintained in 1991 when no fewer than seven players – the others were Sampras ($1,908,413), Courier ($1,748,171), Lendl ($1,438,983), Stich ($1,217,636), Becker ($1,216,568) and Forget ($1,072,252) – surpassed the million dollar mark, three more than in 1990, which had also been a record.

Curiously enough, however, although a record 143 players finished with more than $100,000, Amos Mansdorf, at 50th in the list a year earlier, had earned slightly more than the $243,346 collected by Jim Grabb in the same slot in 1991.

It was also interesting to note how many of the top 50 prize money winners earned more from doubles than singles – an opportunity not always fully appreciated. Not surprisingly, Anders Jarryd, who won no fewer than eight doubles titles, six of them with John Fitzgerald, including the French Open, Wimbledon, the US Open and the world championships in Johannesburg that marked South Africa's return to international tennis, figured prominently on this list.

Of Jarryd's total prize money of $752,514, the Swede won $573,893 from doubles alone although that was $1,000 'pocket money' less than Fitzgerald's doubles-only income from additional events he had played with other partners. Robert Seguso, David Pate, Scott Davis, Glenn Michibata, Grant Connell and Todd Woodbridge were others who cashed in lucratively through their talent in doubles, while Laurie Warder finished 71st in the prize money order of merit with $186,346 from doubles alone. Although Fitzgerald and Jarryd were clearly the doubles team of the year, there was an exciting finish to the race for the final places for Johannesburg. There was doubt until the last tournament in Birmingham when Holland's Tom Nijssen and Czechoslovakia's Cyril Suk, brother of Helena Sukova, just edged out Udo Riglewski and Michael Stich for the eighth spot.

In a year when two of the previous season's most formidable partnerships, Rick Leach and Jim Pugh plus Piet Aldrich and Danie Visser, went their separate ways, Fitzgerald and Jarryd also overhauled Scott Davis and David Pate during the last few weeks in the team rankings race. In the Johannesburg final they beat Ken Flach and Seguso, another pair who had successfully resurrected their partnership.

Overall it was a good year for the Tour with most of its objectives, particularly on the financial front, achieved. Whether the overall circuit is any stronger now than it was – or would have been – under the old system, is debatable. With the exception of the ill-judged introduction of the Best of 14 rule, whereby players are no longer necessarily punished for bad losses, it has been a case of 'steady as she goes'.

From 1993 onwards, that may not be so. The reorganised Championship Series programme, with its proposed nine single-week events each offering a staggering $1.7m, will obviously be attractive to some. But the long-term impact on double-up week tournaments, which will no longer be guaranteed any of the top players (the projection is that they will have one of the top eight), but WILL be able to pay guarantees, may not be so constructive. And for World Series tournaments, which will presumably find life in the appearance money market even tougher, the future could be distinctly bleak.

I hope I am wrong, but ATP's belief that the changes will mark the start of a new period of expansion and prosperity, even though tennis has escaped the ravages of commercial recession better than most sports, may prove to have been overoptimistic. Instead it could be the first step towards contraction.

IBM/ATP TOUR 1991 – POINTS EXPLANATION

The tables below show the ranking points to be won at the four Grand Slam Championships and all tournaments on the IBM/ATP Tour – including Challengers with minimum prize money of $25,000. Points are also awarded at the Masters events of the Satellite circuits organised by member nations of the ITF. A player's ranking alone decides whether or not he is accepted into the main draw or the qualifying event at all Tour tournaments.

Identical points are awarded for singles and doubles. No points are awarded until a player has completed a match. Anyone who reaches the second round via a bye and then loses is considered to have lost in the first round and receives one point, but he does receive second round prize money. There are additional 'Bonus Points' awarded for beating players ranked between 1 and 200 in singles, or a team ranked between 2 and 400 in doubles. In addition to the points won in any tournament, a player or doubles team winning a place in the main draw via qualifying also receives half the points awarded to the second round loser in that tournament. Lucky Losers receive no qualifying points.

POINTS ALLOCATION

Category	Total Prize Money (All US$)	W	F	S	Q	16	32	64	128
Grand Slams	4.0 Million	520	390	260	130	65	33	17	1
	3.5 Million	500	375	250	125	63	32	16	1
	3.0 Million	480	360	240	120	60	30	15	1
	2.5 Million	460	345	230	115	50	29	15	1
	2.0 Million	440	330	220	110	55	28	14	1
Championship	1,875,000	300	225	150	75	38	19	10	1
Series	1,750,000	290	218	145	73	37	19	10	1
	1,625,000	280	210	140	70	35	18	9	1
	1,500,000	270	203	135	68	34	17	9	1
	1,375,000	260	195	130	65	33	17	1	–
	1,250,000	250	188	125	63	32	16	1	–
	1,125,000	240	180	120	60	30	15	1	–
	1,000,000	230	173	115	58	29	15	1	–
	875,000	220	165	110	55	28	14	1	–
	750,000	210	158	105	53	27	14	1	–
	625,000	200	150	100	50	25	13	1	1
World Series	675,000	170	128	85	43	22	11	1	–
	600,000	170	120	80	40	20	10	1	–
	525,000	150	113	75	38	19	10	1	–
	450,000	140	105	70	35	18	9	1	–
	375,000	130	98	65	33	17	9	1	–
	300,000	120	90	60	30	15	8	1	–
	225,000	110	83	55	28	14	7	1	–
	150,000	100	75	50	25	13	1	–	–
Challenger*	100,000+H	80	60	40	20	10	1	–	–
Series	100,000	70	53	35	18	9	1	–	–
	75,000	60	45	30	15	8	1	–	–
	50,000	50	38	25	13	7	1	–	–
	25,000	40	30	20	5	1	1	–	–

* Any Challenger providing hospitality will receive the points of the next highest prize money level. Monies shown are on-site amounts.

BONUS POINTS

Singles		*Doubles* Team	
Ranking	Bonus Points	Ranking	Bonus Points
2–3	50	2–3	50
4–10	45	4–10	45
11–20	36	11–20	36
21–30	18	21–40	24
31–50	12	41–60	18
51–75	6	61–100	12
76–100	3	101–150	6
101–150	2	151–200	3
151–200	1	201–300	2
		300–400	1

GRAND SLAM CHAMPIONSHIPS AND IBM/ATP TOUR 1991

DATE	VENUE	SINGLES FINAL	DOUBLES WINNERS
31 Dec–6 Jan	Wellington	R. Fromberg d. L. Jonsson 6-1 6-4 6-4	L. Mattar/N. Pereira
31 Dec–6 Jan	Adelaide	N. Kulti d. M. Stich 6-3 1-6 6-2	W. Ferreira/S. Kruger
7–13 Jan	Sydney	G. Forget d. M. Stich 6-3 6-4	S. Davis/D. Pate
7–13 Jan	Auckland	K. Novacek d. J. Fleurian 7-6 7-6	S. Casal/E. Sanchez
14–21 Jan	Melbourne (Australian Open)	B. Becker d. I. Lendl 1-6 6-4 6-4 6-4	S. Davis/D. Pate
4–10 Feb	Milan	A. Volkov d. C. Caratti 6-1 7-5	O. Camporese/G. Ivanisevic
4–10 Feb	San Francisco	D. Cahill d. B. Gilbert 6-2 3-6 6-4	W. Masur/J. Stoltenberg
4–10 Feb	Guaruja	P. Baur d. M. Roese 6-2 6-3	O. Delaitre/R. Gilbert
11–17 Feb	Philadelphia	I. Lendl d. P. Sampras 5-7 6-4 6-4 4 3-6 6-3	R. Leach/J. Pugh
11–17 Feb	Brussels	G. Forget d. A. Cherkasov 6-3 7-5 3-6 7-6	T. Woodbridge/M. Woodforde
18–24 Feb	Stuttgart	S. Edberg d. J. Svensson 6-2 3-7 5-7 6-2	S. Casal/E. Sanchez
18–24 Feb	Memphis	I. Lendl d. M. Stich 7-5 6-3	U. Riglewski/M. Stich
25 Feb–3 March	Rotterdam	O. Camporese d. I. Lendl 3-6 7-6 7-6	P. Galbraith/A. Jarryd
25 Feb–3 March	Chicago	J. McEnroe d. P. McEnroe 3-6 7-6 7-6	S. Davis/D. Pate
4–10 March	Indian Wells	J. Courier d. G. Forget 4-6 6-3 4-6 6-3 7-6	J. Courier/J. Sanchez
4–10 March	Copenhagen	J. Svensson d. A. Jarryd 6-7 6-2 6-2	T. Woodbridge/M. Woodforde
15–24 March	Key Biscayne	J. Courier d. D. Wheaton 4-6 6-3 6-4	W. Ferreira/P. Norval
1–7 April	Estoril	R. Bruguera d. K. Novacek 7-6 6-1	P. Haarhuis/M. Koevermans
1–7 April	Hong Kong	R. Krajicek d. W. Masur 7-6 6-1	P. Galbraith/T. Witsken
8–14 April	Orlando	A. Agassi d. D. Rostagno 6-2 1-6 6-3	L. Jensen/N. Melville
8–14 April	Tokyo	S. Edberg d. I. Lendl 6-1 7-5 6-0	S. Edberg/T. Woodbridge
8–14 April	Barcelona	E. Sanchez d. S. Bruguera 6-4 7-6 6-2	H. De la Pena/D. Nargiso
15–21 April	Nice	M. Jaite d. G. Prpic 3-6 7-6 6-3	R. Bergh/J. Gunnarsson
15–21 April	Seoul	P. Baur d. J. Tarango 6-4 1-6 7-6	A. Antonitsch/G. Bloom
22–28 April	Monte Carlo	S. Bruguera d. B. Becker 5-7 6-4 7-6 7-6	L. Jensen/L. Warder
22–28 April	Singapore	J. Siemerink d. G. Bloom 6-4 6-3	G. Connell/G. Michibata
29 April–5 May	Madrid	J. Arrese d. M. Filippini 6-2 6-4	G. Luza/C. Motta
29 April–5 May	Munich	M. Gustafsson d. G. Perez-Roldan 3-6 6-3 4-3 ret'd	P. Galbraith/T. Witsken
29 April–5 May	Tampa	M. Reneberg d. P. Korda 4-6 6-4 6-2	K. Flach/R. Seguso
6–12 May	Hamburg	K. Novacek d. M. Gustafsson 6-3 6-3 5-7 0-6 6-1	S. Casal/E. Sanchez
6–12 May	Charlotte	J. Yzaga d. J. Arias 6-3 7-5	R. Leach/J. Pugh
13–19 May	Rome	E. Sanchez d. A. Mancini 6-3 6-1 3-0 ret'd	O. Camporese/G. Ivanisevic
13–19 May	Umag	D. Poliakov d. J. Sanchez 6-4 6-4	G. Bloom/J. Sanchez
20–26 May	Bologna	P. Cane d. J. Gunnarsson 5-7 6-3 7-5	L. Jensen/L. Warder
27 May–9 June	Paris (French Open)	J. Courier d. A. Agassi 3-6 6-4 2-6 6-1 6-4	J. Fitzgerald/A. Jarryd
10–16 June	Queen's Club	S. Edberg d. D. Wheaton 6-2 6-3	T. Woodbridge/M. Woodforde
10–16 June	Rosmalen	T. Muster d. H. Skoff 6-2 6-7 6-4	H. Davids/P. Haarhuis
10–16 June	Florence	C. Saceanu d. M. Schapers 6-1 3-6 7-5	O. Jonsson/M. Larsson
17–23 June	Genova	C. Steeb d. J. Arrese 6-3 6-4	M. Gorriz/A. Mora
17–23 June	Manchester	G. Ivanisevic d. P. Sampras 6-4 6-4	O. Camporese/G. Ivanisevic
24 June–7 July	London (Wimbledon)	M. Stich d. B. Becker 6-4 7-6 6-4	J. Fitzgerald/A. Jarryd
8–14 July	Gstaad	E. Sanchez d. S. Bruguera 6-1 6-4 6-4	G. Muller/D. Visser

DATE	VENUE	SINGLES FINAL	DOUBLES WINNERS
8-14 July	Bastad	M. Gustafsson d. A. Mancini 6-1 6-2	R. Bathman/R. Bergh
8-14 July	Newport	B. Shelton d. J. Frana 3-6 6-4 6-4	G. Pozzi/B. Steven
15-21 July	Stuttgart	M. Stich d. A. Mancini 1-6 7-6 6-4 6-2	W. Masur/E. Sanchez
15-21 July	Washington	A. Agassi d. P. Korda 6-3 6-4	S. Davis/D. Pate
22-28 July	Montreal	A. Chesnokov d. P. Korda 3-6 6-4 6-3	P. Galbraith/T. Witsken
22-28 July	Hilversum	M. Gustafsson d. J. Arrese 5-7 7-6 2-6 6-1 6-0	R. Krajicek/J. Semerink
29 July-4 Aug	Kitzbuhel	K. Novacek d. M. Gustafsson 7-6 7-6 6-2	T. Carbonell/F. Roig
29 July-4 Aug	Los Angeles	P. Sampras d. B. Gilbert 6-2 6-7 6-3	J. Frana/J. Pugh
29 July-4 Aug	San Marino	G. Perez-Roldan d. F. Fontang 6-3 6-1	J. Arrese/C. Costa
5-11 Aug	Cincinnati	G. Forget d. P. Sampras 2-6 7-6 6-4	V. Flegl/C. Suk
5-11 Aug	Prague	K. Novacek d. M. Gustafsson 7-6 6-2	K. Flach/R. Seguso
12-18 Aug	Indianapolis	P. Sampras d. B. Becker 7-6 3-6 6-3	K. Flach/R. Seguso
12-18 Aug	New Haven	P. Korda d. G. Ivanisevic 6-4 6-2	K. Korda/W. Masur
19-25 Aug	Long Island	I. Lendl d. S. Edberg 6-3 6-2	E. Jelen/C. Steeb
19-25 Aug	Schenectady	M. Stich d. E. Sanchez 6-2 6-4	J. Sanchez/T. Woodbridge
26 Aug-8 Sept	New York (US Open)	S. Edberg d. J. Courier 6-2 6-4 6-0	J. Fitzgerald/A. Jarryd
9-15 Sept	Bordeaux	G. Forget d. O. Delaitre 6-1 6-3	A. Boetsch/G. Forget
9-15 Sept	Brasilia	A. Gomez d. J. Sanchez 6-4 3-6 6-3	K. Kinnear/R. Smith
9-15 Sept	Geneva	T. Muster d. H. Skoff 6-2 6-4	S. Bruguera/M. Rosset
23-29 Sept	Basel	J. Hlasek d. J. McEnroe 7-6 6-0 6-3	J. Hlasek/J. McEnroe
23-29 Sept	Palermo	F. Fontang d. E. Sanchez 1-6 6-3 6-3	J. Eltingh/T. Kempers
23-29 Sept	Brisbane	G. Pozzi d. A. Krickstein 6-3 7-6	T. Woodbridge/M. Woodforde
30 Sept-6 Oct	Sydney	S. Edberg d. B. Gilbert 6-2 6-2 6-2	J. Grabb/R. Reneberg
30 Sept-6 Oct	Toulouse	G. Forget d. A. Mansdorf 6-2 7-6	T. Nijssen/C. Suk
30 Sept-6 Oct	Athens	S. Bruguera d. J. Arrese 7-5 6-3	J. Eltingh/M. Koevermans
7-13 Oct	Tokyo	S. Edberg d. D. Rostagno 6-3 1-6 6-2	J. Grabb/R. Reneberg
7-13 Oct	Berlin	P. Korda d. A. Boetsch 6-3 6-4	P. Korda/K. Novacek
7-13 Oct	Tel Aviv	L. Lavalle d. C. Van Rensburg 6-2 3-6 6-3	D. Riki/M. Schapers
14-20 Oct	Lyon	P. Sampras d. O. Delaitre 6-1 6-1	T. Nijssen/C. Suk
14-20 Oct	Vienna	M. Stich d. J. Siemerink 6-4 6-4 6-4	A. Jarryd/G. Muller
21-27 Oct	Stockholm	B. Becker d. S. Edberg 3-6 6-4 1-6 6-2 6-2	J. Fitzgerald/A. Jarryd
21-27 Oct	Guaruja	J. Frana d. M. Zoecke 2-6 7-6 6-3	J. Eltingh/P. Haarhuis
28 Oct-3 Nov	Paris	G. Forget d. P. Sampras 7-6 4-6 5-7 6-4 6-4	J. Fitzgerald/A. Jarryd
28 Oct-3 Nov	Buzios	J. Arrese d. J. Oncins 1-6 6-4 6-0	S. Casal/E. Sanchez
4-10 Nov	Birmingham	M. Chang d. G. Raoux 6-3 6-2	J. Eltingh/P. Wekesa
4-10 Nov	Moscow	A. Cherkasov d. J. Hlasek 7-6 3-6 7-6	E. Jelen/C. Steeb
4-10 Nov	Sao Paulo	C. Miniussi d. J. Oncins 2-6 6-3 6-4	A. Gomez/J. Oncins
11-17 Nov	Frankfurt (ATP Finals)	P. Sampras d. J. Courier 3-6 7-6 6-3 6-4	
18-24 Nov	Johannesburg (ATP Doubles Finals)		A. Fitzgerald/A. Jarryd
10-15 Dec	Munich (Grand Slam Cup)	D. Wheaton d. M. Chang 7-5 6-2 6-4	

PLAYER NATIONALITIES AND BIRTHDAYS

The following players have competed in the 1991 Grand Slam Tournaments and the ATP Tour:

Name and Nationality	Date of Birth	Name and Nationality	Date of Birth
Acioly, Ricardo (BRA)	04/02/64	Carlsson, Johan (SWE)	29/01/66
Adams, Chuck (USA)	23/04/71	Casal, Sergio (ESP)	08/09/62
Adams, David (AUS)	05/01/70	Cash, Pat (AUS)	27/05/65
Aerts, Nelson (BRA)	25/04/63	Cask, Jason (AUS)	07/02/71
Agassi, Andre (USA)	29/04/70	Castle, Andrew (GBR)	15/11/63
Agenor, Ronald (HAI)	13/11/64	Chamberlin, Paul (USA)	26/03/62
Aguilera, Juan (ESP)	22/03/62	Champion, Thierry (FRA)	31/08/66
Albano, Pablo (ARG)	11/04/67	Chang, Eui-Jong (KOR)	01/04/69
Aler, Ian (USA)	11/11/65	Chang, Michael (USA)	22/02/72
Allgardh, Christer (SWE)	20/02/67	Cherkasov, Andrei (URS)	04/07/70
Altur, Jose-Francisco (ESP)	24/03/68	Chesnokov, Andrei (URS)	02/02/66
Anderson, Johan (AUS)	29/09/71	Cierro, Massimo (ITA)	07/05/64
Annacone, Paul (USA)	20/03/63	Clavet, Francisco (ESP)	24/10/68
Antonitsch, Alex (AUT)	06/02/66	Conde, Jose-Antonio (ESP)	13/03/70
Aparisi, Jose-Luis (ESP)	11/03/69	Connell, Grant (CAN)	17/11/65
Apell, Jan (SWE)	04/11/69	Connors, Jimmy (USA)	02/09/52
Arbanas, John (AUS)	07/02/70	Costa, Carlos (ESP)	24/04/68
Ardinghi, Massimo (ITA)	06/03/71	Courier, Jim (USA)	17/08/70
Arias, Jimmy (USA)	16/08/64	Couto, Emanuel (POR)	06/08/73
Arnold, Patricio (ARG)	20/10/71	Crow, Pat (USA)	04/11/64
Araya, Pablo (PER)	21/10/61	Cunha-Silva, Joao (POR)	27/11/67
Arrese, Jordi (ESP)	29/08/64	Curren, Kevin (USA)	02/03/58
Arriens, Carsten (GER)	11/04/69	Daher, Jose (BRA)	20/04/66
Azar, Roberto (ARG)	21/03/66	Damm, Martin (TCH)	01/08/72
Baguena, Juan-Carlos (ESP)	07/01/67	Davids, Hendrik-Jan (HOL)	30/01/69
Bailey, Chris (GBR)	29/04/68	Davin, Franco (ARG)	11/01/70
Baron, Ivan (USA)	12/11/72	Davis, Scott (USA)	27/08/62
Barrientos, Felix (PHI)	20/11/67	De La Pena, Horacio (ARG)	01/08/66
Bates, Jeremy (GBR)	19/06/62	Delaitre, Olivier (FRA)	01/06/67
Baur, Patrick (GER)	03/05/65	Denman, Heath (AUS)	17/01/71
Bavelas, Tasos (GRE)	27/02/68	Derlin, Bruce (NZL)	28/11/61
Becker, Boris (GER)	22/11/67	Devening, Brian (USA)	16/07/67
Bengoechea, Eduardo (ARG)	02/07/59	Devries, Steve (USA)	08/12/64
Benhabiles, Tarik (FRA)	05/02/65	Doohan, Peter (AUS)	02/05/61
Berger, Jay (USA)	26/11/66	Dosedel, Ctislav (TCH)	14/01/70
Bergh, Rikard (SWE)	14/06/66	Doumbia, Yahiya (SEN)	25/08/63
Bergstrom, Christian (SWE)	19/07/67	Doyle, Grant (AUS)	09/01/74
Bjorkman, Jonas (SWE)	23/03/72	Duncan, Lawson (USA)	26/10/64
Black, Byron (ZIM)	06/10/69	Dyke, Broderick (AUS)	31/12/60
Bloom, Gilad (ISR)	01/03/67	Dzelde, Girts (URS)	16/07/63
Boetsch, Arnaud (FRA)	01/04/69	Edberg, Stefan (SWE)	19/01/66
Borg, Bjorn (SWE)	06/06/56	Eltingh, Jacco (HOL)	29/08/70
Borwick, Neil (AUS)	15/09/67	Engel, David (SWE)	17/10/67
Bouteyre, Pierre (FRA)	07/10/71	Enqvist, Thomas (SWE)	13/03/74
Braasch, Karsten (GER)	14/07/67	Evans, Keith (USA)	22/03/69
Brown, Jimmy (USA)	28/04/65	Evernden, Kelly (NZL)	21/09/62
Brown, Nick (GBR)	03/09/61	Faria, Rodrigo (BRA)	30/06/72
Bruguera, Sergi (ESP)	16/01/71	Farrow, Buff (USA)	28/05/67
Bryan, Steve (USA)	10/08/70	Fernandez, Jose-Antonio (CHI)	26/01/65
Buchmayer, Thomas (AUT)	14/02/71	Fernandez, Oliver (MEX)	07/12/72
Cahill, Darren (AUS)	02/10/65	Ferreira, Wayne (RSA)	15/09/71
Camargo, Ricardo (BRA)	14/05/68	Fetterlein, Frederik (DEN)	11/07/70
Camporese, Omar (ITA)	08/05/68	Filippini, Marcelo (URU)	04/08/67
Cancellotti, Francesco (ITA)	27/02/63	Fitzgerald, John (AUS)	28/12/60
Cane, Paolo (ITA)	09/04/65	Flach, Ken (USA)	24/05/63
Canter, Jonathan (USA)	04/06/65	Fleurian, Jean (FRA)	11/09/65
Caratti, Cristiano (ITA)	23/04/70	Fontang, Frederic (FRA)	16/03/70
Carbonell, Tomas (ESP)	23/08/68	Forget, Guy (FRA)	04/01/65

Name and Nationality	Date of Birth	Name and Nationality	Date of Birth
Frana, Javier (ARG)	25/12/66	Krumrey, Florian (GER)	
Fromberg, Richard (AUS)	28/04/70	Kucera, Karol (TCH)	04/03/74
Furlan, Renzo (ITA)	17/05/70	Kuhnen, Patrick (GER)	11/02/66
Furusho, Eduardo (JPN)	06/07/68	Kulti, Nicklas (SWE)	22/04/71
Gabrichidze, Vladimir (URS)	16/05/68	Kyriakos, William (BRA)	03/09/72
Garner, Chris (USA)	07/04/69	La Reau, Sebastien (CAN)	27/04/73
Garnett, Bret (USA)	02/07/67	Larsson, Magnus (SWE)	25/03/70
Garrow, Brian (USA)	08/04/68	Laurendeau, Martin (CAN)	10/07/64
Gaudenzi, Andrea (ITA)	30/07/73	Lavalle, Leonardo (MEX)	14/07/67
Geserer, Michael (GER)		Layendecker, Glenn (USA)	09/05/61
Gilbert, Brad (USA)	09/08/61	Leach, Rick (USA)	28/12/64
Gilbert, Rodolphe (FRA)	11/12/68	Leconte, Henri (FRA)	04/07/63
Gisbert, Juan (ESP)	13/04/74	Lendl, Ivan (TCH)	07/03/60
Goldie, Dan (USA)	03/10/63	Lopez, German (ESP)	29/12/71
Gomez, Andres (ECU)	27/02/60	Luna, Fernando (ESP)	24/04/58
Gorriz, Marco-Aurelio (ESP)	04/03/64	Lundgren, Peter (SWE)	29/01/65
Grabb, Jim (USA)	14/04/64	MacPherson, David (AUS)	07/03/67
Guardiola, Thierry (FRA)	07/08/71	Madsen, Bertrand (HAI)	18/05/72
Gunnarsson, Jan (SWE)	30/05/62	Mancini, Alberto (ARG)	20/05/69
Gustafsson, Magnus (SWE)	03/01/67	Mandl, Gerald (AUT)	12/11/70
Guy, Steve (NZL)	15/03/59	Mansdorf, Amos (ISR)	20/10/65
Haarhuis, Paul (HOL)	19/02/68	Marcelino, Danilo (BRA)	08/03/66
Haas, Rudiger (GER)	15/12/69	Markus, Gabriel (ARG)	31/03/70
Henricsson, Per (SWE)	09/08/69	Marques, Nuno (POR)	09/04/70
Herrera, Luis (MEX)	27/08/71	Martin, Todd (USA)	08/07/70
Hirszon, Sasa (YUG)	14/07/72	Masso, Eduardo (BEL)	11/01/64
Hlasek, Jakob (SUI)	12/11/64	Masuda, Kentaro (JPN)	26/08/71
Ho, Tommy (USA)	17/06/73	Masur, Wally (AUS)	13/05/63
Hocevar, Alexandre (BRA)	19/02/63	Matsuoka, Shuzo (JPN)	06/11/67
Hogstedt, Thomas (SWE)	21/09/63	Mattar, Luiz (BRA)	18/08/63
Holm, Henrik (SWE)	22/08/68	Matuszewski, Richard (USA)	07/09/64
Hombrecher, Alexis (USA)	29/01/71	Mayotte, Tim (USA)	03/08/60
Ingaramo, Marcelo (ARG)	13/10/62	McEnroe, John (USA)	16/02/59
Ivanisevic, Goran (CRO)	13/09/71	McEnroe, Patrick (USA)	01/07/66
Jabali, Roberto (BRA)	26/05/70	Medvedev, Andrei (URS)	31/08/74
Jaite, Martin (ARG)	09/10/64	Meligeni, Fernando (ARG)	12/04/71
Jarryd, Anders (SWE)	13/07/61	Melville, Scott (USA)	04/08/66
Jelen, Eric (GER)	11/03/65	Menezes, Mauro (BRA)	27/07/63
Ji, Seung-Ho (KOR)	28/04/68	Mercer, Tom (USA)	10/11/64
Jones, Kelly (USA)	31/03/64	Merinov, Andrei (URS)	23/04/71
Jonsson, Lars (SWE)	27/06/70	Merz, Miguel (ESA)	09/06/67
Joyce, Michael (USA)	01/02/73	Mezzadri, Claudio (SUI)	10/06/65
Kalovelonis, George (GRE)	23/08/59	Michibata, Glenn (CAN)	13/06/62
Kaplan, Mark (RSA)	20/12/67	Middleton, Todd (USA)	02/05/68
Karbacher, Bernd (GER)	03/04/68	Miniussi, Christian (ARG)	05/07/67
Keil, Mark (USA)	03/06/67	Moine, Silvio (ITA)	21/06/67
Kim, Bong-Soo (KOR)	30/11/62	Montana, Francisco (USA)	05/11/69
Kim, Jae-Sik (KOR)	17/05/67	Mordegan, Federico (ITA)	01/02/70
Kinnear, Kent (USA)	30/01/66	Morgan, Jamie (AUS)	08/06/71
Kist, Cesar (BRA)	22/10/64	Motta, Cassio (BRA)	22/02/60
Knowles, Mark (BAH)	04/09/71	Mronz, Alexander (GER)	07/04/65
Kodes, Jan (TCH)	11/03/72	Muller, Gary (RSA)	24/12/64
Koevermans, Mark (HOL)	03/02/68	Muster, Thomas (AUT)	02/10/67
Korda, Petr (TCH)	23/01/68	N'Goran, Clement (CIV)	07/08/69
Koslowski, Lars (GER)	22/05/71	Nargiso, Diego (ITA)	15/03/70
Kowalski, Wojtek (POL)	10/10/67	Nastase, Mihnea (ROM)	07/02/67
Krajicek, Richard (HOL)	06/12/71	Nelson, Todd (USA)	18/03/61
Kratzmann, Mark (AUS)	17/05/66	Nemecek, Libor (TCH)	26/10/68
Krickstein, Aaron (USA)	02/08/67	Nestor, Daniel (CAN)	04/09/72
Kriek, Johan (USA)	05/04/58	Netter, Jason (USA)	29/03/69
Krishnan, Ramesh (IND)	05/06/61	Nijssen, Tom (HOL)	01/10/64
Kroon, Niclas (SWE)	05/02/66	Nizet, Alex (USA)	22/02/67

Name and Nationality	Date of Birth	Name and Nationality	Date of Birth
Noah, Yannick (FRA)	18/05/60	Sanchez, Javier (ESP)	01/02/68
Noszaly, Sandor (HUN)	16/03/72	Santoro, Fabrice (FRA)	09/12/72
Novacek, Karel (TCH)	30/03/65	Sapsford, Danny (GBR)	03/04/69
Nyborg, Peter (SWE)	12/12/69	Schaeffl, Martin (AUT)	13/12/69
O'Brien, Alex (USA)	07/03/70	Schapers, Michiel (HOL)	11/10/59
Odizor, Nduka (NGR)	09/08/58	Schmidt, Richard (USA)	31/01/65
Olhovsky, Andrei (URS)	15/04/66	Seguso, Robert (USA)	01/05/63
Oncins, Jaime (BRA)	16/06/70	Sela, Ofer (ISR)	22/07/72
Ondruska, Marcos (RSA)	18/12/72	Shelton, Bryan (USA)	12/12/65
Oosting, Menno (HOL)	17/05/64	Shin, Han-Cheol (KOR)	23/03/70
Oresar, Bruno (YUG)	21/04/67	Siemerink, Jan (HOL)	14/04/70
Orsanic, Daniel (ARG)	11/06/68	Silberberg, Fabio (BRA)	25/03/69
Paes, Leander (IND)	17/06/73	Simian, Stephane (FRA)	28/06/67
Palmer, Jared (USA)	02/07/71	Sinner, Martin (GER)	07/02/68
Paloheimo, Veli (FIN)	13/12/67	Skakun, Sergei (URS)	26/03/70
Pambianco, Paolo (ITA)	11/07/67	Skoff, Horst (AUT)	22/08/68
Pate, David (USA)	16/04/62	Smith, Roger (BAH)	20/01/64
Pearce, Brad (USA)	21/03/66	Sobel, John (USA)	15/02/64
Pereira, Nicolas (VEN)	20/09/70	Solomon, Harold (USA)	17/09/52
Perez, Diego (URU)	09/02/62	Solves, Vicente (ESP)	08/02/69
Perez-Roldan, Guillermo (ARG)	20/10/69	Soresini, Sebastian (ITA)	11/03/68
Perkiss, Shahar (ISR)	14/10/62	Soules, Olivier (FRA)	24/03/67
Pernfors, Mikael (SWE)	16/07/63	Soulie, Serge (FRA)	29/06/69
Pescariu, Dinu (ROM)	12/04/74	Srejber, Milan (TCH)	30/12/63
Pescosolido, Stefano (ITA)	13/06/71	Stafford, Grant (RSA)	27/05/71
Petchey, Mark (GBR)	01/08/70	Stankovic, Branislav (TCH)	30/05/65
Pimek, Libor (BEL)	03/08/63	Stark, Jonathan (USA)	03/04/71
Pioline, Cedric (FRA)	15/06/69	Steeb, Carl-Uwe (GER)	01/09/67
Pistolesi, Claudio (ITA)	25/08/67	Steel, Bruce (USA)	
Poliakov, Dimitri (URS)	19/01/68	Steven, Brett (NZL)	27/04/69
Pozzi, Gian-Luca (ITA)	17/06/65	Stich, Michael (GER)	18/10/68
Prades, Laurent (FRA)	19/07/68	Stimpson, John (USA)	09/04/68
Pridham, Chris (CAN)	11/04/65	Stolle, Sandon (AUS)	13/07/70
Prpic, Goran (CRO)	04/05/64	Stoltenberg, Jason (AUS)	04/04/70
Pugh, Jim (USA)	05/02/64	Strelba, Martin (TCH)	22/03/67
Raffa, Roberto (ITA)		Stringari, Martin (ARG)	09/10/71
Rafter, Patrick (AUS)	28/12/72	Suk, Cyril (TCH)	29/01/67
Rahnasto, Olli (FIN)	28/12/65	Sullivan, John (USA)	22/12/66
Rahunen, Aki (FIN)	24/12/71	Svensson, Jonas (SWE)	21/10/66
Raoux, Guillaume (FRA)	14/02/70	Sznajder, Andrew (CAN)	25/05/67
Rasberger, Emanuel (YUG)	03/06/72	Tanizawa, Hidehiko (JPN)	05/12/71
Rebolledo, Pedro (CHI)	17/12/60	Tarango, Jeff (USA)	20/11/68
Reichel, Alex (USA)	09/03/71	Tauson, Michael (DEN)	25/06/66
Reneberg, Richey (USA)	05/10/65	Theine, Torben (GER)	10/07/68
Richardson, Bret (AUS)	23/01/71	Thomas, Lukas (TCH)	20/01/73
Riglewski, Udo (GER)	28/07/66	Thoms, Arne (GER)	01/01/71
Rikl, David (TCH)	27/02/71	Thorne, Kenny (USA)	24/01/66
Rive, Joey (USA)	08/07/63	Trneny, Milen (TCH)	06/03/71
Rivera, Felipe (CHI)	10/05/71	Tsuchihashi, Toshihisa (JPN)	18/10/66
Robertson, Michael (RSA)	02/07/63	Tsujino, Ryuso (JPN)	24/02/69
Rodriguez, Jose-Antonio (ESP)	05/05/62	Tulasne, Thierry (FRA)	12/07/63
Roese, Fernando (BRA)	24/08/65	Vacek, Daniel (TCH)	01/04/71
Roig, Francisco (ESP)	01/04/68	Vajda, Marian (TCH)	24/03/65
Ross, John (USA)	29/02/64	Van Herck, Johan (BEL)	24/05/74
Rosset, Marc (SUI)	07/11/70	Van Rensburg, Christo (RSA)	23/10/62
Rostagno, Derrick (USA)	25/10/65	Vasek, Radomir (TCH)	23/09/72
Roubicek, Vaclav (TCH)	13/12/67	Velev, Milen (BUL)	04/09/71
Ruah, Maurice (VEN)	19/02/71	Visconti, Mario (ITA)	23/10/68
Saceanu, Christian (GER)	08/07/68	Visser, Danie (RSA)	26/07/61
Saliola, Marcelo (BRA)	31/12/73	Viver, Raul-Antonio (ECU)	17/03/61
Sampras, Pete (USA)	12/08/71	Vogel, Richard (TCH)	13/08/64
Sanchez, Emilio (ESP)	29/05/65	Vojtischek, Paul (TCH)	13/06/63

Name and Nationality	Date of Birth	Name and Nationality	Date of Birth
Vojtisek, Pavel (GER)	13/06/63	Witsken, Todd (USA)	04/11/63
Volkov, Alexander (URS)	03/03/67	Witt, David (USA)	02/06/73
Vysand, Andres (URS)	10/03/66	Woehrmann, Jens (GER)	08/09/67
Wahlgren, Lars (SWE)	24/08/66	Woodbridge, Todd (AUS)	02/04/71
Walker, Michael (HKG)	21/04/65	Woodforde, Mark (AUS)	23/09/65
Washington, Malivai (USA)	20/06/69	Wostenholme, Martin (CAN)	11/10/62
Wawra, Reinhard (AUT)	07/02/73	Wuyts, Bart (BEL)	15/09/69
Weidenfeld, Raviv (ISR)	12/10/70	Yamamoto, Yasufumi (JPN)	03/05/71
Weinberg, Ohad (ISR)	19/03/71	Youl, Simon (AUS)	01/07/65
Weiss, Robbie (USA)	01/12/66	Yunis, Francisco (ARG)	12/08/64
Wekesa, Paul (KEN)	02/07/67	Yzaga, Jaime (PER)	23/10/67
Wheaton, David (USA)	02/06/69	Zdrazila, Tomas (TCH)	24/06/70
Wilander, Mats (SWE)	22/08/64	Zillner, Marcus (GER)	19/03/70
Wilkinson, Chris (GBR)	05/01/70	Zivojinovic, Slobodan (YUG)	23/07/63
Williamson, Phillip (USA)	29/05/65	Zoecke, Markus (GER)	10/05/68
Winogradsky, Eric (FRA)	22/04/66	Zwetsch, Joao (BRA)	12/11/68

The tall Dutchman with the powerful serve, Richard Krajicek, shot to prominence in 1991 with a first Tour title in Hong Kong, and a victory over Stefan Edberg which contributed to a year-end world ranking of 40. (R. Adams)

CHAMPIONSHIP SERIES

US PRO INDOOR TENNIS CHAMPIONSHIPS ($1,000,000)

PHILADELPHIA, 11–17 FEBRUARY

MEN'S SINGLES – 1st round: I. Lendl (1) – bye; G. Raoux d. D. Goldie (Q) 6–4 7–6; R. Furlan d. V. Paloheimo 4–6 7–5 6–4; G. Muller (15) – bye; D. Rostagno (10) – bye; C. Adams (Q) d. G. Stafford (Q) 6–2 6–2; C. Caratti (WC) d. J. Tarango (Q) 7–5 6–4; M. Stich (7) – bye; B. Gilbert (3) – bye; T. Carbonell d. G. Bloom (WC) 6–1 6–1; U. Riglewski d. G. Layendecker (Q) 6–3 6–7 6–0; P. Haarhuis (14) – bye; D. Cahill (11) – bye; T. Hogstedt d. R. Krishnan 6–3 6–1; K. Curren d. M. Kratzmann 6–3 6–7 6–4; J. Berger (5) – bye; J. Courier (6) – bye; J. Grabb d. P. Kuhnen 6–4 6–4; A. Rahunen d. G. Connell 7–6 7–5; M. Koevermans (12) – bye; W. Masur (13) – bye; C. Van Rensburg d. B. Pearce 6–2 6–1; A. Mronz d. H. De la Pena 6–2 6–2; J. McEnroe (4) (WC) – bye; T. Mayotte (8) – bye; W. Ferreira (Q) d. J. Fleurian 7–5 6–4; J. Yzaga d. A. Jarryd 6–3 6–3; P. Korda (9) – bye; P. McEnroe (16) (WC) – bye; M. Washington d. A. Antonitsch 7–6 4–6 6–0; M. Srejber d. S. Davis 6–4 6–7 6–3; P. Sampras (2) – bye.

2nd round: Lendl (1) d. Raoux 6–1 7–5; Muller (15) d. Furlan 6–7 6–3 6–4; Adams (Q) d. Rostagno (10) 7–5 6–3; Stich (7) d. Caratti (WC) 6–2 6–4; Gilbert (3) d. Carbonell 6–3 6–3; Haarhuis (14) d. Riglewski 6–1 6–3; Cahill (11) d. Hogstedt 6–4 6–2; Curren d. Berger (5) 6–1 6–2; Grabb d. Courier (6) 6–2 6–4; Rahunen d. Koevermans (12) 6–1 6–2; Masur (13) d. Van Rensburg 4–6 7–6 7–6; McEnroe (4) (WC) d. Mronz 6–1 6–2; Ferreira (Q) d. Mayotte (8) 6–4 6–2; Korda (9) d. Yzaga 6–4 6–3; Washington d. McEnroe (16) (WC) 6–0 6–3; Sampras (2) d. Srejber 6–2 7–5.

3rd round: Lendl (1) d. Muller (15) 7–6 6–3; Stich (7) d. Adams (Q) 6–4 6–4; Gilbert (3) d. Haarhuis (14) 7–6 6–1; Curren d. Cahill (11) 6–7 6–3 7–6; Rahunen d. Grabb 6–7 6–1 6–3; McEnroe (4) (WC) d. Masur (13) 7–6 6–4; Korda (9) d. Ferreira (Q) 7–5 7–6; Sampras (2) d. Washington 6–3 7–6.

Quarter-finals: Lendl (1) d. Stich (7) 6–2 7–6; Gilbert (3) d. Curren 4–6 6–3 6–0; McEnroe (4) (WC) d. Rahunen 7–5 6–3; Sampras (2) d. Korda (9) 6–4 6–0.

Semi-finals: Lendl (1) d. Gilbert (3) 6–4 3–6 6–4; Sampras (2) d. McEnroe (4) (WC) 6–2 6–4.

Final: Lendl (1) d. Sampras (2) 5–7 6–4 6–3 6–3.

MEN'S DOUBLES – Final: R. Leach/J. Pugh (2) d. Riglewski/Stich (7) 6–4 6–4.

DONNAY INDOOR CHAMPIONSHIP ($600,000)

BRUSSELS, 9–17 FEBRUARY

MEN'S SINGLES – 1st round: B. Becker (1) d. A. Volkov 6–4 3–6 6–3; E. Jelen (Q) d. C. Dosedel (Q) 7–6 6–3; A. Boetsch (Q) d. H. Skoff 6–4 2–6 6–4; M. Chang (7) d. T. Woodbridge 6–4 6–3; C. Saceanu (Q) d. A. Agassi (3) 6–3 7–6; A. Cherkasov (WC) d. J. Aguilera 6–2 6–2; G. Prpic d. H. Leconte 6–7 6–4 6–2; A. Chesnokov (6) d. C. Bergstrom (LL) 3–6 6–4 6–4; M. Rosset d. J. Svensson (5) 6–0 6–4; R. Agenor d. C. Steeb 6–2 7–5; E. Masso (WC) d. R. Fromberg 6–3 6–7 6–3; G. Forget (4) d. A. Mansdorf 4–6 6–3 6–3; J. Hlasek (8) d. M. Larsson 6–3 6–2; M. Wilander d. O. Camporese 6–4 7–6; P. Cash (WC) d. K. Novacek 2–6 7–6 6–3; S. Edberg (2) d. M. Gustafsson 6–0 6–4.

2nd round: Becker (1) d. Jelen (Q) 7–6 7–6; Chang (7) d. Boetsch (Q) 6–3 6–2; Cherkasov (WC) d. Saceanu (Q) 6–4 6–2; Chesnokov (6) d. Prpic 6–4 7–6; Rosset d. Agenor 6–4 6–3; Forget (4) d. Masso (WC) 6–1 6–2; Hlasek (8) d. Wilander 6–1 7–5; Edberg (2) d. Cash (WC) 3–6 6–1 6–4.

Quarter-finals: Becker (1) d. Chang (7) 7–5 6–1; Cherkasov (WC) d. Chesnokov (6) 7–5 6–1; Forget (4) d. Rosset 6–2 7–5; Edberg (2) d. Hlasek (8) 6–1 6–2.

Semi-finals: Cherkasov (WC) d. Becker (1) 2–6 6–3 2–2 ret.; Forget (4) d. Edberg (2) 3–6 6–0 6–3.

Final: Forget (4) d. Cherkasov (WC) 6–3 7–5 3–6 7–6.

MEN'S DOUBLES – Final: Woodbridge/M. Woodforde (4) d. L. Pimek/M. Schapers 6–3 6–0.

EUROCARD CLASSICS ($1,000,000)

STUTTGART, 18–24 FEBRUARY

MEN'S SINGLES – 1st round: C. Bergstrom (LL) d. J. Gunnarsson (Q) 6–4 3–6 6–3; K. Novacek d. J. Arrese 7–6 6–4; P. Baur (Q) d. N. Kulti 6–3 7–6; J. Svensson (7) d. R. Fromberg 6–7 6–1 6–0; G. Ivanisevic (3) d. A. Volkov 6–1 6–2; E. Jelen (WC) d. C. Steeb 6–3 6–4; J. Hlasek d. S. Zivojinovic (WC)

6–3 3–6 7–6; G. Forget (6) d. J. Aguilera 6–2 6–3; E. Sanchez (5) d. A. Mansdorf 7–6 6–3; A. Cherkasov d. P. Kuhnen (WC) 5–7 6–2 7–6; J. Siemerink (Q) d. H. Skoff 6–1 6–0; S. Bruguera d. T. Muster (4) 6–2 6–3; A. Chesnokov (8) d. M. Larsson 6–4 6–4; M. Gustafsson d. M. Rosset 6–4 6–1; O. Camporese d. R. Agenor 6–4 6–2; S. Edberg (2) d. M. Zoecke 6–4 7–6.
2nd round: Novacek d. Bergstrom (LL) 6–1 6–3; Svensson (7) d. Baur (Q) 6–4 6–2; Ivanisevic (3) d. Jelen (WC) 6–4 6–4; Forget (6) d. Hlasek 7–6 7–6; Cherkasov d. Sanchez (5) 6–4 6–4; Siemerink (Q) d. Bruguera 6–2 6–3; Gustafsson d. Chesnokov (8) 4–6 6–3 7–6; Edberg (2) d. Camporese 6–3 7–6.
Quarter-finals: Svensson (7) d. Novacek 7–6 6–2; Forget (6) d. Ivanisevic (3) 7–5 7–6; Siemerink (Q) d. Cherkasov 7–6 7–5; Edberg (2) d. Gustafsson 6–2 6–3.
Semi-finals: Svensson (7) d. Forget (6) 2–6 7–6 6–2; Edberg (2) d. Siemerink (Q) 6–4 6–4.
Final: Edberg (2) d. Svensson (7) 6–2 3–6 7–5 6–2.
MEN'S DOUBLES – Final: S. Casal/Sanchez (2) d. J. Bates/N. Brown 6–3 7–5.

VOLVO TENNIS INDOOR ($750,000)

MEMPHIS, 18–24 FEBRUARY
MEN'S SINGLES – 1st round: I. Lendl (1) (WC) – bye; W. Ferreira (Q) d. L. Herrera (Q) 6–7 7–6 6–3; G. Muller d. J. Arias 6–7 7–6 6–4; P. Haarhuis (16) – bye; P. Korda (9) – bye; P. McEnroe (WC) d. H. De la Pena 6–2 6–2; B. Garrow (LL) d. R. Krishnan 7–6 3–6 7–6; D. Cahill (8) – bye; A. Gomez (3) – bye; T. Mayotte d. P. Lundgren 6–3 6–4; G. Raoux d. R. Furlan 7–6 1–6 6–3; C. Caratti (13) (Q) – bye; D. Rostagno (11) – bye; M. Kratzmann d. M. Filippini 7–6 1–6 6–4; K. Curren d. V. Paloheimo 6–4 6–1; J. Courier (6) – bye; M. Chang (5) – bye; J. Fleurian d. J. Grabb 6–4 7–5; G. Connell (Q) d. S. Davis 6–2 7–6; L. Mattar (12) – bye; W. Masur (14) – bye; D. Goldie (WC) d. J. Yzaga 6–3 4–6 7–6; A. Rahunen d. R. Schmidt (WC) 6–4 2–6 6–4; J. Tarango (LL) – bye; M. Stich (7) – bye; A. Antonitsch d. T. Carbonell 3–6 7–6 7–6; M. Wilander d. M. Ondruska (Q) 7–6 5–7 6–2; D. Wheaton (10) – bye; M. Koevermans (15) – bye; G. Bloom d. C. Van Rensburg 3–6 6–3 6–3; C. Garner (Q) d. B. Pearce 7–6 6–2; P. Sampras (2) – bye.
2nd round: Lendl (1) (WC) d. Ferreira (Q) 6–3 3–6 7–5; Haarhuis (16) d. Muller 6–3 6–1; McEnroe (WC) d. Korda (9) 2–6 6–1 7–5; Cahill (8) d. Garrow 6–4 6–2; Mayotte d. Gomez (3) 6–4 6–2; Caratti (13) (Q) d. Raoux 7–5 7–6; Rostagno (11) d. Kratzmann 7–6 7–6; Courier (6) d. Curren 6–3 6–4; Chang (5) d. Fleurian 6–4 3–6 6–2; Connell (Q) d. Mattar (12) 6–3 6–0; Masur (14) d. Goldie (WC) 6–7 7–5 6–2; Tarango (LL) d. Rahunen 6–3 1–6 6–2; Stich (7) d. Antonitsch 6–2 6–3; Wilander d. Wheaton (10) 6–4 6–3; Koevermans (15) d. Bloom 6–3 6–4; Sampras (2) d. Garner (Q) 7–6 6–3.
3rd round: Lendl (1) (WC) d. Haarhuis (16) 6–2 6–1; Cahill (8) d. McEnroe (WC) 6–3 6–4; Caratti (13) (Q) d. Mayotte 3–6 7–6 6–2; Rostagno (11) d. Courier (6) 6–1 6–4; Chang (5) d. Connell (Q) 7–6 6–7 6–4; Tarango (LL) d. Masur (14) 7–6 6–4; Stich (7) d. Wilander 6–3 6–3; Koevermans (15) d. Sampras (2) 2–6 1–1 ret.
Quarter-finals: Lendl (1) (WC) d. Cahill (8) 7–6 6–3; Rostagno (11) d. Caratti (13) (Q) 6–7 6–2 6–0; Chang (5) d. Tarango (LL) 6–3 7–5; Stich (7) d. Koevermans (15) 6–4 6–2.
Semi-finals: Lendl (1) (WC) d. Rostagno (11) 6–3 6–2; Stich (7) d. Chang (5) 6–2 6–2.
Final: Lendl (1) (WC) d. Stich (7) 7–5 6–3.
MEN'S DOUBLES – Final: Riglewski/Stich (8) d. J. Fitzgerald/L. Warder 7–5 6–3.

NEWSWEEK CHAMPIONS CUP ($1,000,000)

INDIAN WELLS, 4–10 MARCH
MEN'S SINGLES – 1st round: S. Edberg (1) – bye; M. Jaite d. D. Wheaton 7–5 5–7 6–4; D. Cahill d. V. Paloheimo 6–3 6–4; S. Bryan (Q) d. J. Aguilera (15) 6–3 6–1; M. Chang (9) d. M. Filippini 6–1 6–1; J. Arias d. H. Leconte 7–6 6–3; W. Ferreira (Q) d. J. Fleurian 6–4 6–4; A. Gomez (8) – bye; G. Forget (3) – bye; T. Carbonell d. G. Muller 6–4 6–1; D. Rostagno d. D. Goldie (Q) 6–4 7–5; M. Rosset (14) d. P. Lundgren 7–6 6–4; J. McEnroe (12) d. W. Masur 7–6 2–6 7–5; J. Grabb d. G. Bloom 7–6 2–6 6–1; S. Davis d. J. Sanchez 7–6 7–5; T. Muster (6) – bye; G. Ivanisevic (5) (WC) – bye; F. Santoro d. A. Rahunen 6–1 6–4; G. Layendecker (WC) d. K. Jones (Q) 4–6 6–3 6–3; M. Stich (11) d. T. Mayotte 6–3 6–1; A. Volkov (13) d. T. Champion 6–7 6–3 6–4; R. Reneberg d. K. Curren 6–7 7–6 7–6; R. Furlan (Q) d. C. Caratti (WC) 6–1 5–7 7–6; F. Clavet (LL) – bye; E. Sanchez (7) – bye; S. Bruguera d. T. Witsken 7–5 7–6; L. Mattar d. B. Pearce (Q) 6–4 6–2; A. Cherkasov (10) d. P. Korda 7–5 6–1; J. Courier (16) d. G. Raoux (WC) 6–4 3–6 6–2; B. Black (WC) d. M. Vajda 6–1 3–6 6–3; G. Prpic d. M. Ruah (Q) 6–3 6–1; A. Agassi (2) – bye.
2nd round: Edberg (1) d. Jaite 6–3 6–2; Cahill d. Bryan (Q) 7–6 6–2; Chang (9) d. Arias 6–4 4–6 6–1; Ferreira (Q) d. Gomez (8) 6–4 7–6; Forget (3) d. Carbonell 6–1 6–3; Rostagno d. Rosset (14) 7–5 6–1; Grabb d. McEnroe (12) 7–6 7–5; Davis d. Muster (6) 6–3 6–2; Santoro d. Ivanisevic (5) (WC) 6–0 6–2; Stich (11) d. Layendecker 6–3 7–6; Reneberg d. Volkov (13) 6–7 7–6 2–6 4; Clavet d. Furlan (Q) 6–0 6–7 6–2; Sanchez (7) d. Bruguera 6–4 6–4; Cherkasov (10) d. Mattar 7–5 6–7 7–6 4; Courier (16) d. Black 6–1 7–6; Agassi (2) d. Prpic 6–3 6–4.
3rd round: Edberg (1) d. Cahill 3–6 7–5 6–2; Chang (9) d. Ferreira (Q) 6–3 3–6 6–4; Forget (3) d

Rostagno 6–3 6–1; Davis d. Grabb 6–4 6–4; Stich (11) d. Santoro 4–6 6–3 6–4; Reneberg d. Clavet 2–6 6–3 6–0; Sanchez (7) d. Cherkasov (10) 6–3 7–6; Courier (16) d. Agassi (2) 2–6 6–3 6–4.
Quarter-finals: Edberg (1) d. Chang (9) 1–6 6–2 7–5; Forget (3) d. Davis 7–5 6–1; Stich (11) d. Reneberg 6–0 2–6 6–4; Courier (16) d. Sanchez (7) 6–2 6–3.
Semi-finals: Forget (3) d. Edberg (1) 6–4 6–4; Courier (16) d. Stich (11) 6–3 6–2.
Final: Courier (16) d. Forget (3) 4 6 6 3 4 6 6 3 7 6.
MEN'S DOUBLES – Final: Courier/J. Sanchez d. Forget/Leconte 7–6 3–6 6–3.

LIPTON INTERNATIONAL PLAYERS CHAMPIONSHIPS ($1,500,000)

KEY BISCAYNE, 15–24 MARCH
MEN'S SINGLES – 1st round: S. Edberg (1) – bye; B. Derlin (Q) d. H. Solomon (WC) 6–2 6–3; G. Muller d. S. Davis 7–6 6–4; G. Prpic (31) – bye; J. Aguilera (18) – bye; J. Oncins d. A. Hombrecher (Q) 6–3 6–3; D. Witt (WC) d. C. Motta 6–1 7–6; M. Stich (15) – bye; M. Chang (10) – bye; J. Yzaga d. B. Garrow 6–4 3–6 6–1; F. Clavet d. S. Pescosolido (Q) 4–6 6–4 6–1; H. Leconte (23) – bye; D. Cahill (25) – bye; V. Paloheimo d. R. Furlan 6–2 6–4; J. Tarango (Q) d. J. Carlsson (Q) 7–5 6–3; E. Sanchez (7) – bye; A. Agassi (3) – bye; F. Santoro d. G. Raoux 2–6 6–2 7–6; T. Witsken d. A. Mronz 6–4 1–6 6–3; M. Gustafsson (29) – bye; A. Krickstein (20) – bye; K. Curren d. M. Vajda 6–3 6–1; D. Wheaton d. J. Grabb 6–3 3–6 6–1; G. Perez-Roldan (14) – bye; J. Hlasek (12) – bye; N. Marques d. C. Steeb 6–2 6–2; A. Boetsch (Q) d. G. Bloom 3–6 6–3 7–6; S. Bruguera (21) – bye; C. Caratti (28) – bye; J. Connors (WC) d. U. Riglewski 6–4 6–4; R. Gilbert (LL) d. T. Champion 7–6 6–1; P. Sampras (5) – bye; F. Roig (LL) – bye; J. Sanchez d. M. Filippini 6–3 2–6 6–0; W. Ferreira (Q) d. H. De la Pena 6–3 ret.; F. Davin (27) – bye; D. Rostagno (22) – bye; R. Krishnan d. P. Lundgren 6–4 6–4; T. Mayotte d. M. Washington 7–5 6–2; A. Cherkasov (11) – bye; J. Courier (13) – bye; L. Herrera d. B. Pearce 6–3 6–0; P. Haarhuis d. M. Kratzmann 6–3 6–2; K. Novacek (19) – bye; M. Jaite (30) – bye; J. Arias d. J. Fleurian 1–6 6–4 6–3; D. Goldie d. A. Sznajder 7–5 6–7 6–3; G. Forget (4) – bye; A. Gomez (8) – bye; T. Carbonell d. T. Hogstedt 6–2 6–0; J. Gunnarsson d. C. Garner (Q) 6–2 6–2; H. Skoff (26) – bye; R. Reneberg (24) – bye; P. Korda d. R. Krajicek 1–6 6–3 6–2; J. Siemerink (Q) d. J. Stoltenberg 7–6 3–6 7–6; B. Gilbert (9) – bye; A. Volkov (16) – bye; S. Matsuoka (Q) d. K. Evernden 3–6 6–1 6–2; P. Baur (Q) d. L. Mattar 7–6 6–3; M. Rosset (17) – bye; P. McEnroe (32) – bye; K. Jones (Q) d. G. Connell 6–4 6–4; S. Devries (Q) d. A. Rahunen 6–3 6–2; B. Becker (2) – bye.
2nd round: Edberg (1) d. Derlin (Q) 6–2 6–3; Prpic (31) d. Muller 6–4 6–0; Aguilera (18) d. Oncins 6–3 3–6 7–5; Stich (15) d. Witt (WC) 6–2 1–6 6–2; Chang (10) d. Yzaga 6–3 6–2; Leconte (23) d. Clavet 7–5 2–4 6–6 6–4; Cahill (25) d. Paloheimo 6–0 3–6 6–1; Sanchez (7) d. Tarango 6–7 7–6 6–3; Agassi (3) d. Santoro 7–6 4–6 7–5; Gustafsson (29) d. Witsken 6–3 2–6 6–1; Curren d. Krickstein (20) 6–2 6–4; Wheaton d. Perez-Roldan (14) 4–4 ret.; Hlasek (12) d. Marques 7–5 6–3; Bruguera (21) d. Boetsch (Q) 6–4 7–6; Caratti (28) d. Connors (WC) 6–4 6–3; Gilbert (LL) d. Sampras (5) 6–4 6–2; Sanchez d. Roig (LL) 7–6 6–2; Ferreira (Q) d. Davin (27) 7–6 1–0 ret.; Rostagno (22) d. Krishnan 6–7 6–4 6–3; Mayotte d. Cherkasov (11) 6–4 6–1; Courier (13) d. Herrera 7–6 3–6 6–3; Haarhuis d. Novacek (19) 6–4 6–4; Arias d. Jaite (30) 7–6 7–6; Forget (4) d. Goldie 6–1 6–3; Carbonell d. Gomez (8) 6–4 2–6 6–4; Skoff (26) d. Gunnarsson 6–2 6–0; Reneberg (24) d. Korda 6–7 7–6 6–3; Siemerink (Q) d. Gilbert (9) 6–7 6–4 6–3; Matsuoka (Q) d. Volkov (16) 6–3 7–5; Rosset (17) d. Baur (Q) 6–4 6–4; McEnroe (32) d. Jones (Q) 7–5 6–0; Becker (2) d. Devries (Q) 5–7 6–3 7–6.
3rd round: Edberg (1) d. Prpic (31) 6–4 6–2; Stich (15) d. Aguilera (18) 6–4 6–2; Chang (10) d. Leconte (23) 4–6 6–3 6–3; Sanchez (7) d. Cahill (25) 7–6 6–1; Agassi (3) d. Gustafsson (29) 6–7 6–2 7–5; Wheaton d. Curren 0–6 7–6 7–5; Bruguera (21) d. Hlasek (12) 6–1 6–2; Caratti (28) d. Gilbert (LL) 6–4 4–6 6–3; Ferreira (Q) d. Sanchez 6–1 6–3; Rostagno (22) d. Mayotte 6–7 6–4 6–3; Courier (13) d. Haarhuis 7–5 3–6 6–3; Forget (4) d. Arias 6–1 6–1; Carbonell d. Skoff (26) 0–6 6–1 6–2; Reneberg (24) d. Siemerink (Q) 7–6 6–4; Rosset (17) d. Matsuoka (Q) 6–4 6–4; McEnroe (32) d. Becker (2) 6–4 6–4.
4th round: Edberg (1) d. Stich (15) 6–4 2–6 6–4; Sanchez (7) d. Chang (10) 5–7 6–3 6–4; Wheaton d. Agassi (3) 6–0 7–5; Caratti (28) d. Bruguera (21) 6–7 6–3 7–6; Rostagno (22) d. Ferreira (Q) 6–3 1–6 6–4; Courier (13) d. Forget (4) 7–6 6–3; Reneberg (24) d. Carbonell 7–6 7–6; Rosset (17) d. McEnroe (32) 7–6 6–1.
Quarter-finals: Edberg (1) d. Sanchez (7) 6–2 7–6; Wheaton d. Caratti (28) 6–7 6–2 6–0; Courier (13) d. Rostagno (22) 6–0 6–3; Reneberg (24) d. Rosset (17) 7–6 3–6 6–3.
Semi-finals: Wheaton d. Edberg (1) 6–3 6–4; Courier (13) d. Reneberg (24) 6–4 6–3.
Final: Courier (13) d. Wheaton 4–6 6–3 6–4.
MEN'S DOUBLES – Final: Ferreira/P. Norval d. K. Flach/R. Seguso 5–7 7–6 6–2.

SUNTORY JAPAN OPEN TENNIS CHAMPIONSHIP ($1,000,000)

TOKYO, 8–14 APRIL
MEN'S SINGLES – 1st round: S. Edberg (1) – bye; K. Evernden (Q) d. G. Raoux 6–3 6–3; J. Connors (WC) d. J. Pugh (Q) 1–6 6–4 6–0; W. Masur (16) d. E. Masso 6–4 6–3; A. Jarryd (10) d. J. Stoltenberg 6–0 6–3; L. Herrera d. J. Eltingh 6–2 6–2; T. Mayotte d. G. Muller 7–6 4–6 6–3; M. Stich (7) – bye; B. Gilbert

(3) – bye; G. Connell d. J. Apell (Q) 7–6 3–6 7–6; A. Sznajder d. A. Antonitsch 6–2 6–3; P. Cash (14) d. T. Tsuchihashi (WC) 6–2 7–5; D. Pate d. T. Woodbridge 1–6 6–3 6–3; P. Baur d. G. Pozzi (Q) 6–4 6–4; J. Fitzgerald (Q) d. R. Krajicek 6–1 6–4; M. Chang (5) – bye; J. McEnroe (6) – bye; S. Zivojinovic (Q) d. B. Garrow 6–0 7–6; T. Witsken d. E. Furusho (WC) 6–1 6–3; A. Mansdorf (11) d. G. Bloom 6–2 6–1; D. Goldie d. J. Siemerink (13) 6–4 3–6 7–6; J. Stimpson (Q) d. K. Masuda (WC) 6–1 6–1; J. Grabb d. J. Tarango 4–6 6–3 7–6; J. Courier (4) – bye; J. Hlasek (8) – bye; U. Riglewski d. M. Kratzmann 6–4 6–2; A. Mronz d. Y. Yamamoto (WC) 6–1 6–2; P. Kuhnen d. A. Krickstein (9) 6–2 7–5; S. Matsuoka d. K. Curren (15) 7–6 6–2; J. Yzaga d. C. Van Rensburg 7–5 6–4; R. Krishnan d. T. Hogstedt 6–1 6–3; I. Lendl (2) – bye.

2nd round: Edberg (1) d. Evernden (Q) 6–2 7–6; Connors (WC) d. Masur (16) 3–6 7–6 7–5; Jarryd (10) d. Herrera 6–1 6–0; Stich (7) d. Mayotte 7–5 6–4; Gilbert (3) d. Connell 6–1 7–6; Cash (14) d. Sznajder 6–2 6–4; Pate d. Baur 6–1 6–4; Chang (5) d. Fitzgerald (Q) 6–0 6–0; McEnroe (6) d. Zivojinovic (Q) 6–1 6–4; Witsken d. Mansdorf (11) 6–2 1–6 6–3; Goldie d. Stimpson (Q) 6–3 7–6; Courier (4) d. Grabb 7–6 6–2 6–3; Hlasek (8) d. Riglewski 7–6 6–4; Mronz d. Kuhnen 6–4 6–4; Yzaga d. Matsuoka 6–1 7–6; Lendl (2) d. Krishnan 6–3 6–2.

3rd round: Edberg (1) d. Connors (WC) 6–4 6–7 6–1; Stich (7) d. Jarryd (10) 7–6 6–2; Cash (14) d. Gilbert (3) 6–4 1–6 6–3; Chang (5) d. Pate 6–4 7–6; McEnroe (6) d. Witsken 3–6 7–6 6–4; Courier (4) d. Goldie 6–3 6–4; Hlasek (8) d. Mronz 6–1 6–7 7–5; Lendl (2) d. Yzaga 7–5 6–3.

Quarter-finals: Edberg (1) d. Stich (7) 7–6 6–3; Chang (5) d. Cash (14) 6–4 6–1; Courier (4) d. McEnroe (6) 6–2 6–2; Lendl (2) d. Hlasek (8) 6–1 6–4.

Semi-finals: Edberg (1) d. Chang (5) 7–6 5–2; Lendl (2) d. Courier (4) 6–4 6–1.

Final: Edberg (1) d. Lendl (2) 6–1 7–5 6–0.

MEN'S DOUBLES – Final: Edberg/Woodbridge d. Fitzgerald/Jarryd 6–4 5–7 6–4.

TROFEO CONDE DE GODO ($650,000)

BARCELONA, 8–14 APRIL

MEN'S SINGLES – 1st round: B. Becker (1) – bye; J. Fleurian d. F. Davin 4–6 7–6 7–5; C. Steeb d. E. Jelen 7–6 6–2; S. Bruguera (15) d. M. Woodforde 6–0 6–0; M. Rosset (10) d. C. Mezzadri (Q) 6–7 6–1 6–4; J. Sanchez d. J. Altur 6–2 7–5; R. Azar d. J. Aparisi (Q) 7–6 3–6 6–4; A. Chesnokov (8) – bye; A. Agassi (3) (WC) – bye; G. Prpic d. T. Carbonell 6–3 6–1; A. Rahunen d. J. Cunha Silva 6–4 6–4; K. Novacek (14) d. C. Costa 6–3 1–6 6–4; G. Perez-Roldan (11) d. L. Jonsson 6–3 6–4; G. Lopez (Q) d. D. Nargiso 6–3 6–7 6–3; M. Filippini d. H. Skoff 7–6 6–3; A. Gomez (6) – bye; J. Svensson (5) (WC) – bye; M. Jaite d. P. Haarhuis 6–3 6–2; R. Furlan d. H. Leconte 6–1 6–2; M. Gustafsson d. J. Aguilera (12) 6–4 6–0; A. Volkov (13) d. F. Luna 7–6 6–7 6–4; F. Clavet d. M. Wilander 6–3 6–2; V. Paloheimo d. A. Mancini (Q) 6–4 2–6 6–4; G. Ivanisevic (4) – bye; E. Sanchez (7) – bye; D. Perez (Q) d. M. Koevermans 7–6 6–1; F. Roig d. V. Solves (Q) 3–6 6–2 7–6; A. Cherkasov (9) d. T. Benhabiles 2–6 6–2 6–1; O. Camporese (16) d. T. Champion 6–1 3–6 6–1; H. De La Pena d. R. Fromberg 6–4 6–4; J. Arrese d. M. Vajda 6–2 7–5 6–4; G. Forget (2) (WC) – bye.

2nd round: Becker (1) d. Fleurian 7–5 6–1; Bruguera (15) d. Steeb 6–4 6–1; Sanchez d. Rosset (10) 3–6 6–3 3–4 ret.; Chesnokov (8) d. Azar 7–5 6–2; Agassi (3) (WC) d. Prpic 6–7 6–4 7–5; A. Rahunen d. Novacek (14) 0–6 6–2 6–2; Perez-Roldan (11) d. Lopez 7–5 1–6 6–4; Filippini d. Gomez (6) 5–7 6–4 6–4; Jaite d. Svensson (5) (WC) 7–5 4–6 6–2; Gustafsson d. Furlan 6–3 6–1; Clavet d. Volkov (13) 6–0 6–1; Paloheimo d. Ivanisevic (4) 6–3 6–3; Sanchez (7) d. Perez (Q) 4–6 6–1 6–1; Cherkasov (9) d. Roig 6–2 7–5; Camporese (16) d. De la Pena 3–6 6–1 6–2; Arrese d. Forget (2) (WC) 2–6 6–3 7–5.

3rd round: Bruguera (15) d. Becker (1) 6–2 6–4; Chesnokov (8) d. Sanchez 5–7 7–5 6–4; Agassi (3) (WC) d. Rahunen 6–2 6–3; Perez-Roldan (11) d. Filippini 6–1 6–0; Jaite d. Gustafsson 6–3 0–6 7–5; Paloheimo d. Clavet 5–7 6–3 6–4; Sanchez (7) d. Cherkasov (9) 5–7 7–6 7–5; Camporese (16) d. Arrese 6–3 7–5.

Quarter-finals: Bruguera (15) d. Chesnokov (8) 6–2 7–5; Perez-Roldan (11) d. Agassi (3) (WC) 6–0 6–7 7–6; Jaite d. Paloheimo 6–1 4–6 6–3; Sanchez (7) d. Camporese (16) 7–6 4–6 7–5.

Semi-finals: Bruguera (15) d. Perez-Roldan (11) 6–4 6–4; Sanchez (7) d. Jaite 7–5 6–2.

Final: Sanchez (7) d. Bruguera (15) 6–4 7–6 6–2.

MEN'S DOUBLES – Final: De la Pena/Nargiso d. Becker/Jelen 3–6 7–6 6–4.

VOLVO MONTE CARLO OPEN ($1,000,000)

MONTE CARLO, 22–28 APRIL

MEN'S SINGLES – 1st round: S. Edberg (1) – bye; M. Larsson d. D. Rikl (Q) 6–3 6–1; M. Gustafsson d. U. Riglewski (Q) 6–7 6–2 6–4; G. Perez-Roldan (15) d. T. Tulasne (Q) 6–0 6–4; S. Bruguera (9) d. R. Furlan 6–3 6–7 6–3 (Q); C. Caratti d. H. Leconte 7–5 2–6 6–1; A. Mancini (WC) d. J. Arias 6–2 7–6; E. Sanchez (7) – bye; A. Agassi (4) – bye; H. Skoff d. J. Fleurian 4–6 6–4 6–2; J. Aguilera d. P. Lundgren 6–1 6–4; C. Pistolesi (Q) d. M. Rosset (13) 7–6 5–7 6–3; V. Paloheimo (Q) d. T. Muster (11) 6–7, 6–2 6–1; M. Koevermans d. L. Mattar 6–3 6–2; D. Pescariu (Q) d. F. Davin 6–4 1–0 ret.; J. Svensson (6) – bye; G. Ivanisevic (5) – bye; J. Arrese d. B. Borg (WC) 6–2 6–3; C. Steeb (WC) d. T. Champion (WC) 2–6 6–4

6–3; O. Camporese d. A. Gomez (12) 6–3 3–6 6–1; G. Prpic d. K. Novacek (14) 6–2 6–4; R. Fromberg d. M. Jaite 6–3 6–2; P. Haarhuis d. C. Bergstrom 6–3 6–2; G. Forget (3) – bye; A. Chesnokov (8) – bye; M. Wilander d. M. Woodforde (WC) 6–0 6–3; R. Agenor d. N. Kulti 2–6 7–6 7–6; A. Cherkasov (10) d. E. Jelen 6–0 6–2; A. Volkov (16) d. H. De la Pena 5–7 6–3 7–5; F. Santoro d. T. Guardiola (Q) 6–3 6–1; J. Sanchez d. M. Filippini 6–1 6–1; B. Becker (2) – bye.

2nd round: Larsson d. Edberg (1) 5 7 6 3 7 6; Gustafsson d. Perez Roldan (15) 6–4 6–3; Bruguera (9) d. Caratti 6–1 7–5; Mancini (WC) d. Sanchez (7) 6–3 6–3; Skoff d. Agassi (4) 6–0 6–7 6–3; Pistolesi (Q) d. Aguilera 6–3 1–6 7–5; Paloheimo (Q) d. Koevermans 7–5 6–4; Svensson (6) d. Pescariu (Q) 6–3 4–6 6–4; Ivanisevic (5) d. Arrese 7–6 7–6; Steeb (WC) d. Camporese 6–4 6–3; Prpic d. Fromberg 6–1 6–4; Forget (3) d. Haarhuis 7–5 6–4; Chesnokov (8) d. Wilander 7–6 6–2; Cherkasov (10) d. Agenor 7–6 6–3; Volkov (16) d. Santoro 2–6 6–1 6–4; Becker (2) d. Sanchez 6–7 6–3 6–3.

3rd round: Gustafsson d. Larsson 7–6 6–4; Bruguera (9) d. Mancini (WC) 6–1 6–4; Skoff d. Pistolesi (Q) 6–2 7–5; Svensson (6) d. Paloheimo (Q) 6–1 4–6 6–3; Steeb (WC) d. Ivanisevic (5) 2–6 6–0 6–2; Prpic d. Forget (3) 6–2 6–0; Chesnokov (8) d. Cherkasov (10) 6–1 6–0; Becker (2) d. Volkov (16) 3–6 6–1 6–1.

Quarter-finals: Bruguera (9) d. Gustafsson 7–5 7–5; Skoff d. Svensson (6) 6–3 6–3; Prpic d. Steeb (WC) 6–4 6–2; Becker (2) d. Chesnokov (8) 6–1 6–3.

Semi-finals: Bruguera (9) d. Skoff 6–1 6–4; Becker (2) d. Prpic 6–3 6–3.

Final: Bruguera (9) d. Becker (2) 5–7 6–4 7–6 7–6.

MEN'S DOUBLES – Final: L. Jensen/L. Warder d. Haarhuis/Koevermans (4) 5–7 7–6 6–4.

PANASONIC GERMAN OPEN ($1,000,000)

HAMBURG, 6–12 MAY

MEN'S SINGLES – 1st round: S. Edberg (1) – bye; A. Mronz (WC) d. P. Kuhnen (WC) 6–2 7–5; R. Agenor d. N. Kulti 6–4 7–6; A. Krickstein d. M. Rosset (16) 4–6 6–2 6–3; M. Stich (9) d. T. Carbonell 1–6 6–3 7–5; P. Haarhuis d. T. Nijssen (Q) 3–6 6–4 7–6; F. Clavet (Q) d. A. Mansdorf 7–6 6–2; E. Sanchez (8) – bye; P. Sampras (3) – bye; H. Skoff d. T. Muster 7–5 6–2; O. Camporese d. R. Haas (Q) 7–6 6–4; K. Novacek (13) d. C. Steeb (WC) 6–4 7–6; F. Davin d. A. Gomez (11) 6–4 6–3; M. Koevermans d. M. Vajda 6–3 6–2; M. Jaite d. E. Jelen 7–5 6–3; S. Bruguera (5) – bye; J. Courier (6) – bye; H. De la Pena d. C. Bergstrom 6–2 3–6 6–2; J. Arrese d. J. Aguilera 6–2 7–5; G. Prpic d. A. Chesnokov (12) 6–4 6–3; A. Volkov (14) d. G. Bloom 6–1 7–6; A. Boetsch (Q) d. A. Jarryd 4–6 6–1; L. Mattar d. U. Riglewski (WC) 6–1 6–4; G. Ivanisevic (4) – bye; J. Svensson (7) – bye; C. Caratti d. C. Pistolesi (Q) 6–3 6–3; M. Gustafsson d. D. Engel (Q) 6–4 6–2; A. Cherkasov (10) d. H. Leconte 7–6 6–3; M. Larsson d. W. Ferreira (LL) 6–2 3–6 6–3; Y. Noah (WC) d. R. Fromberg 7–6 6–0; R. Furlan (Q) d. M. Filippini 6–3 6–3; I. Lendl (2) – bye.

2nd round: Edberg (1) d. Mronz (WC) 6–3 6–1; Agenor d. Krickstein 7–5 0–6 6–2; Stich (9) d. Haarhuis 7–5 6–0; Clavet (Q) d. Sanchez (8) 6–3 4–6 6–4; Sampras (3) d. Skoff 6–3 4–6 6–4; Novacek (13) d. Camporese 6–3 6–2; Koevermans d. Davin 6–4 6–4; Bruguera (5) d. Jaite 6–3 6–1; De la Pena d. Courier (6) 6–7 6–2 6–4; Prpic d. Arrese 6–3 6–3; Volkov (14) d. Boetsch (Q) 7–6 7–6; Ivanisevic (4) d. Mattar 6–1 6–1; Caratti d. Svensson (7) 6–2 6–2; Gustafsson d. Cherkasov (10) 3–6 6–4 6–4; Noah (WC) d. Larsson 6–4 1–6 6–3; Furlan (Q) d. Lendl (2) 7–5 6–4.

3rd round: Edberg (1) d. Agenor 6–2 6–1; Stich (9) d. Clavet (Q) 6–1 6–4; Novacek (13) d. Sampras (3) 6–4 6–2; Koevermans d. Bruguera (5) 6–4 6–3; Prpic d. De la Pena 6–3 6–4; Ivanisevic (4) d. Volkov (14) 6–1 6–3; Gustafsson d. Caratti 7–5 3–6 6–2; Noah (WC) d. Furlan (Q) 1–6 6–4 6–3.

Quarter-finals: Stich (9) d. Edberg (1) 6–2 7–6; Novacek (13) d. Koevermans 4–6 6–4 6–2; Prpic d. Ivanisevic (4) 7–5 3–0 ret.; Gustafsson d. Noah (WC) 6–1 6–4.

Semi-finals: Novacek (13) d. Stich (9) 6–3 2–6 7–6; Gustafsson d. Prpic 6–2 1–6 7–6.

Final: Novacek (13) d. Gustafsson 6–3 6–3 5–7 0–6 6–1.

MEN'S DOUBLES – Final: S. Casal/E. Sanchez (1) d. C. Motta/D. Visser (8) 4–6 6–3 6–2.

XLVII CAMPIONATI INTERNAZIONALI D'ITALIA ($1,280,000)

ROME, 13–19 MAY

MEN'S SINGLES – 1st round: C. Pioline (LL) d. M. Rosset 7–5 6–3; C. Caratti d. M. Jaite 4–6 7–5 7–6; R. Fromberg d. P. McEnroe 4–6 7–6 6–2; A. Volkov (15) d. J. Siemerink 6–7 6–3 6–2; E. Sanchez (9) d. T. Woodbridge 6–1 6–1; H. Skoff d. L. Mattar 6–1 6–1; W. Ferreira (Q) d. T. Carbonell 6–4 2–6 6–4; M. Woodforde d. B. Gilbert (8) 3–6 6–2 6–4; P. Haarhuis d. G. Ivanisevic (4) 3–6 7–5 6–3; T. Muster d. A. Mansdorf 6–4 6–2; G. Prpic d. M. Filippini 6–0 2–6 6–1; J. Hlasek (13) d. P. Cane (WC) 3–6 6–2 6–4; A. Cherkasov (11) d. A. Antonitsch 6–2 6–4; S. Pescosolido (WC) d. R. Krajicek (Q) 6–1 6–2; N. Kulti d. O. Camporese 7–5 4–6 6–4; J. Courier (6) d. J. Arrese 6–4 4–6 6–3; S. Bruguera (5) d. C. Costa (Q) 3–6 6–2 7–6; Y. Noah (WC) d. A. Mronz 6–1 6–3; A. Krickstein d. C. Pistolesi (WC) 4–6 7–6 7–6; C. Miniussi (Q) d. G. Perez-Roldan (12) 6–7 6–4 6–1; M. Gustafsson (14) d. M. Wilander 7–6 6–1; H. Leconte d. F. Fontang (Q) 6–2 4–6 6–2; F. Santoro d. M. Larsson 6–4 6–1; P. Sampras (3) d. V. Gabrichidze (Q) 7–6 4–6 6–2; J. Svensson (7) d. F. Davin 6–4 3–6 6–4; A. Mancini (Q) d. R. Agenor 6–4 6–4; J. Aguilera d. P. Cash 3–6 6–4 6–1; M. Koevermans d. M. Stich (10) 4–6 6–4 6–4; M. Cierro (Q) d. K. Novacek (16) 6–0 6–3; H. De la

Pena d. P. Lundgren 6–2 6–2; R. Furlan d. J. Yzaga 6–4 6–0; E. Jelen d. A. Agassi (2) (WC) 6–3 7–6.
2nd round: Caratti d. Pioline 6–4 7–5; Fromberg d. Volkov (15) 7–5 6–3; Sanchez (9) d. Skoff 6–4 6–3;
Ferrelra (Q) d. Woodforde /–6 6–4; Muster d. Haarhuis 6–4 6–2; Prpic d. Hlasek (13) 6–1 7–5;
Cherkasov (11) d. Pescosolido 6–7 6–2 7–6; Courier (6) d. Kulti 6–0 6–3; Bruguera (5) d. Noah (WC) 6–1
6–3; Miniussi (Q) d. Krickstein 6–2 6–4; Leconte d. Gustafsson (14) 6–0 6–3; Santoro d. Sampras (3)
6–2 4–6 7–5; Mancini (Q) d. Svensson (7) 4–6 7–5 7–5; Koevermans d. Aguilera 6–2 6–2; De la Pena d.
Cierro (Q) 7–5 6–1; Jelen d. Furlan 2–6 6–3 7–6.
3rd round: Fromberg d. Caratti 7–5 6–0; Sanchez (9) d. Ferreira (Q) 6–2 6–2; Prpic d. Muster 3–6 6–3
6–2; Cherkasov (11) d. Courier (6) 4–6 6–1 6–2; Bruguera (5) d. Miniussi (Q) 6–1 6–2; Santoro d.
Leconte 6–4 5–7 7–6; Mancini (Q) d. Koevermans 6–0 4–6 7–6; De la Pena d. Jelen 7–6 6–1.
Quarter-finals: Sanchez (9) d. Fromberg 6–2 6–2; Prpic d. Cherkasov (11) 7–6 7–5; Bruguera (5) d.
Santoro 6–4 7–6; Mancini (Q) d. De la Pena 6–4 6–2.
Semi-finals: Sanchez (9) d. Prpic 6–4 6–2; Mancini (Q) d. Bruguera (5) 6–3 6–1.
Final: Sanchez (9) d. Mancini (Q) 6–3 6–1 3–0 ret.
MEN'S DOUBLES – Final: Camporese/Ivanisevic d. L. Jensen/L. Warder (7) 6–2 6–3.

MERCEDES CUP ($1,000,000)

STUTTGART, 15–21 JULY
MEN'S SINGLES – 1st round: M. Stich (1) – bye; F. Santoro d. U. Riglewski (WC) 6–0 6–1; J. Sanchez
d. M. Larsson 6–3 6–0; J. Arrese (16) – bye; H. Skoff (9) – bye; H. De la Pena d. K. Curren 6–4 6–4; R.
Krajicek d. F. Davin 6–2 6–4; M. Gustafsson (8) – bye; G. Ivanisevic (4) – bye; A. Gomez d. R. Furlan 2–6
6–2 6–1; F. Clavet d. T. Muster 6–1 6–3; O. Camporese (13) – bye; A. Volkov (12) – bye; J. Woehrmann
(Q) d. J. Siemerink 7–6 4–6 6–3; C. Pioline (Q) d. Y. Noah (WC) 6–3 6–2; K. Novacek (6) – bye; A.
Cherkasov (5) – bye; A. Mancini d. P. Haarhuis 6–4 6–2; C. Costa (Q) d. M. Koevermans 6–3 6–7 6–0; G.
Perez-Roldan (11) – bye; R. Agenor (14) – bye; M. Rosset d. M. Naewie (Q) 6–2 6–4; G. Lopez (Q) d. T.
Champion (WC) 6–7 6–3 6–2; E. Sanchez (3) – bye; G. Prpic (7) – bye; M. Filippini d. N. Kulti 6–2 4–6
7–5; E. Jelen d. C. Steeb (WC) 0–6 6–3 6–2; J. Svensson (10) – bye; M. Jaite (15) – bye; L. Koslowski (Q)
d. F. Roig (LL) 7–6 7–6; W. Masur d. M. Vajda 4–6 6–3 6–3; G. Forget (2) – bye.
2nd round: Stich (1) d. Santoro 6–3 7–6; Sanchez d. Arrese (16) 4–6 6–1 6–4; Skoff (9) d. De la Pena 6–0
6–3; Krajicek d. Gustafsson (8) 7–6 5–7 7–6; Gomez d. Ivanisevic (4) 4–6 6–3 7–6; Clavet d. Camporese
(13) 7–5 6–0; Volkov (12) d. Woehrmann (Q) 6–2 6–3; Pioline (Q) d. Novacek (6) 6–1 1–6 6–3; Mancini d.
Cherkasov (5) 4–6 6–4 6–2; Perez-Roldan (11) d. Costa (Q) 3–6 2–6; Agenor (14) d. Rosset 6–1 3–6 6–3;
Lopez (Q) d. Sanchez (3) 7–6 7–6; Prpic (7) d. Filippini 7–6 6–2; Jelen d. Svensson (10) 7–6 6–1;
Koslowski (Q) d. Jaite (15) 6–3 6–4; Forget (2) d. Masur 5–7 7–6 7–6.
3rd round: Stich (1) d. Sanchez 6–3 6–3; Krajicek d. Skoff (9) 6–3 6–4; Clavet d. Gomez 6–3 6–3; Pioline
d. Volkov (12) 6–2 4–6 6–3; Mancini d. Perez-Roldan (11) 7–6 6–3; Lopez (Q) d. Agenor (14) 6–2 6–3;
Prpic (7) d. Jelen 6–3 2–6 6–2; Koslowski (Q) d. Forget (2) 7–6 7–6.
Quarter-finals: Stich (1) d. Krajicek 6–4 3–6 7–6; Clavet d. Pioline (Q) 6–3 6–7 6–1; Mancini d. Lopez (Q)
6–3 6–3; Koslowski (Q) d. Prpic (7) 6–2 2–6 7–5.
Semi-finals: Stich (1) d. Clavet 6–4 6–2; Mancini d. Koslowski (Q) 4–6 6–1 6–3.
Final: Stich (1) d. Mancini 1–6 7–6 6–4 6–2.
MEN'S DOUBLES – Final: Masur/E. Sanchez (7) d. Camporese/Ivanisevic (6) 4–6 6–3 6–4.

SOVRAN BANK CLASSIC ($550,000)

WASHINGTON, 15–21 JULY
MEN'S SINGLES – 1st round: A. Agassi (1) – bye; D. Pate d. K. Thorne (Q) 6–3 4–6 7–6; C. Adams d. J.
Ross (WC) 5–7 6–3 7–6; P. Baur (15) d. G. Raoux 6–4 7–6; P. Lundgren (9) d. J. Morgan 6–4 6–2; J.
Carlsson (Q) d. C. Garner 6–7 6–2 6–4; S. Matsuoka d. J. Tarango 6–4 6–2; T. Witsken (8) – bye; R.
Reneberg (4) – bye; G. Layendecker d. T. Ho 2–6 6–3 7–6; G. Stafford (Q) d. M. Laurendeau 6–3 4–6 6–2;
S. Davis (14) d. D. Orsanic 6–4 7–6; M. Washington (11) d. J. Frana 6–3 6–7 6–1; C. Pridham d. F. Roese
7–6 6–1; M. Knowles (Q) d. B. Pearce 6–4 6–0; J. Yzaga (6) – bye; D. Rostagno (5) (WC) – bye; S. Youl d. D.
Goldie 7–6 6–4; B. Garnett (Q) d. R. Seguso (Q) 4–6 6–4 6–2; P. Korda (12) d. N. Pereira (WC) 4–6 6–3 6–2;
G. Connell (13) d. M. Wostenholme 6–7 6–4 6–4; A. Sznajder d. H. Holm 5–7 7–5 7–5; J. Sullivan (Q) d. J.
Brown 6–3 6–2; B. Gilbert (3) – bye; A. Krickstein (7) – bye; M. Zoecke d. N. Borwick 7–6 6–4; A. Mronz d.
C. Dosedel 6–3 7–5; J. Arias (10) d. M. Woodforde 6–4 5–7 6–4; L. Herrera d. J. Eltingh (16) 7–5 7–6; J.
Grabb d. I. Baron (WC) 6–3 6–3; B. Garrow d. J. Palmer (WC) 6–3 6–3; J. McEnroe (2) – bye.
2nd round: Agassi (1) d. Pate 6–4 6–3; Adams d. Baur 6–4 6–3; Carlsson (Q) d. Lundgren (9) 1–6
6–2 6–4; Matsuoka d. Witsken (8) 6–3 6–1; Reneberg (4) d. Layendecker 5–7 6–3 6–4; Stafford (Q) d.
Davis (14) 5–7 7–5 6–0; Washington (11) d. Pridham 6–3 6–3; Yzaga (6) d. Knowles (Q) 7–5 6–1;
Rostagno (5) (WC) d. Youl 6–3 4–6 6–4; Korda (12) d. Garnett (Q) 7–6 7–6; Connell (13) d. Sznajder 6–3
7–5; Gilbert (3) d. Sullivan (Q) 4–6 6–2 6–2; Zoecke d. Krickstein (7) 6–7 6–2 7–6; Arias (10) d. Mronz 6–4
7–5; Herrera d. Grabb 6–4 3–6 6–3; McEnroe (2) d. Garrow 6–3 7–5.

3rd round: Agassi (1) d. Adams 6–2 6–2; Carlsson (Q) d. Matsuoka 7–6 7–6; Reneberg (4) d. Stafford (Q) 7–6 6–0; Yzaga (6) d. Washington (11) 6–4 6–4; Korda (12) d. Rostagno (5) (WC) 6–1 6–4; Gilbert (3) d. Connell (13) 6–3 6–2; Zoecke d. Arias (10) 6–3 6–4; Herrera d. McEnroe (2) 3–6 6–2 6–2.
Quarter-finals: Agassi (1) d. Carlsson (Q) 7–5 6–2; Yzaga (6) d. Reneberg (4) 6–3 6–4; Korda (12) d. Gilbert (3) 7–6 7–6; Zoecke d. Herrera 4–6 6–3 6–3.
Semi-finals. Agassi (1) d. Yzaga (6) 0–3 0–2, Korda (12) d. Zoecke 4–0 0–2 0–4.
Final: Agassi (1) d. Korda (12) 6–3 6–4.
MEN'S DOUBLES – Final: Davis/Pate (1) d. K. Flach/Seguso (5) 6–4 6–2.

PLAYERS INTERNATIONAL CANADIAN OPEN ($1,200,00)

MONTREAL, 22–28 JULY
MEN'S SINGLES – 1st round: I. Lendl (1) – bye; G. Bloom d. B. Pearce 6–4 6–1; J. Tarango d. A. Sznajder (WC) 6–4 6–3; W. Masur (15) d. M. Woodforde 6–3 6–4; R. Reneberg (9) d. T. Mayotte 6–3 6–1; J. Grabb d. J. Morgan (Q) 4–6 6–4 7–6; A. Mronz d. S. Davis 6–4 6–3; B. Gilbert (8) – bye; P. Sampras (4) (WC) – bye; S. Matsuoka d. A. Boetsch 6–7 7–6 6–3; C. Garner (Q) d. P. Baur 4–6 6–4 7–6; P. McEnroe (13) d. T. Witsken 6–1 6–1; A. Chesnokov (12) d. D. Goldie 6–1 6–2; S. Lareau (WC) d. I. Aler (Q) 3–6 7–6 6–4; S. Pescosolido d. H. Holm 7–5 6–4; M. Chang (5) – bye; J. Hlasek (6) – bye; N. Borwick (Q) d. J. Kriek 6–3 6–4; S. Youl (Q) d. L. Herrera 6–3 6–7 7–6; C. Pridham (WC) d. C. Caratti (11) 6–3 3–6 7–5; G. Raoux d. J. Yzaga (14) 6–3 1–6 6–3; M. Laurendeau (WC) d. J. Brown (LL) 6–2 7–5; P. Korda d. G. Pozzi (Q) 3–6 6–3 7–6; A. Agassi (3) – bye; J. McEnroe (7) – bye; J. Arias d. G. Connell 7–6 7–6; T. Hogstedt d. J. Fleurian 6–3 6–2; D. Rostagno (10) d. D. Pate 3–6 7–5 6–2; A. Mansdorf (16) d. H. Krishnan 6–2 6–2; P. Lundgren d. C. Dosedel (Q) 6–4 3–6 7–6; M. Washington d. M. Zoecke 6–4 6–4; J. Courier (2) – bye.
2nd round: Lendl (1) d. Bloom 4–6 6–4 6–4; Masur (15) d. Tarango 6–7 6–1 6–4; Grabb d. Reneberg (9) 6–7 6–2 7–5; Gilbert (8) d. Mronz 6–3 7–5; Matsuoka d. Sampras (4) (WC) 2–6 6–4 7–6; McEnroe (13) d. Garner (Q) 6–2 6–4; Chesnokov (12) d. Lareau (WC) 4–6 6–1 6–3; Pescosolido d. Chang (5) 7–6 3–6 6–3; Hlasek (6) d. Borwick (Q) 2–6 6–4 6–4; Youl (Q) d. Pridham (WC) 1–6 6–3 7–5; Raoux d. Laurendeau (WC) 3–6 7–5 6–0; Korda d. Agassi (3) 7–6 6–2; McEnroe (7) d. Arias 6–1 6–2; Rostagno (10) d. Hogstedt 6–3 6–1; Mansdorf (16) d. Lundgren 6–4 6–7 6–1; Courier (2) d. Washington 7–5 6–3.
3rd round: Lendl (1) d. Masur (15) 6–3 3–6 6–4; Grabb d. Gilbert (8) 4–6 6–3 6–4; Matsuoka d. McEnroe (13) 6–4 6–3; Chesnokov (12) d. Pescosolido 6–4 6–4; Hlasek (6) d. Youl (Q) 7–6 6–4; Korda d. Raoux 6–2 6–3; Rostagno (10) d. McEnroe (7) 6–2 1–6 7–6; Courier (2) d. Mansdorf (16) 6–3 3–6 6–3.
Quarter-finals: Lendl (1) d. Grabb 7–6 6–7 7–5; Chesnokov (12) d. Matsuoka 6–2 3–6 7–5; Korda d. Hlasek (6) 7–6 6–4; Courier (2) d. Rostagno (10) 6–3 6–3.
Semi-finals: Chesnokov (12) d. Lendl (1) 7–6 7–5; Korda d. Courier (2) 3–6 7–6 6–2.
Final: Chesnokov (12) d. Korda 3–6 6–4 6–3.
MEN'S DOUBLES – Final: Galbraith/Witsken (3) d. Connell/Michibata (2) 6–4 3–6 6–1.

THRIFTWAY ATP CHAMPIONSHIPS ($1,200,000)

CINCINNATI, 5–11 AUGUST
MEN'S SINGLES – 1st round: B. Becker (1) (WC) – bye; J. Fleurian d. J. Grabb 7–5 4–6 6–3; M. Washington d. R. Fromberg 6–3 6–4; A. Krickstein d. R. Reneberg (15) 7–6 3–6 7–6; A. Cherkasov (10) d. T. Woodbridge 7–6 6–1; P. Lundgren d. A. Chesnokov 7–6 4–6 6–3; A. Gomez (WC) d. S. Pescosolido 5–7 6–4 7–6; D. Wheaton (8) – bye; I. Lendl (3) (WC) – bye; P. McEnroe d. K. Curren 6–3 7–5; C. Garner (Q) d. C. Caratti 6–2 7–6; D. Rostagno (14) d. G. Bloom 6–2 6–3; J. Hlasek (11) d. J. Arias 6–1 6–1; G. Pozzi (Q) d. T. Witsken 6–4 6–2; M. Ondruska (Q) d. M. Woodforde 6–3 6–3; G. Forget (6) – bye; A. Agassi (5) – bye; P. Korda d. G. Connell 6–3 6–1; J. Yzaga d. F. Roese (Q) 6–3 6–1; B. Gilbert (12) d. B. Pearce 7–5 6–3; M. Chang (13) d. R. Gilbert 4–6 6–2 6–1; D. Visser (Q) d. R. Agenor 6–4 3–6 7–6; M. Pernfors d. D. Pate 6–3 7–5; J. Courier (4) – bye; P. Sampras (7) – bye; W. Masur d. G. Muller 6–7 6–4 7–6; W. Ferreira d. R. Krishnan 6–1 6–3; J. Stoltenberg d. E. Sanchez (9) 6–3 6–4; A. Jarryd d. J. Svensson (16) 6–7 7–5 6–4; A. Mansdorf d. S. Davis 6–4 6–4; G. Stafford (Q) d. S. Devries (Q) 6–4 6–3; S. Edberg (2) – bye.
2nd round: Becker (1) (WC) d. Fleurian 6–3 6–3; Washington d. Krickstein 6–1 6–4; Cherkasov (10) d. Lundgren 6–4 6–2; Wheaton (8) d. Gomez (WC) 7–5 6–2; Lendl (3) (WC) d. McEnroe 6–1 6–3; Rostagno (14) d. Garner (Q) 4–6 6–3 6–4; Pozzi (Q) d. Hlasek (11) 6–4 7–5; Forget (6) d. Ondruska (Q) 6–2 6–2; Agassi (5) d. Korda 7–5 2–6 6–2; Gilbert (12) d. Yzaga 6–2 7–5; Chang (13) d. Visser (Q) 6–1 6–3; Courier (4) d. Pernfors 6–3 6–1; Sampras (7) d. Masur 7–6 6–4; Ferreira d. Stoltenberg 6–2 3–6 6–2; Mansdorf d. Jarryd 6–4 6–1; Edberg (2) d. Stafford (Q) 6–2 6–0.
3rd round: Becker (1) (WC) d. Washington 6–4 6–4; Cherkasov (10) d. Wheaton (8) 6–3 6–2; Rostagno (14) d. Lendl (3) (WC) 7–6 3–6 6–3; Forget (6) d. Pozzi (Q) 6–4 6–4; Gilbert (12) d. Agassi (5) 7–6 6–7 6–4; Courier (4) d. Chang (13) 7–5 6–2; Sampras (7) d. Ferreira 6–1 6–4; Edberg (2) d. Mansdorf 6–1 6–2.
Quarter-finals: Becker (1) (WC) d. Cherkasov (10) 7–6 6–3; Forget (6) d. Rostagno (14) 7–6 6–4; Courier

(4) d. Gilbert (12) 6–3 6–3; Sampras (7) d. Edberg (2) 6–3 6–3.
Semi-finals: Forget (6) d. Becker (1) (WC) 7–6 4–6 6–3; Sampras (7) d. Courier (4) 6–2 7–5.
Final: Forget (6) d. Sampras (7) 2–6 7–6 6–4.
MEN'S DOUBLES – Final: K. Flach/R. Seguso d. Connell/G. Michibata (3) 6–7 6–4 7–5

GTE US HARD COURT CHAMPIONSHIPS ($1,000,000)

INDIANAPOLIS, 12–18 AUGUST
MEN'S SINGLES – 1st round: B. Becker (1) – bye; D. Pate d. A. Sznajder 6–4 7–5; N. Marques d. B. Farrow (Q) 6–4 6–4; C. Bergstrom (16) d. W. Ferreira 6–3 6–3; J. Hlasek (9) d. G. Connell 7–6 6–3; R. Weiss d. B. Black (Q) 6–3 6–0; J. Stoltenberg d. J. Sanchez 7–5 6–4; E. Sanchez (7) – bye; A. Agassi (3) – bye; K. Kinnear (Q) d. J. Altur 6–3 6–7 7–6; C. Pioline d. N. Borwick 6–3 6–1; F. Santoro (14) d. I. Carbonell 6–2 6–2; S. Bryan (WC) d. A. Jarryd (11) 7–6 6–1; C. N'Goran (Q) d. K. Evernden 6–7 7–5 7–6; A. Krickstein d. J. Stark (Q) 6–3 4–6 6–4; D. Wheaton (6) – bye; P. Sampras (5) – bye; G. Stafford (Q) d. P. Lundgren 4–6 6–3 6–2; S. Pescosolido d. R. Leach (WC) 6–3 6–3; P. McEnroe (12) d. B. Pearce 7–5 6–1; B. Steven (Q) d. R. Agenor (13) 4–6 6–4 7–6; R. Fromberg d. S. Davis 6–4 6–2; T. Mayotte d. J. Brown 6–4 6–2; G. Forget (4) – bye; A. Cherkasov (8) – bye; T. Witsken d. R. Krishnan 6–1 4–6 6–1; S. Matsuoka d. D. Witt (WC) 7–5 3–6 6–3; A. Volkov (10) d. G. Muller 3–6 6–2 6–3; F. Clavet (15) d. G. Raoux 7–5 6–2; R. Gilbert d. T. Martin (WC) 6–7 6–4 6–4; J. Pugh (WC) d. K. Curren 7–6 5–7 6–3; J. Courier (2) – bye.
2nd round: Becker (1) d. Pate 6–3 6–2; Bergstrom (16) d. Marques 7–6 6–3; Hlasek (9) d. Weiss 7–5 3–6 7–5; Stoltenberg d. Sanchez (7) 7–6 6–3; Agassi (3) d. Kinnear (Q) 7–6 7–5; Santoro (14) d. Pioline 6–4 5–7 6–2; Bryan (WC) d. N'Goran 6–2 3–6 7–6; Wheaton (6) d. Krickstein 6–4 7–5; Sampras (5) d. Stafford (Q) 6–4 6–2; McEnroe (12) d. Pescosolido 7–6 ret.; Fromberg d. Steven (Q) 6–2 6–2; Mayotte d. Forget (4) 7–6 6–1; Cherkasov (8) d. Witsken 2–6 7–6 6–2; Volkov (10) d. Matsuoka 7–6 6–2; Clavet (15) d. Gilbert 6–3 6–3; Courier (2) d. Pugh (WC) 6–4 6–4.
3rd round: Becker (1) d. Bergstrom (16) 6–2 6–2; Hlasek (9) d. Stoltenberg 6–3 6–4; Santoro (14) d. Agassi (3) 2–6 7–5 6–2; Wheaton (6) d. Bryan (WC) 6–3 7–5; Sampras (5) d. McEnroe (12) 6–3 6–4; Fromberg d. Mayotte 6–1 7–5; Cherkasov (8) d. Volkov (10) 7–6 7–5; Courier (2) d. Clavet (15) 6–2 6–1.
Quarter-finals: Becker (1) d. Hlasek (9) 7–5 7–5; Wheaton (6) d. Santoro (14) 6–1 6–4; Sampras (5) d. Fromberg 7–6 6–2; Courier (2) d. Cherkasov (8) 6–2 7–5.
Semi-finals: Becker (1) d. Wheaton (6) 7–6 6–4; Sampras (5) d. Courier (2) 6–3 7–6.
Final: Sampras (5) d. Becker (1) 7–6 3–6 6–3.
MEN'S DOUBLES – Final: K. Flach/R. Seguso d. Kinnear/S. Salumaa 7–6 6–4.

VOLVO NEW HAVEN ($1,000,000)

NEW HAVEN, 12–18 AUGUST
MEN'S SINGLES – 1st round: S. Edberg (1) (WC) – bye; M. Washington d. J. Connors (WC) 6–4 6–2; G. Bloom d. P. Arraya 6–7 6–1 4–0 ret.; R. Krajicek (15) d. C. Van Rensburg 3–6 6–3 6–4; D. Rostagno (9) d. B. Garrow 6–3 6–4; A. O'Brien (Q) d. J. Kriek 7–5 6–2; P. Haarhuis d. T. Ho (Q) 6–3 6–0; A. Chesnokov (8) (WC) – bye; J. McEnroe (4) – bye; L. Mattar d. A. Gomez 6–2 6–3; F. Roese d. J. Arias 6–4 6–4; B. Shelton d. T. Woodbridge (14) 7–6 6–3; J. Siemerink d. A. Castle (LL) 6–1 6–4; C. Dosedel d. T. Nelson (Q) 7–5 2–6 6–2; G. Pozzi (LL) d. T. Hogstedt 6–0 1–0 ret.; G. Ivanisevic (5) (WC) – bye; R. Reneberg (6) – bye; P. Annacone (Q) d. C. Adams 3–6 7–6 6–3; J. Frana d. M. Vajda 6–2 6–3; P. Korda (11) d. J. Fleurian 6–3 6–3; O. Camporese (13) d. W. Masur 4–6 6–4 6–4; L. Herrera d. J. Oncins 6–3 6–2; D. Marcelino d. L. Paes (Q) 6–4 7–5; B. Gilbert (3) – bye; J. Svensson (7) – bye; M. Kaplan (Q) d. D. Goldie 3–6 6–3 7–6; A. Mansdorf d. M. Petchey (Q) 6–4 6–2; M. Chang (10) (WC) d. M. Pernfors 6–3 5–7 6–2; M. Rosset (16) d. M. Woodforde 6–4 6–2; O. Delaitre d. C. Garner 6–4 7–6; A. Boetsch d. J. Grabb 6–1 4–6 6–4; I. Lendl (2) – bye.
2nd round: Edberg (1) (WC) d. Washington 6–4 6–4; Krajicek (15) d. Bloom 7–5 6–3; Rostagno (9) d. O'Brien (Q) 7–6 6–2; Haarhuis d. Chesnokov (8) (WC) 7–6 3–6 7–5; McEnroe (4) d. Mattar 4–6 6–3 6–4; Roese d. Shelton 7–5 2–6 6–4; Siemerink d. Dosedel 6–3 6–1; Ivanisevic (5) (WC) d. Pozzi (LL) 7–6 4–6 6–2; Reneberg (6) d. Annacone (Q) w/o; Korda (11) d. Frana 7–6 6–3; Camporese (13) d. Herrera 6–4 7–6; Marcelino d. Gilbert (3) 6–4 4–6 6–4; Svensson (7) d. Kaplan (Q) 6–4 6–3; Chang (10) (WC) d. Mansdorf 7–5 6–2; Rosset (16) d. Delaitre 6–3 6–1; Lendl (2) d. Boetsch 6–2 6–2.
3rd round: Krajicek (15) d. Edberg (1) (WC) 4–6 6–3 6–3; Rostagno (9) d. Haarhuis 6–3 7–5; McEnroe (4) d. Roese 6–0 6–3; Ivanisevic (5) (WC) d. Siemerink 6–2 6–4; Korda (11) d. Reneberg (6) 6–3 7–6; Camporese (13) d. Marcelino 6–2 6–2; Chang (10) (WC) d. Svensson (7) 6–3 3–6 6–3; Rosset (16) d. Lendl (2) 6–4 6–4.
Quarter-finals: Rostagno (9) d. Krajicek (15) 3–6 2–1 ret.; Ivanisevic (5) (WC) d. McEnroe (4) 6–4 6–2; Korda (11) d. Camporese (13) 6–4 6–1; Rosset (16) d. Chang (10) (WC) 6–2 6–3.
Semi-finals: Ivanisevic (5) (WC) d. Rostagno (9) 6–4 7–5; Korda (11) d. Rosset (16) 6–4 6–3.
Final: Korda (11) d. Ivanisevic (5) (WC) 6–4 6–2.
MEN'S DOUBLES – Final: Korda/Masur (8) d. J. Brown/S. Melville (6) 7–5 6–3.

UNCLE TOBY'S AUSTRALIAN INDOOR TENNIS CHAMPIONSHIPS ($1,000,000)

SYDNEY, 30 SEPTEMBER–6 OCTOBER

MEN'S SINGLES – 1st round: S. Edberg (1) – bye; P. Lundgren d. G. Muller 7–6 6–3; M. Woodforde d. G. Doyle (WC) 6–2 6–1; W. Masur (15) – bye; A. Chesnokov (10) – bye; G. Pozzi d. P. Cane 7–5 1–6 6–1; N. Kroon (Q) d. T. Hogstedt 7–6 7–6; M. Chang (8) – bye; A. Agassi (4) – bye; J. Stoltenberg d. C. Dosedel 7–5 6–3; J. Tarango d. R. Weiss 4–6 6–0 6–3; M. Washington (14) – bye; R. Reneberg (11) – bye; S. Stolle (Q) d. T. Zdrazila 3–6 6–4 6–4; S. Youl (Q) d. R. Fromberg 4–6 6–2 6–3; G. Ivanisevic (6) – bye; D. Wheaton (5) – bye; N. Borwick (WC) d. J. Morgan (WC) 6–1 7–5; G. Connell d. C. Wilkinson (Q) 6–7 6–3 7–6; A. Krickstein (12) – bye; T. Woodbridge (13) – bye; J. Grabb d. A. Olhovskiy 7–5 6–3; T. Nelson (Q) d. S. Matsuoka 3–6 6–3 6–4; P. Sampras (3) – bye; D. Rostagno (7) – bye; D. Marcelino d. L. Herrera 6–2 6–1; J. Fitzgerald (WC) d. J. Anderson 6–2 6–3; B. Gilbert (9) – bye; W. Ferreira (16) – bye; D. Poliakov d. D. Pate 6–0 3–6 6–3; S. Davis d. D. Orsanic (Q) 6–1 6–0; I. Lendl (2) – bye.

2nd round: Edberg (1) d. Lundgren 6–3 6–4; Woodforde d. Masur (15) 6–2 4–6 7–6; Pozzi d. Chesnokov (10) 6–1 6–4; Chang (8) d. Kroon (Q) 6–3 6–4; Agassi (4) d. Stoltenberg 6–2 6–2; Washington (14) d. Tarango 7–6 6–2; Reneberg (11) d. Stolle (Q) 4–6 7–5 7–6; Ivanisevic (6) d. Youl (Q) 6–4 6–3; Wheaton (5) d. Borwick (WC) 6–2 6–3; Connell d. Krickstein (12) 6–4 7–6; Woodbridge (13) d. Grabb 6–3 4–6 6–2; Sampras (3) d. Nelson (Q) 4–6 6–1 6–4; Marcelino d. Rostagno (7) 6–4 6–4; Gilbert (9) d. Fitzgerald (WC) 6–2 6–2; Ferreira (16) d. Poliakov 6–4 7–5; Lendl (2) d. Davis 6–4 6–7 7–5.

3rd round: Edberg (1) d. Woodforde 6–4 6–2; Chang (8) d. Pozzi 6–1 6–2; Agassi (4) d. Washington (14) 6–3 6–1; Ivanisevic (6) d. Reneberg (11) 6–3 6–2; Wheaton (5) d. Connell 7–5 6–2; Sampras (3) d. Woodbridge (13) 6–2 6–1; Gilbert (9) d. Marcelino 6–1 6–2; Ferreira (16) d. Lendl (2) 6–4 2–6 6–3.

Quarter-finals: Edberg (1) d. Chang (8) 6–4 7–5; Ivanisevic (6) d. Agassi (4) 7–5 7–6; Sampras (3) d. Wheaton (5) 6–3 4–6 6–4; Gilbert (9) d. Ferreira (16) 6–1 6–4.

Semi-finals: Edberg (1) d. Ivanisevic (6) 4–6 7–6 7–6; Gilbert (9) d. Sampras (3) 1–6 7–5 6–3.

Final: Edberg (1) d. Gilbert (9) 6–2 6–2 6–2.

MEN'S DOUBLES – Final: Grabb/Reneberg d. L. Jensen/L. Warder (5) 6–4 6–4.

SEIKO SUPER TENNIS ($1,000,000)

TOKYO, 7–13 OCTOBER

MEN'S SINGLES – 1st round: S. Edberg (1) – bye; D. Pate d. J. Sobel (Q) 6–3 6–4; G. Muller d. C. Dosedel 7–5 7–6; F. Fontang (15) – bye; A. Chesnokov (9) – bye; P. Cane d. H. Tanizawa (WC) 6–3 6–4; M. Woodforde d. P. Lundgren 6–1 6–3; M. Chang (8) – bye; A. Agassi (4) – bye; L. Herrera d. D. Marcelino 3–6 6–1 6–4; J. Tarango d. N. Kroon (Q) 6–2 1–6 7–5; W. Ferreira (14) – bye; M. Washington (12) – bye; S. Youl d. T. Hogstedt 7–6 6–1; D. Poliakov d. J. Morgan 3–7 3–5; G. Ivanisevic (6) – bye; D. Wheaton (5) – bye; J. Grabb d. B. Kim (Q) 6–2 6–4; G. Pozzi d. A. Olhovskiy 6–3 7–5; T. Woodbridge (11) – bye; W. Masur (13) – bye; G. Michibata (Q) d. R. Leach (Q) 6–2 6–4; S. Davis d. N. Borwick 7–6 7–6; I. Lendl (3) (WC) – bye; D. Rostagno (7) – bye; J. Stoltenberg d. G. Connell 7–5 6–3; J. Anderson d. R. Tsujino (WC) 6–4 7–5; R. Reneberg (10) – bye; S Matsuoka (16) – bye; R. Weiss d. Y. Yamamoto (WC) 6–2 6–3; J. Gunnarsson d. D. Orsanic (Q) 6–3 6–4; B. Becker (2) – bye.

2nd round: Edberg (1) d. Pate 6–2 6–4; Fontang (15) d. Muller 7–6 6–4; Chesnokov (9) d. Cane 7–5 6–3; Chang (8) d. Woodforde 6–1 6–4; Agassi (4) d. Herrera 7–5 6–1; Tarango d. Ferreira (14) 7–6 6–4; Washington (12) d. Youl 6–4 7–6; Ivanisevic (6) d. Poliakov 6–4 6–2; Wheaton (5) d. Grabb 7–6 3–6 6–2; Pozzi d. Woodbridge (11) 7–6 6–3; Masur (13) d. Michibata (Q) 6–0 6–3; Lendl (3) (WC) d. Davis 6–2 6–3; Rostagno (7) d. Stoltenberg 3–6 6–3 6–2; Reneberg (10) d. Anderson 6–4 7–6; Matsuoka (16) d. Weiss 2–6 6–2 7–6; Becker (2) d. Gunnarsson 6–2 6–4.

3rd round: Edberg (1) d. Fontang (15) 6–2 7–5; Chang (8) d. Chesnokov (9) 6–3 6–4; Agassi (4) d. Tarango 6–4 7–6; Ivanisevic (6) d. Washington (12) 7–6 6–7 6–4; Wheaton (5) d. Pozzi 6–0 6–2; Lendl (3) (WC) d. Masur (13) 6–4 6–7 6–2; Rostagno (7) d. Reneberg (10) 3–6 6–3 6–4; Becker (2) d. Matsuoka (16) 2–6 6–3 6–4.

Quarter-finals: Edberg (1) d. Chang (8) 6–2 6–2; Ivanisevic (6) d. Agassi (4) 6–3 6–4; Lendl (3) (WC) d. Wheaton (5) 7–6 7–5; Rostagno (7) d. Becker (2) 7–6 4–6 6–3.

Semi-finals: Edberg (1) d. Ivanisevic (6) 4–6 7–6 7–5; Rostagno (7) d. Lendl (3) (WC) 7–6 6–2.

Final: Edberg (1) d. Rostagno (7) 6–3 1–6 6–2.

MEN'S DOUBLES – Final: Grabb/Reneberg d. Davis/Pate (1) 7–5 2–6 7–6.

STOCKHOLM OPEN ($1,100,000)

STOCKHOLM, 21–27 OCTOBER

MEN'S SINGLES – 1st round: S. Edberg (1) – bye; P. Lundgren (WC) d. M. Koevermans 6–3 6–2; P. McEnroe d. H. Skoff 6–7 6–3 6–3; B. Gilbert (16) – bye; K. Novacek (9) – bye; W. Masur d. J. Gunnarsson (WC) 6–4 6–4; R. Reneberg d. A. Volkov 6–4 6–2; S. Bruguera (8) – bye; M. Stich (4) – bye; A. Krickstein d. L. Pimek (Q) 6–2 2–6 7–6; J. Siemerink d. T. Champion 7–5 6–3; J. Hlasek (14) – bye; G. Ivanisevic (12)

– bye; M. Larsson d. R. Bergh (Q) 6–2 6–1; R. Agenor d. M. Rosset 6–4 6–3; G. Forget (6) – bye; I. Lendl (5) – bye; T. Woodbridge d. T. Enqvist (WC) 7–6, 6–3; C. Bergstrom d. A. Cherkasov 6–3 7–5; P. Korda (11) – bye; D. Rostagno (13) – bye; A. Jarryd d. H. Holm (Q) 6–3 7–6; C. Steeb d. A. Mancini 6–7 6–3 6–4; J. Courier (3) – bye; P. Sampras (7) – bye; T. Hogstedt (Q) d. J. Svensson 7–5 4–6 6–1; D. Engel (Q) d. N. Kulti 5–7 6–4 6–2; D. Wheaton (10) – bye; G. Prpic (15) – bye; J. Connors (WC) d. M. Jaite 6–3 7–6; O. Camporese d. R. Leach (Q) 6–4 6–2; B. Becker (2) – bye.

2nd round: Edberg (1) d. Lundgren (WC) 6–3 6–4; Gilbert (16) d. McEnroe 6–2 6–2; Novacek (9) d. Masur 6–4 6–7 6–4; Reneberg d. Bruguera (8) 7–6 1–6 6–1; Krickstein d. Stich (4) 6–7 7–6 6–0; Hlasek (14) d. Siemerink 4–6 7–6 7–6; Ivanisevic (12) d. Larsson 7–5 6–7 7–5; Forget (6) d. Agenor 6–3 6–2; Lendl (5) d. Woodbridge 7–5 6–2; Korda (11) d. Bergstrom 6–7 7–6 6–3; Rostagno (13) d. Jarryd 3–0 ret.; Courier (3) d. Steeb 6–4 6–4; Sampras (7) d. Hogstedt (Q) 7–6 6–7 6–3; Engel (Q) d. Wheaton (10) 4–6 6–4 7–6; Prpic (15) d. Connors (WC) 7–6 6–7 6–1; Becker (2) d. Camporese 4–6 7–5 6–3.

3rd round: Edberg (1) d. Gilbert (16) 6–2 6–3; Reneberg d. Novacek (9) 2–6 6–3 6–3; Krickstein d. Hlasek (14) 6–2 3–6 6–2; Ivanisevic (12) d. Forget (6) 7–6 7–6; Korda (11) d. Lendl (5) 5–7 6–1 6–4; Courier (3) d. Rostagno (13) 7–5 6–1; Sampras (7) d. Engel (Q) 6–7 6–2 6–4; Becker (2) d. Prpic (15) 7–6 6–1.

Quarter-finals: Edberg (1) d. Reneberg 6–3 2–6 6–3; Krickstein d. Ivanisevic (12) 7–6 1–0 ret.; Courier (3) d. Korda (11) 6–4 6–4; Becker (2) d. Sampras (7) 7–5 7–5.

Semi-finals: Edberg (1) d. Krickstein 6–2 6–2; Becker (2) d. Courier (3) 6–7 6–3 6–4.

Final: Becker (2) d. Edberg (1) 3–6 6–4 1–6 6–2 6–2.

MEN'S DOUBLES – Final: J. Fitzgerald/Jarryd (1) d. T. Nijssen/C. Suk 7–5 6–2.

PARIS OPEN ($2,000,000)

PARIS, 28 OCTOBER–3 NOVEMBER

MEN'S SINGLES – 1st round: S. Edberg (1) – bye; T. Hogstedt (Q) d. J. Grabb (Q) 3–6 7–5 7–6; R. Gilbert (Q) d. A. Jarryd 2–6 7–5 7–5; M. Chang (16) – bye; P. Korda (9) – bye; J. Stoltenberg (Q) d. A. Mancini 3–6 7–5 7–6; W. Masur (Q) d. C. Steeb 7–6 4–6 6–4; S. Bruguera (7) – bye; W. Ferreira (LL) – bye; A. Boetsch (WC) d. A. Chesnokov 6–4 6–2; A. Volkov d. M. Rosset 6–3 6–4; B. Gilbert (14) – bye; G. Ivanisevic (11) – bye; J. McEnroe d. C. Bergstrom 6–1 7–6; A. Cherkasov d. R. Reneberg 6–4 7–5; P. Sampras (6) – bye; G. Forget (5) – bye; P. McEnroe d. M. Jaite 6–3 7–6; Y. Noah (WC) d. F. Santoro 7–5 6–3; D. Rostagno (12) – bye; J. Hlasek (13) – bye; O. Camporese d. T. Champion 7–6 1–6 6–4; J. Connors (WC) d. R. Agenor 5–7 6–4 6–2; J. Courier (3) – bye; K. Novacek (8) – bye; M. Washington d. T. Woodbridge 6–3 7–6; N. Kulti (Q) d. C. Pioline (WC) 7–6 6–2; D. Wheaton (10) – bye; G. Prpic (15) – bye; J. Svensson d. R. Krajicek 6–3 6–2; H. Skoff d. J. Siemerink 6–2 0–6 6–4; B. Becker (2) – bye.

2nd round: Edberg (1) d. Hogstedt (Q) 6–0 6–7 6–3; Chang (16) d. Gilbert (Q) 7–6 3–6 7–6; Korda (9) d. Stoltenberg (Q) 3–6 6–4 7–6; Bruguera d. Masur (Q) 4–6 7–6 6–2; Boetsch (WC) d. Ferreira (LL) 7–5 6–3; Volkov d. Gilbert (14) 6–2 2–6 6–3; Ivanisevic (11) d. J. McEnroe 6–4 6–4; Sampras (6) d. Cherkasov 7–6 6–2; Forget (5) d. P. McEnroe 6–3 6–2; Rostagno (12) d. Noah (WC) 6–3 6 3; Camporese d. Hlasek (13) 7–6 4–6 6–3; Courier (3) d. Connors (WC) 6–2 6–3; Novacek (8) d. Washington 6–4 6–4; Kulti (Q) d. Wheaton (10) 6–3 6–3; Svensson d. Prpic (15) 6–2 6–2; Becker (2) d. Skoff 6–2 6–4.

3rd round: Chang (16) d. Edberg (1) 2–6 6–1 6–4; Korda (9) d. Bruguera (7) 6–2 6–4; Volkov d. Boetsch (WC) 7–5 6–2; Sampras (6) d. Ivanisevic (11) 6–3 6–7 7–6; Forget (5) d. Rostagno (12) 4–6 6–3 6–1; Camporese d. Courier (3) 7–6 6–3; Novacek d. Kulti (Q) 6–3 6–2; Svensson d. Becker (2) w/o.

Quarter-finals: Chang (16) d. Korda (9) 7–5 6–1; Sampras (6) d. Volkov 6–2 6–3; Forget (5) d. Camporese 6–1 3–6 6–3; Svensson d. Novacek (8) 6–4 6–2.

Semi-finals: Sampras (6) d. Chang (16) 2–6 6–4 6–3; Forget (5) d. Svensson 7–5 6–4.

Final: Forget (5) d. Sampras (6) 7–6 4–6 5–7 6–4 6–4.

MEN'S DOUBLES – Final: J. Fitzgerald/Jarryd (1) d. K. Jones/R. Leach 3–6 6–3 6–2.

WORLD SERIES

BP NATIONAL CHAMPIONSHIPS ($175,000)

WELLINGTON, 31 DECEMBER–6 JANUARY
MEN'S SINGLES – Quarter-finals: C. Bergstrom d. D. Poliakov (Q) 6–2 7–6; R. Fromberg (3) d. R. Krishnan 5–7 6–4 7–5; O. Camporese (6) d. T. Hogstedt 6–3 7–6; L. Jonsson d. A. Sznajder 6–2 6–2.
Semi-finals: Fromberg (3) d. Bergstrom 6–3 5–7 7–6; Jonsson d. Camporese (6) 5–7 6–3 7–6.
Final: Fromberg (3) d. Jonsson 6–1 6–4 6–4.
MEN'S DOUBLES – Final: L. Mattar/N. Pereira (3) d. J. Letts/J. Oncins (Q) 4–6 7–6 6–2.

AUSTRALIAN MEN'S HARDCOURT CHAMPIONSHIPS ($150,000)

ADELAIDE, 31 DECEMBER–6 JANUARY
MEN'S SINGLES – Quarter-finals: M. Larsson d. P. Kuhnen 7–6 3–6 6–3; N. Kulti d. F. Santoro 6–3 6–0; M. Stich (6) d. J. Arias 3–6 6–3 6–3; J. Courier (2) d. M. Sinner (Q) 7–6 6–3.
Semi-finals: Kulti d. Larsson 7–5 6–3; Stich (6) d. Courier (2) 6–4 7–6.
Final: Kulti d. Stich (6) 6–3 1–6 6–2.
MEN'S DOUBLES – Final: W. Ferreira/S. Kruger d. P. Haarhuis/M. Koevermans (4) 6–4 4–6 6–4.

HOLDEN N.S.W. OPEN TOURNAMENT OF CHAMPIONS ($225,000)

SYDNEY, 7–13 JANUARY
MEN'S SINGLES – Quarter-finals: D. Rostagno d. M. Jaite 6–1 6–3; G. Forget (3) d. F. Santoro 6–1 6–2; M. Stich d. J. Anderson 6–3 6–0; M. Gustafsson d. D. Cahill (WC) 7–5 6–4.
Semi-finals: Forget (3) d. Rostagno 6–0 6–2; Stich d. Gustafsson 7–6 6–4.
Final: Forget (3) d. Stich 6–3 6–4.
MEN'S DOUBLES – Final: S. Davis/D. Pate (1) d. Cahill/M. Kratzmann (2) 3–6 6–3 6–2.

BENSON AND HEDGES NEW ZEALAND OPEN ($150,000)

AUCKLAND, 7–13 JANUARY
MEN'S SINGLES – Quarter-finals: J. Fleurian d. E. Sanchez (1) 6–2 7–6; L. Mattar d. C. Bergstrom w/o; K. Novacek (4) d. L. Jonsson w/o; M. Vajda d. P. Kuhnen 4–6 6–3 6–4.
Semi-finals: Fleurian d. Mattar 3–6 6–4 6–3; Novacek (4) d. Vajda 6–4 4–6 6–0.
Final: Novacek (4) d. Fleurian 7–6 7–6.
MEN'S DOUBLES – Final: S. Casal/Sanchez (2) d. G. Connell/G. Michibata (1) 4–6 6–3 6–4.

MURATTI TIME INDOOR CHAMPIONSHIPS ($600,000)

MILAN, 4–10 FEBRUARY
MEN'S SINGLES – Quarter-finals: C. Caratti (WC) d. N. Kulti 6–3 6–1; C. Steeb d. A. Krickstein (6) 6–3 7–6; J. Hlasek (5) d. J. Gunnarsson 6–0 7–6; A. Volkov (8) d. P. Cash 6–4 6–4.
Semi-final: Caratti (WC) d. Steeb 7–6 6–7 6–3; Volkov (8) d. Hlasek (5) 6–4 6–3.
Final: Volkov (8) d. Caratti (WC) 6–1 7–5.
MEN'S DOUBLES – Final: O. Camporese/G. Ivanisevic (3) d. T. Nijssen/C. Suk 6–4 7–6.

VOLVO TENNIS ($250,000)

SAN FRANCISCO, 4–10 FEBRUARY
MEN'S SINGLES – Quarter-finals: A. Agassi (1) d. K. Curren 6–2 6–4; B. Gilbert (3) d. D. Goldie 6–1 5–7 6–4; D. Cahill (6) d. J. McEnroe (WC) 7–6 3–6 6–3; W. Masur (7) d. D. Pate 6–1 4–6 7–6.
Semi-finals: Gilbert (3) d. Agassi (1) 6–1 6–2; Cahill (6) d. Masur (7) 4–6 6–4 7–5.
Final: Cahill (6) d. Gilbert (3) 6–2 3–6 6–4.
MEN'S DOUBLES – Final: Masur/J. Stoltenberg d. R. Bathman/R. Bergh 4–6 7–6 6–4.

CHEVROLET CLASSIC ($150,000)

GUARUJA, 4–10 FEBRUARY
MEN'S SINGLES – Quarter-finals: S. Matsuoka d. R. Gilbert 6–4 6–2; P. Baur d. D. Perez 6–3 7–6; M. Wostenholme d. H. Holm 2–6 6–3 7–5; F. Roese (WC) d. C. Garner 6–3 1–0 ret.
Semi-finals: Baur d. Matsuoka 5–7 6–3 7–6; Roese (WC) d. Wostenholme 6–3 6–4.
Final: Baur d. Roese (WC) 6–2 6–3.
MEN'S DOUBLES – Final: O. Delaitre/Gilbert d. S. Cannon/G. Van Emburgh (2) 6–2 6–4.

ABN/AMRO WERELD TENNIS TOURNAMENT ($500,000)

ROTTERDAM, 25 FEBRUARY–3 MARCH
MEN'S SINGLES – Quarter-finals: I. Lendl (1) d. J. Hlasek (7) 3–6 6–3 7–5; A. Jarryd d. J. Siemerink (SE) 7–6 6–2; P. Haarhuis d. C. Bergstrom 7–5 6–3; O. Camporese d. K. Novacek (8) 6–4 7–5.
Semi-finals: Lendl (1) d. Jarryd 7–5 6–4; Camporese d. Haarhuis 6–7 6–2 7–6.
Final: Camporese d. Lendl (1) 3–6 7–6 7–6.
MEN'S DOUBLES – Final: P. Galbraith/Jarryd (4) d S DeVries/D. Macpherson 7–6 6–2.

VOLVO TENNIS/CHICAGO ($250,000)

CHICAGO, 25 FEBRUARY–3 MARCH
MEN'S SINGLES – Quarter-finals: J. McEnroe (1) d. A. Mronz w/o; M. Washington d. U. Riglewski 4–6 6–3 6–0; G. Connell d. J. Yzaga 6–4 6–4; P. McEnroe (7) (WC) d. R. Reneberg (2) 6–1 7–6.
Semi-finals: McEnroe (1) d. Washington 7–6 6–7 6–4; McEnroe (7) (WC) d. Connell 4–6 6–4 6–4.
Final: McEnroe (1) d. McEnroe (7) (WC) 3–6 6–2 6–4.
MEN'S DOUBLES – Final: S. Davis/D. Pate (1) d. Connell/G. Michibata (2) 6–4 5–7 7–6.

COPENHAGEN OPEN ($150,000)

COPENHAGEN, 4–10 MARCH
MEN'S SINGLES – Quarter-finals: J. Svensson (1) d. C. Bergstrom (7) 6–4 7–5; J. Hlasek (3) d. C. Saceanu (Q) 3–6 6–4 6–4; T. Woodbridge (6) d. K. Novacek (4) 7–6 4–6 6–1; A. Jarryd (8) d. M. Woodforde 6–1 6–3.
Semi-finals: Svensson (1) d. Hlasek (3) 6–2 1–6 6–3; Jarryd (8) d. Woodbridge (6) 6–0 6–4.
Final: Svensson (1) d. Jarryd (8) 6–7 6–2 6–2.
MEN'S DOUBLES – Final: Woodbridge/Woodforde (1) d. M. Bahrami/A. Olhovskiy 6–3 6–1.

SALEM OPEN ($260,000)

HONG KONG, 1–7 APRIL
MEN'S SINGLES – Quarter-finals: G. Muller d. M. Chang (1) 5–7 6–3 7–6; R. Krajicek d. P. Kuhnen 7–6 2–6 6–1; W. Masur d. F. Barrientos (WC) 6–0 6–1; A. Antonitsch d. A. Mronz 3–6 6–3 6–4.
Semi-finals: Krajicek d. Muller 6–2 6–4; Masur d. Antonitsch 4–6 7–6 6–3.
Final: Krajicek d. Masur 6–2 3–6 6–3.
MEN'S DOUBLES – Final: P. Galbraith/T. Witsken (2) d. G. Michibata/R. Van't Hof 6–2 6–4.

PRUDENTIAL-BACHE SECURITIES CLASSIC ($250,000)

ORLANDO, 1–7 APRIL
MEN'S SINGLES – Quarter-finals: A. Agassi (1) d. C. Adams 6–4 7–6; M. Washington d. B. Gilbert (3) 6–2 6–7 6–2; D. Rostagno (4) d. J. Arias (6) 6–1 6–4; P. Sampras (2) d. D. Pate (8) 6–3 6–3.
Semi-finals: Agassi (1) d. Washington 6–4 7–6; Rostagno (4) d. Sampras (2) 7–5 6–4.
Final: Agassi (1) d. Rostagno (4) 6–2 1–6 6–3.
MEN'S DOUBLES – Final: L. Jensen/S. Melville d. N. Pereira/Sampras 6–7 7–6 6–3.

ESTORIL OPEN ($375,000)

ESTORIL, 1–7 APRIL
MEN'S SINGLES – Quarter-finals: K. Novacek (7) d. J. Sanchez 7–5 6–3; M. Vajda d. F. Clavet 6–2 0–6 6–3; A. Chesnokov (3) d. H. Skoff 6–3 6–1; S. Bruguera (8) d. R. Furlan 6–1 6–3.
Semi-finals: Novacek (7) d. Vajda 7–5 6–2; Bruguera (8) d. Chesnokov (3) 6–4 2–6 6–3.
Final: Bruguera (8) d. Novacek (7) 7–6 6–1.
MEN'S DOUBLES – Final: P. Haarhuis/M. Koevermans (3) d. T. Nijssen/C. Suk 6–3 6–3.

PHILIPS OPEN ($250,000)

NICE, 15–21 APRIL
MEN'S SINGLES – Quarter-finals: M. Jaite d. R. Furlan 6–2 6–1; K. Novacek (6) d. A. Mancini (Q) 6–3 7–6; G. Prpic d. H. De la Pena 7–5 6–2; C. Pioline (WC) d. H. Leconte 6–2 6–4.
Semi-finals: Jaite d. Novacek (6) 4–6 6–4 7–6; Prpic d. Pioline (WC) 6–1 6–3.
Final: Jaite d. Prpic 3–6 7–6 6–3.
MEN'S DOUBLES – Final: R. Bergh/J. Gunnarsson d. V. Flegl/V. Utgren 6–4 4–6 6–3.

KAL CUP KOREA TENNIS CHAMPIONSHIPS ($165,000)

SEOUL, 15–21 APRIL
MEN'S SINGLES – Quarter-finals: S. Matsuoka d. J. Siemerink (1) 4–6 6–2 6–4; P. Baur d. R. Krajicek (4) 7–5 6–7 6–2; J. Tarango d. G. Bloom (6) 6–1 7–6; L. Herrera d. A. Antonitsch (2) 6–1 6–2.
Semi-finals: Baur d. Matsuoka 7–6 6–2; Tarango d. Herrera 2–6 7–5 6–2.
Final: Baur d. Tarango 6–4 1–6 7–6.
MEN'S DOUBLES – Final: Antonitsch/Bloom d. K. Kinnear/S. Salumaa (2) 7–6 6–1.

EPSON SINGAPORE SUPER TENNIS ($250,000)

SINGAPORE, 22–28 APRIL
MEN'S SINGLES – Quarter-finals: J. Stoltenberg d. T. Woodbridge (1) 6–2 7–6; G. Bloom d. G. Michibata (Q) 6–3 6–3; G. Connell d. T. Hogstedt (Q) 7–5 6–4; J. Siemerink (2) d. S. Matsuoka (SE) 6–4 6–4.
Semi-finals: Bloom d. Stoltenberg 3–6 6–4 6–3; Siemerink (2) d. Connell 6–2 6–2.
Final: Siemerink (2) d. Bloom 6–4 6–3.
MEN'S DOUBLES – Final: Connell/Michibata (1) d. S. Kruger/C. Van Rensburg 6–4 5–7 7–6.

XX TROFEO GRUPO ZETA VILLA DE MADRID ($500,000)

MADRID, 29 APRIL–5 MAY
MEN'S SINGLES – Quarter-finals: J. Arrese d. T. Champion 6–4 3–2 ret.; K. Novacek (4) d. F. Davin (6) 6–3 3–6 6–1; M. Filippini (5) d. J. Eltingh 6–4 6–2; J. Sanchez d. G. Lopez (WC) 7–5 6–4.
Semi-finals: Arrese d. Novacek (4) 6–4 6–3; Filippini (5) d. Sanchez 7–5 6–1.
Final: Arrese d. Filippini (5) 6–2 6–4.
MEN'S DOUBLES – Final: G. Luza/C. Motta d. L. Mattar/J. Oncins 6–0 7–5.

BMW OPEN ($250,000)

MUNICH, 29 APRIL–5 MAY
MEN'S SINGLES – Quarter-finals: I. Lendl (1) d. T. Witsken 3–6 6–4 7–5; M. Gustafsson d. U. Riglewski (WC) 6–2 7–5; C. Bergstrom d. L. Jonsson 4–6 6–2 6–0; G. Perez-Roldan (7) d. G. Ivanisevic (2) 7–6 6–1.
Semi-finals: Gustafsson d. Lendl (1) 6–4 7–5; Perez-Roldan (7) d. Bergstrom 6–0 6–0.
Final: Gustafsson d. Perez-Roldan (7) 3–6 6–3 4–3 ret.
MEN'S DOUBLES – Final: P. Galbraith/Witsken (3) d. A. Jarryd/D. Visser (2) 7–5 6–4.

USTA MEN'S CLAY COURTS OF TAMPA ($250,000)

TAMPA, FLORIDA, 29 APRIL–5 MAY
MEN'S SINGLES – Quarter-finals: R. Reneberg (1) d. M. Washington 6–3 6–3; P. Arraya d. K. Evernden 6–7 6–4 6–1; P. Korda (4) d. M. Pernfors (WC) 6–3 6–2; C. Garner d. J. Frana (Q) 4–6 7–6 7–6.
Semi-finals: Reneberg (1) d. Arraya 6–3 6–1; Korda (4) d. Garner 6–4 6–4.
Final: Reneberg (1) d. Korda 4–6 6–4 6–2.
MEN'S DOUBLES – Final: K. Flach/R. Seguso (3) d. D. Pate/Reneberg (4) 6–7 6–4 6–1.

USAIR/US MEN'S CLAY COURT CHAMPIONSHIPS ($250,000)

CHARLOTTE, NORTH CAROLINA, 6–12 MAY
MEN'S SINGLES – Quarter-finals: J. Yzaga (7) d. M. Chang (1) 7–6 6–1; M. Washington d. D. Wheaton (3) 6–7 6–1 6–2; J. Arias (5) d. R. Reneberg (4) 6–4 6–2; J. Frana (Q) d. P. Arraya 6–4 ret.
Semi-finals: Yzaga (7) d. Washington 7–5 6–2; Arias (5) d. Frana (Q) 3–6 6–3 7–5.
Final: Yzaga (7) d. Arias (5) 6–3 7–5.
MEN'S DOUBLES – Final: R. Leach/J. Pugh (2) d. B. Garnett/G. Van Emburgh 6–2 3–6 6–3.

YUGOSLAV OPEN ($250,000)

UMAG, 13–19 MAY
MEN'S SINGLES – Quarter-finals: P. Korda d. R. Reneberg (1) 7–5 6–4; J. Sanchez (6) d. B. Oresar (WC) 6–2 7–6; D. Poliakov (Q) d. F. Clavet (5) 7–6 2–6 6–2; J. Fleurian d. M. Vajda 6–3 6–2.
Semi-finals: Sanchez (6) d. Korda 0–6 7–6 7–5; Poliakov (Q) d. Fleurian 4–6 6–4 6–2.
Final: Poliakov (Q) d. Sanchez (6) 6–4 6–4.
MEN'S DOUBLES – Final: G. Bloom/Sanchez (3) d. Reneberg/D. Wheaton (1) 7–6 2–6 6–1.

INTERNAZIONALI DI TENNIS CASSA DI RISPARMIO ($250,000)

BOLOGNA, 20–26 MAY
MEN'S SINGLES – Quarter-finals: J. Tarango d. J. Oncins 4–6 6–3 6–2; P. Cane (WC) d. T. Muster (3) 7–6 7–5; J. Gunnarsson d. E. Masso 6–0 6–2; O. Camporese (2) (WC) d. L. Mattar (8) 6–2 6–1.
Semi-finals: Cane (WC) d. Tarango 6–4 6–4; Gunnarsson d. Camporese (2) (WC) 7–6 6–4.
Final: Cane (WC) d. Gunnarsson 5–7 6–3 7–5.
MEN'S DOUBLES – Final: L. Jensen/L. Warder (1) d. Mattar/J. Oncins 6–4 7–6.

THE STELLA ARTOIS GRASS COURT CHAMPIONSHIPS ($500,000)

LONDON, 10–16 JUNE
MEN'S SINGLES – Quarter-finals: S. Edberg (1) d. P. Cash 6–3 6–4; M. Washington d. J. Fitzgerald 7–5 6–4; D. Wheaton (6) d. M. Chang (4) 6–3 6–3; A. Jarryd (7) d. G. Connell 6–2 6–1.
Semi-finals: Edberg (1) d. Washington 6–4 6–2; Wheaton (6) d. Jarryd (7) 6–3 6–4.
Final: Edberg (1) d. Wheaton (6) 6–2 6–3.
MEN'S DOUBLES – Final: T. Woodbridge/M. Woodforde (5) d. Connell/G. Michibata (3) 6–4 7–6.

THE CONTINENTAL GRASS COURT CHAMPIONSHIPS ($250,000)

ROSMALEN, 10–16 JUNE
MEN'S SINGLES – Quarter-finals: C. Saceanu d. A. Olhovskiy 6–3 6–2; J. Hlasek (4) d. A. Mansdorf 6–4 6–3; M. Schapers (WC) d. D. Nargiso 7–6 7–5; M. Stich (2) d. R. Krajicek 6–4 7–6.
Semi-finals: Saceanu d. Hlasek (4) 6–3 3–6 7–6; Schapers (WC) d. Stich (2) 6–4 7–6.
Final: Saceanu d. Schapers (WC) 6–1 3–6 7–5.
MEN'S DOUBLES – Final: H–J. Davids/P. Haarhuis d. Krajicek/J. Siemerink 6–3 7–6.

TORNEO INTERNAZIONALE 'CITTA' DI FIRENZE ($250,000)

FLORENCE, 10–16 JUNE
MEN'S SINGLES – Quarter-finals: H. Skoff (1) d. G. Markus 6–1 6–7 6–2; E. Masso d. M. Larsson (6) 6–3 4–6 6–1; C. Costa (Q) d. J. Arias 6–4 6–1; T. Muster d. F. Santoro (8) 6–7 6–1 6–1.
Semi-finals: Skoff (1) d. Masso 6–4 6–4; Muster d. Costa (Q) 6–7 6–1 6–3.
Final: Muster d. Skoff (1) 6–2 6–7 6–4.
MEN'S DOUBLES – Final: L. Jonsson/Larsson d. J.C. Baguena/Costa (4) 3–6 6–1 6–1.

IP CUP ($250,000)

GENOVA, 17–23 JUNE
MEN'S SINGLES – Quarter-finals: C. Steeb (7) d. R. Agenor (1) 6–1 6–4; T. Muster d. C. Pioline 4–6 7–6 6–2; J. Arrese (3) d. R. Azar 6–4 7–5; E. Masso d. J. Fleurian (8) 7–5 6–1.
Semi-finals: Steeb (7) d. Muster 7–5 6–4; Arrese (3) d. Masso 7–6 6–3.
Final: Steeb (7) d. Arrese (3) 6–3 6–4.
MEN'S DOUBLES – Final: M. Gorriz/A. Mora (4) d. M. Ardinghi/M. Boscatto 5–7 7–5 6–3.

DIRECT LINE INSURANCE MANCHESTER OPEN ($250,000)

MANCHESTER, 17–22 JUNE
MEN'S SINGLES – Quarter-finals: P. Sampras (1) d. W. Masur 7–5 6–2; V. Paloheimo d. A. Mansdorf 3–6 6–3 6–4; G. Muller d. T. Witsken 3–6 7–6 6–2; G. Ivanisevic (2) (Q) d. A. Thoms (Q) 7–5 6–3.
Semi-finals: Sampras (1) d. Paloheimo 6–4 7–5; Ivanisevic (2) (Q) d. Muller 7–6 7–6.
Final: Ivanisevic (2) (Q) d. Sampras (1) 6–4 6–4.
MEN'S DOUBLES – Final: O. Camporese/Ivanisevic (4) d. N. Brown/A. Castle 6–4 6–3.

RADO SWISS OPEN ($305,000)

GSTAAD, 8–14 JULY
MEN'S SINGLES** – **Quarter-finals: S. Bruguera (1) d. A. Gomez 7–6 7–6; G. Ivanisevic (4) d. H. De la Pena 6–4 6–2; E. Sanchez (5) d. M. Jaite 6–4 7–5; K. Novacek (7) d. M. Stich (2) 6–3 6–4.
Semi-finals: Bruguera (1) d. Ivanisevic (4) 6–1 7–5; Sanchez (5) d. Novacek (7) 6–2 6–1.
Final: Sanchez (5) d. Bruguera (1) 6–1 6–4 6–4.
MEN'S DOUBLES** – **Final: G. Muller/D. Visser (1) d. G. Forget/J. Hlasek (2) 7–6 6–4.

SWEDISH OPEN ($250,000)

BASTAD, 8–14 JULY
MEN'S SINGLES** – **Quarter-finals: A. Mancini (8) d. M. Larsson 4–6 6–3 6–4; A. Volkov (3) d. L. Jonsson 6–2 6–1; C. Bergstrom d. J. Gunnarsson 3–6 6–2 6–2; M. Gustafsson (2) d. P. Arraya 6–1 6–2.
Semi-finals: Mancini (8) d. Volkov (3) 0–6 6–3 6–2; Gustafsson (2) d. Bergstrom 4–6 6–3 6–2.
Final: Gustafsson (2) d. Mancini (8) 6–1 6–2.
MEN'S DOUBLES** – **Final: R. Bergh/R. Bathman (2) d. Gustafsson/A. Jarryd 6–4 6–4.

MILLER LITE HALL OF FAME TENNIS CHAMPIONSHIPS ($175,000)

NEWPORT, 8–14 JULY
MEN'S SINGLES** – **Quarter-finals: T. Martin d. M. Wostenholme 6–1 6–1; B. Shelton d. C. Van Rensburg (5) 6–4 4–6 6–3; M. Kratzmann d. J. Eltingh (4) 6–4 6–7 6–4; J. Frana (7) d. G. Layendecker 6–3 6–4.
Semi-finals: Shelton d. Martin 7–5 6–4; Frana (7) d. Kratzmann 6–2 4–6 7–5.
Final: Shelton d. Frana (7) 3–6 6–4 6–4.
MEN'S DOUBLES** – **Final: G. Pozzi/B. Steven d. Frana/B. Steel 6–4 6–4.

INTERNATIONAL CHAMPIONSHIPS OF THE NETHERLANDS ($250,000)

HILVERSUM, 22–28 JULY
MEN'S SINGLES** – **Quarter-finals: M. Koevermans d. R. Furlan 6–1 6–1; J. Arrese d. T. Muster (WC) 6–4 6–1; M. Gustafsson (4) d. M. Rosset 6–7 6–2 6–4; K. Novacek (2) d. F. Davin 7–6 2–6 6–2.
Semi-finals: Arrese d. Koevermans 6–3 3–6 6–4; Gustafsson (4) d. Novacek (2) 7–6 6–3.
Final: Gustafsson (4) d. Arrese 5–7 7–6 2–6 6–1 6–0.
MEN'S DOUBLES** – **Final: R. Krajicek/J. Siemerink d. F. Clavet/Gustafsson 7–5 6–4.

PHILIPS AUSTRIAN OPEN ($375,000)

KITZBUHEL, 29 JULY–4 AUGUST
MEN'S SINGLES** – **Quarter-finals: F. Clavet (7) d. M. Zillner (Q) 6–2 6–3; K. Novacek (3) d. H. Skoff (5) 7–5 0–6 7–5; M. Gustafsson (4) d. T. Champion (12) 4–6 6–3 6–1; M. Jaite (8) d. E. Sanchez (2) 6–3 3–6 6–3.
Semi-finals: Novacek (3) d. Clavet (7) 6–3 6–7 6–2; Gustafsson (4) d. Jaite (8) 6–2 6–2.
Final: Novacek (3) d. Gustafsson (4) 7–6 7–6 6–2.
MEN'S DOUBLES** – **Final: T. Carbonell/F. Roig (6) d. P. Arraya/D. Poliakov 6–7 6–2 6–4.

INTERNATIONAL CHAMPIONSHIPS OF SAN MARINO ($250,000)

SAN MARINO, 29 JULY–4 AUGUST
MEN'S SINGLES** – **Quarter-finals: G. Perez-Roldan (1) d. C. Costa 5–7 6–2 6–1; R. Furlan (5) d. F. Davin (4) 6–2 6–3; R. Azar (6) d. N. Kulti (3) (WC) 3–6 7–5 6–4; F. Fontang d. C. Mezzadri (WC) 6–4 6–0.
Semi-finals: Perez-Roldan (1) d. Furlan (5) 6–2 6–2; Fontang d. Azar (6) 6–2 6–2.
Final: Perez-Roldan (1) d. Fontang 6–3 6–1.
MEN'S DOUBLES** – **Final: J. Arrese/Costa d. C. Miniussi/D. Perez (3) 6–3 3–6 6–3.

LOS ANGELES ($250,000)

LOS ANGELES, 29 JULY–4 AUGUST
MEN'S SINGLES** – **Quarter-finals: S. Edberg (1) d. A. Krickstein (7) 6–4 7–5; B. Gilbert (4) d. S. Bryan (Q) 6–1 6–3; S. Pescosolido d. S. Davis 7–6 6–3; P. Sampras (2) d. A. Mansdorf (8) 6–3 6–4.
Semi-finals: Gilbert (4) d. Edberg (1) 7–6 6–7 6–4; Sampras (2) d. Pescosolido 6–3 6–1.
Final: Sampras (2) d. Gilbert (4) 6–2 6–7 6–3.
MEN'S DOUBLES** – **Final: J. Frana/J. Pugh (4) d. G. Michibata/B. Pearce 7–5 2–6 6–4.

CZECHOSLOVAK OPEN TENNIS CHAMPIONSHIPS ($350,000)

PRAGUE, 5–11 AUGUST
MEN'S SINGLES – Quarter-finals: M. Gustafsson (1) d. A. Boetsch 6–2 6–2; G. Perez-Roldan (6) d. H. Skoff (4) 3–6 6–4 7–6; T. Muster d. M. Larsson 6–3 6–0; K. Novacek (2) d. H. De la Pena (7) 6–0 6–4.
Semi-finals: Gustafsson (1) d. Perez-Roldan (6) 7–5 6–7 6–2; Novacek (2) d. Muster 6–1 2–6 7–5.
Final: Novacek (2) d. Gustafsson (1) 7–6 6–2.
MEN'S DOUBLES – Final: V. Flegl/C. Suk (1) d. L. Pimek/D. Vacek (2) 6–4 6–2.

NORSTAR BANK CHALLENGE CUP ($250,000)

LONG ISLAND, NEW YORK, 19–25 AUGUST
MEN'S SINGLES – Quarter-finals: S. Edberg (1) d. J. Connors (WC) 6–3 4–6 6–4; O. Delaitre (Q) d. T. Champion 6–4 6–4; J. McEnroe (4) d. L. Mattar 6–3 6–1; I. Lendl (2) (WC) d. O. Camporese (8) 7–6 6–3.
Semi-finals: Edberg (1) d. Delaitre (Q) 6–1 7–6; Lendl (2) (WC) d. McEnroe (4) 6–3 7–5.
Final: Lendl (2) (WC) d. Edberg (1) 6–3 6–2.
MEN'S DOUBLES – Final: E. Jelen/C. Steeb (WC) d. D. Flach/D. Nargiso 0–6 6–4 7–6.

OTB INTERNATIONAL ($150,000)

SCHENECTADY, 19–25 AUGUST
MEN'S SINGLES – Quarter-finals: M. Stich (1) d. T. Woodbridge (7) 6–4 6–2; H. Skoff (6) (WC) d. A. Cherkasov (4) 6–7 6–3 7–6; E. Sanchez (3) d. A. Volkov (5) 6–1 7–5; F. Clavet (8) d. S. Bruguera (2) (WC) 6–1 6–4.
Semi-finals: Stich (1) d. Skoff (6) (WC) 7–5 6–1; Sanchez (3) d. Clavet (8) 7–5 6–1.
Final: Stich (1) d. Sanchez (3) 6–2 6–4.
MEN'S DOUBLES – Final: J. Sanchez/T. Woodbridge (1) d. A. Gomez/E. Sanchez (3) 3–6 7–6 7–6.

GRAND PRIX PASSING SHOT BORDEAUX ($300,000)

BORDEAUX, 9–15 SEPTEMBER
MEN'S SINGLES – Quarter-finals: G. Forget (1) (WC) d. L. Jonsson 6–3 6–3; C. Pioline (5) d. F. Santoro (3) 6–3 3–6 6–4; T. Champion (4) d. A. Boetsch 6–2 7–6; O. Delaitre d. A. Mronz (8) 4–6 6–3 6–0.
Semi-finals: Forget (1) (WC) d. Pioline (5) 6–3 6–1; Delaitre d. Champion (4) 6–3 6–1.
Final: Forget (1) (WC) d. Delaitre 6–1 6–3.
MEN'S DOUBLES – Final: Boetsch/Forget (4) d. P. Kuhnen/Mronz 6–2 6–2.

BARCLAY OPEN ($250,000)

GENEVA, 9–15 SEPTEMBER
MEN'S SINGLES – Quarter-finals: T. Muster d. S. Bruguera (1) 4–6 6–4 6–4; A. Medvedev (WC) d. C. Miniussi (Q) 6–4 5–7 7–5; H. Skoff (4) d. H. De la Pena 7–6 4–6 6–1; J. Arrese d. J. Oncins 4–6 6–4 7–5.
Semi-finals: Muster d. Medvedev (WC) 7–6 7–6; Skoff (4) d. Arrese 7–6 6–2.
Final: Muster d. Skoff (4) 6–2 6–4.
MEN'S DOUBLES – Final: Bruguera/M. Rosset d. P. Henricusson/O. Jonsson 3–6 6–3 6–2.

ABERTO DA REPUBLICA ($250,000)

BRASILIA, 9–15 SEPTEMBER
MEN'S SINGLES – Quarter-finals: B. Shelton (9) d. S. Stolle 7–5 6–4; J. Sanchez (5) d. T. Martin (14) 6–2 6–2; A. Gomez (11) d. M. Jaite (4) 6–3 6–3; D. Marcelino (8) d. F. Montana (16) 6–2 6–1.
Semi-finals: Sanchez (5) d. Shelton (9) 1–6 7–6 7–6; Gomez (11) d. Marcelino (8) 6–4 7–6.
Final: Gomez (11) d. Sanchez (5) 6–4 3–6 6–3.
MEN'S DOUBLES – Final: K. Kinnear/R. Smith (4) d. R. Acioly/M. Menezes (8) 6–4 6–3.

SWISS INDOOR CHAMPIONSHIPS ($750,000)

BASEL, 23–29 SEPTEMBER
MEN'S SINGLES – Quarter-finals: J. McEnroe (8) d. C. Bergstrom (1) 7–6 6–4; J. Connors (WC) d. A. Mansdorf 6–3 6–2; J. Hlasek (6) d. K. Curren 6–3 6–4; A. Volkov (7) d. K. Novacek (2) 6–1 6–7 6–3.
Semi-finals: McEnroe (8) d. Connors (WC) 6–1 6–3; Hlasek (6) d. Volkov (7) 7–6 6–7 7–6.
Final: Hlasek (6) d. McEnroe (8) 7–6 6–0 6–3.
MEN'S DOUBLES – Final: Hlasek/P. McEnroe (1) d. Korda/J. McEnroe 3–6 7–6 7–6.

INTERNATIONAL CHAMPIONSHIPS OF SICILY ($300,000)

PALERMO, 23–29 SEPTEMBER
MEN'S SINGLES – Quarter-finals: E. Sanchez (1) d. T. Muster (8) 6–3 7–6; M. Vajda d. D. Nargiso 2–6 7–6 6–3; J. Arrese d. Y. Noah (WC) 6–2 4–6 6–4; F. Fontang d. M. Cierro (WC) 6–1 7–6.
Semi-finals: Sanchez (1) d. Vajda 6–1 6–2; Fontang d. Arrese 6–3 2–6 7–6.
Final: Fontang d. Sanchez (1) 1–6 6–3 6–3.
MEN'S DOUBLES – Final: J. Eltingh/T. Kempers d. E. Sanchez/J. Sanchez (1) 3–6 6–3 6–3.

QUEENSLAND OPEN ($250,000)

BRISBANE, 23–29 SEPTEMBER
MEN'S SINGLES – Quarter-finals: J. Stoltenberg d. B. Gilbert (1) 6–3 6–1; G. Pozzi d. J. Grabb 6–3 1–6 6–3; A. Krickstein (3) d. W. Ferreira (5) 6–4 6–3; A. Chesnokov (2) d. R. Fromberg (8) 6–4 6–4.
Semi-finals: Pozzi d. Stoltenberg 6–3 6–1; Krickstein (3) d. Chesnokov (2) 7–5 6–4.
Final: Pozzi d. Krickstein (3) 6–3 7–6.
MEN'S DOUBLES – Final: T. Woodbridge/M. Woodforde (2) d. J. Fitzgerald/G. Michibata (1) 7–6 6–3.

GRAND PRIX DE TOULOUSE ($300,000)

TOULOUSE, 30 SEPTEMBER–6 OCTOBER
MEN'S SINGLES – Quarter-finals: G. Forget (1) d. M. Rosset (7) 3–6 6–3 6–3; R. Krajicek d. J. McEnroe (6) 6–4 6–4; A. Volkov (5) d. C. Pioline 5–7 7–6 6–2; A. Mansdorf d. C. Bergstrom 6–4 6–4.
Semi-finals: Forget (1) d. Krajicek 7–6 3–6 6–4; Mansdorf d. Volkov (5) 7–5 5–7 6–1.
Final: Forget (1) d. Mansdorf 6–2 7–6.
MEN'S DOUBLES – Final: T. Nijssen/C. Suk (2) d. J. Bates/K. Curren 4–6 6–3 7–6.

ATHENS INTERNATIONAL ($150,000)

ATHENS, 30 SEPTEMBER–6 OCTOBER
MEN'S SINGLES – Quarter-finals: S. Bruguera (1) d. R. Furlan 6–2 6–2; T. Muster (4) d. G. Perez-Roldan (6) 6–3 3–6 7–6; F. Clavet (5) d. L. Jonsson 7–6 6–1; J. Arrese (8) d. M. Koevermans 2–6 6–3 6–4.
Semi-finals: Bruguera (1) d. Muster (4) 1–6 6–2 6–0; Arrese (8) d. Clavet (5) 7–5 6–2.
Final: Bruguera (1) d. Arrese (8) 7–5 6–3.
MEN'S DOUBLES – Final: J. Eltingh/Koevermans (2) d. M. Oosting/O. Rahnasto (3) 5–7 7–6 7–5.

EUROPEAN INDOOR ($300,000)

BERLIN, 7–13 OCTOBER
MEN'S SINGLES – Quarter-finals: A. Jarryd (7) d. M. Stich (1) 6–4 7–6; P. Korda (4) d. A. Volkov (5) 6–3 5–7 6–1; A. Boetsch (Q) d. J. Fleurian 6–0 6–3; P. Kuhnen d. C. Pioline 7–6 6–3.
Semi-finals: Korda (4) d. Jarryd (7) 6–3 1–6 6–2; Boetsch (Q) d. Kuhnen 6–3 6–2.
Final: Korda (4) d. Boetsch (Q) 6–3 6–4.
MEN'S DOUBLES – Final: Korda/K. Novacek d. J. Siemerink/D. Vacek 3–6 7–5 7–5.

RIKLIS CLASSIC ($150,000)

TEL AVIV, 7–12 OCTOBER
MEN'S SINGLES – Quarter-finals: L. Lavalle (Q) d. A. Cherkasov (1) 7–5 6–7 6–3; B. Shelton d. P. Nyborg (Q) 7–6 6–4; C. Van Rensburg d. O. Delaitre (5) 6–3 6–3; G. Bloom d. J. Carlsson (Q) 6–3 7–5.
Semi-finals: Lavalle (Q) d. Shelton 6–4 7–6; Van Rensburg d. Bloom 6–3 2–6 6–3.
Final: Lavalle (Q) d. Van Rensburg 6–2 3–6 6–3.
MEN'S DOUBLES – Final: D. Rikl/M. Schapers (2) d. J. Frana/Lavalle (1) 6–2 6–7 6–3.

LYON GRAND PRIX ($500,000)

LYON, 14–20 OCTOBER
MEN'S SINGLES – Quarter-finals: O. Delaitre (WC) d. J. Kriek 6–2 7–6; S. Bruguera (3) d. K. Curren 6–0 7–6; B. Gilbert (4) d. A. Mancini (6) 6–2 6–2; P. Sampras (2) d. J. Svensson (7) 6–2 6–2.
Semi-finals: Delaitre (WC) d. Bruguera (3) 6–4 6–4; Sampras (2) d. Gilbert (4) 6–1 6–2.
Final: Sampras (2) d. Delaitre (WC) 6–1 6–1.
MEN'S DOUBLES – Final: T. Nijssen/C. Suk d. S. Devries/D. MacPherson 7–6 6–3.

C.A. TENNIS TROPHY ($250,000)

VIENNA, 14 20 OCTOBER
MEN'S SINGLES – Quarter-finals: M. Stich (1) d. A. Jarryd (8) 6–2 6–1; P. Korda (3) d. A. Krickstein 4–6
6–2 6–1; C. Steeb d. J. Frana 7–6 7–5; J. Siemerink d. H. Skoff (7) 6–3 6–1.
Semi-finals: Stich (1) d. Korda (3) 6–4 2–6 6–2; Siemerink d. Steeb 6–3 6–4.
Final: Stich (1) d. Siemerink 6–4 6–4 6–4.
MEN'S DOUBLES – Final: Jarryd/G. Muller (2) d. J. Hlasek/P. McEnroe (1) 6–4 7–5.

BLISS CUP ($150,000)

GUARUJA, 21–27 OCTOBER
MEN'S SINGLES – Quarter-finals: F. Roig d. B. Wuyts 4–6 6–1 6–4; J. Frana d. M. Ruah (Q) 4–6 6–4
7–6; C. Costa d. A. Gomez (WC) 4–6 6–1 6–3; M. Zoecke d. G. Lopez 6–3 4–6 7–5.
Semi-finals: Frana d. Roig 1–6 6–3 6–0; Zoecke d. Costa 6–4 6–2.
Final: Frana d. Zoecke 2–6 7–6 6–3.
MEN'S DOUBLES – Final: J. Eltingh/P. Haarhuis (3) d. B. Garnett/T. Nelson 6–3 7–5.

KOLYNOS CUP ($175,000)

BUZIOS, RIO DE JANEIRO, 28 OCTOBER–3 NOVEMBER
MEN'S SINGLES – Quarter-finals: J. Oncins d. M. Zoecke 6–4 6–2; F. Roig (SE) d. T. Muster (4) 4–6
6–3 6–3; J. Sanchez (3) d. F. Clavet (6) 6–7 6–4 6–2; J. Arrese (2) d. G. Perez-Roldan (8) 6–7 7–5 3–1 ret.
Semi-finals: Oncins d. Roig (SE) 6–4 6–4; Arrese (2) d. Sanchez (3) 6–2 7–6.
Final: Arrese (2) d. Oncins 1–6 6–4 6–0.
MEN'S DOUBLES – Final: S. Casal/E. Sanchez (1) d. J. Frana/L. Lavalle (3) 4–6 6–3 6–4.

DIET PEPSI INDOOR CHAMPIONSHIPS ($500,000)

BIRMINGHAM, 4–10 NOVEMBER
MEN'S SINGLES – Quarter-finals: M. Chang (1) d. R. Agenor 4–2 ret.; R. Reneberg (3) d. W. Ferreira
(5) 6–4 6–4; T. Champion (6) d. M. Washington (4) 6–4 6–4; G. Raoux d. T. Nijssen (Q) 6–7 7–5 6–3.
Semi-finals: Chang (1) d. Reneberg (3) 4–6 6–1 6–2; Raoux d. Champion (6) 6–3 6–4.
Final: Chang (1) d. Raoux 6–3 6–2.
MEN'S DOUBLES – Final: J. Eltingh/P. Wekesa d. R. Bathman/R. Bergh 7–5 7–5.

KREMLIN CUP ($330,000)

MOSCOW, 4–10 NOVEMBER
MEN'S SINGLES – Quarter-finals: M. Gorriz d. C. Steeb 2–6 6–2 7–6; A. Cherkasov (4) d. M. Rosset
4–6 6–1 7–5; J. Hlasek (3) d. J. Siemerink (5) 6–7 6–2 6–2; A. Volkov (8) d. J. Grabb 7 6 4 6 6 3.
Semi-finals: Cherkasov (4) d. Gorriz 6–3 6–4; Hlasek (3) d. Volkov (8) 6–4 6–2.
Final: Cherkasov (4) d. Hlasek (3) 7–6 3–6 7–6.
MEN'S DOUBLES – Final: E. Jelen/Steeb d. Cherkasov/Volkov 6–4 7–6.

BANESPA OPEN ($250,000)

SAO PAULO, 4–10 NOVEMBER
MEN'S SINGLES – Quarter-finals: F. Clavet (7) d. E. Masso 6–1 6–1; J. Oncins d. D. Marcelino (WC)
6–3 7–6; C. Miniussi (LL) d. G. Markus 4–6 6–0 6–4; A. Gomez (WC) d. F. Rivera (Q) 6–4 6–4.
Semi-finals: Oncins d. Clavet (7) 6–4 6–3; Miniussi (LL) d. Gomez (WC) 6–4 6–4.
Final: Miniussi (LL) d. Oncins 2–6 6–3 6–4.
MEN'S DOUBLES – Final: A. Gomez/Oncins (4) d. J. Lozano/C. Motta 7–5 6–4.

IBM/ATP TOUR WORLD CHAMPIONSHIP

Andrew Longmore

It must be a constant source of frustration to the German television companies, whose money was so instrumental in bringing the year-end championships from New York to Frankfurt, that the title of ATP Tour World Champion has not yet left America. In the first year of the new-style end-of-season honeypot, Andre Agassi of Las Vegas made off with the sweetest prize; 12 months later, it was Pete Sampras of Los Angeles who scooped the jar, ending a season of mixed fortunes with a lucrative flourish.

To add insult to injury, the two home champions, Boris Becker and Michael Stich, fell foul of the mathematical complications of their round robin group and were both eliminated before the semi-finals. The Wimbledon champion, Stich, in particular, seemed out of sorts with his game and with the Frankfurt public, who had sided noisily but never unpleasantly with Becker in their group match.

In beating his long-time friend Jim Courier 3–6 7–6 6–3 6–4 in the first all-American year-end final since 1979, Sampras not only added $1,020,000 to his considerable bank balance, but also silenced the whispers which had grown to a clamour during a miserable first half of the year, that winning the US Open had been no more than a fluke. Even after his latest triumph, questions about his concentration and determination remain, but few who watched Sampras's casual dismantling of Ivan Lendl in the semi-final can have any doubts that the Californian has the ability and the style to be a worthy successor to Stefan Edberg, if he puts his mind to it.

Like the Swede, Sampras's game is based on a whiplash serve delivered with the minimum of effort and a fine touch on the volley, but he can be equally devastating from the back of the court, particularly on the backhand, as Lendl and Courier found to their cost. 'He wasn't missing too much from the baseline and when he's not missing from there, together with the serve, he's awfully tough to beat. Not many have beaten him over the past two months,' Courier explained. Only Becker managed to do so in Frankfurt, in the final group match, which at least salvaged some of the German's pride.

The misfortune for organisers and public was that Sampras could not match his best against Edberg, the world number one, who had been forced to pull out at the last minute with a knee injury, prolonged into the New Year by an injured forearm, which was a bad enough blow on its own, but his withdrawal badly unbalanced the two round robin groups as well. Most of the flair was shoehorned into the John Newcombe group of Becker, Stich, Agassi and Sampras, while the less glamorous quartet of Courier, Lendl, Guy Forget and Karel Novacek, rather inappropriately made up the Ilie Nastase Group.

Without Edberg, Courier was thrust into the role of top seed on his debut in the Championships, which was a tall order even for a man of Courier's phlegmatic temperament. Though beaten by Lendl in a group match, the French Open champion coped well with the pressure without ever quite dispelling the impression that his mind had strayed ahead of his body to a planned holiday in Hawaii.

There was a flutter of controversy even before ball had been struck, which centred inevitably on the impish figure of Agassi. The defending champion had managed to sneak into the original top eight (before Edberg pulled out) by virtue of the 420 points he had won 12 months earlier in becoming ATP champion. Many, including Agassi himself, thought it unfair that the points, which were only available to eight players anyway, should be carried over from 1990 into a championships based on performances in 1991. Without those points Agassi would have been below Novacek, ranked nine, Bruguera, Korda and Gustafsson.

The climax of a fine second half to the year for Pete Sampras was the American's spectacular success at the IBM/ATP World Championship in Frankfurt where he beat his old friend Jim Courier in the final.   (T. Hindley)

The ATP's convenient and ingenuous response was that they had simply forgotten to change the rules which apply to every other tournament on the tour – namely, that points come off immediately after, not before, the event. They will, however, be reviewing the system for 1992. Clearly, the fairest solution would be to return to the format of the old Masters and have no points at all, but television want the Agassis of this world rather more than the Gustafssons and they want an open race for the number one position more than both, so points there will be. Realistically, few could argue with the make-up of the field and, in a way, it was fitting that Novacek, who played more tournaments than anyone else and who epitomises the workhorse ethic encouraged by the ATP, should get his reward when Edberg pulled out.

The big Czech very nearly created an early surprise too, nicking the first set of the opening Nastase Group match off Courier in a tight tie-break. On a court very much faster than he liked, Novacek was a break up in the second set before the top seed found his length and began to pummel those huge forehands down the line. As two big men launched groundstrokes at each other, there was little for the artistically minded to ponder. Courier won because his forehand was marginally more accurate and more powerful than Novacek's.

Lendl's defeat of Guy Forget, based on a rock solid serve, was rather more incisive, but a mere sideshow to the main bout of the first evening, which pitted Agassi against Becker. Due to the combined demands of a television game show called the Wheel of Fortune, which the nation wanted to watch more than the tennis, and the German appetite, which could not wait, there was a delay of 70 minutes between the first and second matches, so the final pair did not get on court until nearly ten o'clock and played until well after midnight. Becker was not very happy with his late night sitting nor with his 6–3 7–5 loss, his fifth defeat in a row at the hands of the quicksilver American. 'He is my dark horse,' Becker said. 'He is doing all the things he is not supposed to do.' More importantly, Becker does not do what he should do: get to the net and force Agassi to pass.

The next night Michael Stich followed his countryman to defeat, Sampras serving too consistently for the Wimbledon champion, who looked very tired and disconsolate at the end of a long, hard year. Stich rallied to force the second set into a tie-break but the mid-summer confidence with which he had won four tie-breaks against Edberg and Becker at Wimbledon, had deserted him by early winter and after losing 6–2 8–6 he was left to contemplate the prospect of an all-or-nothing confrontation with Becker, the local hero, in the third group of round robin matches.

In the meantime, Lendl, playing his 12th consecutive 'Masters', had given one of his best performances of a year hit by injury in trouncing Courier 6–2 6–3. Admittedly, the American never found any sort of rhythm and, at times, looked a little disinterested in proceedings, but this was the commanding Lendl of old, infallible from the back of the court, dominant on serve. Courier had not taken a set off Lendl in their three previous meetings and never threatened to do so. Lendl's victory ensured his place in Saturday's semi-final, while Courier had to beat Guy Forget on Friday night to claim his spot, the Frenchman having beaten Novacek 6–3 7–6 in the first match of the evening. So the scene was set for the heavyweight bout all Germany had been anticipating Stich v Becker. Ideally, it should have been the final, but there was still a lot at stake, survival for the winner, almost certain elimination for the loser, revenge, pride, popularity. Though both men tried to play down the significance of the occasion, no one inside the Festhalle or in the German press was going to miss such a heaven-sent opportunity. A survey in a national newspaper had suggested that, despite his defeat at Wimbledon (perhaps even because of it), nine out of ten Germans preferred Becker to Stich, and the overwhelming support for the past over the present Wimbledon champion on the night bore out the statistics and clearly unnerved Stich in much the same way Becker himself had been mentally unable to cope with an all-German final on Wimbledon's centre court. 'There were 8,500 people out there and 8,000 of them were cheering for Boris,' Stich said after his 7–6 6–3 defeat. 'I think that's very sad. It is not a good feeling as a German.'

Stich admitted that he was as interested in the popularity contest as in the tennis and there was a feeling, later accepted by Stich, that he had over-reacted to the crowd's response, which was pro-Becker rather than anti-Stich. After all, Becker was a national hero when Stich was still winning the German junior championships and he is regarded as the local boy in Frankfurt. In Hamburg, Stich's home town, the reaction might have been very different. Other nations could only envy the Germans the luxury of being able to squabble over two Wimbledon champions.

Statistically, the story of Becker's win is simply told. Aces: Becker 11, Stich 6. Double-faults: 1 to 6. First serve percentage: 79 to 45. Stich did not have one break point and once he had lost the tie-break 7–1 and missed a crucial volley to go a break down in the second set, his head dropped lower and lower as the support for Becker grew louder and louder. 'He clearly couldn't take the fact that the crowd were all on my side,' Becker said. In fact, it was a night for national championships, Sampras defeating Agassi 6–3 1–6 6–3 in an explosive repeat of their all-American US Open final 14 months before, and Lendl disposing of the hapless Novacek in a match which might have played to packed houses in Prague but died a death in Frankfurt. Lendl had already qualified at the expense of his countryman anyway. Agassi simply pressed the self-destruct button in the final set, missing several straightforward forehands. Faced by Sampras's unworldly calm, Agassi scurried hither and thither, squeaking like a hyper-active mouse and his errors smacked of overeagerness. He could, though, console himself with the thought that he had lost to Edberg on the way to winning the title 12 months earlier.

By now, the mathematics were becoming tortuous. The two players with the highest percentage of sets won would go through. With Stich's elimination, Germany's hopes rested on Becker, who needed to beat Sampras in straight sets to keep his chances alive. Not one to bother overmuch about the details of life, Sampras discovered from his courtesy car driver that he needed to win one set to qualify and he duly did so with a brilliant series of passing shots in the second set tie-break. I doubt if a better tie-break has been played in such difficult circumstances because the American had been under pressure for the whole match yet suddenly produced a series of flashing returns which stunned Becker and silenced his supporters. Typically, having won the tie-break 7–3 to ensure his semi-final place, the American won just two more points off the Becker serve in the third set, which he lost in 23 minutes. 'He is a phenomenal player,' said Sampras of Becker. 'For me, he is the number one in the world. He has everything.' Fulsome compliments, though, were not going to help Becker's cause. In a Wagnerian twist to the tale, only the tormented Stich could come to the rescue by beating Agassi in the final group match. It proved a false hope. Hard though he tried, Stich could not squeeze one more win from his slender frame against Agassi, who had played 42 fewer singles matches than his opponent during the year. Three players were therefore tied on four points, but Agassi (5 sets out of 7) and Sampras (5 out of 8) had better winning set percentages than the unlucky Becker (4 out of 7) and went through to face Courier, who had narrowly beaten Forget to claim his place, and Lendl respectively. Three Americans and Lendl, who is due to become an American citizen in April 1992.

Plenty of smart money was being put on Lendl, who had been so imperious in qualifying, but, like last year against Edberg at the same stage, he found no answer to a serve-and-volleyer touching perfection. Had he not summoned a vestige of pride to win three of the last four games, his worst beating in 12 year-end championships could have ended in downright humiliation as the Californian, raining down huge serves and peppering the baseline with majestic groundstrokes, won 10 out of 11 games from 1–1 to lead 6–2 5–0. 'Everything I hit turned to gold,' said Sampras.

The other semi-final, a repeat of the French Open final on a rather quicker surface, was a lot more competitive, not least because they are both graduates of the Nick Bollettieri academy in Florida. Courier had enjoyed a marvellous year, winning three titles, including the French, and rising in the rankings from 25 to 2, while Agassi was heading in the opposite direction after a lacklustre year, Wimbledon and Paris excepted. Courier had won both their meetings in 1991, yet the defending champion was the fresher of the two and was highly fancied to reach the final.

Though tired, the sight of Agassi clearly stirred Courier to one last effort. Almost from the opening game he imposed his will on the match, never allowing Agassi to find any rhythm on the service returns or on his groundstrokes. While Courier invariably found the lines, Agassi, to his evident frustration, could not quite master the angles or get the range right. 'Everything clicked today and it feels good because I haven't hit the ball that clean in a while,' Courier said.

Before the final, Courier must have been worried that, after his US Open mauling by Edberg, he might have to face another torrid afternoon against an inspired serve-and-volleyer. But Sampras could not repeat the devastating form of his semi-final and, though he won comfortably enough in the end, he was broken three times in a row in the opening set as Courier tried desperately to prick Sampras's bubble and get in a blow first. Had he won the second set tie-break, he might well have managed it but, in contrast to their semi-final at the US Open, Sampras had the edge, serving two double-faults. By the time Edberg had arrived at courtside ready to collect his prize of a diamond-studded tennis ball, the reward for being the year-end number one, Courier was struggling further and when he missed a routine backhand volley to drop his service in the fourth set, there was no possible way back for the Floridian. Victory, by 3–6 7–6 6–3 6–4, made Sampras, at 20 years and three months, the youngest winner of the year-end championships since John McEnroe in 1979 and earned him $1,020,000. It also capped a remarkable second half of the year for the American, who won 36 of his 42 matches since August 1. Courier too must have been pleased with his week's work which yielded a cheque for $395,000 and another 225 ranking points.

Further riches will be in store for the top 10 players in 1993 when a new series of nine super tournaments, each worth $1.7m, will replace the present championship events. In an effort to strengthen the fields for the major ATP events and provide television with an international series representative of the best, the top 10 will be offered bonuses totalling $5m to play eight out of the nine events, Mark Miles, chief executive of the ATP, announced in Frankfurt. But players will be penalised heavily for not fulfilling their commitment, even if they are injured. Whether these draconian measures will be greeted warmly by the players, who still complain they want to play less, remains to be seen, but the fact that nine tournaments – five in Europe, four in north America – were prepared to increase their prize money suggests that even in a time of recession, the finances of tennis remain healthy. In another announcement, Miles confirmed that two world series events had been scheduled for South Africa in 1992, in addition to the world doubles championships.

ATP TOUR WORLD CHAMPIONSHIP ($2,270,000)

FRANKFURT, 11–17 NOVEMBER
***ROUND ROBIN SECTION – Ilie Nastase Group:* 1st: I. Lendl (TCH)** d. Forget 6–2 6–4; d. Courier 6–2 6–3; d. Novacek 6–2 6–2. **2nd: J. Courier (USA)** d. Novacek 6–7 7–5 6–4; d. Forget 7–6 6–4. **3rd: G. Forget (FRA)** d. Novacek 0 0 7 0. **4th: K. Novacek (TCH).** *John Newcombe Group:* **1st: A. Agassi (USA)** d. Becker 6–3 7–5; d. Stich 7–5 6–3. **2nd: P. Sampras (USA)** d. Stich 6–2 7–6; d. Agassi 6–3 1–6 6–3. **3rd: B. Becker (GER)** d. Stich 7–6 6–3; Sampras 6–4 6–7 6–1. **4th: M. Stich (GER).**
PLAY-OFFS – Semi-finals: Courier d. Agassi 6–3 7–5; Sampras d. Lendl 6–2 6–3. *Final:* Sampras d. Courier 3–6 7–6 6–3 6–4.

PRIZE MONEY and (POINTS): Sampras $1,020,000 (420); Courier $395,000 (245); Lendl $235,000 (180); Agassi $175,000 (120); Becker $175,000 (120); Forget $115,000 (60); Novacek $55,000; Stich $55,000.
TWO ALTERNATES – $25,000 each.

ATP TOUR WORLD DOUBLES FINAL ($1,000,000)

JOHANNESBURG, 18–24 NOVEMBER
***ROUND ROBIN SECTION – Group 1:* 1st: J. Fitzgerald (AUS)/A. Jarryd (SWE)** d. Nijssen/Suk 6–3 6–4; d. Connell/Michibata 7–6 6–4; d. Galbraith/Witsken 6–1 2–6 7–6. **2nd: G. Connell/G. Michibata (CAN)** d. Galbraith/Witsken 6–3 3–6 7–5; d. Nijssen/Suk 4–6 /–6 /–6. **3rd: P. Galbraith/T. Witsken (USA)** d. Nijssen/Suk 7–6 6–2. **4th: T. Nijssen (HOL)/C. Suk (TCH).** *Group 2:* **1st: K. Flach/R. Seguso** (USA) d. Woodbridge/Woodforde 7–6 7–6; d. Jensen/Warder 7–6 6–3; d. Davis/Pate 6–4 6–4. **2nd: T. Woodbridge/M. Woodforde (AUS)** d. Davis/Pate 6–7 6–4 6–4; d. Jensen/Warder 7–6 3–6 6–4. **3rd: L. Jensen (USA)/L. Warder (AUS)** d. Davis/Pate 6–4 6–3. **4th: S. Davis/D. Pate (USA).**
PLAY-OFFS – Semi-finals: Flach/Seguso d. Connell/Michibata 7–6 7–6; Fitzgerald/Jarryd d. Woodbridge/Woodforde 7–5 6–2. *Final:* Fitzgerald/Jarryd d. Flach/Seguso 6–4 6–4 2–6 6–4.

PRIZE MONEY and (POINTS) per pair: Fitzgerald/Jarryd $225,000 (477); Flach/Seguso $125,000 (305); Woodbridge/Woodforde $50,000 (120); Connell/Michibata $50,000 (120); Galbraith/Witsken; $25,000 (60); Jensen/Warder $ 25,000 (60).
ALTERNATE TEAM – $10,000.

BONUSES (based on season-ending points standings):
1. Fitzgerald/Jarryd $100,000; 2. Flach Seguso $80,000; 3. Davis/Pate $70,000; 4. Connell/Michibata $60,000; 5. Woodbridge/Woodforde $55,000; 6. Galbraith/Witsken $50,000; 7. Nijssen/Suk $40,000; 8. Jensen/Warder $25,000.

KRAFT GENERAL FOODS WORLD TOUR

TOUR REVIEW
POINTS EXPLANATION
KRAFT GENERAL FOODS SERIES TOURNAMENTS
VIRGINIA SLIMS CHAMPIONSHIPS

A remarkably consistent year saw Arantxa Sanchez-Vicario of Spain win one title, reach the final of four others (including the French Open where she had beaten Steffi Graf 6–0 6–2) and the semi-finals of eight more to end the year ranked No. 5. (R. Adams)

With earnings in 1991 of more than $1.1 million, Argentina's Gabriela Sabatini took her career prize money beyond $4 million, the fifth woman to pass this landmark since open tennis began in 1968. *(Professional Sport)*

THE KRAFT GENERAL FOODS WORLD TOUR

Barry Wood

The year was dominated by Monica Seles, who confirmed the potential she showed in 1990 by taking over the number one ranking from Steffi Graf on March 11, thus ending the German's record 186 weeks at the top. Although Graf temporarily regained the top spot for two short periods, Seles finished 1991 firmly established as the world's greatest player.

In achieving that, the amazing young Yugoslav, who did not become 18 until after the season had ended in December, set a remarkable record of reaching the final of every tournament she entered. Only Graf had trodden that path before, in 1987 (13 events, 11 titles) and 1989 (16 events, 14 titles). Seles played 16 tournaments, winning 10.

Those titles included three legs of the Grand Slam. Only Wimbledon eluded her, with her late and (at the time) unexplained withdrawal from that event resulting in a storm of outrage and scorn. It was the first time since 1980, when Chris Evert did not play the Australian Open, that the number one player had missed a Grand Slam.

Her elusive behaviour and refusal then to state the reason for her absence, and eventual explanation that she was suffering from a shin splint injury and was afraid of the seriousness of her condition, did not convince everyone of her sincerity. Her image was further tarnished when she withdrew from the Yugoslav *Federation Cup* team at the 11th hour, claiming she was unfit, only to play both the week before in an exhibition, and the week after in San Diego.

It was a sad and unfortunate situation to see the world's number 1 player flouting the rules, and being fined not only for her Wimbledon withdrawal, but for playing exhibitions at Mahwah in July and Las Palmas in October.

None of it however prevented her surpassing Martina Navratilova's record single-year earnings of $2,173,556, set in 1984, during the final tournament of the year, the Virginia Slims Championships. Seles finished with $2,457,758.

Navratilova, however, would have been unconcerned at losing that record for she gained another when, by reaching the Milan final, she overcame Evert's record 1,209 career wins. She then went on to equal Evert's 157 career titles, defeating the world number 1 Seles 6–3 3–6 6–3 in the final of the Virginia Slims of California. Breaking that record eluded her in her next tournament, the Virginia Slims Championships, but no one doubted that she would be able to claim it once the 1992 season got under way.

Graf, having endured a wretched year in 1990, both personally and professionally, managed eventually to pull herself around again, but it was too late to make up the ground she had lost to Seles. The 21-year-old German won her first title of the year, ironically against Seles, at the US Hardcourt Championships in San Antonio. She added the Citizen Cup in Hamburg, then defeated Arantxa Sanchez-Vicario in the German Open final in Berlin and, soon after her 22nd birthday, regained her Wimbledon title at the expense of Gabriela Sabatini, saving two match points in the process. That last victory was especially sweet, for it ended a dismal run of 5 consecutive defeats against her most persistent adversary.

Further titles followed at Leipzig (where she became the youngest player to win 500 matches), Zurich and Brighton. However, she parted company from her coach, Pavel Slozil, in November, after a period of five years.

'It was a little bit tiring for both of us, and you need sometimes to see different faces and hear different ideas,' she explained at the Virginia Slims Championships.

Sabatini, who had re-charged a flagging career during 1990 by enlisting the coaching skills of Carlos Kirmayr and then winning her first Grand Slam title at the US Open, began 1991 with great, but ultimately unfulfilled, promise.

Of the seven tournaments she played between the Australian and Italian Opens, she won five and was runner-up in a sixth. But having been in a position to take over the number 1 ranking during May and August, Sabatini's game slumped instead. She struggled through the second part of the year, blaming her loss of form on being mentally tired after winning so many earlier events.

Her 3rd round loss to Anke Huber in Berlin the day after celebrating her 21st birthday produced the first hiccup. She then reached the semi-finals in Roland Garros and narrowly lost the Wimbledon final to Graf, 6–4 3–6 8–6.

It was following that defeat that her game fell away. She retired with blisters from her Canadian Open semi-final against Jennifer Capriati, and then lost to Kimiko Date in the semi-finals in Los Angeles. Two further defeats by Capriati followed, at the US Open and Philadelphia (although she stopped the run at the Virginia Slims Championships), and she also lost to Nathalie Tauziat in Zurich.

Capriati, who was quick to engage Slozil once he had parted from Graf, continued to develop, rising to 6 in the world. Her quarter-final win over Navratilova at Wimbledon was her first over a top 4 player, and marked the first time since 1977 that Navratilova had lost there before the semi-finals.

Capriati went on to win two successive titles, but received more than a little assistance along the way. Conchita Martinez, who had beaten her in the 4th round of the French Open, pulled a hamstring during their semi-final in San Diego and limped to a 6–4 6–0 defeat. And Sabatini, as previously stated, withdrew in the 2nd set of their semi-final in Toronto.

However, no one could deny the remarkable 15-year-old the credit she deserved for overcoming Seles 4–6 6–1 7–6 in the San Diego final, and Katerina Maleeva 6–2 6–3 in Toronto.

Another top 4 win came at the US Open, where she beat Sabatini in the quarters (she did so again in the Philadelphia semis). Seles gained revenge for San Diego in the US Open semis however, defeating her 6–3 3–6 7–6 in arguably the best match of the year, and again in the Philadelphia final, 7–5 6–1.

Mary Joe Fernandez had a steady year generally free of injury worries, a novelty for her. She reached 10 semi-finals, advancing to 2 finals, both of which she lost to Seles.

Sanchez-Vicario enjoyed a remarkably consistent year, reaching 13 semi-finals in her 16 tournaments. She was runner-up in four events, including the French Open, before ending a title drought that had lasted more than a year by defeating Katerina Maleeva in Washington. She also helped Spain to win the *Federation Cup* for the first time.

Several players outside the top 10 made headlines through the year, and Navratilova was the unfortunate victim of three of them. Tauziat continued to develop, and gained three victories over top 5 players. Having beaten Mary Joe Fernandez in Boca Raton, she overcame Navratilova in Barcelona and then Sabatini at the European Indoor Championships, where she eventually lost in the final to Graf.

Navratilova was also frustrated, by Huber, at Filderstadt, where she lost the Porsche Tennis Grand Prix final 2–6 6–2 7–6. Navratilova, who celebrated her 35th birthday during the week, had not lost to an unseeded player in eight years.

Indeed, she had lost only four times to unseeded players since becoming number one in 1978. The other upsets came against Betsy Nagelsen and Claudia Kohde-Kilsch in 1981, and Kathleen Horvath in the 4th round of the French Open in 1983, her only defeat of that year.

An interesting fact is that by the time Huber was born, on 4 December 1974, Navratilova had already played 37 tournaments as a professional and completed 96 matches. The most remarkable aspect of Huber's victory was that she defeated four players from the top 20 on the way to the final – Lori McNeil, Natalia Zvereva, Zina Garrison and Helena Sukova.

Navratilova also lost to Leila Meskhi in Hilton Head. The Soviet player had already defeated Capriati, and after finishing off Navratilova in a quarter-final suspended overnight because of rain at one set all, she added Zvereva to her list of victims.

Incidentally, Zvereva acted as Meshki's translator at their post-match press conference, which caused much amusement as Meshki revealed to Zvereva the tactics she had used against her. But then, exhausted by her efforts, Meskhi was an easy victim for Sabatini in the final, and was beaten 6–1 6–1.

Other highlights of 1991 included Novotna's victory in Sydney, followed by her quarter-final defeat of Graf at the Australian Open in Melbourne and a first appearance in a Grand Slam singles final where she lost to Seles. Seles, incidentally, first had to save a match point against Mary Joe Fernandez in the semi-finals before winning 6–3 0–6 9–7. Novotna later took the title at Oklahoma, and reached the final in Leipzig.

Elsewhere, history was made when Magdalena Maleeva became the third Maleeva sister to reach a final, although she was defeated 6–4 3–6 7–5 by Sandra Cecchini in Bol, Yugoslavia.

Cecchini and Navratilova, incidentally, are the only active players to have won at least one title in each of the last nine years.

On the same day that Cecchini defeated Magdalena, Manuela was engaged in a final in Barcelona, where she lost to Martinez. That was not the first occasion that two of the Maleeva sisters had played finals on the same day, however. It had also happened on 1 April 1990, when Katerina had defeated Sanchez-Vicario in Houston and Manuela had lost to Seles in San Antonio.

The promising Czech newcomer Andrea Strnadova, 19, reached two consecutive finals, Auckland and Wellington, to build upon a solid Australian Open, and improved her ranking during the year by more than 100 places. That left the former world junior champion just outside the top 30.

And Kimiko Date established herself. Although defeated by Seles in the Los Angeles final after leading the world number 1 by 3–0, she had excelled by qualifying, and then upsetting Sabatini in the semis. Her ranking leapt from 112 to 32, but the rules meant she was still required to qualify for the US Open the following week.

Players who won their first career titles were Veronika Martinek (Brazil), Eva Sviglerova (Auckland), Yayuk Basuki (Pattaya), and the first ever tour victory by an Indonesian, Emanuel Zardo (Taranto), Mary Pierce (Palermo), Katia Piccolini (Republic of San Marino), Isabelle Demongeot (Westchester), and at 24 the oldest since Anne White in 1987 to win her first title, Brenda Schultz (Schenectady), Larisa Savchenko (St Petersburg), Julie Halard (San Juan) and Sabine Appelmans (who won Pheonix and then Nashville the following week).

Few new players appeared. Rather, those who had already shown promise, such as Huber, Appelmans, Rachel McQuillan and Magdalena Maleeva, consolidated their positions. However, Date's exploits in Los Angeles elevated her to a new level, and Strnadova comfortably made the transition from outstanding junior to the adult circuit.

It was Basuki though, playing her first year at the top level, who perhaps made the biggest impact, as she jumped from 266 to the top 40 in the space of a few months.

As the year ended, the Women's Tennis Association announced their intention of breaking away from the Women's International Professional Tennis Council, before the present contracts with sponsors expire, to operate their own tour in 1993 with ten major tournaments offering $1 million in prize money and another ten offering half that sum. Executive Director Gerry Smith explained that they were acting in an effort to give the women's game a more readily identifiable image. They hoped to generate better marketing possibilities and expected to retain a greater portion of the revenue from television rights.

The WIPTC responded by agreeing to set up a working group to examine possibilities for the growth of women's tennis in the future. The WTA Board went along with this compromise which will give them three of the six places on the working group and said they will, after all, honour the present commitments to sponsors.

KRAFT GENERAL FOODS WORLD TOUR 1991

DATE	VENUE	SINGLES FINAL	DOUBLES WINNERS
26 Nov–2 Dec	Sao Paulo	V. Martinek d. D. Faber 6–2 6–4	B. Fulco/E. Sviglerova
31 Dec–6 Jan	Brisbane	H. Sukova d. A. Kijimuta 6–4 6–3	G. Fernandez/J. Novotna
7–13 Jan	Sydney	J. Novotna d. A. Sanchez-Vicario 6–4 6–2	A. Sanchez-Vicario/H. Sukova
14–27 Jan	Melbourne (Australian Open)	M. Seles d. J. Novotna 5–7 6–3 6–1	G. Fernandez/P. Fendick
28 Jan–3 Feb	Tokyo	G. Sabatini d. M. Navratilova 2–6 6–2 6–4	K. Jordan/E. Smylie
28 Jan–3 Feb	Auckland	E. Sviglerova d. A. Strnadova 6–2 0–6 6–1	P. Fendick/L. Savchenko
4–10 Feb	Oslo	C. Lindqvist d. R. Reggi 6–3 6–0	C. Kohde-Kilsch/S. Meier
4–10 Feb	Wellington	L. Meskhi d. Strnadova 3–6 7–6 6–2	J. Faull/J. Richardson
11–17 Feb	Chicago	M. Navratilova d. Z. Garrison 6–1 6–2	G. Fernandez/Z. Garrison
11–17 Feb	Aurora	L. McNeil d. M. Bollegraf 6–3 6–4	L. Gregory/G. Magers
11–17 Feb	Linz	M. Maleeva-Fragnière d. P. Langrova 6–4 7–6	M. Maleeva-Fragnière/R. Reggi
18–24 Feb	Oklahoma City	J. Novotna d. A. Smith 3–6 6–3 6–2	M. McGrath/A. Smith
25 Feb–3 March	Palm Springs	M. Navratilova d. M. Seles 6–2 7–6	—
4–10 March	Boca Rotan	G. Sabatini d. S. Graf 6–4 7–6	L. Savchenko/N. Zvereva
15–24 March	Key Biscayne	M. Seles d. G. Sabatini 6–3 7–5	M.J. Fernandez/Z. Garrison
25–31 March	San Antonio	S. Graf d. M. Seles 6–4 6–3	P. Fendick/M. Seles
25–31 March	Tarpon Springs, FL	—	G. Fernandez/H. Sukova
1–7 April	Hilton Head	G. Sabatini d. L. Meskhi 6–1 6–1	C. Kohde-Kilsch/N. Zvereva
8–14 April	Amelia Island	G. Sabatini d. S. Graf 7–5 7–6	A. Sanchez-Vicario/H. Sukova
8–14 April	Tokyo	L. McNeil d. S. Appelmans 2–6 6–2 6–1	A. Frazier/M. Kidowaki
15–21 April	Houston	M. Seles d. M.J. Fernandez 6–4 6–3	J. Hetherington/K. Rinaldi
15–21 April	Pattaya	Y. Basuki d. N. Sawamatsu 6–2 6–2	N. Miyagi/S. Wibowo
22–28 April	Barcelona	C. Martinez d. M. Maleeva-Fragnière 6–4 6–1	M. Navratilova/A. Sanchez-Vicario
22–28 April	Bol	S. Cecchini d. Mag. Maleeva 6–4 3–6 7–5	L. Golarsa/Mag. Maleeva
29 April–5 May	Hamburg	S. Graf d. M. Seles 5–7 7–6 6–3	J. Novotna/L. Savchenko
29 April–5 May	Taranto	E. Zardo d. P. Ritter 7–5 6–2	A. Dechaume/F. Labat
6–12 May	Rome	G. Sabatini d. M. Seles 6–3 6–2	J. Capriati/M. Seles
13–19 May	Berlin	S. Graf d. A. Sanchez-Vicario 6–3 4–6 7–6	L. Savchenko/N. Zvereva
20–26 May	Geneva	M. Maleeva-Fragnière d. H. Kelesi 6–3 3–6 6–3	N. Provis/E. Smylie
20–26 May	Strasbourg	R. Zrubakova d. R. McQuillan 7–6 7–6	L. McNeil/S. Rehe
27 May–9 June	Paris (French Open)	M. Seles d. A. Sanchez-Vicario 6–3 6–4	G. Fernandez/J. Novotna
10–16 June	Birmingham	M. Navratilova d. N. Zvereva 6–4 7–6	N. Provis/E. Smylie
17–22 June	Eastbourne	M. Navratilova d. A. Sanchez-Vicario 6–4 6–4	L. Savchenko/N. Zvereva
23 June–7 July	London (Wimbledon)	S. Graf d. G. Sabatini 6–4 3–6 8–6	L. Sachenko/N. Zvereva

DATE	VENUE	SINGLES FINAL	DOUBLES WINNERS
8–14 July	Palermo	M. Pierce d. S. Cecchini 6–0 6–3	P. Langrova/M. Pierce
15–21 July	Kitzbuhel	C. Martinez d. J. Wiesner 6–1 2–6 6–3	B. Fulco/N. Jagerman
15–21 July	San Marino	K. Piccolini d. S. Farina 6–2 6–3	K. Guse/A. Nishiya
22–28 July	Westchester	I. Demongeot d. L. McNeil 6–4 6–4	R. Fairbank/L. Gregory
29 July–4 Aug	San Diego	J. Capriati d. M. Seles 4–6 6–1 7–6	J. Hetherington/K. Rinaldi
5–11 Aug	Toronto	J. Capriati d. K. Maleeva 6–2 6–3	L. Savchenko/N. Zvereva
5–11 Aug	Albuquerque	G. Fernandez d. J. Halard 6–0 6–2	K. Adams/I. Demongeot
12–18 Aug	Manhattan Beach	M. Seles d. K. Date 6–3 6–1	L. Savchenko/N. Zvereva
19–24 Aug	Washington DC	A. Sanchez-Vicario d. K. Maleeva 6–2 7–5	J. Novotna/L. Savchenko
19–25 Aug	Schenectady	B. Schultz d. A. Dechaume 7–6 6–2	R. McQuillan/C. Porwik
26 Aug–8 Sept	New York (US Open)	M. Seles d. M. Navratilova 7–6 6–1	P. Shriver/N. Zvereva
16–22 Sept	Tokyo	M. Seles d. M.J. Fernandez 6–1 6–1	M.J. Fernandez/P. Shriver
16–22 Sept	Paris	C. Martinez d. I. Gorrochategui 6–0 6–3	P. Langrova/R. Zrubakova
23–29 Sept	Bayonne	M. Maleeva-Fragnière d. L. Meskhi 4–6 6–3 6–4	P. Tarabini/N. Tauziat
23–29 Sept	St Petersburg	L. Savchenko d. B. Rittner 3–6 6–3 6–4	E. Brioukhovets/N. Medvedeva
30 Sept–6 Oct	Milan	M. Seles d. M. Navratilova 6–3 3–6 6–4	S. Collins/L. McNeil
30 Sept–6 Oct	Leipzig	S. Graf d. J. Novotna 6–3 6–3	M. Bollegraf/I. Demongeot
7–13 Oct	Zurich	S. Graf d. N. Tauziat 6–4 6–4	J. Novotna/A. Strnadova
14–20 Oct	Filderstadt	A. Huber d. M. Navratilova 2–6 6–2 7–6	M. Navratilova/J. Novotna
21–27 Oct	Brighton	S. Graf d. Z. Garrison 5–7 6–4 6–1	P. Shriver/N. Zvereva
21–27 Oct	San Juan	J. Halard d. A. Coetzer 7–5 7–5	R. Hiraki/F. Labat
28 Oct–3 Nov	Phoenix	S. Appelmans d. C. Rubin 7–5 6–1	P. Harper/C. McGregor
4–10 Nov	Oakland	M. Navratilova d. M. Seles 6–3 3–6 6–3	P. Fendick/G. Fernandez
4–10 Nov	Brentwood	S. Appelmans d. K. Adams 6–2 6–4	S. Collins/E. Reinach
11–17 Nov	Philadelphia	M. Seles d. J. Capriati 7–5 6–1	J. Novotna/L. Savchenko
11–17 Nov	Indianapolis	K. Maleeva d. A. Keller 7–6 6–2	P. Fendick/G. Fernandez
18–24 Nov	Madison Square Gardens (Virginia Slims Champs)	M. Seles d. M. Navratilova 6–4 3–6 7–5 6–0	M. Navratilova/P. Shriver

KRAFT GENERAL FOODS WORLD TOUR 1991 – POINTS EXPLANATION

The Kraft General Foods World Tour is the equivalent of the men's IBM/ATP Tour. The 1991 women's tour began on 26th November 1990 with the tournament in Sao Paolo, Brazil and ended with the $1 million Virginia Slims Championships in New York in November 1991, where the $2 million bonus pool was distributed to the top 50 singles players and 10 doubles players. Altogether 60 tournaments (including the four Grand Slam Championships) were staged in 19 countries, plus the season-ending Championships for the top 16 players and the top eight pairs on the Kraft General Foods points table. The player who heads that table at the end of the Championships is automatically declared the official World Champion.

Events carrying points on the 1991 Kraft General Foods World Tour were:

Grand Slam Championships: The Championships of Australia, France, Great Britain and the United States.

Virginia Slims Championships: With $1 million in prize money and $2 million in the Virginia Slims Bonus Pool.

Lipton International Players Championships: A ten-day tournament with minimum prize money for women of $750,000 and a 96 main draw.

OTHER TOURNAMENTS (All of which receive guaranteed WTA player designations)

Tier I: Five tournaments, approved by the Women's International Professional Tennis Council with prize money of $500,000.

Tier II: Fifteen tournaments approved by the WIPTC with prize money of $350,000.

Tier III: Six tournaments approved by the WIPTC with prize money of $225,000.

Tier IV: Twelve tournaments approved by the WIPTC with prize money of $150,000. Additional tournaments in this category will not carry the WTA player designation.

Tier V: Tournaments approved by the WIPTC with prize money of $75,000 or $100,000. The number of tournaments allowed in this category is at the discretion of the WIPTC.

POINTS TABLE (Equal points are awarded for singles and doubles)

Category	Winner	Finalist	Semi-finalist	Quarter-finalist	9–16	17–32	33–64	Round of 128
Grand Slams	820	575	370	190	100	50	25	13
VS Champs(s)	820	575	370	190	100	—	—	—
Lipton Int.	470	330	210	110	55	25	13	6
Tier I	375	265	170	85	45	23	11	—
Tier II	300	210	135	70	35	18	9	—
Tier III	240	170	110	55	30	14	7	—
Tier IV	190	135	85	45	20	10	5	—
Tier V	110	75	50	25	10	6	3	—

Note: In both singles and doubles, no points are awarded to a player until she has completed a match.

1991 BONUS POOLS (US$ – TOTAL $2 million)

Singles ($1,508,000) **1** 500,000; **2** 350,000; **3** 200,000; **4** 100,000; **5** 50,000; **6** 40,000; **7** 35,000; **8** 30,000; **9** 25,000; **10** 20,000; **11** 17,000; **12** 15,000; **13** 12,000; **14** 10,000; **15** 7,000; **16** 6,000; **17** 5,000; **18** 5,000; **19** 4,000; **20** 4,000.
Players 21–30 $3,500
Players 31–40 $2,500
Players 41–50 $1,300

Doubles ($117,000) **1** 50,000; **2** 25,000; **3** 10,000; **4** 10,000; **5** 5,000; **6** 5,000; **7** 4,000; **8** 4,000; **9** 2,000; **10** 2,000.

Incentive Bonus Pool ($200,500) Special prizes for winners of Tier IV and Tier V events, provided they have completed the required number of tournaments.

Special Incentive Fund ($375,000) Designed to encourage top 20 players to play tournaments above their minimum commitment when a tournament does not have its commitment. Payments are made as follows: Players listed 1 and 2 – $75,000; players listed 3 and 4 – $50,000; players listed 5 to 8 – up to $25,000; players listed 9 to 12 – up to $10,000; players listed 13 to 20 – up to $5,000.

FINAL 1991 BONUS POOL PAYOUTS

Monica Seles finished first in the 1991 $2 Million Virginia Slims Bonus Pool Earnings with $550,000 following the conclusiong of the Virginia Slims Championships at Madison Square Garden.

A total of $1,882,775 was paid of a possible $2,208,500 to the top eligible players on the year-long Kraft General Foods World Tour, a total of 61 events. The Bonus Pool is broken down into three categories: Singles, Doubles and Special Incentive Fund.

Of players who accumulated the most Kraft General Foods World Tour points in 1991 and met Bonus Pool eligibility requirements, Seles finished first, Graf was second ($350,000) and Sabatini was third ($200,000).

	Player	Singles	Doubles	Special Incentive Fund	Total
1.	Seles, Monica	$500,000	–	$50,000	$550,000
2.	Graf, Steffi	350,000	–	–	350,000
3.	Sabatini, Gabriela	200,000	–	–	200,000
4.	Navratilova, Martina	100,000	–	8,000	108,000
5.	Fernandez, Mary Joe	40,000	$5,000	25,000	70,000
6.	Garrison, Zina	12,000	5,000	50,000	67,000
7.	Novotna, Jana	30,000	25,000	8,000	63,000
8.	Zvereva, Natalia	4,000	50,000	–	54,000
9.	Sanchez-Vicario, Arantxa	50,000	2,000	–	52,000
10.	Sukova, Helena	10,000	4,000	33,000	47,000
11.	Maleeva-Fragnière, Manuela	25,000	–	21,500	46,500
12.	Fernandez, Gigi	4,000	10,000	13,000	27,000
13.	Maleeva, Katerina	17,000	–	8,000	25,000
14.	Appelmans, Sabine	5,000	–	16,000	21,000
15.	McNeil, Lori	6,000	–	14,000	20,000
16.	Martinez, Conchita	10,000 (50%)	–	6,750	16,750
17.	Savchenko, Larisa	–	10,000	6,000	16,000
18.	Tauziat, Nathalie	15,000	–	–	15,000
19.	Halard, Julie	7,000	–	7,500	14,500
20.	Zrubakova, Radka	3,500	–	8,000	11,500
21.	Meski, Leila	5,000	–	5,000	10,000
22.	Lindqvist, Catarina	3,500	–	6,000	9,500
23.	Capriati, Jennifer	8,750 (25%)	–	–	8,750
24.	Schultz, Brenda	3,500	–	5,000	8,500
25.	Sviglerova, Eva	2,500	–	5,000	7,500
26.	Shriver, Pam	2,500	4,000	–	6,500
27.	Demongeot, Isabelle	–	–	6,000	6,000
T28.	Gildemeister, Laura	3,500	–	–	3,500
	Frazier, Amy	3,500	–	–	3,500
	Kelesi, Helen	3,500	–	–	3,500
	McQuillan, Rachel	3,500	–	–	3,500
	Harvey-Wild, Linda	3,500	–	–	3,500
T33.	Martinek, Veronika	– (50%)	–	2,500	2,500
	Rajchrtova, Regina	2,500	–	–	2,500
	Werdel, Marianne	2,500	–	–	2,500
	Strnadova, Andrea	2,500	–	–	2,500
	Sawamatsu, Naoko	2,500	–	–	2,500
	Paz, Mercedes	2,500	–	–	2,500
	Minter, Anne	2,500	–	–	2,500
T40.	Huber, Anke	1,750 (50%)	–	–	1,750
	Wiesner, Judith	1,750 (50%)	–	–	1,750
42.	Fendick, Patty	650 (50%)	1,000	–	1,650
T43.	Whitlinger, Tami	1,300	–	–	1,300
	Helgeson, Ginger	1,300	–	–	1,300
	Provis, Nicole	1,300	–	–	1,300
	Cunningham, Carrie	1,300	–	–	1,300
	Reinach, Elna	1,300	–	–	1,300
	Durie, Jo	1,300	–	–	1,300
	Hy, Patricia	1,300	–	–	1,300
50.	Cecchini, Sandra	1,250 (50%)	–	–	1,250
51.	Habsudova, Karina	650 (50%)	–	–	650
52.	Paulus, Barbara	625 (25%)	–	–	625
	TOTAL				$1,882,775

NOTE: Mary Pierce, Emanuela Zardo and Katia Piccolini were ineligible for Bonus Pool distribution because they did not meet eligibility requirements pertaining to minimum number of primary tournaments played. Capriati, Martinez, Fendick, Martinek, Huber, Wiesner, Cecchini, Paulus and Habsudova were eligible but only received a certain percentage of their bonus pool distribution due to the fact that Martinez, Fendick, Martinek, Wiesner, Cecchini and Habsudova were one tournament short and Capriati and Paulus were two tournaments short of the minimum requirement.

* Numbers above are rounded off to the nearest dollar.

PLAYER NATIONALITIES AND BIRTHDAYS

The following players have competed in the 1991 Grand Slam Tournaments and Kraft General Foods World Tour:

Name and Nationality	Date of Birth	Name and Nationality	Date of Birth
Aallonen, Anne (FIN)	15/07/67	Casini, Cristina (SUI)	15/02/68
Adams, Katrina (USA)	05/08/68	Caverzasio, Cathy (SUI)	28/09/72
Albinus, Sofie (DEN)	21/09/72	Cecchini, 'Sandra' (ITA)	27/02/65
Alexander, Jillian (CAN)	02/04/68	Chabalgoity, Claudia (BRA)	13/03/71
Allen, Louise (USA)	07/01/62	Chladkova, Regina (TCH)	25/12/71
Alter, Rene (CAN)	14/01/66	Cioffi, Halle (USA)	05/08/69
Amiach, Sophie (FRA)	10/11/63	Coetzer, Amanda (RSA)	22/10/71
Antonoplis, Lea (USA)	20/01/59	Cohen, Celine (SUI)	05/03/67
Apostoli, Julia (URS)	13/08/64	Collins, Sandy (USA)	13/10/58
Appelmans, Sabine (BEL)	12/04/72	Coorengel, Gaby (HOL)	27/11/69
Arendt, Nicole (USA)	26/08/69	Cordwell, Belinda (NZL)	21/09/65
Attili, Susanna (ITA)	07/03/73	Corsato, Luciana (BRA)	21/01/66
Auer, Sabine (GER)	02/10/66	Cruells-Lopez, Marta (ESP)	01/07/75
Avila, 'Neus' (ESP)	26/07/71	Cueto, Isabel (GER)	03/12/68
Babol, Moike (GER)	22/11/74	Cunningham, Carrie (USA)	28/04/72
Bacheva, Lubomira (BUL)	07/03/75	Dahlman, Cecilia (SWE)	24/07/68
Bakkum, Carin (HOL)	25/07/62	Dahlman, Nanne (FIN)	07/09/70
Ballet, Nathalie (FRA)	05/05/67	Daniels, Mary-Lou (USA)	06/08/61
Baranski, Renata (POL)	24/02/65	Date, Kimiko (JPN)	28/09/70
Barclay, Catherine (AUS)	12/06/73	Davenport, Lindsay (USA)	08/06/76
Barnard, Linda (RSA)	10/08/68	De Gionni, Anne (FRA)	14/03/71
Bartlett, Lindsay (USA)	31/07/62	De Lone, Erika (USA)	14/10/72
Bartlett, Shelley (USA)	21/04/65	De Swardt, Mariaan (RSA)	18/03/71
Bartos, Csilla (SUI)	29/03/66	Dechaume, Alexia (FRA)	03/05/70
Bastian, Kristi (USA)	10/09/69	Delisle, Caroline (CAN)	
Basuki, 'Yayuk' (INA)	30/11/70	Della-Casa, Luciana (BRA)	24/02/71
Batut, Valerie (FRA)	12/10/69	Demongeot, Isabelle (FRA)	18/09/66
Baudone, Nathalie (ITA)	12/07/72	Derly, Emmanuelle (FRA)	30/04/70
Benjamin, Camille (USA)	22/06/66	Devries, Ann (BEL)	27/02/70
Bentley, Sarah (GBR)	08/03/73	Dobrovits, Nike (AUT)	02/12/73
Berger, Ilana (ISR)	31/12/65	Dopfer, Sandra (AUT)	25/05/70
Bernard, Melanie (CAN)	14/09/74	Drake, Maureen (CAN)	21/03/71
Bes, Eva (ESP)	14/01/73	Driehuis, Ingelise (HOL)	17/09/67
Bielsa, Rosa (ESP)	09/01/66	Duell, Katharina (GER)	09/04/73
Birch, Sandra (USA)	03/09/69	Dunn, Leisa (AUS)	06/11/70
Biriukova, Eugenia (URS)	18/12/52	Durie, Jo (GBR)	27/07/60
Blumberga, Agnesse (URS)	09/04/71	Edelman, Deborah (USA)	29/11/70
Bobkova, Radka (TCH)	12/02/73	Ekstrand, Maria (SWE)	03/02/70
Bollegraf, Manon (HOL)	10/04/64	Emmons, Jessica (USA)	13/09/70
Bonder-Kreiss, Lisa (USA)	16/10/65	Endo, Mana (JPN)	06/02/71
Bonsignori, Federica (ITA)	20/11/67	Ercegovic, Nadin (YUG)	02/02/73
Boogert, Kristie (HOL)	16/12/73	Etchemendy, Pascale (FRA)	06/06/66
Borneo, Belinda (GBR)	10/11/66	Exum, Julie (USA)	10/05/72
Bottini, Estefania (ESP)	03/02/74	Faber, Donna (USA)	05/07/71
Bowes, Beverly (USA)	09/09/65	Fairbank-Nideffer, Ros (USA)	02/11/60
Brioukhovets, Elena (URS)	08/06/71	Farina, Silvia (ITA)	27/04/72
Brusati, Emanuela (ITA)	19/04/73	Farley, Andrea (USA)	30/09/71
Budarova, Iva (TCH)	31/07/60	Fauche, Christelle (SUI)	09/06/73
Burgin, Elise (USA)	05/03/62	Faull, Jo-Anne (AUS)	13/01/71
Bykova, Natalie (URS)	13/09/66	Fendick, Patty (USA)	31/03/65
Cacic, Sandra (USA)	10/09/74	Fernandez, Gigi (USA)	22/02/64
Callens, Els (BEL)	20/08/70	Fernandez, Mary Joe (USA)	19/08/71
Canapi, Antonella (ITA)	09/12/57	Ferrando, Linda (ITA)	12/01/66
Capriati, Jennifer (USA)	29/03/76	Field, Louise (AUS)	25/02/67
Carotini, Ana (BRA)	20/05/71	Field, Robyn (RSA)	27/06/66
Casale-Telford, Pam (USA)	20/12/63	Foeldenyi, Anna-Maria (HUN)	22/08/74
Casals, Rosie (USA)	16/09/48	Foeldenyi, Diana (HUN)	18/08/76

Name and Nationality	Date of Birth	Name and Nationality	Date of Birth
Foltz, Shawn (USA)	21/12/67	Italiano, Suzanne (CAN)	19/03/73
Fortuni, Federica (ITA)	30/09/74	Jachia, Lorenza (ITA)	24/10/68
Frankl, Silke (GER)	29/05/70	Jackson-Nobrega, Michelle (USA)	28/12/73
Frazier, Amy (USA)	19/09/72	Jagerman-Muns, Nicole (HOL)	23/07/67
Fuchs, Jennifer (USA)	02/07/67	Jaggard, Michelle (AUS)	06/05/69
Fulco, Bettina (ARG)	23/10/68	Jankovska, Ivana (TCH)	17/11/63
Fusai, Alexandra (FRA)	22/11/73	Javer, Monique (GBR)	22/07/67
Gaddie, Rikki (RSA)	02/09/71	Jeyaseelan, Sonya (CAN)	24/04/76
Gadroen, Susan (HOL)	04/05/69	Jonerup, Jonna (SWE)	22/07/69
Gallardo, Aranzazu (MEX)	30/09/73	Jones, Danielle (AUS)	04/03/69
Garrison, Zina (USA)	16/11/63	Jonsson, Amy (NOR)	08/06/67
Garrone, Laura (ITA)	15/11/67	Jordan, Kathy (USA)	03/12/59
Gavaldon, Angelica (MEX)	03/10/73	Kadzidroga, Henrike (GER)	31/05/71
Gerke, Sabine (GER)	15/11/71	Kamio, Yone (JPN)	22/11/71
Gildemeister, Laura (PER)	12/01/64	Kamstra, Petra (HOL)	18/03/74
Giusto, Sabrina (BRA)	31/08/71	Kanellopoulou, Angeliki (GRE)	18/12/65
Glitz, Laura (USA)	17/05/67	Kelesi, Helen (CAN)	15/11/69
Godridge, Kristin (AUS)	07/02/73	Keller, Audra (USA)	17/11/71
Golarsa, Laura (ITA)	27/11/67	Keller, Lisa (AUS)	15/07/69
Gomer, Sara (GBR)	13/05/64	Kerek, Angela (GER)	25/01/72
Gooden, Akiko (USA)	14/02/72	Kidowaki, Maya (JPN)	17/05/69
Goodling, Jennifer (USA)	26/04/62	Kijimuta, Akiko (JPN)	01/05/68
Gorrochategui, Ines (ARG)	13/06/73	Kochta, Marketa (GER)	14/07/75
Graf, Steffi (GER)	14/06/69	Kohde-Kilsch, Claudia (GER)	11/12/63
Graham, 'Debbie' (USA)	25/08/70	Koizumi, Yukie (JPN)	24/01/58
Grande, Rita (ITA)	23/03/75	Komleva, Svetlana (URS)	15/12/73
Graveraux, Olivia (FRA)	27/04/73	Kratochvilova, Monika (TCH)	27/02/74
Green, Lisa (USA)	18/07/68	Kschwendt, Karin (LUX)	14/09/68
Gregory, Lise (RSA)	29/08/63	Kuhlman, Caroline (USA)	25/08/66
Griffiths, Barbara (GBR)	20/05/72	La Fratta, Silvia (ITA)	05/11/67
Grossman, Ann (USA)	13/10/70	Labat, Florencia (ARG)	12/06/71
Grousbeck, Anne (USA)	05/02/66	Lake, Valda (GBR)	11/10/68
Grunfeld, Amanda (GBR)	01/03/67	Langrova, Petra (TCH)	27/06/70
Guerree, Nathalie (FRA)	07/07/68	Lapi, Laura (ITA)	10/09/70
Guse, Kerry-Anne (AUS)	04/12/72	Laskova, Leona (TCH)	07/04/70
Habsudova, Karina (TCH)	02/08/73	Laval, Maider (FRA)	18/05/70
Hack, Sabine (GER)	07/12/69	Leand, Andrea (USA)	18/01/64
Hakami, Elly (USA)	25/08/69	Lentini, Federica (ITA)	08/09/69
Halard, Julie (FRA)	10/09/70	Limmer, Joanne (AUS)	29/03/74
Hand, Kaye (GBR)	04/10/68	Lindqvist, Catarina (SWE)	13/06/63
Harper, 'Peanut' (USA)	15/08/60	Lindstrom, Maria (SWE)	07/03/63
Harvey-Wild, Linda (USA)	11/02/71	Llorca, Marie-Jose (ESP)	03/04/70
Haumuller, Federica (ARG)	05/12/72	Lohmann, Sabine (GER)	13/03/73
Hausschildt, Tanja (GER)	28/12/72	London, Nicole (USA)	03/02/76
Helgeson, Ginger (USA)	14/09/68	Loosemore, Sarah (GBR)	15/06/71
Henricksson, Ann (USA)	31/10/59	Lucchi, Sabrina (ITA)	15/08/68
Herman, Dierdre (USA)	11/10/71	Ludloff, Heather (USA)	11/06/61
Herreman, Nathalie (FRA)	28/03/66	Ludwig, Audrey (FRA)	16/01/76
Hetherington, Jill (CAN)	27/10/64	Lugina, Olga (URS)	08/01/74
Hiraki, Rika (JPN)	06/12/71	Macgregor, Cammy (USA)	11/10/68
Hodder, Justine (AUS)	10/03/72	Macgregor, Cynthia (USA)	26/03/64
Holubova, Petra (TCH)	12/10/68	Mager, Penny (USA)	11/04/64
Housset, Nathalie (FRA)	29/07/68	Magers, Gretchen (USA)	07/02/64
Huber, Anke (GER)	04/12/74	Makarova, Elena (URS)	01/02/73
Hudson, Laura (USA)	10/12/68	Maleeva, Katerina (BUL)	07/05/69
Humphreys-Davies, Virginia (GBR)	06/01/72	Maleeva, Magdalena (BUL)	01/04/75
Hy, Patricia (CAN)	22/08/65	Maleeva-Fragnière, Manuela (SUI)	14/02/67
Ignatieva, Tatiana (URS)	11/06/74	Malkova, Zdenka (TCH)	19/01/75
Iida, Ei (JPN)	09/09/67	Mall, Anne (USA)	10/12/74
Ingram, Jeri (USA)	11/12/70	Maniokova, Eugenia (URS)	17/05/68
Instebo, Cathrine (NOR)	28/11/73	Marchl, Anke (GER)	27/04/67
Isidori, Simona (ITA)	10/10/67	Marsikova, Regina (TCH)	11/12/58

Name and Nationality	Date of Birth	Name and Nationality	Date of Birth
Martin, Stacey (USA)	13/11/70	Palaversic, Maia (YUG)	24/03/73
Martinek, Veronika (GER)	03/04/72	Pampoulova-Wagner, Elena (BUL)	17/05/72
Martinez, Conchita (ESP)	16/04/72	Papadaki, Christina (GRE)	24/02/73
Martinez, Maite (ESP)	24/11/67	Paquet, Virginie (FRA)	06/05/67
Maruska, Marion (AUT)	15/12/72	Paradis Mangon, Pascale (FRA)	24/04/66
Massart, Virginie (FRA)	18/04/76	Parkhomenko, Svetlana (URS)	08/10/62
Mawdsley, Robyn (AUS)	03/05/71	Paulus, Barbara (AUT)	01/09/70
May, Alycia (USA)	31/01/71	Paz, Mercedes (ARG)	27/06/66
May-Paben, Kathy (USA)	18/06/56	Perez, Pilar (ESP)	22/09/73
McCarthy, Shannon (USA)	19/05/70	Perez-Roldan, Mariana (ARG)	07/11/67
McDonald, Kate (AUS)	21/03/70	Pfaff, Eva (GER)	10/02/61
McGrath, Meredith (USA)	28/04/71	Phebus, Keri (USA)	01/05/74
McNeil, Lori (USA)	18/12/63	Piccini, Claudia (ITA)	30/05/68
McQuillan, Rachel (AUS)	02/12/71	Piccolini, Katia (ITA)	15/01/73
Medvedeva, Natalia (URS)	15/11/71	Pierce, Mary (FRA)	15/01/75
Meier, Silke (GER)	13/07/68	Pizzichini, Gloria (ITA)	24/07/75
Melicharova, Eva (TCH)	20/02/70	Pleming, Louise (AUS)	22/06/67
Meskhi, Leila (URS)	05/06/68	Po, Kimberly (USA)	20/10/71
Milnedland, Allegra (USA)	13/01/72	Podlahova, Sylvia (TCH)	09/03/70
Miller, Patricia (URU)	31/01/72	Popp, Anouschka (GER)	19/07/72
Milvidskaia, Viktoria (URS)	20/04/67	Porwik, Claudia (GER)	14/11/68
Minter, Anne (AUS)	03/04/63	Pospisilova, Jana (TCH)	23/03/70
Miro, Gisele (BRA)	01/11/68	Pratt, Nicole (AUS)	05/03/73
Miyagi, Nana (JPN)	10/04/71	Prausa, Wendy (USA)	29/09/60
Miyauchi, Misumi (JPN)	06/09/71	Price, Tessa (RSA)	
Mizokuchi, Miki (JPN)	13/05/65	Priller, Ulrike (AUT)	06/01/73
Monami, Dominique (BEL)	31/05/73	Probst, Wiltrud (GER)	29/05/69
Moore, Joanne (GBR)	09/03/76	Provis, Nicole (AUS)	22/09/69
Moreno, Jorgelina (ARG)	05/05/70	Quentrec, Karine (FRA)	21/10/69
Moreno, Paulette (HKG)	12/03/69	Quintana, Ana-Belen (ESP)	22/10/71
Moros, Cristina (USA)	10/02/77	Radford, Kristine (AUS)	03/03/70
Morton, Tracey (AUS)	18/12/67	Rajchrtova, Regina (TCH)	05/02/68
Mosca, Gabriela (ARG)	12/08/69	Raymond, Lisa (USA)	10/08/73
Mothes, Catherine (FRA)	07/06/70	Reece, Stephanie (USA)	24/04/70
Mueller, Andrea (GER)	21/08/65	Reggi Concato, Raffaella (ITA)	27/11/65
Mulej, Barbara (YUG)	29/05/74	Rehe, Stephanie (USA)	05/11/69
Na, Hu (USA)	16/04/63	Rehmke, Stefanie (GER)	23/11/70
Nabors, Lynn (USA)	18/10/66	Reichel, Sandra (AUT)	24/06/71
Nagano, Hiromi (JPN)	20/07/71	Reinach, Elna (RSA)	02/12/68
Nagatsuka, Kyoko (JPN)	22/02/74	Reinstadler, Beate (AUT)	20/05/67
Nagelsen, Betsy (USA)	23/10/56	Reis, Ronni (USA)	10/05/66
Navarro, Barbara (ESP)	09/04/73	Richardson, Julie (NZL)	30/03/67
Navratilova, Martina (USA)	18/10/56	Rinaldi, Kathy (USA)	24/03/67
Nelson, Pam (USA)	01/07/75	Ritter, Petra (AUT)	24/05/72
Nelson, Wendy (USA)	01/10/68	Rittner, Barbara (GER)	25/04/73
Niox-Chateau, Sybille (FRA)	19/10/69	Romand, Agnes (FRA)	10/03/69
Nishiya, Akemi (JPN)	11/03/65	Romano, Barbara (ITA)	14/01/65
Nohakova, Alice (TCH)	20/06/67	Romano, Francesca (ITA)	07/02/71
Novelo, 'Lupita' (MEX)	05/05/67	Rossides, Eleni (HOL)	23/10/67
Novotna, Jana (TCH)	02/10/68	Rottier, Stephanie (NED)	12/01/74
Nowak, Katarzyna (POL)	13/01/69	Ruano, Virginia (ESP)	21/09/73
O'Reilly, Christine (USA)	18/01/68	Rubin, Chanda (USA)	18/02/76
O'Reilly, Patty (USA)	18/01/68	Sabas, Sylvie (FRA)	19/02/72
O'Reilly, Terri (USA)	18/01/68	Sabatini, Gabriela (ARG)	16/05/70
Oeljeklaus, Katja (GER)	10/02/71	Salmon, Julie (GBR)	08/07/65
Ohlsson, Sheila		Salvi, Cristina (ITA)	15/05/70
Okagawa, Emiko (JPN)	26/12/64	Sampras, Stella (USA)	09/03/69
Okamoto, Kumiko (JPN)	19/02/65	Sanchez-Vicario, Arantxa (ESP)	18/12/71
Ordinaga, Elena (ESP)	23/04/69	Santrock, Jennifer (USA)	26/02/69
Oremans, Miriam (HOL)	19/09/72	Savchenko-Neiland, Larisa (URS)	21/07/66
Ortuno, Alicia (ESP)	02/05/76	Savoldi, Elena (ITA)	11/11/72
Paganini, Marcia (BRA)	26/10/73	Sawamatsu, Naoko (JPN)	23/03/73

Name and Nationality	Date of Birth	Name and Nationality	Date of Birth
Schefflin, Stacey (USA)	19/03/68	Tella, Luciana (BRA)	31/12/69
Schenck, Sylvia (USA)	27/01/64	Temesvari, Andrea (HUN)	26/04/66
Schett, Barbara (AUT)	10/03/76	Ter Riet, Hellas (HOL)	21/06/68
Scheuer-Larsen, Tine (DEN)	13/03/66	Tessi, Cristina (ARG)	20/07/72
Schilder, Simone (HOL)	07/04/67	Testud, Sandrine (FRA)	03/04/72
Schneider, Caroline (GER)	06/01/73	Thampensri, Orawan (THA)	25/05/70
Schultz, Brenda (HOL)	28/12/70	Thompson, Clare (AUS)	10/06/63
Schwartz, Amy (USA)	02/09/69	Thoren, Petra (FIN)	08/08/69
Scott, Alison (AUS)	08/02/68	Tiezzi, Andrea (ARG)	26/11/64
Seemann, Lisa (USA)	08/01/62	Tokiwa, Shizuka (JPN)	14/06/74
Segal, Yael (ISR)	21/07/72	Toleafoa, Claudine (NZL)	28/02/70
Segura, Ana (ESP)	05/02/69	Toschi, Giulia (ITA)	18/01/72
Seles, Monica (YUG)	02/12/73	Trupia, Maria-Antonietta (ITA)	19/04/66
Sharpe, Kirrily (AUS)	25/02/73	Tschan, Natalie (SUI)	13/10/71
Shiflet, Julie (USA)	07/10/72	Van Buuren, Amy (HOL)	20/05/69
Shriver, Pam (USA)	04/07/62	Van Den Berg, Helen (HOL)	20/02/72
Singer, Christina (GER)	27/07/68	Van Lottum, Noelle (FRA)	12/07/72
Sloane-Lundy, Susan (USA)	05/12/70	Van Wijk, Jackie (HOL)	28/10/64
Smashnova, Anna (ISR)	16/07/76	Varas, Inmaculada (ESP)	08/12/64
Smith, Anne (USA)	01/07/59	Vasquez, Pilar (PER)	15/05/63
Smith, Samantha (GBR)	27/11/71	Vieira, Andrea (BRA)	05/02/71
Smoller, Jill (USA)	04/09/64	Vildova, Helena (TCH)	19/03/72
Smylie, Elizabeth (AUS)	11/04/63	Viqueira, Emilie (USA)	21/03/69
Sodupe, Niurka (USA)	19/04/69	Vis, Caroline (HOL)	04/03/70
Sommerville, Betsy (USA)	27/11/67	Wamelenk, Dorien (HOL)	24/12/70
Souto, Janet (ESP)	22/11/67	Wasserman, Sandra (BEL)	10/03/70
Souto, Ninoska (ESP)	09/12/68	Watanabe, Jolene (USA)	31/08/68
Spadea, Diana (USA)	29/10/75	Weerasuriya, Lihini (SRI)	20/02/72
Spadea, Luanne (USA)	28/12/72	Werdel, Marianne (USA)	17/10/67
Spirlea, Irina (ROM)	26/03/74	White, Anne (USA)	28/09/61
Sprung, Heidi (AUT)	10/01/69	White, Robin (USA)	10/12/63
Stacey, Louise (AUS)	10/01/72	Whitlinger, Tami (USA)	13/11/68
Stafford, Shaun (USA)	13/12/68	Whitlinger, Teri (USA)	13/11/68
Steinmetz, Kim (USA)	22/12/57	Whittington, Tammy (USA)	12/10/65
Strandlund, Maria (SWE)	17/08/69	Wibowo, Suzanna (INA)	25/11/63
Strnadova, Andrea (TCH)	28/05/72	Wiesner, Judith (AUT)	02/03/66
Strnadova, Jana (TCH)	25/05/72	Wittke, Maya (GER)	17/07/74
Strnadova, Nikola (TCH)	28/05/75	Wood, Clare (GBR)	08/03/68
Stubbs, Rennae (AUS)	26/03/71	Wood, Jane (GBR)	20/03/68
Studnicka, Petra (GER)	01/01/75	Woolcock, Angie (AUS)	02/02/73
Suire, Catherine (FRA)	15/09/59	Wreem, Michele (USA)	06/06/66
Sukova, Helena (TCH)	23/02/65	Yanagi, Masako (JPN)	11/11/59
Sviglerova, Eva (TCH)	13/07/71	Yokobori, Miki (JPN)	13/05/75
Szabova, Denisa (TCH)	18/11/68	Zajacova, Katerina (TCH)	25/07/75
Takagi, Tamaka (JPN)	30/12/65	Zaltz, Limor (ISR)	08/07/73
Tanaka, Yuka (JPN)	21/08/74	Zardo, Emanuela (SUI)	24/04/70
Tanvier, Catherine (FRA)	28/05/65	Zivec-Skulj, Maja (GER)	25/09/73
Tarabini, Patricia (ARG)	06/08/68	Zrubakova, 'Radka' (TCH)	26/12/70
Tauziat, Nathalie (FRA)	17/10/67	Zugasti, Agnes (FRA)	15/05/72
Taylor, Jane (AUS)	07/11/72	Zvereva, Natalia (URS)	16/04/71

A quarter-finalist in Sydney, the eldest of the three Maleeva sisters, Manuela, 25, is married to Swiss coach François Fragnière and has been a member of the exclusive top ten club since 1984. *(R. Adams)*

KRAFT GENERAL FOODS WORLD TOUR

Tournaments with prize money of $225,000 and above

THE HOLDEN NSW OPEN ($225,000)

SYDNEY, 7–13 JANUARY

WOMEN'S SINGLES – 1st round: M.J. Fernandez (1) – bye; P. Hy d. M. Paz 6–4 6–2; C. Tanvier d. E. Reinach 7–5 6–3; R. Rajchrtova d. C. Porwik (15) 6–7 7–5 7–6; J. Wiesner (9) d. A. Gavaldon 6–1 6–0; S. Hack d. N. Medvedeva 6–4 7–6; P. Langrova d. R. McQuillan 6–3 5–7 6–2; J. Novotna (6) – bye; M. Maleeva-Fragnière (3) – bye; C. Caverzasio d. C. Lindqvist 6–4 6–3; A. Minter d. S. Stafford 6–3 7–6; S. Appelmans (11) d. G. Fernandez 6–2 6–2; P. Shriver d. I. Cueto (14) 7–6 6–4; K. Godridge d. P. Tarabini 3–6 7–5 7–6; T. Whitlinger d. G. Magers 6–4 6–3; B. Paulus (7) – bye; N. Zvereva (5) bye; P. Fendick d. J. Durie 4–6 6–2 6–4; J. Halard d. C. Wood 6–3 6–3; W. Probst d. R. Reggi (12) 6–4 3–6–3; R. Fairbank (13) d. B. Schultz 4–6 6–2 6–2; N. Herreman d. D. Faber 6–2 7–6; K. Rinaldi d. R. White 4–6 6–2 6–3; Z. Garrison (4) – bye; A. Frazier (8) – bye; E. de Lone d. C. Kohde-Kilsch 6–3 5–7 6–3; N. Provis d. L. McNeil 6–2 6–4; A. Grossman d. N. Sawamatsu (16) 6–1 7–5; L. Gildemeister (10) d. A. Huber 1–6 6–2 6–1; C. Cunningham d. M. Bollegraf 7–6 6–4; A. Dechaume d. E. Smylie 7–6 2–6 6–4; A. Sanchez-Vicario (2) – bye.
2nd round: Fernandez (1) d. Hy 6–4 6–1; Rajchrtova d. Tanvier 6–2 6–3; Wiesner (9) 6–1 1–0 ret.; Novotna (6) d. Langrova 1–6 6–4 6–2; Maleeva-Fragnière (3) d. Caverzasio 6–2 6–1; Appelmans (11) 6–0 6–2; Godridge d. Shriver 7–6 4–6 6–4; Paulus (7) d. Whitlinger 7–5 2–6 6–0; Zvereva (5) d. Fendick 6–2 6–2; Halard d. Probst 6–1 6–0; Fairbank (13) d. Herreman 6–2 3–6 6–4; Garrison (4) d. Rinaldi 6–1 6–3; Frazier (8) d. de Lone 3–6 7–5 6–3; Provis d. Grossman 6–4 6–7 6–2; Cunningham d. Gildemeister (10) 6–1 6–1; Sanchez-Vicario (2) d. Dechaume 6–3 6–1.
3rd round: Fernandez (1) d. Rajchrtova 6–3 6–0; Novotna (6) d. Wiesner (9) 3–6 0–1 ret.; Maleeva-Fragnière (3) d. Appelmans (11) 6–2 3–6 6–2; Paulus (7) d. Godridge 6–1 6–1; Zvereva (5) d. Halard 7–5 7–5; Garrison (4) d. Fairbank (13) 6–3 6–3; Provis d. Frazier (8) 7–5 6–4; Sanchez-Vicario (2) d. Cunningham 6–1 6–1.
Quarter-finals: Novotna (6) d. Fernandez (1) 7–5 6–3; Paulus (7) d. Maleeva-Fragnière (3) 7–6 6–4; Garrison (4) d. Zvereva (5) 6–4 6–3; Sanchez-Vicario (2) d. Provis 7–5 6–2.
Semi-finals: Novotna (6) d. Paulus (7) 7–5 7–6; Sanchez-Vicario (2) d. Garrison (4) 6–2 7–5.
Final: Novotna (6) d. Sanchez-Vicario (2) 6–4 6–2.
WOMEN'S DOUBLES – Final: Sanchez-Vicario/H. Sukova (2) d. G. Fernandez/Novotna (1) 6–1 6–4.

PAN PACIFIC OPEN ($350,000)

TOKYO, 29 JANUARY–3 FEBRUARY

WOMEN'S SINGLES – 1st round: S. Graf (1) – bye; A. Huber d. E. Smylie 6–1 6–4; P. Louie Harper d. A. Kijimuta 6–4 6–2; G. Sabatini (5) d. R. McQuillan 6–7 7–6 6–3; M.J. Fernandez (4) – bye; A. May d. M. Werdel 7–6 6–3; N. Miyagi d. M. Lindstrom 6–2 6–2; K. Date d. N. Sawamatsu (8) 6–4 7–5; P. Shriver d. N. Zvereva (6) 6–2 6–0; R. White d. T. Takagi 2–6 7–6 6–4; J. Durie d. M. Javer 6–3 6–4; M. Navratilova (3) – bye; L. Gildemeister (7) d. K. Okamoto 7–6 7–5; M. Endo d. A. Leand 2–6 6–4 6–3; K. Rinaldi d. M. Kidowaki 3–6 7–5 6–2; Y. Koizumi – bye.
2nd round: Graf (1) d. Huber 6–2 6–3; Sabatini (5) d. Louie Harper 6–4 6–1; Fernandez (4) d. May 6–0 ret.; Miyagi d. Date 7–5 6–1; White d. Shriver 7–5 7–6; Navratilova (3) d. Durie 6–3 4–6 6–2; Gildemeister (7) d. Endo 4–6 7–5 6–3; Rinaldi d. Koizumi 7–5 6–2.
Quarter-finals: Sabatini (5) d. Graf (1) 4–6 6–1 7–6; Fernandez (4) d. Miyagi 6–2 6–0; Navratilova (3) d. White 6–2 6–3; Gildemeister (7) d. Rinaldi 5–7 6–4 6–3.
Semi-finals: Sabatini (5) d. Fernandez (4) 6–3 6–4; Navratilova (3) d. Gildemeister (7) 6–2 7–6.
Final: Sabatini (5) d. Navratilova (3) 2–6 6–2 6–4.
WOMEN'S DOUBLES – Final: K. Jordan/E. Smylie (1) d. M.J. Fernandez/R. White (2) 4–6 6–0 6–3.

VIRGINIA SLIMS OF CHICAGO ($350,000)

CHICAGO, 11–17 FEBRUARY

WOMEN'S SINGLES – 1st round: M. Navratilova (1) – bye; P. Shriver d. M. McGrath 6–2 6–3; A.

Smith d. M.L. Daniels 6–2 7–6; N. Tauziat (8) d. E. Smylie 6–2 6–7 7–5; J. Capriati (4) – bye; T. Whitlinger d. R. White 7–6 6–0; K. Rinaldi d. M. Werdel 6–0 6–2; H. Sukova (6) d. K. Adams 6–4 6–2; A. Frazier (7) d. L. Meskhi 6–2 6–7 6–4; B. Schultz d. C. Lindqvist 7–6 6–3; H. Kelesi d. A. Strnadova 6–4 7–5; J. Novotna (3) – bye; Z. Garrison (5) d. L. Harvey-Wild 6–3 6–3; R. Fairbank d. A. Gavaldon 6–4 6–2; A. Grossman d. G. Fernandez 2–6 7–5 6–3; K. Maleeva (2) – bye.
2nd round: Navratilova (1) d. Shriver 7–6 6–1; Smith d. Tauziat (8) 3–6 7–6 6–3; Capriati (4) d. Whitlinger 6–4 6–1; Sukova (6) d. Rinaldi 6–2 6–2; Frazier (7) d. Schultz 6–3 6–4; Kelesi d. Novotna (3) 2–6 7–6 7–6; Garrison (5) d. Fairbank 6–2 6–2; Maleeva (2) d. Grossman 6–3 6–1.
Quarter-finals: Navratilova (1) d. Smith 6–1 6–2; Sukova (6) d. Capriati (4) 6–4 6–4; Kelesi d. Frazier (7) 7–5 6–3; Garrison (5) d. Maleeva (2) 6–2 1–6 6–1.
Semi-finals: Navratilova (1) d. Sukova (6) 6–3 6–2; Garrison (5) d. Kelesi 6–1 6–2.
Final: Navratilova (1) d. Garrison (5) 6–1 6–2.
WOMEN'S DOUBLES – Final: G. Fernandez/Novotna (1) d. Navratilova/Shriver 6–2 6–4.

VIRGINIA SLIMS OF PALM SPRINGS ($350,000)

PALM SPRINGS, 25 FEBRUARY–3 MARCH

WOMEN'S SINGLES – 1st round: M. Seles (1) – bye; M. Javer d. C. Kuhlman 6–4 6–1; A. Keller d. E. Reinach 2–6 6–0 6–0; S. Appelmans (11) d. L. Harvey-Wild 6–3 6–4; A. Minter d. Mag. Maleeva (16) 3–6 7–5 6–1; P. Hy d. B. Rittner 6–2 7–5; C. Dahlman d. L. Field 7–6 5–7 7–6; A. Frazier (5) – bye; H. Sukova (4) – bye; P. Louie Harper d. P. Fendick 7–6 3–2 ret.; P. Nelson d. Hu Na 7–5 6–4; C. Lindqvist (13) d. N. Miyagi 6–4 6–2; R. Fairbank (10) d. N. Herreman 6–2 6–2; I. Demongeot d. K. Phebus 5–7 6–3 6–4; C. Wood d. M. Pierce 7–6 6–4; H. Kelesi (8) – bye; N. Tauziat (7) – bye; K. Date d. B. Reinstadler 6–3 6–3; K. Kschwendt d. A. Strnadova 6–4 6–4; L. McNeil (12) d. P. Vasquez 7–6 6–3; S. Martin d. M. Werdel (14) 7–5 6–4; T. Takagi d. K. Rinaldi 3–6 6–2 6–4; P. Paradis d. C. Benjamin 6–3 6–4; K. Maleeva (3) – bye; B. Paulus (6) – bye; S. Rehe d. J. Durie 4–6 6–4 6–4; A. Temesvari d. A. Henricksson 7–5 6–4; J. Halard (15) d. J. Watanabe 7–5 4–6 6–3; A. Huber (9) d. R. Simpson 6–3 4–6 6–1; G. Helgeson d. A. Dechaume 6–2 6–2; A. Coetzer d. T. Whitlinger 3–6 7–5 6–0; M. Navratilova (2) – bye.
2nd round: Seles (1) d. Javer 6–3 6–1; Appelmans (11) d. Keller 6–2 6–4; Hy d. Minter 6–1 6–4; Frazier (5) d. Dahlman 6–3 7–5; Louie Harper d. Sukova (4) 7–6 3–6 7–6; Lindqvist (13) d. Nelson 6–1 6–3; Fairbank (10) d. Demongeot 6–7 6–3 6–1; Kelesi (8) d. Wood 6–4 6–4; Tauziat (7) d. Date 6–2 6–2; Kschwendt d. McNeil (12) 2–6 7–6 7–6; Martin d. Takagi 6–3 7–5; Maleeva (3) d. Paradis 6–1 2–0 ret.; Paulus (6) d. Rehe 6–3 6–3; Halard (15) d. Temesvari 6–2 7–5; Helgeson d. Huber (9) 2–6 6–3 6–2; Navratilova (2) d. Coetzer 6–2 6–2.
3rd round: Seles (1) d. Appelmans (11) 6–3 6–0; Hy d. Frazier (5) 4–6 6–4 6–3; Louie Harper d. Lindqvist (13) 3–6 6–4 6–3; Kelesi (8) d. Fairbank (10) 6–2 6–4; Tauziat (7) d. Kschwendt 6–3 6–3; Maleeva (3) d. Martin 6–0 6–2; Halard (15) d. Paulus (6) 3–6 6–2 6–4; Navratilova (2) d. Helgeson 6–0 6–2.
Quarter-finals: Seles (1) d. Hy 7–5 6–2; Kelesi (8) d. Louie Harper 6–4 3–6 6–2; Tauziat (7) d. Maleeva 7–6 7–6; Navratilova (2) d. Halard (15) 6–2 7–5.
Semi-finals: Seles (1) d. Kelesi (8) 6–0 6–3; Navratilova (2) d. Tauziat (7) 6–3 7–6.
Final: Navratilova (2) d. Seles (1) 6–2 7–6.
WOMEN'S DOUBLES – cancelled.

VIRGINIA SLIMS OF FLORIDA ($500,000)

BOCA RATON, 4–10 MARCH

WOMEN'S SINGLES – 1st round: S. Graf (1) – bye; C. Dahlman d. S. Smith 6–0 6–0; A. Strnadova d. J. Halard 6–4 7–5; A. Huber (14) d. N. Herreman 6–3 7–5; M. McGrath (16) d. M.L. Daniels 6–2 6–0; L. Harvey-Wild d. L. Allen 6–4 6–1; L. Bonder-Kreiss d. S. Stafford 6–4 6–1; B. Paulus (6) – bye; M.J. Fernandez (3) – bye; A. Coetzer d. I. Demongeot 6–1 3–0 ret.; L. Ferrando d. E. Pampoulova 6–0 4–6 6–3; L. Gildemeister (12) d. K. Habsudova 6–4 6–3; B. Fulco d. S. Cecchini (10) 6–1 6–0; P. Hy d. J. Durie 6–7 6–1 7–5; P. Louie Harper d. J. Shiflet 7–5 4–6 6–2; N. Tauziat (8) – bye; C. Martinez (5) – bye; C. Porwik d. A. Dechaume 2–6 7–5 6–4; H. Cioffi d. E. Brioukhovets 6–1 6–0; H. Kelesi (9) d. C. Caverzasio 6–1 3–6 6–2; G. Fernandez d. R. Fairbank (13) 4–6 6–4 6–2; S. Martin d. S. Gomer 6–4 6–4; K. Kschwendt d. A. Grossman 6–3 7–5; J. Capriati (4) – bye; N. Zvereva (7) – bye; L. Savchenko d. B. Schultz 7–5 3–6 6–3; R. Rajchrtova d. M. Jackson 6–2 7–6; M. Werdel d. A. Smith (11) 7–5 6–4; N. Medvedeva d. T. Whitlinger 6–3 7–5; E. de Lone d. B. Rittner 3–6 6–1 7–6; G. Sabatini (2) – bye.
2nd round: Graf (1) d. Dahlman default; Huber (14) d. Strnadova 6–2 7–5; McGrath (16) d. Harvey-Wild 3–6 6–3 6–0; Bonder-Kreiss d. Paulus (6) 6–4 6–2; Fernandez (3) d. Coetzer 6–4 6–1; Gildemeister (12) d. Ferrando 7–5 6–4; Hy d. Fulco 7–6 6–2; Tauziat (8) d. Louie Harper 6–0 6–3; Porwik d. Martinez (5) 6–4 3–6 7–6; Kelesi (9) d. Cioffi 6–3 6–1; Fernandez d. Martin 6–3 6–4; Capriati (4) d. Kschwendt 6–7 6–1 6–1; Zvereva (7) d. Suire 7–6 6–4; Rajchrtova d. Savchenko 6–4 7–5; Werdel d. Medvedeva 6–4 4–6 7–5; Sabatini (2) d. de Lone 6–2 6–2.

3rd round: Graf (1) d. Huber (14) 6–0 6–1; McGrath (16) d. Bonder-Kreiss 6–4 6–3; Fernandez (3) d. Gildemeister (12) 7–5 6–4; Tauziat (8) d. Hy 6–2 6–4; Porwik d. Kelesi (9) 6–4 7–5; Capriati (4) d. Fernandez 6–3 6–2; Rajchrtova d. Zvereva (7) 6–3 6–3; Sabatini (2) d. Werdel 6–3 6–0.
Quarter-finals: Graf (1) d. McGrath (16) 6–3 6–1; Tauziat (8) d. Fernandez (3) 6–1 7–5; Capriati (4) d. Porwik 6–1 6–4; Sabatini (2) d. Rajchrtova 6–2 6–2.
Semi-finals: Graf (1) d. Tauziat (8) 6–1 6–2; Sabatini (2) d. Capriati (4) 7–5 6–2.
Final: Sabatini (2) d. Graf (1) 6–4 7–6.
WOMEN'S DOUBLES – Final: Savchenko/Zvereva (2) d. McGrath/A. Smith (4) 6–4 7–6.

LIPTON INTERNATIONAL PLAYERS CHAMPIONSHIPS ($750,000)

KEY BISCAYNE, 15–24 MARCH

WOMEN'S SINGLES – 1st round: S. Graf (1) – bye; E. de Lone d. C. Suire 6–0 6–3; M.L. Daniels d. C. Benjamin 2–6 6–0 6–1; G. Magers (21) – bye; M. Werdel (27) – bye; Mag. Maleeva d. C. MacGregor 2–6 6–4 6–1; C. Wood d. P. Kamstra 6–2 7–5; H. Kelesi (11) – bye; R. Reggi (16) – bye; L. Savchenko d. K. Habsudova 6–2 6–3; L. Ferrando d. N. Medvedeva 6–4 0–6 6–2; M. McGrath (23) – bye; C. Lindqvist (19) – bye; D. Faber d. E. Pampoulova 6–3 7–6; B. Schultz d. S. Martin 7–6 6–4; M. Maleeva-Fragnière (7) – bye; G. Sabatini (3) – bye; A. Henricksson d. S. Schefflin 6–4 6–1; C. Rubin d. M. Laval 6–4 7–5; M. Bollegraf (18) – bye; J. Halard (25) – bye; C. Toleafoa d. P. Vasquez 6–4 6–2; P. Hy d. R. White 6–2 6–0; N. Tauziat (10) – bye; R. Fairbank (14) – bye; M. Pierce d. P. Louie Harper 6–2 6–0; B. Rittner d. S. Loosemore 7–5 6–3; W. Probst (29) – bye; E. Smylie (32) – bye; D. Graham d. K. Date 7–6 3–6 7–5; N. Miyagi d. A. Dechaume 6–4 5–7 6–4; Z. Garrison (5) – bye; N. Zvereva (8) – bye; G. Helgeson d. J. Durie 6–3 6–3; T. Whitlinger d. S. Wasserman 6–3 6–0; E. Sviglerova (30) – bye; R. Rajchrtova (22) – bye; M. Javer d. T. Takagi 6–3 6–2; M. Maruska d. P. Thoren 3–6 6–2 7–6; A. Frazier (12) – bye; L. Gildemeister (13) – bye; C. Dahlman d. C. Mothes 6–2 6–1; P. Shriver d. M. Oremans 6–3 7–5; C. Caverzasio (28) – bye; L. McNeil (17) – bye; K. Quentrec d. I. Demongeot 3–6 6–3 7–5; A. Keller d. K. Rinaldi 7–6 6–3; M.J. Fernandez (4) – bye; J. Capriati (6) – bye; G. Fernandez d. Y. Segal 6–4 6–1; S. Smith d. L. Bonder-Kreiss 6–1 7–5; A. Grossman (26) – bye; S. Rehe (31) – bye; C. Porwik d. L. Harvey-Wild 7–5 6–2; S. Gomer d. N. Herreman 6–4 6–3; B. Paulus (9) – bye; N. Sawamatsu (15) – bye; A. Coetzer d. E. Brioukhovets 7–5 6–4; F. Labat d. N. Housset 7–6 6–2; C. Cunningham (24) – bye; S. Sloane (20) – bye; K. Kschwendt d. R. Simpson 6–3 6–4; H. Cioffi d. P. Fendick 6–4 6–3; M. Seles (2) – bye.
2nd round: Graf (1) d. de Lone 6–1 6–2; Magers (21) d. Daniels 7–5 6–4; Werdel (27) d. Maleeva 6–2 7–5; Wood d. Kelesi (11) 7–5 2–6 7–5; Reggi (16) d. Savchenko 3–6 6–3 6–4; McGrath (23) d. Ferrando 2–6 6–2 6–3; Faber d. Lindqvist (19) 2–6 7–6 6–3; Maleeva-Fragnière (7) d. Schultz 6–3 7–6; Sabatini (3) d. Henricksson 6–1 6–1; Rubin d. Bollegraf (18) 6–2 6–0; Toleafoa d. Halard (25) 2–6 6–1 7–5; Tauziat (10) d. Hy 6–3 6–4; Pierce d. Fairbank (14) 6–2 7–6; Rittner d. Probst (29) 7–6 6–2; Smylie (32) d. Graham 6–3 3–6 6–3; Garrison (5) d. Miyagi 5–7 6–4 7–5; Helgeson d. Zvereva (8) 6–2 6–3; Sviglerova (30) d. Whitlinger 6–7 7–5 6–4; Rajchrtova (22) d. Javer 3–6 6–4 6–1; Gildemeister (13) d. Dahlman 6–3 6–3; Shriver d. Caverzasio (28) 6–1 6–4; McNeil (17) d. Quentrec 6–3 7–5; Fernandez (4) d. Keller 6–3 6–2; Capriati (6) d. Fernandez 6–3 6–2; Grossman (26) d. Smith 7–5 6–4; Porwik d. Rehe (31) 7–6 6–1; Paulus (9) d. Gomer 6–3 5–7 6–2; Sawamatsu (15) d. Coetzer 4–6 6–2 7–5; Labat d. Cunningham (24) 4–6 6–4 6–0; Kschwendt d. Sloane (20) 4–6 6–1 6–4; Seles (2) d. Cioffi 6–1 6–3.
3rd round: Graf (1) d. Magers (21) 6–3 6–0; Werdel (27) d. Wood 6–3 6–1; Reggi (16) d. McGrath (23) 1–6 6–1 6–0; Maleeva-Fragnière (7) d. Faber 6–2 6–3; Sabatini (3) d. Rubin 6–1 6–3; Tauziat (10) d. Toleafoa 6–2 3–6 6–2; Pierce d. Rittner 6–3 6–2; Garrison (5) d. Smylie (32) 6–4 6–1; Helgeson d. Sviglerova (30) 6–3 6–0; Rajchrtova (22) d. Frazier (12) 7–6 2–6 6–4; Shriver d. Gildemeister (13) 6–3 6–2; Fernandez (4) d. McNeil (17) 6–1 6–2; Capriati (6) d. Grossman (26) default; Paulus (9) d. Porwik 6–3 6–2; Labat d. Sawamatsu (15) 1–6 7–6 6–2; Seles (2) d. Kschwendt 6–0 6–1.
4th round: Graf (1) d. Werdel (27) 6–0 6–1; Maleeva-Fragnière (7) d. Reggi (16) 6–0 6–4; Sabatini (3) d. Tauziat (10) 6–3 6–1; Garrison (5) d. Pierce 6–3 6–4; Helgeson d. Rajchrtova (22) 4–6 6–3 6–3; Fernandez (4) d. Shriver 6–2 6–4; Capriati (6) d. Paulus (9) 6–1 6–3; Seles (2) d. Labat 7–5 6–0.
Quarter-finals: Graf (1) d. Maleeva-Fragnière (7) 6–1 6–3; Sabatini (3) d. Garrison (5) 6–3 6–2; Fernandez (4) d. Helgeson 6–1 6–0; Seles (2) d. Capriati (6) 2–6 6–1 6–4.
Semi-finals: Sabatini (3) d. Graf (1) 0–6 7–6 6–1; Seles (2) d. Fernandez (4) 6–1 6–3.
Final: Seles (2) d. Sabatini (3) 6–3 7–5.
WOMEN'S DOUBLES – Final: M.J. Fernandez/Garrison (4) d. G. Fernandez/Novotna (1) 7–5 6–2.

US WOMEN'S HARDCOURT CHAMPIONSHIPS ($225,000)

SAN ANTONIO, TEXAS, 25–31 MARCH

WOMEN'S SINGLES – 1st round: M. Seles (1) d. F. Labat 6–0 6–1; C. Porwik d. J. Emmons (Q) 6–4 6–4; E. de Lone (WC) d. S. Martin 6–3 6–0; R. Zrubakova d. G. Magers (8) 6–4 2–6 7–6; M.

Maleeva-Fragnière (3) d. A. May (Q) 6–1 6–2; I. Demongeot d. R. Baranski 7–6 6–2; P. Fendick d. K. Rinaldi 6–0 1–0 ret.; L. McNeil (6) d. C. Benjamin 6–3 6–1; A. Dechaume d. L. Gildemeister (5) 6–4 6–2; J. Halard d. P. Thoren (Q) 6–1 2–6 6–1; E. Sviglerova d. C. Cunningham 6–3 7–5; P. Shriver d. R. Reggi (4) 6–3 6–3; S. Sloane (7) d. N. Herreman 6–2 6–1; A. Henricksson d. L. Ferrando 6–3 6–4; M. Javer d. C. Kuhlman (Q) 6–3 6–1; S. Graf (2) (WC) d. A. Keller 6–2 6–1.
3nd round: Seles (1) d. Porwilt G 1 G 1; de Lone (WC) d. Zrubukovu 0 4 0 4, Mulceva Fragnière (3) d. Demongeot 6–2 6–2; McNeil (6) d. Fendick 6–4 6–3; Halard d. Dechaume 6–1 6–3; Sviglerova d. Shriver 2–6 7–6 6–3; Sloane (7) d. Henricksson 6–3 6–1; Graf (2) (WC) d. Javer 6–3 6–1.
Quarter-finals: Seles (1) d. de Lone (WC) 6–2 6–0; Maleeva-Fragnière (3) d. McNeil (6) 6–3 6–4; Halard d. Sviglerova 6–1 6–2; Graf (2) (WC) d. Sloane (7) 6–1 6–1.
Semi-finals: Seles (1) d. Maleeva-Fragnière (3) 6–2 2–6 6–2; Graf (2) (WC) d. Halard 6–0 6–1.
Final: Graf (2) (WC) d. Seles (1) 6–4 6–3.
WOMEN'S DOUBLES – **Final:** Fendick/Seles (1) d. Hetherington/Rinaldi (2) 7–6 6–2.

FAMILY CIRCLE MAGAZINE CUP ($500,000)

HILTON HEAD ISLAND, 1–7 APRIL

WOMEN'S SINGLES – **1st round:** M. Navratilova (1) – bye; A. Coetzer d. S. Frankl (Q) 6–1 7–6; M. De Swardt (Q) d. L. Garrone 6–1 6–1; P. Langrova d. K. Piccolini (15) 6–2 6–2; L. Meskhi (9) d. V. Martinek 6–4 7–5; R. Zrubakova d. E. Brioukhovets 3–6 6–3 6–4; A. Keller d. M.L. Daniels 7–6 3–6 6–2; J. Capriati (6) – bye; J. Novotna (4) – bye; C. Kohde-Kilsch d. L. Corsato (LL) 6–2 5–7 6–3; A. Kerek (Q) d. L. Lapi 6–4 6–1; F. Labat d. R. Rajchrtova (13) 6–0 6–0; S. Cecchini (11) d. K. Adams (Q) 6–1 6–0; B. Bowes (Q) d. C. Tessi 3–6 6–4 6–2; D. Faber d. S. Meier 7–6 7–6; N. Zvereva (8) – bye; K. Maleeva (5) – bye; F. Bonsignori d. P. Tarabini 6–4 6–2; R. Baranski d. E. Hakami (Q) 7–5 6–1; S. Hack (16) d. T. Whitlinger 6–2 6–1; I. Cueto (12) d. L. Allen (Q) 6–0 6–2; H. Cioffi d. A. Kanellopoulou 6–0 7–6; B. Fulco d. S. Schefflin (WC) 6–4 6–4; A. Sanchez-Vicario (3) – bye; H. Sukova (7) – bye; G. Helgeson (WC) d. S. Martin 5–7 7–6 7–6; A. Temesvari d. S. Collins (WC) 6–3 3–6 6–3; M. Paz (14) d. L. Laskova (Q) 6–4 6–2; H. Kelesi (10) d. S. Wasserman 7–5 6–4; C. Benjamin d. C. Caverzasio 7–5 2–6 7–6; L. Harvey-Wild d. S. Smith 6–3 6–2; G. Sabatini (2) – bye.
2nd round: Navratilova (1) d. Coetzer 6–2 7–5; Langrova d. De Swardt (Q) 6–1 6–2; Meskhi (9) d. Zrubakova 6–3 6–2; Capriati (6) d. Keller 7–5 6–1; Novotna (4) d. Kohde-Kilsch 6–1 6–2; Labat d. Kerek (Q) 7–5 6–2; Cecchini (11) d. Bowes (Q) 6–4 6–0; Zvereva (8) d. Faber 6–1 6–3; Bonsignori d. Maleeva (5) 6–7 6–2 6–4; Hack (16) d. Baranski 6–1 6–1; Cioffi d. Cueto (12) 6–1 4–6 6–4; Sanchez-Vicario (3) d. Fulco 6–2 6–3; Sukova (7) d. Helgeson (WC) 6–2 6–1; Paz (14) d. Temesvari 6–3 6–1; Kelesi (10) d. Benjamin 6–1 1–6 6–2; Sabatini (2) d. Harvey-Wild 6–0 6–0.
3rd round: Navratilova (1) d. Langrova 6–3 6–4; Meskhi (9) d. Capriati (6) 3–6 6–3 6–3; Novotna (4) d. Labat 6–1 6–1; Zvereva (8) d. Cecchini (11) 7–6 6–3; Bonsignori d. Hack (16) 6–2 6–4; Sanchez-Vicario (3) d. Cioffi 6–1 ret.; Sukova (7) d. Paz (14) 6–4 6–0; Sabatini (2) d. Kelesi (10) 6–3 6–2.
Quarter-finals: Meskhi (9) d. Navratilova (1) 6–4 2–6 6–4; Zvereva (8) d. Novotna (4) 7–6 6–4; Sanchez-Vicario (3) d. Bonsignori 6–3 6–2; Sabatini (2) d. Sukova (7) 6–0 6–1.
Semi-finals: Meskhi (9) d. Zvereva (8) 6–3 3–6 6–4; Sabatini (2) d. Sanchez-Vicario (3) 4–6 6–4 6–3.
Final: Sabatini (2) d. Meskhi (9) 6–1 6–1.
WOMEN'S DOUBLES – **Final:** Kohde-Kilsch/Zvereva (4) d. Daniels/Gregory (5) 6–4 6–0.

BAUSCH & LOMB CHAMPIONSHIPS ($350,000)

AMELIA ISLAND, 8–14 APRIL

WOMEN'S SINGLES – **1st round:** S. Graf (1) – bye; R. Simpson d. A. Kerek (Q) 6–3 6–1; M. De Swardt (Q) d. E. Brioukhovets 6–2 6–1; I. Cueto (9) d. C. Toleafoa 6–3 6–2; V. Martinek (14) d. A. Keller 4–6 7–6 6–3; P. Langrova d. C. Benjamin 5–7 6–4 ret.; J. Emmons (Q) d. S. Smith 6–7 6–4 6–3; N. Zvereva (6) – bye; Z. Garrison (4) – bye; L. Garrone d. S. Meier 6–3 6–3; S. Frankl (LL) d. S. Cacic (Q) 6–2 6–3; A. Kanellopoulou d. S. Sloane (10) 6–1 2–6 6–1; P. Tarabini d. S. Hack (12) 3–2 ret.; P. Fendick d. D. Faber 6–2 6–1; B. Schultz d. F. Labat 7–6 6–3; S. Cecchini (8) – bye; L. Meskhi (7) – bye; A. Temesvari d. J. Exum (WC) 7–5 6–3; B. Fulco d. R. Baranski 6–1 6–1; T. Whitlinger d. M. Paz (11) 3–6 6–3 6–2; H. Cioffi d. P. Hy (16) 6–2 4–6 6–4; R. Zrubakova d. C. Tessi 7–5 5–7 6–3; L. Harvey-Wild d. S. Farina (Q) 7–5 6–3; A. Sanchez-Vicario (3) – bye; H. Sukova (5) – bye; C. Rubin (WC) d. S. Wasserman 3–6 7–6 6–3; G. Helgeson d. L. Corsato 6–4 6–7 6–2; C. Kohde-Kilsch (13) d. M. Lindstrom (Q) 6–0 6–2; C. Kuhlman (Q) d. S. Rehe (15) 7–6 6–1; L. Spadea (Q) d. C. MacGregor 6–3 6–4; F. Bonsignori d. L. Lapi 6–0 6–1; G. Sabatini (2) – bye.
2nd round: Graf (1) d. Simpson (LL) 6–4 6–0; Cueto (9) d. De Swardt (Q) 6–7 6–2 6–4; Martinek (14) d. Langrova 6–3 6–3; Zvereva (6) d. Emmons (Q) 6–1 6–2; Garrison (4) d. Garrone 7–6 6–3; Kanellopoulou d. Frankl (LL) 6–0 6–2; Fendick d. Tarabini 6–3 0–6 6–1; Schultz d. Cecchini (8) 6–3 6–0; Meskhi (7) d.

Temesvari 6–0 6–0; Whitlinger d. Fulco 2–6 6–2 6–3; Cioffi d. Zrubakova 6–2 6–4; Sanchez-Vicario (3) d. Harvey-Wild 6–3 6–0; Sukova (5) d. Rubin (WC) 6–7 7–5 6–2; Helgeson d. Kohde-Kilsch (13) 6–3 6–7 6–4; Spadea (Q) d. Kuhlman (Q) 6–4 1–6 6–4; Sabatini (2) d. Bonsignori 6–1 6–0.
3rd round: Graf (1) d. Cueto (9) 6–1 6–1; Zvereva (6) d. Martinek (14) 1–6 6–2 6–1; Garrison (4) d. Kanellopoulou 6–2 6–4; Fendick d. Schultz 6–3 6–4; Meskhi (7) d. Whitlinger 6–0 6–1; Sanchez-Vicario (3) d. Cioffi 6–3 6–1; Sukova (5) d. Helgeson 6–4 6–7 6–2; Sabatini (2) d. Spadea (Q) 6–0 6–1.
Quarter-finals: Graf (1) d. Zvereva (6) 6–0 6–2; Fendick d. Garrison (4) 6–1 6–4; Sanchez-Vicario (3) d. Meskhi (7) 6–1 7–6; Sabatini (2) d. Sukova (5) 6–2 6–1.
Semi-finals: Graf (1) d. Fendick 6–0 6–1; Sabatini (2) d. Sanchez-Vicario (3) 6–2 2–6 6–4.
Final: Sabatini (2) d. Graf (1) 7–5 7–6.
WOMEN'S DOUBLES – Final: Sanchez-Vicario/Sukova (1) d. Paz/Zvereva (2) 4–6 6–2 6–2.

VIRGINIA SLIMS OF HOUSTON ($350,000)

HOUSTON, 15–21 APRIL

WOMEN'S SINGLES – 1st round: M. Seles (1) – bye; R. Zrubakova d. P. Langrova 6–2 6–2; P. Tarabini d. S. Rehe 7–6 6–2; F. Bonsignori d. S. Sloane (7) 6–0 6–0; K. Maleeva (4) – bye; C. Papadaki (WC) d. P. Hy 6–4 6–3; C. MacGregor (LL) d. L. Allen (Q) 6–2 6–3; S. Cecchini (6) d. P. Nelson (WC) 6–4 6–2; T. Whitlinger d. G. Magers 6–4 1–6 6–4; L. Harvey-Wild d. G. Mosca (Q) 6–1 4–6 6–1; G. Fernandez d. M.L. Daniels 4–6 7–5 6–4; Z. Garrison (Q) – bye; S. Smith (Q) d. M. Paz (8) 6–3 6–1; A. Grossman d. S. La Fratta (Q) 6–1 3–6 7–6; H. Cioffi d. L. Garrone 1–6 6–3 6–1; M.J. Fernandez (2) – bye.
2nd round: Seles (1) d. Zrubakova 6–0 6–2; Bonsignori d. Tarabini 6–4 6–4; Maleeva (4) d. Papadaki (WC) 6–3 6–2; Cecchini (6) d. MacGregor (LL) 6–1 6–3; Harvey-Wild d. Whitlinger 6–4 6–3; Fernandez d. Garrison (3) 6–7 6–1 7–5; Grossman d. Smith (Q) 6–4 6–1; Fernandez (2) d. Cioffi default.
Quarter-finals: Seles (1) d. Bonsignori 6–1 6–0; Cecchini (6) d. Maleeva (4) 3–6 6–4 6–1; Harvey-Wild d. Fernandez 6–4 6–1; Fernandez (2) d. Grossman 7–5 7–5.
Semi-finals: Seles (1) d. Cecchini (6) 6–0 6–2; Fernandez (2) d. Harvey-Wild 6–0 6–3.
Final: Seles (1) d. Fernandez (2) 6–4 6–3.
WOMEN'S DOUBLES – Final: Hetherington/Rinaldi d. Fendick/M.J. Fernandez (1) 6–1 2–6 6–1.

INTERNATIONAL CHAMPIONSHIPS OF SPAIN ($225,000)

BARCELONA, 22–28 APRIL

WOMEN'S SINGLES – 1st round: M. Navratilova (1) – bye; S. Farina d. C. Bakkum 3–6 6–3 6–2; M. Strandlund d. A. Gooden 6–3 6–2; K. Piccolini (9) d. V. Milvidskaia 6–2 6–2; A. Dechaume (15) d. A. Kijimuta 6–1 6–3; N. Housset d. B. Bowes 5–7 6–3 6–2; A. Niox-Chateau d. I. Varas (WC) 6–2 6–3; N. Tauziat (5) – bye; C. Martinez (4) – bye; S. Wasserman d. A. Kanellopoulou 6–3 6–3; N. Avila (WC) d. K. Duell 6–0 6–3; R. McQuillan (11) d. E. Pampoulova 6–1 6–1; C. Tanvier (13) d. S. Auer 6–0 4–6 7–5; N. Van Lottum d. P. Perez 6–1 6–2; E. Bottini (WC) d. I. Demongeot 7–5 6–1; J. Halard (8) – bye; I. Cueto (7) – bye; C. Chabalgoity d. S. Lucchi 6–3 7–6; C. Tessi d. T. Morton 6–4 6–3; E. Zardo (14) d. M. Martinez 6–2 6–1; W. Probst (10) d. A. Vieira 6–0 6–4; S. Frankl d. C. Mothes 5–7 6–3 6–1; N. Jagerman d. M. Laval 6–2 6–7 7–6; M. Maleeva-Fragnière (3) – bye; J. Wiesner (6) – bye; P. Etchemendy d. K. Oeljeklaus 6–4 3–6 6–1; N. Guerree d. C. Cohen 6–3 6–0; K. Quentrec (12) d. A. Segura 6–4 7–5; B. Fulco d. F. Labat (16) 7–5 7–6; N. Herreman d. S. Gomer 6–2 6–4; M. Kidowaki d. D. Monami 7–5 6–3; A. Sanchez-Vicario (2) – bye.
2nd round: Navratilova (1) d. Farina 6–1 6–2; Piccolini (9) d. Strandlund 4–6 7–6 6–3; Dechaume (15) d. Housset 6–1 6–0; Tauziat (5) d. Niox-Chateau 6–4 6–2; Martinez (4) d. Wasserman 6–2 6–1; McQuillan (11) d. Avila (WC) 6–4 6–4; Van Lottum d. Tanvier (13) 6–3 7–5; Halard (8) d. Bottini (WC) 6–1 6–1; Cueto (7) d. Chabalgoity 6–3 6–2; Zardo (14) d. Tessi 6–4; Frankl d. Probst (10) 6–4 3–6 6–3; Maleeva-Fragnière (3) d. Jagerman 7–5 6–3; Wiesner (6) d. Etchemendy 6–4 0–6 7–5; Quentrec (12) d. Guerree 6–2 4–6 6–4; Fulco d. Herreman 6–3 6–4; Sanchez-Vicario (2) d. Kidowaki 6–0 6–0.
3rd round: Navratilova (1) d. Piccolini (9) 6–0 6–2; Tauziat (5) d. Dechaume (15) 6–3 6–3; Martinez (4) d. McQuillan (11) 6–4 6–3; Halard (8) d. Van Lottum 7–5 6–0; Zardo (14) d. Cueto (7) 2–6 6–1 6–2; Maleeva-Fragnière (3) d. Frankl 6–0 6–1; Wiesner (6) d. Quentrec (12) 1–6 6–2 6–0; Sanchez-Vicario (2) d. Fulco 6–1 6–2.
Quarter-finals: Tauziat (5) d. Navratilova (1) 6–1 6–4; Martinez (4) d. Halard (8) 1–6 6–4 6–4; Maleeva-Fragnière (3) d. Zardo (14) 6–3 7–5; Sanchez-Vicario (2) d. Wiesner (6) 6–3 6–2.
Semi-finals: Martinez (4) d. Tauziat (5) 6–1 4–6 6–1; Maleeva-Fragnière (3) d. Sanchez-Vicario (2) 2–6 7–5 6–3.
Final: Martinez (4) d. Maleeva-Fragnière (3) 6–4 6–1.
WOMEN'S DOUBLES – Final: Navratilova/Sanchez-Vicario (1) d. Tauziat/Wiesner (2) 6–1 6–3.

CITIZEN CUP ($350,000)

HAMBURG, 29 APRIL–5 MAY

WOMEN'S SINGLES – 1st round: M. Seles (1) – bye; A. Leand d. E. Pfaff 6–2 2–6 6–4; N. Guerree d. C. Tanvier 7–6 6–4; R. Rajchrtova (13) d. M. Jaggard 6–3 6–1; N. Provis d. W. Probst (16) 7–6 6–1; E. Brioukhovets d. N. Durunski 0–0 0–0, C. Tessi d. K. Quentrec 0–0 0–1, II. Sukova (6) – bye, A. Sanchez-Vicario (3) – bye; E. Reinach d. P. Langrova 6–1 6–3; R. McQuillan d. M. Strandlund 6–3 6–4; A. Huber (10) d. B. Rittner 7–5 6–3; I. Cueto (11) d. S. Smith 6–3 6–3; K. Kschwendt d. M. Kidowaki 6–1 2–6 7–6; C. Porwik d. H. ter Riet 6–4 6–4; L. Meskhi (7) – bye; J. Wiesner (8) – bye; S. Meier d. L. Field 6–3 5–7 6–1; S. Dopfer d. A. Coetzer 7–5 5–7 6–4; C. Lindqvist (15) d. P. Vasquez 6–4 6–4; P. Tarabini d. E. Sviglerova (12) 6–2 6–2; E. Pampoulova d. M. Babel 4–6 6–3 6–2; L. Savchenko d. N. Jagerman 6–2 6–2; J. Novotna (4) – bye; K. Maleeva (5) – bye; S. Frankl d. L. Corsato 6–2 6–4; D. Szabova d. C. Toleafoa 6–2 6–0; R. Zrubakova d. H. Kelesi (9) 6–4 6–1; J. Halard (14) d. C. Cohen 6–0 6–3; R. Simpson d. B. Fulco 2–6 6–0 6–2; M. Kochta d. A. Temesvari 7–6 6–4; S. Graf (2) – bye.

2nd round: Seles (1) d. Leand 6–1 6–1; Rajchrtova (13) d. Guerree 6–2 3–1 ret.; Brioukhovets d. Provis 6–1 6–4; Sukova (6) d. Tessi 6–3 6–2; Sanchez-Vicario (3) d. Reinach 6–1 3–6 6–2; Huber (10) d. McQuillan 6–7 7–6 6–4; Kschwendt d. Cueto (11) 6–2 6–2; Meskhi (7) d. Porwik 6–4 6–3; Wiesner (8) d. Meier 6–4 6–2; Lindqvist (15) d. Dopfer 6–3 6–2; Tarabini d. Pampoulova 6–1 4–6 6–1; Novotna (4) d. Savchenko 6–0 6–1; Maleeva (5) d. Frankl 6–2 6–2; Zrubakova d. Szabova 6–3 4–6 6–3; Halard (14) d. Simpson 2–6 6–1 6–2; Graf (2) d. Kochta 6–1 6–3.

3rd round: Seles (1) d. Rajchrtova (13) 6–3 6–0; Sukova (6) d. Brioukhovets 6–4 6–2; Sanchez-Vicario (3) d. Huber (10) 6–2 6–3; Meskhi (7) d. Kschwendt 6–4 6–0; Wiesner (8) d. Lindqvist (15) 6–2 6–1; Novotna (4) d. Tarabini default; Maleeva (5) d. Zrubakova 6–3 6–0; Graf (2) d. Halard (14) 6–2 6–3.

Quarter-finals: Seles (1) d. Sukova (6) 6–0 6–1; Sanchez-Vicario (3) d. Meskhi (7) 6–2 6–1; Wiesner (8) d. Novotna (4) 6–1 6–3; Graf (2) d. Maleeva (5) 6–3 6–3.

Semi-finals: Seles (1) d. Sanchez-Vicario (3) 6–2 6–4; Graf (2) d. Wiesner (8) 6–0 6–1.

Final: Graf (2) d. Seles (1) 5–7 7–6 6–3.

WOMEN'S DOUBLES – Final: Novotna/Savchenko (1) d. Sanchez-Vicario/Sukova (2) 7–5 6–1.

PEUGEOT ITALIAN OPEN ($500,000)

ROME, 6–12 MAY

WOMEN'S SINGLES – 1st round: M. Seles (1) – bye; N. Provis d. L. Golarsa 6–4 6–1; K. Piccolini d. S. Testud (LL) 6–2 7–6; K. Quentrec d. S. Cecchini (11) 6–4 7–5; R. Fairbank d. N. Baudone 6–2 6–3; A. Kijimuta d. A. Grossman 6–4 2–6 7–6; L. Ferrando d. C. Lindqvist 6–2 6–1; L. Meskhi (8) – bye; M.J. Fernandez (4) – bye; L. Jachia (Q) d. H. Cioffi 6–7 6–2 6–3; N. Herreman d. R. Grande 6–2 6–1; P. Ritter d. F. Bonsignori (16) 6–2 6–3; B. Fulco (Q) d. M. Paz (14) 6–1 6–4; E. Maniokova (Q) d. I. Demongeot (Q) 7–5 6–1; F. Labat d. S. Lucchi (Q) 6–3 1–6 6–3; M. Maleeva-Fragnière (6) – bye; C. Martinez (5) – bye; S. Martin (Q) d. S. Loosemore 6–2 6–4; R. McQuillan d. F. Fortuni (Q) 6–2 6–0; H. Kelesi (12) d. G. Helgeson 6–2 6–0; A. Huber (13) d. A. Dechaume 6–1 6–3; L. Garrone d. E. Sviglerova 2–6 7–6 7–5; E. Reinach d. R. Rajchrtova 7–5 4–6 6–4; M. Navratilova (3) – bye; J. Capriati (7) – bye; C. Tessi d. C. Kohde-Kilsch 6–2 6–4; C. Cunningham d. S. Farina 7–5 6–4; J. Halard d. M. Maleeva (15) 3–6 6–4 7–6; N. Tauziat (9) d. R. Alter (Q) 6–2 6–7 6–4; A. Strnadova d. J. Durie 6–4 7–5; A. Coetzer d. F. Romano 6–2 6–4; G. Sabatini (2) – bye.

2nd round: Seles (1) d. Provis 6–3 6–1; Piccolini d. Quentrec 6–2 6–3; Kijimuta d. Fairbank 6–3 4–6 7–5; Meskhi (8) d. Ferrando 7–6 6–0; Fernandez (4) d. Jachia (Q) 7–5 6–3; Ritter d. Herreman 6–4 5–7 7–6; Fulco (Q) d. Maniokova (Q) 7–6 6–4; Maleeva-Fragnière (6) d. Labat 6–2 6–1; Martinez (5) d. Martin (Q) 6–3 6–3; Kelesi (12) d. McQuillan 6–2 6–3; Huber (13) d. Garrone 6–4 1–6 2; Navratilova (3) d. Reinach 6–3 6–0; Capriati (7) d. Tessi 7–5 7–6; Halard d. Cunningham 3–6 6–0 6–2; Tauziat (9) d. Strnadova 3–6 6–3 6–3; Sabatini (2) d. Coetzer 6–2 6–2.

3rd round: Seles (1) d. Piccolini 6–3 6–1; Meskhi (8) d. Kijimuta 6–1 6–7 6–1; Fernandez (4) d. Ritter 6–1 6–3; Fulco (Q) d. Maleeva-Fragnière (6) 2–6 6–4 6–1; Martinez (5) d. Kelesi (12) 6–1 6–1; Navratilova (3) d. Huber (13) 3–6 6–1 6–3; Capriati (7) d. Halard 6–2 6–4; Sabatini (2) d. Tauziat (9) 6–0 6–1.

Quarter-finals: Seles (1) d. Meskhi (8) 6–0 6–1; Fernandez (4) d. Fulco (Q) 6–3 6–2; Martinez (5) d. Navratilova (3) 6–3 6–4; Sabatini (2) d. Capriati (7) 6–0 6–2.

Semi-finals: Seles (1) d. Fernandez (4) 7–5 2–6 6–4; Sabatini (2) d. Martinez (5) 6–1 6–0.

Final: Sabatini (2) d. Seles (1) 6–3 6–2.

WOMEN'S DOUBLES – Final: Capriati/Seles (5) d. Provis/Reinach (2) 7–5 6–2.

LUFTHANSA CUP – GERMAN OPEN (£500,000)

BERLIN, 13–20 MAY

WOMEN'S SINGLES – 1st round: S. Graf (1) – bye; N. Jagerman (Q) d. K. Kschwendt 7–5 1–0 ret.; E. Brioukhovets d. S. Rehe 6–3 2–6 7–6; M. Maleeva d. J. Wiesner (13) 6–0 6–3; R. Zrubakova d. L. Meskhi

(9) 6–2 6–2; H. Cioffi d. K. Duell 6–2 6–1; A. Coetzer (Q) d. V. Martinek 6–3 6–3; K. Maleeva (6) – bye; J. Novotna (4) – bye; R. McQuillan d. A. Popp (Q) 6–1 7–6; A. Grossman d. C. Dahlman 6–1 6–1; S. Cecchini (12) d. S. Meier (Q) 6–2 6–0; M. Paz (16) d. E. Sviglerova 6–4 6–4; G. Helgeson d. L. Savchenko 6–3 6–0; F. Labat d. I. Cueto 6–1 6–4; H. Sukova (8) – bye; J. Capriati (7) – bye; S. Martin (Q) d. K. Rinaldi 6–2 6–3; W. Probst d. P. Ritter 6–3 7–6; N. Zvereva (11) d. C. Kohde-Kilsch 6–1 6–2; J. Halard d. N. Tauziat (10) 6–0 6–1; F. Bonsignori d. B. Fulco (Q) 2–6 7–6 5–1 ret.; B. Rittner d. R. Rajchrtova 6–1 7–6; M.J. Fernandez (3) – bye; A. Sanchez-Vicario (5) – bye; A. Kijimuta (Q) d. J. Durie 6–3 6–2; N. Provis d. M. Kochta 4–6 6–1 7–6; L. Gildemeister (15) d. F. Romano (Q) 6–3 6–1; A. Huber (14) d. P. Langrova 6–4 6–0; L. Garrone d. K. Piccolini 7–6 6–1; N. Sawamatsu d. R. Fairbank 6–3 6–0; G. Sabatini (2) – bye.
2nd round: Graf (1) d. Jagerman (Q) 6–2 6–3; Brioukhovets d. Maleeva 2–6 6–2 6–3; Zrubakova d. Cioffi 2–6 6–4 6–1; Coetzer (Q) d. Maleeva (6) 6–2 7–6; Novotna (4) d. McQuillan 6–4 6–4; Cecchini (12) d. Grossman 6–2 6–2; Helgeson d. Paz (16) 7–6 6–3; Sukova (8) d. Labat 3–6 6–2 6–1; Capriati (7) d. Martin (Q) 6–2 6–4; Zvereva (11) d. Probst 7–5 7–5; Halard d. Bonsignori 6–1 6–0; Fernandez (3) d. Rittner 6–4 6–7 6–2; Sanchez-Vicario (5) d. Kijimuta (Q) 6–2 6–0; Provis d. Gildemeister (15) 6–2 7–6; Huber (14) d. Garrone 6–3 6–1; Sabatini (2) d. Sawamatsu 6–1 6–0.
3rd round: Graf (1) d. Brioukhovets 6–0 6–1; Zrubakova d. Coetzer (Q) 7–6 0–6 6–1; Novotna (4) d. Cecchini (12) 6–3 3–6 6–3; Helgeson d. Sukova (8) 6–4 6–3; Capriati (7) d. Zvereva (11) 6–2 6–3; Halard d. Fernandez (3) 6–0 5–7 6–3; Sanchez-Vicario (5) d. Provis 6–1 6–1; Huber (14) d. Sabatini (2) 7–5 6–3.
Quarter-finals: Graf (1) d. Zrubakova 6–3 6–2; Novotna (4) d. Helgeson 6–1 6–2; Capriati (7) d. Halard 6–3 6–2; Sanchez-Vicario (5) d. Huber (14) 6–0 6–2.
Semi-finals: Graf (1) d. Novotna (4) 6–1 6–0; Sanchez-Vicario (5) d. Capriati (7) 7–5 5–7 6–4.
Final: Graf (1) d. Sanchez-Vicario (5) 6–3 4–6 7–6.
WOMEN'S DOUBLES – Final: Savchenko/Zvereva (3) d. Provis/Reinach (4) 6–3 6–3.

PILKINGTON GLASS LADIES CHAMPIONSHIPS ($350,000)
EASTBOURNE, 17–22 JUNE
WOMEN'S SINGLES – 1st round: M. Navratilova (1) d. A. Coetzer 6–0 6–1; L. Golarsa d. G. Helgeson 6–2 6–3; B. Schultz d. A. Minter 7–5 6–2; R. McQuillan (12) d. A. Temesvari 6–3 4–6 6–4; R. Fairbank (15) d. N. Provis 6–2 6–2; S. Smith d. C. Dahlman 6–3 6–2; H. Ludloff (Q) d. L. Harvey-Wild 1–6 6–3 6–3; N. Tauziat (7) d. P. Fendick 7–6 3–6 6–2; M.J. Fernandez (3) d. N. Herreman (Q) 6–3 2–6 6–1; S. Gomer d. P. Louie Harper 6–4 6–4; K. Godridge d. A. Grunfeld 6–2 6–4; H. Kelesi (10) d. E. Brioukhovets 6–3 6–4; J. Halard (13) d. C. Wood 7–6 6–2; E. Reinach d. M. Javer 7–6 6–2; Y. Basuki d. S. Stafford 6–0 6–3; C. Kohde-Kilsch d. A. Henricksson (Q) 6–4 7–6; J. Durie d. A. Frazier (8) 6–2 6–3; S. Martin (LL) d. E. de Lone 6–3 4–6 6–1; G. Fernandez d. D. Wamelink (Q) 6–7 6–4 6–2; A. Dechaume d. M. Werdel (14) 7–6 6–2; L. McNeil (11) d. P. Paradis (LL) 6–3 6–4; T. Whitlinger d. T. Whittington (Q) 6–4 6–1; R. White d. C. Lindqvist 6–3 6–2; J. Novotna (4) d. A. Kijimuta 6–2 6–2; H. Sukova (6) d. K. Quentrec 6–1 7–6; P. Shriver d. L. Savchenko 6–2 6–4; D. Faber d. E. Pfaff (Q) 2–6 6–4 6–1; P. Hy d. M. Maniokova (LL) 6–2 5–7 6–1; G. Magers (16) d. B. Borneo (Q) 6–1 6–4; E. Smylic d. S. Rche 7–5 7–6; A. Strnadova d. S. Loosemore 6–1 6–4; A. Sanchez-Vicario (2) d. C. Porwik 6–1 6–4.
2nd round: Navratilova (1) d. Golarsa 6–0 6–0; Schultz d. McQuillan (12) 6–3 6–2; Fairbank (15) d. Smith 6–3 7–5; Ludloff (Q) d. Tauziat (7) 3–6 7–0 6–3; Fernandez (3) d. Gomer 6–2 6–2; Kelesi (10) d. Godridge 6–3 6–3; Halard (13) d. Reinach 1–6 6–4 6–4; Basuki d. Kohde-Kilsch 6–3 6–2; Durie d. Martin (LL) default; Fernandez d. Dechaume 6–4 6–3; McNeil (11) d. Whitlinger 6–3 6–7 6–1; Novotna (4) d. White 6–1 6–3; Shriver d. Sukova (6) 6–3 6–4; Hy d. Faber 6–0 6–2; Smylie d. Magers (16) 7–6 7–6; Sanchez-Vicario (2) d. Strnadova 6–3 6–2.
3rd round: Navratilova (1) d. Schultz 6–1 6–2; Ludloff (Q) d. Fairbank (15) 7–6 4–6 6–3; Fernandez (3) d. Kelesi (10) 6–2 6–4; Basuki d. Halard (13) 7–5 7–6; Fernandez d. Durie 6–3 6–3; Novotna (4) d. McNeil (11) 6–2 7–6; Shriver d. Hy 6–2 6–3; Sanchez-Vicario (2) d. Smylie 6–3 6–3.
Quarter-finals: Navratilova (1) d. Ludloff (Q) 6–1 6–1; Fernandez (3) d. Basuki 6–2 6–1; Fernandez d. Novotna (4) 7–6 6–4; Sanchez-Vicario (2) d. Shriver 6–0 6–1.
Semi-finals: Navratilova (1) d. Fernandez (3) 6–3 6–0; Sanchez-Vicario (2) d. Fernandez 6–1 6–1.
Final: Navratilova (1) d. Sanchez-Vicario (2) 6–4 6–4.
WOMEN'S DOUBLES – Final: Savchenko/Zvereva (2) d. G. Fernandez/Novotna (1) 2–6 6–4 6–4.

MAZDA TENNIS CLASSIC ($225,000)
SAN DIEGO, 29 JULY–4 AUGUST
WOMEN'S SINGLES – 1st round: M. Seles (1) – bye; P. Shriver d. J. Durie 6–3 6–4; A. Kijimuta d. J. Emmons (Q) 6–4 1–6 6–4; A. Minter d. L. Gildemeister (8) 6–3 6–4; M. Maleeva-Fragnière (3) – bye; K. Po (Q) d. P. Louie Harper 6–3 6–3; A. May d. N. Herreman (LL) 6–3 6–1; N. Tauziat (6) d. K. Rinaldi 6–3 4–6 6–4; Z. Garrison (5) d. R. Fairbank 6–3 6–4; K. Quentrec d. C. Kohde-Kilsch 6–4 5–7 6–4; L. McNeil d. N. Sawamatsu 3–6 6–1 6–1; J. Capriati (4) – bye; B. Paulus (7) d. C. Papadaki 6–2 6–3; D. Graham (Q) d. E. de Lone (Q) 6–1 6–0; M. Werdel d. H. Cioffi 0–6 6–1 6–1; C. Martinez (2) – bye.

2nd round: Seles (1) d. Shriver 6–2 6–2; Minter d. Kijimuta 6–3 5–7 7–5; Maleeva-Fragnière (3) d. Po (Q) 6–7 6–3 6–2; Tauziat (6) d. May 6–3 6–4; Garrison (5) d. Quentrec 6–2 6–1; Capriati (4) d. McNeil 6–2 6–1; Graham (Q) d. Paulus (7) 6–3 6–4; Martinez (2) d. Werdel 6–3 6–1.
Quarter-finals: Seles (1) d. Minter 6–0 6–3; Tauziat (6) d. Maleeva-Fragnière (3) 6–3 6–3; Capriati (4) d. Garrison (5) 6–1 6–4; Martinez (2) d. Graham (Q) 6–0 7–5.
Semi-finals. Seles (1) d. Tauziat (6) 6–1 6–2; Capriati (4) d. Martinez (2) 6–4 6–0.
Final: Capriati (4) d. Seles (1) 4–6 6–1 7–6.
WOMEN'S DOUBLES – Final: J. Hetherington/Rinaldi (3) d. G. Fernandez/Tauziat (1) 6–4 3–6 6–2.

CANADIAN OPEN ($500,000)

TORONTO, 5–11 AUGUST

WOMEN'S SINGLES – 1st round: G. Sabatini (1) – bye; S. Farina d. M. Lindstrom (Q) 6–4 4–6 6–3; K. Date d. S. Jeyaseelen 6–4 4–6 6–3; H. Kelesi (11) d. M. Bernard 6–3 4–6 6–3; L. Savchenko d. C. Kohde-Kilsch (15) 4–6 6–4 7–6; M. Endo d. B. Cordwell 6–3 4–6 6–3; M. Strandlund d. J. Durie 3–6 6–2 6–2; H. Sukova (6) – bye; J. Capriati (3) – bye; E. de Lone d. H. Nagano (Q) 6–4 6–7 6–0; S. Gomer d. S. Italiano (Q) 6–3 6–2; M. Werdel (13) d. A. Keller 6–2 6–7 7–6; N. Zvereva (9) d. Y. Segal (LL) 6–1 6–3; P. Hy d. S. Dopfer 1–6 6–0 6–1; J. Watanabe (Q) d. C. Benjamin (Q) 6–1 6–2; J. Salmon (LL) bye; N. Tauziat (5) – bye; A. Minter d. R. Baranski 7–5 7–5; K. Rinaldi d. L. Field 6–4 6–2; L. Gildemeister (10) d. A. Henricksson 7–5 5–7 6–4; N. Sawamatsu (12) d. C. Dahlman 6–2 6–4; P. Thoren d. S. Loosemore (Q) 6–2 6–3; Mag. Maleeva d. A. Leand 6–1 ret.; K. Maleeva (4) – bye; A. Frazier (8) – bye; N. Provis d. M. Drake (Q) 6–1 6–0; D. Graham d. E. Smylie 6–0 6–1; J. Emmons d. K. Piccolini (14) 1–6 6–3 6–2; R. Rajchrtova (6) d. E. Pfaff 6–2 7–5; R. Alter d. A. Kijimuta 1–6 7–6 6–1; R. Hiraki d. S.0; Amiach (Q) 7–5 6–3; M. Maleeva-Fragnière (2) – bye.
2nd round: Sabatini (1) d. Farina 6–0 6–0; Kelesi (11) d. Date 6–4 6–4; Endo d. Savchenko 6–1 6–1; Sukova (6) d. Strandlund 7–6 6–4; Capriati (3) d. de Lone 6–4 6–0; Gomer d. Werdel (13) 6–3 7–5; Zvereva (9) d. Hy 5–7 6–1 7–5; Watanabe (Q) d. Salmon (LL) 6–0 6–1; Tauziat (5) d. Minter 6–1 6–0; Gildemeister (10) d. Rinaldi 6–2 7–6; Sawamatsu (12) d. Thoren 6–4 5–7 6–2; Maleeva (4) d. Maleeva-Fragnière (2) d. Hiraki 7–5 6–0.
3rd round: Sabatini (1) d. Kelesi (11) 7–6 6–2; Sukova (6) d. Endo 6–1 6–0; Capriati (3) d. Gomer 6–2 6–3; Zvereva (9) d. Watanabe (Q) 7–6 6–0; Gildemeister (10) d. Tauziat (5) 6–3 4–6 6–4; Maleeva (4) d. Sawamatsu (12) 6–1 6–3; Frazier (8) d. Graham 6–3 1–6 6–1; Maleeva-Fragnière (2) d. Rajchrtova (6) 6–1 6–2.
Quarter-finals: Sabatini (1) d. Sukova (6) 6–3 6–2; Capriati (3) d. Zvereva (9) 6–1 6–1; Maleeva (4) d. Gildemeister (10) 6–2 6–2; Maleeva-Fragnière (2) d. Frazier (8) 6–2 7–6.
Semi-finals: Capriati (3) d. Sabatini (1) 6–4 2–3 ret.; Maleeva (4) d. Maleeva-Fragnière (2) 6–4 1–0 ret.
Final: Capriati (3) d. Maleeva (4) 6–2 6–3.
WOMEN'S DOUBLES – Final: Savchenko/Zvereva (1) d. Kohde-Kilsch/Sukova (2) 1–6 7–5 6–2.

VIRGINIA SLIMS OF LOS ANGELES ($350,000)

MANHATTAN BEACH, 12–18 AUGUST

WOMEN'S SINGLES – 1st round: M. Seles (1) – bye; E. Reinach d. C. Wood 5–7 6–1 6–3; R. White d. P. Fendick 6–0 6–2; A. Coetzer d. R. Rajchrtova (14) 6–4 7–5; N. Provis d. A. Minter (16) 6–3 4–6 6–1; M. Paz d. E. de Lone 6–1 3–6 6–3; L. Ferrando d. S. Gomer (Q) 6–3 6–4; A. Frazier (7) – bye; A. Sanchez-Vicario (3) – bye; I. Demongeot d. A. May 7–6 6–3; S. Martin (Q) d. J. Faull (LL) 6–3 6–1; P. Paradis d. R. Fairbank 1–6 6–3 6–3; M. Pierce (11) d. P. Tarabini 6–2 4–6 6–0; N. Van Lottum d. S. Stafford 6–3 6–4; N. Herreman (Q) d. C. Toleafoa (Q) 6–3 6–1; H. Sukova (6) – bye; L. Meskhi (5) – bye; K. Date (Q) d. C. Dahlman 6–2 6–2; A. Grossman d. L. Savchenko 6–0 6–0; Y. Basuki (10) d. C. Porwik 2–6 6–2 6–4; G. Magers d. T. Whitlinger (13) 6–3 6–7 6–4; G. Helgeson d. M. Javer 7–5 6–2; J. Durie d. P. Harper 2–6 6–3 6–3; Z. Garrison (4) – bye; L. McNeil (8) – bye; S. Rottier (Q) d. M. Endo (Q) 6–2 6–3; A. Dechaume d. K. Po 6–1 6–1; C. Lindqvist (15) d. C. Benjamin 7–5 6–3; D. Graham d. S. Sloane (12) 6–1 2–1 ret.; P. Kamstra (Q) d. C. Suire 4–6 7–5 6–1; P. Hy d. H. Ludloff (LL) 6–4 7–5; G. Sabatini (2) – bye.
2nd round: Seles (1) d. Reinach 6–1 6–0; Coetzer d. White 6–4 6–4; Paz d. Provis 3–6 7–6 6–3; Frazier (7) d. Ferrando 6–4 6–2; Sanchez-Vicario (3) d. Demongeot 6–2 6–3; Paradis d. Martin (Q) 6–3 3–6 6–4; Pierce (11) d. Van Lottum 6–2 6–2; Sukova (6) d. Herreman (Q) 6–0 6–4; Date (Q) d. Meskhi (5) 6–4 6–1; Basuki (10) d. Grossman 6–3 6–4; Magers d. Helgeson 6–4 7–5; Durie d. Garrison (4) 6–3 6–7 7–5; McNeil (8) d. Rottier (Q) 6–1 6–4; Lindqvist (15) d. Dechaume 2–6 6–1 6–2; Graham d. Kamstra (Q) 6–1 6–0; Sabatini (2) d. Hy 6–3 6–0.
3rd round: Seles (1) d. Coetzer 6–4 6–1; Paz d. Frazier (7) 3–6 7–6 6–1; Sanchez-Vicario (3) d. Paradis 6–1 6–3; Sukova (6) d. Pierce (11) 6–7 6–2 6–2; Date (Q) d. Basuki (10) 6–2 6–2; Durie d. Magers 6–3 6–4; McNeil (8) d. Lindqvist (15) 6–7 6–0 6–1; Sabatini (2) d. Graham 6–3 6–1.

Quarter-finals: Seles (1) d. Paz 6–2 6–2; Sanchez-Vicario (3) d. Sukova (6) 4–6 6–4 6–0; Date (Q) d. Durie 6–4 6–1; Sabatini (2) d. McNeil (8) 6–3 4–6 7–5.
Semi-finals: Seles (1) d. Sanchez-Vicario (3) 6–7 6–4 6–4; Date (Q) d. Sabatini (2) 3–6 6–1 6–4.
Final: Seles (1) d. Date (Q) 6–3 6–1.
WOMEN'S DOUBLES – Final: Savchenko/Zvereva (1) d. Magers/R. White (5) 6–1 2–6 6–2.

VIRGINIA SLIMS OF WASHINGTON ($350,000)

WASHINGTON D.C., 19–24 AUGUST

WOMEN'S SINGLES – 1st round: J. Wiesner – bye; R. Zrubakova d. N. Zvereva 6–4 7–5; P. Shriver d. E. Reinach 6–2 6–3; K. Maleeva (6) d. C. Cunningham 6–4 6–0; M.J. Fernandez (3) – bye; M. De Swardt d. R. Fairbank 6–3 7–6; G. Fernandez d. S. Stafford 6–7 6–3 7–6; A. Strnadova d. N. Tauziat (8) 6–4 7–5; L. Meskhi (7) d. L. Ferrando 6–3 4–4 ret.; A. Minter d. R. White 6–4 6–1; L. Gildemeister d. G. Magers 3–6 6–2 6–2; J. Novotna (4) – bye; Z. Garrison (5) d. C. Tessi 6–2 6–2; Mag. Maleeva d. C. Lindqvist 6–4 6–3; R. Rajchrtova d. H. Kelesi 7–5 6–4; A. Sanchez-Vicario (2) – bye.
2nd round: Wiesner d. Zrubakova 1–6 6–2 6–3; Maleeva (6) d. Shriver 7–6 3–6 6–1; Fernandez (3) d. De Swardt 6–4 6–1; Fernandez d. Strnadova 6–0 7–5; Meskhi (7) d. Minter 4–6 6–1 6–4; Novotna (4) d. Gildemeister 6–1 6–1; Garrison (5) d. Maleeva 6–3 2–6 6–1; Sanchez-Vicario (2) d. Rajchrtova 6–4 6–4.
Quarter-finals: Maleeva (6) d. Wiesner 6–4 6–2; Fernandez (3) d. Fernandez 6–4 3–6 6–3; Meskhi (7) d. Novotna (4) 6–2 2–6 6–4; Sanchez-Vicario (2) d. Garrison (5) 6–3 6–2.
Semi-finals: Maleeva (6) d. Fernandez (3) 6–3 6–4; Sanchez–Vicario (2) d. Meskhi (7) 6–0 6–1.
Final: Sanchez-Vicario (2) d. Maleeva (6) 6–2 7–5.
WOMEN'S DOUBLES – Final: Novotna/Savchenko (2) d. Fernandez/Zvereva (1) 5–7 6–1 7–6.

NICHIREI INTERNATIONAL CHAMPIONSHIPS ($350,000)

TOKYO, 16–22 SEPTEMBER

WOMEN'S SINGLES – 1st round: M. Seles (1) – bye; R. Hiraki d. M. Miyauchi (Q) 4–6 6–4 6–0; M. Kidowaki d. C. Tessi 6–2 6–1; C. Cunningham d. K. Date (8) 2–6 6–4 7–5; A. Frazier (4) – bye; N. Sawamatsu d. M. Endo 3–6 6–1; P. Harper d. L. Harvey-Wild 3–6 7–6 6–1; D. Graham d. P. Shriver (6) 7–5 6–4; L. Gildemeister (5) d. Y. Basuki 7–5 7–5; A. Kijimuta d. M. Javer 6–3 2–6 6–1; A. Strnadova d. E. Iida (Q) 6–7 6–3 6–4; K. Maleeva (3) – bye; M. Werdel (7) d. N. Miyagi (Q) 6–4 6–3; A. Minter d. M. Mizokuchi (Q) 6–2 6–3; P. Hy d. E. Smylie 6–0 7–5; M.J. Fernandez (2) – bye.
2nd round: Seles (1) d. Hiraki 6–3 6–4; Kidowaki d. Cunningham 5–7 6–1 6–1; Frazier (4) d. Sawamatsu 6–1 0–6 6–3; Graham d. Harper 6–4 6–4; Gildemeister (5) d. Kijimuta 6–1 6–2; Maleeva (3) d. Strnadova 6–1 6–2; Werdel (7) d. Minter 7–5 7–6; Fernandez (2) d. Hy 6–1 6–1.
Quarter-finals: Seles (1) d. Kidowaki 6–0 6–0; Frazier (4) d. Graham 7–5 6–1; Maleeva (3) d. Gildemeister (5) 6–3 3–6 6–1; Fernandez (2) d. Werdel (7) 6–2 6–3.
Semi-finals: Seles (1) d. Frazier (4) 6–4 6–0; Fernandez (2) d. Maleeva (3) 3–6 6–1 6–4.
Final: Seles (1) d. Fernandez (2) 6–1 6–1.
WOMEN'S DOUBLES – Final: Fernandez/Shriver (1) d. Cunningham/Gildemeister 6–3 6–3.

MILANO LADIES INDOOR ($225,000)

MILAN, 30 SEPTEMBER–6 OCTOBER

WOMEN'S SINGLES – 1st round: M. Seles (1) – bye; L. Garrone d. S. Cecchini 6–1 2–1 ret.; C. Lindqvist d. L. Golarsa 6–3 1–6 6–2; H. Sukova (6) d. H. Ludloff (Q) 6–2 6–3; C. Martinez (4) – bye; K. Habsudova d. H. Kelesi 2–6 6–4 6–4; N. Herreman (Q) d. P. Paradis 1–6 7–5 7–5; G. Fernandez (7) d. S. Collins (Q) 6–4 6–3; Mag. Maleeva d. L. Bacheva (LL) 3–6 6–3 6–1; S. Wasserman (Q) d. I. Gorrochategui 3–6 6–3 7–6; C. Kohde-Kilsch d. L. Ferrando 6–1 6–2; M.J. Fernandez (3) – bye; L. McNeil (8) d. P. Tarabini 7–5 6–3; S. Appelmans d. N. Housset (LL) 6–2 6–2; R. McQuillan d. R. Reggi 6–2 6–2; M. Navratilova (2) – bye.
2nd round: Seles (1) d. Garrone 6–0 6–1; Sukova (6) d. Lindqvist 6–0 6–2; Martinez (4) d. Habsudova 6–4 6–1; Fernandez (7) d. Herreman (Q) 4–6 6–2 6–1; Maleeva d. Wasserman (Q) 7–6 6–4; Fernandez (3) d. Kohde-Kilsch 6–2 6–0; Appelmans d. McNeil (8) 6–3 6–2; Navratilova (2) d. McQuillan 6–7 6–0 6–0.
Quarter-finals: Seles (1) d. Sukova (6) 6–3 6–4; Martinez (4) d. Fernandez (7) 6–1 7–5; Fernandez (3) d. Maleeva 5–7 6–3 6–4; Navratilova (2) d. Appelmans 6–2 6–3.
Semi-finals: Seles (1) d. Martinez (4) 6–3 6–3; Navratilova (2) d. Fernandez (3) 6–2 3–6 6–4.
Final: Seles (1) d. Navratilova (2) 6–3 3–6 6–4.
WOMEN'S DOUBLES – Final: Collins/McNeil (4) d. Appelmans/Reggi 7–6 6–3.

VOLKSWAGEN CUP ($225,000)

LEIPZIG, 30 SEPTEMBER–6 OCTOBER

WOMEN'S SINGLES – 1st round: S. Graf (1) – bye; P. Langrova d. K. Boogert (Q) 6–2 6–4; C. Porwik
(Q) d. K. Kschwendt 6–3 6–1; J. Wiesner (6) d. E. Brioukhovets 7–6 6–3; K. Maleeva (4) – bye; E.
Sviglerova d. A. Strnadova 6–4 4–6 6–2; R. Zrubakova d. L. Harvey-Wild 6 3 6 7 6 1; B. Paulus (8) d. R.
Rajchrtova 6–1 6–7 6–2; A. Huber (7) d. K. Nowak (Q) 6–2 6–1; I. Demongeot d. M. Paz 7–6 6–4; N.
Ercegovic d. W. Probst 7–6 6–2; J. Novotna (3) – bye; L. Meskhi (5) d. M. Bollegraf 6–3 6–4; B. Rittner d.
K. Rinaldi 6–4 6–1; M. Kochta d. V. Milvidskaia (Q) 6–4 6–4; A. Sanchez-Vicario (2) – bye.
2nd round: Graf (1) d. Langrova 6–0 6–1; Wiesner (6) d. Porwik 6–2 7–5; Maleeva (4) d. Sviglerova 6–4
6–3; Paulus (8) d. Zrubakova 7–6 6–1; Huber (7) d. Demongeot 7–6 6–3; Novotna (3) d. Ercegovic 6–4
6–4; Rittner d. Meskhi (5) 6–2 6–3; Sanchez-Vicario (2) d. Kochta 7–6 6–1.
Quarter-finals: Graf (1) d. Wiesner (6) 6–1 7–6; Paulus (8) d. Maleeva (4) 7–6 0–6 7–6; Novotna (3) d.
Huber (7) 3–6 6–3 6–4; Sanchez-Vicario (2) d. Rittner 6–1 6–1.
Semi-finals: Graf (1) d. Paulus (8) 6–1 6–1; Novotna (3) d. Sanchez-Vicario (2) 6–3 6–2.
Final: Graf (1) d. Novotna (3) 6–3 6–3.
WOMEN'S DOUBLES – Final: Bollegraf/Demongeot (2) d. Hetherington/Rinaldi (1) 6–4 6–3.

BMW EUROPEAN INDOORS ($350,000)

ZURICH, 7–13 OCTOBER

WOMEN'S SINGLES – 1st round: S. Graf (1) d. E. Pfaff (Q) 6–1 7–6; A. Strnadova d. K. Boogert 6–2
6–3; M. Kochta (Q) d. C. Fauche 6–4 6–4; G. Fernandez (8) d. E. Zardo 6–3 7–6; J. Novotna (3) d. W.
Probst 6–2 6–4; C. Kohde-Kilsch d. B. Schultz 7–6 6–2; P. Shriver d. H. Kelesi 6–3 6–2; H. Sukova (5) d.
G. Helgeson 6–2 6–3; J. Wiesner (7) d. C. Tanvier 6–4 6–4; L. McNeil d. A. Frazier 7–6 6–3; I. Berger (Q)
d. K. Kschwendt 6–7 6–4 6–4; M. Maleeva-Fragnière (4) d. K. Habsudova 6–3 6–2; N. Tauziat (6) d. N.
Medvedeva 6–2 6–3; L. Harvey-Wild d. R. McQuillan 7–5 3–6 6–4; N. Zvereva d. E. Brioukhovets 6–2
6–2; G. Sabatini (2) d. E. Maniokova (Q) 6–3 7–5.
2nd round: Graf (1) d. Strnadova 6–2 6–4; Kochta (Q) d. Fernandez (8) 6–1 4–6 6–0; Novotna (3) d.
Kohde-Kilsch 6–3 6–1; Sukova (5) d. Shriver 3–6 7–6 6–4; Wiesner (7) d. McNeil 4–6 6–4 6–1;
Maleeva-Fragnière (4) d. Berger (Q) 6–2 6–1; Tauziat (6) d. Harvey-Wild 6–1 6–0; Sabatini (2) d. Zvereva
6–3 6–2.
Quarter-finals: Graf (1) d. Kochta (Q) 6–2 6–1; Sukova (5) d. Novotna (3) 3–6 6–2 6–4; Maleeva-
Fragnière (4) d. Wiesner (7) 7–6 6–2; Tauziat (6) d. Sabatini (2) 7–6 6–3.
Semi-finals: Graf (1) d. Sukova (5) 6–4 6–3; Tauziat (6) d. Maleeva-Fragnière (4) 7–6 7–6.
Final: Graf (1) d. Tauziat (6) 6–4 6–4.
WOMEN'S DOUBLES – Final: Novotna/Strnadova d. Garrison/McNeil 6–4 6–3.

PORSCHE TENNIS GRAND PRIX ($350,000)

FILDERSTADT, 14–20 OCTOBER

WOMEN'S SINGLES – 1st round: M. Navratilova (1) d. M. Babel (Q) 6–4 6–2; E. Reinach d. B. Paulus
7–6 6–3; M. Bollegraf d. K. Kschwendt 6–3 7–5; N. Tauziat (8) d. P. Shriver 5–7 6–3 6–1; J. Novotna (4)
d. K. Oeljeklaus 6–3 6–3; N. Medvedeva d. H. Kelesi 3–6 6–4 6–4; J. Wiesner d. C. Lindqvist 6–2 6–2; L.
Meskhi (6) d. R. McQuillan 6–2 7–5; Z. Garrison (5) d. G. Helgeson (Q) 6–4 4–6 6–1; B. Schultz d. A.
Temesvari (LL) 6–0 7–6; A. Huber d. L. McNeil 6–4 6–1; N. Zvereva d. C. Martinez (3) 7–6 7–5; H.
Sukova (7) d. W. Probst (Q) 7–6 7–6; A. Frazier d. E. Pfaff 6–2 6–1; R. Zrubakova d. R. Reggi 6–1 6–2;
M.J. Fernandez (2) d. K. Habsudova (Q) 6–0 6–4.
2nd round: Navratilova (1) d. Reinach 6–4 7–5; Tauziat (8) d. Bollegraf default; Novotna (4) d.
Medvedeva 6–4 6–4; Wiesner d. Meskhi (6) 6–1 1–6 6–4; Garrison (5) d. Schultz 6–3 4–6 6–2; Huber d.
Zvereva 6–2 6–2; Sukova (7) d. Frazier 6–7 7–5 6–3; Fernandez (2) d. Zrubakova 6–1 6–1.
Quarter-finals: Navratilova (1) d. Tauziat (8) 6–4 7–5; Wiesner d. Novotna (4) 7–6 6–3; Huber d.
Garrison (5) 6–2 6–1; Sukova (7) d. Fernandez (2) 5–7 6–3 6–3.
Semi-finals: Navratilova (1) d. Wiesner 6–2 7–6; Huber d. Sukova (7) 6–3 7–6.
Final: Huber d. Navratilova (1) 2–6 6–2 7–6.
WOMEN'S DOUBLES – Final: Navratilova/Novotna (1) d. Shriver/Zvereva (2) 6–2 5–7 6–4.

MIDLAND BANK CHAMPIONSHIPS ($350,000)

BRIGHTON, 22–27 OCTOBER

WOMEN'S SINGLES – 1st round: S. Graf (1) d. K. Adams (Q) 7–6 6–3; A. Strnadova d. R. McQuillan
6–3 6–4; E. Maniokova (Q) d. W. Probst 6–2 3–6 6–2; L. McNeil (7) d. B. Schultz 6–4 6–3; N. Tauziat (4)
d. S. Gomer 6–3 7–6; P. Paradis d. K. Kschwendt 6–2 6–3; M. Javer d. D. Monami (Q) 6–1 6–0; B.

Paulus (5) d. N. Jagerman 7–5 6–2; R. Zrubakova (8) d. C. Tanvier 7–6 6–2; Mag. Maleeva d. A. Temesvari 6–1 6–0; R. Fairbank d. P. Shriver 7–6 6–2; Z. Garrison (3) d. E. Pfaff (Q) 6–1 6–3; N. Zvereva (6) d. E. Reinach 6–4 6–2; C. Lindqvist d. C. Wood (LL) 6–0 7–5; J. Durie d. R. Reggi 4–6 6–1 6–0; K. Maleeva (2) d. P. Langrova 6–4 6–3.
2nd round: Graf (1) d. Strnadova 6–2 6–3; McNeil (7) d. Maniokova 7–6 6–3; Tauziat (4) d. Paradis 6–4 6–3; Paulus (5) d. Javer 2–6 6–2 6–2; Zrubakova (8) d. Maleeva 6–2 6–4; Garrison (3) d. Fairbank 6–4 6–4; Lindqvist d. Zvereva (6) 6–4 6–4; Maleeva (2) d. Durie 6–4 6–4.
Quarter-finals: Graf (1) d. McNeil (7) 7–5 6–2; Paulus (5) d. Tauziat (4) default; Garrison (3) d. Zrubakova (8) 6–3 6–2; Lindqvist d. Maleeva (2) 6–2 7–6.
Semi-finals: Graf (1) d. Paulus (5) 7–5 6–1; Garrison (3) d. Lindqvist 6–1 1–0 ret.
Final: Graf (1) d. Garrison (3) 5–7 6–4 6–1.
WOMEN'S DOUBLES – Final: Shriver/Zvereva (1) d. Garrison/McNeil (2) 6–1 6–2.

VIRGINIA SLIMS OF CALIFORNIA ($350,000)

OAKLAND, 4–10 NOVEMBER

WOMEN'S SINGLES – 1st round: M. Seles (1) – bye; M. Javer d. B. Schultz 6–0 6–4; L. Harvey-Wild d. R. Fairbank 2–6 6–4 6–3; G. Fernandez (5) d. G. Helgeson 6–3 6–3; M. Maleeva-Fragnière (3) – bye; M. Paz d. D. Graham 7–5 6–3; M. Werdel d. P. Hy 4–6 6–3 7–5; A. Frazier (7) d. A. Leand 6–3 6–3; L. McNeil (6) d. S. McCarthy 7–5 6–3; P. Fendick d. S. Stafford 6–3 6–3; S. Rehe d. G. Magers 6–4 6–0; Z. Garrison (4) – bye; M. Pierce (8) d. P. Louie-Harper 6–3 3–6 7–5; R. White d. V. Lake 6–2 2–6 6–2; T. Whitlinger d. H. Ludloff 5–7 7–6 6–0; M. Navratilova (2) – bye.
2nd round: Seles (1) d. Javer 6–2 6–0; Harvey-Wild d. Fernandez (5) 3–6 6–3 6–0; Maleeva-Fragnière (3) d. Paz 6–2 6–3; Frazier (7) d. Werdel 7–6 6–4; McNeil (6) d. Fendick 6–4 7–6; Rehe d. Garrison (4) 6–2 6–3; Pierce (8) d. White 6–3 6–3; Navratilova (2) d. Whitlinger 6–1 7–5.
Quarter-finals: Seles (1) d. Harvey-Wild 6–0 6–2; Maleeva-Fragnière (3) d. Frazier (7) 6–3 6–2; McNeil (6) d. Rehe 7–6 6–2; Navratilova (2) d. Pierce (8) 6–2 6–2.
Semi-finals: Seles (1) d. Maleeva-Fragnière (3) 6–2 6–1; Navratilova (2) d. McNeil (6) 6–3 6–2.
Final: Navratilova (2) d. Seles (1) 6–3 3–6 6–3.
WOMEN'S DOUBLES – Final: Fendick/Fernandez (1) d. Navratilova/Shriver (2) 6–4 7–5.

VIRGINIA SLIMS OF PHILADELPHIA ($350,000)

PHILADELPHIA, 11–17 NOVEMBER

WOMEN'S SINGLES – 1st round: M. Seles (1) – bye; M. Werdel d. L. Savchenko 4–6 6–4 7–6; N. Provis d. R. Fairbank 3–6 6–2; Z. Garrison (8) d. J. Moore 6–0 6–0; A. Sanchez-Vicario (3) – bye; T. Whitlinger d. S. Stafford 6–0 7–5; P. Harper d. M. Wreem 6–3 6–0; B. Schultz d. M.J. Fernandez (5) 6–1 2–6 6–4; M. Maleeva-Fragnière (7) d. E. Smylie 6–1 6–2; A. Frazier d. G. Helgeson 6–0 6–2; L. McNeil d. E. Sviglerova 6–1 1–6 6–2; J. Capriati (4) – bye; C. Martinez (6) d. C. Lindqvist 6–2 6–4; H. Sukova d. E. Brioukhovets 6–3 6–4; N. Zvereva d. S. Appelmans 6–4 6–2; G. Sabatini (2) – bye.
2nd round: Seles (1) d. Werdel 7–5 6–1; Garrison (8) d. Provis 6–4 6–4; Sanchez-Vicario (3) d. Whitlinger 6–0 3–6 6–2; Schultz d. Harper 6–3 6–4; Maleeva-Fragnière (7) d. Frazier 6–3 6–3; Capriati (4) d. McNeil 7–6 6–7 6–2; Martinez (6) d. Sukova 6–3 6–2; Sabatini (2) d. Zvereva 7–6 2–6 6–2.
Quarter-finals: Seles (1) d. Garrison (8) 7–6 6–0; Sanchez-Vicario (3) d. Schultz 6–7 6–1 6–4; Capriati (4) d. Maleeva-Fragnière (7) 6–3 6–2; Sabatini (2) d. Martinez (6) 6–3 6–0.
Semi-finals: Seles (1) d. Sanchez-Vicario (3) 6–1 6–2; Capriati (4) d. Sabatini (2) 6–3 6–4.
Final: Seles (1) d. Capriati (4) 7–5 6–1.
WOMEN'S DOUBLES – Final: Novotna/Savchenko (1) d. Fernandez/Garrison (4) 6–2 6–4.

A happy return to form in 1991 for new WTA President Pam Shriver, who achieved victories at the US Open with Zvereva and the US Championships with her old partner Navratilova. *(R. Adams)*

KRAFT GENERAL FOODS WORLD TOUR

Tournaments with prize money below $225,000

NIVEA CUP ($75,000)

SAO PAULO, 29 NOVEMBER–2 DECEMBER 1990

WOMEN'S SINGLES – Quarter-finals: L. Corsato d. E. Sviglerova (1) 6–2 6–2; V. Martinek (5) d. C. Mothes (3) 3–6 7–6 6–4; F. Labat (8) d. C. Tessi 6–2 6–1; D. Faber (6) d. S. Smith 3–6 6–4 6–2.
Semi-finals: Martinek (5) d. Corsato 6–3 6–2; Faber (6) d. Labat (8) 3–6 6–3 6–2.
Final: Martinek (5) d. Faber (6) 6–2 6–4.
WOMEN'S DOUBLES – Final: B. Fulco/E. Sviglerova (4) d. M. Pierce/L. Spadea (1) 7–5 6–4.

DANONE WOMEN'S OPEN ($150,000)

BRISBANE, 31 DECEMBER–6 JANUARY

WOMEN'S SINGLES – Quarter-finals: L. Savchenko d. S. Appelmans (5) 6–4 2–6 6–4; A. Kijimuta d. R. McQuillan (9) 6–2 6–7 6–3; L. Harvey-Wild d. J. Wiesner (4) 6–1 6–4; H. Sukova (2) d. C. Tessi 6–2 6–1.
Semi-finals: Kijimuta d. Savchenko 6–2 5–7 6–2; Sukova (2) d. Harvey-Wild 6–1 6–1.
Final: Sukova (2) d. Kijimuta 6–4 6–3.
WOMEN'S DOUBLES – Final: G. Fernandez/J. Novotna (1) d. P. Fendick/Sukova (2) 6–3 6–1.

NUTRI-METICS BENDON CLASSIC ($100,000)

AUCKLAND, 28 JANUARY–3 FEBRUARY

WOMEN'S SINGLES – Quarter-finals: A. Strnadova (Q) d. L. Savchenko (8) 6–4 6–1; C. Tessi d. D. Faber 6–4 7–6; E. Sviglerova d. S. Hack (7) 6–7 7–5 6–1; M. Paz (2) d. P. Kamstra (Q) 4–3 ret.
Semi-finals: Strnadova (Q) d. Tessi 6–0 6–4; Sviglerova d. Paz (2) 6–2 6–3.
Final: Sviglerova d. Strnadova (Q) 6–2 0–6 6–1.
WOMEN'S DOUBLES – Final: P. Fendick/Savchenko (1) d. J. Faull/J. Richardson (3) 6–3 6–3.

OSLO OPEN ($75,000)

OSLO, 5–10 FEBRUARY

WOMEN'S SINGLES – Quarter-finals: S. Appelmans (1) d. N. Herreman (5) 6–2 6–1; C. Lindqvist (3) d. C. Tanvier (7) 6–0 3–2 ret.; P. Paradis d. C. Dahlman (8) 6–3 6–0; R. Reggi (2) d. B. Reinstadler 6–3 6–4.
Semi-finals: Lindqvist (3) d. Appelmans (1) 6–2 6–2; Reggi (2) d. Paradis 7–5 6–1.
Final: Lindqvist (3) d. Reggi (2) 6–3 6–0.
WOMEN'S DOUBLES – Final: C. Kohde-Kilsch/S. Meier d. Appelmans/Reggi (2) 3–6 6–2 6–4.

FERNLEAF BUTTER CLASSIC ($100,000)

WELLINGTON, 4 10 FEBRUARY

WOMEN'S SINGLES – Quarter-finals: L. Meskhi (1) d. E. Sviglerova 6–3 6–4; K. Quentrec d. S. Hack (4) 0–6 6–2 6–3; K. Godridge d. B. Rittner 6–2 6–3; A. Strnadova d. L. Field 7–6 7–5.
Semi-finals: Meskhi (1) d. Quentrec 6–2 6–3; Strnadova d. Godridge 6–4 7–6.
Final: Meskhi (1) d. Strnadova 3–6 7–6 6–2.
WOMEN'S DOUBLES – Final: J. Faull/J. Richardson (1) d. B. Borneo/C. Wood 2–6 7–5 7–6.

COLORADO TENNIS CLASSIC ($100,000)

AURORA, 11–17 FEBRUARY

WOMEN'S SINGLES – Quarter-finals: C. Cunningham (5) d. S. Sloane (1) 6–2 6–4; L. McNeil (4) d. A. Leand 6–2 6–1; P. Fendick (6) d. H. Cioffi 1–6 7–6 6–4; M. Bollegraf (2) d. P. Louie Harper (7) 7–6 7–5. *Semi-finals:* McNeil (4) d. Cunningham (5) 6–4 6–2; Bollegraf (2) d. Fendick (6) 6–2 6–2.
Final: McNeil (4) d. Bollegraf (2) 6–3 6–4.
WOMEN'S DOUBLES – Final: L. Gregory/G. Magers (2) d. Fendick/McNeil (1) 6–4 6–4.

AUSTRIAN TENNIS GRAND PRIX ($100,000)

LINZ, 11–17 FEBRUARY

WOMEN'S SINGLES – Quarter-finals: M. Maleeva-Fragnière (1) d. E. Maniokova (Q) 6–2 6–2; R. Rajchrtova (4) d. P. Paradis 6–4 6–4; C. Kohde-Kilsch (5) d. R. Reggi (3) 7–6 6–3; P. Langrova d. M. Maruska 6–3 6–1.
Semi-finals: Maleeva-Fragnière (1) d. Rajchrtova (4) 2–6 6–3 6–4; Langrova d. Kohde-Kilsch (5) 3–6 6–1 6–4.
Final: Maleeva-Fragnière (1) d. Langrova 6–4 7–6.
WOMEN'S DOUBLES – Final: Maleeva-Fragnière/Reggi (2) d. Langrova/R. Zrubakova (3) 6–4 1–6 6–3.

VIRGINIA SLIMS OF OKLAHOMA ($150,000)

OKLAHOMA CITY, 18–24 FEBRUARY

WOMEN'S SINGLES – Quarter-finals: J. Novotna (1) d. C. Lindqvist (7) 6–3 6–1; L. Bonder-Kreiss (Q) d. R. Baranski (Q) 6–0 6–3; A. Smith (5) d. A. Minter 6–0 6–4; M. Bollegraf (8) d. C. Martinez (2) 6–4 6–1.
Semi-finals: Novotna (1) d. Bonder-Kreiss (Q) 6–4 6–1; Smith (5) d. Bollegraf (8) 6–3 6–2.
Final: Novotna (1) d. Smith (5) 3–6 6–3 6–2.
WOMEN'S DOUBLES – Final: M. McGrath/Smith (2) d. K. Adams/J. Hetherington (3) 6–2 6–4.

LIGHT 'N LIVELY DOUBLES ($200,000)

TARPON SPRINGS, FLORIDA, 28–31 MARCH

WOMEN'S DOUBLES – Final: G. Fernandez/H. Sukova (1) d. L. Savchenko/N. Zvereva (2) 4–6 6–4 7–6.

SUNTORY JAPAN OPEN ($150,000)

TOKYO, 8–14 APRIL

WOMEN'S SINGLES – Quarter-finals: L. McNeil (7) d. A. Frazier (1) 6–3 6–3; L. Gildemeister (5) d. K. Okamoto (Q) 6–4 6–4; R. Hiraki (Q) d. E. Sviglerova (6) 6–7 6–4 6–4; S. Appelmans (2) d. M. Werdel (8) 6–3 3–6 6–1.
Semi-finals: McNeil (7) d. Gildemeister (5) 7–6 6–3; Appelmans (2) d. Hiraki (Q) 6–4 6–4.
Final: McNeil (7) d. Appelmans (2) 2–6 6–2 6–1.
WOMEN'S DOUBLES – Final: Frazier/M. Kidowaki (4) d. Y. Kamio/A. Kijimuta (Q) 6–2 6–4.

VOLVO WOMEN'S OPEN ($75,000)

PATTAYA, THAILAND, 15–21 APRIL

WOMEN'S SINGLES – Quarter-finals: R. Hiraki (WC) d. S. Loosemore (8) 6–0 6–2; Y. Basuki d. K. Kschwendt (6) 5–7 6–3 6–4; M. Werdel (4) d. M. Miyauchi 7–6 6–0; N. Sawamatsu (2) d. M. Javer (7) 6–2 6–3.
Semi-finals: Basuki d. Hiraki (WC) 3–6 6–1 6–2; Sawamatsu (2) d. Werdel (4) 6–1 6–3.
Final: Basuki d. Sawamatsu (2) 6–2 6–2.
WOMEN'S DOUBLES – Final: N. Miyagi/S. Wibowo d. Hiraki/A. Nishiya 6–1 6–4.

CROATIAN LOTTERY CUP – BOL LADIES OPEN ($100,000)

BOL, 22–28 APRIL

WOMEN'S SINGLES – Quarter-finals: H. Kelesi (1) d. A. Foldenyi 7–5 6–1; Mag. Maleeva (3) d. L. Garrone (7) 6–3 7–5; S. Testud d. C. Bartos (8) 6–2 6–2; S. Cecchini (2) d. A. Strnadova (6) 6–4 6–4.
Semi-finals: Maleeva (3) d. Kelesi (1) 6–4 7–5; Cecchini (2) d. Testud default.
Final: Cecchini (2) d. Maleeva (3) 6–4 3–6 7–5.
WOMEN'S DOUBLES – Final: L. Golarsa/Maleeva (3) d. Cecchini/Garrone (1) 6–3 1–6 6–4.

TROFEO ILVA-COPPA MANTEGAZZA ($100,000)

TARANTO, ITALY, 30 APRIL–5 MAY

WOMEN'S SINGLES – Quarter-finals: P. Ritter d. F. Bonsignori (1) 6–1 0–6 6–4; S. Farina d. F. Labat 2–6 6–3 6–4; N. Dahlman (LL) d. P. Thoren (Q) 6–2 3–6 6–3; E. Zardo d. N. Van Lottum 5–7 6–3 6–2.
Semi-finals: Ritter d. Farina 3–6 6–1 6–0; Zardo d. Dahlman (LL) 6–0 6–3.
Final: Zardo d. Ritter 7–5 6–2.
WOMEN'S DOUBLES – Final: A. Dechaume/Labat (3) d. L. Golarsa/A. Grossman (2) 6–2 7–5.

GENEVA EUROPEAN OPEN ($150,000)

GENEVA, 20–26 MAY

WOMEN'S SINGLES – Quarter-finals: C. Martinez (1) d. C. Fauche 6–3 6–3; H. Kelesi (4) d. G. Helgeson 6–7 7–5 6–1; T. Whitlinger (LL) d. M. Kidowaki 6–4 7–6; M. Maleeva-Fragnière (2) d. S. Stafford (Q) 6–4 6–3.
Semi-finals: Kelesi (4) d. Martinez (1) 6–4 6–7 6–2; Maleeva-Fragnière (2) d. Whitlinger (LL) 6–1 6–3.
Final: Maleeva-Fragnière (2) d. Kelesi (4) 6–3 3–6 6–3.
WOMEN'S DOUBLES – Final: N. Provis/E. Smylie (1) d. C. Caverzasio/Maleeva-Fragnière (4) 6–1 6–2.

INTERNATIONAUX DE STRASBOURG ($150,000)

STRASBOURG, 20–26 MAY

WOMEN'S SINGLES – Quarter-finals: R. McQuillan d. J. Wiesner (1) 6–4 7–6; N. Sawamatsu d. C. Kohde-Kilsch 6–3 6–1; R. Zrubakova d. L. Gildemeister (4) 6–0 6–3; A. Minter d. L. McNeil (2) 6–1 7–6.
Semi-finals: McQuillan d. Sawamatsu 6–4 6–3; Zrubakova d. Mintor 6–1 6–3.
Final: Zrubakova d. McQuillan 7–6 7–6.
WOMEN'S DOUBLES – Final: McNeil/S. Rehe (4) d. M. Bollegraf/M. Paz (1) 6–7 6–4 6–4.

THE DOW CLASSIC ($150,000)

BIRMINGHAM, 10–16 JUNE

WOMEN'S SINGLES – Quarter-finals: M. Navratilova (1) d. L. McNeil (5) 6–3 6–2; B. Schultz d. C. Suire (LL) 6–3 6–2; N. Zvereva (4) d. M. Bollegraf (8) 6–4 6–7 6–2; Z. Garrison (2) d. M. De Swardt 6–3 6–4.
Semi-finals: Navratilova (1) d. Schultz 6–3 6–2; Zvereva (4) d. Garrison (2) 2–6 7–6 8–6.
Final: Navratilova (1) d. Zvereva (4) 6–4 7–6.
WOMEN'S DOUBLES – Final: N. Provis/E. Smylie (2) d. S. Collins/E. Reinach (8) 6–3 6–4.

TORNEO INTERNAZIONALE FEMMINILE DI PALERMO ($75,000)

PALERMO, 8–14 JULY

WOMEN'S SINGLES – Quarter-finals: S. Cecchini (1) d. C. Tessi 6–4 7–5; E. Zardo (3) d. S. Frankl 6–2 6–2; S. Wasserman (Q) d. M. Laval (Q) 6–0 6–1; M. Pierce d. C. Mothes 6–1 6–0.
Semi-finals: Cecchini (1) d. Zardo (3) 6–3 7–6; Pierce d. Wasserman 6–1 6–1.
Final: Pierce d. Cecchini (1) 6–0 6–3.
WOMEN'S DOUBLES – Final: P. Langrova/Pierce (2) d. L. Garrone/M. Paz (1) 6–3 6–7 6–3.

CITROEN AUSTRIAN LADIES OPEN ($150,000)

KITZBUHEL, 15–21 JULY

WOMEN'S SINGLES – Quarter-finals: C. Martinez (1) d. E. Sviglerova 6–2 4–6 7–5; R. Zrubakova (6) d. S. Cecchini (3) 6–3 2–6 6–3; J. Wiesner (4) d. F. Labat 6–2 6–4; N. Jagerman d. M. Maruska 6–3 6–3.
Semi-finals: Martinez (1) d. Zrubakova (6) 7–5 6–4: Wiesner (4) d. Jagerman 6–2 6–3.
Final: Martinez (1) d. Wiesner (4) 6–1 2–6 6–3.
WOMEN'S DOUBLES – Final: B. Fulco/Jagerman (4) d. Cecchini/P. Tarabini (2) 7–5 6–4.

VOLVO SAN MARINO OPEN ($75,000)

SAN MARINO, ITALY, 15–21 JULY

WOMEN'S SINGLES – Quarter-finals: S. Farina d. R. Reggi (1) 6–1 7–5; E. Pampoulova d. S. Hack (4) 6–2 2–0 ret.; D. Szabova d. C. Cunningham (3) 6–2 6–3; K. Piccolini (2) d. E. Maniokova 3–6 7–6 6–4.
Semi–final: Farina d. Pampoulova 6–2 7–6; Piccolini (2) d. Szabova 6–2 6–1.
Final: Piccolini (2) d. Farina 6–2 6–3.
WOMEN'S DOUBLES – Final: K. Guse/A. Nishiya (4) d. L. Garrone/M. Paz (1) 6–0 6–3.

WESTCHESTER LADIES CUP ($100,000)

WESTCHESTER, NEW YORK, 22–28 JULY

WOMEN'S SINGLES – Quarter-finals: L. Gildemeister (1) d. M. Kochta 6–2 6–4; I. Demongeot d. C. Cunningham (6) 7–6 6–3; R. Fairbank (5) d. L. Raymond (Q) 6–3 6–3; L. McNeil (2) d. D. Graham (8) 7–5 6–0.
Semi-finals: Demongeot d. Gildemeister (1) 6–1 6–1; McNeil (2) d. Fairbank (5) 5–7 6–2 6–1.
Final: Demongeot d. McNeil (2) 6–4 6–4.
WOMEN'S DOUBLES – Final: Fairbank/L. Gregory (2) d. K. Adams/McNeil (1) 7–5 6–4.

VIRGINIA SLIMS OF ALBUQUERQUE ($150,000)

ALBUQUERQUE, 5–11 AUGUST

WOMEN'S SINGLES – Quarter-finals: J. Halard (1) d. K. Adams (Q) 6–2 4–6 6–0; E. Reinach (6) d. M. Pierce (3) 6–2 6–0; S. Sloane (4) d. S. Testud 6–3 6–3; G. Fernandez (2) d. L. Ferrando (7) 6–4 7–6.
Semi-finals: Halard (1) d. Reinach (6) 6–3 3–6 6–4; Fernandez (2) d. Sloane (4) 6–3 57 6–2.
Final: Fernandez (2) d. Halard (1) 6–0 6–2.
WOMEN'S DOUBLES – Final: Adams/I. Demongeot (2) d. L. Gregory/P. Louie Harper (3) 6–7 6–4 6–3.

OTB INTERNATIONAL TENNIS OPEN ($100,000)

SCHENECTADY, 19–25 AUGUST

WOMEN'S SINGLES – Quarter-finals: A. Dechaume d. A. Huber (1) 6–3 6–4; M. Werdel (3) d. N. Sawamatsu (5) 6–3 6–2; B. Schultz (7) d. R. McQuillan (4) 4–6 6–4 6–2; N. Provis d. F. Labat 7–5 6–3.
Semi-finals: Dechaume d. Werdel (3) 6–1 6–3; Schultz (7) d. Provis 5–7 7–5 6–3.
Final: Schultz (7) d. Dechaume 7–6 6–2.
WOMEN'S DOUBLES – Final: McQuillan/C. Porwik (4) d. N. Arendt/S. McCarthy 6–2 6–4.

OPEN CLARINS ($150,000)

PARIS, 16–22 SEPTEMBER

WOMEN'S SINGLES – Quarter-finals: C. Martinez (1) d. E. Zardo (6) 6–4 6–2; J. Halard (4) d. V. Martinek 6–4 6–3; M. Paz d. N. Jagerman 1–6 7–5 6–3; I. Gorrochategui d. S. Meier (LL) 6–3 7–5.
Semi-finals: Martinez (1) d. Halard (4) 6–4 2–6 7–5; Gorrochategui d. Paz 6–2 6–3.
Final: Martinez (1) d. Gorrochategui 6–0 6–3.
WOMEN'S DOUBLES – Final: Langrova/Zrubakova (3) d. Dechaume/Halard 6–4 6–4.

OPEN WHIRLPOOL – VILLE DE BAYONNE ($150,000)

BAYONNE, FRANCE, 23–29 SEPTEMBER

WOMEN'S SINGLES – Quarter-finals: M. Maleeva-Fragnière (1) d. J. Halard (5) 6–3 6–4; R. McQuillan (7) d. R. Zrubakova (4) 4–6 6–1 6–3; N. Tauziat (3) d. E. Sviglerova (8) 6–4 6–1; L. Meskhi (2) d. C. Porwik 6–4 6–3.
Semi-finals: Maleeva-Fragnière (1) d. McQuillan (7) 7–6 6–4; Meskhi (2) d. Tauziat (3) 6–2 7–5.
Final: Maleeva-Fragnière (1) d. Meskhi (2) 4–6 6–3 6–4.
WOMEN'S DOUBLES – Final: Tarabini/Tauziat (4) d. McQuillan/Tanvier (1) 6–3 ret.

ST PETERSBURG LADIES OPEN ($100,000)

ST PETERSBURG, 23–29 SEPTEMBER

WOMEN'S SINGLES – Quarter-finals: L. Savchenko (5) d. E. Brioukhovets (1) 6–0 6–3; J. Durie (7) d. I. Demongeot (4) 6–2 6–2; B. Rittner (3) d. S. Testud 7–6 6–2; K. Oeljeklaus d. A. Henricksson 6–7 6–3 6–3.
Semi-finals: Savchenko (5) d. Durie (7) 6–4 6–4; Rittner (3) d. Oeljeklaus 3–6 6–3 6–4.
Final: Savchenko (5) d. Rittner (3) 3–6 6–3 6–4.
WOMEN'S DOUBLES – Final: Brioukhovets/N. Medvedeva (2) d. Demongeot/Durie (1) 7–5 6–3.

PUERTO RICAN OPEN LADIES CHAMPIONSHIPS ($150,000)

SAN JUAN, PUERTO RICO, 21–27 OCTOBER

WOMEN'S SINGLES – Quarter-finals: A. Coetzer d. G. Fernandez (1) 6–4 6–2; S. Appelmans (3) d. S. Sloane (6) 6–4 6–1; M. Pierce (4) d. C. Cunningham 3–6 6–1 6–2; J. Halard (2) d. B. Rittner (5) 5–7 6–1 7–6.
Semi-finals: Coetzer d. Appelmans (3) 3–6 6–3 7–5; Halard (2) d. Pierce (4) 7–5 6–1.
Final: Halard (2) d. Coetzer 7–5 7–5.
WOMEN'S DOUBLES – Final: R. Hiraki/F. Labat d. Appelmans/C. Benjamin (1) 6–3 6–3.

ARIZONA CLASSIC ($150,000)

PHOENIX, 28 OCTOBER–3 NOVEMBER

WOMEN'S SINGLES – Quarter-finals: C. Rubin (Q) d. G. Helgeson 6–3 7–5; K. Habsudova d. K. Po (Q) 4–6 6–1 6–3; S. Appelmans (3) d. N. Provis 6–4 6–4; J. Halard (2) d. P. Fendick 4–6 6–4 6–1.
Semi-finals: Rubin (Q) d. Habsudova 6–2 6–4; Appelmans (3) d. Halard (2) 3–6 6–3 6–3.
Final: Appelmans (3) d. Rubin (Q) 7–5 6–1.
WOMEN'S DOUBLES – Final: P. Harper/C. McGregor d. S. Collins/E. Reinach (3) 7–5 3–6 6–3.

VIRGINIA SLIMS OF NASHVILLE ($150,000)

BRENTWOOD, TENNESSEE, 4–10 NOVEMBER

WOMEN'S SINGLES – Quarter-finals: K. Habsudova d. Y. Basuki (8) 6–4 6–2; S. Appelmans (4) d. M.L. Daniels (Q) 6–4 6–4; K. Adams d. T. Whittington (Q) 7–5 6–1; N. Medvedeva (7) d. I. Demongeot 3–6 7–5 6–2.
Semi-finals: Appelmans (4) d. Habsudova 6–3 6–4; Adams d. Medvedeva (7) 7–6 5–7 6–4.
Final: Appelmans (4) d. Adams 6–2 6–4.
WOMEN'S DOUBLES – Final: S. Collins/E. Reinach (4) d. Basuki/C. Vis 5–7 6–4 7–6.

JELL-O TENNIS CLASSIC ($150,000)

INDIANAPOLIS, 11–16 NOVEMBER

WOMEN'S SINGLES – Quarter-finals: K. Maleeva (1) d. S. Sloane 6–3 6–3; M. Paz d. M.L. Daniels 6–4 6–3; R. Zrubakova (4) d. L. Harvey-Wild 6–4 6–4; A. Keller d. P. Thoren 6–2 6–3.
Semi-finals: Maleeva (1) d. Paz 6–2 6–1; Keller d. Zrubakova (4) 6–2 6–4.
Final: Maleeva (1) d. Keller 7–6 6–2.
WOMEN'S DOUBLES – Final: Fendick/Fernandez (1) d. Adams/Paz (2) 6–4 6–2.

With her victory in the season-ending Virginia Slims Championships Monica Seles, aged 17 years 11 months, became the youngest-ever official world champion. Her earnings of $2,457,758 were $284,202 ahead of Navratilova's record set in 1984. (T. Hindley)

MADISON SQUARE GARDENS, NEW YORK, 18–24 NOVEMBER
1st round: M. Seles (1) d. J. Halard 6–1 6–0; M.J. Fernandez (7) d. H. Sukova 2–6 7–6 2–2 ret.; G. Sabatini (3) d. K. Maleeva 6–2 7–6; J. Capriati (6) d. N. Tauziat 5–7 6–0 7–6; A. Sanchez–Vicario (5) d. Z. Garrison 4–6 6–1 6–0; M. Navratilova (4) d. L. McNeil 6–4 7–5; J. Novotna (8) d. M. Maleeva–Fragnière 6–0 3–6 6–3; S. Graf (2) d. C. Martinez 6–0 6–3.
Quarter-finals: Seles (1) d. Fernandez (7) 6–3 6–2; Sabatini (3) d. Capriati (6) 6–1 6–4; Navratilova (4) d. Sanchez–Vicario (5) 1–6 6–4 6–2; Novotna (8) d. Graf (2) 6–3 3–6 6–1.
Semi-finals: Seles (1) d. Sabatini (3) 6–1 6–1; Navratilova (4) d. Novotna (8) 6–1 6–4.
Final: Seles (1) d. Navratilova (4) 6–4 3–6 7–5 6–0.
DOUBLES – Final: Navratilova/P. Shriver d. G. Fernandez/Novotna (1) 4–6 7–5 6–4.

PRIZE MONEY TOTAL $3 MILLION (including Bonus Pool of $2 million and a contribution of $70,000 to the WTA).

SINGLES – Winner $250,000; Runner-up $120,000; Semi-finalists $53,000; Quarter-finalists $26,000; Round of 16 $14,000.

DOUBLES (per pair) – Winners $90,000; Runners-up $46,000; Semi-finalists $25,000; First Round $13,000.

VIRGINIA SLIMS CHAMPIONSHIPS

Barry Wood

Monica Seles completed her supremely successful year by retaining the Virginia Slims Championships title with a 6–4 3–6 7–5 6–0 victory over Martina Navratilova. In doing so, she confirmed herself as the outstanding player of 1991 and, with bonus pool money included, she added $800,000 to her earnings for the year.

What separated the 5-time former champion and Seles was the Yugoslav's return of serve. Seles was far superior in that area, either hitting outright winners or returning the ball to Navratilova's feet as she rushed the net. There was only one break point in the opening set but it came at a decisive moment, giving Seles a 5–4 lead.

Seles had chances to win the second set too, holding a break point for 3–2 and three more for 4–3, but it was Navratilova who eventually took the lead, in the 8th game, before serving out for the set. But with Seles continuing her relentless groundstroke barrage, Navratilova continued to find herself under extreme pressure.

Seles took a 3–0 lead in the third set, and then broke to love to lead 5–3. Navratilova was not quite ready to lie down, however, and won the next two games, breaking Seles to 30 and holding for 5–5 with her 10th ace. Yet another winning return from Seles, though, gave the top seed another break and the third set.

Stamina was always likely to play a part in the outcome of the only best of five sets match in the women's calendar, for there was surely a limit to what Navratilova, now 35, could muster in defiance of the advancing years. 'She puts more pressure on you from the baseline than anyone I've played against. It comes from both sides so there is no rest.'

And so it proved. Youth triumphed in the end, with 17-year-old Seles romping through the 4th set in 20 minutes, for the loss of just 10 points. Afterwards, however, the winner did admit that she had been far from fresh. Revealing that she was worried about the onset of cramp Seles said, 'I was just hoping it wouldn't have to go to a fifth set.'

Right from the first night the tennis did not disappoint. Steffi Graf, lacking for the first time the guidance of her banished coach, Pavel Slozil, nevertheless reached the second round quite comfortably, defeating Conchita Martinez 6–0 6–3. In truth the score flatters, borne out by the fact that Navratilova took less time to overcome Lori McNeil 6–4 7–5, despite that match containing seven more games.

Martinez has attained her lofty status largely by playing weaker events where she is virtually guaranteed the title, although she certainly has the ability to challenge the best by using her racquet to paint strokes of genius. Graf overcame her artistry by applying a little uncharacteristic serve-and-volley at the right moments, which both surprised and unsettled the frustrated Spaniard, and Graf hinted afterwards that there may be more of that kind of thing from her in the future.

Gabriela Sabatini overcame Katerina Maleeva 6–2 7–6 on the second night, although the margin between success and failure was narrow indeed. Sabatini twice served for the second set and victory, but then found herself down 1–4 in the tiebreak. Had she lost that, Maleeva might well have succeeded, for she was solid from the back and willing to attack when the opportunity was there. But Sabatini showed a greater command of the net, was more agile and athletic, and so deserved her place in the second round.

There were wins too for Arantxa Sanchez-Vicario, who overcame Zina Garrison 4–6 6–1 6–0, Jana Novotna, who defeated Manuela Maleeva 6–0 3–6 6–3, and Mary Joe Fernandez, who progressed when Helena Sukova withdrew in tears at 2–2 in the final set after suffering a hamstring strain.

Sanchez-Vicario totally dominated a dispirited Garrison after a superbly contested first set, during which both played with great intelligence and skill. Their fine running, aggressive rallying from the baseline, and their ability to hit the lines with pinpoint accuracy, was excellent entertainment but Garrison was unable to maintain such a high standard against a more resilient opponent.

On the third night, while Seles dismissed Julie Halard 6–1 6–0 in just 37 minutes, Jennifer Capriati was taken to the brink of defeat by Nathalie Tauziat. Part of the reason for Capriati's difficulty in winning 5–7 6–0 7–6 could be blamed on a groin strain, which made it difficult for her to move wide to the ball.

But Tauziat is also a very able opponent who had earned wins over three top 5 players during the year. Her forehand is a formidable weapon, but she is hindered by a lack of consistency and concentration. Instead of consolidating her position after winning the first set, she lost eight successive games. But once she had regained control of an errant backhand Tauziat renewed her challenge, and six times was within two points of victory.

'In the second set I wanted to win the point too early and tried to play too fast. In the third set I slowed down and put more volleys in the court,' Tauziat explained.

The first upset came in the quarter-finals. Novotna defeated Graf, who rarely looked capable of overcoming what was a competent but by no means exceptional Czech performance, 6–3 3–6 6–1. It took Graf 67 minutes to earn her first, and only, break point of the match, and she fell away quite dramatically in the final set, offering only a muted challenge. The German's errant forehand, and Novotna's ability to pressure her backhand, meant that Graf never looked comfortable.

But a new Graf may rise from the ashes. 'I have to look at my tennis differently, be more positive and a little looser. I take it too seriously now and have to enjoy it more,' she said.

Martina Navratilova's 1–6 6–4 6–2 victory over Sanchez-Vicario was remarkable for the fact that she was so overwhelmed in the first set that she draped a white towel over her racquet and raised it in surrender. The Spaniard assaulted her with a barrage of stunning groundstrokes and service return winners that left Navratilova helpless.

But she immediately responded to the loss of the first set by breaking serve as the second got under way. That was enough to level the match, and she played almost flawlessly in the final set to claim what had seemed an unlikely place in the semi-finals.

Navratilova was joined there by Sabatini, who avenged three consecutive defeats by Capriati, reversing the tide with a 6–1 6–4 win. Capriati broke to take the lead in each set, but lacked discipline and made careless errors. Sabatini was far from perfect, but steadier.

'Mentally I wasn't really there. Because of my injury I cut down on practice and wasn't really prepared,' said Capriati.

Fernandez was beaten 6–3 6–2 in the remaining quarter-final, despite mixing her game up to keep Seles guessing. But she could not cope with constantly having to run down the fiercely struck groundstrokes of her opponent.

The most significant aspect of the semi-finals was not the fact that Seles and Navratilova won, but the ease of their victories. Seles took only 48 minutes to dismiss Sabatini 6–1 6–1.

'I didn't even have a chance to lose my confidence,' Sabatini admitted. 'She just hits the ball so deep on both sides, and puts her whole body into it. I didn't feel I had a chance.'

Navratilova would have overcome Novotna just as comprehensively if she had not had a quite absurd lapse of concentration late in the second set. Instead, she had to be content with winning 6–1 6–4 in 55 minutes. Novotna was sluggish and totally out of touch. Had the American not self-destructed on her serve in the second set, then Novotna would have been totally humiliated.

Navratilova was far more ready for business, and made her statement by dropping only one point in the first three games. Novotna, the broodiest of players, responded by going into a sulk, which even Navratilova's second set wobble failed to lift. Three times Navratilova lost her serve, and three times Novotna allowed her to break straight back, the last occasion from 40–0 for victory.

The week, which drew a new record of more than 100,000 enthusiastic spectators to Madison Square Garden, was another example of the improvement in the image of the women's game. At their best, the women are every bit as entertaining as the men. They proved it again this year.

OTHER OFFICIAL PRO TOURNAMENTS

MEN'S CHALLENGER SERIES
MEN'S SATELLITE CIRCUITS
ITF WOMEN'S FUTURES CIRCUIT

Paul Haarhuis's victory in the Lagos Challenger was the start of a fine year for the Dutchman who beat the entire German Davis Cup team (Jelen, Becker and Steeb) at the US Open before losing narrowly to Connors in the last eight. (R. Adams)

MEN'S CHALLENGER SERIES 1991

Tournaments with minimum prize money of $25,000 that are immediately below the ATP Tour and carry ATP ranking points.

FINALS

HEILBRONN (GER) 21–27 JANUARY
Singles: D. Nargiso (ITA) d. M. Zoecke (GER) 3–6 7–6 6–3. **Doubles:** Nargiso/S. Pescosolido (ITA) d. C. Saceanu (GER)/M. Schapers (HOL) 6–2 6–2

VINA DEL MAR (CHI) 21–27 JANUARY
Singles: G. Giussani (ARG) d. G. Markus (ARG) 4–6 6–2 6–0. **Doubles:** J-A. Pino (CUB)/M. Tabares (CUB) d. Markus/F. Yunis (ARG) 6–3 6–2

BANGALORE (IND) 28 JANUARY–3 FEBRUARY
Singles: F. Dennhardt (GER) d. V. Gabrichidze (URS) 3–6 6–4 6–4. **Doubles:** Gabrichidze/M. Nastase (ROM) d. S. Cole (GBR)/M. Zumpft (GER) 2–6 7–5 6–3

BENIN CITY (NGR) 28 JANUARY–3 FEBRUARY
Singles: U. Colombini (ITA) d. Y. Doumbia (SEN) 6–4 3–6 6–4. **Doubles:** M. Keil (USA)/S. Patridge (USA) d. T. Middleton (USA)/T. Scherman (USA) 7–5 6–7 7–5

JAKARTA I (INA) 4–10 FEBRUARY
Singles: V. Roubicek (TCH) d. S. Youl (AUS) 6–3 3–6 6–3. **Doubles:** M. Ardinghi (ITA)/M. Boscatto (ITA) d. P. Carter (AUS)/N. Kroon (SWE) 5–7 6–4 7–6

LAGOS (NGR) 4–10 FEBRUARY
Singles: P. Haarhuis (HOL) d. T. Middleton (USA) 6–3 6–3. **Doubles:** U. Colombini (ITA)/P. Wekesa (KEN) d. D. Marco (ESP)/C. N'Goran (CIV) 7–5 6–1

TELFORD (GBR) 4–10 FEBRUARY
Singles: J. Siemerink (HOL) d. M. Laurendeau (CAN) 6–3 6–4. **Doubles:** Laurendeau/L. Lavalle (MEX) d. P. Nyborg (SWE)/Siemerink 7–6 6–3

SAO PAULO I (BRA) 11–17 FEBRUARY
Singles: G. Markus (ARG) d. J. Cunha-Silva (POR) 4–6 6–4 6–4. **Doubles:** H. Holm (SWE)/N. Holm (SWE) d. J. Letts (USA)/T. Mercer (USA) 5–7 6–4 6–4

AMERICANA (BRA) 18–24 FEBRUARY
Singles: S. Matsuoka (JPN) d. R. Gilbert (FRA) 6–4 4–6 6–1. **Doubles:** A. Hocevar (BRA)/M. Hocevar (BRA) d. J. Daher (BRA)/F. Roese (BRA) 7–6 6–4

GUADELOUPE (GUD) 25 FEBRUARY–3 MARCH
Singles: O. Delaitre (FRA) d. S. Pescosolido (ITA) 6–2 7–6. **Doubles:** J. Cunha-Silva (POR) d. N. Marques (POR)/d. Delaitre/R. Gilbert (FRA) 6–3 6–1

INDIAN WELLS (USA) 25 FEBRUARY–3 MARCH
Singles: C. Caratti (ITA) d. J. Arias (USA) 6–7 6–4 6–2. **Doubles:** J. Rive (USA)/R. Van't Hof (USA) d. M. Davis (USA)/T. Witsken (USA) 6–4 7–6

SANTIAGO (CHI) 11–17 MARCH
Singles: A. Mancini (ARG) d. P. Rebolledo (CHI) 6–3 6–3. **Doubles:** G. Garetto (ARG)/M. Ingaramo (ARG) d. H. Gildemeister (CHI)/F. Rivera (CHI) 6–2 4–6 6–4

MARSEILLE (FRA) 25–31 MARCH
Singles: R. Agenor (HAI) d. M. Strelba (TCH) 5–7 6–4 6–2. **Doubles:** M. Boscatto (ITA)/S. Pescosolido (ITA) d. T. Kempers (HOL)/T. Nijssen (HOL) 6–2 2–6 6–3

SAN LUIS POTOSI (MEX) 25–31 MARCH
Singles: P. Arraya (PER) d. J. Morgan (AUS) 6–1 5–7 6–3. **Doubles:** M. Hadad (COL) /D. Orsanic (ARG) d. S. Patridge (USA)/K. Thorne (USA) 6–4 3–6 6–3

ZARAGOZA (ESP) 1–7 APRIL
Singles: J-F. Altur (ESP) d. K. Braasch (GER) 5–7 7–6 6–4. **Doubles:** M. Cierro (ITA)/S. Pescosolido (ITA) d. J-C. Baguena (ESP)/D. De Miguel (ESP) 6–2 6–4

PARIOLI (ITA) 8–14 APRIL
Singles: S. Pescosolido (ITA) d. B. Wuyts (BEL) 6–3 6–4. *Doubles:* M-A. Gorriz (ESP)/A. Olhovsky (URS) d. M. Damm (TCH)/D. Rikl (TCH) 7–5 2–6 6–2

MEXICO CITY (MEX) 15–21 APRIL
Singles: F. Roese (BRA) d. F. Maciel (MEX) 7–6 4–6 6–4. *Doubles:* R. Acioly (BRA)/P. Albano (ARG) d. F. Montana (USA)/L. Shiras (USA) 6–3 6–3

OPORTO I (POR) 15–21 APRIL
Singles: S. Pescosolido (ITA) d. R. Azar (ARG) 6–1 6–1. *Doubles:* D. Poliakov (URS)/T. Zdrazila (TCH) d. P. Haarhuis (HOL)/M. Koevermans (HOL) 3–6 6–3 6–4

TAIPEI (TPE) 15–21 APRIL
Singles: M. Zoecke (GER) d. K. Jones (USA) 6–3 6–3. *Doubles:* Jones/T. Woodbridge (AUS) d. M. Kratzmann (AUS)/J. Stoltenberg (AUS) 7–6 6–3

BIRMINGHAM (USA) 22–28 APRIL
Singles: M. Ingaramo (ARG) d. G. Markus (ARG) 3–6 6–3 6–2. *Doubles:* M. Keil (USA)/D. Randall (USA) d. N. Aerts (BRA)/D. Marcelino (BRA) 1–6 7–6 6–2

LISBON (POR) 22–28 APRIL
Singles: B. Wuyts (BEL) d. N. Marques (POR) 6–2 6–4. *Doubles:* D. Adams (AUS)/J. Oncins (BRA) d. T. Benhabiles (FRA)/O. Delaitre (FRA) 5–7 6–2 6–3

NAGOYA (JPN) 22–28 APRIL
Singles: J. Stimpson (USA) d. J. Apell (SWE) 6–1 6–3. *Doubles:* G. Layendecker (USA)/S. Youl (AUS) d. N. Odizor (NGR)/S. Stolle (AUS) 3–6 7–6 7–6

KUALA LUMPUR (MAS) 29 APRIL–5 MAY
Singles: G. Layendecker (USA) d. N. Borwick (AUS) 6–4 6–4. *Doubles:* A. Castle (GBR)/P. Wekesa (KEN) d. G. Dzelde (URS)/J. Turner (GBR) 7–6 6–3

PRAGUE (TCH) 29 APRIL–5 MAY
Singles: J. Kodes (TCH) d. T. Enqvist (SWE) 5–7 6–4 6–1. *Doubles:* S. Devries (USA)/R. Vogel (TCH) d. M. Damm (TCH)/D. Rikl (TCH) 2–6 6–1 6–4

SAO PAULO II (BRA) 29 APRIL–5 MAY
Singles: F. Roese (BRA) d. G. Markus (ARG) 6–4 6–3. *Doubles:* R. Acioly (BRA)/M. Menezes (BRA) d. N. Aerts (BRA)/Roese 6–3 3–6 6–3

LJUBLJANA (YUG) 6–12 MAY
Singles: S. Zivojinovic (YUG) d. A. Olhovsky (URS) 6–7 7–6 6–3. *Doubles:* Olhovsky/ Zivojinovic d. D. Vacek (TCH)/R. Vogel (TCH) 7–5 6–3

RIBEIRAO PRETO (BRA) 6–12 MAY
Singles: R. Jabali (BRA) d. F. Rivera (CHI) 6–3 4–6 7–6. *Doubles:* R. Acioly (BRA)/M. Menezes (BRA) d. S. Bryan (USA)/T. Middleton (USA) 6–3 6–4

BIELEFELD (GER) 27 MAY–2 JUNE
Singles: D. Poliakov (URS) d. L. Koslowski (GER) 6–4 6–1. *Doubles:* C. Limberger (AUS)/F. Segarceanu (ROM) d. M. Keil (USA)/F. Montana (USA) 6–3 6–2

FURTH (GER) 3–9 JUNE
Singles: M-A. Gorriz (ESP) d. D. Poliakov (URS) 6–2 3–0 ret. *Doubles:* Gorriz/M. Ruah (VEN) d. J. Morgan (AUS)/S. Stolle (AUS) 6–2 6–4

TURIN (ITA) 3–9 JUNE
Singles: P. Cane (ITA) d. R. Azar (ARG) 6–2 6–3. *Doubles:* O. Camporese (ITA)/R. Furlan (ITA) d. S. Salumaa (USA)/T. Svantesson (SWE) 7–5 3–6 6–4

COLOGNE (GER) 10–16 JUNE
Singles: M. Gustafsson (SWE) d. M-A. Gorriz (ESP) 6–2 4–6 6–2. *Doubles:* B. Haygarth (RSA)/B. Talbot (RSA) d. Gustafsson/A. Mronz (GER) 7–5 6–4

ITU (BRA) 10–16 JUNE
Singles: L. Nemecek (TCH) d. B. Madsen (HAI) 5–7 6–4 6–3. *Doubles:* R. Acioly (BRA)/M. Menezes (BRA) d. J. Daher (BRA)/D. Furusho (JPN) 7–6 6–3

SALZBURG (AUT) 24–30 JUNE
Singles: M. Rackl (GER) d. M. Sinner (GER) 1–6 6–3 6–4. *Doubles:* J. Carlsson (SWE)/D. Engel (SWE) d. B. Derlin (NZL)/Sinner 7–6 6–2

SEVILLE (ESP) 24–30 JUNE
Singles: L. Koslowski (GER) d. T. Nydahl (SWE) 6–2 3–6 7–6. *Doubles:* D. Rikl (TCH)/E. Winogradsky (FRA) d. J. Cihak (TCH)/T. Zdrazila (TCH) 6–1 6–7 6–3

NYON (SUI) 1–7 JULY
Singles: M. Naewie (GER) d. V. Gabrichidze (URS) 6–3 7–5. *Doubles:* M. Damm (TCH)/B. Stankovic (TCH) d. O. Smith (USA)/V. Van Gelderen (HOL) 6–1 7–6

OPORTO II (POR) 1–7 JULY
Singles: B. Wuyts (BEL) d. M. Wostenholme (CAN) 6–3 7–5. *Doubles:* J. Cihak (TCH)/T. Zdrazila (TCH) d. J-C. Baguena (ESP)/A. Gomez (ECU) 7–5 6–2

SALERNO (ITA) 1–7 JULY
Singles: G. Perez-Roldan (ARG) d. D. Rikl (TCH) 4–6 6–1 6–3. *Doubles:* M. Ondruska (RSA)/N. Pereira (VEN) d. E. Alvarez (ESP)/P. Pennisi (ITA) 6–4 6–4

BRISTOL (GBR) 8–14 JULY
Singles: J. Fitzgerald (AUS) d. P. Nyborg (SWE) 6–3 7–5. *Doubles:* N. Odizor (NGR)/M. Schapers (HOL) d. P. Hand (GBR)/B. Stankovic (TCH) 4–6 7–5 7–6

GRAMADO (BRA) 8–14 JULY
Singles: L. Prades (FRA) d. F. Roese (BRA) 7–5 6–7 6–4. *Doubles:* N. Aerts (BRA)/Roese d. B. Madsen (HAI)/G. Martinez (MEX) 6–4 6–4

KAKEGAWA (JPN) 8–14 JULY
Singles: M. Ardinghi (ITA) d. F. Krumrey (GER) 7–5 6–3. *Doubles:* S. Cole (GBR)/E. Collins (IRL) d. Krumrey/R. Ward (USA) 7–6 7–6

NEW HAVEN (USA) 8–14 JULY
Singles: A. O'Brien (USA) d. S. Simian (FRA) 6–4 6–4. *Doubles:* R.Deppe (RSA)/T. Middleton (USA) d. I. Baron (USA)/B. MacPhie (USA) 6–4 5–7 6–4

NEU ULM (GER) 8–14 JULY
Singles: R. Gilbert (FRA) d. T. Nydahl (SWE) 6–2 6–4. *Doubles:* T. Benhabiles (FRA)/O. Delaitre (FRA) d. C. Limberger (AUS)/D. Nargiso (ITA) 6–4 7–6

CAMPOS DO JORDAO (BRA) 15–21 JULY
Singles: Y. Doumbia (SEN) d. M. Menezes (BRA) 6–1 6–3. *Doubles:* Doumbia/J-P. Fleurian (FRA) d. N. Aerts (BRA)/D. Marcelino (BRA) 6–3 6–3

NEWCASTLE (GBR) 15–21 JULY
Singles: C. Van Rensburg (RSA) d. M. Schapers (HOL) 6–4 6–0. *Doubles:* N. Fulwood (GBR)/P. Nyborg (SWE) d. J. De Jager (RSA)/Van Rensburg 7–6 6–1

TAMPERE (FIN) 15–22 JULY
Singles: C. Pistolesi (ITA) d. V. Paloheimo (FIN) 7–6 6–4. *Doubles:* T. Carbonell (ESP)/M-A. Gorriz (ESP) d. D. Adams (AUS)/A. Olhovsky (URS) 6–4 6–2

APTOS (USA) 22–28 JULY
Singles: C. Adams (USA) d. B. Shelton (USA) 6–3 6–4. *Doubles:* N. Odizor (NGR)/Shelton d. M. Nido (PUR)/F. Roese (BRA) 6–4 6–3

FORTALEZA (BRA) 22–28 JULY
Singles: O. Fernandez (MEX) d. C. Weis (GER) 6–3 6–4. *Doubles:* N. Aerts (BRA)/D. Marcelino (BRA) d. Fernandez/G. Martinez (MEX) 6–3 6–4

HANKO (FIN) 22–28 JULY
Singles: J. Apell (SWE) d. C. Mezzadri (SUI) 6–2 6–4. *Doubles:* Apell/O. Rahnasto (FIN) d. P. Albertsson (SWE)/J. Windahl (SWE) w/o

WARSAW (POL) 22–28 JULY
Singles: M. Damm (TCH) d. D. Rikl (TCH) 3–6 7–5 6–4. *Doubles:* G. Dzelde (URS)/A. Vysand (URS) d. Damm/Rikl 6–4 2–6 6–3

LINS (BRA) 29 JULY–4 AUGUST
Singles: N. Pereira (VEN) d. G-L. Lobo (ARG) 2–6 6–3 7–6. *Doubles:* R. Acioly (BRA)/M. Menezes (BRA) d. D. Furusho (JPN)/J. Zwetsch (BRA) 2–6 7–5 7–5

SALOU (ESP) 29 JULY–4 AUGUST
Singles: L. Lavalle (MEX) d. F. Sanchez (ESP) 7–5 6–4. *Doubles:* M. Jensen (USA)/F. Montana (USA) d. W. Arthurs (AUS)/C. Limberger (AUS) 5–7 6–2 7–5

WINNETKA (USA) 29 JULY–4 AUGUST
Singles: B. Black (ZIM) d. T. Martin (USA) 6–4 4–6 6–2. *Doubles:* Black/S. Melville (USA) d. K. Evans (USA)/D. Randall (USA) 6–4 4–6 6–2

CERVIA (ITA) 5–11 AUGUST
Singles: C. Mezzadri (SUI) d. F. Fontang (FRA) 6–3 6–3. *Doubles:* C. Miniussi (ARG)/D. Perez (URU) d. J. Cunha-Silva (POR)/D. Orsanic (ARG) 6–3 6–4

SAO PAULO III (BRA) 5–11 AUGUST
Singles: N. Pereira (VEN) d. M. Stringari (ARG) 6–3 6–2. *Doubles:* P. Albano (ARG)/G-L. Lobo (ARG) d. R. Camargo (BRA)/J. Daher (BRA) 7–5 7–6

SEGOVIA (ITA) 5–11 AUGUST
Singles: J. Sanchez (ESP) d. F. Montana (USA) 6–3 6–2. *Doubles:* F. Clavet (ESP)/Sanchez d. J-C. Baguena (ESP)/J. Clavet (ESP) 7–6 6–2

PESCARA (ITA) 12–18 AUGUST
Singles: V. Gabrichidze (URS) d. M. Strelba (TCH) 7–5 6–4. *Doubles:* J. Cihak (TCH)/T. Zdrazila (TCH) d. J. Donar (SWE)/J. Sobel (USA) 6–3 6–4

GENEVA (SUI) 19–25 AUGUST
Singles: M-A. Gorriz (ESP) d. D. Pescariu (ROM) 6–3 6–2. *Doubles:* V. Gabrichidze (URS)/M. Strelba (TCH) d. R. Arguello (ARG)/C. Miniussi (ARG) 1–6 6–3 6–4

JAKARTA II (INA) 19–25 AUGUST
Singles: M. Visconti (ITA) d. D. Giewald (SWE) 6–3 1–6 6–2. *Doubles:* M. Briggs (USA)/T. Kronemann (USA) d. J. Sullivan (USA)/V. Van Gelderen (HOL) 5–7 6–3 7–5

MERANO (ITA) 26 AUGUST-1 SEPTEMBER
Singles: F. Fontang (FRA) d. C. Costa (ESP) 6–3 6–3. *Doubles:* Costa/C. Miniussi (ARG) d. J. Cihak (TCH)/T. Zdrazila (TCH) 6–3 6–3

GRAZ (AUT) 2–8 SEPTEMBER
Singles: T. Buchmayer (AUT) d. T. Guardiola (FRA) 6–3 6–2. *Doubles:* J. Apell (SWE)/R. Weidenfeld (ISR) d. S. Le Blanc (CAN)/M. Naewie (GER) 6–3 6–3

ISTANBUL (TUR) 2–8 SEPTEMBER
Singles: O. Delaitre (FRA) d. B. Black (ZIM) 6–1 6–4. *Doubles:* H. Holm (SWE)/N. Holm (SWE) d. G. Pozzi (ITA)/O. Rahnasto (FIN) 5–7 7–5 6–4

VENICE (ITA) 2–8 SEPTEMBER
Singles: C. Costa (ESP) d. A. Mancini (ARG) 6–3 7–5. *Doubles:* J. Arrese (ESP)/F. Roig (ESP) d. F. Davin (ARG)/M. Filippini (URU) 6–3 6–2

AZORES (POR) 9–15 SEPTEMBER
Singles: M. Ondruska (RSA) d. H. Holm (SWE) 6–3 6–2 7–6. *Doubles:* B. Black (ZIM)/T. Middleton (USA) d. Holm/P. Nyborg (SWE) 6–3 4–6 7–6

BOGOTA (COL) 16–22 SEPTEMBER
Singles: R. Saad (ARG) d. X. Daufresne (BEL) 6–3 3–6 6–4. *Doubles:* G. Guerrero (ARG)/Saad d. J. Daher (BRA)/C. Kist (BRA) 6–4 6–4

BUCHAREST (ROM) 16–22 SEPTEMBER
Singles: M. Filippini (URU) d. G. Markus (ARG) 6–3 6–4. *Doubles:* L. Koslowski (GER)/T. Nydahl (SWE) d. G. Cosac (ROM)/F. Segarceanu (ROM) 6–3 2–6 6–3

MADEIRA (POR) 16–22 SEPTEMBER
Singles: B. Black (ZIM) d. N. Pereira (VEN) 6–3 6–4. *Doubles:* J. De Jager (RSA)/B. Talbot (RSA) d. Black/T. Middleton (USA) 2–6 7–6 6–4

MESSINA (ITA) 16–22 SEPTEMBER
Singles: M. Valeri (ITA) d. G. Lopez (ESP) 4–6 6–1 7–6. *Doubles:* R. Furlan (ITA)/G. Perez-Roldan (ARG) d. J. Apell (SWE)/M. Naewie (GER) 6–4 6–2

SINGAPORE (SIN) 16–22 SEPTEMBER
Singles: M. Woodforde (AUS) d. C. Van Rensburg (RSA) 6–1 6–4. *Doubles:* M. Briggs (USA)/T. Kronemann (USA) d. D. Adams (AUS)/S. Patridge (USA) 6–3 6–4

WHISTLER MOUNTAIN (CAN) 16–22 SEPTEMBER
Singles: F. Silberberg (BRA) d. D. Witt (USA) 7–5 6–3. *Doubles:* S. Devries (USA)/P. Galbraith (USA) d. D. Randall (USA)/K. Thorne (USA) 6–4 6–4

CALI (COL) 23–29 SEPTEMBER
Singles: X. Daufresne (BEL) d. M. Stringari (ARG) 6–4 6–3. *Doubles:* G. Guerrero (ARG)/R. Saad (ARG) d. G. Garetto (ARG)/M. Ingaramo (ARG) 6–4 7–6

MICHIGAN (USA) 23–29 SEPTEMBER
Singles: C. Pridham (CAN) d. T. Ho (USA) 6–3 6–4. *Doubles:* S. Devries (USA)/M. Lucena (USA) d. D. Eisenman (USA)/T. Scherman (USA) 6–4 6–3

JERUSALEM (ISR) 30 SEPTEMBER–6 OCTOBER
Singles: C. Van Rensburg (RSA) d. C. Marsh (RSA) 2–6 6–2 6–3. *Doubles:* J. De Jager (RSA)/Van Rensburg d. N. Odizor (NGR)/B. Shelton (USA) 6–2 6–4

PONTE VEDRA (USA) 30 SEPTEMBER–6 OCTOBER
Singles: J. Stark (USA) d. K. Evernden (NZL) 6–3 6–1. *Doubles:* S. Devries (USA)/K. Thorne (USA) d. S. Cannon (USA)/R. Smith (BAH) 7–5 7–6

SAO PAULO IV (BRA) 30 SEPTEMBER–5 OCTOBER
Cancelled

SIRACUSA (ITA) 30 SEPTEMBER–6 OCTOBER
Singles: C. Costa (ESP) d. S. Pescosolido (ITA) 6–3 7–6. *Doubles:* M. Boscatto (ITA)/C. Brandi (ITA) d. D. Nargiso (ITA)/Pescosolido 3–6 7–6 7–6

CASABLANCA (MAR) 7–13 OCTOBER
Singles: J. Woehrmann (GER) d. B. Mota (POR) 6–3 6–1. *Doubles:* M. Goellner (GER)/B. Madsen (HAI) d. T. Benhabiles (FRA)/G. Garetto (ARG) 6–0 6–2

CHERBOURG (FRA) 7–13 OCTOBER
Singles: J. Bates (GBR) d. B. Black (ZIM) 7–5 1–6 7–6. *Doubles:* S. Groen (HOL)/B. Talbot (RSA) d. M. Daniel (ISR)/B. Devening (USA) 3–6 6–3 7–5

PEMBROKE PINES (USA) 7–13 OCTOBER
Singles: R-A. Viver (ECU) d. J. Brown (USA) 6–3 1–6 7–6. *Doubles:* R. Saad (ARG)/T. Svantesson (SWE) d. G. Layendecker (USA)/B. Pearce (USA) 4–6 6–3 6–2

REGGIO CALABRIA (ITA) 7–14 OCTOBER
Singles: L. Koslowski (GER) d. S. Hirszon (YUG) 6–4 6–2. *Doubles:* C. Brandi (ITA)/F. Mordegan (ITA) d. M. Boscatto (ITA)/E. Rossi (ITA) 7–5 6–3

CAIRO (EGY) 14–20 OCTOBER
Singles: B. Shelton (USA) d. J. Eltingh (HOL) 7–6 7–6. *Doubles:* M. Damm (TCH)/D. Rikl (TCH) d. B. Black (ZIM)/M. Ondruska (RSA) 6–2 6–3

ILHEUS (BRA) 14–20 OCTOBER
Singles: J. Oncins (BRA) d. F. Roese (BRA) 6–4 6–4. *Doubles:* L. Mattar (BRA)/Oncins d. J-I. Garat (ARG)/M. Saliola (BRA) 6–4 6–4

BREST (FRA) 21–27 OCTOBER
Singles: F. Santoro (FRA) d. C. Pioline (FRA) 6–4 7–5. *Doubles:* L. Koslowski (GER)/A. Thoms (GER) d. P. Kuhnen (GER)/A. Mronz (GER) 6–2 1–6 6–3

AACHEN (GER) 28 OCTOBER–3 NOVEMBER
Singles: A. Mronz (GER) d. M. Strelba (TCH) 6–4 6–3. *Doubles:* M. Keil (USA)/B. Talbot (RSA) d. J. Gunnarsson (SWE)/M. Larsson (SWE) 6–3 3–6 6–3

HELSINKI (FIN) 4–10 NOVEMBER
Singles: M. Schapers (HOL) d. A. Antonitsch (AUT) 7–6 4–6 7–5. *Doubles:* T.Benhabiles (FRA)/H. Leconte (FRA) d. Antonitsch/G. Layendecker (USA) 7–5 7–6

HOBART (AUS) 4–10 NOVEMBER
Singles: S. Stolle (AUS) d. F. Wibier (HOL) 7–5 6–4. *Doubles:* M. Brown (AUS)/A. Kratzmann (AUS) d. B. Richardson (AUS)/S. Youl (AUS) 3–6 6–3 7–6

CHRISTCHURCH (NZL) 11–7 NOVEMBER
Singles: M. Petchey (GBR) d. F. Wibier (HOL) 7–5 7–6. *Doubles:* N. Borwick (AUS)/S. Youl (AUS) d. J. Morgan (AUS)/S. Stolle (AUS) 7–5 7–6

SAO PAULO V (BRA) 11–17 NOVEMBER
Singles: R-A. Viver (ECU) d. G. Markus (ARG) 7–6 3–6 6–3. *Doubles:* F. Montana (USA)/G. Van Emburgh (USA) d. J. Burillo (ESP)/D. De Miguel (ESP) 3–6 6–4 6–1

SAO PAULO VI (BRA) 18–24 NOVEMBER
Singles: C. Motta (BRA) d. F. Roese (BRA) 6–4 6–3. *Doubles:* J. Cunha-Silva (POR)/Roese d. P. Albano (ARG)/G-L. Lobo (ARG) 7–5 4–6 6–3

MUNICH (GER) 18–24 NOVEMBER
Singles: A. Thoms (GER) d. M. Naewie (GER) 4–6 6–3 6–4. *Doubles:* T. Kempers (HOL)/C. Pridham (CAN) d. R. Haas (GER)/Thoms 7–6 6–4

AUCKLAND (NZL) 18–24 NOVEMBER
Singles: S. Youl (AUS) d. P. Rafter (AUS) 3–6 6–3 6–1. *Doubles:* B. Derlin (NZL)/C. Limberger (AUS) d. D. Adams (AUS)/P. Hand (GBR) 6–4 7–5

BOSSONENS (SUI) 25 NOVEMBER–1 DECEMBER
Singles: C. Van Rensburg (RSA) d. P. Baur (GER) 6–4 7–6. *Doubles:* A. Antonitsch (AUT)/M. Oosting (HOL) d. M. Schapers (HOL)/D. Vacek (TCH) 6–3 6–2

JOHANNESBURG (RSA) 25 NOVEMBER–1 DECEMBER
Singles: T. Witsken (USA) d. W. Ferreira (RSA) 4–6 6–3 6–4. *Doubles:* K. Curren (RSA)/R. Deppe (RSA) d. S. Kruger (RSA)/D. Visser (RSA) 7–5 6–2

PUEBLA (MEX) 25 NOVEMBER–1 DECEMBER
Singles: K. Kinnear (USA) d. L. Herrera (MEX) 6–1 7–5. *Doubles:* O. Fernandez (MEX)/Herrera d. D. Eisenman (USA)/D. Randall (USA) 6–4 7–6

HONG KONG (HKG) 9 DECEMBER–15 DECEMBER
Singles: B. Karbacher (GER) d. G. Rusedski (CAN) 6–2 3–6 6–1. *Doubles:* L. Jensen (USA)/M. Jensen (USA) d. M. Briggs (USA)/T. Kronemann (USA) w/o

GUAM (GUM) 16 DECEMBER–22 DECEMBER
Singles: R. Matuszewski (USA) d. J. Morgan (AUS) 6–4 ret. *Doubles:* J. Canter (USA)/K. Thorne (USA) d. D. Adams (AUS)/D. Eisenman (USA) 6–1 6–2

MEN'S SATELLITE CIRCUITS 1991

There were 73 satellite circuits for men in 47 countries during 1991, all offering prize money. These circuits, consisting of three tournaments followed by a Masters, are organised and run by member nations of the International Tennis Federation. Below are listed the players who led the points tables at the end of each circuit. In three instances two players were level on singles points.

CIRCUIT	START	SINGLES WINNER	DOUBLES WINNNERS
American	25–03	M. Ondruska (RSA)	J. Ireland (AUS)/A. Kratzmann (AUS)
	29–04	R. Schmidt (USA)	B. Curry (RSA)/J. De Jager (RSA)
	03–06	G. Stafford (RSA)	M. Briggs (USA)/T. Kronemann (USA)
	01–07	D. Bosse (RSA)	E. Ferreira (RSA)/K. Ullyett (RSA)
	21–10	A. Sznajder (CAN)	M. Lucena (USA)/B-O. Pedersen (NOR)
Argentinian	18–11	A. Garizzio (ARG)	P. Quijano (MEX)/P. Williamson (USA)
Australian	10–02	A. Kratzmann (AUS)	G. Doyle (AUS)/J. Eagle (AUS)
	26–08	J. Cask (AUS)	P. Rafter (AUS)/P. Tramacchi (AUS)
	07–10	A. Finnberg (GER)	D. Adams (AUS)/C. Eagle (AUS)
Austrian	05–08	A. Merinov (URS)	R. Janecek (CAN)/S. Le Blanc (CAN)
Bangladeshi/Pakistan	04–11	L. Tieleman (ITA)	M. Avedikian (USA)/L. Tieleman (ITA)
Bolivian	21–10	M. Rebolledo (CHI)	A. Aramburu (PER)/A. Moreno (MEX)
Brazilian	18–03	R. Jabali (BRA)	J-I. Garat (ARG)/M. Saliola (BRA)
	15–04	J. Zwetsch (BRA)	D. Del Rio (ARG)/H. Gumy (ARG)
	13–05	H. Gumy (ARG)	C. Zwetsch (BRA)/J. Zwetsch (BRA)
	17–06	A. Dalboni (ITA)	N. Becerra (ARG)/G. Guerrero (ARG)
	15–07	R. Saad (ARG)	J. Ayala (MEX)/R. Saad (ARG)
	02–09	O. Della (BRA)	J-P. Etchecoin (BRA)/A. Ferreira (BRA)
British	18–02	B. Joelson (USA)	C. Banducci (RSA)/E. Zinn (RSA)
	22–04	P. Norval (RSA)	L. Bale (RSA)/B. Richardson (AUS)
Canadian	10–06	M. Hadad (COL)	M. Bauer (USA)/A. Preovolas (USA)
Caribbean	01–04	T. Buchmayer (AUT)	S. Cole (GBR)/E. Collins (IRL)
	29–04	J. Rios (PUR)	S. Cole (GBR)/J. Winnink (HOL)
Cen. African	30–09	D. Isaak (USA)	D. Clark (USA)/B. Curry (RSA)
Cen. American	18–02	O. Fernandez (MEX)	O. Fernandez (MEX)/G. Martinez (MEX)
Colombian	19–08	A. Jordan (COL)	M. Rincon (COL)/M. Tobon (COL)
Czechoslavakian	26–08	T. Gollwitzer (GER)	M. Trneny (TCH)/P. Vizner (TCH)
Dutch	24–06	T. Guardiola (FRA)	T. Kempers (HOL)/F. Wibier (HOL)
Ecuadorian/Peruvian	23–09	O. Bustos (CHI)	E. Diaz (CHI)/M. Rebolledo (CHI)
Finnish	10–06	M. Srdanovic (YUG)	M. Lucena (USA)/B-O. Pedersen (NOR)
French	04–03	M. Laurendeau (CAN)	M. Damm (TCH)/V. Flegl (TCH)
	22–07	O. Soules (FRA)	B. Mota (POR)/M. Rodriguez (ARG)
	09–09	E. Winogradsky (FRA)	S. Sansoni (FRA)/E. Winogradsky (FRA)
German	04–02	K. Braasch (GER)	M. Damm (TCH)/R. Vasek (TCH)
	15–04	D. Dier (GER)	L. Koslowski (GER)/D. Leppen (GER)
	27–05	S. Cortes (CHI)	Q-H. Meng (CHN)/J-P. Xia (CHN)
Hong Kong/Ch. Taipei	05–08	E-J. Chang (KOR)	E-J. Chang (KOR)/C-W. Kim (KOR)
Hungarian	03–06	J. Kroschko (URS)	A. Lanyi (HUN)/T. Toth (TCH)
Indonesian	26–08	N-J. Bae (KOR)	B. Wiryawan (INA)/J-P. Xia (CHN)
Indian	31–12–90	V. Gabrichidze (URS)	V. Gabrichidze (URS)/S. Vasudevan (ITA)
Irish	20–05	D. Farren (USA)	D. Ison (GBR)/M. Petchey (GBR)
Israeli	22–07	O. Casey (IRL)/ O. Weinberg (ISR)	O. Casey (IRL)/A. Hombrecher (USA)
	04–11	G. Rusedski (CAN)	M. Michulka (USA)/M. Penman (RSA)
Italian	31–12–90	P. Pech (FRA)	N. Bruno (ITA)/S. Colombo (ITA)
	08–07	C.Rigagnoli (ITA)	P. Pennisi (ITA)/E. Rossetti (ITA)
	14–10	A. Corretja (ESP)	M. Tillstroem (SWE)/S. Touzil (GER)
Japanese	04–11	A. Castle (GBR)	A. Castle (GBR)/M. Nastase (ROM)
Korean	20–05	E-J. Chang (KOR)	E-J. Chang (KOR)/S-H. Ji (KOR)
Malaysian	11–02	J-P. Xia (CHN)	J-W. Lodder (HOL)/V. Van Gelderen (HOL)
	15–07	J. Bates (GBR)	J. Bates (GBR)/C. Wilkinson (GBR)

CIRCUIT	START	SINGLES WINNER	DOUBLES WINNNERS
Mexican	06–05	F. Maciel (MEX)	O. Fernandez (MEX)/G. Martinez (MEX)
	01–06	P. Crow (USA)	J. Frantz (USA)/K. Kuperstein (USA)
	30–09	B. Farrow (USA)/	M. Petchey (GBR)/D. Sapsford (GBR)
		M. Tabares (CUB)	
Moroccan	02–09	L. Orsini (FRA)	I. Damiani (AUS)/B. Larkham (AUS)
N. African	30–09	F. Garcia-Berro (ARG)	A. Portas (ESP)/D. Salvador (ESP)
Philippino/Thai	11–02	F. Barrientos (PHI)/	E-J. Chang (KOR)/C-W. Kim (KOR)
		E-J. Chang (KOR)	
Portuguese	14–01	M. Barba (USA)	M. Barnard (RSA)/B. Talbot (RSA)
	06–05	Couto (POR)	E. Couto (POR)/B. Mota (POR)
	30–09	C. Falk (SWE)	O. Casey (IRL)/D. Collins (GBR)
Romanian	23–09	G. Cosac (ROM)	A. Marcu (ROM)/A. Pavel (ROM)
Spanish	07–01	R. Weidenfeld (ISR)	P. Koscielski (USA)/S. Simian (FRA)
	04–02	J. Manteca (ESP)	J-L. Aparisi (ESP)/G. Lopez (ESP)
	04–03	G. Lopez (ESP)	D. Eisenman (USA)/J. Gisbert (ESP)
	22–04	E. Alvarez (ESP)	R. Weidenfeld (ISR)/A. Thoms (GER)
	20–05	F. Sanchez (ESP)	G. Bastie (FRA)/M. Huning (GER)
	17–06	F. Sanchez (ESP)	G. Bastie (FRA)/M. Huning (GER)
	15–07	B. Larkham (AUS)	R. Kroll (GER)/J. Renzenbrink (HOL)
	19–08	A. Berasategui (ESP)	V. Solves (ESP)/J. Vila (ESP)
Swedish	13–05	X. Daufresne (BEL)	M. Renstroem (SWE)/M. Tillstroem (SWE)
Swiss	28–10	S. Sansoni (FRA)	D. Prinosil (GER)/J. Woehrmann (GER)
Turkish	27–05	V. Van Gelderen (HOL)	H. Ishii (JPN)/K. Warwick (AUS)
West African	28–10	S. Soresini (ITA)	U. Colombini (ITA)/S. Sorensini (ITA)
Yugoslavian	08–04	D. Buljevic (YUG)	J. Bulant (TCH)/I. Saric (YUG)

REEBOK

After a promising start to the year, the 19-year-old American Michael Chang slipped to No. 15 in the world rankings, but ended the season gloriously by reaching the final of the Compaq Grand Slam Cup *— his reward $1 million.* (T. Hindley)

ITF WOMEN'S FUTURES CIRCUIT

The Kraft Tour is the major professional circuit for women and consists of some 66 tournaments offering prize money of US $75,000 or more, rising to a minimum of $100,000 in 1992, totalling approximately $23 million, plus Bonus Pool Points as authorised by the Women's International Professional Tennis Council (WIPTC). The Tour year culminates in November at the Virginia Slims Championships in New York.

Acceptance into Tour events is based on a player's position on the Virginia Slims Rankings computed regularly by the Women's Tennis Association (WTA). It is therefore essential for all players who wish to compete that they earn computer ranking points.

A series of lower level prize money tournaments exists as an apprenticeship circuit to the Kraft Tour. This level has been in existence for over a decade, funded and co-ordinated by Regional and National Associations responsible for development of the grass roots game in their respective countries. In 1990 this worldwide initiative became known as the ITF FUTURES CIRCUIT; it is run under Regulations promulgated by the International Tennis Federation, the governing body of the National Associations. In 1991 this Circuit comprised 175 events offering a total in excess of $2.5 million in prize money. With an additional 25 Futures Events scheduled on the calendar, this represents a 27% growth in the total amount of prize money that had been on offer in 1990. Eligible for WTA computer credit, ITF Futures Events fall into the following categories:–

$20,000 Development Circuits:
A Circuit of three tournaments, each offering $5,000 in prize money, plus a Masters tournament offering $5,000 for the most successful players. Total prize money available is $20,000 over four weeks. Players receive computer points for the Main Draw of the Masters event only and therefore these Circuits, which are suitable for national unranked players, provide essential match play experience under professional conditions allowing players to begin earning an initial ranking.

$40,000 Satellite Circuits:
A Circuit of three tournaments, each of $10,000 in prize money, plus a Masters tournament also of $10,000 for the most successful players. Players receive computer credit for each tournament played if they reach the Main Draw, and these Circuits provide essential match-play experience under more international conditions.

$10,000 Satellite Tournaments:
Individual tournaments of $10,000 in prize money. Players receive computer points for the Main Draw only. These events therefore help them achieve their minimum three tournaments required to appear on the ranking list, and improve the position of players ranked below 200 on the computer.

$25,000/$50,000 Challenger Tournaments:
Individual tournaments of $25,000 or $50,000 in prize money. Players receive computer credit for the last three rounds of Qualifying and the Main Draw. These events help those ranked higher than 200 on the computer to improve their ranking towards acceptance into Kraft Tour events.

During 1991, ITF Futures Circuit tournaments were staged in no fewer than 46 countries spanning 5 continents.

Further information on the ITF Futures Circuit is available on request from the Director of Women's Tennis at the ITF office.

1991 ITF FUTURES CIRCUIT – RESULTS
$20,000 – DEVELOPMENT CIRCUITS

MEXICO, TABASCO (MASTERS) – APRIL 24–28
SINGLES: X. Escobedo (MEX) d. I. Petrov (MEX) 7–5 6–4
DOUBLES: R. Pichardo (CUB)/B. Rodriguez (CUB) d. O. Limon (MEX)/I. Petrov (CUB) 6–4 5–7 7–6

$40,000 – SATELLITE CIRCUITS

AUSTRALIA, MILDURA (CIRUIT I) – FEBRUARY 13–17
SINGLES: T. Morton (AUS) d. L. Stacey (AUS) 6–3 6–4
DOUBLES: Radford (AUS)/C. Thompson (AUS) d. G. Novelo (MEX)/B. Somerville (USA) 7–6 6–2

AUSTRALIA, WODONGA (CIRCUIT II) – FEBRUARY 20–24
SINGLES: K. Radford (AUS) d. R. Bolodis (AUS) 6–1 4–6 6–3
DOUBLES: T. Morton (AUS)/A. Scott (AUS) d. K. Radford (AUS)/C. Thompson (AUS) 6–4 4–6 7–6

AUSTRALIA, LYNEHAM (CIRCUIT III) – FEBRUARY 27–MARCH 3
SINGLES: J. Limmer (AUS) d. C. Thompson (AUS) 7–5 6–4
DOUBLES: G. Novelo (MEX)/B. Sommerville (USA) d. T. Morton (AUS)/A. Scott (AUS) 7–5 3–6 6–4

AUSTRALIA, NEWCASTLE (MASTERS) – MARCH 6–10
SINGLES: C. Thompson (AUS) d. T. Morton (AUS) 6–3 6–2
DOUBLES: G. Novelo (MEX)/B. Sommerville (USA) d. K. Radford (AUS)/C. Thompson (AUS) 6–2 7–5

ISRAEL, HAIFA (CIRCUIT I) – JULY 29–AUGUST 4
SINGLES: T. Price (RAS) d. T. Shapovalova (URS) 6–2 6–0
DOUBLES: K. Dryer (USA)/T. Price (RSA) d. J. Humphreys (RSA)/E. Nortje (RSA) 6–1 6–0

ISRAEL, RAMAT HASHARON (CIRCUIT II) – AUGUST 5–10
SINGLES: I. Berger (ISR) d. J. Humphreys (RSA) 6–3 6–3
DOUBLES: I. Berger (ISR)/R. Field (RSA) d. J. Humphreys (RSA)/E. Nortje (RSA) 6–0 6–1

ISRAEL, ASHKELON (CIRCUIT III) – AUGUST 12–17
SINGLES: T. Price (RSA) d. I. Berger (ISR) 7–6 6–7 6–3
DOUBLES: I. Berger (ISR)/R. Field (RSA) d. K. Dreyer (USA)/T. Price (RSA) W/O

ISRAEL, JERUSALEM (MASTERS) – AUGUST 20–24
SINGLES: I. Berger (ISR) d. T. Price (RSA) 6–3 6–7 6–4
DOUBLES: B. Griffiths (GBR)/J. Wood (GBR) d. I. Berger (ISR)/R. Field (RSA) 6–3 7–6 6–1

CHINESE TAIPEI, TAIWAN (CIRCUIT I) – AUGUST 5–11
SINGLES: S-T. Wang (TPE) d. I-S. Kim (KOR) 4–6 6–4 6–3
DOUBLES: I-S. Kim (KOR)/M-A. Sohn (KOR) d. J-M. Lee (KOR)/H-J. Jeong (KOR) 7–5 6–2

CHINESE TAIPEI, TAIWAN (CIRCUIT II) – AUGUST 13–18
SINGLES: S-T. Wang (TPE) d. M-A. Sohn (KOR) 6–2 6–3
DOUBLES: J-S. Choi (KOR)/J. Choi (KOR) d. H-J. Pyo (KOR)/S-H. Park (KOR) 6–2 6–3

CHINESE TAIPEI, TAIWAN (CIRCUIT III) – AUGUST 20–25
SINGLES: S-T. Wang (TPE) d. I-S. Kim (KOR) 6–2 2–6 6–2
DOUBLES: I-S. Kim (KOR)/M-A. Sohn (KOR) d. J-M. Lee (KOR)/H-J. Jeong (KOR) 6–0 7–6

CHINESE TAIPEI, YANG MING SHAN (MASTERS) – AUGUST 26–SEPTEMBER 1
SINGLES: S-T. Wang (TPE) d. Y-S. Kim (KOR) 3–6 6–3 6–1
DOUBLES: I-S. Kim (KOR)/M-A. Sohn (KOR) d. S-H. Park (KOR)/H-J. Pyo (KOR) 7–5 6–4

JAPAN, IBARAKI (CIRCUIT I) – SEPTEMBER 25–29
SINGLES: F. Li (CHN) d. N. Kijimuta (JPN) 6–3 6–4
DOUBLES: N. Kinoshita (JPN)/E. Takahashi (JPN) d. F. Li (CHN)/M. Tang (CHN) 5–7 6–3 6–4

JAPAN, IBARAKI (CIRCUIT II) – OCTOBER 2–6
SINGLES: L. Chen (CHN) d. S-H. Park (KOR) 6–2 6–4
DOUBLES: Y. Koizumi (JPN)/M. Mizokuchi (JPN) d. F. Li (CHN)/M. Tang (CHN) 6–1 3–6 6–3

JAPAN, MATSUYAMA (CIRCUIT III) – OCTOBER 7–12
SINGLES: F. Li (CHN) d. L. Chen (CHN) 6–4 6–3
DOUBLES: J. Byrne (AUS)/P. Moreno (HKG) d. J. Saret (PHI)/J-Q. Yi (CHN) 1–6 6–4 6–4

JAPAN, KYOTO (MASTERS) – OCTOBER 17–20
SINGLES: F. Li (CHN) d. H. Yoshihara (JPN) 7–6 6–4
DOUBLES: F. Li (CHN)/M. Tang (CHN) d. D. Gardner (USA)/P. Moreno (HKG) 6–4 7–5

There were also 104 $10,000 Satellite tournaments held in 37 countries. Final round results may be obtained from the ITF office in London (see page 408 for address).

$25,000 – CHALLENGERS

U.S.A., MIDLAND, MI – JANUARY 29–FEBRUARY 3
SINGLES: H. Kelesi (CAN) d. M. McGrath (USA) 6–2 6–2
DOUBLES: M. McGrath (USA)/A. Smith (USA) d. K. Adams (USA)/H. Kelesi (CAN) 7–5 7–5

INDONESIA, JAKARTA – FEBRUARY 4–10
SINGLES: Y. Basuki (INA) d. M. Miyauchi (JPN) 6–2 6–2
DOUBLES: J. Hodder (AUS)/K.-A. Guse (AUS) d. E. Iida (JPN)/M. Miyauchi (JPN) 7–6 7–5

U.S.A., KEY BISCAYNE, FL – FEBRUARY 11–16
SINGLES: J. Emmons (USA) d. N. Sodupe (USA) 6–4 7–5
DOUBLES: P. Mager (USA)/S. Smith (GBR) d. R. Simpson-Alter (CAN)/H. Terriet (HOL) 7–5 6–2

FRANCE, MOULINS – APRIL 3–7
SINGLES: M. Kochta (GER) d. C. Suire (FRA) 6–3 6–4
DOUBLES: C. Suire (FRA)/S. Testud (FRA) d. I. Driehuis (HOL)/L. Pleming (AUS) 6–3 6–4

ITALY, MONCALIERI – APRIL 7–14
SINGLES: J. Wiesner (AUT) d. C. Bargagni (ITA) 6–2 6–4
DOUBLES: V. Ruano (ESP)/E. Bes (ESP) d. H. Vildova (TCH)/L. Ludvigova (TCH) 6–7 6–1 6–3

FRANCE, LIMOGES – APRIL 9–14
SINGLES: A. Fusai (FRA) d. E. Maniokova (URS) 7–5 5–7 6–4
DOUBLES: E. Maniokova (URS)/A. Aallonen (FIN) d. J. Souto (ESP)/R. Bielsa (ESP) 6–3 1–6 7–5

ITALY, CASERTA – APRIL 16–24
SINGLES: E. Zardo (SUI) d. A. Segura (ESP) 6–7 7–6 6–1
DOUBLES: I. Gorrochategui (ARG)/A. Vieira (BRA) d. J. Fuchs (USA)/M. Strandlund (SWE) 6–2 6–2

ISRAEL, ASHKELON – APRIL 22–27
SINGLES: M. de Swardt (RSA) d. I. Berger (ISR) 6–3 4–6 6–2
DOUBLES: I. Berger (ISR)/J. Salmon (GBR) d. A. Aallonen (FIN)/S. Schilder (HOL) 6–4 6–4

POLAND, KATOWICE – MAY 22–26
SINGLES: R. Bobkova (TCH) d. N. Dubrovits (AUT) 6–4 4–6 6–3
DOUBLES: M. Mroz (POL)/H. Vildova (TCH) d. I. Jankovska (TCH)/E. Melicharova (TCH) 6–4 6–7 6–0

ITALY, BRINDISI – MAY 28–JUNE 2
SINGLES: I. Gorrochategui (ARG) d. F. Perfetti (ITA) 7–5 6–3
DOUBLES: I. Gorrochategui (ARG)/P. Miller (URU) d. I. Spirlea (ROM)/K. Studenicova (TCH) 6–1 7–6

ITALY, MILAN – JUNE 3–9
SINGLES: I. Spirlea (ROM) d. A. Zugasti (FRA) 6–4 7–5
DOUBLES: N. Baudone (ITA)/F. Romano (ITA) d. R. Bielsa (ESP)/J. Souto (ESP) 6–4 7–5

LUXEMBOURG, MONDORF – JUNE 5–9
SINGLES: N. Ercegovic (YUG) d. R. Bobkova (TCH) 7–6 7–5
DOUBLES: A. Segura (ESP)/R. Bobkova (TCH) d. D. Szabova (TCH)/H. Kadzidroga (GER) 6–1 6–4

ITALY, MANTOVA – JUNE 9–16
SINGLES: C. Mothes (FRA) d. C. Hofmann (GER) 6–1 6–0
DOUBLES: V. Ruano (ESP)/M. Maruska (AUT) d. H. Nagano (JPN)/Y. Kamio (JPN) 3–6 6–4 6–3

ITALY, MODENA – JUNE 17–23
SINGLES: S. Niox-Chateau (FRA) d. R. De Los Rios (PAR) 6–0 6–1
DOUBLES: I. Pospisilova (TCH)/D. Szabova (TCH) d. S. Rottier (HOL)/Y. Grubben (HOL) 6–4 6–4

U.S.A., ST. SIMONS ISLAND, GA – JUNE 17–23
SINGLES: B. Bowes (USA) d. S. McCarthy (USA) 6–2 5–7 7–5
DOUBLES: L. Allen (USA)/S. Amiach (FRA) d. C. O'Reilly (USA)/P. O'Reilly (USA) 6–3 6–7 7–3

SWEDEN, RONNEBY – JUNE 25–29
SINGLES: S. Albinus (DEN) d. A. Narbe (SWE) 6–2 6–3
DOUBLES: M. Lindstrom (SWE)/J. Emmons (USA) d. J. Jonerup (SWE)/S. Schilder (HOL) 3–6 6–2 6–4

ITALY, CALTAGIRONE – JUNE 26–30
SINGLES: S. Farina (ITA) d. A. Devries (BEL) 7–5 6–3
DOUBLES: S. Farina (ITA)/M. Miyauchi (JPN) d. O. Gravereaux (FRA)/A. Fusai (FRA) 6–7 6–4 6–4

GERMANY, VAIHINGEN – JULY 3–7
SINGLES: S. Frankl (GER) d. K. Oeljeklaus (GER) 6–0 7–5
DOUBLES: L. Seeman (USA)/H. Sprung (GER) d. P. Miller (URU)/H. Kadzidroga (GER) 7–6 6–1

GERMANY, ERLANGEN – JULY 8–14
SINGLES: M. Zivec-Skulj (GER) d. D. Szobova (TCH) 7–5 1–6 6–1
DOUBLES: V. Milvidskaia (URS)/M. Zivec-Skulj (GER) d. L. Stacey (AUS)/A. Woolcock (AUS) 6–4 6–4

U.S.A., EVANSVILLE, IN – JULY 15–21
SINGLES: K. Po (USA) d. I. Demongeot (FRA) 2–6 6–4 6–1
DOUBLES: A. Hirose (JPN)/E. Iida (JPN) d. A. Farley (USA)/K. Foxworth (USA) 6–3 2–6 6–4

GERMANY, DARMSTADT – JULY 17–21
SINGLES: M. Pawlik (GER) d. M. Zivec-Skulj (GER) 1–6 6–3 7–6
DOUBLES: A. Woolcock (AUS)/L. Stacey (AUS) d. L. Seeman (USA)/M. Pawlik (GER) 6–1 6–2

AUSTRIA, SCHWARZACH – JULY 20–27
SINGLES: B. Mulej (YUG) d. H. Sprung (AUT) 6–2 6–1
DOUBLES: K. Studenikova (TCH)/K. Habsudova (TCH) d. A. Blumberga (URS)/H. Sprung (AUT) 6–3 6–1

ITALY, SEZZE – JULY 23–28
SINGLES: G. Mugnaini (ITA) d. G. Pizzichini (ITA) 6–3 6–2
DOUBLES: L. Plemming (AUS)/D. Jones (AUS) d. J. Hodder (AUS)/I. Driehuis (HOL) 6–3 6–2

GERMANY, RHEDA-WIEDENBRUECK – JULY 29–AUGUST 4
SINGLES: F. Curpene (ROM) d. H. Sprung (GER) 6–3 6–2
DOUBLES: C. Bernstein (SWE)/A. Narbe (SWE) d. M. Babel (GER)/I. Spirlea (ROM) 6–3 7–5

ITALY, ACIREALE – JULY 30–AUGUST 4
SINGLES: F. Li (CHN) d. J. Pospisilova (TCH) 6–0 7–5
DOUBLES: J. Hodder (AUS)/D. Jones (AUS) d. K. Johnson (USA)/G. Boschiero (ITA) 6–4 6–4

SPAIN, VIGO – AUGUST 6–11
SINGLES: C. Mothes (FRA) d. E. Bes (ESP) 6–3 6–0
DOUBLES: E. Bes (ESP)/V. Ruano (ESP) d. B. Borneo (GBR)/A. Aallonen (FIN) 7–6 7–5

ITALY, PISTICCI – AUGUST 13–18
SINGLES: N. Baudone (ITA) d. K. Nowak (POL) 6–0 6–1
DOUBLES: J. Hodder (AUS)/M. Muric (YUG) d. R. Dragomir (ROM)/I. Spirlea (ROM) 6–4 3–6 6–3

U.S.A., YORK, PA – AUGUST 12–18
SINGLES: S. Loosemore (GBR) d. T. Whittington (USA) 6–2 6–3
DOUBLES: S. Gilchrist (USA)/V. Paynter (USA) d. B. Bowes (USA)/S. McCarthy (USA) 2–6 7–6 6–3

INDONESIA, JAKARTA – AUGUST 18–25
SINGLES: J. Byrne (AUS) d. T. Soemarno (INA) 6–0 6–2
DOUBLES: T. Trayono (INA)/A. Wibisono (INA) d. D. Fortuna (INA)/V. Rogi (INA) 6–2 6–4

BULGARIA, SOFIA – SEPTEMBER 18–22
SINGLES: M. Kiene (HOL) d. M. Babel (GER) 7–5 6–3
DOUBLES: M. Babel (GER)/V. Lake (GBR) d. I. Havrilkova (TCH)/K. Kroupova (TCH) 7–5 6–0

U.S.A., CHICAGO, IL – SEPTEMBER 23–29
SINGLES: L. Allen (USA) d. A. Keller (USA) 6–1 6–2
DOUBLES: K. Adams (USA)/M-L. Daniels (USA) d. B. Bowes (USA)/C. MacGregor (USA) 6–3 6–4

U.S.A., SALISBURY, MD – SEPTEMBER 30–OCTOBER 6
SINGLES: A. Keller (USA) d. E. Burgin (USA) 6–1 2–6 6–2
DOUBLES: A. Keller (USA)/S. Schefflin (USA) d. B. Bowes (USA)/S. McCarthy (USA) 6–3 3–6 7–6

JAPAN, OITA – OCTOBER 23–27
SINGLES: F. Li (CHN) d. K. Radford (AUS) 6–3 6–0
DOUBLES: K. Radford (AUS)/L. Novello (MEX) d. M. Ekstrand (SWE)/S. Lohmann (GER) 6–1 7–5

PORTUGAL, MADEIRA – OCTOBER 28–NOVEMBER 3
SINGLES: M. Babel (GBR) d. B. Malej (YUG) 6–0 6–2
DOUBLES: M. Babel (YUG)/C. Bakkum (HOL) d. R. Belisa (ESP)/J. Souto (ESP) 6–3 6–2

JAPAN, SAGA – OCTOBER 28–NOVEMBER 3
SINGLES: E. Iida (JPN) d. F. Li (CHN) 6–3 6–3
DOUBLES: L. Novelo (MEX)/K. Radford (AUS) d. F. Li (CHN)/M. Tang (CHN) 5–7 6–2 7–5

AUSTRALIA, PORT PIRIE – NOVEMBER 4–10
SINGLES: L. Field (AUS) d. J. Byrne (AUS) 6–4 6–4
DOUBLES: M. Jaggard (AUS)/J. Faull (AUS) d. K-A. Guse (AUS)/J. Hodder (AUS) 6–2 7–5

Four players with a winning feeling in 1991. **Above (left)** *Natalia Zvereva and her partner Larissa Savchenko* **(right)** *won the Wimbledon doubles.* **Below (left)** *Helena Sukova won the singles at Brisbane, and Elna Reinach* **(right)** *won the Nashville doubles with Sandy Collins.* (R. Adams)

JAPAN, CHIBA – NOVEMBER 6–10
SINGLES: M. Endo (JPN) d. S T. Wang (TPE) 6–4 6–0
DOUBLES: L. Novelo (MEX)/K. Radford (AUS) d. Y. Kamio (JPN)/A. Hirose (JPN) 6–4 5–7 6–4

GREAT BRITAIN, MANCHESTER – NOVEMBER 5–9
SINGLES: A. Grunfeld (GBR) d. S. Smith (GBR) 4–6 6–4 6–2
DOUBLES: A. Grunfeld (GBR)/J. Salmon (GBR) d. L. Bacheva (BUL)/B. Griffiths (GBR) 7–6 6–1

AUSTRALIA, MT. GAMBIA – NOVEMBER 11–17
SINGLES: J. Byrne (AUS) d. K. Godridge (AUS) 0–6 6–4 6–4
DOUBLES: K. Godridge (AUS)/N. Pratt (AUS) d. L. Pleming (AUS)/I. Driehuis (HOL) 6–7 6–3 6–4

GREAT BRITAIN, SWINDON – NOVEMBER 12–16
SINGLES: E. Callens (BEL) d. C. Dahlman (SWE) 3–6 7–5 6–4
DOUBLES: I. Berger (ISR)/T. Price (RSA) d. E. Callens (BEL)/M. Strebel (SUI) 6–2 7–5

AUSTRALIA, NURIOOTPA – NOVEMBER 18–24
SINGLES: L. Stacey (AUS) d. N. Pratt (AUS) 3–6 6–4 7–5
DOUBLES: J. Faull (AUS)/R. Stubbs (AUS) d. L. Novelo (MEX)/T. O'Reilly (USA) 6–4 7–5

NIGERIA, OKADA – NOVEMBER 18–24
SINGLES: A. Gima (ROM) d. S. Nicholson (IRE) 6–1 6–3
DOUBLES: C. Billingham (GBR)/V. Humphries-Davies (GBR) d. A. Evans (GBR)/A. Gima (ROM) 1–6 6–4 6–4

BRAZIL, PORTO ALEGRE – NOVEMBER 28–DECEMBER 2
SINGLES: L. Reynarez (ARG) d. N. Avila (ESP) 6–1 6–3
DOUBLES: S. Niox-Chateau (FRA)/S. Ramon (ESP) d. L. Corsato (BRA)/A. Vieira (BRA) 6–4 6–3

ISRAEL, RAMAT HASHARON – NOVEMBER 25–30
SINGLES: T. Price (RSA) d. A. Smashnova (ISR) 6–4 6–3
DOUBLES: Unfinished due to rain

AUSTRALIA, MILDURA – NOVEMBER 25–DECEMBER 1
SINGLES: R. Stubbs (AUS) d. M. Jaggard (AUS) 6–4 1–6 7–6
DOUBLES: C. Barclay (AUS)/L. Stacey (AUS) d. L. Pleming (AUS)/I. Driehuis (HOL) 6–4 6–3

MEXICO, SAN LUIS POTOSI – DECEMBER 2–8
SINGLES: A. Gavaldon (MEX) d. S. Italiano (CAN) 6–2 6–2
DOUBLES: X. Escobedo (MEX)/A. Galvadon (MEX) d. J-M. Lozano (USA)/C. Grunes (GER) 6–2 7–6

FRANCE, LE HAVRE – DECEMBER 2–8
SINGLES: K. Boogert (HOL) d. N. Perez (ESP) 6–1 6–4
DOUBLES: N. Herreman (GER)/E. Maniokova (URS) d. G. Coorengel (HOL)/A. Van Buuren (HOL) 6–3 6–4

$50,000 – CHALLENGERS

PORTUGAL, OPORTO – MAY 5–11
SINGLES: M. De Swardt (RSA) d. I. Gorrochategui (ARG) 6–1 6–2
DOUBLES: V. Ruano (ESP)/E. Bes (ESP) d. M. de Swardt (RSA)/Y. Segal (ISR) 6–3 7–5

CZECHOSLOVAKIA, KARLOVY VARY – JULY 16–21
SINGLES: Z. Malkuva (TCH) d. K. Oeljeklaus (GER) 6–4 2–6 7–6
DOUBLES: R. Bobkova (TCH)/K. Habsudova (TCH) d. K. Kroupova (TCH)/M. Stuskova (TCH) 6–1 6–3

ITALY, SPOLETO – AUGUST 20–25
SINGLES: F. Bonsignor (ITA) d. C. Salvi (ITA) 6–4 6–3
DOUBLES: A. Segura (ITA)/J. Souto (ESP) d. I. Driehuis (HOL)/L. Pleming (AUS) 3–6 7–6 6–4

ITALY, ARZACHENA SEPTEMBER 2 9
SINGLES: K. Piccolini (ITA) d. S. Smith (GBR) 6–2 6–7 6–4
DOUBLES: J. Pospisilova (TCH)/N. Dahlmann (FIN) d. I. Berger (ISR)/L. Pleming (AUS) 3–6 6–3 6–1

FRANCE, VAL D'OISE – DECEMBER 9–15
SINGLES: N. Tauziat (FRA) d. I. Demongeot (FRA) 3–6 6–3 6–1
DOUBLES: C. Suire (FRA)/E. Pfaff (GER) d. P. Paradis (FRA)/S. Testud (FRA) 4–6 6–3 6–4

MEXICO, VERACRUZ (CIRCUIT III) – APRIL 15–21
SINGLES: I. Petrov (MEX) d. X. Escobedo (MEX) 6–4 6–2
DOUBLES: I. Petrov (MEX)/O. Limon (CUB) d. I. Concepcion (MEX)/J. Montesions (CUB) 6–3 6–2

Katerina Maleeva of Bulgaria had the doubtful pleasure of beating both her sisters – Manuela and Magdalena – to reach the final of the Canadian Open, where she lost to Jennifer Capriati.
(R. Adams)

INTERNATIONAL TEAM COMPETITIONS

EUROPEAN CUPS
WORLD TEAM CUP
MAUREEN CONNOLLY BRINKER TROPHY

Magnus Gustafsson's win over Goran Prpic in Dusseldorf was the prelude to a Swedish success in the Peugeot World Team Cup which they had last won in 1988.   *(T. Hindley)*

OTHER INTERNATIONAL TEAM EVENTS

Henry Wancke

EUROPEAN CUP – MEN

Purported to be one of the major events in European tennis, the men's European Cup regrettably did not live up to expectations. Run on a shoestring budget and reliant on local sponsorship, plus the goodwill of local volunteers, it is more reminiscent of a Club event than an international competition for senior representative national teams. Crowded calendars, busy player schedules and, of course, more tempting financial rewards in other parts of the world – all these factors contrive to keep the stronger players away.

However, the European Cup has a valuable role to play in professional tennis, for it certainly gives the competing nations an opportunity to test players for international duty. Great Britain fielded their full *Davis Cup* team but grasped the opportunity to initiate newcomer Neil Broad. Nikki Pilic, the German national team captain, admitted he was looking at prospective *Davis Cup* players with his line-up, whilst France brought what many thought was their fourth string team. The only nation to bring a player in the top 50 was Holland. He was their No. 1 Richard Krajicek who, ranked at 40, was the classiest player on show. At the other end of the scale, the Soviet Union, no doubt with troubles back home, fielded a 2-man team headed by Andrei Rybalko, ranked 699.

Germany, The Netherlands and Great Britain were in one Round Robin Group, with Czechoslovakia, France and the Soviets contesting the other. The Soviets, despite showing some tenacity, were overwhelmed 3–0 in both their ties. The Czechs were seeded 2, with Martin Damm, David Rikl, Tomas Zdrazila and Radek Vasek as their players – the first three ranked between 144 and 175. The French had only Thierry Guardiola (150) and Olivier Soules (192) ranked in the top 200 but, despite that, they put on a brave performance before finally capitulating in the doubles to give the Czechs a 2–1 win and a place in the final.

In Group A Germany, as the defending champions and top seeds, were upset by Britain in their first match. Mark Petchey (253) lost to Patrik Kuhnen (86) in straight sets but did not disgrace himself, despite playing under the influence of a heavy cold and a temperature. Jeremy Bates (162) then beat Markus Zoecke (56) 6–4 6–7 (5–7) 6–1 to level the tie in a match which had many moments of high quality, punctuated by several disputes. In the doubles, Bates, partnering Neil Broad, captured the tie with a straight sets victory over Eric Jelen and Udo Riglewski.

The Germans went on to beat The Netherlands 2–1, with Krajicek providing the Dutch with their solitary point. So the finalists from Group A would be decided by the eventual score at the conclusion of the tie between Holland and Great Britain. The British had high hopes, but with Petchey still recovering from his bout of influenza, they went behind as Tom Kempers beat him 6–1 6–2. Bates, however, kept British hopes alive as he overwhelmed Krajicek in the first set of the second rubber. But as Krajicek's service form returned the Dutchman emerged a 2–6 6–1 6–3 victor, giving the Netherlands a winning lead. Britain could still make the final if they won the doubles in straight sets and looked en route to achieve this when Bates and Broad snatched the first 6–4. But again Krajicek took control and lead his partner to a 4–6 6–3 6–4 victory. The 3–0 clean sweep for the Dutch put them in the final, and consigned Britain to the relegation tie.

As it was, Britain retained Division 1 status by defeating the Soviet Union 2–0, with the doubles being cancelled. The Czechs went on to win the European Cup 2–1 against The Netherlands, the Dutch forced to play without Krajicek, who was sidelined with an aggravated shoulder injury sustained the previous night in the doubles against Britain.

Kempers took the first rubber 3–6 7–5 6–1 against Rikl, but Fernon Wibier, called up to replace Krajicek, could not make any impression on Damm, a player with solid and powerful ground strokes, who levelled the tie with his 6–3 5–7 6–1 victory. Wibier and Kempers then teamed up for the doubles against Damm and Zdrazila who, combining well, never allowed the Dutch pair an opportunity to get into the match and ran out easy winners 6–3 6–3.

Changes in the European Cup are expected for 1992, and it is to be hoped they will help to restore to the competition a status more in keeping with its title. The event must not be lost for it makes a valuable contribution to European tennis, as the 1991 competition proved.

Division 1 LENGNAU, 5–8 DECEMBER
Group 1: Great Britain d. Germany 2–1 (M. Petchey lost to P. Kuhnen 5–7 4–6; J. Bates d. M. Zoecke 6–4 6–7 6–1; Bates/N. Broad d. E. Jelen/U. Riglewski 6–2 7–6); **Germany d. Netherlands 2–1** (Kuhnen d. F. Wibier 7–5 6–4; Zoeke lost to R. Krajicek 5–7 7–6 7–6; Jelen/Riglewski d. T. Kempers/Krajicek 6–4 6–4); **Netherlands d. Great Britain 3–0** (Kempers d. Petchey 6–1 6–2; Krajicek d. Bates 2–6 6–1 6–3; Kempers/Krajicek d. Bates/Broad 4–6 6–3 6–4).
Group 2: France d. USSR 3–0 (O. Soules d. O. Ogorodov 6–7 6–3 6–2; T. Guardiola d. A. Rybalko 6–1 6–1; Guardiola/Soules d. Ogorodov/Rybalko 6–0 6–4); **Czechoslovakia d. USSR 3–0** (D. Rikl d. Ogorodov 6–1 6–2; M. Damm d. Rybalko 6–3 6–4; R. Vasek/T. Zdrazila d. Ogorodov/Rybalko 6–1 6–4); **Czechoslovakia d. France 2–1** (Rikl d. Soules 7–6 5–7 7–6; Damm lost to Guardiola 6–1 6–7 3–6; Rikl/Zdrazila d. Guardiola/Soules 6–7 7–5 6–3).
FINAL: Czechoslovakia d. Netherlands 2–1 (Rikl lost to Kempers 6–3 5–7 1–6; Damm d. Wibier 6–4 6–1; Damm/Zdrazila d. Kempers/Wibier 6–3 6–3).
RELEGATION PLAY-OFF: Great Britain d. USSR 2–0 (Petchey d. Ogorodov 6–4 7–6; Bates d. Rybalko 6–3 2–6 7–5; doubles not played).

EUROPEAN CUP – WOMEN

For the fourth consecutive year the French city of Nantes successfully hosted the top division of the Women's European Cup, involving defending champions the Soviet Union and their challengers – Great Britain, Italy, France, Belgium and The Netherlands.

The format of playing in two groups was again employed, but the weakness of having three nations in each group was highlighted when the Soviets failed to make an appearance! Regrettably they had been unable to obtain visas for the trip. As a consequence Group A could stage only one match, The Netherlands versus the hosts, France. This tie was decided by the doubles rubber when Oremans and Kiene beat Dechaume and Suire 6–2 6–3. This was a great start for the newly promoted nation, for with the Soviets defaulting, they went straight into the final! It was also very unlucky for the French who had no second chance to make an impression on the proceedings, unlike the other eventual finalist.

In Group B Great Britain, runners-up for the last two years, were defeated by Belgium 2–1, saving face by winning the doubles. The British team of Monique Javer, Sam Smith and Clare Wood then came out the following day to beat the Italians. Sam Smith, making her international debut at senior level, lost to Linda Ferrando 6–4 6–1. Javer however, showing gritty determination, outdrove Katia Piccolini 7–5 6–4 thereby giving Wood and Smith a chance to clinch victory with the doubles. This they achieved to give Britain their first victory at this year's event, and maintain their unbeaten record against the Italians in European Cup competition. Britain then had to await the result of the Belgium versus Italy tie before knowing whether they would proceed. Mathematically, if Italy defeated Belgium 2–1, Britain would have a third chance at the European title. As it turned out, the Italians won 3–0 and Britain, having lost one more rubber, failed to make the Championship match stage! Ironically, it had all turned on Piccolini beating Sabine Appelmans 6–3 6–2, the one match everyone wanted to go the other way.

Having reached the final by a very different route to the Dutch, the Italians could not be blamed for feeling confident with their team more match tight. However they hadn't allowed for the young Stephanie Rottier who adeptly hit winners off both wings with immense regularity. Linda Ferrando dealt with the problem by approaching the net but a pulled stomach muscle then hampered her and the first rubber went to the Dutch 6–1 3–6 7–5. Katie Piccolini's reputation did not deter Miriam Oremans who gained the second winning rubber for the Dutch, 6–4 6–2. The doubles was not played.

The organisers' main concern was what to do about the non-appearance of the Soviet

Union. Sue Livingston, Executive Director of the European Championships was requesting a full explanation before deciding on what action to take. 'As I see it,' she said, 'there are three possibilities: a total ban for one or more years; instant relegation to Division 2; or requiring them to appear as a new team in Division 4 in 1992.' Ultimately it was decided to relegate the USSR to Division 2, for no relegation match could be played. The Czechoslovak team will replace them, having beaten Switzerland 2–0 in the second division. Poland drop down to Division 3 and Germany replace them from that division. All this applies if the European Tennis Association continue with the current format, but they will be meeting in February 1992 to discuss possible changes. These might involve three groups of eight teams with two nations being relegated and replaced from the lower group. To help the organisers out of their awkward situation at this year's event, and to give the public some tennis, Britain and France staged an exhibition match, which was won by the visitors.

Division 1 NANTES, France 28 NOVEMBER–1 DECEMBER
GROUP A: Netherlands bt France 2–1 (M. Oremans lost to A. Dechaume 6–7 2–6; S. Rottier bt P. Paradis 6–7 6–3 6–3; Oremans/M. Kiene bt Dechaume/C. Suire 6–2 6–3) No other matches possible as USSR failed to appear.
GROUP B: Belgium bt Great Britain 2–1 (S. Appelmans bt M. Javer 6–4 6–3; D. Monami bt C. Wood 6–1 5–7 6–4; Appelmans/Monami lost to S. Smith/Wood 6–7 2–6); ***Great Britain bt Italy 2–1*** (Javer bt K. Piccolini 7–5 6–4; Smith lost to L. Ferrando 4–6 1–6; Smith/Wood bt S. Farina/Ferrando 7–6 4–6 6–4) ***Italy bt Belgium 3–0*** (Piccolini bt Appelmans 6–3 6–2; Ferrando bt Monami 6–4 6–4; Farina/Ferrando bt Appelmans/Monami 6–2 7–6).
FINAL: Netherlands bt Italy 2–0 (Oremans bt Piccolini 6–4 6–2; Rottier bt Ferrando 6–1 3–6 7–5) Doubles not played. Relegation Match – not played. USSR relegated.

PEUGEOT WORLD TEAM CUP

DUSSELDORF, 20–26 MAY
RED GROUP RESULTS: Sweden d. Argentina 2–1 (M. Gustafsson d. F. Davin 6–4 7–6; S. Edberg d. H. De La Pena 6–4 6–2; Edberg/Gustafsson lost to De La Pena/J. Frana 6–2 4–6 4–6); ***Spain d. USSR 2–1*** (E. Sanchez d. A. Cherkasov 6–3 3–6 7–6; J. Aguilera lost to A. Volkov 4–6 6–7; S. Casal/Sanchez d. Cherkasov/Volkov 6–3 6–2); ***Sweden d. Spain 3–0*** (Gustafsson d. Aguilera 6–3 6–3; Edberg d. Sanchez 6–4 6–4; Edberg/Gustafsson d. Sanchez/Casal 7–5 6–1); ***USSR d. Argentina 2–1*** (Cherkasov d. De La Pena 3–6 6–2 6–2; Volkov d. Davin 6–0 6–2; Cherkasov/Volkov lost to De La Pena/Frana 4–6 6–3 3–6); ***USSR d. Sweden 2–1*** (Cherkasov d. Edberg 6–4 6–1; Volkov lost to Gustafsson 2–6 2–6; Cherkasov/Volkov d. Edberg/Gustafsson 6–0 6–0); ***Spain d. Argentina 2–1*** (Sanchez d. G. Perez-Roldan 7–6 6–3; Aguilera lost to Davin 2–6 4–6; Casal/Sanchez d. De La Pena/Frana 6–3 6–1).
1st: Sweden 2 wins. ***2nd:*** USSR 2 wins. ***3rd:*** Spain 2 wins. ***4th:*** Argentina 0 wins.
BLUE GROUP RESULTS: Switzerland d. Germany 2–1 (J. Hlasek d. M. Stich 6–4 6–4; M. Rosset lost to E. Jelen 3–6 1–6; Hlasek/Rosset d. U. Riglewski/Stich 4–6 6–1 6–4); ***Yugoslavia d. USA 2–1*** (G. Ivanisevic d. B. Gilbert 7–6 6–3; G. Prpic lost to A. Krickstein 6–7 6–3 4–6; Ivanisevic/S. Zivojinovic d. R. Leach/J. Pugh 6–3 5–7 7–6); ***Yugoslavia d. Germany 2–1*** (Ivanisevic lost to Stich 3–6 4–6; Prpic d. Jelen 6–4 6–2; Ivanisevic/Zivojinovic d. Riglewski/Stich 6–3 6–7 7–5); ***Switzerland d. USA 2–1*** (Hlasek d. Gilbert 6–0 6–4; Rosset lost to Krickstein 3–6 2–6; Hlasek/Rosset d. Leach/Pugh 1–6 6–3 7–6); ***Yugoslavia d. Switzerland 2–1*** (Ivanisevic d. Hlasek 6–4 6–3; Prpic d. Rosset 6–3 6–4; Ivanisevic/Zivojinovic lost to Hlasek/Rosset 6–3 1–6 6–7); ***USA d. Germany 2–1*** (Gilbert lost to Stich 3–6 4–6; Krickstein d. C-U. Steeb 6–4 6–0; Leach/Pugh d. Riglewski/Stich 7–5 6–7 7–5).
1st: Yugoslavia 3 wins. ***2nd:*** Switzerland 2 wins. ***3rd:*** USA 1 win. ***4th:*** Germany 0 wins.
Final: Sweden d. Yugoslavia 2–1 (Gustafsson d. Prpic 6–2 3–6 6–4; Edberg d. Ivanisevic 6–4 7–5; Edberg/Gustafsson lost to Prpic/Zivojinovic 6–3 3–6 4–6.

MAUREEN CONNOLLY BRINKER TROPHY

Women's under 21 team competition between USA and Great Britain
NATIONAL SPORTS CENTRE FOR WALES, 6–8 DECEMBER
USA d. Great Britain 9–2 *(U.S. names first)* (J. Emmons d. S. Bentley 7–5 6–2; S. McCarthy d. C. Hall 7–6 6–4; A. Keller d. S. Smith 6–4 2–6 8–6; L. Albano/Emmons d. Hall/S. Loosemore 6–2 7–6; Albano lost V. Humphreys-Davies 6–3 2–6 3–6; A. Frazier d. Loosemore 6–2 6–4; Emmons d. Hall 6–3 6–0; McCarthy d. Bentley 6–4 6–4; Keller lost to Loosemore 2–6 6–2 5–7; Frazier d. Smith 6–2 3–0 (retd); Frazier/McCarthy d. Humphreys-Davis/Smith 6–3 7–5).

RANKINGS

WORLD RANKINGS
ATP RANKINGS AND PRIZE MONEY
VIRGINIA SLIMS RANKINGS AND PRIZE MONEY

By beating Steffi Graf twice in 1991 – to reach the Australian final in January and the semi-finals of the Virginia Slims Championships in November – the athletic Czech, Jana Novotna, lifted her year-end ranking to No. 7, her best yet.			*(R. Adams)*

WORLD RANKINGS

John Barrett

1991 WORLD RANKINGS (last year's position in brackets)

MEN	WOMEN
1 Stefan Edberg (SWE) (1)	1 Monica Seles (YUG) (2)
2 Jim Courier (USA) (–)	2 Steffi Graf (GER) (1)
3 Boris Becker (GER) (5)	3 Gabriela Sabatini (ARG) (3)
4 Michael Stich (GER) (–)	4 Martina Navratilova (USA) (4)
5 Ivan Lendl (TCH) (2)	5 Arantxa Sanchez-Vicario (ESP) (8)
6 Guy Forget (FRA) (–)	6 Mary Joe Fernandez (USA) (5)
7 Andre Agassi (USA) (3)	7 Jennifer Capriati (USA) (10)
8 Pete Sampras (USA) (4)	8 Jana Novotna (TCH) (–)
9 Karel Novacek (TCH) (–)	9 Conchita Martinez (ESP) (–)
10 Petr Korda (TCH) (–)	10 Manuela Maleeva-Fragnière (BUL) (9)

If there had been any doubts about Stefan Edberg's right to be acclaimed as the No. 1 player for 1991, the athletic Swede dispelled them magnificently in his destruction of Jim Courier, his doggedly persistent pursuer, in the final of the US Open. Edberg had also beaten the American en route to the semi-finals in Australia, and at Wimbledon he was also a semi-finalist when Courier fell a round earlier. Even though Courier did score a magnificent first Grand Slam success in Paris, his three other tournament wins and an appearance in the final of the ATP Tour Championships (where the injured Edberg did not play) could not match the Swede's six wins. It had been a close call but, in the end, a decisive margin separated them – as the ITF's panel of former champions also agreed.

Becker's year was almost a great one but after winning in Australia he faltered at the French Open and at Wimbledon – that unexpectedly one-sided loss to Stich taking a heavy toll on his confidence. Two tournament wins from five finals was not quite enough to dislodge Courier.

Michael Stich's fairytale success at Wimbledon, plus a semi-final finish in Paris and a run to the quarter-finals in New York – together with three other tournament wins, was enough to keep him ahead of Ivan Lendl.

The self-exiled Czech, whose American naturalisation is expected to be confirmed in 1992, had his worst year since falling from the No.1 ranking in 1990. Injuries were largely to blame – a problem with his hand preventing him from challenging in Paris where he usually excels. Nevertheless he did reach the final in Australia and was a semi-finalist at the US Open, successes which kept him marginally ahead of newcomer Guy Forget. The Frenchman's six titles and contribution to his country's *Davis Cup* success give him clear priority over Andre Agassi whose only star performances occurred in Paris, where he was again the beaten finalist, and at Wimbledon where he scored a personal triumph with the young fans and reached his quarter-final place with admirable poise.

Sampras had a disappointing year, though he recovered a little self-respect by claiming the ATP Championships after winning two summer tournaments in America and reaching the quarter-finals in New York. Two Czech newcomers, Karel Novacek and Petr Korda, had impressive wins on European clay and might climb higher in 1992.

Monica Seles was out on her own among the women. Winning the three Grand Slam Championships she entered, as well as the Virginia Slims Championships among her ten titles for the year, the only blemish on a near perfect record was her mysterious non-appearance at Wimbledon.

Steffi Graf's recapture of her Wimbledon crown was the highlight of a year of rehabilitation which kept the German ahead of her final round victim there, Gabriela Sabatini. The South American beauty was certainly a better player than Martina Navratilova in 1991 – but only just.

She was a semi-finalist in Paris and reached the last eight both in Melbourne and New York, while the 35-year-old left-hander did well to reach the US Open final after falling disappointingly to Capriati in the quarters at Wimbledon.

Arantxa Sanchez-Vicario had her most consistent year to date and thumped Graf decisively in Paris to reach the final again but could make no impression on Seles. One semi-final and two quarter-final placings at the other Grand Slams kept her ahead of Mary Joe Fernandez who continues to promise so much but has so far failed to deliver.

The excitement Capriati generated at Wimbledon by reaching the semi-finals at the age of 15 was almost equalled at the US Open where she was again a semi-finalist and gave Seles a wonderful run. Her year was slightly better than that of Jana Novotna who reached the Australian final but could never reproduce that form thereafter.

JOHN BARRETT'S WORLD RANKINGS 1972–1990

MEN

1972		1973		1974		1975		1976	
1	Smith	1	Nastase	1	Connors	1	Ashe	1	Connors
2	Nastase	2	Newcombe	2	Rosewall	2	Orantes	2	Borg
3	Rosewall	=3	Kodes	3	Newcombe	3	Borg	3	Nastase
4	Laver	=3	Smith	4	Borg	4	Connors	4	Vilas
5	Newcombe	5	Connors	5	Smith	5	Nastase	5	Panatta
6	Ashe	6	Okker	6	Vilas	6	Vilas	6	Dibbs
7	Orantes	7	Rosewall	7	Nastase	7	Ramirez	7	Ramirez
8	Okker	8	Ashe	8	Orantes	8	Laver	8	Solomon
9	Drysdale	9	Laver	9	Ashe	9	Tanner	9	Tanner
10	Riessen	10	Orantes	=10	Tanner	10	Roche	10	Orantes
				=10	Kodes				

1977		1978		1979		1980		1981	
1	Borg	1	Connors	1	Borg	1	Borg	1	McEnroe
2	Vilas	2	Borg	2	McEnroe	2	McEnroe	2	Borg
3	Connors	3	Gerulaitis	3	Connors	3	Connors	3	Connors
4	Gottfried	4	McEnroe	4	Gerulaitis	4	Lendl	4	Lendl
5	Stockton	5	Ramirez	5	Tanner	5	Mayer G.	5	Clerc
6	Gerulaitis	6	Dibbs	6	Vilas	6	Vilas	6	Mayer G.
7	Orantes	7	Gottfried	7	DuPre	7	Solomon	7	Vilas
8	Dent	8	Barazzutti	8	Dibbs	8	Gerulaitis	8	Gerulaitis
9	Ramirez	9	Vilas	9	Pecci	9	Gottfried	9	Pecci
10	Nastase	10	Solomon	10	Solomon	10	Clerc	10	Tanner

1982		1983		1984		1985		1986	
1	Connors	1	McEnroe	1	McEnroe	1	Lendl	1	Lendl
2	Lendl	2	Connors	2	Lendl	2	Wilander	2	Becker
3	McEnroe	3	Wilander	3	Connors	3	Edberg	3	Edberg
4	Vilas	4	Lendl	4	Wilander	4	Becker	4	Leconte
5	Wilander	5	Noah	5	Gomez	5	McEnroe	5	Nystrom
6	Gerulaitis	=6	Arias	6	Cash	6	Connors	6	Mecir
7	Mayer G.	=6	Higueras	7	Sundstrom	7	Jarryd	7	Wilander
8	Noah	8	Solomon	8	Jarryd	8	Leconte	8	Noah
9	Clerc	9	Clerc	9	Nystrom	9	Nystrom	9	McEnroe
10	Higueras	10	Teltscher	10	Arias	=10	Gunthardt	10	Gomez
						=10	Noah		

1987		1988		1989		1990	
1	Lendl	1	Wilander	1	Becker	1	Edberg
2	Edberg	2	Edberg	2	Lendl	2	Lendl
3	Wilander	3	Lendl	3	Edberg	3	Agassi
4	Cash	4	Becker	4	McEnroe J.	4	Sampras
5	Mecir	5	Agassi	5	Chang	5	Becker
6	Connors	6	Mayotte	6	Gilbert	6	Gomez
7	Becker	7	Mecir	7	Krickstein	7	Muster
8	Noah	8	Carlsson K.	8	Mecir	8	Ivanisovic
9	Mayotte	9	Cash	9	Mayotte	9	Sanchez
10	Gomez	=10	Leconte	10	Agassi	10	McEnroe J.
		=10	Svensson				

WOMEN

1972		**1973**		**1974**		**1975**		**1976**	
1	King	1	Court	1	Evert	1	Evert	1	Evert
2	Court	2	Evert	2	King	2	King	2	Goolagong
3	Evert	=3	Goolagong	3	Goolagong	3	Goolagong	3	Wade
4	Goolagong	=3	King	4	Morozova	4	Navratilova	4	Barker
5	Gunter	5	Melville	5	Wade	5	Wade	5	Casals
6	Melville	6	Masthoff	6	Melville	6	Court	6	Navratilova
7	Casals	7	Casals	7	Navratilova	7	Morozova	7	Jausovec
8	Wade	8	Wade	8	Heldman	8	Melville Reid	8	Durr
9	Durr	9	Morozova	9	Masthoff	9	Stove	9	Fromholtz
10	Stove	10	Gunter	10	Casals	10	Sawamatsu	10	Tomanova

1977		**1978**		**1979**		**1980**		**1981**	
1	Evert Lloyd	1	Evert Lloyd	1	Navratilova	1	Evert Lloyd	=1	Evert Lloyd
2	Wade	2	Navratilova	2	Austin	2	Austin	=1	Austin
3	King	3	Goolagong	3	Evert Lloyd	3	Navratilova	3	Mandlikova
4	Stove	4	Wade	4	Goolagong	4	Goolagong	4	Navratilova
5	Navratilova	5	Turnbull	5	King	5	Mandlikova	5	Jaeger
6	Barker	6	Ruzici	6	Fromholtz	6	Jaeger	6	Turnbull
7	Turnbull	7	King	7	Wade	7	Turnbull	7	Shriver
8	Casals	=8	Austin	8	Turnbull	8	Ruzici	8	Ruzici
9	Jausovec	=8	Shriver	9	Melville Reid	9	Fromholtz	9	Hanika
10	Melville Reid	10	Jausovec	10	Ruzici	10	Shriver	10	Jausovec

1982		**1983**		**1984**		**1985**		**1986**	
1	Navratilova	1	Navratilova	1	Navratilova	1	Navratilova	1	Navratilova
2	Evert Lloyd	2	Evert Lloyd	2	Evert Lloyd	2	Evert Lloyd	2	Evert
3	Jaeger	3	Jaeger	3	Mandlikova	3	Mandlikova	3	Graf
4	Mandlikova	4	Durie	4	Shriver	4	Garrison	4	Sukova
5	Austin	5	Shriver	5	Bassett	5	Kohde-Kilsch	5	Mandlikova
6	Ruzici	6	Mandlikova	6	Maleeva Man	6	Sukova	6	Sabatini
7	Bunge	7	Turnbull	7	Garrison	7	Shriver	7	Shriver
8	Shriver	8	Hanika	8	Jordan K.	8	Graf	8	Garrison
9	Potter	9	Temesvari	9	Turnbull	9	Maleeva Man	9	Maleeva Man
10	Garrison	10	Potter	10	Kohde-Kilsch	=10	Rinaldi	10	Rinaldi
10	Turnbull					=10	Sabatini		

1987		**1988**		**1989**		**1990**	
1	Graf	1	Graf	1	Graf	1	Graf
2	Navratilova	2	Sabatini	2	Navratilova	2	Seles
3	Evert	3	Navratilova	3	Sanchez-Vicario	3	Sabatini
4	Mandlikova	4	Evert	4	Sabatini	4	Navratilova
5	Sabatini	5	Shriver	5	Seles	5	Fernandez
6	Shriver	6	Sukova	6	Evert	6	Maleeva K.
7	Sukova	7	Zvereva	7	Garrison	7	Garrison
8	Kohde-Kilsch	8	Garrison	8	Sukova	8	Sanchez-Vicario
9	Maleeva-Fragnière	9	Maleeva-Fragnière	9	Maleeva-Fragnière	9	Maleeva-Fragnière
10	McNeil	10	Kohde-Kilsch	10	Lindqvist	10	Capriati

IBM/ATP TOUR RANKINGS AND PRIZE MONEY 1991

The following tables show the rankings of the top 250 in singles, the top 100 in doubles and the top 200 men on the prize money list. For the first time this year, the season is deemed to have ended on 25th November rather than the 31st December. Nevertheless, points earned by players who took part in Challenger and Satellite events between the November date and the end of the year still had them added to subsequent lists.

Besides the four Grand Slam Championships, all official IBM/ATP Tour tournaments, including Championship Series, World Series and Challenger Series events, as well as the Satellite Circuits administered by member nations of the ITF, were eligible for ranking purposes. Rankings for 1991, adjusted every week, were based on a player's best 14 results (including bonus points) during a moving twelve-month period. Somewhat controversially, in 1991 points were also given for the season-ending IBM/ATP Tour World Championships – a decision with which some of the players themselves did not agree.

(Statistics supplied by IBM/ATP Tour)

SINGLES
(As at 25th November 1991)

		T'MENTS	POINTS			T'MENTS	POINTS
1	Stefan Edberg (SWE)	20	3515	32	Javier Sanchez (ESP)	29	833
2	Jim Courier (USA)	18	3205	33	Horst Skoff (AUT)	29	825
3	Boris Becker (GER)	15	2822	34	Aaron Krickstein (USA)	19	803
4	Michael Stich (GER)	23	2675	35	Thomas Muster (AUT)	22	780
5	Ivan Lendl (TCH)	20	2565	36	Patrick McEnroe (USA)	20	778
6	Pete Sampras (USA)	20	2492	37	Paul Haarhuis (HOL)	26	773
7	Guy Forget (FRA)	23	2392	38	Cristiano Caratti (ITA)	23	769
8	Karel Novacek (TCH)	30	1599	39	Carl-Uwe Steeb (GER)	28	746
9	Petr Korda (TCH)	24	1550	40	Richard Krajicek (HOL)	22	744
10	Andre Agassi (USA)	18	1519	41	Olivier Delaitre (FRA)	25	737
11	Sergi Bruguera (ESP)	25	1504	42	Guillermo Perez-Rol (ARG)	20	736
12	Magnus Gustafsson (SWE)	21	1462	43	Fabrice Santoro (FRA)	24	715
13	Derrick Rostagno (USA)	23	1392	44	Christian Bergstrom (SWE)	23	709
14	Emilio Sanchez (ESP)	25	1388	45	Anders Jarryd (SWE)	22	701
15	Michael Chang (USA)	20	1363	46	Martin Jaite (ARG)	24	697
16	Goran Ivanisevic (CRO)	22	1352	47	Thierry Champion (FRA)	29	653
17	David Wheaton (USA)	19	1289	48	Jimmy Connors (USA)	13	650
18	Goran Prpic (CRO)	27	1178	49	Malivai Washington (USA)	21	645
19	Brad Gilbert (USA)	20	1129	50	Wayne Ferreira (RSA)	23	637
20	Jakob Hlasek (SUI)	25	1109	51	Cedric Pioline (FRA)	25	609
21	Andrei Cherkasov (CIS)	30	1099	52	Renzo Furlan (ITA)	31	607
22	Alberto Mancini (ARG)	21	1067	53	Jaime Yzaga (PER)	17	606
23	Jordi Arrese (ESP)	26	960	54	Arnaud Boetsch (FRA)	21	606
24	Omar Camporese (ITA)	26	929	55	Carlos Costa (ESP)	22	559
25	Alexander Volkov (CIS)	30	910	56	Marcus Zoecke (GER)	24	558
26	Jan Siemerink (HOL)	24	885	57	Wally Masur (AUS)	25	545
27	Richey Reneberg (USA)	18	883	58	Kevin Curren (USA)	22	538
28	John McEnroe (USA)	18	866	59	Frederic Fontang (FRA)	27	538
29	Jonas Svensson (SWE)	23	865	60	Marc Rosset (SUI)	28	537
30	Francisco Clavet (ESP)	29	837	61	Magnus Larsson (SWE)	22	525
31	Andrei Chesnokov (CIS)	23	835	62	Amos Mansdorf (ISR)	26	519

		T'MENTS	POINTS			T'MENTS	POINTS
63	Jimmy Arias (USA)	22	518	121	Paolo Cane (ITA)	14	301
64	Jaime Oncins (BRA)	22	517	122	Byron Black (ZIM)	15	301
65	Gabriel Markus (ARG)	23	516	123	Danilo Marcelino (BRA)	24	292
66	Javier Frana (ARG)	17	510	124	Gilad Bloom (ISR)	27	291
67	Shuzo Matsuoka (JAP)	21	504	125	Massimo Cierro (ITA)	21	286
68	Andres Gomez (ECU)	22	500	126	Claudio Mezzadri (SUI)	15	285
69	Stefano Pescosolido (ITA)	24	499	127	Thomas Hogstedt (SWE)	31	283
70	Mark Koevermans (HOL)	26	498	128	Francisco Roig (ESP)	20	281
71	Bryan Shelton (USA)	20	495	129	Henrik Holm (SWE)	22	275
72	Gianluca Pozzi (ITA)	24	486	130	Karsten Braasch (GER)	20	274
73	Jean-Philippe Fleurian (FRA)	29	485	131	Chris Pridham (CAN)	18	265
74	Ronald Agenor (HAI)	30	485	132	Leonardo Lavalle (MEX)	15	257
75	Jason Stoltenberg (AUS)	23	482	133	Todd Martin (USA)	10	256
76	Christian Saceanu (GER)	29	478	134	Steve Bryan (USA)	16	256
77	Todd Woodbridge (AUS)	25	468	135	Glenn Layendecker (USA)	16	255
78	Lars Jonsson (SWE)	23	465	136	Todd Witsken (USA)	16	255
79	Nicklas Kulti (SWE)	25	462	137	Francisco Montana (USA)	21	255
80	German Lopez (ESP)	21	455	138	Luis Herrera (MEX)	23	254
81	Christian Miniussi (ARG)	15	436	139	Andrei Olhovskiy (URS)	25	253
82	Grant Connell (CAN)	20	428	140	Marcos Ondruska (RSA)	16	252
83	Jim Grabb (USA)	22	428	141	Peter Lundgren (SWE)	24	252
84	Christo Van Rensburg (RSA)	19	427	142	Simon Youl (AUS)	18	251
85	Michiel Schapers (HOL)	15	426	143	Slobodan Zivojinovic (YUG)	11	250
86	Patrik Kuhnen (GER)	27	421	144	Martin Damm (TCH)	22	248
87	Lars Koslowski (GER)	16	417	145	Johan Anderson (AUS)	20	247
88	Bart Wuyts (BEL)	31	417	146	Nicolas Pereira (VEN)	18	245
89	Darren Cahill (AUS)	7	412	147	Chris Garner (USA)	22	244
90	Roberto Azar (ARG)	24	408	148	Nuno Marques (POR)	24	243
91	Rodolphe Gilbert (FRA)	24	408	149	David Engel (SWE)	19	242
92	Jan Gunnarsson (SWE)	19	407	150	Thierry Guardiola (FRA)	20	239
93	Richard Fromberg (AUS)	21	401	151	Joao Cunha-Silva (POR)	30	236
94	Eduardo Masso (BEL)	24	400	152	Martin Wostenholme (CAN)	19	234
95	Tomas Carbonell (ESP)	30	398	153	Markus Naewie (GER)	20	231
96	Patrick Baur (GER)	26	391	154	Martin Laurendeau (CAN)	16	228
97	Veli Paloheimo (FIN)	25	389	155	Scott Davis (USA)	21	227
98	Marian Vajda (TCH)	27	386	156	Vladimir Gabrichidze (URS)	23	224
99	Fernando Roese (BRA)	18	384	157	Mats Wilander (SWE)	10	220
100	Horacio de la Pena (ARG)	19	383	158	David Pate (USA)	17	220
101	Mark Woodforde (AUS)	22	382	159	Henri Leconte (FRA)	13	219
102	Diego Nargiso (ITA)	26	370	160	Jimmy Brown (USA)	17	218
103	Dimitri Poliakov (UKR)	23	361	161	David Rikl (TCH)	21	218
104	Guillaume Raoux (FRA)	27	361	162	Jeremy Bates (GBR)	11	215
105	Alexander Mronz (GER)	29	358	163	Oliver Fernandez (MEX)	17	214
106	Jeff Tarango (USA)	23	357	164	Ramesh Krishnan (IND)	22	214
107	Marcelo Filippini (URU)	25	356	165	Vaclav Roubicek (TCH)	25	212
108	Gary Muller (RSA)	24	353	166	Arne Thoms (GER)	10	211
109	Chuck Adams (USA)	24	347	167	Dinu Pescariu (ROM)	21	208
110	Jacco Eltingh (HOL)	27	346	168	Udo Riglewski (GER)	23	206
111	Franco Davin (ARG)	16	344	169	Sandon Stolle (AUS)	21	203
112	Luiz Mattar (BRA)	28	344	170	Jan Apell (SWE)	16	201
113	Pat Cash (AUS)	12	343	171	Neil Borwick (AUS)	17	201
114	Tim Mayotte (USA)	14	338	172	Marcus Zillner (GER)	14	200
115	Alex Antonitsch (AUT)	22	336	173	Markus Rackl (GER)	14	196
116	Claudio Pistolesi (ITA)	26	328	174	Jamie Morgan (AUS)	20	196
117	Eric Jelen (GER)	26	324	175	Tomas Zdrazila (TCH)	24	196
118	Marcos Aurelio Gorriz (ESP)	17	322	176	Jose Daher (BRA)	21	193
119	Martin Strelba (TCH)	24	316	177	Diego Perez (URU)	20	192
120	Pablo Arraya (PER)	24	302	178	Tarik Benhabiles (FRA)	28	191

		T'MENTS	POINTS			T'MENTS	POINTS
179	Martin Stringari (ARG)	13	190	215	Roberto Jabali (BRA)	18	145
180	Johan Carlsson (SWE)	17	189	216	John Fitzgerald (AUS)	10	144
181	Felipe Rivera (CHI)	18	189	217	Lan Bale (RSA)	12	143
182	Grant Stafford (RSA)	10	188	218	Daniele Balducci (ITA)	12	142
183	Peter Nyborg (SWE)	14	188	219	Marcelo Ingaramo (ARG)	22	142
184	Jose Francisco Altur (ESP)	23	188	220	Chris Wilkinson (GBR)	13	141
185	Dan Goldie (USA)	17	18€	221	Andres Vysand (URS)	19	140
186	Raul Antonio Viver (ECU)	8	185	222	Glenn Michibata (CAN)	8	139
187	Luis Lobo (ARG)	15	185	223	Marc Goellner (GER)	6	138
188	Daniel Orsanic (ARG)	21	183	224	Tomas Nydahl (SWE)	17	137
189	Nicola Bruno (ITA)	18	179	225	Brett Steven (NZL)	13	136
190	Yannick Noah (FRA)	7	172	226	Andrei Medvedev (URS)	9	135
191	Xavier Daufresne (BEL)	11	172	227	Thomas Buchmayer (AUT)	11	135
192	Olivier Soules (FRA)	11	171	228	Yahiya Doumbia (SEN)	10	131
193	Niclas Kroon (SWE)	16	168	229	Thomas Enqvist (SWE)	10	130
194	Stephane Simian (FRA)	12	167	230	Kelly Jones (USA)	9	127
195	Kelly Evernden (NZL)	20	165	231	Dirk Dier (GER)	12	127
196	Nicolas Becerra (ARG)	14	164	232	Raviv Weidenfeld (ISR)	11	125
197	Andrew Sznajder (CAN)	21	160	233	Paolo Pambianco (ITA)	13	125
198	Massimo Valeri (ITA)	7	158	234	Alex Corretja (ESP)	6	124
199	Roberto Saad (ARG)	8	158	235	Tommy Ho (USA)	11	122
200	Martin Sinner (GER)	15	158	236	Laurent Prades (FRA)	5	119
201	Mark Keil (USA)	21	158	237	Bruno Oresar (CRO)	10	119
202	Ctislav Dosedel (TCH)	22	158	238	David Prinosil (GER)	10	118
203	Fernando Meligeni (ARG)	18	156	239	Mikael Pernfors (SWE)	13	118
204	Felix Barrientos (PHI)	11	154	240	Brian Joelson (USA)	15	117
205	Federico Sanchez (ESP)	10	153	241	Tom Nijssen (HOL)	8	116
206	Fabio Silberberg (BRA)	12	152	242	Stephane Sansoni (FRA)	7	115
207	John Stimpson (USA)	19	151	243	Jonathan Stark (USA)	7	114
208	Mark Kratzmann (AUS)	18	150	244	Bernardo Mota (POR)	8	114
209	Libor Nemecek (TCH)	16	149	245	Francisco Maciel (MEX)	6	112
210	Andrew Castle (GBR)	16	149	246	Sasa Hirszon (YUG)	8	112
211	Carl Limberger (AUS)	17	149	247	Daniel Nestor (CAN)	11	112
212	Jens Woehrmann (GER)	17	149	248	T. J. Middleton (USA)	14	110
213	Aki Rahunen (FIN)	22	147	249	Pedro Rebolledo (CHI)	21	110
214	Cassio Motta (BRA)	15	145	250	Mario Tabares (CUB)	9	109

DOUBLES
(As at 25th November 1991)

		T'MENTS	POINTS				T'MENTS	POINTS
1	John Fitzgerald (AUS)	21	3452	51	Kevin Curren (USA)		22	894
2	Anders Jarryd (SWE)	18	3346	52	Brad Pearce (USA)		29	890
3	David Pate (USA)	24	2354	53	Cassio Motta (BRA)		22	878
4	Scott Davis (USA)	25	2336	54	Jacco Eltingh (HOL)		22	872
5	Ken Flach (USA)	19	2183	55	Ronnie Bathman (SWE)		21	862
6	Robert Seguso (USA)	16	2121	56	Andres Gomez (ECU)		18	859
7	Todd Woodbridge (AUS)	24	2086	57	Daniel Vacek (TCH)		32	847
8	Glenn Michibata (CAN)	25	2066	58	Michiel Schapers (HOL)		28	843
9	Patrick Galbraith (USA)	24	1900	59	Libor Pimek (TCH)		33	835
10	Grant Connell (CAN)	22	1877	60	Jan Siemerink (HOL)		21	795
11	Mark Woodforde (AUS)	25	1814	61	Charles Beckman (USA)		30	795
12	Laurie Warder (AUS)	34	1792	62	Mark Kratzmann (AUS)		24	789
13	Emilio Sanchez (ESP)	22	1784	63	Petr Korda (TCH)		16	777
14	Rick Leach (USA)	21	1708	64	Jim Courier (USA)		9	776
15	Todd Witsken (USA)	23	1687	65	Luiz Mattar (BRA)		25	772
16	Luke Jensen (USA)	30	1680	66	Scott Melville (USA)		27	738
17	Paul Haarhuis (HOL)	26	1557	67	Tomas Carbonell (ESP)		27	734
18	Cyril Suk (TCH)	33	1511	68	Vojtech Flegl (TCH)		28	723
19	Piet Norval (RSA)	25	1486	69	Diego Nargiso (ITA)		27	686
20	Sergio Casal (ESP)	17	1459	70	Stefan Kruger (RSA)		27	664
21	Javier Frana (ARG)	20	1452	71	Diego Perez (URU)		22	657
22	Jim Grabb (USA)	19	1414	72	Jeff Brown (USA)		35	655
23	Goran Ivanisevic (CRO)	20	1383	73	Karel Novacek (TCH)		25	651
24	Wayne Ferreira (RSA)	22	1380	74	Richard Krajicek (HOL)		15	649
25	Tom Nijssen (HOL)	30	1370	75	Nicolas Pereira (VEN)		20	646
26	Leonardo Lavalle (MEX)	23	1359	76	Henrik Jan Davids (HOL)		22	642
27	Michael Stich (GER)	22	1343	77	Eric Jelen (GER)		13	638
28	Patrick McEnroe (USA)	18	1330	78	Jan Gunnarsson (SWE)		15	633
29	Udo Riglewski (GER)	30	1327	79	Gustavo Luza (ARG)		22	633
30	Jim Pugh (USA)	17	1307	80	Paul Wekesa (KEN)		20	627
31	Omar Camporese (ITA)	21	1299	81	Shelby Cannon (USA)		34	622
32	Mark Koevermans (HOL)	22	1278	82	Jorge Lozano (MEX)		23	617
33	Wally Masur (AUS)	22	1224	83	Christian Miniussi (ARG)		19	616
34	Gary Muller (RSA)	27	1217	84	Guy Forget (FRA)		15	603
35	Danie Visser (RSA)	24	1210	85	Stefan Edberg (SWE)		7	598
36	Javier Sanchez (ESP)	32	1205	86	Brian Garrow (USA)		20	595
37	Kelly Jones (USA)	16	1193	87	Byron Talbot (RSA)		23	590
38	Steve Devries (USA)	33	1116	88	Gilad Bloom (ISR)		18	588
39	Jakob Hlasek (SUI)	21	1100	89	Menno Oosting (HOL)		25	587
40	David Macpherson (AUS)	32	1074	90	Tobias Svantesson (SWE)		26	585
41	Richey Reneberg (USA)	17	1021	91	Boris Becker (GER)		10	584
42	Sven Salumaa (USA)	30	1019	92	Greg van Emburgh (USA)		32	582
43	Jeremy Bates (GBR)	20	1012	93	Ola Jonsson (SWE)		28	569
44	Neil Broad (GBR)	27	997	94	Pablo Albano (ARG)		22	564
45	Jason Stoltenberg (AUS)	26	992	95	Andrei Olhovskiy (URS)		28	563
46	Rikard Bergh (SWE)	24	991	96	Sergi Bruguera (ESP)		10	557
47	David Wheaton (USA)	12	969	97	Simon Youl (AUS)		23	557
48	Nick Brown (GBR)	21	916	98	Broderick Dyke (AUS)		23	549
49	Kent Kinnear (USA)	28	905	99	Roger Smith (BAH)		32	540
50	Jamie Oncins (BRA)	20	903	100	Pete Sampras (USA)		7	537

PRIZE MONEY (As at 25th November 1991)

Despite the worldwide economic recession, the escalation in levels of prize money continued unabated in 1991 and was reflected in players' earnings. Stefan Edberg won more than $2 million for the first time and six other players exceeded $1 million, two more than in 1990. Altogether 17 players earned more than $500,000 (up from 12 in 1990), 38 banked over $300,000 (32), 60 earned more than $200,000 (curiously, ten fewer than in 1990) and there were 140 men with earnings above the $100,000 plateau (132).

All this without considering the $6 million that was distributed to the 16 men who competed in the *Compaq Grand Slam Cup*! (A combined earnings list appears at the end of this section.)

Note: Prize money figures include earnings from tournaments, circuit bonuses and play-offs, plus team events where entry is based purely on merit. They do not include earnings from *Davis Cup* ties, invitation tournaments, exhibitions or special events, nor do they include income from commercial contracts or endorsements.

		PRIZE MONEY			PRIZE MONEY
1	Stefan Edberg (SWE)	$2,363 575	43	Marc Rosset (SUI)	278,258
2	Pete Sampras (USA)	1,908,413	44	Robert Seguso (USA)	272,553
3	Jim Courier (USA)	1,748,171	45	Francisco Clavet (ESP)	259,384
4	Ivan Lendl (TCH)	1,438,983	46	Todd Witsken (USA)	257,196
5	Boris Becker (GER)	1,228,708	47	Carl-Uwe Steeb (GER)	253,273
6	Michael Stich (GER)	1,220,116	48	Jordi Arrese (ESP)	252,860
7	Guy Forget (FRA)	1,101,772	49	Glenn Michibata (CAN)	249,445
8	Andre Agassi (USA)	986,611	50	Jim Grabb (USA)	243,348
9	Anders Jarryd (SWE)	752,514	51	Horst Skoff (AUT)	239,168
10	Emilio Sanchez (ESP)	672,071	52	Javier Frana (ARG)	232,306
11	Karel Novacek (TCH)	650,350	53	Richard Krajicek (HOL)	231,590
12	John Fitzgerald (AUS)	616,493	54	Thierry Champion (FRA)	229,336
13	Petr Korda (TCH)	573,970	55	Mark Koevermans (HOL)	227,213
14	Jakob Hlasek (SUI)	573,642	56	Cristiano Caratti (ITA)	224,943
15	Goran Ivanisevic (CRO)	562,795	57	Jimmy Connors (USA)	224,319
16	Magnus Gustafsson (SWE)	538,792	58	Aaron Krickstein (USA)	224,005
17	Sergi Bruguera (ESP)	527,320	59	Gary Muller (RSA)	211,242
18	David Wheaton (USA)	479,239	60	Malivai Washington (USA)	208,210
19	Michael Chang (USA)	461,730	61	Kevin Curren (USA)	199,111
20	Goran Prpic (CRO)	411,068	62	Tomas Carbonell (ESP)	198,403
21	Alexander Volkov (URS)	404,046	63	Arnaud Boetsch (GER)	197,844
22	Omar Camporese (ITA)	399,959	64	Rick Leach (USA)	195,639
23	Derrick Rostagno (USA)	399,729	65	Jason Stoltenberg (AUS)	195,459
24	Andrei Cherkasov (URS)	382,327	66	Fabrice Santoro (FRA)	195,252
25	Todd Woodbridge (AUS)	366,959	67	Patrick Galbraith (USA)	191,802
26	Jonas Svensson (SWE)	347,659	68	Christ. Bergstrom (SWE)	190,549
27	Brad Gilbert (USA)	343,803	69	Thomas Muster (AUT)	189.840
28	Scott Davis (USA)	338,781	70	Udo Riglewski (GER)	189,506
29	Andrei Chesnokov (URS)	337,810	71	Laurie Warder (AUS)	186,346
30	Javier Sanchez (ESP)	336,292	72	Andres Gomez (ECU)	181,740
31	Richey Reneberg (USA)	333,121	73	Guillermo P-Roldan (ARG)	180,995
32	David Pate (USA)	330,191	74	Jaime Yzaga (PER)	179,190
33	Patrick McEnroe (USA)	328,114	75	Jaime Oncins (BRA)	179,024
34	Grant Connell (CAN)	326,046	76	Nicklas Kulti (SWE)	177,517
35	John McEnroe (USA)	321,209	77	Jan Gunnarsson (SWE)	177,102
36	Paul Haarhuis (HOL)	312.082	78	Jacco Eltingh (HOL)	176,969
37	Wayne Ferreira (RSA)	302,205	79	Luke Jensen (USA)	176,828
38	Wally Masur (AUS)	301,160	80	Martin Jaite (ARG)	172,827
39	Mark Woodforde (AUS)	295,250	81	Olivier Delaitre (FRA)	172,292
40	Alberto Mancini (ARG)	290,375	82	Luiz Mattar (BRA)	171,228
41	Ken Flach (USA)	284,373	83	Eric Jelen (GER)	168,822
42	Jan Siemerink (HOL)	280,559	84	Amos Mansdorf (ISR)	168,488

85	Cedric Pioline (FRA)	165,850	143	Cassio Motta (BRA)	96,861
86	Jim Pugh (USA)	165,219	144	Pablo Arraya (PER)	95,682
87	Tom Nijssen (HOL)	163,640	145	Tim Mayotte (USA)	95,251
88	Ronald Agenor (HAI)	163,165	146	Kelly Evernden (NZL)	94,288
89	Leonardo Lavalle (MEX)	161,797	147	Nuno Marques (POR)	93,453
90	Patrik Kuhnen (GER)	161,479	148	David Macpherson (AUS)	92,001
91	Magnus Larsson (SWE)	160,700	149	Juan Aguilera (ESP)	91,645
92	Guillaume Raoux (FRA)	160,182	150	Danilo Marcelino (BRA)	91,120
93	Cyril Suk (TCH)	159,226	151	German Lopez (ESP)	90,715
94	Peter Lundgren (SWE)	157,044	152	Fernando Roese (BRA)	90,398
95	Horacio de la Pena (ARG)	156,195	153	Nick Brown (GBR)	89,615
96	Richard Fromberg (AUS)	155,274	154	Alex Antonitsch (AUT)	88,826
97	Renzo Furlan (ITA)	153,920	155	Glenn Layendecker (USA)	88,417
98	Jean-Phil. Fleurian (FRA)	151,668	156	Roberto Azar (ARG)	88,104
99	Alexander Mronz (GER)	151,292	157	Claudio Pistolesi (ITA)	87,794
100	Slobodan Zivojinovic (YUG)	150,921	158	Marco Aurelio Gorriz (ESP)	87,774
101	Christian Saceanu (GER)	150,632	159	Diego Perez (URU)	87,696
102	Gilad Bloom (ISR)	147,217	160	David Engel (SWE)	87,523
103	Gianluca Pozzi (ITA)	147,145	161	Francisco Roig (ESP)	87,482
104	Stefano Pescosolido (ITA)	147,066	162	Todd Martin (USA)	86,949
105	Carlos Costa (ESP)	143,585	163	Paolo Cane (ITA)	86,894
106	Diego Nargiso (ITA)	141,178	164	Henrik Holm (SWE)	84,428
107	Jimmy Arias (USA)	138,710	165	Jose Francisco Altur (ESP)	84,277
108	Bryan Shelton (USA)	137,584	166	Aki Rahunen (FIN)	80,620
109	Christo V Rensburg (RSA)	137,509	167	Tarik Benhabiles (FRA)	79,992
110	Sergio Casal (ESP)	136,766	168	Chuck Adams (USA)	79,120
111	Marian Vajda (TCH)	134,360	169	Ctislav Dosedel (TCH)	78,043
112	Franco Davin (ARG)	133,870	170	Neil Borwick (AUS)	77,635
113	Frederic Fontang (FRA)	132,480	171	Nicolas Pereira (VEN)	77,517
114	Marcelo Filippini (URU)	129,790	172	Brian Garrow (USA)	77,081
115	Christian Miniussi (ARG)	129,116	173	Joao Cunha-Silva (POR)	77,079
116	Michiel Schapers (HOL)	127,814	174	Lars Koslowski (GER)	75,125
117	Shuzo Matsuoka (JAP)	126,790	175	Kent Kinnear (USA)	75,079
118	Dimitri Poliakov (URS)	126,014	176	Marcos Ondruska (RSA)	74,103
119	Jeff Tarango (USA)	125,260	177	Daniel Vacek (TCH)	73,336
120	Patrick Baur (GER)	125,202	178	Neil Broad (GBR)	73,248
121	Rodolphe Gilbert (FRA)	125,110	179	Rikard Bergh (SWE)	71,735
122	Brad Pearce (USA)	124,209	180	Ramesh Krishnan (IND)	71,723
123	Pat Cash (AUS)	123,817	181	Jeff Brown (USA)	71,366
124	Darren Cahill (AUS)	118,050	182	Scott Melville (USA)	71,319
125	Jeremy Bates (GBR)	117,892	183	Sven Salumaa (USA)	70,081
126	Piet Norval (RSA)	116,567	184	Mats Wilander (SWE)	69,967
127	Bart Wuyts (BEL)	115,195	185	Claudio Mezzadri (SUI)	69,025
128	Mark Kratzmann (AUS)	114,919	186	Charles Beckman (USA)	68,466
129	Gabriel Markus (ARG)	114,645	187	Yannick Noah (FRA)	66,445
130	Veli Paloheimo (FIN)	112,705	188	Byron Black (ZIM)	63,156
131	Henri Leconte (FRA)	110,399	189	Andrew Castle (GBR)	63,007
132	Steve Devries (USA)	108,719	190	Johan Anderson (AUS)	62,786
133	Kelly Jones (USA)	107,851	191	Dan Goldie (USA)	62,410
134	Lars Jonsson (SWE)	107,633	192	Francisco Montana (USA)	62,263
135	Danie Visser (RSA)	106,850	193	Andrew Sznajder (CAN)	62,262
136	Eduardo Masso (BEL)	106,682	194	Massimo Cierro (ITA)	59,839
137	Andrei Olhovskiy (URS)	103,754	195	Daniel Orsanic (ARG)	59,619
138	Simon Youl (AUS)	103,111	196	Chris Garner (USA)	59,490
139	Luis Herrera (MEX)	101,889	197	Ronnie Bathman (SWE)	59,370
140	Markus Zoecke (GER)	101,775	198	Martin Laurendeau (CAN)	58,972
141	Libor Pimek (TCH)	100,638	199	Niclas Kroon (SWE)	58,360
142	Thomas Hogstedt (SWE)	99,110	200	Sandon Stolle (AUS)	57,264

COMBINED EARNINGS

The combined earnings of the 16 men who contested the second *Compaq Grand Slam Cup*, plus the alternate (Javier Sanchez), were:

		IBM/ATP TOUR	COMPAQ GRAND SLAM CUP	TOTAL
1	David Wheaton (USA)	$ 479,239	$2,000,000	$2,479,239
2	Ivan Lendl (TCH)	1,438,983	450,000	1,888,985
3	Jim Courier (USA)	1,748,171	100,000	1,848,171
4	Michael Stich (GER)	1,220,116	450,000	1,670,116
5	Michael Chang (USA)	461,730	1,000,000	1,461,730
6	Guy Forget (FRA)	1,101,772	300,000	1,401,772
7	Jacob Hlasek (SUI)	573,642	300,000	873,642
8	Todd Woodbridge (AUS)	366,959	300,000	666,959
9	Patrick McEnroe (USA)	328,114	300,000	628,114
10	Goran Prpic (CRO)	411,068	100,000	511,068
11	Paul Haarhuis (HOL)	312,082	100,000	412,082
12	Javier Sanchez (ESP)	336,292	50,000	386,292
13	Thierry Champion (FRA)	229,336	100,000	329,336
14	Cristiano Caratti (ITA)	224,943	100,000	324,943
15	Jimmy Connors (USA)	224,319	100,000	324,319
16	Aaron Krickstein (USA)	224,005	100,000	324,005
17	Jaime Yzaga (PER)	179,190	100,000	279,190

Apart from the following seven players, everyone in the above list also appears in the list of Millionaires below. The career earnings of the seven are: **Jaime Yzaga (PER)** $975,001; **Goran Prpic (CRO)** $906,203; **Andrei Cherkasov (URS)** $879,614; **Paul Haarhuis (HOL)** $732,744; **Thierry Champion (FRA)** $709,566; **Christian Bergstrom (SWE)** $684,954; **Cristiano Caratti (ITA)** $412,063.

THE MILLIONAIRES

Below is a list of players who by 25th November had won more than $1 million in career prize money. The list includes earnings at the two *Compaq Grand Slam Cup* tournaments in 1990 and 1991.
* Denotes players who appear in the list for the first time.

1	Ivan Lendl (TCH)	$18,961,061	26	Tim Mayotte (USA)	2,660,152
2	John McEnroe (USA)	11,586,545	27	Miloslav Mecir (TCH)	2,632,538
3	Stefan Edberg (SWE)	11,097,271	28	Henri Leconte (FRA)	2,614,220
4	Boris Becker (GER)	9,376,755	29	John Fitzgerald (AUS)	2,462,764
5	Jimmy Connors (USA)	8,432,004	30	Aaron Krickstein (USA)	2,439,388
6	Mats Wilander (SWE)	7,377,193	31	Johan Kriek (USA)	2,374,814
7	Pete Sampras (USA)	5,012,138	32	Raul Ramirez (MEX)	2,213,671
8	Guillermo Vilas (ARG)	4,904,922	33	Ilie Nastase (RUM)	2,076,761
9	Brad Gilbert (USA)	4,561,749	34	Joakim Nystrom (SWE)	2,074,947
10	Andre Agassi (USA)	4,255,449	35	Michael Stich (GER)	*2,065,592
11	Andres Gomez (ECU)	4,240,425	36	Eddie Dibbs (USA)	2,016,426
12	Anders Jarryd (SWE)	3,986,703	37	Peter Fleming (USA)	1,986,529
13	Tomas Smid (TCH)	3,696,243	38	Jose-Luis Clerc (ARG)	1,984,461
14	Bjorn Borg (SWE)	3,609,896	39	Robert Seguso (USA)	1,851,935
15	David Wheaton (USA)	3,410,951	40	Scott Davis (USA)	1,816,378
16	Yannick Noah (FRA)	3,395,395	41	Harold Solomon (USA)	1,802,769
17	Guy Forget (FRA)	3,289,554	42	Goran Ivanisevic (CRO)	1,796,457
18	Emilio Sanchez (ESP)	3,247,148	43	Jonas Svensson (SWE)	1,781,592
19	Michael Chang (USA)	3,203,354	44	Stan Smith (USA)	1,774,811
20	Jakob Hlasek (SUI)	3,192,962	45	Martin Jaite (ARG)	1,741,163
21	Kevin Curren (USA)	2,892,780	46	Jimmy Arias (USA)	1,710,050
22	Brian Gottfried (USA)	2,782,514	47	Roscoe Tanner (USA)	1,696,108
23	Vitas Gerulaitis (USA)	2,778,748	48	David Pate (USA)	1,688,869
24	Wojtek Fibak (POL)	2,725,133	49	Eliot Teltscher (USA)	1,653,997
25	Jim Courier (USA)	*2,693,074	50	Pat Cash (AUS)	1,653,203

51	Sherwood Stewart (USA)	1,602,565	79	Paul McNamee (AUS)	1,232,825
52	Ken Rosewall (AUS)	1,600,300	80	John Alexander (AUS)	1,214,079
53	Thomas Muster (AUT)	1,594,041	81	Jan Gunnarsson (SWE)	1,212,031
54	Ken Flach (USA)	1,588,298	82	Ramesh Krishnan (IND)	1,211,093
55	Arthur Ashe (USA)	1,584,909	83	Jim Grabb (USA)	*1,186,145
56	Rod Laver (AUS)	1,564,213	84	Magn.Gustafsson (SWE)	*1,171,512
57	Jim Pugh (USA)	1,550,299	85	Robert Lutz (USA)	1,165,276
58	Heinz Gunthardt (SUI)	1,550,007	86	Darren Cahill (AUS)	1,152,379
59	Andrei Chesnokov (URS)	1,493,395	87	Tim Gullikson (USA)	1,120,570
60	Paul Annacone (USA)	1,477,533	88	Petr Korda (TCH)	*1,107,269
61	Mark Edmondson (AUS)	1,450,890	89	Javier Sanchez (ESP)	*1,105,228
62	Balazs Taroczy (HUN)	1,437,443	90	Todd Witsken (USA)	*1,096,887
63	Wally Masur (AUS)	1,436,685	91	Danie Visser (RSA)	*1,089,891
64	Slo. Zivojinovic (YUG)	1,436,054	92	Steve Denton (USA)	1,084,214
65	Bill Scanlon (USA)	1,427,007	93	Alberto Mancini (ARG)	*1,077,248
66	Brian Teacher (USA)	1,426,244	94	Derrick Rostagno (USA)	*1,070,423
67	Sergio Casal (ESP)	1,412,026	95	Eric Jelen (GER)	*1,068,364
68	Karel Novacek (TCH)	*1,409,037	96	Dick Stockton (USA)	1,063,385
69	Jose Higueras (ESP)	1,406,355	97	John Newcombe (AUS)	1,062,408
70	Manuel Orantes (ESP)	1,398,303	98	Thierry Tulasne (FRA)	1,058,412
71	Amos Mansdorf (ISR)	1,382,687	99	Sandy Mayer (USA)	1,057,783
72	Gene Mayer (USA)	1,381,562	100	Patrick McEnroe (USA)	*1,049,105
73	Chris. V Rensburg (RSA)	1,374,926	101	Sergi Bruguera (ESP)	*1,046,145
74	Guil'mo P-Roldan (ARG)	1,336,430	102	Peter McNamara (AUS)	1,046,145
75	Vijay Amritraj (IND)	1,325,833	103	Mark Woodforde (AUS)	1,042,769
76	Tim Wilkison (USA)	1,284,815	104	Horst Skoff (AUT)	*1,033,729
77	Rick Leach (USA)	1,262,814	105	Ronald Agenor (HAI)	*1,013,692
78	Tom Okker (HOL)	1,257,200	106	Todd Woodbridge (AUS)	*1,005,576

ATP TOUR BOARD OF DIRECTORS (Chief Executive Officer: Mark Miles)

Tournament representatives:
Franco Bartoni (Europe)
Graham Lovett (International Group)
Charlie Pasarell (North America)

Player Representatives:
Vijay Amritraj
Steve Meister
Larry Scott

ADDRESSES

United States:
200 ATP Tour Boulevard,
Ponte Vedra Beach,
Florida,
32082, U.S.A.
Tel: 1–904–285 8000
Fax: 1–904–285 5966

Europe:
Monte Carlo Sun,
74 Boulevard D'Italie,
98000, Monaco
Tel: 33–93–159 565
Fax: 33–93–159 794

International Group:
Suite 2, Level 32,
NORTHPOINT
100 Miller Street,
North Sydney,
N.S.W. 2060
Australia
Tel: 61–2–956 7888
Fax: 61–2–956 7773

VIRGINIA SLIMS RANKINGS AND PRIZE MONEY 1991

RANKINGS

The following tables show the season-ending rankings in singles and doubles. The rankings, updated weekly, are based on points won on the Kraft General Foods World Tour. Where players appear to have equal points the complete figures contain the fractional differences. These are not included here. (Statistics supplied by VIRGINIA SLIMSTAT SYSTEM.)

SINGLES

		T'MENTS	AVGE POINTS			T'MENTS	AVGE POINTS
1	Monica Seles (YUG)	16	277	40	Eva Sviglerova (TCH)	19	25
2	Steffi Graf (GER)	15	219	41	Linda Harvey-Wild (USA)	20	24
3	Gabriela Sabatini (ARG)	16	200	42	Debbie Graham (USA)	12	24
4	Martina Navratilova (USA)	14	191	43	Barbara Rittner (GER)	17	24
5	Arantxa Sanchez-Vicar. (ESP)	16	153	44	Marianne Werdel (USA)	19	23
6	Jennifer Capriati (USA)	13	143	45	Nicole Provis (AUS)	19	23
7	Jana Novotna (TCH)	17	109	46	Caterina Lindqvist (SWE)	23	23
8	Mary Joe Fernandez (USA)	18	101	47	Karine Quentrec (FRA)	13	23
9	Conchita Martinez (ESP)	15	95	48	Larisa Savchenko (URS)	17	23
10	Manuela Maleeva-Frag. (SUI)	17	88	49	Manon Bollegraf (HOL)	13	23
11	Katerina Maleeva (BUL)	17	75	50	Federica Bonsignori (ITA)	13	23
12	Zina Garrison (USA)	18	66	51	Carrie Cunningham (USA)	19	22
13	Nathalie Tauziat (FRA)	20	65	52	Tami Whitlinger (USA)	18	22
14	Anke Huber (GER)	14	62	53	Marianne de Swardt (RSA)	10	22
15	Leila Meskhi (URS)	15	61	54	Karina Habsudova (TCH)	16	21
16	Judith Wiesner (AUT)	14	59	55	Patty Fendick (USA)	18	21
17	Helena Sukova (TCH)	19	57	56	Florencia Labat (ARG)	18	21
18	Sabine Appelmans (BEL)	16	51	57	Patricia Hy (CAN)	17	20
19	Lori McNeil (USA)	23	46	58	Ginger Helgeson (USA)	19	20
20	Julie Halard (FRA)	24	45	59	Anne Minter (AUS)	21	19
21	Natalia Zvereva (URS)	18	44	60	Jo Durie (GBR)	18	19
22	Gigi Fernandez (USA)	19	43	61	Isabelle Demongeot (FRA)	19	19
23	Radka Zrubakova (TCH)	21	40	62	Katia Piccolini (ITA)	13	19
24	Laura Gildemeister (PER)	17	39	63	Anne Smith (USA)	5	19
25	Barbara Paulus (AUT)	13	39	64	Veronika Martinek (GER)	15	18
26	Mary Pierce (FRA)	11	38	65	Akiko Kijimuta (JAP)	17	18
27	Sandra Cecchini (ITA)	14	36	66	Nicole Jagerman (HOL)	12	18
28	Amy Frazier (USA)	18	36	67	Amanda Coetzer (RSA)	19	18
29	Helen Kelesi (CAN)	20	34	68	Sylvia Farina (ITA)	13	18
30	Brenda Schultz (HOL)	20	30	69	Mercedes Paz (ARG)	22	17
31	Emanuela Zardo (SUI)	12	30	70	Ines Gorrochategui (ARG)	11	17
32	Kimiko Date (JAP)	12	29	71	Peanut Harper (USA)	16	17
33	Naoko Sawamatsu (JAP)	16	27	72	Alexia Dechaume (FRA)	18	17
34	Andrea Strnadova (TCH)	18	27	73	Maya Kidowaki (JAP)	14	17
35	Yayuk Basuki (INA)	14	27	74	Pascale Paradis-Mangon (FRA)	14	16
36	Rachel McQuillan (AUS)	20	27	75	Raffaella Reggi Concato (ITA)	11	16
37	Pam Shriver (USA)	18	26	76	Petra Ritter (AUT)	12	16
38	Magdalena Maleeva (BUL)	15	25	77	Susan Sloane-Lundy (USA)	15	16
39	Regina Rajchrtova (TCH)	18	25	78	Claudia Porwick (GER)	20	15

	T'MENTS	AVGE POINTS			T'MENTS	AVGE POINTS
79 Marketa Kochta (GER)	14	15	138 Nadin Ercegovic (YUG)	13	8
80 Elna Reinach (RSA)	22	15	139 Heather Ludloff (USA)	13	8
81 Bettina Fulco (ARG)	17	15	140 Radka Bobkova (TCH)	14	8
82 Natalia Medvedeva (URS)	10	15	141 Ann Henricksson (USA)	18	8
83 Chanda Rubin (USA)	14	15	142 Meike Babel (GER)	12	8
84 Claudia Kohde-Kilsch (GER)	19	15	143 Barbara Mulej (YUG)	7	8
85 Petra Langrova (TCH)	19	15	144 Nana Miyagi (JAP)	18	8
86 Kristin Godridge (AUS)	20	14	145 Sybile Niox-Chateau (FRA)	15	8
87 Halle Cioffi (USA)	19	14	146 Noelle Van Lottum (FRA)	20	8
88 Karin Kschwendt (GER)	18	14	147 Maria Strandlund (SWE)	12	8
89 Ann Grossman (USA)	19	14	148 Miriam Oremans (HOL)	13	8
90 Sabine Hack (GER)	15	14	149 Kataryna Nowak (POL)	13	8
91 Ros Fairbank-Nideffer (USA)	20	14	150 Louise Allen (USA)	17	8
92 Donna Faber (USA)	21	14	151 Jessica Emmons (USA)	18	7
93 Katrina Adams (USA)	17	14	152 Anna-Maria Foldenyi (HUN)	15	7
94 Cristina Tessi (ARG)	20	14	153 Fang Li (CHN)	19	7
95 Laura Garrone (ITA)	14	13	154 Stephanie Rottier (HOL)	16	7
96 Linda Ferrando (ITA)	12	13	155 Csilla Bartos (SUI)	10	7
97 Audra Keller (USA)	21	13	156 Beverly Bowes (USA)	17	7
98 Elena Brioukhovets (URS)	18	13	157 Andrea Temesvari (HUN)	15	7
99 Petra Thoren (FIN)	19	13	158 Tamaka Takagi (JAP)	16	7
100 Katja Oeljeklaus (GER)	12	12	159 Nanne Dahlman (FIN)	15	7
101 Robin White (USA)	14	12	160 Tammy Whittington (USA)	15	7
102 Shaun Stafford (USA)	17	12	161 Ilana Berger (ISR)	18	7
103 Kimberly Po (USA)	8	12	162 Meredith McGrath (USA)	6	7
104 Rika Hiraki (JAP)	15	12	163 Stacey Martin (USA)	27	7
105 Kathy Rinaldi (USA)	12	12	164 Cammy MacGregor (USA)	14	7
106 Catherine Mothes (FRA)	15	12	165 Amanda Grunfeld (GBR)	15	6
107 Eugenia Maniokova (TCH)	15	11	166 Alysia May (USA)	13	6
108 Erika de Lone (USA)	17	11	167 Jenny Byrne (AUS)	5	6
109 Marion Maruska (AUT)	12	11	168 Kristine Radford (AUS)	16	6
110 Lisa Bonder-Kreiss (USA)	7	11	169 Nathalie Housset (FRA)	14	6
111 Catherine Tanvier (FRA)	10	11	170 Agnes Zugasti (FRA)	18	6
112 Monique Javer (GBR)	18	11	171 Maureen Drake (CAN)	16	6
113 Gretchen Magers (USA)	15	11	172 Beate Reinstadler (AUT)	14	6
114 Catherine Suire (FRA)	17	11	173 Els Callens (BEL)	15	6
115 Elizabeth Smylie (AUS)	16	11	174 Sarah Loosemore (GBR)	16	6
116 Patricia Tarabini (ARG)	13	11	175 Shannan McCarthy (USA)	11	6
117 Mana Endo (JAP)	10	11	176 Cristina Salvi (ITA)	15	6
118 Sandrine Testud (FRA)	18	11	177 Christiane Hofmann (GER)	12	6
119 Isabel Cueto (GER)	11	11	178 Nathalie Guerree (FRA)	14	6
120 Samantha Smith (GBR)	18	11	179 Natalia Baudone (ITA)	17	6
121 Petra Kamstra (HOL)	15	11	180 Cecilia Dahlman (SWE)	21	6
122 Silke Frankl (GER)	13	10	181 Andrea Leand (USA)	10	6
123 Sara Gomer (GBR)	13	10	182 Cathy Caverzasio (SUI)	14	6
124 Nathalie Herreman (FRA)	23	10	183 Kumiko Okamoto (JAP)	7	6
125 Stephanie Rehe (USA)	13	10	184 Alexandra Fusai (FRA)	15	6
126 Mary Lou Daniels (USA)	10	10	185 Shi-Ting Wang (TPE)	10	6
127 Christelle Fauche (SUI)	13	10	186 Luciana Corsato (BRA)	16	6
128 Wiltrud Probst (GER)	18	10	187 Sofie Albinus (DEN)	13	6
129 Dominique Monami (BEL)	11	9	188 Caroline Kuhlman (USA)	20	6
130 Clare Wood (GBR)	16	9	189 Simone Schilder (HOL)	13	6
131 Sandra Wasserman (BEL)	16	9	190 Zdenka Malkova (TCH)	9	6
132 Maja Zivec-Skulj (GER)	12	9	191 Yael Segal (ISR)	11	5
133 Denisa Szabova (TCH)	15	9	192 Christen Torrens-Valero (ESP)	12	5
134 Elena Pamp.-Wagner (BUL)	12	9	193 Monique Kiene (HOL)	11	5
135 Rene Alter (CAN)	15	9	194 Estefania Bottini (ESP)	16	5
136 Silke Meier (GER)	17	8	195 Louise Field (AUS)	20	5
137 Misumi Miyauchi (JAP)	12	8	196 Sandra Dopfer (AUT)	12	5

		T'MENTS	AVGE POINTS			T'MENTS	AVGE POINTS
197	Claudia Chabalgoity (BRA)	9	5	199	Jo-Anne Faull (AUS)	18	5
198	Michelle Jaggard (AUS)	15	5	200	Renata Baranski (USA)	22	5

DOUBLES

		T'MENTS	AVGE POINTS			T'MENTS	AVGE POINTS
1	Jana Novotna (TCH)	19	376	26	Sandy Collins (USA)	20	112
2	Larisa Savchenko (URS)	19	342	27	Robin White (USA)	16	108
3	Natalia Zvereva (URS)	22	330	28	Lise Gregory (RSA)	21	108
4	Gigi Fernandez (USA)	20	320	29	Raffaella Reggi Concato (ITA)	9	108
5	Mary Joe Fernandez (USA)	18	245	30	Gretchen Magers (USA)	17	107
6	Martina Navratilova (USA)	11	241	31	Rachel McQuillan (AUS)	19	104
7	Arantxa Sanchez-Vicario (ESP)	16	222	32	Catherine Tanvier (FRA)	10	103
8	Helena Sukova (TCH)	20	209	33	Jennifer Capriati (USA)	9	102
9	Pam Shriver (USA)	19	201	34	Manuela Maleeva-Fragn. (SUI)	10	102
10	Patty Fendick (USA)	20	188	35	Meredith McGrath (USA)	5	101
11	Anne Smith (USA)	9	176	36	Andrea Strnadova (TCH)	17	100
12	Zina Garrison (USA)	21	174	37	Leila Meskhi (URS)	16	98
13	Jill Hetherington (CAN)	22	146	38	Nathalie Tauziat (FRA)	17	97
14	Elizabeth Smylie (AUS)	18	142	39	Sabine Appelmans (BEL)	11	93
15	Mercedes Paz (ARG)	19	141	40	Patricia Tarabini (ARG)	13	91
16	Katrina Adams (USA)	19	138	41	Judith Wiesner (AUT)	10	90
17	Elna Reinach (RSA)	20	138	42	Maya Kidowaki (JAP)	13	86
18	Nicole Provis (AUS)	18	136	43	Mary Lou Daniels (USA)	11	82
19	Lori McNeil (USA)	19	135	44	Peanut Harper (USA)	15	80
20	Kathy Rinaldi (USA)	21	135	45	Stephanie Rehe (USA)	9	78
21	Kathy Jordan (USA)	8	133	46	Yayuk Basuki (INA)	15	74
22	Monica Seles (YUG)	5	132	47	Ros Fairbank-Nideffer (USA)	20	72
23	Manon Bollegraf (HOL)	18	123	48	Sandra Cecchini (ITA)	12	72
24	Claudia Kohde-Kilsch (GER)	13	121	49	Mary Pierce (FRA)	10	71
25	Isabelle Demongeot (FRA)	16	116	50	Caroline Vis (HOL)	9	69

PRIZE MONEY

The following table shows the prize money (including bonuses) won at all recognised tournaments which adopt the WTA guidelines and where direct entry is based solely on merit. Figures supplied by VIRGINIA SLIMSTAT SYSTEM.

		PRIZE MONEY			PRIZE MONEY
1	Monica Seles (YUG)	$2,457,758	51	Gretchen Magers (USA)	98,606
2	Steffi Graf (GER)	1,468,336	52	Naoko Sawamatsu (JAP)	94,996
3	Gabriela Sabatini (ARG)	1,192,971	53	Mary Pierce (FRA)	94,582
4	Martina Navratilova (USA)	989,986	54	Isabelle Demongeot (FRA)	94,359
5	Arantxa Sanchez-Vic. (ESP)	799,340	55	Yayuk Basuki (INA)	92,631
6	Jana Novotna (TCH)	766,369	56	Ginger Helgeson (USA)	91,288
7	Mary Joe Fernandez (USA)	672,035	57	Carrie Cunningham (USA)	91,142
8	Natalia Zvereva (URS)	558,002	58	Jill Hetherington (CAN)	90,353
9	Jennifer Capriati (USA)	535,617	59	Anne Smith (USA)	87,745
10	Gigi Fernandez (USA)	455,228	60	Elena Brioukhovets (URS)	86,509
11	Zina Garrison (USA)	435,859	61	Magdalena Maleeva (BUL)	85,607
12	Helena Sukova (TCH)	396,824	62	Anne Minter (AUS)	85,583
13	Larisa Savchenko (URS)	374,540	63	Patricia Hy (CAN)	84,720
14	Manuela Maleeva-Frag. (SUI)	316,003	64	Petra Langrova (TCH)	81,608
15	Conchita Martinez (ESP)	304,790	65	Nathalie Herreman (FRA)	80,536
16	Katerina Maleeva (BUL)	299,693	66	Shaun Stafford (USA)	79,654
17	Pam Shriver (USA)	292,561	67	Peanut Harper (USA)	79,601
18	Nathalie Tauziat (FRA)	280,304	68	Maya Kidowaki (JAP)	79,524
19	Lori McNeil (USA)	253,565	69	Kimiko Date (JAP)	79,299
20	Leila Meskhi (URS)	223,168	70	Florencia Labat (ARG)	76,511
21	Anke Huber (GER)	196,629	71	Claudia Porwick (GER)	75,510
22	Sabine Appelmans (BEL)	192,871	72	Ann Grossman (USA)	75,150
23	Julie Halard (FRA)	187,677	73	Akiko Kijimuta (JAP)	74,188
24	Patty Fendick (USA)	186,473	74	Barbara Rittner (GER)	74,178
25	Radka Zrubakova (TCH)	171,430	75	Karina Habsudova (TCH)	74,040
26	Judith Wiesner (AUT)	167,361	76	Barbara Paulus (AUT)	73,540
27	Laura Gildemeister (PER)	162,462	77	Sandy Collins (USA)	72,851
28	Elizabeth Smylie (AUS)	162,357	78	Bettina Fulco (ARG)	72,074
29	Rachel McQuillan (AUS)	159,681	79	Wiltrud Probst (GER)	71,942
30	Brenda Schultz (HOL)	151,578	80	Alexia Dechaume (FRA)	71,109
31	Elna Reinach (RSA)	149,469	81	Karin Kschwendt (GER)	70,455
32	Mercedes Paz (ARG)	149,359	82	Amanda Coetzer (RSA)	70,293
33	Amy Frazier (USA)	148,935	83	Emanuela Zardo (SUI)	69,076
34	Helen Kelesi (CAN)	139,843	84	Audra Keller (USA)	66,399
35	Manon Bollegraf (HOL)	139,278	85	Debbie Graham (USA)	65,932
36	Nicole Provis (AUS)	132,000	86	Kristin Godridge (AUS)	65,446
37	Jo Durie (GBR)	130,071	87	Clare Wood (GBR)	60,660
38	Kathy Rinaldi (USA)	129,580	88	Laura Garrone (ITA)	60,243
39	Andrea Strnadova (TCH)	128,758	89	Andrea Temesvari (HUN)	59,950
40	Caterina Lindqvist (SWE)	124.791	90	Nicole Jagerman (HOL)	59,181
41	Regina Rajchrtova (TCH)	120,665	91	Mariaan de Swardt (RSA)	58,219
42	Sandra Cecchini (ITA)	119,156	92	Catherine Suire (FRA)	57,652
43	Robin White (USA)	110,767	93	Donna Faber (USA)	57,478
44	Claudia Kohde-Kilsch (GER)	108,507	94	Halle Cioffi (USA)	57,275
45	Ros Fairbank-Nideffer (USA)	108,388	95	Monique Javer (GBR)	56,577
46	Linda Harvey-Wild (USA)	107,721	96	Linda Ferrando (ITA)	56,371
47	Tami Whitlinger (USA)	105,896	97	Lise Gregory (RSA)	55,842
48	Eva Sviglerova (TCH)	105,339	98	Meredith McGrath (USA)	55,786
49	Katrina Adams (USA)	102,322	99	Eva Pfaff (GER)	64,666
50	Marianne Werdel (USA)	100,551	100	Cathy Caverzasio (SUI)	54,429

MILLIONAIRES

Players who have won more than $1 million in prize money.

1	Martina Navratilova (USA)	$17,664,593	20	Kathy Jordan (USA)	1,592,111
2	Chris Evert (USA)	8,896,195	21	Virginia Wade (GBR)	1,542,278
3	Steffi Graf (GER)	8,641,534	22	Evonne Goolagong (AUS)	1,399,431
4	Gabriela Sabatini (ARG)	4,849,107	23	Gigi Fernandez (USA)	1,392,402
5	Pam Shriver (USA)	4,616,058	24	Katerina Maleeva (BUL)	1,387,112
6	Monica Seles (YUG)	4,349,041	25	Andrea Jaeger (USA)	1,379,066
7	Helena Sukova (TCH)	3,869,921	26	Barbara Potter (USA)	1,376,580
8	Hana Mandlikova (AUS)	3,340,959	27	Rosie Casals (USA)	1,364,955
9	Zina Garrison (USA)	3,219,629	28	Ros Fairbank-Nidef. (USA)	1,338,683
10	Wendy Turnbull (AUS)	2,769,024	29	Sylvia Hanika (GER)	1,296,560
11	Man. Maleeva-Frag. (SUI)	2,282,682	30	Elizabeth Smylie (AUS)	1,242,946
12	Claudia Kohde-Kilsch (GER)	2,143,048	31	Larisa Savchenko (URS)	1,239,741
13	Jana Novotna (TCH)	2,116,473	32	Virginia Ruzici (RUM)	1,183,728
14	Arantxa Sanchez-Vic. (ESP)	2,059,757	33	Anne Smith (USA)	1,158,767
15	Billie Jean King (USA)	1,966,487	34	Bettina Bunge (USA)	1,126,424
16	Tracy Austin (USA)	1,925,415	35	Catarina Lindqvist (SWE)	1,057,117
17	Natalia Zvereva (URS)	1,706,135	36	Betty Stove (HOL)	1,047,356
18	Mary Joe Fernandez (USA)	1,647,613	37	Jo Durie (GBR)	1,023,148
19	Lori McNeil (USA)	1,646,629			

WTA ANNUAL AWARDS, New York, 26 August 1991

PLAYER OF THE YEAR	Monica Seles
DOUBLES TEAM OF THE YEAR	Gigi Fernandez/Jana Novotna
MOST IMPROVED PLAYER	Gabriela Sabatini
MOST IMPRESSIVE NEWCOMER	Andrea Strnadova
COMEBACK PLAYER OF THE YEAR	Stephanie Rehe
TED TINLING MEDIA AWARD	Thomas Bonk
KAREN KRANTZCKE SPORTSMANSHIP	Judith Wiesner
PLAYER SERVICE	Kathy Jordan
DAVID GRAY SPECIAL SERVICE	Jane Brown

WTA BOARD OF DIRECTORS (Voted in, August 1991)

PRESIDENT	Pam Shriver	**ADDRESS**
VICE-PRESIDENT	Kathy Jordan	133 First Street N.E.
SECRETARY	Wendy Turnbull	St Petersburg,
TREASURER	Elise Burgin	Florida, 33701.
Members	Katrina Adams	U.S.A.
	Sandy Collins	Tel: 813–895 5000
	Chris Evert	Fax: 813–894 1982
	Zina Garrison	Telex: 441761
	Martina Navratilova	
	Elizabeth Smylie	
	Judith Wiesner	
	Natalia Zvereva	
Business Advisors	Marvin Koslow	
	Loretta McCarthy	

SENIOR WTA EXECUTIVE STAFF

EXECUTIVE DIRECTOR AND C.E.O.	Gerard Smith
DIRECTOR OF INTERNATIONAL OPERATIONS	Peachy Kellmeyer
DIRECTOR OF FINANCE AND ADMINISTRATION	Jay Meder
DIRECTOR OF PUBLIC RELATIONS	Ana Leaird
DIRECTOR OF MANAGEMENT INFORMATION SYSTEMS	Gene Beckwith

WOMEN'S INTERNATIONAL PROFESSIONAL TENNIS COUNCIL

ADDRESS: 215 Park Avenue South, Suite 1715, New York, N.Y., 10003, U.S.A.
TEL: 212–228 4400; FAX: 212–228 4800; TELEX: 510–6004566.

MANAGING DIRECTOR:	Ann Person
ITF REPRESENTATIVES:	J. Howard Frasor, USTA
	Heinz Grimm, ETA
	Brian Tobin, ITF
	Deborah Jevans, ITF
PLAYER REPRESENTATIVES:	Kathy Jordan
	Wendy Turnbull
	Peachy Kellmeyer
	Gerard Smith
TOURNAMENT REPRESENTATIVES:	William Goldstein, U.S.A.
	George Hendon, Europe
	Sara Fornaciari, U.S.A.
	Geoffrey Pollard, Rest of the World
KRAFT GENERAL FOODS REPRESENTATIVES:	Tom Keim, Edy McGoldrick
VIRGINIA SLIMS REPRESENTATIVES:	Ina Broeman, Leo McCullagh

Nearing the end of her distinguished career, the British No. 1, Joe Durie, added the Australian mixed doubles title to the 1987 Wimbledon title she had won with the same partner, Jeremy Bates. (T. Hindley)

REFERENCE SECTION

BIOGRAPHIES
ALL-TIME GREATS
CHAMPIONSHIP ROLLS

At Wimbledon Martina Navratilova had lifted her career earnings to a record $17 million and by defeating Monica Seles at Oakland in November, the 35-year-old, Czech-born American equalled Chris Evert's record of 157 tournament victories. But her year-end ranking slipped to 4, her lowest since 1976. (T. Hindley)

Attempting a return to the main men's circuit almost ten years after his first retirement, the great Swedish champion Bjorn Borg (34), using his old wooden rackets, was soundly beaten in the first round at Monte Carlo by Jordi Arrese of Spain. (T. Hindley)

BIOGRAPHIES

Christine Forrest

Men and women who appear in the top 100 on the ATP and WTA computer rankings are included below, as well as leading doubles players, a few prominent players who compete less than usual nowadays, plus some newcomers. We gratefully acknowledge the assistance of the ATP Tour, Virginia Slims and WTA in supplying additional biographical information.

The final ranking for each year is shown in brackets following the year.

1990 doubles ranking is shown in brackets after 1991 ranking where applicable.

Note: 1991 rankings for women are season-end rankings, and those for men are as at 25 November 1991.

Career prize money of all players who have exceeded earnings of $1 million can be found on pages 209–12 (men) and 216–17 (women).

KATRINA ADAMS (USA)
Born Chicago, 5 August 1968, and lives there; RH; 5ft 5in; 143lb; final 1991 WTA ranking 93 singles, 16 doubles; 1991 prize money $102,322.
1986: (393) Won NCAA doubles with Donnelly. **1987:** (158). **1988:** (105) Upset Fendick *en route* to 1st VS f in Wellington and upset Hanika to reach last 16 Wimbledon. **1989:** (86) Upset Manuela Maleeva and Fendick *en route* to sf US HC. In doubles won 8 titles with different partners. **1990:** (254) Reached 1 f and 10 sf in doubles but won no title on the main tour. **1991:** In singles r/u VS Nashville and qf VS Albuquerque (d. Fendick). In doubles won VS Albuquerque with Demongeot and reached 3 more f with various partners. **1991 HIGHLIGHTS – SINGLES:** *r/u* VS Nashville (d. Langrova 7–6 7–6, Thoren 6–3 2–6 6–3, Whittington 7–5 6–1, Medvedeva 7–6 5–7 6–4, lost Appelmans 6–2 6–4). **1991 HIGHLIGHTS – DOUBLES:** [Demongeot] **won** VS Albuquerque (d. Gregory/Louie Harper 6–7 6–4 6–3); [Hetherington] *r/u* VS Oklahoma (lost McGrath/A. Smith 6–2 6–4), [McNeil] *r/u* Westchester (lost Fairbank-Nideffer/Gregory 7–5 6–4), [Paz] *r/u* Indianapolis (lost Fendick/G. Fernandez 6–4 6–2).

ANDRE AGASSI (USA)

Born Las Vegas, 29 April 1970, and lives there; RH; 2HB; 5ft 11in; 175lb; final 1991 ATP ranking 10; 1991 prize money $982,611.

Suffered from Osgood Schlatter's disease, which causes a bone in the knee to grow improperly. Coached from age 13 by Nick Bollettieri and from 1989 by Pat Etchenbery for movement, trained by Gil Reyes in 1990. *1984.* Ranked 4 in US Boys' 14s and won Nat 14s. *1985:* (618) Receiving expert council from brother-in-law Pancho Gonzales, he tested the waters of men's circuit. *1986:* (91) Downed Mayotte and S. Davis on way to qf Stratton Mountain. *1987:* (25) Reached first GP f at Seoul, won his 1st GP title at Itaparica at end of season and d. Jarryd *en route* to sf Basel. *1988:* (3) Began the year by winning 2nd consecutive tourn at Memphis, adding US CC, Tourn of Champs, Stuttgart, Stratton Mountain and Livingston during the year. After reaching 1st GS sf in Paris, he took a month's rest, missing Wimbledon. Made D Cup début and qualified for Masters, but was restricted by a hand injury. *1989:* (7) Could not maintain the high standards of 1988, having to wait until Orlando in Oct. for his 1st title for 14 months. R/u Italian Open; reached 2nd GS sf at US Open and appeared in 4 other sf to qualify for Masters, but won no match there. *1990:* (4) His year finished on a high note when he beat world No. 1, Edberg, to win ATP Tour World Champ in Nov. Reached 1st GP f at French Open, where he shocked traditionalists with his lurid outfits, which included luminous cycling shorts under black denim shorts. Did not play Wimbledon or Australian Open, but was also r/u at US Open, where he was fined $3,000 for his conduct in 3r match v Korda. In autumn was fined 20% of total earnings on ATP tour (excluding GS) for falling 2 tourns short of his commitment to the tour and was fined a further $25,000 at end of year of withdrawing from GS Cup after submitting an entry. Won San Francisco, LIPC, Washington; r/u Indian Wells; and played in US D Cup team that d. Australia 3–2 in f but withdrew with pulled stomach muscle in 4th rubber. *1991:* Reached his 3rd GS final at French Open, but in losing to Courier, he again cast doubts on his ability to win a title at the highest level. Known generally for his garish outfits, he delighted both officials and crowds at Wimbledon with his pristine white attire and his enthusiasm. He reached sf there, but disappointed at US Open, falling in ss 1r to Krickstein. At ATP World Champ he reached sf but again fell to Courier to finish the ATP year with just 2 titles – Orlando and Washington. Again led USA to f D Cup with 2 s wins in 3–2 victory over Germany in sf and d. Forget in opening rubber of f v France in Lyon where Fr. win in 4th rubber caused his match v Leconte to be abandoned. *1991 HIGHLIGHTS – SINGLES: r/u French Open* seed 4 (d. Rosset 3–6 7–5 6–4, Korda 6–1 6–2 6–2, P. McEnroe 6–2 6–2 6–0, Mancini 6–3 6–3 5–7 6–1, Hlasek 6–3 6–1 6–1, Becker [seed 2] 7–5 6–3 6–1, lost Courier [seed 9] 3–6 6–4 2–6 6–1 6–4), *Wimbledon* qf, seed 5 (d. Connell 4–6 6–1 6–7 7–5 6–3, Prpic 7–6 3–6 6–4 6–2, Krajicek 7–6 6–3 7–6, Eltingh 6–3 3–6 6–3 6–4, lost Wheaton 6–2 0–6 3–6 7–6 6–2), *US Open* 1r, seed 8 (lost Krickstein 7–5 7–6 6–2); *won* Orlando (d. Garrow 6–2 6–4, Engel 6–4 6–4, Adams 6–4 7–6, Washington 6–4 7–6, Rostagno 6–2 1–6 6–3), *won* Washington (d. Pate 6–4 6–3, Adams 6–2 6–2, Carlsson 7–5 6–2, Yzaga 6–3 6–2, Korda 6–3 6–4); *sf* San Francisco (d. Tarango 7–6 6–3, Riglewski 3–6 6–4 6–3, Curren 6–2 6–4, lost B. Gilbert 6–1 6–2), *sf* ATP World Champ (d. Becker 6–3 7–5, Stich 7–5 6–3, lost Sampras in rr, lost Courier 6–3 7–5). *CAREER HIGHLIGHTS – SINGLES: French Open – r/u 1990* (d. Wostenholme, Woodbridge, Boetsch, Courier 6–7 6–1 6–4 6–1, Chang 6–1 6–2 4–6 6–2, Svensson 6–1 6–4 3–6 6–3, lost Gomez 6–3 2–6 6–4 6–4), *r/u* 1991, *sf 1988* (d. Perez-Roldan 6–2 6–2 6–4, lost Wilander 4–6 6–2 7–5 5–7 6–0); *US Open – r/u 1990* (d. Connell, Korda, Davin, Berger 7–5 6–0 6–2, Cherkasov 6–2 6–2 6–3, Becker 6–7 6–3 6–2 6–3, lost Sampras 6–4 6–3 6–2), *sf 1988* (d. Chang 7–5 6–3 6–2, Connors 6–2 7–6 6–1, lost Lendl 4–6 6–2 6–3), *sf 1989* (d. Weiss, Broad, Johnson 6–1 7–5 6–2, Grabb 6–1 7–5 6–3, Connors 6–1 4–6 0–6 6–3 6–4, lost Lendl 7–6 6–1 3–6 6–1); *Wimbledon – sf 1991; LIPC – won 1990* (d. Jones, Gunnarsson, Gomez 6–7 6–2 6–3, Courier 4–6 6–3 6–1, Berger 5–7 6–1 6–1, Edberg 6–1 6–4 0–6 6–2); *ATP World Champ – won 1990* (d. Becker 6–2 6–4, d. Edberg 5–7 7–6 7–5 6–2); *sf 1991.*

RONALD AGENOR (Haiti)

Born Rabat, Morocco, 13 November 1964; lives Bordeaux, France and Monte Carlo; RH; 5ft 11in; 163lb; final 1991 ATP ranking 74; 1991 prize money $163,165.

Lived some time in Zaire. Works with Patrice Hagelauer. *1985:* (50) With a stream of steady results including six qf showings on GP tour, he moved up 366 places on ATP computer. *1986:* (74) Performing solidly on clay again, he beat Pate, Arias, Tulasne and Jaite among others and reached sf Bordeaux. *1987:* (44) Took Lendl to 4s French Open before reaching his 1st GP f at Gstaad and being r/u again in Bordeaux and Basel. *1988:* (28) Last 16 French Open (d. Gomez) and US Open; r/u Bordeaux (d. Noah), sf Italian Open (d. Wilander). *1989:*

(37) Won his 1st GP title at Athens, upset Agassi at Tokyo Seiko and was a surprise quarter-finalist at French Open. *1990:* (29) Won Genova and at Berlin took his 1st title on a surface other than clay; sf Gstaad (upset Gomez), Bordeaux and Toulouse. *1991:* Upset Gomez again at Estoril, reached qf Genova and won Marseille Challenger. *1991 HIGHLIGHTS – SINGLES:* French Open 2r (d. Matsuoka 6–2 6–3 6–7 6–3), *US Open* 1r (lost Laurendeau 7–5 7–6 3–6 7–5); *won* Marseille Challenger (d. Strelba 5–7 6–4 6–2). *CAREER HIGHLIGHTS – SINGLES: French Open – qf 1989* unseeded (d. Limberger, Mayotte 3–6 7–5 5–7 7–5 6–2, Pistolesi 1–6 6–1 6–4 6–3, Bruguera 2–6 3–6 6–3 6–1 6–2, lost Chang 6–4 2–6 6–3 6–3).

KARIM ALAMI (Morocco)
Born 24 May 1973; final 1991 ATP ranking 405.
1991: In Jun tennis was r/u US Open singles to Paes, winning doubles there with De Jager and Wimbledon with Rusedski, to finish the year No. 1 in Jun doubles rankings and No. 2 in the singles behind Enqvist.

SABINE APPELMANS (Belgium)
Born Aalst, 22 April 1972; lives Erembonegen; LH; 2HB; 5ft 5in; 120lb; final 1991 WTA ranking 18; 1991 prize money $192,871.
1987: (283). *1988:* (215) Enjoyed some success on the European satellite circuits and upset Burgin 1r French Open. *1989:* (149) Reached her 1st primary circuit qf at Taipei. *1990:* (22) R/u Auckland (d. Cordwell) and reached sf Wellington and Singapore, breaking into top 100 and finishing the year in the top 25. *1991:* Won her 1st singles title at Phoenix, following with VS Nashville; r/u Tokyo Suntory; sf Oslo and Puerto Rico; reached last 16 Australian Open and French Open and appeared in 3 doubles f. *1991 HIGHLIGHTS – SINGLES: Australian Open* last 16, seed 16 (d. Paz 6–0 6–1, Tarabini 7–5 6–1, Kamstra 6–4 6–3, lost M. J. Fernandez [seed 3] 6–3 6–3), *French Open* last 16, unseeded (d. Bowes 6–1 3–6 7–5, Coetzer 6–3 5–7 6–1, Rajchrtova 6–2 6–0, lost Graf [seed 2] 6–2 6–2), *Wimbledon* 1r (lost Graf [seed 1] 6–2 6–2), *US Open* 1r (lost Garrison [seed 12] 7–5 6–4); *won* Phoenix (d. Gavaldon 7–5 6–3, Cunningham 7–5 6–0, Provis 7–6 6–4, Halard 3–6 6–3 6–3, Rubin 7–5 6–1), *won* VS Nashville (d. Sloane Lundy 7–5 3–6 6–4, Cunningham 6–4 6–3, Daniels 6–4 6–4, Habsudova 6–3 6–4, Adams 6–2 6–4); *r/u* Tokyo Suntory (d. Yanagi 6–3 6–2, Endo 6–3 6–1, Werdel 6–3 3–6 6–1, Hiraki 6–4 6–4, lost McNeil 2–6 6–2 6–1); *sf* Oslo (d. Mueller 6–3 6–1, Van Lottum 7–5 6–3, Herreman 6–2 6–1, lost Lindqvist 6–2 6–2), *sf* Puerto Rico (d. Hiraki 7–5 6–2, Faber 6–4 6–1, Sloane Lundy 6–4 6–1, lost Coetzer 3–6 6–3 7–5). *1991 HIGHLIGHTS – DOUBLES:* (with Reggi unless stated) *r/u* Oslo (lost Kohde-Kilsch/Meier 3–6 6–2 6–4), *r/u* Milan (lost Collins/McNeil 7–6 6–3), [Benjamin] *r/u* Puerto Rico (lost Hiraki/Labat 6–3 6–3)

JIMMY ARIAS (USA)
Born Buffalo, NY, 16 August 1964, and lives there; RH; 5ft 9in; 145lb; final 1991 ATP ranking 63; 1991 prize money $138,710.
Wife Gina (married Dec. 1989). Does not employ a coach, preferring to work alone. *1981:* (81) Under guidance of Nick Bollettieri, climbed into top 100, beat Teltscher on USTA Penn circuit and won French Open mixed doubles with A. Jaeger. *1982:* (20) Beaten in 1r of 6 of first 8 tournaments, he then made tremendous surge to reach f Washington and US CC and won his first GP event (Japan Asian Open) in autumn. *1983:* (6) Won 4 tourns, including Italian Open and US CC; sf US Open. *1984:* (14) Reached qf French Open and 6 sf. *1985:* (21) Had disappointing results until end of year when he reached sf Canadian Open, f Japan Open and sf South African Open. *1986:* (48) Helped US past Ecuador in D Cup. *1987:* (34) After D Cup loss in Paraguay he consulted sports psychologist Jim Loehe, who helped him to improve his attitude, enjoy his tennis more and reach f Monte Carlo. Yet, still lacking motivation, he took 3 months off from Aug. *1988:* (106) Still only a shadow of his former self, he lost 1r 5 consecutive tourns before reaching f US CC. *1989:* (92) Qf Memphis. *1990:* (60) R/u Adelaide; qf Auckland, San Francisco and Hamburg. *1991:* Upset Chesnokov 1r Australian Open; r/u US CC and reached qf Adelaide, Orlando and Florence. *1991 HIGHLIGHTS – SINGLES: Australian Open* 3r (d. Chesnokov [seed 9] 6–0 6–3 4–6 2–6 6–4, Wuyts 6–3 6–1 6–2, lost Yzaga 3–6 7–6 6–1 6–3), *French Open* 2r (d. Rebolledo 6–0 3–6 6–0 6–2, lost Forget [seed 7] 6–3 6–2 5–7 7–6), *US Open* 2r (d. Lundgren 7–5 7–5 3–6 6–3, lost Courier [seed 4] 6–3 6–2 6–0); *r/u* US CC (d. Hogstedt 6–3 6–3, Perez 6–1 6–4, Reneberg 6–4 6–2, Frana 3–6 6–3 7–5, lost Yzaga 6–3 7–5). *CAREER HIGHLIGHTS – MIXED DOUBLES:* (with A. Jaeger) *French Open – won 1981* (d. McNair/Stove 7–6 6–4).

JORDI ARRESE (Spain)
Born Barcelona, 29 August 1964, and lives there; RH; 5ft 9in; 142lb; final 1991 ATP ranking 23; 1991 prize money $252,860.
Coached by Roberto Vizcaino. *1986:* (97) With a sf showing in his first tournament of the season at Nice, he set the tone for a successful year. *1987:* (128) Qf Palermo. *1988:* (33) Won 2 Challenger titles before reaching 1st SS of at Hamburg and qf Kitzbuhol. *1989:* (44) Reached 1st GP f at Madrid despite being restricted by a back injury during the last 3 matches, for which he wore a neck brace. Upset Krickstein *en route* to sf Italian Open. *1990:* (39) Won San Remo in Aug., following with Prague the next week; sf Estoril and Athens. *1991:* Won Madrid and Buzios; r/u Genova, Hilversum (d. Muster) and Athens; sf Geneva (d. Cherkasov), Palermo and upset Forget at Barcelona. *1991 HIGHLIGHTS –* **SINGLES: French Open** 1r (lost Becker [seed 2] 6–2 7–5 6–2), **Wimbledon** 1r (lost Muller 6–2 6–3 6–3); **won** Madrid (d. Conde 6–3 6–2, Altur 6–4 6–7 7–6, Champion 6–4 3–2 ret'd, Novacek 6–4 6–3, Filippini 6–2 6–4), **won** Buzios (d. Matsuoka 6–1 6–3, Daher 7–6 1–6 6–4, Perez-Roldan 6–7 7–5 3–1 ret'd, J. Sanchez 6–2 7–6, Oncins 1–6 6–4 6–0); **r/u** Genova (d. Cunha-Silva 6–3 7–5, Costa 3–6 6–2 6–3, Azar 6–4 7–5, Masso 7–6 6–3, lost Steeb 6–3 6–4), **r/u** Hilversum (d. Delaitre 6–0 6–2, Skoff 3–6 7–6 6–2, Muster 6–4 6–1, Koevermans 3–3 6–4, lost Gustafsson 5–7 7–6 2–6 6–1 6–0), (**r/u** Athens (d. Theine 7–6 6–1, Markus 6–2 6–4, Koevermans 2–6 6–3 6–4, Clavet 7–5 6–2, lost Bruguera 7–5 6–3); **sf** Geneva (d. Cherkasov 6–4 4–6 6–1, Paloheimo 6–2 3–6 7–5, Oncins 4–6 6–4 7–5, lost Skoff 7–6 6–2), **sf** Palermo (d. J. Sanchez 6 4 2 6 7 5, Conde 6–3 6–4, Noah 6–2 4–6 6–4, lost Fontang 6–3 2–6 7–6). *1991 HIGHLIGHTS – DOUBLES:* (with Costa) **won** San Marino (d. Miniussi/Perez 6–3 3–6 6–3).

ROBERTO AZAR (Argentina)
Born Lincoln, 12 March 1966; lives Buenos Aires; LH; 6ft 1in; 170lb; final 1991 ATP ranking 90; 1991 prize money $88,104.
Coached by Raul Perez-Roldan. *1987:* (228). *1988:* (180). *1989:* (147). Reached his 1st f at San Marino and sf Bologna. *1990:* (106) Sf showing at San Remo and qf Casablanca and Umag took him briefly into top 100 1st time. *1991:* Reached sf San Marino and qf Genova. *1991 HIGHLIGHTS – SINGLES:* US Open 1r (lost Hlasek 6–3 7–5 6–3); **sf** San Marino (d. Cierro 6–3 6–1, Orsanic 6–4 2–6 6–4, Kulti 3–6 7–5 6–4, lost Fontang 6–2 6–2).

CATHERINE BARCLAY (Australia)
Born Sydney, 12 June 1973; lives Kingsford, Sydney; RH; 5ft 9in; final 1991 WTA ranking 386; 1991 prize money $13,248.
1991: Won Wimbledon Jun doubles with Zaltz. *1991 HIGHLIGHTS – SINGLES: Australian Open* 1r (lost S. Martin 6–1 6–1).

YAYUK BASUKI (Indonesia)
Born Yogyakarta, 30 November 1970, and lives there; RH; 5ft 4½in. 122lb; final 1991 WTA ranking 35; 1991 prize money $92,631.
Coached by Mien Gondowiljoyo. *1986:* Joined her country's Fed Cup team. *1988:* (284). *1989:* (377) Made her mark on the satellite circuits. *1990:* (266) Continued to enjoy success on the satellite circuits. *1991:* At Pattaya City, she became 1st native Indonesian to win a primary circuit title; upset Kohde-Kilsch *en route* to qf Eastbourne and reached the same stage at VS Nashville. *1991 HIGHLIGHTS – SINGLES: French Open* 1r (lost Rehe 7–5 6–3), **Wimbledon** 3r (d. Henricksson 6–4 7–6, Herreman 6–4 6–4, lost Graf [seed 1] 6–2 6–3), **US Open** 2r (d. Keller 6–4 6–3, lost Martinez [seed 8] 6–3 6–4); **won** Pattaya City (d. Field 6–2 7–5, Lindqvist 6–4 6–2, Kschwendt 5–7 6–3 6–4, Hiraki 3–6 6–1 6–2, Sawamatsu 6–2 6–2), **won** Jakarta Challenger (d. Miyauchi 6–2 6–2). *1991 HIGHLIGHTS – DOUBLES:* (with Vis) **r/u** VS Nashville (lost Collins/E. Reinach 5–7 6–4 7–6).

JEREMY BATES (Great Britain)
Born Solihull, 19 June 1962; lives London; RH; 5ft 11in; 160lb; final 1991 ATP ranking 162; 1991 prize money $117,892.
Coached by Warren Jacques. *1982:* (329) Joined British D Cup squad. *1983:* (256). *1984:* (185). *1985:* (99) Sf Tel Aviv, qf Bristol. *1986:* (187) Qf Bristol. *1987:* (89) Sf Hong Kong and won Wimbledon mixed doubles with Durie. *1988:* (152) Qf Guaruja, Lyon and Rye Brook; r/u Australian Open doubles with Lundgren. *1989:* (96) Reached sf Johannesburg and qf Nancy; upset Gilbert at Tel Aviv. *1990:* (126) Won Durban Challenger and in doubles won Queen's with Curren. *1991:* At Australian Open won a second GS mixed doubles title with Durie and in singles he won Cherbourg Challenger. *1991 HIGHLIGHTS – SINGLES:* **Australian Open** 1r (lost Becker [seed 2] 6–4 6–2 6–3), **Wimbledon** 2r (d. Altur 6–4 6–4

6–2, lost Mayotte 6–3 3–6 6–4 7–6); **won** Cherbourg Challenger (d. Black 7–5 1–6 7–6). **1991 HIGHLIGHTS – DOUBLES:** [N. Brown] **r/u** Stuttgart Eurocard (lost Casal/E. Sanchez 6–3 7–5), [Curren] **r/u** Toulouse (lost Nijssen/Suk 4–6 6–3 7–6). **MIXED DOUBLES:** (with Durie) **won Australian Open** (d. Davis/R. White 2–6 6–4 6–4). **CAREER HIGHLIGHTS – DOUBLES:** (with Lundgren) **Australian Open – r/u 1988** (lost R. Leach/Pugh 6–3 6–2 6–3). **MIXED DOUBLES:** (with Durie) **Australian Open – won 1991; Wimbledon – won 1987** (d. Cahill/Provis 7–6 6–3).

PATRICK BAUR (Germany)
Born Radolfzell, 3 May 1965; lives Bochum; RH; 6ft 3in; 165lb; final 1991 ATP ranking 96; 1991 prize money $131,597.
1986: (346). **1987:** (215) Won Furth Challenger. **1988:** (178) Qf Adelaide and Tel Aviv in singles and won Bastad doubles with Riglewski. **1989:** (192) In singles reached qf Wellington and won Manchester Challenger; in doubles teamed with Bates to win Tel Aviv. **1990:** (136) Qf Rio de Janeiro. **1991:** Won 1st tour title at Guaruja Chevrolet, following with Seoul in April. **1991 HIGHLIGHTS – SINGLES: French Open** 1r (lost Kulti 6–4 3–6 6–4 6–2), **Wimbledon** 1r (lost Pate 4–6 6–7 6–4 6–2 6–3), **US Open** 1r (lost Rostagno 6–0 6–2 6–3); **won** Guaruja Chevrolet (d. Delaitre 6–3 4–6 6–2, Markus 4–6 7–6 6–2, Perez 6–3 7–6, Matsuoka 5–7 6–3 7–6, Roese 6–2 6–3), **won** Seoul (d. Mronz 7–6 6–0, Melville 6–2 6–1, Krajicek 7–5 6–7 6–2, Matsuoka 7–6 6–2, Tarango 6–4 1–6 7–6).

BORIS BECKER (Germany)
Born Leimen, 22 November 1967; lives there and Monte Carlo; RH; 6ft 3in; 187lb; final 1991 ATP ranking 3 singles, 91 (28) doubles; 1991 prize money $1,228,708.
Coached by Bob Brett until Feb. 1991 and by Nikki Pilic until May 1991. Thereafter worked with Tomas Smid. **1982:** Won first of three consecutive German Nat Jun Champs. **1983:** (564) R/u Orange Bowl 16s. **1984:** (65) R/u US Open Jun and qf Australian Open in first big men's showing. **1985:** (6) Won Queen's Club, Wimbledon, at 17 yrs 7 mths becoming youngest men's titlist, the first German, and the first unseeded player to capture the world's most prestigious event. Won Cincinnati and closed year with D Cup wins over Edberg and Wilander in f as Germany lost 3–2 to Sweden. Won inaugural Young Masters and was voted ATP Most Improved Player. **1986:** (2) Won tournaments in Chicago, Toronto, Sydney and Paris Indoor, but most notably won Wimbledon again in even more convincing fashion, dismissing Lendl in f without loss of a set and still younger than any other champ. Closed year with streak of 3 straight tournaments and 21 matches in a row before losing Masters f to Lendl. Won Young Masters in Jan. and Dec. **1987:** (5) Split with coach Gunther Bosch Jan; trained by Frank Dick. At end of year Bob Brett became coach. Missed LIPC suffering from a form of typhus which seemed to weaken him and restrict his performance for several weeks, and he was further restricted by tendonitis of left knee for last 5 months of year. Won only 3 titles all year and going for his third consecutive Wimbledon singles title, fell 2r to Doohan. After US Open took time off in Germany with his family, returning refreshed in Oct. and qualified for Masters where he extended Lendl to 3s, but lost his Young Masters title. **1988:** (4) He was again plagued by injury problems, withdrawing from Toronto and the Olympics and playing Masters only 10 days after his foot had been removed from plaster following injury in Stockholm sf. He still won Indian Wells, WCT Finals, Queen's, Indianapolis, Tokyo Seiko and Stockholm and finished the year by taking his 1st Masters title in a thrilling f v Lendl, as well as leading West Germany to victory over Sweden in D Cup f in Gothenburg. At Wimbledon he was r/u to Edberg and reached last 16 in French Open. **1989:** (2) The high spot of his year was a convincing third title at Wimbledon where he beat Lendl in a stirring sf and Edberg in f, followed by his first triumph at US Open, where he d. Lendl in f, and r/u spot at Masters to Edberg. He won in Milan and on clay reached the f in Monte Carlo and sf in French Open. He also won 3 other titles and led FRG to victory in World Team Cup, and in D Cup where he won 2 singles and doubles (with Jelen) as Germany d. Sweden 3–2 in Stuttgart. Voted ATP Player of the Year. **1990:** (2) R/u Wimbledon to Edberg, sf US Open, qf Australian Open, but his 1r loss to Ivanisevic at French Open was his 1st at that stage in GS. Strongly challenged Edberg for the No. 1 spot at end of year, especially after a stunning performance at Stockholm where he d. the Swede in f, a result that took his indoor match record since 1988 to 77–5. However, in f Paris Open he had to withdraw v the same player with a pulled left thigh, which was still undergoing treatment when he began play on 2nd day of ATP World Champ, where he fell to Agassi in sf. Won Brussels, Stuttgart, Indianapolis, Sydney Indoor and Stockholm, reaching 4 more f. **1991:** Reached No. 1 on computer 1st time on 28 Jan. after winning his 1st Australian Open; his 5hr 22min match in 3r with Camporese

was the longest ever played there and lasted only 1 minute less than the marathon at Wimbledon in 1969 between Gonzales and Pasarell. He was overtaken again by Edberg on 18 Feb., after retiring v Cherkasov at Brussels with a right thigh strain, but returned to the top after his appearance in f Wimbledon, where he lost in ss to countryman Stich. His disappointing 3r loss to Haarhuis at US Open saw him slip again to No. 2, and by year's end he had fallen to 3 behind Courier, having narrowly failed to qualify for sf ATP World Champ in Frankfurt. However, he played his best ever CC season, although he again failed to win his 1st title on that surface, losing f Monte Carlo to Bruguera, who had also beaten him at Barcelona. Withdrew from Italian Open with back trouble, but played French Open, where he reached sf for 3rd time. He outlasted Edberg in 5s f Stockholm in Oct. for only his 2nd title of the year; also reached f Indianapolis and sf Brussels and Cincinnati. *1991* *HIGHLIGHTS – SINGLES: won Australian Open* seed 2 (d. Bates 6–4 6–2 6–3, Vajda 6–4 6–1 6–3, Camporese 7–6 7–6 0–6 4–6 14–12, Ferreira 6–4 7–6 6–4, Forget [seed 10] 6–2 7–6 6–3, P. McEnroe 7–6 6–3 4–6 4–6 6–2, Lendl [seed 3] 1–6 6–4 6–4 6–4), *French Open* sf, seed 2 (d. Arrese 6–2 7–5 6–2, Woodbridge 5–7 1–6 6–4 6–4 6–4, Masur 6–3 6–3 6–2, Clavet 7–6 6–4 6–3, Chang [seed 10] 6–4 6–4 6–2, lost Agassi [seed 4] 7–5 6–3 3–6 6–1), *r/u Wimbledon*, seed 2 (d. Steeb 6–4 6–2 6–4, Lundgren 7–6 7–5 7–5, Olkhovskiy 6–1 6–4 3–6 6–3, Bergstrom 6–4 6–7 6–1 7–6, Forget [seed 7] 6–7 7–6 6–2 7–6, Wheaton 6–4 7–6 7–5, lost Stich 6–4 7–6 6–4), *US Open* 3r, seed 1 (d. Jaite 7–6 6–4 6–4, Volkov 6–0 7–6 6–1, lost Haarhuis 6–3 6–4 6–2); *won* Stockholm (d. Camporese 4–6 7–5 6–3, Prpic 7–6 6–1, Sampras 7–5 7–5, Courier 6–7 6–3 6–4, Edberg 3–6 6–4 1–6 6–2 6–2); *r/u* Monte Carlo (d. J. Sanchez 6–7 6–3 6–3, Volkov 3–6 6–1 6–1, Chesnokov 6–1 6–3, Prpic 6–3 6–3, lost Bruguera 5–7 6–4 7–6 7–6), *r/u* Indianapolis (d. Pate 6–3 6–2, Bergstrom 6–2 6–2, Hlasek 7–5 7–5, Wheaton 7–6 6–4, lost Sampras 7–6 3–6 6–3); *sf* Brussels (d. Volkov 6–4 3–6 6–3, Jelen 7–6 7–6, Chang 7–5 6–1, lost Cherkasov 2–6 6–3 2–2 ret'd), *sf* Cincinnati (d. Fleurian 6–3 6–3, Washington 6–4 6–4, Cherkasov 7–6 6–3, lost Forget 7–6 4–6 6–3). *1991* *HIGHLIGHTS – DOUBLES:* (with Jelen) *r/u* Barcelona (lost de la Pena/Nargiso 3–6 7–6 6–4). *CAREER HIGHLIGHTS – SINGLES: Australian Open – won 1991; Wimbledon – won 1985* unseeded (d. Nystrom 3–6 7–6 6–1 4–6 9–7, Mayotte 6–3 4–6 6–7 7–6 6–2, Leconte 7–6 3–6 6–3 6–4, Jarryd 2–6 7–6 6–3 6–3, Curren 6–3 6–7 7–6 6–4), *won 1986* (d. Bengoechea, Tom Gullikson, McNamee, Pernfors 6–3 7–6 6–2, Mecir 6–4 6–2 7–6, Leconte 6–2 6–4 6–7 6–3, Lendl 6–4 6–3 7–5), *won 1989* (d. Shelton 6–1 6–4 7–6, Matuszewski 6–3 7–5 6–4, Gunnarsson 7–5 7–6 6–3, Krickstein 6–4 6–4 7–5, Chamberlin 6–1 6–2 6–0, Lendl 7–6 6–7 2–6 6–4 6–3, Edberg 6–0 7–6 6–4), *r/u 1988* (d. Annacone, Cash 6–4 6–3 6–4, Lendl 6–4 6–3 6–7 6–4, lost Edberg 4–6 7–6 6–4 6–2), *r/u 1990* (d. Herrera, Masur, Goldie, Cash 7–6 6–1 6–4, Gilbert 6–4 6–4 6–1, Ivanisevic 4–6 7–6 6–0 7–6, lost Edberg 6–2 6–2 3–6 3–6 6–4), *r/u 1991*; *US Open – won 1989* (d. Pate 6–1 6–3 6–1, Rostagno 1–6 6–7 6–3 7–6 6–3, Mecir 6–4 3–6 6–3, Pernfors 5–7 6–3 6–2 6–1 Noah 6–3 6–3 6–2, Krickstein 6–4 6–3 6–4, Lendl 7–6 1–6 6–3 7–6), *sf 1986* (d. Michibata Motta, Casal, Donnelly 6–4 6–3 6–7 6–4, Srejber 6–3 6–2 6–1, lost Mecir 4–6 6–3 6–4 3–6 6–3), *sf 1990* (d. Aguilera, Noah, Carbonell, Cahill 2–6 6–2 6–3 3–6 6–4, Krickstein 3–6 6–3 6–3 6–3, lost Agassi 6–7 6–3 6–2 6–3); *Nabisco Masters – won 1988* (d. Wilander Leconte, lost Edberg in rr, d. Hlasek 7–6 7–6, Lendl 5–7 7–6 3–6 6–2 7–6), *r/u 1985* (lost Lendl 6–2 7–6 6–1), *r/u 1986* (d. Nystrom, Leconte, Wilander 6–3 fs, Edberg 6–4 6–4, lost Lendl 6–4 6–4 6–4), *r/u 1989* (d. Gilbert, Agassi, Edberg in rr, J. McEnroe 6–4 6–4, lost Edberg 2–6 7–6 6–3 6–1); *French Open – sf 1987* (d. Connors 6–3 6–3 7–5, lost Wilander 6–4 6–1 6–2), *sf 1989* (d. Pugh, Winogradsky, Bates, Perez-Roldan 3–6 6–4 6–2 4–6 7–5 Berger 6–3 6–4 6–1, lost Edberg 6–3 6–4 5–7 3–6 6–2), *sf 1991, qf 1986* (d. Potier, Oresar Teltscher, E. Sanchez 6–0 4–6 4–6 6–4 6–2, lost Pernfors 2–6 6–4 6–2 6–0).

CHRISTIAN BERGSTROM (Sweden)
Born Gothenburg, 19 July 1967; lives Monte Carlo; RH; 5ft 11in; 150lb; final 1991 ATF ranking 44; 1991 prize money $190,549.
Coached by Tim Klein. *1984:* (606) Nat Jun Champ. *1985:* (410) European Jun Champ for 2nd year and No. 2 in ITF Jun rankings. *1986:* (120) Won Tampere Challenger. *1987:* (69) Qf Nancy; won Porto Challenger. *1988:* (71) Working with sports psychologist Lars Ryberg, he reached 1st GP sf at Bastad and upset Leconte *en route* to same stage at Toulouse. *1989:* (106) Qf Milan, Bastad and Toulouse. *1990:* (80) A qualifier at the French Open, he was 2 sets up v Chang before losing 3r; at Wimbledon he upset Forget *en route* to qf, unseeded, and in sf Wembley was 4–0 up fs v Chang but lost 7–2 on t-b. Played GS Cup, lost 1r Lendl (2) 6–4 6–0. *1991:* Scored some useful upsets during the year in which he reached sf Wellington (d. Cherkasov), Munich (d. Muster) and Bastad; qf Rotterdam Copenhagen, Toulouse and Basel (d. Stich); and in GS upset B. Gilbert *en route* to last 16

Wimbledon, unseeded. *1991 HIGHLIGHTS – SINGLES: Australian Open* 2r (d. Pioline 6–4 6–2 1–6 7–6, lost Woodbridge 6–1 0–6 6–2 7–6), *French Open* 1r (lost Davin 6–3 6–4 6–1), *Wimbledon* last 16, unseeded (d. Masso 6–1 7–5 6–3, Holm 7–5 6–0 6–4, B. Gilbert 6–3 6–2 3–6 6–3, lost Becker [seed 2] 6–4 6–7 6–1 7–6), *US Open* 2r (d. Montana 6–7 4–6 6–3 6–0 6–3, lost Boetsch 6–2 6–3 2–1 ret'd); *sf* Wellington (d. Cherkasov 7–6 7–6, P. McEnroe 6–3 6–2, Poliakov 6–2 7–6, lost Fromberg 6–3 5–7 7–6), *sf* Munich (d. Muster 6–1 2–6 6–4, Vajda 6–2 6–4, Jonsson 4–6 6–2 6–0, lost Perez-Roldan 6–0 6–0), *sf* Bastad (d. Rahunen 6–1 6–2, Kulti 6–2 6–1, Gunnarsson 3–6 6–2 6–2, lost Gustafsson 4–6 6–3 6–2), *CAREER HIGHLIGHTS – SINGLES: Wimbledon – qf 1990* unseeded (d. Wilkison, Broad, Grabb, Forget 6–4 3–6 6–3 7–5, lost Edberg 6–3 6–2 6–4).

EVA BES (Spain)
Born Zaragoza, 14 January 1973, and lives there; RH; 5ft 7in; 125lb; final 1991 WTA ranking 223; 1991 prize money $12,061.
1991: Won French Open Jun doubles with Gorrochategui.

ARNAUD BOETSCH (France)
Born Meulam, 1 April 1969; lives Strasbourg; RH; 6ft; 168lb; final 1991 ATP ranking 54; 1991 prize money $197,844.
Coached by Francis Rawsthorne. *1985:* European Jun Champ and won Orange Bowl. *1988:* (275). *1989:* (212). *1990:* (176) Made his mark on the Challenger circuit, although he won no title. *1991:* A wild-card, he reached last 16 French Open, unseeded, and upset Korda at US Open. Played his 1st tour f at Berlin after qualifying and reached qf Prague. Fourth member of winning French D Cup team v USA in Lyon where their 3–1 victory was first French success since 1932. *1991 HIGHLIGHTS – SINGLES: French Open* last 16, unseeded (d. Mattar 6–4 6–3 6–1, Kulti 6–3 6–3 6–3, Markus 5–7 7–6 6–3 6–2, lost Davin 7–6 4–6 6–3 6–1, *Wimbledon* 3r (d. Dyke 6–3 7–6 6–3, Pozzi 4–6 7–6 7–6 6–4, lost Courier 6–2 6–2 6–0), *US Open* 3r (d. Korda [seed 15] 6–1 3–6 6–3 6–2, Bergstrom 6–2 6–3 2–1 ret'd, lost Steeb 3–6 6–3 6–4 6–4); *r/u* Berlin (d. Bergstrom 6–4 6–2, Svensson 6–2 6–1, Fleurian 6–0 6–3, Kuhnen 6–3 6–2, lost Korda 6–3 6–4). *1991 HIGHLIGHTS – DOUBLES:* [Forget] *won* Bordeaux (d. Kuhnen/Mronz 6–2 6–2).

MANON BOLLEGRAF (Netherlands)
Born Den Bosch, 10 April 1964; lives Ermelo; RH; 2HB; 5ft 8in; 140lb; final 1991 WTA ranking 49 singles, 23 doubles; 1991 prize money $137,278.
Coached by Auke Dijkstra. *1986:* (148) Qf Singapore. *1987:* (120) Qf Little Rock. *1988:* (117) Qf Brisbane. *1989:* (38) In singles won 1st primary circuit title at Oklahoma, reached sf Brussels and Nashville and upset McNeil 2r French Open. In doubles won 4 women's titles plus French Open mixed with Nijssen. *1990:* (32) In singles r/u VS Oklahoma and reached sf Strasbourg. Appeared in 5 doubles f with various partners, winning Wichita with McGrath and Zurich with Pfaff. *1991:* R/u Colorado and sf Oklahoma in singles, won Leipzig with Demongeot in doubles and took US Open mixed with Nijssen. *1991 HIGHLIGHTS – SINGLES: Australian Open* 1r (lost Stafford 6–4 6–4), *French Open* 1r (lost E. Reinach 6–0 6–2), *Wimbledon* 3r (d. Humphreys-Davies 6–4 6–4, Durie 6–3 5–7 6–3, lost A. Huber [seed 14] 6–3 6–7 6–0), *US Open* 1r (lost K. Maleeva [seed 11] 6–3 6–4); *r/u* Colorado (d. Kuhlman 6–2 6–2, Keller 6–1 6–0, Louie Harper 7–6 7–5, Fendick 6–2 6–3, lost McNeil 6–3 6–4); *sf* VS Oklahoma (d. Stubbs 6–1 6–4, Smylie 6–4 6–2, Martinez 6–4 6–1, lost A. Smith 6–3 6–2). *1991 HIGHLIGHTS – DOUBLES:* [Demongeot] *won* Leipzig (d. Hetherington/Rinaldi 6–4 6–3); [Paz] *r/u* Strasbourg (lost McNeil/Rehe 6–7 6–4 6–4). *MIXED DOUBLES:* (with Nijssen) *won US Open* (d. Sanchez-Vicario/E. Sanchez 6–2 7–6). *CAREER HIGHLIGHTS – MIXED DOUBLES:* (with Nijssen) *US Open – won 1991.*

FEDERICA BONSIGNORI (Italy)
Born Rome, 20 November 1967, and lives there; RH; 2HB; 5ft 4in; 117lb; final 1991 WTA ranking 50; 1991 prize money $52,896.
Coached by Martin Simek. *1984:* (145). *1985:* (188) Sf Bastad. *1986:* (123) Qf Athens. *1987:* (88) Reached sf Paris Open and upset M. Maleeva *en route* to qf Belgian Open. *1988:* (99) Upset McNeil 1r LIPC. *1989:* (141) Upset Cueto at Athens. *1990:* (76) Won her first primary circuit title at Estoril, reached sf Athens and returned to the top 100 in July. *1991:* Her best showings were qf FC Cup (d. K. Maleeva) and VS Houston (d. Sloane). *1991 HIGHLIGHTS – SINGLES: French Open* 2r (d. Herreman 6–3 6–4, lost A. Huber [seed 16] 6–0 6–2), *Wimbledon* 1r (lost R. White 6–1 6–1).

ELENA BRIOUKHOVETS (USSR)
Born Odessa, 8 June 1971, and lives there; RH; 5ft 4in; 132lb; final 1991 WTA ranking 98; 1991 prize money $86,509.
Coached by Bahtchevan Valeriy. **1989:** (175) Enjoyed some success on the satellite circuits. **1990:** (73) Upset Magers to reach her 1st tour f at Moscow, taking her place in the top 100 in Oct. and won 2 doubles titles. **1991:** Reached no qf in singles, but won St Petersburg doubles with Medvedeva. **1991 HIGHLIGHTS – SINGLES: Australian Open** 1r (lost McQuillan 2–6 6–4 6–1), **French Open** 3r (d. Dechaume 1–6 6–2 7–5, Caverzasio 6–2 6–2, lost Novotna [seed 6] 7–6 6–2), **Wimbledon** 3r (d. Nagelsen 6–2 6–1, Provis 7–6 6–4, lost Schultz 5–7 6–4 7–5), **US Open** 2r (d. Bonder Kreiss 6–3 6–0, lost Herreman 3–6 7–6 7–6). **1991 HIGHLIGHTS – DOUBLES:** (with Medvedeva) **won** St Petersburg (d. Demongeot/Durie 7–5 6–3).

SERGI BRUGUERA (Spain)
Born Barcelona, 16 January 1971, and lives there; RH; 6ft 1in; 160lb; final 1991 ATP ranking 11; 1991 prize money $527,320.
Coached by his father, Luis. **1987:** (333) Nat Jun Champ. **1989:** (26) Upset Gomez and Connors *en route* to 1st GP sf at Italian Open, following with his 2nd and 3rd at Gstaad and Stuttgart, as well as reaching last 16 French Open. Voted ATP Newcomer of the Year. **1990:** (28) Recorded some big upsets during the year. Removed top seed Edberg in ss 1r French Open; r/u Gstaad (d. Chesnokov) and Geneva; sf Adelaide (took Muster to 3s and Paris Open (d. Gomez). Won 2 doubles titles. **1991:** Enjoyed an extraordinary month in April, when he upset Chesnokov at Estoril *en route* to his 1st career title, upset the same player and Becker back-to-back in reaching f Barcelona and beat Becker again in f Monte Carlo, these triumphs taking him into top 10 1st time. He also won Athens (d. Muster); r/u Gstaad (d. Gomez and Ivanisevic); sf Italian Open and Lyon. **1991 HIGHLIGHTS – SINGLES: Australian Open** 1r (lost Ivanisevic [seed 5] 6–4 0–6 6–1 6–4), **French Open** 2r, seed 5 (d. S. Davis 6–2 6–2 6–1, lost Camporese 1–6 2–6 6–4 1–0 ret'd); **won** Estoril (d. Koevermans 6–3 6–3, Bengoechea 6–3 6–7 6–3, Furlan 6–1 6–3, Chesnokov 6–4 2–6 6–3, Novacek 7–6 6–1), **won** Monte Carlo (d. Furlan 6–3 6–7 6–3, Caratti 6–1 7–5, Mancini 6–1 6–4, Gustafsson 7–5 7–5, Skoff 6–1 6–4, Becker 5–7 6–4 7–6 7–6), **won** Athens (d. Kuhnen 6–2 7–5, Kowalski 6–2 6–1, Furlan 6–2 6–2, Muster 1–6 6–2 6–0, Arrese 7–5 6–3); r/u Barcelona (d. Woodforde 6–0 6–0, Steeb 6–4 6–1, Becker 6–2 6–4, Chesnokov 6–2 7–5, Perez-Roldan 6–4 6–4, lost E. Sanchez 6–4 7–6 6–2), r/u Gstaad (d. Masur 7–6 6–4, Agenor 6–4 6–0, Gomez 7–6 7–6, Ivanisevic 6–1 7–5, lost E. Sanchez 6–1 6–4 6–4); sf Italian Open (d. Costa 3–6 6–2 7–6, Noah 6–1 6–3, Miniussi 6–1 6–2, Santoro 6–4, 7–6, lost Mancini 6–3 6–1), sf Lyon (d. Boetsch 3–6 6–3 6–4, Raoux 7–6 7–6, Curren 6–0 7–6, lost Delaitre 6–4 6–4). **1991 HIGHLIGHTS – DOUBLES:** (with Rosset) **won** Geneva (d. Henricsson/Jonsson 3–6 6–3 6–2).

DARREN CAHILL (Australia)
Born Adelaide, 2 October 1965; lives there and Tampa, Fla.; RH; 6ft 2in; 165lb; final 1991 ATP ranking 89; 1991 prize money $118,050.
1985: (132). **1986:** (132) Formed an effective doubles partnership with Kratzmann, reaching f Queen's. **1987:** (82) Sf Kitzbuhel and Hong Kong. Broke into top 100 in Aug. and underwent a knee operation at end of year. **1988:** (20) Upset Krickstein and Becker to reach sf US Open; won 1st GP title at Gstaad and reached sf Stratton Mountain and Queen's (d. Cash and Curren back-to-back). Won 4 doubles titles with 3 different partners. **1989:** (53) Sf Rotterdam and Tokyo Seiko; upset Hlasek 1r Australian Open and took J. McEnroe to 8–6 5s at the same stage at Wimbledon. In doubles was r/u Australian Open with Kratzmann and won 3 titles, qualifying for Masters, where they lost sf to Jarryd and Fitzgerald. **1990:** (57) R/u Newport then, unseeded, he upset Ivanisevic to reach last 16 US Open, where he extended Becker to 5s. In doubles with Kratzmann won 3 titles and qualified for IBM/ATP World Doubles. Member of Aust. D Cup team beaten 3–2 by USA in f. **1991:** Upset Cherkasov at Australian Open and surprised J. McEnroe and B. Gilbert as he took his 2nd career singles title at San Francisco. Underwent knee surgery in summer. **1991 HIGHLIGHTS – SINGLES: Australian Open** 3r (d. Canter 6–1 6–4 6–3, Cherkasov [seed 14] 4–6 2–6 6–3 7–5 7–5, lost Krajicek 6–7 6–3 6–3 7–6); **won** San Francisco (d. Hogstedt 6–2 6–3, Raoux 5–7 6–4 6–3, J. McEnroe 7–6 3–6 6–3, Masur 4–6 6–4 7–5, B. Gilbert 6–2 3–6 6–4). **1991 HIGHLIGHTS – DOUBLES:** (with Kratzmann) r/u Sydney NSW (lost S. Davis/Pate 3–6 6–3 6–2). **CAREER HIGHLIGHTS – SINGLES: US Open – sf 1988** (d. Becker 6–3 6–3 6–2, Krickstein 6–2 5–7 7–6 5–7 6–3, lost Wilander 6–4 6–4 6–2). **CAREER HIGHLIGHTS – DOUBLES:** (with Kratzmann) **Australian Open – r/u 1989** (lost R. Leach/Pugh 6–4 6–4 6–4).

OMAR CAMPORESE (Italy)
Born Bologna, 8 May 1968, and lives there; RH; 6ft 2in; 172lb; final 1991 ATP ranking 24; 1991 prize money $399,959.
1986: (766) Won Italian Jun and r/u European Jun Champs. *1987:* (283) R/u Mediterranean Games. *1988:* (216) Qf Bologna and won Vienna Challenger. *1989:* (49) Won Vienna Challenger again and upset Mecir *en route* to qf Italian Open. *1990:* (45) Reached 1st tour f at San Marino; sf Florence, Genova and Hilversum and upset Berger *en route* to qf Italian Open. In doubles with various partners reached 4 f, winning Milan and Madrid. *1991:* Returning from a 3-month lay-off with a knee injury, he reached sf Wellington in Jan. then extended Becker to 14–12 5s in epic 5hr 22min match in 3r at Australian Open – the longest ever played at the tourn and only 1 minute shorter than the marathon between Gonzales and Pasarell at Wimbledon in 1969. Followed in March with the title at Rotterdam, where he d. Lendl in f, reached sf Bologna, and finished the year by upsetting Hlasek and Courier *en route* to qf Paris Open. Won 3 doubles titles from 4 f with Ivanisevic. *1991 HIGHLIGHTS – SINGLES: Australian Open* 3r (d. Zoecke 3–6 6–2 7–6 6–4, Haarhuis 7–5 7–5 3–6 6–3, lost Becker [seed 2] 7–6 7–6 0–6 4–6 14–12), *French Open* 3r (d. Riglewski 6–4 6–2 6–2, Bruguera [seed 5] 1–6 6–2 6–4 1–0 ret'd, lost Miniussi 2–6 3–6 6–1 6–3), *Wimbledon* 3r (d. Pistolesi 6–1 6–3 2–6 6–3, Michibata 7–5 6–2 6–1, lost Stich [seed 6] 7–6 6–2 6–7 6–4), *US Open* 2r (d. Mansdorf 5–7 6–4 7–5 3–6 6–3, lost Washington 4–6 6–1 6–1 6–4); *won* Rotterdam (d. Jelen 6–2 2–6 6–2, Antonitsch 6–3 6–4, Novacek 6–4 7–5, Haarhuis 6–7 6–2 7–6, Lendl 3–6 7–6 7–6); *sf* Wellington (d. Garrow 6–1 6–1, Zoecke 6–4 6–0, Hogsteth 6–3 7–6, lost Jonsson 5–7 6–3 7–6), *sf* Bologna (d. Nargiso 6–1 3–6 6–2, Cunha-Silva 6–2 6–3, Mattar 6–2 6–1, lost Gunnarsson 7–6 6–4). *1991 HIGHLIGHTS – DOUBLES:* (with Ivanisevic) *won* Milan (d. Nijssen/Suk 6–4 7–6), *won* Italian Open (d. Jensen/Warder 6–2 6–3), *won* Manchester (d. Brown/Castle 6–4 6–3); *r/u* Stuttgart Mercedes (lost Masur/E. Sanchez 4–6 6–3 6–4).

JENNIFER CAPRIATI (USA)
Born New York, 29 March 1976; lives Saddlebrook, Fla.; RH; 2HB; 5ft 7in; 135lb; 1991 WTA ranking 6; 1991 prize money $535,617.
Coached by her father, Stefano; formerly coached by Jimmy Evert, and working with Pavel Slozil from Dec. 1991. *1988:* Won Nat 18s. *1989:* (—) Won French Open Jun (lost no set and d. Sviglerova 6–4 6–0 in f), US Open Jun (d. McQuillan 6–2 6–3), plus Wimbledon and US Open Jun doubles with McGrath as well as 18s HC and CC. At 13 yrs 6 mths was youngest to play W Cup, making a sparkling début with a 6–0 6–0 drubbing of Wood, but was still too young to compete on the pro tour until March 1990. *1990:* (8) At age 13 she became the first female to reach f of her first pro tourn at VS Florida, Boca Raton. She upset Sukova there and at LIPC, where she reached last 16, stunned Sanchez-Vicario and Zvereva *en route* to 2nd tour f at FC Cup, and in Oct. beat Garrison at Puerto Rico to win her 1st tour title. Reached sf in 1st GS tourn at French Open, becoming youngest (at 14 yrs 66 days) to reach that stage; youngest seed at Wimbledon, where she reached last 16; youngest to win singles match at US Open where she reached same stage; and youngest to qualify for VS Champs, where she lost 1r to Graf. She was a member of the winning US Fed Cup team and won WTA Most Impressive Newcomer award. *1991:* Caused the upset of the Championships when she stunned Navratilova in ss to become youngest semi-finalist at Wimbledon, and d. Sabatini to reach the same stage at US Open, where she took Seles to 3s t-b. She had earlier upset the No. 1 as she won San Diego, following with Toronto and r/u VS Philadelphia. Also reached sf VS Florida and Berlin and qualified for VS Champs, where she lost qf to Sabatini. In doubles won Italian Open with Seles. Played Fed Cup, winning all her matches as USA reached f. *1991 HIGHLIGHTS – SINGLES: French Open* last 16, seed 10 (d. Piccolini 6–2 7–5, Temesvari 2–6 6–1, Kidowaki 6–3 6–0, lost Martinez [seed 7] 6–3 6–3), *Wimbledon* sf, seed 10 (d. Stafford 6–0 7–5, Zrubakova 6–2 6–3, Probst 6–3 1–6 6–3, Schultz 3–6 6–1 6–1, Navratilova [seed 4] 6–4 7–5, lost Sabatini [seed 2] 6–4 6–4), *US Open* sf, seed 7 (d. Pfaff 6–1 6–0, Ritter 6–3 6–0, Hy 6–1 6–4, Durie 6–1 6–2, Sabatini [seed 3] 6–3 7–6, lost Seles [seed 2] 3–6 6–3 7–6); *won* San Diego (d. McNeil 6–2 6–1, Garrison 6–1 6–3, Martinez 6–4 6–0, Seles 4–6 6–1 7–6), *won* Toronto (d. de Lone 6–4 6–0, Gomer 6–2 6–3, Zvereva 6–1 6–1, Sabatini 6–4 2–3 ret'd, K. Maleeva 6–2 6–3); *r/u* VS Philadelphia (d. McNeil 7–6 6–7 6–2, Maleeva Fragnière 6–3 6–2, Sabatini 6–3 6–4, lost Seles 7–5 6–1); *sf* VS Florida (d. Kschwendt 6–3 6–2, G. Fernandez 6–3 6–4, Porwik 6–1 6–4, lost Sabatini 7–5 6–2), *sf* Berlin (d. S. Martin 6–2 6–4, Zvereva 6–2 6–3, Halard 6–3 6–2, lost Sanchez-Vicario 7–5 5–7 6–4). *1991 HIGHLIGHTS – DOUBLES:* (with Seles) *won* Italian Open (d. Provis/E. Reinach 7–5 6–2). *CAREER HIGHLIGHTS – SINGLES: French Open – sf 1990* unseeded (d. Testud, Cammy MacGregor, Wiesner 6–4 6–4, Paz 6–0 6–3, M. J. Fernandez 6–2 6–4, lost Seles 6–2 6–2); *Wimbledon – sf 1991; US Open – sf 1991.*

CRISTIANO CARATTI (Italy)
Born Acqui Terme, 24 May 1970, and lives there; RH; 5ft 10in; 145lb; final 1991 ATP ranking 38; 1991 prize money $324,943.
1989: (232) R/u Dublin Challenger. *1990:* (98) Won Winnetka Challenger; qf New Haven and extended Berger to 5s 3r US Open after qualifying. *1991:* Reached qf Australian Open, unseeded, then followed with an appearance in f Milan, upsetting Lendl on the way and breaking into top 50 for 1st time. He followed with back-to-back upsets of B. Gilbert and Bruguera *en route* to qf LIPC. *1991 HIGHLIGHTS – SINGLES: Australian Open* qf, unseeded (d. Dyke 6–2 3–6 6–4 6–3, Engel 3–6 6–2 6–3 6–4, Layendecker 6–4 6–4 5–7 4–6 7–5, Krajicek 6–3 6–4 6–7 3–6 6–4, lost P. McEnroe 7–6 6–3 4–6 4–6 6–2), *French Open* 2r (d. Lopez 2–6 2–6 6–3 6–3 6–4, lost Carbonell 6–1 7–5 3–6 6–1), *Wimbledon* 1r (lost Holm 7–6 6–3 6–4), *US Open* 2r (d. Bloom 4–6 3–6 6–2 6–2 6–4, lost Mattar 2–6 6–3 6–0 7–6); *won* Indian Wells Challenger (d. Arias 6–7 6–4 6–2); *r/u* Milan (d. Lundgren 6–1 7–6 6–2, Lendl 6–4 1–6 7–6, Kulti 6–3 6–1, Steeb 7–6 6–7 6–3, lost Volkov 6–1 7–5). *CAREER HIGHLIGHTS – SINGLES: Australian Open – qf 1991.*

TOMAS CARBONELL (Spain)
Born Barcelona, 23 August 1968; lives Cabrera de Mar; RH; 5ft 10in; 158lb; final 1991 ATP ranking 95; 1991 prize money $198,403.
Coached by Juan Avendano. *1985:* Nat Jun champ. *1986:* No. 1 in ITF Jun Doubles World Rankings. Won US Open Jun (with J. Sanchez), Wimbledon Jun (with Korda) and r/u French Open Jun (with J. Sanchez). *1987:* (242) Qf Barcelona and won Buenos Aires doubles with Casal. *1988:* Qf Bologna and Athens. *1989:* (77) Reached 1st GP sf at Hilversum, following with St Vincent, and won 2 doubles titles. *1990:* (76) Reached sf Casablanca and Itaparica and won 2 doubles titles again. *1991:* His best performance was his qf appearance at LIPC, having upset Gomez. *1991 HIGHLIGHTS – SINGLES: French Open* 3r (d. Gunnarsson 5–7 6–2 6–3 6–1, Caratti 6–1 7–5 3–6 6–1, lost Hlasek 7–6 4–6 6–4 6–3), *Wimbledon* 1r (lost Leconte 6–3 6–1 7–6), *US Open* 1r (lost Bruguera 3–6 4–6 6–3 7–6 6–3). *1991 HIGHLIGHTS – DOUBLES:* [Roig] *won* Kitzbuhel (d. Arraya/Poliakov 6–7 6–2 6–4).

SERGIO CASAL (Spain)
Born Barcelona, 8 September 1962, and lives there; RH; 6ft 1in; 167lb; final 1991 ATP ranking 811 singles, 20 (13) doubles; 1991 prize money $138,851.
Coached by Pato (Bill) Alvarez. *1980:* Stopped S. Giammalva and Wilander to reach qf Orange Bowl. *1982:* (159) Joined Spanish D Cup squad. *1985:* (38) Won first GP at Florence and reached sf Kitzbuhel. Started successful partnership with E. Sanchez, winning Kitzbuhel, Geneva and Barcelona and reaching 4 other f. *1986:* (62) Had great run to final of new Paris tourn, won 5 doubles titles with E. Sanchez, and won US Open mixed doubles with Reggi. *1987:* (92) Qf Munich and Itaparica; with E. Sanchez won 6 doubles titles, r/u Wimbledon and sf Masters. *1988:* (77) Underwent wrist surgery after French Open, returning in July. Sf Gstaad and qf Madrid in singles. In doubles with E. Sanchez won US Open and r/u Masters, winning 7 other titles plus Olympic silver medal. *1989:* (184) In singles reached sf Madrid, upsetting E. Sanchez. In doubles, injuries to his regular partner E. Sanchez prevented the success of previous years, but he teamed with J. Sanchez to win Bologna. *1990:* (263) In action again with E. Sanchez, won French Open and 5 other titles, plus a 7th with J. Sanchez. R/u IBM/ATP World Doubles with E. Sanchez. *1991:* Although he and E. Sanchez had a quieter year, they won 4 tour titles together. *1991 HIGHLIGHTS – DOUBLES:* (with E. Sanchez) *won* Auckland (d. Connell/Michibata 4–6 6–3 6–4), *won* Stuttgart Eurocard (d. Bates/Brown 6–3 7–5), *won* Hamburg (d. Motta/Visser 4–6 6–3 6–2), *won* Buzios (d. Frana/Lavalle 4–6 6–3 6–4). *CAREER HIGHLIGHTS – DOUBLES:* (with E. Sanchez) *French Open – won 1990* (d. Ivanisevic/Korda 7–5 6–3); *US Open – won 1988* (d. R. Leach/Pugh w.o.); *Wimbledon – r/u 1987* (lost Flach/Seguso 7–6 6–1 6–4); *Masters – r/u 1988* (lost R. Leach/Pugh 6–4 6–3 2–6 6–0); *IBM/ATP World Doubles r/u 1990* (lost Forget/Hlasek 6–4 7–6 5–7 6–4); *Olympics – silver medal 1988* (lost Flach/Seguso 6–3 6–4 6–7 6–7 9–7). *MIXED DOUBLES:* (with Reggi) *US Open – won 1986* (d. Navratilova/Fleming 6–4 6–4).

PAT CASH (Australia)
Born Melbourne, 27 May 1965; lives London; RH; 6ft; 185lb; final 1991 ATP ranking 113; 1991 prize money $120,585.
Coached by Ian Barclay, trainer Anne Quinn. Separated from former girlfriend Anne-Britt Kristiansen May 1989; son Daniel (born May 1986), daughter Mia (born April 1988). Married

Emily Bendit in Jamaica, 22 July 1990. ***1982:*** (44) In Melbourne he became the youngest to win a GP title (Krickstein broke the record the following year); earlier in year he won Wimbledon and US Open Jun. ***1983:*** (38) Won Brisbane and led Australia to victory in D Cup. ***1984:*** (8) Sf Wimbledon and US Open, where he had m-p in sf with Lendl, upset Connors in dead rubber D Cup match and reached f Melbourne. ***1985:*** (67) Sidetracked by back injuries, he achieved his best effort to reach sf Brussels. R/u Wimbledon doubles 2nd straight year. ***1986:*** (24) Only 3 weeks after having emergency appendectomy he reached qf Wimbledon with win over Wilander and later in year he led Australia to victory over Sweden in D Cup f. ***1987:*** (7) After reaching f Australian Open (d. Lendl sf), where he took Edberg to 5s, won Nancy for 1st title since 1983. He followed in tremendous style by winning 1st GS title at Wimbledon (d. Lendl in ss in f), becoming 1st Australian to win the singles there since Newcombe in 1971 and the only player to d. Lendl twice in 1987. Won Johannesburg and qualified for Masters 1st time. ***1988:*** (20) Began the year in style as r/u Australian Open, losing 8–6 5s to Wilander, but after arthroscopic surgery on right knee in Feb., fell in last 16 French Open, qf Wimbledon and missed US Open with Achilles tendon injury. In other tourns reached sf Indian Wells and qf Toronto. ***1989:*** (368) Feb. injury to right elbow kept him off court until Suntory Tokyo in April where, v Scanlon in 2r and leading 4–2 1st set, he ruptured Achilles tendon and was sidelined for 7 months. ***1990:*** (81) Returned to action in Jan. playing doubles only at Sydney and winning the title with Kratzmann. In his 4th tourn he was r/u Seoul and the following week won both singles and doubles (with Masur) at Hong Kong. It was his 1st singles title since Johannesburg in Nov. 1987 and, at 243, he became the lowest-ranked player to win a tour title. At Wimbledon, still not ranked high enough to be seeded, he reached qf. ***1991:*** Qf Tokyo Suntory and Queen's. ***1991 HIGHLIGHTS – SINGLES: Australian Open*** 3r (d. Novacek 6–2 6–4 6–1, Van Rensburg 7–6 6–4 6–4, lost Edberg [seed 1] 7–6 7–5 6–2), ***French Open*** 2r (d. Noszaly 6–4 7–6 6–3, lost Cherkasov 6–7 6–1 6–3 6–7 6–3), ***Wimbledon*** 2r (d. Tarango 6–4 6–3 6–3, lost Champion 7–5 6–7 4–6 6–1 12–10). ***CAREER HIGHLIGHTS – SINGLES: Wimbledon – won 1987*** (d. Freeman, McNamee, Schapers, Forget 6–2 6–3 6–4, Wilander 6–3 7–5 6–4, Connors 6–4 6–4 6–1, Lendl 7–6 6–2 7–5), ***sf 1984*** unseeded (d. Wilander, Motta, Curren, Gomez, lost McEnroe 6–3 7–6 6–4), ***qf 1986*** unseeded (d. Vilas, Simpson, Lapidus, Wilander 4–6 6–4 7–5 6–3, lost Leconte 4–6 7–6 7–6 6–3), ***qf 1988*** (d. Fitzgerald, Olhovsky, lost Becker 6–4 6–3 6–4), ***qf 1990*** (d. Azar, Anderson, Aguilera 6–1 6–1 6–4, lost Becker 7–6 6–1 6–4); ***Australian Open – r/u 1987*** (d. Pistolesi, Testerman, Annacone, Noah 6–4 6–2 2–6 6–0, Lendl 7–6 5–7 7–6 6–4, lost Edberg 6–3 6–4 3–6 5–7 6–3), ***r/u 1988*** (d. Muster, Svensson 6–1 6–4 6–1, Schapers 6–1 6–4 6–2, Lendl 6–4 2–6 6–2 4–6 6–2, lost Wilander 6–3 6–7 2–6 6–1 8–6), ***qf 1984*** (lost Kriek 7–5 6–1 7–6); ***US Open – sf 1984*** (d. Wilander, lost Lendl 3–6 6–3 6–4 6–7 7–6 after having 1 m-p). ***CAREER HIGHLIGHTS – DOUBLES:*** (with Fitzgerald unless stated) ***Wimbledon –*** [McNamee] ***r/u 1984*** (lost McEnroe/Fleming 6–2 5–7 6–2 3–6 6–3), ***r/u 1985*** (d. McEnroe/Fleming, lost Gunthardt/Taroczy 6–4 6–3 4–6 6–3); ***Australian Open – sf 1984*** (lost Nystrom/Wilander 6–4 6–4 2–6 6–3).

ANNA MARIA (SANDRA) CECCHINI (Italy)

Born Bologna, 27 February 1965; lives Ceriva and Monte Carlo; RH; 5ft 6½in; 130lb; final 1991 WTA ranking 27; 1991 prize money $119,156.

Prefers to be known by her nickname, Sandra. ***1983:*** R/u to Spence at Orange Bowl 18s, ranked second among world juniors and third among Italy's women. ***1984:*** (49) Won Rio de Janeiro. ***1985:*** (49) Reached qf French Open and won Barcelona, restoring herself after 8 consecutive 1r losses early in year. ***1986:*** (76) Produced the upset of the year when she stunned Evert Lloyd in Fed Cup, the first time the American had lost in the international team competition. ***1987:*** (18) Extended Graf to 3s sf Berlin, won VS Arkansas and reached f Strasbourg. ***1988:*** (21) Won Strasbourg and Nice and reached f Bastad. ***1989:*** (26) Won Paris Open in singles and doubles; r/u Estoril, sf Tampa and Bastad in singles and won 2 other doubles titles with Tarabini. ***1990:*** (20) Won Bastad; sf Berlin (upset Sabatini), Kitzbuhel and Clarins. ***1991:*** At French Open, unseeded, she upset A. Huber to reach last 16, where she was the only player to take a set off Seles. Won Bol, r/u Palermo, sf Houston and reached 2 doubles f. ***1991 HIGHLIGHTS – SINGLES: French Open*** last 16, unseeded (d. Cueto 6–3 3–6 7–6, Suire 6–2 6–2, A. Huber [seed 16] 6–3 6–4, lost Seles 3–6 6–3 6–0), ***Wimbledon*** 1r, seed 16 (lost Smylie 6–3 3–6 6–1), ***US Open*** 2r (d. Javer 7–6 6–1, lost Garrison [seed 12] 6–1 6–1); ***won*** Bol (d. Dahlman 6–3 6–1, Nowak 6–2 7–5, Strnadova 6–4 6–4, Testud def., Magdalena Maleeva 6–4 3–6 7–5); ***r/u*** Palermo (d. Labat 6–3 6–1, Caverzasio 6–2 6–1, Tessi 6–4 7–5, Zardo 6–3 7–6, lost Pierce 6–0 6–3); ***sf*** VS Houston (d. Nelson 6–4 6–2, Cammy MacGregor 6–1 6–3, K. Maleeva 3–6 6–4 6–1, lost Seles 6–0

6–2). *1991 HIGHLIGHTS – DOUBLES:* [Garrone] *r/u* Bol (lost Golarsa/Magdalena Maleeva 6–3 1–6 6–4), [Tarabini] *r/u* Kitzbuhel (lost Fulco/Jagerman 7–5 6–4). *CAREER HIGHLIGHTS – SINGLES: French Open – qf 1985* (lost Navratilova 6–2 6–2).

THIERRY CHAMPION (France)
Born Bagnolet sur Seine, 31 August 1966; lives Paris; RH; 6ft; 155lb; final 1991 ATP ranking 47; 1991 prize money $329,336.
Coached by Bernard Pestre. Wife Juliette Coupel (married Aug. 1991). Won Nat 16s and 18s. *1985:* (190). *1986:* (128) Qf Bordeaux. *1987:* (105) Qf Bordeaux again. *1988:* (125) Appeared in 1st GP singles f at St Vincent (d. Jaite) and sf Bari. Broke into top 100 briefly in late summer. *1989:* (404) Reached qf Athens but then was sidelined for months with a broken wrist and was close to retiring. *1990:* (59) Became the first qualifier to reach qf French Open in the open era, despite being hampered by right hip injury. Reached sf Palermo and finished the year at his highest-ever ranking. *1991:* Upset Sampras at French Open, and Cash as he moved unexpectedly to qf Wimbledon. Sf Bordeaux and Birmingham; qf Madrid, Kitzbuhel and Long Island. *1991 HIGHLIGHTS – SINGLES: Australian Open* 1r (lost Svensson [seed 8] 6–3 6–4 6–1), *French Open* 3r (d. Rahunen 7–6 7–5 1–6 6–1, Sampras [seed 6] 6–3 6–1 6–1, lost Santoro 6–2 6–0 6–4), *Wimbledon* qf, unseeded (d. Wilkinson 6–4 6–2 3–6 6–4, Cash 7–5 6–7 4–6 6–1 12–10, N. Brown 7–6 1–6 7–5 6–3, Rostagno 6–7 6–2 6–1 3–6 6–3, lost Edberg [seed 1] 6–3 6–2 7–5), *US Open* 2r (d. Pistolesi 3–6 4–6 6–3 6–2 6–2, lost Jarryd 7–5 6–2 1–1 ret'd); *sf* Bordeaux (d. Raoux 6–2 6–1, Riglewski 6–1 6–1, Boetsch 6–2 7–6, lost Delaitre 6–3 6–1), *sf* Birmingham (d. Gunnarsson 6–2 6–2, Bates 6–7 7–5 6–1, Washington 6–4 6–4, lost Raoux 6–3 6–4). *CAREER HIGHLIGHTS – SINGLES: French Open – qf 1990* (d. Prpic, Aguilera, Forget 6–4 6–7 6–4 5–7 6–3, Novacek 6–4 4–6 3–6 7–6 6–3, lost Gomez 6–3 6–3 6–4); *Wimbledon – qf 1991.*

MICHAEL CHANG (USA)
Born Hoboken, NJ, 22 February 1972; lives Placentia, Cal.; RH; 5ft 8in; 145lb; final 1991 ATP ranking 15; 1991 prize money $1,461,730.
Parents from Taipei. Coached by his father, Joe, and José Higueras and at end of 1990 by Phil Dent. *1987:* (163) At 15 yrs 6 mths was youngest player to compete in men's singles at US Open since 1918, and was the youngest ever to win a match in GS tourn, having been granted a wild card after winning US 18s at Kalamazoo. At 15 yrs 7 mths was youngest to win a pro tourn at Las Vegas Challenger and was youngest-ever GP semi-finalist at Scottsdale. *1988:* (30) At 16 yrs 4 mths he was the youngest for 60 years to win a match in Wimbledon main draw, and when he won his 1st title at San Francisco at 16 yrs 7 mths, he was youngest to win an SS event and second-youngest after Krickstein to win a GP title. Upset Svensson *en route* to last 16 US Open and reached qf Washington and Cincinnati. *1989:* (5) The highlight of his career to date came at the French Open where, at 17 yrs 3 mths, he became the youngest known male winner of a GS tourn and the 1st American since Trabert in 1955 to win that title. In 5s of his 4r match v Lendl, he was so badly affected with cramp that he had to serve underarm. Won Wembley and r/u Los Angeles, last 16 Wimbledon and US Open to qualify for 1st Masters, where he failed to win a match. Was the youngest to play D Cup for USA, making his début v Paraguay, and the youngest to break into top 5. *1990:* (15) Out until March with stress fracture of cup of left hip suffered Dec. 1989. He did not reach the heights of the previous year, but won 1st HC title at Canadian Open, was r/u Los Angeles and Wembley and reached sf Washington. His best showing in GS was qf French Open. In winning US D Cup team, in sf coming back from 2 sets to 1 down v Skoff to take US into f where he d. Cahill in 2nd rubber in 3–2 win v Australia. Reached sf GS Cup. Semi-finalist in inaugural Compaq Grand Slam Cup losing to eventual winner Sampras. *1991:* He had slipped so far down the rankings that he was not seeded at US Open, wherre he reached last 16. At French open reached qf, but at Wimbledon Mayotte inflicted his 1st loss in 12 GS tourns. He had to wait until Nov. before winning his 1st title of the year at Birmingham, having earlier reached sf Memphis, Tokyo Suntory and Paris Open – upsetting Edberg – and reached 7 more qf. Runner-up to Wheaton in Compaq Grand Slam Cup, winning $1 million. *1991 HIGHLIGHTS – SINGLES: French Open* qf, seed 10 (d. Siemerink 6–2 6–0 6–3, Jonsson 7–6 4–6 6–4 3–6 6–3, Connors 4–6 7–5 6–2 4–6 0–15 ret'd, Forget [seed 7] 6–1 6–1 4–6 6–3, lost Becker [seed 2] 6–4 6–4 6–2), *Wimbledon* 1r (lost Mayotte 6–7 4–6 6–1 7–6 6–2), *US Open* last 16, unseeded (d. Woodforde 6–3 6–0 6–2, Witsken 6–3 6–0 6–2, J. McEnroe [seed 16] 6–4 4–6 7–6 2–6 6–3, lost Edberg [seed 2] 7–6 7–5 6–3); *won* Birmingham (d. Vajda 6–1 6–2, Connell 5–7 6–3 6–1, Agenor 4–2 ret'd, Reneberg 4–6 6–1 6–2, Raoux 6–3 6–2); *r/u* Compaq Grand Slam Cup (d. Lendl in s/f 2–6 4–6 6–4 7–6 9–7, lost Wheaton 7–5 6–2 6–4);

sf Memphis (d. Fleurian 6–4 3–6 6–2, Connell 7–6 6–7 6–4, Tarango 6–3 7–5, lost Stich 6–2 6–2), *sf* Tokyo Suntory (d. Fitzgerald 6–0 6–0, Pate 6–4 7–6, Cash 6–4 6–1, lost Edberg 7–5 6–2), *sf* Paris Open (d. R. Gilbert 7–6 3–6 7–6, Edberg 2–6 6–1 6–4, Korda 7–5 6–1, lost Sampras 2–6 6–4 6–3). *CAREER HIGHLIGHTS – SINGLES: French Open – won 1989* (d. Masso 6–7 6–3 6–0 6–3, Sampras 6–1 6–1 6–1, Roig 6–0 7–5 6–3, Lendl 4–6 4–6 6–3 6–3, Agenor 6–4 2–6 6–4 7–6, Chesnokov 6–1 5–7 7–6 7–5, Edberg 6–1 2–6 4–6 6–4 6–2), *qf 1990* (d. Motta, Rosset, Bergstrom, E. Sanchez 6–4 6–4 6–2, lost Agassi 6–1 6–2 4–6 6–2), *qf 1991*.

ANDREI CHERKASOV (USSR)
Born Ufa, 4 July 1970; lives Moscow; RH; 5ft 10in; 160lb; final 1991 ATP ranking 21; 1991 prize money $382,327.
Coached by Natalia Rogova. *1986:* (870) R/u to Courier at Orange Bowl. *1987:* (409) No. 3 in ITF Jun rankings; r/u to Wheaton at US Open Jun and to Courier at Orange Bowl again. *1988:* (236). *1989:* (82) Broke into top 100 after qf showing at Milan and top 50 after winning 2 Challenger titles. At Sydney reached f, having never before reached GP qf. *1990:* (21) Upset Gomez *en route* to his 1st GS qf at Australian Open, and Chang in reaching same stage at US Open, unseeded both times. Won his 1st tour title at Moscow in Oct.; sf Nice (d. Berger) and Umag. Played in GS Cup but lost Sampras 1r. *1991:* Won Moscow, r/u Brussels (d. Chesnokov) and reached last 16 at French Open, he reached last 16, upsetting J. McEnroe 1r. *1991 HIGHLIGHTS – SINGLES: Australian Open* 2r, seed 14 (d. Rostagno 3–6 6–4 6–1 4–6 10–8, lost Cahill 4–6 2–6 7–3 7–5 7–5), *French Open* last 16, unseeded (d. J. McEnroe [seed 15] 2–6 6–4 7–5 7–6, Cash 6–7 6–1 6–3 3–6 7–5, Yzaga 7–5 3–6 6–3 6–3, lost Edberg [seed 1] 7–6 6–4 6–3, *Wimbledon* 1r, seed 12 (lost Reneberg) 6–4 6–3 6–4), *US Open* 1r, seed 13 (lost Svensson 7–6 6–2 6–2); *won* Moscow (d. Krumrey 6–3 6–4, Medvedev 6–1 6–2, Rosset 4–6 6–1 7–5, Gorriz 6–3 6–4, Hlasek 7–6 3–6 7–6); *r/u* Brussels (d. Aguilera 6–2 6–2, Saceanu 6–4 6–2, Chesnokov 7–5 6–1, Becker 2–6 6–3 2–2 ret'd, lost Forget 6–3 7–5 3–6 7–6). *1991 HIGHLIGHTS – DOUBLES:* (with Volkov) *r/u* Moscow (lost Jelen/Steeb 6–4 7–6). *CAREER HIGHLIGHTS – SINGLES: Australian Open – qf 1990* (d. Matsuoka 6–2 4–6 4–6 6–0 6–2, Layendecker, Fleurian, Gomez 2–6 6–3 7–6 7–6, lost Lendl 6–3 6–2 6–3); *US Open – qf 1990* (d. Seguso, Leconte, Chang 6–4 6–4 6–3, Van Rensburg, lost Agassi 6–2 6–2 6–3).

ANDREI CHESNOKOV (USSR)
Born Moscow, 2 February 1966, and lives there; RH; 2HB; 6ft 2in; 167lb; final 1991 ATP ranking 31; 1991 prize money $337,810.
Coached by Tatiana Naoumko. *1980:* Won Russian Nat Jun Champ. *1982:* Won Russian Nat Jun Champ again. *1984:* Beat Glickstein and Perkis in D Cup. *1985:* (136) Upset Teltscher at French Open. *1986:* (36) Reached qf French Open, upsetting No. 2 seed Wilander in 3r, and last 16 US Open. *1987:* (52) Reached last 16 US Open and won his 1st GP title in his 1st f at Florence, becoming 1st from his country to win a title since Metreveli won S Orange in 1974. *1988:* (14) Won Orlando, r/u Wellington, Sydney and Toulouse. In GS reached qf both Australian Open and French Open (d. Cash). *1989:* (22) Upset Wilander *en route* to sf French Open after winning Nice and Munich back-to-back in spring. *1990:* (12) Won Monte Carlo (d. E. Sanchez and Muster) and Tel Aviv; r/u Auckland and Italian Open (d. E. Sanchez again); sf Barcelona and New Haven. *1991:* Upset Lendl in ss *en route* to the title at Montreal, as well as reaching sf Estoril and Brisbane. *1991 HIGHLIGHTS – SINGLES: Australian Open* 1r, seed 9 (lost Arias 6–0 6–3 4–6 2–6 6–4), *French Open* 3r (d. Koevermans 7–5 6–2 6–7 2–6 6–3, Kuhnen 4–6 6–3 3–6 6–3 8–6, lost Edberg [seed 1] 6–1 6–4 6–3), *US Open* 2r (d. Pernfors 6–2 6–2 6–3, lost Haarhuis 6–1 4–6 6–2 7–6); *won* Montreal (d. Goldie 6–1 6–2, Lareau 4–6 6–1 6–3, Pescosolido 6–4 6–4, Matsuoka 6–2 3–6 7–5, Lendl 7–6 7–5, Korda 3–6 6–4 6–3); *sf* Estoril (d. de la Pena 6–4 6–2, Mezzadri 5–7 7–5 6–1, Skoff 6–3 6–1, lost Bruguera 6–4 2–6 6–3), *sf* Brisbane (d. Rafter 6–4 6–1, Weiss 3–6 6–2 6–0, Fromberg 6–4 6–4, lost Krickstein 7–5 6–4). *CAREER HIGHLIGHTS – SINGLES: French Open – sf 1989* unseeded (d. Arraya, Steeb 3–6 6–1 7–5 6–3, Courier 2–6 3–6 7–6 6–2 7–5, Wilander 6–4 6–0 7–5, lost Chang 6–1 5–7 7–6 7–5), *qf 1986* unseeded (d. Svensson 6–3 2–6 6–4 6–2, Osterthun, Wilander 6–2 6–3 6–2, Maciel, lost Leconte 6–3 6–4 6–3), *qf 1988* (d. Cash, lost Leconte 6–2 6–3 7–6); *Australian Open – qf 1988* (d. Mansdorf 6–3 4–6 7–5 6–2, Benhabiles, Kratzmann, Steeb, lost Edberg 4–6 7–6 6–4 6–4).

HALLE CIOFFI (USA)
Born Cleveland, Ohio, 5 August 1969; lives Knoxville, Tenn.; RH; 2HB; 5ft 7½in; 130lb; final 1991 WTA ranking 87; 1991 prize money $57,275.
Coached by Mike DePalmer. *1985:* (177) Sidelined 6 months with back problems. *1986:*

(145). **1987:** (55) Won VS Indianapolis. Out of action 4 months in summer with back problems. **1988:** (47) Upset Garrison *en route* to sf Tampa, and reached the same stage at Cincinnati. **1989:** (50) Sf Schenectady; and won Evansville Challenger. **1990:** (108). **1991:** Qf Colorado was her best showing. **1991 HIGHLIGHTS – SINGLES: French Open** 2r (d. L. Ferrando 7–5 4–6 6–0, lost E. Reinach 6–3 6–1), **Wimbledon** 1r (lost Wiesner [seed 9] 6–1 6–2), **US Open** 1r (lost de Lone 6 2 6 7 6 3).

FRANCISCO CLAVET (Spain)
Born Aranjuez, 24 October 1968; lives Madrid; LH; 6ft; 156lb; final 1991 ATP ranking 30; 1991 prize money $259,384.
Elder brother of José. **1987:** (638). **1988:** (290). **1989:** (188) Qf Kitzbuhel. **1990:** (90) Won his 1st tour title at Hilversum as a lucky loser, upsetting Jaite on the way. **1991:** Reached sf Stuttgart Mercedes (d. Muster and Gomez), Kitzbuhel, Schenectady, Athens and Sao Paulo, reaching 3 more qf and last 16 French Open, unseeded. **1991 HIGHLIGHTS – SINGLES: Australian Open** 2r (d. Castle 6–7 6–2 6–1 6–2, lost Svensson [seed 8] 6–2 7–5 3–6 6–1), **French Open** last 16, unseeded (d. Evernden 6–4 6–0 6–2, Pioline 6–2 6–3 7–6, Delaitre 4–6 6–2 6–3 6–4, lost Becker [seed 2] 7–6 6–4 6–3), **Wimbledon** 1r (lost Gustafsson 7–6 6–3 6–3), **US Open** 3r (d. Reneberg 7–6 6–7 6–4 6–2, Raoux 6–1 6–1 6–4, lost Krickstein 6–4 6–4 6–7 7–6); **sf** Stuttgart Mercedes (d. Muster 6–1 6–3, Camporese 7–5 6–0, Gomez 6–3 6–3, Pioline 6–3 6–7 6–1, lost Stich 6–4 6–2), **sf** Kitzbuhel (d. Kuhnen 1–6 6–4 6–4, de la Pena 6–4 6–2, Zillner 6–2 6–3, lost Novacek 6–3 6–7 6–2), **sf** Schenectady (d. Simian 7–5 7–6, Knowles 6–3 6–0, Bruguera 6–1 6–4, lost E. Sanchez 7–5 6–1), **sf** Athens (d. Masso 7–6 6–3, Azar 4–6 6–4 6–0, Jonsson 7–6 6–1, lost Arrese 7–5 6–2), **sf** Sao Paulo (d. Wuyts 6–3 6–4, Motta 6–2 6–2, Masso 6–1 6–1, lost Oncins 6–4 6–3). **1991 HIGHLIGHTS – DOUBLES:** [Gustafsson] **r/u** Hilversum (lost Krajicek/Siemerink 7–5 6–4).

AMANDA COETZER (South Africa)
Born Hoopstad, 22 October 1971, and lives there; RH; 2HB; 5ft 2in; 115lb; final 1991 WTA ranking 67; 1991 prize money $70,293.
1987: (442). **1988:** (153) Won 4 titles on the satellite circuits. **1989:** (63) Made an unexpected appearance in last 16 French Open and reached sf VS Arizona. **1990:** (75) Qf VS Florida, Geneva and VS Albuquerque. **1991:** Upset K. Maleeva at Berlin and G. Fernandez *en route* to her 1st primary circuit f at Puerto Rico. **1991 HIGHLIGHTS – SINGLES: French Open** 2r (d. A. Minter 5–7 7–5 6–3, lost Appelmans 6–3 5–7 6–1), **Wimbledon** 2r (d. F. Romano 7–6 6–2), **US Open** 1r (lost Halard 7–5 6–1); **r/u** Puerto Rico (d. Viquera 6–1 6–0, Alter 6–2 6–2, G. Fernandez 6–4 6–2, Appelmans 3–6 6–3 7–5, lost Halard 7–5 7–5).

RAFAELLA REGGI CONCATO (Italy)
Born Faenza, 27 November 1965; lives Monte Carlo; RH; 2HB; 5ft 7in; 127lb; final 1991 WTA ranking 75; 1991 prize money $50,297.
Coached by Ferruccio Bonetti; fitness coach Daniele Gatti. Husband Maurizio Concato (married Sept. 1991). **1981:** one of the most spirited performers in the sport, an unwavering competitor, she won Orange Bowl 16s and was ranked No. 1 in Italian 16s. **1982:** (127) Moved up to No. 3 among Italian women and joined Fed Cup Team. **1983:** (48) No. 1 in Italy. **1984:** (62) Sf Swiss Open and qf Italian Open. **1985:** (42) Won Taranto and r/u Barcelona. **1986:** (26) Won Puerto Rican Open and Lugano with victories over Bunge and M. Maleeva, reached last 16 Wimbledon and US Open both unseeded, and won US Open mixed doubles with Casal. Qualified for VS Champ Nov. **1987:** (17) Beat Sukova *en route* to qf French Open, reached last 16 Wimbledon and won VS San Diego. Qualified for VS Champs again. **1988:** (23) At Olympics upset Kohde-Kilsch and Evert to reach qf; r/u Brussels, sf Oklahoma and Filderstadt. **1989:** (21) In GS reached last 16 Australian Open, upset 1988 finalist Zvereva at French Open and held 2 mps v Sanchez at Wimbledon. R/u Eastbourne and VS Indianapolis, sf Oklahoma and Bayonne to qualify for VS Champs (lost Sukova 1r), and in doubles reached 3f. **1990:** (23) Won Taranto and reached last 16 Australian Open. **1991:** In singles r/u Oslo; in doubles won Linz with Maleeva Fragnière and reached 2 more f with Appelmans. **1991 HIGHLIGHTS – SINGLES: Australian Open** 1r (lost Whitlinger 6–7 6–2 6–2); **r/u** Oslo (d. Testud 6–1 2–6 6–4, Gerke 6–2 6–3, Reinstadler 6–3 6–4, Paradis 7–5 6–1, lost Lindqvist 6–3 6–0). **1991 HIGHLIGHTS – DOUBLES:** (with Appelmans unless stated) [Maleeva Fragnière] **won** Linz (d. Langrova/Zrubakova 6–4 1–6 6–3); **r/u** Oslo (lost Kohde-Kilsch/Meier 3–6 6–2 6–4), **r/u** Milan (lost Collins/McNeil 7–6 6–3). **CAREER HIGHLIGHTS – SINGLES: French Open – qf 1987** (lost Evert 6–2 6–2). **MIXED DOUBLES:** (with Casal) **US Open – won 1986** (d. Navratilova/Fleming 6–4 6–4).

GRANT CONNELL (Canada)

Born Regina, Saskatchewan, 17 November 1965; lives Vancouver; LH; 6ft 1in; 175lb; final 1991 ATP ranking 82 singles, 10 (101) doubles; 1991 prize money $326,046.
1983: Nat Jun Singles Champ. ***1985:*** (570) All American at Texas A & M. ***1986:*** (191) Won 1st of 3 straight Nat doubles titles. ***1987:*** (123) Won Vancouver Challenger and r/u Nancy doubles with Scott. ***1988:*** (134) Qf Sydney and Tokyo Seiko; won Livingston in doubles with his D Cup partner, Michibata. ***1989:*** (94) Reached qf Montreal and broke into top 100 Aug. ***1990:*** (92) In singles reached f Auckland, Hong Kong and Sydney Indoor. In doubles with Michibata r/u Australian Open, won 2 titles and reached 2 other f to qualify for IBM/ATP World Doubles. ***1991:*** In singles reached sf Singapore and Chicago, as well as upsetting Lendl at Queen's. In doubles with Michibata won Singapore and reached 5 more f to qualify for ATP Doubles Champ, where they reached sf. ***1991 HIGHLIGHTS – SINGLES: Australian Open*** 3r (d. Kroon 6–1 6–4 6–2, Jarryd 6–1 7–5 6–2, lost Woodforde 6–4 3–6 7–5 6–3), ***French Open*** 1r (lost Muller 6–4 4–6 6–4 6–7 6–0), ***Wimbledon*** 1r (lost Agassi [seed 5] 4–6 6–1 6–7 7–5 6–3), ***US Open*** 1r (lost Stoltenberg 6–4 7–6 6–2); ***sf*** Singapore (d. Canter 6–4 2–6 6–4, Antonitsch 6–4 6–4, Hogstedt 7–5 6–4, lost Siemerink 6–2 6–2), ***sf*** Chicago (d. Grabb 6–1 6–4, Mattar 6–1 6–7 6–3, Yzaga 6–4 6–4, lost P. McEnroe 4–6 6–4 6–4). ***1991 HIGHLIGHTS – DOUBLES:*** (with Michibata) ***won*** Singapore (d. Kruger/Van Rensburg 6–4 5–7 7–6); ***r/u*** Auckland (lost Casal/E. Sanchez 4–6 6–3 6–4), ***r/u*** Chicago (lost S. Davis/Pate 6–4 5–7 7–6), ***r/u*** Queen's (lost Woodbridge/Woodforde 6–4 7–6), ***r/u*** Montreal (lost Galbraith/Witsken 6–4 3–6 6–1), ***r/u*** Cincinnati (lost Flach/Seguso 6–7 6–4 7–5). ***CAREER HIGHLIGHTS – DOUBLES:*** (with Michibata) ***Australian Open – r/u 1990*** (lost Aldrich/Visser 6–4 4–6 6–1 6–4).

JIMMY CONNORS (USA)

Born East St Louis, Ill., 2 September 1952; lives Belleville, Ill. and Santa Ynez, Cal., LH; 2HB; 5ft 10in; 155lb; final 1991 ATP ranking 48; 1991 prize money $324,319.
Wife Patti; son Brett (born 1979); daughter Aubrie-Leigh (born Dec. 1984). One of the game's greatest players, he was taught by his mother and grandmother, growing up outside St Louis in Bellville, Ill. Moving to California, he received expert tutelage from the two great Panchos – Gonzales and Segura – during his crucial late teenage years. His exceptional record from the mid-70s into the mid-80s is an enormous tribute to his skill and willpower. ***1971:*** Won NCAA title as UCLA freshman. ***1972:*** Won first pro title in Jacksonville and made Wimbledon début, upsetting 7th seed Hewitt *en route* to qf, where he lost to Nastase. ***1973:*** Won first important title – US Pro – signalling that he was ready to take over American tennis when he stopped Smith in 1r and Ashe in f. Won Wimbledon doubles with Nastase. ***1974:*** (1) Rose to No. 1 in world, winning Wimbledon, US and Australian Opens and 99 of 103 matches. ***1975:*** (1) He slipped to No. 2 in minds of most experts, losing in f Wimbledon, US and Australian Opens, falling to Ashe in most critical match of the year in Wimbledon f. Won US Open doubles with Nastase. ***1976:*** (1) Won second US Open crown (on clay this time). ***1977:*** (1) Beaten again in Wimbledon and US Open f by Borg and Vilas, but salvaged year with triumph at Masters. ***1978:*** (1) Avenged Wimbledon f loss to Borg at US Open. ***1979:*** (2) Beaten in sf Wimbledon by Borg and sf US Open by McEnroe, he slipped to third in world on most experts' lists. ***1980:*** (3) Ousted by McEnroe in both Wimbledon and US semis he nevertheless played with renewed inspiration and conviction. ***1981:*** (3) Lost Wimbledon and US semis to Borg and returned briefly to represent US in D Cup for first time since Dec. 75. ***1982:*** (2) Despite No. 2 computer ranking behind McEnroe, he was everyone else's choice for No. 1 as he won second Wimbledon and fourth US Open crowns and 7 of 18 tournaments entered; was deservedly awarded ITF World Champion's award. ***1983:*** (3) Took fifth US Open title after disappointment of 4r loss to Curren at Wimbledon, the first time in 12 years he had failed to reach qf. ***1984:*** (2) Reached fifth Wimbledon and joined forces with McEnroe to lead US into D Cup f where they lost to Sweden. Won Seiko Tokyo. ***1985:*** (4) For first time since 1972, did not win a singles title but he appeared in his 12th consecutive US Open sf. ***1986:*** (8) Again did not win a title but reached 4 f. Missed the Masters and suffered first Wimbledon 1r loss in 15 years, then beaten in 3r at US Open after an early-year suspension had kept him out of French Open. ***1987:*** (4) After taking a 3-month break Nov–Jan, he played a lighter winter schedule and, with the pressure off him to win, he enjoyed his best season for 4 years, reaching f 3 times, with a win–loss record of 52–16 going into Masters for which he qualified a record 11th time. Played superbly and with tremendous spirit to reach sf Wimbledon, coming back from 1–6 1–6 1–4 to d. Pernfors in last 16; sf US Open, qf French Open, r/u Memphis, Orlando and Queen's and reached sf 5 more times. ***1988:*** (7) At Washington in July won his 1st title since 1984 and followed with his record 107th career

title at Toulouse, also reaching f LIPC and Milan, sf Toronto and Basle and qf US Open. However, he was plagued by injury throughout the year and withdrew from Masters to undergo surgery on a growth between 2 toes on his left foot and a long-standing problem with the ball on his right foot. In Oct. he slipped from top 10 for 2 weeks for 1st time since ATP rankings began in 1973, a record approached by no other man. During that time he was No. 1 for a record total of 263 weeks. *1989:* (14) Returned to action in Feb., reaching qf Memphis. Won Toulouse and Tel Aviv during the year and achieved his best showing in GS at US Open, where he d. Edberg to reach qf, narrowly losing to Agassi. *1990:* (936) Returning after foot surgery in Dec. the previous year, he suffered an injury to his left wrist in his 1st tourn at Milan, and although he returned in autumn, he lost 2 consecutive matches and eventually underwent surgery in Oct. *1991:* As determined as ever, and enjoying his tennis all the more in his 20th pro season, this remarkable man confounded all those who had written him off. He beat Riglewski 1r LIPC for his 1st match victory since Oct 1989, then at French Open, in only his 5th tourn back, he reached 3r but was forced to retire in 5s v Chang, suffering from exhaustion and back problems. When he played Krickstein at Wimbledon, where he reached 3r, he became the 1st man to play 100 matches there, and followed at Long Island with his 1st qf appearance since 1989. The triumph of his year, though, came at the US Open where, ranked 174, he was given a wild-card entry. He delighted the crowds by reaching sf at age 39 (oldest to reach that stage since Rosewall in 1974), recovering from 2 sets and 0–3 down v P. McEnroe 1r and outlasting Krickstein in another 5s contest in 4r, both matches lasting more than 4 hours. He followed with sf appearance at Basel. *1991 HIGHLIGHTS – SINGLES: French Open* 3r (d. Witsken 6–3 6–3 7–5, Agenor 6–4 6–2 3–6 0–6 6–4, lost Chang [seed 10] 4–6 7–5 6–2 4–6 0–15 ret'd), *Wimbledon* 3r (d. Paloheimo 6–2 6–0 7–5, Krickstein 6–3 6–2 6–3, lost Rostagno 7–6 6–1 6–4), *US Open* sf, unseeded (d. P. McEnroe 4–6 6–7 6–4 6–2 6–4, Schapers 6–2 6–3 6–2, Novacek [seed 10] 6–1 6–4 6–3, Krickstein 3–6 7–6 1–6 6–3 7–6, Haarhuis 4–6 7–6 6–4 6–2, lost Courier [seed 4] 6–3 6–3 6–2); *sf* Basel (d. Prades 6–3 6–1, Korda 6–3 6–4, Mansdorf 6–3 6–2, lost J. McEnroe 6–1 6–3). *CAREER HIGHLIGHTS – SINGLES: Australian Open – won 1974* (d. Dent 7–6 6–4 4–6 6–3), *r/u 1975* (lost Newcombe 7–5 3–6 6–4 7–6); *Wimbledon– won 1974* (d. Rosewall 6–1 6–1 6–4), *won 1982* (d. Alexander 7–6 4s, Gitlin 7–5 4s, G. Mayer 6–1 6–2 7–6, Edmondson 6–4 6–3 6–1, McEnroe 3–6 6–3 6–7 7–6 6–4), *r/u 1975* (lost Ashe 6–1 6–1 5–7 6–4), *r/u 1977* (lost Borg 3–6 6–2 6–1 5–7 6–4), *r/u 1978* (lost Borg 6–2 6–2 6–3), *r/u 1984* (d. Lendl 6–7 6–3 7–5 6–1, lost McEnroe 6–1 6–1 6–2), *sf 1979* (lost Borg 6–2 6–3 6–2), *sf 1980* seed 3 (lost McEnroe 6–3 3–6 6–3 6–4), *sf 1981* (d. V. Amritraj 2–6 5–7 6–4 6–3 6–2, lost Borg 0–6 4–6 6–3 6–0 6–4), *sf 1985* (lost Curren 6–2 6–2 6–1), *sf 1987* (lost Cash 6–4 6–4 6–1); *US Open – won 1974* (d. Rosewall 6–1 6–0 6–1), *won 1976* (d. Borg 6–4 3–6 7–6 6–4), *won 1978* (d. McEnroe 6–2 6–2 7–5, Borg 6–4 6–2 6–2), *won 1982* (d. Arias 6–4 4–6 6–4 6–1, Nastase 6–3 6–3 6–4, Harmon 6–1 3–6 6–4, Vilas 6–1 3–6 6–2 6–3, Lendl 6–3 6–2 4–6 6–4), *won 1983* (d. Lendl 6–3 6–7 7–5 6–0), *r/u 1975* (lost Orantes 6–4 6–3 6–3), *r/u 1977* (lost Vilas 2–6 6–3 7–6 6–0), *sf 1979* (lost McEnroe 6–3 6–3 7–5), *sf 1980* seed 3 (lost McEnroe 6–4 5–7 0–6 6–3 7–6), *sf 1981* (lost Borg 6–2 7–5 6–4), *sf 1984* (lost McEnroe 6–4 4–6 7–5 4–6 6–3), *sf 1985* (lost Lendl 6–2 6–3 7–5), *sf 1987* (lost Lendl 6–4 6–2 6–2), *sf 1991; Masters – won 1978* (d. Borg 6–4 1–6 6–4), *sf 1979* seed 3 (lost Gerulaitis 7–5 6–2), *sf 1980* seed 4 (lost Borg 6–4 6–7 6–3), *sf 1982* (lost Lendl 6–3 6–1), *sf 1983* (lost Lendl 3–6 6–4), *sf 1984* (lost Lendl 7–6 5–7 7–5); *WCT Finals – won 1977* (d. Stockton 6–7 6–1 6–4 6–3), *won 1980* seed 2 (d. Scanlon, Lendl, McEnroe 2–6 7–6 6–1 6–2); *US CC – won 1974* (d. Borg 5–7 6–3 6–4), *won 1976* (d. Fibak 6–2 6–4) *won 1978* (d. Higueras 7–5 6–1), *won 1978* (d. Vilas 6–1 2–6 6–4), *r/u 1972* (lost Hewitt 6–1 7–6), *r/u 1977* (lost Orantes 6–1 6–3); *US Pro Indoor – won 1976* (d. Borg 7–6 6–4 6–0), *won 1978* (d. Tanner 6–4 6–2 6–3), *won 1979* (d. Ashe 6–3 6–4 6–1), *won 1980* (d. McEnroe 6–3 2–6 6–3 3–6 6–4); *US Indoor – won 1973* (d. Meiler), *won 1974* (d. McMillan), *won 1975* (d. Gerulaitis 6–1 fs), *won 1978* (d. Tim Gullikson 7–6 6–3), *won 1979* (d. Ashe 6–4 5–7 6–3), *won 1983* (d. G. Mayer 7–5 6–0), *won 1984* (d. Leconte 6–3 4–6 7–5); *South African Open – won 1973* (d. Ashe), *won 1974* (d. Ashe); *French Open – sf 1979* seed 2 (lost Pecci 7–6 6–4 5–7 6–3), *sf 1980* (lost Gerulaitis 6–1 3–6 6–7 6–2 6–4), *qf 1982* (lost Clerc 4–6 6–2 4–6 7–5 6–0), *sf 1985* (d. Edberg, lost Lendl 6–2 6–3 6–1). *CAREER HIGHLIGHTS – DOUBLES:* (with Nastase) *Wimbledon – won 1973* (d. Cooper/Fraser 3–6 6–3 6–4 8–9 6–1); *US Open – won 1975* (d. Okker/Riessen); *French Open – r/u 1973* (lost Newcombe/Okker 6–4 fs). *MIXED DOUBLES:* (with Evert) *US Open – r/u 1974* (lost Masters/Teeguarden 6–1 7–6).

CARLOS COSTA (Spain)

Born Barcelona, 22 April 1968, and lives there; RH; 6ft; 162lb; final 1991 ATP ranking 55; 1991 prize money $143,585.
Coached by Robert Vizcaino. *1986:* Nat Jun Champ. *1988:* (243). *1989:* (201) Won Madrid

doubles with Carbonell. *1990:* (151) Won Zaragoza Challenger; upset Korda and Cherkasov at Barcelona. *1991:* Reached sf Florence and sf Guaruja Bliss; won Venice and Siracusa Challengers. Reached 2 doubles, winning San Marino with Arrese. *1991 HIGHLIGHTS – SINGLES: French Open* 3r (d. Eltingh 6–2 6–3 6–3, Benhabiles 7–5 6–1 6–2, lost Stich 3–6 7–5 7–6 6–2); *won* Venice Challenger (d. Mancini 6–3 7–5), *won* Siracusa Challenger (d. Pescosolido 6–3 7–6); *sf* Florence (d. Azar 6–3 6–4, Fromberg 6–3 5–7 6–4, Arias 6–4 6–1, lost Muster 6–7 6–1 6–3), *sf* Guaruja Bliss (d. Herrera 7–5 3–6 6–4, Clavet 7–6 3–6 6–3, Gomez 4–6 6–1 6–3, lost Zoecke 6–4 6–2). *1991 HIGHLIGHTS – DOUBLES:* [Arrese] *won* San Marino (d. Miniussi/Perez 6–3 3–6 6–3); [Baguena] *r/u* Florence (d. Jonsson/Larsson 3–6 6–1 6–1).

JIM COURIER (USA)

Born Sanford, Fla., 17 August 1970; lives Dade City, Fla.; RH; 6ft 1in; 173lb; final 1991 ATP ranking 2; 1991 prize money $1,848,171.
Started at Nick Bollettieri Tennis Academy. Coached by José Higueras from Nov. 1990. *1986:* Played on US Jun World Cup team r/u to AUS; won Orange Bowl. *1987:* Won French Open Jun doubles with Stark and was ranked 4 in Jun singles, winning Orange Bowl. *1988:* (43) Sf US CC and Stockholm (d. Jarryd and Pernfors back-to-back); qf Stratton Mountain and Detroit. R/u US Nat 18s to Chang. *1989:* (24) Upset Agassi *en route* to last 16 French Open and beat Edberg to win his 1st GP title at Basle in autumn. In doubles won Italian Open and qualified for Masters with Sampras. *1990:* (25) Sf Indian Wells; qf Milan, Philadelphia, LIPC, Munich, Gstaad and Cincinnati. *1991:* He began an extraordinary year by extending Edberg to 5s in last 16 Australian Open, then in March won both singles and doubles (with J. Sanchez) at Indian Wells, following immediately with the title at LIPC over Wheaton, which took him into top 10 for 1st time. Played first D Cup tie in March v Mexico (away) and lost line singles to Herrera and dead one to Lavalle. Then followed the high spot of his career to date, when he won the French Open, beating Edberg *en route* and overpowering Agassi to win his 1st GS final, replacing him as No. 4 in the world. He made a qf appearance at Wimbledon, losing to eventual champion Stich, then swept to f US Open, ending Connors' romantic run in sf, but was completely outplayed by Edberg at the last hurdle. That performance took him to No. 3 behind Edberg and Becker and by Nov. he had edged Becker aside to take 2nd place, a position confirmed by his progress to f ATP World Champ, where he lost to Sampras. Also reached sf Adelaide, Tokyo Suntory, Montreal, Cincinnati, Indianapolis and Stockholm. *1991 HIGHLIGHTS – SINGLES: Australian Open* last 16, seed 16 (d. Gunnarsson 6–3 6–4 6–2, Bloom 6–2 6–3 6–2, Oncins 6–3 6–1 6–1, lost Edberg [seed 1] 4–6 6–0 6–4 5–7 6–2), *won French Open* seed 9 (d. Rostagno 6–3 6–3 6–0, Ferreira 6–2 6–3 6–4, Larsson 6–3 4–6 4–6 7–5 6–2, Martin 6–2 6–3 6–3, Edberg [seed 1] 6–4 2–6 6–3 6–4, Stich 6–2 6–7 6–2 6–4, Agassi 3–6 6–4 2–6 6–1 6–4), *Wimbledon* qf, seed 4 (d. R. Gilbert 6–4 6–2 7–6, Grabb 6–4 7–6 2–6 4–6 6–3, Boetsch 6–2 6–2 6–0, Novacek [seed 14] 6–3 6–4 6–2, lost Stich [seed 6] 6–3 7–6 6–2), *r/u US Open*, seed 4 (d. Kulti 6–3 6–4 6–4, Arias 6–3 6–2 6–0, Jarryd 6–3 6–2 6–2, E. Sanchez [seed 14] 6–4 6–4 6–3, Sampras [seed 6] 6–2 7–6 7–6, Connors 6–3 6–3 6–2, lost Edberg [seed 2] 6–2 6–4 6–0); *won* Indian Wells (d. Raoux 6–4 3–6 6–2, Black 6–1 7–6, Agassi 2–6 6–3 6–4, E. Sanchez 6–2 6–3, Stich 6–3 6–2, Forget 4–6 6–3 4–6 6–3 7–6), *won* LIPC (d. Herrera 7–6 3–6 6–3, Haarhuis 7–5 3–6 6–3, Forget 7–6 6–3, Rostagno 6–0 6–3, Reneberg 6–4 6–3, Wheaton 6–3 6–4); *r/u* ATP World Champ (d. Novacek 6–7 7–5 6–4, Forget 7–6 6–4, lost Lendl 6–2 6–3 in rr, d. Agassi 6–3 7–5, lost Sampras 3–6 7–6 6–3 6–4); *sf* Adelaide (d. Mronz 3–6 6–2 6–1, Haarhuis 6–4 6–4, Sinner 7–6 6–3, lost Stich 6–4 7–6), *sf* Tokyo Suntory (d. Grabb 6–7 6–2 6–3, Goldie 6–3 6–4, J. McEnroe 6–2 6–2, lost Lendl 6–4 6–1), *sf* Montreal (d. Washington 7–5 6–3, Mansdorf 6–3 3–6 6–3, Rostagno 6–3 6–3, lost Korda 3–6 7–6 6–2), *sf* Cincinnati (d. Pernfors 6–3 6–1, Chang 7–5 6–2, B. Gilbert 6–3 6–3, lost Sampras 6–2 7–5), *sf* Indianapolis (d. Pugh 6–4 6–4, Clavet 6–2 6–1, Cherkasov 6–2 7–5, lost Sampras 6–3 7–6), *sf* Stockholm (d. Steeb 6–4 6–4, Rostagno 7–5 6–1, Korda 6–4 6–4, lost Becker 6–7 6–3 6–4). *1991 HIGHLIGHTS – DOUBLES:* (with J. Sanchez) *won* Indian Wells (d. Forget/Leconte 7–6 3–6 6–3). *CAREER HIGHLIGHTS – SINGLES: French Open – won 1991; US Open – r/u 1991; ATP World Champ – r/u 1991; Wimbledon – qf 1991.*

CARRIE CUNNINGHAM (USA)

Born Southfield, Mich., 28 April 1972; lives Livonia, Mich.; LH; 5ft 5in; 112lb; final 1991 WTA ranking 51; 1991 prize money $91,142.
Coached by Joe Fodell. *1986:* Won Nat 14s. *1987:* Won Nat 16s. *1988:* (138) Won US Open Jun over McQuillan. Qf Schenectady. *1989:* (88) Upset K. Maleeva *en route* to sf VS

Houston. **1990:** (70) Reached sf Puerto Rico and qf San Antonio. **1991:** Sf Colorado and qf San Marino, Westchester and Puerto Rico. **1991 HIGHLIGHTS – SINGLES: Australian Open** 3r (d. Pratt 6–1 6–1, Lindqvist 6–1 6–0, lost Frazier [seed 13] 3–6 6–2 6–2), **French Open** 3r (d. S. Martin 6–2 6–2, Halard 6–2 7–5, lost Martinez [seed 7] 6–1 6–4), **Wimbledon** 2r (d. Helgeson 7–6 6–4, lost Strnadova 6–1 6–3), **US Open** 1r (lost Durie 6–4 6–2); **sf** Colorado (d. Santrock 6–3 6–1, A. Minter 6–2 5–7 6–1, Sloane 6–2 6–4, lost McNeil 6–4 6–2). **1991 HIGHLIGHTS – DOUBLES:** [Gildemeister] **r/u** Tokyo Nicherei (lost M. J. Fernandez/Shriver 6–3 6–3).

KEVIN CURREN (USA)
Born Durban, South Africa, 2 March 1958; lives Austin, Tex.; RH; 2HB; 6ft 1in; 170lb; final 1991 ATP ranking 58 singles, 51 doubles; 1991 prize money $199,111.
Coached by Robert Trogolo. Became US citizen in 1985. **1979:** (195) A huge server with a two-handed forehand (a shot he has since abandoned), he won NCAA champs while attending University of Texas. **1980:** (47) Last 16 Wimbledon, coached by Warren Jacques. **1981:** (57) Won Johannesburg in spring; last 16 US Open. **1982:** (17) Won Cologne singles, US Open doubles with Steve Denton and 2nd straight US Open mixed and Wimbledon mixed with A. Smith. **1983:** (9) R/u Milan and reached sf Wimbledon, upsetting Connors in last 16. **1984:** (15) R/u to Wilander at Australian Open (d. Lendl). **1985:** (10) R/u to Becker at Wimbledon (d. McEnroe and Connors) and won Toronto Indoor. **1986:** (18) Won his 1st SS title in Atlanta and was one of only four players to beat Lendl, upsetting world No. 1 at Canadian Open. **1987:** (37) Reached qf only 3 times in singles but won 3 doubles titles. **1988:** (23) At Toronto reached 1st GP f since Scottsdale 1986, and appeared in sf Memphis, LA, Scottsdale and Vienna. Out with torn calf muscle from March to June, and then again with twisted ankle from Wimbledon to end Aug. **1989:** (20) Won his 1st title for 3 years at Frankfurt, despite being restricted all autumn by knee problems, and reached sf Memphis, LIPC, Singapore and San Francisco. In doubles with various partners reached 5 f, winning Tokyo Seiko. **1990:** (71) Reached qf Wimbledon and last 16 US Open, both unseeded. In doubles with various partners reached 4 f, winning Queen's with Bates. Played GS Cup, losing 1r to Ivanisevic. **1991:** Qf San Francisco, Philadelphia, Basel and Lyon. **1991 HIGHLIGHTS – SINGLES: Wimbledon** 2r (d. Roese 6–3 6–3 6–1, lost Frana 7–6 6–2 6–2), **US Open** 2r (d. Santoro 3–6 2–6 6–3 6–3 6–3, lost Simian 6–3 6–7 7–6 6–4). **1991 HIGHLIGHTS – DOUBLES:** [Bates] **r/u** Toulouse (lost Nijssen/Suk 4–6 6–3 7–6). **CAREER HIGHLIGHTS – SINGLES: Australian Open – r/u 1984** (d. Lendl, S. Davis, Testerman, lost Wilander 6–7 6–4 7–6 6–2); **Wimbledon – r/u 1985** (d. Edberg 7–6 6–3 7–6, McEnroe 6–2 6–2 6–4, Connors 6–2 6–2 6–1, lost Becker 6–3 6–7 7–6 6–4), **sf 1983** (d. Connors 6–3 6–7 6–3 7–6, Mayotte, lost C. Lewis 6–7 6–4 7–6 8–6). **CAREER HIGHLIGHTS – DOUBLES:** (with Denton) **US Open – won 1982** (d. Amaya/Pfister 6–2 6–7 5–7 6–2 6–4); **US CC – won 1980** (d. Fibak/Lendl 3–6 7–6 6–4), **won 1981** (d. Ramirez/Winitsky 7–5 fs); **US Pro Indoor – won 1983** (d. McEnroe/Fleming 6–4 7–6); **Australian Open – sf 1981** (lost Edmondson/Warwick); **Wimbledon – sf 1982** (lost McEnroe/Fleming 6–2 6–4 2–6 6–3), **sf 1983** (lost Tim/Tom Guillikson 7–6 6–7 7–6 6–3). **MIXED DOUBLES:** (with A. Smith) **Wimbledon – won 1982** (d. Lloyd/Turnbull 2–6 6–3 7–5); **US Open – won 1981** (d. Denton/Russell 6–4 7–6), **won 1982** (d. Taygan/Potter 6–3 7–6).

KIMIKO DATE (Japan)
Born Kyoto, 28 September 1970; lives Amagasaki City; RH; 5ft 4in; 113lb; final 1991 WTA ranking 32; 1991 prize money $79,299.
Coached by Takeshi Koura. Although she plays right-handed, she writes and eats left-handed. **1988:** (321) Won 2 titles on Japanese satellite circuit. **1989:** (120) Qf Tokyo Suntory and Birmingham; won 3 titles on British satellite circuit in May, and played Fed Cup. **1990:** (78) Upset Fairbank-Nideffer at Brisbane and then surprised Shriver at Australian Open to become the 1st Japanese woman since 1973 to reach last 16 there, a performance which took her into the top 100. Appeared in qf Tokyo Suntory again. **1991:** Upset Meskhi and Sabatini as she swept to her 1st primary circuit f at VS Los Angeles. **1991 HIGHLIGHTS – SINGLES: Australian Open** 2r (d. Herreman 6–2 6–1, lost Provis 4–6 6–0 6–4), **Wimbledon** 1r (lost Ferrando 6–4 3–6 6–2), **US Open** 2r (d. Tami Whitlinger 7–6 6–4, lost Zrubakova 7–5 6–7 6–3); **r/u** VS Los Angeles (d. Dahlman 6–2 6–2, Meskhi 6–4 6–1, Basuki 6–2 6–2, Durie 6–4 6–1, Sabatini 3–6 6–1 6–4, lost Seles 6–3 6–1).

SCOTT DAVIS (USA)
Born Santa Monica, Cal., 27 August 1962; lives Newport Beach, Cal.; RH; 6ft 2in; 170lb; final 1991 ATP ranking 155 singles, 4 (8) doubles; 1991 prize money $338,781.

1977–80: No. 1 US Jun in his age group. *1980:* (457) Broke Dick Stockton's previous record of 20 US Nat Jun titles, concluding jun career with 24. *1983:* (24) Graduated from Stanford, turned pro, won Maui (first GP title), r/u Seiko Tokyo (d. Leconte, Gomez, Connors, lost Lendl 6–4 fs), Newport and Taipei. Won Columbus doubles with Teacher. *1984:* (48) Married Suzy Jaeger (sister of Andrea). Reached last 16 Wimbledon, extending Lendl to 7–5 in 5s, and qf Australian Open. *1985:* (17) Finalist LIPC and sf at US Pro Indoor and Chicago; won Japan Open and qualified for Masters first time. Won doubles at Stratton Mountain, Japan Open (with Pate) and LA (with Van't Hof). *1986:* (39) An off year in which injuries and bad draws contributed to his woes. Began working with Australian Bob Brett in autumn in effort to build up stamina and confidence and finished on a high note as r/u WCT Houston. *1987:* (59) Beat Mecir and Connors to reach sf Tokyo. Continued to work with Bob Brett until end of year. *1988:* (111) Qf Tel Aviv and won Cherbourg Challenger. *1989:* (70) R/u Schenectady and sf Los Angeles. In doubles won 3 titles with different partners. *1990:* (44) Started the year by winning Auckland for his 1st singles title since 1985, then upset Chesnokov for a 2nd time and J. McEnroe *en route* to sf Cincinnati. In doubles with Pate won 5 titles to qualify for IBM/ATP World Doubles. *1991:* In partnership with Pate won a 1st GS title at Australian Open and r/u US Open, as well as winning 3 other titles to qualify for ATP Doubles Champ. R/u Australian Open mixed doubles with R. White and in singles reached qf Indian Wells. *1991 HIGHLIGHTS – SINGLES: Australian Open* 2r (d. Antonitsch 3–6 6–2 6–4 6–3, lost Lendl [seed 3] 7–6 6–3 6–2), *French Open* 1r (lost Bruguera [seed 5] 6–2 6–2 6–1), *Wimbledon* 1r (lost Saceanu 6–4 7–6 6–4, *US Open* 1r (lost Novacek [seed 10] 6–3 5–7 6–1 6–3). *1991 HIGHLIGHTS – DOUBLES:* (with Pate) *won Australian Open* (d. P. McEnroe/Wheaton 6–7 7–6 6–3 7–5), *r/u US Open* (lost Fitzgerald/Jarryd 6–3 3–6 6–3 6–3); *won* Sydney NSW (d. Cahill/Kratzmann 3–6 6–3 6–2), *won* Chicago (d. Connell/Michibata 6–4 5–7 7–6), *won* Washington (d. Flach/Seguso 6–4 6–2); *r/u* Tokyo Seiko (lost Grabb/Reneberg 7–5 2–6 7–6). *MIXED DOUBLES:* (with R. White) *r/u Australian Open* (lost Bates/Durie 2–6 6–4 6–4). *CAREER HIGHLIGHTS – DOUBLES:* (with Pate) *Australian Open – won 1991; US Open – r/u 1991*.

ALEXIA DECHAUME (France)
Born La Rochelle, 3 May 1970; lives Bologne; 5ft 4½in; 124lb; RH; 2HB; final 1991 WTA ranking 72; 1991 prize money $71,109.
Coached by Patrick Favière. *1986:* (225). *1987:* (127) Qf Athens. *1988:* (127) Qf Taranto and won Bayonne on French satellite circuit, breaking into top 100 in June. In doubles with Derly won Paris Open, French Open Jun and r/u Wimbledon Jun. *1989:* (173). *1990:* (84) Reached her first primary circuit f at Taranto and broke into the top 100 in Sept. *1991:* In singles her best showing was qf Barcelona; in doubles she reached 2 f, winning Taranto with Labat. *1991 HIGHLIGHTS – SINGLES: Australian Open* 3r (d. Godridge 7–3 7–5, Martinek 6–2 6–3, lost Garrison 6–2 6–4), *French Open* 1r (lost Brioukhovets 1–6 6–2 7–5), *Wimbledon* 1r (lost Grunfeld 6–4 6–4), *US Open* 1r (lost Wiesner 4–6 6–3 6–3). *1991 HIGHLIGHTS – DOUBLES:* [Labat] *won* Taranto (d. Golarsa/Grossman 6–2 7–5); [Halard] *r/u* Clarins (lost Langrova/Zrubakova 6–4 6–4).

JOHN DE JAGER (South Africa)
Born 17 March 1973.
1991: Won US Open Jun Doubles with Alami.

OLIVIER DELAITRE (France)
Born Metz, 1 June 1967; lives Luxembourg; RH; 5ft 8in; 150lb; final 1991 ATP ranking 41; 1991 prize money $172,292.
Wife Emmanuelle Willay (married Oct. 1991). *1987:* (298). *1988:* (129) Enjoyed some success on the satellite circuits. *1989:* (111) Reached 1st GP sf at Sydney (upsetting Svensson), with qf Nancy and Basle, breaking into top 100 in Jan. *1990:* (152)) Qf Hilversum, won Brasilia Challenger and extended Ivanisevic to 5s 2r Wimbledon. *1991:* Returning to the top 100, he broke into the top 50 with his 1st GP r/u showings at Bordeaux and Lyon (d. Forget and Bruguera), sf Long Island and 2 Challenger titles. Member of winning French D Cup team v USA in Lyon but did not play. *1991 HIGHLIGHTS – SINGLES: French Open* 3r (d. Perez-Roldan 6–2 6–1 6–1, Lundgren 6–2 6–7 6–4 6–2, lost Clavet 4–6 6–2 6–3 6–4); *won* Guadeloupe Challenger (d. Pescosolido 6–2 7–6), *won* Istanbul Challenger (d. Black 6–1 6–4); *r/u* Bordeaux (d. Markus 5–7 6–2 6–3, Svensson 7–6 6–3, Mronz 4–6 6–3 6–0, Champion 6–3 6–1, lost Forget 6–1 6–3), *r/u* Lyon (d. Forget 1–6 6–4 6–3, Pioline 6–2 6–7 7–6, Kriek 6–2 7–6, Bruguera 6–4 6–4, lost Sampras 6–1 6–1); *sf* Long Island (d. Agenor 1–6 7–6 6–2, Larsson 6–0 2–6 6–1, Champion 6–4 6–4, lost

Edberg 6–1 7–6).*1991 HIGHLIGHTS – DOUBLES:* (with R. Gilbert) *won* Guaruja Chevrolet (d. Cannon/Van Emburgh 6–2 6–4).

HORACIO DE LA PENA (Argentina)
Born Buenos Aires, 1 August 1966, and lives there; LH; 5ft 11in; 138lb; final 1991 ATP ranking 100; 1991 prize money $156,195.
Has twin sister, Nuria. Coached by Roy Emerson whose daughter Heidi he married 8 March 1990. *1984:* (90) Won two satellite events, beginning to fulfil promise he had exhibited in sweeping Nat 12, 14 16 and 18 jun crowns. *1985:* (70) Joined Argentine D Cup team. Won GP Marbella and reached sf Buenos Aires. *1986:* (38) Producing superior CC results, he reached last 16 at French Open, was r/u at Bari, and reached sf Boston (d. Tulasne). *1987:* (88) Sf Bari, qf Buenos Aires and stunned McEnroe 1r French Open. *1988:* (52) R/u Sao Paulo, sf Rye Brook, Geneva and Boston, where he upset Wilander in ss. *1989:* As a qualifier he won Florence for his 1st title since 1985 but thereafter suffered bouts of patellar tendonitis and bursitis. *1990:* (63) Returning from injury, he was obliged to play qualifying in the early tourns. Won Kitzbuhel in Aug, upsetting Gilbert and E. Sanchez, and reached sf Umag and Prague. *1991:* In singles he reached qf at Nice, Italian Open, Gstaad, Geneva and Prague, but progressed no further. In doubles won Barcelona with Nargiso. *1991 HIGHLIGHTS – SINGLES: French Open* 1r (lost Jonsson 7–6 6–3 2–0 ret'd). *1991 HIGHLIGHTS – DOUBLES:* (with Nargiso) *won* Barcelona (d. Becker/Jelen 3–6 7–6 6–4)

ISABELLE DEMONGEOT (France)
Born Gassin, 18 September 1966; lives St Tropez; RH; 5ft 7in; 134lb; final 1991 WTA ranking 61; 1991 prize money $94,359.
Coached by Regis DeCamaret. *1983:* (245) No. 1 player on Israeli satellite circuit. *1984:* (165) No. 15 in ITF World Jun rankings. R/u French Nat. *1985:* (135) Won Chicago on USTA satellite circuit and reached sf Hilversum. *1986:* (64) Reached last 16 Wimbledon and qf Mahwah. *1987:* (54) Played Fed Cup; qf San Francisco and San Diego. *1988:* (44) Sf Geneva (d. M. Maleeva) and Nice. In doubles with Tauziat won Berlin and Zurich and qualified for VS Champs. *1989:* (46) Upset Manuela Maleeva Fragnière to reach qf LIPC and in doubles with Tauziat won Hamburg. *1990:* (77) Qf Indian Wells and Barcelona. *1991:* Upset Lindqvist, Gildemeister and McNeil in taking her 1st tour title at Westchester, and surprised Halard on her way to qf VS Nashville. In doubles won VS Albuquerque with Adams and Leipzig with Bollegraf. *1991 HIGHLIGHTS – SINGLES: French Open* 1r (lost Niox-Chateau 6–4 6–4), *Wimbledon* 1r (lost Lindqvist 6–1 6–0); *won* Westchester (d. Lindqvist 6–4 5–7 6–4, Amiach 6–4 6–3, Cunningham 7–6 6–3, Gildemeister 6–1 6–1, McNeil 6–4 6–4). *1991 HIGHLIGHTS – DOUBLES:* [Adams] *won* VS Albuquerque (d. Gregory/Louie Harper 6–7 6–4 6–3), [Bollegraf] *won* Leipzig (d. Hetherington/Rinaldi 6–4 6–3); [Durie] *r/u* St Petersburg (lost Brioukhovets/Medvedeva 7–5 6–3).

MARIAAN DE SWARDT (South Africa)
Born Johannesburg, 18 March 1971; lives Pretoria; RH; 5ft 8in; 149lb; final 1991 WTA ranking 53; 1991 prize money $58,219
1988: (167) Won Vereeniging on the South African satellite circuit for the second straight year. *1989:* (306). *1990:* (158) Won 3 titles on the satellite circuits. *1991:* Upset McGrath *en route* to qf Birmingham and won Oporto Challenger. *1991 HIGHLIGHTS – SINGLES: French Open* 2r (d. Fusai 6–7 7–6 6–1, lost Seles [seed 1] 6–0 6–2), *Wimbledon* 2r (d. Rehe 6–3 3–6 6–4, lost Gildemeister 6–4 6–1), *US Open* 2r (d. Suire 6–1 6–7 6–3, lost K. Maleeva [seed 11] 6–3 6–4; *won* Oporto Challenger (d. Gorrochategui 6–1 6–2).

GRANT DOYLE (Australia)
Born Glenfield, 9 January 1974, and lives there; RH; 5ft 11in; 165lb; final 1991 ATP ranking 627.
Coached by Chris Kachel and Brad Guan. *1991:* Won Australian Open Jun with Eagle.

JO DURIE (Great Britain)
Born Bristol, 27 July 1960; lives London; RH; 6ft; 150lb; final 1991 WTA ranking 60; 1991 prize money $130,071.
Coached by Alan Jones. *1978:* Top-ranked British jun. *1979:* (73) Sf Wimbledon Plate. *1980:* (53) Out of action 8 months following back surgery. Sf German Indoor Open. *1981:* (31) Last 16 US Open; won British HC. *1982:* (28) No. 1 in Great Britain, taking over from Wade. *1983:* (6) Best year of career when she reached sf US and French Opens, qf Australian Open, and won Sydney and Mahwah. *1984:* (24). *1985:* (26) Sf Brighton (d. Graf). *1986:* (23) Played 17 tournaments and W and Fed Cups, winning 24 of 44 matches,

beating McNeil, Lindqvist and K. Jordan, but best showing was sf Mahwah in summer. *1987:* (73) In W Cup ended 23-match winning streak by US when she d. Garrison, and won Wimbledon mixed doubles with Bates, but otherwise suffered a poor year. *1988:* (61) Qf San Diego and California Open. Missed Fed Cup with shoulder injury. *1989:* (118) Sf Auckland. A back injury forced her to withdraw from Wimbledon. *1990:* (64) An appearance in f VS Newport was her best showing since Brighton 1983. *1991:* Reached sf St Petersburg, qf Los Angeles and upset Sukova on her way to an unexpected appearance in last 16 US Open. In mixed doubles won Australian Open with Bates. Won 6th British Nat. singles since beating V. Wade for first win in 1983. *1991: HIGHLIGHTS – SINGLES: Australian Open* 2r (d. Morton 6–1 3–6 7–5, lost Strnadova 6–3 6–2), *French Open* 1r (lost Hack 6–4 7–5), *Wimbledon* 2r (d. Kelesi 6–3 6–2, lost Bollegraf 6–3 5–7 7–3), *US Open* last 16, unseeded (d. Cunningham 6–4 6–2, Fulco 6–4 6–0, Sukova [seed 15] 6–4 2–6 6–1, lost Capriati [seed 7] 6–1 6–2); *sf* St Petersburg (d. Smashnova 6–1 6–4, Reinstadler 6–0 6–7 6–2); Demongeot 6–2 6–2, lost Savchenko 6–4 6–4). *1991 HIGHLIGHTS – DOUBLES:* [Demongeot] *r/u* St Petersburg (lost Brioukhovets/Medvedeva 7–5 6–3). *1991 HIGHLIGHTS – MIXED DOUBLES:* (with Bates) *won Australian Open* (d. Davis/R. White 2–6 6–4 6–4). *CAREER HIGHLIGHTS – SINGLES: French Open – sf 1983* (d. Moulton, Shriver, Rinaldi, Austin 6–0 fs, lost Jausovec 6–2 fs); *US Open – sf 1983* (d. Madruga Osses 6–2 6–2, lost Evert Lloyd 6–4 6–4); *Australian Open – qf 1983* (lost Navratilova 4–6 6–3 6–4). *CAREER HIGHLIGHTS – DOUBLES:* (with Hobbs unless stated) *Australian Open – sf 1985* (lost Navratilova/Shriver 7–6 6–2); *French Open – sf 1983* (lost Fairbank/Reynolds 6–3 6–2); *Wimbledon – sf 1983* (lost Navratilova/Shriver 6–3 7–5), [Evert Lloyd] *qf 1985* (d. Bunge/Pfaff, lost Navratilova/Shriver 6–4 6–2). *MIXED DOUBLES:* (with Bates) *Australian Open – won 1991; Wimbledon – won 1987* (d. Cahill/Provis 7–6 6–3).

JOSHUA EAGLE (Australia)
Born 10 May 1973.
1991: Won Australian Open Jun doubles with Doyle.

STEFAN EDBERG (Sweden) Official World Champion
Born Vastervik, 19 January 1966; lives London, RH; 6ft 2in; 170lb; final 1991 ATP ranking 1; 1991 prize money $2,363,575.
Coached by Tony Pickard. Girlfriend Annette Olssen. *1983:* (53) Won jun Grand Slam, proving prowess on 3 different surfaces, and played 11 events on men's tour. *1984:* (20) Won Milan and contributed crucial triumph in D Cup f as Sweden d. USA with doubles win alongside Jarryd over McEnroe/Fleming, repeating their success over that duo at US Open, where they were r/u. *1985:* (5) Reached top 5 with first GS men's success, upending Lendl and Wilander for Australian Open title. Also won San Francisco, Basle and Memphis. *1986:* (5) Won Gstaad, Basle and Stockholm, lost four other finals (two to Becker, one to McEnroe, one to Gilbert) and reached sf US Open. In doubles with Jarryd won Masters and r/u French Open. *1987:* (2) Won 2nd Australian singles title, sf Wimbledon and US Open, won titles in Memphis, Rotterdam, Tokyo (2), Cincinnati and Stockholm, reached 4 more f and achieved win-loss singles record of 70–11 going into Masters, where he reached sf. In doubles with Jarryd won Australian and US Opens, and reached sf Masters. *1988:* (5) Won Wimbledon over Becker, sf Australian Open and last 16 French and US Opens. Won Rotterdam and Basel, reached 4 other f and took Olympic bronze medal. Played virtually no doubles and was restricted at Masters by tendonitis in left knee, falling to Lendl in sf. *1989:* (3) Finished the year in triumph with his 1st Masters title, beating Lendl in sf and Becker in f. R/u French Open and Wimbledon, but fell last 16 US Open to Connors and withdrew qf Australian Open with back injury which kept him out for 5 weeks. His only other title came at Tokyo Suntory, but he reached f Scottsdale, Cincinnati, Basle and Paris Open. *1990:* (1) Won a 2nd Wimbledon title and on 13 Aug took over No. 1 ranking for 1st time from Lendl, holding off a strong late challenge from Becker to finish the year in that position. He was forced to retire during f Australian Open with stomach muscle injury, suffered during sf match, which kept him out for 4 weeks. He was without his coach, Pickard, who was recovering from a hip operation, from end Australian Open to beginning French, where, as top seed, he lost 1r to Bruguera, suffering similarly at the hands of Volkov at the same stage US Open. Altogether in 1990 won 7 titles and reached 5 other finals including ATP World Champ, where he lost to Agassi, having beaten him in rr. Fined 15% of total earnings on ATP tour (excluding GS) for falling 2 tourns short of commitment to the tour. Seeded No.1 GS Cup but lost Chang 1r. Voted Player of the Year. *1991:* Lost his No. 1 ranking to Becker for 3 weeks from 28 Jan after falling to Lendl in sf

Australian Open, but regained the top position 18 Feb after the German was forced to retire in sf Brussels. His unexpected loss to Stich in sf Wimbledon cost him the top ranking again until his 1st US Open title, which he won by playing the best tennis of his life v Courier in f. This took him back to No. 1, where he finished the year. In addition to US Open he won Stuttgart Eurocard, Tokyo Suntory, Queen's (at his 6th attempt), Sydney Indoor and Tokyo Seiko, as well as reaching 2 more f and 4 sf and leading Sweden to victory in World Team Cup. His 6 titles during the year were equalled in the men's game only by Forget. Missed ATP Champs with knee injury, caused by playing too heavy a schedule. *1991 HIGHLIGHTS – SINGLES: Australian Open* sf, seed 1 (d. Poliakov 6–1 7–6 6–2, Masso 6–1 6–2 6–3, Cash 7–6 7–5 6–2, Courier 4–6 6–0 6–4 5–7 6–2, Yzaga 6–2 6–3 6–2, lost Lendl [seed 3] 6–4 5–7 3–6 7–6 6–4), *French Open* qf, seed 1 (d. Wuyts 6–2 6–2 6–3, Skoff 6–4 5–7 7–6 6–3, Chesnokov 6–1 6–4 6–3, Cherkasov 7–6 6–4 6–4, lost Courier [seed 9] 6–4 2–6 6–3 6–4), *Wimbledon* sf, seed 1 (d. Rosset 6–4 6–4 6–4, Pate 6–2 6–2 6–3, Van Rensburg 6–1 6–3 6–2, J. McEnroe [seed 16] 7–6 6–1 6–4, Champion 6–3 6–2 7–5, lost Stich [seed 6] 4–6 7–6 7–6 7–6), *won US Open*, seed 2 (d. Shelton 6–4 2–6 7–6 6–1, Tarango 6–3 7–5 6–0, Grabb 7–6 4–6 6–3 6–4, Chang 7–6 7–5 6–3, J. Sanchez 6–3 6–2 6–3, Lendl [seed 5] 6–3 6–3 6–4, Courier [seed 4] 6–2 6–4 6–0); *won* Stuttgart Eurocard (d. Zoecke 6–4 7–6, Camporese 6–3 7–6, Gustaffson 6–2 6–3, Siemerink 6–4 6–4, Svensson 6–2 3–6 7–5 6–2), *won* Tokyo Suntory (d. Evernden 6–2 7–6, Connors 6–4 6–7 6–1, Stich 7–6 6–3, Chang 7–5 6–2, Lendl 6–1 7–5 6–0), *won* Queen's (d. Boetsch 6–4 6–3, Stoltenberg 6–4 6–4, Cash 6–3 6–4, Washington 6–4 6–2, Wheaton 6–2 6–3), *won* Sydney Indoor (d. Lundgren 6–3 6–4, Woodforde 6–4 6–2, Chang 6–4 7–5, Ivanisevic 4–6 7–6 7–6, B. Gilbert 6–2 6–2 6–2, *won* Tokyo Seiko (d. Pate 6–2 6–4, Fontang 6–2 7–5, Chang 6–2 6–2, Ivanisevic 4–6 7–6 7–5, Rostagno 6–3 1–6 6–2); *r/u* Long Island (d. Garner 6–1 6–1, Lundgren 6–3 6–3, Connors 6–3 4–6 6–4, Delaitre 6–1 7–6, lost Lendl 6–3 6–2), *r/u* Stockholm (d. Lundgren 6–3 6–4, Gilbert 6–2 6–3, Reneberg 6–3 2–6 6–3, Krickstein 6–2 6–2, lost Becker 3–6 6–4 1–6 6–2 6–2); *sf* Brussels (d. Gustafsson 6–0 6–4, Cash 3–6 6–1 6–4, Hlasek 6–1 6–2, lost Forget 3–6 6–0 6–3), *sf* Indian Wells (d. Jaite 6–3 6–2, Cahill 1–6 6–2 7–5, lost Forget 6–4 6–4), *sf* LIPC (d. Derlin 6–2 6–3, Prpic 6–4 6–2, Stich 6–4 2–6 6–4, E. Sanchez 6–2 7–6, lost Wheaton 6–3 6–4), *sf* Los Angeles (d. Krishman 6–4 6–3, Lundgren 6–3 6–4, Krickstein 6–4 7–5, lost B. Gilbert 7–6 6–7 6–4). *1991 HIGHLIGHTS – DOUBLES:* (with Woodbridge) *won* Tokyo Suntory (d. Fitzgerald/Jarryd 6–4 5–7 6–4). *CAREER HIGHLIGHTS – SINGLES: Australian Open – won 1985* (d. Masur 6–7 2–6 7–6 6–4 6–2 [saving 2 mps], Schapers, Lendl 6–7 7–5 6–1 4–6 9–7, Wilander 6–4 6–3 6–3), *won 1987* (d. Mecir 6–1 6–4 6–4, Masur 6–2 6–4 7–6, Cash 6–3 6–4 3–6 5–7 6–3), *r/u 1990* (d. Anderson, Kuhnen, Chamberlain, Svensson 6–2 6–4, Wheaton 7–5 7–6 3–6 6–4, Wilander 6–1 6–1 6–2, lost Lendl 4–6 7–6 5–2 ret'd), *sf 1988* (d. Chesnokov 4–6 7–6 6–4 6–4, lost Wilander 6–0 6–7 6–3 3–6 6–1), *sf 1991; Wimbledon – won 1988* (d. Forget, Reneberg, K. Flach, Youl 6–2 6–4 6–4, Kuhnen 6–3 4–6 6–1 7–6, Mecir 4–6 2–6 6–4 6–3 6–4, Becker 4–6 7–6 6–4 6–2), *won 1990* (d. Dyke, Mecir, Mansdorf 6–4 5–7 3–6 6–2 9–7, Chang 6–3 6–2 6–1, Bergstrom 6–3 6–2 6–4, Lendl 6–1 7–6 6–3, Becker 6–2 6–2 3–6 3–6 6–4), *r/u 1989* (d. Pridham, Woodbridge 6–4 6–4 1–6 7–6, S. Davis 6–3 6–4 4–6 6–2, Mansdorf 6–4 6–3 6–2, Mayotte 7–6 7–6 6–3, J. McEnroe 7–5 7–6 7–6, lost Becker 6–0 7–6 6–4), *sf 1987* (lost Lendl 3–6 6–4 7–6 6–4), *sf 1991; US Open – won 1991, sf 1986* (d. Curren, Krishnan, Goldie, Wilkison 6–3 6–3 6–3, lost Lendl 7–6 6–2 6–3), *sf 1987* (lost Wilander 6–4 3–6 6–3 6–4); *Masters – won 1989* (d. Agassi, Gilbert, Becker in rr, Lendl 7–6 7–5, Becker 4–6 7–6 6–3 6–1); *French Open – r/u 1989* (d. Vajda, Pereira, Arias 6–4 6–4 6–4, Ivanisevic 7–5 6–3 6–3, Mancini 6–1 6–3 7–6, Becker 6–3 6–4 6–3, lost Chang 6–1 3–6 4–6 7–6 4–6 6–2), *qf 191; ATP World Champ – r/u 1990* (d. E. Sanchez, Agassi, Sampras in rr, Lendl 6–4 6–2, lost Agassi 5–7 7–6 7–5 6–2); *LIPC – r/u 1990* (d. Smith, Mansdorf, Steeb, Hlasek 6–7 7–6 7–6, E. Sanchez 6–1 7–5, lost Agassi 6–1 6–4 0–6 6–2); *Olympics – bronze medal 1988* (d. Skoff, Moreno, Hlasek 6–2 6–4 7–6, Cane 6–1 7–5 6–4, lost Mecir 3–6 6–0 1–6 6–4 6–2). *CAREER HIGHLIGHTS – DOUBLES:* (with Jarryd) *Australian Open – won 1987* (d. Doohan/Warder 6–4 6–4 7–6); *US Open – won 1987* (d. Flach/Seguso 7–6 6–2 4–6 5–7 7–6), *r/u 1984* (d. McEnroe/Fleming 3–6 7–6 5–7 7–6, lost Fitzgerald/Smid 7–6 6–3 6–3); *Masters – won 1985* (d. Wilander/Nystrom 4–6 6–2 6–3), *won 1986* (d. Forget/Noah 6–3 7–6 6–3); *French Open – r/u 1986* (lost Fitzgerald/Smid 6–3 4–6 6–3 6–7 14–12).

TOMAS ENQVIST (Sweden)
Born Stockholm, 13 March, 1974, and lives there; RH; 6ft 3in; 185lb; final 1991 ATP ranking 229.
Coached by Martin Bohm. *1990:* R/u French Open Jun to Gaudenzi. *1991:* In Jun singles

won Australian Open over Gleeson, Wimbledon over Joyce and was r/u French Open to Medvedev to finish the year at No. 1 in the ITF Jun singles rankings. In Jun doubles won French Open with Martinelle.

DONNA FABER (USA)
Born East Orange, NJ, 5 July 1971; lives Hilton Head Island, Fla., LH; 2HB; 5ft 4in; 120lb; final 1991 WTA ranking 92; 1991 prize money $57,478.
Coached by her mother, Ofelia. *1987:* (216) R/u Nat 18s. *1988:* (137) Qf Guaruja. *1989:* (60) Sf Auckland then, unseeded, she reached last 16 both Australian Open and US Open, upsetting Mandlikova at Flushing Meadow. *1990:* (114) Made an unexpected appearance in last 16 Australian Open with an upset of Fairbank. *1991:* Appeared in her 1st main tour f at Sao Paulo, reached qf Auckland and upset Lindqvist at LIPC. *1991 HIGHLIGHTS – SINGLES: Australian Open* 3r (d. de Lone 5–7 6–3 6–2, Probst 6–2 6–0, lost K. Maleeva [seed 5] 6–3 6–2), *French Open* 1r (lost Zvereva [seed 15] 6–0 6–0), *Wimbledon* 2r (d. Caverzasio 6–3 6–7 6–2, lost G. Fernandez 7–5 7–5), *US Open* 2r (d. Helgeson 6–4 6–4, lost Magers 6–3 6–3); *r/u* Sao Paulo (d. Spadea 6–3 6–0, Giusto 6–2 5–7 7–6, S. Smith 3–6 6–4 6–2, Labet 3–6 6–3 6–2, lost Martinek 6–2 6–4).

ROSALYN FAIRBANK-NIDEFFER (USA)
Born Durban, South Africa, 2 November 1960; lives San Diego, Cal.; RH; 5ft 8in; 140lb; final 1991 WTA ranking 91; 1991 prize money $108,388.
Married her coach, sports psychologist Bob Nideffer (May 1989) and became a US citizen. *1978:* Seemingly shy and somewhat portly, she displayed extraordinary court sense and a fine flat forehand in her drive to f Orange Bowl, losing to A. Jaeger. *1979:* Established herself firmly on women's tour, winning 22 of 23 matches on Australian satellite tour and reaching f NSW Open. *1980:* (33) Won Wimbledon Plate. *1981:* (43) Won French Open doubles with Harford. *1982:* (17) Won Indianapolis, sf Detroit and Fort Myers. *1983:* (26) Won Richmond. *1984:* (32) Sf VS LA. *1985:* (38) Beat Rehe in San Diego. *1986:* (30) Sf Canadian Open (d. Sabatini) and Brighton, r/u French Open mixed doubles with Edmondson, and sf Wimbledon and US Open doubles with Burgin. *1987:* (37) Reached last 16 Wimbledon, extending Evert to 7–5 fs. *1988:* (37) Reached qf Wimbledon, upsetting McNeil and Zvereva and extending Navratilova to 7–5 3s; sf San Diego and Newport. *1989:* (22) Unseeded, she reached qf Wimbledon again (upset Sabatini and M. J. Fernandez) and last 16 US Open. Sf Eastbourne and Newport in singles and in doubles reached 6 f, winning San Diego. *1990:* (24) Surprised Novotna *en route* to sf San Antonio and G. Fernandez in reaching the same stage at Birmingham. *1991:* Her best performances came at Westchester where she reached sf singles and won the doubles with Gregory. *1991 HIGHLIGHTS – SINGLES: Australian Open* 3r, seed 14 (d. G. Fernandez 6–3 6–2, Tami Whitlinger 6–4 6–1, lost Magdalena Maleeva 6–4 6–3), *Wimbledon* 1r (lost Ily 6–2 3–6 6–0), *US Open* 1r (lost Ritter 6–4 7–6); *sf* Westchester (d. Keller 6–0 6–2, De Lone 7–5 6–1, Raymond 6–3 6–3, lost McNeil 6–3 6–1). *1991 HIGHLIGHTS – DOUBLES:* (with Gregory) *won* Westchester (D. Adams/McNeil 7–5 6–4). *CAREER HIGHLIGHTS – DOUBLES:* (with Harford unless stated) *French Open – won 1981* (d. Reynolds/P. Smith 6–1 6–3), [Reynolds] *won 1983* (d. K. Jordan/A. Smith 5–7 7–5 6–2); *US Open –* [Reynolds] *r/u 1983* (lost Navratilova/Shriver 6–7 6–1 6–3). *MIXED DOUBLES:* (with Edmondson) *French Open – r/u 1986* (lost Flach/K. Jordan 3–6 7–6 6–3).

SILVIA FARINA (Italy)
Born Milan, 27 April 1970, and lives there; RH; 5ft 7½in; final 1991 WTA ranking 68; 1991 prize money $46,412.
1989: (165) Qf Taranto. *1990:* (192). *1991:* Upset Reggi *en route* to her 1st primary circuit f at San Marino and reached sf Taranto. *1991 HIGHLIGHTS – SINGLES: French Open* 1r (lost Novotna [seed 6] 7–5 6–2), *US Open* 1r (lost Rubin 6–4 6–0); *r/u* San Marino (d. Jachia 3–6 6–1 6–2, Tessi 6–2 6–1, Reggi 6–1 7–5, Pampoulova Wagner 6–2 7–6, lost Piccolini 6–2 6–3); *sf* Taranto (d. Piccolini 6–3 6–4, Oremans 6–3 6–3, Labat 2–6 6–3 6–4, lost Ritter 3–6 6–1 6–0).

PATTY FENDICK (USA)
Born Sacramento, Cal., 31 March 1965, and lives there; RH; 5ft 5in; 117lb; final 1991 WTA ranking 55 singles, 10 doubles; 1991 prize money $186,473.
Scar tissue in her eye from an old injury expands and restricts her vision in brightness, obliging her to wear a baseball cap to play tennis. *1983:* Won Wimbledon Jun doubles with Hy, and Orange Bowl 18s singles and doubles. *1984:* Member US Jun Fed Cup team. All-American for Stanford, playing No. 1 on that team. *1985:* (83). *1986:* (94) Sf Wimbledon

doubles with Hetherington and won NCAA singles. *1987:* (78) NCAA Champ for second time. While out of action at end of year with intestinal flu, she worked on the mental aspect of her game with John Whittlinger. *1988:* (22) Won her 1st pro title in Auckland, following with Japan Open, and reached sf on 5 other occasions. Last 16 US Open singles, and r/u in doubles with Hetherington, with whom she won 5 of 6 titles during the year and qualified for VS Champs. *1989:* (31) Out 3 months March–June with shoulder injury, returning to reach last 16 Wimbledon. Won Auckland in both singles and doubles with Hetherington, with whom she was r/u Australian Open and won VS California. *1990:* (42) In singles she upset Novotna and Paulus to reach qf Australian Open and, again unseeded, appeared in last 16 Wimbledon. In doubles was r/u Australian Open with M. J. Fernandez, but was less fortunate at US Open, where both her women's and mixed partners withdrew. With various partners she reached 4 other doubles f, winning 2. Played in winning US Fed Cup team. *1991:* Reached sf Colorado and Amelia Island. In doubles she won her 1st GS title, taking Australian Open with M. J. Fernandez and going on to reach 7 more f, winning 4 with 3 different partners. *1991 HIGHLIGHTS – SINGLES: Australian Open* 1r (lost Takagi 6–2 3–6 6–3), *French Open* 2r (d. Kanellopoulou 6–4 6–2, lost Quentrec 6–1 4–6 6–3), *Wimbledon* 2r (d. Hetherington 7–6 4–6 6–1, lost Ferrando 4–6 6–1 7–5), *US Open* 3r (d. Thoren 6–1 6–4, Habsudova 6–2 6–3, lost Martinez 7–5 6–3); *sf* Colorado (d. S. Martin 6–2 6–1, Collins 6–3 6–4, Cioffi 1–6 7–6 6–4, lost Bollegraf 6–2 6–3), *sf* Amelia Island (d. Faber 6–2 6–1, Tarabini 6–3 0–6 6–1, Schultz 6–3 6–4, Garrison 6–1 6–4, lost Graf 6–0 6–1). *1991 HIGHLIGHTS – DOUBLES:* (with M. J. Fernandez unless stated) *won Australian Open* (d. G. Fernandez/Novotna 7–6 6–1); [Savchenko] *won* Auckland (d. Faull/Richardson 6–3 6–3), [Seles] *won* San Antonio (d. Hetherington/Rinaldi 7–6 6–2), [G. Fernandez] *won* VS California (d. Navratilova/Shriver 6–4 7–5), [G. Fernandez] *won* Indianapolis (d. Adams/Paz 6–4 6–2), [Sukova] *r/u* Brisbane (lost G. Fernandez/Novotna 6–3 6–1), [McNeil] *r/u* Colorado (lost Gregory/Magers 6–4 6–4), *r/u* VS Houston (lost Hetherington/Rinaldi 6–1 2–6 6–1). *CAREER HIGHLIGHTS DOUBLES:* (with M. J. Fernandez unless stated) *Australian Open – won 1991,* [Hetherington] *r/u 1989* (lost Navratilova/Shriver 3–6 6–3 6–2), *r/u 1990* (lost Novotna/Sukova 7–6 7–6); *US Open –* [Hetherington] *r/u 1988* (lost G. Fernandez/R. White 6–4 6–1).

GIGI FERNANDEZ (USA)

Born Puerto Rico, 22 February 1964; lives Aspen, Col.; 5ft 7in; 145lb; final 1991 WTA ranking 22 singles, 4 doubles; 1991 prize money $455,228.
Coached by Julie Anthony. *1983:* (84) Narrowly beaten 7–6 fs by Herr in f AIAW. *1984:* (27) Buoyed by praise she received from Navratilova after coming within two points of upsetting Shriver at Wimbledon, she reached f Newport as 'Lucky Loser' and pushed Navratilova to 2s tb. *1985:* (64) Won LIPC doubles with Navratilova. *1986:* (62) Qualified with R. White for VS Champ doubles in Nov. and in singles won her 1st primary circuit title at Singapore. *1987:* (39) Reached last 16 Wimbledon unseeded, qf VS Florida and San Diego and won 3 doubles titles with McNeil. *1988:* (52) In doubles won US Open and Japan Open with R. White, reaching 7 other f with various partners and qualifying for VS Champs. *1989:* (23) R/u Puerto Rico, sf Eastbourne and Newport in singles; in doubles with various partners reached 8 f, winning 4. *1990:* (36) In singles appeared in last 16 US Open plus sf Puerto Rico and qf Tokyo, San Antonio and Birmingham. In doubles won US Open with Navratilova and with various partners took 4 other titles, reaching 3 more f. Played in winning US Fed Cup team. *1991:* At VS Albuquerque she won her 1st singles title since 1986 and reached sf Eastbourne (d. Novotna); qf US Open, unseeded; upset Sukova 1r Wimbledon and Garrison at VS Houston. Voted WTA Doubles Team of the Year with Novotna: together they won French Open, r/u Australian Open, Wimbledon and VS Champs and reached 5 other f, winning 2. In addition she reached 5 more f with 4 different partners, winning a further 3 to bring a total of 6 titles from 14 f. *1991 HIGHLIGHTS – SINGLES: Australian Open* 1r (lost Fairbank-Nideffer [seed 14] 6–3 6–2), *French Open* 2r (d. Takagi 7–6 6–2, lost McQuillan 6–2 6–2), *Wimbledon* 3r (d. Sukova [seed 11] 4–6 6–1 6–4, Faber 7–5 7–5, lost A. Minter 6–3 6–3), *US Open* qf, unseeded (d. Frankl 6–0 6–4, Rinaldi 6–4 6–1, Meskhi [seed 13] 7–6 6–7 7–6, Zrubakova 6–2 6–2, lost Seles [seed 2] 6–1 6–2); *won* VS Albuquerque (d. O'Reilly 5–7 6–1 6–4, Cioffi 6–4 7–5, L. Ferrando 6–4 7–6, Sloane 6–3 5–7 6–2, Halard 6–0 6–2); *sf* Eastbourne (d. Wamelink 6–7 6–4 6–2, Dechaume 6–4 6–3, Durie 6–3 6–3, Novotna 7–6 6–4, lost Sanchez-Vicario 6–1 6–1). *1991 HIGHLIGHTS – DOUBLES:* (with Novotna unless stated) *r/u Australian Open* (lost Fendick/M. J. Fernandez 7–6 6–1), *won French Open* (d. Savchenko/Zvereva 6–4 6–0), *r/u Wimbledon* (lost Savchenko/Zvereva 6–4 3–6 6–4); *won* Brisbane (d. Fendick/Sukova 6–3 6–1), *won* VS Chicago (d. Navratilova/Shriver 6–2 6–4), [Sukova] *won* Tarpon Springs (d. Savchenko/Zvereva 4–6 6–4 7–6), [Fendick] *won* VS California (d. Navratilova/Shriver 6–4

7–5), [Fendick] **won** Indianapolis (d. Adams/Paz 6–4 6–2); **r/u** Sydney (lost Sanchez-Vicario/Sukova 6–1 6–4), **r/u** LIPC (lost M. J. Fernandez/Garrison 7–5 6–2, **r/u** Eastbourne (lost Savchenko/Zvereva 2–6 6–4 6–4), [Tauziat] **r/u** San Diego (lost Hetherington/Rinaldi 6–4 3–6 6–2), [Zvereva] **r/u** VS Washington (lost Novotna/Savchenko 5–7 6–1 7–6), **r/u** VS Champs (lost Navratilova/Shriver 4–6 7–5 6–4). *CAREER HIGHLIGHTS – DOUBLES:* (with Novotna unless stated) *French Open – won 1991; US Open –* [R. White] *won 1988* (d. Fendick/Hetherington 6–4 6–1), [Navratilova] *won 1990* (d. Novotna/Sukova 6–2 6–4); *Australian Open – r/u 1991; Wimbledon – r/u 1991; VS Champs – r/u 1991; LIPC – r/u 1991.*

MARY JOE FERNANDEZ (USA)

Born Dominican Republic, 19 August 1971; lives Miami, Fla.; RH; 2HB; 5ft 10in; 130lb; final 1991 WTA ranking 8 singles, 5 doubles; 1991 prize money $672,035.
Coached by Dean Goldfeen. *1982:* Won Orange Bowl 12s, beating Sabatini in f. *1983:* Won Orange Bowl 14s, beating Sabatini in sf. *1984:* Won Orange Bowl 16s, US Nat 16, US 16 CC and was ranked 1 in US 16s. *1985:* (99) Won Orange Bowl 18s, ranked second behind Rehe in US 18s. *1986:* (27) Demonstrating her uncanny court sense, her excellent anticipation, her extraordinary determination and formidable flat forehand and two-handed backhand, she stopped 4th-seeded Kohde-Kilsch to reach qf French Open; had other good CC wins over Rehe and Sabatini during year. *1987:* (20) Reached last 16 Wimbledon, qf Geneva and Filderstadt. *1988:* (15) Last 16 Wimbledon and upset Sabatini *en route* to sf both LIPC and Eastbourne. *1989:* (12) Upset Sabatini *en route* to sf French Open; r/u Filderstadt and sf Pan Pacific Open. In doubles r/u US Open with Shriver, and with various partners reached 4 other f, winning VS Dallas. Qualified for VS Champs for 1st time but lost 1r to Navratilova. *1990:* (4) Her year began on a high note at Australian Open, where she was r/u to Graf in singles and r/u with Fendick in doubles. She continued to do well in GS, reaching qf French Open and sf US Open, having missed Wimbledon. In Sept. won her 1st career title at Tokyo Nicherei, following with Filderstadt in Oct. In other tourns she reached sf VS Florida, Barcelona, VS Los Angeles, VS New England and VS Champs to finish the year in the top 5, ahead of Sabatini. *1991:* Reached sf Wimbledon and Australian Open, where she extended Seles to 9–7 fs as she suffered the 1st of 6 defeats during the year at the hands of the new No. 1. R/u VS Houston, Tokyo Ariake; sf Tokyo Pan Pacific, LIPC, Italian Open, Eastbourne, VS Washington and Milan; and qualified for VS Champs, where she lost qf to Seles. Won her 1st GS title when she took Australian Open doubles with Fendick and from 5 more f with various partners she won LIPC with Garrison, with whom she qualified for VS Champs. Recruited Ion Tiriac to improve her game and image, feeling that although she was ranked in the top 5 she was relatively little known. *1991 HIGHLIGHTS – SINGLES: Australian Open* sf, seed 3 (d. Gomer 6–1 6–0, F. Romano 6–1 6–2, Sawamatsu 6 3 6 3, Appelmans [seed 16] 6 3 6 3, K. Maleeva [seed 5] 6 3 6 2, lost M. Seles [seed 2] 6–3 0–6 9–7), *Wimbledon* sf, seed 6 (d. Kamstra 6–2 6–4, Keller 7–6 6–1, Shriver 6–3 7–5, Wiesner [seed 9] 6–0 7–5, Sanchez-Vicario [seed 3] 6–2 7–5, lost Graf [seed 1] 6–2 6–4), *US Open* 3r, seed 5 (d. Savchenko 6–3 6–3, Schultz 7–6 6–3, lost Zrubakova 6–1 6–2); **r/u** VS Houston (d. Cioffi def., Grossman 7–5 7–5, Harvey-Wild 6–0 6–3, lost Seles 6–4 6–3), **r/u** Tokyo Ariake (d. Hy 6–1 6–1, Werdel 6–2 6–3, K. Maleeva 3–6 6–1 6–4, lost Seles 6–1 6–1); **sf** Tokyo Pan Pacific (d. May 6–0 ret'd, Miyagi 6–2 6–0, lost Sabatini 6–3 6–4), **sf** LIPC (d. Keller 6–3 6–2, McNeil 6–1 6–2, Shriver 6–2 6–4, Helgeson 6–1 6–0, lost Seles 6–1 6–0), **sf** Italian Open (d. Jachia 7–5 6–3, Rittner 6–1 6–3, Fulco 6–3 6–2, lost Seles 7–5 2–6 6–4), **sf** Eastbourne (d. Herreman 6–3 2–6 6–1, Gomer 6–2 6–2, Kelesi 6–2 6–4, Basuki 6–2 6–1, lost Navratilova 6–3 6–0), **sf** VS Washington (d. de Swardt 6–4 6–1, G. Fernandez 6–4 3–6 6–3, lost K. Maleeva 6–3 6–4), **sf** Milan (d. Kohde-Kilsch 6–2 6–0, Magdalena Maleeva 5–7 6–3 6–4, lost Navratilova 6–2 3–6 6–4). *1991 HIGHLIGHTS – DOUBLES:* (with Garrison unless stated) [Fendick] *won Australian Open* (d. G. Fernandez/Novotna 7–6 6–1); **won** LIPC (d. G. Fernandez/Novotna 6–5 6–2); [R. White] **r/u** Tokyo Pan Pacific (lost K. Jordan/Smylie 4–6 6–0 6–3), [Fendick] **r/u** VS Houston (lost Hetherington/Rinaldi 6–1 2–6 6–1), [Shriver] **r/u** Tokyo Ariake (d. Cunningham/Gildemeister 6–3 6–3), **r/u** VS Philadelphia (lost Novotna/Savchenko 6–2 6–4). *CAREER HIGHLIGHTS – SINGLES: Australian Open – r/u 1990* (d. Jaggard, Rinaldi, Halard 6–0 3–6 6–3, Faber 6–4 6–2, Garrison 1 6 6 2 8 6, Porwik 6 2 6 1, lost Graf 6–3 6–4), **sf 1991; French Open – sf 1989** (d. Herreman, Farley, Dias, Sabatini 6–4 6–4, Kelesi 6–2 7–5, lost Sanchez-Vicario 6–2 6–2), **qf 1986** (d. Temesvari, Hobbs, Kohde-Kilsch 7–6 7–5, lost Sukova 6–2 6–4), **qf 1990** (d. McDonald, Pierce, Cueto, Grossman 6–3 6–2, lost Capriati 6–2 6–4); *Wimbledon – sf 1991; US Open – sf 1990* (d. Henricksson, Oremans, R. White, Wiesner 6–3 6–2, Maleeva Fragnière 7–5 3–6 6–3, lost Sabatini 7–5 5–7 6–3); *VS Champs*

– *sf 1990* (d. Tauziat, Maleeva Fragnière 6–2 6–4, lost Seles 6–3 6–4). *CAREER HIGHLIGHTS – DOUBLES:* (with Fendick unless stated) *Australian Open – won 1991, r/u 1990* (lost Novotna/Sukova 7–6 7–6; [Garrison] *LIPC – won 1991; US Open –* [Shriver] *r/u 1989* (lost Mandlikova/Navratilova 5–7 6–4 6–4).

LINDA FERRANDO (Italy)
Born Genova, 12 January 1966, and lives there; RH; 5ft 7in; 127lb; final 1991 WTA ranking 96; 1991 prize money $56,371.
Coached by her elder brother, Paulo. *1984:* (294). *1985:* (217) Qf Bastad. *1986:* (253). *1987:* (154). *1988:* (67) Sf Taranto. *1989:* (44) Sf Mahwah; qf Tampa and US HC, where she upset Zvereva. *1990:* (67) Having never before passed 2s in GS, she upset Seles at US Open and advanced to last 16, unseeded. *1991:* Qf VS Albuquerque was her best showing. *1991 HIGHLIGHTS – SINGLES: French Open* 1r (lost Cioffi 7–5 4–6 6–0), *Wimbledon* 3r (d. Date 6–4 3–6 6–2, Fendick 4–6 6–1 7–5, lost Tauziat [seed 12] 6–1 6–1), *US Open* 1r (lost Sawamatsu 6–4 6–2).

WAYNE FERREIRA (South Africa)
Born Johannesburg, 15 September 1971, and lives there; RH; 6ft; 163lb; final 1991 ATP ranking 50; 1991 prize money $302, 205.
1989: (229) Finished the year No. 1 doubles player in ITF Jun Rankings, having won US Open Jun with Stafford and r/u Wimbledon Jun with De Jager. *1990:* (173) Upset Noah 1r Wimbledon. *1991:* In singles reached last 16 Australian Open after qualifying and played qf Sydney Indoor (d. Lendl), Brisbane and Birmingham. In doubles s/f Wimbledon with Norval, winning LIPC with him and Adelaide with Kruger. *1991 HIGHLIGHTS – SINGLES: Australian Open* last 16, unseeded (d. Luna 6–1 6–3 6–2, Wahlgren 6–2 6–4 7–6, Eltingh 6–2 6–4 6–2, lost Becker [seed 2] 6–4 7–6 6–4), *French Open* 2r (d. Steeb 6–4 6–1 6–4, lost Courier [seed 9] 6–2 6–3 6–4), *Wimbledon* 2r (d. Aguilera 6–4 6–3 6–3, lost Van Rensburg 6–4 7–5 6–2), *US Open* 2r (d. Pioline 7–6 4–6 6–2 2–6 6–3, lost Sampras 6–1 6–2 2–2 ret'd). *1991 HIGHLIGHTS – DOUBLES:* (with Norval unless stated) [Kruger] *won* Adelaide (d. Haarhuis/Koevermans 6–4 4–6 6–4), *won* LIPC (d. Flach/Seguso 5–7 7–6 6–2). *CAREER HIGHLIGHTS – DOUBLES:* (with Norval) *LIPC – won 1991*.

JOHN FITZGERALD (Australia)
Born Cummins, 28 December 1960; lives Newport Beach, Cal.; RH; 6ft 1in; 170lb; final 1991 ATP ranking 216 singles, 1 (42) doubles; 1991 prize money $616,493.
Wife Jenny, daughters Elizabeth Jean (born July 1988) and Bridget (born Aug. 1990). *1979:* (301). *1980:* (136) Won $25,000 tourn in Tokyo. *1981:* (60) Last 16 Wimbledon and won Kitzbuhel over Vilas. *1982:* (78) Won Australian Open doubles with Alexander, and in singles won Hawaii and r/u Sydney. *1983:* (35) Last 16 Australian Open, where he won mixed doubles with Sayers, and won Newport and Stowe. Member of winning Australian D Cup team. *1984:* (29) Won Sydney NSW and r/u Melbourne; sf Australian Open doubles with Cash. *1985:* (91) In doubles won Auckland with C. Lewis, Las Vegas with Cash and Sydney Indoor with Jarryd, also reaching f Wimbledon (d. McEnroe/Fleming) and Queens Club, both with Cash. *1986:* (102) Won French Open doubles with Smid. In victorious Australian D Cup squad, winning doubles in f over Edberg/Jarryd with Cash. Married Jenny Harper 18 Nov. *1987:* (73) Underwent shoulder surgery in Feb. Reached 1st f in 3 years at Hong Kong and d. Connors 2r Tokyo Seiko. *1988:* (25) Finally free from his nagging shoulder injury, he enjoyed his best season, winning Sydney. *En route* to f Philadelphia, he upset Lendl, being the 1st player outside the top 50 to do so since F. Gonzalez in Aug. 1984. Beat Gomez and Edberg back-to-back to reach f Tokyo Seiko and appeared in sf Adelaide, Wembley and Brussels. In doubles r/u French Open and Wimbledon with Jarryd, won 4 titles with different partners and qualified for Masters doubles with Jarryd, losing sf to Casal/E. Sanchez. Missed US Open with calf injury. *1989:* (117) Took a 2-month break mid Feb. to April, returning to reach sf Seoul. The high spot of his year came at Wimbledon, where he upset Gilbert to reach last 16 singles and won the doubles with Jarryd, with whom he was also r/u Masters. *1990:* (188) Out 4 weeks April–May with torn calf muscle. In singles reached sf Brisbane; in doubles reached 2 f with Jarryd and was r/u Wimbledon mixed with Smylie. Won doubles (with Cash) in Aust. D Cup wins over France, New Zealand and Argentina but lost vital 3rd rubber in f during 2–3 loss to USA. *1991:* In singles reached qf Queen's and won Bristol Challenger. In doubles with Jarryd, he finished the year with three-quarters of a Grand Slam, having won French Open, Wimbledon and a first US Open, plus ATP Doubles Champ and 2 other titles. *1991 HIGHLIGHTS – SINGLES: Australian Open* 1r (lost Mronz 6–4 6–4 6–4); *won* Bristol Challenger (d. Nyborg 6–2 7–5). *1991 HIGHLIGHTS – DOUBLES:* (with Jarryd unless stated) *won French Open*

(d. R. Leach/Pugh 6–0 7–6), **won Wimbledon** (d. Frana/Lavalle 6–3 6–4 6–7 6–1), **won US Open** (d. Davis/Pate 6–3 3–6 6–3 6–3); **won** Stockholm (d. Nijssen/Suk 7–5 6–2), **won** Paris Open (d. Jones/Leach 3–6 6–3 6–2), **won** ATP Doubles Champ (d. Flach/Seguso 6–4 6–4 2–6 6–4); [Warder] **r/u** Memphis (lost Riglewski/Stich 7–5 6–3), **r/u** Tokyo Suntory (lost Edberg/Woodbridge 6–4 5–7 6–4), [Michibata] **r/u** Brisbane (lost Woodbridge/ Woodforde 7–6 6–3). **CAREER HIGHLIGHTS – DOUBLES:** (with Jarryd unless stated) **Australian Open –** [Alexander] **won 1982** (d. Taygan/Rennert, Andrews/Sadri 6–4 7–6), [Cash] **sf 1984** (lost Nystrom/Wilander 6–4 6–4 2–6 6–3); **French Open –** [Smid] **won 1986** (d. Edberg/Jarryd 6–3 4–6 6–3 6–7 14–12), **won 1991, r/u 1988** (lost Gomez/E. Sanchez 6–3 6–7 6–4 6–3); **Wimbledon – won 1989** (d. R. Leach/Pugh 3–6 7–6 6–4 7–6), **won 1991,** [Cash] **r/u 1985** (d. McEnroe/Fleming, lost Gunthardt/Taroczy), **r/u 1988** (lost Flach/Seguso 6–4 2–6 6–4 7–6); **US Open – won 1991; Masters/ATP Doubles Champ – won 1991, r/u 1989** (lost Grabb/P. McEnroe 7–5 7–6 5–7 6–3); **LIPC – won 1988** (d. Flach/Seguso 7–6 6–1 7–5).

KEN FLACH (USA)
Born St Louis, 24 May 1963, and lives there; RH; 6ft 1in; 165lb; final 1991 ATP ranking 561 singles, 5 (76) doubles; 1991 prize money $284,373.
Wife Sandra, son Dylan Eliot (born Feb. 1988); daughter Madison Lynn (born April 1990). **1983:** All-American at Southern Ill. Univ. with Seguso. **1984:** (154) In doubles with Seguso won Italian Open, US Pro, US CC, Los Angeles, Hong Kong, Taipei and WCT London. **1985:** (60) With Seguso won US Open, Fort Myers, WCT Forest Hills, Queen's Club, US CC, Canadian Open, Tokyo Seiko. **1986:** (223) Won mixed doubles with K. Jordan at French Open and Wimbledon. Married Sandra Freeman 9 Sept. **1987:** (100) Last 16 US Open and qf Livingston in singles; won Wimbledon and r/u US Open and Masters in doubles with Seguso. **1988:** (203) In doubles with Seguso won Wimbledon, Olympic gold medal and 3 other tourns; qualified for Masters but failed to make the knockout rounds. **1989:** (11) In doubles with Seguso r/u US Open and won 2 titles, but tore ankle ligament at Wembley and was forced to withdraw from Masters. **1990:** (222). **1991:** At Tampa in May, the old partnership of Flach/Seguso won their first title since 1989, following with Cincinnati and Indianapolis to qualify for ATP Doubles Champ, where they reached f. Recalled, with Seguso, to D Cup duty for f v France in Lyon but lost to inspired Leconte and Forget 6–1 6–4 4–6 6–2 as France win 3–1. This was only their second defeat in 12 D Cup rubbers since 1985 (not selected 1990). **1991 HIGHLIGHTS – DOUBLES:** (with Seguso unless stated) **won** Tampa (d. Pate/Reneberg 6–7 6–4 6–1), **won** Cincinnati (d. Connell/Michibata 6–7 6–4 7–5), **won** Indianapolis (d. Kinnear/Salumaa 7–6 6–4); **r/u** LIPC (lost Ferreira/Norval 5–7 7–6 6–2), **r/u** Washington (lost Davis/Pate 6–4 6–2), [Nargiso] **r/u** Long Island (lost Jelen/Steeb 0–6 6–4 7–6), **r/u** ATP Doubles Champ (lost Fitzgerald/Jarryd 6–4 6–4 2–6 6–4) **CAREER HIGHLIGHTS – DOUBLES:** (with Seguso) **Wimbledon – won 1987** (d. Casal/E. Sanchez 3–6 6–7 7–6 6–1 6–4), **won 1988** (d. Fitzgerald/Jarryd 6–4 2–6 6–4 7–6); **US Open – won 1985** (d. Noah/Leconte 7–6 6–7 7–6 6–0), **r/u 1987** (lost Edberg/Jarryd 7–6 6–2 4–6 5–7 7–6), **r/u 1989** (lost J. McEnroe/Woodforde 6–4 4–6 6–3 6–3); **Olympics – gold medal 1988** (d. Casal/E. Sanchez 6–3 6–4 6–7 6–7 9–7); **Masters/ATP Doubles Champ – r/u 1987** (d. Mecir/Smid 6–4 7–5 6–7 6–3, **r/u 1991**; **LIPC – r/u 1991. MIXED DOUBLES:** (with K. Jordan) **French Open – won 1986** (d. Edmondson/Fairbank 3–6 6–7 6–3); **Wimbledon – won 1986** (d. Gunthardt/Navratilova 6–3 7–6).

JEAN-PHILIPPE FLEURIAN (France)
Born Paris, 11 September 1965, and lives there; RH; 6ft 1in; 175lb; final 1991 ATP ranking 73; 1991 prize money $151,668.
1985: (151). **1986:** (78) R/u Itaparica in 1st GP f. **1987:** (129) Sf Seoul. **1988:** (108) Gained his best results on the Challenger circuit. **1989:** (78) Sf Bordeaux and Sao Paulo. **1990:** (67) Reached sf Adelaide and scored 2 big upsets, removing E. Sanchez 1r Australian Open and Becker 3r LIPC. **1991:** R/u Auckland (upsetting E. Sanchez) and sf Umag. **1991 HIGHLIGHTS – SINGLES: Australian Open** 2r (d. Furlan 6–1 6–0 6–0, lost Eltingh 6–1 3–6 7–6 3–6 6–1), **French Open** 1r (lost Korda 4–6 6–4 6–2 6–4), **Wimbledon** 3r (d. Mronz 6–4 6–0 6–3, Skoff 6–2 6–0 6–3, lost J. McEnroe [seed 16] 6–2 7–6 6–1), **US Open** 1r (lost Simian 6–1 6–7 3–6 6–4 6–2); **r/u** Auckland (d. Steven 2–6 6–1 6–2, Jelen 6–3 6–1, E. Sanchez 6–2 7–6, Mattar 3–6 6–4 6–3, lost Novacek 7–6 7–6); **sf** Umag (d. Fernandez 6–2 7–6, R. Gilbert 6–3 6–2, Vajda 6–3 6–2, lost Poliakov 4–6 6–4 6–2).

FREDERIC FONTANG (France)
Born Casablanca, Morocco, 18 March 1970; lives Paris; RH; 5ft 11in; 143lb; final 1991 ATP ranking 59; 1991 prize money $131,440.

1989: (371) Won North African Satellite circuit. *1990:* (215) Made his mark on the Challenger circuit, but without taking a title. *1991:* At San Marino, having won his 1st main draw match, he went all the way to f, upsetting Arrese on the way, and followed in September with his first GP title at Palermo, where he d. E. Sanchez in f. *1991 HIGHLIGHTS – SINGLES: French Open* 1r (lost Ivanisevic [seed 8] 6–4 1–6 6–3 6–1); *won* Palermo (d. Medvedev 4–6 6–3 6–4, Furlan 6–2 6–3, Cierro 6 1 7 6, Arrese 6 3 2 6 7–6, E. Sanchez 1–6 6–3 6–3), *won* Merano Challenger (d. Costa 6–3 6–3); *r/u* San Marino (d. Nastase 6–3 6–4, Arrese 6–3 6–0, Mezzadri 6–4 6–0, Azar 6–2 6–2, lost Perez-Roldan 6–3 6–1).

GUY FORGET (France)
Born Casablanca, Morocco, 4 January 1965; lives Marseilles and Neuchatel, Switzerland; LH; 6ft 3in; 177lb; final 1991 ATP ranking 7 singles, 84 doubles; 1991 prize money $1,401,772.
Wife Isabelle (married May 1989); son Mathieu (born Oct. 1989). *1982:* (70) Was world's second best Jun, winning Orange Bowl in Dec. and making presence felt on GP tour. *1983:* (188) String of 1r losses as he joined men's tour. *1984:* (36) Confidence restored by reaching 3r Wimbledon and last 16 Australian Open where he beat V. Amritraj (seed 15). Qf Queen's, Bordeaux, Stockholm and Wembley where he beat Jarryd and Becker. *1985:* (61) Despite sf appearances in Gstaad and Toulouse, he suffered a hard year. *1986:* (25) Reached last 16 French Open where he held m-p before bowing to Vilas. Won Toulouse, as his grandfather (1946) and father (1966) had done, and lifted his ranking again. R/u Masters doubles with Noah. *1987:* (54) Last 16 Wimbledon, d. his doubles partner Noah, with whom he was r/u French Open and won 5 titles. *1988:* (48) Sf Nice and Queen's and upset Zivojinovic at Olympics. In doubles won 3 titles with different partners. *1989:* (36) Won Nancy for 1st title since Toulouse 1986. Underwent surgery on his left knee in April, returning to action at Geneva in Sept. and upset J. McEnroe *en route* to f Wembley in Nov. *1990:* (16) Broke into top 20 in his most successful year to date in which he reached last 16 Wimbledon and won Bordeaux, overcoming the trauma of the death of his father before qf and funeral before sf and playing on at the insistence of his mother. Also reached f Nice and sf Hamburg and Long Island. In Feb. formed a successful doubles duo with Hlasek, with whom he won IBM/ATP World Doubles (for which both shaved their heads) and 4 other titles (plus a 6th with Becker). *1991:* Improving even on his previous year's performance, and feeling more relaxed, he broke into the top 10 for the 1st time and in April moved as high as 4. He won Sydney NSW, Brussels (upset Edberg), Cincinnati (d. Becker and Sampras as he took his 1st title in US), Bordeaux (where he also won the doubles with Boetsch), Toulouse, and Paris Open (d. Sampras), taking more titles during the year than any other man. In GS reached qf both Australian Open and Wimbledon but progressed no further and in ATP World Champ he did not pass rr. Won decisive 4th rubber v Sampras 7–6 3–6 6–3 6–4 to clinch 3–1 French victory in D Cup f v USA in Lyon after nervously losing opening rubber to Agassi 6–7 6–2 6–1 6–2. This was first French success since 1932. *1991 HIGHLIGHTS – SINGLES: Australian Open* qf, seed 10 (d. Skoff 7–6 6–2 6–4, Mronz 6–7 6–4 6–4 6–2, Stich 7–6 7–6 4–6 6–3, Woodbridge 6–3 3–6 6–3 6–4, lost Becker [seed 2] 6–2 7–6 6–3), *French Open* last 16, seed 7 (d. Washington 7–5 2–6 7–5 1–6 7–5, Arias 6–3 6–2 5–7 7–6, Ondruska 6–1 6–4 3–6 6–3, lost Chang [seed 10] 6–1 6–1 4–6 6–3), *Wimbledon* qf, seed 7 (d. Bloom 2–6 7–6 7–5 6–7 6–4, Gustafsson 6–4 6–3 6–4, Leconte 3–6 4–6 6–1 4–1 ret'd, Mayotte 6–7 7–5 6–2 6–4, lost Becker [seed 2] 6–7 7–6 6–2 7–6), *US Open* 2r, seed 7 (d. Ondruska 7–5 6–3 6–1, lost Siemerink 4–6 6–3 6–2 7–6); *won* Sydney NSW (d. S. Davis 6–3 6–3, Woodbridge 6–1 6–0, Santoro 6–1 6–2, Rostagno 6–0 6–2, Stich 6–3 6–4), *won* Brussels (d. Mansdorf 4–6 6–3 6–3, Masso 6–1 6–2, Rosset 6–2 7–5, Edberg 3–6 6–0 6–3, Cherkasov 6–3 7–5 3–6 7–6), *won* Cincinnati (d. Ondruska 6–2 6–2, Pozzi 6–4 6–4, Rostagno 7–6 6–4, Becker 7–6 4–6 6–3, Sampras 2–6 7–6 6–4), *won* Bordeaux (d. R. Gilbert 6–2 6–1, Kuhnen 6–3 6–2, Jonsson 6–3 6–3, Pioline 6–3 6–4, Delaitre 6–1 6–3), *won* Toulouse (d. Carlsson 6–4 6–4, Champion 6–1 3–6 6–3, Rosset 3–6 6–3 6–3, Krajicek 7–6 3–6 6–4, Mansdorf 6–2 7–6), *won* Paris Open (d. P. McEnroe 6–3 6–2, Rostagno 4–6 6–3 6–1, Camporese 6–1 3–6 6–3, Svensson 7–5 6–4, Sampras 7–6 4–6 5–7 6–4 6–4); *r/u* Indian Wells (d. Carbonell 6–1 6–3, Rostagno 6–3 6–1, S. Davis 7–5 6–1, Edberg 6–4 6–4, lost Courier 4–6 6–3 4–6 6–3 7–6); *sf* Stuttgart Eurocard (d. Aguilera 6–2 6–3, Hlasek 7–6 7–6, Ivanisevic 7–5 7–6, lost Svensson 2–6 7–6 6–2). *1991 HIGHLIGHTS – DOUBLES:* [Boetsch] *won* Bordeaux (d. Kuhnen/Mronz 6–2 6–2); [Leconte] *r/u* Indian Wells (lost Courier/J. Sanchez 7–6 3–6 6–3), [Hlasek] *r/u* Gstaad (lost Muller/Visser 7–6 6–4). *CAREER HIGHLIGHTS – SINGLES: Australian Open – qf 1991; Wimbledon – qf 1991. CAREER HIGHLIGHTS – DOUBLES: French Open –* [Noah]

r/u 1987 (lost Jarryd/Seguso 6–7 6–7 6–3 6–4 6–2); ***IBM/ATP World Doubles –*** [Hlasek] ***won 1990*** (d. Casal/E. Sanchez 6–4 7–6 5–7 6–4).

MANUELA MALEEVA FRAGNIÈRE (Switzerland)
Born Sofia, Bulgaria, 14 February 1967; lives Bourg-Dessous; RH; 2HB; 5ft 8in; 127lb; final 1991 WTA ranking 10; 1991 prize money $316,003.
Coached by her husband, Swiss coach François Fragnière (married Dec. 1987). Daughter of Yulia Berberian, 9 times Bulgarian women's champion; sister of Katerina and Magdalena. Played for Switzerland from Jan. 1990. ***1981:*** Won Orange Bowl 14s. ***1982:*** (60) This stylish groundstroker made inroads in women's events but concluded jun career on sad note when her mother ordered her of the court as she trailed Bassett 3–6 3–4 in Orange Bowl f at Miami Beach. ***1983:*** (31) Upsets of Mandlikova and Bunge signalled her swift advance. ***1984:*** (6) In her most productive season, she won 5 tourns, including Italian Open, on the last day of which she completed qf win over Ruzici and then dismissed Bassett and Evert Lloyd. Voted Most Impressive Newcomer. ***1985:*** (7) Won Tokyo Pacific to close year with her only singles title. ***1986:*** (8) Reached qf or better in 11 of 22 tournaments entered, including US Open qf, and joined sister Katerina and mother Yulia to represent Bulgaria in Fed Cup at Prague. ***1987:*** (8) Upset Evert FC Cup and at Wild Dunes won 1st Tourn since 1985, qualifying for VS Champs, where she reached sf. ***1988:*** (6) Won Kansas and Arizona, qf US Open and VS Champs and won Olympic bronze medal. ***1989:*** (9) Won Indian Wells and Geneva; sf VS Dallas, Brighton and VS Chicago. At VS Champs lost qf to Sanchez-Vicario. In GS reached qf French Open and US Open. ***1990:*** (9) Reached qf French Open, where she took Seles to 3s, and same stage US Open, upsetting Navratilova on the way. R/u VS Chicago, San Antonio and San Diego and appeared in 5 more sf. Qualified for VS Champs, where she fell in qf to M. J. Fernandez. ***1991:*** Won her 1st title for 2 years at Linz, where she took both singles and doubles, and followed with Geneva and Bayonne. R/u Barcelona (upset Sanchez-Vicario); sf San Antonio (extended Seles to 3s), Toronto and VS California. Qualified for VS Champs, where she lost Novotna 1r. ***1991 HIGHLIGHTS – SINGLES: Australian Open*** 2r, seed 8 (d. Faull 6–2 6–0, lost A. Huber 6–4 6–4), ***French Open*** 2r, seed 9 (d. N. Dahlman 6–2 6–2, lost Rajchrtova 6–4 6–0), ***US Open*** last 16, seed 10 (d. Birch 6–3 6–1, Strnadova 7–5 6–2, Pierce 4–6 6–1 5–1 ret'd, lost Navratilova [seed 6] 7–6 1–6 6–2); ***won*** Linz (d. Mothes 6–0 6–1, Thoren 6–1 6–3, Maniokova 6–2 6–2, Rajchrtova 6–2 6–3, Langrova 6–4 7–6), ***won*** Geneva (d. Habsudova 6–1 2–6 6–1, Stafford 6–4 6–3, Tami Whitlinger 6–1 6–3, Kelesi 6–3 3–6 6–3), ***won*** Bayonne (d. Housset 6–0 6–1, Kohde-Kilsch 6–0 6–2, Halard 6–3 6–4, McQuillan 7–6 6–4, Meskhi 4–6 6–3 6–4); ***r/u*** Barcelona (d. Jagerman 7–5 6–3, Frankl 6–0 6–1, Zardo 6–3 7–5, Sanchez-Vicario 2–6 7–5 6–3, lost Martinez 6–4 6–1); ***sf*** San Antonio (d. May 6–1 6–2, Demongeot 6–2 6–2, McNeil 6–3 6–4, lost Seles 6–2 2–6 6–2), ***sf*** Toronto (d. Hiraki 7–5 6–0, Rajchrtova 6–1 6–2, Frazier 6–2 7–6, lost K. Maleeva 6–4 1–0 ret'd), ***sf*** VS California (d. Paz 6–2 6–3, Frazier 6–3 6–2, lost Seles 6–2 6–1). ***1991 HIGHLIGHTS – DOUBLES:*** [Reggi] ***won*** Linz (d. Langrova/Zrubakova 6–4 1–6 6–3); [Caverzasio] ***r/u*** Geneva (lost Provis/Smylie 6–1 6–2). ***CAREER HIGHLIGHTS – SINGLES: Olympics – bronze medal 1988*** (d. Reggi 6–3 6–4, lost Sabatini 6–1 6–1); ***VS Champs –*** sf 1987 (lost Sabatini 6–3 4–6 6–3); ***Australian Open –*** qf 1985 (lost Evert Lloyd 6–3 6–3); ***French Open –*** qf 1985 (lost Sabatini 6–3 3–6 6–1), ***qf 1989*** (d. Smylie, Wasserman, Savchenko 6–1 6–2, J. Thompson 7–6 6–2, lost Seles 6–3 7–5); ***Wimbledon –*** qf 1984 (lost Navratilova 6–3 6–2); ***US Open –*** qf 1986 (d. Kohde-Kilsch 6–2 2–6 7–6, lost Evert Lloyd 6–2 6–2), ***qf 1988*** (d. Potter 6–3 6–2, lost Evert 3–6 6–4 6–2), ***qf 1989*** (d. Werdel, Cueto, Tauziat, Zvereva 6–2 6–0, lost Navratilova 6–0 6–0).

JAVIER FRANA (Argentina)
Born Rafaela, 25 December 1966; lives Buenos Aires; LH; 6ft; 164lb; final 1991 ATP ranking 66; 1991 prize money $232,306.
Coached by Ricardo Cano. ***1986:*** (143). ***1987:*** (137) Won Santiago Challenger. ***1988:*** (85) R/u Itaparica (d. E. Sanchez), qf Florence and Sao Paulo. ***1989:*** (174) Sf Charleston. ***1990:*** (184) Enjoyed his greatest success in doubles, winning Guaruja with Luza and won all 3 doubles matches for ARG in World Team Cup. ***1991:*** Came from behind in 3 matches at Guaruja Bliss in Oct. to win 1st GP singles title; he had already broken into top 100 during summer, following r/u Newport and sf US CC. Reached 4 doubles f with 3 different partners, winning in Los Angeles with Pugh. ***1991 HIGHLIGHTS – SINGLES: Australian Open*** 1r (lost Dosedel 7–5 2–6 6–3 6–3), ***Wimbledon*** 3r (d. Roese 3–6 2–6 6–3 6–3 6–3, Curren 7–6 6–2 6–2, lost Novacek [seed 14] 6–4 6–4 5–7 6–4), ***US Open*** 2r (d. Engel 6–3 6–4 6–4, lost Larsson 4–6 6–4 6–2 6–4); ***won*** Guaruja Bliss (d. Marcelino 7–6 6–2,

Perez-Roldan 6–2 7–6, Ruah 4–6 6–4 7–6, Roig 1–6 6–3 6–0, Zoecke 2–6 7–6 6–3); *r/u* Newport (d. Mercer 7–5 6–2, Palmer 6–1 6–3, Layendecker 6–3 6–4, Kratzmann 6–2 4–6 7–5, lost Shelton 3–6 6–4 6–4); *sf* US CC (d. Garrow 7–6 6–3, Pearce 6–4 6–2, Arraya 6–4 ret'd, lost Arias 3–6 6–3 7–5). *1991 HIGHLIGHTS – DOUBLES:* (with Lavalle unless stated) *r/u Wimbledon* (lost Fitzgerald/Jarryd 6–3 6–4 6–7 6–1); [Pugh] **won** Los Angeles (d. Michibata/Pearce 7–5 2–6 6–4); [Stool] *r/u* Newport (lost Pozzi/Steven 6–4 6–4), *r/u* Tel Aviv (lost Rikl/Schapers 6–2 6–7 6–3), *r/u* Buzios (lost Casel/E. Sanchez 4–6 6–3 6–4).

AMY FRAZIER (USA)
Born St Louis, Mo., 19 September 1972; lives Rochester Hills, Mich.; RH; 2HB; 5ft 8in; 130lb; final 1991 WTA ranking 28; 1991 prize money $148,936.
Won 7 Nat Jun titles. *1986:* (331). *1987:* (202) Won Kona on USTA circuit. *1988:* (55) Sf Guaruja; qf LA (d. Shriver and Magers), Kansas and Indianapolis (d. Kelesi). *1989:* (33) Won 1st primary circuit singles title at VS Kansas; sf Albuquerque (d. Maleeva Fragnière) and VS Indianapolis. *1990:* (16) Won VS Oklahoma and was r/u Tokyo Nicherei, where she beat Seles and K. Maleeva back-to-back and extended M. J. Fernandez to 3s. In other tourns reached sf Indian Wells and Sydney, where she upset Novotna and took Zvereva to 3s, and upset Fairbank Nideffer at Wimbledon. *1991:* Reached sf Tokyo Nicherei; qf VS Chicago, Tokyo Suntory, Toronto and VS California; last 16 Australian Open and Wimbledon. *1991 HIGHLIGHTS – SINGLES: Australian Open* last 16, [seed 13] (d. McDonald 6–3 6–4, Leand 6–3 6–0, Cunningham 3–6 6–2 6–2, lost Sanchez-Vicario [seed 6] 6–3 6–2), *Wimbledon* last 16, [seed 15] (d. Kschwendt 7–6 6–4, R. White 7–5 6–4, Werdel 6–2 6–1, lost Graf [seed 1] 6–2 6–1), *US Open* 2r (d. Wood 6–3 7–6, lost Labat 2–6 7–5 6–2); *sf* Tokyo Nicherei (d. Sawamatsu 6–1 0–6 6–3, Graham 7–5 6–1, lost Seles 6–4 6–0). *1991 HIGHLIGHTS – DOUBLES:* (with Kidowaki) **won** Tokyo Suntory (d. Kamio/Kijimuta 6–2 6–4).

RICHARD FROMBERG (Australia)
Born Ulverstone, Tas., 28 April 1970; lives Newtown, Tas.; RH; 6ft 3in; 168lb; final 1991 ATP ranking 93; 1991 prize money $155,274.
Played in winning World Youth Cup team in 1985 and 1986. Member BP Achiever Squad. Coach Ray Ruffels. *1988:* (103) Qf Brisbane and r/u Australian Open Jun doubles with J. Anderson. *1989:* (126) Won Bahia Challenger. *1990:* (32) Reached f Singapore then won 1st tour title at Bologna, following with Bastad. Joined Australian D Cup squad for f v USA, where he took Agassi to 5s in 1st rubber and beat Chang in dead 5th rubber. *1991:* Began the year in style by winning Wellington, followed by qf showing at Italian Open. Sidelined for 5 weeks in July/August with rotator cuff tendonitis, he returned to reach qf Indianapolis and Brisbane. *1991 HIGHLIGHTS – SINGLES: Australian Open* 2r (d. Doohan 6–4 7–6 7–5, lost Gilbert [seed 7] 4–6 6–4 6–4 4–6 6–0), *French Open* 1r (lost Filippini 6–4 3–6 6–1 6–2), *Wimbledon* 1r (lost Lundgren 6–4 7–6 6–2), *US Open* 1r (lost Wheaton [seed 11] 6–0 4–6 7–6 6–3); **won** Wellington (d. Herrera 7–5 6–2, Vajda 6–2 6–2, Krishnan 5–7 6–4 7–5, Bergstrom 6–3 5–7 7–6, Jonsson 6–1 6–4 6–4).

BETTTINA FULCO (Argentina)
Born Mar Del Plata, 23 October 1968; lives there and Key Biscayne, Fla.; RH; 5ft 3in; 120lb; final 1991 WTA ranking 81; 1991 prize money $72,074.
Coached by Patricio Apey. Husband Pablo Villella (married Nov. 1991). *1986:* (118) Won 3 singles title on Italian circuit. *1987:* (46) Sf Wild Dunes, qf Argentine Open. *1988:* (24) Upset Mandlikova *en route* to qf French Open; reached f Barcelona and 5 sf. *1989:* (47) Sf Hamburg (d. Manuela Maleeva) and Italian Open (d. Reggi). *1990:* (127) Last 16 LIPC was her best showing. *1991:* Upset Cecchini at VS Florida, surprised Paz and Maleeva Fragnière *en route* to qf Italian Open and won 2 doubles titles. *1991 HIGHLIGHTS – SINGLES: French Open* 3r (d. Smylie 6–4 6–0, Tessi 6–2 6–2, lost Sanchez-Vicario [seed 5] 6–1 6–1), *Wimbledon* 2r (d. de Lone 2–6 6–2 6–4, lost Shriver 6–0 6–3), *US Open* 2r (d. E. Reinach 6–2 4–6 7–6, lost Durie 6–4 6–0). *1991 HIGHLIGHTS – DOUBLES:* [Sviglerova] **won** Sao Paulo (d. Pierce/Spadea 7–5 6–4), [Jagerman] **won** Kitzbuhel (d. Cecchini/Tarabini 7–5 6–4). *CAREER HIGHLIGHTS – SINGLES: French Open – qf 1988* (d. Mandlikova 6–4 6–3, Zrubakova, Martinez 6–2 6–4, lost Graf 6–0 6–1).

RENZO FURLAN (Italy)
Born Conegliano, 17 May 1970; lives Codogne; RH; 5ft 8in; 150lb; final 1991 ATP ranking 52; 1991 prize money $153,920.
1988: (374). *1989:* (222) Qf San Marino. *1990:* (77) Won Tampere Challenger; qf San Remo (d. Agenor) San Marino and Geneva. *1991:* Reached his 1st GP sf at San Marino,

plus qf Estoril, Nice, Athens and Hilversum. Upset E. Sanchez 1r Madrid and Lendl 2r Hamburg. *1991 HIGHLIGHTS – SINGLES: Australian Open* 1r (lost Fleurian 6–1 6–0 6–0), *French Open* 1r (lost Dosedel 6–3 6–0 6–2), *Wimbledon* 1r (lost Rostagno 6–0 6–3 6–4); *sf* San Marino (d. Miniussi 6–3 6–1, Pambianco 6–4 6–2, Davin 6–2 6–3, lost Perez-Roldan 6–2 6–2).

PATRICK GALBRAITH (USA)
Born Tacoma, Wash., 16 April 1967, and lives there; RH; 6ft; 160lb; final 1991 ATP ranking 670 singles, 9(20) doubles; 1991 prize money $191,802.
A 3-time All-American at UCLA in doubles with Garrow, with whom he won NCAA doubles in 1988. *1989:* (438) Won Newport doubles with Garrow. *1990:* (581) Playing with various partners, he reached 3 doubles f, winning 2. *1991:* Continuing to make his mark in doubles, he won 3 titles with Witsken and a 4th with Jarryd. Qualified with Witsken for ATP Doubles Champ, but they were eliminated after rr. *1991 HIGHLIGHTS – DOUBLES:* (with Witsken unless stated) [Jarryd] *won* Rotterdam (d. Devries/MacPherson 7–6 6–2), *won* Hong Kong (d. Michibata/Van't Hof 6–2 6–4), *won* Munich (d. Jarryd/Visser 7–5 6–4), *won* Montreal (d. Connell/Michibata 6–4 3–6 6–1).

ZINA GARRISON (USA)
Born Houston, 16 November 1963, and lives there; RH; 5ft 4½in; 128lb; final 1991 WTA ranking 12 singles, 12 doubles; 1991 prize money $435,859.
Husband Willard Jackson Jr (married Sept. 1989). Coached by Willis Thomas until Aug. that year when Angel Lopez took over. During 1990 Sherwood Stewart took on that role. Discovered by John Wilkerson in public parks programme in Houston. *1981:* Won Wimbledon and US Open Jun. *1982:* (16) Qf French Open and last 16 Wimbledon. *1983:* (10) Sf Australian Open, Eastbourne and Detroit. *1984:* (9) Won Zurich; r/u VS Washington and New Orleans. *1985:* (8) Won WTA Champs (d. Mandlikova and Evert Lloyd), sf Wimbledon and r/u US CC. *1986:* (11) Won 48 of 69 matches as she won VS Indianapolis, reached f Tampa and sf Canadian Open. *1987:* (9) Suffering stress fracture to foot, was obliged to pull out of French Open and missed Wimbledon. Won NSW Open and VS California, reached f Canadian Open, 5 sf, and qf Australian Open. In doubles was r/u Australian Open with McNeil and won Australian Open mixed with Stewart. Qualified for VS Champs in singles and doubles. *1988:* (9) Qf Wimbledon, where she won mixed doubles with Stewart, and sf US Open, where she d. Navratilova for 1st time in 22 meetings. At Olympics won bronze medal in singles and gold in doubles with Shriver. Qualified for VS Champs singles, but lost 1r to Sukova. *1989:* (4) Won first singles title for 2 years at VS Cal, following with Newport and Chicago as well as reaching 4 more f. At US Open ended Evert's GS career *en route* to sf, reached qf Australian Open and at VS Champs fell qf to Sabatini. In doubles won 4 titles with K. Adams and in mixed was r/u Australian Open with Stewart. *1990:* (10) The high point of her career came at Wimbledon, where she beat Seles and Graf back-to-back before losing f to Navratilova, becoming the 1st black woman to reach f there since Althea Gibson in 1950. Reached qf Australian Open and US Open; won Birmingham; r/u VS Washington and Puerto Rico; sf VS Chicago, Houston, San Diego, Los Angeles and VS California. In doubles won Washington with Navratilova, San Diego with Fendick and Filderstadt with M. J. Fernandez; in mixed won Wimbledon and r/u Australian Open. Played in winning US Fed Cup team and qualified for VS Champs, where she lost 1r to Martinez. *1991:* Qualified for VS Champs in both singles (lost 1r to Sanchez-Vicario) and doubles (with M. J. Fernandez). Her best showing in GS was qf Wimbledon; r/u VS Chicago and Brighton; sf Sydney, Eastbourne and Birmingham. In doubles won LIPC with M. J. Fernandez and reached 2 more f. *1991 HIGHLIGHTS – SINGLES: Australian Open* last 16, [seed 7] (d. Stubbs 6–2 6–0, Miyagi 2–6 6–0 6–2, Dechaume 6–2 6–4, lost Novotna [seed 10] 7–6 6–4), *French Open* 1r, [seed 8] (lost Sawamatsu 6–4 6–0), *Wimbledon* qf, [seed 8] (d. Gomer 6–3 6–3, Pampoulova 6–3 6–1, Strandlund 6–3 6–3, A. Huber [seed 14] 4–6 6–3 6–0, lost Graf [seed 1] 6–1 6–3, *US Open* last 16 [seed 12] (d. Appelmans 7–5 6–4, Cecchini 6–1 6–1, Rittner 6–2 3–6 6–4, lost Martinez [seed 8] 6–4 6–4); *r/u* VS Chicago (d. Harvey-Wild 6–3 6–3, Fairbank Nideffer 6–2 6–2, K. Maleeva 6–2 1–6 6–1, Kelesi 6–1 6–2, lost Navratilova 6–1 6–2), *r/u* Brighton (d. Pfaff 6–1 6–3, Fairbank Nideffer 6 4 6 4, Zrubakova 6–3 6–2, Lindqvist 6–1 1–0 rct'd, lost Graf 5–7 6–4 6–1); *sf* Sydney (d. Rinaldi 6–1 6–3, Fairbank Nideffer 6–3 6–3, Zvereva 6–4 6–3, lost Sanchez-Vicario 6–2 7–5), *sf* Eastbourne (d. Paradis Mangon 6–4 6–3, Gomer 4–6 6–2 6–4, de Swardt 6–3 6–4, lost Zvereva 2–6 7–6 8–6), *sf* Birmingham (d. Paradis Mangon 6–4 6–3, Gomer 4–6 6–2 6–4, de Swardt 6–3 6–4, lost Zvereva 2–6 7–6 8–6). *1991 HIGHLIGHTS – DOUBLES:* (with M. J. Fernandez unless stated) *won* LIPC (d. G. Fernandez/Novotna 7–5

6–2); [McNeil] **r/u** Brighton (lost Shriver/Zvereva 6–1 6–2), **r/u** VS Philaldephia (lost Novotna/Savchenko 6–2 6–4). **CAREER HIGHLIGHTS – SINGLES: Wimbledon – r/u 1990** (d. S. Smith, Dahlman, Leand, Sukova 6–3 6–3, Seles 3–6 6–3 9–7, Graf 6–3 3–6 6–4, lost Navratilova 6–4 6–1), **sf 1985** (d. Tanvier, Van Nostrand, lost Navratilova 6–4 7–6), **qf 1988** (d. Sabatini 6–1 3–6 6–2, lost Shriver 6–4 6–4), **qf 1991**; **USCC – r/u 1983** (lost Tomosvari 6–2 6–2), **r/u 1985** (lost Tomosvari 7–6 6–3); **Olympics – bronze medal 1988** (lost Graf 6–2 6–0); **Australian Open – sf 1983** (d. Pfaff, Turnbull 6–2 7–6, lost K. Jordan 7–6 6–1), **qf 1985** (d. Henricksson, lost Mandlikova 2–6 6–3 6–3), **qf 1989** (lost Sabatini 6–4 2–6 6–4), **qf 1990** (d. Kijimuta, Thoren, Demongest 5–7 6–3 6–4, Tanvier 6–2 2–0 ret'd, lost M. J. Fernandez 1–6 6–2 8–6); **US Open – sf 1988** (d. Sanchez 4–6 7–5 6–2, Navratilova 6–4 6–7 7–5, lost Sabatini 6–4 7–5), **sf 1989** (d. G. Fernandez, Fendick 6–3 7–5, Faber, Evert 7–6 6–2, lost Navratilova 7–6 6–2), **qf 1985** (d. Gompert, lost Navratilova 6–2 6–3), **qf 1990** (d. Reinstadler, Gavaldon, Meier, Tauziat 6–1 7–5, lost Sanchez-Vicario 6–2 6–2); **French Open – qf 1982** unseeded (d. Bunge, Herr, Jausovec 7–5 6–1, lost Navratilova 6–3 6–2). **CAREER HIGHLIGHTS – DOUBLES: Olympics –** [Shriver] **gold medal 1988** (d. Novotna/Suire 4–6 6–2 10–8); **LIPC –** [M. J. Fernandez] **won 1991**; **Australian Open –** [McNeil] **r/u 1987** (lost Navratilova/Shriver 6–1 6–0); **US Open –** [Rinaldi] **qf 1985** unseeded (d. Bassett/Evert Lloyd, lost Kohde-Kilsch/Sukova 5–7 6–4 6–3). **MIXED DOUBLES:** (with Stewart unless stated) **Australian Open – won 1987** (d. Castle/Hobbs 3–6 7–6 6–3); **Wimbledon – won 1988** (d. Magers/Jones 6–1 7–6), [R. Leach] **won 1990** (d. Smylie/Fitzgerald 7–6 6–2).

LAURA GARRONE (Italy)
Born Milan, 15 November 1967, and lives there; RH; 5ft 5in; 125lb; final 1991 WTA ranking 95; 1991 prize money $60,243.
1985: (108) Won French Open Jun and US Open Jun, was ranked 1 in ITF Jun World Rankings, and 3 in her country behind Reggi and Cecchini. **1986:** (38) Reached last 16 French Open, unseeded, and f Barcelona. **1987:** (87) Sf Belgian Open. **1988:** (60) R/u Taranto. **1989:** (92) Sf Geneva and Athens. **1990:** (65) Still looking for a 1st primary circuit singles title, she reached 3rd f of career at Estoril in July. In doubles with Kschwendt won Palermo and Athens. **1991:** In singles reached qf Bol and in doubles played 3 f. **1991 HIGHLIGHTS – SINGLES: French Open** 1r (lost A. Huber [seed 16] 6–2 6–3), **Wimbledon** 3r (d. Magers 6–4 7–6, Kidowaki 6–4 6–3, lost Navratilova [seed 4] 6–2 6–2, **US Open** 1r (lost Pierce 4–6 6–0 7–6). **1991 HIGHLIGHTS – DOUBLES:** (with Garrone unless stated) [Cecchini] **r/u** Bol (lost Golarsa/Magdalena Maleeva), **r/u** Palermo (lost Langrova/Pierce 6–3 6–7 6–3), **r/u** San Marino (lost Guse/Nishiya 6–0 6–3).

BRAD GILBERT (USA)
Born Oakland, Cal., 9 August 1961; lives there and San Rafael, Cal.; RH; 6ft 1in; 175lb; final 1991 ATP ranking 19; 1991 prize money $343,803.
Coached by Tom Shivington; trained by Mark Grabow. Wife Kim, son Zachary (born 1988). **1982:** (54) The brother of 1978 US CC titlist Dana Gilbert he played for Allan Fox's Pepperdine team in California and reached f NCAA, losing to M. Leach. Won Taipei. **1983:** (62). **1984:** (23) Won Columbus and Taipei and reached last 16 Australian Open. **1985:** (18) Moved into top 20 winning Livingston, Cleveland and Tel Aviv and capping best year with 1r victory over McEnroe at Masters. **1986:** (11) Made further strides, downing Connors and Edberg for US Indoor crown, adding GP titles in Livingston, Israel and Vienna, reaching last 16 Wimbledon and US Open, and playing D Cup. **1987:** (13) Qf US Open, won Scottsdale and reached 4 more f to qualify for Masters, where he d. Connors and Becker. **1988:** (21) Out of action Jan–March with ankle injury and again, missing Wimbledon, after X-rays revealed a massive build-up of scar tissue on the tendon of left ankle as well as ligament damage from a sprain suffered in 1982. Won his 1st tourn of year at Tel Aviv, was Olympic bronze medallist, and reached f Paris Open plus 3 sf. **1989:** (6) Won Memphis, then in late summer captured Stratton Mountain, Livingston and Cincinnati back-to-back, becoming the first player to win 3 titles in consecutive weeks since Becker in 1986. Reached qf or better in 17 of 20 tourns – exceptions being 1r losses at Wimbledon, US Open and Tel Aviv – and qualified for Masters, where he won only one match. **1990:** (19) Won Rotterdam, Orlando and Brisbane; r/u Cincinnati; sf Toronto World Tennis, Tokyo Suntory and Washington; and reached 2nd GS qf at Wimbledon. Won $1m as finalist at GS Cup where he competed as alternate when Agassi withdrew. **1991:** although he won no title, he recorded some significant upsets, beating Sampras to reach f Sydney Indoor, Edberg *en route* to f Los Angeles and Agassi in reaching the same stage at San Francisco and again at Cincinnati. He also reached sf US Pro Indoor and Lyon. **1991 HIGHLIGHTS –**

SINGLES: Australian Open 3r, [seed 7] (d. Wheaton 6–4 4–6 6–3 7–6, Fromberg 4–6 6–4 6–4 4–6 6–0, lost Wilander 7–6 6–1 6–4), *French Open* 1r, [seed 16] (lost Pioline 6–4 2–6 6–1 6–4), *Wimbledon* 3r, [seed 15] (d. Orsanic 7–5 6–1 6–2, Masur 7–5 2–6 6–3 5–7 6–4, lost Bergstrom 6–3 6–2 3–6 6–3), *US Open* 1r (lost Prpic 2–6 6–4 6–2 1–6 6–4); *r/u* San Francisco (d. Kuhnen 6–3 3–6 6–2, Mronz 6–3 6–3, Goldie 6–1 5–7 6–4, Agassi 6–1 6–2, lost Cahill 6–2 3–6 6–4), *r/u* Los Angeles (d. Frana 6–3 7–5, Fleurian 7–6 6–0, Bryan 6–1 6–3, Edberg 7–6, 6–7, 6–4, lost Sampras 6–2 6–7 6–3), *r/u* Sydney Indoor (d. Fitzgerald 6–2 6–2, Marcelino 6–1 6–2, Ferreira 6–1 6–4, Sampras 1–6 7–5 6–3, lost Edberg 6–2 6–2 6–2); *sf* US Pro Indoor (d. Carbonell 6–3 6–3, Haarhuis 7–6 6–1, Curren 4–6 6–3 6–0, lost Lendl 6–4 3–6 6–4), *sf* Lyon (d. Mronz 6–3 7–5, Winogradsky 7–5 6–1, Mancini 6–2 6–2, lost Sampras 6–1 6–2). *CAREER HIGHLIGHTS – SINGLES: Olympics – bronze medal 1988* (d. Jaite, lost Mayotte 6–4 6–4 6–3); *Wimbledon – qf 1990* (d. Oresar, Visser, Haarhuis, Wheaton 6–7 3–6 6–1 6–4 13–11, lost Becker 6–4 6–4 6–1); *US Open – qf 1988* (d. Doohan, Berger 4–6 6–2 6–4 6–3, Forget 6–4 6–7 7–5 6–4, Becker 2–6 6–7 7–6 7–5 6–1, lost Connors 4–6 6–3 6–4 6–0); *Masters – qf 1985* (d. McEnroe 5–7 6–4 6–1, lost Jarryd 6–1 6–2).

RODOLPHE GILBERT (France)
Born Chanteneine, 12 December 1968; lives Paris; LH; 6ft; 150lb; final 1991 ATP ranking 91; 1991 prize money $120,320.
1990: (160) Won Hossegor Challenger. *1991:* Reached qf Guaruja Chevrolet, where he won the doubles with Delaitre, then upset Sampras 2r LIPC as Lucky Loser. On the Challenge circuit he won Neu Ulm. *1991 HIGHLIGHTS – SINGLES: French Open* 1r (lost Davin 6–3 6–4 6–1), *Wimbledon* 1r (lost Courier [seed 4] 6–4 6–2 7–6), *US Open* 2r (d. Palmer 6–1 6–2 5–7 1–6 7–6, lost Rostagno 7–6 6–1 6–3); *won* Neu Ulm Challenger (d. Nydahl 6–2 6–4). *1991 HIGHLIGHTS – DOUBLES:* (with Delaitre) *won* Guaruja Chevrolet (d. Cannon/Van Emburgh 6–2 6–4).

LAURA ARRAYA GILDEMEISTER (Peru)
Born Cordoba, Argentina, 12 January 1964; lives Lima and Miami, Fla.; RH; 2HB; 5ft 8in; 125lb; final 1991 WTA ranking 24; 1991 prize money $162,462.
Coached by her husband, Heinz Gildemeister (married 1984); son Heinz Andre (born June 1988). Having lived in Argentina until age 7, she moved with her family to Peru and became a citizen of that country. *1982:* (69) Burst into her own, beating Bonder, Nagelsen, Temesvari and Horvath. *1983:* (86) R/u Freiburg, qf Hilton Head. *1984:* (34) R/u Tourn of Champs. *1985:* (63) Sf VS Utah and Japan Open; played Fed Cup. *1986:* (31) Upset Lindqvist, M. Maleeva and Kohde-Kilsch during year. *1987:* (46). *1988:* (—) Did not play all year, taking a 9-month break after the birth of her son in June. *1989:* (19) Returned to action at LIPC in March and at Schenectady won 1st primary circuit title for 7 years, following with Puerto Rico (d. Zvereva and G. Fernandez) in Oct. *1990:* (21) R/u Albuquerque and upset Seles in ss *en route* to sf VS Florida. *1991:* Upset K. Maleeva to reach qf Wimbledon, unseeded, and appeared in sf both tourns in Tokyo and Westchester. *1991 HIGHLIGHTS – SINGLES: Australian Open* 2r, [seed 15] (d. Vasquez 6–1 6–1, lost Smylie 6–3 2–6 9–7), *French Open* 2r (d. S. Smith 6–3 2–6 6–1, lost Harvey-Wild 7–6 6–7 11–9), *Wimbledon* qf, unseeded (d. Wood 6–4 6–2, de Swardt 6–4 6–1, Harvey-Wild 2–6 7 ret'd; K. Maleeva [seed 5] 3–6 6–2 6–3, lost Sabatini [seed 2] 6–2 6–1), *US Open* 2r (d. Jagerman 7–6 6–4, lost Meskhi [seed 13] 6–4 3–6 6–0; *sf* Tokyo Pan Pacific (d. Okamoto 7–6 6–5, Endo 4–6 7–5 6–3, Rinaldi 5–7 6–4 6–3, lost Navratilova 6–2 7–6), *sf* Tokyo Suntory (d. Kijimuta 6–4 5–7 7–5, Basuki 3–6 6–3 6–3, Okamoto 6–4 6–4, lost McNeil 7–6 6–3), *sf* Westchester (d. Boogert 6–4 7–5, Field 7–5 6–4, Kochta 6–2 6–4, lost Demongeot 6–1 6–1). *1991 HIGHLIGHTS – DOUBLES:* (with Cunningham) *r/u* Tokyo Nicherei (lost M. J. Fernandez/Shriver 6–3 6–3). *CAREER HIGHLIGHTS – SINGLES: Wimbledon – qf 1991.*

STEPHEN GLEESON (Australia)
Born 7 June 1973.
1991: R/u Australian Open Jun to Enqvist.

KRISTIN GODRIDGE (Australia)
Born Traralgon, 7 February, 1973, and lives there; RH; 2HB; 5ft 4in; 120lb; final 1991 WTA ranking 86; 1991 prize money $65,446.
Coached by Peter Campbell. *1990:* (129) Qf Brisbane. In doubles with Sharpe won US Open Jun and Clarins. *1991:* R/u Australian Open Jun to Pratt, with whom she won US Open Jun doubles, and in the senior game she upset Paz at Wellington *en route* to her 1st sf at that level. *1991 HIGHLIGHTS – SINGLES: Australian Open* 1r (lost Dechaume 6–3

7–5), **French Open** 2r (d. McGrath 6–4 4–6 6–3, lost Sanchez-Vicario [seed 5] 6–1 6–2), **Wimbledon** 1r (lost Faull 6–0 6–2), **US Open** 2r (d. Smylie 6–3 6–4, lost Sanchez-Vicario [seed 4] 6–1 6–1); **sf** Wellington (d. Paz 6–2 7–5, Cordwell 7–5 6–4, Rittner 6–2 6–3, lost Strnadova 6–4 7–6).

ANDRES GOMEZ (Ecuador)
Born Guayaquil, 27 February 1960 and lives there; LH; 6ft 4in; 185lb; final 1991 ATP ranking 68 singles, 56 doubles; 1991 prize money $181,740.
Coached by Patricio Rodriguez. Wife Ana Maria Estrada (married June 1986); sons, Juan Andres (born Dec. 1987), Emilio (born Nov. 1991). *1980:* (43). *1981:* (37) Won first GP title in Bordeaux. *1982:* (15) Won Italian Open and Quito, showing the talent that had been blossoming under the guidance of Harry Hopman. *1983:* (14) Won Dallas GP event. *1984:* (5) Qf French and US Opens and Wimbledon. Won second Italian, US CC, Washington, Nice and Hong Kong. *1985:* (15) Won Hong Kong again and r/u US CC. *1986:* (10) Won US CC, Florence, US Pro and Itaparica in singles and US Open doubles with Zivojinovic. *1987:* (11) Qf French Open, won Tourn of Champs, r/u Frankfurt and reached sf on 5 other occasions, but failed to qualify for Masters. *1988:* (24) Having reached 6 qf, was r/u Stuttgart and Washington back-to-back in July. Won French Open doubles with E. Sanchez. *1989:* (17) Upset Lendl on his way to the title in Barcelona and Wilander to take US Pro; sf Florence and Basle. *1990:* (6) His best tennis came at the beginning of the year, reaching a climax at French Open when, aged 30, he became the 1st Ecuadorian to win a GS title, reaching an all-time high at No. 4 on the computer. Also won Barcelona and Madrid, r/u Philadelphia and sf Italian Open and Cincinnati. Qualified for ATP World Champ at end of year, but failed to reach sf and fell 1r GS Cup to Krickstein. In doubles with J. Sanchez reached 3 f, winning Barcelona. *1991:* He did not pass 2r in any tourn until reaching qf Gstaad in July, and had even dropped out of the top 100. However, he took his 1st title since June 1990 at Brasilia, and with sf Sao Paulo and qf Guaruja Bliss he finished the year on the way up again. *1991 HIGHLIGHTS – SINGLES: US Open* 1r (lost Larsson 4–6 6–3 2–6 6–2 6–3); **won** Brasilia (d. Aerts 4–6 6–3 6–3, Frana 6–7 6–4 6–4, Jaite 6–3 6–3, Marcelino 6–4 7–6, J. Sanchez 6–4 3–6 6–3); **sf** Sao Paulo (d. Koevermans 6–1 6–3, Zoecke 6–2 6–4, Rivera 6–4 6–4, lost Miniussi 2–6 6–3 6–4). *1991 HIGHLIGHTS – DOUBLES:* [Oncins] **won** Sao Paulo (d. Lozano/Motta 7–5 6–4); [E. Sanchez] **r/u** Schenectady (lost J. Sanchez/Woodbridge 3–6 7–6 7–6). *CAREER HIGHLIGHTS – SINGLES: French Open –* **won** *1990* (d. Luna, Filippini, Volkov 6–2 7–5 4–6 6–3, Gustafsson w.o., Champion 6–3 6–3 6–4, Muster 7–5 6–1 7–5, Agassi 6–1 6–4 3–6 6–3), *qf 1984* (lost Lendl 6–3 6–7 6–4 6–3), *qf 1986* (lost Lendl 6–7 7–6 6–0 6–0), *qf 1987* (lost Lendl 5–7 6–4 6–1 6–1); *Italian Open –* **won** *1982* (d. Noah 6–0 fs, Higueras 6–3 fs. Wilander 5–7 6–4 6–3, Teltscher 6–2 6–3 6–2), **won** *1984* (d. Krickstein 2–6 6–1 6–2 6–2); *Wimbledon – qf 1984* (lost Cash 6–4 6–4 6–7 7–6); *US Open – qf 1984* (lost Lendl 6–4 6–4 6–1). *CAREER HIGHLIGHTS – DOUBLES: French Open –* [E. Sanchez] **won** *1988* (d. Fitzgerald/Jarryd 6–3 6–7 6–4 6–3); *US Open –* [Zivojinovic] **won** *1986* (d. Nystrom/Wilander 4–6 6–3 6–3 4–6 6–3); *Italian Open –* [Gildemeister] **won** *1981* (d. Manson/Smid 7–5 6–2).

INES GORROCHATEGUI (Argentina)
Born Cordoba, 13 June 1973, and lives there; RH; 5ft 6½in; 128lb; final 1991 WTA ranking 70; 1991 prize money $30,077.
1991: R/u French Open Jun singles to Smashnova and won Jun doubles there with Bes. In the senior game, in only her 2nd event, she reached f Clarins (d. Cecchini and Paz). *1991 HIGHLIGHTS – SINGLES:* r/u Clarins (d. Cecchini 6–4 6–1, Niox-Chateau 2–6 6–4 6–1, Meier 6–3 7–5, Paz 6–2 6–3, lost Martinez 6–0 6–3).

JIM GRABB (USA)
Born Tucson, Arizona, 14 April 1964, and lives there; RH; 6ft 4in; 180lb; final 1991 ATP ranking 83 singles, 22 doubles; 1991 prize money $243,348.
1984: (313) Sf NCAA Champs. *1985:* (250) Senior year at Stanford; reached sf Livingston. *1986:* (94) Qf San Francisco and Scottsdale. *1987:* (66) Won 1st GP title at Seoul. *1988:* (91) Qf Memphis (d. Edberg) and Philadelphia. In doubles, with 6 different partners, won Stockholm and reached 5 f. *1989:* (35) Sf Stratton Mountain then upset E. Sanchez to make an unexpected appearance in last 16 US Open. In doubles with P. McEnroe won French Open and Masters, r/u LIPC and Washington. *1990:* (72) In singles was r/u Washington (d. Gilbert) and reached sf San Francisco. In doubles with 3 different partners appeared in 5 f, winning Wembley. *1991:* In singles reached qf Montreal (d. B. Gilbert) and Moscow; in doubles won 2 titles with Reneberg. *1991 HIGHLIGHTS – SINGLES: French Open* 1r

(lost Benhabiles 4–6 4–6 6–4 6–2 6–3), **Wimbledon** 2r (d. Marques 7–5 6–7 6–4 6–1, lost Courier [seed 4] 6–4 7–6 2–6 6–4 6–3), **US Open** 3r (d. Koevermans 6–4 7–6 6–2, Stoltenberg /–5 6–4 4–6 /–5, lost Edberg [seed 2] 7–6 4–6 6–3 6–4). **1991 HIGHLIGHTS – DOUBLES:** (with Reneberg) **won** Sydney Indoor (d. Jensen/Warder 6–4 6–4), **won** Tokyo Seiko (d. Davis/Pate 7–5 2–6 7–6). **CAREER HIGHLIGHTS – DOUBLES:** (with P. McEnroe) **French Open – won 1989** (d. Bahrami/Winogradsky 6–4 2–6 6–4 7–6); **Masters – won 1989** (d. Jarryd/Fitzgerald 7–5 7–6 5–7 6–3); **LIPC – r/u 1989** (lost Hlasek/Jarryd 6–3 ret'd).

STEFFI GRAF (Germany)
Born Bruehl, 14 June 1969; lives there and Delray Beach, Fla.; RH; 5ft 9in; 132lb; final 1991 WTA ranking 2; 1991 prize money $1,468,336.
Coached by her father, Peter. Trained by Pavel Slozil until Nov. 1991. **1981:** Won Orange Bowl 12s. **1982:** (214) The youngest at the time to receive a WTA ranking at 13 years 4 months; won European 14-and-under and European circuit Masters. **1983:** (98) Sf Freiburg. **1984:** (22) Won Olympic Demonstration event in LA and reached last 16 Wimbledon. **1985:** (6) Sf US Open and LIPC; last 16 French Open and Wimbledon. **1986:** (3) Won 8 of her last 11 tourns and 52 of her last 55 matches. Won her first pro tourn by beating Evert Lloyd in Hilton Head f, then beat Navratilova in German Open f and had 3 mps in memorable US Open sf loss to Navratilova. Won 4 straight tourns and 23 consecutive matches in the spring. A virus infection affected her performance in Paris and kept her out of Wimbledon, and a freak accident in Prague (a heavy umbrella stand blew over and broke a toe) prevented her from playing in Fed Cup. **1987:** (1) After a 2-month break Dec–Jan, missing Australian Open, she took over No. 2 ranking from Evert Lloyd end Feb., and No. 1 from Navratilova 16 Aug. Won her first GS title at French Open, becoming, at 17 years 11 months and 23 days, the youngest-ever winner of the women's singles there. Unbeaten from 23 Nov 1986 (VS Champs) until Wimbledon f, where she fell to Navratilova, losing to her again in f US Open when suffering from flu. She won 75 of 77 matches to take 11 titles, confirming her No. 1 ranking by taking the VS Champs and being named Official World Champion by virtue of her position at head of VS points table. She became only the 2nd player after Navratilova to earn more than 1m in prize money in a year. **1988:** (1) At the age of 19 she achieved a unique 'Golden Slam', becoming only the 3rd woman, after Connolly and Court, to achieve the traditional Grand Slam, and topping her exceptional year with a gold medal at the Olympics in Seoul. She won 6 other titles, and 71 of 74 matches, losing only to Sabatini – at VS Florida (following a 6-week break) and at Amelia Island – and to Shriver (when suffering from flu) at VS Champs, ending run of 46 winning results. Became the 2nd German woman to win Wimbledon after Cilly Aussem in 1931. In doubles won Wimbledon and LIPC with Sabatini, but was forced to default qf VS Champs. **1989:** (1) A second consecutive GS slipped from her grasp when, feeling unwell after suffering from food poisoning, she lost f French Open to Sanchez-Vicario. However, she retained her titles at Australian Open, Wimbledon and US Open, won VS Champs and took 10 other singles titles. With a record of 82 wins and 2 defeats, losing just 12 sets all year, she was beaten only by Sanchez-Vicario at French Open and Sabatini at Amelia Island in spring. In doubles was r/u French Open with Sabatini. **1990:** (1) Began the year in her usual style by winning Australian Open and recorded a 66-match winning streak (the 2nd-highest in women's tennis), which was broken when she lost to Seles in f Berlin. She lost f French Open (her 13th consecutive GS final) to the same player, Garrison upset her in sf Wimbledon and Sabatini beat her in f US Open and sf VS Champs. These were the only players to beat her in a year in which she won 9 titles. She was out of action from Feb. to April after breaking her thumb ski-ing, and was hampered through the year by allegations concerning her father and by sinus problems, which caused her to withdraw from the Fed Cup team and required an operation after Wimbledon. On 13 Aug. went into her 157th consecutive week at No. 1 (starting 17 Aug., 1987), overtaking Navratilova's women's record of 156 (14 June 1982 – 9 June 1985); 3 weeks later she passed Jimmy Connors' all-time record of 159 weeks. **1991:** Her loss to Novotna in qf Australian Open was her 1st so early in GS since French Open 1986, and until she beat Seles to take San Antonio in April, she had gone 5 tourns since Nov. 1990 without winning a title. She went on to take Hamburg, Berlin, Leipzig, Zurich and Brighton and was r/u VS Florida and Amelia Island. However, she lost her No. 1 ranking to Seles in March, having held that position for a record 86 consecutive weeks, regained it briefly after winning her 3rd Wimbledon in a thrilling final over Sabatini, but lost it again 8 Aug. after losing to Capriati at San Diego. In sf French Open Sanchez-Vicario inflicted her worst defeat (6–0 6–2) and 1st love set since 1984, Navratilova beat her in sf US Open and Novotna removed her in qf VS Champs. When she

d. Wiesner 2r Leipzig, she notched up her 500th career win, the youngest to reach that landmark, being 6 months younger than Evert, although Evert needed only 545 matches to Graf's 568. Split with Slozil in Nov., preferring to work on her own. *1991 HIGHLIGHTS – SINGLES: Australian Open* qf, seed 1 (d. Santrock 6–3 6–0, Kidowaki 6–1 6–0, Provis 6–4 6–2, Habsudova 6–0 6–1, lost Novotna 5–7 6–4 8–6), *French Open* sf, seed 2 (d. Magdalena Maleeva 0–3 7–0, Langrova 0–0 0–1, Stafford 0–0 0–1, Appelmans 0–2 0–2, Tauziat [seed 13] 6–3 6–2, lost Sanchez-Vicario [seed 5] 6–0 6–2), *won Wimbledon*, seed 1 (d. Appelmans 6–2 6–2, Louie Harper 6–0 6–1, Basuki 6–2 6–3, Frazier [seed 15] 6–2 6–1, Garrison [seed 8] 6–1 6–3, M. J. Fernandez [seed 6] 6–2 7–5, Sabatini [seed 2] 6–4 3–6 8–6), *US Open* sf, seed 1 (d. Temesvari 6–1 6–2, Mothes 6–5 6–0, Sviglerova 6–4 7–5 Wiesner 7–5 6–4, Martinez 6–1 6–3, lost Navratilova 7–6 6–7 6–4); *won* San Antonio (d. Keller 6–2 6–1, Javer 6–3 6–1, Sloane 6–1 6–1, Halard 6–0 6–1, Seles 6–4 6–3), *won* Hamburg (d. Kochta 6–1 6–3, Halard 6–2 6–3, K. Maleeva 6–3 6–3, Wiesner 6–0 6–1, Seles 5–7 7–6 6–3), *won* Berlin (d. Jagerman 6–2 6–3, Brioukhovets 6–0 6–1, Zrubakova 6–3 6–2, Novotna 6–1 6–0, Sanchez-Vicario 6–3 4–6 7–6), *won* Leipzig (d. Langrova 6–0 6–1, Wiesner 6–1 7–6, Paulus 6–1 6–1, Novotna 6–3 6–3), *won* Zurich (d. Pfaff 6–1 7–6, Strnadova 6–2 6–4, Kochta 6–2 6–1, Sukova 6–4 6–3, Tauziat 6–4 6–4), *won* Brighton (d. Adams 7–6 6–3, Strnadova 6–2 6–3, McNeil 7–5 6–2, Paulus 7–5 6–1, Garrison 5–7 6–4 6–1); *r/u* VS Florida (d. Dahlman def., A. Huber 6–0 6–1, McGrath 6–3 6–1, Tauziat 6–1 6–2, lost Sabatini 6–4 7–6), *r/u* Amelia Island (d. Simpson Alter 6–4 6–0, Cueto 6–1 6–1, Zvcrova 6 0 6 2, Fendick 6 0 6 1, lost Sabatini 6–0 6–1); *sf* LIPC (d. de Lone 6–1 6–2, Magers 6–3 6–0, Werdel 6–0 6–1, Maleeva Fragnière 6–1 6–3, lost Sabatini 0–6 7–6 6–1). *CAREER HIGHLIGHTS – SINGLES: Olympics – gold medal 1988* (d. Garrison 6–2 6–0, Sabatini 6–3 6–3); *Australian Open – won 1988* (d. Lindqvist 6–0 7–5, Mandlikova 6–2 6–2, Kohde-Kilsch 6–2 6–3, Evert 6–1 7–6), *won 1989* (d. Guse, Simpson, Werdel, Provis 6–4 6–0, Kohde-Kilsch 6–2 6–3, Sabatini 6–3 6–0, Sukova 6–4 6–4), *won 1990* (d. Cunningham, de Lone, Meskhi, Reggi 6–2 6–3, Fendick 6–3 7–5, Sukova 6–3 3–6 6–4, M. J. Fernandez 6–3 6–4), *qf 1991; French Open – won 1987* (d. Novotna, Kelesi, M. Maleeva 6–4 6–1, Sabatini 6–4 4–6 7–5, Navratilova 6–4 4–6 8–6), *won 1988* (d. Tauziat, Fulco, Sabatini 6–3 7–6, Zvereva 6–0 6–0), *r/u 1989* (d. Benjamin, Fulco, Jagerman, La Fratta, Martinez 6–0 6–4, Seles 6–3 3–6 6–3, Novotna 6–1 6–2, lost Sanchez-Vicario 7–6 3–6 7–5), *r/u 1990* (d. Paradis, Santrock, Cecchini, Tauziat 6–1 6–4, Martinez 6–1, 6–3, Novotna 6–1 6–2, lost Seles 7–6 6–4), *sf 1991; Wimbledon – won 1988* (d. M. J. Fernandez 6–2 6–2, Paradis 6–3 6–1, Shriver 6–1 6–2, Navratilova 5–7 6–2 6–1), *won 1989* (d. Salmon, Kessaris, A. Minter, Seles 6–0 6–1, Sanchez-Vicario 7–5 6–1, Evert 6–2 6–1, Navratilova 6–2 6–7 6–1), *won 1991, r/u 1987* (d. Gildemeister, Novotna, Sabatini 4–6 6–1 6–1, Shriver 6–0 6–2, lost Navratilova 7–5 6–3), *sf 1990* (d. Porwik, McGrath, Kohde-Kilsch, Capriati 6–2 6–4, Novotna 7–5 6–2, lost Garrison 6–3 3–6 6–4); *US Open – won 1988* (d. Fendick 6–4 6–2, K. Maleeva 6–3 6–0, Evert w.o., Sabatini 6–3 6–0, Sukova 6–1), *won 1989* (d. Inoue, Herreman, Phelps, Fairbank Nideffer 6–4 6–0, Sukova 6–1 6–1, Sabatini 3–6 6–4 6–2, Navratilova 3–6 7–5 6–1), *r/u 1987* (d. Tarabini, Hanika 7–5 6–2, Shriver 6–4 6–3, McNeil 4–6 6–2 6–4, lost Navratilova 7–6 6–1), *r/u 1990* (d. Drake, McQuillan, E. Rienach, Capriati 6–1 6–2, Novotna 6–3 6–1, Sanchez-Vicario 6–1 6–2, lost Sabatini 6–2 7–6), *sf 1985* (d. M. Maleeva 6–4 6–2, Shriver 7–6 6–7 7–6, lost Navratilova 6–2 6–3), *sf 1986* (d. Mascarin, Temesvari, Bowes, Reggi 6–1 3–6 6–0, Gadusek 6–3 6–1, lost Navratilova 6–1 6–7 7–6), *sf 1991; VS Champs – won 1987* (d. Garrison 6–0 6–3, Sukova 6–2 6–0, Hanika 6–1 6–4, Sabatini 4–6 6–4 6–0 6–4), *won 1989* (d. Novotna 6–3 6–4, Sukova 6–2 6–1, Sabatini 6–3 5–7 6–1, Navratilova 6–4 7–5 2–6 6–2), *r/u Nov. 1986* (d. McNeil 6–3 fs, M. Maleeva 7–5 fs, Sukova 6–1 fs, lost Navratilova 7–6 6–3 6–2), *sf March 1986* (lost Navratilova 6–3 6–2), *sf 1988* (lost Shriver 6–3 7–6), *sf 1990* (d. Capriati 6–3 5–7 6–3, K. Maleeva 6–3 6–0, lost Sabatini 6–4 6–4); *LIPC – won 1988* (d. Kohde-Kilsch 6–3 6–0, Rehe 6–3 6–1, Evert 6–4 6–4), *sf 1991. CAREER HIGHLIGHTS – DOUBLES:* (with Sabatini) *Wimbledon – won 1988* (d. Savchenko/ Zvereva 6–3 1–6 12–10); *LIPC – won 1988* (d. G. Fernandez/Garrison 7–6 6–3); *French Open – r/u 1986* (lost Navratilova/Temesvari 6–1 6–2), *r/u 1987* (lost Navratilova/Shriver 6–2 6–1), *r/u 1989* (lost Savchenko/Zvereva 6–4 6–4).

DEBBIE GRAHAM (USA)
Born Walnut Greek, Cal., 25 August 1970; lives Fountain Valley, Cal.; RH; 2HB; final 1991 WTA ranking 42; 1991 prize money $65,932.
Coached by Bob Hochstadter and Frank Brenna. Did not join the tour full time until she had finished her education. *1986:* Won Nat 16s. *1988:* (139). *1989:* (252) All-American in singles and doubles for 1st of 2 years. *1990:* (121) Qf Clarins and won NCAA singles, playing for Stanford Univ. *1991:* Qf Westchester, San Diego (d. Paulus) and Tokyo Nicherei

(d. Shriver). *1991 HIGHLIGHTS – SINGLES: French Open* 3r (d. Reinstadler 6–1 7–5, Niox-Chateau 6–4 6–0, lost Sawamatsu 5–7 6–2 6–4), *Wimbledon* 1r (lost Werdel 6–3 6–2), *US Open* 2r (d. Davenport 6–3 6–2, lost Navratilova [seed 6] 6–1 6–4).

ANN GROSSMAN (USA)
Born Grove City, Ohio, 13 October 1970, and lives there; RH; 2HB; 5ft 3in; 110lb; final 1991 WTA ranking 89; 1991 prize money $75,150.
Coached by Trevor Nettle. *1986:* Won US Int GC 16s. *1987:* (378) Won Nat 18s. *1988:* (48) Upset Fairbank *en route* to f San Diego. *1989:* (55) Reached qf San Diego and last 16 LIPC and French Open. *1990:* (50) Reached last 16 French Open, unseeded, and upset Magers *en route* to f Strasbourg. *1991:* Upset Zvereva at French Open and reached qf VS Houston. *1991 HIGHLIGHTS – SINGLES: Australian Open* 1r (lost Quentrec 7–6 2–6 7–5), *French Open* 3r (d. Golarsa 7–5 6–0, Zvereva [seed 15] 4–6 6–1 6–4, lost Tami Whitlinger 7–6 6–4), *Wimbledon* 2r (d. Hand 6–0 6–4, lost K. Maleeva [seed 5] 6–4 6–1), *US Open* 1r (lost Novotna [seed 9] 6–3 4–6 6–1). *1991 HIGHLIGHTS – DOUBLES:* [Golarsa] *r/u* Taranto (lost Dechaume/Labat 6–2 7–5).

JAN GUNNARSSON (Sweden)
Born Olofstroem, 30 May 1962; lives Monte Carlo; RH; 6ft 1in; 176lb; final 1991 ATP ranking 92; 1991 prize money $177,102.
Girlfriend Catharin; daughter Anna; twins Elin and Johan born Sept. 1989. *1979:* (392) R/u US Open Jun. *1980:* (247) Sf Pepsi GS Jun; finished 3rd Swedish satellite circuit. *1983:* (100) Qf Bastad and Barcelona. R/u doubles Nancy with Jarryd and Rome with Leach. *1984:* (47) Won Vienna ($25,000), r/u Metz, qf 4 tourns and last 16 French Open. Won doubles at Nice, Bastad, Toulouse with Mortensen. *1985:* (25) Won Vienna and sf LIPC. *1986:* (57) Sf Gstaad and Vienna, last 16 Boca West. *1987:* (39) R/u Stuttgart and d. Wilander, E. Sanchez and Gilbert during the year. *1988:* (84). *1989:* (29) Upset Leconte and Svensson to reach sf Australian Open, unseeded; sf Gstaad. *1990:* (99) His best showing was qf Indian Wells, where he upset Wilander 1r. *1991:* Reached last 16 Wimbledon, unseeded, and r/u Bologna. *1991 HIGHLIGHTS – SINGLES: Australian Open* 1r (lost Courier [seed 16] 6–3 6–4 6–2), *French Open* 1r (lost Carbonell 5–7 6–2 6–3 6–1), *Wimbledon* last 16, unseeded (d. Rebolledo 6–1 7–5 6–2, Jonsson 6–2 6–3 2–6 7–6, Woodbridge 7–6 4–6 6–3 6–4, lost Wheaton 6–4 6–3 6–1); *r/u* Bologna (d. Fromberg 6–3 6–1, Cancellotti 6–2 6–0, Masso 6–0 6–2, Camporese 7–6 6–4, lost Cane 5–7 6–3 7–5). *1991 HIGHLIGHTS – DOUBLES:* (with Bergh) *won* Nice (d. Flegl/Utgren 6–4 4–6 6–3). *CAREER HIGHLIGHTS – SINGLES: Australian Open – sf 1989,* unseeded (d. Leconte 6–4 6–3 6–2, Saceanu 6–1 6–2 6–7 4–6 6–1, Keretic 6–3 6–4 3–6 6–3, Schapers 7–6 6–1 6–2, Svensson 6–0 6–3 4–6 6–4, lost Mecir 7–5 6–2 6–2).

MAGNUS GUSTAFSSON (Sweden)
Born Lund, 3 January 1967; lives Lindome; RH; 6ft 1in; 172lb; final 1991 ATP ranking 12; 1991 prize money $538,792.
Coached by Tim Klein. *1986:* (273) Nat 18 Champ. *1987:* (53) Reached 1st GP sf at Stockholm, won Tampere Challenger and broke into top 50. *1988:* (51) Upset Mayotte to reach last 16 French Open; sf Hilversum and Barcelona (d. Jaite and Leconte). *1989:* (34) Reached last 16 Australian Open; played 1st GP f at Gstaad, then in autumn upset Wilander and Agassi *en route* to 1st SS f at Stockholm. *1990:* (31) Took a break in March, suffering from shin splints. Reached sf Brussels, Stuttgart (d. E. Sanchez and took Lendl to 3s) and upset Agassi at Hamburg. Reached last 16 French Open, but was forced to default to Gomez owing to a knee injury. *1991:* Won 1st GP title at Munich, upsetting Lendl on the way, and followed with Bastad and Hilversum to break into the top 10 in July. R/u Hamburg, Kitzbuhel and Prague; sf Sydney NSW and reached 2 doubles f. Withdrew from US Open with chronic inflammation of the right elbow. *1991 HIGHLIGHTS – SINGLES: Australian Open* 3r (d. Morgan 6–1 6–0 6–3, Masur 7–5 3–6 7–6 6–0, lost Lendl [seed 3] 4–6 6–2 6–3 6–2), *French Open* 3r (d. Novacek [seed 14] 6–2 3–6 5–1 ret'd, Krickstein 6–1 4–6 6–4 6–2, lost Mancini 6–3 3–6 6–2 6–3), *Wimbledon* 2r (d. Clavet 7–7 6–3 6–3, lost Forget [seed 7] 6–4 6–3 6–4); *won* Munich (d. Stich 5–7 6–4 6–3, Skoff 6–1 4–6 6–4, Riglewski 6–2 7–5, Lendl 6–4 7–5, Perez-Roldan 3–6 6–3 4–3 ret'd), *won* Bastad (d. Marques 6–0 7–5, Kroon 6–7 6–1, Arraya 6–1 6–2, Bergstrom 4–6 6–3 6 2, Mancini 6–1 6–2), *won* Hilversum (d. Clavet 7–6 7–6, Jonsson 7–5 7–5, Rosset 6–7 6–2 6–4, Novacek 7–6 6–3, Arrese 5–7 7–6 2–6 6–1 6–0), *won* Cologne Challenger (d. Gorriz 6–2 4–6 6–2); *r/u* Hamburg (d. Engel 6–4 6–2, Cherkasov 3–6 6–4 6–4, Caratti 7–5 3–6 6–2, Noah 6–1 6–4, Prpic 6–2 1–6 7–6, lost Novacek 6–3 6–3 5–7 0–6 6–1), *r/u* Kitzbuhel (d. Nargiso 6–4 7–5, Muster 7–5 2–6 6–4, Champion 4–6 6–3 6–1, Jaite 6–2 6–2, lost Novacek

7–6 7–6 6–2), *r/u* Prague (d. Thomas 6–3 6–2, Costa 6–4 6–1, Boetsch 6–2 6–2, Perez-Roldan 7–5 6–7 6–2, lost Novacek 7–6 6–2); *sf* Sydney NSW (d. Svensson 3–6 6–4 6–4, Mansdorf 7–6 6–3, Cahill 7–5 6–4, lost Stich 7–6 6–4). *1991 HIGHLIGHTS – DOUBLES:* [Jarryd] *r/u* Bastad (lost Bathman/Bergh 6–4 6–4), [Clavet] *r/u* Hilversum (lost Krajicek/Siemerink 7–5 6–4).

PAUL HAARHUIS (Netherlands)
Born Eindhoven, 19 February 1966, and lives there; RH; 6ft 2in; 177lb; final 1991 ATP ranking 37 singles, 17 (34) doubles; 1991 prize money $412,082.
Coached by Henk van Hulst. *1987:* (397) Finished 2nd on Dutch satellite circuit. *1988:* (462). *1989:* (57) After winning Lagos Challenger qualified for French Open, where he upset Zivojinovic 1r, and again as a qualifier upset J. McEnroe at US Open, going on to last 16. Qf Hilversum (d. K. Carlsson) and Itaparica. *1990:* (54) Qf Philadelphia (d. Gilbert and took Gomez to 3s) and Estoril. Reached 4 f in doubles with various partners, winning Moscow. *1991:* He again excelled at US Open, upsetting top seed Becker *en route* to qf, unseeded. Reached sf Rotterdam, won Lagos Challenger and scored some other big upsets – E. Sanchez at Estoril and Ivanisevic at Italian Open and French Open. In doubles reached 5 f, winning 3 with different partners, and was r/u French Open mixed with Vis. *1991 HIGHLIGHTS – SINGLES: Australian Open* 2r (d. J. Sanchez 2–6 6–1 6–2 7–6, lost Camporese 7–5 7–5 3–6 6–3), *French Open* 3r (d. Reneberg 6–3 6–3 6–1, Ivanisevic [seed 8] 6–1 6–4 6–1, lost Martin 6–2 4–6 6–3 6–4), *Wimbledon* 1r (lost Larsson 6–4 1–6 6–3 6–1), *US Open* qf, unseeded (d. Jelen 2–6 6–2 6–1 3–6 6–2, Chesnokov 6–1 4–6 6–2 7–6, Becker [seed 1] 6–3 6–4 6–2, Steeb 6–2 6–3 6–4, lost Connors 4–6 7–6 6–4 6–2); *won* Lagos Challenger (d. Middleton 6–3 6–3); *sf* Rotterdam (d. Svensson 7–5 0–6 6–3, Gustafsson 6–3 3–6 6–1, Bergstrom 7–5 6–3, lost Camporese 6–7 6–2 7–6). *1991 HIGHLIGHTS – DOUBLES:* (with Koevermans unless stated) *won* Estoril (d. Nijssen/Suk 6–3 6–3), [Davids] *won* Rosmalen (d. Krajicek/Siemerink 6–3 7–6), [Etingh] *won* Guaruja Bliss (d. Garnett/Nelson 6–3 7–5); *r/u* Adelaide (lost Ferreira/Kruger 6–4 4–6 6–4), *r/u* Monte Carlo (lost Jensen/Warder 5–7 7–6 6–4). *MIXED DOUBLES:* (with Vis) *r/u French Open* (lost Suk/Sukova 6–4 6–1). *CAREER HIGHLIGHTS – SINGLES: US Open – qf 1991.*

KARINA HABSUDOVA (Czechoslovakia)
Born Bojnice, 2 August 1973; lives Bratislava; RH; 2HB; 5ft 7in; 132lb; final 1991 WTA ranking 54; 1991 prize money $74,040
Coached by Milan Martnec. *1990:* (122) In the Jun game won Wimbledon doubles with Strnadova and finished the year at No. 1 in ITF Jun singles and doubles Rankings. In the senior game she won Katowice Challenger and reached qf Moscow on the main tour. *1991:* Won US Open Jun over Mall and took Australian Open Jun doubles with Rittner. In the senior game she made an unexpected appearance in last 16 Australian Open and reached sf Phoenix and VS Nashville. *1991 HIGHLIGHTS SINGLES: Australian Open* last 16 (d. Tessi 6–2 7–6, A. Smith 7–6 6–2, Smylie 6–0 3–6 8–6, lost Graf [seed 1] 6–0 6–1), *French Open* 1r (lost Halard 6–4 7–5), *Wimbledon* 2r (d. C. Dahlman 6–3 6–2, lost Lindqvist 6–3 6–2), *US Open* 2r (d. Kidowaki 6–1 6–4, lost Fendick 6–2 6–3); *sf* Phoenix (d. Emmone 6–1 7–5, Frazier 6–3 7–6, Po 4–6 6–1 6–3, lost Rubin 6–2 6–4), *sf* VS Nashville (d. Provis 6–2 4–6 6–1, Basuki 6–4 6–2, lost Appelmans 6–3 6–4).

SABINE HACK (Germany)
Born Ulm, 7 December 1969; lives Ravemburg; RH; 5ft 7in; 130lb; final 1991 WTA ranking 90; 1991 prize money $43,134.
1985: (187) Enjoyed some success on the satellite circuits. *1986:* (263). *1987:* (234). *1988:* (141) Qf Athens and Paris Open. *1989:* (73) Reached sf at Bastad and broke into top 100. *1990:* (45) Upset Maleeva Fragnière *en route* to sf Geneva and reached same stage Estoril. *1991:* Qf Auckland, Wellington and San Marino. *1991 HIGHLIGHTS – SINGLES: Australian Open* 1r (lost Seles [seed 2] 6–0 6–0), *French Open* 2r (d. Durie 6–4 7–5, lost M. J. Fernandez [seed 4] 6–4 6–0), *US Open* 1r (lost Paulus 6–7 6–4 6–4).

JULIE HALARD (France)
Born Versailles, 10 September 1970; lives La Baule; RH; 2HB; 5ft 7in; 110lb; final 1991 WTA ranking 20; 1991 prize money $187,677
1986: (—) Won French Open Jun. *1987:* (62) Turned pro June. R/u Wimbledon Jun to Zvereva and reached f Athens. *1988:* (75) Won French Open Jun over Farley. *1989:* (119) Upset Shriver *en route* to qf Moscow. *1990:* (41) Sf Clarins, qf Sydney and Barcelona, and upset Garrison *en route* to last 16 LIPC. *1991:* Won her 1st primary circuit title at Puerto Rico; r/u VS Albuquerque; sf San Antonio, Clarins and Phoenix; and upset M. J. Fernandez

at Berlin. Qualified for her 1st VS Champs, but fell 1r to Seles. *1991 HIGHLIGHTS – SINGLES: Australian Open* 2r (d. Szabova 6–2 6–3, lost Kamstra 6–3 6–4), *French Open* 2r (d. Habsudova 6–4 7–5, lost Cunningham 6–2 7–5), *Wimbledon* 2r (d. Toleafoa 6–2 6–3, lost Werdel 6–2 6–4), *US Open* 2r (d. Coetzer 7–5 6–1, lost Rittner 6–2 6–0); *won* Puerto Rico (d. Hack 6–3 6–4, Kuhlman 6–4 6–4, Rittner 5–7 6–1 7–6, Pierce 7–5 6–1, Coetzer 7–5 7–5); *r/u* VS Albuquerque (d. Jackson Nobrega 6–3 6–3, Van Lottum 6–1 6–1, Adams 6–2 4–6 6–0, E. Reinach 6–3 3–6 6–4, lost G. Fernandez 6–0 6–2); *sf* San Antonio (d. Thoren 6–1 2–6 6–1, Dechaume 6–1 6–3, Sviglerova 6–1 6–2, lost Graf 6–0 6–1), *sf* Clarins (d. Dechaume 6–4 0–6 6–2, Garrone 7–6 6–2, Martinek 6–4 6–3, lost Martinez 6–4 2–6 7–5), *sf* Phoenix (D. Stafford 6–2 3–6 6–4, Grossman 3–6 6–4 6–4, Fendick 4–6 6–4 6–1, lost Appelmans 3–6 6–3 6–3). *1991 HIGHLIGHTS – DOUBLES:* (with Dechaume) *r/u* Clarins (lost Langrova/Zrubakova 6–4 6–4).

MAREEN 'PEANUT' LOUIE HARPER (USA)
Born San Francisco, 15 August 1960, and lives there; RH; 2HB; 5ft 5in; 120lb; final 1991 WTA ranking 71; 1991 prize money $79,601.
1977: One of five children including Marcie Louie (ranked 5 in US in 1975), she was r/u Wimbledon Jun. *1978:* (36) Won San Carlos. *1979:* (80). *1980:* (35) Won Columbus. *1981:* (32) Qf Chicago, Boston. *1982:* (90). *1983:* (52) Qf Hershey. *1984:* (53) Won Durban. *1985:* (22) Her best year, in which she reached sf Fort Lauderdale, sf VS Florida and won VS Denver (d. Sabatini and Garrison). *1986:* (65) Married Tim Harper 31 May. Overcame four consecutive 1r losses at start of season to beat Kelesi and Spence. *1987:* (97). *1988:* (56) Qf VS Kansas and Pan Pacific Open. *1989:* (115) In doubles won VS Arizona with Barg, and in singles upset Kohde-Kilsch 1r US HC. *1990:* (74) Returned to top 100 with sf showing at Wichita. *1991:* In singles reached qf Colorado and Palm Springs (d. Sukova), and reached 2 doubles f, winning Phoenix with Cammy MacGregor. *1991 HIGHLIGHTS – SINGLES: Wimbledon* 2r (d. Porwik 6–4 6–1, lost Graf [seed 1] 6–0 6–1), *US Open* 2r (d. Werdel 6–4 5–7 6–4, lost Novotna [seed 9] 6–1 6–2). *1991 HIGHLIGHTS – DOUBLES:* [Cammy MacGregor] *won* Phoenix (d. Collins/E. Reinach 7–5 3–6 6–3); [Gregory] *r/u* VS Albuquerque (lost Adams/Demongeot 6–7 6–4 6–3).

LINDA HARVEY-WILD (USA)
Born Arlington Heights, Ill., 11 February 1971; lives Hawthorn Woods, Ill.; RH; 5ft 7in; 135lb; final 1991 WTA ranking 41; 1991 prize money $107,721.
Coached by her stepfather, Steve Wild. At Univ. of S. Cal. *1987:* (338). *1988:* (428). *1989:* (153) Won 2 consec. USTA circuit events. *1990:* (83) Qf VS Chicago (upsetting Sanchez-Vicario) and VS Nashville (d. Provis); broke into top 100 in Aug. *1991:* Reached sf Brisbane and VS Houston, upsetting G. Fernandez there and *en route* to qf VS California, and surprised Zvereva 2r Wimbledon. *1991 HIGHLIGHTS – SINGLES: Australian Open* 1r (lost Sabatini [seed 4] 6–3 6–1), *French Open* 3r (d. Baudone 6–4 7–5, Gildemeister 7–6 6–7 11–9, lost Meskhi [seed 14] 6–3 6–1), *Wimbledon* 3r (d. Bonder Kreiss 6–4 6–2, Zvereva [seed 13] 6–4 6–1, lost Gildemeister 2–2 ret'd); *sf* Brisbane (d. R. White 6–0 2–6 6–3, Provis 7–6 3–6 6–2, Porwik 6–3 6–4, Wiesner 6–1 6–4, lost Sukova 6–1 6–1), *sf* VS Houston (d. Mosca 6–1 4–6 6–1, Tami Whitlinger 6–4 6–3, G. Fernandez 6–4 6–1, lost M. J. Fernandez 6–0 6–3).

GINGER HELGESON (USA)
Born St Cloud, Minn., 14 September 1968; lives San Diego, Cal.; RH; 2HB; 5ft 8in; 140lb; final 1991 WTA ranking 58; 1991 prize money $91,228.
Works with anatomical functionist Pete Egoscue. *1991:* Made her mark with some notable upsets on her way to qf LIPC (d. Zvereva, Sviglerova and Rajchrtova), Berlin (d. Paz and Sukova), Geneva and Phoenix (d. G. Fernandez). *1991 HIGHLIGHTS – SINGLES: Australian Open* 1r (lost Zvereva [seed 11] 6–3 6–4), *French Open* 1r (lost Quentrec 7–6 7–6), *Wimbledon* 1r (lost Cunningham 7–6 6–4), *US Open* 1r (lost Faber 6–4 6–4).

JILL HETHERINGTON (Canada)
Born Brampton, 27 October 1964; lives Peterborough and Gainesville, Fla.; RH; 2HB; 5ft 10in; 150lb; final 1991 WTA ranking 240 singles, 13 doubles; 1991 prize money $90,353.
Coached by Andy Brandi. *1983:* Won Orange Bowl 18s doubles with Fendick. *1985:* (335). *1986:* (–) All-American for 3rd consecutive year. *1987:* (203) Won Bethesda on USTA circuit. *1988:* (84) Won 1st major singles title at Wellington. In doubles with Fendick r/u US Open and won 5 titles to qualify for VS Champs. In 1r doubles at Olympics with Bassett Seguso d. Sabatini/Paz 7–6 (10–8) 5–7 20–18 in 4 hr 13 min, the second-longest women's doubles match in Open history. *1989:* (123) In doubles r/u Australian Open with Fendick

and won 3 titles with various partners. *1990:* (243) Won Singapore doubles with Durie. *1991:* Reached 5 doubles f, winning VS Houston and San Diego with Rinaldi, with whom she qualified for VS Champs. *1991 HIGHLIGHTS – SINGLES: Wimbledon* 1r (lost Fendick 7–6 4–6 6–1). *1991 HIGHLIGHTS – DOUBLES:* (with Finaldi unless stated) *won* VS Houston (d. Fendick/M. J. Fernandez 6–1 2–6 6–1), *won* San Diego (d. G. Fernandez/ Tauziat 6–4 3–6 6–2); [Adams] *r/u* VS Oklahoma (lost McGrath/A. Smith 6–2 6–4), *r/u* San Antonio (lost Fendick/Seles 7–6 6–2), *r/u* Leipzig (lost Bollegraf/Demongeot 6–4 6–3). *CAREER HIGHLIGHTS – DOUBLES:* (with Fendick) *Australian Open – r/u 1989* (lost Navratilova/Shriver 3–6 6–3 6–2); *US Open – r/u 1988* (lost G. Fernandez/R. White 6–4 6–1).

JAKOB HLASEK (Switzerland)
Born Prague, Czechoslovakia, 12 November 1964; lives Zurich; 6ft 2in; 165lb; final 1991 ATP ranking 20 singles, 39 doubles; 1991 prize money $873,642.
Family moved to Zurich in 1968. Speaks 6 languages. *1984:* (88) Joined both Olympic and D Cup squads for Switzerland and played prolific schedule including 22 tournaments. *1985:* (33) R/u Rotterdam, sf Milan, Hong Kong and qf 4 times. Won Toulouse doubles with Acuna. *1986:* (32) Played consistent tennis all season, reaching f Hilversum and 8 qf. *1987:* (23) Reached last 16 Wimbledon with 2nd win over Nystrom, sf Toulouse and Wembley (d. Mecir). *1988:* (8) Out of action 3½ months after breaking right wrist and 3 ribs in car accident Jan., when he fell asleep at the wheel. Enjoyed a spectacular 2nd half of year, reaching last 16 US Open, f Gstaad and Basel (d. Connors), before taking 1st GP title at Wembley and following with Johannesburg and r/u finish at Brussels to qualify for 1st Masters, where he reached sf. *1989:* (30) Won Rotterdam and r/u Lyon in singles; in doubles won Milan, Indian Wells, LIPC and Wembley with various partners. Out of action with wrist injury July–Oct. *1990:* (17) In singles won Wembley (d. Chang) and reached sf Rotterdam and Canadian Open. Formed a successful doubles duo with Forget in Feb.; together they won 5 titles, including IBM/ATP World Doubles for which both shaved their heads, and he took another with Stich. *1991:* Upset E. Sanchez *en route* to sf French Open, unseeded, and at Basel won both singles and doubles titles. He was also r/u Moscow, reached sf Milan, Copenhagen and Rosmalen, and played 2 other doubles, f. *1991 HIGHLIGHTS – SINGLES: Australian Open* 1r, seed 11 (lost Stoltenberg 0–6 6–4 7–5 6–4), *French Open* sf, unseeded (d. Pate 6–4 6–1 7–5, E. Sanchez 6–3 4–6 6–2 7–6, Carbonell 7–6 4–6 6–4 6–3, Miniussi 4–6 6–3 5–7 7–5 6–2, lost Agassi [seed 4] 6–3 6–1 6–1), *Wimbledon* 2r, seed 13 (d. Zivojinovic 6–2 3–6 6–3 6–2, lost Woodbridge 6–3 1–6 7–5 6–3), *US Open* 3r (d. Azar 6–3 7–5 6–3, Svensson 6–4 7–5 6–7 6–3, lost Rostagno 6–7 7–6 7–6 7–6); *won* Basel (d. Gunnarsson 6–3 6–2, Steeb 7–6 6–2, Curren 6–3 6–4, Volkov 7–6 6–7 7–6, J. McEnroe 7–6 6–0 6–3); *r/u* Moscow (d. Stankovic 4–6 6–3 7–6, Haas 6–3 6–4, Siemerink 6–7 6–2 6–2, Volkov 6–4 6–2, lost Cherkasov 7–6 3–6 7–6); *sf* Milan (d. Witsken 7–6 6–2, Jarryd 6–3 0–6 6–4, Gunnarsson 6–0 7–6, lost Volkov 6–4 6–3), *sf* Copenhagen (d. Zoecke 2–6 6–4 6–3, Jonsson 6–3 6–4, Saceanu 3–6 6–4 6–4, lost Svensson 6–2 1–6 6–3), *sf* Rosmalen (d. Eltingh 3–6 7–5 7–5, Siemerink 7–6 7–5, Mansdorf 6–4 6–3, lost Saceanu 6–3 3–6 7–6). *1991 HIGHLIGHTS – DOUBLES:* (with P. McEnroe unless stated) *won* Basel (d. Korda/J. McEnroe 3–6 7–6 7–6); [Forget] *r/u* Gstaad (lost Muller/Visser 7–6 6–4), *r/u* Vienna (lost Jarryd/Muller 6–4 7–5). *CAREER HIGHLIGHTS – SINGLES: French Open – sf 1991. CAREER HIGHLIGHTS – DOUBLES:* [Jarryd] *LIPC – won 1989* (d. Grabb/P. McEnroe 6–3 ret'd); *IBM/ATP World Doubles –* [Forget] *won 1990* (d. Casal/E. Sanchez 6–4 7–6 5–7 6–4).

ANKE HUBER (Germany)
Born Bruchsal, 4 December 1974; lives Karlsdorf; RH; 2HB; 5ft 8in; 120lb; final 1991 WTA ranking 14; 1991 prize money $196,629.
Coached by Boris Breskvar, who coached both Becker and Graf in the early stages of their development. *1986:* Won Nat 12s. *1987:* Won Nat 14s. *1988:* Won Nat 16s. *1989:* (203) Won European Jun Champs. *1990:* (34) She showed great fighting spirit in extending Sabatini to 2s tb in their 2r encounter at Wimbledon. At end Aug. won her 1st tour title at Schenectady after qualifying and followed with r/u Bayonne, upsetting Garrison and breaking into top 100, then shooting up to top 50 by Oct. Voted WTA most impressive newcomer. *1991:* Upset Maleeva Fragnière and Zvereva *en route* to qf Australian Open, unseeded, reached last 16 Wimbledon and ended Sabatini's winning run as she reached qf Berlin. The high spot of her year, though, came at Filderstadt in autumn, where she upset Garrison, Sukova and Navratilova in fs tb to take the title. It was the 1st time for 8 years that Navratilova had been beaten by an unseeded player. *1991 HIGHLIGHTS – SINGLES:*

Australian Open qf, unseeded (d. Richardson 6–4 6–1, Maleeva Fragnière 6–4 6–4, Shriver 6–3 7–5, Zvereva [seed 11] 6–3 6–4, lost Seles [seed 2] 6–3 6–1), *French Open* 3r, seed 16 (d. Garrone 6–2 6–3, Federica Bonsignori 6–0 6–2, lost Cecchini 6–3 6–4), *Wimbledon* last 16, seed 14 (d. Martinek 6–1 6–2, Tami Whitlinger 6–2 6–1, Bollegraf 6–3 6–7 6–0, lost Garrison [seed 8] 4–6 6–3 6–0), *US OPEN* 2r seed 16 (d. A. Minter 6–1 4–6 6–1, lost Zvereva 6–2 6–4); *won* Filderstadt (d. McNeil 6–4 6–1, Zvereva 6–2 6–2, Garrison 6–2 6–1, Sukova 6–3 7–6, Navratilova 2–6 6–2 7–6). *CAREER HIGHLIGHTS – SINGLES: Australian Open – qf 1991.*

PATRICIA HY (Canada)
Born Cambodia, 22 August 1965; lives Vancouver; RH; 5ft 4in; 119lb; final 1991 WTA ranking 57; 1991 prize money $84,720.
Coached by her father, Ly. In 1981, living in Kowloon, Hong Kong, she was ranked No. 1 in that country at age 16. *1983:* (65) R/u Wimbledon Jun singles and won doubles there with Fendick. On the senior tour she reached sf Nashville. *1984:* (214) An All-American at UCLA, she won Fort Lauderdale on USTA circuit. *1985:* (308). *1986:* (101) Won Taipei and reached sf Singapore. *1987:* (101) Extended Graf to 3s in Fed Cup. *1988:* (205) Won USTA Detroit. *1989:* (222) Won USTA Chicago. *1990:* (103) Qf Singapore. *1991:* Qf VS Indian Wells and upset Fairbank-Nideffer at Wimbledon. *1991 HIGHLIGHTS – SINGLES: Australian Open* 2r (d. Bowes 6–4 6–3, lost Tanvier 6–7 7–5 6–1), *French Open* 2r (d. Mothes 6–2 6–2, lost Novotna [seed 6] 6–2 6–1), *Wimbledon* 3r (d. Fairbank-Nideffer 6–2 3–6 6–0, Paradis Mangon 4–6 6–4 6–2, lost K. Maleeva [seed 5] 6–3 6–4), *US Open* 3r (d. Strandlund 6–3 6–0, McQuillan 6–1 6–2, lost Capriati [seed 7] 6–1 6–4).

GORAN IVANISEVIC (Croatia)
Born Split, 13 September 1971, and lives there; LH; 6ft 4in; 161lb; final 1991 ATP ranking 16; 1991 prize money $562,795.
Coached from Sept. 1989 by Balazs Taroczy. They parted company end 1990, when Bob Brett took over. *1987:* (954) Won US Open Jun doubles with Nargiso. *1988:* (371) Joined Yugoslav D Cup squad. R/u French Open Jun doubles with Coratti and was ranked No. 3 in ITF Jun singles rankings. *1989:* (40) Qf Australian Open after qualifying and last 16 French Open, unseeded. Upset Leconte *en route* to 1st GP sf at Nice, following with 2nd at Palermo and f Florence. *1990:* (9) Helped his country to win World Team Cup in May, then upset Becker 1r French Open *en route* to qf, following with sf appearance at Wimbledon, both unseeded. Won his 1st career title at Stuttgart; r/u Umag, Long Island, Bordeaux and Basel; 2r GS Cup and broke into the top 10. R/u French Open doubles with Korda. *1991:* After a good year in 1990, his game fell apart at the beginning of 1991, and he withdrew from LIPC with compact fracture of left index finger. But then he played through the qualifying to gain a place at Manchester, where he won both singles and doubles, reached f New Haven, plus sf Gstaad, Sydney Indoor and Tokyo Seiko and after a last 16 showing at US Open, he finished the year still in the top 20. In doubles with Camporese he won 3 titles from 4f. Did not play for Yugoslavia in D Cup and, with Prpic, announced in Tokyo in October that henceforth he wanted to be known as a Croatian. *1991 HIGHLIGHTS – SINGLES: Australian Open* 3r, seed 5 (d. Bruguera 6–4 0–6 6–1 6–4, Krishnan 6–4 3–6 4–6 6–1 6–2, lost Prpic 6–3 6–4 6–3), *French Open* 2r, seed 8 (d. Fontang 6–4 1–6 6–3 6–1, lost Haarhuis 6–1 6–4 6–1), *Wimbledon* 2r, seed 10 (d. Castle 7–6 7–6 6–2, lost N. Brown 4–6 6–3 7–6 6–3), *US Open* last 16, seed 12 (d. Holm 6–7 6–3 6–3 7–6, Prpic 6–1 6–3 6–4, Mattar 6–3 6–2 6–2, lost Lendl [seed 5] 7–5 6–7 6–4 6–2); *won* Manchester (d. Castle 7–5 7–6, Bates 6–3 6–4, Thoms 7–5 6–3, Muller 7–6, Sampras 6–4 6–4); *r/u* New Haven (d. Pozzi 7–6 4–6 6–2, Siemerink 6–2 6–4, J. McEnroe 6–4 6–2, Rostagno 6–4 7–5, lost Korda 6–4 6–2); *sf* Gstaad (d. J. Sanchez 5–7 7–5 6–1, Wheaton 6–4 6–4, de la Pena 6–4 6–2, lost Bruguera 6–1 7–5), *sf* Sydney Indoor (d. Youl 6–4 6–3, Reneberg 6–3 6–2, Agassi 7–5 7–6, lost Edberg 4–6 7–6 7–6), *sf* Tokyo Seiko (d. Poliakov 6–4 6–2, Washington 7–6 6–7 6–4, Agassi 6–3 6–4, lost Edberg 4–6 7–6 7–5). *1991 HIGHLIGHTS – DOUBLES:* (with Camporese) *won* Milan (d. Nijssen/Suk 6–4 7–6), *won* Italian Open (d. Jensen/Warder 6–2 6–3), *won* Manchester (d. Brown/Castle 6–4 6–3); *r/u* Stuttgart Mercedes (lost Masur/E. Sanchez 4–6 6–3 6–4). *CAREER HIGHLIGHTS – SINGLES: Wimbledon – sf 1990,* unseeded (d. Leach, Delaitre, Rostagno, Koevermans 4–6 6–3 6–4 7–6, Curren 4 6 6 4 6–4 6–4 6–7 6–3, lost Becker 4–6 7–6 6–0 7–6); *Australian Open – qf 1989,* unseeded (d. Larsson, Fitzgerald 6–3 4–6 6–3 6–4, Nijssen 6–4 6–4 6–0, Lavelle 3–6 3–6 6–3 6–4 6–1, lost Mecir 7–5 6–0 6–3); *French Open – qf 1990,* unseeded (d. Becker 5–7 6–4 7–5 6–2, Jarryd, Kuhnen, Kroon 6–2 6–4 7–5, lost Muster 6–2 4–6 6–4 6–3). *CAREER HIGHLIGHTS – DOUBLES:* (with Korda) *French Open – r/u 1990* (lost Casal/E. Sanchez 7–5 6–3).

NICOLE JAGERMAN (Netherlands)
Born Amstelveen, 23 July 1967, and lives there; RH; 5ft 10in; 148lb; final 1991 WTA ranking 66; 1991 prize money $59,181.
Coached by Frits Don. *1985:* (259). *1986:* (134) Qf Brazilian Open, Argentine Open (d. Garrison in ss) and Hilversum. *1987:* (146) Joined Fed Cup team. *1988:* (72) Last 16 French Open. *1989:* (83) Sf Arcachon and Brussels. *1990:* (68) In singles reached qf Hamburg and in doubles played 2 f with Bakkum. *1991:* At Kitzbuhel she reached sf singles and won the doubles with Fulco. *1991 HIGHLIGHTS – SINGLES: French Open* 3r (d. Strnadova 6–2 6–4, Provis 6–4 5–7 6–3, lost Tauziat [seed 13] 6–4 6–0), *Wimbledon* 2r (d. Oremans 7–5 6–4, lost Kohde-Kilsch 7–6 6–2), *US Open* 1r (lost Gildemeister 7–6 6–4); *sf* Kitzbuhel (d. Schett 7–6 6–2, Paulus 5–7 7–5 6–3, Maruska 6–3 6–3, lost Wiesner 6–2 6–3). *1991 HIGHLIGHTS – DOUBLES:* (with Fulco) *won* Kitzbuhel (d. Cecchini/Tarabini 7–5 6–4).

MARTIN JAITE (Argentina)
Born Buenos Aires, 9 October 1964; lives there and Barcelona, Spain; RH; 5ft 11in; 155lb; final 1991 ATP ranking 46; 1991 prize money $172,827.
Wife Beatrice (married Nov. 1986). Coached by Daniel Garcia. Lived in Spain 1976–83. *1984:* (54) Burst into top 100 with upset of Gerulaitis at French Open and qf appearances at US CC and Barcelona. *1985:* (20) Won his first tournament of year in Buenos Aires, r/u Boston and Washington, and reached qf French Open over Mecir and Gunthardt. *1986:* (17) Won Bologna and Stuttgart, r/u Boston, sf Forest Hills (d. Becker) and US CC and last 16 French Open. *1987:* (14) Last 16 French Open, r/u Italian Open (d. Nystrom), won Barcelona (d. Wilander) and Palermo back-to-back in autumn. Underwent ankle surgery at end of year. *1988:* (54) R/u Monte Carlo, sf Bologna and Itaparica. *1989:* (11) Won Stuttgart, Madrid, Sao Paulo and Itaparica; r/u Rio de Janeiro and Kitzbuhel. *1990:* (36) Won Guaruja and Gstaad; sf Madrid and Schenectady; reached last 16 French Open and broke into top 10 in July. *1991:* Won Nice (d. Forget and Novacek); sf Barcelona and Kitzbuhel (d. E. Sanchez). *1991 HIGHLIGHTS – SINGLES: Australian Open* 2r (d. Herrera 6–3 6–1 3–6 6–7 6–4, lost Stich 6–3 7–6 7–6), *French Open* 2r (d. Ingaramo 4–6 6–4 5–7 7–5 6–4, lost Davin 6–4 6–3 6–2), *US Open* 1r (lost Becker [seed 1] 7–6 6–4 6–4); *won* Nice (d. Forget 6–2 6–2, Arias 6–2 6–1, Furlan 6–2 6–1, Novacek 4–6 6–4 7–6, Prpic 3–6 7–6 6–3); *sf* Barcelona (d. Haarhuis 6–3 6–2, Svensson 7–5 4–6 6–2, Gustafsson 6–3 0–6 7–5, Paloheimo 6–1 4–6 6–3, lost E. Sanchez 7–5 6–2), *sf* Kitzbuhel (d. Jelen 6–3 6–7 6–2, Bergstrom 6–4 6–3, E. Sanchez 6–3 3–6 6–3, lost Gustafsson 6–2 6–2). *CAREER HIGHLIGHTS – SINGLES: French Open – qf 1985* (d. Mecir 2–6 7–6 6–3 6–4, Gunthardt 6–1 6–2 6–3, lost Lendl 6–4 6–2 6–4).

ANDERS JARRYD (Sweden)
Born Lidkoping, 13 July 1961; lives London and Bastad; RH; 2HB; 5ft 11in; 155lb; final 1991 ATP ranking 45 singles, 2 (52) doubles; 1991 prize money $752,514.
Girlfriend Lotta Sundgren; son Niklas (born Feb. 1988). *1981:* (100). *1982:* (60) Playing second singles in D Cup v US, he stunned Gottfried in straight sets. Won Linz and Ancona. *1983:* (19) Won French Open doubles with H. Simonsson, d. McEnroe in sf Canadian Open, losing f to Lendl, and was r/u Bastad. *1984:* (6) Won 2 GP tourns, including Australian Indoor at Sydney where he d. Lendl in f and was r/u US Open doubles with Edberg. Played on winning Swedish D Cup team, contributing decisive win in doubles with Edberg over McEnroe/Fleming. *1985:* (8) Sf Wimbledon, won Brussels over Wilander; r/u Toronto, Milan and Stockholm and won Masters doubles with Edberg. *1986:* (19) Won WCT Finals in Dallas over Wilander and Becker, and r/u French Open doubles, but slowed down after knee surgery, returning to win Masters doubles with Edberg again in Dec. *1987:* (15) In singles reached qf Australian Open and Wimbledon, r/u Wembley; in doubles won Australian and US Opens with Edberg and French Open with Seguso and sf Masters with Edberg. *1988:* (32) Underwent knee surgery early in year. Qf Australian Open; sf Cincinnati and Frankfurt. In doubles with Fitzgerald r/u French Open and Wimbledon, won LIPC and qualified for Masters, losing sf to Casal/E. Sanchez. *1989:* (31) In singles reached f Rotterdam and San Francisco. In doubles won Wimbledon and r/u Masters with Fitzgerald, taking 3 other titles with various partners. *1990:* (73) Restricted for much of the year by a shoulder injury and persistent cough. However, he upset J. McEnroe and Skoff to win Vienna for his 1st title for 4½ years and won The Hague Challenger. *1991:* A year of rejuvenation. In singles reached f Copenhagen and sf Rotterdam, Queen's and Berlin. In doubles with Fitzgerald finished the year with threequarters of a Grand Slam, having won French Open, Wimbledon and US Open, as well as ATP Doubles Champ. With various partners he played 7 other f, winning 4 to regain his place as one of the world's best

doubles players. ***1991 HIGHLIGHTS – SINGLES: Australian Open*** 2r (d. Muller 6–4 6–3 6–1, lost Connell 6–1 7–5 6–2), ***French Open*** 1r (lost E. Sanchez [seed 11] 6–2 6–3 6–2), ***Wimbledon*** 2r (d. Kroon 6–3 6–4 3–6 6–3, lost Volkov 6–2 3–6 6–4 8–6), ***US Open*** 3r (d. Arraya 6–1 6–3 6–3, Champion 7–5 6–2 1–1 ret'd, lost Courier [seed 4] 6–3 6–2 6–2); ***r/u*** Copenhagen (d. Wuyts 6–3 6–2, Gunnarsson 6–3 6–2, Woodforde 6–1 6–3, Woodbridge 6–0 6–4, lost Svensson 6–7 6–2 6–2); ***sf*** Rotterdam (d. Mansdorf 6–4 6–2, E. Sanchez 6–2 6–2, Siemerink 7–6 6–2, lost Lendl 7–5 6–4), ***sf*** Queen's (d. Pearce 6–3 3–6 6–3, Oncins 6–2 6–1, Connell 6–2 6–1, lost Wheaton 6–3 6–4), ***sf*** Berlin (d. Kriek 6–3 6–2, Santoro 6–3 6–7 6–3, Stich 6–4 7–6, lost Korda 6–3 1–6 6–2). ***1991 HIGHLIGHTS – DOUBLES:*** (with Fitzgerald unless stated) ***won French Open*** (d. R. Leach/Pugh 6–0 7–6), ***won Wimbledon*** (d. Frana/Lavalle 6–3 6–4 6–7 6–1), ***won US Open*** (d. Davis/Pate 6–3 3–6 6–3 6–3); [Galbraith] ***won*** Rotterdam (d. Devries/MacPherson 7–6 6–2), [Muller] ***won*** Vienna (d. Hlasek/P. McEnroe 6–4 7–5), ***won*** Stockholm (d. Nijssen/Suk 7–5 6–2), ***won*** Paris Open (d. Jones/Leach 3–6 6–3 6–2), ***won*** ATP Doubles Champ (d. Flach/Seguso 6–4 6–4 2–6 6–4); ***r/u*** Tokyo Suntory (lost Edberg/Woodbridge 6–4 5–7 6–4), [Visser] ***r/u*** Munich (lost Galbraith/Witsken 7–5 6–4), [Gustafsson] ***r/u*** Bastad (lost Bathman/Bergh 6–4 6–4). ***CAREER HIGHLIGHTS – SINGLES: Wimbledon – sf 1985*** (d. Visser, Gunthardt 6–4 6–3 6–2, lost Becker 2–6 7–6 6–3 6–3). ***CAREER HIGHLIGHTS – DOUBLES:*** (with Fitzgerald unless stated) ***Australian Open –*** [Edberg] ***won 1987*** (d. Doohan/Warder 6–4 6–4 7–6); ***French Open –*** [H. Simonsson] ***won 1983***, seed 8 (d. Edmondson/Stewart 7–6 6–4 6–2), [Seguso] ***won 1987*** (d. Forget/Noah 6–7 6–7 6–3 6–4 6–2), ***won 1991***, [Edberg] ***r/u 1986*** (lost Fitzgerald/Smid 6–3 4–6 6–3 6–7 14–12), ***r/u 1988*** (lost Gomez/E. Sanchez 6–3 6–7 6–4 6–3), [Edberg] ***sf 1985*** (d. Annacone/Van Rensburg, lost Glickstein/H. Simonsson 6–3 6–4 6–1); ***Wimbledon – won 1989*** (d. R. Leach/Pugh 3–6 7–6 6–4 7–6), ***won 1991, r/u 1988*** (lost Flach/Seguso 6–4 2–6 6–4 7–6); ***US Open –*** [Edberg] ***won 1987*** (d. Flach/Seguso 7–6 6–2 4–6 5–7 7–6), ***won 1991***, [Edberg] ***r/u 1984*** (d. McEnroe/Fleming 3–6 7–6 7–5 7–6, lost Fitzgerald/Smid 7–6 6–3 6–3); ***Masters/ATP Doubles Champ –*** [Edberg] ***won 1985*** (d. Nystrom/Wilander 4–6 6–2 6–3), [Edberg] ***won 1986*** (d. Forget/Noah 6–3 7–6 6–3), ***won 1991, r/u 1989*** (lost Grabb/P. McEnroe 7–5 7–6 5–7 6–3); ***LIPC – won 1988*** (d. Flach/Seguso 7–6 6–1 7–5), [Hlasek] ***won 1989*** (d. Grabb/P. McEnroe 6–3 ret'd).

LARS JONSSON (Sweden)
Born Goteborg, 27 June 1970; lives Onsala and Monte Carlo; RH; 6ft 2in; 155lb; final 1991 ATP ranking 78; 1991 prize money $109,303.
Coached by Tim Klein. ***1984:*** Nat Jun Champ. ***1987:*** (897). ***1988:*** (452). ***1989:*** (102) Qf Geneva; won Dublin and Tampere Challengers. ***1990:*** (100) Upset Perez-Roldan *en route* to 1st tour sf at Bastad. ***1991:*** Reached his 1st GP f at Wellington, upsetting Volkov 1r, appeared in qf Munich, Bordeaux and Athens and extended Chang to 5s French Open. ***1991 HIGHLIGHTS – SINGLES: Australian Open*** 1r (lost Wuyts 5–7 5–7 6–4 7–6 9–7), ***French Open*** 2r (d. de la Pena 7–6 6–3 2–0 ret'd, lost Chang [seed 10] 7–6 4–6 6–4 3–6 6–3), ***Wimbledon*** 2r (d. Vajda 7–5 6–3 7–5, lost Gunnarsson 6–2 6–3 2–6 7–6); ***r/u*** Wellington (d. Volkov 6–4 6–2, Oncins 6–2 6–2, Sznajder 6–2 6–2, Camporese 5–7 6–3 7–6, lost Fromberg 6–1 6–4 6–4). ***1991 HIGHLIGHTS – DOUBLES:*** [Larsson] ***won*** Florence (d. Baguena/Costa 3–6 6–1 6–1); [Henricsson] ***r/u*** Geneva (lost Bruguera/Rosset 3–6 6–3 6–2).

KATHY JORDAN (USA)
Born Bryn Mawr, Pa., 3 December 1959; lives King of Prussia, Pa.; RH; 5ft 8in; 130lb; final 1991 WTA ranking 21 doubles; 1991 prize money $52,716.
1977: R/u US Nat 18 Champs. ***1979:*** (11) Won AIAW Champs while at Stanford and came within 2 points of beating eventual champ Tracy Austin in last 16 US Open. ***1980:*** (13) Won Wimbledon and French Open doubles with A. Smith. ***1981:*** (15) Won US and Australian doubles with A. Smith. ***1982:*** (21) Won Boston indoors over Turnbull. ***1983:*** (14) Reached qf Wimbledon, upsetting Evert Lloyd in 3r to hand her fellow-American her first pre-semi final defeat in 35 GS events. R/u Australian Open to Navratilova. ***1984:*** (10) Ranked 5 for 9 months in her finest year, reaching sf Wimbledon with upset of Shriver and f Eastbourne with win over Evert Lloyd. ***1985:*** (19) Won Wimbledon doubles again with Smylie, ending the 109-match winning streak of Navratilova/Shriver in memorable 3s f. ***1986:*** (15) Had first career win in 13 meetings with Navratilova in sf VS Oakland and won French Open and Wimbledon mixed doubles with Flach. ***1987:*** (36) Out of action for first half of year with a string of injuries, returning to form in autumn to be r/u US Open doubles with Smylie and d. Garrison to reach sf Brighton. ***1988:*** (—) Underwent knee surgery in July and was out of action for the next 12 months. ***1989:*** (—) Returned to action at San Diego, playing doubles only and wearing a knee brace; played her first singles match at Albuquerque, where she

lost 1r to Reggi. *1990:* (205) Again concentrating mainly on doubles, was r/u Wimbledon and won VS Champs plus 2 other titles with Smylie, taking a 4th with Savchenko. *1991:* Won Tokyo Pan Pacific with Smylie. *1991 HIGHLIGHTS – DOUBLES:* (with Smylie) *won* Tokyo Pan Pacific (d. M. J. Fernandez/R. White 4–6 6–0 6–3). *CAREER HIGHLIGHTS – SINGLES: Wimbledon – qf 1983* (d. Evert Lloyd 6–1 7–6, lost King), *sf 1984* (d. Shriver 2–0 0–0 0–4, lost Navratilova 6–3 6–1). *CAREER HIGHLIGHTS – DOUBLES:* (with A Smith unless stated) *Australian Open – won 1981* (d. Navratilova/Shriver 6–2 7–5); *French Open – won 1980* (d. Madruga/Villagran 6–1 6–0); *Wimbledon – won 1980* (d. Casals/Turnbull 3–6 7–6 6–1), [Smylie] *won 1985* (d. Navratilova/Shriver 5–7 6–3 6–4), *r/u 1981* (lost Navratilova/Shriver 6–3 7–6), *r/u 1982* (lost Navratilova/Shriver 6–4 6–1), *r/u 1984* (lost Navratilova/Shriver 6–3 6–1), [Smylie] *r/u 1990* (lost Novotna/Sukova 6–3 6–4); *US Open – won 1981* (d. Casals/Turnbull 6–3 6–3), [Smylie] *r/u 1987* (lost Navratilova/Shriver 5–7 6–4 6–2); *VS Champs* – [Smylie] *won 1990* (d. Paz/Sanchez-Vicario 7–6 6–4). *CAREER HIGHLIGHTS – MIXED DOUBLES:* (with Flach) *French Open – won 1986* (d. Edmondson/Fairbank 4–6 7–5 6–3); *Wimbledon – won 1986* (d. Navratilova/Gunthardt 6–3 7–6).

MICHAEL JOYCE (USA)
Born Santa Monica, Ca., 1 February 1973; RH; 5ft 11in; 155lb; final 1991 ATP ranking 606.
Father, Mike, former movie producer. Sister Brigid one of top US juniors. *1987:* Won US National Indoor 14s. *1988:* Won US National Hardcourt 16s. *1989:* won US National Indoor 18s. *1991:* Qf French Open Jun; r/u Wimbledon Jun; won US Nat Junior 18s and earned wild card into US Open where he turned pro.

HELEN KELESI (Canada)
Born Victoria, 15 November 1969; lives Toronto; RH; 2HB; 5ft 5in; 130lb; final 1991 WTA ranking 29; 1991 prize money $139,843.
Coached by her father, Milan. *1985:* (48) The daughter of Czech parents who left that country for Canada a year before her birth, this feisty, gritty backcourt player made her mark on the tour, reaching f VS Central NY. *1986:* (40) Won her first pro event – Japan Open – and d. Mandlikova VS New England. *1987:* (33) Upset Kohde-Kilsch at Amelia Island and Lindqvist at French Open, where she held sp against Graf last 16. Reached qf Canadian Open, played Fed Cup and took over No. 1 ranking in Canada from Bassett Seguso. *1988:* (19) Extended Sabatini to 3s qf French Open and f Italian Open. Upset Maleeva Fragnière twice; won Taranto, r/u Cincinnati and qualified for VS Champs 1st time. *1989:* (13) Qf French Open, r/u Barcelona and VS Nashville, sf Berlin and San Juan to qualify for VS Champs. *1990:* (25) In singles was r/u Geneva and upset Sanchez-Vicario *en route* to sf Italian Open, where she won the doubles with Seles, reaching 2 other f with Reggi. *1991:* R/u Geneva; sf VS Chicago (d. Novotna), Palm Springs and Bol; won Midland Challenger and upset Sukova at French Open. *1991 HIGHLIGHTS – SINGLES: French Open* 3r (d. Rittner 6–0 6–2, Sukova [seed 12] 4–6 7–5 6–0, lost McQuillan 6–4 3–6 6–4), *Wimbledon* 1r (lost Durie 6–3 6–2), *US Open* 2r (d. Van Lottum 6–3 7–5, lost Gomer 6–2 2–6 6–3); *won* Midland Challenger (d. McGrath 6–2 6–2); *r/u* Geneva (d. Mothes 7–5 6–3, Helgeson 6–7 7–5 6–1, Martinez 6–4 6–7 6–2, lost Maleeva Fragnière 6–3 3–6 6–3); *sf* VS Chicago (d. Strnadova 6–4 7–5, Novotna 2–6 7–6 7–6, Frazier 7–5 6–3, lost Garrison 6–1 6–2), *sf* VS Palm Springs (d. C. Wood 6–4 6–4, Fairbank-Nideffer 6–4 3–6 6–2, Louie Harper 6–4 3–6 6–2, lost Seles 6–0 6–3), *sf* Bol (d. Bobkova 6–1 6–4, Thoren 6–1 6–2, Foldenyi 7–5 6–1, lost Magdalena Maleeva 6–4 7–5). *CAREER HIGHLIGHTS – SINGLES: French Open – qf 1988* (d. Manuela Maleeva 6–4 6–2, Jagerman, lost Sabatini 4–6 6–1 6–3), *qf 1989* (d. Zrubakova, Temesvari, Magers 6–4 2–6 6–3, Grossman 6–1 6–2, lost M. J. Fernandez 6–2 7–5).

AUDRA KELLER (USA)
Born Macon, Ga., 17 November 1971; lives Memphis, Tenn.; RH; 2HB; 5ft 8in; 132lb; final 1991 WTA ranking 97; 1991 prize money $66,399.
Coached by Phil Chamberlain. *1988:* Ranked No. 1 in Nat 16s. *1989:* (154) Ranked No. 1 in Nat 18s. *1990:* (94) Upsets of Savchenko and Fendick, followed by a qf appearance at Puerto Rico (d. Kelesi), took her into the top 100 in autumn. *1991:* Although disappointing early performance saw her slip out of the top 100, she returned in Nov. with r/u showing at Indianapolis, upsetting Fendick and Zrubakova on the way. *1991 HIGHLIGHTS – SINGLES: Australian Open* 1r (lost Javer 6–2 6–2), *French Open* 1r (lost Caverzasio 6–4 6–3), *Wimbledon* 2r (d. Golarsa 7–5 6–3, lost M. J. Fernandez [seed 6] 7–6 6–1), *US Open* 1r (lost Basuki 6–1 6–4); *r/u* Indianapolis (d. Fendick 7–5 6–3, Langrova 6–2 6–3, Thoren 6–2 6–3, Zrubakova 6–2 6–4, lost K. Maleeva 7–6 6–2).

MAYA KIDOWAKI (Japan)
Born Kyoto, 17 May 1969; lives Tokyo; RH; 5ft 6in; 125lb; final 1991 WTA ranking 73; 1991 prize money $79,524.
1985: (263). **1986:** (304). **1987:** (219). **1988:** (243) Won 3 titles back-to-back on Japanese satellite circuit. **1989:** (136) Won singles and doubles titles again on the Japanese satellite circuit. **1990:** (89) Made her mark on the primary circuit and broke into the top 100 in April after reaching sf Singapore, where she took Sawamatsu to 3s. **1991:** Reached qf Geneva and Tokyo Nicherei in singles, winning Tokyo Suntory doubles with Frazier. **1991 HIGHLIGHTS – SINGLES: Australian Open** 2r (d. Sharpe 1–6 6–1 6–4, lost Graf [seed 1] 6–1 6–0), **French Open** 3r (d. Schultz 6–4 6–4, Van Lottum 6–3 5–7 8–6, lost Capriati 6–3 6–0), **Wimbledon** 2r (d. Bentley 1–6 7–5 6–1, lost Garrone 6–4 6–3), **US Open** 1r (lost Habsudova 6–1 6–4). **1991 HIGHLIGHTS – DOUBLES:** (with Frazier) **won** Tokyo Suntory (d. Kamio/Kijimuta 6–2 6–4).

AKIKO KIJIMUTA (Japan)
Born Tokyo, 1 May 1968; lives Kanagawa; RH; 2HB; 5ft 4½in; 115lb; final 1991 WTA ranking 65; 1991 prize money $74,188.
1986: (128) Qf Singapore. **1987:** (79) Upset Potter 1r US Open and played Fed Cup. **1988:** Extended Navratilova to 3s at Australian Open. **1989:** (56) Upset Sukova 2r French Open and reached f Singapore. **1990:** (113) Sf Tokyo Pan Pacific. **1991:** R/u Brisbane. **1991 HIGHLIGHTS – SINGLES: Australian Open** 1r (lost Martinek 6–3 6–1), **French Open** 2r (d. Strandlund 6–0 6–4, lost K. Maleeva [seed 11] 6–2 6–3), **Wimbledon** 2r (d. Paz 6–1 6–3, lost Tauziat [seed 12] 3–6 6–2 6–2), **US Open** 1r (lost Schultz 3–6 6–3 6–2); **r/u** Brisbane (d. Shriver 6–4 6–2, Paulus 6–2 6–3, Kidowaki 6–4 6–4, McQuillan 6–2 6–7 6–3, Savchenko 6–2 5–7 6–2, lost Sukova 6–4 6–3). **1991 HIGHLIGHTS – DOUBLES:** (with Kamio) **r/u** Tokyo Suntory (lost Frazier/Kidowaki 6–2 6–4).

MARKETA KOCHTA (Germany)
Born Prague, Czechoslovakia, 14 July 1975; lives Munich; RH; 5ft 7½in; 122lb; final 1991 WTA ranking 79; 1991 prize money $30,206.
Coached by her father, Jiri. **1989:** (442) Won Nat Jun Champs in singles and doubles. **1990:** (172). **1991:** Reached qf Westchester and Zurich. **1991 HIGHLIGHTS – SINGLES: Australian Open** 1r (lost Porwik 7–6 6–3).

MARK KOEVERMANS (Netherlands)
Born Rotterdam, 3 February 1968, and lives there; RH; 6ft 1in; 175lb; final 1991 ATP ranking 70; 1991 prize money $227,213.
Coached by Fritz Don. **1987:** (524). **1988:** (139) Won Salou Challenger and joined the Dutch D Cup squad. **1989:** (63) Broke into top 100 March after being r/u Casablanca and Agadir Challengers. Reached 1st GP sf at Sao Paulo and upset K. Carlsson 1r Italian Open, where he reached qf despite playing with a broken toe suffered two weeks earlier. **1990:** (48) Having appeared in qf Adelaide, Casablanca, Madrid and Genova and won Porto Challenger, he took his 1st tour title at Athens and reached sf Sao Paulo. In GS he reached last 16 Wimbledon, unseeded. **1991:** Upset Sampras *en route* to qf Memphis and Bruguera on his way to sf Hilversum. In doubles won 2 titles with Haarhuis and Eltingh from 4 f. **1991 HIGHLIGHTS – SINGLES: Australian Open** 3r (d. Pate 6–4 6–2 3–6 2–6 6–0, Stoltenberg 6–3 6–3 6–3, lost Siemerink 4–6 6–2 6–4 3–6 6–1), **French Open** 1r (lost Chesnokov 7–5 6–2 6–7 2–6 6–3), **Wimbledon** 1r (lost Washington 6–3 6–2 6–3), **US Open** 1r (lost Grabb 6–4 7–6 6–2); **sf** Hilversum (d. Haarhuis 7–6 6–2, Bruguera 7–5 6–4, Furlan 6–1 6–1, lost Arrese 6–3 3–6 6–4). **1991 HIGHLIGHTS – DOUBLES:** (with Haarhuis unless stated) **won** Estoril (d. Nijssen/Suk 6–3 6–3), [Eltingh] **won** Athens (d. Oosting/Rahnasto 5–7 7–6 7–5); **r/u** Adelaide (lost Ferreira/Kruger 6–4 4–6 6–4), **r/u** Monte Carlo (lost Jensen/Warder 5–7 7–6 6–4).

CLAUDIA KOHDE-KILSCH (Germany)
Born Saarbrucken, 11 December 1963; lives there and Monte Carlo; RH; 6ft 0½in; 150lb; final 1991 WTA ranking 84; 1991 prize money $108,507.
Coached by Bob Rheinberger. **1979:** Ranked in top 10 jun, she won German Int Jun event. **1980:** (78). **1981:** (20) Upset Navratilova 1r VS Oakland and won Swiss Open. **1982:** (19) Won Avon Futures Champs, reached sf Mahwah and r/u Australian Open doubles. **1983:** (24) Adopted by her step-father, Jurgen Kilsch, and added his name to hers. **1984:** (8) Won German Open and r/u Australian and French Open doubles. **1985:** (5) Reached sf French and Australian Opens; upset Navratilova in qf on way to f Canadian Open, won US Open doubles, and r/u French Open and Australian Open doubles with Sukova. **1986:** (7) R/u WTA Champs. **1987:** (10) Sf Australian Open, qf Wimbledon and French and US Opens; won Wimbledon doubles with Sukova and qualified for VS Champs in singles and doubles.

1988: (12) Sf Australian Open, won Birmingham and reached 5 other sf, qualifying for VS Champs in both singles and doubles again. R/u French Open doubles with Sukova and reached 6 other f with various partners. Underwent knee operation in June, missing Wimbledon. *1989:* (36) Still plagued by injuries, she was inconsistent but reached qf Australian Open and sf Birmingham. *1990:* (46) Still struggling to regain her form, she won Kitzbuhel for her 1st title since 1988. *1991:* In singles reached sf Linz and qf Strasbourg. In doubles won Oslo with Meier and FC Cup with Zvereva. *1991 HIGHLIGHTS – SINGLES: Australian Open* 1r (lost Smylie 2–6 6–4 6–4), *French Open* 2r (d. Loosemore 6–1 6–3, lost Meskhi [seed 14] 7–5 6–1), *Wimbledon* 3r (d. Griffiths 6–1 6–3, Jagerman 7–6 6–2, lost Wiesner [seed 9] 7–6 6–2), *US Open* 1r (lost Herreman 4–6 6–4 6–3); *sf* Linz (d. Testud 6–1 7–5, Ritter 6–4 5–7 6–3, Reggi 7–6 6–3, lost Langrova 4–6 6–1 6–4). *1991 HIGHLIGHTS – DOUBLES:* [Meier] *won* Oslo (d. Appelmans/Reggi 3–6 6–2 6–4), [Zvereva] *won* FC Cup (d. Daniels/Gregory 6–4 6–0); [Sukova] *r/u* Toronto (lost Savchenko/Zvereva 1–6 7–5 6–2). *CAREER HIGHLIGHTS – SINGLES: French Open – sf 1985* (d. Mandlikova 6–4 6–4, lost Navratilova 6–4 6–4); *Australian Open – sf 1985* (lost Evert Lloyd 6–1 7–6), *sf 1987* (d. Hanika, Smylie 7–6 4–6 6–2, lost Mandikova 6–1 0–6 6–3), *sf 1988* (d. Zrubakova 3–6 6–0 6–3, A. Minter 6–2 6–4, lost Graf 6–2 6–3); *US Open – sf 1985* (lost Evert Lloyd 6–3 6–3). *CAREER HIGHLIGHTS – DOUBLES:* (with Sukova unless stated) *Wimbledon – won 1987* (d. Nagelsen/Smylie 6–4 6–7 6–4); *US Open – won 1985* (d. Navratilova/Shriver 6–7 6–2 6–3); *Australian Open –* [Pfaff] *r/u 1982* (lost Navratilova/Shriver 6–4 6–2), *r/u 1984* (lost Navratilova/Shriver 6–3 6–4), *r/u 1985* (lost Navratilova/Shriver 6–3 6–4); *French Open –* [Mandlikova] *r/u 1984* (lost Navratilova/Shriver 5–7 6–3 6–2), *r/u 1985* (lost Navratilova/Shriver 4–6 6–2 6–2), *r/u 1988* (lost Navratilova/Shriver 6–2 7–5); *VS Champs – r/u 1984–85* (lost Navratilova/Shriver 6–7 6–4 7–6), *r/u 1985–86* (lost Mandlikova/Turnbull 6–4 6–7 6–3), *r/u Nov. 1986* (lost Navratilova/Shriver 7–6 6–3), *r/u 1987* (lost Navratilova/Shriver 6–1 6–1).

PETR KORDA (Czechoslovakia)
Born Prague, 23 January 1968, and lives there; LH; 6ft 3in; 145lb; final 1991 ATP ranking 9 singles, 63 doubles; 1991 prize money $573,970.
1986: (511) Won Wimbledon Jun doubles with Carbonell. *1987:* (87) Won Budapest Challenger; qf Prague (d. Srejber). *1988:* (188) Broke into top 100 in May and upset E. Sanchez in his 1st tourn on grass at Wimbledon. In doubles won Gstaad and Prague. Out of action with shoulder and ankle injuries following a car accident. *1989:* (59) Reached his 1st GP f at Frankfurt in autumn after sf showing at Vienna. In doubles won Stuttgart and reached 3 other f. *1990:* (38) Reached sf Philadelphia, Munich (d. Chang) and Moscow, and upset Gomez at Toronto World Tennis. In doubles r/u French Open with Ivanisevic and reached 3 more f, winning Monte Carlo with Smid. *1991:* Made tremendous strides as he moved into the top 10 in autumn. Won his 1st tour singles title at New Haven, following with Berlin and also winning the doubles at both tourns. R/u Tampa, Washington (d. B. Gilbert), Montreal (d. Agassi and Courier); sf Umag and Vienna, and upset Lendl *en route* to qf Stockholm. *1991 HIGHLIGHTS – SINGLES: Australian Open* 2r (d. Volkov 6–1 1–6 1–6 6–4 7–5), lost Krajicek 4–6 7–6 6–3 6–4), *French Open* 2r (d. Fleurian 4–6 6–4 6–2 6–4, lost Agasssi [seed 4] 6–1 6–2 6–2), *Wimbledon* 1r (lost Wheaton 7–6 6–7 6–4 6–2), *US Open* 1r, seed 15 (lost Boetsch 6–1 6–3 3–6 6–2); *won* New Haven (d. Fleurian 6–3 6–3, Frana 7–6 6–3, Reneberg 6–3 7–6, Camporese 6–4 6–1, Rosset 6–4 6–3, Ivanisevic 6–4 6–2), *won* Berlin (d. Agenor 6–3 1–6 6–3, Riglewski 7–6 6–3, Volkov 6–3 5–7 6–1, Jarryd 6–3 1–6 6–2, Boetsch 6–3 6–4); *r/u* Tampa (d. Leach 6–3 6–2, J. Brown 6–4 2–6 7–6, Pernfors 6–3 6–2, Garner 6–4 6–4, lost Reneberg 4–6 6–4 6–2), *r/u* Washington (d. Pereira 4–6 6–3 6–2, Garnett 7–6 7–6, Rostagno 6–1 6–4, B. Gilbert 7–6 7–6, Zoecke 6–2 6–4, lost Agassi 6–3 6–4), *r/u* Montreal (d. Pozzi 3–6 6–3 7–6, Agassi 7–6 6–2, Raoux 6–2 6–3, Hlasek 7–6 6–4, Courier 3–6 7–6 6–2, lost Chesnokov 3–6 6–4 6–3); *sf* Umag (d. Champion 6–4 3–6 6–3, Marques 6–2 6–1, Reneberg 7–5 6–4, lost J. Sanchez 0–6 7–6 7–5), *sf* Vienna (d. Hombrecher 4–6 6–1 6–2, Jonsson 6–2 6–4, Krickstein 4–6 6–2 6–1, lost Stich 6–4 2–6 6–2). *1991 HIGHLIGHTS – DOUBLES:* [Masur] *won* New Haven (d. J. Brown/Melville 7–5 6–3), [Novacek] *won* Berlin (d. Siemerink 3–6 7–5 7–5); [J. McEnroe] *r/u* Basel (lost Hlasek/P. McEnroe 3–6 7–6 7–6). *CAREER HIGHLIGHTS – DOUBLES:* (with Ivanisevic) *French Open – r/u 1990* (lost Casal/E. Sanchez 7–5 6–3).

LARS KOSLOWSKI (Germany)
Born Kassel, Germany, 22 May 1971, and lives there; RH; 6ft 2in; 159lb; final 1991 ATP ranking 87; 1991 prize money $76,530.
Coached by Karl Meiler. *1991:* After qualifying for only his 2nd tournament on the main tour at Stuttgart Mercedes, he upset Jaite, Forget and Prpic back-to-back as he swept to sf. On

the Challenger circuit he won Sevilla and Reggio Calabria. *1991 HIGHLIGHTS – SINGLES:* ***won*** Sevilla Challenger (d. Nydahl 6–2 3–6 7–6), ***won*** Reggio Calabria Challenger (d. Hirszon 6–4 6–2), *sf* Stuttgart Mercedes (d. Roig 7–6 7–6, Jaite 6–3 6–4, Forget 7–6 7–6, Prpic 6–2 2–6 7–5, lost Mancini 4–6 6–1 6–3).

RICHARD KRAJICEK (Netherlands)
Born Rotterdam, 6 December 1971; lives The Hague; RH; 6ft 3in; 175lb; final 1991 ATP ranking 40; 1991 prize money $231,590.
Coached by Rohan Goetzke. Won Nat 12s and 14s. *1990:* (129) Won Verona and Casablanca Challengers. *1991:* Reached last 16 Australian Open, unseeded, then at Hong Kong in April he won his 1st tour title in his 1st f. At New Haven upset Edberg *en route* to qf (where he retired) and Hlasek and J. McEnroe in reaching sf Toulouse. At US Open held 2 mps v Lendl 1r before losing in 5s, and in doubles reached 2 f with Siemerink, winning Hilversum. *1991 HIGHLIGHTS – SINGLES: **Australian Open*** last 16, unseeded (d. Santoro 2–6 6–1 6–2 6–3, Kords 4–6 7–6 6–3 6–4, Cahill 6–7 6–3 6–3 7–6, lost Caratti 6–3 6–4 6–7 3–6 6–4), **French Open** 2r (d. Altur 6–0 6–4 6–1, lost Stich 6–7 7–6 6–3 6–2), ***Wimbledon*** 3r (d. Ruah 5–7 6–1 3–6 6–3 6–4, Larsson 6–3 6–4 6–3, lost Agassi [seed 5] 7–6 6–3 7–6), ***US Open*** 1r (lost Lendl [seed 5] 3–6 2–6 6–4 7–6 6–0); ***won*** Hong Kong (d. Borwick 6–4 6–7 6–3, Masso 6–1 6–4, Kuhnen 7–6 2–6 6–1, Muller 6–2 6–4, Masur 6–2 3–6 6–3); *sf* Toulouse (d. Fontang 6–2 6–0, Hlasek 6–2 6–4, J. McEnroe 6–4 6–4, lost Forget 6–2 7–6). *1991 HIGHLIGHTS – DOUBLES:* (with Siemerink) ***won*** Hilversum (d. Clavet/Gustafsson 7–5 6–4); *r/u* Rosamlen (lost Davids/Haarhuis 6–3 7–6).

AARON KRICKSTEIN (USA)
Born Ann Arbor, Mich., 2 August 1967; lives Grosse Pointe, Mich.; RH; 2HB; 6ft; 160lb; final 1991 ATP ranking 34; 1991 prize money $324,005.
Attended Nick Bollettieri Tennis Academy. Coached by Tim Gullikson from 1989. *1982:* Won US Nat 16 at Kalamazoo. *1983:* (94) Won Nat 18 at Kalamazoo and turned pro in autumn, after arriving in last 16 at US Open where he upended Edberg and Gerulaitis in 5s before Noah stopped him. He won his first pro event in Tel Aviv to become youngest ever to capture GP tournament at 16 years, 2 months, 13 days. *1984:* (12) Won US Pro and two other GP titles and reached f Italian Open, including Wilander among his major victims. *1985:* (30) Despite r/u showing in Hong Kong and last 16 French Open, he did not live up to promise of previous two years. *1986:* (26) Made history at US Open with two straight triumphs from two-sets-to-love down against Novacek and Annacone, and added a straight-sets dismissal of Purcell to reach last 16. R/u Tel Aviv and contributed to US D Cup win over Ecuador with win over Viver. *1987:* (61) Reached qf 3 times, but progressed no further. Stress fracture of left tibia kept him out Aug–Sept, and before he could return to action, a rib injury sustained in a motor accident sidelined him until Feb. 1988. *1988:* (15) Qf US Open, upsetting Gomez and Edberg back-to-back, r/u Tel Aviv and Detroit and reached 3 other sf. *1989:* (8) Regained his old form, returning to top 10 in Oct. after sf appearance at US Open. At Sydney in Jan. he won his 1st title since Geneva in Sept. 1984. At Los Angeles in Sept. took his 1st SS title since US Pro in July 1984 and followed with Tokyo Seiko in Oct. (d. Edberg). Qualified for Masters. *1990:* (20) *En route* to f Tokyo Suntory had back-to-back wins v Chang and Lendl (for the 1st time), despite nursing a hamstring injury that forced him to withdraw from Orlando. Also appeared in f Brisbane and sf Sydney, reached qf US Open, and reached 2r GS Cup. *1991:* Switched to a remodelled racket in late summer, which seemed to revive his fortunes. Unseeded at US Open, he upset Agassi *en route* to last 16, where he lost in 5s tb to an inspired Connors. He followed with r/u Brisbane, upsetting Chesnokov, and swept to sf Stockholm with back-to-back upsets of Stich and Hlasek. *1991 HIGHLIGHTS – SINGLES: **Australian Open*** last 16, seed 13 (d. Youl 6–4 6–4 6–4, Mansdorf 7–5 3–6 7–6 6–2, Kuhnen 6–4 6–4 6–1, lost Lendl [seed 3] 6–2 6–2 6–1), **French Open** 2r (d. Masso 6–7 6–4 2–6 6–1 7–5, lost Gustafsson 6–1 4–6 6–4 6–2), ***Wimbledon*** 2r (d. Pescosolido 6–1 6–3 6–7 6–7 7–5, lost Connors 6–3 6–2 2–6 2), ***US Open*** last 16, unseeded (d. Agassi [seed 8] 7–5 7–6 6–2, Yzaga 6–1 3–6 6–1 3–2 ret'd, Clavet 6–4 6–4 6–7 7–6, lost Connors 3–6 7–6 1–6 6–3 7–6); *r/u* Brisbane (d. Fitzgerald 6–3 7–6, Woodforde 6–3 7–5, Ferreira 6–4 6–3, Chesnokov 7 5 6 4, lost Pozzi 6–3 7–6); *sf* Stockholm (d. Pimek 6–2 2–6 7–6, Stich 6–7 7–6 6–0, Hlasek 6–2 3–6 6–2, Ivanisevic 7–6 1–0 ret'd, lost Edberg 6–2 6–2). *CAREER HIGHLIGHTS – SINGLES: **US Open** – sf 1989* (d. Matuszewski, Masur 2–6 6–4 7–6 6–3, Volkov 3–6 3–6 6–4 6–2 6–3, Haarhuis 6–2 6–4 7–5, Berger 3–6 6–4 6–2 1–0 ret'd, lost Becker 6–4 6–3 6–4), *qf 1990* (d. Sznajder, Stoltenberg, Cash, Mansdorf 6–3 6–4 6–4, lost Becker 3–6 6–3 6–3 6–3).

KARIN KSCHWENDT (Luxembourg)
Born Sorengo, Switzerland, 14 September 1968; lives Leuggern, Switzerland; RH; 5ft 8in; 127lb; final 1991 WTA ranking 88; 1991 prize money $70,455.
Speaks six languages. Plays Fed Cup for Luxembourg. *1986:* (415). *1987:* (342). *1988:* (199) Won Palermo on the Italian satellite circuit. *1989:* (169). *1990:* (115) Upset Rinaldi at Wimbledon and in doubles with Garrone won Palormo and Athens. *1991:* Upset Sloane at LIPC and reached qf Pattaya Island. *1991 HIGHLIGHTS – SINGLES: Australian Open* 3r (d. Langrova 2–6 6–3 6–2, Rajchrtova 6–1 6–1, lost Seles [seed 2] 6–1 6–0), *Wimbledon* 1r (lost Frazier [seed 15] 7–6 6–4), *US Open* 1r (lost Magdalena Maleeva 5–7 7–6).

PATRIK KUHNEN (Germany)
Born Puttlingen, 11 February 1966, and lives there; RH; 6ft 2in; 170lb; final 1991 ATP ranking 86; 1991 prize money $161,479.
Coached by Bob Rheinberger. *1987:* (83) Qf Indianapolis and won Bergen on satellite circuit. *1988:* (61) Sprung one of the surprises of the year at Wimbledon, where he upset Connors to reach qf. Sf Brussels and qf Frankfurt. *1989:* (69) R/u Adelaide. *1990:* (82) Sf Hong Kong, qf Stuttgart and Seoul. *1991:* Reached sf Berlin, and qf Adelaide, Auckland and Hong Kong. *1991 HIGHLIGHTS – SINGLES: Australian Open* 3r (d. Raoux 7–5 6–4 7–6, Dosedel 6–2 6–4 6–4, lost Krickstein [seed 13] 6–4 6–4 6–1), *French Open* 2r (d. Raoux 4–6 6–2 6–4 6–4, lost Chesnokov 4–6 6–3 3–6 6–3 8–6), *Wimbledon* 3r (d. Rahunen 6–4 6–3 6–4, Petchey 6–2 6–4 6–3, lost Mayotte 3–6 6–2 7–6 6–4), *US Open* 2r (d. Youl 7–6 6–7 6–4 6–2, lost Lendl [seed 5] 6–3 6–2 6–4); *sf* Berlin (d. Mronz 6–3 6–4, Mayotte 3–6 7–5 6–4, Pioline 7–6 6–3, lost Boetsch 6–3 6–2). *1991 HIGHLIGHTS – DOUBLES:* [Mronz] *r/u* Bordeaux (lost Boetsch/Forget 6–2 6–2).

NICKLAS KULTI (Sweden)
Born Stockholm, 22 April 1971 and lives there; RH; 6ft 3in; 172lb; final 1991 ATP ranking 79; 1991 prize money $177,517.
Coached by Martin Bohm. Won 11 nat junior titles. *1988:* (176) R/u US Open Jun to Pereira. *1989:* (118) In jun tennis won Australian Open and Wimbledon, r/u US Open to Stark and finished the year ranked No. 1 in ITF Jun rankings. On the senior tour reached sf Bastad. *1990:* (57) Reached 1st tour f at Prague and sf San Marino. *1991:* Won his 1st tour title at Adelaide. *1991 HIGHLIGHTS – SINGLES: Australian Open* 1r (lost Mattar 6–4 7–5 6–7 6–3), *French Open* 2r (d. Baur 6–4 3–6 6–4 6–2, lost Boetsch 6–3 6–3 6–3), *Wimbledon* 1r (lost Yzaga 6–2 7–5 5–7 6–1), *US Open* 1r (lost Courier [seed 4] 6–3 6–4 6–4); *won* Adelaide (d. Rahunen 6–4 6–0, Gustafsson 4–6 6–1 6–1, Santoro 6–3 6–0, Larsson 7–5 6–3, Stich 6–3 1–6 6–2).

FLORENCIA LABAT (Argentina)
Born Buenos Aires, 12 June 1971, and lives there; LH; 5ft 7in; 135lb; final 1991 WTA ranking 56; 1991 prize money $76, 511.
Coached by Roberto Graets. *1987:* Won S American Jun Champs. *1988:* (389) No. 3 in ITF Jun rankings. *1989:* (70) Won S American Jun Champs again. On the pro tour she reached qf Arcachon and VS Arizona as well as upsetting Lindqvist 1r US Open. *1990:* (118) Qf Strasbourg and Puerto Rico and joined her country's Fed Cup team. *1991:* Reached her 1st sf on the main tour at Sao Paulo, appeared in qf Taranto, Kitzbuhel (d. Kelesi) and Schenectady and upset Tauziat at US Open. In doubles won Taranto with Dechaume and Puerto Rico with Hiraki. *1991 HIGHLIGHTS – SINGLES: French Open* 2r (d. Rottier 1–6 7–5 6–1, lost Stafford 6–3 7–5), *US Open* 3r (d. Tauziat [seed 14] 7–5 6–4, Frazier 2–6 7–5 6–2, lost Wiesner 6–4 7–5); *sf* Sao Paulo (d. Fulco 6–0 6–4, Miro 7–5 6–3, Tessi 6–2 6–1, lost Faber 3–6 6–3 6–2). *1991 HIGHLIGHTS – DOUBLES:* [Dechaume] *won* Taranto (d. Golarsa/Grossman 4–6 7–6 6–4), [Hiraki] *won* Puerto Rico (d. Appelmans/Benjamin 3–6 3–3).

PETRA LANGROVA (Czechoslovakia)
Born Prostejov, 27 June 1970, and lives there; RH; 5ft 8in; 143lb; final 1991 WTA ranking 85; 1991 prize money $81,608.
Coached by Radim Paveler. *1987:* (412). *1988:* (106) Won satellite events in Bournemouth and Oporto and took 1st title on main tour at Paris Open in Sept. Won European Champs doubles. *1989:* (78) Sf Paris Open and qf Tampa (d. Zvereva). *1990:* (79) Reached qf Hamburg, Clarins and Kitzbuhel, where she won the doubles with Zrubakova. *1991:* Upset Zrubakova and Kohde-Kilsch as she swept to f Linz and won doubles titles at Palermo and Clarins. *1991 HIGHLIGHTS – SINGLES: Australian Open* 1r (lost Kschwendt 2–6 6–3 6–2), *French Open* 2r (d. Testud 6–2 0–6 9–7, lost Graf [seed 2] 6–0 6–1), *Wimbledon* 1r (lost McNeil 6–4 7–5), *US Open* 1r (lost A. Smith 6–4 7–5); *r/u* Linz (d. Frankl 6–2 6–2, Zrubakova 6–3 6–1, Maruska 6–3 6–1, Kohde-Kilsch 3–6 6–1 6–4, lost Maleeva Fragnière

6–4 7–6). *1991 HIGHLIGHTS – DOUBLES:* (with Zrubakova unless stated) [Pierce] *won* Palermo (d. Garrone/Paz 6–3 6–7 6–3), *won* Clarins (d. Dechaume/Halard 6–4 6–4); *r/u* Linz (lost Maleeva Fragnière/Reggi 6–4 1–6 6–3).

MAGNUS LARSSON (Sweden)
Born Olofstrom, 25 March 1970; lives Vaxjo and Monte Carlo; RH; 6ft 3in; 172lb; final 1991 ATP ranking 61; 1991 prize money $160,700.
Coached by Martin Bohm. *1986:* Won European Jun doubles with Kulti. *1988:* (381) R/u French Open Jun to Pereira. *1989:* (145) Won Genova Challenger. *1990:* (56) Won Florence after qualifying, r/u Bastad and won Ljubliana Challenger. *1991:* He sprung some big upsets during the year, surprising Becker *en route* to sf Adelaide, Edberg at Monte Carlo, Gomez at US Open and Cherkasov on his way to qf Bastad. He reached the same stage at Prague and Florence and extended Courier to 5s French Open, at one stage being 2 sets to 1 ahead. *1991 HIGHLIGHTS – SINGLES: Australian Open* 1r (lost Berger [seed 12] 6–4 6–4 6–0), *French Open* 3r (d. Marques 6–1 6–3 6–2, Dosedel 7–5 6–2 6–4, lost Courier 6–3 4–6 4–6 7–5 6–2), *Wimbledon* 2r (d. Haarhuis 6–4 1–6 6–3 6–1, lost Krajicek 6–3 6–4 6–3), *US Open* 3r (d. Gomez 4–6 6–3 2–6 6–2 6–3, Frana 4–6 6–4 6–2 6–4, lost J. Sanchez 7–6 6–0 6–3); *sf* Adelaide (d. Becker 6–4 3–6 7–6, Zivojinovic 7–6 7–6, Kuhnen 7–6 3–6 6–3, lost Kulti 7–5 6–3). *1991 HIGHLIGHTS – DOUBLES:* (with Jonsson) *won* Florence (d. Baguena/Costa 3–6 6–1 6–1).

LEONARDO LAVALLE (Mexico)
Born Mexico City, 14 July 1967, and lives there; LH; 6ft 2in; 175lb; final 1991 ATP ranking 132; 1991 prize money $161,797.
Coached by Heinz Gildemeister. *1984:* (741) Won US Open Jun doubles with Nastase. *1985:* (87) Won Wimbledon Jun singles; reached qf Geneva and Hong Kong. *1986:* (105) Upset Edberg at Philadelphia and Cash in 5s at US Open and helped Mexico d. West Germany in D Cup. *1987:* (224) Won Bancen Challenger. *1988:* (64) Upset Leconte and Jarryd to reach 1st GP f at Frankfurt. *1989:* (132) Unseeded, he reached last 16 Australian Open and extended Hlasek to 5s at French Open. *1990:* (183) Won Rotterdam doubles with Nargiso. *1991:* In singles won his 1st main tour title at Tel Aviv, after qualifying, and took Salou on the Challenger circuit. In doubles with Frana was r/u Wimbledon and reached 2 other f. *1991 HIGHLIGHTS – SINGLES: Australian Open* 1r (lost Lundgren 7–6 3–6 7–6 6–1), *French Open* 1r (lost Wilander 6–4 6–3 6–2); *won* Tel Aviv (d. Eltingh 4–6 6–3 6–4, Pridham 6–4 7–6, Cherkasov 7–5 6–7 6–3, Shelton 6–4 7–6, Van Rensburg 6–2 3–6 6–3), *won* Salou Challenger (d. J. Sanchez 7–5 6–4). *1991 HIGHLIGHTS – DOUBLES:* (with Frana) *r/u Wimbledon* (lost Fitzgerald-Jarryd 6–3 6–4 6–7 6–1); *r/u* Tel Aviv (lost Rikl/ Schapers 6–2 6–7 6–3), *r/u* Buzios (lost Casal/E. Sanchez 4–6 6–3 6–4).

RICK LEACH (USA)
Born Arcadia, Cal., 28 December 1964; lives Laguna Beach, Cal.; LH; 6ft 2in; 175lb; final 1991 ATP ranking 402 singles, 14 (5) doubles; 1991 prize money $195,639.
1986: (201) Coached by father, Dick, at USC, when he was All American; won NCAA doubles with Pawsat and 3 singles titles on USTA circuit. *1987:* (148) Won NCAA doubles again (with Melville) and won 2 GP doubles titles. *1988:* (258) In doubles with Pugh won Australian Open and Masters doubles on 1st appearance there but, suffering from flu and food poisoning, was forced to default US Open doubles f. Won 6 other titles (1 with Goldie). *1989:* (195) In doubles with Pugh won Australian Open, r/u Wimbledon and took 4 other titles to qualify for Masters, where they surprisingly took only 6th place. *1990:* (279) In doubles with Pugh won a 1st Wimbledon title, plus LIPC and Philadelphia, to qualify for IBM/ATP World Doubles Final, where they failed to reach sf, and played together in winning US D Cup team. In mixed doubles with Garrison won Wimbledon and r/u US Open. *1991:* Won 2 doubles titles with Pugh and r/u French Open. *1991 HIGHLIGHTS – SINGLES: US Open* 1r (lost Mattar 6–3 3–6 7–6 6–2). *1991 HIGHLIGHTS – DOUBLES:* (with Pugh unless stated) *r/u French Open* (lost Fitzgerald/Jarryd 6–0 7–6); *won* US Pro Indoor (d. Riglewski/Stich 6–4 6–4), *won* US CC (d. Garnett/Van Emburgh 6–2 3–6 6–3); [Jones] *r/u* Paris Open (lost Fitzgerald/Jarryd 3–6 6–3 6–2). *CAREER HIGHLIGHTS – DOUBLES:* (with Pugh) *Australian Open – won 1988* (d. Bates/Lundgren 6–3 6–2 6–3), *won 1989* (d. Cahill/Kratzmann 6–4 6–4 6–4); *Wimbledon – won 1990* (d. Aldrich/Visser 7–6 7–6 7–6), *r/u 1989* (lost Fitzgerald/Jarryd 3–6 7–6 6–4 7–6); *Masters – won 1988* (d. Casal/E. Sanchez 6–4 6–3 2–6 6–0); *French Open – r/u 1991; US Open – r/u 1988* (lost Casal/E. Sanchez def.). *MIXED DOUBLES:* (with Garrison) *Wimbledon – won 1990* (d. Smylie/Fitzgerald 7–5 6–2).

HENRI LECONTE (France)
Born Lilliers, 4 July 1963; lives Geneva, Switzerland; LH; 6ft 1in; 175lb; final 1991 ATP ranking 159; 1991 prize money $110,399.
Coached by Patrice Hagelauer. Separated from wife Brigitte 1989; son Maxim (born March 1986), daughter Edoli. *1982:* (28) Won Stockholm Open over Wilander and played No. 2 singles on D Cup team behind Noah as France lost to US in f. Beat Borg in 2r Monte Carlo as the Swede attempted a come-back. *1983:* (30) Beat Lendl twice (on clay at WCT Forest Hills and indoors at Sydney) and was r/u at Kitzbuhel and Sydney. *1984:* (27) Won Stuttgart (d. Borg in 2r), r/u to Connors at Memphis and won French Open doubles with Noah. *1985:* (16) Won Nice and Sydney NSW as well as reaching qf French Open and Wimbledon and last 16 US Open. R/u US Open doubles with Noah. *1986:* (6) Won Geneva and Hamburg, qualified for Masters first time, reached sf French Open and Wimbledon and qf US Open, finally arriving as expected in world's top 10. *1987:* (21) Underwent laser surgey Feb. to repair herniated disc, and was not fully fit until Wimbledon, where he reached qf again and followed with last 16 US Open. But then he was sidelined again in Oct. suffering from an illness similar to mononucleosis, returning to reach 1st sf of year at Paris Open. *1988:* (9) At Nice won 1st GP title title since 1986 and finished the year by taking Brussels to qualify for Masters, where he retired v Becker in 1r with injured ankle. Delighted and disappointed the Paris crowds as he swept to f French Open, where he lost to Wilander; reached last 16 Wimbledon and was r/u Hamburg. *1989:* (115) Out of action from May, when he underwent back surgery again to repair disc hernia, returning in Sept. to reach qf Barcelona, Bordeaux and Tokyo Seiko. *1990:* (30) A wild-card entry at French Open, he upset Chesnokov *en route* to qf. Reached sf Monte Carlo (d. Gomez), Stuttgart (d. Chesnokov again) and Hamburg, where he extended Becker to 3s. Reached 2r GS Cup (d. Muster (7) 6–3 6–4, lost Chang 7–6 6–3). *1991:* Dropped out of the top 100 in a disappointing year in which he was plagued by injury and underwent back surgery in summer, missing US Open. However, he finished in tremendous style in Lyon D Cup f where he was the hero, first in beating Sampras 6–4 7–5 6–4 in 2nd rubber and then, with Forget, beating Flach and Seguso 6–1 6–4 4–6 6–2 for a 2–1 lead. When Forget beat Sampras for 3–1 victory Leconte's rubber v Agassi was abandoned. This was first French win since 1932. *1991 HIGHLIGHTS – SINGLES: French Open* 2r (d. R. Gilbert 6–2 6–1 6–1, lost Vajda 3–6 6–4 7–6 6–4), *Wimbledon* 3r (d. Carbonell 6–3 6–1 7–6, Yzaga 6–4 6–2 6–3, lost Forget 3–6 4–6 6–1 4–1 ret'd). *1991 HIGHLIGHTS – DOUBLES:* (with Forget) *r/u* Indian Wells (lost Courier/J. Sanchez 7–6 3–6 6–3). *CAREER HIGHLIGHTS – SINGLES: French Open – r/u 1988* (d. de la Pena 6–4 7–5 6–1, Becker 6–7 6–3 6–1 5–7 6–4, Chesnokov 3–6 2–7 6–3, Svensson 7–6 6–2 6–1, lost Wilander 7–5 6–2 6–1), *sf 1986* (d. Chesnokov 6–3 6–4 6–3, lost Pernfors 2–6 7–5 7–6 6–3), *qf 1985* (d. Gomez, Noah 6–3 6–4 6–7 4–6 6–1, lost Wilander 6–4 7–6 6–7 7–5), *qf 1990* unseeded (d. Agenor, Oresar, Davin, Chesnokov 6–4 6–3 4–6 2–6 6–3, lost Svensson 3–6 7–5 6–3 6–4); *Wimbledon – sf 1986* (d. Fitzgerald, Cash 4–6 7–6 7–6 6–3, lost Becker 6–2 6–4 6–7 6–3), *qf 1985* (d. Lendl 3–6 6–4 6–3 6–1, lost Becker 7–6 3–6 6–3 6–4), *qf 1987* (d. Gomez, lost Lendl 7–6 6–3 7–6); *US Open – qf 1986* (d. Krickstein 6–3 7–5 6–4, lost Lendl 7–6 6–1 1–6 6–1). *CAREER HIGHLIGHTS – DOUBLES:* (with Noah) *French Open – won 1984* (d. Slozil/Smid 6–4 2–6 3–6 6–3 6–2); *US Open – r/u 1985* (lost Flach/Seguso 7–6 6–7 7–6 6–0).

IVAN LENDL (USA)
Born Ostrava, Czechoslovakia, 7 March 1960; lives Greenwich, Conn.; RH; 6ft 2in; 175lb; final 1991 ATP ranking 5; 1991 prize money $1,888,985.
Coached by Tony Roche with Chris Lewis (NZL) as hitting partner. Wife Samantha Frankl (married 16 Sept. 1989); daughters, Marike Lee (born May 1990) and twins Caroline and Isabelle (born July 1991). *1977:* Won Orange Bowl 18s. *1978:* (74) Won Wimbledon, French, Italian Jun and became first ITF World Jun Champ. *1979:* (20) R/u Brussels. *1980:* (6) Won Houston, Toronto, Barcelona, Basel, Tokyo, Hong Kong, Taipei, beating world No.1 Borg in Toronto and Basel. *1981:* (2) Won Stuttgart, Las Vegas, Montreal, Madrid, Barcelona, Basel, Vienna, Cologne, Buenos Aires, Masters, closing season with seven straight tourn wins and 35 straight matches, a streak which ended at 44 in Feb. 1982. *1982:* (3) Won 15 of 23 tourns and 106 of 115 matches, taking Frankfurt, Washington, North Conway, Cincinnati, WCT Delray Beach, WCT Genoa, WCT Munich, Strasbourg, Houston, Dallas, Forest Hills, LA, Naples, Hartford, Masters and r/u US Open. *1983:* (2) Won Detroit, Milan, Houston, Hilton Head, Montreal, San Francisco, Tokyo, r/u US Open and Australian Open. *1984:* (3) Won French Open for first GS success in 5 finals, coming from two-sets-to-love down to oust McEnroe in f. Won Wembley and Luxembourg and reached sf Wimbledon and f US Open. *1985:* (1) Won 84 of 91 matches (31 consecutively

from US Open to sf Australian Open) and 11 of 18 tournaments, capturing first US Open in fourth straight f and third Masters to cement his status as No. 1 in the world. *1986:* (1) Won 74 of 80 matches and 9 of 15 tournaments to take second consecutive US Open, second French Open, second consecutive Nabisco Masters and fourth in all, being beaten by only Becker, Noah, Edberg and Curren all year. *1987:* (1) Underwent arthroscopic knee surgery March, returning to win Hamburg in May. Still vulnerable on grass, he fell in sf Australian Open and 2nd consecutive Wimbledon f, both to Cash. However, he won 3rd French Open, 3rd US Open crown, a record 5th Masters, 5 other titles and finished the year undisputed No. 1 for 3rd consecutive year. *1988:* (2) In an injury-plagued year, a fractured bone in his right foot kept him out for 6 weeks in spring, and he underwent arthroscopic surgery on his right shoulder after US Open, returning for Masters, where he lost thrilling f to Becker. Won no GS, losing sf Australian Open to Cash, qf French Open to Svensson, sf Wimbledon to Becker and f US Open to Wilander. Lost to Fitzgerald in Philadelphia – the 1st time he had been beaten by a player outside the top 50 since losing to F. Gonzalez Aug. 1984 – and then to R. Smith at Stratton Mountain in July – the 1st time he'd lost to a player ranked as low as 150 since losing 1r Wimbledon to Fancutt in 1981. After US Open he lost the No. 1 ranking to Wilander, having held that position continuously for 156 weeks, just 3 weeks short of Connors's record of 159 weeks. However, he won Monte Carlo, Italian Open and Toronto during the year. *1989:* (1) Regained the No. 1 ranking after winning his 1st Australian Open. At Queen's won his 1st GP title on grass but failed again to win Wimbledon, lost 5s sf to Becker, and was r/u to the same player at US Open. Won a total of 10 titles and in autumn he achieved the highest No. 1 average ever in the history of the ATP computer rankings (208.5385). Was the 1st to qualify for Masters, but failed for 1st time in 10 appearances to reach f, falling in sf to an inspired Edberg. *1990:* (3) Won Australian Open but missed French Open (1st GS he'd missed since Australian Open 1982) to prepare for Wimbledon. He looked to be on course to achieve his greatest ambition of winning there when he beat Becker for 1st time on grass to win Queen's, but at Wimbledon he never looked secure and fell to Edberg in sf. On 13 Aug. lost No. 1 ranking to Edberg, having held that position for 80 weeks since 30 Jan. 1989, and on 20 Aug. slipped to No. 3 behind Becker for 1st time since 1 April 1985. At US Open, seeded 3 for 1st time since 1983, he fell to Sampras in qf. Won a total of 5 titles, reached 1 other f and 3 sf, including ATP World Champ, and 2r GS Cup (lost Wheaton). Fined 15% of total earnings on ATP tour (excluding GS) for falling 2 tourns short of commitment to ATP. *1991:* He began the year well as r/u Australian Open, where he d. Edberg but lost to Becker. Underwent surgery to remove callouses from racket hand 10 May, missing Italian Open and French Open when scar tissue in the palm of his hand became infected and failed to heal as rapidly as expected. He was again disappointed at Wimbledon, losing in 3r to Wheaton, and in July he was overtaken in the rankings by Stich, slipping from the top 3 for the 1st time since Aug. 1982. In Aug. he slipped to No. 5 behind Courier and was seeded only 5 at US Open, where he lost to Edberg in sf. Won US Pro Indoor, Memphis and Long Island to maintain a 12-year record of winning 3 or more titles, r/u Rotterdam and Tokyo Suntory and reached 4 other sf, including ATP World Champ, where he won all rr matches but lost to Sampras. Ended year with disappointing s/f loss to Chang in Compaq Grand Slam Cup after winning first two sets. *1991 HIGHLIGHTS – SINGLES: r/u Australian Open* seed 3 (d. Benhabiles 6–1 6–1 6–3, S. Davis 7–6 6–3 6–2, Gustafsson 4–6 6–2 6–3 6–2, Krickstein [seed 13] 6–2 6–2 6–1, Prpic 6–0 7–6 7–6, Edberg [seed 1] 6–2 6–3 6–2, lost Becker [seed 2] 1–6 4–6 6–0 7–6, *Wimbledon* 3r, seed 3 (d. Evernden 6–2 7–5 7–6, Washington 4–6 2–6 6–4 6–4 7–5, lost Wheaton 6–3 3–6 7–6 6–3), *US Open* sf, seed 5 (d. Krajicek 3–6 2–6 6–4 7–6 6–0, Kuhnen 6–3 6–2 6–4, Woodbridge 3–6 6–3 6–4 6–3, Ivanisevic [seed 12] 7–5 6–7 6–4 6–2, Stich [seed 3] 6–3 3–6 4–6 7–6 6–1, lost Edberg [seed 2] 6–3 6–3 6–4; *won* US Pro Indoor (d. Raoux 6–1 7–5, Muller 7–6 6–3, Stich 6–2 7–6, B. Gilbert 6–3 6–6 6–4, Sampras 5–7 6–4 6–3 6–3), *won* Memphis (d. Ferreira 6–3 3–6 7–5, Haarhuis 6–2 6–1, Cahill 7–6 6–3, Rostagno 6–3 6–2, Stich 7–5 6–3), *won* Long Island (d. Steeb 6–4 3–6 6–3, Jelen 6–2 6–0, Camporese 7–6 6–3, J. McEnroe 6–3 7–5, Edberg 6–3 6–2); *r/u* Rotterdam (d. Nijssen 6–3 6–1, Kulti 6–4 6–0, Hlasek 3–6 6–3 7–5, Jarryd 7–5 6–4, lost Camporese 3–6 7–6 7–6), *r/u* Tokyo Suntory (d. Krishnan 6–3 6–2, Yzaga 7–5 6–3, Hlasek 6–1 6–4, Courier 6–4 6–1, lost Edberg 6–1 7–5 6–0); *sf* Munich (d. Mronz 6–2 6–2, Prpic 3–6 6–4 6–2, Witsken 3–6 6–4 7–5, lost Gustafsson 6–4 7–5), *sf* Montreal (d. Bloom 4–6 6–4 6–4, Masur 6–3 3–6 6–4, Grabb 7–6 6–7 7–5, lost Chesnokov 7–6 7–5), *sf* Tokyo Seiko (d. Davis 6–2 6–3, Masur 6–4 6–7 6–2, Wheaton 7–6 7–5, lost Rostagno 7–6 6–2), *sf* ATP World Champs (d. Forget 6–2 6–4, Courier 6–2 6–3, Novacek 6–2 6–2 in rr, lost Sampras 6–2 6–3), *sf* Compaq Grand Slam Cup (lost Chang 2–6 4–6 6–4 7–6 9–7). *CAREER HIGHLIGHTS – SINGLES: Australian Open – won 1989* (d. Mronz, Steeb, Kulti, Mansdorf

7–6 6–4 6–2, J. McEnroe 7–6 6–2 7–6, Muster 6–2 6–4 5–7 7–5, Mecir 6–2 6–2 6–2), *won* *1990* (d. Pugh, Carbonell, Novacek, Youl, Cherkasov 6–3 6–2 6–3, Noah 6–4 6–1 6–2, Edberg 4–6 7–6 5–2 ret'd), *r/u 1983* (d. Mayotte 6–1 7–6 6–3, lost Wilander 6–1 6–4 6–4), *r/u 1991, sf 1985* (lost Edberg 6–7 7–5 6–1 4–6 9–7), *sf 1987* (d. Jarryd 7–6 6–1 6–3, lost Cash 7–6 5–7 7–6 6–4), *sf 1988* (d. Woodforde, Masur 7–5 6–4 6–4, Witsken 6–2 6–1 7–6, lost Cash 6–4 2–6 6–2 4–6 6–2); *Frenoh Open – won 1984* (d. Wilander, J. McEnroe 3–6 2–6 6–4 7–5 7–5), *won 1986* (d. Westphal, Hlasek, Miniussi, Keretic, Gomez 6–7 7–6 6–0 6–0, Kriek 6–2 6–1 6–0, Pernfors 6–3 6–2 6–4), *won 1987* (d. Agenor, Canter, Tulasne, Nystrom 6–1 5–7 6–0 6–2, Gomez 5–7 6–4 6–1 6–1, Mecir 6–3 6–3 7–6), *r/u 1981* (d. McNamee 6–2 4–6 7–6 7–6, J. McEnroe 6–4 6–4 7–5, Clerc 3–6 6–4 4–6 7–6 6–2, lost Borg 6–1 4–6 6–2 3–6 6–1), *r/u 1985* (lost Wilander 3–6 6–4 6–2 6–2), *qf 1988* (lost Svensson 7–6 7–5 6–2); *US Open – won 1985* (d. Noah, Connors 6–2 6–3 7–5, J. McEnroe 6–2 6–3 6–4), *won 1986* (d. Svensson, Gilbert, Leconte, Edberg 7–6 6–3 6–3, Mecir 6–4 6–2 6–0), *won 1987* (d. Moir, Fleurian, Pugh, Jarryd 6–2 7–6 6–4, J. McEnroe 6–4 7–6 6–3, Connors 6–4 6–2 6–2), *r/u 1982* (d. J. McEnroe 6–4 6–4 7–6, lost Connors 6–3 6–2 0–6 6–4), *r/u 1983* (d. Wilander, Arias 6–2 7–6 6–1, lost Connors 6–3 6–7 7–5 6–0), *r/u 1984* (d. Cash 3–6 6–3 6–4 6–7 7–6 [saving 1 mp], lost J. McEnroe 6–3 6–4 6–4), *r/u 1988* (d. Hlasek, Rostagno, Agassi 4–6 6–2 6–3 6–4, lost Wilander 6–4 4–6 6–3 5–7 6–4), *r/u 1989* (d. Perez, Fitzgerald, Courier, Chesnokov 6–3 4–6 1–6 6–4 6–3, Mayotte 6–4 6–0 6–1, Agassi 7–6 6–1 3–6 6–1, lost Becker 7–6 1–6 6–3 7–6), *sf 1991, qf 1990* (d. Laurendeau, Stich, Antonitsch, Bloom 6–0 6–3 6–4, lost Sampras 6–4 7–6 3–6 6–4 6–2); *Masters/ATP World Champ – won 1981* (d. Gerulaitis, Vilas in rr, J. McEnroe 6–4 6–2, Gerulaitis 6–7 2–6 7–6 6–2 6–4), *won 1982* (d. Noah 6–4 7–5, Connors 6–3 6–1, J. McEnroe 6–4 6–4 6–2), *won 1985* (d. Becker 6–2 7–6 6–3), *won 1986* (d. Gomez, Edberg, Noah 6–4 6–4, Wilander 6–4 6–2, Becker 6–4 6–4 6–4), *won 1987* (d. Gilbert 6–2 6–4, Wilander 6–2 6–2 6–3), *r/u 1980* (d. Mayer 6–3 6–4, lost Borg 6–4 6–2 6–2), *r/u 1983* (d. Connors 6–3 6–4, lost J. McEnroe 6–3 6–4 6–4), *r/u 1984* (d. Connors, lost J. McEnroe 7–5 6–0 6–4), *r/u 1988* (d. Edberg 6–3 7–6, lost Becker 5–7 7–6 3–6 6–2 7–6), *sf 1989* (d. Chang, Krickstein, J. McEnroe in rr, lost Edberg 7–6 7–5), *sf 1991*; *Wimbledon – r/u 1986* (d. Lavelle, Freeman, Mansdorf, Anger, Mayotte 6–4 4–6 6–4 3–6 9–7, Zivojinovic 6–2 6–7 6–3 6–7 6–4, lost Becker 6–4 6–3 7–5), *r/u 1987* (d.Saceanu, Cane, Reneberg, Kreik, Leconte 7–6 6–3 7–6, Edberg 3–6 6–4 7–6 6–4, lost Cash 7–6 6–2 7–5), *sf 1983* (d. Tanner, lost J. McEnroe 7–6 6–4 6–4), *sf 1984* (lost Connors 6–7 6–3 7–6 6–1), *sf 1988* (d. Woodforde 7–5 6–7 6–7 7–5 10–8, Mayotte 7–6 7–6 6–3, lost Becker 6–4 6–3 6–7 6–4), *sf 1989* (d. Pereira 7–6 4–6 6–3 6–7 6–1, Bathman 6–7 6–3 6–2 6–2, Carbonell 7–6 6–3 6–1, Lundgren 1–6 7–6 6–2 6–4, Goldie 7–6 7–6 6–0, lost Becker 7–5 6–7 2–6 6–4 6–3), *sf 1990* (d. Miniussi, Hlasek, Shelton, Antonitsch 3–6 6–4 3–6 6–4; Pearce 6–4 6–4 5–7 6–4, lost Edberg 6–1 7–6 6–3); *D Cup – 1980 winning team* TCH.

CATARINA LINDQVIST (Sweden)
Born Kristinehamn, 13 June 1963; lives Holviksnas and London; RH; 5ft 5in; 125lb; final 1991 WTA ranking 46; 1991 prize money $124,791.
Husband Bill Ryan of IMG (married 16 July 1988). *1983:* (114). *1984:* (18) Won Hershey and Filderstadt and reached sf Canadian Open. *1985:* (13) Won Ginny Champs, and using superior topspin groundstrokes off both sides she upset Shriver at Australian Open, to reach qf, and Mandlikova at Key Biscayne. *1986:* (16) R/u to Graf at Brighton, had 4mps v Navratilova qf Filderstadt, reached first Wimbledon qf and won Bastad. *1987:* (16) Sf Australian Open, last 16 Wimbledon and US Open, r/u Bastad and qualified for VS Champs. *1988:* (42) Last 16 Australian Open; sf Oklahoma and Taipei, and upset Shriver and Manuela Maleeva during the year. *1989:* (16) Upset Shriver *en route* to qf Australian Open, and at Wimbledon upset Zvereva and Sukova *en route* to sf, becoming the first Swedish woman to reach that stage. At Sydney reached 1st f since Bastad 1987 and qualified for VS Champs, but fell 1r to Sanchez-Vicario. *1990:* (38) At Tokyo Suntory she won her 1st primary circuit title since 1984, also reaching sf Brighton and qf Italian Open. *1991:* Won Oslo and reached sf Brighton (d. Zvereva and K. Maleeva), where she def. ill. She also appeared in last 16 Wimbledon, unseeded, and qf VS Oklahoma. *1991 HIGHLIGHTS – SINGLES: Australian Open* 2r (d. Cammy MacGregor 7–5 4–6 6–3, lost Cunningham 6–1 6–0), *Wimbledon* last 16, unseeded (d. Demongeot 6–1 6–0, Habsudova 6–3 6–2, Smylie 6–1 7–6, lost Navratilova [seed 4] 6–1 6–3), *US Open* 2r (d. Alter 6–3 6–3, lost Sviglerova 6–2 6–2); *won* Oslo (d. Laval 6–2 6–1, Nowak 6–0 6–0, Tanvier 6–0 3–2 ret'd, Appelmans 6–2 6–2, Reggi 6–3 6–0); *sf* Brighton (d. Wood 6–0 7–5, Zvereva 6–4 6–4, K. Maleeva 6–2 7–6, lost Garrison 6–1 1–0 ret'd). *CAREER HIGHLIGHTS – SINGLES: Australian Open – sf 1987* (d. Manuela Maleeva 6–3 6–3, Shriver 6–3 6–1, lost Navratilova 6–3 6–2), *qf 1985*

(d. Shriver, lost Kohde-Kilsch 6–4 6–0), *qf 1989* (d. Shriver 1–6 6–3 6–4, Wiesner 7–5 6–2, lost Cordwell 6–2 2–6 6–1); *Wimbledon – sf 1989* (d. Cammy MacGregor, Demongeot, Zvereva 7–6 4–6 6–4, Sukova 6–4 7–6, Fairbank-Nideffer 7–5 7–5, lost Navratilova /–6 6–2), *qf 1986* (d. Rush, Kelesi, E. Minter, Balestrat 7–6 7–5, lost Sabatini 6–2 6–3).

GERMAN LOPEZ (Spain)
Born Barcelona, 29 December 1971, and lives there; RH; 6ft 4in; 168lb; final 1991 ATP ranking 80; 1991 prize money $90,715.
Coached by Javier Duarte. *1990:* (166) Made his mark on the Challenger circuit. *1991:* Qf Madrid and Stuttgart Mercedes. *1991 HIGHLIGHTS – SINGLES: French Open* 1r (lost Caratti 2–6 2–6 6–3 6–3 6–4).

SUSAN SLOANE LUNDY (USA)
Born Lexington, Ky, 5 December 1970, and lives there; RH; 2HB; 5ft 5in; 120lb; final 1991 WTA ranking 77; 1991 prize money $44,550.
Husband Duane Lundy (married Sept. 1991). Coached by Fritz Nau and Nick Bollettieri. *1984:* R/u Orange Bowl 14s. *1985:* Ranked 3 in US 18s. *1986:* (88) Qf Indianapolis. *1987:* (111) Qf Arkansas. *1988:* (31) Upset McNeil *en route* to 1st tour singles title at Nashville, reached sf Arizona and 4 other qf. *1989:* (39) Sf VS Kansas, VS Houston (upsetting McNeil) and VS Nashville. *1990:* (27) R/u VS Nashville (d. Reggi); sf Wichita and VS Albuquerque. *1991:* Reached VS Albuquerque plus qf Colorado, San Antonio and Puerto Rico. *1991: HIGHLIGHTS – SINGLES: Wimbledon* 1r (lost Suire 6–2 6–2), *US Open* 1r (lost Rittner 6–4 6–1); *sf* VS Albuquerque (d. Coetzer 6–4 6–4, Takagi 7–5 6–4, Testud 6–3 6–3, lost G. Fernandez 6–3 5–7 6–2).

JOHN McENROE (USA)
Born Wiesbaden, West Germany, 16 February 1959; lives New York and Malibu, Cal.; LH; 5ft 11in; 165lb; final 1991 ATP ranking 28; 1991 prize money $321,209.
Wife Tatum O'Neal (married Aug. 1986); sons Kevin (born May 1986) and Sean Timothy (born Sept. 1987), daughter Emily Catherine (born May 1991). As youth, coached at Pt. Washington Tennis Academy by Harry Hopman. Later by Tony Palafox. Works with Madonna's former trainer, Bob Parr. *1976:* (264) R/u to Larry Gottfried at US Nat 18 Champs and won Orange Bowl 18s. *1977:* (21) Stunned tennis world by reaching sf Wimbledon as qualifier and taking set off Connors. *1978:* (4) Turned pro in June after winning NCAA title as Stanford freshman. Won Hartford, San Francisco, Stockholm and Wembley in autumn, led US D Cup triumph, and closed year by saving 2 mps to beat Ashe in Masters f. *1979:* (3) Won US Open, WCT Finals, New Orleans, Milan, San José, Queen's Club, South Orange, San Francisco, Stockholm and Wembley and again led US D Cup triumph. *1980:* (2) Lost epic Wimbledon f to Borg after saving 7 mps in 4s, finally falling 8–6 5s. Won second straight US Open with 5s triumph over Borg as well as Richmond, Memphis, Milan, Queen's Club, Brisbane, Sydney, Wembley and WCT Montreal. *1981:* (1) Became first male player since Connors in 1974 to win Wimbledon and US Open in same year, stopping Borg in both f to replace the Swede as the No. 1 player in the world. Led US to D Cup victory. *1982:* (1) Lost to Connors in 5s Wimbledon f, coming within three points of victory at 4–3 in 4s tb. After losing to Lendl in sf US Open and f Masters, he was regarded by many experts as No. 3 behind Connors and Lendl. Led US to D Cup victory for 4th time in 5 years and won US Pro Indoor, San Francisco, Sydney, Tokyo and Wembley. *1983:* (1) Won his second Wimbledon and Masters titles, beating Lendl in sf former and f latter. Also won US Pro Indoor, WCT Dallas, Forest Hills, Sydney and Wembley to become undisputed No. 1. *1984:* (1) Won 13 of 15 tournaments and 79 of 82 matches, losing only to Lendl in f French Open, V. Amritraj at Cincinnati and Sundstrom in D Cup f. For the second time he won Wimbledon and US Open, producing glorious form to rout Connors in Wimbledon f and dismissing Lendl with relative ease 6–3 6–4 6–1 in US Open f. Only his loss to Lendl from 2 sets to 0 ahead in f French Open spoiled a nearly perfect year. *1985:* (2) Won Philadelphia, Houston, Chicago, Milan, Atlanta, Stratton, Montreal and Stockholm, but was soundly beaten by Curren in qf Wimbledon and Lendl in f US Open. When he lost to Gilbert in 1r Masters, he elected to take a 6-month sabbatical from the game. *1986:* (14) Returning to competition in Stratton Mountain in July, he lost to Becker in sf after holding 4 mps, then lost to Seguso in 3r Canadian Open and suffered his first 1r defeat at US Open to Annacone. He rebounded with three straight tourn wins (LA, San Francisco and Scottsdale), but was beaten thereafter by Casal in qf of Paris Indoor and Cash in 1r Wembley. *1987:* (10) In f World Team Cup v Mecir he walked off the court following two disputed umpiring decisions, later claiming that a back injury had prompted his withdrawal, and avoided threatened suspension when MIPTC accepted that he was indeed injured.

However, following US Open, when he accumulated fines exceeding $7,500 for the second time in the year, he was suspended for 2 months from 28 Sept. Continuing to be plagued by injuries, and missing Wimbledon with a leg injury, he began working with physical trainers Dae-Shik Seo and Chuck Debus. Reached f 5 times but won no title. *1988:* (11) Won Tokyo for his 71st title and his 1st since Oct. 1986, following win Detroit, and was r/u Indianapolis. Formed a successful partnership with Woodforde in autumn. Coached by Peter Fleming until end of year. *1989:* (4) Playing with renewed confidence he won WCT Finals for record fifth time (d. Lendl for 1st time in 4 years), Lyon and Indianapolis. Missed French Open with back trouble and prepared enthusiastically for Wimbledon, where he reached sf, but fell 2r US Open to qualifier Haarhuis. However, he won the doubles title there with Woodforde. Played Masters for 1st time since losing to Gilbert 1r in 1985, and reached sf (lost Becker). *1990:* (13) At Australian Open became the 1st player since Willy Alvarez at French Open in 1963 to be disqualified from a GS tourn, following a third code of conduct warning for verbal abuse in 4r match v Pernfors. He was fined $6,000 for extreme verbal abuse, although he claimed that he believed GS events were still run on the basis of four warnings. Out nearly 4 months to June with a shoulder injury and lacking motivation, and fell 1r Wimbledon to Rostagno. His ranking dropped to 21 until, unseeded for the 1st time in 12 years, he reached sf US Open. Returned to top 10 for a while, having also won Basel, to become only the 2nd player after Sherwood Stewart to win titles in 3 decades. Sf Milan, Toronto World Tennis, Queen's and Long Island. Reunited during the year with his former coach, Tony Palafox. *1991:* Won Chicago, beating his brother in f, *r/u* Basel and reached sf US Pro Indoor and Long Island. He missed French Open to be present at the birth of his daughter in May and his best showing in GS was last 16 Wimbledon. *1991 HIGHLIGHTS – SINGLES: French Open* 1r, seed 15 (lost Cherkasov 2–6 6–4 7–5 7–6), *Wimbledon* last 16, seed 16 (d. Oncins 6–1 6–2 6–4, Stolle 7–5 5–7 6–0 7–6), Fleurian 6–2 7–6 6–1, lost Edberg 7–6 6–1 6–4), *US Open* 3r, seed 16 (d. Layendecker 6–4 6–3 6–3, Laurendeau 6–3 6–4 6–2, lost Chang 6–4 4–6 7–6 2–6, 6–3); *won* Chicago (d. Bloom 6–2 6–1, Krishnan 7–5 6–3, Mronz w.o., Washington 7–6 6–7 6–4, P. McEnroe 3–6 6–2 6–4); *r/u* Basel (d. Guardiola 6–2 6–4, P. McEnroe 6–2 6–4, Bergstrom 7–6 6–4, Connors 6–1 6–3, lost Hlasek 7–6 6–0 6–3); *sf* US Pro Indoor (d. Mronz 6–1 6–2, Masur 7–6 6–4, Rahunen 7–5 6–3, lost Sampras 6–2 6–4), *sf* Long Island (d. Bloom 6–4 4–6 6–1, Arnold 6–1 6–3, Mattar 6–3 6–1, lost Lendl 6–3 7–5). *1991 HIGHLIGHTS – DOUBLES:* [Korda] *r/u* Basel (lost Hlasek/P. McEnroe 3–6 7–6 7–6). *CAREER HIGHLIGHTS – SINGLES: Wimbledon – won 1981* (d. Ramirez, Smith, Kriek, Frawley 7–6 6–4 7–5, Borg 4–6 7–6 7–6 6–4), *won 1983* (d. Lendl 6–4 6–4, C. Lewis 6–2 6–2 6–2), *won 1984* (d. Connors 6–1 6–1 6–2), *r/u 1980* (d. Connors 6–3 3–6 6–3 6–4, lost Borg 1–6 7–5 6–3 6–7 8–6), *r/u 1982* (lost Connors 3–6 6–3 6–7 7–6 6–4), *sf 1977* (lost Connors 6–3 6–3 4–6 6–4), *sf 1989* (d. Cahill 4–6 4–6 6–2 6–3 8–6, Reneberg 6–3 3–6 6–3 7–5, Pugh 6–3 6–4 6–2, Fitzgerald 6–3 0–6 6–4 6–4, Wilander 7–6 3–6 6–3 6–4, lost Edberg 7–5 7–6 7–6); *US Open – won 1979* (d. Connors 6–3 6–3 7–5, Gerulaitis 7–5 6–4 6–3), *won 1980* (d. Lendl 4–6 6–3 6–2 7–5, Connors 6–4 5–7 0–6 6–3 7–6, Borg 7–6 6–1 6–7 5–7 6–4), *won 1981* (d. Gerulaitis 5–7 6–3 6–2 4–6 6–3, Borg 4–6 6–2 6–4 6–3), *won 1984* (d. Connors 6–4 4–6 7–5 4–6 6–3, Lendl 6–3 6–4 6–4), *r/u 1985* (d. Wilander 3–6 6–4 4–6 6–3 6–3, lost Lendl 7–6 6–3 6–4), *sf 1982* (lost Lendl 6–4 4–7 7–6), *sf 1990* (d. J Sanchez, Engel, Chesnokov 6–3 7–5 6–4, E. Sanchez 7–6 3–6 4–6 6–3, Wheaton 6–1 6–4 6–4, lost Sampras 6–2 6–4 3–6 6–3); *Masters – won 1979* (d. Ashe 6–7 6–3 7–5), *won 1983* (d. Wilander 6–2 7–5, Lendl 6–3 6–4 6–4), *won 1984* (d. Wilander 6–1 6–1, Lendl 7–5 6–0 6–4), *r/u 1982* (d. Vilas, lost Lendl 6–4 6–4 6–2), *sf 1989* (d. Krickstein, Chang, lost Lendl in rr, lost Becker 6–4 6–4); *WCT Finals – won 1979* (d. Connors 6–1 6–4 6–4, Borg 7–5 4–6 6–2 7–6), *won 1981* (d. Kriek 6–1 6–2 6–4), *won 1983* (d. Lendl 6–2 4–6 6–7 7–6), *won 1984* (d. Connors 6–1 6–2 6–3), *won 1989* (d. Lendl 6–7 7–6 6–2 7–5, Gilbert 6–3 6–3 7–6); *French Open – r/u 1984* (lost Lendl 3–6 2–6 6–4 7–5 7–5, *sf 1985* (lost Wilander 6–1 7–5 7–5). *CAREER HIGHLIGHTS – DOUBLES:* (with Fleming unless stated) *Wimbledon – won 1979* (d. Gottfried/Ramirez 6–2 4s), *won 1981* (d. Smith/Lutz 6–4 6–4 6–4), *won 1983* (d. Tim/Tom Gullikson 6–4 6–3 6–4), *won 1984* (d. Cash/McNamee 6–2 5–7 6–2 3–6 6–3), *r/u 1978* (lost Hewitt/McMillan 6–1 6–4 6–2), *r/u 1982* (lost McNamara/McNamee 6–3 6–1), *sf 1980* (lost McNamara/McNamee 6–3 6–3 6–3), *sf 1985* (lost Cash/Fitzgerald 7–6 2–6 6–1 6–4); *US Open – won 1979* (d. Smith/Lutz), *won 1981* (d. Newcombe/Stolle 6–2 6–2 6–7 5–7 7–6, McNamara/Gunthardt def.), *won 1983* (d. Buehning/Winitsky 6–3 6–4 6–2), [Woodforde] *won 1989* (d. Flach/Seguso 6–4 4–6 6–3 6–3); *Masters – won 1978* (d. Lutz/Smith 6–4 6–2 6–4), *won 1979* (d. Fibak/Okker 6–4 6–2 6–4), *won 1980* (d. McNamara/McNamee 6–4 6–4), *won 1981* (d. Curren/Denton 6–3 6–3), *won 1982* (d. Stewart/Taygan 7–5 6–3), *won 1983* (d. Slozil/Smid 6–2 6–2), *won 1984* (d. Edmondson/Stewart 6–3 6–1).

PATRICK McENROE (USA)
*Born Manhasset, NY, 1 July 1966; lives Oyster Bay, NY; RH; 2HB; 6ft; 160lb; final 1991
AIP ranking 36 singles, 28 doubles; 1991 prize money $628,114.*
Brother of John. Coached by Carlos Goffi. *1983:* R/u US Nat 18s. *1984:* Won Nat GC 18s.
1987: (452) Won San Francisco doubles with Grabb. *1988:* (494) Graduated from Stanford
and in winning NCAA team. 3 times All-American in singles (1986–8). R/u US Open mixed
doubles with Smylie. *1989:* (356) Won French Open and Masters doubles with Grabb.
Elected ATP Tour Council. *1990:* (120) In singles reached qf Hong Kong and Singapore
before appearing in his 1st tour sf at Rosmalen. In doubles with Grabb won Wembley and
reached 2 more f. *1991:* Played the tennis of his life at Australian Open where, unseeded, he
reached sf singles before falling to Becker in 4s, and was r/u doubles with Wheaton. He
followed with his 1st singles f at Chicago, where he took his brother to 3s, and broke into top
50, before upsetting Becker at LIPC and E. Sanchez at Wimbledon. He reached 2 more
doubles f with Hlasek, winning Basel. *1991 HIGHLIGHTS – SINGLES: Australian Open* sf,
unseeded (d. Hogstedt 4–6 4–6 6–3 6–1 6–3, Anderson 6–3 6–3 5–7 6–1, Berger [seed 12]
6–1 7–5 7–5, Woodforde 6–2 6–4 6–1, Caratti 7–6 6–3 4–6 4–6 6–2, lost Becker [seed 2] 6–7
6–4 6–1 6–4), *French Open* 3r (d. Bloom 7–5 6–4 7–6, Stoltenberg 7–6 6–3 6–4, lost Agassi
[seed 4] 6–2 6–2 6–0), *Wimbledon* 2r (d. E. Sanchez [seed 11] 6–3 7–6 6–1, lost Eltingh 7–6
2–6 1–6 6–4 12–10), *US Open* 1r (lost Connors 4–6 6–7 6–4 6–2 6–4); *r/u* Chicago (d. Pearce
6–1 6–7 7–6, Pereira 6–4 7–6, Reneberg 6–1 7–6, Connell 4–6 6–4 6–4, lost J. McEnroe 3–6
6–2 6–4). *1991 HIGHLIGHTS – DOUBLES:* (with Hlasek unless stated) [Wheaton] *r/u
Australian Open* (lost S. Davis/Pate 6–7 7–6 6–3 7–5); *won* Basel (d. Korda/J/McEnroe 3–6
7–6 7–6); *r/u* Vienna (lost Jarryd/Muller 6–4 7–5). *CAREER HIGHLIGHTS – SINGLES:
Australian Open – sf 1991. CAREER HIGHLIGHTS – DOUBLES:* (with Grabb unless
stated) *French Open – won 1989* (d. Bahrami/Winogradsky 6–4 2–6 6–4 7–6); *Masters –
won 1989* (d. Jarryd/Fitzgerald 7–5 7–6 5–7 6–3); *Australian Open –* [Wheaton] *r/u 1991;
LIPC – r/u 1989* (lost Hlasek/Jarryd 6–3 ret'd).

LORI McNEIL (USA)
*Born San Diego, Cal., 18 December 1963; lives Houston, Texas; RH; 5ft 7in; 135lb; final
1991 WTA ranking 19 singles, 19 (22) doubles; 1991 prize money $253,565.*
Coached by Willis Thomas. *1983:* Member US Jun Fed Cup team, ranked 8 US Intercolle-
giate list and 4 on USTA satellite circuit. *1984:* (97) Reached last 16 US Open and led
Mandlikova by a set and 4–2 before losing. *1985:* (93). *1986:* (14) Burst out of the pack and
established herself as one of top 15 players in world. Won Tampa – over Garrison in first VS
Series final between two black women – and VS Tulsa back-to-back in Sept. Ably coached
by John Wilkerson, who was also Garrison's instructor, she reached qf Wimbledon
unseeded and qualified first time for VS Champs in Nov., clearly the most improved
fast-court player in the world. *1987:* (11) Qf Australian Open and sf US Open, where she
spoiled Evert's record of winning at least one GS event each year by beating her in qf. Won
no singles title but reached f Oklahoma, New Orleans and New Jersey. In doubles r/u
Australian Open with Garrison, won 6 titles and r/u 7 more with 5 different partners.
Qualified for VS Champs in singles and doubles. *1988:* (13) Won Oklahoma and Newport in
singles, took 5 doubles titles with different partners, and won French Open mixed with
Lozano. Qualified for VS Champs in both singles and doubles. *1989:* (37) Upset Evert *en
route* to f Pan Pacific Open in Tokyo, where she took Navratilova to 3s tb, then won her first
singles title for 13 months at Albuquerque. In doubles with various partners she reached 8
f, winning 5. *1990:* (52) Upset Sabatini and G. Fernandez *en route* to sf San Antonio and
reached the same stage at Eastbourne. Qualified for VS Champs doubles with K. Adams,
upsetting Savchenko/Zvereva to reach sf. *1991:* at Colorado, she won her 1st title for 18
months, following with Tokyo Suntory in April; r/u Westchester and sf VS California to
qualify for VS Champs, where she lost 1r to Navratilova. Reached 5 doubles f with different
partners, winning Strasbourg with Rehe and Milan with Collins. *1991 HIGHLIGHTS –
SINGLES: Australian Open* 3r (d. Rinaldi 5–7 7–6 6–1, Savchenko 6–3 4–6 6–3, lost
Sanchez-Vicario [seed 6] 6–4 3–6 6–0), *French Open* 1r (lost Sanchez-Vicario [seed 5] 6–2
6–2), *Wimbledon* 3r (d. Langrova 6–4 7–5, Sawamatsu 3–6 6–2 6–2, lost Sanchez-Vicario
[seed 3] 6–2 6–4), *US Open* 2r (d. R. White 6–2 6–2, lost Pierce 6–3 3–6 7–6); *won*
Colorado (d. Field 6–7 6–1 6–2, Shiflet 6–2 3–6 6–2, Leand 6–2 6–1, Cunningham 6–4 6–2,
Bollegraf 6–3 6–4), *won* Tokyo Suntory (d. Vasquez 6–1 6–4, Cunningham 6–3 6–4, Frazier
6–3 6–3, Gildemeister 7–6 6–3, Appelmans 2–6 6–2 6–1); *r/u* Westchester (d. Pratt 6–3
7–5, Farley 6–7 6–3 7–6, Graham 7–5 6–0, Fairbank-Nideffer 5–7 6–2 6–1, lost Demongeot
6–4 6–4); *sf* VS California (d. McCarthy 7–5 6–3, Fendick 6–4 7–6, Rehe 7–6 6–2, lost
Navratilova 6–3 6–2). *1991 HIGHLIGHTS – DOUBLES:* [Rehe] *won* Strasbourg

(d. Bollegraf/Paz 6–1 6–4), [Collins] **won** Milan (d. Appelmans/Reggi 7–6 6–3); [Fendick] **r/u** Colorado (lost L. Gregory/Magers 6–4 6–4), [Adams] **r/u** Westchester (Fairbank-Nideffer/Gregory 7–5 6–4), [Garrison] **r/u** Brighton (lost Shriver/Zvereva 6–1 6–2). **CAREER HIGHLIGHTS – SINGLES: US Open – sf 1987** (d. Provis, Garrison 7–6 3–6 7–5, Evert 3–6 6–2 6–4, lost Graf 4–6 6–2 6–4); **Wimbledon – qf 1986** (d. Bryant, Mesker, Burgin 6–3 6–2, Nagelsen 7–5 6–1, lost Mandlikova 0–7 0–0 0 2); **Australian Open qf 1987** (lost Mandlikova 6–0 6–0). **CAREER HIGHLIGHTS – DOUBLES:** (with Garrison) **Australian Open – r/u 1987** (lost Navratilova/Shriver 6–1 6–0). **MIXED DOUBLES:** (with Lozano) **French Open – won 1988** (d. Schultz/Schapers 7–5 6–2).

RACHEL McQUILLAN (Australia)
Born Waratah, NSW, 2 December 1971; lives Newcastle, NSW; RH; 2HB; 5ft 7in; 132lb; final 1991 WTA ranking 36; 1991 prize money $159,681.
Coached by Ken Richardson and Terry Rocivert. **1987:** (448) In winning World Youth Cup team. **1988:** (202) Won Australian Open and Wimbledon Jun doubles with Faull; r/u US Open Jun to Cunningham. Ranked No. 2 in ITF Jun doubles and No. 5 in singles. **1989:** (79) Qf Adelaide and Hamburg, then upset Cecchini *en route* to f Athens. R/u US Open Jun to Capriati. **1990:** (39) Upset Wiesner twice to make surprise appearances in f Brisbane and Kitzbuhel. In GS overturned Kelesi *en route* to last 16 Australian Open, unseeded, and in doubles reached 2 f with Faull. **1991:** Unseeded she reached last 16 Australian Open (d. Paulus) and French Open (d. Kelesi). R/u Strasbourg (d. Wiesner), sf Bayonne and won Schenectady doubles with Porwik. **1991 HIGHLIGHTS – SINGLES: Australian Open** last 16, unseeded (d. Brioukhovets 2–6 6–4 6–1, Paulus [seed 12] 6–4 6–7 6–4, Schefflin 6–4 6–0, lost Sabatini [seed 4] 6–3 6–1), **French Open** last 16, unseeded (d. Bartos 6–3 7–5, G. Fernandez 6–2 6–2, Kelesi 6–4 2–6 6–4, lost Sabatini [seed 3] 6–3 6–0), **Wimbledon** 1r (lost Zrubakova 7–6 6–2), **US Open** 2r (d. Niox-Chateau 6–4 3–6 6–0, lost Hy 6–1 6–2); **r/u** Strasbourg (d. Golarsa 6–0 7–6, Langrova 6–1 6–1, Wiesner 6–4 7–6, Sawamatsu 6–4 6–3, lost Zrubakova 7–6 7–6); **sf** Bayonne (d. Ruano 6–1 6–0, Paradis Mangon 6–2 7–6, Zrubakova 4–6 6–1 6–3, lost Maleeva Fragnière 7–6 6–4). **1991 HIGHLIGHTS – DOUBLES:** [Porwik] **won** Schenectady (d. Arendt/McCarthy 6–2 6–4); [Tanvier] **r/u** Bayonne (lost Tarabini/Tauziat 6–3 30–40 ret'd).

ELENA MAKAROVA (USSR)
Born 1 February 1973; RH; 5ft 6in; 120lb; final WTA ranking 465; 1991 prize money $3,856.
1991: R/u Wimbledon Jun to Rittner and finished the year at No. 3 in the ITF Jun rankings.

KATERINA MALEEVA (Bulgaria)
Born Sofia, 7 May 1969, and lives there; RH; 2HB; 5ft 6in; 122lb; final 1991 WTA ranking 11; 1991 prize money $299,693.
Coached by her mother, 9 times Bulgarian champion Yulia Berberian. Sister of Manuela and Magdalena. **1984:** (93) Won US Open Jun and was r/u to Sabatini at both Orange Bowl and French Open Jun while making her mark in women's play as well. **1985:** (28) Won Seabrook Island and Hilversum and stopped some of the big names in the sport like Shriver, Sukova and Garrison. **1986:** (28) Did not pass qf in 20 tournaments but won 26 of 47 matches. Played Fed Cup again with sister and mother. **1987:** (13) Beat Sukova 3r Mahwah, won Japan/Asian Open for first title since 1985, following with Athens and qualifying for VS Champs 1st time. **1988:** (11) Upset Sukova to reach f US HC and again *en route* to qf US Open. After reaching f Hamburg, won 1st primary circuit title at Indianapolis, beating Garrison in f. Qualified for VS Champs again. **1989:** (15) Won Bastad, Bayonne and VS Indianapolis; r/u Sofia. **1990:** (6) Won VS Houston (d. Navratilova and Sanchez-Vicario back-to-back), r/u Tampa (d. Sanchez-Vicario) and Canadian Open (d. Sabatini and took Graf to 3s), and appeared in 5 more sf. In GS reached qf Australian Open, French Open and Wimbledon. Broke into the top 10, overtaking her elder sister in the rankings in June, and qualified for VS Champs, where she lost qf to Graf. **1991:** Finished the season in style by taking the title at Indianapolis, although she then fell 1r VS Champs to Sabatini. She was also r/u Toronto and VS Washington (d. M. J. Fernandez), sf Tokyo Nicherei and reached 5 more qf, including Australian Open. **1991 HIGHLIGHTS – SINGLES: Australian Open** qf, seed 5 (d. Schultz 6–1 6–3, S. Martin 6–2 6–0, Faber 6–3 6–2, Magdalena Maleeva 6–3 6–2, lost M. J. Fernandez [seed 3] 6–3 6–2), **French Open** 3r, seed 11 (d. Jaggard 6–3 6–4, Kijimuta 6–2 6–3, lost E. Reinach 6–4 6–4), **Wimbledon** last 16 [seed 5] (d. Salmon 7–5 6–3, Grossman 6–4 6–1, Hy 6–3 6–4, lost Gildemeister 3–6 6–2 6–3), **US Open** 3r, seed 11 (d. Bollegraf 6–3 6–4, de Swardt 6–3 6–4, lost Rajchrtova 2–6 6–3 6–3); **won** Indianapolis (d. Ignatieva 6–1 6–3, Cioffi 6–1 6–1, Sloane Lundy 6–4 6–3, Paz 6–2 6–1, Keller 7–6 5–2); **r/u** Toronto (d. Magdalena Maleeva 6–3 6–3, Sawamatsu 6–1 6–3, Gildemeister 6–2 6–2,

Maleeva Fragnière 6–4 1–0 ret'd, lost Capriati 6–2 6–3), *r/u* VS Washington (d. Cunningham 6–4 6–0, Shriver 7–6 3–6 6–1, Wiesner 6–4 6–2, M. J. Fernandez 6–3 6–4, lost Sanchez-Vicario 6–2 7–5), *sf* Tokyo Nicherei (d. Strnadova 6–1 6–2, Gildemeister 6–3 3–6 6–1, lost M. J. Fernandez 3–6 6–1 6–4). *CAREER HIGHLIGHTS – SINGLES: Australian Open – qf 1990* (d. McNeil, McDonald, Jagerman, McQuillan 3–6 6–4 6–1, lost Sukova 6–4 6–3), *qf 1991*; *French Open – qf 1990* (d. Appelmans, Faber, Halard, Provis 3–6 6–3 6–3, lost Novotna 4–6 6–2 6–4); *Wimbledon – qf 1990* (d. B. Romano, Date, DeVries, Herreman 6–3 6–0, lost Navratilova 6–1 6–1); *US Open – qf 1988* (d. Sukova 6–1 6–3, lost Graf 6–3 6–0).

MAGDALENA MALEEVA (Bulgaria)
Born Sofia, 1 April 1975, and lives there; RH; 2HB; 5ft 6in; 109lb; final 1991 WTA ranking 38; 1991 prize money $85,607.
Coached by Jan Kurtz and her mother, Yulia Berberian. Sister of Manuela and Katerina. *1988:* Won Orange Bowl 12s. *1989:* (211) R/u Bari on Italian satellite circuit in first pro tourn. *1990:* (72) In Jun singles won Australian Open (over Stacey), French Open (over Ignatieva) and US Open (over Van Lottum). On the senior tour reached qf Wellington and after upsetting Lindqvist at Wimbledon she moved into the top 100. *1991:* Upset Fairbank-Nideffer on her way to an unexpected appearance in last 16 Australian Open and in April upset Kelesi *en route* to her 1st tour f at Bol, where she also teamed with Golarsa to win the doubles. *1991 HIGHLIGHTS – SINGLES: Australian Open* last 16, unseeded (d. Jaggard 6–4 5–7 7–4, Toleafoa 6–0 6–3, Fairbank-Nideffer [seed 14] 6–4 6–3, lost K. Maleeva [seed 5] 6–3 6–2), *French Open* 1r (lost Graf [seed 2] 6–3 7–6), *Wimbledon* 1r (lost Tami Whitlinger 6–1 6–3), *US Open* 2r (d. Kschwendt 5–7 7–6, lost Shriver 6–7 6–1 6–2); *r/u* Bol (d. Maniokova 7–5 6–1, Rottier 6–3 6–4, Garrone 6–3 7–5, Kelesi 6–4 7–5, lost Cecchini 6–4 3–6 7–5). *1991 HIGHLIGHTS – DOUBLES:* (with Golarsa) *won* Bol (d. Cecchini/Garrone 6–3 1–6 6–4).

ZDENKA MALKOVA (Czechoslovakia)
Born Pardubice, 19 January 1975; lives Prague; RH; 5ft 3in; 111lb; final 1991 WTA ranking 190; 1991 prize money $13,761.
Coached by Ladislav Travnicek. *1991:* R/u Fench Open Jun doubles with Martincova and finished the year top of the ITF Jun rankings.

ANNE MALL (USA)
Born 10 December 1974; RH; 5ft 6in; 120lb; final 1991 WTA ranking 474; 1991 prize money $3,388.
1991: R/u US Open Jun to Habsudova.

ALBERTO MANCINI (Argentina)
Born Misiones, 20 May 1969; lives Buenos Aires; RH; 5ft 11in; 164lb; final 1991 ATP ranking 22; 1991 prize money $290,375.
Coached by Francisco (Pancho) Mastelli. *1987:* (130). *1988:* (49) Emerging from the satellite circuits, he won 1st GP title at Bologna and reached sf Madrid, St Vincent and Buenos Aires. Beat E. Sanchez twice during the year. *1989:* (9) Beat Wilander and Becker back-to-back to win Monte Carlo, then followed with Italian Open, saving mp to beat Agassi in f. These performances plus qf showing at French Open and last 16 at US Open took him into the top 10. *1990:* Suffered a difficult year, dropping out of the top 100 and he could manage no better than 2 qf showings at Italian Open and Madrid, although in doubles he won Nice with Noah. *1991:* Returning to form he reached qf Nice and then, as a qualifier, appeared in f Italian Open, where he was forced to retire v E. Sanchez. He reached last 16 French Open as a wild-card entry and followed with r/u Bastad and Stuttgart Mercedes. *1991 HIGHLIGHTS – SINGLES: French Open* last 16, unseeded (d. Jelen 7–5 6–4 6–2, Prpic 1–6 7–6 6–4 1–6 6–2, Gustafsson 6–3 3–6 6–2 6–3, lost Agassi [seed 4] 6–3 6–3 5–7 6–1), *US Open* 1r (lost J. Brown 6–2 6–4 3–6 6–7 6–2); *won* Santiago Challenger (d. Rebolledo 6–3 6–3); *r/u* Italian Open (d. Agenor 6–4 6–4, Svensson 4–6 7–5 7–5, Koevermans 6–0 4–6 7–6, de la Pena 6–4 6–2, Bruguera 6–3 6–1, lost E. Sanchez 6–3 6–1 3–0 ret'd), *r/u* Bastad (d. Bjorkman 6–3 6–1, Pistolesi 3–6 6–3 6–4, Larsson 4–6 6–3 6–4, Volkov 0–6 6–3 6–2, lost Gustafsson 6–1 6–2), *r/u* Stuttgart Mercedes (d. Haarhuis 6–4 6–2, Cherkasov 4–6 6–4 6–2, Perez-Roldan 7–5 6–2, Lopez 6–3 6–3, Koslowski 4–6 6–1 6–3, lost Stich 1–6 7–6 6–4 6–2). *CAREER HIGHLIGHTS – SINGLES: French Open – qf 1990* (d. Youl, Jaite, Haarhuis, Hlasek 6–4 6–4 4–6 2–6 6–4, lost Edberg 6–1 6–3 7–6).

PASCALE PARADIS MANGON (France)
Born Troyes, 24 April 1966; lives Paris; RH; 5ft 9in; 135lb; final 1991 WTA ranking 74; 1991 prize money $50,648.

Coached by Patrick Favière. Husband Xavier Mangon (married April 1991). *1981:* Won French Open Jun. *1983:* (87) Won French and Wimbledon Jun, reached last 16 US Open in main draw and won Austrian Open. *1984:* (28) R/u Indianapolis and Pittsburgh; sf Brisbane and Brighton. *1985:* (46) Beat Hanika and Turnbull to reach last 16 Wimbledon. Played Fed Cup. *1986:* (129). *1987:* (102). *1988:* (20) Having appeared in no qf since 1984, she did so at Brisbane, Kansas and VS Florida, going on to sf Eastbourne and the highlight of her year with qf showing at Wimbledon. Upset Sukova (twice), M. Maleeva, Potter and Reggi during the year and was voted WTA Comeback Player of the Year. *1989:* (121) Qf Mahwah. *1990:* (169) Qf Bayonne and on the French satellite circuit won Limoges. *1991:* Upset Kohde-Kilsch and Dahlman in reaching sf Oslo and appeared in qf Linz. *1991 HIGHLIGHTS – SINGLES: French Open* 1r (lost Suire 6–2 6–3), *Wimbledon* 2r (d. Radford 6–3 6–3, lost Hy 4–6 6–4 6–2), *US Open* 1r (lost Maekhi [seed 13] 3–6 6–3 6–2); *sf* Oslo (d. Kohde-Kilsch 7–5 6–1, Jaggard 6–3 7–5, Dahlman 6–3 6–0, lost Reggi 7–5 6–1).

AMOS MANSDORF (Israel)
Born Tel Aviv, 20 October 1965, and lives there; RH; 5ft 9in; 158lb; final 1991 ATP ranking 62; 1991 prize money $168,488.
Coached by Guenther Bresnik. *1984:* (268) Joined Israeli Olympic team; qf US Open Jun. *1985:* (84) R/u Tel Aviv. *1986:* (37) Won first GP title in Johannesburg. *1987:* (27) Beat Mecir and Novacek as he led his country to major upset of TCH in D Cup, d. Connors and Gilbert to win Tel Aviv, and appeared in top 20 in Nov. *1988:* (26) Won Auckland and Paris Open, sf Tel Aviv; upset Becker at Orlando and took Lendl to 5s 1r US Open. *1989:* (39) R/u Auckland and Singapore; last 16 Australian Open and Wimbledon. *1990:* (33) Won his 1st title on grass at Rosmalen, r/u Tel Aviv, sf Auckland and Toulouse. Upset Gilbert *en route* to last 16 US Open, and in 3r Wimbledon took eventual champion Edberg to 9–7 5s. *1991:* Experienced a quieter year in which his best showing was r/u Toulouse; qf Rosmalen, Manchester and Los Angeles. *1991 HIGHLIGHTS – SINGLES: Australian Open* 2r (d. Sznajder 6–0 6–3 6–3, lost Krickstein 7–5 3–6 7–6 6–2), *Wimbledon* 1r (lost Masur 6–3 1–6 7–6 6–4), *US Open* 1r (lost Camporese 5–7 6–4 7–5 3–6 6–3); *r/u* Toulouse (d. Gustafsson 6–4 6–1, Mronz 7–5 4–6 6–2, Bergstrom 6–4 6–4, Volkov 7–5 5–7 6–1, lost Forget 6–2 7–6).

GABRIEL MARKUS (Argentina)
Born Buenos Aires, 31 March 1970, and lives there; RH; 5ft 11in; 155lb; final 1991 ATP ranking 65; 1991 prize money $114,650.
1989: (207) Won Santos Challenger. *1990:* (205). *1991:* Reached his 1st tour qf at Florence, following with the same stage at Sao Paulo, where he also won the Challenger tourn, and broke into the top 100 after an unexpected appearance in last 16 US Open. *1991 HIGHLIGHTS – SINGLES: French Open* 3r (d. Sznajder 6–1 7–5 6–4, Perez 2–6 2–6 7–6 6–4 6–4 6–3, lost Boetsch 5–7 7–6 6–3 6–2), *US Open* last 16, unseeded (d. Nargiso 7–6 7–6 7–6, Pescosolido 6–2 1–6 4–6 7–6 6–2, Siemerink 6–4 6–4 1–6 6–7 7–6, lost J. Sanchez 6–4 6–2 6–3); *won* Sao Paulo Challenger (d. Cunha-Silva 4–6 6–4 6–4).

EVA MARTINCOVA (Czechoslovakia)
Born Brno, 4 March 1975, and lives there; RH; 5ft 5in; 114lb; final 1991 WTA ranking 416; 1991 prize money $3,141.
1991: With consistent rather than spectacular results, she finished the year ranked No. 1 in the ITF Jun doubles rankings.

VERONIKA MARTINEK (Germany)
Born Usti Nad Laben, Czechoslovakia, 3 April 1972; lives Nuremberg; RH; 2HB; 5ft 3in; 120lb; final 1991 WTA ranking 64; 1991 prize money $39,304.
Coached by her father, Vladimir, and travels with her mother, Jaroslava. Her family defected to West Germany from Czechoslovakia in 1980. *1987:* (397). *1988:* (115) Sf Taranto. *1989:* (157) Won Cava dei Tirreni on the Italian satellite circuit. *1990:* (111) Qf Strasbourg and Kitzbuhel and broke into the top 100 in autumn. *1991:* Won her 1st main tour title at Sao Paulo. *1991 HIGHLIGHTS – SINGLES: French Open* 2r (d. Porwik 6–1 6–0, lost Pierce 6–3 6–0), *Wimbledon* 1r (lost A. Huber [seed 14] 6–1 6–2); *won* Sao Paulo (d. Ter Riet 6–2 7–6, Haumuller 7–5 6–3, Mothes 3–6 7–6 6–4, Corsato 6–3 6–2, Faber 6–2 6–4).

MAGNUS MARTINELLE (Sweden)
Born 8 February 1973.
1991: Won French Open Jun doubles with Enqvist.

CONCHITA MARTINEZ (Spain)
Born Monzon, 16 April 1972; lives Barcelona; RH; 5ft 7in; 132lb; final 1991 WTA ranking 9; 1991 prize money $304,790.

Coached by Eric van Harpen in Switzerland. *1988:* (40) Upset McNeil *en route* to last 16 French Open after qualifying and won 1st pro title in both singles and doubles (with Paulus) at Sofia. Won Nat Champs over Sanchez and played Fed Cup. *1989:* (7) Won her 2nd tour singles title at Wellington, following with Tampa (d. Sabatini) and VS Arizona; r/u Geneva and Bayonne; qf French Open and qualified for 1st VS Champs. Voted WTA Most Impressive Newcomer. *1990:* (11) Won Clarins and Indianapolis; sf LIPC (d. Sabatini), Tampa and Leipzig; qf French Open again. *1991:* Won Barcelona, Kitzbuhel and Clarins and reached sf Italian Open (d. Navratilova qf), Geneva, San Diego and Milan. Played in the successful Spanish Fed Cup team, and qualified for VS Champs, where she fell 1r to Graf. In GS reached qf French Open and US Open. *1991 HIGHLIGHTS – SINGLES: Australian Open* 2r (d. Kijimuta 6–3 6–1, lost Dechaume 6–2 6–2), *French Open* qf, seed 7 (d. Wiesner 6–4 6–3, Rehe 6–1 7–6, Cunningham 6–1 6–4, Capriati [seed 10] 6–3 6–3, lost Seles [seed 1] 6–0 7–5), *US Open* qf seed 8 (d. C. Dahlman 6–1 6–1, Basuki 6–3 6–4, Fendick 7–5 6–3, Garrison [seed 12] 6–4 6–4, lost Graf [seed 1] 6–1 6–3); *won* Barcelona (d. Wasserman 6–2 6–1, McQuillan 6–4 6–3, Halard 1–6 6–4 6–4, Tauziat 6–1 4–6 6–1, Maleeva Fragnière 6–4 6–1), *won* Kitzbuhel (d. Tarabini 6–1 6–3, Strandlund 6–3 6–1, Sviglerova 6–2 4–6 7–5, Zrubakova 7–5 6–4, Wiesner 6–1 2–6 6–3), *won* Clarins (d. Tarabini 6–1 6–3, Hack 6–0 6–3, Zardo 6–4 6–2, Halard 6–4 2–6 7–5, Gorrochategui 6–0 6–3); *sf* Italian Open (d. Stacey Martin 6–3 6–3, Kelesi 6–1 6–1, Navratilova 3–6 6–4, lost Sabatini 6–1 6–0), *sf* Geneva (d. Ferrando 6–0 6–2, Fauche 6–3 6–3, lost Kelesi 6–4 6–7 6–2), *sf* San Diego (d. Werdel 6–3 6–1, Graham 6–0 7–5, lost Capriati 6–4 6–0), *sf* Milan (d. Habsudova 6–4 6–1, G. Fernandez 6–1 7–5, lost Seles 6–3 6–3). *CAREER HIGHLIGHTS – SINGLES: French Open – qf 1989* (d. Herr, Pospisilova, Amiach 6–3 6–3, K. Maleeva 6–0 6–1, lost Graf 6–0 6–4), *qf 1990* (d. Thompson, Etchemendy, Zrubakova, Probst 6–3 6–3, lost Graf 6–1 6–3), *qf 1991*; *US Open – qf 1991*.

EDUARDO MASSO (Belgium)
Born Cordoba, Argentina, 11 January 1964; lives Brussels; LH; 5ft 10in; 172lb; final 1991 ATP ranking 94; 1991 prize money $103,917.
His wife, Mabille, is Belgian and he has taken dual Argentinian/Belgian nationality, playing D Cup for Belgium. *1982:* Argentinian Nat Jun champ. *1986:* (208). *1987:* (185) Enjoyed some success on the Challenger circuit. *1988:* (87) Sf Lyon after qualifying, qf Madrid and Bristol, and broke into top 100 1st time. *1989:* (305) Sf Nancy, but was forced out for 4½ months with side injury suffered at French Open. *1990:* (125) Upset E. Sanchez at Hilversum as he swept to f in only his 2nd tourn of year after qualifying, and was undefeated in 4 D Cup matches. *1991:* Sf Florence and Geneva, qf Bologna. *1991 HIGHLIGHTS – SINGLES: Australian Open* 2r (d. Pearce 6–1 6–7 6–3 8–6, lost Edberg [seed 1] 6–1 6–2 6–3), *French Open* 1r (lost Krickstein 6–7 6–4 2–6 6–1 7–5), *Wimbledon* 1r (lost Bergstrom 6–1 7–5 6–3); *sf* Florence (d. Arrese 6–2 5–7 6–1, J. Sanchez 6–3 7–6, Larsson 6–3 4–6 6–1, lost Skoff 6–4 6–4), *sf* Genova (d. Cancellotti 6–2 7–5, Koevermans 6–4 6–4, Fleurian 7–5 6–1, lost Arrese 7–6 6–3).

WALLY MASUR (Australia)
Born Southampton, England, 13 May 1963; lives Sydney; RH; 5ft 11in; 167lb; final 1991 ATP ranking 57; 1991 prize money $301,160.
Wife Sue Steel (married 17 Dec. 1989). *1981:* (287) Won Australian Open Jun. *1982:* (125). *1983:* (66) Qf Australian Open and won Hong Kong. *1984:* (106) R/u Taipei. *1985:* (101) R/u Auckland. *1986:* (87) Sf Livingston and Auckland. *1987:* (35) In Adelaide won first tourn since 1983, then upset Becker *en route* to sf Australian Open. *1988:* (46) Won Newport, r/u Adelaide and reached last 16 Australian Open and Wimbledon (d. McEnroe 2r). *1989:* (42) Sf Singapore, Brisbane and Wembley. *1990:* (53) In singles was r/u Memphis; in doubles won Tokyo Suntory with Kratzmann and Hong Kong with Cash. In D Cup won singles v FRA, NZ and ARG, but was dropped from the team that lost 2–3 in f to USA. *1991:* In singles he reached f Hong Kong (upset Hlasek), sf San Francisco, and upset Lendl 1r Sydney. In doubles he won 3 titles with different partners. *1991 HIGHLIGHTS – SINGLES: Australian Open* 2r (d. Stolle 6–1 6–2 6–2, lost Gustafsson 7–5 3–6 7–6 6–0), *French Open* 3r (d. Cunha-Silva 7–6 6–1 6–4, Oncins 6–1 7–6 7–5, lost Becker [seed 2] 6–3 6–3 6–2), *Wimbledon* 2r (d. Mandsdorf 6–3 1–6 7–6 6–4, lost B. Gilbert 7–5 2–6 6–3 5–7 6–4), *US Open* 3r (d. Williamson 4–6 6–3 6–3 6–2, Joyce 6–4 6–3 3–6 6–3, lost E. Sanchez [seed 14] 6–4 7–6 7–6; *r/u* Hong Kong (d. Hlasek 6–4 7–6, Michibata 6–3 6–2, Barrientos 6–0 6–1, Antonitsch 4–6 7–6 6–3, lost Krajicek 6–2 3–6 6–3); *sf* San Francisco (d. Pearce 6–1 6–4, Krishnan 6–3 6–3, Pate 6–1 4–6 7–6, lost Cahill 4–6 6–4 7–5). *1991 HIGHLIGHTS – DOUBLES:* [Stoltenberg] *won* San Francisco (d. Bathman/Bergh 4–6 7–6 6–4),

[E. Sanchez] **won** Stuttgart Mercedes (d. Camporese/Ivanisevic 4–6 6–3 6–4), [Korda] **won** New Haven (d. J. Brown/Melville 7–5 6–3). **CAREER HIGHLIGHTS – SINGLES: Australian Open – sf 1987** (d. Becker 4–6 7–6 6–4 6–7 6–2, Evernden, lost Edberg 6–2 6–4 7–6), **qf 1983** (d. Flach, Jarryd 6–3 6–3 4–6 6–1, lost J. McEnroe 6–2 6–1 6–2).

SHUZO MATSUOKA (Japan)
Born Tokyo, 6 November 1967, and lives there; RH; 6ft 1in; 176lb; final 1991 ATP ranking 67; 1991 prize money $126,790.
Coached by Alvarez Betancur. Father played D Cup for Japan. **1986:** (370) R/u Nat Champs. **1987:** (260). **1988:** (82) Upset Mecir *en route* to 1st GP qf in Tokyo, where he took McEnroe to 2 t-b (10–9 and 9–7), and then reached sf Brisbane in Oct. **1989:** (181) Won his 1st GP title at Wellington and took Auckland doubles with Guy, but was then out of action for 3 months following surgery on both knees in April. **1990:** (144) Reached qf Seoul, but was out again from Oct. with ligament damage to ankle. **1991:** Returning after 3½ months, he reached sf Guaruja Chevrolet and Seoul, won Brazil Challenger and upset Sampras at Montreal. **1991 HIGHLIGHTS – SINGLES: French Open** 1r (lost Agenor 6–2 6–3 6–7 6–3), **Wimbledon** 1r (lost Mattar 6–4 4–6 6–7 7–5 7–5); **won** Brazil Challenger (d. R. Gilbert 6–4 4–6 6–1); **sf** Guaruja Chevrolet (d. Altur 2–6 6–3 6–4, Eltingh 6–4 6–2, R. Gilbert 6–4 6–2, lost Baur 5–7 6–3 7–6), **sf** Seoul (d. Kuhnen 7–5 4–6 6–4, Dzelde 6–2 6–1, Siemerink 4–6 6–2 6–4, lost Baur 7–6 6–2).

ANDREI MEDVEDEV (USSR)
Born Kiev, 31 August 1974, and lives there; RH; 6ft 3in; 178lb; final 1991 ATP ranking 402; 1991 prize money $226.
Coach Youri Cherepov. Turned pro 1991. **1990:** Won Orange Bowl over Fernandez. **1991:** Won French Open Jun over Enqvist.

NATALIA MEDVEDEVA (USSR)
Born Kiev, 15 November 1971, and lives there; RH; 2HB; 5ft 8in; 142lb; final 1991 WTA ranking 82; 1991 prize money $36,778.
Known as Natasha in USSR. **1987:** (196) ITF Jun Champ in doubles; won French Open and Wimbledon Jun doubles with Zvereva. In autumn won 3 consec. titles on LTA British circuit. **1988:** (305). **1989:** (66) Sf Moscow and extended Sanchez-Vicario to 3s at French Open. **1990:** (56) In singles won her 1st tour title at VS Nashville in Oct. and followed the next week with sf showing at Indianapolis. In doubles won Auckland and Wellington at the beginning of the year with Meskhi, with whom she upset Novotna/Sukova at VS Champs, and also took Puerto Rico with Brioukhovets in Oct. **1991:** Reached sf Nashville in singles and won St Petersburg doubles with Brioukhovets. **1991 HIGHLIGHTS – SINGLES: Australian Open** 1r (lost Sanchez-Vicario [seed 6] 6–0 6–2); **sf** VS Nashville (d. E. Reinach 6–1 6–2, Porwik 6–1 7–6, Demongeot 3–6 7–5 6–2, lost Adams 7–6 5–7 6–4). **1991 HIGHLIGHTS – DOUBLES:** (with Brioukhovets) **won** St Petersburg (d. Demongeot/Durie 7–5 6–3).

LEILA MESKHI (USSR)
Born Tbilisi, 5 January 1968, and lives there; RH; 2HB; 5ft 4½in; 120lb; final 1991 WTA ranking 15; 1991 prize money $223,168.
Coached by Temuraz Kakulia and Olga Morozova. Husband Pavil Nadibaidze (married July 1989). **1986:** (241) No. 1 in ITF Jun doubles world rankings. In singles r/u Wimbledon Jun; in doubles won French Open Jun (with Zvereva), r/u Wimbledon (with Zvereva) and US Open Jun (with Brioukhovets). **1987:** (44) Reached 1st sf at VS Indianapolis, qf Athens and Chicago, and upset Bunge 2r Hamburg. **1988:** (46) R/u Singapore, sf Japan Open and Nashville (d. Potter) and stunned Shriver 2r US Open. **1989:** (30) Won VS Nashville (d. K. Maleeva and Kelesi); r/u VS Oklahoma. Joined her country's Fed Cup team. **1990:** (19) In singles she won Auckland and Moscow, was r/u Wellington and Indianapolis (upset K. Maleeva) and, after surprising Zvereva *en route* to qf US Open, she broke into the top 20. In doubles with Medvedeva won 2 titles and upset Novotna/Sukova at VS Champs. **1991:** After winning Wellington and surprising Navratilova *en route* to f FC Cup, she found herself poised just outside the top 10, but despite also reaching f Bayonne and sf Washington, she was still unable to break in. **1991 HIGHLIGHTS – SINGLES: French Open** last 16, seed 14 (d. Dopfer 6–2 6–2, Kohde-Kilsch 7–5 6–1, Harvey-Wild 6–3 6–1, lost Novotna [seed 6] 6–0 7–6), **US Open** 3r, seed 13 (d. Paradis Mangon 3–6 6–3 6–2, Gildemeister 6–4 3–6 6–0, lost G. Fernandez 7–6 6–7 7–6); **won** Wellington (d. Pratt 6–2 6–2, Cammy McGregor 6–3 7–6, Sviglerova 6–3 6–4, Quentrec 6–2 6–3, Strnadova 3–6 7–6 6–2); **r/u** FC Cup (d. Martinek 6–4 7–5, Zrubakova 6–3 6–2, Capriati 3–6 6–3 6–3, Navratilova 6–4 2–6 6–4, Zvereva 6–3 3–6 6–4, lost Sabatini 6–1 6–1), **r/u** Bayonne (d. Probst 7–5 6–4, Herreman

6–3 6–2, Porwik 6–4 6–3, Tauziat 6–2 7–5, lost Maleeva Fragnière 4–6 6–3 6–4); *sf* VS Washington (d. Ferrando 6–3 4–4 ret'd, A. Minter 4–6 6–1 6–4, Novotna 6–2 2–6 6–4, lost Sanchez-Vicario 6–0 6–1). *CAREER HIGHLIGHTS – SINGLES: US Open – qf 1990* (d. Kijimuta, Zvereva 6–4 6–0, Piccolini 6–2 4–6 7–6, Ferrando 7–6 6–1, lost Sabatini 7–6 6–4).

GLENN MICHIBATA (Canada)
Born Toronto, 13 June 1962; lives Islington, Ontario; RH; 5ft 9in; 152lb; final 1991 ATP ranking 222 singles, 8 (10T) doubles; 1991 prize money $249,445.
Wife Angie. Nat champ in 14s, 16s, 18s and 21s. *1982:* (172) Qf Japan Open. *1983:* (79) Nat Jun champ for 3rd year. Qf Tokyo Seiko, Maui and Taipei. *1984:* (163). *1985:* (76). *1986:* (206) Broke into top 50 in April. *1987:* (178) Qf Adelaide. *1988:* (102) Won Livingston doubles with Connell. *1989:* (152) Sf Wellington and Schenectady. *1990:* (481) In doubles with Connell r/u Australian Open, won Seoul and Washington and reached 2 more f, qualifying for IBM/ATP World Doubles Final. *1991:* Again excelled in doubles, reaching 9 f, 6 of them with Connell, with whom he won his only title at Singapore, where he also reached qf in singles. Qualified with Connell for ATP Doubles Champ, where they fell sf to Flach and Seguso. *1991 HIGHLIGHTS – SINGLES: Wimbledon* 2r (d. Stoltenberg 5–7 6–4 3–6 7–6 6–4, lost Camporese 7–5 6–2 6–1), *US Open* 1r (lost Marques 6–3 6–4 7–6). *1991 HIGHLIGHTS – DOUBLES:* (with Connell unless stated) *won* Singapore (d. Kruger/Van Rensburg 6–4 5–7 7–6); *r/u* Auckland (lost Casal/E. Sanchez 4–6 6–3 6–4), *r/u* Chicago (lost Davis/Pate 6–4 5–7 7–6), [Van't Hof] *r/u* Hong Kong (lost Galbraith/Witsken 6–2 6–4), *r/u* Queen's (lost Woodbridge/Woodforde 6–4 7–6), [Pearce] *r/u* Los Angeles (lost Frana/Pugh 7–5 2–6 6–4), *r/u* Montreal (lost Galbraith/Witsken 6–4 3–6 6–1), [Fitzgerald] *r/u* Brisbane (lost Woodbridge/Woodforde 7–6 6–3), *r/u* Cincinnnati (lost Flach/Seguso 6–7 6–4 7–5). *CAREER HIGHLIGHTS – DOUBLES:* (with Connell) *Australian Open – r/u 1990* (lost Aldrich/Visser 6–4 4–6 6–1 6–4).

CRISTIAN MINIUSSI (Argentina)
Born Buenos Aires, 5 July 1967, and lives there; RH; 6ft 1in; 165lb; final 1991 ATP ranking 81; 1991 prize money $129,116.
1981–82: Won Banana Bowl. *1984:* (186) Upset Gerulaitis at Bordeaux. *1985:* (308) Won Buenos Aires doubles with Jaite. *1986:* (96) Sf Geneva. *1987:* (125) Qf St Vincent and Palermo. *1988:* (179) Qf Bari and upset Vilas at Munich, but made his mark mainly on the Challenger circuit. *1990:* (163) Won 2 Challenger titles in Nairobi. *1991:* Won Sao Paulo as a lucky loser, reached qf Geneva and took Hlasek to 5s in last 16 French Open after qualifying. *1991 HIGHLIGHTS – SINGLES: French Open* last 16, unseeded (d. Baguena 6–4 3–6 2–6 6–3, Filippini 1–6 6–2 4–4 ret'd, Camporese 2–6 3–6 1 6–3, lost Hlasek 4–6 6–3 5–7 7–5 6–2); *won* Sao Paulo (d. Frana 6–4 6–3, Lopez w.o., Markus 4–6 6–0 6–4, Gomez 6–4 6–4, Oncins 2–6 6–3 6–4). *1991 HIGHLIGHTS – DOUBLES:* [Perez] *r/u* San Marino (lost Arrese/Costa 6–3 3–6 6–3).

ANNE MINTER (Australia)
Born Ballarat, 3 April 1963; lives Melbourne and Deerfield Beach, Fla.; RH; 5ft 5in; 120lb; final 1991 WTA ranking 59; 1991 prize money $85,583.
Married her coach, Graeme Harris (Nov. 1988). Sister of Elizabeth. Plays flute to state orchestra standard. *1980:* Won Australian Open Jun and was ranked 5 on ITF world Jun list. *1981:* Australian Jun champ. *1982:* (77) Won Goldair on Australian satellite circuit. *1983:* (95). *1984:* (43) Sf Salt Lake City and Newport in singles, qf Australian Open doubles with her sister. Joined Fed Cup team. *1985:* (72) Qf Marco Island. *1986:* (82) Won 20 of 40 matches, upsetting Lindqvist 1r VS LA. *1987:* (38) Won her first major title at Taipei, following with Singapore a week later and d. Sukova 2r Canadian Open. *1988:* (26) Upset Shriver to reach qf Australian Open and Mandlikova to reach last 16 Wimbledon; won Puerto Rico, sf Wellington. *1989:* (34) Won Taipei, sf Tokyo and Toronto (upset Evert). *1990:* (85) Sf Moscow; qf Wichita, VS Oklahoma and Albuquerque. *1991:* Began the year with an upset of Meskhi in Auckland, reached sf Strasbourg, qf VS Oklahoma and San Diego (d. Gildemeister) and made an unscheduled appearance in last 16 Wimbledon, where she took Sanchez-Vicario to 3s. *1991 HIGHLIGHTS – SINGLES: Australian Open* 1r (lost Novotna [seed 10] 7–6 6–2), *French Open* 1r (lost Coetzer 5–7 7–5 6–3), *Wimbledon* last 16, unseeded (d. S. Martin 6–4 6–0, Faull 6–3 6–2, G. Fernadez 6–3 6–3, lost Sanchez-Vicario [seed 3] 7–5 3–6 6–1), *US Open* 1r (lost A. Huber [seed 16] 6–1 4–6 6–1); *sf* Strasbourg (d. Cueto 0–6 7–6 6–3, Quentrec 6–2 6–2, McNeil 6–1 7–6, lost Zrubakova 6–1 6–3). *CAREER HIGHLIGHTS – SINGLES: Australian Open – qf 1988* (d. Shriver 6–2 6–4, lost Kohde-Kilsch 6–2 6–4).

THOMAS MUSTER (Austria)
Born Leibnitz, 2 October 1967; lives there and Monte Carlo; LH; 5ft 11in; 165lb; final 1991 ATP ranking 35; 1991 prize money $189,840.
Coached by Ronald Leitgeb until end 1990 when he became business manager only. *1985:* (98) Won Banana Bowl, r/u French Open Jun and Rolex. Became a member of Austrian D Cup squad and finished 6 on Austrian satellite circuit. *1986:* (47) Won first GP title in Hilversum. *1987:* (56) Sf Vienna (d. E. Sanchez) and won Young Masters. *1988:* (16) Upset Jaite 1r Italian Open and then in the space of 5 weeks won Boston (playing in his 1st GP f), Bordeaux and Prague, following with Bari later in year. *1989:* (21) Reached 1st GS sf at Australian Open. On 1 April, 2 hours after beating Noah to reach f LIPC, which took him into top 10 for 1st time, he was knocked down by a drunken driver in Miami and suffered 2 torn ligaments and torn cartilage in his left knee, requiring reconstructive surgery. In plaster 1½ months and was expected to be out of action for about 10 months, but in May he was already practising in a specially designed wheelchair. In Sept., after only 4 months' rehabilitation, he played doubles at Geneva then reached qf Barcelona in singles, following with sf Vienna. *1990:* (7) At Adelaide in Jan. won 1st tour title since injury 10 months earlier, following with Casablanca in March, Italian Open in May and reaching sf French Open to regain his place in the top 10. R/u Monte Carlo and Munich; sf Vienna; qualified for ATP World Champ but failed to reach sf and fell 1r GS Cup to Leconte. Still in pain and advised by doctors to concentrate on CC tourns in 1990. Suspended 5 weeks from 22 Oct. and fined $15,000 (reduced on appeal from a ten-week suspension from US Open plus $25,000 fine) by ATP for 'violation of best efforts' and 'unsportsmanlike conduct' – after accepting guarantee to play at Prague he pulled out after just 1 game, having previously expressed his intention to do so. Voted Comeback Player of the Year. *1991:* Underwent arthroscopic surgery on his left knee in March and won no match in his 1st 6 tourns until Italian Open, where he reached 3r, following with qf Bologna. Having dropped out of top 100 for the 1st time since April 1986, he returned after taking the title at Florence, following with Geneva and beating Skoff in f both times. He also reached sf Genova, Prague and Athens. *1991 HIGHLIGHTS – SINGLES: French Open* 1r (lost Sampras 4–6 4–6 6–4 6–1 6–4); *won* Florence (d. Rebolledo 1–6 6–4 6–0, Champion 4–6 6–3 6–2, Santoro 6–7 6–1 6–1, Costa 6–7 6–1 6–3, Skoff 6–2 6–7 6–4), *won* Geneva (d. Vajda 6–3 7–5, Perez-Roldan 4–6 6–1 6–2, Bruguera 4–6 6–4 6–4, Medvedev 7–6 7–6, Skoff 6–2 6–4); *sf* Genova (d. Champion 4–6 6–0 6–3, Pescosolido 6–4 6–3, Pioline 4–6 7–6 6–2, lost Steeb 7–5 6–4), *sf* Prague (d. Nargiso 6–4 6–2, Arrese 6–2 6–3, Larsson 6–3 6–0, lost Novacek 6–1 2–6 7–5), *sf* Athens (d. Eltingh 6–4 6–3, Yunis 6–4 6–3, Perez-Roldan 6–3 3–6 7–6, lost Bruguera 1–6 6–2 6–0). *CAREER HIGHLIGHTS – SINGLES: LIPC – r/u 1989* (d. Odizor, Michibata 7–5 7–6 6–2, Sznajder 6–1 3–6 6–3 7–6, Bengoechea 6–1 6–1 6–1, Grabb 7–5 7–6 1–6 6–0, Noah 5–7 3–6 6–3 6–3 6–2, lost Lendl def.); *Australian Open – sf 1989* (d. Rive, Wekesa, Visser 6–3 3–6 6–3 11–9, Gustafsson 6–3 6–2 7–5, Edberg w.o., lost Lendl 6–2 6–4 5–7 7–5); *French Open – sf 1990* (d. Jonsson, Winogradsky, Haarhuis, Jaite 7–6 6–3 6–2, Ivanisevic 6–2 4–6 6–4 6–3, lost Gomez 7–6 6–1 7–5).

MARTINA NAVRATILOVA (USA)
Born Prague, Czechoslovakia, 18 October 1956; lives Fort Worth, Texas and Aspen, Colo.; LH; 5ft 8in; 145lb; final 1991 WTA ranking 4 singles, 6 (4) doubles; 1991 prize money $989,986.
Coached by Craig Kardon and B. J. King (1990). *1973:* Displaying enormous promise, she reached qf French Open and extended Goolagong to 7–6 6–4 in memorable match after eliminating 1968 champion Nancy Richey. *1974:* Won first major tournament in Orlando and was r/u to Evert at Italian Open. *1975:* (3) Led Czechoslovakia to Fed Cup title (d. Goolagong in f), and was r/u to Evert at VS Champs, French and Italian Opens, reaching f in 13 of 25 tourns. The day after losing to Evert in US Open sf Forest Hills she announced her defection from Czechoslovakia. *1976:* (4) Reached first sf at Wimbledon and won first doubles there with Evert, but made tearful exit from US Open after losing 1r. *1977:* (3) Won 6 tourns and reached f of 5 other events in 20 appearances. *1978:* (1) Ranked 1 on computer in close race with Evert, whom she beat to win first Wimbledon singles title. Won 80 of 89 matches and 11 of 20 tourns, including 37-match winning streak as she won 7 straight VS tourns in winter. *1979:* (1) Defended Wimbledon title safely and won 11 of 23 tourns, reaching f of 19 events and closing year with resounding victory over Austin at TS Champs. *1980:* (3) Won 11 of 24 tourns but no majors. *1981:* (3) Linking with Renee Richards at US Open, she received sound technical and tactical advice, leading to sf win there over Evert Lloyd, another f Australian Open, and sucess in 8 of 19 tourns. Became US citizen 21 July. *1982:* (1) Won 15 of 18 tourns, 90 of 93 matches, including 41 straight from

March until September, with third Wimbledon singles and first French Open. *1983:* (1) Won 16 of 17 tourns, including first US Open and fourth Wimbledon, and 86 of 87 matches, closing season with streak of 50 straight match victories, her only defeat being by Kathleen Horvath in last 16 of French Open. Her 0.988 winning percentage set an 'Open Tennis' record for men and women. *1984:* (1) Won 78 of 80 matches, 13 of 15 tourns, and set modern pro record of 74 straight matches won, beginning immediately after her 54-match streak was broken at start of season by Mandlikova at VS Oakland. Won bonus of $1m from ITF for achieving a modern GS, culminating with French Open where she played possibly the best match of her career to beat Evert Lloyd in f. She extended her GS streak to six with her fifth Wimbledon and second US Open victories, but her bid for traditional GS, as well as her 74-match winning streak, were stopped by Sukova in sf Australian Open. *1985:* (1) Won her 6th Wimbledon and 3rd Australian titles, 84 of 89 matches and 12 of 17 tourns. Was challenged for No. 1 ranking by Evert Lloyd, who took over top spot for virtually half the year, but Martina clinched No. 1 with 3s triumph over Chris in Australian f. *1986:* (1) Won 14 of 17 tourns and 89 of 92 matches, including 5th straight Wimbledon (the first since Lenglen 1919–23 to achieve that feat) and her 3rd US Open. Won two VS Champs and closed season with streak of 53 straight matches. Won 1,000th match in Filderstadt. *1987:* (2) Coached by Randy Crawford Jan. to March, Virginia Wade Jan. to May and by Renee Richards to end of year. Losing Australian Open f to Mandlikova, French Open f to Graf, who also beat her in sf LIPC, she won no singles tournament from Nov. 1986 until triumphing over Graf at Wimbledon. This was her longest spell without a win since mid 1970s and cost her the No. 1 computer ranking which she had held continuously since July 1985. However, she won her 1st triple crown at US Open, her 2 GS singles titles confirming her as No. 1 in some eyes until she fell to Sabatini in qf VS Champs. In doubles, won 3rd GS with Shriver in Paris and their 6th VS Champs together. *1988:* (2) Coached by Tim Gullikson, with Craig Kardon taking over for 1989. For the first time in 8 years she won no GS title, falling in sf Australian Open to Evert, last 16 French Open to Zvereva, f Wimbledon to Graf and qf US Open to Garrison. Nor did she find consolation at VS Champs, where she fell in qf to Sukova. In doubles won Australian, French Open and VS Champs with Shriver, but failed in both women's and mixed at Wimbledon, leaving there empty-handed for the first time since 1981. However, she won 9 singles titles and her 1,100th career victory at Amelia Island, remaining firmly in the No. 2 position. *1989:* (2) Again won no GS singles title, falling qf Australian Open to Sukova, missing French Open to prepare for Wimbledon, where she was r/u to Graf, and losing f US Open also to Graf, despite having been ahead 6–3 4–2. However, she won 8 singles titles, was r/u VS Champs to Graf and lost to no one else from April. Took 7 doubles titles, including Australian Open and VS Champs with Shriver and US Open with Mandlikova after ending her partnership with Shriver in July. Called on Billie Jean King mid-season to help her overcome a crisis of confidence and to 'get the fun back' into her game. *1990:* (3) Achieved her primary aim of winning a 9th Wimbledon – without dropping a set – to pass Helen Wills Moody's record, and setting a new record of 99 singles victories there, passing Chris Evert's 97. In her only other GS tourn, at US Open, found motivation hard to maintain and lost in last 16 to Maleeva Fragnière, who beat her again in qf Tokyo Nicherei. Won her 150th title at FC Cup in April, also taking VS Chicago, Washington, Indian Wells and Eastbourne; r/u Italian Open, Los Angeles and VS California, losing each time to Seles, while Sanchez-Vicario beat her in sf Hamburg and K. Maleeva at same stage Houston. She was overtaken in the rankings by Seles and finished the year ranked 3 for the first time since 1981. In doubles she won US Open with G. Fernandez and took four other titles with various partners. *1991:* Missed Australian Open after undergonig knee surgery and returned to reach f Tokyo Pan Pacific end Jan. However, it was her least successful year since 1976, with Sabatini, Sanchez-Vicario and M. J. Fernadez all overtaking her at times in the rankings, and she slipped out of the top 3 for the 1st time since 1977. By anyone else's standards, though she enjoyed an excellent year, wining VS Chicago, Palm Springs, Birmingham, Eastbourne, VS California and r/u Tokyo Pan Pacific, Milan, Filderstadt and VS Champs. In doubles she reached 3 f, winning Barcelona with Sanchez-Vicario, Filderstadt with Novotna and a seventh VS Champs with Shriver. When she d. Seles at Palm Springs, it was the 1st time since 1987 that she'd beaten a player above her in the rankings and she repeated the performance in winning VS California to equal Evert's record of 157 career titles. In beating Reinach 1r Wimbledon – recovering from 4–6 6–2 3–4 0–30 down – she recorded a record 100th single win there, and during the tourn she also passed Evert's record of 111 singles matches played there. She has already set a new record of 1,310 career match wins when she d. M. J. Fernandez in Milan. However, she failed to take a 10th Wimbledon title, falling in ss to Capriati in qf, and at US Open she was seeded as low as 6. However, she belied that assessment by beating Graf to reach f, which she lost to Seles, who also beat her in 4s f VS Champs. *1991 HIGHLIGHTS – SINGLES: Wimbledon* qf, seed 4 (d. Reinach 4–6 6–2 6–4, Grunfeld 6–3 6–1, Garrone 6–2 6–2, Lindqvist 6–1 6–3, lost Capriati [seed 10] 6–4 7–5), *r/u US Open*, seed 6 (d. Tarabini 6–2 6–2, Graham 6–1 6–4, Shriver 7–5 6–1, Malccva Fragnièrc [seed 10] 7 6 1 6 6 2, Sanchez-Vicario [seed 4] 6–7 7–6 6–2, Graf [seed 1] 7–6 6–7 6–4, lost Seles [seed 2] 7–6 6–1); *won* VS Chicago (d. Shriver 7–6 6–1, A. Smith 6–1 6–2, Sukova 6–3 6–2, Garrison 6–1, 6–2), *won* Palm Springs (d. Coetzer 6–0 6–2, Helgeson 6–0 6–2, Halard 6–2 7–5, Tauziat 6–3 7–6, Seles 6–2 7–6), *won* Birmingham (d. Basuki 6–2 6–3, Kidowaki 6–0 6–2, McNeil 6–3 6–2, Schultz 6–3 6–2, Zvereva 6–4 7–6), *won* Eastbourne (d. Coetzer 6–0 6–1, Golarsa 6–0 6–0, Schultz 6–1 6–2, Ludloff 6–1 6–1, M. J. Fernandez 6–3 6–0, Sanchez-Vicario 6–4 6–4), *won* VS California (d. Tami Whitlinger 6–1 7–5, Pierce 6–2 6–2, McNeil 6–3 6–2, Seles 6–3 3–6 6–3); *r/u* Tokyo Pan Pacific (d. Durie 6–3 4–6 6–2, R. White 6–2 6–3, Gildemeister 6–2 7–6, lost Sabatini 2–6 6–2 6–4), *r/u* Milan (d. McQuillan 6–7 6–0 6–0, Appelmans 6–2 6–3, M. J. Fernandez 6–2 3–6 6–4, lost Seles 6–3 3–6 6–4), *r/u* Filderstadt (d. Babel 6–4 6–2, E. Reinach 6–4 7–5, Tauziat 6–4 7–5, Wiesner 6–2 7–6, lost A. Huber 2–6 6–2 7–6), *r/u* VS Champs (d. McNeil 6–4 7–5, Sanchez-Vicario 1–6 6–4 6–2, Novotna 6–1 6–4, lost Seles 6–4 3–6 7–5 6–0). *1991 HIGHLIGHTS – DOUBLES:* (with Shriver unless stated) [Sanchez-Vicario] *won* Barcelona (d. Tauziat/Wiesner 6–1 6–3), [Novotna] *won* Filderstadt (d. Shriver/Zvereva 6 2 5 7 6–4), *won* VS Champs (d. G. Fernandez/Novotna 4–6 7–5 6–4); *r/u* VS Chicago (lost G. Fernandez/Novotna 6–2 6–4), *r/u* VS California (lost Fendick/G. Fernandez 6–4 7–5). *CAREER HIGHLIGHTS – SINGLES: Australian Open – won 1981* (d. Tobin, K. Jordan, Goolagong Cawley, Shriver, Evert Lloyd 6–7 6–4 7–5), *won 1983* (d. Durie 4–6 6–3 6–4, Shriver 6–4 6–3, K. Jordan 6–2 7–6), *won 1985* (d. Mandlikova 6–7 6–1 6–4, Evert Lloyd 6–2 4–6 6–2), *r/u 1982* (d. Shriver 6–3 6–4, lost Evert Lloyd 6–3 2–6 6–3), *r/u 1987* (d. Garrison 6–0 6–3, Lindqvist 6–3 6–2, lost Mandlikova 7–5 7–6); *French Open – won 1982* (d. Mandlikova 6–0 6–2, Jaeger 7–6 6–1), *won 1984* (d. Mandlikova 3–6 6–2 6–2, Evert Lloyd 6–3 6–1), *r/u 1975* (lost Evert 2–6 6–2 6–0), *r/u 1985* (lost Evert Lloyd 6–3 6–7 7–5), *r/u 1986* (d. Cecchini, Savchenko, Porwik, Garrone 6–1 6–2, Rinaldi 7–5 6–4, Sukova 4–6 7–6 6–2, lost Evert Lloyd 2–6 6–3 6–3), *r/u 1987* (d. Huber, Hanika, Kohde-Kilsch 6–1 6–2, Evert 6–2 6–2, lost Graf 6–4 4–6 8–6); *Wimbledon – won 1978* (d. Goolagong Cawley 2–6 6–4 6–4, Evert 2–6 6–4 7–5), *won 1979* (d. Austin 7–5 6–1, Evert Lloyd 6–4 6–4), *won 1982* (d. Russell 6–3 6–4, Bunge 6–2 6–2, Evert Lloyd 6–1 3–6 6–2), *won 1983* (d. Vermaak 6–1 6–1, Jaeger 6–0 6–3), *won 1984* (d. Evert Lloyd 7–6 6–2), *won 1985* (d. Garrison 6–4 7–6, Evert Lloyd 4–6 6–3 6–2), *won 1986* (d. Dingwall, Forman, Kinney, Demongeot 6–3 6–3, Bunge 6–1 6–3, Sabatini 6–2 5–7 6–4, Mandlikova 7–6 6–3), *won 1987* (d. G. Fernandez 6–3 6–1, Balestrat, Evert 6–2 5–7 6–4, Graf 7–5 6–3), *won 1990* (d. Amiach, A. Smith, Kschwendt, Wiesner 6–3 6–3, K. Maleeva 6–1 6–1, Sabatini 6–3 6–4, Garrison 6–4 6–1), *r/u 1988* (d. Savchenko 6–4 6–2, Fairbank 4–6 6–4 7–5, Evert 6–1 4–6 7–5, lost Graf 5–7 6–2 6–1), *r/u 1989* (d. Hetherington, Radford 3–6 6–3 6–3, Provis, Mandlikova 6–3 6–2, Magers 6–1 6–2, Lindqvist 7–6 6–2, lost Graf 6–2 6–7 6–1); *US Open – won 1983* (d. Hanika 6–0 6–3, Shriver 6–2 6–1, Evert Lloyd 6–1 6–3), *won 1984* (d. Evert Lloyd 4–6 6–4 6–4), *won 1986* (d. Holikova, Nagelsen, Horvath, Sabatini 6–4 6–2, Shriver 6–2 6–4, Graf 6–1 6–7 7–6, Sukova 6–3 6–2), *won 1987* (d. Lindqvist 6–0 6–4, Sabatini 7–5 6–3, Sukova 6–2 6–2, Graf 7–6 6–1), *r/u 1981* (d. K. Jordan, A. Smith, Evert Lloyd, lost Austin 1–6 7–6 7–6), *r/u 1985* (d. Garrison, Graf, lost Mandlikova 7–6 1–6 7–6), *r/u 1989* (d. Iida, Halard 6–1 6–0, Goles 6–4 6–0, Rajchrtova 6–2 6–0, Manuela Maleeva 6–0 6–0, Garrison 7–6 6–2, lost Graf 3–6 7–5 6–1), *r/u 1991*; *VS Champs – won 1978* (d. Goolagong Cawley 7–6 6–4), *won 1984* (d. Evert Lloyd 6–3 7–5 6–1), *won 1985* (d. Mandlikova, Sukova 6–3 7–5 6–4), *won 1985–86* (d. Mandlikova 6–2 6–0 3–6 6–1), *won 1986* (d. Shriver 6–2 4–6 6–4, Graf 7–6 6–3 6–2), *r/u 1975* (lost Evert Lloyd 6–4 6–2), *r/u 1989* (d. M. J. Fernandez 6–2 6–3, Seles 6–3 5–7 7–5, Sanchez-Vicario 6–2 6–2, lost Graf 6–4 7–5 2–6 6–2), *r/u 1991*; *Avon Champs – won 1979* (d. Austin 6–3 3–6 6–2), *won 1981* (d. Jaeger 6–3 7–6), *r/u 1982* (lost Hanika 1–6 6–3 6–4); *TS Final – won 1982* (d. Evert Lloyd 4–6 6–1 6–2), *r/u 1981* (lost Austin 2–6 6–4 6–2); *Italian Open – r/u 1974* (lost Evert 6–3 6–3), *r/u 1975* (lost Evert 6–1 6–0); *CS Finals – r/u 1978* (lost Evert 6–3 6–3). *CAREER HIGHLIGHTS – DOUBLES:* (with Shriver unless stated) *Australian Open –* [Nagelsen] *won 1980* (d. Kiyomura/Reynolds), *won 1982* (d. Kohde/Pfaff 6–4 6–2), *won 1983* (d. Hobbs/Turnbull 6–4 6–7 6–2), *won 1984* (d. Kohde-Kilsch/Sukova 6–3 6–4), *won 1987* (d. Garrison/McNeil 6–1 6–0), *won 1988* (d. Evert/Turnbull 6–0 7–5), *won 1989* (d. Fendick/Hetherington 3–6 6–3 6–2), [Tomanova] *r/u 1974, r/u 1981* (lost

K. Jordan/A. Smith 6–2 7–5); *French Open* – [Evert] *won 1975* (d. Anthony/Morozova), [A. Smith] *won 1982* (d. Casals/Turnbull 6–3 6–4), *won 1984* (d. Kohde-Kilsch/Mandlikova 5–7 6–3 6–2), *won 1985* (d. Kohde-Kilsch/Sukova 4–6 6–2 6–2), [Temesvari] *won 1986* (d. Graf/Sabatini 6–1 6–2), *won 1987* (d. Graf/Sabatini 6–2 6–1), *won 1988* (d. Kohde-Kilsch/Sukova 6–2 7–5); *Wimbledon* – [Evert] *won 1976* (d. King/Stove 6–1 3–6 7–5), [King] *won 1979* (d. Stove/Turnbull 5–7 6–3 6–2), *won 1981* (d. K. Jordan/A. Smith 6–3 7–6), *won 1982* (d. K. Jordan/A. Smith 6–4 6–1), *won 1983* (d. Casals/Turnbull 6–2 6–2), *won 1984* (d. K. Jordan/A. Smith 6–3 6–4), *won 1986* (d. Mandlikova/Turnbull 6–1 6–3), *r/u 1985* (lost K. Jordan/Smylie 5–7 6–3 6–4); *US Open* – [Stove] *won 1977* (d. Richards/Stuart), [King] *won 1978* (d. Stove/Turnbull 7–6 6–4), [King] *won 1980* (d. Shriver/Stove 7–6 7–5), *won 1983* (d. Reynolds/Fairbank 6–7 6–1 6–3), *won 1984* (d. Turnbull/Hobbs 6–2 6–4), *won 1986* (d. Mandlikova/Turnbull 6–4 3–6 6–3), *won 1987* (d. K. Jordan/Smylie 5–7 6–4 6–2), [Mandlikova] *won 1989* (d. M. J. Fernandez/Shriver 5–7 6–4 6–4), [G. Fernandez] *won 1990* (d. Novotna/Sukova 6–2 6–4), [King] *r/u 1979* (lost Stove/Turnbull), *r/u 1985* (lost Kohde-Kilsch/Sukova 6–7 6–2 6–3); *Italian Open* – [Evert] *won 1975* (d. Barker/Coles), [Tomanova] *r/u 1973* (lost Wade/Morozova 7–5 fs); *CS Finals* – [King] *won 1978* (d. Reid/Turnbull), [King] *won 1979* (d. Casals/Evert Lloyd); *TS Champs* – *won 1981* (d. Casals/Turnbull 6–3 6–4), *won 1982* (d. Reynolds/P. Smith); *VS Champs* – *won 1984* (d. Durie/Kiyomura 6–3 6–1), *won 1985–86* (d. Kohde-Kilsch/Sukova 6–7 6–4 7–6), *won 1986* (d. Kohde-Kilsch/Sukova 7–6 6–3), *won 1987* (d. Kohde-Kilsch/Sukova 6–1 6–1), *won 1988* (d. Savchenko/Zvereva 6–3 6–4), *won 1989* (d. Savchenko/Zvereva 6–3 6–2), *won 1991*; *Avon Champs* – *won 1980* (d. Casals/Turnbull 6–3 fs), [King] *won 1981* (d. Potter/Walsh 6–0 7–6), *won 1982* (d. K. Jordan/A. Smith). *MIXED DOUBLES:* (with J. Sanchez) *US Open* – *won 1987* (d. Nagelsen/Annacone 6–4 6–7 7–6).

TOM NIJSSEN (Netherlands)
Born Maastricht, 1 October 1964; lives Sittard; RH; 5ft 9in; 148lb; final 1991 ATP ranking 241 singles, 25 doubles; 1991 prize money $163,640.
Coached by Ron Timmermans. *1981:* Won Nat 18s *1985:* (225) Won 3 doubles titles. *1986:* (396). *1987:* (103) Won his 1st GP singles match at US Pro, going on to qf. *1988:* (114) Won Bergen Challenger, qf Brussels and took 3 doubles titles with different partners. *1989:* (99) Sf Frankfurt; won French Open mixed doubles with Bollegraf. *1990:* (194) Qf Hong Kong. *1991:* In mixed doubles with Bollegraf won US Open, and in partnership with Temesvari played the longest set (56 games) and longest match in games (77) in history of Wimbledon mixed doubles when losing 6–3 5–7 29–27 to Schapers/Schultz. In men's doubles with Suk reached 5 f, winning Toulouse and Lyon and qualifying for ATP Doubles Champ, although they won no match there. *1991 HIGHLIGHTS – DOUBLES:* (with Suk) *won* Toulouse (d. Bates/Curren 4–6 6–3 7–6), *won* Lyon (d. Devries/MacPherson 7–6 6–3); *r/u* Milan (lost Camporese/Ivanisevic 6–4 7–6), *r/u* Estoril (lost Haarhuis/Koevermans 6–3 6–3), *r/u* Stockholm (lost Fitzgerald/Jarryd 7–5 6–2). *MIXED DOUBLES:* (with Bollegraf) *won US Open* (d. Sanchez-Vicario/E. Sanchez 6–2 7–6). *CAREER HIGHLIGHTS – MIXED DOUBLES:* (with Bollegraf) *US Open – won 1991.*

PIET NORVAL (South Africa)
Born Belville, 7 April 1991; lives Cape Town; RH; 6ft; 165lb; final 1991 ATP ranking 437 singles, 19 (89) doubles; 1991 prize money $116,932.
1987: (356) Nat Jun Champ. *1988:* (194) Nat Jun Champ again. *1989:* (273) Out of action for 7 months with arm and wrist injuries. Won Johannesburg Challenger. *1990:* (427). *1991:* In doubles with Ferreira he won LIPC and reached s/f Wimbledon. *1991 HIGHLIGHTS – DOUBLES:* (with Ferreira) *won* LIPC (d. Flach/Seguso 5–7 7–6 6–2).

KAREL NOVACEK (Czechoslovakia)
Born Prostejov, 30 March 1965; lives Prevov; RH; 6ft 3in; 180lb; final 1991 ATP ranking 8; 1991 prize money $650,350.
Wife Maya (married July 1990). Won Nat 12s, 14s, 18s. *1984:* Joined Olympic team. *1985:* (158) Sf Madrid. *1986:* (33) R/u Vienna and captured his first GP title in Washington. Czech Nat champ. *1987:* (76) Reached qf French Open unseeded (d. Jaite); r/u Palermo. *1988:* (127) Qf Nice, Athens and Bastad. *1989:* (74) After splitting with former coach Petr Hutka, he won his 2nd GP title at Hilversum (d. E. Sanchez). *1990:* (34) Scored some major upsets during the year, beating Krickstein and Muster to win Munich, upsetting Krickstein again to reach last 16 French Open and removing Antonitsch, Becker and Skoff back-to-back to reach f Kitzbuhel, as well as appearing in sf Wellington. *1991:* In his best year to date, he broke into the top 20 in April and top 10 in autumn, taking the last berth at ATP World Champ when Edberg withdrew, although he lost all his rr matches there. Won Auckland,

Hamburg (d. Sampras), Kitzbuhel and Prague, as well as reaching f Estoril and sf Nice, Madrid, Gstaad (d. Stich) and Hilversum. *1991 HIGHLIGHTS – SINGLES: Australian Open* 1r (lost Cash 6–2 6–4 6–1), *French Open* 1r, seed 14 (lost Gustafsson 6–2 3–6 5–1 ret'd), *Wimbledon* last 16, seed 14 (d. Riglewski 7–6 6–3 6–4, J. Sanchez 6–0 6–1 7–6, Frana 6–4 6–4 5–7 6–4, lost Courier [seed 4] 6–3 6–4 6–2), *US Open* 3r, seed 10 (d. Davis 6–3 5–7 6–1 6–3, Marques 6–7 7–0 0–4 0–0 0–0, lost Connors 6–1 6–4 6–3); *won* Auckland (d. Mronz 3–6 7–5 6–3, Connell 6–4 6–4, Jonsson w.o., Vajda 6–4 4–6 6–0, Fleurian 7–6 7–6, *won* Hamburg (d. Steeb 6–4 7–6, Camporese 6–3 6–2, Sampras 6–4 6–2, Koevermans 4–6 6–4 6–2, Stich 6–3 2–6 7–6, Gustafsson 6–3 6–3 5–7 0–6 6–1), *won* Kitzbuhel (d. Braasch 6–2 6–3, Vajda 6–1 7–6, Skoff 7–5 0–6 7–5, Clavet 6–3 6–7 6–2, Gustafsson 7–6 7–6 6–2), *won* Prague (d. Paloheimo 6–4 6–3, Furlan 4–6 6–4 7–6, de la Pena 6–0 6–4, Muster 6–1 2–6 7–5, Gustafsson 7–6 6–2); *r/u* Estoril (d. Camporese 6–1 6–3, Prpic 6–2 7–5, J. Sanchez 7–5 6–3, Vajda 7–5 6–2, lost Bruguera 6–6 6–1); *sf* Nice (d. Fleurian 6–2 6–3, Steeb 3–6 7–5 6–4, Mancini 6–3 7–6, lost Jaite 4–6 6–4 7–6), *sf* Madrid (d. Nargiso 6–3 7–6, Motta 6–3 7–5, Davin 6–3 3–6 6–1, lost Arrese 6–4 6–3), *sf* Gstaad (d. Chesnokov 6–0 6–2, Mezzadri 6–3 6–2, Stich 6–3 6–4, lost E. Sanchez 6–2 6–1), *sf* Hilversum (d. Mancini 5–7 6–3 6–1, Pioline 6–4 6–4, Davin 7–6 2–6 6–2, lost Gustafsson 7–6 6–3). *1991 HIGHLIGHTS – DOUBLES:* [Korda] *won* Berlin (d. Siemerink/Vacek 3–6 7–5 7–5).

JANA NOVOTNA (Czechoslovakia)
Born Brno, 2 October 1968, and lives there; RH; 5ft 8½in; 145lb; final 1991 WTA ranking 7 singles, 1 (2) doubles; 1991 prize money $766,369.
Coached by Mike Estep until after 1990 Wimbledon when Hana Mandlikova took over. **1986:** (182) Won US Open Jun doubles with Zrubakova. **1987:** (49) Reached last 16 Wimbledon and US Open, qf VS Kansas. In doubles formed a formidable partnership with Suire, qualifying for VS Champs and taking a set off Navratilova/Shriver. **1988:** (45) Reached her 1st VS final at Brisbane and upset Sabatini 1r Filderstadt. In doubles won Olympic silver medal with Sukova and took 5 titles with 3 different partners. In mixed doubles with Pugh won Australian and US Open. **1989:** (11) In singles won Adelaide, Eastbourne, Strasbourg, r/u Hamburg and Zurich and reached 4 more sf as well as qf French Open to qualify for VS Champs in both singles (lost Graf 1r) and doubles for 1st time. In doubles won 6 women's titles, including Wimbledon and LIPC with Sukova, plus Australian Open and Wimbledon mixed with Pugh. Won Most Improved Player award. **1990:** (13) She continued her successful doubles partnership with Sukova, with whom she won 8 of her 9 titles across the year. The duo were unbeaten until US Open, but, having won Australian Open, French Open and Wimbledon, failed in their bid for a GS when they lost f US Open to Navratilova/G. Fernandez. They were also disappointed at VS Champs, where they fell 1r to Medvedeva/Meskhi. In singles she upset Sabatini and K. Maleeva *en route* to her 1st GS sf at French Open and followed with qf Wimbledon and US Open. Won VS Albuquerque and extended Navratilova to 3s *en route* to sf Eastbourne, Qualified for VS Champs in both singles and doubles, losing 1r singles to Sabatini. **1991:** Showing the benefits the partnership with her new coach, Mandlikova, she made a tremendous start to the year, upsetting Garrison, Graf and Sanchez-Vicario back-to-back in ss to reach her 1st GS singles f at Australian Open, where she took the 1st set off Seles. Won Sydney and VS Oklahoma; r/u Leipzig; sf Berlin and VS Champs, upsetting Graf on the way; and qf French Open. Was voted WTA Doubles Team of the year with G. Fernandez, with whom she won French Open and was r/u Australian Open, Wimbledon and VS Champs. She completed a full hand of GS doubles f, being r/u US Open with Savchenko, and appeared in 14 f altogether, winning 3 with Fernandez, 3 with Savchenko and 1 with Navratilova. *1991 HIGHLIGHTS – SINGLES: r/u Australian Open,* seed 10 (d. A. Minter 7–6 6–2, Quentrec 6–2 6–2, Stafford 6–7 6–1 8–6, Garrison [seed 7] 7–6 6–4, Graf [seed 1] 5–7 6–4 8–6, Sanchez-Vicario [seed 6] 6–2 6–4, lost Seles 5–7 6–3 6–1), *French Open* qf, seed 6 (d. Farina 7–5 6–2, Hy 6–2 6–1, Brioukhovets 7–6 6–2, Meskhi [seed 14] 6–0 7–6, lost Sabatini 5–7 7–6 6–0), *US Open* last 16, seed 9 (d. Grossman 6–3 4–6 6–1, Louie Harper 6–2 6–3, Monami 6–1 6–2, lost Sabatini [seed 3] 6–4 7–6); *won* Sydney (d. Langrova 1–6 6–4 6–2, Wiesner 3–6 0–1 ret'd, M. J. Fernandez 7–5 6–3, Paulus 7–5 7–6, Sanchez-Vicario 6–4 6–2), *won* VS Oklahoma (d. Cunningham 7–6 6–3, E. Reinach 6–1 6–2, Lindqvist 6–3 6–1, Bonder Kreiss 6–4 6–1, A. Smith 3–6 6–3 6–2); *r/u* Leipzig (d. Ercegovic 6–4 6–4, Huber 3–6 6–3 6–4, Sanchez-Vicario 6–3 6–2, lost Graf 6–3 6–3); *sf* Berlin (d. McQuillan 6–4 6–4, Cecchini 6–3 3–6 6–3, Helgeson 6–1 6–2, lost Graf 6–1 6–0), *sf* VS Champs (d. Maleeva Fragnière 6–0 3–6 6–3, Graf 6–3 3–6 6–1, lost Navratilova 6–1 6–4). *1991 HIGHLIGHTS – DOUBLES:* (with G. Fernandez unless stated) *r/u Australian Open* (lost Fendick/M. J. Fernandez 7–6 6–1), *won French Open* (d. Savchenko/Zvereva 6–4 6–0), *r/u Wimbledon*

(lost Savchenko/Zvereva 6–4 3–6 6–4), [Savchenko] *r/u US Open* (lost Shriver/Zvereva 6–4 4–6 7–6); *won* Brisbane (d. Fendick/Sukova 6–3 6–1), *won* VS Chicago (d. Navratilova/Shriver 6–2 6–4), [Savchenko] *won* Hamburg (d. Sanchez-Vicario/Sukova 7–5 6–1), [Savchenko] *won* VS Washington (d. G. Fernandez/Zvereva 5–7 6–1 7–6), [Navratilova] *won* Filderstadt (d. Shriver/Zvereva 6–2 5–7 6–4), [Savchenko] *won* VS Philadelphia (d. M. J. Fernandez/Sabatini 6–2 6–4); *r/u* Sydney (lost Sanchez-Vicario/Sukova 6–1 6–4), *r/u* LIPC (lost M. J. Fernandez/Garrison 7–5 6–2), *r/u* Eastbourne (lost Savchenko/Zvereva 2–6 6–4 6–4), *r/u* VS Champs (lost Navratilova/Shriver 4–6 7–5 6–4). *CAREER HIGHLIGHTS – SINGLES: Australian Open – r/u 1991; French Open – sf 1990* (d. Demongeot 6–0 6–7 10–8, Schultz, Sviglerova, Sabatini 6–4 7–5, K. Maleeva 4–6 6–2 6–4, lost Graf 6–1 6–2), *qf 1989* (d. Halard, Porwik 6–3 7–5, Simpson 6–1 6–0, Hanika 6–1 6–4, lost Sanchez-Vicario 6–2 6–2), *qf 1991*; *VS Champs – sf 1991*; *Wimbledon – qf 1990* (d. Golarsa 3–6 7–6 6–2, Cunningham, Faull, Fendick 6–2 6–4, lost Graf 7–5 6–2); *US Open – qf 1990* (d. Lapi, Rinaldi, Gildemeister, K. Maleeva 6–4 6–2, lost Graf 6–3 6–1). *CAREER HIGHLIGHTS – DOUBLES:* (with Sukova unless stated) *Australian Open – won 1990* (d. Fendick/M. J. Fernandez 7–6 7–6), [G. Fernandez] *r/u 1991*; *French Open – won 1990* (d. Savchenko/Zvereva 6–4 7–5), [G. Fernandez] *won 1991*; *Wimbledon – won 1989* (d. Savchenko/Zvereva 6–1 6–2), *won 1990* (d. K. Jordan/Smylie 6–3 6–4), [G. Fernandez] *r/u 1991*; *LIPC – won 1989* (d. G. Fernandez/McNeil 7–6 6–4), *won 1990* (d. Nagelsen/R. White 6–4 6–3), [G. Fernandez] *r/u 1991*; *US Open – r/u 1990* (lost G. Fernandez/Navratilova 6–2 6–4), [Savchenko] *r/u 1991*; *VS Champs –* [G. Fernandez] *r/u 1991*; *Olympics – silver medal 1988* (lost Shriver/Garrison 4–6 6–2 10–8). *MIXED DOUBLES:* (with Pugh) *Australian Open – won 1988* (d. Navratilova/Gullikson 5–7 6–2 6–4), *won 1989* (d. Stewart/Garrison 6–3 6–4); *Wimbledon – won 1989* (d. Kratzmann/Byrne 6–4 5–7 6–4); *US Open – won 1988* (d. Smylie/P. McEnroe 7–5 6–3).

KATJA OELJEKLAUS (Germany)
Born Munster, 10 February 1971; lives Ladbergen; RH; 5ft 7in; 134lb; final 1991 WTA ranking 100; 1991 prize money $19,417.
Coached by Ute Strakersahn. *1989:* (447). *1990:* (199) Won Lisbon on the Portuguese satellite circuit. *1991:* Upset Medvedeva on her way to qf St Petersburg.

JAIME ONCINS (Brazil)
Born Sao Paulo, 16 June 1970, and lives there; RH; 6ft 4in; 165lb; final 1991 ATP ranking 64; 1991 prize money $179,024.
Coached by Paulo Cleto. *1988:* (314). *1989:* (263) Won Lins Challenger. *1990:* (113) Making his mark again on the Challenger circuit, he reached f in 4 tourns, winning Campos and Sao Paulo. *1991:* Won Sao Paulo Challenger again and at end Oct. he reached his 1st tour f at Buzios, following the next week with his 2nd at Sao Paulo to add to his qf showings at Bologna and Geneva. He had overtaken Mattar as No. 1 in his country by end of year. In doubles he reached 4 f with 3 different partners. *1991 HIGHLIGHTS – SINGLES: Australian Open* 3r (d. Arbanas 6–3 6–3 7–5, Marques 6–3 6–0 6–2, lost Courier [seed 16] 6–3 6–1 6–1), *French Open* 2r (d. J. Sanchez 5–7 6–4 6–4 6–3, lost Masur 6–1 7–6 7–5), *Wimbledon* 1r (lost J. McEnroe [seed 16] 6–1 6–2 6–4), *US Open* 1r (lost Washington 6–2 6–2 6–1); *won* Sao Paulo Challenger (d. Roese 6–4 6–4); *r/u* Buzios (d. Fleurian 7–6 6–3, Delaitre 7–6 6–4, Zoecke 6–4 6–2, Roig 6–4 6–4, lost Arrese 1–6 6–4 6–0), *r/u* Sao Paulo (d. Filippini 7–5 6–2, Carbonell 6–7 6–2 6–1, Marcelino 6–3 7–6, Clavet 6–4 6–3, lost Miniussi 2–6 6–3 6–4). *1991 HIGHLIGHTS – DOUBLES:* (with Mattar unless stated) [Gomez] *won* Sao Paulo (d. Lozano/Motta 7–5 6–4); [Letts] *r/u* Wellington (lost Mattar/Pereira 4–6 7–6 6–2), *r/u* Madrid (lost Luza/Mattar 6–0 7–5), *r/u* Bologna (lost Jensen/Warder 6–4 7–6).

LEANDER PAES (India)
Born Calcutta, 16 June 1973; lives there and Tampa, Fla.; RH; 5ft 9in; 150lb; final 1991 WTA ranking 275; 1991 prize money $13,924.
Coached by David O'Meara. *1990:* Won Wimbledon Jun over Ondruska. *1991:* Won US Open Jun over Alami. Joined India's D Cup Squad.

VELI PALOHEIMO (Finland)
Born Tampere, 13 December 1967, and lives there; RH; 6ft; 168lb; final 1991 ATP ranking 97; 1991 prize money $112,705.
Coached by Jari Hedman. Has won 4 Nat singles titles. *1986:* (418) Joined Finnish D Cup squad. *1987:* (515). *1988:* (117) Won Helsinki Challenger. *1989:* (109) Sf Adelaide and won 2 Challenger titles. *1990:* (69) Sf Basel, qf Memphis and Bastad. Upset Steeb 1r *en route* to last 16 Australian Open, unseeded, becoming the first Finn to appear at that stage of any GS tourn. *1991:* Reached sf Manchester and qf Barcelona. *1991 HIGHLIGHTS –*

SINGLES: French Open 2r (d. Tarango 6–2 6–2 6–1, lost Ondruska 3–6 6–1 6–1 2–6 6–0), *Wimbledon* 1r (lost Connors 6–2 6–0 7–5), *US Open* 1r (lost Witsken 6–3 5–7 6–4 6–1); *sf* Manchester (d. Siemerink 7–6 6–2, Bloom 6–7 6–4 7–5, Mansdorf 3–6 6–3 6–4, lost Sampras 6–4 7–5).

DAVID PATE (USA)
Born Los Angeles, 16 April 1962; lives Las Vegas; RH; 6ft; 170lb; final 1991 ATP ranking 158 singles, 3 (6) doubles; 1991 prize money $330,191.
Coached, as a young man, by Pancho Gonzales. Wife Debra, sons Dakota (born 1989) and Cotton (born March 1991). *1981:* (662) A two-time All-American at Texas Christian University, he won NCAA doubles title with Richter. *1982:* (203). *1983:* (130). *1984:* (31) Won first GP event – Japan Open in Tokyo. *1985:* (26) R/u La Quinta to Stefanki and sf Newport and Wembley where he d. Edberg and Nystrom. *1986:* (30) Sf Atlanta and Scottsdale and 7 qfs. *1987:* (18) Had his biggest wins of the year at Tokyo, where he beat Lendl on his way to f, and at LA where he beat Edberg *en route* to his first title since Tokyo 1984. *1988:* (47) Upset Connors *en route* to sf Orlando; qf Memphis and Tokyo. *1989:* (157) Reached 4 doubles f, winning 2. *1990:* (94) Sf Orlando and Lyon in singles. In doubles reached 7 f, winning 5 titles with S. Davis, with whom he qualified for IBM/ATP World Doubles Final. *1991:* In partnership with S. Davis won a 1st GS title at Australian Open and r/u US Open, winning 3 other titles and qualifying for ATP Doubles Champ. In singles upset Gomez *en route* to qf San Francisco and reached the same stage at Orlando. *1991 HIGHLIGHTS – SINGLES: Australian Open* 1r (lost Koevermans 6–4 6–2 3–6 2–6 6–0), *French Open* 1r (lost Hlasek 6–4 6–1 7–5), *Wimbledon* 2r (d. Ferreira 4–6 6–7 6–4 6–2 6–3, lost Edberg 6–2 6–2 6–3), *US Open* 1r (lost Pescosolido 7–6 6–7 6–2 6–3). *1991 HIGHLIGHTS – DOUBLES:* (with S. Davis unless stated) *won Australian Open* (d. P. McEnroe/Wheaton 6–7 7–6 6–3 7–5), *r/u US Open* (lost Fitzgerald/Jarryd 6–3 3–6 6–3 6–3); *won* Sydney NSW (d. Cahill/Kratzmann 3–6 6–3 6–2), *won* Chicago (d. Connell/Michibata 6–4 5–7 7–6), *won* Washington (d. Flach/Seguso 6–4 6–2); [Reneberg] *r/u* Tampa (lost Flach/Seguso 6–7 6–4 6–1), *r/u* Tokyo/Seiko (lost Grabb/Reneberg 7–5 2–6 7–6). *CAREER HIGHLIGHTS – DOUBLES:* (with S. Davis) *Australian Open – won 1991*; *US Open – r/u 1991.*

BARBARA PAULUS (Austria)
Born Vienna, 1 September 1970; lives Hinterbruehl; RH; 5ft 9½in; 134lb; final 1991 WTA ranking 25; 1991 prize money $73,540.
Coached by Peter Eipeldauer. *1982:* Won Nat 12s 2nd time. *1985:* Won Nat 18s. *1986:* (187) Won Nat Indoor and Outdoor; qf Bregenz and played Fed Cup. *1987:* (96). Qf Guaruja. *1988:* (25) Won her 1st primary circuit title at Geneva over McNeil, r/u Sofia and upset Kohde-Kilsch 1r Filderstadt. *1989:* (24) R/u Arcachon, sf Geneva (d. Evert) and surprised Novotna *en route* to last 16 US Open. *1990:* (15) Won Geneva; r/u Sydney, Palermo and Filderstadt (d. Garrison and Sabatini); sf San Diego and Leipzig and reached last 16 Australian Open. *1991:* Reached sf Sydney (d. Maleeva Fragnière), Leipzig (d. K. Maleeva) and Brighton, where she was forced to def. ill. *1991 HIGHLIGHTS – SINGLES: Australian Open* 2r, seed 12 (d. Thoren 6–3 6–3, lost McQuillan 6–4 6–7 6–4), *US Open* 2r (d. Hack 6–7 6–4 6–4, lost Sabatini [seed 3] 6–3 4–6 5–1 ret'd); *sf* Sydney (d. Whitlinger 7–5 2–6 6–0, Godridge 6–1 6–1, Maleeva Fragnière 7–6 6–4, lost Novotna 7–5 7–6), *sf* Leipzig (d. Rajchrtova 6–1 6–7 6–2, Zrubakova 7–6 6–1, K. Maleeva 7–6 0–6 7–6, lost Graf 6–1 6–1), *sf* Brighton (d. Jagerman 7–5 6–2, Javer 2–6 6–2 6–2, lost Tauziat def.)

MERCEDES PAZ (Argentina)
Born Tucuman, 27 June 1966, and lives there; RH; 5ft 10in; 164lb; final 1991 WTA ranking 69 singles, 15 (14) doubles; 1991 prize money $149,359.
Coached by Jorge Todero. *1984:* Won Rolex Jun Port Washington and US Open Jun doubles and Orange Bowl 18 doubles with Sabatini. *1985:* (115) Won Sao Paulo and was ranked 2 in Argentina. *1986:* (59) Last 16 French Open, r/u Singapore, sf USCC. *1987:* (91) Qf Belgian Open. *1988:* (43) Won Guaruja at end of year, r/u Puerto Rico and reached 5 other qf. *1989:* (87) R/u Brussels and sf Arcachon in singles; won 4 doubles titles with different partners. Won WTA Player Service award. *1990:* (37) Following a new fitness regime from early in year, she won Strasbourg and then upset Sanchez-Vicario *en route* to last 16 French Open, unseeded. In doubles won 5 titles with 3 different partners and was r/u VS Champs with Sanchez-Vicario. Won Karen Krantzcke Sportsmanship award. *1991:* In singles reached sf Auckland, Clarins and Indianapolis. In doubles appeared in 5 f with 4 different partners, but won no title. *1991 HIGHLIGHTS – SINGLES: Australian Open* 1r (lost Appelmans [seed 16] 6–0 6–1), *French Open* 1r (lost Zardo 6–3 6–2), *Wimbledon* 1r (lost Kijimuta 6–1 6–3), *US Open* 1r (lost Rinaldi 6–7 6–4 6–1); *sf* Auckland (d. Godridge

7–6 5–7 6–4, Quentrec 6–3 6–2, Kamstra 4–3 ret'd, lost Sviglerova 6–2 6–3), *sf* Clarins (d. Langrova 6–2 6–4, Zrubakova 7–6 6–2, Jagerman 1–6 7–5 6–3, Lost Gorrochategui 6–2 6–3), *sf* Indianapolis (d. Toleafoa 6–2 6–2, Henricksson 7–5 6–2, Daniels 6–4 6–3, lost K. Maleeva 6–2 6–1). *1991 HIGHLIGHTS – DOUBLES:* (with Garrone unless stated) [Zvereva] *r/u* Amelia Island (lost Sanchez-Vicario/Sukova 4–6 6–2 6–2), [Bollegraf] *r/u* Strasbourg (lost McNeil/Rehe 6–7 6–4 6–4), *r/u* Palermo (lost Langrova/Pierce 6–3 6–7 6–3), *r/u* San Marino (lost Guse/Nishiya 6–0 6–3), [Adams] *r/u* Indianapolis (lost Fendick/G. Fernandez 6–4 6–2). *CAREER HIGHLIGHTS – DOUBLES:* (with Sanchez-Vicario) *VS Champs – r/u 1990* (lost K. Jordan/Smylie 7–6 6–4).

GUILLERMO PEREZ-ROLDAN (Argentina)
Born Tandil, Buenos Aires, 20 October 1969, and lives there; RH; 5ft 10in; 173lb; final 1991 ATP ranking 42; 1991 prize money $180,995.
Coached by his father, Raul. Won Nat. and S American 14s, 16s, 18s. Brother of Mariana. *1985:* (485). *1986:* (109) Sf St Vincent and Buenos Aires and won French Open Jun singles and doubles. *1987:* (19) When he won Munich aged 17 years, 6 months, 10 days he became the second-youngest at the time (after Krickstein) to win a GP title, following with Athens 7 weeks later and Buenos Aires in Nov. to take him into top 20. Won French Open Jun singles again over Stoltenberg. *1988:* (18) Confirmed his CC ability by winning Munich again, taking Lendl to 5s f Italian Open, upsetting Edberg *en route* to qf French Open and also reaching f Hilversum, Prague and Buenos Aires. *1989:* (32) Won Palermo in autumn, r/u Geneva and sf Bologna. *1990:* (14) Won San Marino; r/u Casablanca, Barcelona and Stuttgart; sf Bordeaux and Palermo and reached last 16 French Open. *1991:* Following a slow start to the year with knee and ankle injuries, he won San Marino; upset Ivanisevic *en route* to f Munich, where he was forced to retire in f v Gustafsson; and appeared in sf Barcelona (d. Agassi) and Prague. *1991 HIGHLIGHTS – SINGLES: French Open* 1r (lost Delaitre 6–2 6–1 6–1); *won* San Marino (d. Perez 6–0 6–1, Oosting 2–6 6–0 7–6, Costa 5–7 6–2 6–1, Furlan 6–2 6–2, Fontang 6–3 6–1), *won* Salerno Challenger (d. Pistolesi 4–6 6–1 6–3); *r/u* Munich (d. Aguilera 6–3 6–0, Engel 7–5 6–2, Ivanisevic 7–6 6–1, Bergstrom 6–0 6–0, lost Gustafsson 3–6 6–3 4–3 ret'd); *sf* Barcelona (d. Jonsson 6–3 6–4, Lopez 7–5 1–6 6–4, Filippini 6–1 6–0, Agassi 6–0 6–7 7–6, lost Bruguera 6–4 6–4), *sf* Prague (d. Altur 6–4 6–4, Steeb 6–4 6–0, Skoff 3–6 6–4 7–6, lost Gustafsson 7–5 6–7 6–2).

STEFANO PESCOSOLIDO (Italy)
Born Sora, 13 June 1971; lives Rome; RH; 6ft 1in; 180lb; final 1991 ATP ranking 69; 1991 prize money $149,106.
Coached by Tonino Zugarelli. *1987:* Won Nat 16s. *1988:* R/u Orange Bowl and won Nat 18s. *1989:* (225) Won Parioli Challenger. *1990:* (141) Upset Gunnarsson 1r Australian Open. *1991:* Upset Chang at Montreal and again the following week at Los Angeles, where he reached his 1st GP sf. Enjoyed success on the Challenger circuits at the beginning of the year, winning Parioli and Oporto and being r/u at Guadeloupe. At Wimbledon he extended Krickstein to 7–5 5s 1r. *1991 HIGHLIGHTS – SINGLES: Wimbledon* 1r (lost Krickstein 6–1 6–3 6–7 6–7 7–5), *US Open* 2r (d. Pate 7–6 6–7 3–6 6–2 6–3, lost Markus 6–2 1–6 4–6 7–6 6–2); *won* Parioli Challenger (d. Wuyts 6–3 6–4), *won* Oporto Challenger (d. Azar 6–1 6–1); *sf* Los Angeles (d. Woodforde 6–4 6–4, Chang 4–6 6–2 6–4, Davis 7–6 6–3, lost Sampras 6–3 6–1).

KATIA PICCOLINI (Italy)
Born L'Aquile, 15 January 1973, and lives there; RH; 5ft 11in; 107lb; final 1991 WTA ranking 62; 1991 prize money $52,834.
1988: (300) On Italian satellite circuit reached 3 consec. f, winning Subiaco. *1989:* (171) Sf Estoril. *1990:* (47) Qf Taranto, Palermo and Estoril (upset Cecchini), then in Sept. reached her first tour f at Athens. Broke into top 100 in June and top 50 in Sept. *1991:* Won her 1st title on the main tour at San Marino and reached qf Barcelona. *1991 HIGHLIGHTS – SINGLES: French Open* 1r (lost Capriati [seed 10] 6–2 7–5), *US Open* 1r (lost Sanchez-Vicario [seed 4] 6–0 6–1); *won* San Marino (d. Perez-Roldan 6–4 6–1, Golarsa 6–2 6–1, Maniokova 3–6 7–6 6–4, Szabova 6–2 6–1, Farina 6–2 6–3).

MARY PIERCE (France)
Born Montrêal, Canada, 15 January 1975; lives Villeneuve Loubet; RH; 2HB; 5ft 9in; 137lb; final 1991 WTA ranking 26; 1991 prize money $94,582.
Coached by her father, Jim. *1989:* (236) At 14 years 2 months at Hilton Head she was the youngest to make her pro début – a record broken the following year by Capriati. *1990:* (106) Sf Athens. Moved to France and represented that country in Fed Cup. *1991:* At

Palermo she won both singles and doubles for her 1st career title, which took her into the top 50. Upset Fairbank-Nideffer *en route* to last 16 LIPC and appeared in sf Puerto Rico. *1991 HIGHLIGHTS – SINGLES: French Open* 3r (d. Dahlman 7–6 6–0, Martinek 6–3 6–0, lost Sabatini 6–2 6–1), *US Open* 3r (d. Garrone 4–6 6–0 7–6, McNeil 6–3 3–6 7–6, lost Maleeva Fragnière [seed 10] 4–6 5–1 ret'd); *won* Palermo (d. Bonsignori 6–4 7–5, Langrova 6–1 6–0, Mothes 6 1 6 0, Wasserman 6–1 6–1, Cecchini 6–0 6–3); *sf* Puerto Rico (d. Grossman 6–3 6–1, Rehe 6–3 0–6 6–2, lost Halard 7–5 6–1). *1991 HIGHLIGHTS – DOUBLES:* [Langrova] *won* Palermo (d. Garrone/Paz 6–3 6–7 6–3); [Spadea] *r/u* Sao Paulo (lost Fulco/Sviglerova 7–5 6–4).

CEDRIC PIOLINE (France)
Born Neuilly sur Seine, 15 June 1969; lives Paris; RH; 6ft 2in; 175lb; final 1991 ATP ranking 51; 1991 prize money $185,850.
Coached by Henri Dumont. *1987:* R/u Nat Jun Champ. *1988:* (461). *1989:* (202). *1990:* (118) Sf Genova and won Brest Challenger. *1991:* Broke into top 100 after reaching sf Nice (d. Volkov and Leconte back-to-back), following with same stage Bordeaux; qf Genova, Stuttgart Mercedes and Toulouse. *1991 HIGHLIGHTS – SINGLES: Australian Open* 1r (lost Bergstrom 6–4 6–2 1–6 7–6), *French Open* 2r (d. B. Gilbert 6–4 2–6 6–1 6–4, lost Clavet 6–2 6–3 7–6), *Wimbledon* 2r (d. Layendecker 4–6 6–3 6–4 7–6, lost Wheaton 6–4 6–7 6–3 6–3), *US Open* 1r (lost Ferreira 7–6 4 6 6–2 2–6 6–3); *sf* Nice (d. Santoro 3–6 6–1 6–4, Volkov 6–4 6–3, Leconte 6–2 6–4, lost Pripic 6–1 6–3), *sf* Bordeaux (d. Dosedel 6–3 1–6 6–3, Bouteyre 6–3 6–4, Santoro 6–3 3–6 6–4, lost Forget 6–3 6–1).

CLAUDIA PORWIK (Germany)
Born Coburg, 14 November 1968; lives Furth; RH; 5ft 10in; 138lb; final 1991 WTA ranking 78; 1991 prize money $75,510.
Works with Nic Marschand. *1985:* (244) Won Mexico. *1986:* (95) Won 20 of 28 matches. Underwent operation to remove cysts from right wrist end of year. *1987:* (103) Reached first f at Taipei. *1988:* (68) Beat Potter to make an unscheduled appearance in qf Australian Open. *1989:* (74) Qf Oklahoma and Bayonne. *1990:* (29) Taking advantage of an injury to Sabatini, who had to retire when a set up in their 3r match, she reached her 1st GS sf at Australian Open, unseeded, Qf LIPC and Sydney. *1991:* Appeared in qf VS Florida and Bayonne and won Schenectady doubles with McQuillan. *1991 HIGHLIGHTS – SINGLES: Australian Open* 2r (d. Kochta 7–6 6–3, lost Zvereva [seed 11] 7–6 6–4), *French Open* 1r (lost Martinek 6–1 6–0), *Wimbledon* 1r (lost Louie Harper 6–4 6–1), *US Open* 1r (lost Strnadova 6–3 6–2). *1991 HIGHLIGHTS – DOUBLES:* (with McQuillan) *won* Schenectady (d. Arendt/McCarthy 6–1 6–7 7–5). *CAREER HIGHLIGHTS – SINGLES: Australian Open – sf 1990* (d. Celine Cohen, Wiesner, Sabatini 2–6 0–1 ret'd, Van Rensburg 7–6 3–6 6–4, Gavaldon 6–4 6–3, lost M. J. Fernandez 6–2 6–1), *qf 1988* (d. Potter 7–6 7–5, lost Evert 6–3 6–1).

GIANLUCA POZZI (Italy)
Born Bari, 17 June 1965, and lives there; LH; 5ft 11in; 165lb; final 1991 ATP ranking 72; 1991 prize money $147,175.
1987: (153) Won Dublin Challenger. *1988:* (165). *1989:* (179) Again made his mark on the Challenger circuit, but won no title. *1990:* (185). *1991:* Emerging from the satellite circuits, he won his 1st GP singles title at Brisbane in Sept. and in doubles with Steven took Newport. *1991 HIGHLIGHTS – SINGLES: Wimbledon* 2r (d. Pearce 4–6 6–3 6–2 6–2, lost Boetsch 4–6 7–6 7–6 6–4); *won* Brisbane (d. Stolle 7–6 4–6 6–4, Woodbridge 6–4 0–6 6–1, Grabb 6–3 1–6 6–3, Stoltenberg 6–3 6–1, Krickstein 6–3 7–6). *1991 HIGHLIGHTS – DOUBLES:* (with Steven) *won* Newport (d. Frana/Steel 6–4 6–4).

NICOLE PRATT (Australia)
Born Mackay, 5 March 1973; RH; 2HB; 5ft 4in; 123lb; final 1991 WTA ranking 241; 1991 prize money $22,184.
1990: R/u Futures Adelaide and Melbourne. *1991:* Won Australian Open Jun over Godridge, with whom she took US Open Jun doubles. *1991 HIGHLIGHTS – SINGLES: Australian Open* 1r (lost Cunningham 6–1 6–1), *Wimbledon* 1r (lost Novotna [seed 7] 6–3 6–0).

NICOLE PROVIS (Australia)
Born Melbourne, 22 September 1969; lives Sandringham, Vic.; RH; 5ft 9in; 141lb; final 1991 WTA ranking 45 singles, 18 (26) doubles; 1991 prize money $132,000.
Coached by Ken Richardson. *1986:* (105) R/u French Open Jun. *1987:* (77) R/u Australian Open Jun to Jaggard; won doubles with Devries. On senior tour qf Auckland and r/u Wimbledon mixed doubles with Cahill. *1988:* (33) Reached sf Strasbourg and qf North California and Berlin, but the high spot of her year came at the French Open, where

unseeded, she upset Kohde-Kilsch, Hanika and Sanchez, before taking Zvereva to 7–5 3s in sf. *1989:* (61) Reached last 16 Australian Open and sf VS Arizona. *1990:* (49) Reached last 16 French Open, unseeded, and qf VS Washington and Indianapolis. In doubles won Berlin and Strasbourg with Reinach, with whom she qualified for VS Champs, and was r/u French Open mixed with Visser. *1991:* In singles reached sf Schenectady, qf Sydney and upset Gildemeister at Berlin and Martinez at VS Nashville. Reached 4 doubles f, winning Geneva and Birmingham with Smylie, with whom she qualified for VS Champs. *1991 HIGHLIGHTS – SINGLES: Australian Open* 3r (d. E. Reinach 6–2 6–0, Date 4–6 6–0 6–4, lost Graf [seed 1] 6–4 6–2), *French Open* 2r (d. Hiraki 4–6 7–6 6–2, lost Jagerman 6–4 5–7 6–3), *Wimbledon* 2r (d. S. Smith 3–6 6–4 6–2, lost Brioukhovets 7–6 6–3), *US Open* 1r (lost Sabatini [seed 3] 7–6 6–3); *sf* Schenectady (d. Cioffi 4–6 6–1 6–3, Halard 5–7 6–2 6–2, Labat 7–5 6–3, lost Schultz 5–7 7–5 6–3). *1991 HIGHLIGHTS – DOUBLES:* (with Smylie unless stated) *won* Geneva (d. Caverzasio/Maleeva Fragnière 6–1 6–2), *won* Birmingham (d. Collins/E. Reinach 6–3 6–4); [E. Reinach] *r/u* Italian Open (lost Capriati/Seles 7–5 6–2), [E. Reinach] *r/u* Berlin (lost Savchenko/Zvereva 6–3 6–3). *CAREER HIGHLIGHTS – SINGLES: French Open – sf 1988* (d. Kohde-Kilsch 1–6 6–4 7–5, Hanika 7–6 7–6, Sanchez 7–5 3–6 6–4, lost Zvereva 6–3 6–7 7–5).

GORAN PRPIC (Croatia)
Born Zagreb, 4 May 1964, and lives there; RH; 5ft 11in; 165lb; final 1991 ATP ranking 18; 1991 prize money $511,068.
Wife Andrea, son Tin (born 1988). *1980:* Nat Jun champ. *1982:* Won Rolex Jun. *1985:* (139) Qf Bologna (d. Vilas), Bastad (d. Svensson) and Palermo. Upset Noah and Leconte in D Cup. *1986:* (870) Severe knee injury suffered at LIPC sidelined him for nearly 2 years. *1988:* (226) Returned to play D Cup. *1989:* (28) Broke into top 100 in April after success on the Challenger circuit, upset Mecir *en route* to 1st GP f at Stuttgart and reached sf Kitzbuhel. Voted ATP Comeback Player of the Year. *1990:* (55) Played a major part in Yugoslavia winning first World Team Cup with a 4–0 singles record. Won 1st tour title at Umag (d. Ivanisevic) and reached sf Casablanca and Prague. *1991:* Scored some big upsets during the year in reaching qf Australian Open, unseeded (d. Ivanisevic, whom he also beat 1r Milan), f Nice, sf Monte Carlo (d. Forget), Hamburg (d. Chesnokov) and Italian Open (d. Hlasek, Muster and Cherkasov). Did not play for Yugoslavia in D Cup and, with Ivanisevic, announced in Tokyo in October that henceforth he wanted to be known as a Croatian. *1991 HIGHLIGHTS – SINGLES: Australian Open* qf, unseeded (d. Pugh 6–3 6–2 3–6 6–2, Mattar 6–3 6–1 6–1, Ivanisevic [seed 5] 6–3 6–4 6–3, Siemerink 7–6 6–7 6–0 7–6, lost Lendl [seed 3] 6–0 7–6 7–6), *French Open* 2r (d. Robertson 7–6 6–3 6–3, lost Mancini 1–6 7–5 6–4 1–6 6–2), *Wimbledon* 2r (d. Siemerink 6–4 3–6 6–3 3–6 10–8), lost Agassi [seed 5] 7–6 3–6 6–4 6–2), *US Open* 2r (d. B. Gilbert 2–6 6–4 6–2 1–6 6–4, lost Ivanisevic [seed 12] 6–1 6–3 6–4); *r/u* Nice (d. Wilander 6–3 6–1, Perez-Roldan 6–1 4–6 6–1, de la Pena 7–5 6–2, Pioline 6–1 6–3, lost Jaite 3–6 7–6 6–3); *sf* Monte Carlo (d. Novacek 6–2 6–4, Fromberg 6–1 6–4, Forget 6–2 6–0, Steeb 6–4 6–2, lost Becker 6–3 6–3), *sf* Hamburg (d. Chesnokov 6–4 6–3, Arrese 6–3 6–3, de la Pena 6–3 6–2, Ivanisevic 7–5 3–0 ret'd, lost Gustafsson 6–2 1–6 7–6), *sf* Italian Open (d. Filippini 6–0 2–6 6–1, Hlasek 6–1 7–5, Muster 3–6 6–3 6–2, Cherkasov 7–6 7–5, lost E. Sanchez 6–4 6–2.

JIM PUGH (USA)
Born Burbank, Cal., 5 February 1964; lives Rancho Palos Verdes, Cal.; RH; 2HF and 2HB; 6ft 4in; 180lb; final 1991 ATP ranking 399 singles, 30 doubles; 1991 prize money $165,219.
1982: Suffered severe shoulder injury, amazingly cured by taking thyroid tablets. *1983:* All-American at UCLA. *1985:* (344). *1986:* (99) Won Istanbul Challenger. *1987:* (45) Stunned Cash 1r French Open and reached first GP f at Schenectady, following with San Francisco (d. Mayotte). *1988:* (63) Sf Auckland, Scottsdale and Frankfurt in singles. Was a major force in doubles with R. Leach, winning Australian Open and Masters, and being forced to default US Open f to Casal/E. Sanchez because of Leach's illness. Took 5 other titles, and in mixed doubles with Novotna won Australian and US Opens. *1989:* (60) Won his 1st GP singles title at Newport and reached f Stratton Mountain. He continued his success in doubles with R. Leach, winning Australian Open, r/u Wimbledon and taking 4 other titles to qualify for Masters, where they surprisingly took only 6th place. In mixed doubles with Novotna won Australian Open and Wimbledon. *1990:* (121) In singles reached qf Newport and upset Mayotte at LIPC. In doubles with R. Leach won 1st Wimbledon title, plus LIPC and Philadelphia to qualify for IBM/ATP World Doubles Final. In mixed doubles with Zvereva won Australian Open and r/u US Open. Was a member of the victorious US D Cup team winning doubles with Leach. *1991:* In doubles with Leach r/u French Open and won 2

titles, taking a 3rd with Frana. *1991 HIGHLIGHTS – SINGLES: Australian Open* 1r (lost Prpic 6–3 6–2 3–6 6–2), *Wimbledon* 1r (lost Petchey 4–6 4–6 6–3 6–3 8–6), *US Open* 1r (lost Stafford 6–3 6–7 7–6 3–6 6–3). *1991 HIGHLIGHTS – DOUBLES:* (with R. Leach unless stated) *r/u French Open* (lost Fitzgerald/Jarryd 6–0 7–6); *won* US Pro Indoor (d Riglewski/Stich 6–4 6–4), *won* US CC (d. Garnett/Van Emburgh 6–2 3–6 6–3), [Frana] *won* Los Angeles (d. Michibata/Pearce 7–5 2–0 0–4). *CAREER HIGHLIGHTS DOUBLES:* (with R. Leach) *Australian Open – won 1988* (d. Bates/Lundgren 6–3 6–2 6–3), *won 1989* (d. Cahill/Kratzmann 6–4 6–4 6–4); *Wimbledon – won 1990* (d. Aldrich/Visser 7–6 7–6 7–6), *r/u 1989* (lost Fitzgerald/Jarryd 3–6 7–6 6–4 7–6); *Masters – won 1988* (d. Casal E. Sanchez 6–4 6–3 2–6 6–0); *LIPC – won 1990* (d. Becker/Motta 6–4 3–6 6–3); *French Open – r/u 1991; US Open – r/u 1988* (lost Casal/Sanchez def.). *MIXED DOUBLES:* (with Novotna unless stated) *Australian Open – won 1988* (d. Navratilova/Gullikson 5–7 6–2 6–4), *won 1989* (d. Stewart/Garrison 6–3 6–4), [Zvereva] *won 1990* (d. R. Leach/Garrison 4–6 6–2 6–3); *Wimbledon – won 1989* (d. Kratzmann/Byrne 6–4 5–7 6–4); *US Open – won 1988* (d. Smylie/P. McEnroe 7–5 6–3).

KARINE QUENTREC (France)
Born Marseilles, 21 October 1969, and lives there; RH; 5ft 4½in; 132lb; final 1991 WTA ranking 47; 1991 prize money $49,289.
1988: (145) Won Moulins back-to-back on the French satellite circuit and played Fed Cup. *1989:* (64) Won her 1st tour title at Taranto and upset Kohde-Kilsch 1r French Open *1990:* (104) Reached sf Strasbourg and qf VS Albuquerque. *1991:* Appeared in sf Wellington *1991 HIGHLIGHTS – SINGLES: Australian Open* 2r (d. Grossman 7–6 2–6 7–5, lost Novotna [seed 10] 6–2 6–2), *French Open* 3r (d. Helgeson 7–6 7–6, Fendick 6–1 4–6 6–3, lost Seles 6–1 6–2), *Wimbledon* 2r (d. Stubbs 6–2 6–2, lost Sabatini [seed 2] 6–4 6–2); *sf* Wellington (d. Zardo 6–3 6–2, Oremans 6–4 1–6 7–5, Hack 0–6 6–2 6–3, lost Meskhi 6–2 6–3)

REGINA RAJCHRTOVA (Czechoslovakia)
Born Havlickuv Brod, 5 February 1968; lives Prague; RH; 6ft; 148lb; final 1991 WTA ranking 39; 1991 prize money $120,665.
Coached by Zdenek Zofka and Jan Soukup. *1985:* (282). *1986:* (226). *1987:* (89) Reached 4 on satellite circuits, winning Mald. *1988:* (217). *1989:* (40) Reached her 1st tour f at Paris Open and made an unexpected appearance in last 16 US Open. *1990:* (54) Upset Gildemeister and Garrison to reach sf FC Cup. *1991:* Sf Linz; upset Maleeva Fragnière 2r French Open and K Maleeva *en route* to last 16 US Open, unseeded. *1991 HIGHLIGHTS – SINGLES: Australian Open* 2r (d. Stacey 4–6 7–5 8–6, lost Kschwendt 6–1 6–1), *French Open* 3r (d. Probst 6–4 6–3, Maleeva Fragnière [seed 9] 6–4 6–0, lost Appelmans 6–2 6–0), *Wimbledon* 1r (lost Tauziat [seed 12] 6–4 7–5), *US Open* last 16, unseeded (d. Bartos 6–1 6–3, Sawamatsu 6–2 6–4, K. Maleeva [seed 11] 2–6 6–3 6–3, lost Seles [seed 2] 6–1 6–1); *sf* Linz (d. Corsato 6–2 6–0, Celine Cohen 6–1 6–0, Paradis 6–4 6–4, lost Maleeva Fragnière 2–6 6–3 6–4).

ELNA REINACH (South Africa)
Born Pretoria, 2 December 1968, and lives there; RH; 5ft 11½in; 145lb; final 1991 WTA ranking 80 singles, 17 (19) doubles; 1991 prize money $149,469.
Coached by her mother, Elna. Sister of Monica. *1984:* R/u Wimbledon Jun, won South African Int Jun event and South African satellite circuit Masters. *1985:* Won Wimbledon Plate and 2 tourns on satellite circuits. *1986:* (55) Upset Rinaldi at Mahwah. *1987* (93). *1988:* (28) Qf Birmingham, Oklahoma, Filderstadt and LIPC, where she upset Garrison, and reached last 16 US Open with upset of M. J. Fernandez. *1989:* (57) Sf Birmingham and reached 3 doubles f, winning Albuquerque. Ranked No. 1 in her country for 3rd straight year. *1990:* (86) In singles reached sf VS Nashville and qf Schenectady; in doubles with Provis won Berlin and Strasbourg, qualifying for VS Champs. *1991:* At 6–4 2–6 4–3 30–0 up against Navratilova 1r Wimbledon she was close to pulling off the upset of the year, but won no more games. Upset K. Maleeva *en route* to last 16 French Open, unseeded, and reached sf VS Albuquerque. In doubles played 5 f, winning VS Nashville with Collins. *1991 HIGHLIGHTS – SINGLES: Australian Open* 1r (lost Provis 6–2 6–0), *French Open* last 16, unseeded (d. Bollegraf 6–0 6–2, Cioffi 6–3 6–1, K. Maleeva [seed 11] 6–4 6–4, lost M. J Fernandez [seed 4] 6–4 7–6), *Wimbledon* 1r (lost Navratilova [seed 4] 6–6 2–6 4), *US Open* 1r (lost Fulco 6–2 4–6 7–6); *sf* VS Albuquerque (d. Demongeot 6–4 3–6 6–4 Dechaume 6–1 2–6 6–0, Pierce 6–2 6–0, lost Halard 6–3 3–6 6–4). *1991 HIGHLIGHTS – DOUBLES:* (with Collins unless stated) *won* VS Nashville (d. Basuki/Vis 5–7 6–4 7–6) [Provis] *r/u* Italian Open (lost Capriati/Seles 7–5 6–2), [Provis] *r/u* Berlin (lost Savchenko Zvereva 6–3 6–3), *r/u* Birmingham (lost Provis/Smylie 6–3 6–4), *r/u* Phoenix (lost Louie Harper/Cammy MacGregor 7–5 3–6 6–3).

RICHEY RENEBERG (USA)
Born Phoenix, Ariz., 5 October 1965; lives Houston, Texas; RH; 5ft 11in; 170lb; final 1991 ATP ranking 27 singles, 41 doubles; 1991 prize money $333,121.
1985: (794) All American at Southern Methodist Univ. for 1st of 3 straight years. **1986:** (337) R/u NCAA singles to Goldie. **1987:** (79) Qf Indianapolis and was voted ATP Newcomer of the Year. No. 1 Collegiate player in US. **1988:** (103) Qf US CC and Vienna. **1989:** (80) Reached 1st GP sf at Auckland and upset Noah *en route* to the same stage at Washington. **1990:** (23) Shot up the rankings into the top 25 with r/u showing at Wellington (d. Chesnokov), plus sf Rosmalen, Indianapolis (d. Sampras) and Tokyo Seiko, and an upset of J. McEnroe at Philadelphia. **1991:** Sidelined at start of year with rotator cuff tendonitis in his right shoulder, he missed the indoor season, but returned to make a surprise appearance in sf LIPC. He went on to win his 1st career singles title at Tampa, breaking into the top 20 in May, and following with sf Birmingham and a surprise defeat of Cherkasov 1r Wimbledon. In doubles won 2 titles with Grabb and reached 2 more f with different partners. **1991 HIGHLIGHTS – SINGLES: French Open** 1r (lost Haarhuis 6–3 6–3 6–1), **Wimbledon** 2r (d. Cherkasov [seed 12] 6–4 6–3 6–4, lost Laurendeau 3–6 6–4 6–7 6–4 6–2), **US Open** 1r (lost Clavet 7–6 6–7 6–4 6–2); **won** Tampa (d. Duncan 7–6 6–2, Oresar 6–3 6–4, Washington 6–3 6–3, Arraya 6–3 6–1, Korda 4–6 6–4 6–2); **sf** LIPC (d. Korda 6–7 7–6 6–3, Siemerink 7–6 6–4, Carbonell 7–6 7–6, Rosset 7–6 3–6 6–3, lost Courier 6–4 6–3), **sf** Birmingham (d. Jonsson 4–6 6–3 6–3, Muller 7–6 6–3, Ferreira 6–4 6–4, lost Chang 4–6 6–1 6–2). **1991 HIGHLIGHTS – DOUBLES:** (with Grabb unless stated) **won** Sydney Indoor (d. Jensen/Warder 6–4 6–4), **won** Tokyo Seiko (d. Davis/Pate 7–5 2–6 7–6); [Pate] **r/u** Tampa (lost Flach/Seguso 6–7 6–4 6–1), [Wheaton] **r/u** Umag (lost Bloom/J. Sanchez 7–6 2–6 6–1).

KATHY RINALDI (USA)
Born Stuart, Fla, 24 March 1967; lives Amelia Island, Fla; RH; 2HB; 5ft 6in; 121lb; final 1991 WTA ranking 105 singles, 20 doubles; 1991 prize money $129,580.
Coached by Andy Brandi. **1979:** Quietly precocious, she became first to win a US Girls' 12 GS, winning Indoor, HC, CC and Nat Champ. **1980:** Won Nat Girls' 14 CC and was ranked 3rd in division. **1981:** (33) Youngest to reach qf French Open and youngest to win a match at Wimbledon (14 years and 3 months). Turned pro in July. Voted WTA Most Impressive Newcomer. **1982:** (12) R/u German Open and San Diego. **1983:** (16) Sf US CC and WTA Champs, last 16 Wimbledon and French Open, and played W Cup. **1984:** (23) Sf Fort Lauderdale. **1985:** (11) Sf Wimbledon, won Mahwah over Graf and had wins over Sukova, Kohde-Kilsch and Mandlikova. **1986:** (9) Had a strong start with qf French Open, overcame mid-season injuries and returned to win VS Arkansas at end of year. **1987:** (26) Qf Washington. Suffered a fractured thumb at French Open, which kept her out of action for 11 months. **1988:** (88) Returned at Amelia Island, playing only doubles and losing 1r. **1989:** (52) Reached sf Bayonne and was voted WTA Comeback Player of Year. **1990:** (69) Suffered a poor year in which she reached no qf. **1991:** Qf Tokyo Pan Pacific was her best showing in singles, but in doubles with Hetherington she won VS Houston and San Diego from 4 f to qualify for VS Champs. **1991 HIGHLIGHTS – SINGLES: Australian Open** 1r (lost McNeil 5–7 7–6 6–1), **French Open** 2r (d. Laskova 6–2 6–3, lost Tami Whitlinger 6–4 6–0), **Wimbledon** 1r (lost Herreman 7–5 6–2), **US Open** 2r (d. Paz 6–7 6–4 6–1, lost G. Fernandez 6–4 6–1). **1991 HIGHLIGHTS – DOUBLES:** (with Hetherington) **won** VS Houston (d. Fendick/M. J. Fernandez 6–1 2–6 6–1), **won** San Diego (d. G. Fernandez/Tauziat 6–4 3–6 6–2); **r/u** San Antonio (lost Fendick/Seles 7–6 6–2), **r/u** Leipzig (lost Bollegraf/Demongeot 6–4 6–3). **CAREER HIGHLIGHTS – DOUBLES:** (with Garrison) **US Open – sf 1985** (lost Kohde-Kilsch/Sukova 6–3 fs).

PETRA RITTER (Austria)
Born Vienna, 24 May 1972, and lives there; RH; 2HB; 5ft 8½in; 134lb; final 1991 WTA ranking 76; 1991 prize money $33,902.
Coached by Peter Eipeldauer. **1988:** (174) European Jun champ in singles and doubles. **1989:** (151). **1990:** (145) Reached her 1st tour sf Taranto. **1991:** She again produced her best performance at Taranto, where an appearance in her 1st tour f took her into the top 100. **1991 HIGHLIGHTS – SINGLES: Australian Open** 1r (lost Cueto 6–4 2–6 7–5), **US Open** 2r (d. Fairbank-Nideffer 6–4 7–6, lost Capriati [seed 7] 6–3 6–0); **r/u** Taranto (d. Kuhlman 6–3 6–0, Dechaume 6–2 2–6 6–2, Federica Bonsignori 6–1 0–6 6–4, Farina 3–6 6–1 6–0, lost Zardo 7–5 6–2).

BARBARA RITTNER (Germany)
Born Krefeld, 25 April 1973; lives Odenthal; RH; 2HB; 5ft 8in; 145lb; final 1991 WTA ranking 43; 1991 prize money $74,178.

Coached by Lutz Steinhofel. **1989:** (349). **1990:** (107) Enjoyed some success on the satellite circuits. **1991:** Won Wimbledon Jun over Makarova and Australian Open Jun doubles with Habsudova. In the senior game she reached her 1st tour f at St Petersburg and appeared in qf Wellington, Puerto Rico and Leipzig. **1991 HIGHLIGHTS – SINGLES: Australian Open** 2r (d. Loosemore 4–6 6–3 6–1, lost Sawamatsu 6–3 6–3), **French Open** 1r (lost Kelesi 6 0 6 2), **Wimbledon** 1r (lost Sanchez Vicario [seed 2] 6 1 6 2), **US Open** 3r (d. Sloane 6–4 6–1, Halard 6–2 6–0, lost Garrison [seed 12] 6–2 3–6 6–4); **r/u** St Petersburg (d. Dopfer 6–2 6–3, Mulej 4–6 6–3 6–1, Testud 7–6 6–2, Oeljeklaus 3–6 6–3 6–4, lost Savchenko 3–6 6–3 6–4).

FERNANDO ROESE (Brazil)
Born Novo Hamburgo, 24 August 1965, and lives there; RH; 6ft 3in; 170lb; final 1991 ATP ranking 99; 1991 prize money $90,398.
A doubles specialist who has enjoyed most of his success on the Challenger circuit in his native Brazil. **1988:** (148). **1989:** (219). **1990:** (252) Won Itaparica doubles with Menezes. **1991:** A wild-card entry, he was r/u Guaruja Chevrolet, and on the Challenger circuit he won Mexico City and Sao Paulo. **1991 HIGHLIGHTS – SINGLES: Wimbledon** 1r (lost Curren 6–3 6–3 6–1); **won** Mexico City Challenger (d. Maciel 7–6 4–6 6–4), **won** Sao Paulo Challenger (d. Markus 6–4 6–3); **r/u** Guaruja Chevrolet (d. Carlsson 6–4 7–6, Marcelino 6–2 7–6, Garner 6–3 1–0 ret'd, Wostenholme 6–3 6–4, lost Baur 6–2 6–3).

MARC ROSSET (Switzerland)
Born Geneva, 7 November 1970, and lives there; RH; 6ft 5in; 184lb; final 1991 ATP ranking 60; 1991 prize money $278,258.
Coached by Stephane Oberer. **1988:** Won Orange Bowl and was No. 4 on ITF Jun Rankings. **1989:** (45) On Challenger circuit reached qf or better in 10 tourns, winning 2. Broke into top 100 after winning Geneva in Sept. **1990:** (22) Broke into the top 25 in autumn, following some big upsets during the year. Won his 1st tour title at Lyon (d. Wilander); r/u Madrid (d. E. Sanchez) and Bologna; sf Nice (d. Noah), Gstaad (d. E. Sanchez) and Geneva. **1991:** Sf New Haven (d. Lendl and Chang back-to-back); qf Brussels, LIPC and Hilversum. **1991 HIGHLIGHTS – SINGLES: Australian Open** 1r, seed 15 (lost Wahlgren 4–6 2–6 7–6 6–3 9–7), **French Open** 1r (lost Agassi [seed 4] 3–6 7–5 6–4 6–3), **Wimbledon** 1r (lost Edberg [seed 1] 6–4 6–4 6–4), **US Open** 1r (lost Raoux 5–7 6–3 6–3 4–6 6–3); **sf** New Haven (d. Woodforde 6–4 6–2, Delaitre 6–3 6–1, Lendl 6–4 6–4, Chang 6–2 6–3, lost Korda 6–4 6–3). **1991 HIGHLIGHTS – DOUBLES:** [Bruguera] **won** Geneva (d. Henricsson/Jonsson 3–6 6–3 6–2).

DERRICK ROSTAGNO (USA)
Born Los Angeles, 25 October 1965; lives Pacific Palisades, Cal. and St Augustine, Fla.; RH; 6ft 1in; 165lb; final 1991 ATP ranking 13; 1991 prize money $399,729.
Coached by Mike Conroy. **1983:** Won New Zealand Masters satellite circuit. **1984:** Played in Olympic demonstration event in Los Angeles. **1985:** (427). **1986:** (70) Sf Houston, qf LA. **1987:** (60) Reached last 16 Australian Open, sf Auckland and Frankfurt, with wins across the year over Gilbert, Becker and Gomez. **1988:** (36) Upset Mayotte *en route* to an unexpected appearance in qf US Open, took Connors to 7–5 fs Wimbledon and reached sf Bristol and Washington. **1989:** (89) Sf Queen's. **1990:** (47) Upset Mayotte and Chesnokov *en route* to his 1st tour title at New Haven and removed J. McEnroe 1r Wimbledon. **1991:** Continued to score some significant upsets as he swept into the top 20. R/u Orlando (d. Sampras) and Tokyo Seiko (d. Becker and Lendl back-to-back and extended Edberg to 3s); sf Sydney NSW, Memphis (d. Courier) and New Haven; last 16 Wimbledon (d. Sampras) and US Open (d. Hlasek), unseeded both times. **1991 HIGHLIGHTS – SINGLES: Australian Open** 1r (lost Cherkasov [seed 14] 3–6 6–4 6–1 4–6 10–8), **French Open** 1r (lost Courier [seed 9] 6–3 6–3 6–0), **Wimbledon** last 16, unseeded (d. Furlan 6–0 6–3 6–4, Sampras [seed 8] 6–4 3–6 7–6 6–4, Connors 7–6 6–1 6–4, lost Champion 6–7 6–2 6–1 3–6 6–3), **US Open** last 16, unseeded (d. Baur 6–0 6–2 6–3, R. Gilbert 7–6 6–1 6–3, Hlasek 6–7 7–6 7–6 7–6, lost Stich [seed 3] 6–3 3–6 6–1 7–6); **r/u** Orlando (d. Connors 6–1 6–4, Hogstedt 4–6 6–2 6–2, Arias 6–1 6–4, Sampras 7–5 6–4, lost Agassi 6–2 1–6 6–3), **r/u** Tokyo Seiko (d. Stoltenberg 3–6 6–3 6–2, Reneberg 3–6 6–3 6–4, Becker 7–6 4–6 6–3, Lendl 7–6 6–2, lost Edberg 6–3 1–6 6–2); **sf** Sydney NSW (d. Skoff 6–2 6–2, Masur 6–4 7–6, Jaite 6–1 6–3, lost Forget 6–0 6–2), **sf** Memphis (d. Kratzmann 7–6 7–6, Courier 6–1 6–4, Caratti 6–7 6–2 6–0, lost Lendl 6–3 6–2), **sf** New Haven (d. Garrow 6–3 6–4, O'Brien 7–6 6–2, Krajicek 3–6 2–1 ret'd, lost Ivanisevic 6–4 7–5).

CHANDA RUBIN (USA)
*Born Lafayette, La, 18 February 1976, and lives there; RH; 2HB; 5ft 6in; 128lb; final 1991
WTA ranking 83; 1991 prize money $39,818.*
Coached by Ashley Rhoney. *1988:* Won Nat 12s and Orange Bowl in same age group.
1989: Won Nat 14s. *1990:* (522). *1991:* She announced her presence on the senior tour by
upsetting Bollegraf at LIPC in spring, and at end of year borke into the top 100 after
reaching her 1st tour f at Phoenix. *1991 HIGHLIGHTS – SINGLES: US Open* 2r (d. Farina
6–4 6–0, Monami 6–4 6–3); *r/u* Phoenix (d. Smylie 6–3 6–0, Louie Harper 6–7 6–0 6–3,
Helgeson 6–3 7–5, Habsudova 6–2 6–4, lost Appelmans 7–5 6–1).

GREG RUSEDSKI (Canada)
Born 6 September 1973.
1991: Won Wimbledon Jun doubles with Alami.

GABRIELA SABATINI (Argentina)
*Born Buenos Aires, 16 May 1970; lives there and Key Biscayne, Fla.; 5ft 8in; 130lb; final
1991 WTA ranking 3; 1991 prize money $1,192,971.*
Coached by Angel Gimenez for 5 years until, in June 1990, she turned to the Brazilian,
Carlos Kirmayr, who restored her joy in the game. Trained by Omar Carminatti and works
with sports psychologist Jim Loehr. *1984:* (74) Top of ITF Jun rankings, she won French
and Italian Jun and Orange Bowl 18s, where she conceded only 9 games in 6 matches.
Meanwhile she tested the waters in women's tennis and reached 3r US CC and US Open,
where she was youngest to win a match. *1985:* (12) Youngest sf at French Open, won
Japan Open and was r/u to Evert Lloyd at Hilton Head, following big wins over Garrison,
Shriver and M. Maleeva. *1986:* (10) Youngest sf to date at Wimbledon and qf or better in 12
of 21 tournaments. Established a successful doubles partnership with Graf, r/u French
Open. *1987:* (6) With a win-loss record of 56–16, she was one of the few players to trouble
Graf during the year, frequently taking her to 3s but never beating her. Sf French Open, r/u
Italian Open and won her first major titles at Tokyo and Brighton in autumn. R/u VS Champs
where she d. Navratilova in ss and took Graf to 4s. R/u French Open doubles with Graf.
1988: (4) Won VS Champs over Shriver, Argentine Open, Italian Open, Montreal and VS
Florida, where she beat Evert and achieved a first-ever win over Graf, ending the No. 1's
30-match winning streak. She upset her again at Amelia Island, and was the only player to
inflict 2 defeats on the World Champion during the year. Reached sf French Open and last
16 Wimbledon, then at US Open became 1st Argentine to reach GS f where she took Graf
to 3s, following an Olympic silver medal. In doubles with Graf won Wimbledon and LIPC,
but they were forced to default sf VS Champs owing to Graf's illness. *1989:* (3) Did not
progress beyond sf in any GS, reaching that stage in Australian Open and US Open but
falling to M. J. Fernandez in last 16 French Open and to Fairbank 2r Wimbledon. However,
she was r/u French Open with Graf. In singles won LIPC, Italian Open, Amelia Island (d.
Navratilova and Graf) and Filderstadt, reaching 3 other f and sf VS Champs. Was 1 of only 2
players to beat Graf during the year. *1990:* (5) Following her loss to Novotna in last 16
French Open, she sacked her coach, Angel Gimenez, and working with new coach Carlos
Kirmayr and sports psychologist Jim Loehr, she developed a serve and volley game with
which she beat Graf at US Open to win a 1st GS title in her 8th f. Earlier had snapped a
tendon in her ankle 3r Australian Open, which kept her out until March, when she returned
to win VS Florida at Boca Raton, following with sf Wimbledon, r/u VS New England and
Zurich, plus 4 more sf showings. At VS Champs she beat Graf again in sf, but lost f in 5s to
Seles. *1991:* At Tokyo Pan Pacific upset Graf, M. J. Fernandez and Navratilova back-to-
back for the title, then beat Graf again at VS Florida, LIPC and Amelia Island to take to 5 her
consec. victories over the German. That run ended in her 1st Wimbledon f, where she lost
8–6 fs to Graf in a thrilling match after serving for it twice. In other GS she lost sf French
Open to Seles, qf Australian Open to Sanchez-Vicario and qf US Open to Capriati. Her year
featured wins in Tokyo Pan Pacific, VS Florida, FC Cup, Amelia Island, Italian Open; r/u
LIPC; sf Toronto, VS Los Angeles, VS Philadelphia and VS Champs. After Amelia Island she
passed Navratilova in the rankings to take up 3rd place behind Graf and won the WTA Most
Improved Player award. Concentrating on her challenge for the No. 1 spot, she chose to
rest rather than play Fed Cup, thus forfeiting her right to play in the 1992 Olympics. *1991
HIGHLIGHTS – SINGLES: Australian Open* qf, seed 4 (d. Harvey-Wild 6–3 6–1, Ekstrand
6–1 6–1, Strnadova 6–1 6–1, McQuillan 6–3 6–1, lost Sanchez-Vicario [seed 6] 6–1 6–3),
French Open sf, seed 3 (d. Werdel 6–1 6–1, Zardo 6–1 6–1, Pierce 6–2 6–1, McQuillan 6–3
6–0, Novotna [seed 6] 5–7 7–6 6–0, lost Seles 6–4 6–1), *r/u Wimbledon*, seed 2 (d. Javer
6–4 6–0, Quentrec 6–2 6–2, Strnadova 6–1 6–3, Tauziat [seed 12] 7–6 6–3, Gildemeister

6–2 6–1, Capriati [seed 10] 6–4 6–4, lost Graf [seed 1] 6–4 3–6 8–6), **US Open** qf, seed 3 (d. Provis 7–6 6–3, Paulus 6–3 4–6 5–1 ret'd, Magers 6–3 6–4 6–4, Novotna [seed 9] 6–4 7–6, lost Capriati [seed 7] 6–3 7–6); **won** Tokyo Pan Pacific (d. McQuillan 6–7 7–6 6–3, Louie Harper 6–4 6–1, Graf 4–6 6–4 7–6, M. J. Fernandez 6–3 6–4, Navratilova 2–6 6–2 6–4), **won** VS Florida (d. de Lone 6–2 6–2, Werdel 6–3 6–0, Rajchrtova 6–2 6–2, Capriati 7–5 6–2, Graf 6–1 6–2), **won** FC Cup (d. Harvey-Wild 6–3 6–2, Kelesi 6–3 6–2, Sukova 6–0 6–1, Sanchez-Vicario 4–6 6–4 6–3, Meskhi 6–1 6–1), **won** Amelia Island (d. Federica Bonsignori 6–1 6–0, Spadea 6–0 6–1, Sukova 6–2 6–1, Sanchez-Vicario 6–2 2–6 6–4, Graf 7–5 7–6), **won** Italian Open (d. Coetzer 6–2 6–2, Tauziat 6–0 6–1, Capriati 6–0 6–2, Martinez 6–1 6–0, Seles 6–3 6–2); **r/u** LIPC (d. Henricksson 6–1 6–1, Rubin 6–1 6–3, Tauziat 6–3 6–2, Garrison 6–3 6–2, Graf 0–6 7–6 6–1, lost Seles 6–3 7–5); **sf** Toronto (d. Farina 6–0 6–0, Kelesi 7–6 6–2, Sukova 6–3 6–2, lost Capriati 6–4 3–2 ret'd), **sf** VS Los Angeles (d. Hy 6–3 6–0, Graham 6–3 6–1, McNeil 6–3 4–6 7–5, lost Date 3–6 6–1 6–4), **sf** VS Philadelphia (d. Zvereva 7–6 2–6 6–2, Martinez 6–3 6–0, lost Capriati 6–3 6–4), **sf** VS Champs (d. K. Maleeva 6–2 7–6, Capriati 6–1 6–4, lost Seles 6–1 6–1). **CAREER HIGHLIGHTS – SINGLES: US Open – won 1990** (d. Jordan, Demongeot, Appelmans, Sukova 6–2 6–1, Meskhi 7–6 6–4, M. J. Fernandez 7–5 5–7 6–3, Graf 6–2 7–6), **r/u 1988** (d. Rehe, Savchenko 4–6 6–4 6–1, Garrison 6–4 7–5, lost Graf 6–3 3–6 6–1), **sf 1989** (d. Porwik, Caverzasio, Meskhi 6–2 6–0, Martinez 6–1 6–1, Sanchez-Vicario 3–6 6–4 6–1, lost Graf 3–6 6–4 6–2), **qf 1991**; **VS Champs – won 1988** (d. K. Maleeva, Zvereva 6–1 6–1, Sukova 6–4 6–2, Shriver 7–5 6–2 6–2), **r/u 1987** (d. Bunge, Navratilova 6–4 7–5, lost Graf 7–5 4 6 6 0), **r/u 1990** (d. Novotna 6–1 5–7 7–6, Martinez 6–4 1–6 6–1, Graf 6–4 6–4, lost Seles 6–4 5–7 4–6 6–4 6–2), **sf 1989** (d. Magers 6–4 6–1, Garrison 6–3 5–7 6–3, lost Graf 6–3 5–7 6–1), **sf 1991**; **Wimbledon – r/u 1991, sf 1986** (d. Jolissaint, Suire, Gerken, Reggi 6–4 1–6 6–3, Lindqvist 6–2 6–3, lost Navratilova 6–2 6–2), **sf 1990** (d. Burgin, Huber, Tanvier, Tauziat 6–2 7–6, Zvereva 6–2 2–6 8–6, lost Navratilova 6–3 6–4); **LIPC – r/u 1991; Olympics – silver medal 1988** (d. Zvereva, Manuela Maleeva 6–1 6–1, lost Graf 6–3 6–3); **Australian Open – sf 1989** (d. Dahlman, Martinez 3–6 6–1 6–2, Benjamin 6–0 6–0, Reggi 6–0 4–6 6–1, Garrison 6–4 2–6 6–4, lost Graf 6–3 6–0), **qf 1991**; **French Open – sf 1985** (d. Manuela Maleeva 6–1 fs, lost Evert Lloyd 6–4 6–1), **sf 1987** (d. Schimper, Sanchez, lost Graf 6–4 4–6 7–5), **sf 1988** (d. Kelesi 4–6 6–1 6–3, lost Graf 6–3 7–6), **sf 1991**. **CAREER HIGHLIGHTS – DOUBLES:** (with Graf) **Wimbledon – won 1988** (d. Savchenko/Zvereva 6–3 1–6 12–10); **LIPC – won 1988** (d. G. Fernandez/Garrison 7–6 6–3); **French Open – r/u 1986** (lost Navratilova/Temesvari 6–1 6–2), **r/u 1987** (lost Navratilova/Shriver 6–2 6–1), **r/u 1989** (lost Savchenko/Zvereva 6–4 6–4).

CHRISTIAN SACEANU (Germany)

Born Klausenburg, Romania, 8 July 1968; lives Neuss; RH; 6ft 3in; 176lb; final 1991 ATP ranking 76; 1991 prize money $147,192.
Coached by Martin Simek. **1986:** (239) Won Nat singles and ranked No. 1 in nat 18s. **1987:** (84) Won Graz Challenger, Valkenswaard Challenger and reached 1st GP f at Livingston. **1988:** (88) Won 1st GP title at Bristol, reached last 16 US Open, qf Rotterdam and Lorraine and upset Svensson at Brussels. **1989:** (160) Qf Newport. **1990:** (153) Won Bristol and Croydon Challengers. Fined $15,000 and suspended 10 weeks from US Open for defaulting from Prague after 2r win to play in a special event the next day. **1991:** Won Rosmalen on the main tour and Hong Kong Challenger. **1991 HIGHLIGHTS – SINGLES: Australian Open** 2r (d. Tarango 2–6 6–3 6–2 3–6 7–5, lost Wilander 7–6 6–3 3–6 4–6 6–4), **French Open** 1r (lost Woodbridge 6–4 7–6 6–4), **Wimbledon** 3r (d. Davis 6–4 7–6 6–4, Muller 7–6 6–4 3–6 7–5, lost Eltingh 6–3 4–6 6–4 7–5), **US Open** 2r (d. Vajda 2–6 7–6 6–4 6–4, lost Woodbridge 6–2 6–3 6–3); **won** Rosmalen (d. Rosset 6–3 6–3, Nelson 6–3 6–2, Olkhovskiy 6–3 6–2, Hlasek 6–3 3–6 7–6, Schapers 6–1 3–6 7–5), **won** Hong Kong Challenger (d. Barrientos 6–4 6–1).

PETE SAMPRAS (USA)

Born Washington, DC, 12 August 1971; lives Bradenton, Fla.; RH; 6ft; 165lb; final 1991 ATP ranking 6; 1991 prize money $1,908,413.
Mother Georgia, father Sam, son of Greek immigrants. Brother Gus sometimes trains with him. In 1985 changed from 2HB to 1HB on the advice of his then coach, Dr Pete Fischer, with whom he split in 1989. Robt. Lansdof had coached him on forehand, Larry Easley on volleying and Del Little for footwork. Went to Bollettieri Academy and worked with Joe Brandi but parted in Dec. 1990 and started working with Pat Etchenbury for strength at Bollettieri Academy. Reunited with Brandi Jan. 1991. **1988:** (97) Sf Schenectady and upset Mayotte *en route* to qf Detroit. **1989:** (81) Reached qf Adelaide and upset Wilander *en*

route to last 16 US Open. In doubles with Courier won Italian Open, and took 7th place at Masters. *1990:* (5) Upset Mayotte in 70-game struggle 1r Australian Open *en route* to last 16, unseeded, and in Feb. won his 1st tour title at Philadelphia, which took him into top 20. He followed with Manchester, but the crescendo of his year came in Sept, when he won his 1st GS title at US Open and moved into the top 10. At 19 years 28 days he was the youngest champion there (the previous youngest was Oliver Campbell, who won in 1890 aged 19 years 6 months). Also reached sf Milan, Canadian Open, Los Angeles and Stockholm, but withdrew from Paris Open suffering from shin splints, which had been troubling him since US Open. He was able to play ATP World Champ, but did not progress beyond rr. Won inaugural GS Cup and first prize $2m. Voted Most Improved Player of Year. *1991:* Suffered a string of injuries to shin, foot and hamstring, returning to action in Feb. He finished the year in tremendous style by winning ATP World Champ in Frankfurt, the youngest since J. McEnroe in 1979 to win year-end Champ, beating Courier in f and losing only to Becker in rr. In between he won Los Angeles, Indianapolis, and Lyon; r/u US Pro Indoor, Manchester, Cincinnati and Paris Open; sf Orlando and Sydney Indoor. In GS he was disappointing at French Open and Wimbledon, but reached qf US Open. After Frankfurt sacked Brandi again and sought new coach on eve of D Cup f v France in Lyon where, in his first ever tie, was humiliated by inspired Leconte on opening day 6–4 7–5 6–4 and lost decisive 3rd rubber to Forget 7–6 3–6 6–3 6–4. *1991 HIGHLIGHTS – SINGLES: French Open* 2r, seed 6 (d. Muster 4–6 4–6 6–4 6–1 6–4, lost Champion 6–3 6–1 6–1), *Wimbledon* 2r, seed 8 (d. Marcelino 6–1 6–2 6–2, lost Rostagno 6–4 3–6 7–6 6–4), *US Open* qf, seed 6 (d. Van Rensburg 6–0 6–3 6–2, Ferreira 6–1 6–2 2–2 ret'd, Simian 7–6 6–4 6–3, Wheaton [seed 11] 3–6 6–2 6–2 6–4, lost Courier [seed 4] 6–2 7–6 7–6); *won* Los Angeles (d. Bloom 6–0 6–2, Matsuoka 6–3 6–4, Mansdorf 6–3 6–4, Pescosolido 6–3 6–1, Gilbert 6–2 6–7 6–3), *won* Indianapolis (d. Stafford 6–4 6–2, P. McEnroe 6–3 6–4, Fromberg 7–6 6–2, Courier 6–3 7–6, Becker 7–6 6–4), *won* Lyon (d. Nijssen 6–3 6–2, Champion 6–1 6–3, Svensson 6–2 6–2, B. Gilbert 6–1 6–2, Delaitre 6–1 6–1), *won* ATP World Champ (d. Stich 6–2 7–6, Agassi 6–3 1–6 6–3, lost Becker 6–4 6–7 6–1 in rr, Lendl 6–2 6–3, Courier 4–6 7–6 6–3 6–4); *r/u* US Pro Indoor (d. Strejber 6–2 7–5, Washington 6–3 7–6, Korda 6–4 6–0, J. McEnroe 6–2 6–4, lost Lendl 5–7 6–4 6–4 6–3), *r/u* Manchester (d. Bergstrom 7–5 4–6 6–2, Washington 7–6 4–6 6–2, Masur 7–5 6–2, Paloheimo 6–4 7–5, lost Ivanisevic 6–4 6–4), *r/u* Cincinnati (d. Masur 7–6 6–4, Ferreira 6–1 6–4, Edberg 6–3 6–3, Courier 6–2 7–5, lost Forget 2–6 7–6 6–4), *r/u* Paris Open (d. Cherkasov 7–6 6–2, Ivanisevic 6–3 6–7 7–6, Volkov 6–2 6–3, Chang 2–6 6–4 6–3, lost Forget 7–6 4–6 5–7 6–4 6–4); *sf* Orlando (d. Pearce 6–2 6–2, Nargiso 6–3 7–6, Pate 6–3 6–3, lost Rostagno 7–5 6–4), *sf* Sydney Indoor (d. Nelson 4–6 6–1 6–4, Woodbridge 6–2 6–1, Wheaton 6–3 4–6 6–4, lost B. Gilbert 1–6 7–5 6–3). *1991 HIGHLIGHTS – DOUBLES:* (with Pereira) *r/u* Orlando (lost Jensen/Melville 6–7 7–6 6–3). *CAREER HIGHLIGHTS – SINGLES: US Open – won 1990* (d. Goldie, Lundgren, Hlasek, Muster 6– / /–6 6–4 6–3, Lendl 6–4 7–6 3–6 4–6 6–2, J. McEnroe 6–2 6–4 3–6 6–3, Agassi 6–4 6–3 6–2), *qf 1991; ATP World Champ – won 1991.*

EMILIO SANCHEZ (Spain)
Born Madrid, 29 May 1965; lives Barcelona; RH; 5ft 10in; 164lb; final 1991 ATP ranking 14 singles, 13 (9) doubles; 1991 prize money $672,071.
Coached by Pato (Bill) Alvarez. Brother of Javier and Arantxa. *1983:* (208) R/u Orange Bowl and won Spanish Champs. *1984:* (112) Last 16 French Open. *1985:* (64) Upset Nystrom and Jarryd and reached 7 f doubles with Casal, winning 3 titles. *1986:* (16) Emerged as the most improved slow-court player, winning Nice, Munich and Bastad, r/u Italian Open reaching 5 sfs and twice stopping Wilander and also claiming Becker and Edberg as his victims. *1987:* (17) In singles won Gstaad, Bordeaux, Kitzbuhel, Madrid and reached last 16 French Open and Wimbledon. In doubles with Casal r/u Wimbledon, won 6 titles and qualified for Masters, reaching sf. In mixed doubles won French Open and US Open with Navratilova. *1988:* (17) In doubles won French Open with Gomez and Bologna with his brother Javier, while regular partner Casal was undergoing wrist surgery. With Casal won US Open and 7 other titles, plus Olympic silver medal and r/u Masters to R. Leach and Pugh. In singles won Hilversum, reached 3 more f, upset Noah *en route* to qf French Open and d. Mecir to reach same stage at US Open. *1989:* (19) Missed French Open with knee injury which kept him out for 2 months. Won Kitzbuhel in singles and doubles and was r/u Hilversum and Bordeaux. *1990:* (8) In singles won Wellington and Estoril; sf LIPC (d. Lendl), Barcelona, Monte Carlo (d. Becker), Italian Open, Stuttgart, Hilversum and Kitzbuhel. Qualified for ATP World Champ, but won no match there. In doubles reached 9 f, winning 5 with Casal, including French Open, and 1 with Zivojinovic.

Qualified with Casal for IBM/ATP World Doubles Final, where they were r/u to Forget/ Hlasek. *1991:* In singles he won Barcelona, Italian Open and Gstaad; r/u Schenectady and Palermo. In doubles won 4 titles with Casal and 1 with Masur, reaching 2 more f with different partners, and in mixed doubles was r/u US Open with his sister, Arantxa. *1991 HIGHLIGHTS – SINGLES: Australian Open* 1r, seed 6 (lost Woodforde 0–6 7–5 7–6 6–2), *French Open* 2r, seed 11 (d. Jarryd 0–2 0–3 0–2, lost Hlasek 0–3 4–0 0–2 7–0), *Wimbledon* 1r, seed 11 (lost P. McEnroe 6–3 7–6 6–1), *US Open* last 16, seed 14 (d. Witt 6–4 6–4 3–6 6–3, Castle 6–3 6–2 6–2, Masur 6–4 7–6 7–6, lost Courier [seed 4] 6–4 6–4 6–3); *won* Barcelona (d. Perez 4–6 6–1 6–1, Cherkasov 5–7 7–5 6–3, Camporese 7–6 4–6 7–5, Jaite 7–5 6–2, Bruguera 6–4 7–6 6–2), *won* Italian Open (d. Woodbridge 6–1 6–1, Skoff 6–4 6–3, Ferreira 6–2 6–2, Fromberg 6–2 6–2, Prpic 6–4 6–2, Mancini 6–3 6–1 3–0 ret'd, *won* Gstaad (d. Hirszon 6–2 6–4, Krickstein 6–3 6–2, Jaite 6–4 7–5, Novacek 6–2 6–1, Bruguera 6–1 6–4 6–4); *r/u* Schenectady (d. Adams 6–4 6–4, Volkov 6–1 7–5, Clavet 7–5 6–1, lost Stich 6–2 6–4), *r/u* Palermo (d. Perez 6–4 6–0, Jaite 2–6 7–6 6–4, Muster 6–3 7–6, Vajda 6–1 6–2, lost Fontang 1–6 6–3 6–3). *1991 HIGHLIGHTS – DOUBLES:* (with Casal unless stated) *won* Auckland (d. Connell/Michibata 4–6 6–3 6–4), *won* Stuttgart Eurocard (d. Bates/Brown 6–3 7–5), *won* Hamburg (d. Motta/Visser 4–6 6–3 6–2), [Masur] *won* Stuttgart Mercedes (d. Camporese/Ivanisevic 4–6 6–3 6–4), *won* Buzios (d. Frana/Lavalle 4–6 6–3 6–4); [Gomez] *r/u* Schenectady (lost J. Sanchez/Woodbridge 3–6 7–6 7–6), [J. Sanchez] *r/u* Palermo (lost Eltingh/Kempers 3–6 6–3 6–3). *MIXED DOUBLES:* (with Sanchez Vicario) *r/u US Open* (lost Bollegraf/Nijssen 6–2 7–6). *CAREER HIGHLIGHTS – DOUBLES:* (with Casal unless stated) *French Open* – [Gomez] *won 1988* (d. Fitzgerald/ Jarryd 6–3 6–7 6–4 6–3), *won 1990* (d. Ivanisevic/Kulti 7–5 6–3); *US Open – won 1988* (d. R. Leach/Pugh w.o.); *Wimbledon – r/u 1987* (lost Flach/Seguso 3–6 6–7 7–6 6–1 6–4); *Olympics – silver medal 1988* (lost Flach/Seguso 6–3 6–4 6–7 6–7 9–7); *Masters – r/u 1988* (lost R. Leach/Pugh 6–4 6–3 2–6 6–0); *IBM/ATP World Doubles Final – r/u 1990* (lost Forget/Hlasek 6–4 7–6 5–7 6–4). *MIXED DOUBLES: French Open* – [Shriver] *won 1987* (d. McNeil/Stewart 6–3 7–6); *US Open* – [Navratilova] *won 1987* (d. Nagelsen/ Annacone 6–4 6–7 7–6).

JAVIER SANCHEZ (Spain)
Born Pamplona, 1 February 1968; lives Barcelona; RH; 5ft 10in; 155lb; final 1991 ATP ranking 32 singles, 36 doubles; 1991 prize money $386,292.
Coached by Pato (Bill) Alvarez. Brother of Emilio and Arantxa. *1986:* No. 1 in ITF Jun world rankings. Won Orange Bowl 18s, US Open Jun singles and doubles (with Carbonell), r/u Wimbledon Jun singles and French Open Jun doubles (with Carbonell). *1987:* (110) R/u Madrid to his brother, Emilio. *1988:* (55) Won 1st GP titles at Buenos Aires in both singles and doubles; sf Itaparica and qf Bologna. *1989:* (51) Won both singles and doubles at Bologna, r/u Sao Paulo singles and took 3 more doubles titles with various partners. *1990:* (70) Reached sf Madrid and last 16 French Open, unseeded. In doubles with various partners reached 6 f, winning 3. *1991:* R/u Umag and Brasilia; sf Buzios and Madrid, upsetting Bruguera there and *en route* to qf US Open, unseeded. In doubles won 3 titles with different partners. *1991 HIGHLIGHTS – SINGLES: Australian Open* 1r (lost Haar- huis 2–6 6–1 6–2 7–6), *French Open* 1r (lost Oncins 5–7 6–4 6–4 6–3), *Wimbledon* 2r (d. Kriek 6–4 6–4 6–7, 6–3, lost Novacek [seed 14] 6–0 6–1 7–6), *US Open* qf, unseeded (d. Mronz 6–2 6–3 3–1 ret'd, Bruguera [seed 9] 7–6 6–3 6–0, Larsson 7–6 6–0 6–3, Markus 6–4 6–2 6–3, lost Edberg [seed 2] 6–3 6–2 6–3); *won* Segovia Challenger (d. Montana 6–3 6–2); *r/u* Umag (d. Cunha-Silva 6–2 4–6 6–2, Benhabiles 6–0 6–3, Oresar 6–2 7–6, Korda 0–6 7–6 7–5, lost Poliakov 6–4 6–4), *r/u* Brasilia (d. Meligeni 6–7 6–4 6–4, Damm 7–6 6–4, Martin 6–2 6–2, Shelton 1–6 7–6 7–6); *sf* Madrid (d. Benhabiles 7–6 6–4, Bruguera 3–6 6–1 6–4, Lopez 7–6 6–4, lost Filippini 7–5 6–1), *sf* Buzios (d. Carbonell 6–4 6–4, Herrera 2–6 6–2 7–5, Clavet 6–7 6–4 6–2, lost Arrese 6–2 7–6). *1991 HIGHLIGHTS – DOUBLES:* [Courier] *won* Indian Wells (d. Forget/Leconte 7–6 3–6 6–3), [Bloom] *won* Umag (d. Reneberg/Wheaton 7–6 2–6 6–1), [Woodbridge] *won* Schenectady (d. E. Sanchez/ Woodbridge 3–6 7–6 7–6); [E. Sanchez] *r/u* Palermo (lost Eltingh/Kempers 3–6 6–3 6–3).

ARANTXA SANCHEZ-VICARIO (Spain)
Born Barcelona, 18 December 1971, livs Andorra; RH; 2HB; 5ft 6½in; 110lb; final 1991 WTA ranking 5 singles, 7 (8) doubles; 1991 prize money $799,340.
Sister of Emilio and Javier. Coached by Eduardo Osta. Travels with her mother, Marisa, whose family name, Vicario, she added to her own after 1989 French Open. *1986:* (124) Emerging from satellite circuit, she reached sf Spanish Open and played Fed Cup. *1987:* (47) Qf French Open in first GS appearance. *1988:* (18) Upset Evert (suffering from a foot

injury) at French Open *en route* to qf again and reached last 16 US Open. Won her 1st pro singles title at Brussels and was r/u Tampa. *1989:* (5) At 17 yrs 6 mths became the youngest woman and the first Spaniard to win French Open women's title. Qf Wimbledon and US Open, won Barcelona and was r/u Italian Open and Canadian Open, qualifying for 1st VS Champs, where she reached sf. Voted WTA most Improved Player for 2nd year running. *1990:* (7) In some disappointing performances she fell to Harvey-Wild 1r VS Chicago, to Paz 2r French Open and to Nagelsen 1r Wimbledon. Her 1st singles title came at Barcelona in April, followed by VS Newport; r/u Tokyo Toray, VS Houston, Amelia Island, Leipzig and Hamburg, where she d. Navratilova and took Graf to 3s. She lost 1r VS Champs to K. Maleeva and in GS her best showing was sf US Open, but she won French Open mixed doubles with Lozano. In women's doubles won 1 title with Navratilova and 3 with Paz, with whom she was r/u VS Champs. *1991:* Upset Sabatini *en route* to sf Australian Open and Graf on her way to f French Open, inflicting on the former No. 1 her worst defeat and 1st love set since 1984. In other GS lost qf Wimbledon to M. J. Fernandez and same round US Open to Navratilova, who also stopped her at that stage VS Champs. Had to wait until late Aug. to win her 1st title of the year at VS Washington, although she had reached qf or better in all 13 tourns until then. R/u Sydney, Berlin, Eastbourne, VS Philadelphia; sf FC Cup, Amelia Island, Barcelona, Hamburg, VS Los Angeles and Leipzig. Played in the winning Spanish Fed Cup Team, winning all her matches. In doubles won Barcelona with Navratilova and took Sydney and Amelia Island with Sukova, with whom she qualified for VS Champs. In mixed doubles r/u US Open with her brother, Emilio. *1991 HIGHLIGHTS – SINGLES: Australian Open* sf, seed 6 (d. Medvedeva 6–0 6–2, Javer 4–6 6–4 6–2, McNeil 6–4 3–6 6–0, Frazier [seed 13] 6–3 6–2, Sabatini [seed 4] 6–1 6–3, lost Novotna 6–2 6–4), *r/u French Open*, seed 5 (d. McNeil 6–2 6–2, Godridge 6–1 6–2, Fulco 6–1 6–1, Tami Whitlinger 6–2 6–1, M. J. Fernandez [seed 4] 6–3 6–2, Graf [seed 2] 6–0 6–2, lost Seles 6–3 6–4), *Wimbledon* qf, seed 3 (d. Rittner 6–1 6–2, Coetzner 6–4 6–1, McNeil 6–2 6–2, A. Minter 7–5 3–6 6–1, lost M. J. Fernandez [seed 6] 6–2 7–5), *US Open* qf, seed 4 (d. Piccolini 6–0 6–1, Godridge 6–1 6–1, Herreman 6–2 6–2, Zvereva 6–3 7–6, lost Navratilova [seed 6] 7–6 6–7 6–4); *won* VS Washington (d. Rajchrtova 6–4 6–4, Garrison 6–3 6–2, Meskhi 6–0 6–1, K. Maleeva 6–2 7–5); *r/u* Sydney (d. Dechaume 6–3 6–1, Cunningham 6–1 6–1, Provis 7–5 6–2, Garrison 6–2 7–5, lost Novotna 6–4 6–2), *r/u* Berlin (d. Kijimuta 6–2 6–0, Provis 6–1 6–1, A. Huber 6–0 6–2, Capriati 7–5 5–7 6–4, lost Graf 6–3 4–6 7–6), *r/u* Eastbourne (d. Porwik 6–1 6–4, Strnadova 6–3 6–2, Smylie 6–3 6–3, Shriver 6–2 6–3, G. Fernandez 6–1 6–1, lost Navratilova 6–4 6–4), *r/u* VS Philadelphia (d. Tami Whitlinger 6–0 3–6 6–2, Schultz 6–7 6–1 6–4, lost Seles 6–1 6–2); *sf* FC Cup (d. Fulco 6–2 6–3, Cioffi 6–1 ret'd, Federica Bonsignori 6–3 6–2, lost Sabatini 4–6 6–4 6–3), *sf* Amelia Island (d. Harvey-Wild 6–3 6–0, Cioffi 6–3 6–1, Meskhi 6–1 7–6, lost Sabatini 7–5 7–6), *sf* Barcelona (d. Kidowaki 6–0 6–0, Fulca 6–1, 6–2, Wiesner 6–3 6–2, lost Maleeva Fragnière 2–6 7–5 6–3), *sf* Hamburg (d. E. Reinach 6–1 3–6 6–2, A. Huber 6–2 6–1, Meskhi 6–2 6–1, lost Seles 6–2 6–4), *sf* VS Los Angeles (d. Demongeot 6–2 6–3, Paradis Mangon 6–1 6–3, Sukova 4–6 6–4 6–0, lost Seles 6–4 7–6 4–6 6–4), *sf* Leipzig (d. Kochta 7–6 6–1, Rittner 6–1 6–1, lost Novotna 6–3 6–2). *1991 HIGHLIGHTS – DOUBLES:* (with Sukova unless stated) *won* Sydney (d. G. Fernandez/Novotna 6–1 6–4), *won* Amelia Island (d. Paz/Zvereva 4–6 6–2 6–2), [Navratilova] *won* Barcelona (d. Tauziat/Wiesner 6–1 6–3); [Sukova] *r/u* Hamburg (lost Novotna/Savchenko 7–5 6–1). *MIXED DOUBLES:* [E. Sanchez] *r/u US Open* (lost Bollegraf/Nijssen 6–2 7–6). *CAREER HIGHLIGHTS – SINGLES: French Open – won 1989* (d. Rajchrtova, Demongeot Medvedeva 6–0 3–6 6–2, Coetzer 6–3 6–2, Novotna 6–2 6–2, M. J. Fernandez 6–2 6–2, Graf 7–6 3–6 7–5), *r/u 1991*, *qf 1987* (lost Sabatini 6–4 6–0), *qf 1988* (d. Evert 6–1 7–6, Tanvier 6–2 6–0, lost Provis 7–5 3–6 6–4; *Australian Open – sf 1991*; *US Open – sf 1990* (d. Provis, Kuhlman, Fendick, Paulus 6–4 6–3, Garrison 6–2 6–2, lost Graf 6–1 6–2), *qf 1989* (d. Faull, Cammy MacGregor, Wasserman 6–1 2–6 6–4, Paulus 6–2 6–2, lost Sabatini 3–6 6–4 6–1, *qf 1991. Wimbledon – qf 1989* (d. Pospisilova, Halard, Reggi 4–6 6–3 7–5, McNeil 6–3 2–6 6–1, lost Graf 7–5 6–1). *CAREER HIGHLIGHTS – DOUBLES:* (with Paz) *VS Champs – r/u 1990* (lost K. Jordan/ Smylie 7–6 6–4). *CAREER HIGHLIGHTS – MIXED DOUBLES:* (with Lozano) *French Open – won 1990* (d.Provis/Visser 7–6 7–6).

FABRICE SANTORO (France)
Born Tahiti, 7 December 1972; lives Toulon; RH; 5ft 10in; 148lb; final 1991 ATP ranking 43; 1991 prize money $195,252.

Nat champ in 12s, 14s and 16s. *1988:* (571) Won Orange Bowl 16s. *1989:* (235) Won French Open Jun over Palmer and was No. 2 in ITF Jun rankings. Upset Gomez at Stuttgart. *1990:* (62) Won Telford Challenger and then upset Gomez again *en route* to his 1st tour f at

Toulouse. Qf Nice (d. Chesnokov) and Bordeaux. Voted Newcomer of the Year. *1991:* Won Barcelona, upsetting Bruguera, and Brest Challenger; qf Adelaide, Sydney, Italian Open, Florence, Indianapolis and Bordeaux; last 16 French Open, unseeded. *1991 HIGHLIGHTS – SINGLES: Australian Open* 1r (lost Krajicek 2–6 6–1 6–2 6–3), *French Open* last 16, unseeded (d. Mronz 6–3 7–5 6–1, Wilander 6–2 6–3 6–2, Champion 6–2 6–0 6–4, lost Stich 6–3 6–1 6–2), *US Open* 1r (lost Curren 3–6 2–6 6 3–6 3–6 3); *won* Barcelona (d. Perez 4–6 6–1 6–1, Cherkasov 5–7 7–5 6–3, Camporese 7–6 4–6 7–5, Jaite 7–5 6–2, Bruguera 6–4 7–6 6–2), *won* Brest Challenger (d. Pioline 6–4 7–5).

LARISA SAVCHENKO (USSR)
Born Lvov, Ukraine, 21 July 1966; lives Urmala, Latvia; RH; 5ft 6½in; 138lb; final 1991 WTA ranking 48 singles, 2 (7) doubles; 1991 prize money $374,540.
Husband Alex Neland, manager of USSR Nat tennis team (married Dec. 1989). *1983:* Ranked 10 on ITF Jun list after reaching qf Wimbledon Jun and first Wimbledon doubles qf with Parkhomenko. *1984:* (138) Wimbledon doubles qf again. *1985:* (55) Third Wimbledon doubles qf and sf VS Denver in singles. Joined Fed Cup team. *1986:* (35) Showed affinity for grass courts, reaching sf Birmingham, qf Eastbourne, and upsetting Rehe at Wimbledon. Qualified with Parkhomenko for VS Champ doubles March and Nov. *1987:* (24) Won 4 doubles titles with Parkhomenko and ousted Navratilova/Shriver *en route* to sf Wimbledon. *1988:* (16) Upset Mandlikova and Sabatini as she swept to f VS California, upset Zvereva *en route* to sf Pan Pacific Open and Kohde-Kilsch *en route* to qf Eastbourne. Reached the same stage at US Open and Olympics and last 16 Wimbledon. In doubles with Zvereva r/u Wimbledon and VS Champs for which she qualified in both singles and doubles. *1989:* (20) Upset Navratilova *en route* to f VS California but then, frustrated by her poor form in singles, she talked of retiring after US Open. However, there she reached last 16, upsetting Shriver, and followed up with sf Moscow and r/u VS Chicago. In doubles won French Open and r/u Wimbledon and VS Champs with Zvereva, reaching 9 more f and winning 4. *1990:* (87) In singles qf Tokyo Toray and Birmingham. In doubles r/u French Open and won 3 titles with Zvereva, taking another with K. Jordan. Qualified for VS Champs with Zvereva but lost 1r to Adams/McNeil. *1991:* Won her 1st singles at St Petersburg and reached sf Brisbane, upsetting Novotna. In doubles played 8 f with Zvereva, winning Wimbledon plus 5 others and r/u French Open to qualify for VS Champs; reached another 4 f with Novotna, winning 3 and r/u US Open; and won Auckland with Fendick. *1991 HIGHLIGHTS – SINGLES: Australian Open* 2r (d. D. Jones 6–2 6–2, lost McNeil 6–3 4–6 6–3), *French Open* 2r (d. Housset 6–1 6–4, lost Thoren 6–3 3–6 7–5), *Wimbledon* 2r (d. Temesvari 6–2 6–7 8–6, lost Wiesner 6–3 6–0), *US Open* 1r (lost M. J. Fernandez [seed 5] 7–6 6–3); *won* St Petersburg (d. Zivec Skulj 5–7 6–4 6–1, Miyagi 6–4 6–4, Brioukhovets 6–0 6–3, Durie 6–4 6–4, Rittner 3–6 6–3 6–4); *sf* Brisbane (d. Pfaff 6–3 7–6, Magdalena Maleeva 6–1 6–2, Novotna 6–2 6–4, Appelmans 6–4 2–6 6–4, lost Kijimuta 6–2 5–7 6–2). *1991 HIGHLIGHTS – DOUBLES:* (with Zvereva unless stated) *r/u French Open* (lost G. Fernandez/Novotna 6–4 6–0), *won Wimbledon* (d. G. Fernandez/Novotna 6–4 3–6 6–4), [Novotna] *r/u US Open* (lost Shriver/Zvereva 4–6 6–4 6 7–6); [Fendick] *won* Auckland (d. Faull/Richardson 6–3 6–3), *won* VS Florida (d. McGrath/A. Smith 6–4 7–6), [Novotna] *won* Hamburg (d. Sanchez-Vicario/Sukova 7–5 6–1), *won* Berlin (d. Provis/E. Reinach 6–3 6–3), *won* Eastbourne (d. G. Fernandez/Novotna 2–6 6–4 6–4), *won* Toronto (d. Kohde-Kilsch/Zvereva 1–6 7–5 6–2), *won* VS Los Angeles (d. Magers/R. White 6–1 2–6 6–2), [Novotna] *won* VS Washington (d. G. Fernandez/Zvereva 5–7 6–1 7–6), [Novotna] *won* VS Philadelphia (d. M. J. Fernandez/Garrison 6–2 6–4); *r/u* Tarpon Springs (lost G. Fernandez/Sukova 4–6 6–4 7–6). *CAREER HIGHLIGHTS – DOUBLES:* (with Zvereva unless stated) *French Open – won 1989* (d. Graf/Sabatini 6–4 6–4), *r/u 1990* (lost Novotna/Sukova 6–4 7–5), *r/u 1991; Wimbledon – won 1991, r/u 1988* (lost Graf/Sabatini 6–3 1–6 12–10), *r/u 1989* (lost Novotna/Sukova 6–1 6–2); *US Open –* [Novotna] *r/u 1991; VS Champs – r/u 1988* (lost Navratilova/Shriver 6–3 6–4), *r/u 1989* (lost Navratilova/Shriver 6–3 6–2).

NAOKO SAWAMATSU (Japan)
Born Nishinomiya, 23 March 1973, and lives there; RH; 5ft 6in; 130lb; final 1991 WTA ranking 33; 1991 prize money $94,996.
Coached by Hiroyuki Bamba. Niece of Kazuko Sawamatsu, the 1975 Wimbledon doubles titlist. *1988:* Nat champ. *1989:* (256) Won Nagasaki on satellite circuit. *1990:* (31) Won Moulins Challenger, then, a wild-card entry, she beat 3 seeded players to win Singapore, having reached sf Tokyo Suntory 2 weeks earlier. These results saw her break into the top 100 and then top 50 in April. *1991:* Unseeded, she upset Garrison 1r French Open *en route*

to last 16, where she took Tauziat to 12–10 fs; r/u Pattaya City and reached sf Strasbourgb.
1991 HIGHLIGHTS – SINGLES: Australian Open 3r (d. Burgin 6–4 6–3, Rittner 6–3 6–3,
lost M. J. Fernandez 6–3 6–3), *French Open* last 16, unseeded (d. Garrison [seed 8] 6–4
6–0, Baranski 6–0 7–6, Graham 5–7 6–2 6–4, lost Tauziat [seed 13] 7–5 2–6 12–10),
Wimbledon 2r (d. Bartos 6–2 6–2, lost McNeil 3–6 6–2 6–2), *US Open* 2r (d. Ferrando 6–4
6–2, lost Rajchrtova 6–2 6–4); *r/u* Pattaya City (d. Pratt 6–1 2–6 6–0, Kamstra 4–6 5–0
ret'd, Javer 6–2 6–3, Werdel 6–1 6–3, lost Basuki 6–2 6–2); *sf* Strasbourg (d. Testud 5–7
6–4 6–2, Appelmans 6–4 6–3, Kohde-Kilsch 6–3 6–1, lost McQuillan 6–4 6–3).

MICHIEL SCHAPERS (Netherlands)
*Born Rotterdam, 11 October 1959; lives Eemnes; RH; 6ft 7in; 182lb; final 1991 ATP
ranking 85; 1991 prize money $131,064.*
Coached by Martin Simek. Wife Carole de Bruin, a physician (married Sept. 1990). *1982:*
Won Dutch Nat Indoor. *1983:* (107) Won Dutch Nat Outdoor. *1984:* (78) *1985:* (100) Upset
Becker *en route* to qf Australian Open. *1986:* (84) Sf Metz. *1987:* (49) R/u Auckland, sf
Adelaide, Bristol, Paris Open. *1988:* (50) Upset Noah *en route* to qf Australian Open,
extended Lendl to 5s at Wimbledon and upset Chesnokov *en route* to qf Olympics; r/u
Lorraine and sf Rotterdam. *1989:* (79) R/u Nancy, sf Bristol and reached last 16 Australian
Open. *1990:* (169) His best performances came in doubles in which he reached 2 f. *1991:*
In partnership with Schultz, won the longest set (56 games) and longest match in games
(77) ever recorded in Wimbledon mixed doubles when they beat Nijssen/Temesvari 6–3
5–7 29–27. In singles r/u Rosmalen, upsetting Stich, and in men's doubles won Tel Aviv
with Rikl. *1991 HIGHLIGHTS – SINGLES: Australian Open* 2r (d. Sinner 6–3 6–2 2–6 6–2,
lost Yzaga 7–6 6–4 6–2), *US Open* 2r (d. Altur 4–6 6–4 6–2 6–1, lost Connors 6–2 6–3 6–2);
r/u Rosmalen (d. Prpic 6–4 6–3, Thoms 4–6 6–3 6–2, Nargiso 7–6 7–5, Stich 6–4 7–6, lost
Saceanu 6–1 3–6 7–5). *1991 HIGHLIGHTS – DOUBLES:* [Rikl] *won* Tel Aviv (d. Frana/
Lavalle 6–2 6–7 6–3); [Pimek] *r/u* Brussels (lost Woodbridge/Woodforde 6–3 6–0).
CAREER HIGHLIGHTS – MIXED DOUBLES: (with Henricksson) *LIPC – won 1988* (d.
Pugh/Novotna 6–4 6–4).

BRENDA SCHULTZ (Netherlands)
*Born Haarlem, 28 December 1970; lives Heemstede; RH; 6ft 2in; 170lb; final 1991 WTA
ranking 30; 1991 prize money $151,578.*
Coached by Lada Travnicek. *1987:* (150) Won Chicago on USTA circuit, qf Paris Open.
1988: (39) Won Wimbledon Jun over Derly and on the senior tour was a finalist at
Oklahoma and Taipei. Upset Cecchini to reach last 16 French Open and also scored upsets
during the year over Lindqvist, Hanika, Reggi and Fendick. *1989:* (85) Reached f Brisbane
and last 16 Australian Open. *1990:* (43) Reached last 16 Wimbledon, unseeded; sf
Brisbane (d. Rinaldi); qf Tokyo Toray and Oklahoma (d. Reggi). *1991:* Produced some
excellent results on grass, upsetting Kohde-Kilsch and Tauziat on her way to sf Birmingham and then surprising Novotna *en route* to an unexpected appearance in last 16
Wimbledon, where she extended Capriati to 3s. Then went on in Aug. to win her 1st main
tour title at Schenectady. In partnership with Schapers, won longest set (56 games) and
longest match in games (77) ever recorded in Wimbledon mixed doubles when they beat
Temesvari/Nijssen 6–3 5–7 29–27). *1991 HIGHLIGHTS – SINGLES: Australian Open* 1r
(lost K. Maleeva 6–1 6–3), *French Open* 1r (lost Kidowaki 6–4 6–4), *Wimbledon* last 16,
unseeded (d. Reinstadler 6–3 6–0, Novotna [seed 7] 4–6 7–6 6–4, Brioukhovets 5–7 6–4
7–5, lost Capriati [seed 10] 3–6 6–1 6–1), *US Open* 2r (d. Kijimuta 3–6 6–3 6–2, lost
M. J. Fernandez [seed 5] 7–6 6–3); *won* Schenectady (d. Teri Whitlinger 6–1 6–1, Probst
6–3 6–2, McQuillan 4–6 6–4 6–2, Provis 5–7 7–5 6–3, Dechaume 7–6 6–2); *sf* Birmingham
(d. Kohde-Kilsch 6–4 6–1, Temesvari 7–6 6–2, Tauziat 6–3 7–5, Suire 6–3 6–2, lost
Navratilova 6–3 6–2).

ROBERT SEGUSO (USA)
*Born Minneapolis, 1 May 1963; lives Boca Raton, Fla; 6ft 3in; 180lb; final 1991 ATP
ranking 811 singles, 6 (95) doubles; 1991 prize money $272,553.*
Wife Carling Bassett (married Sept. 1987); son Holden John (born March 1988) and
daughter Carling Robbie Sean (born March 1991). *1983:* (146) All-American with Flach at
Southern Ill. Univ. *1984:* (208). *1985:* (56) Sf Stratton Mountain, last 16 Wimbledon and
won US Open doubles with Flach. *1986:* Beat Connors at Wimbledon and McEnroe at
Canadian Open; sf Queen's. Knee surgery postponed after US Open. *1987:* (135) Under-
went knee surgery in Jan. in an attempt to solve problems caused by scar tissue. Last 16
Australian Open; in doubles won French Open with Karryd, Wimbledon with Flach and r/u
Masters with Flach. *1988:* (37) In singles qf Memphis and Indianapolis. In doubles with

Flach won Wimbledon and Olympic gold medal plus 3 other titles to qualify for Masters, but failed to reach knockout rounds. *1989:* (86) Qf US Pro Indoor and Wembley in singles. In doubles with Flach r/u US Open and won 2 titles to qualify for Masters, but had to withdraw owing to an injury to Flach. *1990:* (367) Suffering from knee problems, he had a quieter year. *1991:* At Tampa the old partnership of Flach/Seguso won their 1st title since 1989, following with Cincinnati and Indianapolis to qualify for ATP Doubles Champ, where they reached f. Recalled, with Flach, to D Cup duty for f v France in Lyon but lost to inspired Leconte and Forget 6–1 6–4 4–6 6–2 as France won 3–1. This was only their second defeat in 12 D Cup rubbers since 1985 (not selected 1990). *1991 HIGHLIGHTS – DOUBLES:* (with Flach) *won* Tampa (d. Pate/Reneberg 6–7 6–4 6–1), *won* Cincinnati (d. Connell/Michibata 6–7 6–4 7–5), *won* Indianapolis (d. Kinnear/Salumaa 7–6 6–4); *r/u* LIPC (lost Ferreira/Norval 5–7 7–6 6–2), *r/u* Washington (lost Davis/Pate 6–4 6–2), *r/u* ATP Doubles Champ (lost Fitzgerald/Jarryd 6–4 6–4 2–6 6–4). *CAREER HIGHLIGHTS – DOUBLES:* (with Flach unless stated) *French Open –* [Jarryd] *won 1987* (d. Forget/Noah 6–7 6–7 6–3 6–4 6–2); *Wimbledon – won 1987* (d. Casal/E. Sanchez 3–6 6–7 7–6 6–1 6–4), *won 1988* (d. Fitzgerald/Jarryd 6–4 2–6 6–4 7–6); *US Open – won 1985* (d. Leconte/Noah 7–6 6–7 7–6 6–0), *r/u 1987* (lost Edberg/Jarryd 7–6 6–2 4–6 5–7 7–6), *r/u 1989* (lost J. McEnroe/Woodforde 6–4 4–6 6–3 6–3); *Olympics – gold medal 1988* (d. Casal/E. Sanchez 6–3 6–4 6–7 6–7 9–7); *Masters (/ATP Doubles Champ) – r/u 1987* (lost Mecir/Smid 6–4 7–5 6–7 6–3), *r/u 1991*.

MONICA SELES (Yugoslavia) **Official World Champion**

Born Novi Sad, 2 December 1973; lives Sarasota, Fla.; LH; 2HF; 2HB; 5ft 9in; 118lb; final 1991 WTA ranking 1; 1991 prize money $2,457,758.
Coached by her father Karolj; a cartoonist; travels with him and her mother Esther. Brother Zoltan (26) also trains her. Discovered by Nick Bollettieri at 1985 Orange Bowl; family moved to USA from Yugoslavia in 1986. Grew 5in between French Opens of 1989 and 1990. *1983:* At age 9, reached last 16 Sport Goofy singles. *1984:* Won Sport Goofy singles. *1985:* Won Sport Goofy singles and doubles. *1988:* (86) Upset Kelesi at VS Florida in 1st pro match, took Sabatini to 1s tb 1r LIPC and upset Magers and McNeil to reach sf New Orleans. *1989:* (6) Upset Savchenko and Manuela Maleeva at VS Washington, but had to default sf owing to injury, then won Houston over Evert and was r/u VS Dallas and Brighton. Unseeded at French Open she upset Garrison and Manuela Maleeva before extending Graf to 3s sf; reached last 16 Wimbledon and US Open and qualified for 1st VS Champs, where she lost qf to Navratilova. *1990:* (2) Following her acrimonious split in March with Bollettieri, who she considered was spending too much time coaching Agassi, she was coached only by her father. At 16 years 6 months became the youngest French Open women's champion and second-youngest GS champion (after Lottie Dod, who was 15 years 10 months when she won Wimbledon in 1897). She went into the French Open having won 5 consec. tourns without dropping a set, but her unbeaten run of 36 matches was ended by Garrison in qf Wimbledon. She in turn had ended Graf's 66-match unbeaten run at Berlin, which she won in addition to LIPC, San Antonio, Tampa, Italian Open, Los Angeles and VS California – plus VS Champs, where she finished the season triumphantly by beating Sabatini in 5s in f. She beat Graf twice and Navratilova three times and by year's end had displaced Navratilova to finish ranked 2. Won WTA Most Improved Player award. *1991:* Enjoyed a spectacular year in which she reached f in all 16 tourns she entered, winning Australian Open, French Open, US Open, VS Champs, LIPC, VS Houston, VS Los Angeles, Tokyo Nicherei, Milan and VS Philadelphia. At 17 years 2 months she became the youngest to take the Australian Open, being 4 months younger than Margaret Smith in 1960, and in March, she ousted Graf from the top ranking to become the youngest (17 years 3 months) to reach that spot (Tracy Austin had been 1 month older). Although the German overtook her again briefly on and off during the summer, Seles finished the year firmly fixed at the top and was voted WTA Singles Player of the Year. She caused much controversy during the year, notably when she pulled out of Wimbledon 72 hours before the start, failing to give a satisfactory explanation and losing her chance of completing a GS, with Australian and French Opens already under her belt. Various explanations were offered, the first being that she had suffered a 'minor accident' but eventually she claimed she had panicked after being given conflicting advice that the shin splints from which she was suffering might keep her out of the game for six months or a year. She was fined $6,000 for withdrawing and $20,000 for subsequently appearing in an exhibition tournament. She also missed Fed Cup, claiming injury, although she played an exhibition tournament at the same time. *1991 HIGHLIGHTS – SINGLES: won Australian Open*, seed 2 (d. Hack 6–0 6–0, Caverzasio 6–1 6–0, Kschwendt 6–3 6–1, Tanvier 6–2 6–1, Huber

6–3 6–1, M. J. Fernandez [seed 3] 6–3 0–6 9–7, Novotna [seed 10] 5–7 6–3 6–1), **won French Open**, seed 1 (d. Zrubakova 6–3 6–0, de Swardt 6–0 6–2, Quentrec 6–1 6–2, Cecchini 3–6 6–3 6–0, Martinez [seed 7] 6–0 7–5, Sabatini 6–4 6–1, Sanchez-Vicario 6–3 6–4), **won US Open**, seed 2 (d. Arendt 6–2 6–0, Zardo 7–5 6–1, Gomer 6–1 6–4, Rajchrtova 6–1 6–1, G. Fernandez 6–2 6–2, Capriati [seed 7] 6–3 3–6 7–6, Navratilova [seed 6] 7–6 6–1); **won** LIPC (d. Cioffi 6–1 6–3, Kschwendt 6–0 6–1, Labat 7–5 6–0, Capriati 2–6 6–1 6–4, M. J. Fernandez 6–1 6–3, Sabatini 0–6 7–6 6–1), **won** VS Houston (d. Zrubakova 6–0 6–2, Federica Bonsignori 6–1 6–0, Cecchini 6–0 6–2, M. J. Fernandez 6–4 6–3), **won** VS Los Angeles (d. E. Reinach 6–1 6–0, Coetzer 6–4 6–1, Paz 6–2 6–2, Sanchez-Vicario 6–7 6–4 6–4, Date 6–3 6–1), **won** Tokyo Nicherei (d. Hiraki 6–3 6–4, Kidowaki 6–0 6–0, Frazier 6–4 6–0, M. J. Fernandez 6–1 6–1), **won** Milan (d. Garrone 6–0 6–1, Sukova 6–3 6–4, Martinez 6–3 6–3, Navratilova 6–3 3–6 6–4), **won** VS Philadelphia (d. Werdel 7–5 6–1, Garrison 7–6 6–0, Sanchez-Vicario 6–1 6–2, Capriati 7–5 6–1), **won** VS Champs (d. Halard 6–1 6–0, M. J. Fernandez 6–3 6–2, Sabatini 6–1 6–1, Navratilova 6–4 3–6 7–5 6–0); *r/u* VS Palm Springs (d. Javer 6–3 6–1, Appelmans 6–3 6–0, Hy 7–5 6–2, Kelesi 6–0 6–3, lost Navratilova 6–2 7–6), *r/u* San Antonio (d. Labat 6–0 6–1, Porwik 6–1 6–4, de Lone 6–2 6–0, Maleeva Fragnière 6–2 2–6 6–2, lost Graf 6–4 6–3), *r/u* Hamburg (d. Leand 6–1 6–1, Rajchrtova 6–3 6–0, Sukova 6–1 6–1, Sanchez-Vicario 6–4 6–4, lost Graf 5–7 7–6 6–3), *r/u* Italian Open (d. Provis 6–3 6–1, Piccolini 6–3 6–1, Meskhi 6–0 6–1, M. J. Fernandez 7–5 2–6 6–4, lost Sabatini 6–3 6–2), *r/u* San Diego (d. Shriver 6–2 6–2, A. Minter 6–0 6–3, Tauziat 6–1 6–2, lost Capriati 4–6 6–1 7–6), *r/u* VS California (d. Javer 6–2 6–0, Harvey-Wild 6–0 6–2, Maleeva Fragnière 6–2 6–1, lost Navratilova 6–3 3–6 6–3). *1991* **HIGHLIGHTS – DOUBLES:** [Capriati] **won** Italian Open (d. Provis/Reinach 7–5 6–2), [Fendick] **won** San Antonio (d. Hetherington/Rinaldi 7–6 6–2). **CAREER HIGHLIGHTS – SINGLES: Australian Open – won 1991**; **French Open – won 1990** (d. Piccolini, Kelesi 4–6 6–4 6–4, Meskhi 7–6 7–6, Gildemeister 6–4 6–0, Maleeva Fragnière 3–6 6–1 7–5, Capriati 6–2 6–2, Graf 7–6 6–4), **won 1991, sf 1989** (d. Reis, S. Martin, Garrison 6–3 6–2, Faull 6–3 6–2, Maleeva Fragnière 6–3 7–5, lost Graf 6–3 3–6 6–3); **US Open – won 1991**; **VS Champs – won 1990** (d. Paulus, Sanchez-Vicario 5–7 7–6 6–4; M. J. Fernandez 6–3 6–4, Sabatini 6–4 5–7 4–6 6–4), **won 1991**; **LIPC – won 1990** (d. Harvey-Wild, Lapi, Fairbank-Nideffer 6–3 6–4, Herreman 6–3 6–1, Tauziat 6–3 6–1, Wiesner 6–1 6–2), **won 1991**; **Wimbledon – qf 1990** (D. Strandlund, Benjamin, A. Minter 6–3 6–3, Henriksson 6–1 6–0, lost Garrison 6–3 3–6 6–4).

BRYAN SHELTON (USA)

Born Huntsville, Ala., 22 December 1965; lives Atlanta, Ga.; RH; 6ft 1in; 170lb; final 1991 ATP ranking 71; 1991 prize money $137,584.
Coached by Bill Tym. *1988:* (455) *1989:* (164). *1990:* (123) Won Tampa Challenger; qf New Haven. *1991:* Won 1st tour title at Newport, becoming the 1st black American to win a title since Ashe took Los Angeles in 1978; sf Brasilia and Tel Aviv and won Cairo Challenger. *1991 HIGHLIGHTS – SINGLES: Australian Open* 2r (d. Cane 7–6 4–6 6–3 6–4, lost Woodforde 7–6 6–3 6–3), *US Open* 1r (lost Edberg [seed 2] 6–4 2–6 7–6 6–1); **won** Newport (d. Baur 7–5 1–6 7–5, Stark 6–4 6–4, Van Rensburg 6–4 4–6 6–3, Martin 7–5 6–4, Frana 3–6 6–4 6–4), **won** Cairo Challenger (d. Eltingh 7–6 7–6); *sf* Brasilia (d. Ho 6–3 6–4, Roese 7–5 7–6, Stolle 7–5 6–4, lost J. Sanchez 1–6 7–6 7–6), *sf* Tel Aviv (d. Jonsson 6–3 7–6, Weidenfeld 6–3 6–1, Nyborg 7–6 6–4, lost Lavalle 6–4 7–6).

PAM SHRIVER (USA)

Born Baltimore, Md, 4 July 1962, and lives there; RH; 6ft; 150lb; final 1991 WTA ranking 37 singles, 9 doubles; 1991 prize money $292,561.
Coached by Don Candy. *1978:* (13) At age 16 upset top-seeded Navratilova to become youngest finalist in US Open. *1979:* (33) Troubled by nagging shoulder injury, lost 1r US Open. *1980:* (9) Won La Costa and r/u Sydney (d. Navratilova). *1981:* (7) Won first Wimbledon doubles title with Navratilova, sf Wimbledon and Australian Open singles (d. Austin in both) and won Perth. *1982:* (6) Sf US Open (d. Navratilova). *1983:* (4) Sf US Open and won Brisbane. *1984:* (4) Won VS Chicago and r/u Mahwah. *1985:* (4) Won Sydney, Melbourne and Birmingham. Completed double GS with Navratilova by collecting 8th straight GS title in Paris, but record 109-match winning streak broken in f Wimbledon by Jordan/Smylie. *1986:* (6) Won 5th Wimbledon doubles title in 6 years with Navratilova. Won Birmingham and Newport and reached sf VS Champs in Nov. *1987:* (4) Played no singles from March until June, returning to win Edgbaston, Canadian Open (d. Evert 1st time), VS Newport and New England, beating Evert again. With Navratilova won Australian and French Opens for 3rd GS in doubles, won US Open doubles, VS Champs for the 6th

time and won French Open mixed doubles with E. Sanchez. *1988:* (5) In singles won Brisbane, Sydney, Pan Pacific Open and Zurich and reached 4 more f, including VS Champs, where she beat Evert in qf and Graf (suffering from flu) in sf. In doubles won Australian Open, French Open and 7th VS Champs with Navratilova and Olympic gold medal with Garrison. However, a form of mononucleosis restricted her performance at Wimbledon, and she lost 2r US Open to Meskhi. *1989.* (17) Struggling to find motivation, she suffered a lacklustre year in singles with r/u Newport her best showing and failed to reach VS Champs in singles, although she qualified again in doubles with Navratilova. Won 8 doubles titles with various partners, including Australian Open and VS Champs with Navratilova, who ended their partnership before US Open, where Shriver was r/u with M. J. Fernandez. Teamed with Navratilova again in winning US Fed Cup team v Spain. *1990:* (66) Out of action from March having fractured her toe when she kicked a chair in frustration after a bad call and missed shot v Van Rensburg at Boca Raton. She then withdrew from Wimbledon following arthroscopic surgery for a shoulder injury suffered the previous Dec. Sf VS Chicago. *1991:* Returning after a 9-month absence and aiming to return to top 25 after her ranking had dropped a low as 116, she was unseeded at Australian Open in 1st GS for a year. Reached last 16 LIPC, upsetting Caverzasio and Gildemeister then d. Reggi at San Antonio and Sukova *en route* to qf Eastbourne. In doubles she reached 7 f, winning US Open and Brighton with Zvereva, a 7th VS Champs with Navratilova and Tokyo Nicherei with M. J. Fernandez. *1991 HIGHLIGHTS – SINGLES: Australian Open* 3r (d. Van Lottum 6–3 6–1, Pfaff 6–3 7–6, lost A. Huber 6–3 7–5), *Wimbledon* 3r (d. Leand 6–0 7–5, Fulco 6–0 6–3, lost M. J. Fernandez [seed 6] 6–3 7–5), *US Open* 3r (d. Hiraki 6–1 6–1, Magdalena Maleeva 6–7 6–1 6–2, lost Navratilova [seed 6] 7–5 6–1). *1991 HIGHLIGHTS – DOUBLES:* (with Zvereva unless stated) *won US Open* (d. Novotna/Savchenko 6–4 4–6 7–6); [M. J. Fernandez] *won* Tokyo Nicherei (d. Cunningham/Gildemeister 6–3 6–3), *won* Brighton (d. Garrison/McNeil 6–1 6–2), [Navratilova] *won* VS Champs (d. G. Fernandez/Novotna 4–6 7–5 6–4); [Navratilova] *r/u* VS Chicago (lost G. Fernandez/Novotna 6–2 6–4), *r/u* Filderstadt (lost Navratilova/Novotna 6–2 5–7 6–4), [Navratilova] *r/u* VS California (lost Fendick/G. Fernandez 6–4 7–5). *CAREER HIGHLIGHTS – SINGLES: US Open – r/u 1978* (d. Reid, Hunt, Navratilova 7–6 7–6, lost Evert 7–5 6–4), *sf 1982* (d. Navratilova 1–6 7–6 6–2, lost Mandlikova 6–4 2–6 6–2), *sf 1983* (d. Jaeger 7–6 6–3, lost Navratilova 6–2 6–1); *VS Champs – r/u 1988* (d. Hanika, Evert 7–5 6–4, Graf 6–3 7–6, lost Sabatini 7–5 6–2 6–2), *sf 1984* (d. Mandlikova, lost Navratilova), *sf 1986* (lost Navratilova 6–2 4–6 6–4); *Australian Open – sf 1981* (d. Desfor, Durie, Austin 7–5 7–6, lost Navratilova 6–3 7–5), *sf 1982* (lost Navratilova 6–3 6–4), *sf 1983* (d. Bassett 6–0 6–1, lost Navratilova 6–4 6–3); *Wimbledon – sf 1981*, (d. Ekblom, Little, Coles, Durie, Austin 7–5 6–4, lost Evert Lloyd 6–3 6–1), *sf 1987* (d. Hanika, Sukova 4–6 7–6 10–8, lost Graf 6–0 6–2), *sf 1988* (d. K. Maleeva, Garrison 6–4 6–4, lost Graf 6–1 6–2). *CAREER HIGHLIGHTS – DOUBLES:* (with Navratilova unless stated) *Australian Open – won 1982* (d. Kohde-Kilsch/Pfaff 6–4 6–2), *won 1983* (d. Hobbs/Turnbull 6–4 6–7 6–2), *won 1984* (d. Kohde-Kilsch/Sukova 6–3 6–4), *won 1985* (d. Kohde-Kilsch/Sukova 6–3 6–4), *won 1987* (d. Garrison/McNeil 6–1 6–0), *won 1988* (d. Evert/Turnbull 6–0 7–5), *won 1989* (d. Fendick/Hetherington 3–6 6–3 6–2), *r/u 1981* (lost K. Jordan/A. Smith 6–2 7–5); *French Open – won 1984* (d. Kohde-Kilsch/Mandlikova 5–7 6–3 6–2), *won 1985* (d. Kohde-Kilsch/Sukova 4–6 6–2 6–2), *won 1987* (d. Graf/Sabatini 6–2 6–1), *won 1988* (d. Kohde-Kilsch/Sukova 6–2 7–5); *Wimbledon – won 1981* (d. K. Jordan/A. Smith 6–3 7–6), *won 1982* (d. K. Jordan/A. Smith 6–4 6–1), *won 1983* (d. Casals/Turnbull 6–2 6–2), *won 1984* (d. K. Jordan/A. Smith 6–3 6–4), *won 1986* (d. Mandlikova/Turnbull 6–1 6–3), *r/u 1985* lost K. Jordan/Smylie 5–7 6–3 6–4); *US Open – won 1983* (d. Fairbank/Reynolds 6–7 6–1 6–3), *won 1984* (d. Turnbull/Hobbs 6–2 6–4), *won 1986* (d. Mandlikova/Turnbull 6–4 3–6 6–3), *won 1987* (d. K. Jordan/Smylie 5–7 6–4 6–2), [Zvereva] *won 1991*, [Stove] *r/u 1980* (lost King/Navratilova 7–6 7–5), *r/u 1985* (lost Kohde-Kilsch/Sukova 6–7 6–2 6–3), [M. J. Fernandez] *r/u 1989* (lost Mandlikova/Navratilova 5–7 6–4 6–4); *Olympics –* [Garrison] *gold medal 1988* (d. Novotna/Sukova 4–6 6–2 10–8); *TS Champs – won 1982* (d. P. Smith/Reynolds 6–4 7–5); *VS Champs – won 1984* (d. Durie/Kiyomura 6–3 6–1), *won 1985–6* (d. Kohde-Kilsch/Sukova 6–7 6–4 7–6), *won 1986* (d. Kohde-Kilsch/Sukova 7–6 6–3), *won 1987* (d. Kohde-Kilsch/Sukova 6–1 6–1), *won 1988* (d. Savchenko/Zvereva 6–3 6–4), *won 1989* (d. Savchenko/Zvereva 6–3 6–2), *won 1991. MIXED DOUBLES:* (with E. Sanchez) *French Open – won 1987* (d. McNeil/Stewart 6–3 7–6).

JAN SIEMERINK (Netherlands)
Born Rijnsburg, 14 April 1970, and lives there; LH; 6ft; 156lb; final 1991 ATP ranking 26; 1991 prize money $280,559.

Coached by Rohan Goetze, trained by Fritz Don. *1988:* Nat 18s Champ. *1989:* (477). *1990:* (135) Appeared in his 1st GP sf at Singapore after qualifying. *1991:* Moved into the top 100 with an unscheduled appearance in last 16 Australian Open, then shot through the rankings with his 1st GP title in his 1st f at Singapore in April and r/u placing at Vienna in Oct. (d. Hlasek and Skoff). In addition, he upset Forget at US Open, reached sf Stuttgart Eurocard and won Telford Challenger. From 3 doubles f he won Hilversum with Krajicek. *1991 HIGHLIGHTS – SINGLES: Australian Open* last 16, unseeded (d. Altur 6–3 6–3, Steeb 6–2 5–7 4–6 6–4 6–2, Koevermans 4–6 6–2 6–4 3–6 6–1, lost Prpic 7–6 6–7 6–0 7–6), *French Open* 1r (lost Chang [seed 10] 6–2 6–0 6–3), *Wimbledon* 1r (lost Prpic 6–4 3–6 6–3 3–6 10–8), *US Open* 3r (d. Poliakov 5–7 7–5 3–6 6–4 6–4, Forget [seed 7] 4–6 6–3 6–2 7–6, lost Markus 6–4 6–4 1–6 6–7 7–6); *won* Singapore (d. Kratzmann 3–6 7–6 6–2, Herrera 7–6 7–6, Matsuoka 6–4 6–4, Connell 6–2 6–2, Bloom 6–4 6–3), *won* Telford Challenger (d. Laurendeau 6–3 6–4); *r/u* Vienna (d. Vojtischek 6–4 6–3, Hlasek 6–7 7–6 6–3, Skoff 6–3 6–1, Steeb 6–3 6–4, lost Stich 6–4 6–4); *sf* Stuttgart Eurocard (d. Skoff 6–1 6–0, Bruguera 6–2 6–3, Cherkasov 7–6 7–5, lost Edberg 6–4 6–4). *1991 HIGHLIGHTS – DOUBLES:* (with Krajicek unless stated) *won* Hilversum (d. Clavet/Gustafsson 7–5 6–4); *r/u* Rosmalen (lost Davids/Haarhuis 6–3 7–6), [Vacek] *r/u* Berlin (lost Korda/Novacek 3–6 7–5 7–5).

HORST SKOFF (Austria)
Born Klagenfurt, 22 August 1968; lives Vienna and Monte Carlo; RH; 5ft 9in; 155lb; final 1991 ATP ranking 33; 1991 prize money $239,168.
Coached by Hakan Dahlbo. *1984:* (555) Won Orange Bowl 16s. *1985:* (299) Won Austrian Nat Indoor and Orange Bowl 18s. *1986:* (42) Won Austrian Nat Indoor Champ and Orange Bowl again, sf Barcelona, qf Kitzbuhel and Stuttgart. *1987:* (63) Upset Noah and Gomez *en route* to sf Monte Carlo. *1988:* (45) Won 1st GP title at Athens, following with Vienna. *1989:* (25) R/u Hamburg (d. Becker), Prague and Barcelona. *1990:* (26) At Geneva won 1st tour title since 1988; also reached f Vienna and sf Kitzbuhel, upsetting Muster both times, and won 2 Challenger titles. *1991:* R/u Florence and Geneva; sf Monte Carlo (d. Agassi) and Schenectady. *1991 HIGHLIGHTS – SINGLES: Australian Open* 1r (lost Forget [seed 10] 7–6 6–2 6–4), *French Open* 2r (d. Wheaton 6–2 6–7 3–6 6–2 6–4, lost Edberg [seed 1] 6–4 5–7 6–3 6–3), *Wimbledon* 2r (d. Mronz 6–4 6–4 6–3, lost Fleurian 6–2 6–3), *US Open* 2r (d. Evernden 6–4 6–4 3–6 6–3, lost Wheaton [seed 11] 6–1 6–2 6–2); *r/u* Florence (d. Pioline 6–4 6–2, Wuyts 6–3 5–7 6–1, Markus 6–1 6–7 6–2, Masso 6–4 6–4, lost Muster 6–2 6–7 6–4), *r/u* Geneva (d. Lopez 6–2 6–0, Merz 6–2 6–0, de la Pena 7–6 4–6 6–1, Arrese 7–6 6–2, lost Muster 6–2 6–4); *sf* Monte Carlo (d. Fleurian 4–6 6–4 6–2, Agassi 6–0 6–7 6–3, Pistolesi 6–2 7–5, Svensson 6–3 6–3, lost Bruguera 6–1 6–4), *sf* Schenectady (d. Ferreira 6–3 6–7 6–2, Adams 5–7 6–2 7–6, Cherkasov 6–7 6–3 7–6, lost Stich 7–5 6–1).

ANNA SMASHNOVA (Israel)
Born 16 July 1976. Final 1991 WTA ranking 347; 1991 prize money $5,803.
1991: Won French Open Jun over Gorrochategui.

ANNE SMITH (USA)
Born Dallas, 1 July 1959, and lives there; RH; 5ft 5in; 120lb; final 1991 WTA ranking 63 singles, 17 doubles; 1991 prize money $87,745.
1976: R/u Orange Bowl. *1977:* Won Orange Bowl and became 1st American to win French Open Jun. *1978:* (20) Last 16 US Open. *1979:* (24) Last 16 US Open. *1980:* (24) With K. Jordan won French Open and Wimbledon doubles. *1981:* (16) With Jordan won US and Australian Opens and r/u Wimbledon. Won US Open mixed with Curren. *1982:* (13) R/u Washington, qf Wimbledon singles. With Jordan won French Open and r/u Wimbledon. In mixed won Wimbledon and US Open with Curren. *1983:* (28) After r/u French Open with Jordan, took a 6-month break to coach at Trinity Univ. *1984:* (Not ranked) Still coaching, but with Jordan won WTA Champs, r/u Wimbledon; with Curren won French Open mixed. Played Fed Cup. *1985:* (Not ranked) Playing sparingly, she reached last 16 Wimbledon. *1986:* (79) Won only 8 of 21 singles matches. *1987:* (40) At VS Indianapolis reached 1st f since 1982. *1988:* (53) Following rotator cuff surgery on her racket arm, she was out of action for 9 months, returning in July and reaching qf North California Open in her 2nd tourn, then in Oct. upset Lindqvist and Potter to reach f New Orleans. *1989:* (42) Sf VS Dallas (d. Shriver and Fairbank) and VS New England (d. Kelesi and Martinez). *1990:* (33) Sf VS Newport and Albuquerque; qf VS Washington and Birmingham in singles. In doubles with different partners reached 4 f, winning 3. *1991:* The high spot of her year came at VS Oklahoma, where she was r/u in singles, taking Novotna to 3s in f, and won the doubles with McGrath. *1991 HIGHLIGHTS – SINGLES: Australian Open* 2r (d. Sviglerova 6–3

6–4, lost Habsudova 7–6 6–2), **Wimbledon** 1r (lost Provis 3–6 6–4 6–2), **US Open** 2r (d. Langrova 6–4 7–5, lost Po 6–2 6–4); **r/u** VS Oklahoma (d. Fendick 6–1 7–6, Suire 6–3 6–4, A. Minter 6–0 6–4, Bollegraf 6–3 6–2, lost Novotna 3–6 6–3 6–2). **1991 HIGHLIGHTS – DOUBLES:** (with McGrath) **won** VS Oklahoma (d. Adams/Hetherington 6–2 6–4); **r/u** VS Florida (lost Savchenko/Zvereva 6–4 7–6). **CAREER HIGHLIGHTS – DOUBLES:** (with K. Jordan unless stated) **Australian Open – won 1981** (d. Navratilova/Shriver 6–2 7–5); **French Open – won 1980** (d. Madruga/Villagran 6–1 6–0), [Navratilova] **won 1982** (d. Casals/Turnbull 6–3 6–4), **r/u 1983** (lost Reynolds/Fairbank 5–7 7–5 6–2); **Wimbledon – won 1980** (d. Casals/Turnbull 3–6 7–6 6–1), **r/u 1981** (lost Navratilova/Shriver 6–3 7–6), **r/u 1982** (lost Navratilova/Shriver 7–5 6–1), **r/u 1984** (lost Navratilova/Shriver 6–3 6–4); **US Open – won 1981** (d. Casals/Turnbull 6–3 6–3). **MIXED DOUBLES:** (with Curren unless stated) **French Open** – [Stockton] **won 1984** (d. A. Minter/Warder 6–2 6–4); **Wimbledon – won 1982** (d. Turnbull/J. Lloyd 7–5 fs); **US Open – won 1981** (d. Denton/Russell 6–4 7–6), **won 1982** (d. Potter/Taygan 7–6 fs).

ELIZABETH SAYERS SMYLIE (Australia)
Born Perth, 11 April 1963; lives Sydney; RH; 5ft 7in; 129lb; final 1991 WTA ranking 115 singles, 14 (10) doubles; 1991 prize money $162,357.
Coached by her husband, Peter (married Nov. 1984). **1981:** Among world's top 10 jun. **1982:** (115) Won Sardinia on Italian satellite circuit and was ranked 7 in Australia. **1983:** (70) Won Kansas City. **1984:** (36) Ranked 2 in Australia behind Turnbull and played Fed Cup. **1985:** (43) Joined K. Jordan to beat Navratilova/Shriver in Wimbledon f, ending the record 109-match winning streak by world's top pair. **1986:** (80) Won only 6 of 20 singles matches including 7 straight 1r losses at start of year. Won LIPC mixed doubles with Fitzgerald. **1987:** (27) Qf Australian Open and won VS Oklahoma in Feb. in first singles f since Nov. 1984. In doubles r/u Wimbledon with Nagelsen and US Open with K. Jordan. **1988:** (172) Suffered a poor year in singles but won Eastbourne doubles with Pfaff. **1989:** (67) In singles reached f Tokyo and in doubles with various partners played 10 f, winning 5. **1990:** (53) In doubles with K. Jordan won VS Champs and r/u Wimbledon, taking 2 other titles plus a 4th with G. Fernandez; in mixed won US Open with Woodbridge and was r/u Wimbledon with Fitzgerald. Her best showing in singles was r/u Tokyo Suntory. Voted WTA Comeback Player of the Year. **1991:** Upset Magers at Eastbourne, Gildemeister at Australian Open and Cecchini at Wimbledon. In doubles won Tokyo with K. Jordan and Geneva and Birmingham with Provis, with whom she qualified for VS Champs doubles. Teamed with Fitzgerald again to win a 1st Wimbledon mixed title. **1991 HIGHLIGHTS – SINGLES: Australian Open** 3r (d. Kohde-Kilsch 2–6 6–4 6–4, Gildemeister [seed 15] 6–3 2–6 9–7, lost Habsudova 6–0 3–6 8–6), **French Open** 1r (lost Fulco 6–4 6–0), **Wimbledon** 3r (d. Cecchini [seed 16] 6–3 3–6 6–1, Suire 6–3 6–4, lost Lindqvist 6–1 7–6), **US Open** 1r (lost Godridge 6–3 6–4). **1991 HIGHLIGHTS – DOUBLES:** (with Provis unless stated) [K. Jordan] **won** Tokyo Pan Pacific (d. M. J. Fernandez/R. White 4–6 6–0 6–3), **won** Geneva (d. Caverzasio/Maleeva Fragnière 6–1 6–2), **won** Birmingham (d. Collins/E. Reinach 6–3 6–4). **MIXED DOUBLES:** (with Fitzgerald) **won Wimbledon** (d. Pugh/Zvereva 7–6 6–2). **CAREER HIGHLIGHTS – SINGLES: Australian Open – qf 1987** (d. R. White, Sukova 7–5 3–6 7–5, lost Kohde-Kilsch 7–6 4–6 6–2). **CAREER HIGHLIGHTS – DOUBLES:** (with K. Jordan unless stated) **Wimbledon – won 1985** (d. Navratilova/Shriver 5–7 6–3 6–4), [Nagelsen] **r/u 1987** (lost Kohde-Kilsch/Sukova 7–5 7–5), **r/u 1990** (lost Novotna/Sukova 6–3 6–4); **VS Champs – won 1990** (d. Paz/Sanchez-Vicario 7–6 6–4); **US Open – r/u 1987** (lost Navratilova/Shriver 5–7 6–4 6–2). **MIXED DOUBLES:** (with Fitzgerald unless stated) **Wimbledon – won 1991; US Open – won 1983** (d. Taygan/Potter 3–6 6–3 6–4), [Woodbridge] **won 1990** (d. Zvereva/Pugh 6–4 6–2).

CARL-UWE (CHARLIE) STEEB (Germany)
Born Aalen, 1 September 1967; lives Stuttgart; LH; 5ft 11in; 165lb; final 1991 ATP ranking 39; 1991 prize money $263,273.
1985: (363). **1986:** (150) Won Hauptfeld and r/u Harren on German satellite circuit; qf Buenos Aires. **1987:** (41) Upset Krickstein, Forget and Leconte to reach first GP sf in Stuttgart; qf Munich and Hilversum. **1988:** (73) Upset Zivojinovic *en route* to last 16 Australian Open and Jarryd to reach qf Olympics; sf Lorraine, qf Milan and Munich. Finished the year in style, beating Wilander in 5s as West Germany d. Sweden in D Cup f. **1989:** (15) Won his 1st GP title at Gstaad (d. Krickstein) and reached f Tokyo Seiko. **1990:** (46) Upset Becker and Wilander back-to-back *en route* to f Sydney in Jan.; reached the same stage at Brussels and sf Brisbane, where he d. Wilander again. Pulled out of Paris Open in Oct. with a foot injury, requiring surgery. **1991:** In singles he won Genova, reached

sf Milan (d. Chang and Krickstein) and Vienna, made an unexpected appearance in last 16 US Open and upset Ivanisevic at Monte Carlo. In doubles with Jelen he won 2 titles. *1991 HIGHLIGHTS – SINGLES: Australian Open* 2r (d. Pistolesi 6–2 6–2 6–3, lost Siemerink 6–2 5–7 4–6 6–4 6–2), *French Open* 1r (lost Ferreira 6–4 6–1 6–4), *Wimbledon* 1r (lost Becker [seed 2] 6–4 6–2 6–4), *US Open* last 16, unseeded (d. Adams 6–2 7–5 6–3, Stafford 6–0 7–6 6–1, Boetsch 3–6 6–3 6–4 6–4, lost Haarhuis 6–2 6–3 6–4); *won* Genova (d. Benhabiles 6–1 6–1, Wuyts 6–3 2–6 6–1, Agenor 6–1 6–4, Muster 7–5 6–4, Arrese 6–3 6–4); *sf* Milan (d. Chang 6–1 7–5, Novacek 4–6 7–6 6–4, Krickstein 6–3 7–6, lost Caratti 7–6 6–7 6–3), *sf* Vienna (d. Engel 6–4 6–3, Volkov 6–2 6–7 6–3, Frana 7–6 7–5, lost Siemerink 6–3 6–4). *1991 HIGHLIGHTS – DOUBLES:* (with Jelen) *won* Long Island (d. Flach/Nargiso 0–6 6–4 7–6), *won* Moscow (d. Cherkasov/Volkov 6–4 7–6).

MICHAEL STICH (Germany)
Born Pinneberg, 18 October 1968; lives Elmshorn; RH; 6ft 4in; 175lb; final 1991 ATP ranking 4; 1991 prize money $1,670,116.
Coached by Mark Lewis, brother of the 1983 Wimbledon finalist, Chris Lewis. An all-round sportsman who took to tennis aged 18, waiting to turn pro until he had finished his exams and gained a place at university. Unlike Becker, he has completed his National Service. *1986:* Nat Jun champ. *1987:* (795). *1988:* (269) Won Munster Challenger. *1989:* (100) Played his 1st GP qf at Queen's, where he took Lendl to 3s, and reached the same stage at Bristol and Frankfurt. *1990:* (42) Won his 1st tour title at Memphis, upsetting Chesnokov *en route* to becoming the 1st unseeded finalist there, and upset Volkov and Hlasek *en route* to qf Washington. In doubles reached 6 f, winning Munich and Vienna with Riglewski and Rosmalen with Hlasek. *1991:* Began a remarkable year by reaching f Adelaide and Sydney NSW and following with Memphis. He reached his 1st GS sf at French Open, breaking into the top 10, but the triumph of his year was his straight-sets victory over Becker on grass to win Wimbledon – only the second title of his career – which took him to No. 4 ahead of Courier and Agassi. After winning Stuttgart Mercedes (on clay) he replaced Lendl at No. 3, but was overtaken by Courier. With titles also at Schenectady (HC) and Vienna (Supreme), he became the 1st player since Mecir in 1987 to win titles on 4 different surfaces. With those successes plus sf showings at Indian Wells, Hamburg (d. Edberg) and Rosmalen, he qualified for ATP World Champ in Frankfurt, but, shaken by the overwhelming support for his opponent when he played Becker, he won none of his rr matches. Ended year by reaching sf Compaq Grand Slam Cup where Wheaton beat him. *1991 HIGHLIGHTS – SINGLES: Australian Open* 3r (d. Washington 4–6 5–7 7–6 6–1 6–4, Jaite 6–3 7–6 7–6, lost Forget 7–6 7–6 4–6 6–3), *French Open* sf, seed 12 (d. Pearce 6–3 6–3 7–5, Krajicek 6–7 7–6 6–3 6–2, Costa 3–6 7–5 7–6 6–2, Santoro 6–3 6–1 6–2, Davin 6–4 6–4 6–4, lost Courier [seed 8] 6–2 6–7 6–2 6–4), *Wimbledon* seed 6 (d. Goldie 6–4 6–1 6–2, Nargiso 6–3 6–4 6–7 6–2, Camporese 7–6 6–2 6–7 6–4, Volkov 4–6 6–3 7–6 1–6 7–5, Courier [seed 4] 6–3 7–6 6–2, Edberg [seed 1] 4–6 7–6 7–6 7–6, Becker [seed 2] 6–4 7–6 6–4), *US Open* qf, seed 3 (d. Eltingh 7–6 6–1 6–0, J. Brown w.o., Washington 5–7 7–5 6–2 4–6 6–3, Rostagno 6–2 3–6 6–1 7–6, lost Lendl [seed 5] 6–3 3–6 4–6 7–6 6–1); *won* Stuttgart Mercedes (d. Santoro 6–3 7–6, J. Sanchez 6–3 6–3, Krajicek 6–4 3–6 7–6, Clavet 6–4 6–3, Mancini 1–6 7–6 6–4 6–2), *won* Schenectady (d. Woodforde 7–6 6–3, Carbonell 6–1 6–2, Woodbridge 6–4 6–2, Skoff 7–5 6–1, E. Sanchez 6–2 6–4), *won* Vienna (d. Lavalle 6–3 6–4, P. McEnroe 7–5 6–3, Jarryd 6–2 6–1, Korda 6–4 2–6 6–2, Siemerink 6–4 6–4 6–4); *r/u* Adelaide (d. Fleurian 6–4 6–4, Bloom 7–5 6–1, Arias 3–6 6–3 6–3, Courier 6–4 7–6, lost Kulti 6–3 1–6 6–2), *r/u* Sydney NSW (d. Volkov 6–4 6–3, Hlasek 3–6 7–6 6–4, Anderson 6–3 6–0, Gustafsson 7–6 6–4, lost Forget 3–6 6–4), *r/u* Memphis (d. Antonitsch 6–2 6–3, Wilander 6–3 6–3, Koevermans 6–4 6–2, Chang 6–2 6–2, lost Lendl 7–5 6–3); *sf* Indian Wells (d. Mayotte 6–3 6–1, Layendecker 6–3 7–6, Santoro 4–6 6–3 6–4, Reneberg 6–0 2–6 6–4, lost Courier 6–3 6–2), *sf* Hamburg (d. Carbonell 1–6 6–3 7–5, Haarhuis 7–5 6–0, Clavet 6–1 6–4, Edberg 6–2 7–6, lost Novacek 6–3 2–6 7–6), *sf* Rosmalen (d. Youl 7–6 6–3, Haarhuis 6–3 6–3, Krajicek 6–4 7–6, lost Schapers 6–4 7–6), *sf* Compaq Grand Slam Cup (lost Wheaton 7–6 7–6 7–6). *1991 HIGHLIGHTS – DOUBLES:* (with Riglewski) *won* Memphis (d. Fitzgerald/Warder 7–5 6–3); *r/u* US Pro Indoor (lost R. Leach/Pugh 6–4 6–4). *CAREER HIGHLIGHTS – SINGLES: Wimbledon – won 1991; French Open – sf 1991; US Open – qf 1991.*

JASON STOLTENBERG (Australia)
Born Narrabri, 4 April 1970; lives Newcastle; RH; 6ft 1in; 177lb; final 1991 ATP ranking 75; 1991 prize money $195,459.

Coached by Gavin Hopper. **1987:** (413) 1st to become ITF Jun Champ in both singles and doubles in the same year. Won Australian Open Jun singles and Australian and Wimbledon Jun doubles (with Woodbridge); r/u French Open and Wimbledon Jun singles. **1988:** (70) In Jun doubles won Australian Open, French Open and Wimbledon, all with Woodbridge. In the senior game reached last 16 Australian Open and qf Rye Brook and Brisbane. **1989:** (84) Upset Chang en route to his 1st GP f at Livingston. **1990.** (100) In singles reached qf Orlando and Los Angeles. In doubles won 2 titles with Kratzmann and 1 with Woodbridge. **1991:** Sf Singapore and Brisbane singles and took San Francisco doubles with Masur. **1991 HIGHLIGHTS – SINGLES: Australian Open** 2r (d. Hlasek 0–6 6–4 7–5 6–4, lost Koevermans 6–3 6–3 6–3), **French Open** 2r (d. Soules 6–2 7–6 7–5, lost P. McEnroe 7–6 6–3 6–4), **Wimbledon** 1r (lost Michibata 5–7 6–4 3–6 7–6 6–4), **US Open** 2r (d. Connell 6–4 7–6 6–2, lost Grabb 7–5 6–4 4–6 7–5); **sf** Singapore (d. Krajicek 6–2 6–2, Grabb 6–4 6–2, Woodbridge 6–2 7–6, lost Bloom 3–6 6–4 6–3), **sf** Brisbane (d. Muller 6–7 6–2 6–2, Morgan 6–3 6–1, B. Gilbert 6–3 6–1, lost Pozzi 6–3 6–1). **1991 HIGHLIGHTS – DOUBLES:** (with Masur) **won** San Francisco (d. Bathman/Bergh 4–6 7–6 6–4).

ANDREA STRNADOVA (Czechoslovakia)
Born Prague, 28 May 1972, and lives there; 5ft 9in; 130lb; RH; 2HB; final 1991 WTA ranking 34; 1991 prize money $128,758.
1988: (374). **1989:** (199) Won Wimbledon Jun singles (d. McGrath 6–2 6–3) and in Jun doubles with Sviglerova won Australian Open and r/u Wimbledon to finish No. 1 in ITF Jun doubles rankings. In the senior game won Darmstadt on the German satellite circuit. **1990:** (144) Won Wimbledon Jun singles over Sharpe and took doubles with Habsudova. Qf Leipzig and won Karlov Vary Challenger in the senior game. **1991:** Upset Savchenko en route to 1st tour f at Auckland, and beat the same player to reach the same stage at Wellington the following week. Won WTA Most Impressive Newcomer award. **1991 HIGHLIGHTS – SINGLES: Australian Open** 3r (d. Wasserman 7–6 6–4, Durie 6–3 6–2, lost Sabatini [seed 4] 6–1 6–1), **French Open** 1r (lost Jagerman 6–2 6–4), **Wimbledon** 3r (d. Loosemore 6–4 7–5, Cunningham 6–1 6–3, lost Sabatini [seed 2] 6–1 6–3), **US Open** 2r (d. Porwik 6–3 6–2, lost Maleeva Fragnière [seed 10] 7–5 6–2); **r/u** Auckland (d. Toleafoa 6–0 6–2, A. Minter 6–2 7–5, Savchenko 6–4 6–1, Tessi 6–0 6–4, lost Sviglerova 6–2 0–6 6–1), **r/u** Wellington (d. Savchenko 6–4 3–6 6–4, A. Minter 6–4 6–1, Field 7–6 7–5, Godridge 6–4 7–6, lost Meskhi 3–6 7–6 6–2).

CYRIL SUK (Czechoslovakia)
Born Prague, 29 January 1967, and lives there; RH; 5ft 11in. 158lb; final 1991 ATP ranking 532 singles, 18 (75) doubles; 1991 prize money $159,226.
Brother of Helena Sukova; son of the 1962 Wimbledon finalist, the late Vera Sukova, and Cyril Suk, former President of Czech Tennis Federation. **1985:** No. 1 in Jun doubles rankings with Korda. **1988:** (184). **1989:** (231) Won St Vincent doubles with Cihak. **1990:** (288). **1991:** Reached 6 doubles f, winning Prague with Flegl and Toulouse and Lyon with Nijssen, with whom he qualified for ATP Doubles Champ. In mixed doubles won French Open with his sister, Helena. **1991 HIGHLIGHTS – DOUBLES:** (with Nijssen unless stated) **won** Toulouse (d. Bates/Curren 4–6 6–3 7–6), [Flegl] **won** Prague (d. Pimek/Vacek 6–4 6–2), **won** Lyon (d. Devries/MacPherson 7–6 6–3); **r/u** Milan (lost Camporese/Ivanisevic 6–4 7–6), **r/u** Estoril (lost Haarhuis/Koevermans 6–3 6–3), **r/u** Stockholm (lost Fitzgerald/Jarryd 7–5 6–2). **MIXED DOUBLES:** (with Sukova) **won French Open** (d. Haarhuis/Vis 3–6 6–4 6–1). **CAREER HIGHLIGHTS – MIXED DOUBLES:** (with Sukova) **French Open – won 1991.**

HELENA SUKOVA (Czechoslovakia)
Born Prague, 23 February 1965, and lives there; RH; 6ft 2in; 150lb; final 1991 WTA ranking 17 singles, 8 (1) doubles; 1991 prize money $396,824.
Coached by Jaramir Jirik. Daughter of 1962 Wimbledon finalist, the late Vera Sukova, and Cyril Suk, former President of Czech Tennis Federation. Brother also named Cyril. **1981:** (74) Beat Anne Smith and Barbara Potter to reach last 16 Australian Open at age 16. **1982:** (24) Qf Swiss Open, r/u US CC and Avon Futures Champs. **1983:** (17) Sf Sydney. **1984:** (7) R/u Australian Open (d. Navratilova) and won Brisbane. **1985:** (9) R/u VS Champ and Eastbourne. Qf Australian Open. Voted WTA Most Improved Player. **1986:** (5) Won Canadian Open and Hilversum and r/u US Open (d. Evert Lloyd first time in 15 career meetings). **1987:** (7) Sf US Open, qf Wimbledon, won Eastbourne (d. Evert and Navratilova back-to-back) and New Jersey in singles and Wimbledon doubles with Kohde-Kilsch. Qualified for VS Champs in singles and doubles. **1988:** (8) In singles qf Australian Open, French Open and Wimbledon; r/u Sydney, Pan Pacific Open and Berlin. In doubles r/u

French Open with Kohde-Kilsch, won Olympic silver medal with Novotna, took 4 titles and reached 7 other f with various partners. Qualified for VS Champs in singles and doubles, reaching sf in both and beating Navratilova in qf singles. *1989:* (8) At Brisbane she won her 1st title for 18 months, following with r/u Australian Open (d. Navratilova qf), qf US Open and 5 sf to qualify for VS Champs, where she reached qf. Tore cartilage in right knee at Eastbourne, which kept her out for 2 months, although she played Wimbledon with knee taped and won doubles there with Novotna. Appeared in 7 other doubles f, winning 4. *1990:* (14) Reached sf Australian Open, where she extended Graf to 3s, and was r/u Indian Wells, Birmingham and Brighton. Out for most of CC season undergoing treatment for Achilles' tendon problems, missing French Open singles and playing doubles there only at the request of her partner Novotna, with whom she won 8 of her 10 titles. They captured Australian Open, French Open and Wimbledon, but missed a GS in doubles when they lost US Open f to G. Fernandez/Navratilova. Qualified for VS Champs in both singles and doubles, losing 1r singles to K. Maleeva and 1r doubles to Medvedeva/Meskhi. *1991:* In singles won Brisbane and reached sf VS Chicago (d. Capriati) and Filderstadt (d. M. J. Fernandez), but failed to pass 3r in GS. Qualified for VS Champs in singles and doubles (with Sanchez-Vicario) but was forced to retire 3s v M. J. Fernandez 1r. In women's doubles won 3 titles from 6 f with 4 different partners, and in mixed doubles won French Open with her brother, Cyril. *1991 HIGHLIGHTS – SINGLES: Australian Open* 3r, seed 9 (d. Cordwell 6–2 6–1, Cueto 6–2 7–5, lost Tanvier 4–6 6–1 6–4), *French Open* 2r, seed 12 (d. Sviglerova 6–0 6–1, lost Kelesi 4–6 7–6 6–0), *Wimbledon* 1r, seed 11 (lost G. Fernandez 4–6 6–1 6–4), *US Open* 3r, seed 15 (d. Emmons 6–0 4–6 6–2, de Lone 6–1 6–3, lost Durie 6–4 2–6 6–1); *won* Brisbane (d. Jaggard 6–2 6–3, Halard 6–4 6–4, Tessi 6–2 6–1, Kijimuta 6–1 6–1); *sf* VS Chicago (d. Adams 6–4 6–2, Rinaldi 6–2 6–2, Capriati 6–4 6–4, lost Navratilova 6–3 6–2), *sf* Filderstadt (d. Probst 7–6 7–6, Frazier 6–7 7–5 6–3, M. J. Fernandez 5–7 6–3 6–3, lost Huber 6–3 7–6). *1991 HIGHLIGHTS – DOUBLES:* (with Sanchez-Vicario unless stated) *won* Sydney (d. G. Fernandez/Novotna 6–1 6–4), [G. Fernandez] *won* Tarpon Springs (d. Savchenko/Zvereva 4–6 6–4 7–6), *won* Amelia Island (d. Paz/Zvereva 4–6 6–2 6–2); [Fendick] *r/u* Brisbane (lost G. Fernandez/Novotna 6–3 6–1), *r/u* Hamburg (lost Novotna/Savchenko 7–5 6–1), [Kohde-Kilsch] *r/u* Toronto (lost Savchenko/Zvereva 1–6 7–5 6–2). *MIXED DOUBLES:* (with Suk) *won French Open* (d. Haarhuis/Vis 3–6 6–4 6–1). *CAREER HIGHLIGHTS – SINGLES: Australian Open – r/u 1984* (d. Kohde-Kilsch, Shriver, Navratilova 1–6 6–3 7–5, lost Evert Lloyd 6–7 6–1 6–3), *r/u 1989* (d. Richardson, Ludloff, O'Neil, Tanvier 7–5 6–4, Navratilova 6–2 3–6 9–7, Cordwell 7–6 4–6 6–2, lost Graf 6–4 6–4), *sf 1990* (d. Morton, Medvedeva, Loosemore 6–3 4–6 6–3, Date 6–4 6–3, K. Maleeva 6–4 6–3, lost Graf 6–3 3–6 6–4); *US Open – r/u 1986* (d. Drescher, Gomer, Bonder, Garrison 6–4 2–6 6–4, Turnbull 6–4 6–0, Evert Lloyd 6–2 6–4, lost Navratilova 6–3 6–2), *sf 1987* (d. Hobbs, Kohde-Kilsch 6–1 6–3, lost Navratilova 6–2 6–2), *qf 1984* (d. K. Jordan, lost Navratilova), *qf 1989* (d. Langrova, Magers 6–2 6–7 6–2, A. Minter 1–6 6–2 6–1, Savchenko 4–6 6–1 6–2, lost Graf 6–1 6–1); *VS Champs – r/u 1985–86* (lost Navratilova 6–3 7–5 6–4), *sf 1986* (lost Graf 7–6 3–6 6–1); *Wimbledon – qf 1986* (d. Parnell, Betzner, A. Minter, R. White 6–3 6–0, lost Evert Lloyd 7–6 4–6 6–4). *CAREER HIGHLIGHTS – DOUBLES:* (with Kohde-Kilsch unless stated) *Australian Open* – [Novotna] *won 1990* (d. Fendick/M. J. Fernandez 7–6 7–6), *r/u 1984* (lost Navratilova/Shriver 6–3 6–4), *r/u 1985* (lost Navratilova/Shriver 6–3 6–4); *French Open* – [Novotna] *won 1990* (d. Savchenko/Zvereva 6–4 7–5), *r/u 1985* (lost Navratilova/Shriver 4–6 6–2), *r/u 1988* (lost Navratilova/Shriver 6–2 7–5); *Wimbledon – won 1987* (d. Nagelsen/Smylie 7–5 7–5), [Novotna] *won 1989* (d. Savchenko/Zvereva, 6–1 6–2), [Novotna] *won 1990* (d. K. Jordan/Smylie 6–2 7–6); *US Open – won 1985* (d. Navratilova/Shriver 6–7 6–2 6–3); *LIPC* – [Novotna] *won 1990* (d. G. Fernandez/McNeil 7–6 6–4), [Novotna] *won 1990* (d. Nagelsen/R. White 6–4 6–3); *VS Champs – r/u 1984–85* (lost Navratilova/Shriver 6–1 6–4 7–6), *r/u 1985–86* (lost Mandlikova/Turnbull 6–4 6–7 6–3), *r/u 1986* (lost Navratilova/Shriver 7–6 6–3), *r/u 1987* (lost Navratilova/Shriver 6–1 6–1); *Olympics* – [Novotna] *silver medal 1988* (lost Shriver/Garrison 4–6 6–2 10–8). *MIXED DOUBLES:* (with Suk) *French Open – won 1991.*

JONAS SVENSSON (Sweden)
Born Gothenburg, 21 October 1966; lives Kungsbaka; RH; 6ft 2in; 168lb; final 1991 ATP ranking 29; 1991 prize money $347,659.
Coach Tim Klein, psychologist Lars Ryberg. Fiancée Anne Galopp. *1978:* Won Swedish Nat. 12s outdoor and indoor. *1983:* (445) Sf Wimbledon Jun. *1984:* (741). *1985:* (122) Won Swiss Satellite and became full-time pro. *1986:* (21) Clearly the most improved player in the top 25, winning Cologne, narrowly losing to Noah in f Wembley, r/u Stuttgart and

beating Jarryd, Zivojinovic and Mecir. *1987:* (30) Shortly after starting to work with psychologist Lars Ryberg, he reached last 16 US Open, won 1st GP title in Vienna and reached f Stockholm and Young Masters. *1988:* (22) Last 16 Australian Open, then reached his 1st GS sf in Paris, upsetting Lendl in ss, but was hampered in his performance at Wimbledon by a mystery virus infection. Won Lorraine and r/u Munich and Wembley. *1989:* (41) Upset Becker *en route* to qf Australian Open and reached sf Lyon. *1990:* (11) Enjoyed his best year to date, in which he reached last 16 Australian Open, then swept to sf French Open, unseeded on both occasions. Won Toulouse; r/u Rotterdam; sf Stuttgart, Munich and Paris Open, where he d. Lendl and E. Sanchez back-to-back; played GS Cup but lost Gilbert 1r. *1991:* Won Copenhagen, r/u Stuttgart, sf Paris Open and upset Cherkasov at US Open. *1991 HIGHLIGHTS – SINGLES: Australian Open* 3r, seed 8 (d. Champion 6–3 6–4 6–1, Clavet 6–2 7–5 3–6 6–1, lost Woodbridge 7–5 6–2 6–1), *US Open* 2r (d. Cherkasov [seed 13] 7–6 6–2 6–2, lost Hlasek 6–4 7–5 6–7 6–3); *won* Copenhagen (d. Strelba 7–6 6–2, Fetterlein 6–3 2–6 6–2, Bergstrom 6–4 7–5, Hlasek 6–2 1–6 6–3, Jarryd 6–7 6–2 6–2); *r/u* Stuttgart Eurocard (d. Fromberg 6–7 6–1 6–0, Baur 6–4 6–2, Novacek 7–6 6–2, Forget 2–6 7–6 6–2, lost Edberg 6–2 3–6 7–5 6–2); *sf* Paris Open (d. Krajicek 6–3 6–2, Prpic 6–2 6–2, Becker w.o., Novacek 6–4 6–2, lost Forget 7–5 6–4). *CAREER HIGHLIGHTS – SINGLES: French Open – sf 1988* (d. Miniussi, Champion, Nystrom 6–7 6–4 4–6 6–3 6–2, K. Carlsson 5–7 7–6 1–6 6–4 6–2, Lendl 7–6 7–5 6–2, lost Leconte 7–6 6–2 6–3), *sf 1990* (d. Potier, Bruguera 2–6 2–6 6–4 6–4 6–0, Azar 5–7 6–4 6–1 7–6, Perez-Roldan 2–6 6–4 6–2 6–2, Leconte 3–6 7–5 6–3 6–4, lost Agassi 6–1 6–4 3–6 6–).

EVA SVIGLEROVA (Czechoslovakia)
Born Plzen, 13 July 1971 and lives there; RH; 2HB; 5ft 7in; 134lb; final 1991 WTA ranking 40; 1991 prize money $105,339.
Coached by Jiri Hrdina. *1988:* (254). *1989:* (135) Sf Barcelona and r/u French Open Jun (lost Capriati 6–4 6–0) in singles. In Jun doubles with Strnadova won Australian Open and r/u Wimbledon. *1990:* (95) Reached sf Tokyo Suntory and broke into the top 100 in Sept. *1991:* Won her 1st primary circuit title at Auckland and reached qf Wellington, San Antonio, Tokyo Suntory and Kitzbuhel. *1991 HIGHLIGHTS – SINGLES: Australian Open* 1r (lost A. Smith 6–3 6–4), *French Open* 1r (lost Sukova [seed 12] 6–0 6–1), *Wimbledon* 1r (lost Probst 7–6 7–5), *US Open* 3r (d. Caverzasio 6–4 6–1, Lindqvist 6–2 6–2, lost Graf [seed 1] 6–4 7–5); *won* Auckland (d. Bartos 6–1 6–2, Rittner 3–6 6–4 6–4, Hack 6–7 7–5 6–1, Paz 6–2 6–3, Strnadova 6–2 0–6 6–1). *1991 HIGHLIGHTS – DOUBLES:* (with Fulco) *won* Sao Paulo (d. Pierce/Spadea 7–5 6–4).

NATHALIE TAUZIAT (France)
Born Bangui, Africa, 17 October 1967; lives St Tropez; RH; 5ft 5in; 120lb; final 1991 WTA ranking 13; 1991 prize money $280,304.
Coached by Regis DeCamaret. *1985:* (112) Reached 3r French Open, upsetting 16th seed Casale, and played Fed Cup. *1986:* (67) Qf Hilversum. *1987:* (25) Last 16 French Open, sf Strasbourg, San Diego and Zurich and d. Rinaldi to reach qf LIPC. *1988:* (27) Last 16 French Open, r/u Nice and upset Zvereva and K. Maleeva *en route* to f Mahwah. In doubles with Demongeot upset Kohde-Kilsch/Sukova to win both Berlin and Zurich and qualified for VS Champs. *1989:* (25) Sf Italian Open (d. Manuela Maleeva) and San Diego. *1990:* (18) In GS reached last 16 French Open, Wimbledon and US Open. Won her 1st primary circuit title at Bayonne; r/u Wichita and reached sf LIPC, Birmingham and Canadian Open (d. Maleeva Fragnière). Qualified for VS Champs, where she lost 1r to M. J. Fernandez. *1991:* Appeared in her 1st GS qf at French Open and last 16 Wimbledon. In other tourns she scored some major upsets in reaching f Zurich (d. Sabatini), sf VS Palm Springs, VS Florida (d. M. J. Fernandez), Barcelona (d. Navratilova), San Diego and Bayonne and was close to beating Capriati at VS Champs, eventually losing their 1r match in 3s tb. Reached 3 doubles f, winning Bayonne with Tarabini. *1991 HIGHLIGHTS – SINGLES: French Open* qf, seed 13 (d. Etchemendy 6–3 6–1, Guerree 6–2 6–1, Jagerman 6–4 6–0, Sawamatsu 7–5 2–6 12–10, lost Graf [seed 2] 6–3 6–2), *Wimbledon* last 16, seed 12 (d. Rajchrtova 6–4 7–5, Kijimuta 3–6 6–2 6–2, L. Ferrando 6–1 6–1, lost Sabatini [seed 2] 7–6 6–3), *US Open* 1r, seed 14 (lost Labat 7–5 6–4); *r/u* Zurich (d. Medvedeva 6–2 6–3, Harvey-Wild 6–1 6–0, Sabatini 7–6 6–3, Maleeva Fragnière 7–6 7–6, lost Graf 6–4 6–3); *sf* VS Palm Springs (d. Date 6–2 6–2, Kschwendt 6–3 6–3, K. Maleeva 7–6 7–6, lost Navratilova 6–2 7–6), *sf* VS Florida (d. Louie Harper 6–0 6–3, Hy 6–2 6–4, M. J. Fernandez 6–1 7–5, lost Graf 6–1 6–2), *sf* Barcelona (d. Niox-Chateau 6–4 6–2, Dechaume 6–3 6–3, Navratilova 6–1 6–4, lost Martinez 6–1 4–6 6–1), *sf* San Diego (d. Rinaldi 6–3 4–6 6–4, May 6–3 6–4, Maleeva Fragnière 6–3 6–3, lost Seles 6–1 6–2), *sf* Bayonne (d. Zugasti 6–4 4–6 7–6, Habsudova

6–4 6–3, Sviglerova 6–4 6–1, lost Meskhi 6–2 7–5). *1991 HIGHLIGHTS – DOUBLES:* [Tarabini] *won* Bayonne (d. McQuillan/Tanvier 6–3 30–40 ret'd); [Wiesner] *r/u* Barcelona (lost Navratilova/Sanchez-Vicario 6–1 6–3), [G. Fernandez] *r/u* San Diego (lost Hetherington/Rinaldi 6–4 3–6 6–2). *CAREER HIGHLIGHTS – SINGLES: French Open – qf 1991.*

ANDREA TEMESVARI (Hungary)
Born Budapest, 26 April 1966; lives there and Marbella, Spain; RH; 2HB; 5ft 11in; 129lb; final 1991 WTA ranking 157; 1991 prize money $59,950.
Coached by her father, Otto. Married to rock musician and composer Andras Trunkos (May 1988). *1980:* Won European 18s and Orange Bowl 14s. *1981:* (146). *1982:* (33) Voted WTA Most Impressive Newcomer after winning Pennsylvania and reaching f Swiss Open. *1983:* (11) Won Italian Open, US CC and Hittfield. *1984:* (14) Sf US CC, Brighton and Zurich. *1985:* (16) Won 1st tourn for 2 years at US CC. *1986:* (44) Disappointed in singles, reaching just 2 qf, but in doubles won French Open with Navratilova. *1987:* (—) Ranked 1 in her country for 5th straight year. *1988:* (—) Out of action for 20 months in 1987 and 1988 with shoulder and ankle injuries, undergoing 3 operations. *1989:* (43) Qf Berlin then at Mahwah reached 1st f for 4 years. Won WTA Comeback Player of the Year Award. *1990:* (116) Reached no qf all year. *1991:* In partnership with Nijssen, won longest set (56 games) and longest match in games (77) ever recorded in Wimbledon mixed doubles when they lost to Schapers/Schultz (6–3 5–7 29–27). *1991 HIGHLIGHTS – SINGLES: French Open* 2r (d. Miyagi 6–1 6–3, lost Capriati [seed 10] 6–2 6–1), *Wimbledon* 1r (lost Savchenko 6–2 6–7 8–6), *US Open* 1r (lost Graf [seed 1] 6–1 6–2). *CAREER HIGHLIGHTS – DOUBLES:* (with Navratilova) *French Open – won 1986* (d. Graf/Sabatini 6–1 6–2).

CRISTINA TESSI (Argentina)
Born Buenos Aires, 20 July 1972, and lives there; RH; 5ft 5in; 115lb; final 1991 WTA ranking 94; 1991 prize money $52,351.
Coached by her brother, Richardo. *1988:* (286) No. 1 in ITF Jun singles rankings and joined her country's Fed Cup team. *1989:* (197). *1990:* (126) Qf Guaruja and won Darmstadt Challenger. *1991:* Reached her 1st main tour sf at Auckland and appeared in qf Sao Paulo, Brisbane and Palermo. *1991 HIGHLIGHTS – SINGLES: Australian Open* 1r (lost Habsudova 6–2 7–6, *French Open* 2r (d. C. Wood 6–4 6–1, lost Fulco 6–2 6–2), *Wimbledon* 1r (lost Zvereva [seed 13] 7–6 6–4), *US Open* 1r (lost Stafford 6–3 6–3); *sf* Auckland (d. Porwik 6–1 7–6, Cammy McGregor 6–4 5–7 6–4, Faber 6–4 7–6, lost Strnadova 6–0 6–4).

PETRA THOREN (Finland)
Born Tammisaari, 8 August 1969; lives Helsinki; RH; 2HB; 5ft 8in; 132lb; final 1991 WTA ranking 99; 1991 prize money $51,379.
Coached by Pawel Bojarski. *1987:* (410). *1988:* (318). *1989:* (176) Won 2 titles on the British satellite circuits. *1990:* (170) Again made her mark on the satellite circuits and reached qf Athens on the main tour. *1991:* Upset Savchenko at French Open and reached qf Taranto. *1991 HIGHLIGHTS – SINGLES: Australian Open* 1r (lost Paulus 6–3 6–3), *French Open* 3r (d. Javer 6–2 6–2, Savchenko 6–3 3–6 7–5, lost M. J. Fernandez 6–4 6–3), *US Open* 1r (lost Fendick 6–1 6–4).

MARIAN VAJDA (Czechoslovakia)
Born Povazska, 24 March 1965; lives Bratislava; RH; 5ft 8in; 150lb; final 1991 ATP ranking 98; 1991 prize money $136,080.
Coached by Vladimir Zednik. Wife Ingrid (married 1988); daughter Nicole (born Jan. 1989). *1985:* (52) A former Czech Nat Jun Champ, he came from nowhere to reach sf Kitzbuhel and qf Geneva. *1986:* (88) Qf Nice, Hilversum, Itaparica. *1987:* (46) After qualifying at Munich he upset Kriek and Nystrom in ss *en route* to f, following in Aug. with 1st GP title at Prague. *1988:* (72) Won Geneva (d. Carlsson in f) and reached qf Kitzbuhel. *1989:* (123) Reached f Bari and qf Kitzbuhel but slipped out of the top 100 for 1st time since 1984. *1990:* (83) Qf Palermo, then in Oct. upset Muster *en route* to sf Athens. *1991:* Sf Auckland (d. Chesnokov), Estoril and Palermo. *1991 HIGHLIGHTS – SINGLES: Australian Open* 2r (d. Garrow 2–6 6–4 7–5 6–3, lost Becker [seed 2] 6–4 6–1 6–3), *French Open* 3r (d. Kroon 3 6 6 3 6–1 6–3, Leconte 3–6 6–4 7–6 6–4, lost Davin 6–2 2–6 6–4 3–6 6–4), *Wimbledon* 1r (lost Jonsson 7–5 6–3 7–5), *US Open* 1r (lost Saceanu 2–6 7–6 6–4 6–4); *sf* Auckland (d. Weiss 6–1 6–3, Chesnokov 6–1 5–7 7–5, Kuhnen 4–6 6–3 6–4, lost Novacek 6–4 4–6 6–0), *sf* Estoril (d. Aguilera 7–5 3–6 6–2, Marques 4–6 7–5 6–3, Clavet 6–2 0–6 6–3, lost Novacek 7–5 6–2), *sf* Palermo (d. Filippini 6–3 2–6 6–2, Perez-Roldan 6–2 6–4, Nargiso 2–6 7–6 6–3, lost E. Sanchez 6–1 6–2).

CHRISTO VAN RENSBURG (South Africa)
Born Uitenhage, 23 October 1962; lives Indian Wells, Cal.; RH; 6ft 1in; 160lb; final 1991 ATP ranking 84 singles, 105 doubles; 1991 prize money $137,507.
Coached by Peter Fishbach. No relation to Dinky. *1983:* (291) Won South African Jun. *1984:* (120) Formed partnership with Annacone in Dec. *1985:* (252) Moved into top 10 in doubles after winning 4 GP titles with Annacone, including first GS success at Australian Open. *1986:* (69) Reached sf Wimbledon doubles with Annacone but his appearance in last 16 singles there was more surprising. *1987:* (29) Won Orlando over Mayotte and Connors in 1st GP f. *1988:* (35) R/u Johannesburg, sf Sydney, Philadelphia and Tel Aviv. *1989:* (27) Won Johannesburg, r/u Queen's and reached last 16 both Australian Open and Wimbledon. Won 2 doubles titles with Annacone and qualified for Masters. *1990:* (61) R/u Orlando; qf Queen's, Manchester and San Francisco; reached last 16 US Open, unseeded, and won 2 doubles titles. *1991:* R/u Tel Aviv and on the Challenger circuit won Newcastle and Jerusalem. *1991 HIGHLIGHTS – SINGLES: Australian Open* 2r (d. Kratzmann 6–3 6–1 7–5, lost Cash 7–6 6–4 6–4), *Wimbledon* 3r (d. Witsken 6–1 7–6 4–6 6–4, Ferreira 6–4 7–5 6–2, lost Edberg [seed 1] 6–1 6–3 6–2), *US Open* 1r (lost Sampras [seed 6] 6–0 6–3 6–2); *won* Newcastle Challenger (d. Schapers 6–4 6–0), *won* Jerusalem Challenger (d. Marsh 2–6 6–2 6–3); *r/u* Tel Aviv (d. Mansdorf 6–3 6–2, Holm 7–6 6–1, Delaitre 6–3 6–3, Bloom 6–3 2–6 6–3, lost Lavalle 6–2 3–6 6–3). *1991 HIGHLIGHTS – DOUBLES:* (with Kruger) *r/u* Singapore (lost Connell/Michibata 6–4 5–7 7–6). *CAREER HIGHLIGHTS – DOUBLES:* (with Annacone) *Australian Open – won 1985* (d. Edmondson/Warwick 3–6 7–6 6–4 6–4); *LIPC – won 1987* (d. Flach/Seguso 6–2 6–4 6–4).

CAROLINE VIS (Netherlands)
Born Vlaardingen, 4 March 1970, and lives there; RH; 5ft 11in; 158lb; final 1991 WTA ranking 417; 1991 prize money $35,333.
Coached by Don Frits. *1989:* (253). *1990:* (209) Upset Savchenko at VS Nashville. *1991:* R/u French Open mixed doubles with Haarhuis. *1991 HIGHLIGHTS – DOUBLES:* (with Basuki) *r/u* VS Nashville (lost Collins/E. Reinach 5–7 6–4 7–6). *1991 HIGHLIGHTS – MIXED DOUBLES:* (with Haarhuis) *r/u French Open* (lost Suk/Sukova 3–6 6–4 6–1).

ALEXANDER VOLKOV (USSR)
Born Kaliningrad, 3 March 1967, and lives there; LH; 6ft 2in; 175lb; final 1991 ATP ranking 25; 1991 prize money $404,046.
In separate childhood accidents he broke each wrist. Originally played right-handed, then with either hand, and from 1985, when he broke right wrist, he has played left-handed. *1986:* (529) R/u Nat Champs. *1987:* (104) Upset Gilbert *en route* to last 16 Wimbledon after qualifying, surprised Jaite at Paris Open and broke into top 100 Nov. *1988:* (79) Qf Sydney and won Munich Challenger. *1989:* (50) Sf Adelaide and Munich, then broke into top 50 after reaching 1st GP f at Milan. *1990:* (24) R/u Rosmalen and Berlin; sf Vienna and Stockholm (d. E. Sanchez). In GS reached last 16 Wimbledon, unseeded, and upset top seed Edberg 1r US Open. *1991:* Won his 1st GP title at Milan, breaking into the top 20, and at Wimbledon made an unexpected appearance in last 16, where he took eventual champion Stich to 5s. Reached sf Bastad, Basel, Toulouse and Moscow. *1991 HIGHLIGHTS – SINGLES: Australian Open* 1r (lost Korda 6–1 1–6 1–6 6–4 7–5), *French Open* 1r (lost Lundgren 6–3 7–6 6–7 7–5), *Wimbledon* last 16, unseeded (d. Wuyts 6–1 6–2 6–2, Jarryd 6–2 3–6 6–4 8–6, Laurendeau 6–1 6–2 6–1, lost Stich [seed 6] 4–6 6–3 7–5 1–6 7–5), *US Open* 2r (d. Herrera 7–6 6–3 3–6 6–4, lost Becker [seed 1] 6–0 7–6 6–1); *won* Milan (d. Pioline 6–4 6–7 6–4, Jelen 6–3 3–6 7–6, Cash 6–4 6–4, Hlasek 6–4 6–3, Caratti 6–1 7–5); *sf* Bastad (d. Paloheimo 6–4 6–4, Pernfors 6–4 4–6 6–4, Jonsson 6–2 6–1, lost Mancini 0–6 6–3 6–2), *sf* Basel (d. Raoux 6–3 6–4, Carbonell 6–3 6–4, Novacek 6–1 6–7 6–3, lost Hlasek 7–6 6–7 7–6), *sf* Toulouse (d. Kulti 6–3 6–2 6–3, Nijssen 7–5 4–6 6–4, Pioline 5–7 7–6 6–2, lost Mansdorf 7–5 5–7 6–1), *sf* Moscow (d. Nargiso 6–3 3–6 6–3, Poliakov 7–5 6–3, Grabb 7–6 4–6 6–3, lost Hlasek 6–4 6–2). *1991 HIGHLIGHTS – DOUBLES:* (with Cherkasov) *r/u* Moscow (lost Jelen/Steeb 6–4 7–6).

LAURIE WARDER (Australia)
Born Sydney, 23 October 1962, and lives there; RH; 6ft; 165lb; final 1991 ATP ranking 12 (83) doubles; 1991 prize money $186,346.
1985: (339). *1986:* (281). *1987:* (311) A formidable doubles player he was r/u Australian Open with Doohan and reached 5 other f, winning Indianapolis with Willenborg. *1988:* (379) Won Hamburg with Cahill and Bristol with Doohan. *1989:* (1072) Reached 3 doubles f, winning Wellington with Doohan. *1990:* (—). *1991:* Reached 5 doubles f, winning Monte Carlo and Bologna with Jensen, with whom he qualifiedf for ATP Doubles Champ. *1991*

HIGHLIGHTS – DOUBLES: (with Jensen unless stated) ***won*** Monte Carlo (d. Haarhuis/ Koevermans 5–7 7–6 6–4), ***won*** Bologna (d. Mattar/Oncins 6–4 7–6); [Fitzgerald] ***r/u*** Memphis (lost Riglewski/Stich 7–5 6–3), ***r/u*** Italian Open (lost Camporese/Ivanisevic 6–2 6–3), ***r/u*** Sydney Indoor (lost Grabb/Reneberg 6–4 6–4).

MALIVAI WASHINGTON (USA)
Born Glen Cove, NY, 20 June 1969; lives Swartz Creek, Mich.; RH; 5ft 11in; 175lb; final 1991 ATP ranking 49; 1991 prize money $208,210.
Coached by his father, William. ***1987:*** R/u Easter Bowl. ***1988:*** (329) All-American at Univ. of Michigan. ***1989:*** (199) Won Seattle Challenger. ***1990:*** (93) Reached sf Orlando after qualifying and appeared at same stage US CC. Upset Lendl in ss 1r New Haven in Aug. ***1991:*** Sf Chicago, Orlando (d. B. Gilbert), US CC (d. Wheaton) and Queen's. In GS he extended Forget to 7–5 5s at French Open and handed the same treatment to Lendl at Wimbledon. ***1991 HIGHLIGHTS – SINGLES: Australian Open*** 1r (lost Stich 4–6 5–7 7–6 6–1 6–4), French Open 1r (lost Forget [seed 7] 7–5 2–6 7–5 1–6 7–5), ***Wimbledon*** 2r (d. Koevermans 6–3 6–2 6–1, lost Lendl [seed 3] 4–6 2–6 6–4 6–4 7–5), ***US Open*** 3r (d. Oncins 6–2 6–2 6–1, Camporese 4–6 6–1 6–1 6–4, lost Stich [seed 3] 5–7 7–5 6–2 4–6 6–3); ***sf*** Chicago (d. Vajda 6–1 6–1, Korda 6–4 7–6, Riglewski 4–6 6–3 6–0, lost J. McEnroe 7–6 6–7 6–4), ***sf*** Orlando (d. Herrera 4–6 7–5 6–4, Pereira 6–1 6–3, B. Gilbert 6–2 6–7 6–2, lost Agassi 6–4 7–6), ***sf*** US CC (d. Leach 6–1 7–6, Saceanu 3 6–4, Wheaton 6–7 6–1 6–2, lost Yzaga 7–5 6–2), ***sf*** Queen's (d. S. Davis 7–6 6–4, Bates 7–5 6–1, Keil 6–7 6–3 6–2, Fitzgerald 7–5 6–4, lost Edberg 6–4 6–2).

MARIANNE WERDEL (USA)
Born Los Angeles, Cal., 17 October 1967; lives Bakersfield, Cal.; RH; 2HB; 5ft 10in; 144lb; final 1991 WTA ranking 44; 1991 prize money $100,551.
Coached by Tommy Tucker. ***1983:*** (221) R/u US Open Jun. ***1985:*** (122) Won USTA Key Biscayne and Fayetteville. ***1986:*** (32) Sf Puerto Rico, played Jun Fed Cup and was All-American at Stanford. ***1987:*** (59) Qf VS New Orleans and Tokyo and upset Shriver 1r VS Washington. ***1988:*** (103) After reaching sf Japan Open was sidelined for 2 months recovering from partially herniated disc. ***1989:*** (95) R/u Schenectady. ***1990:*** (48) Uspet Savchenko and Paz *en route* to f Schenectady. ***1991:*** Reached sf Pattaya City and Schenectady. ***1991 HIGHLIGHTS – SINGLES: French Open*** 1r (lost Sabatini [seed 3] 6–1 6–1), ***Wimbledon*** 3r (d. Graham 6–3 6–2, Halard 6–2 6–4, lost Frazier [seed 15] 6–2 6–1), ***US Open*** 1r (lost Louie Harper 6–4 5–7 6–4); ***sf*** Pattaya City (d. Driehuis 6–1 6–2, Faull 6–4 6–0, Miyauchi 7–6 6–0, lost Sawamatsu 6–1 6–3), ***sf*** Schenectady (d. Paz 4–6 6–2 7–6, Paradis Mangon 6–2 4–6 7–5, Sawamatsu 6–3 6–2, lost Dechaume 6–1 6–3).

DAVID WHEATON (USA)
Born Minneapolis, Minn., 2 June 1969; lives Lake Minnetonka, Minn.; RH; 6ft 4in; 185lb; final 1991 ATP ranking 17; 1991 prize money $2,479,239.
Coached by Jerry Noyce. Spent time at Nick Bollettieri Tennis Academy. Travels with brother John, a lawyer. ***1985–87:*** Member of US Jun D Cup squad. ***1986:*** A freshman at Stanford, was r/u Nat Jun Champs. ***1987:*** (345) Extended Lendl to 3s at Washington and won US Open Jun singles over Cherkasov and US Nat 18s clay court over Courier. ***1988:*** (441). Played No. 1 singles and doubles for Stanford's NCAA winning team. ***1989:*** (66) Upset Agassi *en route* to sf Stratton Mountain and won Brasilia Challenger. ***1990:*** (27) Reached qf Australian Open and US Open and last 16 Wimbledon (lost Gilbert 13–11 5s), all unseeded, and with Annacone reached f doubles at US Open. Out of action 10 weeks early in year with stress fracture of leg, returning in May to win 1st tour title at US CC and broke into top 50. Reached sf inaugural GS Cup. ***1991:*** Following 4 1r losses at beginning of the year, he enjoyed his best season yet, upsetting Agassi and Edberg *en route* to f LIPC, Lendl and Agassi *en route* to sf Wimbledon, unseeded. He was also r/u Queen's and sf Indianapolis and in doubles with P. McEnroe he reached f Australian Open. Ended year with first Compaq Grand Slam Cup title, winning $2 million. ***1990 HIGHLIGHTS – SINGLES: Australian Open*** 1r (lost Gilbert [seed 7] 6–4 4–6 6–3 7–6), ***French Open*** 1r (lost Skoff 6–2 6–7 3–6 6–2 6–4), ***Wimbledon*** sf, unseeded (d. Korda 7–6 6–7 6–4 6–2, Pioline 6–4 6–7 6–3 6–3, Lendl [seed 3] 6–3 3–6 7–6 6–3, Gunnarsson 6–4 6–3 6–1, Agassi [seed 5] 6–2 0–6 3–6 7–6 6–2, lost Becker [seed 2] 6–4 7–6 7–5), ***US Open*** last 16, seed 11 (d. Fromberg 6–0 4–6 7–6 6–3, Skoff 6–1 6–2 6–2, Martin 7–6 4–6 6–3 6–4, lost Sampras [seed 6] 3–6 6–2 6–2 6–4); ***won*** Compaq Grand Slam Cup (d. Stich in s/f 7–6 7–6 7–6, Chang 7–5 6–2 6–4); ***r/u*** LIPC (d. Grabb 6–3 3–6 6–1, Perez-Roldan 4–4 ret'd, Curren 0–6 7–6 7–5, Agassi 6–0 7–5, Caratti 6–7 6–2 6–0, Edberg 6–3 6–4, lost Courier 4–6 6–3 6–4), ***r/u*** Queen's (d. Black 6–1 3–6 6–3, Kuhnen 6–4 7–5, Chang 6–3 6–3, Jarryd 6–3 6–4, lost

Edberg 6–2 6–3); *sf* Indianapolis (d. Krickstein 6–4 7–5, Bryan 6–3 7–5, Santoro 6–1 6–4, lost Becker 7–6 6–4). *1991 HIGHLIGHTS – DOUBLES:* [P. McEnroe] *r/u Australian Open* (lost S. Davis/Pate 6–7 7–6 6–3 7–5); [Reneberg] *r/u* Umag (lost Bloom/J. Sanchez 7–6 2–6 6–1). *CAREER HIGHLIGHTS – SINGLES: Compaq Grand Slam Cup – won 1991; LIPC – r/u 1991; Wimbledon – sf 1991; Australian Open – qf 1990,* unseeded (d. Ivanisevic, Larsson, Woodforde, Krickstein 7 6 6 4 6–3, lost Edberg 7–5 7–6 3 6 6–2); *US Open – qf 1990,* unseeded (d. Arrese, Svensson, Annacone, Curren 7–5 7–6 4–6 6–4, lost J. McEnroe 6–1 6–4 6–4). *CAREER HIGHLIGHTS – DOUBLES:* (with Annacone) *US Open – r/u 1990* (lost Aldrich/Visser 6–2 7–6 6–2).

ROBIN WHITE (USA)
Born San Diego, Cal., 10 December 1963; lives Del Mar, Cal.; RH; 5ft 4½in; 125lb; final 1991 WTA ranking 101 singles, 27 (12) doubles; 1991 prize money $110,767.
Formerly coached by John Lloyd. *1984:* (105) R/u Wimbledon Plate. *1985:* (32) Last 16 US Open with win over Gadusek and won VS Hershey. *1986:* (20) Won 24 of 42 matches, upsetting Mandlikova and Sabatini to reach sf Eastbourne, and reaching last 16 Wimbledon. Qualified for VS Champ Nov. doubles with G. Fernandez. *1987:* (56) Qf New Orleans in singles and won 4 doubles titles. *1988:* (38) Upset Fendick to reach f North California Open. In doubles with G. Fernandez won US Open and Japan Open, reaching f on 4 other occasions to qualify for VS Champs. *1989:* (90) Qf San Diego was her best showing in singles, but in doubles she took 3 titles with G. Fernandez and won US Open mixed with Cannon. *1990:* (59) In singles reached sf Auckland and in doubles appeared in 6 f with different partners, winning 2 titles. *1991:* Qf Tokyo Pan Pacific in singles, reached 2 f in women's doubles and r/u Australian Open mixed with Davis. *1991 HIGHLIGHTS – SINGLES: Australian Open* 1r (lost Kamstra 6–4 6–2), *Wimbledon* 2r (d. Federica Bonsignori 6–1 6–1, lost Frazier [seed 15] 7–5 6–4), *US Open* 1r (lost McNeil 6–2 6–2). *1991 HIGHLIGHTS – DOUBLES:* [M. J. Fernandez] *r/u* Tokyo Pan Pacific (lost K. Jordan/Smylie 4–6 6–0 6–3), [Magers] *r/u* VS Los Angeles (lost Savchenko/Zvereva 6–1 2–6 6–2). *1991 HIGHLIGHTS – MIXED DOUBLES:* (with Davis) *r/u Australian Open* (lost Bates/Durie 2–6 6–4 6–4). *CAREER HIGHLIGHTS – DOUBLES:* (with G.Fernandez) *US Open – won 1988* (d. Fendick/Hetherington 6–4 6–1). *MIXED DOUBLES:* (with Cannon) *US Open – won 1989* (d. McGrath/R. Leach 6–7 7–5 6–4).

TAMI WHITLINGER (USA)
Born Neenah, Wis., 13 November 1968, and lives there; RH; 2HB; 5ft 6in; 118lb; final 1991 WTA ranking 52; 1991 prize money $105,896.
Coached by her father, Warren, and Ted Thomsen. Has an identical twin, Teri, who plays collegiate tennis at Stanford and has joined her sister on the circuit. A second sister, Tori (15), and a brother, Tate (12), also play tennis. *1986:* Won Nat 18s. *1988:* (626). *1989:* (129) Won 2 titles on USTA circuit and upset McNeil 1r Los Angeles. An All-American for 2nd year at Stanford, she won Rolex Collegiate singles. *1990:* (81) Qf VS Chicago and VS Nashville and broke into top 100 1st time in Feb. *1991:* Reached sf Geneva, made an unexpected appearance in last 16 French Open and upset Magers at VS Houston. *1991 HIGHLIGHTS – SINGLES: Australian Open* 2r (d. Reggi 6–7 6–2 6–2, lost Fairbank-Nideffer [seed 14] 6–4 6–1), *French Open* last 16, unseeded (d. de Lone 6–1 7–6, Rinaldi 6–4 6–0, Grossman 7–6 6–4, lost Sanchez-Vicario [seed 5] 6–2 6–1), *Wimbledon* 2r (d. Magdalena Maleeva 6–1 6–3, lost A. Huber [seed 14] 6–2 6–1), *US Open* 1r (lost Date 7–6 6–4); *sf* Geneva (d. Piccolini 6–3, Kidowaki 6–4 7–6, lost Maleeva Fragnière 6–1 6–3).

JUDITH POLZL WIESNER (Austria)
Born Hallein, 2 March 1966; lives Salzburg; RH; 5ft 7in; 138lb; final 1991 WTA ranking 16; 1991 prize money $167,361.
Husband Heinz (married April 1987). Coached by Karel Safarik. *1985:* (305). *1986:* (142) R/u Kitzbuhel and played Fed Cup. *1987:* (34) Sf Bastad and Athens and d. Bunge *en route* to both qf VS Arizona and 2r Italian Open. *1988:* (36) Upset Zvereva to reach f Strasbourg, Cecchini and Hanika as she won her 1st pro singles title at Aix-en-Provence, Kohde-Kilsch to reach sf Italian Open and McNeil *en route* to last 16 US Open. *1989:* (35) Reached last 16 Australian Open and won Arcachon. In doubles won Strasbourg and reached 2 other f. *1990:* (17) The high spot of her year came when she beat Novotna, Maleeva Fragnière and Martinez to make an unexpected appearance in f LIPC; also reached sf Brisbane, Sydney, Barcelona, Hamburg and Kitzbuhel to qualify for VS Champs, where she lost 1r to Maleeva Fragnière. *1991:* R/u Kitzbuhel, upset Novotna twice *en route* to sf Hamburg and Filderstadt, and reached last 16 Wimbledon and US Open. Won the Karen Krantzcke Sportsmanship Award. *1991 HIGHLIGHTS – SINGLES: French Open* 1r (lost Martinez

6–4 6–3), **Wimbledon** last 16, seed 9 (d. Cioffi 6–1 6–2, Savchenko 6–3 6–0, Kohde-Kilsch 3–6 7–5 6–1, lost M. J. Fernandez 6–0 7–5), **US Open** last 16, unseeded (d. Dechaume 4–6 6–3 6–3, Stafford 3–6 6–1 6–4, Labat 6–4 7–5, lost Graf [seed 1] 7–5 6–4); **r/u** Kitzbuhel (d. Sprung 6–3 7–6, Kschwendt 2–6 6–2 6–4, Labat 6–2 6–4, Jagerman 6–2 6–3, lost Martinez 6–1 2–6 6–3); **sf** Hamburg (d. Meier 6–4 6–2, Lindqvist 6–2 6–1, Novotna 6–1 6–3, lost Graf 6–0 6–1), **sf** Filderstadt (d. Lindqvist 6–2 6–2, Meskhi 6–1 1–6 6–4, Novotna 7–6 6–3, lost Navratilova 6–2 7–6). **1991 HIGHLIGHTS – DOUBLES:** [Tauziat] **r/u** Barcelona (lost Navratilova/Sanchez-Vicario 6–1 6–3). **CAREER HIGHLIGHTS – SINGLES: LIPC – r/u 1990** (d. Werdel 7–6 0–6 6–3, Phelps 6–1 5–7 6–2, Novotna 7–5 5–7 6–3, Maleeva Fragnière 2–6 6–1 6–2, Martinez 7–6 6–2, lost Seles 6–1 6–2).

TODD WITSKEN (USA)
Born Indianapolis, 4 November 1963; lives Carmel, Ind.; 5ft 11in; 165lb; final 1991 ATP ranking 136 singles, 15 (21) doubles; 1991 prize money $257,196.
Wife Lisa (married Nov. 1990), son Tyler Martin (born Aug. 1991). **1983–84:** Member of US Jun D Cup squad and All American at USC. **1985:** (218) Played three GP tournaments in time off from college. **1986:** (55) Stunned Connors in straight sets 3r US Open – the first time Connors had lost there before qf since 1972. **1987:** (158) Qf Washington. **1988:** (67) Qf Australian Open (d. Leconte), sf Indianapolis. In doubles with Lozano won 3 titles and reached 5 more f to qualify for Masters, where they fell sf to R. Leach/Pugh. **1989:** (54) Sf Rio de Janeiro and Washington in singles. Won 4 doubles titles with 3 different partners, qualifying for Masters with Lozano, where they took 5th place. **1990:** (58) R/u San Francisco (d. Krickstein); qf Washington (d. Mayotte) and Canadian Open (d. Gilbert). Reached 2 doubles f with Lozano, but won no title. **1991:** Upset J. McEnroe 1r Hong Kong, and reached qf Munich and Manchester. Won 3 doubles titles with Galbraith to qualify for ATP Doubles Champ. **1991 HIGHLIGHTS – SINGLES: Australian Open** 2r (d. Larsson 6–0 6–1 6–0, lost Berger [seed 12] 6–1 6–3 6–0), **French Open** 1r (lost Connors 6–3 7–5), **Wimbledon** 1r (lost Van Rensburg 6–1 7–6 4–6 6–4), **US Open** 2r (d. Paloheimo 6–3 5–7 6–4 6–1, lost Chang 6–3 6–0 6–2). **1991 HIGHLIGHTS – DOUBLES:** (with Galbraith) **won** Hong Kong (d. Michibata/Van't Hof 6–2 6–4), **won** Munich (d. Jarryd/Visser 7–5 6–4), **won** Montreal (d. Connell/Michibata 6–4 3–6 6–1).

TODD WOODBRIDGE (Australia)
Born Sydney, 2 April 1971; lives Woolooware; RH; 5ft 10in; 158lb; final 1991 ATP ranking 77 singles, 7 (25) doubles; 1991 prize money $666,959.
Coached by Ray Ruffels. **1987:** (420) R/u Australian Open Jun to Stoltenberg with whom he won the doubles there and at Wimbledon. **1988:** (213) Won Tasmania and in Jun doubles with Stoltenberg won Australian Open, French Open and Wimbledon. **1989:** (131) Won Brisbane Challenger, upset Fitzgerald *en route* to sf GP event there and finished the year by winning Hobart Challenger. In Jun doubles won Australian and French Open with J. Anderson and in Jun singles r/u Wimbledon to Kulti. **1990:** (50) Upset Chang *en route* to 1st tour f at New Haven and Gilbert *en route* to sf Sydney Indoor. In doubles with various partners reached 4 f, winning 2, and took US Open mixed with Smylie. **1991:** Upset Svensson *en route* to last 16 Australian Open, unseeded, and at French Open extended Becker to 5s. In doubles won 6 titles, 4 with Woodforde, with whom he qualified for ATP Doubles Champ. **1991 HIGHLIGHTS – SINGLES: Australian Open** last 16, unseeded (d. Kaplan 1–6 6–3 6–3 6–1, Bergstrom 6–1 0–6 6–2 7–6, Svensson [seed 8] 7–5 6–2 6–1, lost Forget [seed 10] 6–4 3–6 6–3 6–4), **French Open** 2r (d. Saceanu 6–4 7–6 6–4, lost Becker [seed 2] 5–7 1–6 6–4 6–4 6–4), **Wimbledon** 3r (d. Arraya 2–6 6–2 6–3 6–1, Hlasek [seed 13] 6–3 1–6 7–5 6–3, lost Gunnarsson 7–6 4–6 6–3 6–4), **US Open** 3r (d. Madsen 6–2 6–0 6–2, Saceanu 6–2 6–3 6–3, lost Lendl [seed 5] 3–6 6–3 6–4 6–3); **sf** Copenhagen (d. Henricsson 6–2 7–5, Hogstedt 6–3 6–0, Novacek 7–6 4–6 6–1, lost Jarryd 6–0 6–4). **1991 HIGHLIGHTS – DOUBLES:** (with Woodforde unless stated) **won** Brussels (d. Pimek/Schapers 6–3 6–0), **won** Copenhagen (d. Beckman/MacPherson 6–3 6–1), [Edberg] **won** Tokyo Suntory (d. Fitzgerald/Jarryd 6–4 3–6 6–1), **won** Queen's (d. Connell/Michibata 6–4 7–6), [J. Sanchez] **won** Schenectady (d. E. Sanchez/Gomez 3–6 7–6 7–6), **won** Brisbane (d. Fitzgerald/Michibata 7–6 6–3). **CAREER HIGHLIGHTS – MIXED DOUBLES:** (with Smylie) **US Open – won 1990** (d. Zvereva/Pugh 6–4 6–2).

MARK WOODFORDE (Australia)
Born Adelaide, 23 September 1965, and lives there; LH; 6ft 2in; 165lb; final 1991 ATP ranking 101 singles, 10 doubles; 1991 prize money $295,250.
Coached by Barry Phillips-Moore. **1984:** (385). **1985:** (127). **1986:** (181) Won 1st pro title at Auckland, sf Bristol. **1987:** (67) Last 16 US Open (d. Mayotte) after qualifying. **1988:** (42)

Enjoyed a remarkable year, with success on all surfaces, in which he extended Lendl to 5 close sets in 4¾-hour 4r match at Wimbledon, conceding only 10–8 in 5s, upset Edberg and J. McEnroe to reach sf Toronto and beat McEnroe again *en route* to last 16 US Open, unseeded. Formed a useful doubles partnership with J. McEnroe in autumn. *1989:* (75) In singles won Adelaide and r/u Brisbane. In doubles won US Open with J. McEnroe and Monte Carlo with Smid. *1990:* (101) Upset Chesnokov 2r Australian Open, but was forced to retire in 3r v Wheaton when he tore 2 ligaments in his ankle, requiring surgery. Out of action until June, when he progressed to last 16 Wimbledon, unseeded and a wild card, and in Aug. reached sf New Haven. *1991:* Upset E. Sanchez *en route* to last 16 Australian Open (unseeded), Chesnokov in reaching qf Copenhagen and Korda 1r Moscow. Won 4 doubles titles with Woodbridge to qualify for ATP Doubles Champ. *1991 HIGHLIGHTS – SINGLES: Australian Open* last 16, unseeded (d. E. Sanchez [seed 6] 0–6 7–5 7–6 6–2, Shelton 7–6 6–3 6–3, Connell 6–4 3–6 7–5 6–3, lost P. McEnroe 6–2 6–4 6–1), *French Open* 1r (lost Perez 6–1 6–7 6–1 6–3), *Wimbledon* 1r (lost Nargiso 6–4 7–6 7–6), *US Open* 1r (lost Chang 6–3 6–0 6–2). *1991 HIGHLIGHTS – DOUBLES:* (with Woodbridge) *won* Brussels (d. Pimek/Schapers 6–3 6–0), *won* Copenhagen (d. Beckman/MacPherson 6–3 6–1), *won* Queen's (d. Connell/Michibata 6–4 7–6), *won* Brisbane (d. Fitzgerald/Michibata 7–6 6–3). *CAREER HIGHLIGHTS – DOUBLES:* (with J. McEnroe) *US Open – won 1989* (d. Flack/Seguso 6–4 4–6 6–3 6–3).

ANGIE WOOLCOCK (Australia)
Born Launceston, 2 February 1973; lives Relbia; RH; 5ft 11in; final 1991 WTA ranking 403; 1991 prize money $8,344.
Coached by Ken Richardson. *1991:* R/u Australian Open Jun and Wimbledon Jun doubles with Limmer.

BART WUYTS (Belgium)
Born Leuven, 15 September 1969, and lives there; RH; 5ft 10in; 150lb; final 1991 ATP ranking 88; 1991 prize money $119,245.
1985: Nat 18s Champ. *1988:* (221) Joined Belgian D Cup squad. *1989:* (206). *1990:* (145). *1991:* As in previous years, he played mainly on the Challenger circuit, where he won Lisbon and Oporto. At end of year reached qf Guaruja Bliss on main tour. *1991 HIGHLIGHTS – SINGLES: Australian Open* 2r (d. Jonsson 5–7 5–7 6–4 7–6 9–7, lost Arias 6–3 6–1 6–2), *French Open* 1r (lost Edberg 6–2 6–2 6–3), *Wimbledon* 1r (lost Volkov 6–1 6–2 6–2), *US Open* 1r (lost Castle 0–6 7–5 6–4 7–5); *won* Lisbon Challenger (d. Marques 6–2 6–4), *won* Oporto Challenger (d. Wostenholme 6–3 7–5).

JAIME YZAGA (Peru)
Born Lima, 23 October 1967, and lives there; RH; 5ft 7in; 134lb; final 1991 ATP ranking 53; 1991 prize money $279,190.
Coached by Colon Nunez. Has suffered from recurring shoulder injury since 1982. *1981:* Won S. American 16s. *1983:* Won S. American 18s. *1984:* Joined Peruvian D Cup squad. *1985:* (45) Won French Jun and Wimbledon Jun doubles before bursting into last 16 US Open, after qualifying, where he was the only player to take a set off Lendl. Voted Newcomer of the Year. *1986:* (64) Played D Cup for Peru, scored wins over Hlasek, Pecci and Pate and reached sf Tokyo. *1987:* (70) Won first GP singles title at Schenectady, following with Sao Paulo. *1988:* (65) Finished the year on a high note by winning Itaparica. Upset Gilbert at US Open and reached qf Italian Open, Florence and Sao Paulo. *1989:* (23) Upset Chang *en route* to f Tourn of Champs and Mecir at LIPC, as well as reaching sf Guaruja, Bordeaux, Orlando (d. E. Sanchez) and Itaparica. *1990:* (87) R/u Sao Paulo and upset Berger at Monte Carlo. *1991:* Won US CC, upsetting Chang; sf Washington; and made an unexpected appearance in qf Australian Open. *1991 HIGHLIGHTS – SINGLES: Australian Open* qf, unseeded (d. Vacek 6–4 6–4 6–2, Schapers 7–6 6–4 6–2, Arias 3–6 7–6 6–1 6–3, Wilander 7–5 2–6 6–1 3–6 6–1, lost Edberg 6–2 6–3 6–2), *French Open* 3r (d. Cash 6–1 4–6 6–4 6–2, Pescariu 6–2 6–2 6–0, lost Cherkasov 7–5 3–6 6–3), *Wimbledon* 2r (d. Kulti 6–2 7–5 5–7 6–1, lost Leconte 6–4 6–2 6–3), *US Open* 2r (d. Mayotte 7–5 7–5 7–5, lost Krickstein 6–1 3–6 6–1 3–2 ret'd); *won* US CC (d. Garner 7–6 6–3, J. Brown 6–4 6–4, Chang 7–6 6–1, Washington 7–5 6–2, Arias 6–3 7–5); *sf* Washington (d. Knowles 7–5 6–1, Washington 6–4 6–4, Reneberg 6–3 6–4, lost Agassi 6–3 6–2).

LIMOR ZALTZ (Israel)
Born Haifa, 8 July 1973, and lives there; 5ft 8in; 123lb; final 1991 WTA ranking 516; 1991 prize money $3,421.
Coached by Sharon Casiff. *1991:* Won Wimbledon Jun doubles with Barclay.

EMANUEL ZARDO (Switzerland)
Born Bellinzona, 24 April 1970; lives Giubiasco; LH; 2HB; 5ft 4½in; 114lb; final 1991 WTA ranking 31, 1991 prize money $69,076.
1986: (294) Won Nat Jun Champ. **1987:** (254) Won 3 titles on satellite circuits and joined Swiss Fed Cup team. **1988:** (296). **1989:** (140) Won Oporto on Portuguese satellite circuit. **1990:** (63) Reached sf Geneva, qf Wellington, Palermo and Estoril, and broke into the top 100 in June. **1991:** Moved into the top 50 when she won her 1st primary circuit title at Taranto, playing her 1st f. In addition she reached sf Palermo, won Caserta Challenger and took a set off Seles 2r US Open. **1991 HIGHLIGHTS – SINGLES: Australian Open** 1r (lost Magers 6–4 6–2), **French Open** 2r (d. Paz 6–3 6–2, lost Sabatini [seed 3] 6–1 6–1), **Wimbledon** 2r (d. Miyagi 6–0 6–3, lost Strandlund 6–4 6–4), **US Open** 2r (d. Nowak 7–5 6–1, lost Seles [seed 2] 6–0 4–6 6–0); **won** Taranto (d. Maruska 6–1 6–3, Rottier 6–3 6–1, Van Lottum 5–7 6–3 6–2, Dahlman 6–3, Ritter 7–5 6–2), **won** Caserta Challenger (d. Segura 6–7 7–6 6–1); **sf** Palermo (d. Thoren 6–1 4–6 6–1, Paz 6–7 6–4 7–5, Frankl 6–2 6–2, lost Cecchini 6–3 7–6.

MARKUS ZOECKE (Germany)
Born Berlin, 10 May 1968, and lives there; RH; 6ft 5in; 190lb; final 1991 ATP ranking 56; 1991 prize money $101,775.
1989: (108) Qf Tel Aviv. **1990:** (167) Out for 6 weeks in spring with an arm injury. **1991:** Appeared in his 1st tour f at Guaruja Bliss; reached sf Washington, qf Buzios and won Taiwan Challenger. Upset Prpic at Athens, Arrese at Guaruja, E. Sanchez at Buzios and Mancini at Sao Paulo. **1991 HIGHLIGHTS – SINGLES: Australian Open** 1r (lost Camporese 3–6 6–2 7–6 6–4); **won** Taiwan Challenger (d. Jones); **r/u** Guaruja Bliss (d. Nestor 6–3 6–4, Arrese 6–1 6–7 6–3, Lopez 6–3 4–6 7–5, Costa 6–4 6–2, lost Frana 2–6 7–6 6–3); **sf** Washington (d. Borwick 7–6 6–4, Krickstein 6–7 6–2 7–6, Arias 6–3 6–4, Herrera 4–6 6–3 6–3, lost Korda 6–2 6–4).

RADKA ZRUBAKOVA (Czechoslovakia)
Born Bratislava, 26 December 1970, and lives there; RH; 2HB; 5ft 6½in; 138lb; final 1991 WTA ranking 23; 1991 prize money $171,430.
1985: In Jun doubles with Holikova won US Open and r/u French Open. **1986:** (409) Won US Open Jun doubles with Novotna. **1987:** (143) Won Helsinki on satellite circuit. **1988:** (35) Last 16 Australian Open, sf Hamburg, qf Taranto, Berlin (d. Mandlikova) and Filderstadt. **1989:** (32) Won 1st tour singles title at Brussels, reached sf Adelaide and upset Sukova at Filderstadt. **1990:** (57) Sf Bastad, upset Sukova again *en route* to qf Sydney and surprised Wiesner in reaching same stage at VS California. In doubles won Kitzbuhel with Langrova. **1991:** Upset Magers at San Antonio, Kelesi at Hamburg and Meshki *en route* to qf Berlin, before sweeping to the title at Strasbourg, surprising Gildemeister in the process. She then continued her upsetting ways by disposing of M. J. Fernandez to reach last 16 US Open, unseeded, and reached sf Kitzbuhel and Indianapolis. In doubles with Langrova won Clarins and r/u Linz. **1991 HIGHLIGHTS – SINGLES: French Open** 1r (lost Seles 6–3 6–0), **Wimbledon** 2r (d. McQuillan 7–6 6–2, lost Capriati [seed 10] 6–2 6–3), **US Open** last 16, unseeded (d. Baranski 6–2 7–6, Date 7–5 6–7 6–3, M. J. Fernandez [seed 5] 6–1 6–2, lost G. Fernandez 6–2 6–2); **won** Strasbourg (d. Paz 6–3 6–3, de Swardt 7–6 6–1, Gildemeister 6–0 6–3, A. Minter 6–1 6–3, McQuillan 7–6 7–6); **sf** Kitzbuhel (d. Reinstadler 6–3 6–7 6–0, Thoren 7–6 7–6, Cecchini 6–3 2–6 6–3, lost Martinez 7–5 6–4), **sf** Indianapolis (d. Bastien 6–0 6–0, McCarthy 6–4 6–0, Harvey-Wild 6–4 6–4, lost Keller 6–2 6–4). **1991 HIGHLIGHTS – DOUBLES:** (with Langrova) **won** Clarins (d. Dechaume/Halard 6–4 6–4); **r/u** Linz (lost Maleeva Fragnière/Reggi 6–4 1–6 6–3).

NATALIA ZVEREVA (USSR)
Born Minsk, 16 April 1971, and lives there; RH; 2HB; 5ft 8in; 138lb; final 1991 WTA ranking 21 singles, 3 (5) doubles; 1991 prize money $558,002.
Nicknamed Natasha. Coached by her father, Marat Zverev. **1985:** Won Bethesda on USTA circuit and World Jun Champs. **1986:** (92) In singles won Soviet Nat Champs (d. Savchenko), won Wimbledon Jun singles, USTA Bethesda, and was r/u to Rinaldi at VS Arkansas after qualifying, becoming youngest player to reach f of VS Series event, at 15 years 7 months. In doubles won French Open Jun and r/u Wimbledon Jun with Meskhi. **1987:** (19) ITF Jun Champ; won Nat Champ, Jun singles at French Open, Wimbledon and US Open and Jun doubles at French Open and Wimbledon with Medvedeva. Did not compete in Australian Open Jun. Last 16 Wimbledon, beating McNeil and extending Sabatini to 3s; won Taranto on Italian satellite and reached f in Arkansas and Chicago in consecutive weeks. **1988:** (7) Played her best tennis to upset Navratilova last 16 French

Open, but disappointed in her 1st GS f there, being totally outclassed 6–0 6–0 in 32 minutes by Graf. Last 16 Wimbledon, qf Olympics, r/u Eastbourne, New England and Montreal (d. Navratilova and Shriver back-to-back). In doubles with Savchenko r/u Wimbledon and won 2 titles. At VS Champs reached qf in singles and r/u in doubles. Voted WTA Newcomer of the Year. *1989:* (27) Was less successful in singles, winning no title, although she reached f FC Cup (d. Navratilova) and Moscow plus 3 more sf. However, in doubles with Savchenko she won French Open, was r/u Wimbledon and VS Champs and reached 7 other f, winning 4. *1990:* (12) Won 1st senior singles title at Brisbane (upset Sukova qf), following with Sydney the next week. Sf Washington, FC Cup, Amelia Island (extending Graf to 3s) and Berlin; qf Wimbledon. In doubles with Savchenko r/u French Open and won 3 titles; in mixed with Pugh won Australian Open and r/u US Open. Qualified for VS Champs in singles and doubles, losing 1r singles to Sanchez-Vicario and 1r doubles to Adams/McNeil. *1991:* In singles r/u Birmingham, sf FC Cup and reached last 16 Australian Open and US Open. In doubles GS won Wimbledon and r/u French Open with Savchenko and teamed with Shriver 1st time to win US Open. She also won VS Florida, Berlin, Eastbourne, Toronto and Los Angeles with Savchenko, Brighton with Shriver and FC Cup with Kohde-Kilsch, as well as reaching 4 more f with various partners, qualifying for VS Champs with Savchenko. In mixed doubles, r/u Wimbledon with Pugh. *1991 HIGHLIGHTS – SINGLES: Australian Open* last 16, seed 11 (d. Helgeson 6–3 6–4, Porwik 7–6 6–4, Wood 6–1 6–3, lost A. Huber 6–3 6–4), *French Open* 2r, seed 15 (d. Faber 6–0 6–0, lost Grossman 4 6–1 6–4), *Wimbledon* 2r, seed 13 (d. Tessi 7–6 6–4, lost Harvey-Wild 6–4 6–1), *US Open* last 16, unseeded (d. Probst 6–1 7–6, A. Huber [seed 16] 6–2 6–4, Po 6–1 3–6 6–2, lost Sanchez-Vicario [seed 4] 6–3 7–6); *r/u Birmingham* (d. Cammy McGregor 6–7 7–6 6–4, Date 6–3 6–1, Bollegraf 6–4 6–7 6–2, Garrison 2–6 7–6 8–6, lost Navratilova 6–4 7–6); *sf* FC Cup (d. Faber 6–1 6–3, Cecchini 7–6 6–3, Novotna 7–6 6–4, lost Meskhi 6–3 3–6 6–4). *1991 HIGHLIGHTS – DOUBLES:* (with Savchenko unless stated) *r/u French Open* (lost G. Fernandez/Novotna 6–4 6–0), *won Wimbledon* (d. G. Fernandez/Novotna 6–4 3–6 6–4), [Shriver] *won US Open* (d. Novotna/Savchenko 6–4 4–6 7–6); *won* VS Florida (d. McGrath/A. Smith 6–4 7–6), [Kohde-Kilsch] *won* FC Cup (d. Daniels/Gregory 6–4 6–0), *won* Berlin (d. Provis/E. Reinach 6–3 6–3), *won* Eastbourne (d. G. Fernandez/Novotna 2–6 6–4 6–4), *won* Toronto (d. Kohde-Kilsch/Sukova 1–6 7–5 6–2), *won* VS Los Angeles (d. Magers/R. White 6–1 2–6 6–2), [Shriver] *won* Brighton (d. Garrison/McNeil 6–1 6–2); *r/u* Tarpon Springs (d. G. Fernandez/Sukova 4–6 6–4 7–6), [Paz] *r/u* Amelia Island (lost Sanchez-Vicario/Sukova 4–6 6–2 6–2), [G. Fernandez] *r/u* Washington (lost Novotna/Savchenko 5–7 6–1 7–6), [Shriver] *r/u* Filderstadt (lost Navratilova/Novotna 6–2 5–7 6–4). *MIXED DOUBLES:* (with Pugh) *r/u Wimbledon* (lost Fitzgerald/Smylie 7–6 6–2). *CAREER HIGHLIGHTS – SINGLES: French Open –* r/u 1988 (d. Golarsa, Field, Gurney, Navratilova 6–3 7–6, Sukova 6–2 6–3, Provis 6–3 6–7 7–5, lost Graf 6–0 6–0); *Wimbledon – qf 1990* (d. Harper, G. Fernandez, Magers 2–6 6–2 6–4, Schultz 6–2 6–2, lost Sabatini 6–2 2–6 8–6). *CAREER HIGHLIGHTS – DOUBLES:* (with Savchenko unless stated) *French Open – won 1989* (d. Graf/Sabatini 4 6–4), *r/u 1990* (lost Novotna/Sukova 6–4 7–5), *r/u 1991; Wimbledon – won 1991, r/u 1988* (lost Graf/Sabatini 6–3 1–6 12–10), *r/u 1989* (lost Novotna/Sukova 6–1 6–2); *US Open –* [Shriver] *won 1991; VS Champs – r/u 1988* (lost Navratilova/Shriver 6–3 6–4), *r/u 1989* (lost Navratilova/Shriver 6–3 6–2). *CAREER HIGHLIGHTS – MIXED DOUBLES:* (with Pugh) *Australian Open – won 1990* (d. R. Leach/Garrison 4–6 6–2 6–3).

ALL-TIME GREATS

David Gray and John Barrett

WILMER LAWSON ALLISON (USA)

Born 8/1/04. Died 30/4/77. One of the greatest and most spectacular of American doubles specialists, he also gained some notable singles successes. Possessing a fierce smash, a serve 'with the kick of a Texas mustang', considerable power on the volley, and a fine backhand drive, he found an ideal doubles partner in John Van Ryn. They won at Wimbledon in **1929–30** and were runners-up in **1935.** They took the US title in **1931** and **1935** and reached the final in **1930/32/34/36.** His singles form was less consistent, but on his day could play brilliantly. He defeated Perry to win the US title in **1935,** and in **1930,** after beating Cochet, he was runner-up to Tilden at Wimbledon. Between **1929–35** he played in 45 D Cup rubbers, winning 18 out of 29 singles and 14 of his 16 doubles.

JOSEPH ASBOTH (Hungary)

Born 18/9/17. A stylish righthander whose victory in the **1947** French singles, when he beat Petra, Tom Brown and Sturgess, was Hungary's most important tennis success before their victory in the Saab King's Cup in 1976; 7 times nat champ; 6 times winner of the Hungarian int title; he played 1st at Wimbledon in **1939** and impressed those who saw him against Austin in 1 r. Lost to Bromwich in the **1948** sfs. From **1938–57** he played 41 D Cup rubbers in 16 ties.

ARTHUR ROBERT ASHE (USA)

Born 10/7/43. A cool, thoughtful, dogged competitor, he was the first black American to win the Wimbledon men's singles title and, in **1968,** playing as an amateur, he became the first US Open champion. Always happier on fast courts, he tried hard to succeed on clay but endured regular disappointments in Paris and never progressed further than the semi-finals **(1971)** in Rome. He was a semi-finalist at Wimbledon **1968–69** before surprising Connors in the **1975** final. He defeated Okker to win the US title in **1968** but in **1972** lost to Nastase after leading by two sets to one and 4–2 in the final. He won Australian singles **1970** and the WCT title **1975.** Refused a visa to South Africa in 1970, he broke through apartheid laws to play in Johannesburg **1973,** losing to Connors in the final and winning the doubles with Okker. After missing most of the 1977 season, he regained his place among the leaders of the circuit in **1978** and reached match-point against McEnroe in the Masters final. Between **1963–78,** he appeared in 18 *D Cup* ties, winning 27 out of 32 singles and one of two doubles. US *D Cup* captain **1980–85,** following his retirement from active play owing to a heart condition that had necessitated triple by-pass surgery.

CILLY AUSSEM (Germany)

Born 4/1/09. Died 22/3/63. Later the Contessa della Corta Brae. The first German to win the women's singles at Wimbledon. Her strokes were not strong but she was a model of steadiness and persistence. 'Quite small and more of a girl in appearance with round brown eyes and a cherub face', wrote Helen Wills. 'Her agility on court and the distance that she covers in spite of her shortness are really astonishing.' **1931** – when the Californian did not compete – was her best year. She beat Betty Nuthall in the French f and then defeated Hilde Krahwinkel in Wimbledon's only all-German final. That was a disappointing match, because both women were handicapped by blistered feet. Her victory compensated for an unlucky failure in **1930.** Then she slipped and sprained an ankle at 4–4 in the fs of her sf against Elizabeth Ryan and had to be carried from the court.

HENRY WILFRED AUSTIN (Great Britain)
Born 20/8/06. Bunny Austin's Wimbledon record was remarkable (and unlucky), but his most important contribution to British tennis was in the D Cup. The possessor of elegant groundstrokes, which compensated for a lack of power in his serving and smashing, he played many of the crucial singles, alongside Perry, in Britain's successful campaigns in the 1930s. A former Cambridge Univ captain, he played in 24 ties between *1929–37*, winning 36 of his 48 rubbers, all singles. He won 8 rubbers out of 12 and 5 out of 8 'live' rubbers in his 6 Challenge Rounds. At Wimbledon he failed only once to reach the qf or go further between *1929–39*. R/u to Vines *1932* and Budge *1938*, in sf *1929* and *1936/37*, and r/u to Henkel in *1937* French singles.

WILFRED BADDELEY (Great Britain)
Born 11/1/1872. Died 30/1/1929. Youngest winner – at 19 years, 5 months and 23 days – of Wimbledon singles in *1891* until Becker in 1985. Also won singles in *1892/95*, and doubles (with twin brother Herbert) *1891/94/95/96*.

MARCEL BERNARD (France)
Born 18/6/14. Shrewd and stylish, a canny lefthander with considerable touch, he is one of only two French players to have won in Paris since the days of the 'Musketeers' (the other is Noah, 1983); demonstrated his promise early, reaching the French singles sf and, with Boussus, the doubles in *1932*, still in sufficient form to be chosen for the French D Cup team in *1956*. In *1946* he won 5 set matches against Petra in the sf and Drobny in the final to take the French title; in sf on 3 other occasions; won the doubles with Borotra *(1936)* and with Petra *(1946)* and the mixed with Lollette Payot *(1935)* and Billie Yorke *(1936)*. Between *1935–56* he played 42 D Cup rubbers in 25 ties and he has also served as president of the French Tennis Federation.

PAULINE MAY BETZ (USA)
Born 6/8/19. Now Mrs Addie. An agile, athletic competitor, who might have gained many more titles if the war had not interrupted international competition. She was ranked eighth in the US in *1939* and was the most successful player in wartime competitions there, winning the national title from *1942–44*. She won Wimbledon at a cost of only 20 games in *1946*, defeating Louise Brough 6–2 6–4 in the final. She and Miss Hart were runners-up to Miss Brough and Miss Osborne in the doubles and, if she was disappointed in Paris, where Miss Osborne beat her 1–6 8–6 7–5 in the final, after saving two match-points with drop-shots at 5–6 in the second set, she asserted her supremacy again at Forest Hills by defeating Doris Hart 11–9 6–3 in the final. Soon afterwards she turned professional.

BLANCHE BINGLEY (Great Britain)
Born 3/11/1863. Died 6/8/1946. Became Mrs Hillyard. One of the determined pioneers of women's tennis. She competed in the first women's tournament at Wimbledon in *1884* and lost to Maud Watson, the eventual champion, in sfs. The following year Miss Watson defeated her in f, but she avenged those failures by beating the champion in the challenge round in *1886*. That was the first of her six victories. Further successes followed in *1889/94/97/99* and *1900*. Only Lottie Dod, who retired in 1893, troubled her until Mrs Sterry ended her supremacy in 1901. Like many early players, her game was founded on a powerful forehand and strict command of length. A reluctant volleyer who invariably ran round her backhand, she was so quick and so fit that she was difficult to outmanoeuvre. She wore white gloves to give her a better grip and her follow-through on the forehand was said to have been so complete 'that her left shoulder was often a mass of bruises from the impact of the racket'. She married Commander G. W. Hillyard, secretary of the All England Club from 1907–24; altogether she competed in the championships 24 times.

PENELOPE DORA HARVEY BOOTHBY (Great Britain)
Born 2/8/1881. Died 22/2/1970. Became Mrs Green. One of the group of players from the county of Middlesex who dominated the early years of women's tennis at Wimbledon. She

won one of the most exciting of the pre-1914 f, defeating Miss A. M. Morton 6–4 4–6 8–6 ('Few closer or more interesting struggles have ever been witnessed on the famous old court', wrote G. W. Hillyard) in *1909,* and lost the most dismal in the history of the championships to Mrs Lambert Chambers, who beat her 6–0 6–0, in the *1911* challenge round. Mrs Lambert Chambers had beaten her by the same score at the Beckenham tournament two weeks earlier and had allowed her only four games in the challenge round in *1910.* Somewhat fortunately she and Mrs McNair became Wimbledon's first women's doubles champions in 1913. They were down 2–6 2–4 to Mrs Lambert Chambers and Mrs Sterry in the final when Mrs Sterry fell and retired with a torn tendon. She and Mrs McNair were also semi-finalists in *1922.*

BJORN BORG (Sweden)
Born 6/6/56. One of the coolest match players the game has ever known, he matured early, winning his first important title, the *1974* Italian Open, shortly before his 18th birthday and the first of his six French Championships just after it. With fierce topspin on both his forehand and his double-handed backhand, a powerful serve and speedy court coverage plus an indomitable will to win, he was virtually invincible on European clay between *1974–81* adding the French Open in *1975/78/79/80/81* and a second Italian title in *1978* as well as the US Pro Championship on US clay in *1974/75/76.* Never an instinctive volleyer, he confounded those observers who thought his game was unsuited to grass by setting a modern record at Wimbledon where he won five successive titles between *1976–80.* Only William Renshaw, in the days of the Challenge Round, won more (1881–86). He learned to win indoors, taking the WCT title in *1976* and the Masters twice *(1979/80)* and leading Sweden to their first D Cup success, a 3–2 victory over Czechoslovakia in Stockholm in *1975.* But he never solved the problems of the high, fast bounce and positive foothold of US hard courts. Four times he was beaten in the US Open final, twice by Connors *(1976/78)* and twice by McEnroe *(1980/81),* the last three being on asphalt at Flushing Meadow. By the autumn of *1981* this great champion felt burnt out and virtually retired from the mainstream, restricting his play to exhibitions and special events. Although he attempted two comebacks, in *1982/84,* he could no longer make the total commitment that had once made him supreme and turned to other interests. Seven years later he again attempted a return but fell in his first match to Jordi Arrese in Monte Carlo and competed no more in 1991. His legacy to Swedish tennis is immeasurable for he sparked the flame that has burned so brightly ever since through Wilander, Sundstrom, Jarryd, Nystrom and Edberg. His style of errorless, counter-attacking topspin inspired a whole generation of players around the world.–J.B.

JEAN BOROTRA (France)
Born 13/8/1898. A brilliantly agile volleyer and a shrewd player. One of the 'Four Musketeers' who won the D Cup for France from *1927–32.* Enthusiastic and popular, he continued to play competitive lawn tennis long past his 80th year, regularly appearing for France in International Club matches against Britain. Won Wimbledon singles *1924/26* and doubles (with R. Lacoste) *1925* and (with J. Brugnon) *1932/33.* French singles *1924/31,* and doubles *1924/25/28/29/34/36.* Won Australian singles and doubles *1928.* Had long and spectacular covered court record, winning French singles title 12 times, British 11, and US 4. Played 54 D Cup rubbers *1922–47,* winning 36 in 32 ties.

MAUREEN CONNOLLY BRINKER (USA)
Born 17/9/34. Died 21/6/69. The most determined and concentrated of post-war women's champions she hit her groundstrokes with remorseless accuracy. Won US singles in *1951* at the age of 16 and thereafter lost only 4 matches – 2 to Doris Hart, one to Shirley Fry, and another to Beverley Fleitz – before she broke her leg in a riding accident in 1954 and retired. She was never beaten in singles at Wimbledon, winning *1952/53/54.* US singles *1951/52/ 53.* French singles *1953/54* and (with Mrs H. C. Hopman) doubles *1954.* Australian singles and doubles (with Julie Sampson) *1953.* Italian singles *1954.* She won all 9 of her W Cup

rubbers and in *1953* she was the first woman to bring off the Grand Slam of the 4 major singles titles in the same year.

JOHN EDWARD BROMWICH (Australia)
Born 14/11/18. A gracefully unorthodox player whose career might have been even more successful if it had not been interrupted by World War II. Ambidextrous but using both hands on the forehand, he used a very light, softly strung racket to control the ball with great subtlety. He won the Australian singles in *1939* and regained the title from Quist in *1946.* Those were his only major singles victories, although he was agonisingly close to success in f of *1948* Wimbledon when he lost to Falkenburg after leading 5–2 in the fs and holding three match-points. But it was in doubles, mostly with Quist or Sedgman, that he earned most honours. He won at Wimbledon in *1948* (with Sedgman) */50* (with Quist), took the US title three times, and he and Quist ruled in Australia from *1938–40* and *1946–50.* Won the Wimbledon mixed with Louise Brough, *1947/48,* and played in 53 D Cup rubbers between *1937–50.*

SIR NORMAN EVERARD BROOKES (Australia)
Born 14/11/1877. Died 10/1/1968. The first overseas winner of men's singles at Wimbledon. Left-handed and a notable volleyer, he lost to H. L. Doherty in Challenge Round on first visit to Wimbledon 1905. Won singles and doubles (with A. F. Wilding) *1907* and *1914* and Australian singles in *1911* and doubles in *1924* with J. O. Anderson. With Wilding won the D Cup for Australasia in *1907.* Between *1905–20* he played 39 rubbers and was 6 times a member of a side which won the Challenge Round. Returned to Wimbledon in *1924* at 46 and reached the 4r.

ALTHEA LOUISE BROUGH (USA)
Born 11/3/23. Now Mrs Clapp. An aggressive server and volleyer, she played a major part in establishing American domination of women's tennis immediately after World War II. Won Wimbledon singles *1948/49/50* and again in *1955* after the retirement of Maureen Connolly (who beat her in *1952* and *1954* f), US in *1947,* and Australian, *1950.* She and Margaret Osborne du Pont formed a redoubtable doubles partnership, winning 5 times at Wimbledon and 3 times in Paris, and holding the US title from *1942–50* and *1955–57.* She was mixed doubles champ at Wimbledon *1946/47/48/50* and took all 3 titles in *1948* and *1950.* She played 22 W Cup rubbers between *1946–57* and was never beaten.

JACQUES BRUGNON (France)
Born 11/6/1895. Died 20/3/1978. The doubles specialist of the 'Four Musketeers', he gained most of his early success with Cochet and then formed a partnership with Borotra, which was still capable of reaching the *1939* French f, when he was 44 and Borotra 40, and coming three times within a point of the title. He and Borotra returned to Wimbledon and reached the 3r in *1948.* Won Wimbledon doubles *1926/28* (Cochet) */32/33* (Borotra). Between *1927–34* won French doubles 3 times with Cochet and twice with Borotra. Also Australian doubles (with Borotra) in *1928.* Reached singles sf at Wimbledon, *1926.* Played 31 D Cup doubles and 6 singles *1921–34.*

JOHN DONALD BUDGE (USA)
Born 13/6/15. The first player to bring off the Grand Slam of the 4 historic singles titles in one year – *1938.* A relentless competitor with a majestic backhand he won all 3 titles at Wimbledon in *1937* and *1938.* Won doubles (with G. Mako) and mixed (with Alice Marble). US singles *1937/38* and doubles (with Mako) *1936/38.* French and Australian singles *1938* and between *1935–38* won 25 out of 29 D Cup rubbers in 11 ties. Turned professional in *1938.*

MARIA ESTHER ANDION BUENO (Brazil)
Born 11/10/39. The most gracefully artistic of post-war women's champions. For nearly a decade her rivalry with Margaret Court provided the principal excitement of the women's

game, but at the end she was plagued by injury. Won Wimbledon singles **1959/60/64,** and doubles (with Althea Gibson) **1958,** (with Darlene Hard) **1960/63,** (with Billie Jean King) **/65,** and (with Nancy Gunter) **/66.** US singles **1959/63/64/66** and doubles (with Darlene Hard) **1960/62,** (with Nancy Gunter) **/66,** and (with Margaret Court) **/68.** French doubles (with Darlene Hard) **1960.** Australian doubles (with Christine Truman) **1960.** Italian singles, **1958/61/65.**

MAY SUTTON BUNDY (USA)
Born in Plymouth, England, 25/9/1886. Died 4/10/1975. In **1905** the first overseas player to win a Wimbledon title. The seventh and youngest child of a British naval officer, Captain A. de G. Sutton, she learnt tennis on asphalt courts after her family moved to California in 1893. She was forceful and vigorous with a disconcerting top-spin forehand. F. R. Burrow commented: 'She took a deep breath before every stroke and then hit the ball with all her force to the accompaniment of a very audible expiration.' After winning the US singles and doubles in **1904** she went, aged 18, to Wimbledon **1905** and defeated the holder, Miss Douglass, in the Challenge Round. Miss Douglass regained the title the following year, but then lost a third battle with the Californian in **1907.** After winning the US Clay Court singles **1912,** Miss Sutton married Thomas Bundy, 3 times a US doubles champ. She played doubles in the **1925** W Cup and in **1929** returned to Wimbledon at 42 to defeat Eileen Bennett, seeded 4, and reach the qf. She was still playing 44 years later. Her daughter Dorothy represented the US 3 times in the W Cup and won the Australian singles 1938, and a nephew, John Doeg, was US champ in 1930.

DOROTHEA LAMBERT CHAMBERS (Great Britain)
Born 3/9/1878. Died 7/1/1960. Née Douglass. The most successful British woman player before 1914, she won Wimbledon singles 7 times and lost dramatically to Suzanne Lenglen in **1919** Challenge Round after holding 2 match-points. Played in **1926** W Cup – 23 years after first success at Wimbledon. The daughter of an Ealing vicar, she became a coach in **1928.** Won Wimbledon singles **1903/04/06/10/11/13/14.**

HENRI COCHET (France)
Born 14/12/01. Died April 1987. The great instinctive genius of lawn tennis, swift and imaginative, a master of the volley and half-volley, whose play could rise to dizzy heights and sometimes slip to unexpected disaster. Won Wimbledon singles **1927/29** and doubles (with J. Brugnon) **1926/28.** US singles **1928.** French singles **1922/26/28/30/32** and doubles (with Brugnon) **1927/30/32.** With the other 'Musketeers', he played successfully in 6 Challenge Rounds. Between **1922** and **1933,** when he turned professional, he won 44 D Cup rubbers out of 58 in 26 ties. After the war reinstated as an amateur.

ASHLEY JOHN COOPER (Australia)
Born 15/9/36. A strong and determined competitor who maintained Australia's command of the international game after Hoad and Rosewall turned professional. After being overwhelmed by Hoad in the **1957** f at Wimbledon, he returned to beat Fraser in a stern test of endurance in **1958.** He was US champion **1958** and won Australia **1957–58.** His doubles victories included Australia **1958,** France **1957–58** and US **1958.** He played singles when Australia successfully defended the D Cup in **1957** and **1958,** winning one rubber in each match. He beat Seixas and lost to Mackay **1957** and beat Mackay and lost to Olmedo **1958.**

CHARLOTTE COOPER (Great Britain)
Born 22/9/1870. Died 10/10/1970. Became Mrs Sterry. One of the first successful women volleyers, she won at Wimbledon **1895/96/98/1901/08.** Overshadowed at first by Mrs Hillyard – her first three victories were gained in years when the older player did not compete – she defeated her at last in **1901,** the year of her marriage, after losing to Mrs Hillyard in four previous matches at the championships. In **1902** she lost in the famous re-played challenge round to Muriel Robb (they stopped at 4–6 13–11 on the first evening,

then began again and Miss Robb won 7–5 6–1) and then regained the title in *1908* after beating Mrs Lambert Chambers in the quarter-finals. She reached the all-comers' final in *1912* and took Mrs McNair to 9–7 in the third set of a qf in *1913*. Her attacking spirit delighted her contemporaries. 'Her smiling good temper and sportsmanship made her as popular a player as ever went on to the Centre Court', wrote Burrow. 'She had a constitution like the proverbial ostrich. She never knew what it was to be tired and was never sick or sorry', said Hillyard.

BARON GOTTFRIED VON CRAMM (Germany)
Born 7/7/09. Died in car accident in Egypt 9/11/76. An elegant stylist and Germany's most successful player. Won French singles *1934/36* and doubles (with H. Henkel) *1937,* and German singles *1932/33/34/35/48/49* and doubles *1948/49/53/55.* Like F. S. Stolle, he was losing singles finalist at Wimbledon for 3 successive years – 1935–37. Won Wimbledon mixed (with Hilda Krahwinkel) *1933* and US doubles (with Henkel) *1937.* Won 82 D Cup rubbers out of 102 in 37 ties between *1932–53.*

JOHN HERBERT CRAWFORD (Australia)
Born 22/3/08. Died 10/9/91. Classic stylist, he beat H. E. Vines in *1933* in one of the greatest of all Wimbledon f. Won Wimbledon doubles (with A. K. Quist) *1935.* French singles *1933* and doubles (with Quist) *1935,* Australian singles *1931/33* and doubles (with H. C. Hopman) *1929/30,* (with E. F. Moon) *1932,* and (with V. B. McGrath) *1935.* Won 36 out of 58 D Cup rubbers between *1928–37.*

DWIGHT FILLEY DAVIS (USA)
Born 5/7/1879. Died 28/11/1945. The donor of the D Cup, the trophy at stake in the international team championship. A Harvard undergraduate, he played against the British Isles in the first two matches of that competition, winning a single and partnering Holcombe Ward successfully in the doubles in *1900* and, with Ward again, losing to the Dohertys in the doubles in *1902.* A lefthander, he won the US doubles with Ward from *1899–1901,* retiring undefeated, and also the all-comers' final at Wimbledon in *1901,* only to fall to the Dohertys. He was President of the US LTA in *1923,* US Secretary of War 1925–29 and later Governor-General of the Philippines.

MAX DECUGIS (France)
Born 24/9/1882. Died 6/9/1978. The first great French player. He spent his schooldays in England and won his first tournaments there. Short, quick, and wiry, he was an aggressive competitor, whom Lawrie Doherty described as 'the most promising young player in the world'. He dominated French tennis from *1903,* when he won in Paris for the first time, to the outbreak of World War I, winning the singles title 8 times in 12 years and the doubles from *1902–14* and again in *1920* when the Champs were resumed. He was still playing well enough to reach the singles final in *1923* when he was 41. By that time the age of the 'Musketeers' was dawning. Although he competed regularly at Wimbledon, he never progressed beyond the singles sf *(1911/12)* but, with Gobert, he gained France's first title by winning the doubles in *1911.*

CHARLOTTE DOD (Great Britain)
Born 24/9/1871. Died 27/6/1960. The first lawn tennis prodigy. Won the first of 5 Wimbledon titles in *1887* at the age of 15 years and 10 months. When she retired, she became an international golfer and hockey player. Nicknamed the 'Little Wonder', she won Wimbledon singles *1887/88/91/92/93.*

HUGH LAWRENCE DOHERTY (Great Britain)
Born London, 8/10/1875. Died 21/8/1919. Learnt game with elder brother, Reginald Frank ('Reggie'), at Westminster School. Played for Cambridge Univ against Oxford in 1896–98 and developed into one of the most spectacular, aggressive, stylish, and successful of British players. 'Lawrie' Doherty was celebrated for smashing and volleying, and for speed

about the court. With his brother, formed one of the greatest doubles partnerships in the history of the game. Won all-comers' singles at Wimbledon, *1898,* and singles champ *1902–06.* Doubles champ (with R. F. Doherty) *1897–1901, 1903–05.* First overseas player to win US singles, *1903,* and doubles, *1902/03.* In 5 D Cup challenge rounds, *1902–06,* he was never beaten, winning 7 singles rubbers and 5 doubles.

REGINALD FRANK DOHERTY (Great Britain)
Born London, 14/10/1872. Died 29/12/1910. The senior partner of the great Doherty combination and the most notable stylist of early lawn tennis. Contemporary observers called his backhand, produced with back swing, full follow-through and remarkable touch, 'a model of perfection'. Was Wimbledon singles champ *1897–1900* and doubles champ *1897–1901* and *1903–05.* Reached the doubles challenge round at Wimbledon for first time with H. A. Nisbet in 1896. Thereafter he and his brother, H. L. Doherty, were beaten only by S. H. Smith and F. L. Riseley at Wimbledon. They lost to this pair in 1902, then beat them in the next three challenge rounds before falling to them again in 1906. The Dohertys won the US doubles in *1902/03.* Won South African singles and doubles *1909.*

JAROSLAV DROBNY (Great Britain)
Born 12/10/21. Exiled himself from Czechoslovakia in 1949, became Egyptian subject in 1950 and a naturalised Briton in 1960. One of the great post-war clay court competitors with tremendous left-hand serve and smash, and delicate touch, he played in some of Wimbledon's most dramatic and emotional matches and eventually won the singles in *1954* at the age of 33. In *1946* he beat Kramer, the favourite; he lost to Schroeder in the *1949* f; in *1950* he let a two-set lead slip against Sedgman; Mottram surprised him in *1951;* he fell to Sedgman again in the *1952* f; and in *1953* he never recovered from beating Patty 8–6 16–18 3–6 8–6 12–10 in Wimbledon's second longest singles. The following year, when his chance seemed to be slipping away, he beat Rosewall, then 19, in f. He won in Paris in *1951/52* (after another series of dramatic failures), Italy *1950/51/53* and Germany *1950.* In *1946/47/48/49* he played in 43 D Cup rubbers, and won 37.

FRANCOISE DURR (France)
Born 25/12/42. Now Mrs Browning. The outstanding French woman player of the 1960s and 1970s. Shrewd and unorthodox, particularly in her serve and on the backhand, she excelled in doubles. She gained her major singles successes in *1967* when she won the French and German titles and reached the US semi-finals, but in doubles won a host of titles with a variety of partners, including five successive French victories – with Gail Sheriff (later Mrs Chanfreau and now Mrs Lovera) *1967* and *1970/71,* and with Ann Jones, *1968/69.* Won US doubles *1972* with Betty Stove, and Italian and South African titles *1969* with Jones. She failed, however, in six Wimbledon doubles finals between *1965–75.* Won Wimbledon mixed doubles with Tony Roche *1976* and the French with Jean-Claude Barclay in *1968/71/73.*

ROY STANLEY EMERSON (Australia)
Born 3/11/36. A remarkable athlete, 'lean, keen, and trained to the last ounce', who led Australia's international challenge for five years after Laver turned professional in 1962. A Queenslander, he won Wimbledon singles *1964/65* but injury in 1966 spoilt his chance of equalling Perry's record of three successive titles. Won the doubles with Fraser *1959/61,* US singles *1961/64* and doubles *1959/60* (with Fraser) and *1965/66* (with Stolle), Australian singles *1961* and *1963/64/65/66/67* and doubles *1960/66.* On clay courts won the French singles *1963/67,* Italian *1959/61/66* and German *1967* and his most interesting doubles achievement was to take the French title from *1960/61/ 63/64/65* with five different partners, Fraser *1960/62,* Laver *1961,* Santana *1963,* Fletcher *1964,* and Stolle *1965.* He won 36 of his 40 D Cup rubbers and played in 9 successive challenge rounds between *1959–67.*

CHRISTINE MARIE EVERT (USA)

Born Fort Lauderdale, Fl., 21/12/54. Now Mrs Andy Mill (married 30th July 1988). Coached by father Jimmy in Fort Lauderdale to become the most consistent back-court player of her generation: she won at least one Grand Slam singles title every year from **1974** to **1986** during which period her friendly rivalry with Martina Navratilova dominated the women's game. When she and Jimmy Connors (who were engaged at the time) won the two Wimbledon singles titles in **1974** with their double-handed backhands they legitimised the stroke and set a fashion that became a world trend. Her metronomic consistency, unshakeable concentration and fearless resolve to go for her shots were legendary and earned her more professional titles (157) than any other player, male or female, during the open era plus a fortune in prize money ($8,896,195). She competed for 19 consecutive years at the US Open and reached 9 finals, 8 semi-finals and was twice beaten in the quarter-finals, including her last year **1989** when she won her 101st match at these Championships, a record. As a sixteen-year-old, in **1971**, she reached the first of four consecutive semi-finals on grass at Forest Hills. In **1975/76/77** she won the title there on US clay and repeated that success on hard courts at Flushing Meadow in **1978/80/82**, by which time her first husband, John Lloyd (married 17th April 1979, divorced April 1987) had helped her to become a much better volleyer. In 13 challenges in Paris between 1973 and 1988 she won seven of the nine finals she contested (**1974/75/79/80/83/85/86**) and only in her last year failed to reach the semi-final, losing in the third round to Arantxa Sanchez-Vicario. She competed at Wimbledon every year from **1972–89** and only in **1983** (when she was ill and lost to Kathy Jordan) did she fail to reach the semi-finals. She was the champion 3 times (**1974/76/81**), a finalist 7 times (**1973/78/79/80/82/84/85**) and a semi-finalist 7 times (**1972/75/77/86/87/88/89**). She competed in the Australian Open six times between **1974–88**, winning the title in **1982** and **1984** and reaching the final in **1974/81/85/88**. Her 18 Grand Slam singles titles place her third behind Margaret Court (26) and Helen Wills Moody (19) on the list of great champions. Her streak of 125 consecutive wins on clay courts August **1973** – May **1979** is an all-time record and her prodigious achievement in reaching the semi-finals or better at 52 of her last 56 Grand Slams is unlikely ever to be equalled. She represented the United States eight times in the *Fed Cup* and won all but two of her 42 singles rubbers and 16 of 18 doubles rubbers in 42 ties between **1977–89**. She was unbeaten in 26 W Cup singles rubbers and won 8 of the 12 doubles rubbers she contested in 13 ties between **1971–85**.–J.B.

ROBERT FALKENBURG (USA)

Born 29/1/26. Won the US Junior Championship in **1943–44** and came to Europe in **1947** with the reputation of possessing the fastest service in the US. He won at Queen's Club, but lost to Pails in qf at Wimbledon and then won the doubles with Kramer, defeating Mottram and Sidwell in f. The following year he won one of Wimbledon's most dramatic f, defeating Bromwich 7–5 0–6 6–2 3–6 7–5 after saving three match-points as 3–5 in 5s. He was born in New York, learnt most of his tennis in Los Angeles and moved to Brazil, for whom he played in D Cup on a residential qualification.

NEALE ANDREW FRASER (Australia)

Born 3/10/33. A consistently aggressive lefthander, with a plain, direct serve-and-volley game, he was trained by Hopman, winning 18 of 21 D Cup rubbers between **1958** and **1963,** and later captained the Australian team which recaptured the trophy at Cleveland in **1973** and at Melbourne in **1978/83**. Fraser started his Wimbledon career in the qualifying competition and ended by winning the singles in **1960** after a remarkable escape in the qf. Buchholz, who had held 5 match-points against him, retired with cramp. He won the doubles with Emerson **1959/61** and mixed with du Pont in **1962** – the year in which he and his brother, John, a Melbourne doctor, both reached the singles sf. Neither got through to the f. He won the US singles **1959/60** and doubles **1957/59/60,** the French doubles **1958/60/62,** and Australian doubles **1957/58/62**.

SHIRLEY JUNE FRY (USA)
Born 30/6/27. Now Mrs Irvin. A persistent competitor, whose most notable performances were in doubles. She was first ranked in the top ten in the US in 1944, but she did not gain her two major singles successes until *1956* when she won both Wimbledon and Forest Hills. Until then she had always been thwarted by fellow-Americans. She won the Wimbledon doubles from *1951–53* with Doris Hart, losing only four games in capturing the title in *1953* and beat Helen Fletcher and Jean Quertier 6–0 6–0 in sf and Julie Sampson and Maureen Connolly by the same score in f. They won the US title *1951–54.* Her other successes included the Wimbledon mixed, with Seixas, *1956,* the Australian singles and doubles, with Althea Gibson, *1957,* and the French singles, *1951,* and doubles, with Hart, *1950–53.* She played in six W Cup contests, winning 10 matches and losing twice.

ALTHEA GIBSON (USA)
Born 25/8/27. The first black player to dominate international lawn tennis, relying on fierce serving and considerable strength and reach. Won Wimbledon singles *1957/58* and (doubles (with Angela Buxton) *1957* and (with Maria Bueno) */58.* US singles *1957/58.* French singles and doubles (with Angela Buxton) *1956.* Australian doubles (with Shirley Fry) *1957.* Italian singles *1956.* W Cup *1957/58,* turned professional *1958.*

ANDRE HENRI GOBERT (France)
Born 30/9/1890. Died 6/12/1951. Wallis Myers described him as 'perhaps the greatest indoor player of all time'. With Decugis, he gained France's first Wimbledon title by defeating the holders, Ritchie and Wilding, in *1911.* Although they were beaten by Dixon and Roper Barrett the following year, the brilliant Gobert's compensation was a place in the all-comers' singles f in which he lost to the experienced A. W. Gore. He won the French covered court title from *1911–13* and again in *1920* and the British covered court event in *1911–12* and again from *1920–22.* He first played in D Cup in *1911* and his career ended when the 'Musketeers' arrived in *1922.* He also won two Olympic gold medals in *1912.*

RICHARD (PANCHO) GONZALES (USA)
Born 9/5/28. A dramatic and spectacular competitor, who was undoubtedly the best player in the world for most of the 1950s. He turned pro in 1949 after winning the US singles in *1948/49,* taking the US Clay Court title *1948/49,* the US indoor title *1949,* and winning the doubles in Paris and at Wimbledon – in his only amateur appearances there – in *1949* with Parker. Thereafter he played his brilliant, angry tennis away from the main arenas of the game until, at last, open competition was allowed. By then he was 40, but he played one last great match for the Wimbledon crowd. In *1969* he beat Pasarell 22–24 1–6 16–14 6–3 11–9 in 5hr 12min – the longest singles seen at Wimbledon.

EVONNE FAY GOOLAGONG (Australia)
Born 31/7/51. Now Mrs Roger Cawley (married in 1975). One of the most naturally gifted of champions, she was the first of her Aborigine race to excel at the game. Suddenly in *1971* at the age of 19, 3 years before her coach Vic Edwards had forecast she would, she swept through both the French Championships and Wimbledon on a cloud of inspiration to win her first major titles. Although she reached the Wimbledon final again the following year and twice more, in *1975* and *1976*, it was not until *1980* that she won again – four years after the birth of her daughter, Kelly. This was the first win by a mother since Dorothea Lambert Chambers's success in 1914. The nine-year gap between her championships was also the greatest since Bill Tilden's wins in 1921 and 1930. She was always more at home on faster surfaces where her beautifully instinctive volleying paid handsome dividends and she won her native Australian Open on that surface four times – *1974/75/76/78*. She was always a competent player on clay but tended to be rather erratic as her famous 'walkabouts' led to extravagant errors. Nevertheless, besides the French Open in *1971* she also won the Italian title in *1973*. The other highlights of her singles career were the victories in the South African Championships *(1972)* and the Virginia Slims Champs *(1974/76)*. She was a good doubles player and won once at Wimbledon *(1974)*, four times in Melbourne *(1971/74/75/*

76) and twice in Johannesburg *(1971/72)*. In seven years of Fed Cup duty for Australia from *1971–82* she won 33 of the 38 rubbers she contested in 24 ties. – J.B.

ARTHUR WENTWORTH GORE (Great Britain)
Dorn 2/1/1060. Died 1/12/1038. Wimbledon's oldest champ and probably the most persistent and industrious competitor in the history of the Champs. He played there for the first time in 1888 and although the Dohertys, Brookes, and Wilding were among his contemporaries, won the singles 3 times *1901* and *1908/09* and, at the age of 44 years and 6 months, won the right to challenge Wilding for the title in *1912.* That was his seventh appearance in the challenge round in 13 years. He was almost entirely a forehand player, hitting the ball flat with the racket in a dead line with his outstretched arm. His lightness of foot enabled him to protect his backhand which was no more than a safe push. He competed at every Wimbledon between *1888–1927* and captained the first British D Cup team at Boston in 1900, reaching sf US Champs on that trip.

KAREN HANTZE (USA)
Born 11/12/42. Now Mrs Susman. One of the new generation of aggressive Californians who arrived on the international scene at the start of the 1960s, she won the doubles at Wimbledon with the 17-year-old Billie Jean Moffitt in *1961* and then defeated Vera Sukova in the *1962* singles final. Marriage and motherhood restricted her tennis, but she won US doubles (again with Moffitt) *1964.* She played W Cup *1960–62* and *1965,* winning six of her nine matches, and *Fed Cup 1965.*

DARLENE R. HARD (USA)
Born 6/1/36. An energetic volleyer, a shrewd tactician, and one of the best doubles players of her generation, she won the US singles in *1960/61* and the French singles *1960,* but she failed in both her Wimbledon finals, losing to Althea Gibson in *1957* and Maria Bueno *1960.* She won the Wimbledon doubles, with Gibson *1957*, Jeanne Arth *1959*, and twice with Bueno *(1960/63)* and the mixed in *1957* (with Rose), *1959–60* (with Laver). She won the US doubles six times and the French doubles three times. Perhaps her most surprising American success came in *1969,* some years after she had retired from regular competition, when she and Francoise Durr defeated Margaret Court and Virginia Wade 0–6 6–3 6–4 in f.

DORIS HART (USA)
Born 20/6/25. In spite of childhood illness which impeded her movement, she became one of the subtlest and most graceful of post-war competitors. Won Wimbledon singles *1951,* doubles (with Pat Todd) *1947* and (with Shirley Fry) *1951/52/53.* US singles *1954/55* and doubles (with Shirley Fry) *1951/52/53/54.* French singles *1950/52* and doubles (with Pat Todd) *1948* and (with Shirley Fry) *1950/51/53.* Australian singles *1949* and doubles (with Louise Brough) *1950.* Italian singles *1951/53* and South African singles *1952.* Also won many mixed titles, notably with E. V. Seixas at Wimbledon *1953/54/55.* Turned professional *1955.*

ADRIANNE (ANN) SHIRLEY HAYDON (Great Britain)
Born 17/10/38. Now Mrs Jones. A shrewd, persistent lefthander, who reached sf at Wimbledon 7 times in 10 years, she captured the title at last in *1969* after beating Margaret Court in sf and Billie Jean King, to whom she had been r/u in *1967,* in f. She achieved international fame as a table tennis player, but decided to concentrate on lawn tennis after being r/u in three events in the 1957 World Table Tennis Champs. She won the French title in *1961/66,* Rome in *1966* and was twice r/u at Forest Hills *1961/67.* She took the French doubles (with Francoise Durr) in *1968/69* and won the Wimbledon mixed with Stolle in *1969.* Her W Cup record – 15 successful rubbers out of 32 in 12 matches – is another remarkable illustration of her tenacity and consistency.

ROBERT ANTHONY JOHN HEWITT (South Africa)

Born in Sydney, Australia, 12/1/40. He moved to South Africa in the early 1960s and started to represent that country when his residential qualification matured in 1967. A big brooding volcano of a man, he had a deceptively fine touch and became one of the greatest right-court returners of the serve of modern times. He enjoyed two careers – first with fellow-Australian Fred Stolle and then with South Africa's Frew McMillan. With Stolle he won Wimbledon twice *(1962/64)* the Australian Championship twice *(1963/64)* and the Italian twice *(1963/64)* and with McMillan he added three more Wimbledon crowns *(1967/72/78)*, two German *(1967/70)*, one French *(1972)*, one US *(1977)*, one Masters *(1977)* and one WCT *(1974)* title as well as the Italian in *1967* and four at home in South Africa *(1967/70/72/74)*. He registered four major mixed doubles successes with three different partners, winning in Australia with Jan Lehane in *1961*, in Paris with Billie Jean King in *1970* and twice at Wimbledon with his pupil, Greer Stevens, in *1977/79*. He represented South Africa in D Cup *1967–74* and was a member of the successful team of *1974* that won by default from India. – J.B.

LEWIS ALAN HOAD (Australia)

Born 23/11/34. Capable of generating fierce power with great ease, he was one of the 'boy wonders' Harry Hopman produced to beat the US in the *1953* D Cup match. The other was Rosewall, 21 days his senior, who was to thwart his attempt on the Grand Slam in *1956* by beating him at Forest Hills, in the last of the 4 great f. That year Hoad had won the Australian and French titles, and had beaten Rosewall at Wimbledon. In *1957* he defeated Ashley Cooper in one of the most devastating Wimbledon f ever and then turned professional, but constant back trouble spoilt his pro career and also ended his attempt to return to the circuit when the game was opened to the pros. He won the Wimbledon doubles in *1953/55/56,* the US doubles in *1956,* the French doubles in *1953,* and the Australian doubles in *1953/56/57*. He won 17 rubbers out of 21 in D Cup play between *1953–56.*

HAZEL HOTCHKISS (USA)

Born 20/12/1886. Died 5/12/1974. Became Mrs G. Wightman. One of the most remarkable and enthusiastic competitors that the game has known. She was the donor of the W Cup and a considerable influence in American tennis for more than 60 years. She gained the first of her four US singles titles *(1909/10/11/19)* in 1909 and won the US indoor doubles for the 10th *(1919/21/24/27/28/29/30/31/33/43)* and last time in 1943. A remarkable volleyer with great speed about the court, she and Helen Wills were never beaten in doubles. They won the Wimbledon doubles in *1924* and the US doubles – a title which she had won on 4 other occasions – in *1924–28.* She captained the first US W Cup team in 1923 and between *1923–31* won 3 doubles rubbers in 5 matches.

HELEN HULL JACOBS (USA)

Born 6/8/08. A tenacious competitor, notable for duels with fellow-Californian, Helen Wills Moody, 5 times a Wimbledon finalist between *1929–39* but won only in *1936.* US singles *1932/33/34/35* and doubles (with Sarah Palfrey Fabyan) *1930/34/35.* Italian singles *1934.*

WILLIAM JOHNSTON (USA)

Born 2/11/1894. Died 1/6/1946. 'Little Bill', a Californian, small in physique but a brilliant volleyer and the possessor of a formidable top-spin forehand, was 'Big Bill' Tilden's principal rival at home in the first half of the 1920s. He defeated McLoughlin to win the US singles in *1915,* the first year at Forest Hills, lost to Williams in the *1916* final and then regained the title by beating Tilden in straight sets in *1919.* Tilden gained his revenge the following year and, although Johnston reached the final five times between *1920* and *1925,* Tilden always frustrated him. He beat Hunter in the *1923* Wimbledon final, losing only one set in the tournament. He won the US doubles with Griffin *1915/16* and *1920* and played in eight D Cup challenge rounds, winning 18 of his 21 D Cup rubbers.

BILLIE JEAN MOFFITT KING (USA)
Born 22/11/43. Perhaps the most important single figure in the history of tennis, as player, stateswoman, innovator and entrepreneur (usually with lawyer husband Larry King, whom she married in 1965), she has worked tirelessly to gain recognition and respect for the women's game. One of the founders of the women's pro tour in *1970*, twice President of the Women's Tennis Association, and the prime mover behind Team Tennis, she has been involved in most aspects of the game. As a player her natural exuberance and bubbling personality suited her attacking serve-and-volley game and made her a fearsome opponent. She will best be remembered for her 'Battle of the Sexes' against Bobby Riggs at the Houston Astrodome on 20 September, *1973* where the world's largest-ever crowd of 30,492 and some 50 million more around the world on TV, saw her win 6–4 6–3 6–3. In *1979* she achieved her 20th Wimbledon title to pass the record she had jointly shared with fellow-Californian Elizabeth Ryan who, ironically, had died on the eve of that unique achievement. Her unparalleled record comprises 6 singles – *1966/67/68/72/73/75*; 10 women's doubles – *1961/62/65/67/68/70/71/72/73/79*; 4 mixed doubles – *1967/71/73/74*. She first played at Wimbledon in *1961* and won the doubles with Karen Hantze. At her last appearance in *1983* she was competing for the 22nd year (she had not entered in *1981*) and reached the mixed doubles final with Steve Denton when she played her 265th and last match at Wimbledon. It was also her 29th final and, as they lost to John Lloyd and Wendy Turnbull 7–5 in the final set, she was losing at that stage for only the 9th time. She was almost as successful in her own US Championships where she won 13 titles, 4 in singles – *1967/71/72/74*, five in doubles – *1964/67/74/78/80* and four in mixed – *1967/71/73/76* and, in addition she became the only woman to win US National titles on all four surfaces – grass, clay, hard and indoor – a feat she repeated in doubles with Rosie Casals with whom she had most of her major doubles successes. She won the French Open singles and doubles in *1972* and the mixed in *1967/70* and was successful in singles and mixed at the Australian Open in *1968*, the first year of open tennis. Her 39 Grand Slam titles put her second only to Margaret Court who won 62. She was also the singles and doubles champion of Italy *(1970)* and of Germany *(1971)* and won the South African title 3 times *1966/67/69)*. With 21 winning rubbers from 26 played in 9 W Cup matches between *1961–78*, plus 52 wins from 58 rubbers in 6 years of Fed Cup play from *1963–79* she contributed hugely to American dominance in those team competitions. – J.B.

JAN KODES (Czechoslovakia)
Born 1/3/46. A dogged, industrious player with great strength and determination. He won his first major victories on clay, winning the French singles *1970/71* and reaching the Italian final *1970/71/72*, but he won the Wimbledon singles in the boycott year of *1973* and was runner-up in the US Champs *1971/73*. Having served his apprenticeship in European junior team competitions (he was on a winning Galea Cup team), he first represented Czechoslovakia in D Cup in *1966*, took them to the final in *1975* and was a member of their winning team in *1980*.

HILDE KRAHWINKEL (West Germany)
Born 26/3/08. Died 7/3/81. Became Mrs Sperling. A tall German, later Danish by marriage, whose dogged ability to retrieve from the back of the court turned her matches into long tests of endurance. She won the German indoor title in *1929* and then, emerging rapidly as an international player, lost to Cilly Aussem in the only all-German women's f at Wimbledon *1931*. She reached the final again in *1936*, losing 6–2 4–6 7–5 to Helen Jacobs, and altogether she was in qf (or better) 8 times. She won the French singles *1935–37*, defeating Mrs Mathieu in each of the three f, the Italian title *1935* and she was German singles champ *1933/35/37/39*. (There was no competition in 1936.) Her last important victory was in the Scandinavian indoor final in *1950*.

JACK ALBERT KRAMER (USA)
Born 1/8/21. A methodical and powerful exponent of the serve-and-volley game. Played for the US in the last pre-war D Cup challenge round against Australia. Won Wimbledon

singles title in *1947* after losing dramatically to the then unknown Jaroslav Drobny in 1946. Won doubles *1946/47*. Won US singles *1946/47* and doubles *1940/41/43/47*. Turned pro *1947* and then controlled pro tennis for 15 years. Still appears occasionally as a television commentator and was executive director of ATP Sept. 1972–April 1975.

RENE LACOSTE (France)

Born 2/7/04. In spite of ill health, he became the best groundstroke player and most astute tactician of pre-war lawn tennis. Won Wimbledon singles *1925/28* and doubles (with J. Borotra) *1925*. Won US singles *1926/27,* French singles *1925/27/29* and French doubles (with Borotra) *1924/25/29.* Played in 51 D Cup rubbers between *1923–28* and won the crucial rubbers of the *1927* challenge round which brought France the trophy for the first time, when he beat Tilden and Johnston in the singles.

ARTHUR D. LARSEN (USA)

Born 6/4/25. A graceful, elegant lefthander with exquisite touch and some notable eccentricities, he was famous for his dressing-room superstitions, his physical twitches and his rituals on court. He was known as Tappy because he would have a lucky number for the day and would always tap the baseline, the umpire's chair – even his own toe – with his racket the required number of times before continuing. He won US singles *1950,* US Clay Courts *1952* and US Indoor *1953.* A motor-cycle accident in which he suffered severe head injuries ended his career in 1957.

RODNEY GEORGE LAVER (Australia)

Born 9/8/38. The first player to achieve the Grand Slam twice and the master of the old professional circuit, with Rosewall as his great rival, in its last days. A lefthander, red-haired like Budge, with a spectacularly aggressive style, he brought off the slam of the four major singles titles, as an amateur, in *1962* and then, as a professional, in *1969.* Disciplined, unassuming, quick and light in movement, he could produce sudden bombardments of shots, heavy with spin, which totally disconcerted his opponents. Born at Rockhampton, Queensland, 'Rocket' was a perfect nickname for the first tennis millionaire. If he had not turned professional in 1963, he would have won many more of the traditional titles. As it was, he won the singles at Wimbledon *1961/62* and *1968/69,* the doubles with Emerson *1971* and the mixed, with Darlene Hard, *1959/60.* He took the US singles and French singles *1962* and *1969,* also winning the French doubles with Emerson and the mixed with Hard in *1961.* His Australian singles victories came in *1960/62/69,* with doubles *1959/61* (Mark) and *1969* (Emerson). He was Italian singles champion *1962* and *1971,* German champion *1961/62* and a member of the undefeated D Cup team from *1959–62.* He returned to D Cup in *1973,* collecting three more rubbers in Australia's 5–0 victory over the US in the final at Cleveland.

SUZANNE LENGLEN (France)

Born 24/5/1899. Died 4/7/1938. The most exciting, and successful of women players. She survived 2 match-points to win at Wimbledon in *1919* against Mrs Lambert Chambers and thereafter lost only in a controversial match to Molla Mallory (US) in 1921 US Champs until her retirement in 1926. Quarrelled with the Wimbledon referee in 1926 and turned pro. Won Wimbledon singles and doubles (with Elizabeth Ryan) *1919/20/21/22/23/25*. French singles and doubles (with various partners) *1920/21/22/23/25/26.*

KATHLEEN McKANE (Great Britain)

Born 7/5/1896. Now Mrs Godfree. A fine match-player with a quick, aggressive game, she achieved the notable distinction of winning the Wimbledon singles twice – even though she was a contemporary of Suzanne Lenglen and Helen Wills. In Lenglen's absence, she beat the Californian (a feat which no other player achieved in the next 14 years at Wimbledon) in the *1924* final after trailing by a set and 1–4, and in *1926* she regained the title after being within a point of 1–4 in the third set against Lili d'Alvarez. She won the Wimbledon mixed (with Gilbert) in *1924* and in *1926* (with her husband, Leslie Godfree).

She was r/u to Miss Wills at Forest Hills in 1925 after beating Elizabeth Ryan and Molla Mallory, and she won the US doubles in *1923* (with Mrs Covell) */27* (with Miss Harvey). She won 7 rubbers out of 17 in 7 W Cup matches between *1923–34.*

CHARLES ROBERT McKINLEY (USA)
Born 5/1/41. Died 11/8/86. An energetic and athletic match-player, who won the Wimbledon singles title in *1963* without meeting another seeded player in the course of the tournament. He was runner-up to Laver in *1961,* a disappointing competitor in *1962* but in *1963* bounced back to take the title. In the US Championships he never progressed further than the semi-finals, failing three times at that stage, but, with Ralston, he won the doubles in *1961* and *1963–64.* He played in 16 D Cup matches between *1960–65* and won 29 of his 38 rubbers.

MAURICE EVANS McLOUGHLIN (USA)
Born 7/1/1890. Died 10/12/1957. The 'Californian Comet' was the first notable exponent of the cannonball service. Fiercely effective with volley and smash, he was US champ in *1912–13* and his appearance at Wimbledon was, as a contemporary remarked, a sign of the way the modern game was developing. His spectacular style had considerable appeal. When he met Wilding for the title in *1913,* 'there was such an indecent crush round the barriers of the Centre Court that, to avoid serious injury, several ladies had to be lifted over by policemen into the security of the arena'. Wilding beat him 8–6 6–3 10–8, but McLoughlin had the consolation of winning 2 rubbers in the American capture of the D Cup from Britain at Wimbledon. In the *1914* challenge round at Forest Hills he beat both Brookes and Wilding, but Australasia took the trophy. He did not play after the war. His aggressive style was said to have burnt him out.

FREW DONALD McMILLAN (South Africa)
Born in Springs, a small Transvaal town, 20/5/42. A gifted and unusual doubles player who invariably wore a peaked white cloth cap and held the racket with two hands on both sides to produce just the right blend of disguise, finesse and power. His partnership with expatriate Australian Bob Hewitt was particularly fruitful and they became one of the three greatest pairs of the post-Second World War years. Together they won their native South African title four times *(1967/70/72/74)* and succeeded at Wimbledon three times *(1967/72/78).* They won once each the French *(1972),* the US *(1977),* the Masters *(1977* played in Jan '78), the WCT *(1974)* and the Italian *(1967)* titles and won the German twice *(1967/70).* But it was in mixed doubles that he won his first and last major championships. In *1966* he partnered Annette Van Zyl to the French title and in *1981* he captured the Wimbledon mixed for the second time with Betty Stove, with whom he had been successful in 1978 – the same year they won a second US Open together *(1977/78).* He played D Cup from *1965–76* and was a member of the only team ever to win the famous trophy by default – from India in 1974. – J.B.

ALICE MARBLE (USA)
Born 28/9/13. Died 13/12/90. A brilliant server and volleyer whose career was interrupted by ill health and the war. Won Wimbledon singles *1939* and doubles (with Sarah Palfrey Fabyan) *1938/39.* US singles *1936/38/39/40* and doubles (with Sarah Palfrey Fabyan) *1937/38/39/40.* Turned pro *1941.*

SIMONE MATHIEU (France)
Born 31/1/08. Died 7/1/80. A formidable clay court player, she succeeded Lenglen as the leader of the women's game in France. She was junior champ – as a married woman – at 18, and 3 years later reached the French f, losing 6–3 6–4 to Wills. She was r/u again in *1933/36/37* before she won at last in *1938,* defeating Landry, and then retained her title *1939* against Jedrzejowska. She won the French doubles 6 times and the Wimbledon doubles twice with Ryan *1933/34* and once with Yorke *1937.* Her soundness from the baseline carried her 4 times to the singles sf.

HELEN WILLS MOODY (USA)

Born 6/10/05. Later Mrs A. Roark. Lenglen's successor as ruler of Wimbledon, A relentless baseliner, she won the singles 8 times in 9 attempts, losing only to Kitty McKane in 1924. Between *1927–32* she won all the major singles champs, except Australia, without losing a set. Won Wimbledon singles *1927/28/29/30/32/33/35/38* and doubles (with Hazel Wightman) *1924* and (with Elizabeth Ryan) */27/30*. US singles *1923/24/25/27/28/29/31,* and doubles (with Mrs J. B. Jessup) *1922,* (with Hazel Wightman) */24/28,* and (with Mary K. Browne) */25*. French singles *1928/29/30/32* and doubles (with Elizabeth Ryan) *1930/ 31/32.*

ANGELA MORTIMER (Great Britain)

Born 21/4/32. Now Mrs Barrett. Britain's first post-war Wimbledon singles champ. Coached by Arthur Roberts at Torquay, she used an armoury of firmly controlled groundstrokes most effectively and considerable determination enabled her to overcome a certain frailty of physique. Her first notable success was the capture of the French title in *1955* – the first British victory in Paris since Peggy Scriven won in 1934 – and in the same year she won the Wimbledon doubles (with Anne Shilcock). She won the Australian title in *1958,* after travelling there to recover from illness, and 6 months later was r/u to Althea Gibson at Wimbledon. She won the title in *1961* by beating Christine Truman in the first all-British f of the modern Wimbledon. She won 5 rubbers out of 16 in 6 W Cup matches and became W Cup captain *1964–70* and *Fed Cup* captain *1967–70.*

ILLIE NASTASE (Rumania)

Born 19/8/46. One of the most gifted shot-makers and fluid movers in the game's history, he never quite fulfilled his enormous potential. His two Grand Slam titles were won on different surfaces – on grass in New York in *1972* and on clay in Paris the following year. He could also play beautifully indoors as his four Masters titles in *1971/72/73/75* testify. Sadly for his many admirers, a childlike and sometimes mischievous streak was his undoing on many occasions, particularly towards the end of his playing days when he fell foul of authority for his behaviour. Throughout his career the showman in him struggled constantly with the athlete so that there was often a lack of steel about his match play. This failing, and an inability to put the ball away with his somewhat lightweight volleys, cost him two chances to win the Wimbledon title – in *1972* when Smith beat him and in *1976* when Borg won the first of his five titles. His lightning reflexes made him an excellent doubles player and he won major titles in Paris *(1970)* and Rome *(1970/72),* at Wimbledon *(1973)* and in New York *(1975)*. He also won two mixed titles at Wimbledon with Rosie Casals *1970/72)*. His biggest disappointment was his failure to lead Rumania to victory in the *1972* D Cup final against the Americans on clay in Bucharest where his loss to Smith in the opening rubber proved decisive. – J.B.

JOHN DAVID NEWCOMBE (Australia)

Born 23/5/44. The supreme exponent of the simple, rugged style in modern tennis. Splendidly confident and with great strength of personality, Newcombe relied upon a heavy service, forceful volleying and solid, powerful groundstrokes. His best singles successes were on grass – Wimbledon *1967/70/71,* US Championships *1967/73,* and Australia *1973/75* – but he also won, by doggedness and determination, the German *1968)* and Italian *(1969)* titles. He and Roche formed the most successful of modern doubles partnerships, winning Wimbledon in *1965, 1968–70,* and *1974*. When Roche was injured in *1966,* Fletcher replaced him at short notice and he and Newcombe won the title. He won the US doubles with Roche *1967,* with Taylor *1971,* and with Davidson *1973,* France twice with Roche *(1967/69)* and once with Okker *(1973)* and Australia four times with Roche *(1965/67/71/76)* and once with Anderson *(1973)*. In *1981,* aged 37, he and Stolle (42) took McEnroe/Fleming to 5s tie-break in US Open sf. He first played in the *D Cup* in *1963* and finally against Italy in Rome, *1976,* but perhaps his best performance was in *1973* when he and Laver inflicted a 5–0 defeat upon the United States at Cleveland.

BETTY NUTHALL (Great Britain)
Born 23/6/11. Died 8/11/83. Became Mrs Shoemaker. An aggressive and attractive competitor, with a remarkable record as a junior, she never progressed beyond qf at Wimbledon but gained her most impressive victories abroad. At 16, after beating Molla Mallory, No. 6 seed, at Wimbledon in *1927,* she astonished the tennis world by reaching f at F Hills, where Helen Wills beat her 6–1 6–4. In *1930* she became the first British player to win that title with 6–4 6–1 victory over Mrs Harper. She won the US doubles *1930/31/33* and mixed *1929/31* and the French doubles *1931* and mixed *1931/32.* Her only British success in a nat singles event was the capture of the HC title in *1927.* She won the HC doubles *1926/28/31/32* and the mixed in *1927.* She played in 8 W Cup matches between *1927–39,* winning 6 rubbers and losing 7.

ALEJANDRO OLMEDO (USA)
Born 24/3/36. The son of a groundsman in Peru, this superb natural athlete rose like a comet in *1958* to win D Cup for America in Brisbane almost single-handed. Selected by the captain, Perry T. Jones, Olmedo had rewarded him with two singles wins and a share with Ham Richardson in the doubles win that had sealed the victory. Success in the Australian Championships confirmed the quality of his play as he beat Neale Fraser in four sets. Six months later 'The Chief', as he was popularly known, won the *1959* Wimbledon from Rod Laver for the loss of only two sets, with one of the most competent displays of power tennis seen since the war. After taking part in the unsuccessful defence of D Cup where he lost to Fraser but beat Laver again, he reached the final of the US Championships but failed once more against Fraser. Immediately he turned professional. – J.B.

MANUEL ORANTES (Spain)
Born 6/2/49. A consummate artist on European clay whose exquisite touch and gentle, generous manners made him an international favourite. A left-hander who, after leading Spain to two Galea Cup victories in *1968/69,* won his first two important titles in *1972* – the German and Italian Opens. His best year was *1975* for, besides winning a second German title, the Canadian Open and the first of his two US Clay Court crowns (he won the second in *1977*), he was triumphant on the clay at Forest Hills. After recovering miraculously to defeat Vilas in a night-time semi-final, having trailed one set to two and 0–5 in the fourth, he was back on court 15 hours later to thrash Jimmy Connors 6–4 6–3 6–3 in a near-perfect display of the clay-court art. In *1976* he won the Spanish Open and at the year's end won Masters in Houston against Fibak with another brave recovery, coming back from one set to two and 1–4. He played in the losing Spanish team in the D Cup challenge round of *1967* in Brisbane but led his country to victory in the World Team Cup in Dusseldorf 11 years later. – J.B.

MARGARET OSBORNE (USA)
Born 4/4/18. Now Mrs du Pont. One of the finest of American doubles players and a formidably successful competitor in singles. With her splendidly consistent serving and her strength and skill at the net, she did much to set the pattern for the period of American supremacy in women's tennis, which began in 1946. Won Wimbledon singles in *1947,* Forest Hills *1948/49/50* and Paris in *1946/49.* She and Louise Brough won the Wimbledon doubles in *1946/48/49/50/54.* They ruled the US doubles from *1942–50* and *1955–57,* and held the French title *1946/47/49.* She won the Wimbledon mixed with Neale Fraser in *1962* – 15 years after her first singles victory.

SARAH PALFREY (USA)
Born 18/9/12. Now Mrs Danzig, formerly Mrs Fabyan, and Mrs Cooke. A fine volleyor with a sweeping backhand and a notable doubles player, she partnered Alice Marble to victory at Wimbledon in *1938/39* and won the US doubles title with a variety of partners – Betty Nuthall, Helen Jacobs (3 times), Alice Marble (4 times) and Margaret Osborne – 9 times between *1930–41.* She won the US singles in *1941/45* and was r/u to Helen Jacobs

in *1934/35*. She was the US mixed champion on 4 occasions. She played in 10 W Cup matches and won 14 rubbers out of 21.

ADRIANO PANATTA (Italy)
Born 9/7/50. Without doubt, 1976 was the *annus mirabilis* of Panatta's career. Until then he had always been dashing and stylish, but had never made full use of his talent. In *1976*, however, he lived dangerously and survived brilliantly. In Rome he became the first home player to win in Italy for 15 years after frustrating Warwick no fewer than 11 times at m-p in the first round. In Paris, against Hutka, he again faced a first-round m-p and again went on to take the championship. Four months later, when Italy won D Cup for the first time, Panatta played a major role in their victory. Paris, Rome and D Cup – this was Panatta's year! He was also the leading player in the Italian teams which reached the *1977/79/80* D Cup finals. He reached the French sf in *1973/75* and was runner-up in Rome *1978* and Hamburg *1972*.

GERALD L. PATTERSON (Australia)
Born 17/12/1895. Died 13/6/1967. Formidably aggressive with a cannonball service modelled on McLoughlin's, he was the dominating player when international competition was resumed in 1919. After being r/u to O'Hara Wood in the *1914* Australian singles, he became Wimbledon's first post-war champ by defeating Brookes in *1919*. He lost his Wimbledon title to Tilden in *1920* but regained it against Lycett in *1922*. R/u doubles in *1922* (O'Hara Wood) and *1928* (Hawkes) and won the mixed with Suzanne Lenglen in *1920*. He won the Australian singles in his fourth final in *1927*. Between *1919–28* he played 46 D Cup rubbers for Australia and Australasia and won 4 out of 12 challenge round rubbers. He was a nephew of Dame Nellie Melba and was the first man to win the Wimbledon singles by playing through when the challenge round was abolished there in 1922.

J. EDWARD PATTY (USA)
Born 11/2/24. An American who lived in Paris and developed his game there, 'Budge' Patty, with his elegant, effective forehand volley, was one of the great post-war sty-lists. *1950* – when he won both the Wimbledon and French singles – was the peak of his career, but his rivalry with Drobny captured the public's imagination. The most notable of their long and dramatic matches was in the third round at Wimbledon in 1953. After 4½ hours Patty lost 8–6 16–18 3–6 8–6 12–10 after holding 6 m-ps. He had beaten the Czech at Wimbledon in *1947* and 3 years later by 6–1 6–2 3–6 5–7 7–5 in his French f. The last of their meetings was in *1954*. Drobny, on his way to the title, won a 4-set sf. Patty won his last title there in *1957* when he and Mulloy, then aged 43, beat Hoad and Fraser to take the men's doubles. He won the Italian singles *1954,* and the German singles *1953/54* and doubles *1953/54/55.*

FRANK A. PARKER (USA)
Born 31/1/16. Shrewd, persistent, and accurate in spite of a certain lightness of shot, he shared with Trabert the distinction, rare for an American, of winning the French title twice. At his best on slow courts, he was ranked in the first 10 in the US for 17 consecutive years between *1933,* the year of the first of his 5 US Clay Court victories, and *1949* when he turned pro. His victories in Paris were in *1948/49*, and in *1949* he won the doubles in Paris and Wimbledon with Gonzales. He won the US singles in *1944/45* as an Army sergeant and the doubles with Kramer in *1943*. He played in the D Cup challenge round against Britain in *1937* when the US regained the trophy after 10 years and in the *1939* and *1948* challenge rounds. He was beaten only twice in 14 D Cup rubbers.

FREDERICK JOHN PERRY (Great Britain)
Born 18/5/09. A US citizen. The most successful modern British player, an aggressive competitor with boundless self-confidence and a remarkable running forehand. Won Wimbledon singles *1934/35/36* – the first player since A. F. Wilding (1910–13) to take the title 3 years in succession – and mixed (with Dorothy Round) *1935/36.* US singles

1933/34/36. French singles *1935* and doubles (with G. P. Hughes) *1933.* Australian singles *1934* and doubles (with Hughes) *1934.* Won 45 out of 52 D Cup rubbers, 34 out of 38 singles, between *1931–36.* Turned pro in *1936.*

YVON FRANÇOIS MARIE PETRA (France)
Born 8/3/16 in Indo-China. Died 11/9/84. Wimbledon's first post-war men's singles champion. Reached mixed f at Wimbledon *1937* with Simone Mathieu and won French doubles *1938* with Destremau, defeating Budge and Mako in f. Between 1942, when he was released from a prisoner-of-war camp, and 1945, he consolidated his reputation as France's most aggressive competitor in wartime domestic competitions. At Wimbledon, *1946,* his strength, flair and, notably, the consistency of his heavy serving gained this formidably built player an unexpected title. Drobny beat Kramer, the favourite, in 4r. Petra disposed of Pails, the other expected finalist, in qf and then won 5s matches against Tom Brown and Geoff Brown. That was the peak of his career. Marcel Bernard beat him in the French sf – played in July that year – and his consolation was a doubles victory, partnered by Bernard, over Morea and Segura in f. Patty beat him easily on the second day at Forest Hills and in *1947* he lost to Tom Brown in qf at Wimbledon.

NICOLA PIETRANGELI (Italy)
Born 11/9/33. A master of the European clay court style, he was born in Tunis (of a French father and Russian mother) and between *1954–72* played in 163 D Cup rubbers for Italy, more than anyone in history. Won most rubbers (120), played most singles (109) and won most (78), played most doubles (54) and won most (42), and played in most ties (66). Appeared in the *1960/61* challenge rounds against Australia, but won only one 'dead' singles. Won French singles *1959/60* and doubles (with Sirola), Italian singles *1957/61,* and German singles *1960.* Reached sf at Wimbledon, *1960,* and doubles final (with Sirola) *1956.*

DR JOSHUA PIM (Ireland)
Born 20/6/1869. Died 13/4/1942. A robust, adventurous competitor, regarded by contemporary critics as one of the great geniuses of early tennis. 'When Pim was at his best he was virtually unplayable', wrote Wallis Myers. 'It is scarcely exaggerating to say that he could hit a coin placed anywhere on the court.' He reached sf at Wimbledon *1890,* losing to Hamilton, who became Wimbledon's first Irish champ, then lost in *1891* to Wilfred-Baddeley in the all-comers' f and again in *1892* challenge round. He gained his revenge, however, by beating Baddeley in the 2 following Wimbledon f. Pim won the Irish title for the 3rd and last time in *1895* but then played little first-class tennis until he was controversially picked for the D Cup match against USA at New York in 1902. He was preferred to Lawrie Doherty, lost both his singles badly and the British Isles were beaten 3–2. 'Although still very good, Pim had no more than a shadow of his former skill, but alas! a great deal more than the shadow of his former weight', wrote Commander Hillyard.

ADRIAN KARL QUIST (Australia)
Born 4/8/13. Died 17/11/91. A shrewd, graceful doubles player, whose victories at Wimbledon were separated by a gap of 15 years. Won with J. H. Crawford in *1935* and, when almost a veteran, with J. E. Bromwich *1950.* Held Australian title from *1936–50,* winning twice with D. P. Turnbull and 8 times with Bromwich. Won US doubles (with Bromwich) *1939,* French doubles (with J. H. Crawford) *1935,* and Australian singles *1936/40/48.* Won 42 out of 55 D Cup rubbers in 28 ties between *1933–48.*

WILLIAM CHARLES RENSHAW (Great Britain)
Born 3/1/1861. Died 12/8/1904. The first great champ. Learnt on asphalt at school at Cheltenham with twin brother, Ernest, a more graceful but less determined competitor. They were the first spectacular players and their skill – particularly in volleying and smashing – brought crowds to Wimbledon and contributed considerably to the development of lawn tennis as a spectator sport. 'Willie' Renshaw was singles champ at Wimbledon from

1881–86 and in *1889.* He held the doubles, with Ernest, in *1884/85/86/88/89.* Ernest won the singles title in *1888* and was beaten by William in the challenge rounds of 1882 and 1883.

NANCY ANN RICHEY (USA)
Born 23/8/42. Later Mrs Gunter. A Texan, famous for her shorts and peaked cap, she was, like her brother, George Clifford Richey, a tenacious baseliner, impressive on clay. Her determination occasionally brought unexpected success on grass. She reached the *1969* US final, losing 6–2 6–2 to Margaret Court. She won Australia *1967,* beating Lesley Turner, another clay-court specialist, in the final. At Wimbledon she reached qf seven times in nine years *1964–72* but was semi-finalist only in *1968.* She won Wimbledon doubles with Maria Bueno *1966.* On clay she won French singles *1968,* beating Ann Jones to avenge a defeat in the *1966* final, but the best evidence of her quality was her record in US Clay Courts. She won Indianapolis from *1963–68* and even as late as *1975* led Chris Evert 7–5 5–0 in the semi-finals there, twice reaching m-p before retiring with cramp at 2–4 in the final set. She played W Cup from *1962–68* and *Fed Cup 1964–69.*

ROBERT LARIMORE RIGGS (USA)
Born 25/2/18. A shrewd, confident match-player, with remarkable versatility of shot, he won all 3 titles on his first appearance at Wimbledon in *1939.* He also won Forest Hills in *1939,* but lost to McNeill in the French f. He turned pro in 1941 and later became a notable competitor in veterans' events, but his greatest fame came at the age of 55. Profiting from the Women's Lib controversy, he challenged and beat Margaret Court 6–2 6–1 in a singles match in Ramona, Cal, and then lost to Billie Jean King 6–4 6–3 6–3, before a record television audience of almost 50 million and 30,492 paying spectators at the Houston Astrodome in September 1973.

ANTHONY DALTON ROCHE (Australia)
Born 17/6/45. Strong, rugged and a fine volleyer, he was the lefthander in one of Wimbledon's most successful doubles partnerships. He won the doubles with John Newcombe in *1965,* from *1968–70* (the first hat-trick of titles since the Dohertys 1903–5) and in *1974.* Other doubles victories included US *1967,* French *1967–69,* Australia *1965/67/71/76/77* and Italy *1965/71*; and Wimbledon mixed doubles with Francoise Durr *1976*. He did not achieve as much as expected in singles, partly because of injury. The extraordinary operation on his left elbow, performed without knife or anaesthetic in the Philippines by a faith healer, received worldwide publicity. He never reached an Australian final in spite of numerous attempts, but was runner-up to Laver at Wimbledon in *1968* and lost two US Open finals: *1969* when Laver beat him to complete the Grand Slam and *1970* to Rosewall. His most successful year was *1966* when he won French and Italian titles. Played Davis Cup *1964–78* but did not play singles in a final until he beat Panatta in the opening match *1977.*

KENNETH ROBERT ROSEWALL (Australia)
Born 2/11/34. For a quarter of a century Rosewall's grace and easy, economical style delighted the connoisseurs and the only regret about his long and distinguished career is that, in spite of four finals over a period of 20 years, he never won the Wimbledon singles title. He began as a Hopman prodigy and it was not until the end of *1979* that he retired from Grand Prix tennis. In *1953,* aged 18, he won the Australian and French singles and, with Hoad, the French and Wimbledon doubles. In *1954* he lost to Drobny in the Wimbledon final. Hoad beat him in the *1956* Wimbledon final, but Rosewall avenged that defeat in the US final, frustrating Hoad in the last leg of his attempt on the Grand Slam. Turning professional in *1957,* he took over the leadership of the professional circuit from Gonzales until Laver's arrival in *1963.* Rosewall's skills endured. In *1968* he won the first open tournament at Bournemouth and then recaptured some of his former titles. He re-gained the French singles and doubles (with Stolle) in *1968.* In *1970* – after 14 years and aged 35 – he won the US title again and reached his fourth final at Forest Hills in *1974.* The gap

between his Australian successes was even wider. After his victories in **1953/55,** he won again in **1971/72.** But Wimbledon always eluded him. Newcombe beat him in **1970,** his third final, and Connors overwhelmed him in the **1974** final.

DOROTHY EDITH ROUND (Great Britain)
Born 13/7/09. Died 12/11/82. Became Mrs Little. Determined and efficient, possessing a fine forehand drive and shrewd drop-shot, she was one of the two British women's singles champs at Wimbledon between the wars. She gained her first notable victory there against Lili d'Alvarez in **1931,** was r/u to Helen Wills Moody in **1933,** then beat Helen Jacobs to win the title in **1934** and regained it against Jadwiga Jedrzejowska in **1937.** She won the Australian singles in **1935** and the Wimbledon mixed in **1934** (with Miki) and **1935/36** (with Perry). She won 4 of her 13 W Cup rubbers between **1931–36.**

ELIZABETH RYAN (USA)
Born 5/2/1892. Died 6/7/1979. Suzanne Lenglen's doubles partner and the winner of 19 Wimbledon titles – 12 doubles and 7 mixed. A determined competitor with a cunningly chopped forehand and a great appetite for match-play, she was regarded by contemporaries as 'the best player never to win a great singles championship'. With a variety of partners, she won the Wimbledon doubles **1914/19/20/21/22/23/25/26/27/30/33/34** and the mixed **1919/21/23/27/28/30/32.** US doubles in **1926,** the French doubles **1930/ 32/33/34.**

JOHN WILLIAM VAN RYN (USA)
Born 30/6/05. Formed one of the most famous of all doubles partnerships with Wilmer Allison. Pat Hughes described their combination as 'a perfect blending of styles . . . Van Ryn dipped the ball over from the right court and his partner stepped in at the psychological moment for the final volley.' George Lott thought that their deep personal friendship and knowledge of each other's movements and reactions played an important part in their success. With Allison, Van Ryn succeeded at Wimbledon in **1929–30** and took the US title in **1931/35.** He won Paris and Wimbledon with Lott in **1931.** In the **1929** D Cup challenge round he and Allison beat Cochet and Borotra and in the **1932** match they defeated Cochet and Brugnon. He was a member of the US team from **1929–36** and won 29 of his 32 rubbers in 24 matches. He lost only two of his 24 D Cup doubles.

MANUEL SANTANA (Spain)
Born 10/5/38. Learnt the game as a ballboy and, after a period in which he was the most admired clay court player in Europe, won US singles **1965,** and Wimbledon singles **1966.** Possesed a remarkable forehand and great delicacy of touch. Won French singles **1961/ 64,** defeating Pietrangeli in both finals, and doubles (with Emerson) **1963,** and South African singles **1967.** The most successful Spanish player in history, he won 91 D Cup rubbers out of 119 between **1958–73.**

RICHARD SAVITT (USA)
Born 4/3/27. His talent was discovered in the classic fashion by a complete stranger who saw him playing in a public park, and after a modest junior career he became a powerful exponent of the serve-and-volley game. Concentrating on tennis after a basketball injury in 1949, he rose rapidly on the US ranking-list, moving up from 16th to 6th after reaching sf at Forest Hills, **1950,** with victories over Seixas and Bromwich. His remarkable year was **1951.** He won both the Australian and Wimbledon titles, defeating McGregor in both finals. This was his first trip to Europe and he never achieved the same kind of success again, although he played some memorable matches, notably sf against Rosewall at Forest Hills, **1956,** and a vain defence of his US indoor title in a three-hour f in **1959.** He was a member of the US D Cup team in 1951, but was not chosen to play in the challenge round against Australia.

FREDERICK RUDOLPH SCHROEDER (USA)

Born 20/7/21. A powerful Californian whose aggressive serve-and-volley game brought him much success on fast surfaces. The US National Junior Champion in **1939**, he won the NC Championships from Stanford in **1942** and the same year won the US Championships, defeating Frank Parker in the final. In **1949** he reached the final again but lost in five sets to Pancho Gonzales. Earlier that same year, on his only visit to Wimbledon he had won the singles in heroic fashion after surviving four five-set matches. In the first round he had beaten his doubles partner, Gardnar Mulloy, 7–5 in the fifth (later they reached the doubles final and lost to Gonzales and Parker). In the quarter-finals he had been m-p down to Frank Sedgman and, despite being foot-faulted on his first serve, had followed in his second serve to hit a winning volley and finally won 9–7 in the final set. In all he played 291 games. Only two champions played more – Boris Becker (292) in 1985 and Ashley Cooper (322) in 1958. In doubles he won the US Championships with Jack Kramer in **1940/41/47** and the mixed with Louise Brough in **1942**. A distinguished member of the US D Cup team between **1946–51**, he played in six challenge rounds, winning eight of his 11 singles and one of his four doubles. – J.B.

FRANCIS ARTHUR SEDGMAN (Australia)

Born 29/10/27. A superb volleyer who seemed to glide about the court, he was Australia's first post-war Wimbledon singles champ and, with Ken McGregor, he achieved the grand slam of the 4 major doubles titles in **1953**. Won Wimbledon singles **1952** and doubles (with J. E. Bromwich) **1948** and (with McGregor) **/51/52**. US singles **1951/52** and doubles (with Bromwich) **1950** and (with McGregor) **/51**. French doubles (with McGregor) **1951/52**. Australian singles **1949/50** (with McGregor) doubles **1951/52**. Italian singles and doubles (with McGregor) **1952.** Won 25 D Cup rubbers out of 28 between **1949–52.** Turned pro in **1953.**

FRANCISCO 'PANCHO' SEGURA (Ecuador)

Born 20/6/21. An unorthodox showman who made his reputation in his pro years – he achieved little as an amateur. Won the US Clay Court title in **1944** and the US Indoor in **1946,** but made little mark at Wimbledon, losing to Tom Brown and to Drobny in his two singles appearances. He turned pro in 1947 and immediately became one of the great entertainers of the pro game. With his double-fisted forehand, his deadly lobs, his scuttling speed about the court, and his beaming smile, he was a most popular competitor for 20 years. If he did not win as many titles as he deserved, he was always capable of testing players of the quality of Kramer, Rosewall, and Gonzales.

ELIAS VICTOR SEIXAS (USA)

Born 30/8/23. A doggedly successful American competitor. Won Wimbledon singles **1953** and mixed **1953/54/55/56,** 3 times with Doris Hart and once with Shirley Fry. US singles **1954** and doubles (with M. G. Rose) **1952** and (with M. A. Trabert) **/54**. French doubles (with Trabert) **1954/55**. Played in 7 successive D Cup challenge rounds and won 38 out of 55 rubbers in 19 ties between **1951–57.**

MARGARET SMITH (Australia)

Born 16/7/42. Now Mrs Court. In 1970 she became the second woman to achieve the Grand Slam of the major singles championships, having brought off a unique mixed doubles slam with Fletcher in **1963.** A powerful athlete, superbly fit, with a heavy service, great stamina and a formidable reach on the volley, she won a record number of 62 GS titles – and would have won more if she had not been afflicted by occasional and often inexplicable losses of confidence. Her major singles successes were Wimbledon **1963/65/70**, US Championships **1962/65/69/70/73**, French Championships **1962/64/69/70/73,** and Australia **1960–66, 1969–71** and **1973.** She was also three times the holder of the Italian, German and South African titles. In addition, she won the doubles at Wimbledon twice and the mixed five times, the US doubles five times and the mixed on eight occasions, the French four times in doubles and mixed, and she held eight Australian doubles and two mixed titles. She toured successfully, with the help of her husband, Barry, with two children, but retired in 1977 when she found that she was expecting a third baby.

STANLEY ROGER SMITH (USA)
Born 14/12/46. The very epitome of the All-American boy with his tall straight-backed figure, his fair hair and his clean-cut good looks, he became a national hero in *1972*, as well as the world's No. 1 player, when he won a magnificent Wimbledon final against Nastase and then beat the Rumanian again in the opening rubber of the D Cup final on unfriendly clay in Bucharest to launch the United States towards an improbable victory against the odds. Earlier, in *1969*, he had won the US Nationals and the following year had beaten Laver and Rosewall to capture the first-ever Masters which, that year, was a round-robin competition. When he won the US Open in *1971* on the grass of Forest Hills he was perfecting the serve-and-volley technique that made him such an awkward opponent. Although his groundstrokes were never his strength, he used them intelligently to secure the few breaks of serve that were necessary as he blanketed the net to secure his own service games. His doubles partnership with Lutz was one of the best American pairings there has ever been. They are the only pair to have won US National titles on all four surfaces – grass, clay, hard and indoor. Four times they won the US Open – *1968/74/78/80* and in *1977* they were successful both in South Africa and the US Pro at Boston. In D Cup they are the only American pair to have won three Challenge Round rubbers and two in the Final Round. Overall his D Cup record is 34 wins and 7 losses in 23 ties. – J.B.

FREDERICK SYDNEY STOLLE (Australia)
Born 8/10/38. Former Sydney bank clerk, regarded primarily as doubles specialist, who by diligence and determination became one of the most successful singles players of the 1960s. Powerful serving and volleying, added to dogged consistency in return of service on the backhand, compensated for his lack of mobility and flexibility. Shared with Von Cramm the unlucky distinction of losing in 3 successive Wimbledon singles f, falling to McKinley *(1963)* and Emerson *(1964/65)*. Was also r/u to Lundquist in *1964* Italian f, but won French singles *1965* and US and German titles *1966*. Established himself first as a doubles player with Hewitt. They won Australia *1963/64,* Wimbledon *1962/64* and Italy *1963/64.* With Emerson, who had dominated him in singles, won French and US doubles *1965* and Australia, Italy and US *1966.* In *1981,* aged 42, he and Newcombe (37) took McEnroe/Fleming to 5s tie-break in US Open sf. Became contract professional *1967* and reached Wimbledon doubles f with Rosewall *1968*, and won mixed doubles there with Ann Jones in *1969*. Between *1964–66* he won 13 out of his 16 D Cup rubbers. Coached NY Sets to victory in World Team Tennis competition *1976.*

ERIC WILLIAM STURGESS (South Africa)
Born 10/6/20. South Africa's most successful singles competitor and their nat champ on no fewer than 11 occasions, beginning a sequence of victories in *1939/40* and continuing in *1946, 1948–54,* and *1957*. Outside Johannesburg his major achievement was the capture of the German singles *1952;* r/u in Paris *1947/51* and lost to Gonzales in *1948* US f. Twice he was in Wimbledon sf, but in spite of speed, steadiness, and elegance, he lacked the weight of shot to win in the highest class and his second service was vulnerable. He won the French doubles with Fannin *1947* and a number of mixed titles, notably Wimbledon *1949* (with Sheila Summers) Land and *1950* (with Louise Brough), and F Hills *1949* (with Brough).

WILLIAM F. TALBERT (USA)
Born 4/11/18. An expert in the practice, technique and strategy of doubles. The best right-court player of his generation, his most important victories were gained with Mulloy, with whom he won the US doubles *1942/45/46/48*, and a total of 84 out of 90 tournaments in ten years. With a variety of partners, he won US Clay Court doubles *1942/44/45/46* and the US Indoor Doubles *1949/50/51/52/54*. Abroad, with the young Trabert, also from Cincinnati, he won French and Italian doubles *1950*. He was runner-up to Parker in US singles *1944/45* and US Indoor champion *1948/51*. He won nine of his ten

D Cup rubbers *1946–53*, from *1953–57* he captained the US D Cup team and later became Tournament Director of the US Open. All this was achieved despite the disability of diabetes.

WILLIAM TATUM TILDEN (USA)

Born 10/2/1893. Died 5/6/1953. For many critics the greatest player and student of match-strategy in the history of the game. Tall, with a long reach and a long stride, great strength and versatility of shot, and a powerful sense of drama, Tilden did not win a major title until he was 27. Then won Wimbledon singles *1920/21/30,* and doubles (with F. T. Hunter) *1927,* and US singles *1920/21/22/23/24/25/29,* and doubles *1918/21/22/23/27.* Was first Italian champ in *1930* and played D Cup from *1920–30* winning 34 rubbers out of 41 and 21 out of 28 in challenge rounds. Between *1920–26* won 13 successive challenge round singles. Turned pro in *1931.*

MARION ANTHONY TRABERT (USA)

Born 16/8/30. Won Wimbledon singles *1955* and US singles *1953/55* without losing a set. Won French singles *1954,* and doubles victories included US in *1954* (with E. V. Seixas), French *1950* (with W. F. Talbert) and *1954/55* (with Seixas) and Italian *1950* (with Talbert). Won 27 out of 35 D Cup rubbers between *1951–55.* Turned pro in *1955.*

CHRISTINE CLARA TRUMAN (Great Britain)

Born 16/1/41. Now Mrs Janes. Britain's most popular post-war player. She possessed a powerful forehand, a disconcerting ability to hit her way out of crises, a remarkable capacity for unorthodox volleying, and a temperament and court manners that made her a model for every schoolgirl in the country. She was always regarded as a potential Wimbledon champ and reached sf at the age of 16 at her first Wimbledon, where she lost to Althea Gibson, the eventual winner. Afterwards came a series of spectacular failures until she reached the *1961* f, only to fall to Angela Mortimer. Her best performances were a victory over Miss Gibson in the *1958* W Cup match, which helped to give Britain the trophy for the first time since the war, and the capture of the French and Italian singles titles in *1959.* Won *1960* Australian doubles with Maria Bueno. She and her sister, Nell, formed an aggressively effective – and sometimes erratic – doubles partnership. She won 10 rubbers out of 25 in 11 W Cup matches.

LESLEY ROSEMARY TURNER (Australia)

Born 16/8/42. Now Mrs Bowrey. Clever, strong and persistent, she gained her principal successes on European clay courts. In *1961* on her first European tour she lost to Maria Bueno in the Italian final and was runner-up again *1962/64* before winning the title *1967/68.* She won the French singles *1963,* defeating Ann Jones, and *1965,* beating Margaret Court, and was runner-up *1962/67.* She reached the Australian final *1964/67.* In doubles, with Margaret Court, she won Wimbledon *1964,* Paris *1964/65* and Australia *1965.* Also took the Australian doubles title, with Judy Tegart, *1964/67* and the US doubles, with Darlene Hard, *1961.* Won Wimbledon mixed doubles with Fred Stolle *1961/64.*

H. ELLSWORTH VINES (USA)

Born 28/9/11. The possessor of a fine forehand and one of the fastest services of all time. Defeated Bunny Austin in *1932* 6–4 6–2 6–0 in one of the shortest Wimbledon f and lost title next year in a classic f against Jack Crawford. Won US singles *1931/32* and Australian doubles *1933.* Played D Cup *1932/33,* winning 13 rubbers out of 16. Turned pro *1934.*

SARAH VIRGINIA WADE (Great Britain)

Born 10/7/45. A spectacular and dramatic competitor, at her 16th attempt she finally achieved her ambition of winning the women's singles at Wimbledon in the Centenary year of *1977.* Until then her career had been an extravagant mixture of bitter disappointments, many of the worst endured at Wimbledon, and dazzling successes. Her first major success was gained at US Open *1968* when she defeated Billie Jean King 6–4 6–2 in the final. She won the Australian title, beating Evonne Goolagong, in *1972* and gained her only major clay-court success in *1971*, when she defeated Helga Masthoff in the Italian final. Her best doubles victories – France *1973*, US *1973/75*, Australia *1975* and Italy *1968* – were won with Margaret Court, but she also succeeded in Rome *1971* with Mrs Masthoff and *1973* with Olga Morozova. She also holds the record for the most appearances of any player of any nation in both *Fed Cup* (100 rubbers in 57 ties) and the W Cup (56 rubbers in 20 ties).

ANTHONY FREDERICK WILDING (New Zealand)
Born 31/10/1883. Killed in action in Belgium 9/5/1915. Coached by his father, a notable cricketer, he won the champ of Canterbury, New Zealand, at the age of 17 and went to Cambridge Univ for which he played *1904–05.* He became one of the great heroes of Edwardian tennis, winning the singles champ at Wimbledon *1910/11/12/13.* Won doubles (with N. E. Brookes) in *1907/14* and (with M. J. G. Ritchie) */08/10.* He won 21 of the 30 D Cup rubbers which he played for Australasia between *1905–14.*

SIDNEY BURR BEARDSLEE WOOD (USA)
Born 1/11/11. A nephew of the late Julian Myrick, a former President of the US LTA and the prime mover in 1913 in the development of Forest Hills as the national centre of tennis in the US, he made his first appearance at Wimbledon, aged 15, in *1927,* playing Lacoste on the Centre Court. In *1931,* aged 19 years and 243 days, he became Wimbledon's second youngest champion at the time. He won by default. Frank Shields fell in 4s of his sf against Borotra and damaged an ankle. Shields won, but was not fit enough to play in f. A shrewd strategist and a graceful stroke-maker, Wood was r/u to Allison at Forest Hills in *1935* but lost 6–2 6–2 6–3 in one of the tournament's most disappointing finals.

OBITUARIES 1991

Ian Ayre died rather tragically late last year at the age of 62 while playing tennis. Ian was a rugged Queenslander who had been one of the stalwarts of the post-war Australian game. He was a member of the 1951 *Davis Cup* team (alongside Frank Sedgman, Ken McGregor and Mervyn Rose), which successfully defended the Cup by beating the Americans 3–2 in Sydney. Ian was a fine all-rounder whose amateur career ended when he was signed by Jack Kramer to take part in professional events in Australia. Later, Ian's vast playing experience was passed on to the many hundreds of youngsters he coached while working first for Lester Hancock in Brisbane, and later at the Ken Laffy Tennis Centre at Mount Gravatt. Ian was a familiar figure at tennis events all over Queensland, helping the Queensland Tennis Association with their development work. For many years Ian also contributed regular radio pieces for the ABC on the Queensland Championships and other events. Helpful to the last, Ian died on court while filling in for a friend who had failed to arrive for his doubles match in a local competition.

Jack Crawford, who died on 10th September 1991, at the age of 83, was the greatest of the pre-war Australians and is the subject of a feature elsewhere in these pages, written by his nephew. To many, this elegant strokemaker with the flat-topped racquet, the long-sleeved cricket shirt buttoned at the wrists and the long white flannels, epitomised the stylish game of the 1930s. Jack Crawford was a self-taught genius who grew up in a country district of New South Wales and suddenly, without any coaching or experience of match play, exploded on an unsuspecting game as an outstanding junior who beat even the best of the Australian men. In the course of a few dramatic years he became, quite simply, the finest tennis player in the world. His fluent, easy style set the fashion for a whole generation and earned him four Australian singles and doubles titles, and three in mixed with his wife Marjorie. His winning final at Wimbledon in 1933, a marathon five-setter against the defending champion Ellsworth Vines, was spoken of in awe by those who saw it. That same year he had claimed the third of his Australian titles and had also won in France so that when he reached the final in New York he was one match away from winning the four great titles in the same year. He was beaten that day by Fred Perry in five sets and it was not until 1938 that the Grand Slam was at last accomplished by America's Don Budge. Crawford was also a fine doubles player and won five Australian titles with three different partners – Harry Hopman, Gar Moon and Vivian McGrath – as well as the French and Wimbledon crowns in 1935 with Adrian Quist. Jack contributed 36 winning Davis Cup rubbers from the 58 he contested for Australia and he made a sentimental return to Wimbledon in 1947, after his retirement from the mainstream, but lost in the first round.

Susan Noel, who died last November at the age of 79, was the British Open squash champion for three years from 1932 to 1934. In 1933 she had become the first overseas player to win the U.S. Squash Championships. The daughter of Queen's Club's distinguished Secretary, E.B.Noel, Susan was a fine all-round sportswoman and one of the few players who excelled both at squash and lawn tennis. In 1934 Susan teamed with Kitty Godfree to win the British Hard Courts doubles title and two years later reached the fourth round at Wimbledon and the final of the ladies' doubles at the French Championships. When her playing days were over she turned to writing about tennis and squash for the *Sunday Times* and was the author of several books. In 1948 Susan Noel had been one of the founder members of the British Lawn Tennis Writers' Association.

Hans Nusslein died in an Altenkirchen hospital on 28th June, 1991 aged 81. This elegant German had achieved lasting fame for his 1933 victory over Bill Tilden in Berlin that had won him the first German Professional title. 'Hanne' was one of a select band of outstanding teaching professionals in Europe like Roman Najuch, Robert Ramillon, Dan Maskell and Karel Kozeluh, who had never enjoyed an amateur career. His connection with the game had begun in Nuremberg when, aged 15, he had become a ballboy at the leading club there. Three years later he became a tennis teacher by qualifying at the German Association of Tennis Professionals. Always an outstanding natural competitor, 'Hanne' was signed by Tilden in 1933 to join the professional tour in America. Professional tours and tournaments were rare in those days and the only way to make a living was by teaching the game. In 1936 Nusslein became the coach at the famous Rot-Weiss Club in Cologne and began working with Cilly Aussem who in 1931 had become the first German to win a Wimbledon singles title. In 1937 Nusslein was asked by the USLTA to work with the American Davis Cup team which included Don Budge. This led to subsequent appointments with the Australian Davis Cup team and, at last, the strong German team in which Gottfried von Cramm and Henner Henkel were the stars. After the war 'Hanne' had posts in India and Sweden before returning to Germany where he advised Wilhelm Bungert, Dieter Ecklebe and Christian Kuhnke. In 1954 'Hanne' played his last official tournament in Bad Ems where he won the International Tennis Teachers Masters title. In his later years he spent more and more time developing his Hans Nusslein Foundation which he had established to help in the development of German juniors. He was not a rich man when he died, but he always used to say, 'Money corrupts a man's character.' Hans Nusslein remained incorruptible to the end.

Adrian Quist, another of the great pre-war Australians, died in Sydney on 17th November at the age of 78 after a short illness. Quist was a small, lively man with lightning reflexes and fast hands that made him one of the finest of net players. Although remembered mostly as a doubles champion (he won the Australian title every year from 1936 to 1950, the first two with Turnbull, the remainder with Bromwich), Adrian was also a fine singles player and became the Australian champion three times (1936, 1940 and 1948). He also won the French and US doubles titles and his two successes at Wimbledon came 15 years apart. In 1935 he won with Crawford and in 1950 with Bromwich. Most of his working life was spent with the Dunlop Sports Company for whom he was a wonderful ambassador. As a Vice-President of the International Club of Australia, Adrian was also a tireless worker for the game, as well as being a marvellous host and a loyal friend to his old Davis Cup team mates Crawford and Bromwich with whom he kept constantly in touch and encouraged others to do the same. At his happiest in Davis Cup situations, Adrian was a member of the 1939 team that recovered from 0–2 to beat the Americans 3–2 in Philadelphia. His doubles win with Bromwich against Hunt and Kramer and his 5-sets singles victory over the Wimbledon champion Riggs on Labour Day (the day following the outbreak of the Second world War), set the scene for Bromwich's tie-winning success against Parker that brought back the Cup to Australia after a gap of 20 years, their first success as an individual nation. Altogether Quist played in 28 Davis Cup ties between 1933 and 1948, winning 42 of the 55 rubbers he contested.

Michael Westphal's death on 20th June after losing a long fight against a mystery virus with no known cure that he had contracted, probably in Asia or Africa, two years earlier, was one of the saddest events of 1991. Michael, a former German No.1, was only 26 years old when he died. He was a fearless competitor whose greatest moment had come in 1985 when his marathon Davis Cup win against Tomas Smid (6–8 1–6 7–5 11–9 17–15) had enabled Germany to beat Czechoslovakia and so proceed to the final against Sweden in Munich. Michael was an unconventional sportsman, very much an individualist, which was both his strength and weakness. After becoming the European junior champion in 1981, a great future was forecast for him, but he discovered that life held pleasures outside the tennis court and explored them. Known as the laziest tennis professional in the world because of his free and easy life style, Michael's talent was such that he would suddenly produce surprising wins. In 1986 Michael had stopped working with his coach Klaus Hofsaess but in 1988, after two free-wheeling years, he decided to make a new start and returned to work with him in Marbella, determined to improve on his career-high ranking of 49. Sadly, he was not given sufficient time to achieve that new ambition.

CHAMPIONSHIP ROLLS

AUSTRALIAN CHAMPIONSHIPS

MEN'S SINGLES

	CHAMPION	RUNNER-UP	SCORE				
1905	R. W. Heath	A. H. Curtis	4–6	6–3	6–4	6–4	
1906	A. F. Wilding	F. N. Fisher	6–0	6–0	6–4		
1907	H. M. Rice	H. A. Parker	6–3	6–4	6–4		
1908	F. B. Alexander	A. W. Dunlop	3–6	3–6	6–0	6–2	6–3
1909	A. F. Wilding	E. F. Parker	6–1	7–5	6–2		
1910	R. W. Heath	H. M. Rice	6–4	6–3	6–2		
1911	N. E. Brookes	H. M. Rice	6–1	6–2	6–3		
1912	J. C. Parke	A. E. Beamish	3–6	6–2	1–6	6–1	7–5
1913	E. F. Parker	H. A. Parker	2–6	6–1	6–3	6–2	
1914	A. O'Hara Wood	G. L. Patterson	6–4	6–3	5–7	6–1	
1915	F. G. Lowe	H. M. Rice	4–6	6–1	6–1	6–4	
1916–18	*Not held*						
1919	A. R. F. Kingscote	E. O. Pockley	6–4	6–0	6–3		
1920	P. O'Hara Wood	V. Thomas	6–3	4–6	6–8	6–1	6–3
1921	R. H. Gemmell	A. Hedeman	7–5	6–1	6–4		
1922	J. O. Anderson	G. L. Patterson	6–0	3–6	3–6	6–3	6–2
1923	P. O'Hara Wood	C. B. St John	6–1	6–1	6–3		
1924	J. O. Anderson	R. E. Schlesinger	6–3	6–4	3–6	5–7	6–3
1925	J. O. Anderson	G. L. Patterson	11–9	2–6	6–2	6–3	
1926	J. B. Hawkes	J. Willard	6–1	6–3	6–1		
1927	G. L. Patterson	J. B. Hawkes	3–6	6–4	3–6	18–16	6–3
1928	J. Borotra	R. O. Cummings	6–4	6–1	4–6	5–7	6–3
1929	J. C. Gregory	R. E. Schlesinger	6–2	6–2	5–7	7–5	
1930	E. F. Moon	H. C. Hopman	6–3	6–1	6–3		
1931	J. H. Crawford	H. C. Hopman	6–4	6–2	2–6	6 1	
1932	J. H. Crawford	H. C. Hopman	4–6	6–3	3–6	6–3	6–1
1933	J. H. Crawford	K. Gledhill	2–6	7–5	6–3	6–2	
1934	F. J. Perry	J. H. Crawford	6–3	7–5	6–1		
1935	J. H. Crawford	F. J. Perry	2–6	6–4	6–4	6–4	
1936	A. K. Quist	J. H. Crawford	6–2	6–3	4–6	3–6	9–7
1937	V. B. McGrath	J. E. Bromwich	6–3	1–6	6–0	2–6	6–1
1938	J. D. Budge	J. E. Bromwich	6–4	6–2	6–1		
1939	J. E. Bromwich	A. K. Quist	6–4	6–1	6–3		
1940	A. K. Quist	J. H. Crawford	6–3	6–1	6–2		
1941–45	*Not held*						
1946	J. E. Bromwich	D. Pails	5–7	6–3	7–5	3–6	6–2
1947	D. Pails	J. E. Bromwich	4–6	6–4	3–6	7–5	8–6
1948	A. K. Quist	J. E. Bromwich	6–4	3–6	6–3	2–6	6–3
1949	F. A. Sedgman	J. E. Bromwich	6–3	6–2	6–2		
1950	F. A. Sedgman	K. McGregor	6–3	6–4	4–6	6–1	
1951	R. Savitt	K. McGregor	6–3	2–6	6–3	6–1	
1952	K. McGregor	F. A. Sedgman	7–5	12–10	2–6	6–2	
1953	K. R. Rosewall	M. G. Rose	6–0	6–3	6–4		
1954	M. G. Rose	R. N. Hartwig	6–2	0–6	6–4	6–2	
1955	K. R. Rosewall	L. A. Hoad	9–7	6–4	6–4		
1956	L. A. Hoad	K. R. Rosewall	6–4	3–6	6–4	7–5	
1957	A. J. Cooper	N. A. Fraser	6–3	6–4	6–2		
1958	A. J. Cooper	M. J. Anderson	7–5	6–3	6–4		
1959	A. Olmedo	N. A. Fraser	6–1	6–2	3–6	6–3	
1960	R. G. Laver	N. A. Fraser	5–7	3–6	6–3	8–6	8–6
1961	R. S. Emerson	R. G. Laver	1–6	6–3	7–6	6–4	
1962	R. G. Laver	R. S. Emerson	8–6	0–6	6–4	6–4	
1963	R. S. Emerson	K. N. Fletcher	6–3	6–3	6–1		

1964	R. S. Emerson	F. S. Stolle	6–3	6–4	6–2		
1965	R. S. Emerson	F. S. Stolle	7–9	2–6	6–4	7–5	6–1
1966	R. S. Emerson	A. R. Ashe	6–4	6–8	6–2	6–3	FIRST
1967	R. S. Emerson	A. R. Ashe	6–4	6–1	6–4		PRIZE
1968	W. W. Bowrey	J. M. Gisbert	7–5	2–6	9–7	6–4	(US $)
1969	R. G. Laver	A. Gimeno	6–3	6–4	7–5		5,000
1970	A. R. Ashe	R. D. Crealy	6–4	9–7	6–2		3,800
1971	K. R. Rosewall	A. R. Ashe	6–1	7–5	6–3		10,000
1972	K. R. Rosewall	M. J. Anderson	7–6	6–3	7–5		2,240
1973	J. D. Newcombe	O. Parun	6–3	6–7	7–5	6–1	8,750
1974	J. S. Connors	P. Dent	7–6	6–4	4–6	6–3	9,750
1975	J. D. Newcombe	J. S. Connors	7–5	3–6	6–4	7–5	12,489
1976	M. Edmondson	J. D. Newcombe	6–7	6–3	7–6	6–1	32,000
1977	(Jan) R. Tanner	G. Vilas	6–3	6–3	6–3		32,000
1977	(Dec) V. Gerulaitis	J. M. Lloyd	6–3	7–6	5–7	3–6	6–2	28,000
1978	(Dec) G. Vilas	J. Marks	6–4	6–4	3–6	6–3	41,000
1979	(Dec) G. Vilas	J. Sadri	7–6	6–3	6–2		50,000
1980	(Dec) B. Teacher	K. Warwick	7–5	7–6	6–3		65,000
1981	(Dec) J. Kriek	S. Denton	6–2	7–6	6–7	6–4	65,000
1982	(Dec) J. Kriek	S. Denton	6–3	6–3	6–2		70,000
1983	(Dec) M. Wilander	I. Lendl	6–1	6–4	6–4		77,500
1984	(Dec) M. Wilander	K. Curren	6–7	6–4	7–6	6–2	100,000
1985	(Dec) S. Edberg	M. Wilander	6–4	6–3	6–3		100,000
1986	*Not held*						
1987	(Jan) S. Edberg	P. Cash	6–3	6–4	3–6	5–7	6–3	103,875
1988	M. Wilander	P. Cash	6–3	6–7	2–6	6–1	8–6	104,997
1989	I. Lendl	M. Mecir	6–2	6–2	6–2		140,000
1990	I. Lendl	S. Edberg	4–6	7–6	5–2 ret'd		200,000
1991	B. Becker	I. Lendl	6–4	5–7	3–6	7–6	6–4	246,400

WOMEN'S SINGLES

	CHAMPION	RUNNER-UP	SCORE		
1922	Mrs M. Molesworth	Miss E. F. Boyd	6–3	10–8	
1923	Mrs M. Molesworth	Miss E. F. Boyd	6–1	7–5	
1924	Miss S. Lance	Miss E. F. Boyd	6–3	3–6	6–4
1925	Miss D. Akhurst	Miss E. F. Boyd	1–6	8–6	6–4
1926	Miss D. Akhurst	Miss E. F. Boyd	6–1	6–3	
1927	Miss E. F. Boyd	Mrs S. Harper	5–7	6–1	6–2
1928	Miss D. Akhurst	Miss E. F. Boyd	7–5	6–2	
1929	Miss D. Akhurst	Miss L. M. Bickerton	6–1	5–7	6–2
1930	Miss D. Akhurst	Mrs S. Harper	10–8	2–6	7–5
1931	Mrs C. Buttsworth	Mrs J. H. Crawford	1–6	6–3	6–4
1932	Mrs C. Buttsworth	Miss K. Le Messurier	9–7	6–4	
1933	Miss J. Hartigan	Mrs C. Buttsworth	6–4	6–3	
1934	Miss J. Hartigan	Mrs M. Molesworth	6–1	6–4	
1935	Miss D. E. Round	Miss N. M. Lyle	1–6	6–1	6–3
1936	Miss J. Hartigan	Miss N. Wynne	6–4	6–4	
1937	Miss N. Wynne	Mrs V. Westacott	6–3	5–7	6–4
1938	Miss D. M. Bundy	Miss D. Stevenson	6–3	6–2	
1939	Mrs V. Westacott	Mrs H. C. Hopman	6–1	6–2	
1940	Mrs N. Bolton	Miss T. Coyne	5–7	6–4	6–0
1941–45	*Not held*				
1946	Mrs N. Bolton	Miss J. Fitch	6–4	6–4	
1947	Mrs N. Bolton	Mrs H. C. Hopman	6–3	6–2	
1948	Mrs N. Bolton	Miss M. Toomey	6–3	6–1	
1949	Miss D. J. Hart	Mrs N. Bolton	6–3	6–4	
1950	Miss A. L. Brough	Miss D. J. Hart	6–4	3–6	6–4
1951	Mrs N. Bolton	Mrs T. D. Long	6–1	7–5	
1952	Mrs T. D. Long	Miss H. Angwin	6–2	6–3	
1953	Miss M. Connolly	Miss J. Sampson	6–3	6–2	
1954	Mrs T. D. Long	Miss J. Staley	6–3	6–4	
1955	Miss B. Penrose	Mrs T. D. Long	6–4	6–3	
1956	Miss M. Carter	Mrs T. D. Long	3–6	6–2	9–7
1957	Miss S. J. Fry	Miss A. Gibson	6–3	6–4	
1958	Miss A. Mortimer	Miss L. Coghlan	6–3	6–4	
1959	Mrs S. J. Reitano	Miss R. Schuurman	6–2	6–3	
1960	Miss M. Smith	Miss J. Lehane	7–5	6–2	
1961	Miss M. Smith	Miss J. Lehane	6–1	6–4	
1962	Miss M. Smith	Miss J. Lehane	6–0	6–2	
1963	Miss M. Smith	Miss J. Lehane	6–2	6–2	

Year	Champion	Runner-up	Score			First Prize (US $)
1964	Miss M. Smith	Miss L. R. Turner	6–3	6–2		
1965	Miss M. Smith	Miss M. E. Bueno	5–7	6–4	5–2 ret'd	
1966	Miss M. Smith	Miss N. Richey	w.o.			FIRST
1967	Miss N. Richey	Miss L. R. Turner	6–1	6–4		PRIZE
1968	Mrs L. W. King	Mrs B. M. Court	6–1	6–2		(US $)
1969	Mrs B. M. Court	Mrs L. W. King	6–4	6–1		2,000
1970	Mrs B. M. Court	Miss K. Melville	6–1	6–3		700
1971	Mrs B. M. Court	Miss E. Goolagong	2–6	7–5	7–6	1,800
1972	Miss S. V. Wade	Miss E. Goolagong	6–4	6–4		1,200
1973	Mrs B. M. Court	Miss E. Goolagong	6–4	7–5		5,700
1974	Miss E. Goolagong	Miss C. M. Evert	7–6	4–6	6–0	9,000
1975	Miss E. Goolagong	Miss M. Navratilova	6–3	6–2		8,115
1976	Mrs E. Cawley	Miss R. Tomanova	6–2	6–2		12,000
1977 (Jan)	Mrs G. Reid	Miss D. Fromholtz	7–5	6–2		12,000
1977 (Dec)	Mrs E. Cawley	Mrs H. Cawley	6–3	6–0		9,000
1978 (Dec)	Miss C. O'Neil	Miss B. Nagelsen	6–3	7–6		6,000
1979 (Dec)	Miss B. Jordan	Miss S. Walsh	6–3	6–3		10,000
1980 (Dec)	Miss H. Mandlikova	Miss W. M. Turnbull	6–0	7–5		32,000
1981 (Dec)	Miss M. Navratilova	Mrs C. Evert Lloyd	6–7	6–4	7–5	34,000
1982 (Dec)	Mrs C. Evert Lloyd	Miss M. Navratilova	6–3	2–6	6–3	40,000
1983 (Dec)	Miss M. Navratilova	Miss K. Jordan	6–2	7–6		75,000
1984 (Dec)	Mrs J. M. Lloyd	Miss H. Sukova	6–7	6–1	6–3	100,000
1985 (Dec)	Miss M. Navratilova	Mrs J. M. Lloyd	6–2	4–6	6–2	100,000
1986	*Not held*					
1987 (Jan)	Miss H. Mandlikova	Miss M. Navratilova	7–5	7–6		115,000
1988	Miss S. Graf	Miss C. Evert	6–1	7–6		115,000
1989	Miss S. Graf	Miss H. Sukova	6–4	6–4		135,000
1990	Miss S. Graf	Miss M. J. Fernandez	6–3	6–4		190,000
1991	Miss M. Seles	Miss J. Novotna	5–7	6–3	6–1	246,400

MEN'S DOUBLES

	CHAMPIONS	RUNNERS-UP	SCORE				
1905	R. Lycett/T. Tachell	E. T. Barnard/B. Spence	11–9	8–6	1–6	4–6	6–1
1906	R. W. Heath/A. F. Wilding	C. C. Cox/H. A. Parker	6–2	6–4	6–2		
1907	W. A. Gregg/H. A. Parker	H. M. Rice/G. W. Wright	6–2	3–6	6–3	6–2	
1908	F. B. Alexander/A. W. Dunlop	G. G. Sharpe/A. F. Wilding	6–3	6–2	6–1		
1909	J. P. Keane/E. F. Parker	C. Crooks/A. F. Wilding	1–6	6–1	6–1	9–7	
1910	A. Campbell/H. M. Rice	R. W. Heath/J. L. O'Dea	6–3	6–3	6–2		
1911	H. W. Heath/R. Lycett	J. J. Addison/N. E. Brookes	6–2	7–5	6–0		
1912	C. P. Dixon/J. C. Parke	A. E. Beamish/F. G. Lowe	6–0	6–4	6–2		
1913	A. H. Hedemann/E. F. Parker	H. Parker/R. Taylor	8–6	4–6	6–4	6–4	
1914	A. Campbell/G. L. Patterson	R. W. Heath/A. O'Hara Wood	7–5	3–6	6–3	6–3	
1915	H. M. Rice/C. V. Todd	F. G. Lowe/C. St John	8–6	6–4	7–9	6–3	
1916–1918	*Not held*						
1919	P. O'Hara Wood/R. V. Thomas	J. O. Anderson/A. H. Lowe	7–5	6–1	7–9	3–6	6–3
1920	P. O'Hara Wood/R. V. Thomas	H. Rice/R. Taylor	6–1	6–0	7–5		
1921	S. H. Eaton/R. H. Gemmell	E. Stokes/N. Breasly	7–5	6–3	6–3		
1922	J. B. Hawkes/G. L. Patterson	J. O. Anderson/N. Peach	8–10	6–0	6–0	7–5	
1923	P. O'Hara Wood/C. B. St John	H. Rice/J. Bullough	6–4	6–3	3–6	6–0	
1924	J. O. Anderson/N. E. Brookes	P. O'Hara Wood/G. L. Patterson	6–2	6–4	6–3		
1925	P. O'Hara Wood/G. L. Patterson	J. O. Anderson/F. Kalms	6–4	8–6	7–5		
1926	J. B. Hawkes/G. L. Patterson	J. O. Anderson/P. O'Hara Wood	6–1	6–4	6–2		
1927	J. B. Hawkes/G. L. Patterson	I. McInnes/P. O'Hara Wood	8–6	6–2	6–1		
1928	J. Borotra/J. Brugnon	E. F. Moon/J. Willard	6–2	4–6	6–4	6–4	
1929	J. H. Crawford/H. C. Hopman	R. O. Cummings/E. F. Moon	6–1	6–8	4–6	6–1	6–3
1930	J. H. Crawford/H. C. Hopman	J. Fitchett/J. B. Hawkes	8–6	6–1	2–6	6–3	
1931	C. Donohoe/R. Dunlop	J. H. Crawford/H. O. Hopman	8–6	6–2	5–7	7–9	6–4
1932	J. H. Crawford/E. F. Moon	H. C. Hopman/G. L. Patterson	12–10	6–3	4–6	6–4	
1933	K. Gledhill/H. E. Vines	J. H. Crawford/E. F. Moon	6–4	10–8	6–2		
1934	G. P. Hughes/F. J. Perry	A. K. Quist/D. P. Turnbull	6–8	6–3	6–4	3–6	6–3
1935	J. H. Crawford/V. B. McGrath	G. P. Hughes/F. J. Perry	6–4	8–6	6–2		
1936	A. K. Quist/D. P. Turnbull	J. H. Crawford/V. B. McGrath	6–8	6–2	6–1	3–6	6–2
1937	A. K. Quist/D. P. Turnbull	J. E. Bromwich/J. E. Harper	6–2	9–7	1–6	6–8	6–4
1938	J. E. Bromwich/A. K. Quist	H. Henkel/G. Von Cramm	7–5	6–4	6–0		
1939	J. E. Bromwich/A. K. Quist	C. F. Long/D. P. Turnbull	6–4	7–5	6–2		
1940	J. E. Bromwich/A. K. Quist	J. H. Crawford/V. B. McGrath	6–3	7–5	6–1		
1941–1945	*Not held*						
1946	J. E. Bromwich/A. K. Quist	M. Newcombe/L. A. Schwartz	6–4	6–2	6–3		
1947	J. E. Bromwich/A. K. Quist	F. A. Sedgman/G. Worthington	6–1	6–3	6–1		
1948	J. E. Bromwich/A. K. Quist	C. Long/F. A. Sedgman	1–6	6–8	9–7	6–3	8–6

1949	J. E. Bromwich/A. K. Quist	G. Brown/O. W. Sidwell	6–8	7–5	6–2	6–3	
1950	J. E. Bromwich/A. K. Quist	J. Drobny/E. W. Sturgess	6–3	5–7	4–6	6–3	8–6
1951	K. McGregor/F. A. Sedgman	J. E. Bromwich/A. K. Quist	11–9	2–6	6–3	4–6	6–3
1952	K. McGregor/F. A. Sedgman	D. Candy/M. G. Rose	6–4	7–5	6–3		
1953	L. A. Hoad/K. R. Rosewall	D. Candy/M. G. Rose	9–11	6–4	10–8	6–4	
1954	R. N. Hartwig/M. G. Rose	N. A. Fraser/C. Wilderspin	6–3	6–4	6–2		
1955	E. V. Seixas/M. A. Trabert	L. A. Hoad/K. R. Rosewall	6–3	6–2	2–6	3–6	6–1
1956	L. A. Hoad/K. R. Rosewall	D. Candy/M. G. Rose	10–8	13–11	6–4		
1957	N. A. Fraser/L. A. Hoad	M. J. Anderson/A. Cooper	6–3	8–6	6–4		
1958	A. Cooper/N. A. Fraser	R. S. Emerson/R. Mark	6–5	6–8	3–6	6–3	7–5
1959	R. G. Laver/R. Mark	D. Candy/R. N. Howe	9–7	6–4	6–2		
1960	R. G. Laver/R. Mark	R. S. Emerson/N. A. Fraser	1–6	6–2	6–4	6–4	
1961	R. G. Laver/R. Mark	R. S. Emerson/M. F. Mulligan	6–3	7–5	3–6	7–9	6–2
1962	R. S. Emerson/N. A. Fraser	R. A. J. Hewitt/F. S. Stolle	4–6	4–6	6–1	6–4	11–9
1963	R. A. J. Hewitt/F. S. Stolle	K. N. Fletcher/J. D. Newcombe	6–2	3–6	6–3	3–6	6–3
1964	R. A. J. Hewitt/F. S. Stolle	R. S. Emerson/K. N. Fletcher	6–4	7–5	3–6	6–4	14–12
1965	J. D. Newcombe/A. D. Roche	R. S. Emerson/F. S. Stolle	3–6	4–6	13–11	6–3	6–4
1966	R. S. Emerson/F. S. Stolle	J. D. Newcombe/A. D. Roche	7–9	6–3	6–8	14–12	12–10
1967	J. D. Newcombe/A. D. Roche	W. W. Bowrey/O. K. Davidson	3–6	6–3	7–5	6–8	8–6
1968	R. D. Crealy/A. J. Stone	T. Addison/R. Keldie	10–8	6–4	6–3		
1969	R. S. Emerson/R. G. Laver	K. R. Rosewall/F. S. Stolle	6–4	6–4	6–4		
1970	R. C. Lutz/S. R. Smith	J. G. Alexander/P. Dent	6–3	8–6	6–3		
1971	J. D. Newcombe/A. D. Roche	T. S. Okker/M. C. Riessen	6–2	7–6			
1972	O. K. Davidson/K. R. Rosewall	R. Case/G. Masters	3–6	7–6	6–3		
1973	M. J. Anderson/J. D. Newcombe	J. G. Alexander/P. Dent	6–3	6–4	7–6		
1974	R. Case/G. Masters	S. Ball/R. Giltinan	6–7	6–3	6–4		
1975	J. G. Alexander/P. Dent	R. Carmichael/A. J. Stone	6–3	7–6			
1976	J. D. Newcombe/A. D. Roche	R. Case/G. Masters	7–6	6–4			
1977	A. R. Ashe/A. D. Roche	C. Pasarell/E. Van Dillen	6–4	6–4			
1977	(Dec) R. O. Ruffels/A. J. Stone	J. G. Alexander/P. Dent	7–6	7–6			
1978	(Dec) Fibak/K. Warwick	P. Kronk/C. Letcher	7–6	7–5			
1979	(Dec) P. McNamara/P. McNamee	P. Kronk/C. Letcher	7–6	6–2			
1980	(Dec) M. R. Edmondson/K. Warwick	P. McNamara/P. McNamee	7–5	6–4			
1981	(Dec) M. R. Edmondson/K. Warwick	H. Pfister/J. Sadri	6–3	6–7	6–3		
1982	(Dec) J. G. Alexander/J. Fitzgerald	A. Andrews/J. Sadri	6–4	7–6			
1983	(Dec) M. R. Edmondson/P. McNamee	S. Denton/S. E. Stewart	6–3	7–6			
1984	(Dec) M. R. Edmondson/S. E. Stewart	J. Nystrom/M. Wilander	6–2	6–2	7–5		
1985	(Dec) P. Annacone/C. Van Rensburg	M. R. Edmondson/K. Warwick	3–6	7–6	6–4	6–4	
1986	Not held						
1987	(Jan) S. Edberg/A. Jarryd	P. Doohan/L. Warder	6–4	6–4	7–6		
1988	R. Leach/J. Pugh	M. J. Bates/P. Lundgren	6–3	6–2	6–3		
1989	R. Leach/J. Pugh	D. Cahill/M. Kratzmann	6–4	6–4	6–4		
1990	P. Aldrich/D. Visser	G. Connell/G. Michibata	6–4	4–6	6–1	6–4	
1991	S. Davis/D. Pate	P. McEnroe/D. Wheaton	6–7	7–6	6–3	7–5	

WOMEN'S DOUBLES

	CHAMPIONS	RUNNERS-UP	SCORE		
1922	E. F. Boyd/M. Mountain	St George/H. S. Utz	1–6	6–4	7–5
1923	E. F. Boyd/S. Lance	M. Molesworth/H. Turner	6–11	6–4	
1924	D. Akhurst/S. Lance	K. Le Mesurier/P. O'Hara Wood	7–5	6–2	
1925	D. Akhurst/R. Harper	E. F. Boyd/K. Le Mesurier	6–4	6–3	
1926	E. F. Boyd/P. O'Hara Wood	D. Akhurst/M. Cox	6–3	6–8	8–6
1927	L. M. Bickerton/P. O'Hara Wood	E. F. Boyd/R. Harper	6–3	6–3	
1928	D. Akhurst/E. F. Boyd	K. Le Mesurier/D. Weston	6–3	6–1	
1929	D. Akhurst/L. M. Bickerton	R. Harper/P. O'Hara Wood	6–2	3–6	6–2
1930	E. Hood/M. Molesworth	M. Cox/R. Harper	6–3	0–6	7–5
1931	L. M. Bickerton/R. Cozens	A. Lloyd/H. S. Utz	6–0	6–4	
1932	C. Buttsworth/J. H. Crawford	K. Le Mesurier/D. Weston	6–2	6–2	
1933	M. Molesworth/V. Westacott	J. Hartigan/J. Van Ryn	6–3	6–3	
1934	M. Molesworth/V. Westacott	J. Hartigan/U. Valkenborg	6–8	6–4	6–4
1935	E. M. Dearman/N. M. Lyle	L. M. Bickerton/N. Hopman	6–3	6–4	
1936	T. Coyne/N. Wynne	M. Blick/K. Woodward	6–2	6–4	
1937	T. Coyne/N. Wynne	N. Hopman/V. Westacott	6–2	6–2	
1938	T. Coyne/N. Wynne	D. M. Bundy/D. E. Workman	9–7	6–4	
1939	T. Coyne/N. Wynne	M. Hardcastle/V. Westacott	7–5	6–4	
1940	T. Coyne/N. Bolton	J. Hartigan/E. Niemeyer	7–5	6–2	
1941–1945	Not held				
1946	M. Bevis/J. Fitch	Not available			
1947	N. Bolton/T. D. Long	M. Bevis/J. Fitch	6–3	6–3	
1948	N. Bolton/T. D. Long	M. Bevis/N. Jones	6–3	6–3	

949	N. Bolton/T. D. Long	D./M. Toomey	6–0 6–1	
950	L. Brough/D.J. Hart	N. Bolton/T. D. Long	6–3 2–6 6–3	
951	N. Bolton/T. D. Long	J. Fitch/M. Hawton	6–2 6–1	
952	N. Bolton/T. D. Long	R. Baker/M. Hawton	6–1 6–1	
953	M. Connolly/J. Sampson	M. Hawton/B. Penrose	6–3 6–2	
954	M. Hawton/B. Penrose	H. Redick-Smith/J. Wipplinger	6–3 8–6	
955	M. Hopman/B. Penrose	N. Hopman/A. Thiele	7–5 6–1	
956	M. Hawton/T. D. Long	M. Carter/B. Penrose	6–3 5–7 9–7	
957	S. J. Fry/A. Gibson	M. Hawton/F. Muller	6–2 6–1	
958	M. Hawton/T. D. Long	L. Coghlan/A. Mortimer	7–5 6–8 6–2	
959	S. Reynolds/R. Schuurman	L. Coghlan/M. Reitano	7–5 6–4	
960	M. E. Bueno/C. Truman	L. Robinson/M. Smith	6–2 5–7 6–2	
961	M. Reitano/M. Smith	M. Hawton/J. Lehane	6–3 3–6 7–5	
962	R. Ebbern/M. Smith	D. R. Hard/M. Reintano	6–4 6–4	
963	R. Ebbern/M. Smith	J. Lehane/L. R. Turner	6–1 6–3	
964	J. A. M. Tegart/L. R. Turner	R. Ebbern/M. Smith	6–4 6–4	
965	M. Smith/L. R. Turner	R. Ebbern/B. J. Moffitt	1–6 6–2 6–3	
966	C. Graebner/N. Richey	M. Smith/L. R. Turner	6–4 7–5	
967	J. A. M. Tegart/L. R. Turner	L. Robinson/E. Terras	6–0 6–2	
968	K. Krantzcke/K. Melville	J. A. M. Tegart/L. R. Turner	6–4 3–6 6–2	
969	B. M. Court/J. A. M. Tegart	R. Casals/L. W. King	6–4 6–4	
970	B. M. Court/D. Dalton	K. Krantzcke/K. Melville	6–3 6–4	
971	B. M. Court/E. F. Goolagong	J. Emmerson/L. Hunt	6–0 6–0	
972	H. Gourlay/K. Harris	P. Coleman/K. Krantzcke	6–2 6–3	
973	B. M. Court/S. V. Wade	K. Harris/K. Melville	6–4 6–4	
974	E. F. Goolagong/M. Michel	K. Harris/K. Melville	7–5 6–3	
975	E. F. Goolagong/M. Michel	B. M. Court/O. Morozova	7–6 7–6	
976	E. F. Cawley/H. Gourlay	W. W. Bowrey/R. Tomanova	8–1 (one set)	
977	D. Fromholtz/H. Gourlay	B. Nagelsen/G. E. Reid	5–7 6–1 7–5	
977	(Dec) E. F. Cawley/H. Cawley div'd with M. Guerrant/G. E. Reid			
978	(Dec) B. Nagelsen/R. Tomanova	N. Sato/P. Whytcross	7–5 6–2	
979	(Dec) D. D. Chaloner/D. R. Evers	L. Harrison/M. Mesker	6–2 1–6 6–0	
980	(Dec) B. Nagelsen/M. Navratilova	A. Kiyomura/C. Reynolds	6–4 6–4	
981	(Dec) K. Jordan/A. E. Smith	M. Navratilova/P. H. Shriver	6–2 7–5	
982	(Dec) M. Navratilova/P. H. Shriver	C. Kohde/E. Pfaff	6–4 6–2	
983	(Dec) M. Navratilova/P. H. Shriver	A. E. Hobbs/W. M. Turnbull	6–4 6–7 6–2	
984	(Dec) M. Navratilova/P. H. Shriver	C. Kohde-Kilsch/H. Sukova	6–3 6–4	
985	(Dec) M. Navratilova/P. H. Shriver	C. Kohde-Kilsch/H. Sukova	6–3 6–4	
986	*Not held*			
987	(Jan) M. Navratilova/P. H. Shriver	Z. Garrison/L. McNeil	6–1 6–0	
988	M. Navratilova/P. H. Shriver	C. Evert/W. M. Turnbull	6–0 7–5	
989	M. Navratilova/P. H. Shriver	P. Fendick/J. Hetherington	3–6 6–3 6–2	
990	J. Novotna/H. Sukova	P. Fendick/M. J. Fernandez	7–6 7–6	
991	P. Fendick/M. J. Fernandez	G. Fernandez/J. Novotna	7–6 6–1	

MIXED DOUBLES

	CHAMPIONS	RUNNERS-UP	SCORE		
922	J. B. Hawkes/Miss E. F. Boyd	H. S. Utz/Mrs Utz	6–1	6–1	
923	H. M. Rice/Miss S. Lance	C. St John/Miss M. Molesworth	2–6	6–4	6–4
924	J. Willard/Miss D. Akhurst	G. M. Hone/Miss E. F. Boyd	6–3	6–4	
925	J. Willard/Miss D. Akhurst	R. E. Schlesinger/Mrs R. Harper	6–4	6–4	
926	J. B. Hawkes/Miss E. F. Boyd	J. Willard/Miss D. Akhurst	6–2	6–4	
927	J. B. Hawkes/Miss E. F. Boyd	J. Willard/Miss Y. Anthony	6–1	6–3	
928	J. Borotra/Miss D. Akhurst	J. B. Hawkes/Miss E. F. Boyd	w.o		
929	E. F. Moon/Miss D. Akhurst	J. H. Crawford/Miss M. Cox	6–0	7–5	
930	H. C. Hopman/Miss N. Hall	J. H. Crawford/Miss M. Cox	11–9	3–6	6–3
931	J. H. Crawford/Mrs Crawford	A. Willard/Mrs V. Westacott	7–5	6–4	
932	J. H. Crawford/Mrs Crawford	J. Satoh/Mrs P. O'Hara Wood	6–8	8–6	6–3
933	J. H. Crawford/Mrs Crawford	H. E. Vines/Mrs J. Van Ryn	3–6	7–5	13–11
934	E. F. Moon/Miss J. Hartigan	R. Dunlop/Mrs V. Westacott	6–3	6–4	
935	C. Boussus/Miss L. Bickerton	V. G. Kirby/Mrs Bond	1–6	6–3	6–3
936	H. C. Hopman/Mrs Hopman	A. A. Kay/Miss M. Blick	6–2	6–0	
937	H. C. Hopman/Mrs Hopman	D. P. Turnbull/Miss D. Stevenson	3–6	6–3	6–2
938	J. E. Bromwich/Miss J. Wilson	C. Long/Miss N. Wynne	6–3	6–2	
939	H. C. Hopman/Mrs Hopman	J. E. Bromwich/Miss J. Wilson	6–8	6–2	6–3
940	C. Long/Mrs N. Bolton	H. C. Hopman/Mrs Hopman	7–5	2–6	6–4
941–1945	*Not held*				
946	C. Long/Mrs N. Bolton	J. Bromwich/Miss J. Fitch	6–0	6–4	
947	C. Long/Mrs N. Bolton	J. E. Bromwich/Miss J. Fitch	6–3	6–3	
948	C. Long/Mrs N. Bolton	O. W. Sidwell/Mrs T. D. Long	7–5	4–6	8–6

1949 F. A. Sedgman/Miss D. J. Hart	J. E. Bromwich/Miss J. Fitch	6–1	5–7	12–10
1950 F. A. Sedgman/Miss D. J. Hart	E. W. Sturgess/Miss J. Fitch	6–3	2–6	6–3
1951 G. A. Worthington/Mrs T. D. Long	J. May/Miss C. Proctor	4–6	6–3	6–2
1952 G. A. Worthington/Mrs T. D. Long	T. Warhurst/Mrs A. R. Thiele	9–7	7–5	
1953 R. N. Hartwig/Miss J. Sampson	H. Richardson/Miss M. Connolly	6–4	6–3	
1954 R. N. Hartwig/Mrs T. D. Long	J. E. Bromwich/Miss B. Penrose	8–6	9–7	
1955 G. A. Worthington/Mrs T. D. Long	L. A. Hoad/Miss J. Staley	6–2	6–1	
1956 N. A. Fraser/Miss B. Penrose	R. S. Emerson/Mrs M. Hawton	6–2	6–4	
1957 M. J. Anderson/Miss F. Muller	W. A. Knight/Miss J. Langley	7–5	3–6	6–1
1958 R. N. Howe/Mrs M. Hawton	A. Newman/Miss A. Mortimer	9–11	6–1	6–2
1959 R. Mark/Miss S. Reynolds	R. G. Laver/Miss R. Schuurman	4–6	13–11	6–1
1960 T. Fancutt/Miss J. Lehane	R. Mark/Mrs M. Reitano	6–2	7–5	
1961 R. A. J. Hewitt/Miss J. Lehane	J. Pearce/Mrs M. Reitano	9–7	6–2	
1962 F. S. Stolle/Miss L. R. Turner	R. Taylor/Miss D. R. Hard	6–3	9–7	
1963 K. N. Fletcher/Miss M. Smith	F. S. Stolle/Miss L. R. Turner	7–5	5–7	6–4
1964 K. N. Fletcher/Miss M. Smith	M. J. Sangster/Miss J. Lehane	6–1	6–2	
1965 J. D. Newcombe/Miss M. Smith div'd with O. K. Davidson/Miss R. Ebbern				
1966 A. D. Roche/Miss J. A. Tegart	W. W. Bowrey/Miss R. Ebbern	6–1	6–3	
1967 O. K. Davidson/Miss L. R. Turner	A. D. Roche/Miss J. A. M. Tegart	9–7	6–4	
1968 R. D. Crealy/Mrs L. W. King	A. J. Stone/Mrs B. M. Court	6–2	9–7	
1969 M. C. Riessen/Mrs B. M. Court div'd with F. S. Stolle/Mrs P. F. Jones				
1970–1986 Not held				
1987 S. E. Stewart/Miss Z. Garrison	A. Castle/Miss A. E. Hobbs	3–6	7–6	6–3
1988 J. Pugh/Miss J. Novotna	Tim Gullikson/M. Navratilova	5–7	6–2	6–4
1989 J. Pugh/Miss J. Novotna	S. Stewart/Miss Z. Garrison	6–3	6–4	
1990 J. Pugh/Miss N. Zvereva	R. Leach/Miss Z. Garrison	4–6	6–2	6–3
1991 J. Bates/Miss J. Durie	S. Davis/Miss R. White	2–6	6–4	6–4

FRENCH CHAMPIONSHIPS

Up to 1924 entry was restricted to members of French clubs. In 1925 entry was open to all amateurs. The Championship became 'open' in 1968.

MEN'S SINGLES

1891	H. Briggs	1903–04	M. Decugis	1920	A. H. Gobert
1892	J. Schopfer	1905–06	M. Germot	1921	J. Samazeuilh
1893	L. Riboulet	1907–09	M. Decugis	1922	H. Cochet
1894–96	A. Vacherot	1910	M. Germot	1923	P. Blanchy
1897–1900	P. Ayme	1911	A. H. Gobert	1924	J. Borotra
1901	A. Vacherot	1912–14	M. Decugis		
1902	M. Vacherot	1915–19	Not held		

	CHAMPION	RUNNER-UP	SCORE			
1925	R. Lacoste	J. Borotra	7–5	6–1	6–4	
1926	H. Cochet	R. Lacoste	6–2	6–4	6–3	
1927	R. Lacoste	W. T. Tilden	6–4	4–6	5–7	6–3	11–9
1928	H. Cochet	R. Lacoste	5–7	6–3	6–1	6–3
1929	R. Lacoste	J. Borotra	6–3	2–6	6–0	2–6	8–6
1930	H. Cochet	W. T. Tilden	3–6	8–6	6–3	6–1
1931	J. Borotra	C. Boussus	2–6	6–4	7–5	6–4
1932	H. Cochet	G. de Stefani	6–0	6–4	4–6	6–3
1933	J. H. Crawford	H. Cochet	8–6	6–1	6–3	
1934	G. von Cramm	J. H. Crawford	6–4	7–9	3–6	7–5	6–3
1935	F. J. Perry	G. von Cramm	6–3	3–6	6–1	6–3
1936	G. von Cramm	F. J. Perry	6–0	2–6	6–2	2–6	6–0
1937	H. Henkel	H. W. Austin	6–1	6–4	6–3	
1938	J. D. Budge	R. Menzel	6–3	6–2	6–4	
1939	W. D. McNeill	R. L. Riggs	7–5	6–0	6–3	
1940–45	Not held					
1946	M. Bernard	J. Drobny	3–6	2–6	6–1	6–4	6–3
1947	J. Asboth	E. W. Sturgess	8–6	7–5	6–4	
1948	F. A. Parker	J. Drobny	6–4	7–5	5–7	8–6
1949	F. A. Parker	J. E. Patty	6–3	1–6	6–1	6–4
1950	J. E. Patty	J. Drobny	6–1	6–2	3–6	5–7	7–5
1951	J. Drobny	E. W. Sturgess	6–3	6–3	6–3	
1952	J. Drobny	F. A. Sedgman	6–2	6–0	3–6	6–3
1953	K. R. Rosewall	E. V. Seixas	6–3	6–4	1–6	6–2
1954	M. A. Trabert	A. Larsen	6–4	7–5	6–1	
1955	M. A. Trabert	S. Davidson	2–6	6–1	6–4	6–2

1956	L. A. Hoad	S. Davidson	6–4	8–6	6–3			
1957	S. Davidson	H. Flam	6–3	6–4	6–4			
1958	M. G. Rose	L. Ayala	6–3	6–4	6–4			
1959	N. Pietrangeli	I. C. Vermaak	3–6	6–3	6–4	6–1		
1960	N. Pietrangeli	L. Ayala	3–6	6–3	6–4	4–6	6–3	
1961	M. Santana	N. Pietrangeli	4–6	6–1	3–6	6–0	6–2	
1962	R. G. Laver	R. S. Emerson	3–6	2–6	6–3	9–7	6–2	
1963	R. S. Emerson	P. Darmon	3–6	6–1	6–4	6–4		
1964	M. Santana	N. Pietrangeli	6–3	6–1	4–6	7–5		
1965	F. S. Stolle	A. D. Roche	3–6	6–0	6–2	6–3		FIRST
1966	A. D. Roche	I. Gulyas	6–1	6–4	7–5			PRIZE
1967	R. S. Emerson	A. D. Roche	6–1	6–4	2–6	6–2		*(in French francs)*
1968	K. R. Rosewall	R. G. Laver	6–3	6–1	2–6	6–2		15,000
1969	R. G. Laver	K. R. Rosewall	6–4	6–3	6–4			35,000
1970	J. Kodes	Z. Franulovic	6–2	6–4	6–0			56,000
1971	J. Kodes	I. Nastase	8–6	6–2	2–6	7–5		48,000
1972	A. Gimeno	P. Proisy	4–6	6–3	6–1	6–1		48,000
1973	I. Nastase	N. Pilic	6–3	6–3	6–0			70,000
1974	B. Borg	M. Orantes	2–6	6–7	6–0	6–1	6–1	120,000
1975	B. Borg	G. Vilas	6–2	6–3	6–4			120,000
1976	A. Panatta	H. Solomon	6–1	6–4	4–6	7–6		130,000
1977	G. Vilas	B. E. Gottfried	6–0	6–3	6–0			190,000
1978	B. Borg	G. Vilas	6–3	6–1	6–3			210,000
1979	B. Borg	V. Pecci	6–3	6–1	6–7	6–4		208,200
1980	B. Borg	V. Gerulaitis	6–4	6–1	6–2			221,000
1981	B. Borg	I. Lendl	6–1	4–6	6–2	3–6	6–1	250,000
1982	M. Wilander	G. Vilas	1–6	7–6	6–0	6–4		400,000
1983	Y. Noah	M. Wilander	6–2	7–5	7–6			500,000
1984	I. Lendl	J. P. McEnroe	3–6	2–6	6–4	7–5	7–5	1,058,600
1985	M. Wilander	I. Lendl	3–6	6–4	6–2	6–2		1,338,200
1986	I. Lendl	M. Pernfors	6–3	6–2	6–4			1,397,250
1987	I. Lendl	M. Wilander	7–5	6–2	3–6	7–6		1,303,800
1988	M. Wilander	H. Leconte	7–5	6–2	6–1			1,500,240
1989	M. Chang	S. Edberg	6–1	3–6	4–6	6–4	6–2	1,791,390
1990	A. Gomez	A. Agassi	6–3	2–6	6–4	6–4		2,226,100
1991	J. Courier	A. Agassi	3–6	6–4	2–6	6–1	6–4	2,448,000

WOMEN'S SINGLES

1897–99	Mlle F. Masson	1906	Mme F. Fenwick	1915–19	*Not held*
1900	Mlle Y. Prevost	1907	Mme de Kermel	1920–23	Mlle S. Lenglen
1901	Mme P. Girod	1908	Mme F. Fenwick	1924	Mlle D. Vlasto
1902–03	Mlle F. Masson	1909–12	Mlle J. Matthey		
1904–05	Mlle K. Gillou	1913–14	Mlle M. Broquedis		

Up to 1924 entry was restricted to members of French clubs. In 1925 entry was open to all amateurs.

	CHAMPION	RUNNER-UP	SCORE		
1925	Mlle S. Lenglen	Miss K. McKane	6–1	6–2	
1926	Mlle S. Lenglen	Miss M. K. Browne	6–1	6–0	
1927	Mlle K. Bouman	Mrs G. Peacock	6–2	6–4	
1928	Miss H. N. Wills	Miss E. Bennett	6–1	6–2	
1929	Miss H. N. Wills	Mme R. Mathieu	6–3	6–4	
1930	Mrs F. S. Moody	Miss H. H. Jacobs	6–2	6–1	
1931	Frl C. Aussem	Miss B. Nuthall	8–6	6–1	
1932	Mrs F. S. Moody	Mme R. Mathieu	7–5	6–1	
1933	Miss M. C. Scriven	Mme R. Mathieu	6–2	4–6	6–4
1934	Miss M. C. Scriven	Miss H. H. Jacobs	7–5	4–6	6–1
1935	Mrs H. Sperling	Mme R. Mathieu	6–2	6–1	
1936	Mrs H. Sperling	Mme R. Mathieu	6–3	6–4	
1937	Mrs H. Sperling	Mme R. Mathieu	6–2	6–4	
1938	Mme R. Mathieu	Mme N. Landry	6–0	6–3	
1939	Mme R. Mathieu	Miss J. Jedrzejowska	6–3	8–6	
1940–45	*Not held*				
1946	Miss M. E. Osborne	Miss P. M. Betz	1–6	8–6	7–5
1947	Mrs P. C. Todd	Miss D. J. Hart	6–3	3–6	6–4
1948	Mme N. Landry	Miss S. J. Fry	6–2	0–6	6–0
1949	Mrs W. du Pont	Mme N. Adamson	7–5	6–2	
1950	Miss D. J. Hart	Mrs P. C. Todd	6–4	4–6	6–2
1951	Miss S. J. Fry	Miss D. J. Hart	6–3	3–6	6–3
1952	Miss D. J. Hart	Miss S. J. Fry	6–4	6–4	
1953	Miss M. Connolly	Miss D. J. Hart	6–2	6–4	

1954	Miss M. Connolly	Mme G. Bucaille	6–4	6–1			FIRST
1955	Miss A. Mortimer	Mrs D. P. Knode	2–6	7–5	10–8		
1956	Miss A. Gibson	Miss A. Mortimer	6–0	12–10			
1957	Miss S. J. Bloomer	Mrs D. P. Knode	6–1	6–3			
1958	Mrs Z. Kormoczy	Miss S. J. Bloomer	6–4	1–6	6–2		
1959	Miss C. C. Truman	Mrs Z. Kormoczy	6–4	7–5			
1960	Miss D. R. Hard	Miss Y. Ramirez	6–3	6–4			
1961	Miss A. S. Haydon	Miss Y. Ramirez	6–2	6–1			
1962	Miss M. Smith	Miss L. R. Turner	6–3	3–6	7–5		
1963	Miss L. R. Turner	Mrs P. F. Jones	2–6	6–3	7–5		
1964	Miss M. Smith	Miss M. E. Bueno	5–7	6–1	6–2		
1965	Miss L. R. Turner	Miss M. Smith	6–3	6–4			FIRST
1966	Mrs P. F. Jones	Miss N. Richey	6–3	6–1			PRIZE
1967	Mlle F. Durr	Miss L. R. Turner	4–6	6–3	6–4		(in French francs)
1968	Miss N. Richey	Mrs P. F. Jones	5–7	6–4	6–1		5,000
1969	Mrs B. M. Court	Mrs P. F. Jones	6–1	4–6	6–3		10,000
1970	Mrs B. M. Court	Miss H. Niessen	6–2	6–4			17,800
1971	Miss E. Goolagong	Miss H. Gourlay	6–3	7–5			13,500
1972	Mrs L. W. King	Miss E. Goolagong	6–3	6–3			13,500
1973	Mrs B. M. Court	Miss C. M. Evert	6–7	7–6	6–4		25,000
1974	Miss C. M. Evert	Mrs O. Morozova	6–1	6–2			40,000
1975	Miss C. M. Evert	Miss M. Navratilova	2–6	6–2	6–1		40,000
1976	Miss S. Barker	Miss R. Tomanova	6–2	0–6	6–2		30,000
1977	Miss M. Jausovec	Miss F. Mihal	6–2	6–7	6–1		35,000
1978	Miss V. Ruzici	Miss M. Jausovec	6–2	6–2			100,000
1979	Mrs C. Evert Lloyd	Miss W. M. Turnbull	6–2	6–0			126,900
1980	Mrs C. Evert Lloyd	Miss V. Ruzici	6–0	6–3			178,500
1981	Miss H. Mandlikova	Miss S. Hanika	6–2	6–4			200,000
1982	Miss M. Navratilova	Miss A. Jaeger	7–6	6–1			300,000
1983	Mrs C. Evert Lloyd	Miss M. Jausovec	6–1	6–2			375,000
1984	Miss M. Navratilova	Mrs C. Evert Lloyd	6–3	6–1			791,600
1985	Mrs C. Evert Lloyd	Miss M. Navratilova	6–3	6–7	7–5		1,262,700
1986	Mrs C. Evert Lloyd	Miss M. Navratilova	2–6	6–3	6–3		1,278,400
1987	Miss S. Graf	Miss M. Navratilova	6–4	4–6	8–6		1,178,840
1988	Miss S. Graf	Miss N. Zvereva	6–0	6–0			1,463,390
1989	Miss A. Sanchez	Miss S. Graf	7–6	3–6	7–5		1,593,175
1990	Miss M. Seles	Miss S. Graf	7–6	6–4			1,762,900
1991	Miss M. Seles	Miss A. Sanchez-Vicario	6–3	6–4			2,237,000

MEN'S DOUBLES

	CHAMPIONS	RUNNERS-UP	SCORE				
1925	J. Borotra/R. Lacoste	J. Brugnon/H. Cochet	7–5	4–6	6–3	2–6	6–3
1926	H. O. Kinsey/V. Richards	J. Brugnon/H. Cochet	6–4	6–1	4–6	6–4	
1927	J. Brugnon/H. Cochet	J. Borotra/R. Lacoste	2–6	6–2	6–0	1–6	6–4
1928	J. Borotra/J. Brugnon	R. de Buzelet/H. Cochet	6–4	3–6	6–2	3–6	6–4
1929	J. Borotra/R. Lacoste	J. Brugnon/H. Cochet	6–3	3–6	6–3	3–6	8–6
1930	J. Brugnon/H. Cochet	H. C. Hopman/J. Willard	6–3	9–7	6–3		
1931	G. M. Lott/J. Van Ryn	N. G. Farquharson/V. G. Kirby	6–4	6–3	6–4		
1932	J. Brugnon/H. Cochet	M. Bernard/C. Boussus	6–4	3–6	7–5	6–3	
1933	G. P. Hughes/F. J. Perry	V. B. McGrath/A. K. Quist	6–2	6–4	2–6	7–5	
1934	J. Borotra/J. Brugnon	J. H. Crawford/V. B. McGrath	11–9	6–3	2–6	4–6	9–7
1935	J. H. Crawford/A. K. Quist	V. B. McGrath/D. P. Turnbull	6–1	6–4	6–2		
1936	M. Bernard/J. Borotra	G. P. Hughes/C. R. D. Tuckey	6–2	3–6	9–7	6–1	
1937	G. Von Cramm/H. Henkel	N. G. Farquharson/V. G. Kirby	6–4	7–5	3–6	6–1	
1938	B. Destremau/Y. Petra	J. D. Budge/G. Mako	3–6	6–3	9–7	6–1	
1939	C. Harris/W. D. McNeil	J. Borotra/J. Brugnon	4–6	6–4	6–0	2–6	10–8
1940–1945	*Not held*						
1946	M. Bernard/Y. Petra	E. Morea/F. Segura	7–5	6–3	0–6	1–6	10–8
1947	E. Fannin/E. W. Sturgess	T. P. Brown/O. W. Sidwell	6–4	4–6	6–4	6–3	
1948	L. Bergelin/J. Drobny	H. C. Hopman/F. A. Sedgman	8–6	6–1	12–10		
1949	R. A. Gonzales/F. Parker	E. Fannin/E. W. Sturgess	6–3	8–6	5–7	6–3	
1950	W. F. Talbert/M. A. Trabert	J. Drobny/E. W. Sturgess	6–2	1–6	10–8	6–2	
1951	K. McGregor/F. A. Sedgman	G. Mulloy/R. Savitt	6–2	2–6	9–7	7–5	
1952	K. McGregor/F. A. Sedgman	G. Mulloy/R. Savitt	6–3	6–4	6–4		
1953	L. A. Hoad/K. R. Rosewall	M. G. Rose/C. Wilderspin	6–2	6–1	6–1		
1954	E. V. Seixas/M. A. Trabert	L. A. Hoad/K. R. Rosewall	6–4	6–2	6–1		
1955	E. V. Seixas/M. A. Trabert	N. Pietrangeli/O. Sirola	6–1	4–6	6–2	6–4	
1956	D. W. Candy/R. M. Perry	A. J. Cooper/L. A. Hoad	7–5	6–3	6–3		
1957	M. J. Anderson/A. J. Cooper	D. W. Candy/M. G. Rose	6–3	6–0	6–3		
1958	A. J. Cooper/N. A. Fraser	R. N. Howe/A. Segal	3–6	8–6	6–3	7–5	

1959 N. Pietrangeli/O. Sirola	R. S. Emerson/N. A. Fraser	6–3	6–2	14–12	
1960 R. S. Emerson/N. A. Fraser	J. L. Arilla/A. Gimeno	6–2	8–10	7–5	6–4
1961 H. S. Emerson/H. G. Laver	R. N. Howe/R. Mark	3–6	6–1	6–1	6–4
1962 R. S. Emerson/N. A. Fraser	W. P. Bungert/C. Kuhnke	6–3	6–4	7–5	
1963 R. S. Emerson/M. Santana	G. L. Forbes/A. Segal	6–2	6–4	6–4	
1964 R. S. Emerson/K. N. Fletcher	J. D. Newcombe/A. D. Roche	7–5	6–3	3–6	7–5
1965 R. S. Emerson/F. S. Stolle	K. N. Fletcher/R. A. J. Hewitt	6–8	6–3	8–6	6–2
1966 C. E. Graebner/R. D. Ralston	I. Nastase/I. Tiriac	6–3	6–3	6–0	
1967 J. D. Newcombe/A. D. Roche	R. S. Emerson/K. N. Fletcher	6–3	9–7	12–10	
1968 K. R. Rosewall/F. S. Stolle	R. S. Emerson/R. G. Laver	6–3	6–4	6–3	
1969 J. D. Newcombe/A. D. Roche	R. S. Emerson/R. G. Laver	4–6	6–1	3–6	6–4 6–4
1970 I. Nastase/I. Tiriac	A. R. Ashe/C. Pasarell	6–2	6–4	6–3	
1971 A. R. Ashe/M. C. Riessen	T. W. Gorman/S. R. Smith	6–8	4–6	6–3	6–4 11–9
1972 R. A. J. Hewitt/F. D. McMillan	P. Cornejo/J. Fillol	6–3	8–6	3–6	6–1
1973 J. D. Newcombe/T. S. Okker	J. S. Connors/I. Nastase	6–1	3–6	6–3	5–7 6–4
1974 R. D. Crealy/O. Parun	R. C. Lutz/S. R. Smith	6–3	6–2	3–6	5–7 6–1
1975 B. E. Gottfried/R. Ramirez	J. G. Alexander/P. Dent	6–2	2–6	6–2	6–4
1976 F. McNair/S. E. Stewart	B. E. Gottfried/R. Ramirez	7–6	6–3	6–1	
1977 B. E. Gottfried/R. Ramirez	W. Fibak/J. Kodes	7–6	4–6	6–3	6–4
1978 G. Mayer/H. Pfister	J. Higueras/M. Orantes	6–3	6–2	6–2	
1979 A. A./G. Mayer	R. Case/P. Dent	6–4	6–4	6–4	
1980 V. Amaya/H. Pfister	B. E. Gottfried/R. Ramirez	1–6	6–4	6–4	6–3
1981 H. Gunthardt/B. Taroczy	T. Moor/E. Teltscher	6–2	7–6	6–3	
1982 S. E. Stewart/F. Taygan	H. Gildemeister/B. Prajoux	7–5	6–3	1–1 ret'd	
1983 A. Jarryd/H. Simonsson	M. R. Edmondson/S. E. Stewart	7–6	6–4	6–2	
1984 H. Leconte/Y. Noah	P. Slozil/T. Smid	6–4	2–6	3–6	6–3 6–2
1985 M. R. Edmondson/K. Warwick	S. Glickstein/H. Simonsson	6–3	6–4	6–7	6–3
1986 J. Fitzgerald/T. Smid	S. Edberg/A. Jarryd	6–3	4–6	6–3	6–7 14–12
1987 A. Jarryd/R. Seguso	G. Forget/Y. Noah	6–7	6–7	6–3	6–4 6–2
1988 A. Gomez/E. Sanchez	J. Fitzgerald/A. Jarryd	6–3	6–7	6–4	6–3
1989 J. Grabb/P. McEnroe	M. Bahrami/E. Winogradsky	6–4	2–6	6–4	7–6
1990 S. Casal/E. Sanchez	G. Ivanisevic/P. Korda	7–5	6–3		
1991 J. Fitzgerald/A. Jarryd	R. Leach/J. Pugh	6–0	7–6		

WOMEN'S DOUBLES

	CHAMPIONS	RUNNERS-UP	SCORE		
1925	S. Lenglen/D. Vlasto	E. Colyer/K. McKane	6–1	9–11	6–2
1926	S. Lenglen/D. Vlasto	E. Colyer/L. A. Godfree	6–1	6–1	
1927	E. L. Heine/G. Peacock	P. Saunders/P. H. Watson	6–2	6–1	
1928	E. Bennett/P. H. Watson	S. Deve/A. Lafaurie	6–0	6–2	
1929	L. de Alvarez/K. Bouman	E. L. Heine/A. Neave	7–5	6–3	
1930	F. S. Moody/E. Ryan	S. Barbier/S. Mathieu	6–3	6–1	
1931	B. Nuthall/E. F. Whittingstall	C. Aussem/E. Ryan	9–7	6–2	
1932	F. S. Moody/E. Ryan	B. Nuthall/E. F. Whittingstall	6–1	6–3	
1933	S. Mathieu/E. Ryan	S. Henrotin/C. Rosambert	6–1	6–3	
1934	S. Mathieu/E. Ryan	H. H. Jacobs/S. Palfrey	3–6	6–4	6–2
1935	M. C. Scriven/K. Stammers	N. Adamoff/H. Sperling	6–4	6–0	
1936	S. Mathieu/A. M. Yorke	S. Noel/J. Jedrzejowska	2–6	6–4	6–4
1937	S. Mathieu/A. M. Yorke	D. Andrus/S. Henrotin	3–6	6–2	6–2
1938	S. Mathieu/A. M. Yorke	A. Halff/N. Landry	6–3	6–3	
1939	J. Jedrzejowska/S. Mathieu	A. Florian/H. Kovac	7–5	7–5	
1940–1945	*Not held*				
1946	L. Brough/M. Osborne	P. Betz/D. Hart	6–4	0–6	6–1
1947	L. Brough/M. Osborne	D. Hart/P. C. Todd	7–5	6–2	
1948	D. Hart/P. C. Todd	S. Fry/M. A. Prentiss	6–4	6–2	
1949	L. Brough/W. du Pont	J. Gannon/B. Hilton	7–5	6–1	
1950	S. Fry/D. Hart	L. Brough/W. du Pont	1–6	7–5	6–2
1951	S. Fry/D. Hart	B. Bartlett/B. Scofield	10–8	6–3	
1952	S. Fry/D. Hart	H. Redick-Smith/J. Wipplinger	7–5	6–1	
1953	S. Fry/D. Hart	M. Connolly/J. Sampson	6–4	6–3	
1954	M. Connolly/N. Hopman	M. Galtier/S. Schmitt	7–5	4–6	6–0
1955	B. Fleitz/D. R. Hard	S. J. Bloomer/P. Ward	7–5	6–8	13–11
1956	A. Buxton/A. Gibson	D. R. Hard/D. Knode	6–8	8–6	6–1
1957	S. J. Bloomer/D. R. Hard	Y. Ramirez/R. M. Reyes	7–5	4–6	7–5
1958	Y. Ramirez/R. M. Reyes	M. K. Hawton/T. D. Long	6–4	7–5	
1959	S. Reynolds/R. Schuurman	Y. Ramirez/R. M. Reyes	2–6	6–0	6–1
1960	M. E. Bueno/D. R. Hard	R. Hales/A. Haydon	6–2	7–5	
1961	S. Reynolds/R. Schuurman	M. E. Bueno/D. R. Hard	w.o.		
1962	S. Price/R. Schuurman	J. Bricka/M. Smith	6–4	6–4	

1963	P. F. Jones/R. Schuurman	R. A. Ebbern/M. Smith	7–5	6–4	
1964	M. Smith/L. R. Turner	N. Baylon/H. Schultze	6–3	6–1	
1965	M. Smith/L. R. Turner	F. Durr/J. Lieffrig	6–3	6–1	
1966	M. Smith/J. A. M. Tegart	J. Blackman/F. Toyne	4–6	6–1	6–1
1967	F. Durr/G. Sheriff	A. M. Van Zyl/P. Walkden	6–2	6–2	
1968	F. Durr/P. F. Jones	R. Casals/L. W. King	7–5	4–6	6–4
1969	F. Durr/P. F. Jones	M. Court/N. Richey	6–0	4–6	7–5
1970	F. Durr/G. Chanfreau	R. Casals/L. W. King	6–1	3–6	6–3
1971	F. Durr/G. Chanfreau	H. Gourlay/K. Harris	6–4	6–1	
1972	L. W. King/B. Stove	W. Shaw/F. E. Truman	6–1	6–2	
1973	M. Court/S. V. Wade	F. Durr/B. Stove	6–2	6–3	
1974	C. Evert/O. Morozova	G. Chanfreau/K. Ebbinghaus	6–4	2–6	6–1
1975	C. Evert/M. Navratilova	J. Anthony/O. Morozova	6–3	6–2	
1976	F. Bonicelli/G. Lovera	K. Harter/H. Masthoff	6–4	1–6	6–3
1977	R. Marsikova/P. Teeguarden	R. Fox/H. Gourlay	5–7	6–4	6–2
1978	M. Jausovec/V. Ruzici	N. Bowey/G. Lovera	5–7	6–4	8–6
1979	B. Stove/W. M. Turnbull	F. Durr/S. V. Wade	6–4	7–6	
1980	K. Jordan/A. E. Smith	I. Madruga/I. Villagran	6–1	6–0	
1981	R. Fairbank/T. Harford	C. Reynolds/P. Smith	6–1	6–3	
1982	M. Navratilova/A. E. Smith	R. Casals/W. M. Turnbull	6–3	6–4	
1983	R. Fairbank/C. Reynolds	K. Jordan/A. E. Smith	5–7	7–5	6–2
1984	M. Navratilova/P. H. Shriver	C. Kohde-Kilsch/H. Mandlikova	5–7	6–3	6–2
1985	M. Navratilova/P. H. Shriver	C. Kohde-Kilsch/H. Sukova	4–6	6–2	6–2
1986	M. Navratilova/A. Temesvari	S. Graf/G. Sabatini	6–1	6–2	
1987	M. Navratilova/P. H. Shriver	S. Graf/G. Sabatini	6–2	6–1	
1988	M. Navratilova/P. H. Shriver	C. Kohde-Kilsch/H. Sukova	6–2	7–5	
1989	L. Savchenko/N. Zvereva	S. Graf/G. Sabatini	6–4	6–4	
1990	J. Novotna/H. Sukova	L. Savchenko/N. Zvereva	6–4	7–5	
1991	G. Fernandez/J. Novotna	L. Savchenko/N. Zvereva	6–4	6–0	

MIXED DOUBLES

	CHAMPIONS	RUNNERS-UP	SCORE		
1925	J. Brugnon/Miss S. Lenglen	H. Cochet/Miss D. Vlasto	6–2	6–2	
1926	J. Brugnon/Miss S. Lenglen	J. Borotra/Mrs Le Besnerais	6–4	6–3	
1927	J. Borotra/Miss M. Broquedis	W. T. Tilden/Miss L. de Alvarez	6–4	2–6	6–2
1928	H. Cochet/Miss E. Bennett	F. T. Hunter/Miss H. Wills	3–6	6–3	6–3
1929	H. Cochet/Miss E. Bennett	F. T. Hunter/Miss H. Wills	6–3	6–2	
1930	W. T. Tilden/Miss C. Aussem	H. Cochet/Mrs F. Whittingstall	6–4	6–4	
1931	P. D. B. Spence/Miss B. Nuthall	H. W. Austin/Mrs D. C. Shepherd-Barron	6–3	5–7	6–3
1932	F. J. Perry/Miss B. Nuthall	S. B. Wood/Mrs F. S. Moody	6–4	6–2	
1933	J. H. Crawford/Miss M. C. Scriven	F. J. Perry/Miss B. Nuthall	6–2	6–3	
1934	J. Borotra/Miss C. Rosambert	A. K. Quist/Miss E. Ryan	6–2	6–4	
1935	M. Bernard/Miss L. Payot	A. M. Legeay/Mrs S. Henrotin	4–6	6–2	6–4
1936	M. Bernard/Miss A. M. Yorke	A. M. Legeay/Mrs S. Henrotin	7–5	6–3	
1937	Y. Petra/Mrs S. Mathieu	R. Journu/Miss M. Horne	7–5	7–5	
1938	D. Mitic/Mrs S. Mathieu	C. Boussus/Miss N. Wynne	2–6	6–3	6–4
1939	E. T. Cooke/Mrs S. Fabyan	F. Kukuljevic/Mrs S. Mathieu	4–6	6–1	7–5
1940–1945	*Not held*				
1946	J. E. Patty/Miss P. M. Betz	T. P. Brown/Miss D. Bundy	7–5	9–7	
1947	E. W. Sturgess/Mrs S. P. Summers	C. Caralulis/Miss J. Jedrzejowska	6–0	6–0	
1948	J. Drobny/Mrs P. C. Todd	F. A. Sedgman/Miss D. Hart	6–3	3–6	6–3
1949	E. W. Sturgess/Mrs S. P. Summers	G. D. Oakley/Miss J. Quertier	6–1	6–1	
1950	E. Morea/Miss B. Scofield	W. F. Talbert/Mrs P. C. Todd	w.o.		
1951	F. A. Sedgman/Miss D. Hart	M. G. Rose/Mrs T. D. Long	7–5	6–2	
1952	F. A. Sedgman/Miss D. Hart	E. W. Sturgess/Miss S. Fry	6–8	6–3	6–3
1953	E. V. Seixas/Miss D. Hart	M. G. Rose/Miss M. Connolly	4–6	6–4	6–0
1954	L. A. Hoad/Miss M. Connolly	R. N. Hartwig/Mrs J. Patorni	6–4	6–3	
1955	G. L. Forbes/Miss D. R. Hard	L. Ayala/Miss J. Staley	5–7	6–1	6–2
1956	L. Ayala/Mrs T. D. Long	R. N. Howe/Miss D. R. Hard	4–6	6–4	6–1
1957	J. Javorsky/Miss V. Puzejova	L. Ayala/Miss E. Buding	6–3	6–4	
1958	N. Pietrangeli/Miss S. J. Bloomer	R. N. Howe/Miss L. Coghlan	9–7	6–8	6–2
1959	W. A. Knight/Miss R. Ramirez	R. G. Laver/Miss R. Schuurman	6–4	6–4	
1960	R. N. Howe/Miss M. Bueno	R. S. Emerson/Miss A. Haydon	1–6	6–1	6–2
1961	R. G. Laver/Miss D. R. Hard	J. Javorsky/Miss V. Puzejova	6–0	2–6	6–3
1962	R. N. Howe/Miss R. Schuurman	F. S. Stolle/Miss L. R. Turner	3–6	6–4	6–4
1963	K. N. Fletcher/Miss M. Smith	F. S. Stolle/Miss L. R. Turner	6–1	6–2	
1964	K. N. Fletcher/Miss M. Smith	F. S. Stolle/Miss L. R. Turner	6–3	6–4	
1965	K. N. Fletcher/Miss M. Smith	J. D. Newcombe/Miss M. Bueno	6–4	6–4	
1966	F. D. McMillan/Miss A. M. Van Zyl	C. Graebner/Mrs P. F. Jones	1–6	6–3	6–2
1967	O. K. Davidson/Mrs L. W. King	I. Tiriac/Mrs P. F. Jones	6–3	6–1	

1968 J. C. Barclay/Miss F. Durr	O. K. Davidson/Mrs L. W. King	6–1	6–4	
1969 M. C. Riessen/Mrs. B. M. Court	J. C. Barclay/Miss F. Durr	7–5	6–4	
1970 R. A. J. Hewitt/Mrs L. W. King	J. C. Barclay/Miss F. Durr	3–6	6–3	6–2
1971 J. C. Barclay/Miss F. Durr	T. Lejus/Miss W. Shaw	6–2	6–4	
1972 K. Warwick/Miss E. Goolagong	J. C. Barclay/Miss F. Durr	6–2	6–4	
1973 J. C. Barclay/Miss F. Durr	P. Dominguez/Miss B. Stove	6–1	6–4	
1974 I. Molina/Miss M. Navratilova	M. Lara/Mrs R. M. Darmon	6–3	6–3	
1975 T. Koch/Miss F. Bonicelli	J. Fillol/Miss P. Teeguarden	6–4	7–6	
1976 K. Warwick/Miss I. Kloss	C. Dowdeswell/Miss L. Boshoff	5–7	7–6	6–2
1977 J. P. McEnroe/Miss M. Carillo	I. Molina/Miss F. Mihai	7–6	6–3	
1978 P. Slozil/Miss R. Tomanova	P. Dominguez/Miss V. Ruzici	7–6	ret'd	
1979 R. A. J. Hewitt/Miss W. M. Turnbull	I. Tiriac/Miss V. Ruzici	6–3	2–6	6–3
1980 W. Martin/Miss A. E. Smith	S. Birner/Miss R. Tomanova	2–6	6–4	8–6
1981 J. Arias/Miss A. Jaeger	F. D. McNair/Miss B. Stove	7–6	6–4	
1982 J. M. Lloyd/Miss W. M. Turnbull	C. Motta/Miss C. Monteiro	6–2	7–6	
1983 E. Teltscher/Miss B. Jordan	C. Strode/Miss L. Allen	6–2	6–3	
1984 R. L. Stockton/Miss A. E. Smith	L. Warder/Miss A. Minter	6–2	6–4	
1985 H. P. Gunthardt/Miss M. Navratilova	F. Gonzalez/Miss P. Smith	2–6	6–3	6–2
1986 K. Flach/Miss. K. Jordan	M. R. Edmondson/Miss R. Fairbank	3–6	7–6	6–3
1987 E. Sanchez/Miss P. H. Shriver	S. E. Stewart/Miss L. McNeil	6–3	7–6	
1988 J. Lozano/Miss L. McNeil	M. Schapers/Miss B. Schultz	7–5	6–2	
1989 T. Nijssen/Miss M. Bollegraf	H. de la Pena/Miss A. Sanchez-Vicario	6–3	6–7	6–2
1990 J. Lozano/Miss A. Sanchez-Vicario	D. Visser/Miss N. Provis	7–6	7–6	
1991 C. Suk/Miss H. Sukova	P. Haarhuis/Miss C. Vis	3–6	6–4	6–1

WIMBLEDON CHAMPIONSHIPS

For the years 1913, 1914, and 1919–23 inclusive, these records include the 'World's Championship on Grass' granted to the LTA by the ILTF. This title was then abolished. Prior to 1922 the holder did not compete in the Championship but met the winner of the singles in the Challenge Round. The Challenge Round was abolished in 1922 and the holder subsequently played through. Modified 'seeding' was introduced in 1924. Full 'seeding', as we know it today, was first practised in 1927. The Championships became 'open' in 1968. From 1877–1921 the Championships were played at the Worple Road ground. Since 1922 they have been played at the present ground in Church Road.

There was a tie-break at 8–all in the years 1971–1978. Thereafter the tie-break was played at 6–all.

Holders did not defend the title.

MEN'S SINGLES

	CHAMPION	RUNNER-UP	SCORE				
1877	S. W. Gore	W. C. Marshall	6–1	6–2	6–4		
1878	P. F. Hadow	S. W. Gore	7–5	6–1	9–7		
1879*	J. T. Hartley	V. St L. Goold	6–2	6–4	6–2		
1880	J. T. Hartley	H. F. Lawford	6–3	6–2	2–6	6–3	
1881	W. Renshaw	J. T. Hartley	6–0	6–1	6–1		
1882	W. Renshaw	E. Renshaw	6–1	2–6	4–6	6–2	6–2
1883	W. Renshaw	E. Renshaw	2–6	6–3	6–3	4–6	6–3
1884	W. Renshaw	H. F. Lawford	6–0	6–4	9–7		
1885	W. Renshaw	H. F. Lawford	7–5	6–2	4–6	7–5	
1886	W. Renshaw	H. F. Lawford	6–0	5–7	6–3	6–4	
1887*	H. F. Lawford	E. Renshaw	1–6	6–3	3–6	6–4	6–4
1888	E. Renshaw	H. F. Lawford	6–3	7–5	6–0		
1889	W. Renshaw	E. Renshaw	6–4	6–1	3–6	6–0	
1890	W. J. Hamilton	W. Renshaw	6–8	6–2	3–6	6–1	6–1
1891*	W. Baddeley	J. Pim	6–4	1–6	7–5	6–0	
1892	W. Baddeley	J. Pim	4–6	6–3	6–3	6–2	
1893	J. Pim	W. Baddeley	3–6	6–1	6–3	6–2	
1894	J. Pim	W. Baddeley	10–8	6–2	8–6		
1895*	W. Baddeley	W. V. Eaves	4–6	2–6	8–6	6–2	6–3
1896	H. S. Mahony	W. Baddeley	6–2	6–8	5–7	8–6	6–3
1897	R. F. Doherty	H. S. Mahony	6–4	6–4	6–3		
1898	R. F. Doherty	H. L. Doherty	6–3	6–3	2–6	5–7	6–1
1899	R. F. Doherty	A. W. Gore	1–6	4–6	6–2	6–3	6–3
1900	R. F. Doherty	S. H. Smith	6–8	6–3	6–1	6–2	
1901	A. W. Gore	R. F. Doherty	4–6	7–5	6–4	6–4	
1902	H. L. Doherty	A. W. Gore	6–4	6–3	3–6	6–0	
1903	H. L. Doherty	F. L. Riseley	7–5	6–3	6–0		
1904	H. L. Doherty	F. L. Riseley	6–1	7–5	8–6		
1905	H. L. Doherty	N. E. Brookes	8–6	6–2	6–4		
1906	H. L. Doherty	F. L. Riseley	6–4	4–6	6–2	6–3	

							FIRST PRIZE (£)
1907* N. E. Brookes	A. W. Gore	6–4	6–2	6–2			
1908* A. W. Gore	H. Roper Barrett	6–3	6–2	4–6	3–6	6–4	
1909 A. W. Gore	M. J. G. Ritchie	6–8	1–6	6–2	6–2	6–2	
1910 A. F. Wilding	A. W. Gore	6–4	7–5	4–6	6–2		
1911 A. F. Wilding	H. Roper Barrett	6–4	4–6	2–6	6–2	ret'd	
1912* A. F. Wilding	A. W. Gore	6–4	6–4	4–6	6–4		
1913 A. F. Wilding	M. E. McLoughlin	8–6	6–3	10–8			
1914 N. E. Brookes	A. F. Wilding	6–4	6–4	7–5			
1915–18 *Not held*							
1919 G. L. Patterson	N. E. Brookes	6–3	7–5	6–2			
1920 W. T. Tilden	G. L. Patterson	2–6	6–2	6–3	6–4		
1921 W. T. Tilden	B. I. C. Norton	4–6	2–6	6–1	6–0	7–5	
(Challenge Round abolished)							
1922* G. L. Patterson	R. Lycett	6–3	6–4	6–2			
1923* W. M. Johnston	F. T. Hunter	6–0	6–3	6–1			
1924 J. Borotra	R. Lacoste	6–1	3–6	6–1	3–6	6–4	
1925 R. Lacoste	J. Borotra	6–3	6–3	4–6	8–6		
1926 J. Borotra	Howard Kinsey	8–6	6–1	6–3			
1927 H. Cochet	J. Borotra	4–6	4–6	6–3	6–4	7–5	
1928 R. Lacoste	H. Cochet	6–1	4–6	6–4	6–2		
1929 H. Cochet	J. Borotra	6–4	6–3	6–4			
1930 W. T. Tilden	W. L. Allison	6–3	9–7	6–4			
1931* S. B. Wood	F. X. Shields	w.o.					
1932 H. E. Vines	H. W. Austin	6–4	6–2	6–0			
1933 J. H. Crawford	H. E. Vines	4–6	11–9	6–2	2–6	6–4	
1934 F. J. Perry	J. H. Crawford	6–3	6–0	7–5			
1935 F. J. Perry	G. von Cramm	6–2	6–4	6–4			
1936 F. J. Perry	G. von Cramm	6–1	6–1	6–0			
1937* J. D. Budge	G. von Cramm	6–3	6–4	6–2			
1938 J. D. Budge	H. W. Austin	6–1	6–0	6–3			
1939 R. L. Riggs	E. T. Cooke	2–6	8–6	3–6	6–3	6–2	
1940–45 *Not held*							
1946* Y. Petra	G. E. Brown	6–2	6–4	7–9	5–7	6–4	
1947 J. A. Kramer	T. Brown	6–1	6–3	6–2			
1948* R. Falkenburg	J. E. Bromwich	7–5	0–6	6–2	3–6	7–5	
1949 F. R. Schroeder	J. Drobny	3–6	6–0	6–3	4–6	6–4	
1950* J. E. Patty	F. A. Sedgman	6–1	8–10	6–2	6–3		
1951 R. Savitt	K. McGregor	6–4	6–4	6–4			
1952 F. A. Sedgman	J. Drobny	4–6	6–2	6–3	6–2		
1953* E. V. Seixas	K. Nielsen	9–7	6–3	6–4			
1954 J. Drobny	K. R. Rosewall	13–11	4–6	6–2	9–7		
1955 M. A. Trabert	K. Nielsen	6–3	7–5	6–1			
1956* L. A. Hoad	K. R. Rosewall	6–2	4–6	7–5	6–4		
1957 L. A. Hoad	A. J. Cooper	6–2	6–1	6–2			
1958* A. J. Cooper	N. A. Fraser	3–6	6–3	6–4	13–11		
1959* A. Olmedo	R. G. Laver	6–4	6–3	6–4			
1960* N. A. Fraser	R. G. Laver	6–4	3–6	9–7	7–5		
1961 R. G. Laver	C. R. McKinley	6–3	6–1	6–4			
1962 R. G. Laver	M. F. Mulligan	6–2	6–2	6–1			
1963* C. R. McKinley	F. S. Stolle	9–7	6–1	6–4			
1964 R. S. Emerson	F. S. Stolle	6–1	12–10	4–6	6–3		
1965 R. S. Emerson	F. S. Stolle	6–2	6–4	6–4			
1966 M. Santana	R. D. Ralston	6–4	11–9	6–4			
1967 J. D. Newcombe	W. P. Bungert	6–3	6–1	6–1			
1968 R. G. Laver	A. D. Roche	6–3	6–4	6–2			2,000
1969 R. G. Laver	J. D. Newcombe	6–4	5–7	6–4	6–4		3,000
1970 J. D. Newcombe	K. R. Rosewall	5–7	6–3	6–2	3–6	6–1	3,000
1971 J. D. Newcombe	S. R. Smith	6–3	5–7	2–6	6–4	6–4	3,750
1972* S. R. Smith	I. Nastase	4–6	6–3	6–3	4–6	7–5	5,000
1973* J. Kodes	A. Metreveli	6–1	9–8	6–3			5,000
1974 J. S. Connors	K. R. Rosewall	6–1	6–1	6–4			10,000
1975 A. R. Ashe	J. S. Connors	6–1	6–1	5–7	6–4		10,000
1976 B. Borg	I. Nastase	6–4	6–2	9–7			12,500
1977 B. Borg	J. S. Connors	3–6	6–2	6–1	5–7	6–4	15,000
1978 B. Borg	J. S. Connors	6–2	6–2	6–3			19,000
1979 B. Borg	R. Tanner	6–7	6–1	3–6	6–3	6–4	20,000
1980 B. Borg	J. P. McEnroe	1–6	7–5	6–3	6–7	8–6	20,000
1981 J. P. McEnroe	B. Borg	4–6	7–6	7–6	6–4		21,600
1982 J. S. Connors	J. P. McEnroe	3–6	6–3	6–7	7–6	6–4	41,667
1983 J. P. McEnroe	C. J. Lewis	6–2	6–2	6–2			66,600
1984 J. P. McEnroe	J. S. Connors	6–1	6–1	6–2			100,000
1985 B. Becker	K. Curren	6–3	6–7	7–6	6–4		130,000

1986	B. Becker	I. Lendl	6–4	6–3	7–5			140,000
1987	P. Cash	I. Lendl	7–6	6–2	7–5			155,000
1988	S. Edberg	B. Becker	4–6	7–6	6–4	6–2		165,000
1989	B. Becker	S. Edberg	6–0	7–6	6–4			190,000
1990	S. Edberg	B. Becker	6–2	6–2	3–6	3–6	6–4	230,000
1991	M. Stich	B. Becker	6–4	7–6	6–4			240,000

WOMEN'S SINGLES

	CHAMPION	RUNNER-UP	SCORE		
1884	Miss M. Watson	Miss L. Watson	6–8	6–3	6–3
1885	Miss M. Watson	Miss B. Bingley	6–1	7–5	
1886	Miss B. Bingley	Miss M. Watson	6–3	6–3	
1887	Miss C. Dod	Miss B. Bingley	6–2	6–0	
1888	Miss C. Dod	Mrs G. W. Hillyard	6–3	6–3	
1889*	Mrs G. W. Hillyard	Miss H. Rice	4–6	8–6	6–4
1890*	Miss H. Rice	Miss M. Jacks	6–4	6–1	
1891*	Miss C. Dod	Mrs G. W. Hillyard	6–2	6–1	
1892	Miss C. Dod	Mrs G. W. Hillyard	6–1	6–1	
1893	Miss C. Dod	Mrs G. W. Hillyard	6–8	6–1	6–4
1894*	Mrs G. W. Hillyard	Miss L. Austin	6–1	6–1	
1895*	Miss C. Cooper	Miss H. Jackson	7–5	8–6	
1896	Miss C. Cooper	Mrs W. H. Pickering	6–2	6–3	
1897	Mrs G. W. Hillyard	Miss C. Cooper	5–7	7–5	6–2
1898*	Miss C. Cooper	Miss L. Martin	6–4	6–4	
1899	Mrs G. W. Hillyard	Miss C. Cooper	6–2	6–3	
1900	Mrs G. W. Hillyard	Miss C. Cooper	4–6	6–4	6–4
1901	Mrs A. Sterry	Mrs G. W. Hillyard	6–2	6–2	
1902	Miss M. E. Robb	Mrs A. Sterry	7–5	6–1	
1903*	Miss D. K. Douglass	Miss E. W. Thomson	4–6	6–4	6–2
1904	Miss D. K. Douglass	Mrs A. Sterry	6–0	6–3	
1905	Miss M. Sutton	Miss D. K. Douglass	6–3	6–4	
1906	Miss D. K. Douglass	Miss M. Sutton	6–3	9–7	
1907	Miss M. Sutton	Mrs Lambert Chambers	6–1	6–4	
1908*	Mrs A. Sterry	Miss A. M. Morton	6–4	6–4	
1909*	Miss D. P. Boothby	Miss A. M. Morton	6–4	4–6	8–6
1910	Mrs Lambert Chambers	Miss D. P. Boothby	6–2	6–2	
1911	Mrs Lambert Chambers	Miss D. P. Boothby	6–0	6–0	
1912*	Mrs D. R. Larcombe	Mrs A. Sterry	6–3	6–1	
1913*	Mrs Lambert Chambers	Mrs R. J. McNair	6–0	6–4	
1914	Mrs Lambert Chambers	Mrs D. R. Larcombe	7–5	6–4	
1915–18	*Not held*				
1919	Mlle S. Lenglen	Mrs Lambert Chambers	10–8	4–6	9–7
1920	Mlle S. Lenglen	Mrs Lambert Chambers	6–3	6–0	
1921	Mlle S. Lenglen	Miss E. Ryan	6–2	6–0	
(Challenge Round abolished)					
1922	Mlle S. Lenglen	Mrs F. Mallory	6–2	6–0	
1923	Mlle S. Lenglen	Miss K. McKane	6–2	6–2	
1924	Miss K. McKane	Miss H. N. Wills	4–6	6–4	6–4
1925	Mlle S. Lenglen	Miss J. Fry	6–2	6–0	
1926	Mrs L. A. Godfree	Sta E. de Alvarez	6–2	4–6	6–3
1927	Miss H. N. Wills	Sta E. de Alvarez	6–2	6–4	
1928	Miss H. N. Wills	Sta E. de Alvarez	6–2	6–3	
1929	Miss H. N. Wills	Miss H. H. Jacobs	6–1	6–2	
1930	Mrs F. S. Moody	Miss E. Ryan	6–2	6–2	
1931*	Frl C. Aussem	Frl H. Krahwinkel	6–2	7–5	
1932*	Mrs F. S. Moody	Miss H. H. Jacobs	6–3	6–1	
1933	Mrs F. S. Moody	Miss D. E. Round	6–4	6–8	6–3
1934*	Miss D. E. Round	Miss H. H. Jacobs	6–2	5–7	6–3
1935	Mrs F. S. Moody	Miss H. H. Jacobs	6–3	3–6	7–5
1936*	Miss H. H. Jacobs	Mrs S. Sperling	6–2	4–6	7–5
1937	Miss D. E. Round	Miss J. Jedrzejowska	6–2	2–6	7–5
1938*	Mrs F. S. Moody	Miss H. H. Jacobs	6–4	6–0	
1939*	Miss A. Marble	Miss K. E. Stammers	6–2	6–0	
1940–45	*Not held*				
1946*	Miss P. M. Betz	Miss A. L. Brough	6–2	6–4	
1947*	Miss M. E. Osborne	Miss D. J. Hart	6–2	6–4	
1948	Miss A. L. Brough	Miss D. J. Hart	6–3	8–6	
1949	Miss A. L. Brough	Mrs W. du Pont	10–8	1–6	10–8
1950	Miss A. L. Brough	Mrs W. du Pont	6–1	3–6	6–1
1951	Miss D. J. Hart	Miss S. J. Fry	6–1	6–0	

					FIRST PRIZE (£)
1952	Miss M. Connolly	Miss A. L. Brough	6–4	6–3	
1953	Miss M. Connolly	Miss D. J. Hart	8–6	7–5	
1954	Miss M. Connolly	Miss A. L. Brough	6–2	7–5	
1955*	Miss A. L. Brough	Mrs J. G. Fleitz	7–5	8–6	
1956	Miss S. J. Fry	Miss A. Buxton	6–3	6–1	
1957*	Miss A. Gibson	Miss D. R. Hard	6–3	6–2	
1958	Miss A. Gibson	Miss A. Mortimer	8–6	6–2	
1959*	Miss M. E. Bueno	Miss D. R. Hard	6–4	6–3	
1960	Miss M. E. Bueno	Miss S. Reynolds	8–6	6–0	
1961*	Miss A. Mortimer	Miss C. C. Truman	4–6	6–4	7–5
1962	Mrs J. R. Susman	Mrs V. Sukova	6–4	6–4	
1963*	Miss M. Smith	Miss B. J. Moffitt	6–3	6–4	
1964	Miss M. E. Bueno	Miss M. Smith	6–4	7–9	6–3
1965	Miss M. Smith	Miss M. E. Bueno	6–4	7–5	
1966	Mrs L. W. King	Miss M. E. Bueno	6–3	3–6	6–1
1967	Mrs L. W. King	Mrs P. F. Jones	6–3	6–4	
1968	Mrs L. W. King	Miss J. A. M. Tegart	9–7	7–5	
1969	Mrs P. F. Jones	Mrs L. W. King	3–6	6–3	6–2
1970*	Mrs B. M. Court	Mrs L. W. King	14–12	11–9	
1971	Miss E. Goolagong	Mrs B. M. Court	6–4	6–1	
1972	Mrs L. W. King	Miss E. Goolagong	6–3	6–3	
1973	Mrs L. W. King	Miss C. M. Evert	6–0	7–5	
1974	Miss C. M. Evert	Mrs O. Morozova	6–0	6–4	
1975	Mrs L. W. King	Mrs R. A. Cawley	6–0	6–1	
1976*	Miss C. M. Evert	Mrs R. A. Cawley	6–3	4–6	8–6
1977	Miss S. V. Wade	Miss B. F. Stove	4–6	6–3	6–1
1978	Miss M. Navratilova	Miss C. M. Evert	2–6	6–4	7–5
1979	Miss M. Navratilova	Mrs C. Evert Lloyd	6–4	6–4	
1980	Mrs R. A. Cawley	Mrs C. Evert Lloyd	6–1	7–6	
1981	Mrs C. Evert Lloyd	Miss H. Mandlikova	6–2	6–2	
1982	Miss M. Navratilova	Mrs C. Evert Lloyd	6–1	3–6	6–2
1983	Miss M. Navratilova	Miss A. Jaeger	6–0	6–3	
1984	Miss M. Navratilova	Mrs C. Evert Lloyd	7–6	6–2	
1985	Miss M. Navratilova	Mrs C. Evert Lloyd	4–6	6–3	6–2
1986	Miss M. Navratilova	Miss H. Mandlikova	7–6	6–3	
1987	Miss M. Navratilova	Miss S. Graf	7–5	6–3	
1988	Miss S. Graf	Miss M. Navratilova	5–7	6–2	6–1
1989	Miss S. Graf	Miss M. Navratilova	6–2	6–7	6–1
1990	Miss M. Navratilova	Miss Z. Garrison	6–4	6–1	
1991	Miss S. Graf	Miss G. Sabatini	6–4	3–6	8–6

First prize (£) column values:
750, 1,500, 1,500, 1,800, 2,400, 3,000, 7,000, 7,000, 10,000, 13,500, 17,100, 18,000, 18,000, 19,440, 37,500, 60,000, 90,000, 117,000, 126,000, 139,500, 148,500, 171,000, 207,000, 216,000

MEN'S DOUBLES

	CHAMPIONS	RUNNERS-UP	SCORE				
1884	E./W. Renshaw	E. W. Lewis/E. L. Williams	6–3	6–1	1–6	6–4	
1885	E./W. Renshaw	C. E. Farrer/A. J. Stanley	6–3	6–3	10–8		
(Challenge Round instituted)							
1886	E./W. Renshaw	C. E. Farrer/A. J. Stanley	6–3	6–3	4–6	7–5	
1887*	P. Bowes-Lyon/ W. W. Wilberforce	E. Barret-Smith/J. H. Crispe	7–5	6–3	6–2		
1888	E./W. Renshaw	P. Bowes-Lyon/ W. W. Wilberforce	2–6	1–6	6–3	6–4	6–3
1889	E./W. Renshaw	G. W. Hillyard/E. W. Lewis	6–4	6–4	3–6	0–6	6–1
1890*	J. Pim/F. O. Stoker	G. W. Hillyard/E. W. Lewis	6–0	7–5	6–4		
1891	H./W. Baddeley	J. Pim/F. O. Stoker	6–1	6–3	1–6	6–2	
1892	H. S. Barlow/E. W. Lewis	H./W. Baddeley	4–6	6–2	8–6	6–4	
1893	J. Pim/F. O. Stoker	H. W. Barlow/E. W. Lewis	4–6	6–3	6–1	2–6	6–0
1894*	H./W. Baddeley	H. S. Barlow/C. H. Martin	5–7	7–5	4–6	6–3	8–6
1895	H./W. Baddeley	W. V. Eaves/E. W. Lewis	8–6	5–7	6–4	6–3	
1896	H./W. Baddeley	R. F. Doherty/H. A. Nisbet	1–6	3–6	6–4	6–2	6–1
1897	H. L./R. F. Doherty	H./W. Baddeley	6–4	4–6	8–6	6–4	
1898	H. L./R. F. Doherty	C. Hobart/H. A. Nisbet	6–4	6–4	6–2		
1899	H. L./R. F. Doherty	C. Hobart/H. A. Nisbet	7–5	6–0	6–2		
1900	H. L./R. F. Doherty	H. A. Nisbet/H. Roper Barrett	9–7	7–5	4–6	3–6	6–3
1901	H. L./R. F. Doherty	D. F. Davis/H. Ward	4–6	6–2	6–3	9–7	
1902	F. L. Riseley/S. H. Smith	H. L./R. F. Doherty	4–6	8–6	6–3	4–6	11–9
1903	H. L./R. F. Doherty	F. L. Riseley/S. H. Smith	6–4	6–4	6–4		
1904	H. L./R. F. Doherty	F. L. Riseley/S. H. Smith	6–3	6–4	6–3		
1905	H. L./R. F. Doherty	F. L. Riseley/S. H. Smith	6–2	6–4	6–8	6–3	
1906	F. L. Riseley/S. H. Smith	H. L./R. F. Doherty	6–8	6–4	5–7	6–3	6–3
1907*	N. E. Brookes/A. F. Wilding	K. Behr/B. C. Wright	6–4	6–4	6–2		

Year	Winners	Runners-up					Prize
1908*	M. J. G. Ritchie/A. F. Wilding	A. W. Gore/H. Roper Barrett	6–1	6–2	1–6	1–6	9–7
1909*	A. W. Gore/H. Roper Barrett	S. N. Doust/H. A. Parker	6–2	6–1	6–4		
1910	M. J. G. Ritchie/A. F. Wilding	A. W. Gore/H. Roper Barrett	6–1	6–1	6–2		
1911	M. Decugis/A. H. Gobert	M. J. G. Ritchie/A. F. Wilding	9–7	5–7	6–3	2–6	6–2
1912	C. P. Dixon/H. Roper Barrett	M. Decugis/A. H. Gobert	3–6	6–3	6–4	7–5	
1913	C. P. Dixon/H. Roper Barrett	H. Kleinschroth/F. W. Rahe	6–2	6–4	4–6	6–2	
1914	N. E. Brookes/A. F. Wilding	C. P. Dixon/H. Roper Barrett	6–1	6–1	5–7	8–6	
1915–1918	*Not held*						
1919*	P. O'Hara Wood/R. V. Thomas	R. W. Heath/R. Lycett	6–4	6–2	4–6	6–2	
1920*	C. S. Garland/R. N. Williams	A. R. F. Kingscote/J. C. Parke	4–6	6–4	7–5	6–2	
1921*	R. Lycett/M. Woosnam	A. H./F. G. Lowe	6–3	6–0	7–5		
(Challenge Round abolished)							
1922	J. O. Anderson/R. Lycett	P. O'Hara Wood/G. L. Patterson	3–6	7–9	6–4	6–3	11–9
1923	L. A. Godfree/R. Lycett	E. Flaquer/Count de Gomar	6–3	6–4	3–6	6–3	
1924	F. T. Hunter/V. Richards	W. M. Washburn/R. N. Williams	6–3	3–6	8–10	8–6	6–3
1925	J. Borotra/R. Lacoste	R. Casey/J. Hennessey	6–4	11–9	4–6	1–6	6–3
1926	J. Brugnon/H. Cochet	H. Kinsey/V. Richards	7–5	4–6	6–3	6–2	
1927	F. T. Hunter/W. T. Tilden	J. Brugnon/H. Cochet	1–6	4–6	8–6	6–3	6–4
1928	J. Brugnon/H. Cochet	J. B. Hawkes/G. L. Patterson	13–11	6–4	6–4		
1929	W. L. Allison/J. Van Ryn	I. G. Collins/J. C. Gregory	6–4	5–7	6–3	10–12	6–4
1930	W. L. Allison/J. Van Ryn	J. H. Doeg/G. M. Lott	6–3	6–3	6–2		
1931	G. M. Lott/J. Van Ryn	J. Brugnon/H. Cochet	6–2	10–8	9–11	3–6	6–3
1932	J. Borotra/J. Brugnon	G. P. Hughes/F. J. Perry	6–0	4–6	3–6	7–5	7–5
1933	J. Borotra/J. Brugnon	R. Nunoi/J. Satoh	4–6	6–3	6–3	7–5	
1934	G. M. Lott/L. R. Stoefen	J. Borotra/J. Brugnon	6–2	6–3	6–4		
1935	J. H. Crawford/A. K Quist	W. L. Allison/J. Van Ryn	6–3	5–7	6–2	5–7	7–5
1936	G. P. Hughes/C. R. D. Tuckey	C. E. Hare/F. H. D. Wilde	6–4	3–6	7–9	6–1	5–4
1937	J. D. Budge/G. Mako	G. P. Hughes/C. R. D. Tuckey	6–0	6–4	6–8	6–1	
1938	J. D. Budge/G. Mako	H. Henkel/G. von Metaxa	6–4	3–6	6–3	8–6	
1939	E. T. Cooke/R. L. Riggs	C. E. Hare/F. H. D. Wilde	6–3	3–6	6–3	9–7	
1940–1945	*Not held*						
1946	T. Brown/J. A. Kramer	G. E. Brown/D. Pails	6–4	6–4	6–2		
1947	R. Falkenburg/J. A. Kramer	A. J. Mottram/O. W. Sidwell	8–6	6–3	6–3		
1948	J. E. Bromwich/F. A. Sedgman	T. Brown/G. Mulloy	5–7	7–5	7–5	9–7	
1949	R. A. Gonzales/F. A. Parker	G. Mulloy/F. R. Schroeder	6–4	6–4	6–2		
1950	J. E. Bromwich/A. K. Quist	G. E. Brown/O. W. Sidwell	7–5	3–6	6–3	3–6	6–2
1951	K. McGregor/F. A. Sedgman	J. Drobny/E. W. Sturgess	3–6	6–2	6–3	3–6	6–3
1952	K. McGregor/F. A. Sedgman	E. V. Seixas/E. W. Sturgess	6–3	7–5	6–4		
1953	L. A. Hoad/K. R. Rosewall	R. N. Hartwig/M. G. Rose	6–4	7–5	4–6	7–5	
1954	R. N. Hartwig/M. G. Rose	E. V. Seixas/M. A. Trabert	6–4	6–4	3–6	6–4	
1955	R. N. Hartwig/L. A. Hoad	N. A. Fraser/K. R. Rosewall	7–5	6–4	6–3		
1956	L. A. Hoad/K. R. Rosewall	N. Pietrangeli/O. Sirola	7–5	6–2	6–1		
1957	G. Mulloy/B. Patty	N. A. Fraser/L. A. Hoad	8–10	6–4	6–4		
1958	S. Davidson/U. Schmidt	A. J. Cooper/N. A. Fraser	6–4	6–4	8–6		
1959	R. Emerson/N. A. Fraser	R. Laver/R. Mark	8–6	6–3	1–6	9–7	
1960	R. H. Osuna/R. D. Ralston	M. G. Davies/R. K. Wilson	7–5	6–3	10–8		
1961	R. Emerson/N. A. Fraser	R. A. J. Hewitt/F. S. Stolle	6–4	6–8	6–4	6–8	8–6
1962	R. A. J. Hewitt/F. S. Stolle	B. Jovanovic/N. Pilic	6–2	5–7	6–2	6–4	
1963	R. H. Osuna/A. Palafox	J. C. Barclay/P. Darmon	4–6	6–2	6–2	6–2	
1964	R. A. J. Hewitt/F. S. Stolle	R. Emerson/K. N. Fletcher	7–5	11–9	6–4		FIRST
1965	J. D. Newcombe/A. D. Roche	K. N. Fletcher/R. A. J. Hewitt	7–5	6–3	6–4		PRIZE
1966	K. N. Fletcher/J. D. Newcombe	W. W. Bowrey/O. K. Davidson	6–3	6–4	3–6	6–3	*(£ per*
1967	R. A. J. Hewitt/F. D. McMillan	R. Emerson/K. N. Fletcher	6–2	6–3	6–4		*team)*
1968	J. D. Newcombe/A. D. Roche	K. R. Rosewall/F. S. Stolle	3–6	8–6	5–7	14–12	6–3	800
1969	J. D. Newcombe/A. D. Roche	T. S. Okker/M. C. Riessen	7–5	11–9	6–3		1,000
1970	J. D. Newcombe/A. D. Roche	K. R. Rosewall/F. S. Stolle	10–8	6–3	6–1		1,000
1971	R. Emerson/R. Laver	A. R. Ashe/R. D. Ralston	4–6	9–7	6–8	6–4	6–4	750
1972	R. A. J. Hewitt/F. D. McMillan	S. R. Smith/E. Van Dillen	6–2	6–2	9–7		1,000
1973	J. S. Connors/I. Nastase	J. R. Cooper/N. A. Fraser	3–6	6–3	6–4	8–9	6–1	1,000
1974	J. D. Newcombe/A. D. Roche	R. C. Lutz/S. R. Smith	8–6	6–4	6–4		2,000
1975	V. Gerulaitis/A. Mayer	C. Dowdeswell/A. J. Stone	7–5	8–6	6–4		2,000
1976	B. E. Gottfried/R. Ramirez	R. L. Case/G. Masters	3–6	6–3	8–6	2–6	7–6	3,000
1977	R. L. Case/G. Masters	J. G. Alexander/P. C. Dent	6–3	6–4	3–6	8–9	6–4	6,000
1978	R. A. J. Hewitt/F. D. McMillan	P. Fleming/J. P. McEnroe	6–1	6–4	6–2		7,500
1979	P. Fleming/J. P. McEnroe	B. E. Gottfried/R. Ramirez	4–6	6–4	6–2	6–2	8,000
1980	P. McNamara/P. McNamee	R. C. Lutz/S. R. Smith	7–6	6–3	6–7	6–4	8,400
1981	P. Fleming/J. P. McEnroe	R. C. Lutz/S. R. Smith	6–4	6–4	6–4		9,070
1982	P. McNamara/P. McNamee	P. Fleming/J. P. McEnroe	6–3	6–2			16,666
1983	P. Fleming/J. P. McEnroe	T. E./T. R. Gullikson	6–4	6–3	6–4		26,628
1984	P. Fleming/J. P. McEnroe	P. Cash/P. McNamee	6–2	5–7	6–2	3–6	6–3	40,000
1985	H. P. Gunthardt/B. Taroczy	P. Cash/J. Fitzgerald	6–4	6–3	4–6	6–3	47,500
1986	J. Nystrom/M. Wilander	G. Donnelly/P. Fleming	7–6	6–3	6–3		48,500

1987	K. Flach/R. Seguso	S. Casal/E. Sanchez	3–6	6–7	7–6	6–1	6–4	53,730
1988	K. Flach/R. Seguso	J. Fitzgerald/A. Jarryd	6–4	2–6	6–4	7–6		57,200
1989	J. B. Fitzgerald/A. Jarryd	R. Leach/J. Pugh	3–6	7–6	6–4	7–6		65,870
1990	R. Leach/J. Pugh	P. Aldrich/D. Visser	7–6	7–6	7–6			94,230
1991	J. B. Fitzgerald/A. Jarryd	J. Franai/L. Lavalle	6–3	6–4	6–7	6–1		98,330

WOMEN'S DOUBLES

	CHAMPIONS	RUNNERS-UP	SCORE			
1913	R. J. McNair/D. P. Boothby	A. Sterry/D. Lambert Chambers	4–6	2–4	ret'd	
1914	A. M. Morton/E. Ryan	G. Hannam/D. R. Larcombe	6–1	6–3		
1915–1918	*Not held*					
1919	S. Lenglen/E. Ryan	D. Lambert Chambers/D. R. Larcombe	4–6	7–5	6–3	
1920	S. Lenglen/E. Ryan	D. Lambert Chambers/D. R. Larcombe	6–4	6–0		
1921	S. Lenglen/E. Ryan	A. E. Beamish/G. Peacock	6–1	6–2		
1922	S. Lenglen/E. Ryan	K. McKane/A. D. Stocks	6–0	6–4		
1923	S. Lenglen/E. Ryan	J. Austin/E. L. Colyer	6–3	6–1		
1924	H. Wightman/H. N. Wills	B. C. Covell/K. McKane	6–4	6–4		
1925	S. Lenglen/E. Ryan	A. V. Bridge/C. G. McIlquham	6–2	6–2		
1926	M. K. Browne/E. Ryan	L. A. Godfree/E. L. Colyer	6–1	6–1		
1927	H. N. Wills/E. Ryan	E. L. Heine/G. Peacock	6–3	6–2		
1928	P. Saunders/M. Watson	E. Bennett/E. H. Harvey	6–2	6–3		
1929	L. R. C. Michell/M. Watson	B. C. Covell/D. C. Shepherd-Barron	6–4	8–6		
1930	F. S. Moody/E. Ryan	E. Cross/S. Palfrey	6–2	9–7		
1931	D. C. Shepherd-Barron/P. E. Mudford	D. Metaxa/J. Sigart	3–6	6–3	6–4	
1932	D. Metaxa/J. Sigart	H. H. Jacobs/E. Ryan	6–4	6–3		
1933	S. Mathieu/E. Ryan	F. James/A. M. Yorke	6–2	9–11	6–4	
1934	S. Mathieu/E. Ryan	D. B. Andrus/S. Henrotin	6–3	6–3		
1935	F. James/K. E. Stammers	S. Mathieu/H. Sperling	6–1	6–4		
1936	F. James/K. E. Stammers	S. Fabyan/H. H. Jacobs	6–2	6–1		
1937	S. Mathieu/A. M. Yorke	P. King/E. Pittman	6–3	6–3		
1938	S. Fabyan/A. Marble	S. Mathieu/A. M. Yorke	6–2	6–3		
1939	S. Fabyan/A. Marble	H. H. Jacobs/A. M. Yorke	6–1	6–0		
1940–1945	*Not held*					
1946	A. L. Brough/M. E. Osborne	P. M. Betz/D. J. Hart	6–3	2–6	6–3	
1947	D. J. Hart/P. C. Todd	A. L. Brough/M. E. Osborne	3–6	6–4	7–5	
1948	A. L. Brough/W. du Pont	D. J. Hart/P. C. Todd	6–3	3–6	6–3	
1949	A. L. Brough/W. du Pont	G. Moran/P. C. Todd	8–6	7–5		
1950	A. L. Brough/W. du Pont	S. J. Fry/D. J. Hart	6–4	5–7	6–1	
1951	S. J. Fry/D. J. Hart	A. L. Brough/W. du Pont	6–3	13–11		
1952	S. J. Fry/D. J. Hart	A. L. Brough/M. Connolly	8–6	6–3		
1953	S. J. Fry/D. J. Hart	M. Connolly/J. Sampson	6–0	6–0		
1954	A. L. Brough/W. du Pont	S. J. Fry/D. J. Hart	4–6	9–7	6–3	
1955	A. Mortimer/J. A. Shilcock	S. J. Bloomer/P. E. Ward	7–5	6–1		
1956	A. Buxton/A. Gibson	F. Muller/D. G. Seeney	6–1	8–6		
1957	A. Gibson/D. R. Hard	K. Hawton/T. D. Long	6–1	6–2		
1958	M. E. Bueno/A. Gibson	W. du Pont/M. Varner	6–3	7–5		
1959	J. Arth/D. R. Hard	J. G. Fleitz/C. C. Truman	2–6	6–2	6–3	
1960	M. E. Bueno/D. R. Hard	S. Reynolds/R. Schuurman	6–4	6–0		
1961	K. Hantz/B. J. Moffitt	J. Lehane/M. Smith	6–3	6–4		
1962	B. J. Moffitt/J. R. Susman	L. E. G. Price/R. Schuurman	5–7	6–3	7–5	
1963	M. E. Bueno/D. R. Hard	R. A. Ebbern/M. Smith	8–6	9–7		
1964	M. Smith/L. R. Turner	B. J. Moffitt/J. R. Susman	7–5	6–2		FIRST
1965	M. E. Bueno/B. J. Moffitt	F. Durr/J. Lieffrig	6–2	7–5		PRIZE
1966	M. E. Bueno/N. Richey	M. Smith/J. A. M. Tegart	6–3	4–6	6–4	*(£ per*
1967	R. Casals/L. W. King	M. E. Bueno/N. Richey	9–11	6–4	6–2	*team)*
1968	R. Casals/L. W. King	F. Durr/P. F. Jones	3–6	6–4	7–5	500
1969	B. M. Court/J. A. M. Tegart	P. S. A. Hogan/M. Michel	9–7	6–2		600
1970	R. Casals/L. W. King	F. Durr/S. V. Wade	6–2	6–3		600
1971	R. Casals/L. W. King	B. M. Court/E. Goolagong	6–3	6–2		450
1972	L. W. King/B. Stove	D. E. Dalton/F. Durr	6–2	4–6	6–3	600
1973	R. Casals/L. W. King	F. Durr/B. Stove	6–1	4–6	7–5	600
1974	E. Goolagong/M. Michel	H. F. Gourlay/K. M. Krantzcke	2–6	6–4	6–3	1,200
1975	A. Kiyomura/K. Sawamatsu	F. Durr/B. Stove	7–5	1–6	7–5	1,200
1976	C. Evert/M. Navratilova	L. W. King/B. Stove	6–1	3–6	7–5	2,400
1977	H. Gourlay-Cawley/J. C. Russell	M. Navratilova/B. Stove	6–3	6–3		5,200
1978	G. E. Reid/W. Turnbull	M. Jausovec/V. Ruzici	4–6	9–8	6–3	6,500
1979	L. W. King/M. Navratilova	B. Stove/W. M. Turnbull	5–7	6–3	6–2	6,930
1980	K. Jordan/A. E. Smith	R. Casals/W. M. Turnbull	4–6	7–5	6–1	7,276
1981	M. Navratilova/P. H. Shriver	K. Jordan/A. E. Smith	6–3	7–6		7,854
1982	M. Navratilova/P. H. Shriver	K. Jordan/A. E. Smith	6–4	6–1		14,450

983 M. Navratilova/P. H. Shriver	R. Casals/W. M. Turnbull	6–2 6–2		23,100
984 M. Navratilova/P. H. Shriver	K. Jordan/A. E. Smith	6–3 6–4		34,700
985 K. Jordan/E. Smylie	M. Navratilova/P. H. Shriver	5–7 6–3 6–4		41,100
986 M. Navratilova/P. H. Shriver	H. Mandlikova/W. M. Turnbull	6–1 6–3		42,060
987 C. Kohde-Kilsch/H. Sukova	B. Nagelsen/E. Smylie	7–5 7–5		46,500
988 S. Graf/G. Sabatini	L. Savchenko/N. Zvereva	6–3 1–6 12–10		49,500
989 J. Novotna/H. Sukova	L. Savchenko/N. Zvereva	6–1 6–2		56,970
990 J. Novotna/H. Sukova	K. Jordan/E. Smylie	6–3 6–4		81,510
991 L. Savchenko/N. Zvereva	G. Fernandez/J. Novotna	6–4 3–6 6–4		85,060

MIXED DOUBLES

	CHAMPIONS	RUNNERS-UP	SCORE		
913	Hope Crisp/Mrs C. O. Tuckey	J. C. Parke/Mrs D. R. Larcombe	3–6 5–3 ret'd		
914	J. C. Parke/Mrs D. R. Larcombe	A. F. Wilding/Mlle M. Broquedis	4–6 6–4 6–2		
915–1918	*Not held*				
919	R. Lycett/Miss E. Ryan	A. D. Prebble/Mrs D. Lambert Chambers	6–0 6–0		
920	G. L. Patterson/Mlle S. Lenglen	R. Lycett/Miss E. Ryan	7–5 6–3		
921	R. Lycett/Miss E. Ryan	M. Woosnam/Miss P. L. Howkins	6–3 6–1		
922	P. O'Hara Wood/Mlle S. Lenglen	R. Lycett/Miss E. Ryan	6–4 6–3		
923	R. Lycett/Miss E. Ryan	L. S. Deane/Mrs D. C. Shepherd-Barron	6–4 7–5		
924	J. B. Gilbert/Miss K. McKane	L. A. Godfree/Mrs D. C. Shepherd-Barron	6–3 3–6 6–3		
925	J. Borotra/Mlle S. Lenglen	H. L. de Morpurgo/Miss E. Ryan	6–3 6–3		
926	L. A./Mrs Godfree	H. Kinsey/Miss M. K. Browne	6–3 6–4		
927	F. T. Hunter/Miss E. Ryan	L. A./Mrs Godfree	8–6 6–0		
928	P. D. B. Spence/Miss E. Ryan	J. H. Crawford/Miss D. Akhurst	7–5 6–4		
929	F. T. Hunter/Miss H. N. Wills	I. G. Collins/Miss J. Fry	6–1 6–4		
930	J. H. Crawford/Miss E. Ryan	D. Prenn/Frl H. Krahwinkel	6–1 6–3		
931	G. M. Lott/Mrs L. A. Harper	I. G. Collins/Miss J. C. Ridley	6–3 1–6 6–1		
932	E. Maier/Miss E. Ryan	H. C. Hopman/Mlle J. Sigart	7–5 6–2		
933	G. von Cramm/Frl H. Krahwinkel	N. G. Farquharson/Miss M. Heeley	7–5 8–6		
934	R. Miki/Miss D. E. Round	H. W. Austin/Mrs D. C. Shepherd-Barron	3–6 6–4 6–0		
935	F. J. Perry/Miss D. E. Round	H. C./Mrs Hopman	7–5 4–6 6–2		
936	F. J. Perry/Miss D. E. Round	J. D. Budge/Mrs S. Fabyan	7–9 7–5 6–4		
937	J. D. Budge/Miss A. Marble	Y. Petra/Mme S. Mathieu	6–4 6–1		
938	J. D. Budge/Miss A. Marble	H. Henkel/Mrs S. Fabyan	6–1 6–4		
939	R. L. Riggs/Miss A. Marble	F. H. D. Wilde/Miss N. B. Brown	9–7 6–1		
940–1945	*Not held*				
946	T. Brown/Miss A. L. Brough	G. E. Brown/Miss D. Bundy	6–4 6–4		
947	J. E. Bromwich/Miss A. L. Brough	C. F. Long/Mrs N. M. Bolton	1–6 6–4 6–2		
948	J. E. Bromwich/Miss A. L. Brough	F. A. Sedgman/Miss D. J. Hart	6–2 3–6 6–3		
949	E. E. Sturgess/Mrs S. P. Summer	J. E. Bromwich/Miss A. L. Brough	9–7 9–11 7–5		
950	E. W. Sturgess/Miss A. L. Brough	G. E. Brown/Mrs P. C. Todd	11–9 1–6 6–4		
951	F. A. Sedgman/Miss D. J. Hart	M. G. Rose/Mrs N. M. Bolton	7–5 6–2		
952	F. A. Sedgman/Miss D. J. Hart	E. Morea/Mrs T. D. Long	4–6 6–3 6–4		
953	E. V. Seixas/Miss D. J. Hart	E. Morea/Miss S. J. Fry	9–7 7–5		
954	E. V. Seixas/Miss D. J. Hart	K. R. Rosewall/Mrs W. du Pont	5–7 6–4 6–3		
955	E. V. Seixas/Miss D. J. Hart	E. Morea/Miss A. L. Brough	8–6 2–6 6–3		
956	E. V. Seixas/Miss S. J. Fry	G. Mulloy/Miss A. Gibson	2–6 6–2 7–5		
957	M. G. Rose/Miss D. R. Hard	N. A. Fraser/Miss A. Gibson	6–4 7–5		
958	R. N. Howe/Miss L. Coghlan	K. Nielsen/Miss A. Gibson	6–3 13–11		
959	R. Laver/Miss D. R. Hard	N. A. Fraser/Miss M. E. Bueno	6–4 6–3		
960	R. Laver/Miss D. R. Hard	R. N. Howes/Miss M. E. Bueno	13–11 3–6 8–6		
961	F. S. Stolle/Miss L. R. Turner	R. N. Howe/Miss E. Buding	11–9 6–2		
962	N. A. Fraser/Mrs W. du Pont	R. D. Ralston/Miss A. S. Haydon	2–6 6–3 13–11		
963	K. N. Fletcher/Miss M. Smith	R. A. J. Hewitt/Miss D. R. Hard	11–9 6–4		
964	F. S. Stolle/Miss L. R. Turner	K. N. Fletcher/Miss M. Smith	6–4 6–4		FIRST
965	K. N. Fletcher/Miss M. Smith	A. D. Roche/Miss J. A. M. Tegart	12–10 6–3		PRIZE
966	K. N. Fletcher/Miss M. Smith	R. D. Ralston/Mrs L. W. King	4–6 6–3 6–3		*(£ per*
967	O. K. Davidson/Mrs L. W. King	K. N. Fletcher/Miss M. E. Bueno	7–5 6–0		*team)*
968	K. N. Fletcher/Mrs B. M. Court	A. Metreveli/Miss O. Morozova	6–1 14–12		450
969	F. S. Stolle/Mrs P. F. Jones	A. D. Roche/Miss J. A. M. Tegart	6–3 6–2		500
970	I. Nastase/Miss R. Casals	A. Metreveli/Miss O. Morozova	6–3 4–6 9–7		500
971	O. K. Davidson/Mrs L. W. King	M. C. Rieseen/Mrs B. M. Court	3–6 6–2 15–13		375
972	I. Nastase/Miss R. Casals	K. Warwick/Miss E. Goolagong	6–4 6–4		500
973	O. K. Davidson/Mrs L. W. King	Mr. Ramirez/Miss J. Newberry	6–3 6–2		500
974	O. K. Davidson/Mrs L. W. King	M. J. Farrell/Miss L. J. Charles	6–3 9–7		1,000
975	M. C. Riessen/Mrs B. M. Court	A. J. Stone/Miss B. Stove	6–4 7–5		1,000
976	A. D. Roche/Miss F. Durr	R. L. Stockton/Miss R. Casals	6–3 2–6 7–5		2,000
977	R. A. J. Hewitt/Miss G. R. Stevens	F. D. McMillan/Miss B. Stove	3–6 7–5 6–4		3,000
978	F. D. McMillan/Miss B. Stove	R. O. Ruffels/Mrs L. W. King	6–2 6–2		4,000

1979	R. A. J. Hewitt/Miss G. R. Stevens	F. D. McMillan/Miss B. Stove	7–5	7–6		4,200
1980	J. R. Austin/Miss T. Austin	M. R. Edmondson/Miss D. L. Fromholtz	4–6	7–6	6–3	4,42●
1981	F. D. McMillan/Miss B. Stove	J. R. Austin/Miss T. Austin	4–6	7–6	6–3	4,77●
1982	K. Curren/Miss A. E. Smith	J. M. Lloyd/Miss W. M. Turnbull	2–6	6–3	7–5	6,75●
1983	J. M. Lloyd/Miss W. M. Turnbull	S. Denton/Mrs L. W. King	6–7	7–6	7–5	12,00●
1984	J. M. Lloyd/Miss W. M. Turnbull	S. Denton/Miss K. Jordan	6–3	6–3		18,00●
1985	P. McNamee/Miss M. Navratilova	J. Fitzgerald/Mrs E. Smylie	7–5	4–6	6–2	23,40●
1986	K. Flach/Miss K. Jordan	H. P. Gunthardt/Miss M. Navratilova	6–3	7–6		25,20●
1987	M. J. Bates/Miss J. M. Durie	D. Cahill/Miss N. Provis	7–6	6–3		27,90●
1988	S. E. Stewart/Miss Z. Garrison	K. Jones/Mrs G. Magers	6–1	7–6		29,70●
1989	J. Pugh/Miss J. Novotna	M. Kratzmann/Miss J. Byrne	6–4	5–7	6–4	34,20●
1990	R. Leach/Miss Z. Garrison	J. Fitzgerald/Mrs E. Smylie	7–5	6–2		40,00●
1991	J. B. Fitzgerald/Mrs E. Smylie	J. Pugh/Miss N. Zvereva	7–6	6–2		41,72●

US NATIONAL CHAMPIONSHIPS 1881–1969

Holders did not defend the title.

MEN'S SINGLES

	CHAMPION	RUNNER-UP	SCORE				
1881	R. D. Sears	W. E. Glyn	6–0	6–3	6–2		
1882	R. D. Sears	C. M. Clark	6–1	6–4	6–0		
1883	R. D. Sears	J. Dwight	6–2	6–0	9–7		
(Challenge Round instituted)							
1884	R. D. Sears	H. A. Taylor	6–0	1–6	6–0	6–2	
1885	R. D. Sears	G. M. Brinley	6–3	4–6	6–0	6–3	
1886	R. D. Sears	R. L. Beeckman	4–6	6–1	6–3	6–4	
1887	R. D. Sears	H. W. Slocum	6–1	6–3	6–2		
1888*	H. W. Slocum	H. A. Taylor	6–4	6–1	6–0		
1889	H. W. Slocum	Q. A. Shaw	6–3	6–1	4–6	6–2	
1890	O. S. Campbell	H. W. Slocum	6–2	4–6	6–3	6–1	
1891	O. S. Campbell	C. Hobart	2–6	7–5	7–9	6–1	6–2
1892	O. S. Campbell	F. H. Hovey	7–5	3–6	6–3	7–5	
1893*	R. D. Wrenn	F. H. Hovey	6–4	3–6	6–4	6–4	
1894	R. D. Wrenn	M. F. Goodbody	6–8	6–1	6–4	6–4	
1895	F. H. Hovey	R. D. Wrenn	6–3	6–2	6–4		
1896	R. D. Wrenn	F. H. Hovey	7–5	3–6	6–0	1–6	6–1
1897	R. D. Wrenn	W. V. Eaves	4–6	8–6	6–3	2–6	6–2
1898*	M. D. Whitman	D. F. Davis	3–6	6–2	6–2	6–1	
1899	M. D. Whitman	J. P. Paret	6–1	6–2	3–6	7–5	
1900	M. D. Whitman	W. A. Larned	6–4	1–6	6–2	6–2	
1901*	W. A. Larned	B. C. Wright	6–2	6–8	6–4	6–4	
1902	W. A. Larned	R. F. Doherty	4–6	6–2	6–4	8–6	
1903	H. L. Doherty	W. A. Larned	6–0	6–3	10–8		
1904*	H. Ward	W. J. Clothier	10–8	6–4	9–7		
1905	B. C. Wright	H. Ward	6–2	6–1	11–9		
1906	W. J. Clothier	B. C. Wright	6–3	6–0	6–4		
1907*	W. A. Larned	R. LeRoy	6–2	6–2	6–4		
1908	W. A. Larned	B. C. Wright	6–1	6–2	8–6		
1909	W. A. Larned	W. J. Clothier	6–1	6–2	5–7	1–6	6–1
1910	W. A. Larned	T. C. Bundy	6–1	5–7	6–0	6–8	6–1
1911	W. A. Larned	M. E. McLoughlin	6–4	6–4	6–2		
(Challenge Round abolished)							
1912	M. E. McLoughlin	W. F. Johnson	3–6	2–6	6–2	6–4	6–2
1913	M. E. McLoughlin	R. N. Williams	6–4	5–7	6–3	6–1	
1914	R. N. Williams	M. E. McLoughlin	6–3	8–6	10–8		
1915	W. M. Johnston	M. E. McLoughlin	1–6	6–0	7–5	10–8	
1916	R. N. Williams	W. M. Johnston	4–6	6–4	0–6	6–2	6–4
1917†	R. L. Murray	N. W. Niles	5–7	8–6	6–3	6–3	
1918	R. L. Murray	W. T. Tilden	6–3	6–1	7–5		
1919	W. M. Johnston	W. T. Tilden	6–4	6–4	6–3		
1920	W. T. Tilden	W. M. Johnston	6–1	1–6	7–5	5–7	6–3
1921	W. T. Tilden	W. F. Johnson	6–1	6–3	6–1		
1922	W. T. Tilden	W. M. Johnston	4–6	3–6	6–2	6–3	6–4
1923	W. T. Tilden	W. M. Johnston	6–4	6–1	6–4		
1924	W. T. Tilden	W. M. Johnston	6–1	9–6	6–2		
1925	W. T. Tilden	W. M. Johnston	4–6	11–9	6–3	4–6	6–3
1926	R. Lacoste	J. Borotra	6–4	6–0	6–4		
1927	R. Lacoste	W. T. Tilden	11–9	6–3	11–9		

928	H. Cochet	F. T. Hunter	4–6	6–4	3–6	7–5	6–3
929	W. T. Tilden	F. T. Hunter	3–6	6–3	4–6	6–2	6–4
930	J. H. Doeg	F. X. Shields	10–8	1–6	6–4	16–14	
931	H. E. Vines	G. M. Lott	7–9	6–3	9–7	7–5	
932	H. E. Vines	H. Cochet	6–4	6–4	6–4		
933	F. J. Perry	J. H. Crawford	6–3	11–13	4–6	6–0	6–1
934	F. J. Perry	W. L. Allison	6–4	6–3	1–6	8–6	
935	W. L. Allison	S. B. Wood	6–2	6–2	6–3		
936	F. J. Perry	J. D. Budge	2–6	6–2	8–6	1–6	10–8
937	J. D. Budge	C. Von Cramm	6–1	7–9	6–1	3–6	6–1
938	J. D. Budge	G. Mako	6–3	6–8	6–2	6–1	
939	R. L. Riggs	S. W. van Horn	6–4	6–2	6–4		
940	W. D. McNeill	R. L. Riggs	4–6	6–8	6–3	6–3	7–5
941	R. L. Riggs	F. Kovacs	5–7	6–1	6–3	6–3	
942	F. R. Schroeder	F. A. Parker	8–6	7–5	3–6	4–6	6–2
943	J. R. Hunt	J. A. Kramer	6–3	3–6	10–8	6–0	
944	F. A. Parker	W. F. Talbert	6–4	3–6	6–3	6–3	
945	F. A. Parker	W. F. Talbert	14–12	6–1	6–2		
946	J. A. Kramer	T. P. Brown	9–7	6–3	6–0		
947	J. A. Kramer	F. A. Parker	4–6	2–6	6–1	6–0	6–3
948	R. A. Gonzales	E. W. Sturgess	6–2	6–3	14–12		
949	R. A. Gonzales	F. R. Schroeder	16–18	2–6	6–1	6–2	6–4
950	A. Larsen	H. Flam	6–3	4–6	5–7	6–4	6–3
951	F. A. Sedgman	E. V. Seixas	6–4	6–1	6–1		
952	F. A. Sedgman	G. Mulloy	6–1	6–2	6–3		
953	M. A. Trabert	E. V. Seixas	6–3	6–2	6–3		
954	E. V. Seixas	R. N. Hartwig	3–6	6–2	6–4	6–4	
955	M. A. Trabert	K. R. Rosewall	9–7	6–3	6–3		
956	K. R. Rosewall	L. A. Hoad	4–6	6–2	6–3	6–3	
957	M. J. Anderson	A. J. Cooper	10–8	7–5	6–4		
958	A. J. Cooper	M. J. Anderson	6–2	3–6	4–6	10–8	8–6
959	N. A. Fraser	A. Olmedo	6–3	5–7	6–2	6–4	
960	N. A. Fraser	R. G. Laver	6–4	6–4	9–7		
961	R. S. Emerson	R. G. Laver	7–5	6–3	6–2		
962	R. G. Laver	R. S. Emerson	6–2	6–4	5–7	6–4	
963	R. H. Osuna	F. Froehling	7–5	6–4	6–2		
964	R. S. Emerson	F. S. Stolle	6–4	6–2	6–4		
965	M. Santana	E. C. Drysdale	6–2	7–9	7–5	6–1	
966	F. S. Stolle	J. D. Newcombe	4–6	12–10	6–3	6–4	
967	J. D. Newcombe	C. Graebner	6–4	6–4	8–6		
968	A. R. Ashe	R. C. Lutz	4–6	6–3	8–10	6–0	6–4
969	S. R. Smith	R. C. Lutz	9–7	6–3	6–1		

Played as National Patriotic tournament.

WOMEN'S SINGLES

	CHAMPION	RUNNER-UP	SCORE			
887	Miss E. Hansell	Miss L. Knight	6–1	6–0		
888	Miss B. L. Townsend	Miss E. Hansell	6–3	6–5		
889	Miss B. L. Townsend	Miss L. D. Voorhees	7–5	6–2		
890	Miss E. C. Roosevelt	Miss B. L. Townsend	6–2	6–2		
891	Miss M. E. Cahill	Miss E. C. Roosevelt	6–4	6–1	4–6	6–3
892	Miss M. E. Cahill	Miss E. H. Moore	5–7	6–3	6–4	4–6	6–2
893*	Miss A. Terry	Miss A. L. Schultz	6–1	6–3		
894	Miss H. Hellwig	Miss A. Terry	7–5	3–6	6–0	3–6	6–3
895	Miss J. Atkinson	Miss H. Hellwig	6–4	6–2	6–1	
896	Miss E. H. Moore	Miss J. Atkinson	6–4	4–6	6–2	6–2
897	Miss J. Atkinson	Miss E. H. Moore	6–3	6–3	4–6	3–6	6–3
898	Miss J. Atkinson	Miss M. Jones	6–3	5–7	6–4	2–6	7–5
899*	Miss M. Jones	Miss M. Banks	6–1	6–1	7–5	
900*	Miss M. McAteer	Miss E. Parker	6–2	6–2	6–0	
901	Miss E. H. Moore	Miss M. McAteer	6–4	3–6	7–5	2–6	6–2
902	Miss M. Jones	Miss E. H. Moore	6–1	1–0	ret'd	
903	Miss E. H. Moore	Miss M. Jones	7–5	8–6		
904	Miss M. G. Sutton	Miss E. H. Moore	6–1	6–2		
905*	Miss E. H. Moore	Miss H. Homans	6–4	5–7	6–1	
906*	Miss H. Homans	Mrs M. Barger-Wallach	6–4	6–3		
907*	Miss Evelyn Sears	Miss C. Neely	6–3	6–2		
908	Mrs M. Barger-Wallach	Miss Evelyn Sears	6–3	1–6	6–3	
909	Miss H. Hotchkiss	Mrs M. Barger-Wallach	6–0	6–1		

1910	Miss H. Hotchkiss	Miss L. Hammond	6–4	6–2	
1911	Miss H. Hotchkiss	Miss F. Sutton	8–10	6–1	9–7
1912*	Miss M. K. Browne	Miss Eleanora Sears	6–4	6–2	
1913	Miss M. K. Browne	Miss D. Green	6–2	7–5	
1914	Miss M. K. Browne	Miss M. Wagner	6–2	1–6	6–1
1915*	Miss M. Bjurstedt	Mrs G. W. Wightman	4–6	6–2	6–0
1916	Miss M. Bjurstedt	Mrs L. H. Raymond	6–0	6–1	
1917†	Miss M. Bjurstedt	Miss M. Vanderhoef	4–6	6–0	6–2
1918	Miss M. Bjurstedt	Miss E. E. Goss	6–4	6–3	

(Challenge Round abolished)

1919	Mrs G. W. Wightman	Miss M. Zinderstein	6–1	6–2	
1920	Mrs F. Mallory	Miss M. Zinderstein	6–3	6–1	
1921	Mrs F. Mallory	Miss M. K. Browne	4–6	6–4	6–2
1922	Mrs F. Mallory	Miss H. N. Wills	6–3	6–1	
1923	Miss H. N. Wills	Mrs F. Mallory	6–2	6–1	
1924	Miss H. N. Wills	Mrs F. Mallory	6–1	6–3	
1925	Miss H. N. Wills	Miss K. McKane	3–6	6–0	6–2
1926	Mrs F. Mallory	Miss E. Ryan	4–6	6–4	9–7
1927	Miss H. N. Wills	Miss B. Nuthall	6–1	6–4	
1928	Miss H. N. Wills	Miss H. H. Jacobs	6–2	6–1	
1929	Miss H. N. Wills	Mrs P. H. Watson	6–4	6–2	
1930	Miss B. Nuthall	Mrs L. A. Harper	6–1	6–4	
1931	Mrs F. S. Moody	Mrs F. Whittingstall	6–4	6–1	
1932	Miss H. H. Jacobs	Miss C. A. Babcock	6–2	6–2	
1933	Miss H. H. Jacobs	Mrs F. S. Moody	8–6	3–6	3–0 ret'd
1934	Miss H. H. Jacobs	Miss S. Palfrey	6–1	6–4	
1935	Miss H. H. Jacobs	Mrs S. P. Fabyan	6–2	6–4	
1936	Miss A. Marble	Miss H. H. Jacobs	4–6	6–3	6–2
1937	Miss A. Lizana	Miss J. Jedrzejowksa	6–4	6–2	
1938	Miss A. Marble	Miss N. Wynne	6–0	6–3	
1939	Miss A. Marble	Miss H. H. Jacobs	6–0	8–10	6–4
1940	Miss A. Marble	Miss H. H. Jacobs	6–2	6–3	
1941	Mrs E. T. Cooke	Miss P. M. Betz	7–5	6–2	
1942	Miss P. M. Betz	Miss A. L. Brough	4–6	6–1	6–4
1943	Miss P. M. Betz	Miss A. L. Brough	6–3	5–7	6–3
1944	Miss P. M. Betz	Miss M. E. Osborne	6–3	8–6	
1945	Mrs E. T. Cooke	Miss P. M. Betz	3–6	8–6	6–4
1946	Miss P. M. Betz	Miss P. C. Todd	11–9	6–3	
1947	Miss A. L. Brough	Miss M. E. Osborne	8–6	4–6	6–1
1948	Mrs W. D. du Pont	Miss A. L. Brough	4–6	6–4	15–13
1949	Mrs W. D. du Pont	Miss D. J. Hart	6–4	6–1	
1950	Mrs W. D. du Pont	Miss D. J. Hart	6–4	6–3	
1951	Miss M. Connolly	Miss S. J. Fry	6–3	1–6	6–4
1952	Miss M. Connolly	Miss D. J. Hart	6–3	7–5	
1953	Miss M. Connolly	Miss D. J. Hart	6–2	6–4	
1954	Miss D. J. Hart	Miss A. L. Brough	6–8	6–1	8–6
1955	Miss D. J. Hart	Miss P. E. Ward	6–4	6–2	
1956	Miss S. J. Fry	Miss A. Gibson	6–3	6–4	
1957	Miss A. Gibson	Miss A. L. Brough	6–3	6–2	
1958	Miss A. Gibson	Miss D. R. Hard	3–6	6–1	6–2
1959	Miss M. E. Bueno	Miss C. C. Truman	6–1	6–4	
1960	Miss D. R. Hard	Miss M. E. Bueno	6–4	10–12	6–4
1961	Miss D. R. Hard	Miss A. S. Haydon	6–3	6–4	
1962	Miss M. Smith	Miss D. R. Hard	9–7	6–4	
1963	Miss M. E. Bueno	Miss M. Smith	7–5	6–4	
1964	Miss M. E. Bueno	Mrs C. Graebner	6–1	6–0	
1965	Miss M. Smith	Miss B. J. Moffitt	8–6	7–5	
1966	Miss M. E. Bueno	Miss N. Richey	6–3	6–1	
1967	Mrs L. W. King	Mrs P. F. Jones	11–9	6–4	
1968	Mrs B. M. Court	Miss M. E. Bueno	6–2	6–2	
1969	Mrs B. M. Court	Miss S. V. Wade	4–6	6–3	6–0

† *Played as National Patriotic tournament.*

MEN'S DOUBLES

*Holders did not defend the title.

CHAMPIONS	RUNNERS-UP	SCORE		
1881 C. M. Clark/F. W. Taylor	A. Van Rensselaer/A. E. Newbold	6–5	6–4	6–5
1882 J. Dwight/R. D. Sears	W. Nightingale/G. M. Smith	6–2	6–4	6–4

Year	Winners	Runners-up	Score				
1883	J. Dwight/R. D. Sears	A. Van Rensselaer/A. E. Newbold	6–0	6–2	6–2		
1884	J. Dwight/R. D. Sears	A. Van Rensselaer/W. V. R. Berry	6–4	6–1	8–10	6–4	
1885	J. S. Clark/R. D. Sears	W. P. Knapp/H. W. Slocum	6–3	6–0	6–2		
1886	J. Dwight/R. D. Sears	G. M. Brinley/H. A. Taylor	7–5	5–7	7–5	6–4	
1887	J. Dwight/R. D. Sears	H. W. Slocum/H. A. Taylor	6–4	3–6	2–6	6–3	6–3
1888	O. S. Campbell/V. G. Hall	C. Hobart/E. P. MacMullen	6–4	6–2	6–4		
1889	H. W. Slocum/H. A. Taylor	O. S. Campbell/V. G. Hall	6–1	6–3	6–2		
1890	V. G. Hall/C. Hobart	C. W. Carver/J. A. Ryerson	6–3	4–6	6–2	2–6	6–3
Challenge Round instituted)							
1891	O. S. Campbell/R. P. Huntington	V. G. Hall/C. Hobart	6–3	6–4	8–6		
1892	O. S. Campbell/R. P. Huntington	V. G. Hall/E. L. Hall	6–4	6–2	4–6	6–3	
1893	C. Hobart/F. H. Hovey	O. S. Campbell/R. P. Huntington	6–3	6–4	4–6	6–2	
1894	C. Hobart/F. H. Hovey	C. B. Neel/S. R. Neel	6–3	8–6	6–1		
1895	M. G. Chace/R. D. Wrenn	C. Hobart/F. H. Hovey	7–5	6–1	8–6		
1896*	C. B./S. R. Neel	M. G. Chace/R. D. Wrenn	6–3	1–6	6–1	3–6	6–1
1897	L. E. Ware/G. P. Sheldon	H. S. Mahony/H. A. Nisbet	11–13	6–2	9–7	1–6	6–1
1898	L. E. Ware/G. P. Sheldon	D. F. Davis/H. Ward	1–6	7–5	6–4	4–6	7–5
1899	D. F. Davis/H. Ward	L. E. Ware/G. P. Sheldon	6–4	6–4	6–3		
1900	D. F. Davis/H. Ward	F. B. Alexander/R. D. Little	6–4	9–7	12–10		
1901	D. F. Davis/H. Ward	L. E. Ware/B. C. Wright	6–3	9–7	6–1		
1902	H. L./R. F. Doherty	D. F. Davis/H. Ward	11–9	12–10	6–4		
1903	H. L./R. F. Doherty	L. Collins/L. H. Waldner	7–5	6–3	6–3		
1904*	H. Ward/B. C. Wright	K. Collins/R. D. Little	1–6	6–2	3–6	6–4	6–1
1905	H. Ward/B. C. Wright	F. B. Alexander/H. H. Hackett	6–3	6–1	6–2		
1906	H. Ward/B. C. Wright	F. B. Alexander/H. H. Hackett	6–3	3–6	6–3	6–3	
1907*	F. B. Alexander/B. C. Wright	W. J. Clothier/W. A. Larned	6–3	6–1	6–4		
1908	F. B. Alexander/H. H. Hackett	R. D. Little/B. C. Wright	6–1	7–5	6–2		
1909	F. B. Alexander/H. H. Hackett	G. J. Janes/M. E. McLoughlin	6–4	6–1	6–0		
1910	F. B. Alexander/H. H. Hackett	T. C. Bundy/T. W. Hendrick	6–1	8–6	6–3		
1911	R. D. Little/G. F. Touchard	F. B. Alexander/H. H. Hackett	7–5	13–15	6–2	6–4	
1912	T. C. Bundy/M. E. McLoughlin	R. D. Little/G. F. Touchard	3–6	6–2	6–1	7–5	
1913	T. C. Bundy/M. E. McLoughlin	C. J. Griffin/J. R Strachan	6–4	7–5	6–1		
1914	T. C. Bundy/M. E. McLoughlin	G. M. Church/D. Mathey	6–4	6–2	6–4		
1915	C. J. Griffin/W. M. Johnston	T. C. Bundy/M. E. McLoughlin	6–2	3–6	4–6	6–3	6–3
1916	C. J. Griffin/W. M. Johnston	W. Dawson/M. E. McLoughlin	6–4	6–3	5–7	6–3	
1917	F. B. Alexander/H. A. Throckmorton	H. C. Johnson/I. C. Wright	11–9	6–4	6–4		
Challenge Round abolished)							
1918	V. Richards/W. T. Tilden	F. B. Alexander/B. C. Wright	6–3	6–4	3–6	2–6	6–2
Challenge Round restored)							
1919	N. E. Brookes/G. L. Patterson	V. Richards/W. T. Tilden	8–6	6–3	4–6	6–2	
Challenge Round abolished)							
1920	C. J. Griffin/W. M. Johnston	W. E. Davis/R. Roberts	6–2	6–2	6–3		
1921	V. Richards/W. T. Tilden	W. M. Washburn/R. N. Williams	13–11	12–10	6–1		
1922	V. Richards/W. T. Tilden	P. O'Hara Wood/G. L. Patterson	4–6	6–1	6–3	6–4	
1923	B. I. C. Norton/W. T. Tilden	W. M. Washburn/R. N. Williams	3–6	6–2	6–3	5–7	6–2
1924	H. O./R. G. Kinsey	P. O'Hara Wood/G. L. Patterson	7–5	5–7	7–9	6–3	6–4
1925	V. Richards/R. N. Williams	J. B. Hawkes/G. L. Patterson	6–2	8–10	6–4	11–9	
1926	V. Richards/R. N. Williams	A. H. Chapin/W. T. Tilden	6–4	6–8	11–9	6–3	
1927	F. T. Hunter/W. T. Tilden	W. M. Johnston/R. N. Williams	10–8	6–3	6–3		
1928	J. F. Hennessey/G. M. Lott	J. B. Hawkes/G. L. Patterson	6–2	6–1	6–2		
1929	J. H. Doeg/G. M. Lott	R. B. Bell/L. N. White	10–8	16–14	6–1		
1930	J. H. Doeg/G. M. Lott	W. L. Allison/J. Van Ryn	8–6	6–3	4–6	13–15	6–4
1931	W. L. Allison/J. Van Ryn	R. B. Bell/G. S. Mangin	6–4	8–6	6–3		
1932	K. Gledhill/H. E. Vines	W. L. Allison/J. Van Ryn	6–4	6–3	6–2		
1933	G. M. Lott/L. R. Stoefen	F. A. Parker/F. X. Shields	11–13	9–7	9–7	6–3	
1934	G. M. Lott/L. R. Stoefen	W. L. Allison/J. Van Ryn	6–4	9–7	3–6	6–4	
1935	W. L. Allison/J. Van Ryn	J. D. Budge/G. Mako	6–4	6–2	3–6	2–6	6–1
1936	J. D. Budge/G. Mako	W. L. Allison/J. Van Ryn	6–4	6–2	6–4		
1937	G. Von Cramm/H. Henkel	J. D. Budge/G. Mako	6–4	7–5	6–4		
1938	J. D. Budge/G. Mako	J. E. Bromwich/A. K. Quist	6–3	6–2	6–1		
1939	J. E. Bromwich/A. K. Quist	J. H. Crawford/H. C. Hopman	8–6	6–1	6–4		
1940	J. A. Kramer/F. Schroeder	G. Mulloy/H. J. Prussoff	6–4	8–6	9–7		
1941	J. A. Kramer/F. Schroeder	G. Mulloy/W. Sabin	9–7	6–4	6–2		
1942	G. Mulloy/W. F. Talbert	F. R. Schroeder/S. B. Wood	9–7	7–5	6–1		
1943	J. A. Kramer/F. A. Parker	D. Freeman/W. F. Talbert	6–2	6–4	6–4		
1944	R. Falkenburg/W. D. McNeill	F. Segura/W. F. Talbert	7–5	6–4	3–6	6–1	
1945	G. Mulloy/W. F. Talbert	R. Falkenburg/J. Tuero	12–10	8–10	12–10	6–2	
1946	G. Mulloy/W. F. Talbert	G. Guernsey/W. D. McNeill	3–6	6–4	2–6	6–3	20–18
1947	J. A. Kramer/F. Schroeder	W. F. Talbert/O. W. Sidwell	6–4	7–5	6–3		
1948	G. Mulloy/W. F. Talbert	F. A. Parker/F. R. Schroeder	1–6	9–7	6–3	3–6	9–7
1949	J. Bromwich/O. W. Sidwell	F. A. Sedgman/G. Worthington	6–4	6–0	6–1		
1950	J. Bromwich/F. A. Sedgman	G. Mulloy/W. F. Talbert	7–5	8–6	3–6	6–1	

1951 K. McGregor/F. A. Sedgman	D. Candy/M. G. Rose	10–8	6–4	4–6	7–5	
1952 M. G. Rose/E. V. Seixas	K. McGregor/F. A. Sedgman	3–6	10–8	10–8	6–8	8–6
1953 R. N. Hartwig/M. G. Rose	G. Mulloy/W. F. Talbert	6–4	4–6	6–2	6–4	
1954 E. V. Seixas/M. A. Trabert	L. A. Hoad/K. R. Rosewall	3–6	6–4	8–6	6–3	
1955 K. Kamo/A. Miyagi	G. Moss/W. Quillian	6–3	6–3	3–6	1–6	6–4
1956 † L. A. Hoad/K. R. Rosewall	H. Richardson/E. V. Seixas	6–2	6–2	3–6	6–4	
1957 A. J. Cooper/N. A. Fraser	G. Mulloy/J. E. Patty	4–6	6–3	9–7	6–3	
1958 A. Olmedo/H. Richardson	S. Giammalva/B. McKay	3–6	6–3	6–4	6–4	
1959 R. S. Emerson/N. A. Fraser	E. Buchholz/A. Olmedo	3–6	6–3	5–7	6–4	7–5
1960 R. S. Emerson/N. A. Fraser	R. G. Laver/R. Mark	9–7	6–2	6–4		
1961 C. McKinley/R. D. Ralston	A. Palafox/R. H. Osuna	6–3	6–4	2–6	13–11	
1962 A. Palafox/R. H. Osuna	C. McKinley/R. D. Ralston	6–4	10–12	1–6	9–7	6–3
1963 C. McKinley/R. D. Ralston	A. Palafox/R. H. Osuna	9–7	4–6	5–7	6–3	11–9
1964 C. McKinley/R. D. Ralston	G. Stilwell/M. Sangster	6–3	6–2	6–4		
1965 R. S. Emerson/F. S. Stolle	F. Froehling/C. Pasarell	6–4	10–12	7–5	6–3	
1966 R. S. Emerson/F. S. Stolle	C. Graebner/R. D. Ralston	6–4	6–4	6–4		
1967 J. D. Newcombe/A. D. Roche	O. K. Davidson/W. W. Bowrey	6–8	9–7	6–3	6–3	
1968 R. C. Lutz/S. R. Smith	R. A. J. Hewitt/R. J. Moore	6–4	6–4	9–7		
1969 R. D. Crealy/A. Stone	W. W. Bowrey/C. Pasarell	9–11	6–3	7–5		

† *Played as National Patriotic tournament.*

WOMEN'S DOUBLES

Not recognised as an official championship.

CHAMPIONS	RUNNERS-UP	SCORE				
1887* E. F. Hansell/L. Knight	L. Allderdice/Church	6–0	6–4			
1888* E. C. Roosevelt/G. W. Roosevelt	A. K. Robinson/V. Ward	3–6	6–3	6–4		
1889 M. Ballard/B. L. Townsend	M. Wright/L. Knight	6–0	6–2			
1890 E. C. Roosevelt/G. W. Roosevelt	B. L. Townsend/M. Ballard	6–1	6–2			
1891 M. E. Cahill/Mrs W. F. Morgan	E. C. Roosevelt/G. W. Roosevelt	2–6	8–6	6–4		
1892 M. E. Cahill/A. M. McKinlay	Mrs A. H. Harris/A. R. Williams	6–1	6–3			
1893 H. Butler/A. M. Terry	A. L. Schultz/Stone	6–4	6–3			
1894 J. P. Atkinson/H. R. Hellwig	A. R. Williams/A. C. Wistar	6–4	7–5			
1895 J. P. Atkinson/H. R. Hellwig	E. H. Moore/A. R. Williams	6–2	6–2	12–10		
1896 J. P. Atkinson/E. H. Moore	A. R. Williams/A. C. Wistar	6–4	7–5			
1897 J. P. Atkinson/K. Atkinson	F. Edwards/E. J. Rastall	6–2	6–1	6–1		
1898 J. P. Atkinson/K. Atkinson	C. B. Neely/M. Wimer	6–1	2–6	4–6	6–1	6–
1899 J. W. Craven/M. McAteer	M. Banks/E. J. Rastall	6–1	6–1	7–5		
1900 H. Champlin/E. Parker	M. McAteer/M. Wimer	9–7	6–2	6–2		
1901 J. P. Atkinson/M. McAteer	M. Jones/E. H. Moore	w.o.				
1902§ J. P. Atkinson/M. Jones	M. Banks/N. Closterman	6–2	7–5			
1903 E. H. Moore/C. B. Neely	M. Jones/M. Hall	6–4	6–1	6–1		
1904 M. Hall/M. G. Sutton	E. H. Moore/C. B. Neely	3–6	6–3	6–3‡		
1905 H. Homans/C. B. Neely	V. Maule/M. F. Oberteuffer	6–0	6–1			
1906 Mrs L. S. Coe/Mrs D. S. Platt	C. Boldt/H. Homans	6–4	6–4			
1907 C. B. Neely/M. Wimer	E. Wildey/N. Wildey	6–1	2–6	6–4		
1908 M. Curtis/Evelyn Sears	C. B. Neely/M. Steever	6–3	5–7	9–7		
1909 H. V. Hotchkiss/E. E. Rotch	D. Green/L. Moyes	6–1	6–1			
1910 H. V. Hotchkiss/E. E. Rotch	A. Browning/E. Wildey	6–4	6–4			
1911 H. V. Hotchkiss/Eleanora Sears	D. Green/F. Sutton	6–4	4–6	6–2		
1912 M. K. Browne/D. Green	Mrs M. Barger-Wallach/Mrs F. Schmitz	6–2	5–7	6–0		
1913 M. K. Browne/Mrs R. H. Williams	D. Green/E. Wildey	12–10	2–6	6–3		
1914 M. K. Browne/Mrs R. H. Williams	Mrs E. Raymond/E. Wildey	8–6	6–2			
1915 Eleanora Sears/Mrs G. W. Wightman	Mrs G. L. Chapman/Mrs M. McLean	10–8	6–2			
1916 M. Bjurstedt/E. Sears	Mrs E. Raymond/E. Wildey	4–6	6–2	10–8		
1917 M. Bjurstedt/Eleanora Sears	Mrs R. LeRoy/P. Walsh	6–2	6–4			
1918 E. E. Goss/M. Zinderstein	M. Bjurstedt/Mrs J. Rogge	7–5	8–6			
1919 E. E. Goss/M. Zinderstein	Eleanora Sears/Mrs G. W. Wightman	9–7	9–7			
1920 E. E. Goss/M. Zinderstein	H. Baker/E. Tennant	13–11	4–6	6–3		
1921 M. K. Browne/Mrs R. H. Williams	H. Gilleaudeau/Mrs L. G. Morris	6–3	6–2			
1922 Mrs J. B. Jessup/H. N. Wills	Mrs F. I. Mallory/E. Sigourney	6–4	7–9	6–3		
1923 Mrs B. C. Covell/K. McKane	E. E. Goss/Mrs G. W. Wightman	2–6	6–2	6–1		
1924 Mrs G. W. Wightman/H. N. Wills	E. E. Goss/Mrs J. B. Jessup	6–4	6–3			
1925 M. K. Browne/H. N. Wills	Mrs T. C. Bundy/E. Ryan	6–4	6–3			
1926 E. E. Goss/E. Ryan	M. K. Browne/Mrs A. H. Chapin	3–6	6–4	12–10		
1927 Mrs L. A. Godfree/E. H. Harvey	J. Fry/B. Nuthall	6–1	4–6	6–4		
1928 Mrs G. W. Wightman/H. N. Wills	E. Cross/Mrs L. A. Harper	6–2	6–2			
1929 Mrs L. R. C. Michell/Mrs P. H. Watson	Mrs B. C. Covell/Mrs D. C. Shepherd-Barron	2–6	6–3	6–4		

1930	B. Nuthall/S. Palfrey	E. Cross/Mrs L. A. Harper	3–6	6–3	7–5
1931	B. Nuthall/Mrs E. F. Whittingstall	H. H. Jacobs/D. E. Round	6–2	6–4	
1032	H. H. Jacobs/S. Palfrey	A. Marble/Mrs M. Painter	8–6	6–1	
1933	F. James/B. Nuthall	Mrs F. S. Moody/E. Ryan	w.o.		
1934	H. H. Jacobs/S. Palfrey	Mrs D. B. Andrus/C. A. Babcock	4–6	6–3	6–4
1935	H. H. Jacobs/Mrs M. Fabyan	Mrs D. B. Andrus/C. A. Babcock	6–4	6–2	
1936	C. A. Babcock/Mrs J. Van Ryn	H. H. Jacobs/Mrs M. Fabyan	9–7	2–6	6–4
1937	Mrs M. Fabyan/A. Marble	C. A. Babcock/Mrs J. Van Ryn	7–5	6–4	
1938	Mrs M. Fabyan/A. Marble	J. Jedrzejowska/Mrs R. Mathieu	6–8	6–4	6–3
1939	Mrs M. Fabyan/A. Marble	Mrs S. H. Hammersley/K. E. Stammers	7–5	8–6	
1940	Mrs M. Fabyan/A. Marble	D. M. Bundy/Mrs J. Van Ryn	6–4	6–3	
1941	Mrs E. T. Cooke/M. E. Osborne	D. M. Bundy/D. J. Hart	3–6	6–1	6–4
1942	A. L. Brough/M. E. Osborne	P. M. Betz/D. J. Hart	9–7	6–2	6–1
1943	A. L. Brough/M. E. Osborne	P. M. Betz/D. J. Hart	6–4	6–3	
1944	A. L. Brough/M. E. Osborne	P. M. Betz/D. J. Hart	4–6	6–4	6–3
1945	A. L. Brough/M. E. Osborne	P. M. Betz/D. J. Hart	6–4	6–4	
1946	A. L. Brough/M. E. Osborne	Mrs P. C. Todd/Mrs M. A. Prentiss	6–1	6–3	
1947	A. L. Brough/M. E. Osborne	Mrs P. C. Todd/D. J. Hart	5–7	6–3	7–5
1948	A. L. Brough/Mrs W. D. du Pont	Mrs P. C. Todd/D. J. Hart	6–4	8–10	6–1
1949	A. L. Brough/Mrs W. D. du Pont	S. J. Fry/D. J. Hart	6–4	10–8	
1950	A. L. Brough/Mrs W. D. du Pont	S. J. Fry/D. J. Hart	6–2	6–3	
1951	S. J. Fry/D. J. Hart	N. Chaffee/Mrs P. C. Todd	6–4	6–2	
1952	S. J. Fry/D. J. Hart	A. L. Brough/M. Connolly	10–8	6–4	
1953	S. J. Fry/D. J. Hart	A. L. Brough/Mrs W. D. du Pont	6–2	7–9	9–7
1954	S. J. Fry/D. J. Hart	A. L. Brough/Mrs W. D. du Pont	6–4	6–4	
1955	A. L. Brough/Mrs W. D. du Pont	S. J. Fry/D. J. Hart	6–3	1–6	6–3
1956	A. L. Brough/Mrs W. D. du Pont	Mrs B. R. Pratt/S. J. Fry	6–3	6–0	
1957	A. L. Brough/Mrs W. D. du Pont	A. Gibson/D. R. Hard	6–2	7–5	
1958	J. M. Arth/D. R. Hard	A. Gibson/M. E. Bueno	2–6	6–3	6–4
1959	J. M. Arth/D. R. Hard	S. Moore/M. E. Bueno	6–2	6–3	
1960	M. E. Bueno/D. R. Hard	D. M. Catt/A. A. Haydon	6–1	6–1	
1961	D. R. Hard/L. Turner	E. Buding/Y. Ramirez	6–4	5–7	6–0
1962	M. E. Bueno/D. R. Hard	Mrs R. Susman/B. J. Moffitt	4–6	6–3	6–2
1963	R. Ebbern/M. Smith	M. E. Bueno/D. R. Hard	4–6	10–8	6–3
1964	Mrs R. Susman/B. J. Moffitt	M. Smith/L. Turner	3–6	6–2	6–4
1965	N. Richey/Mrs C. Graebner	Mrs R. Susman/B. J. Moffitt	6–4	6–4	
1966	M. E. Bueno/N. Richey	R. Casals/Mrs L. W. King	6–3	6–4	
1967	R. Casals/Mrs L. W. King	M. A. Eisel/Mrs D. Fales	4–6	6–3	6–4
1968	M. E. Bueno/M. Smith	S. V. Wade/Mrs G. M. Williams	6–3	7–5	
1969	Mrs B. M. Court/S. V. Wade	Mrs P. W. Curtis/V. Ziegenfuss	6–1	6–3	

† *Played as National Patriotic tournament.*
‡ *There is some doubt about the accuracy of this result.*
§ *5-set finals abolished.*

MIXED DOUBLES

Not recognised as an official championship.

	CHAMPIONS	RUNNERS-UP	SCORE			
1887*	J. S. Clark/Miss L. Stokes	E. D. Faries/Miss L. Knight	7–5	6–4		
1888*	J. S. Clark/Miss M. Wright	P. Johnson/Miss A. Robinson	1–6	6–5	6–4	6–3
1889*	A. E. Wright/Miss G. W. Roosevelt	C. T. Lee/Miss B. L. Townsend	6–1	6–3	3–6	6–3
1890*	R. Beach/Miss M. E. Cahill	C. T. Lee/Miss B. L. Townsend	6–2	3–6	6–2	
1891*	M. R. Wright/Miss M. E. Cahill	C. T. Lee/Miss G. W. Roosevelt	6–4	6–0	6–5	
1892	C. Hobart/Miss M. E. Cahill	R. Beach/Miss E. H. Moore	6–1	6–3		
1893	C. Hobart/Miss E. C. Roosevelt	R. N. Willson/Miss Bankson	6–1	4–6	10–8	6–1
1894	E. P. Fischer/Miss J. P. Atkinson	G. Remak/Mrs McFadden	6–2	6–2	6–1	
1895	E. P. Fischer/Miss J. P. Atkinson	M. Fielding/Miss A. R. Williams	4–6	6–1	6–2	
1896	E. P. Fischer/Miss J. P. Atkinson	M. Fielding/Miss A. R. Williams	6–2	6–3	6–3	
1897	D. L. Magruder/Miss L. Henson	R. A. Griffin/Miss M. Banks	6–4	6–3	7–5	
1898	E. P. Fischer/Miss C. B. Neely	J. A. Hill/Miss H. Chapman	Not known			
1899	A. L. Hoskins/Miss E. J. Rastall	J. P. Gardner/Miss J. W. Craven	6–4	6–0	ret'd	
1900	A. Codman/Miss M. J. Hunnewell	G. Atkinson/Miss T. Shaw	11–9	6–3	6–1	
1901	R. D. Little/Miss M. Jones	C. Stevens/Miss M. McAteer	6–4	6–4	7–5	
1902	W. C. Grant/Miss E. H. Moore	A. L. Hoskins/Miss E. J. Rastall	6–2	6–1		
1903	H. F. Allen/Miss H. Chapman	W. H. Rowland/Miss C. B. Neely	6–4	7–5		
1904	W. C. Grant/Miss E. H. Moore	F. B. Dallas/Miss M. Sutton	6–2	6–1		
1905	C. Hobart/Mrs Hobart	E. B. Dewhurst/Miss E. H. Moore	6–2	6–4		
1906	E. B. Dewhurst/Miss S. Coffin	J. B. Johnson/Miss M. Johnson	6–3	7–5		
1907	W. F. Johnson/Miss M. Sayres	H. M. Tilden/Miss N. Wildey	6–1	7–5		

1908	N. W. Niles/Miss E. E. Rotch	R. D. Little/Miss L. Hammond	6–4	4–6	6–4
1909	W. F. Johnson/Miss H. V. Hotchkiss	R. D. Little/Miss L. Hammond	6–2	6–0	
1910	J. R. Carpenter/Miss H. V. Hotchkiss	H. M. Tilden/Miss E. Wildey	6–2	6–2	
1911	W. F. Johnson/Miss H. V. Hotchkiss	H. M. Tilden/Miss E. Wildey	6–4	6–4	
1912	R. N. Williams/Miss M. K. Browne	W. J. Clothier/Miss Evelyn Sears	6–4	2–6	11–9
1913	W. T. Tilden/Miss M. K. Browne	C. S. Rogers/Miss D. Green	7–5	7–5	
1914	W. T. Tilden/Miss M. K. Browne	J. R. Rowland/Miss M. Myers	6–1	6–4	
1915	H. C. Johnson/Mrs G. W. Wightman	I. C. Wright/Miss M. Bjurstedt	6–0	6–1	
1916	W. E. Davis/Miss Evelyn Sears	W. T. Tilden/Miss F. A. Ballin	6–4	7–5	
1917	I. C. Wright/Miss M. Bjurstedt	W. T. Tilden/Miss F. A. Ballin	10–12	6–1	6–3
1918	I. C. Wright/Mrs G. W. Wightman	F. B. Alexander/Miss M. Bjurstedt	6–2	6–4	
1919	V. Richards/Miss M. Zinderstein	W. T. Tilden/Miss F. A. Ballin	2–6	11–9	6–1
1920	W. F. Johnson/Mrs G. W. Wightman	C. Biddle/Mrs F. I. Mallory	6–4	6–3	
1921	W. M. Johnston/Miss M. K. Browne	W. T. Tilden/Miss F. I. Mallory	3–6	6–4	6–3
1922	W. T. Tilden/Mrs F. I. Mallory	H. Kinsey/Miss H. N. Wills	6–4	6–3	
1923	W. T. Tilden/Miss F. I. Mallory	J. B. Hawkes/Miss K. McKane	6–3	2–6	10–8
1924	V. Richards/Miss H. N. Wills	W. T. Tilden/Mrs F. I. Mallory	6–8	7–5	6–0
1925	J. B. Hawkes/Miss K. McKane	V. Richards/Miss E. H. Harvey	6–2	6–4	
1926	J. Borotra/Miss E. Ryan	R. Lacoste/Mrs G. W. Wightman	6–4	7–5	
1927	H. Cochet/Miss E. Bennett	R. Lacoste/Mrs G. W. Wightman	2–6	6–0	6–2
1928	G. M. Lott/Miss B. Nuthall	H. W. Austin/Mrs B. C. Covell	6–3	6–3	
1929	G. M. Lott/Miss B. Nuthall	H. W. Austin/Mrs B. C. Lovell	6–3	6–3	
1930	W. L. Allison/Miss E. Cross	F. X. Shields/Miss M. Morrill	6–4	6–4	
1931	G. M. Lott/Miss B. Nuthall	W. L. Allison/Mrs L. A. Harper	6–3	6–3	
1932	F. J. Perry/Miss S. Palfrey	H. E. Vines/Miss H. H. Jacobs	6–3	7–5	
1933	H. E. Vines/Miss E. Ryan	G. M. Lott/Miss S. Palfrey	11–9	6–1	
1934	G. M. Lott/Miss H. H. Jacobs	L. R. Stoefen/Miss E. Ryan	4–6	13–11	6–2
1935	E. Maier/Miss M. Fabyan	R. Menzel/Miss K. E. Stammers	6–3	3–6	6–4
1936	G. Mako/Miss A. Marble	J. D. Budge/Mrs M. Fabyan	6–3	6–2	
1937	J. D. Budge/Mrs M. Fabyan	Y. Petra/Mme S. Henrotin	6–2	8–10	6–0
1938	J. D. Budge/Miss A. Marble	J. E. Bromwich/Miss T. Coyne	6–1	6–2	
1939	H. C. Hopman/Miss A. Marble	E. T. Cooke/Mrs M. Fabyan	9–7	6–1	
1940	R. L. Riggs/Miss A. Marble	J. A. Kramer/Miss D. M. Bundy	9–7	6–1	
1941	J. A. Kramer/Miss E. T. Cooke	R. L. Riggs/Miss P. M. Betz	4–6	6–4	6–4
1942	F. R. Schroeder/Miss A. L. Brough	A. D. Russell/Mrs P. C. Todd	3–6	6–1	6–4
1943	W. F. Talbert/Miss M. E. Osborne	F. Segura/Miss P. M. Betz	10–8	6–4	
1944	W. F. Talbert/Miss M. E. Osborne	W. D. McNeill/Miss D. M. Bundy	6–2	6–3	
1945	W. F. Talbert/Miss M. E. Osborne	R. Falkenburg/Miss D. J. Hart	6–4	6–4	
1946	W. F. Talbert/Miss M. E. Osborne	R. Kimbrell/Miss A. L. Brough	6–3	6–4	
1947	J. Bromwich/Miss A. L. Brough	F. Segura/Miss G. Morgan	6–3	6–1	
1948	T. P. Brown/Miss A. L. Brough	W. F. Talbert/Mrs W. D. du Pont	6–4	6–4	
1949	E. W. Sturgess/Miss A. L. Brough	W. F. Talbert/Mrs W. D. du Pont	4–6	6–3	7–5
1950	K. McGregor/Mrs W. D. du Pont	F. A. Sedgman/Miss D. J. Hart	6–4	3–6	6–3
1951	F. A. Sedgman/Miss D. J. Hart	M. G. Rose/Miss S. J. Fry	6–3	6–2	
1952	F. A. Sedgman/Miss D. J. Hart	L. A. Hoad/Mrs T. C. Long	6–3	7–5	
1953	E. V. Seixas/Miss D. J. Hart	R. N. Hartwig/Miss J. A. Sampson	6–2	4–6	6–4
1954	E. V. Seixas/Miss D. J. Hart	K. R. Rosewall/Mrs W. D. du Pont	4–6	6–1	6–1
1955	E. V. Seixas/Miss D. J. Hart	L. A. Hoad/Miss S. J. Fry	9–7	6–1	
1956	K. R. Rosewall/Mrs W. D. du Pont	L. A. Hoad/Miss D. R. Hard	9–7	6–1	
1957	K. Nielsen/Miss A. Gibson	R. N. Howe/Miss D. R. Hard	6–3	9–7	
1958	N. A. Fraser/Mrs W. D. du Pont	A. Olmedo/Miss M. E. Bueno	6–3	3–6	9–7
1959	N. A. Fraser/Mrs W. D. du Pont	R. Mark/Miss J. Hopps	7–5	13–15	6–2
1960	N. A. Fraser/Mrs W. D. du Pont	A. Palafox/Miss M. E. Bueno	6–3	6–2	
1961	R. Mark/Miss M. Smith	R. D. Ralston/Miss D. R. Hard	w.o.		
1962	F. S. Stolle/Miss M. Smith	F. Froehling/Miss L. Turner	7–5	6–2	
1963	K. Fletcher/Miss M. Smith	E. Rubinoff/Miss J. Tegart	3–6	8–6	6–2
1964	J. D. Newcombe/Miss M. Smith	E. Rubinoff/Miss J. Tegart	10–8	4–6	6–3
1965	F. S. Stolle/Miss M. Smith	F. Froehling/Miss J. Tegart	5–2	6–2	
1966	O. K. Davidson/Mrs D. Fales	E. Rubinoff/Miss C. A. Aucamp	6–1	6–3	
1967	O. K. Davidson/Mrs L. W. King	S. R. Smith/Miss R. Casals	6–3	6–2	
1968	P. W. Curtis/Miss M. A. Eisel	R. N. Perry/Miss T. A. Fretz	6–4	7–5	
1969	P. Sullivan/Miss P. S. A. Hogan	T. Addison/Miss K. Pigeon	6–4	2–6	12–10

† Played as National Patriotic tournament.

US OPEN CHAMPIONSHIPS

Played at West Side Club, Forest Hills, New York, on grass courts 1968–74, on Har-Tru courts 1975–77.
Played at National Tennis Centre, Flushing Meadow, New York, on cement courts, 1978 on.

MEN'S SINGLES

	CHAMPION	RUNNER-UP	SCORE					WINNER'S PRIZE ($)
1968	A. R. Ashe	T. S. Okker	14–12	5–7	6–3	3–6	6–3	14,000
1969	R. G. Laver	A. D. Roche	7–9	6–3	6–1	6–2		16,000
1970	K. R. Rosewall	A. D. Roche	2–6	6–4	7–6	6–3		20,000
1971	S. R. Smith	J. Kodes	3–6	6–3	6–2	7–6		15,000
1972	I. Nastase	A. R. Ashe	3–6	6–3	6–7	6–4	6–3	25,000
1973	J. D. Newcombe	J. Kodes	6–4	1–6	4–6	6–2	6–3	25,000
1974	J. S. Connors	K. R. Rosewall	6–1	6–0	6–1			22,500
1975	M. Orantes	J. S. Connors	6–4	6–3	6–3			25,000
1976	J. S. Connors	B. Borg	6–4	3–6	7–6	6–4		30,000
1977	G. Vilas	J. S. Connors	2–6	6–3	7–6	6–0		33,000
1978	J. S. Connors	B. Borg	6–4	6–2	6–2			38,000
1979	J. P. McEnroe	V. Gerulaitis	7–5	6–3	6–3			39,000
1980	J. P. McEnroe	B. Borg	7–6	6–1	6–7	5–7	6–4	46,000
1981	J. P. McEnroe	B. Borg	4–6	6–2	6–4	6–3		60,000
1982	J. S. Connors	I. Lendl	6–3	6–2	4–6	6–4		90,000
1983	J. S. Connors	I. Lendl	6–3	6–7	7–5	6–0		120,000
1984	J. P. McEnroe	I. Lendl	6–3	6–4	6–1			160,000
1985	I. Lendl	J. P. McEnroe	7–6	6–3	6–4			187,500
1986	I. Lendl	M. Mecir	6–4	6–2	6–0			210,000
1987	I. Lendl	M. Wilander	6–7	6–0	7–6	6–4		250,000
1988	M. Wilander	I. Lendl	6–4	4–6	6–3	5–7	6–4	275,000
1989	B. Becker	I. Lendl	7–6	1–6	6–3	7–6		300,000
1990	P. Sampras	A. Agassi	6–4	6–3	6–2			350,000
1991	S. Edberg	J. Courier	6–2	6–4	6–0			400,000

WOMEN'S SINGLES

	CHAMPION	RUNNER-UP	SCORE			WINNER'S PRIZE ($)
1968	Miss S. V. Wade	Mrs L. W. King	6–4	6–2		6,000
1969	Mrs B. M. Court	Miss N. Richey	6–2	6–2		6,000
1970	Mrs B. M. Court	Miss R. Casals	6–2	2–6	6–1	7,500
1971	Mrs L. W. King	Miss R. Casals	6–4	7–6		5,000
1972	Mrs L. W. King	Miss K. Melville	6–3	7–5		10,000
1973	Mrs B. M. Court	Miss E. Goolagong	7–6	5–7	6–2	25,000
1974	Mrs L. W. King	Miss E. Goolagong	3–6	6–3	7–5	22,500
1975	Miss C. M. Evert	Mrs R. A. Cawley	5–7	6–4	6–2	25,000
1976	Miss C. M. Evert	Mrs R. A. Cawley	6–3	6–0		30,000
1977	Miss C. M. Evert	Miss W. Turnbull	7–6	6–2		33,000
1978	Miss C. M. Evert	Miss P. Shriver	7–5	6–4		38,000
1979	Miss T. A. Austin	Miss C. M. Evert	6–4	6–3		39,000
1980	Mrs J. M. Lloyd	Miss H. Mandlikova	5–7	6–1	6–1	46,000
1981	Miss T. A. Austin	Miss M. Navratilova	1–6	7–6	7–6	60,000
1982	Mrs J. M. Lloyd	Miss H. Mandlikova	6–3	6–1		90,000
1983	Miss M. Navratilova	Mrs J. M. Lloyd	6–1	6–3		120,000
1984	Miss M. Navratilova	Mrs J. M. Lloyd	4–6	6–4	6–4	160,000
1985	Miss H. Mandlikova	Miss M. Navratilova	7–6	1–6	7–6	187,500
1986	Miss M. Navratilova	Miss H. Sukova	6–3	6–2		210,000
1987	Miss M. Navratilova	Miss S. Graf	7–6	6–1		250,000
1988	Miss S. Graf	Miss G. Sabatini	6–3	3–6	6–1	275,000
1989	Miss S. Graf	Miss M. Navratilova	3–6	7–5	6–1	300,000
1990	Miss G. Sabatini	Miss S. Graf	6–2	7–6		350,000
1991	Miss M. Seles	Miss M. Navratilova	7–6	6–1		400,000

MEN'S DOUBLES

	CHAMPIONS	RUNNERS-UP	SCORE				
1968	R. C. Lutz/S. R. Smith	A. R. Ashe/A. Gimeno	11–9	6–1	7–5		
1969	K. R. Rosewall/F. S. Stolle	C. Pasarell/R. D. Ralston	2–6	7–5	13–11	6–3	
1970	P. Barthes/N. Pilic	R. S. Emerson/R. G. Laver	6–3	7–6	4–6	7–6	
1971	J. D. Newcombe/R. Taylor	S. R. Smith/E. van Dillen	6–7	6–3	7–6	4–6	7–6
1972	E. C. Drysdale/R. Taylor	O. K. Davidson/J. D. Newcombe	6–4	7–6	6–3		
1973	O. K. Davidson/J. D. Newcombe	R. G. Laver/K. R. Rosewall	7–5	2–6	7–5	7–5	
1974	R. C. Lutz/S. R. Smith	P. Cornejo/J. Fillol	6–3	6–3			
1975	J. S. Connors/I. Nastase	T. S. Okker/M. C. Riessen	6–4	7–6			
1976	T. S. Okker/M. C. Riessen	P. Kronk/C. Letcher	6–4	6–4			

1977	R. A. J. Hewitt/F. D. McMillan	B. E. Gottfried/R. Ramirez	6–4	6–0	
1978	R. C. Lutz/S. R. Smith	M. C. Riessen/S. E. Stewart	1–6	7–5	6–3
1979	P. Fleming/J. P. McEnroe	R. C. Lutz/S. R. Smith	6–2	6–4	
1980	R. C. Lutz/S. R. Smith	P. Fleming/J. P. McEnroe	7–6	3–6	6–1 3–6 6–3
1981	P. Fleming/J. P. McEnroe	H. Gunthardt/P. McNamara	w.o.		
1982	K. Curren/S. Denton	V. Amaya/H. Pfister	6–2	6–7	5–7 6–2 6–4
1983	P. Fleming/J. P. McEnroe	F. Buehning/V. Winitsky	6–3	6–4	6–2
1984	J. Fitzgerald/T. Smid	S. Edberg/A. Jarryd	7–6	6–3	6–3
1985	K. Flach/R. Seguso	H. Leconte/Y. Noah	7–6	6–7	7–6 6–0
1986	A. Gomez/S. Zivojinovic	J. Nystrom/M. Wilander	4–6	6–3	6–3 4–6 6–3
1987	S. Edberg/A. Jarryd	K. Flach/R. Seguso	7–6	6–2	4–6 5–7 7–6
1988	S. Casal/E. Sanchez	R. Leach/J. Pugh	w.o.		
1989	J. P. McEnroe/M. Woodforde	K. Flach/R. Seguso	6–4	4–6	6–3 6–3
1990	P. Aldrich/D. Visser	P. Annacone/D. Wheaton	6–2	7–6	6–2
1991	J. B. Fitzgerald/A. Jarryd	S. Davis/D. Pate	6–3	3–6	6–3 6–3

WOMEN'S DOUBLES

	CHAMPIONS	RUNNERS-UP	SCORE		
1968	M. E. Bueno/Mrs B. M. Court	R. Casals/Mrs L. W. King	4–6	9–7	8–6
1969	F. Durr/D. R. Hard	Mrs B. M. Court/S. V. Wade	0–6	6–4	6–4
1970	Mrs B. M. Court/Mrs D. Dalton	R. Casals/S. V. Wade	6–3	6–4	
1971	R. Casals/Mrs D. Dalton	Mrs J. B. Chanfreau/F. Durr	6–3	6–3	
1972	F. Durr/B. Stove	Mrs B. M. Court/S. V. Wade	6–3	1–6	6–3
1973	Mrs B. M. Court/S. V. Wade	R. Casals/Mrs L. W. King	3–6	6–3	7–5
1974	R. Casals/Mrs L. W. King	F. Durr/B. Stove	7–6	6–7	6–4
1975	Mrs B. M. Court/S. V. Wade	R. Casals/Mrs L. W. King	7–5	2–6	7–5
1976	L. Boshoff/I. Kloss	O. Morozova/S. V. Wade	6–1	6–4	
1977	M. Navratilova/B. Stove	R. Richards/B. Stuart	6–1	7–6	
1978	Mrs L. W. King/M. Navratilova	Mrs G. E. Reid/W. M. Turnbull	7–6	6–4	
1979	B. Stove/W. M. Turnbull	Mrs L. W. King/M. Navratilova	7–5	6–3	
1980	Mrs L. W. King/M. Navratilova	P. H. Shriver/B. Stove	7–6	7–5	
1981	K. Jordan/A. E. Smith	R. Casals/W. M. Turnbull	6–3	6–3	
1982	R. Casals/W. M. Turnbull	B. Potter/S. A. Walsh	6–4	6–4	
1983	M. Navratilova/P. H. Shriver	R. Fairbank/C. Reynolds	6–7	6–1	6–3
1984	M. Navratilova/P. H. Shriver	A. E. Hobbs/W. M. Turnbull	6–2	6–4	
1985	C. Kohde-Kilsch/H. Sukova	M. Navratilova/P. H. Shriver	6–7	6–2	6–3
1986	M. Navratilova/P. H. Shriver	H. Mandlikova/W. M. Turnbull	6–4	3–6	6–3
1987	M. Navratilova/P. H. Shriver	K. Jordan/E. Smylie	5–7	6–4	6–2
1988	G. Fernandez/R. White	J. Hetherington/P. Fendick	6–4	6–1	
1989	H. Mandlikova/M. Navratilova	M. J. Fernandez/P. H. Shriver	5–7	6–4	6–4
1990	G. Fernandez/M. Navratilova	J. Novotna/H. Sukova	6–2	6–4	
1991	P. Shriver/N. Zvereva	J. Novotna/L. Savchenko	6–4	4–6	7–6

MIXED DOUBLES

	CHAMPIONS	RUNNERS-UP	SCORE		
1968	Not held				
1969	M. C. Riessen/Mrs B. M. Court	R. D. Ralston/Miss F. Durr	7–5	6–3	
1970	M. C. Riessen/Mrs B. M. Court	F. D. McMillan/Mrs D. Dalton	6–4	6–4	
1971	O. K. Davidson/Mrs L. W. King	R. R. Maud/Miss B. Stove	6–3	7–5	
1972	M. C. Riessen/Mrs B. M. Court	I. Nastase/Miss R. Casals	6–3	7–5	
1973	O. K. Davidson/Mrs L. W. King	M. C. Riessen/Mrs B. M. Court	6–3	3–6	7–6
1974	G. Masters/Miss P. Teeguarden	J. S. Connors/Miss C. M. Evert	6–1	7–6	
1975	R. L. Stockton/Miss R. Casals	F. S. Stolle/Mrs L. W. King	6–3	7–6	
1976	P. Dent/Mrs L. W. King	F. D. McMillan/Miss B. Stove	3–6	6–2	7–5
1977	F. D. McMillan/Miss B. Stove	V. Gerulaitis/Mrs L. W. King	6–2	3–6	6–3
1978	F. D. McMillan/Miss B. Stove	R. O. Ruffels/Mrs L. W. King	6–3	7–6	
1979	R. A. J. Hewitt/Miss G. Stevens	F. D. McMillan/Miss B. Stove	6–3	7–5	
1980	M. C. Riessen/Miss W. M. Turnbull	F. D. McMillan/Miss B. Stove	7–5	6–2	
1981	K. Curren/Miss A. E. Smith	S. Denton/Miss J. Russell	6–4	7–6	
1982	K. Curren/Miss A. E. Smith	F. Taygan/Miss B. Potter	6–7	7–6	7–6
1983	J. Fitzgerald/Miss E. Sayers	F. Taygan/Miss B. Potter	3–6	6–3	6–4
1984	Tom Gullikson/Miss M. Maleeva	J. Fitzgerald/Miss E. Sayers	2–6	7–5	6–4
1985	H. Gunthardt/Miss M. Navratilova	J. Fitzgerald/Miss E. Smylie	6–3	6–4	
1986	S. Casal/Miss R. Reggi	P. Fleming/Miss M. Navratilova	6–4	6–4	
1987	E. Sanchez/Miss M. Navratilova	P. Annacone/Miss B. Nagelsen	6–4	6–7	7–6
1988	J. Pugh/Miss J. Novotna	P. McEnroe/Miss E. Smylie	7–6	6–3	
1989	S. Cannon/Miss R. White	R. Leach/Miss M. McGrath	3–6	6–2	7–5
1990	T. Woodbridge/Mrs E. Smylie	J. Pugh/Miss N. Zvereva	6–4	6–2	
1991	T. Nijssen/Miss M. Bollegraf	E. Sanchez/Miss A. Sanchez-Vicario	6–2	7–6	

ITALIAN CHAMPIONSHIPS

Staged in Milan 1930 to 1934. Moved to the Foro Italico in Rome in 1935. Not held 1936 to 1949 because of the Abyssinia War and World War II. In 1961 the tournament was staged in Turin. Men's and women's events were held at different dates in 1979. In 1980–1985 the women's events moved to Perugia.

MEN'S SINGLES

	CHAMPION	RUNNER-UP	SCORE				
1930	W. T. Tilden	H. L. de Morpurgo	6–1	6–1	6–2		
1931	G. P. Hughes	H. Cochet	6–4	6–3	6–2		
1932	A. Merlin	G. P. Hughes	6–1	5–7	6–0	8–6	
1933	E. Sertorio	A. Martin Legeay	6–3	6–1	6–3		
1934	G. Palmieri	G. de Stefani	6–3	6–0	7–5		
1935	W. Hines	G. Palmieri	6–3	10–8	9–7		
1936–49	*Not held*						
1950	J. Drobny	W. F. Talbert	6–4	6–3	7–9	6–2	
1951	J. Drobny	G. Cucelli	6–3	10–8	6–1		
1952	F. A. Sedgman	J. Drobny	7–5	6–3	1–6	6–4	
1953	J. Drobny	L. A. Hoad	6–2	6–1	6–2		
1954	J. E. Patty	E. Morea	11–9	6–4	6–4		
1955	F. Gardini	G. Merlo	6–1	1–6	3–6	5–6	ret'd
1956	L. A. Hoad	S. Davidson	7–5	6–2	6–0		
1957	N. Pietrangeli	G. Merlo	8–6	6–2	6–4		
1958	M. G. Rose	N. Pietrangeli	5–7	8–6	6–4	1–6	6–2
1959	L. Ayala	N. A. Fraser	6–3	1–6	6–3	6–3	
1960	B. MacKay	L. Ayala	7–5	7–5	0–6	0–6	6–1
1961	N. Pietrangeli	R. G. Laver	6–8	6–1	6–1	6–2	
1962	R. G. Laver	R. S. Emerson	6–1	1–6	3–6	6–3	6–1
1963	M. F. Mulligan	B. Jovanovic	6–2	4–6	6–3	8–6	
1964	J. E. Lundquist	F. S. Stolle	1–6	7–5	6–3	6–1	
1965	M. F. Mulligan	M. Santana	1–6	6–4	6–3	6–1	
1966	A. D. Roche	N. Pietrangeli	11–9	6–1	6–2		
1967	M. F. Mulligan	A. D. Roche	6–3	0–6	6–4	6–1	
1968	T. S. Okker	R. A. J. Hewitt	10–8	6–8	6–1	1–6	6–0
1969	J. D. Newcombe	A. D. Roche	6–3	4–6	6–2	5–7	6–3
1970	I. Nastase	J. Kodes	6–3	1–6	6–3	8–6	
1971	R. G. Laver	J. Kodes	7–5	6–3	6–3		
1972	M. Orantes	J. Kodes	4–6	6–1	7–5	6–2	
1973	I. Nastase	M. Orantes	6–1	6–1	6–1		
1974	B. Borg	I. Nastase	6–3	6–4	6–2		
1975	R. Ramirez	M. Orantes	7–6	7–5	7–5		
1976	A. Panatta	G. Vilas	2–6	7–6	6–2	7–6	
1977	V. Gerulaitis	A. Zugarelli	6–2	7–6	3–6	7–6	
1978	B. Borg	A. Panatta	1–6	6–3	6–1	4–6	6–3
1979	V. Gerulaitis	E. Dibbs	6–7	7–6	6–7	6–4	6–2
1980	G. Vilas	Y. Noah	6–0	6–4	6–4		
1981	J. L. Clerc	V. Pecci	6–3	6–4	6–0		
1982	A. Gomez	E. Teltscher	6–2	6–3	6–2		
1983	J. Arias	J. Higueras	6–2	6–7	6–1	6–4	
1984	A. Gomez	A. Krickstein	2–6	6–1	6–2	6–2	
1985	Y. Noah	M. Mecir	6–3	3–6	6–2	7–6	
1986	I. Lendl	E. Sanchez	7–5	4–6	6–1	6–1	
1987	M. Wilander	M. Jaite	6–3	6–4	6–4		
1988	I. Lendl	G. Perez Roldan	2–6	6–4	6–4	4–6	6–4
1989	A. Mancini	A. Agassi	6–3	4–6	2–6	7–6	6–1
1990	T. Muster	A. Chesnokov	6–1	6–3	6–1		
1991	E. Sanchez	A. Mancini	6–3	6–1	3–0	ret'd	

WOMEN'S SINGLES

	CHAMPION	RUNNER-UP	SCORE		
1930	Miss E. de Alvarez	Miss L. Valerio	3–6	8–6	6–0
1931	Mrs L. Valerio	Mrs D. Andrus	2–6	6–2	6–2
1932	Miss I. Adamoff	Miss L. Valerio	6–4	7–5	

1933	Miss E. Ryan	Miss I. Adamoff	6–1	6–1	
1934	Miss H. Jacobs	Miss L. Valerio	6–3	6–0	
1935	Miss H. Sperling	Miss L. Valerio	6–4	6–1	
1936–49	*Not held*				
1950	Mrs A. Bossi	Miss P. J. Curry	6–4	6–4	
1951	Miss D. J. Hart	Miss S. J. Fry	6–3	8–6	
1952	Miss S. Partridge	Miss M. P. Harrison	6–3	7–5	
1953	Miss D. J. Hart	Miss M. Connolly	4–6	9–7	6–3
1954	Miss M. Connolly	Miss P. E. Ward	6–3	6–0	
1955	Miss P. E. Ward	Miss E. Vollmer	6–4	6–3	
1956	Miss A. Gibson	Mrs S. Kormoczy	6–3	7–5	
1957	Miss S. J. Bloomer	Mrs D. P. Knode	1–6	9–7	6–2
1958	Miss M. E. Bueno	Miss L. Coghlan	3–6	6–3	6–3
1959	Miss C. C. Truman	Miss S. Reynolds	6–0	6–1	
1960	Mrs S. Kormoczy	Miss A. S. Haydon	6–4	4–6	6–1
1961	Miss M. E. Bueno	Miss L. R. Turner	6–4	6–4	
1962	Miss M. Smith	Miss M. E. Bueno	8–6	5–7	6–4
1963	Miss M. Smith	Miss L. R. Turner	6–3	6–4	
1964	Miss M. Smith	Miss L. R. Turner	6–1	6–1	
1965	Miss M. E. Bueno	Miss N. Richey	6–1	1–6	6–3
1966	Mrs P. F. Jones	Miss A. Van Zyl	8–6	6–1	
1967	Miss L. R. Turner	Miss M. E. Bueno	6–3	6–3	
1968	Mrs W. W. Bowrey	Mrs B. M. Court	2–6	6–2	6–3
1969	Miss J. M. Heldman	Miss K. Melville	7 5	6 4	
1970	Mrs L. W. King	Miss J. M. Heldman	6–1	6–3	
1971	Miss S. V. Wade	Mrs H. Masthoff	6–4	6–4	
1972	Miss L. Tuero	Mrs O. Morozova	6–4	6–3	
1973	Miss E. F. Goolagong	Miss C. M. Evert	7–6	6–0	
1974	Miss C. M. Evert	Miss M. Navratilova	6–3	6–3	
1975	Miss C. M. Evert	Miss M. Navratilova	6–1	6–0	
1976	Miss M. Jausovec	Miss L. Hunt	6–1	6–3	
1977	Miss J. Newberry	Miss R. Tomanova	6–3	7–6	
1978	Miss R. Marsikova	Miss V. Ruzici	7–5	7–5	
1979	Miss T. A. Austin	Miss S. Hanika	6–4	1–6	6–3
1980	Mrs J. M. Lloyd	Miss V. Ruzici	5–7	6–2	6–2
1981	Mrs J. M. Lloyd	Miss V. Ruzici	6–1	6–2	
1982	Mrs J. M. Lloyd	Miss H. Mandlikova	6–0	6–3	
1983	Miss A. Temesvari	Miss B. Gadusek	6–1	6–0	
1984	Miss M. Maleeva	Mrs J. M. Lloyd	6–3	6–3	
1985	Miss R. Reggi	Miss V. Nelson	6–4	6–4	
1986	*Not held*				
1987	Miss S. Graf	Miss G. Sabatini	7–5	4–6	6–0
1988	Miss G. Sabatini	Miss H. Kelesi	6–1	6–7	6–1
1989	Miss G. Sabatini	Miss A. Sanchez	6–2	5–7	6–4
1990	Miss M. Seles	Miss M. Navratilova	6–1	6–1	
1991	Miss G. Sabatini	Miss M. Seles	6–3	6–2	

MEN'S DOUBLES

	CHAMPIONS	RUNNERS-UP	SCORE				
1930	W. F. Coen/W. T. Tilden	H. L. de Morpurgo/P. Gaslini	6–0	6–3	6–3		
1931	A. del Bono/G. P. Hughes	H. Cochet/A. Merlin	3–6	8–6	4–6	6–4	6–3
1932	G. P. Hughes/G. de Stafani	J. Bonte/A. Merlin	6–2	6–2	6–4		
1933	J. Lesueur/A. M. Legeay	G. Palmieri/E. Sertorio	6–2	6–4	6–2		
1934	G. Palmieri/G. L. Rogers	G. P. Hughes/G. de Stefani	3–6	6–4	9–7	0–6	6–2
1935	J. H. Crawford/V. B. McGrath	J. Borotra/J. Brugnon	4–6	4–6	6–4	6–2	6–2
1936–49	*Not held*						
1950	W. F. Talbert/M. A. Trabert	J. E. Patty/O. W. Sidwell	6–3	6–1	4–6	ret'd	
1951	J. Drobny/R. Savitt	G. Cucelli/M. Del Bello	6–2	7–9	6–1	6–3	
1952	J. Drobny/F. A. Sedgman	G. Cucelli/M. Del Bello	3–6	7–5	3–6	6–3	6–2
1953	L. A. Hoad/K. R. Rosewall	J. Drobny/J. E. Patty	6–2	6–4	6–2		
1954	J. Drobny/E. Morea	M. A. Trabert/E. V. Seixas	6–4	0–6	3–6	6–3	6–4
1955	A. Larsen/E. Morea	N. Pietrangeli/O. Sirola	6–1	6–4	4–6	7–5	
1956	J. Drobny/L. A. Hoad	N. Pietrangeli/O. Sirola	11–9	6–2	6–3		
1957	N. A. Fraser/L. A. Hoad	N. Pietrangeli/O. Sirola	6–1	6–8	6–0	6–2	
1958	A. Jancso/K. Nielsen	L. Ayala/D. Candy	8–10	6–3	6–2	1–6	9–7
1959	R. S. Emerson/N. A. Fraser	N. Pietrangeli/O. Sirola	8–6	6–4	6–4		
1960	N. Pietrangeli/O. Sirola	R. S. Emerson/N. A. Fraser	3–6	7–5	2–6	11–11 ret'd	
1961	R. S. Emerson/N. A. Fraser	N. Pietrangeli/O. Sirola	6–2	6–4	11–9		
1962	N. A. Fraser/R. G. Laver	K. N. Fletcher/J. D. Newcombe	11–9	6–2	6–4		
1963	R. A. J. Hewitt/F. S. Stolle	N. Pietrangeli/O. Sirola	6–3	6–3	6–1		

1964	R. A. J. Hewitt/F. S. Stolle	A. D. Roche/J. D. Newcombe	7–5	6–3	3–6	7–5
1965	A. D. Roche/J. D. Newcombe	C. Barnes/T. Koch	1–6	6–4	2–6	12–10 ret'd
1966	R. S. Emerson/F. S. Stolle	N. Pietrangeli/C. C. Drysdale	6–4	12–10	6–3
1967	R. A. J. Hewitt/F. D. McMillan	W. W. Bowrey/O. K. Davidson	6–3	2–6	6–3	9–7
1968	T. S. Okker/M. C. Riessen	A. Stone/N. Kalogeropoulos	6–3	6–4	6–2
1969	A. D. Roche/J. D. Newcombe	T. S. Okker/M. C. Riessen	6–4	1–6	ret'd
1970	I. Nastase/I. Tiriac	W. W. Bowrey/O. K. Davidson	0–6	10–8	6–3	6–8	6–1
1971	A. D. Roche/J. D. Newcombe	A. Gimeno/R. Taylor	6–4	6–4
1972	I. Nastase/I. Tiriac	L. A. Hoad/F. D. McMillan	3–6	3–6	6–4	6–3	5–3 ret'd
1973	J. D. Newcombe/T. S. Okker	R. Case/G. Masters	6–3	6–2	6–4
1974	B. E. Gottfried/R. Ramirez	J. Gisbert/I. Nastase	6–3	6–2	6–3
1975	B. E. Gottfried/R. Ramirez	J. S. Connors/I. Nastase	6–4	7–6	2–6	6–1
1976	B. E. Gottfried/R. Ramirez	G. Masters/J. D. Newcombe	7–6	5–7	6–3	3–6	6–3
1977	B. E. Gottfried/R. Ramirez	F. McNair/S. E. Stewart	7–6	6–7	7–5
1978	V. Pecci/B. Prajoux	J. Kodes/T. Smid	6–7	7–6	6–1
1979	P. Fleming/T. Smid	J. L. Clerc/I. Nastase	4–6	6–1	7–5
1980	M. R. Edmondson/K. Warwick	B. Taroczy/E. Teltscher	7–6	7–6
1981	H. Gildemeister/A. Gomez	B. Manson/T. Smid	7–5	6–2
1982	H. Gunthardt/B. Taroczy	W. Fibak/J. Fitzgerald	6–4	4–6	6–3
1983	F. Gonzalez/V. Pecci	J. Gunnarsson/M. Leach	6–2	6–7	6–4
1984	K. Flach/R. Seguso	J. G. Alexander/M. Leach	3–6	6–3	6–4
1985	A. Jarryd/M. Wilander	K. Flach/R. Seguso	4–6	6–3	6–2
1986	G. Forget/Y. Noah	M. R. Edmondson/S. E. Stewart	7–6	6–2
1987	G. Forget/Y. Noah	M. Mecir/T. Smid	6–2	6–7	6–3
1988	J. Lozano/T. Witsken	A. Jarryd/T. Smid	6–3	6–3
1989	J. Courier/P. Sampras	D. Marcelino/M. Menezes	6–4	6–3
1990	S. Casal/E. Sanchez	J. Courier/M. Davis	7–6	7–5
1991	O. Camporese/G. Ivanisevic	L. Jensen/L. Warder	6–2	6–3

WOMEN'S DOUBLES

	CHAMPIONS	RUNNERS-UP	SCORE		
1930	E. de Alvarez/L. Valerio	C. Anet/M. Neufeld	7–5	5–7	7–5
1931	A. Luzzatti/J. Prouse	Mrs D. Andrus Burke/L. Valerio	6–3	1–6	6–3
1932	C. Rosambert/L. Payot	Mrs D. Andrus Burke/L. Valerio	7–5	6–3
1933	I. Adamoff/ Mrs D. Andrus Burke	E. Ryan/L. Valerio	6–3	1–6	6–4
1934	H. H. Jacobs/E. Ryan	I. Adamoff/ Mrs D. Andrus Burke	7–5	9–7
1935	E. M. Dearman/N. Lyle	C. Aussem/E. Ryan	6–2	6–4
1936–49	*Not held*				
1950	J. Quertier/J. Walker-Smith	B. E. Hilton/K. L. A. Tuckey	1–6	6–3	6–2
1951	S. J. Fry/D. J. Hart	L. Brough/T. D. Long	6–1	7–5
1952	N. Hopman/ Mrs T. D. Long	N. Migliori/V. Tonoli	6–2	6–8	6–1
1953	M. Connolly/J. Sampson	S. J. Fry/D. J. Hart	6–8	6–4	6–4
1954	P. E. Ward/E. M. Watson	N. Adamson/G. Bucaille	3–6	6–3	6–4
1955	C. Mercellis/P. E. Ward	M. Muller/B. Penrose	6–4	10–8
1956	M. Hawton/ Mrs T. D. Long	A. Buxton/D. R. Hard	6–4	6–8	9–7
1957	M. Hawton/ Mrs T. D. Long	Y. Ramirez/R. M. Reyes	6–1	6–1
1958	S. J. Bloomer/C. Truman	M. Hawton/ Mrs T. D. Long	6–3	6–2
1959	Y. Ramirez/R. M. Reyes	M. E. Bueno/J. Hopps	4–6	6–4	6–4
1960	M. Hellyer/Y. Ramirez	S. J. Brasher/A. Haydon	6–4	6–4
1961	J. Lehane/L. R. Turner	M. Reitano/M. Smith	2–6	6–1	6–1
1962	M. E. Bueno/D. R. Hard	S. Lazzarino/L. Pericoli	6–4	6–4
1963	R. Ebbern/M. Smith	S. Lazzarino/L. Pericoli	6–2	6–3
1964	L. R. Turner/M. Smith	S. Lazzarino/L. Pericoli	6–1	6–2
1965	M. Schacht/A. Van Zyl	S. Lazzarino/L. Pericoli	2–6	6–2	12–10
1966	N. Baylon/A. Van Zyl	Mrs P. F. Jones/E. Starkie	6–3	1–6	6–2
1967	R. Casals/L. R. Turner	S. Lazzarino/L. Pericoli	7–5	7–5
1968	Mrs B. M. Court/S. V. Wade	A. Van Zyl/P. Walkden	6–2	7–5
1969	F. Durr/ Mrs P. F. Jones	R. Casals/ Mrs L. W. King	6–3	3–6	6–2
1970	R. Casals/L. W. King	F. Durr/S. V. Wade	6–2	3–6	9–7
1971	Mrs H. Masthoff/S. V. Wade	Mrs L. Bowrey/H. Gourlay	5–7	6–2	6–2
1972	L. Hunt/ Mrs O. Morozova	Mrs G. Chanfreau/R. Vido	6–3	6–4
1973	Mrs O. Morozova/S. V. Wade	M. Navratilova/R. Tomanova	3–6	6–2	7–5
1974	C. M. Evert/ Mrs O. Morozova	H. Masthoff/H. Orth	w.o.
1975	C. M. Evert/M. Navratilova	S. Barker/G. Coles	6–1	6–2
1976	L. Boshoff/I. Kloss	M. Simionescu/V. Ruzici	6–1	6–2
1977	B. Cuypers/M. Kruger	B. Bruning/S. A. Walsh	3–6	7–5	6–2
1978	M. Jausovec/V. Ruzici	F. Mihai/B. Nagelsen	6–2	2–6	7–5
1979	B. Stove/W. M. Turnbull	Mrs E. Crawley/G. E. Reid	6–3	6–4
1980	H. Mandlikova/R. Tomanova	I. Madruga/I. Villagran	6–4	6–4

1981	C. Reynolds/P. Smith	Mrs J. M. Lloyd/V. Ruzici	7–5	6–1	
1982	K. Horvath/Y. Vermk	Mrs L. W. King/I. Kloss	2–6	6–4	7–6
1983	V. Ruzici/S. V. Wade	I. Madruga Osses/C. Tanvier	6–3	2–6	6–1
1984	I. Budarova/M. Skuherska	K. Horvath/V. Ruzici	7–6	1–6	6–4
1985	A. M. Cecchini/R. Reggi	P. Murgo/B. Romano	1–6	6–4	6–3
1986	Not held				
1987	M. Navratilova/G. Sabatini	C. Kohde-Kilsch/H. Sukova	6–4	6–1	
1988	J. Novotna/C. Suire	J. Byrne/J. Thompson	6–3	4–6	7–5
1989	E. Smylie/J. Thompson	M. Bollegraf/M. Paz	6–4	6–3	
1990	H. Kelesi/M. Seles	L. Garrone/L. Golarsa	6–3	6–4	
1991	J. Capriati/M. Seles	N. Provis/E. Reinach	7–5	6–2	

MIXED DOUBLES

	CHAMPIONS	RUNNERS-UP	SCORE		
1930	H. L. de Morpurgo/Miss E. de Alvarez	G. P. Hughes/Miss L. Valerio	4–6	6–4	6–2
1931	G. P. Hughes/Miss L. Valerio	A. del Bono/Mrs D. Andrus Burke	6–0	6–1	
1932	J. Bonte/Miss L. Payot	A. del Bono/Mrs D. Andrus Burke	6–1	6–2	
1933	A. M. Legeay/Mrs D. Andrus Burke	E. Gabrowitz/Miss Y. Orlandini	6–4	6–3	
1934	H. M. Culley/Miss E. Ryan	F. Puncec/Miss R. Couquerque	6–1	6–3	
1935	H. C. Hopman/Miss J. Jedrzejowska	G. P. Hughes/Miss E. M. Dearman	6–3	1–6	6–3
1936–49	Not held				
1950	A. K. Quist/Miss G. Moran div'd with G. Cucelli/Miss A. Bossi		6–3	1–1	unf.
1951	F. Ampon/Miss S. J. Fry	L. Bergelin/Miss D. J. Hart	8–6	3–6	6–4
1952	K. Nielsen/Miss A. McGuire	E. Migone/Mrs M. J. de Riba	4–6	6–3	6–3
1953	E. V. Seixas/Miss D. J. Hart	M. G. Rose/Miss M. Connolly	6–4	6–4	
1954	E. V. Seixas/Miss M. Connolly div'd with M. A. Trabert/Miss B. M. Kimbrell		3–6	11–9	3–3 unf.
1955	E. Morea/Miss P. E. Ward div'd with M. G. Rose/Miss B. Penrose				
1956	L. Ayala/Mrs T. D. Long	G. Fachini/Miss S. J. Bloomer	6–4	6–3	
1957	L. Ayala/Mrs T. D. Long	R. N. Howe/Miss S. J. Bloomer	6–1	6–1	
1958	G. Fachini/Miss S. J. Bloomer	L. Ayala/Mrs T. D. Long	4–6	6–2	9–7
1959	F. Contreras/Miss R. M. Reyes	W. A. Knight/Miss Y. Ramirez	9–7	6–1	
1960	Not held				
1961	R. S. Emerson/Miss M. Smith	R. A. J. Hewitt/Miss J. Lehane	6–1	6–1	
1962	F. S. Stolle/Miss L. R. Turner	S. Davidson/Miss M. Schacht	6–4	6–1	
1963	Not held				
1964	J. D. Newcombe/Miss M. Smith	T. Koch/Miss M. E. Bueno	3–6	7–5	6–2
1965	J. E. Mandarino/Miss M. Coronado	V. Zarazua/Miss E. Subirats	6–1	6–1	
1966	Not held				
1967	W. W. Bowrey/Miss L. R. Turner	F. D. McMillan/Miss F. Durr	6–2	7–5	
1968	M. C. Riessen/Mrs B. M. Court	T. S. Okker/Miss S. V. Wade	8–6	6–3	
	Event ceased				

THE DAVIS CUP

The International Men's Team Championship of the World was initiated in 1900 when the British Isles, then comprising Great Britain and Ireland, challenged the United States for the trophy presented by Dwight F. Davis. The competition was enlarged in 1904 when Belgium and France took part. Each tie has comprised two players engaged in reverse singles plus a doubles match with the best of five sets throughout. In 1989 the tie-break was introduced for all sets except the fifth, in all matches.

From 1900 to 1971 the Champion Nation stood out until challenged by the winner of a knock-out competition between the challenging nations and had the choice of venue. The format was changed in 1972 with all nations taking part in a knock-out event. The format was amended in 1981, when the competition became sponsored by NEC. The Champion Nation was the winner of the World Group of 16 nations. Other nations competed in four zonal groups, two European, an American and an Eastern Zone, with the four winners earning promotion to the World Group. The four bottom nations of the top group, as decided by a relegation round, fell back to the zonal competition.

Between 1900 and 1990 the total number of participating nations was 93, including Hawaii and Estonia which have ceased to exist as distinct tennis nations. South Africa withdrew from the competition in 1979 and have not played since.

CHALLENGE ROUNDS (In playing order)
1900 USA d. British Isles 3–0, Boston: M. D. Whitman d. A. W. Gore 6–1 6–3 6–2; D. F. Davis d. E. D. Black 4–6 6–2 6–4 6–4; Davis/H. Ward d. Black/H. Roper Barrett 6–4 6–4 6–4; Davis div'd with Gore 9–7 9–9.
1901 Not held

1902 *USA d. British Isles 3–2, Brooklyn, New York:* W. A. Larned lost to R. F. Doherty 6–2 6–3 3–6 4–6 4–6; M. D. Whitman d. J. Pim 6–1 6–1 1–6 6–0; Larned d. Pim 6–3 6–2 6–3; Whitman d. R. F. Doherty 6–1 7–5 6–4; D. F. Davis/H. Ward lost to R. F./H. L. Doherty 6–3 8–10 3–6 4–6.

1903 *British Isles d. USA 4–1, Boston:* H. L. Doherty d. R. D. Wrenn 6–0 6–3 6–4; R. F. Doherty lost to W. A. Larned ret'd; R. F./H. L. Doherty d. R. D./G. L. Wrenn 7–5 9–7 2–6 6–3; H. L. Doherty d. Larned 6–3 6–8 6–0 2–6 7–5; R. F. Doherty d. R. D. Wrenn 6–4 3–6 6–3 6–8 6–4.

1904 *British Isles d. Belgium 5–0, Wimbledon:* H. L. Doherty d. P. de Borman 6–4 6–1 6–1; F. L. Riseley d. W. Lemaire 6–1 6–4 6–2; R. F./H. L. Doherty d. de Borman/Lemaire 6–0 6–1 6–3; H. L. Doherty w.o. Lemaire; Riseley d. de Borman 4–6 6–2 8–6 7–5.

1905 *British Isles d. USA 5–0, Wimbledon:* H. L. Doherty d. H. Ward 7–9 4–6 6–1 6–2 6–0; S. H. Smith d. W. A. Larned 6–4 6–4 5–7 6–4; R. F./H. L. Doherty d. Ward/B. Wright 8–10 6–2 6–2 4–6 8–6; Smith d. W. J. Clothier 4–6 6–1 6–4 6–3; H. L. Doherty d. Larned 6–4 2–6 6–8 6–4 6–2.

1906 *British Isles d. USA 5–0, Wimbledon:* S. H. Smith d. R. D. Little 6–4 6–4 6–1; H. L. Doherty d. H. Ward 6–2 8–6 6–3; R. F./H. L. Doherty d. Little/Ward 3–6 11–9 9–7 6–1; Smith d. Ward 6–1 6–0 6–4; H. L. Doherty d. Little 3–6 6–3 6–8 6–1 6–3.

1907 *Australasia d. British Isles 3–2, Wimbledon:* N. E. Brookes d. A. W. Gore 7–5 6–1 7–5; A. F. Wilding d. H. Roper Barrett 1–6 6–4 6–3 7–5; Brookes/Wilding lost to Gore/Roper Barrett 6–3 6–4 5–7 2–6 11–13; Wilding lost to Gore 6–3 3–6 5–7 2–6; Brookes d. Roper Barrett 6–2 6–0 6–3.

1908 *Australasia d. USA 3–2, Melbourne:* N. E. Brookes d. F. B. Alexander 5–7 9–7 6–2 4–6 6–3; A. F. Wilding lost to B. Wright 6–3 5–7 3–6 1–6; Brookes/Wilding d. Alexander/Wright 6–4 6–2 5–7 1–6 6–4; Brookes lost to Wright 6–0 6–3 5–7 2–6 10–12; Wilding d. Alexander 6–3 4–6 6–1.

1909 *Australasia d. USA 5–0, Sydney:* N. E. Brookes d. M. E. McLoughlin 6–2 6–2 6–4; A. F. Wilding d. M. H. Long 6–2 7–5 6–1; Brookes/Wilding d. Long/McLoughlin 12–10 9–7 6–3; Brookes d. Long 6–4 7–5 8–6; Wilding d. McLoughlin 3–6 8–6 6–2 6–3.

1910 *Not held*

1911 *Australasia d. USA 5–0, Christchurch, NZ:* N. E. Brookes d. B. Wright 6–4 2–6 6–3 6–3; R. W. Heath d. W. A. Larned 2–6 6–1 7–5 6–2; Brookes/A. W. Dunlop d. Wright/M. E. McLoughlin 6–4 5–7 7–5 6–4; Brookes d. McLoughlin 6–4 3–6 4–6 6–3 6–4; Heath w.o. Wright.

1912 *British Isles d. Australasia 3–2, Melbourne:* J. C. Parke d. N. E. Brookes 8–6 6–3 5–7 6–2; C. P. Dixon d. R. W. Heath 5–7 6–4 6–4 6–4; A. E. Beamish/Parke lost Brookes/A. W. Dunlop 4–6 1–6 5–7; Dixon lost to Brookes 2–6 4–6 4–6; Parke d. Heath 6–2 6–4 6–4.

1913 *USA d. British Isles 3–2, Wimbledon:* M. E. McLoughlin lost to J. C. Parke 10–8 5–7 4–6 6–1 5–7; R. N. Williams d. C. P. Dixon 8–6 3–6 6–2 1–6 7–5; H. Hackett/McLoughlin d. Dixon/H. Roper Barrett 5–7 6–1 2–6 7–5 6–4; McLoughlin d. Dixon 8–6 6–3 6–2; Williams lost to Parke 2–6 7–5 7–5 4–6 2–6.

1914 *Australasia d. USA 3–2, Forest Hills, NY:* A. F. Wilding d. R. N. Williams 7–5 6–2 6–3; N. E. Brookes lost to M. E. McLoughlin 15–17 3–6 3–6; Brookes/Wilding d. T. C. Bundy/McLoughlin 6–3 8–6 9–7; Brookes d. Williams 6–1 6–2 8–10 6–3; Wilding lost to McLoughlin 2–6 3–6 6–2 2–6.

1915–18 *Not held*

1919 *Australasia d. British Isles 4–1, Sydney:* G. L. Patterson d. A. H. Lowe 6–4 6–3 2–6 6–3; J. O. Anderson lost to A. R. F. Kingscote 5–7 2–6 4–6; N. E. Brookes/Patterson d. A. E. Beamish/Kingscote 6–0 6–0 6–2; Patterson d. Kingscote 6–4 6–4 8–6; Anderson d. Lowe 6–4 5–7 6–3 4–6 12–10.

1920 *USA d. Australasia 5–0, Auckland:* W. T. Tilden d. N. E. Brookes 10–8 6–4 1–6 6–4; W. M. Johnston d. G. L. Patterson 6–3 6–1 6–1; Johnston/Tilden d. Brookes/Patterson 4–6 6–4 6–0 6–4; Johnston d. Brookes 5–7 7–5 6–3 6–3; Tilden d. Patterson 5–7 6–2 6–3 6–3.

1921 *USA d. Japan 5–0, Forest Hills, NY:* W. M. Johnston d. I. Kumagae 6–2 6–4 6–2; W. T. Tilden d. Z. Schimidzu 5–7 6–4 6–2 6–1; W. Washburn/R. N. Williams d. Kumagae/Shimidzu 6–2 7–5 4–6 7–5; Tilden d. Kumagae; 9–7 6–4 6–1; Johnston d. Shimidzu 6–3 5–7 6–2 6–4.

1922 *USA d. Australasia 4–1, Forest Hills, NY:* W. T. Tilden d. G. L. Patterson 7–5 10–8 6–0; W. M. Johnston d. J. O. Anderson 6–1 6–2 6–3; V. Richards/Tilden lost to P. O'Hara Wood/Patterson 4–6 0–6 3–6; Johnston d. Patterson 6–2 6–2 6–1; Tilden d. Anderson 6–4 5–7 3–6 6–4 6–2.

1923 *USA d. Australia 4–1, Forest Hills, NY:* W. M. Johnston lost to J. O. Anderson 6–4 2–6 6–2 5–7 2–6; W. T. Tilden d. J. B. Hawkes 6–4 6–2 6–1; Tilden/R. N. Williams d. Anderson/Hawkes 17–15 11–13 2–6 6–3 6–2; Johnston d. Hawkes 6–0 6–2 6–1; Tilden d. Anderson 6–2 6–3 1–6 7–5.

1924 *USA d. Australia 5–0, Philadelphia:* W. T. Tilden d. G. L. Patterson 6–4 6–2 6–3; V. Richards d. P. O'Hara Wood 6–2 6–2 6–4; W. M. Johnston/Tilden d. O'Hara Wood/Patterson 5–7 6–3 6–4 6–1; Tilden d. O'Hara Wood 6–2 6–1 6–1; Richards d. Patterson 6–3 7–5 6–4.

1925 *USA d. France 5–0, Philadelphia:* W. T. Tilden d. J. Borotra 4–6 6–0 2–6 9–7 6–4; W. M. Johnston d. R. Lacoste 6–1 6–1 6–8 6–3; V. Richards/R. N. Williams d. Borotra/Lacoste 6–4 6–4 6–3; Tilden d. Lacoste 3–6 10–12 8–6 7–5 6–2; Johnston d. Borotra 6–1 6–4 6–0.

1926 *USA d. France 4–1, Philadelphia:* W. M. Johnston d. R. Lacoste 6–0 6–4 0–6 6–0; W. T. Tilden d. J. Borotra 6–2 6–3 6–3; V. Richards/R. N. Williams d. J. Brugnon/H. Cochet 6–4 6–4 6–2; Johnston d. Borotra 8–6 6–4 9–7; Tilden lost to Lacoste 6–4 4–6 6–8 6–8.

1927 *France d. USA 3–2, Philadelphia:* R. Lacoste d. W. M. Johnston 6–3 6–2 6–2; H. Cochet lost to W. T. Tilden 4–6 6–2 2–6 6–8; J. Borotra/J. Brugnon lost to F. Hunter/Tilden 6–3 3–6 3–6 6–4 0–6; Lacoste d. Tilden 6–4 4–6 6–3 6–3; Cochet d. Johnston 6–4 4–6 6–2 6–4.

1928 *France d. USA 4–1, Paris:* R. Lacoste lost to W. T. Tilden 6–1 4–6 4–6 6–2 3–6; H. Cochet d. J. Hennessey 5–7 9–7 6–3 6–0; J. Borotra/Cochet d. F. Hunter/Tilden 6–4 6–8 7–5 4–6 6–2; Lacoste d. Hennessey 4–6 6–1 7–5 6–3; Cochet d. Tilden 9–7 8–6 6–4.

1929 *France d. USA 3–2, Paris:* H. Cochet d. W. T. Tilden 6–3 6–1 6–2; J. Borotra d. G. M. Lott 6–1 3–6 6–4 7–5; Borotra/Cochet lost to W. Allison/J. Van Ryn 1–6 6–8 4–6; Cochet d. Lott 6–1 3–6 6–0 6–3; Borotra lost to Tilden 6–4 1–6 4–6 5–7.

1930 *France d. USA 4–1, Paris:* J. Borotra lost to W. T. Tilden 6–2 5–7 4–6 5–7; H. Cochet d. G. M. Lott 6–4 6–2 6–2; J.

Brugnon/Cochet d. W. Allison/J. Van Ryn 6–3 7–5 1–6 6–2; Borotra d. Lott 5–7 6–3 2–6 6–2 8–6; Cochet d. Tilden 4–6 6–3 6–1 7–5.

1931 France d. Great Britain 3–2, Paris: H. Cochet d. H. W. Austin 3–6 11–9 6–2 6–4; J. Borotra lost to F. J. Perry 6–4 8–10 0–6 6–4 4–6; J. Brugnon/Cochet d. G. P Hughes/C. H. Kingsley 6–1 5–7 6–3 8–6; Cochet d. Perry 6–4 1–6 9–7 6–3; Borotra lost to Austin 5–7 3–6 6–3 5–7.

1932 France d. USA 3–2, Paris: H. Cochet d. W. Allison 5–7 7–5 3–6 7–5 6–2; J. Borotra d. H. E. Vines 6–4 6–2 2–6 6–4; J. Brugnon/Cochet lost to Allison/J. Van Ryn 0–0 10–11 5–7 0–4 4–0; Borotra d. Allison 1–6 3–6 0–4 0–2 7–5; Cochet lost to Vines 6–4 6–0 5–7 6–8 2–6.

1933 Great Britain d. France 3–2, Paris: H. W. Austin d. A. Merlin 6–3 6–4 6–0; F. J. Perry d. H. Cochet 8–10 6–4 8–6 3–6 6–1; G. P. Hughes/H. G. N. Lee lost to J. Borotra/J. Brugnon 3–6 6–8 2–6; Austin lost to Cochet 7–5 4–6 6–4 4–6 4–6; Perry d. Merlin 4–6 8–6 6–2 7–5.

1934 Great Britain d. USA 4–1, Wimbledon: F. J. Perry d. S. B. Wood 6–1 4–6 5–7 6–0 6–3; H. W. Austin d. F. X. Shields 6–4 4–6 6–1; G. P. Hughes/H. G. N. Lee lost to G. M. Lott/L. Stoefen 5–7 0–6 6–4 7–9; Perry d. Shields 6–4 4–6 6–2 15–13; Austin d. Wood 6–4 6–0 6–8 6–3.

1935 Great Britain d. USA 5–0, Wimbledon: F. J. Perry d. J. D. Budge 6–0 6–8 6–3 6–4; H. W. Austin d. W. Allison 6–2 2–6 4–6 3–7–5; G. P. Hughes/C. R. D. Tuckey d. Allison/J. Van Ryn 6–2 1–6 6–8 6–3 6–3; Perry d. Allison 4–6 6–4 7–5 6–3; Austin d. Budge 6–2 6–4 6–8 7–5.

1936 Great Britain d. Australia 3–2, Wimbledon: H. W. Austin d. J. H. Crawford 4–6 6–3 6–1 6–1; F. J. Perry d. A. K. Quist 6–1 4–6 7–5 6–2; G. P. Hughes/C. R. D. Tuckey lost to Crawford/Quist 4–6 6–2 5–7 8–10; Austin lost to Quist 4–6 6–3 5–7 2–6; Perry d. Crawford 6–2 6–3 6–3.

1937 USA d. Great Britain 4–1, Wimbledon: F. A. Parker lost to H. W. Austin 3–6 2–6 5–7; J. D. Budge d. C. E. Hare 15–13 6–1 6–2; Budge/G. Mako d. C. R. D. Tuckey/F. H. D. Wilde 6–3 7–5 7–9 12–10; Parker d. Hare 6–2 6–4 6–2; Budge d. Austin 8–6 3–6 6–4 6–3.

1938 USA d. Australia 3–2, Philadelphia: R. L. Riggs d. A. K. Quist 4–6 6–0 8–6 6–1; J. D. Budge d. J. E. Bromwich 6–2 6–3 4–6 7–5; Budge/G. Mako lost to Bromwich/Quist 6–0 3–6 4–6 2–6; Budge d. Quist 8–6 6–1 6–2; Riggs lost to Bromwich 4–6 6–4 0–6 2–6.

1939 Australia d. USA 3–2, Philadelphia: J. E. Bromwich lost to R. L. Riggs 4–6 0–6 5–7; A. K. Quist lost to F. A. Parker 3–6 6–2 4–6 6–1 5–7; Bromwich/Quist d. J. R. Hunt/J. Kramer 5–7 6–2 7–5 6–2; Quist d. Riggs 6–1 6–4 3–6 3–6 6–4; Bromwich d. Parker 6–0 6–3 6–1.

1940–45 Not held

1946 USA d. Australia 5–0, Melbourne: F. R. Schroeder d. J. E. Bromwich 3–6 6–1 6–2 0–6 6–3; J. Kramer d. D. Pails 8–6 6–2 9–7; Kramer/Schroeder d. Bromwich/A. K. Quist 6–2 7–5 6–4; Kramer d. Bromwich 8–6 6–4 6–2 6–4; G Mulloy d. Pails 6–3 6–3 6–4.

1947 USA d. Australia 4–1, Forest Hills, NY: J. Kramer d. D. Pails 6–2 6–1 6–2; F. R. Schroeder d. J. E. Bromwich 6–4 5–7 6–3 6–3; Kramer/Schroeder lost to Bromwich/C. F. Long 4–6 6–2 2–6 4–6; Schroeder d. Pails 6–3 8–6 4–6 9–11 10–8; Kramer d. Bromwich 6–3 6–2 6–2.

1948 USA d. Australia 5–0, Forest Hills, NY: F. A. Parker d. O. W. Sidwell 6–4 6–4 6–4; F. R. Schroeder d. A. K. Quist 6–3 4–6 6–0 6–0; G. Mulloy/W. F. Talbert d. C. F. Long/Sidwell 8–6 9–7 2–6 7–5; Parker d. Quist 6–2 6–2 6–3; Schroeder d. Sidwell 6–2 6–1 6–1.

1949 USA d. Australia 4–1, Forest Hills, NY: F. R. Schroeder d. O. W. Sidwell 6–1 5–7 4–6 6–2 6–3; R. A. Gonzales d. F. A. Sedgman 8–6 6–4 9–7; G. Mulloy/W. F. Talbert lost to J. E. Bromwich/Sidwell 6–3 6–4 8–10 7–9 7–9; Schroeder d. Sedgman 6–4 6–3 6–3; Gonzales d. Sidwell 6–1 6–3 6–3.

1950 Australia d. USA 4–1, Forest Hills, NY: F. A. Sedgman d. T. Brown 6–0 8–6 9–7; K. McGregor d. F. R. Schroeder 13–11 6–3 6–4; J. E. Bromwich/Sedgman d. G. Mulloy/Schroeder 4–6 6–4 6–2 4–6 6–4; Sedgman d. Schroeder 6–2 6–2 6–2; McGregor lost to Brown 11–9 10–8 9–11 1–6 4–6.

1951 Australia d. USA 3–2, Sydney: M. G. Rose lost to E. V. Seixas 3–6 4–6 7–9; F. A. Sedgman d. F. R. Schroeder 6–4 6–3 4–6 6–4; K. McGregor/Sedgman d. Schroeder/M. A. Trabert 6–2 9–7 6–3; Rose lost to Schroeder 4–6 11–13 5–7; Sedgman d. Seixas 6–4 6–2 6–2.

1952 Australia d. USA 4–1, Adelaide: F. A. Sedgman d. E. V. Seixas 6–3 6–4 6–3; K. McGregor d. M. A. Trabert 11–9 6–4 6–1; McGregor/Sedgman d. Seixas/Trabert 6–3 6–4 1–6 6–3; Sedgman d. Trabert 7–5 6–4 10–8; McGregor lost to Seixas 3–6 6–8 8–6 3–6.

1953 Australia d. USA 3–2, Melbourne: L. A. Hoad d. E. V. Seixas 6–4 6–2 6–3; K. R. Rosewall lost to M. A. Trabert 3–6 4–6 4–6; R. Hartwig/Hoad lost to Seixas/Trabert 2–6 4–6 4–6; Hoad d. Trabert 13–11 6–3 2–6 3–6 7–5; Rosewall d. Seixas 6–2 2–6 6–3 6–4.

1954 USA d. Australia 3–2, Sydney: M. A. Trabert d. L. A. Hoad 6–4 2–6 12–10 6–3; E. V. Seixas d. K. R. Rosewall 8–6 6–8 6–4 6–3; Seixas/Trabert d. Hoad/Rosewall 6–2 4–6 6–2 10–8; Trabert lost to Rosewall 7–9 5–7 3–6; Seixas lost to R. Hartwig 6–4 3–6 2–6 3–6.

1955 Australia d. USA 5–0, Forest Hills, NY: K. R. Rosewall d. E. V. Seixas 6–3 10–8 4–6 6–2; L. A. Hoad d. M. A. Trabert 4–6 6–3 6–3 8–6; R. Hartwig/Hoad d. Seixas/Trabert 12–14 6–4 6–3 3–6 7–5; Rosewall d. H. Richardson 6–4 3–6 6–1 6–4; Hoad d. Seixas 7–9 6–1 6–4 6–4.

1956 Australia d. USA 5–0, Adelaide: L. A. Hoad d. H. Flam 6–2 6–3 6–3; K. R. Rosewall d. E. V. Seixas 6–2 7–5 6–3; Hoad/Rosewall d. S. Giammalva/Seixas 1–6 6–1 7–5 6–4; Hoad d. Seixas 6–2 7–5 6–3; Rosewall d. Giammalva 4–6 6–1 8–6 7–5.

1957 Australia d. USA 3–2, Melbourne: A. J. Cooper d. E. V. Seixas 3–6 7–5 6–1 1–6 6–3; M. J. Anderson d. B. MacKay 6–3 7–5 3–6 47–9 6–3; Anderson/M. G. Rose d. MacKay/Seixas 6–4 6–4 8–6; Cooper lost to MacKay 4–6 6–1 6–4 4–6 6–3; Anderson lost to Seixas 3–6 6–4 3–6 6–0 11–13.

1958 USA d. Australia 3–2, Brisbane: A. Olmedo d. M. J. Anderson 8–6 2–6 9–7 8–6; B. MacKay lost to A. J. Cooper 6–4 3–6 2–6 4–6; Olmedo/H. Richardson d. Anderson/N. A. Fraser 10–12 3–6 16–14 6–3 7–5; Olmedo d. Cooper 6–3 4–6 4–6 8–6; MacKay lost to Anderson 5–7 11–13 9–11.

1959 Australia d. USA 3–2, Forest Hills, NY: N. A. Fraser d. A. Olmedo 8–6 6–8 6–4 8–6; R. G. Laver lost to B. MacKay 5–7 4–6 1–6; R. S. Emerson/Fraser d. E. Buchholz/Olmedo 7–5 7–5 6–4; Laver lost to Olmedo 7–9 6–4 8–10 10–12; Fraser d. MacKay 8–6 3–6 6–2 6–4.

1960 *Australia d. Italy 4–1, Sydney:* N. A. Fraser d. O. Sirola 4–6 6–3 6–3 6–3; R. G. Laver d. N. Pietrangeli 8–6 6–4 6–3; R. S. Emerson/Fraser d. Pietrangeli/Sirola 10–8 5–7 6–3 6–4; Laver d. Sirola 9–7 6–2 6–3; Fraser lost to Pietrangeli 9–11 3–6 6–1 2–6.

1961 *Australia d. Italy 5–0, Melbourne:* R. S. Emerson d. N. Pietrangeli 8–6 6–4 6–0; R. G. Laver d. O. Sirola 6–1 6–4 6–3; Emerson/N. A. Fraser d. Pietrangeli/Sirola 6–2 6–3 6–4; Emerson d. Sirola 6–2 6–3 4–6 6–2; Laver d. Pietrangeli 6–3 3–6 4–6 6–3 8–6.

1962 *Australia d. Mexico 5–0, Brisbane:* N. A. Fraser d. A. Palafox 7–9 6–3 6–4 11–9; R. G. Laver d. R. H. Osuna 6–2 6–1 7–5; R. S. Emerson/Laver d. Osuna/Palafox 7–5 6–2 6–4; Fraser d. Osuna 3–6 11–9 6–1 3–6 6–4; Laver d. Palafox 6–1 4–6 6–4 8–6.

1963 *USA d. Australia 3–2, Adelaide:* R. D. Ralston d. J. D. Newcombe 6–4 6–1 3–6 4–6 7–5; C. R. McKinley lost to R. S. Emerson 3–6 6–3 5–7 5–7; McKinley/Ralston d. Emerson/N. A. Fraser 6–3 4–6 11–9 11–9; Ralston lost to Emerson 2–6 3–6 6–3 2–6; McKinley d. Newcombe 10–12 6–2 9–7 6–2.

1964 *Australia d. USA 3–2, Cleveland, Ohio:* F. S. Stolle lost to C. R. McKinley 1–6 7–9 6–4 2–6; R. S. Emerson d. R. D. Ralston 6–3 6–1 6–3; Emerson/Stolle lost to McKinley/Ralston 4–6 6–4 6–4 3–6 4–6; Stolle d. Ralston 7–5 6–3 3–6 9–11 6–4; Emerson d. McKinley 3–6 6–2 6–4 6–4.

1965 *Australia d. Spain 4–1, Sydney:* F. S. Stolle d. M. Santana 10–12 3–6 6–1 6–4 7–5; R. S. Emerson d. J. Gisbert 6–3 6–2 6–2; J. D. Newcombe/A. D. Roche d. J. L. Arilla/Santana 6–3 4–6 7–5 6–2; Emerson lost to Santana 6–2 3–6 4–6 13–15; Stolle d. Gisbert 6–2 6–4 8–6.

1966 *Australia d. India 4–1, Melbourne:* F. S. Stolle d. R. Krishnan 6–3 6–2 6–4; R. S. Emerson d. J. Mukerjea 7–5 6–4 6–2; J. D. Newcombe/A. D. Roche lost to Krishnan/Mukerjea 6–4 5–7 4–6 4–6; Emerson d. Krishnan 6–0 6–2 10–8; Stolle d. Mukerjea 7–5 6–8 6–3 5–7 6–3.

1967 *Australia d. Spain 4–1, Brisbane:* R. S. Emerson d. M. Santana 6–4 6–1 6–1; J. D. Newcombe d. M. Orantes 6–3 6–3 6–2; Newcombe/A. D. Roche d. Orantes/Santana 6–4 6–4 6–4; Newcombe lost to Santana 5–7 4–6 2–6; Emerson d. Orantes 6–1 6–1 2–6 6–4.

1968 *USA d. Australia 4–1, Adelaide:* C. Graebner d. W. W. Bowrey 8–10 6–4 8–6 3–6 6–1; A. R. Ashe d. R. O. Ruffels 6–8 7–5 6–3 6–3; R. C. Lutz/S. R. Smith d. J. G. Alexander/Ruffels 6–4 6–4 6–2; Graebner d. Ruffels 3–6 8–6 2–6 6–3 6–1; Ashe lost to Bowrey 6–2 3–6 9–11 6–8.

1969 *USA d. Rumania 5–0, Cleveland, Ohio:* A. R. Ashe d. I. Nastase 6–2 15–13 7–5; S. R. Smith d. I. Tiriac 6–8 6–3 5–7 6–4 6–4; R. C. Lutz/Smith d. Nastase/Tiriac 8–6 11–9; Smith d. Nastase 4–6 4–6 6–4 6–1 11–9; Ashe d. Tiriac 6–3 8–6 3–6 4–0 ret'd.

1970 *USA d. West Germany 5–0, Cleveland, Ohio:* A. R. Ashe d. W. Bungert 6–2 10–8 6–2; C. Richey d. C. Kuhnke 6–3 6–4 6–2; R. C. Lutz/S. R. Smith d. Bungert/Kuhnke 6–3 7–5 6–4; Richey d. Bungert 6–4 6–4 7–5; Ashe d. Kuhnke 6–8 10–12 9–7 13–11 6–4.

1971 *USA d. Rumania 3–2, Charlotte, NC:* S. R. Smith d. I. Nastase 7–5 6–3 6–1; F. A. Froehling d. I. Tiriac 3–6 1–6 6–1 6–3 8–6; Smith/E. Van Dillen lost to Nastase/Tiriac 5–7 4–6 8–6; Smith d. Tiriac 8–6 6–3 6–0; Froehling lost to Nastase 3–6 1–6 6–1 4–6.

Challenge Round abolished

FINAL ROUND SCORES

1972 *USA d. Rumania 3–2, Bucharest:* S. R. Smith d. I. Nastase 11–9 6–2 6–3; T. Gorman lost to I. Tiriac 6–4 6–2 4–6 3–6 2–6; Smith/E. Van Dillen d. Nastase/Tiriac 6–2 6–0 6–3; Smith d. Tiriac 4–6 6–2 6–4 2–6 6–0; Gorman lost to Nastase 1–6 2–6 7–5 8–10.

1973 *Australia d. USA 5–0, Cleveland, Ohio (indoors):* J. D. Newcombe d. S. R. Smith 6–1 3–6 6–3 3–6 6–4; R. G. Laver d. T. Gorman 8–10 8–6 6–8 6–3 6–1; Laver/Newcombe d. Smith/E. Van Dillen 6–1 6–2 6–4; Newcombe d. Gorman 6–2 6–1 6–3; Laver d. Smith 6–3 6–4 3–6 6–2.

1974 *South Africa w.o. India*

1975 *Sweden d. Czechoslovakia 3–2, Stockholm (indoors):* O. Bengtson lost to J. Kodes 4–6 6–2 5–7 4–6; B. Borg d. J. Hrebec 6–1 6–3 6–0; Bengtson/Borg d. Kodes/V. Zednik 6–4 6–4 6–4; Borg d. Kodes 6–4 6–2 6–2; Bengtson lost to Hrebec 6–1 3–6 1–6 4–6.

1976 *Italy d. Chile 4–1, Santiago:* C. Barazzutti d. J. Fillol 7–5 4–6 7–5 6–1; A. Panatta d. P. Cornejo 6–3 6–1 6–3; P. Bertolucci/Panatta d. Cornejo/Fillol 3–6 6–2 9–7 6–3; Panatta d. Fillol 8–6 6–4 3–6 10–8; A. Zugarelli lost to B. Prajoux 4–6 4–6 2–6.

1977 *Australia d. Italy 3–1, Sydney:* A. D. Roche d. A. Panatta 6–3 6–4 6–4; J. G. Alexander d. C. Barazzutti 6–2 8–6 4–6 6–2; Alexander/P. Dent lost to P. Bertolucci/Panatta 4–6 4–6 5–7; Alexander d. Panatta 6–4 4–6 2–6 8–6 11–9; Roche div'd with Barazzutti 12–12.

1978 *USA d. Great Britain 4–1, Palm Springs, California:* J. P. McEnroe d. J. M. Lloyd 6–1 6–2 6–2; B. E. Gottfried lost to C. J. Mottram 6–4 6–2 8–10 4–6 3–6; R. C. Lutz/S. R. Smith d. M. Cox/D. A. Lloyd 6–2 6–2 6–3; McEnroe d. Mottram 6–2 6–2 6–1; Gottfried d. J. M. Lloyd 6–1 6–2 6–4.

1979 *USA d. Italy 5–0, San Francisco (indoors):* V. Gerulaitis d. C. Barazzutti 6–3 3–2 ret'd; J. P. McEnroe d. A. Panatta 6–2 6–3 6–4; R. C. Lutz/S. R. Smith d. P. Bertolucci/Panatta 6–4 12–10 6–2; McEnroe d. A. Zugarelli 6–4 6–3 6–1; Gerulaitis d. Panatta 6–1 6–3 6–3.

1980 *Czechoslovakia d. Italy 4–1, Prague (indoors):* T. Smid d. A. Panatta 3–6 3–6 6–3 6–4 6–1; I. Lendl d. C. Barazzutti 4–6 6–1 6–1 6–2; Lendl/Smid d. P. Bertolucci/Panatta 3–6 6–3 3–6 6–3 6–4; Smid lost to Barazzutti 6–3 3–6 2–6; Lendl d. G. Ocleppo 6–3 6–3.

1981 *USA d. Argentina 3–1, Cincinnati (indoors):* J. P. McEnroe d. G. Vilas 6–3 6–2 6–2; R. Tanner lost to J. L. Clerc 5–7 3–6 6–8; P. Fleming/McEnroe d. Clerc/Vilas 6 3 4 6 6 4 4 6 11–9; McEnroe d. Clerc 7–5 5–7 6–3 3–6 6–3; Tanner div'd with Vilas 11–10.

1982 *USA d. France 4–1, Grenoble (indoors):* J. P. McEnroe d. Y. Noah 12–10 1–6 3–6 6–2 6–3; G. Mayer d. H. Leconte 6–2 6–2 7–9 6–4; P. Fleming/McEnroe d. Leconte/Noah 6–3 6–4 9–7; Mayer lost to Noah 1–6 0–6; McEnroe d. Leconte 6–2 6–3.

1983 *Australia d. Sweden 3–2, Melbourne:* P. Cash lost to M. Wilander 3–6 4–6 7–9 3–6; J. Fitzgerald d. J. Nystrom 6–4 6–2 4–6 6–4; M. R. Edmondson/P. McNamee d. A. Jarryd/H. Simonsson 6–4 6–4 6–2; Cash d. Nystrom 6–4 6–1 6–1; Fitzgerald lost to Wilander 8–6 0–6 1–6.

1984 *Sweden d. USA 4–1, Gothenburg:* M. Wilander d. J. S. Connors 6–1 6–3 6–3; H. Sundstrom d. J. P. McEnroe 13–11 6–4 6–3; S. Edberg/A. Jarryd d. P. Fleming/McEnroe 7–5 5–7 6–2 7–5; Wilander lost to McEnroe 3–6 7–6 3–6; Sundstrom d. J. Arias 3–6 8–6 6–3.
1985 *Sweden d. West Germany 3–2, Munich:* M. Wilander d. M. Westphal 6–3 6–4 10–8; S. Edberg lost to B. Becker 3–6 6–3 5–7 6–8; Wilander/J. Nystrom d. Becker/A. Maurer 6–4 6–2 6–1; Wilander lost to Becker 3–6 6–2 3–6 3–6; Edberg d. Westphal 3–6 7–5 6–4 6–3.
1986 *Australia d. Sweden 3–2, Melbourne:* P. Cash d. S. Edberg 13–11 13–11 6–4; P. McNamee lost to M. Pernfors 3–6 1–6 3–6; Cash/J. Fitzgerald d. Edberg/A. Jarryd 6–3 6–4 4–6 6–1; Cash d. Pernfors 2–6 4–6 6–3 6–4 6–3; McNamee lost to Edberg 8–10 4–6.
1987 *Sweden d. India 5–0, Gothenburg:* M. Wilander d. R. Krishnan 6–4 6–1 6–3; A. Jarryd d. V. Amritraj 6–3 6–3 6–1; Wilander/J. Nystrom d. An./V. Amritraj 6–3 3–6 6–1 6–2; Jarryd d. Krishnan 6–4 6–3; Wilander d. V. Amritraj 6–2 6–0.
1988 *West Germany d. Sweden 4–1, Gothenburg:* C.-U. Steeb d. M. Wilander 8–10 1–6 6–2 6–4 8–6; B. Becker d. S. Edberg 6–3 6–1 6–4; Becker/E. Jelen d. Edberg/A. Jarryd 3–6 2–6 7–5 6–3 6–2; Steeb lost to Edberg 4–6 6–8; P. Kuhnen w.o. K. Carlsson.
1989 *West Germany d. Sweden 3–2, Stuttgart:* C.-U. Steeb lost to M. Wilander 7–5 6–7 7–6 2–6 3–6; B. Becker d. S. Edberg 6–2 6–2 6–4; Becker/E. Jelen d. A. Jarryd/J. Gunnarsson 7–6 6–4 3–6 6–7 6–4; Becker d. Wilander 6–2 6–0 6–2; Steeb lost to Edberg 2–6 4–6.
1990 *USA d. Australia 3–2, St Petersburg:* A. Agassi d. R. Fromberg 4–6 6–4 4–6 6–2 6–4; M. Chang d. D. Cahill 6–2 7–6 6–0; R. Leach/J. Pugh d. P. Cash/J. Fitzgerald 6–4 6–2 3–6 7–6; Agassi lost to Cahill 4–6 6–4 ret.; Chang lost to Fromberg 5–7 6–2 3–6.
1991 *France d. USA 3–1, Lyon:* G. Forget lost to A. Agassi 7–6 2–6 1–6 2–6; H. Leconte d. P. Sampras 6–4 7–5 6–4; Forget/Leconte d. K. Flach/R. Seguso 6–1 6–4 4–6 6–2; Forget d. Sampras 7–6 3–6 6–3 6–4; Leconte v Agassi not played.

QUALIFIERS FOR WORLD GROUP

| 1991 | Belgium | Canada | Brazil | Netherlands |
| | Great Britain | Italy | Sweden | Switzerland |

FEDERATION CUP

International Women's Team Championship, staged on a knock-out basis at one venue with each tie comprising two singles and one doubles match.

FINAL ROUNDS

1963 *USA d. Australia 2–1, Queen's Club, London, 18–21 June:* D. R. Hard lost to M. Smith 3–6 0–6; B. J. Moffitt d. L. R. Turner 5–7 6–0 6–3; Hard/Moffitt d. Smith/Turner 3–6 13–11 6–3.
1964 *Australia d. USA 2–1, Germanstown Cricket Club, Philadelphia, 2–5 September:* M. Smith d. B. J. Moffitt 6–2 6–3; L. R. Turner d. N. Richey 7–5 6–1; Smith/Turner lost to Moffitt/Mrs J. R. Susman 6–4 5–7 1–6.
1965 *Australia d. USA 2–1, Kooyong Stadium, Melbourne, 12–18 January:* L. R. Turner d. Mrs C. Graebner 6–3 2–6 6–3; M. Smith d. B. J. Moffitt 6–4 8–6; Smith/J. M. Tegart lost to Graebner/Moffitt 5–7 6–4 4–6.
1966 *USA d. West Germany 3–0, Turin, 11–15 May:* J. M. Heldman d. H. Niessen 4–6 7–5 6–1; Mrs L. W. King d. E. Buding 6–3 3–6 6–1; Mrs C. Graebner/Mrs King d. Buding/H. Schultse 6–4 6–2.
1967 *USA d. Great Britain 2–0, Rot-Weiss Club, Berlin, 7–11 June:* R. Casals d. S. V. Wade 9–7 8–6; Mrs L. W. King d. Mrs P. F. Jones 6–3 6–4; Casals/Mrs King div'd with Mrs Jones/Wade 6–8 9–7.
1968 *Australia d. Netherlands 3–0, Stade Roland Garros, Paris, 23–26 May:* K. A. Melville d. M. Jansen 4–6 7–5 6–3; Mrs B. M. Court d. A. Suurbeck 6–1 6–3; Court/Melville d. Suurbeck/L. Venneboer 6–3 6–8 7–5.
1969 *USA d. Australia 2–1, Athens, 19–25 May:* N. Richey d. K. A. Melville 6–4 6–3; J. M. Heldman lost to Mrs B. M. Court 1–6 6–8; J. Bartkowicz/Richey d. Court/J. M. Tegart 6–4 6–4.
1970 *Australia d. West Germany 3–0, Freiburg, Germany, 19–24 May:* K. M. Krantzcke d. Mrs H. Hoesl 6–2 6–3; Mrs D. E. Dalton d. H. Niessen 4–6 6–3 6–3; Dalton/Krantzcke d. Hoesl/Niessen 6–2 7–5.
1971 *Australia d. Great Britain 3–0, Perth, Australia, 26–29 December 1970:* Mrs B. M. Court d. Mrs P. F. Jones 6–8 6–3 6–2; E. F. Goolagong d. S. V. Wade 6–4 6–1; Court/L. Hunt d. W. M. Shaw/Wade 6–4 6–4.
1972 *South Africa d. Great Britain 2–1, Ellis Park, Johannesburg, 19–26 March:* Mrs Q. C. Pretorius lost to S. V. Wade 3–6 2–6; B. Kirk d. W. M. Shaw 4–6 7–5 6–0; Kirk/Pretorius d. Wade/Mrs G. M. Williams 6–1 7–5.
1973 *Australia d. South Africa 3–0, Bad Homburg, Germany, 30 April–6 May:* E. F. Goolagong d. Mrs Q. C. Pretorius 6–0 6–2; P. Coleman d. B. Kirk 10–8 6–0; Goolagong/J. Young d. Kirk/Pretorius 6–1 6–2.
1974 *Australia d. USA 2–1, Naples, 13–19 May:* E. F. Goolagong d. J. M. Heldman 6–1 7–5; D. L. Fromholtz lost to C. M. Evert 6–2 5–7 3–6; Goolagong/J. Young d. Heldman/S. A. Walsh 7–5 8–6.
1975 *Czechoslovakia d. Australia 3–0, Aix-en-Provence, 6–11 May:* M. Navratilova* d. E. F. Goolagong 6–3 6–4; R. Tomanova d. H Gourlay 6–4 6–2; Navratilova/Tomanova d. L. Fromholtz/Gourlay 6–3 6–1.
1976 *USA d. Australia 2–1, Spectrum Stadium, Philadelphia, 22–29 August:* R. Casals lost to Mrs G. Reid 6–1 3–6 5–7; Mrs L. W. King d. Mrs E. Cawley 7–6 6–4; Casals/King d. Cawley/Reid 7–5 6–3.
1977 *USA d. Australia 2–1, Devonshire Park, Eastbourne, 13–18 June:* Mrs L. W. King d. D. L. Fromholtz 6–1 2–6 6–2; C. M. Evert d. Mrs G. Reid 7–5 6–3; Casals/Evert lost to Reid/W. M. Turnbull 3–6 3–6.
1978 *USA d. Australia 2–1, Kooyong Stadium, Melbourne, 27 November–3 December:* T. A. Austin lost to Mrs G. Reid 3–6 3–6; C. M. Evert d. W. M. Turnbull 3–6 6–1 6–1; Evert/Mrs L. W. King d. Reid/Turnbull 4–6 6–1 6–4.
1979 *USA d. Australia 3–0, Madrid, 30 April–6 May:* T. A. Austin d. Mrs G. Reid 6–3 6–0; Mrs J. M. Lloyd d. D. L. Fromholtz 2–6 6–3 8–6; R. Casals/Mrs L. W. King d. Reid/W. M. Turnbull 3–6 6–3 8–6.

1980 USA d. Australia 3–0, Rot-Weiss Club, Berlin, 19–25 May: Mrs J. M. Lloyd d. D. L. Fromholtz 4–6 6–1 6–1; T. A. Austin d. W. M. Turnbull 6–2 6–3; R. Casals/K. Jordan d. Fromholtz/S. Leo 2–6 6–4 6–4.

1981 USA d. Great Britain 3–0, Tokyo, 9–15 November: A. Jaeger d. S. V. Wade 6–3 6–1; Mrs J. M. Lloyd d. S. Barker 6–2 6–1; R. Casals/K. Jordan d. J. M. Durie/Wade 6–4 7–5.

1982 USA d. West Germany 3–0, Santa Clara, California, 19–25 July: Mrs J. M. Lloyd d. C. Kohde 2–6 6–1 6–3; M. Navratilova d. B. Bunge 6–4 6–4; Lloyd/Navratilova d. Bunge/Kohde 3–6 6–1 6–2.

1983 Czechoslovakia d. West Germany 2–1, Zurich, 18–24 July: H. Sukova d. C. Kohde 6–4 2–6 6–2; H. Mandlikova d. B. Bunge 6–2 3–0 ret'd; I. Budarova/M. Skuherska lost to E. Pfaff/Kohde 6–3 2–6 1–6.

1984 Czechoslovakia d. Australia 2–1, Sao Paulo, 15–22 July: H. Sukova lost to A. Minter 5–7 5–7; H. Mandlikova d. E. Sayers 6–1 6–0; Mandlikova/Sukova d. W. Turnbull/Sayers 6–2 6–2.

1985 Czechoslovakia d. USA 2–1, Nagoya, 7–13 October: H. Sukova d. E. Burgin 6–3 6–7 6–4; H. Mandlikova d. K. Jordan 7–5 6–1; A. Holikova/R. Marsikova lost to Burgin/Jordan 2–6 3–6.

1986 USA d. Czechoslovakia 2–1, Prague, 21–27 July: Mrs J. M. Lloyd d. H. Sukova 7–5 7–6; M. Navratilova d. H. Mandlikova 7–5 6–1; Navratilova/P. H. Shriver d. Mandlikova/Sukova 6–4 6–2.

1987 West Germany d. USA 2–1, Vancouver, 27 July–2 August: C. Kohde-Kilsch lost to P. H. Shriver 0–6 6–7; S. Graf d. C. M. Evert 6–2 6–3; Kohde-Kilsch/Graf d. Evert/Shriver 1–6 7–5 6–4.

1988 Czechoslovakia d. USSR 2–1, Melbourne, 7–11 December: R. Zrubakova d. L. Savchenko 6–1 7–6; H. Sukova d. Zvereva 6–3 6–4; J. Novotna/J. Pospisilova lost to Savchenko/Zvereva 6–7 5–7.

1989 USA d. Spain 3–0, Tokyo, 1–8 October: C. Evert d. C. Martinez 6–3 6–2; M. Navratilova d. A. Sanchez 0–6 6–3 6–4; Z. Garrison/P. H. Shriver d. Martinez/Sanchez 7–5 6–1.

1990 USA d. USSR 2-1, Atlanta, 22–29 July: J. Capriati d. L. Meskhi 7–6 6–2; Z. Garrison lost to N. Zvereva 6–4 3–6 3–6; Z. Garrison/G. Fernandez d. N. Zvereva/L. Savchenko 6–4 6–3.

1991 Spain d. USA 2-1, Nottingham, 22–28 July: C. Martinez lost to J. Capriati 6–4 6–7 1–6; A. Sanchez d. M. J. Fernandez 6–3 6–4; Martinez/Sanchez d. G. Fernandez/Z. Garrison 3–6 6–1 6–1.

* M. Navratilova became a US citizen in 1981.

WIGHTMAN CUP

Women's team contest between USA and Great Britain, each match comprising five singles and two doubles, with reverse singles played between the two top players.

1923 USA d. Great Britain 7–0, Forest Hills: H. Wills d. K. McKane 6–2 7–5, d. Mrs R. Clayton 6–2 6–3; Mrs F. Mallory d. Clayton 6–1 8–6, d. McKane 6–2 6–3; E. Goss d. Mrs W. G. Beamish 6–2 0–6 7–5; Mrs G. W. Wightman/Goss d. McKane/Mrs B. C. Covell 10–8 5–7 6–4; Mallory/Wills d. Beamish/Clayton 6–3 6–2.

1924 Great Britain d. USA 6–1, Wimbledon: Mrs B. C. Covell d. H. Wills 6–2 6–4, d. Mrs F. Mallory 6–2 5–7 6–3; K. McKane d. Mallory 6–3 6–3, d. Wills 6–0 6–2; Mrs W. G. Beamish d. E. Goss 6–1 8–10 6–3; Covell/Mrs D. C. Shepherd-Barron d. Mrs M. Z. Jessup/Goss 6–2 6–2; McKane/E. Colyer lost to Mrs G. W. Wightman/Wills 6–2 2–6 4–6.

1925 Great Britain d. USA 4–3, Forest Hills: K. McKane d. Mrs F. Mallory 6–4 5–7 6–0, lost to H. Wills 1–6 6–1 7–9; J. Fry lost to Wills 0–6 5–7, lost to Mallory 3–0 6–3; Mrs R. Lambert Chambers d. Goss 7–5 3–6 6–1; Lambert Chambers/E. H. Harvey d. Mallory/Mrs T. C. Bundy 10–8 6–1; McKane/E. Colyer d. Wills/M. K. Browne 6–0 6–3.

1926 USA d. Great Britain 4–3, Wimbledon: E. Ryan d. J. Fry 6–1 6–3, lost to Mrs L. A. Godfree 1–6 7–5 4–6; M. K. Browne lost to Godfree 1–6 5–7, lost to Fry 6–3 0–6 4–6; Mrs M. Z. Jessup d. Mrs D. C. Shepherd-Barron 6–1 5–7 6–4; Jessup/E. Goss d. Mrs R. Lambert Chambers/Shepherd-Barron 6–4 6–2; Browne/Ryan d. Godfree/E. L. Colyer 3–6 6–2 6–4.

1927 USA d. Great Britain 5–2, Forest Hills: H. Wills d. J. Fry 6–2 6–0, d. Mrs L. A. Godfree 6–1 6–1; Mrs F. Mallory d. Godfree 6–4 6–2, d. J. Fry 6–2 11–9; H. H. Jacobs lost to B. Nuthall 3–6 6–2 1–6; E. Goss/Mrs A. H. Chapin lost to G. Sterry/Mrs J. Hill 7–5 5–7 5–7; Wills/Mrs G. W. Wightman d. Godfree/E. H. Harvey 6–4 4–6 6–3.

1928 Great Britain d. USA 4–3, Wimbledon: Mrs P. H. Watson lost to H. Wills 1–6 2–6, d. Mrs F. Mallory 2–6 6–1 6–2; E. Bennett d. Mallor 6–1 6–3, lost to Wills 3–6 2–6; B. Nuthall lost to H. H. Jacobs 3–6 1–6; E. H. Harvey/P. Saunders d. E. Goss/Jacobs 6–4 6–1; Bennett/Watson d. Wills/P. Anderson 6–2 6–1.

1929 USA d. Great Britain 4–3, Forest Hills: H. Wills d. Mrs P. H. Watson 6–1 6–4, d. B. Nuthall 8–6 8–6; H. H. Jacobs d. Nuthall 7–5 8–6, lost to Watson 3–6 2–6; E. Goss d. Mrs L. R. C. Michell 6–3 3–6 6–3; Wills/Goss lost to Watson/Michell 4–6 1–6; Mrs G. W. Wightman/Jacobs lost to Mrs B. C. Covell/Mrs D. C. Shepherd-Barron 2–6 1–6.

1930 Great Britain d. USA 4–3, Wimbledon: J. Fry lost to H. Wills 1–6 1–6, lost to H. H. Jacobs 0–6 3–6; Mrs P. H. Watson d. Jacobs 2–6 6–2 6–4, lost to Wills 5–7 1–6; P. Mudford d. S. Palfrey 6–0 6–2; Fry/E. H. Harvey d. Palfrey/L. Cross 2–6 6–2 6–4; Watson/Mrs L. A. Godfree d. Jacobs/Wills 7–5 1–6 6–4.

1931 USA d. Great Britain 5–2, Forest Hills: Mrs F. S. Moody d. P. Mudford 6–1 6–4, d. B. Nuthall 6–4 6–2; H. H. Jacobs d. Nuthall 8–6 6–4, d. Mudford 6–4 6–2; Mrs L. A. Harper d. D. E. Round 6–3 4–6 9–7; S. Palfrey/Mrs G. W. Wightman lost to Mudford/Mrs D. C. Shepherd-Barron 4–6 8–10; Moody/Harper lost to Nuthall/Mrs Fearnley Whittingstall 6–8 7–5 3–6.

1932 USA d. Great Britain 4–3, Wimbledon: H. H. Jacobs d. D. E. Round 6–4 6–3, lost to Mrs Fearnley Whittingstall 4–6 6–2 1–6; Mrs F. S. Moody d. Fearnley Whittingstall 6–2 6–4, d. Round 6–2 6–3; Mrs L. A. Harper lost to Mrs M. R. King 6–3 1–6 1–6; Harper/Jacobs d. Mrs L. R. C. Michell/Round 6–4 6–1; Moody/Palfrey lost to Fearnley Whittingstall/B. Nuthall 3–6 6–1 8–10.

1933 USA d. Great Britain 4–3, Forest Hills: H. H. Jacobs d. D. E. Round 6–4 6–2, d. M. Scriven 5–7 6–2 7–5; S. Palfrey d. Scriven 6–3 6–1, lost to Round 4–6 8–10; C. Babcock lost to B. Nuthall 6–1 1–6 3–6; Jacobs/Palfrey d. Round/M. Heeley 6–4 6–2; A. Marble/Mrs J. Van Ryn lost to Nuthall/F. James 5–7 2–6.

1934 USA d. Great Britain 5–2, Wimbledon: S. Palfrey d. D. E. Round 6–3 5–8 6–6, d. M. Scriven 4–6 6–2 8–6; H. H. poJacobs d. Scriven 6–1 6–1, d. Round 6–4 6–4; C. Babcock lost to B. Nuthall 7–5 3–6 4–6; Babcock/J. Cruickshank lost to N. Lyle/E. M. Dearman 5–7 5–7; Jacobs/Palfrey d. Mrs L. A. Godfree/Nuthall 5–7 6–3 6–2.

1935 *USA d. Great Britain 4–3, Forest Hills:* H. H. Jacobs lost to K. Stammers 7–5 1–6 7–9, d. D. E. Round 6–3 6–2
Mrs E. B. Arnold lost to Round 0–6 3–6, d. Stammers 6–2 1–6 6–3; S. Palfrey d. Mrs M. R. King 6–0 6–3
Jacobs/Palfrey d. Stammers/F. James 6–3 6–2; Mrs D. B. Andrus/C. Babcock lost to N. Lyle/E. M. Dearman 6–
A4–6 1–6.

1936 *USA d. Great Britain 4–3, Wimbledon:* H. H. Jacobs lost to K. Stammers 10–12 1–6, lost to D. E. Round 3–6 3–6
S. Palfrey lost to Round 3–6 4–6, d. Stammers 6–3 6–4; C. Babcock d. M. Hardwick 6–4 4–6 6–2; Babcock/Mrs
Van Ryn d. N. Lyle/E. M. Dearman 6–2 1–6 6–3; Jacobs/Palfrey d. Stammers/F. James 1–6 6–3 7–5.

1937 *USA d. Great Britain 6–1, Forest Hills:* A. Marble d. M. Hardwick 4–6 6–2 6–4, d. K. Stammers 3–6 6–1; H. H
Jacobs d. Stammers 6–1 4–6 6–4, d. Hardwick 2–6 6–4 6–2; S. Palfrey d. M. Lumb 6–3 6–1; Marble/Palfrey d
E.M. Dearman/J. Ingram 6–3 6–2; Mrs J. Van Ryn/D. M. Bundy lost to Stammers/F. James 3–6 8–10.

1938 *USA d. Great Britain 5–2, Wimbledon:* A. Marble lost to K. Stammers 3–5–7 3–6, d. M. Scriven 6–3 3–6 6–0
Mrs F. S. Moody d. Scriven 6–0 7–5, d. Stammers 6–2 3–6 6–3; S. Fabyan d. M. Lumb 5–7 6–2 6–3
Marble/Fabyan d. Lumb/F. James 6–4 6–2; Moody/D. Bundy lost to E. M. Dearman/J. Ingram 2–6 5–7.

1939 *USA d. Great Britain 5–2, Forest Hills:* A. Marble d. M. Hardwick 6–3 6–4, d. K. Stammers 3–6 6–4; H. H
Jacobs lost to Stammers 2–6 6–1 3–6, d. Hardwick 6–2 6–2; S. Fabyan lost to V. Scott 3–6 4–6; M. Arnold/D. M
Bundy d. B. Nuthall/N. Brown 6–3 6–1; Marble/Fabyan d. Stammers/Mrs S. H. Hammersley 7–5 6–2.

1940–45 *Not held.*

1946 *USA d. Great Britain 7–0, Wimbledon:* P. M. Betz d. Mrs J. Bostock 6–2 6–4, d. Mrs M. Menzies 6–4 6–4; M
Osborne d. Bostock 6–1 6–4, d. Menzies 6–3 6–2; L. Brough d. J. Curry 8–6 6–2; Brough/Osborne d. Bostock/Mr
M. Halford 6–2 6–1; Betz/D. Hart d. Mrs B. Passingham/M. Lincoln 6–1 6–3.

1947 *USA d. Great Britain 7–0, Forest Hills:* M. Osborne d. Mrs J. Bostock 6–4 2–6 6–2, d. Mrs M. Menzies 7–5 6–2
L. Brough d. Menzies 6–4 6–2, d. Bostock 6–4 6–2; D. Hart d. Mrs B. Hilton 4–6 6–3 7–5; Hart/Mrs P. C. Todd d. J
Gannon/J. Quertier 6–1 6–2; Brough/Osborne d. Bostock/Hilton 6–1 6–4.

1948 *USA d. Great Britain 6–1, Wimbledon:* Mrs W. du Pont d. Mrs J. Bostock 6–4 8–6, d. Mrs B. Hilton 6–3 6–4; L
Brough d. Hilton 6–1 6–1, d. Bostock 6–2 4–6 7–5; D. Hart d. J. Gannon 6–1 6–4; Brough/du Pont d. Mrs M
Menzies/Hilton 6–2 6–2; Hart/Mrs C. Todd lost to Bostock/Mrs N. W. Blair 3–6 4–6.

1949 *USA d. Great Britain 7–0, Merion Cricket Club, Philadelphia:* D. Hart d. Mrs J. Walker-Smith 6–3 6–1, d. Mrs B
Hilton 6–1 6–3; Mrs W. du Pont d. Hilton 6–1 6–3, d. Walker-Smith 6–4 6–2; B. Baker d. J. Quertier 6–4 7–5
Hart/S. Fry d. Quertier/Mrs N. W. Blair 6–1 6–2; G. Moran/Mrs P. C. Todd d. Hilton/K. Tuckey 6–4 8–6.

1950 *USA d. Great Britain 7–0, Wimbledon:* Mrs W. du Pont d. Mrs B. Hilton 6–3 6–4, d. Mrs J. Walker-Smith 6–1
6–2; L. Brough d. Hilton 2–6 6–2 7–5, d. Walker-Smith 6–0 6–0; D. Hart d. J. Curry 6–2 6–4; Hart/Mrs P. C. Todd d
Walker-Smith/J. Quertier 6–2 6–3; Brough/du Pont d. Hilton/K. Tuckey 6–2 6–0.

1951 *USA d. Great Britain 6–1, Longwood Cricket Club, Boston:* D. Hart d. J. Quertier 6–4 6–4, d. Mrs J
Walker-Smith 6–4 2–6 7–5; S. Fry d. Walker-Smith 6–1 6–4; lost to Quertier 3–6 6–8; M. Connolly d. K. Tuckey 6–
6–3; Mrs P. C. Todd/N. Chaffee d. Mrs J. Mottram/P. Ward 7–5 6–3; S. Fry/D. Hart d. Quertier/Tuckey 3–6 3–

1952 *USA d. Great Britain 7–0, Wimbledon:* D. Hart d. Mrs J. Rinkel-Quertier 6–3 6–3, d. Mrs J. Walker-Smith–5 6–2
M. Connolly d. Walker-Smith 3–6 6–1 7–5, d. Rinkel-Quertier 9–7 6–2; S. Fry d. S. Partridge 6–0 8–6; Fry/Hart d. H
Fletcher/Rinkel-Quertier 8–6 6–4; L. Brough/Connolly d. Mrs J. Mottram/P. Ward 6–0 6–3.

1953 *USA d. Great Britain 7–0, Westchester Club, Rye, NY:* M. Connolly d. A. Mortimer 6–1 6–1, d. H. Fletcher 6–
6–1; Hart d. Fletcher 6–4 7–5, d. Mortimer 6–4 7–5; S. Fry d. Rinkel-Quertier 6–2 6–4; L. Brough/Connolly d
Mortimer/A. Shilcock 6–2 6–3; Fry/Hart d. Fletcher/Rinkel-Quertier 6–2 6–1.

1954 *USA d. Great-Britain 6–0, Wimbledon:* M. Connolly d. H. Fletcher 6–1 6–3, d. A. Shilcock 6–2 6–2; Hart d
Shilcock 6–4 6–1, d. Fletcher 6–1 6–8 6–2; L. Brough d. A. Buxton 8–6 6–2; L. Brough/Mrs W. du Pont d. Buxton/P
Hird 2–6 6–4 7–5; S. Fry/Hart v. Fletcher/Shilcock not played.

1955 *USA d. Great Britain 6–1, Westchester Club, Rye, NY:* D. Hart lost to A. Mortimer 4–6 6–1 5–7, d. S. J. Bloome
7–5 6–3; L. Brough d. Bloomer 6–2 6–4, d. Mortimer 6–0 6–2; Mrs D. Knode d. A. Buxton 6–3 6–3; Brough/Mrs W
du Pont d. Bloomer/P. Ward 6–3 6–3; S. Fry/Hart d. Buxton/Mortimer 3–6 6–2 7–5.

1956 *USA d. Great Britain 5–2, Wimbledon:* L. Brough d. A. Mortimer 3–6 6–4 7–5, d. A. Buxton 3–6 6–3 6–4; S. Fry d
Buxton 6–2 6–8 7–5, lost to Mortimer 4–6 3–6; Mrs D. Knode lost to S. J. Bloomer 4–6 4–6; B. Baker/Knode d
Bloomer/P. Ward 6–1 6–4; Brough/Fry d. Buxton/Mortimer 6–2 6–2.

1957 *USA d. Great Britain 6–1, Sewickley, Pennsylvania:* A. Gibson d. S. J. Bloomer 6–4 4–6 6–2, d. C. Truman 6–4
6–2; Mrs D. Knode d. Truman 6–2 11–9, d. Bloomer 5–7 6–1 6–2; D. R. Hard lost to A. Haydon 3–6 6–3 4–6; A
Gibson/Hard d. Bloomer/S. M. Armstrong 6–3 6–4; L. Brough/W. du Pont d. Haydon/A. Shilcock 6–4 6–1.

1958 *Great Britain d. USA 4–3, Wimbledon:* S. J. Bloomer lost to A. Gibson 3–6 4–6, lost to Mrs D. Knode 4–6 2–6; C
Truman d. Knode 6–4 6–4, d. Gibson 2–6 6–3 6–4; A. Haydon d. M. Arnold 6–3 5–7 6–3; Bloomer/Truman d. K
Fageros/Knode 6–2 6–3; A. Shilcock/P. Ward lost to Gibson/J. Jopps 4–6 6–3 3–6.

1959 *USA d. Great Britain 4–3, Sewickley, Pennsylvania:* Mrs B. Fleits d. A. Mortimer 6–2 6–1, d. C. Truman 6–4
6–4; D. R. Hard lost to Truman 4–6 6–2 3–6, d. Mortimer 6–3 6–8 6–4; S. Moore lost to A. Haydon 1–6 1–6; J
Arth/Hard d. S. J. Bloomer/Truman 9–7 9–7; J. Hopps/Moore lost to Haydon/Mortimer 2–6 4–6.

1960 *Great Britain d. USA 4–3, Wimbledon:* A. Haydon d. K. Hantze 2–6 11–9 6–1, lost to D. R. Hard 7–5 2–6 1–6; C
Truman lost to Hard 6–4 3–6 4–6, d. Hantze 7–5 6–3; A. Mortimer d. J. Hopps 6–8 6–4 6–1; Haydon/Mortimer los
to Hard/Hantze 0–6 0–6; S. J. Bloomer/Truman d. Hopps/Mrs D. Knode 6–4 9–7.

1961 *USA d. Great Britain 6–1, Saddle & Cycle Club, Chicago:* K. Hantze d. C. Truman 7–9 6–1 6–1, d. A. Haydon 6–
6–4; B. J. Moffitt d. Haydon 6–4 6–4, lost to Truman 3–6 6–3; J. Bricka d. A. Mortimer 10–8 4–6 6–3
Hantze/Moffitt d. Truman/D. M. Catt 7–5 6–2; Mrs W. du Pont/M. Varner w.o. Mortimer/Haydon.

1962 *USA d. Great Britain 4–3, Wimbledon:* D. R. Hard d. C. Truman 6–2 6–2, d. A. Haydon 6–3 6–8 6–4; Mrs J. R
Susman lost to Haydon 8–10 5–7, d. Truman 6–4 7–5; N. Richey lost to D. M. Catt 1–6 6–3 5–7; Mrs W. du Pont/M
Varner d. Catt/E. Starkie 6–2 3–6 6–2; Hard/B. J. Moffitt lost to Haydon/Truman 4–6 3–6.

1963 *USA d. Great Britain 6–1, Cleveland Skating Club, Cleveland:* D. R. Hard lost to Mrs P. F. Jones 1–6 6–0 6–8
d. C. Truman 6–3 6–0; B. J. Moffitt d. Truman 6–4 19–17, d. Jones 6–4 4–6 6–3; N. Richey d. D. M. Catt 14–12
6–3; Hard/Moffitt d. Truman/Jones 4–6 7–5 6–2; Richey/Mrs D. Fales d. Catt/E. Starkie 6–4 6–8 6–2.

1964 *USA d. Great Britain 5–2, Wimbledon:* N. Richey d. D. M. Catt 4–6 6–4 7–5, d. Mrs P. F. Jones 7–5 11–9; B. J.

Moffitt d. Jones 4–6 6–2 6–3, d. Catt 6–3 4–6 6–3; C. Caldwell d. E. Starkie 6–4 1–6 6–3; Caldwell/Moffitt lost to Catt/Jones 2–6 6–4 0–6; Richey/Mrs D. Fales lost to A. Mortimer/Starkie 6–2 3–6 4–6.

965 *USA d. Great Britain 5–2, Clarke Stadium, Cleveland:* B. J. Moffitt lost to Mrs P. F. Jones 2–6 4–6, d. C. Starkie 6–3 6–2; N. Richey d. Starkie 6–1 6–0, lost to Jones 4–6 6–8; Mrs C. Graebner d. S. V. Wade 3–6 10–8 6–4; Graebner/Richey d. F. E. Truman/Starkie 6–1 6–0; Moffitt/Mrs J. R. Susman d. Jones/Wade 6–3 8–6.

966 *USA d. Great Britain 4–3, Wimbledon:* N. Richey lost to Mrs P. F. Jones 6–2 4–6 3–6, d. S. V. Wade 2–6 6–2 7–5; Mrs L. W. King d. Wade 6–3 6–3, d. Jones 5–7 6–2 6–3; M. A. Eisel lost to W. Shaw 2–6 3–6; King/J. Albert lost to Jones/Wade 5–7 2–6; Richey/Eisel d. R. Bentley/E. Starkie 6–1 6–2.

967 *USA d. Great Britain 6–1, Clarke Stadium, Cleveland:* Mrs L. W. King d. S. V. Wade 6–3 6–2, d. Mrs P. F. Jones 6–1 6–2; N. Richey d. Jones 6–2 6–2, d. Wade 3–6 8–6 6–2; R. Casals lost to C. Truman 6–3 5–7 1–6; Casals/King d. Jones/Wade 10–8 6–4; M. A. Eisel/Mrs C. Graebner d. W. Shaw/Mrs J. Williams 8–6 12–10.

968 *Great Britain d. USA 4–3, Wimbledon:* Mrs C. Janes lost to N. Richey 1–6 6–8, lost to M. A. Eisel 4–6 3–6; S. V. Wade d. Eisel 6–0 6–1, d. Richey 6–4 2–6 6–3; W. Shaw lost to J. Bartkowicz 5–7 6–3 4–6; Shaw/Wade d. Eisel/Richey 5–7 6–4 6–3; Janes/F. E. Truman d. S. De Fina/K. Harter 6–3 2–6 6–3.

969 *USA d. Great Britain 5–2, Clarke Stadium, Cleveland:* J. M. Heldman d. S. V. Wade 3–6 6–1 8–6, d. W. Shaw 6–3 6–4; N. Richey d. Shaw 6–2, lost to Wade 3–6 6–2 4–6; J. Bartkowicz d. Mrs C. Janes 8–6 6–0; Mrs P. Curtis/V. Ziengenfuss lost to Janes/F. E. Truman 1–6 6–3 4–6; Heldman/Bartkowicz d. Shaw/Wade 6–4 6–2.

970 *USA d. Great Britain 4–3, Wimbledon:* Mrs L. W. King d. S. V. Wade 8–6 6–4, d. Mrs P. F. Jones 6–4 6–2; N. Richey lost to Jones 3–6 3–6, lost to Wade 3–6 2–6; J. M. Heldman d. Mrs G. Williams 6–3 6–2; Mrs P. Curtis/Heldman lost to Jones/Williams 3–6 2–6; King/J. Bartkowicz d. W. Shaw/Wade 7–5 6–8 6–2.

971 *USA d. Great Britain 4–3, Clarke Stadium, Cleveland:* C. Evert d. W. Shaw 6–0 6–4, d. S. V. Wade 6–1 6–1; J. M. Heldman lost to Wade 5–7 5–7; V. Ziegenfuss d. Shaw 4–6 6–3, lost to Mrs G. Williams 5–7 6–3 4–6; K. Pigeon lost to Mrs G. Williams 5–7 6–3 4–6; Mrs P. Curtis/Ziegenfuss d. Mrs C. Janes/F. E. Truman 6–1 6–4; Mrs C. Graebner/Evert lost to Wade/Williams 8–10 6–4 1–6.

972 *USA d. Great Britain 5–2, Wimbledon:* W. Overton lost to Mrs G. Williams 3–6 6–3 3–6, lost to S. V. Wade 6–8 5–7; C. Evert d. Wade 6–4 6–4, d. Williams 6–2 6–3; P. S. A. Hogan d. C. Molesworth 6–8 6–4 6–2; Evert/Hogan d. W. Shaw/F. E. Truman 7–5 6–4; Overton/V. Ziegenfuss d. Wade/Williams 6–3 6–3.

973 *USA d. Great Britain 5–2, Longwood Cricket Club, Boston:* C. Evert d. S. V. Wade 6–4 6–2, d. V. Burton 6–3 6–0; P. S. A. Hogan d. Burton 6–4 6–3, lost to Wade 2–6 2–6; L. Tuero d. G. Coles 7–5 6–2; Evert/M. Redondo lost to Coles/Wade 3–6 4–6; J. Evert/Hogan d. L. Beaven/L. Charles 6–3 4–6 8–6.

974 *Great Britain d. USA 6–1, Deeside Leisure Centre, Queensferry, North Wales (indoors):* S. V. Wade d. J. M. Heldman 5–7 9–7 6–4, d. J. Newberry 6–1 6–3; G. Coles d. Newberry 4–6 6–1 6–3, d. Heldman 6–0 6–4; S. Barker d. J. Evert 4–6 6–4 6–1; Barker/Charles d. Newberry/B. Nagelsen 4–6 6–2 6–1; Coles/Wade lost to Heldman/M. Schallau 5–7 4–6.

975 *Great Britain d. USA 5–2, Public Auditorium, Cleveland (indoors):* S. V. Wade d. M. Schallau 6–2 6–2; lost to C. Evert 3–6 5–7; G. Coles lost to Evert 4–6 1–6, d. Schallau 6–3 7–6; S. Barker d. J. Newberry 6–4 7–5; Mrs P. F. Jones/Wade d. Newberry/J. Anthony 6–2 6–3; Coles/Barker d. Evert/Schallau 7–5 6–4.

976 *USA d. Great Britain 5–2, Crystal Palace, London (indoors):* C. Evert d. S. V. Wade 6–2 3–6 6–2, d. S. Barker 2–6 6–2 6–2; R. Casals lost to Barker 6–1 3–6 2–6, lost to Wade 3–6 7–9 ret'd; T. Holladay d. G. Coles 3–6 6–1 6–4; Casals/Evert d. Barker/Wade 6–0 5–7 6–1; Mrs M. Guerrant/A. Kiyomura d. S. Mappin/L. Charles 6–2 6–2.

977 *USA d. Great Britain 7–0, Oakland, California (indoors):* C. Evert d. S. V. Wade 7–5 7–6, d. S. Barker 6–1 6–2; Mrs L. W. King d. Barker 6–1 6–4, d. Wade 3–6 8–6; R. Casals d. M. Tyler 6–2 3–6 6–4; King/J. Russell d. S. Mappin/L. Charles 6–0 6–1; Casals/Evert d. Barker/Wade 6–2 6–4

978 *Great Britain d. USA 4–3, Albert Hall, London (indoors):* S. Barker lost to C. Evert 2–6 1–6, d. T. Austin 6–3 3–6 6–0; S. V. Wade d. Austin 3–6 7–5 6–3, lost to Evert 0–6 1–6; M. Tyler d. P. H. Shriver 5–7 6–2 6–3; S. Mappin/A. E. Hobbs lost to Mrs L. W. King/Austin 2–6 6–4 2–6; Barker/Wade d. Evert/Shriver 6–0 5–7 6–4.

979 *USA d. Great Britain 7–0, Palm Beach West, Florida:* Mrs J. M. Lloyd d. S. Barker 7–5 6–2, d. S. V. Wade 6–1 6–1; T. Austin d. Wade 6–1 6–3, d. Barker 6–4 6–7 6–2; K. Jordan d. A. E. Hobbs 4–6 7–6 2–6; Austin/A. Kiyomura d. J. M. Durie/D. A. Jevans 6–3 6–1; Lloyd/R. Casals d. Barker/Wade 6–0 6–1.

980 *USA d. Great Britain 5–2, Albert Hall, London (indoors):* Mrs J. M. Lloyd d. S. Barker 6–1 6–2, d. S. V. Wade 7–5 3–6 7–5; A. Jaeger d. Wade 3–6 6–3 6–3, lost to Barker 7–5 3–6 3–6; K. Jordan lost to A. E. Hobbs 6–4 4–6 1–6; Lloyd/R. Casals d. Hobbs/G. Coles 6–3 6–3; A. E. Smith/Jordan d. Barker/Wade 6–4 7–5.

981 *USA d. Great Britain 7–0, International Amphitheatre, Chicago (indoors):* T. Austin d. S. Barker 7–5 6–3, d. S. V. Wade 6–3 6–1; Mrs J. M. Lloyd d. Wade 6–1 6–3, d. Barker 6–3 6–3; A. Jaeger d. A. E. Hobbs 6–0 6–0; Jaeger/P. H. Shriver d. J. M. Durie/Hobbs 6–1 6–3; Lloyd/R. Casals d. G. Coles/Wade 6–3 6–3.

982 *USA d. Great Britain 6–1, Albert Hall, London (indoors):* B. Potter d. S. Barker 6–2 6–3, d. J. M. Durie 5–7 7–6 6–2; Mrs J. M. Lloyd d. Durie 6–2 6–2, d. Barker 6–4 6–3; A. E. Smith d. S. V. Wade 3–6 7–5 6–3; R. Casals/Smith lost to Durie/A. E. Hobbs 3–6 6–2 2–3–6; Potter/S. A. Walsh d. Barker/Wade 2–6 6–4 6–4.

983 *USA d. Great Britain 5–2, Williamsburg, Virginia (indoors):* M. Navratilova d. S. Barker 6–2 6–0, d. J. M. Durie 6–3 6–3; P. H. Shriver d. Durie 6–3 6–2, d. Barker 6–0 6–1; K. Rinaldi d. S. V. Wade 6–3 6–2; C. Reynolds/P. Smith lost to Barker/Wade 5–7 6–3 1–6; Navratilova/Shriver d. Durie/A. Croft 6–2 6–1.

984 *USA d. Great Britain 5–2, Albert Hall, London (indoors):* Mrs J. M. Lloyd d. A. E. Hobbs 6–2 6–2; A. Moulton lost to A. Croft 1–6 7–5 4–6; B. Potter lost to J. M. Durie 3–6 6–7; Lloyd/Moulton d. A. Brown/S. V. Wade 6–2 6–2; Potter d. Hobbs 6–1 6–3; Lloyd d. Durie 7–6 6–1; Potter/S. A. Walsh d. Durie/Hobbs 7–6 4–6 9–7.

985 *USA d. Great Britain 7–0, Williamsburg, Virginia (indoors):* Mrs J. M. Lloyd d. J. M. Durie 6–2 6–3; K. Rinaldi d. A. E. Hobbs 7–5 7–5; P. H. Shriver d. A. Croft 6–0 6–0; B. Nagelsen/A. White d. Croft/S. V. Wade 6–2 6–1; Shriver d. Durie 6–4 6–4; Lloyd d. Croft 6–3 6–0; Lloyd/Shriver d. Durie/Hobbs 6–3 6–7 6–2.

986 *USA d. Great Britain 7–0, Albert Hall, London (indoors):* K. Rinaldi d. S. Gomer 6–3 7–6; S. Rehe d. A. Croft 6–3 6–1; B. Gadusek d. J. M. Durie 6–2 6–4; Gadusek/Rinaldi d. Croft/Gomer 6–3 5–7 6–3; Gadusek d. Hobbs 2–6 6–4 6–4; Rinaldi d. Durie 6–4 6–2; E. Burgin/A. White d. Durie/Hobbs 7–6 6–3.

987 *USA d. Great Britain 5–2, Williamsburg, Virginia (indoors):* Z. Garrison d. A. E. Hobbs 7–5 6–2; L. McNeil d. S.

Gomer 6–2 6–1; P. H. Shriver d. J. M. Durie 6–1 7–5; G. Fernandez/R. White d. Gomer/C. Wood 6–4 6–1; Shriver
Hobbs 6–4 6–3; Garrison lost to Durie 6–7 3–6; Garrison/McNeil lost to Durie/Hobbs 6–0 4–6 5–7.

1988 USA d. Great Britain 7–0, Albert Hall, London (indoors): Z. Garrison d. J. M. Durie 6–2 6–4; P. Fendick d. N
Javer 6–2 6–1; L. McNeil d. S. Gomer 6–7 6–4 6–4; McNeil/B. Nagelsen d. Gomer/J. Salmon 6–3 6–2; Garrison
C. Wood 6–3 6–2; McNeil d. Durie 6–1 6–2; G. Fernandez/Garrison d. Durie/Wood 6–1 6–3.

1989 USA d. Great Britain 7–0, Williamsburg, Virginia: L. McNeil d. J. Durie 7–5 6–1; J. Capriati d. C. Wood 6–0 6–0
M. J. Fernandez d. S. Gomer 6–1 6–2; McNeil d. Gomer 6–4 6–2; Fernandez d. Durie 6–1 7–5; B. Nagelse
Fernandez d. Gomer/Wood 6–2 7–6; P. Fendick/McNeil d. Durie/A. Hobbs 6–3 6–3.

EUROPEAN CUP

Formerly King's Cup

International Men's Team Championship on Indoor Courts. It was staged on a knock-out basis 1936–38
1952–74, on a league basis 1976–83 with ties home and away. From 1984 the ties in each division wer
held concurrently at one venue. The Challenge Round system was used in the two opening years, wit
1937 the only Challenge Round.

FINALS

1936 France d. Sweden 4–1, Stockholm: J. Borotra d. K. Schroder 2–6 6–2 6–1 6–3, d. C. Ostberg 6–1 6–3 7–5; F
Destremau d. Schroder 3–6 7–5 6–2 6–4, d. Ostberg 6–2 6–2 6–4; C. Boussus/J. Brugnon lost to Ostber
Schroder 2–6 6–3 4–6 6–3 4–6.

1937 France d. Sweden 5–0, Paris: B. Destremau d. K. Schroder 8–6 1–6 2–6 11–9 8–6, d. N. Rohlsson 1–6 1–6 6–
6–1 6–0; Y. Petra d. Rohlsson 6–1 6–4 6–2, d. Schroder 6–3 3–6 6–3 6–4; H. Bolelli/J. Lesueur d. Schroder/F
Wallen 10–8 6–4 6–4.

1938 Germany d. Denmark 5–0, Hamburg: R. Menzel d. H. Plougmann 6–3 6–2 8–6; H. Henkel d. I. Gerdes 6–4 6–
6–3, d. Plougmann 6–2 6–1 6–3; R. Redl d. Gerdes 6–3 6–3 6–2; Henkel/Menzel d. Gerdes/Plougmann 6–0 6–
6–2.

1939–51 Not held

1952 Denmark d. Sweden 3–2, Stockholm: K. Nielsen lost to S. Davidson 3–6 7–9 4–6; T. Ulrich d. T. Johansson 7–
0–6 6–4 6–2; Nielsen/Ulrich d. Davidson/Johansson 6–2 2–6 4–6 8–6 7–5; Nielsen d. Johansson 6–3 6–4 6–
Ulrich lost to Davidson 6–4 4–6 1–6 6–1 2–6.

1953 Denmark d. Sweden 3–2, Milan: T. Ulrich d. S. Davidson 14–12 11–9 1–6 11–9; J. Ulrich lost to T
Johansson 0–6 2–6 7–9; J. Ulrich/T. Ulrich d. Davidson/N. Rohlsson 6–4 6–4 4–6 3–6 6–3; J. Ulrich lost t
Davidson 3–6 4–6 0–6; T. Ulrich d. Johansson 6–3 2–6 6–4 5–7 6–3.

1954 Denmark d. Italy 3–2, Milan: T. Ulrich d. G. Merlo 7–5 2–6 9–7 9–7; K. Nielsen lost to O. Sirola 5–7 6–8 8–6 6–
3–6; Nielsen/Ulrich d. N. Pietrangeli/Sirola 2–6 2–6 11–9 6–1 12–10; Nielsen lost to Pietrangeli 5–7 6–3 9–7 3–
5–7; Ulrich d. Sirola 7–5 10–8 6–4.

1955 Sweden d. Denmark 4–1, Copenhagen: S. Davidson d. J. Ulrich 7–5 12–10 6–1; U. Schmidt lost to K. Nielse
3–6 2–6 6–4 4–6; Davidson/T. Johansson d. Nielsen/J. Ulrich 11–9 6–3 14–12; Davidson d. Nielsen 8–10 6–2 7–
12–10 7–5; Schmidt d. J. Ulrich 7–9 3–6 6–0 8–6 6–3.

1956 Sweden d. France 4–1, Paris: S. Davidson d. P. Darmon 7–9 6–2 5–7 6–8; U. Schmidt d. R. Haillet 6–1 /6–
6–4; Davidson/Schmidt d. Darmon/P. Remy 8–6 3–6 6–1 6–4; Davidson d. Haillet 6–2 2–6 6–4 6–1; Schmidt d
Darmon 6–1 10–8 6–3.

1957 Sweden d. Denmark 3–2, Copenhagen: J. E. Lundqvist d. K. Nielsen 4–6 6–3 10–8 6–4; U. Schmidt lost to T
Ulrich 4–6 7–9 2–6; Lundqvist/Schmidt d. J. Ulrich/T. Ulrich 6–3 5–7 6–0 6–3; Lundqvist d. T. Ulrich 7–5 6–1 6–2
Schmidt lost to Nielsen 6–4 4–6 2–6 5–7.

1958 Sweden d. Denmark 3–2, Stockholm: B. Folke lost to J. Ulrich 11–13 3–6 4–6; S. Davidson d. K. Nielsen 6–0 6–
6–4; Davidson/T. Johansson d. Nielsen/J. Ulrich 10–8 1–6 6–3 8–6 6–3; Folke lost to Nielsen 4–6 3–6 3–6
Davidson d. J. Ulrich 6–4 6–3 1–6 6–1.

1959 Denmark won, Stockholm: Denmark d. Italy 2–1, lost to Sweden 2–1, d. France 2–1 (12–11 sets); Sweden los
to France 2–1, d. Denmark 2–1, d. Italy 2–1 (10–10 sets); Italy lost to Denmark 2–1, d. France 2–1, lost to Swede
2–1 (11–11 sets); France d. Sweden 2–1, lost to Italy 2–1, lost to France 2–1 (10–11 sets). Danish team: K. Nielse
and J. Ulrich.

1960 Denmark d. West Germany 3–0, Paris: J. Leschly d. B. Nitsche 6–4 8–6; J. Ulrich d. P. Scholl 6–2 6–3; Leschly/J
Ulrich d. Nitsche/Scholl 6–8 6–2 6–0.

1961 Sweden d. Denmark 2–1, Cologne: U. Schmidt d. J. Leschly 6–4 6–2; J. E. Lundqvist d. J. Ulrich 6–3 6–1
Lundqvist/Schmidt lost to Leschly/J. Ulrich 5–7 6–4 5–7.

1962 Denmark d. Italy 3–0, Copenhagen: J. Leschly d. G. Merlo 6–3 8–6; J. Ulrich d. N. Pietrangeli 6–4 6–2; Leschly/J
Ulrich d. Pietrangeli/O. Sirola 9–7 7–5.

1963 Yugoslavia d. Denmark 3–0, Belgrade: Yugoslav team: B. Jovanovic and N. Pilic.

1964 Great Britain d. Sweden 3–0, Stockholm: M. J. Sangster d. J. E. Lundquist 13–15 10–8 12–10; R. Taylor d. B
Holmstrom 6–3 9–7; Sangster/R. K. Wilson d. Holmstrom/L. Olander 4–6 12–10 6–4.

1965 Great Britain d. Denmark 2–1, Torquay: R. K. Wilson lost to J. Leschly 1–6 4–6; M. Cox d. C. Hedelund 6–4 6–3
A. R. Mills/Wilson d. Leschly/Hedelund 3–6 6–2 6–4 12–10.

1966 Great Britain d. Italy 3–0, Milan: R. Taylor d. N. Pietrangeli 6–4 6–4; M. J. Sangster d. G. Maioli 7–9 6–4 11–9
Sangster/R. K. Wilson d. D. di Maso/Maioli 6–4 6–1.

1967 Great Britain d. Sweden 2–1, Stockholm: R. Taylor d. O. Bengtson 2–6 6–3 9–7; R. K. Wilson d. M. Carlstein 8–
6–2; M. Cox/Taylor lost to Bengtson/B. Homstrom 4–6 7–9.

1968 Sweden d. Netherlands 2–1, Bratislava: O. Bengtson lost to T. S. Okker 12–14 4–6; M. Carlstein d. J. Hordij
6–4 6–3; Bengtson/Carlstein d. N. Fleury/Okker 1–6 4–6 7–5 6–3 6–4.

1969 *Czechoslovakia d. Sweden 2–1, Cologne:* V. Zednik d. H. Zahr 6–4, 7–5; J. Kukal d. O. Bengtson 6–1 5–7 11–9; Kukal/Zednik lost to Bengtson/H. Nerell 4–6 4–6.

1970 *France d. Denmark 2–1, Copenhagen:* J. B. Chanfreau d. J. Ulrich 6–3 0–0; G. Goven lost to J. Leschly 1–6 3–6; Chanfreau/Goven d. Ulrich/Leschly 2–6 6–4 7–5.

1971 *Italy d. Spain 2–1, Ancona:* A. Panatta lost to M. Orantes 2–6 3–6; N. Pietrangeli d. J. Gisbert 7–9 8–6 6–4; Panatta/Pietrangeli d. Gisbert/Orantes 4–6 8–6 6–3 6–4.

1972 *Spain d. Hungary 3–0, Madrid:* A. Gimeno d. S. Baranyi 10–8 6–2; J. Gisbert d. B. Taroczy 6–1 7–9 6–3; J. Herrera/A. Munoz d. R. Machan/Taroczy 6–4 3–6 7–5.

1973 *Sweden d. Italy 2–1, Hanover:* L. Johansson d. A. Zugarelli 6–4 6–3; B. Borg d. A. Panatta 4–6 6–2 8–6; Borg/Johansson lost to P. Bertolucci/Zugarelli 6–3 5–7 4–6.

1974 *Italy d. Sweden 3–0, Ancona:* A. Panatta d. R. Norberg 6–3 6–4; A. Zugarelli d. T. Svensson 6–3 6–4; P. Bertolucci/A. Panatta d. B. Andersson/Norberg 6–2 6–4.

1975 *Not held*

1976 *Hungary 11 wins, Great Britain 10 wins* (played entirely as round robin, each tie home and away). Hungarian team: P. Szoke, B. Taroczy. British team: M. Cox, J. M. Lloyd, C. J. Mottram, R. Taylor.

1977 *Sweden d. West Germany 5–1, Berlin:* R. Norberg d. U. Marten 6–2 4–6 6–4; K. Johansson d. K. Meiler 6–4 6–4; O. Bengtson/Norberg d. P. Elter/Meiler 6–2 6–2. *Linkoping:* Norberg d. U. Pinner 7–6 6–2; Johansson d. Meiler 6–7 6–2 6–3; Bengtson/Norberg lost to Elter/Marten 6–3 4–6 4–6.

1978 *Sweden d. Hungary 3–3 (9–7 sets), Uppsala:* T. Svensson d. P. Szoke 6–2 6–4; O. Bengtson lost to B. Taroczy 6–7 6–7; Bengtson/Svensson lost to Szoke/Taroczy 6–7 4–6; *Debrecen:* Svensson d. Szoke 6–2 6–2; Bengtson d. Taroczy 6–4 7–6; Bengtson/Svensson lost to Szoke/Taroczy 3–6 6–3 3–6.

1979 *Czechoslovakia d. Hungary 4–2, Pecs:* I. Lendl lost to J. Benyik 6–7 7–5 6–7; T. Smid d. B. Taroczy 5–7 6–3 6–4; P. Slozil/T. Smid d. P. Szoke/Taroczy 5–4 6–4; *Chrudin:* Lendl lost to Benyik 6–4 2–6 0–6; Smid d. Szoke 6–3 3–6 6–2; Slozil/Smid d. Benyik/Szoke 6–4 6–2.

1980 *Czechoslovakia d. Hungary 5–1, Chrudin:* T. Smid d. R. Machan 6–4 6–2; I. Lendl d. B. Taroczy 6–2 6–1; Smid/P. Slozil d. P. Szoke/Machan 6–4 7–5; *Debreden:* Smid d. J. Benyik 6–2 3–6 6–2; Lendl d. Machan 6–0 6–2; Smid/Slozil lost to Machan/Szoke 6–3 3–6 2–6.

1981 *West Germany d. USSR 3–3 (9–7 sets), Moscow, 2–1, and Hamburg, 1–2.*

1982 *West Germany d. Czechoslovakia 2–1, Dortmund:* K. Eberhard lost to J. Navratil 4–6 1–6; U. Pinnder d. P. Slozilp 6–4 6–4; C. Zipf/H. D. Beutel d. Navratil/Slozil 6–3 6–4.

1983 *West Germany d. Czechoslovakia 2–1, Uppsala:* H. J. Schwaier lost to L. Pimek 6–4 2–6 3–6; M. Westphal d. J. Navratil 3–6 6–2 6–3; E. Jelen/W. Popp d. Navratil/Piimek 6–1 1–6 7–6.

1984 *Czechoslovakia d. Sweden 2–1, Essen:* M. Mecir d. J. Gunnarsson 7–6 6–4; L. Pimek lost to J. Nystrom 3–6 5–7; Pimek/J. Navratil d. Gunnarsson/Nystrom 3–6 6–2 6–4.

1985 *Sweden d. Switzerland 3–0, Essen:* T. Hogstedt d. R. Stadler 6–3 6–2; J. Gunnarsson d. J. Hlasek 7–5 4–6 6–2; S. Simonsson d. Hlasek/Stadler 6–3 3–6 6–3.

1986 *Switzerland d. Czechoslovakia 2–1, Queen's Club, London:* R. Stadler d. M. Vajda 6–4 7–5; J. Hlasek lost L. Pimek 7–5 3–6 5–7; Hlasek/Stadler d. Pimek/P. Korda 6–2 6–3.

1987 *Switzerland d. Great Britain 2–1, Hanover:* R. Stadler lost to M. J. Bates 6–7 2–6; J. Hlasek d. A. Castle 6–3 6–7 6–2; Hlasek/Stadler d. Bates/Castle 3–6 7–5 6–0.

1988 *Czechoslovakia d. Netherlands 2–0, Zurich:* P. Korda d. M. Oosting 6–3 7–6; doubles not played.

1989 *Czechoslovakia d. West Germany 2–1, Ostrava:* P. Korda lost to C.-U. Steeb 3–6 3–6; M. Srejber d. E. Jelen 7–5 6–3; Srejber/Korda d. P. Kuhnen/Jelen 7–6 7–6.

1990 *Germany d. USSR 2–1, Metz:* U. Riglewski lost to D. Poliakov 7–5 3–6 2–6; M. Stich d. A. Cherkasov 6–3 7–6; Stich/Riglewski d. A. Olhovskiy/V. Gabrichidze 6–3 7–6.

1991 *Czechoslovakia d. Netherlands 2–1, Lengnau:* D. Rikl lost to T. Kempers 6–3 5–7 1–6; M. Damm d. F. Wibier 6–4 6–1; Damm/T. Zdrazila d. Kempers/Wibier 6–3 6–3.

WORLD TEAM CUP

Eight-nation men's team event, qualification by individual ATP rating. Formerly Nations Cup.

FINALS

Played at Kingston, Jamaica

1975 *USA d. Great Britain 2–1:* R. Tanner d. R. Taylor 6–3 2–6 6–4; A. R. Ashe lost to C. J. Mottram 5–7 7–5 1–6; Ashe/Tanner d. Mottram/Taylor 6–1 1–6 6–4.

1976–77 *Not held*

Played at Dusseldorf

1978 *Spain d. Australia 2–1:* J. Higueras d. J. D. Newcombe 6–2 6–3; M. Orantes d. P. Dent 6–3 6–4; Higueras/Orantes lost to Dent/Newcombe 6–7 4–6.

1979 *Australia d. Italy 2–1:* J. G. Alexander d. C. Barazzutti 6–2 6–0; P. Dent lost to A. Panatta 3–6 3–6; Alexander/Dent d. P. Bertolucci/Panatta 6–3 7–6.

1980 *Argentina d. Italy 3–0:* G. Vilas d. C. Barazzutti 6–3 6–2; J. L. Clerc d. A. Panatta 7–6 6–3; Clerc/Vilas d. P. A. Bertolucci/Panatta 6–2 6–3.

1981 *Czechoslovakia d. Australia 2–1:* I. Lendl lost to P. McNamara 3–6 4–6; T. Smid d. P. McNamee 6–4 7–6; Lendl/Smid d. McNamara/McNamee 6–4 6–3.

1982 *USA d. Australia 2–1:* G. Mayer d. K. Warwick 7–6 6–2; E. Teltscher d. P. McNamara 6–4 7–6; Mayer/S. E. Stewart lost to M. R. Edmondson/McNamara 1–6 1–6.

1983 *Spain d. Australia 2–1:* J. Higueras d. M. R. Edmondson 6–2 6–4; M. Orantes d. P. Cash 6–3 6–2; A. Gimenez/Higueras lost to Cash/Edmondson 5–7 6–4 1–6.

1984 *USA d. Czechoslovakia 2–1:* J. P. McEnroe d. I. Lendl 6–3 6–2; J. Arias lost to T. Smid 6–4 6–7 4–6; F
Fleming/McEnroe d. Lendl/Smid 6–1 6–2.
1985 *USA d. Czechoslovakia 2–1:* J. P. McEnroe lost to I. Lendl 7–6 6–7 3–6; J. S. Connors d. M. Mecir 6–3 3–6 7–5; K
Flach/R. Seguso d. Lendl/T. Smid 6–3 7–6
1986 *France d. Sweden 2–1:* H. Leconte d. A. Jarryd 6–3 3–6 6–1; T. Tulasne lost to M. Wilander 1–6 4–6; G
Forget/Leconte d. Jarryd/Wilander 6–3 2–6 6–2.
1987 *Czechoslovakia d. USA 2–1:* M. Mecir d. J. P. McEnroe 7–5 2–6 2–1 disqual.; M. Srejber lost to B. Gilbert 4–6 7–5
4–6; Mecir/T. Smid d. Gilbert/R. Seguso 6–3 6–1.
1988 *Sweden d. USA 2–1:* S. Edberg d. T. Mayotte 6–4 6–2; K. Carlsson d. A. Krickstein 6–4 6–3; Edberg/A. Jarryd lost
to K. Flach/R. Seguso 7–6 3–6 6–7.
1989 *West Germany d. Argentina 2–1:* B. Becker d. G. Perez Roldan 6–0 2–6 6–2; C.-U. Steeb lost to M. Jaite 4–6 3–6
Becker/E. Jelen d. J. Frana/G. Luna 6–4 7–5.
1990 *Yugoslavia d. USA 2–1:* G. Prpic d. B. Gilbert 6–4 6–4; G. Ivanisevic d. J. Courier 3–6 7–5 6–1; Prpic/S. Zivojinovic
lost to K. Flach/R. Seguso 5–7 6–7.
1991 *Sweden d. Yugoslavia 2–1:* M. Gustafsson d. G. Prpic 6–2 3–6 6–4; S. Edberg d G. Ivanisevic 6–4 7–5;
Edberg/Gustafsson lost to Prpic/S. Zivojinovic 6–3 3–6 4–6.

GRAND SLAM CUP

A knockout competition held in Munich in December, for the 16 men who have amassed the most points in the four
Grand Slam Championships of Australia, France, Great Britain and the USA. The competition administered by the Grand
Slam Committee (the four Chairmen) and an Administrator, is promoted by an independent German company and offer
prize money of $6 million. A further $2 million goes annually to the Grand Slam Development Fund, administered by the
ITF.

	WINNER	RUNNER-UP	SCORE			FIRST PRIZE
1990	P. Sampras	B. Gilbert	6–3	6–4	6–2	$2,000,000
1991	D. Wheaton	M. Chang	7–5	6–2	6–4	$2,000,000

MEN'S GRAND PRIX WINNERS

	SINGLES	BONUS	DOUBLES	BONUS	SPONSOR
1970	C. Richey	$25,000			Pepsi-Cola
1971	S. R. Smith	$25,000			Pepsi-Cola
1972	I. Nastase	$50,000			Commercial Union
1973	I. Nastase	$55,000			Commercial Union
1974	G. Vilas	$100,000			Commercial Union
1975	G. Vilas	$100,000	J. Gisbert	$25,000	Commercial Union
1976	R. Ramirez	$150,000	R. Ramirez	$40,000	Commercial Union
1977	G. Vilas	$300,000	R. A. J. Hewitt	$85,000	Colgate
1978	J. S. Connors	*$300,000	W. Fibak	$90,000	Colgate
1979	J. P. McEnroe	$300,000	S. E. Stewart	$90,000	Colgate
1980	J. P. McEnroe	$300,000	S. R. Smith	$90,000	Volvo
1981	I. Lendl	$300,000	H. Gunthardt	$90,000	Volvo
1982	J. S. Connors	$600,000	S. E. Stewart	$150,000	Volvo
1983	M. Wilander	$600,000	P. Fleming	$150,000	Volvo
1984	J. P. McEnroe	$600,000	T. Smid	$150,000	Volvo
1985	I. Lendl	$800,000	R. Seguso	$165,000	Nabisco
1986	I. Lendl	$800,000	G. Forget	$165,000	Nabisco
1987	I. Lendl	$800,000	A. Jarryd	$165,000	Nabisco
1988	M. Wilander	$800,000	R. Leach	$165,000	Nabisco
1989	I. Lendl	$800,000	R. Leach	$165,000	Nabisco

* *Neither Connors nor second-placed B. Borg had played enough tournaments to qualify for the bonus payment, which*
was awarded to third-placed E. Dibbs.

MEN'S GRAND PRIX MASTERS WINNERS

SINGLES

	VENUE	WINNER	RUNNER-UP	SCORE	FIRST PRIZE
1970	Tokyo	S. R. Smith	R. G. Laver	Round-Robin	$10,000
1971	Paris	I. Nastase	S. R. Smith	Round-Robin	$15,000
1972	Barcelona	I. Nastase	S. R. Smith	6–3 6–2 3–6 2–6 6–3	$15,000
1973	Boston	I. Nastase	T. S. Okker	6–3 7–5 4–6 6–3	$15,000
1974	Melbourne	G. Vilas	I. Nastase	7–6 6–2 3–6 3–6 6–4	$40,000
1975	Stockholm	I. Nastase	B. Borg	6–2 6–2 6–1	$40,000

1976 Houston	M. Orantes	W. Fibak	5–7 6–2 0–6 7–6 6–1					$40,000
1977* New York	J. S. Connors	B. Borg	6–4 1–6 6–4					$100,000
1978* New York	J. P. McEnroe	A. R. Ashe	6–7 6–3 7–5					$100,000
1979* New York	B. Borg	V. Gerulaitis	6–2 6–2					$100,000
1980* New York	B. Borg	I. Lendl	6–4 6–2 6–2					$100,000
1981* New York	I. Lendl	V. Gerulaitis	6–7 2–6 7–6 6–2 6–4					$100,000
1982* New York	I. Lendl	J. P. McEnroe	6–4 6–4 6–2					$100,000
1983* New York	J. P. McEnroe	I. Lendl	6–3 6–4 6–4					$100,000
1984* New York	J. P. McEnroe	I. Lendl	7–5 6–0 6–4					$100,000
1985* New York	I. Lendl	B. Becker	6–2 7–6 6–3					$100,000
1986 New York	I. Lendl	B. Becker	6–4 6–4 6–4					$200,000
1987 New York	I. Lendl	M. Wilander	6–2 6–2 6–3 ■					$200,000
1988 New York	B. Becker	I. Lendl	5–7 7–6 3–6 6–2 7–6					$150,000
1989 New York	S. Edberg	B. Becker	4–6 7–6 6–3 6–1					$285,000

DOUBLES

	WINNERS	RUNNERS-UP	SCORE				
1970	S. R. Smith/A. R. Ashe	R. G. Laver/J. Kodes	Round-Robin				
1971--74	*Not held*						
1975	J. Gisbert/M. Orantes	J. Fassbender/H. J. Pohmann	Round-Robin				
1976	F. McNair/S. E. Stewart	B. E. Gottfried/R. Ramirez	6–3	5–7	5–7	6–4	6–4
1977*	R. A. J. Hewitt/F. D. McMillan	R. C. Lutz/S. R. Smith	7–5	7–6	6–3		
1978*	P. Fleming/J. P. McEnroe	W. Fibak/T. S. Okker	6–4	6–2	6–4		
1979*	P. Fleming/J. P. McEnroe	W. Fibak/T. S. Okker	6–3	7–6	6–1		
1980*	P. Fleming/J. P. McEnroe	P. McNamara/P. McNamee	6–4	6–3			
1981*	P. Fleming/J. P. McEnroe	K. Curren/S. Denton	6–3	6–3			
1982*	P. Fleming/J. P. McEnroe	S. E. Stewart/F. Taygan	6–2	6–2			
1983*	P. Fleming/J. P. McEnroe	P. Slozil/T. Smid	6–2	6–2			
1984*	P. Fleming/J. P. McEnroe	M. R. Edmondson/S. E. Stewart	6–3	6–1			
1985†	A. Jarryd/S. Edberg	J. Nystrom/M. Wilander	6–1	7–6			
1986†	A. Jarryd/S. Edberg	G. Forget/Y. Noah	6–3	7–6	6–3		
1987†	M. Mecir/T. Smid	K. Flach/R. Seguso	6–4	7–5	7–6	6–3	
1988†	R. Leach/J. Pugh	S. Casal/E. Sanchez	6–4	6–3	2–6	6–0	
1989†	P. McEnroe/J. Grabb	A. Jarryd/J. Fitzgerald	7–5	7–6	5–7	6–3	

■ *Played in January of the following year.*   † *Played separately from the singles at the Royal Albert Hall, London.*

ATP TOUR CHAMPIONSHIP

SINGLES

	VENUE	WINNER	RUNNER-UP	SCORE	FIRST PRIZE
1990	Frankfurt	A. Agassi	S. Edberg	5–7 7–6 7–5 6–2	$950,000
1991	Frankfurt	P. Sampras	J. Courier	3–6 7–6 6–3 6–4	$1,020,000

DOUBLES

	VENUE	WINNERS	RUNNERS-UP		FIRST PRIZE
1990	Sanctuary Cove, Australia	G. Forget/J. Hlasek	S. Casal/E. Sanchez	6–4 7–6 5–7 6–4	$225,000
1991	Johannesburg	J. Fitzgerald/ A. Jarryd	K. Flach/R. Seguso	6–4 6–4 2–6 6–4	$325,000

WOMEN'S WORLD SERIES

	WINNER	BONUS	DOUBLES WINNERS	SPONSOR
1971	Mrs L. W. King	$10,000		Pepsi-Cola
1972	Mrs L. W. King	$20,000		Commerical Union
1973	Miss C. M. Evert	$23,000		Commercial Union
1974–76	*Not held*			
1977	Miss C. M. Evert	$100,000	Miss M. Navratilova/Miss B. Stove	Colgate
1978	Miss C. M. Evert	$100,000	Mrs G. E. Reid/Miss W. M. Turnbull	Colgate
1979	Mrs J. M. Lloyd	$115,000	Miss B. Stove/Miss W. M. Turnbull	Colgate
1980	Miss H. Mandlikova	$115,000	Miss K. Jordan/Miss A. E. Smith	Colgate
1981	Miss M. Navratilova	$125,000	Miss R. Casals/Miss W. M. Turnbull	Toyota
1982	Miss M. Navratilova	$130,000	Miss R. Casals/Miss W. M. Turnbull	Toyota

1983	Miss M. Navratilova	$150,000	Miss M. Navratilova/Miss P. H. Shriver	Virginia Slims
1984	Miss M. Navratilova	$150,000	Miss M. Navratilova/Miss P. H. Shriver	Virginia Slims
1985	Miss M. Navratilova	$150,000	Miss M. Navratilova/Miss P. H. Shriver	Virginia Slims
1986	Miss M. Navratilova	$200,000	Miss M. Navratilova/Miss P. H. Shriver	Virginia Slims
1987	Miss S. Graf	$225,000	Miss M. Navratilova/Miss P. H. Shriver	Virginia Slims
1988	Miss S. Graf	$400,000	Miss M. Navratilova/Miss P. H. Shriver	Virginia Slims
1989	Miss S. Graf	$400,000	Miss J. Novotna/Miss H. Sukova	Virginia Slims
1990	Miss S. Graf	$500,000	Miss J. Novotna/Miss H. Sukova	Kraft General Foods
1991	Miss M. Seles	$500,000	Miss M. Navratilova/Miss P. H. Shriver	Kraft General Foods

WOMEN'S INTERNATIONAL SERIES CHAMPIONSHIPS

SINGLES

	VENUE	WINNER	RUNNER-UP	SCORE			FIRST PRIZE
1977	Palm Springs	Miss C. M. Evert	Mrs L. W. King	6–2	6–2		$75,000
1978	Palm Springs	Miss C. M. Evert	Miss M. Navratilova	6–3	6–3		$75,000
1979*	Landover, Maryland	Miss M. Navratilova	Miss T. A. Austin	6–2	6–1		$75,000
1980*	Palm Springs	Miss T. A. Austin	Miss A. Jaeger	6–2	6–2		$75,000
1981	East Rutherford, NJ	Miss T. A. Austin	Miss M. Navratilova	2–6	6–4	6–2	$75,000
1982	East Rutherford, NJ	Miss M. Navratilova	Mrs J. M. Lloyd	4–6	6–1	6–2	$75,000
1983*	Madison Square Garden, NY	Miss M. Navratilova	Mrs J. M. Lloyd	6–3	7–5	6–1**	$125,000
1984*	Madison Square Garden, NY	Miss M. Navratilova	Miss H. Sukova	6–3	7–5	6–4**	$125,000
1985*	Madison Square Garden, NY	Miss M. Navratilova	Miss H. Mandlikova	6–2 6–1**	6–0	3–6	$125,000
1986	Madison Square Garden, NY	Miss M. Navratilova	Miss S. Graf	7–6	6–3	6–2**	$125,000
1987	Madison Square Garden, NY	Miss S. Graf	Miss G. Sabatini	4–6 6–4**	6–4	6–0	$125,000
1988	Madison Square Garden, NY	Miss G. Sabatini	Miss P. H. Shriver	7–5	6–2	6–2**	$125,000
1989	Madison Square Garden, NY	Miss S. Graf	Miss M. Navratilova	6–4 6–2**	7–5	2–6	$125,000
1990	Madison Square Garden, NY	Miss M. Seles	Miss G. Sabatini	6–4 6–4	5–7	3–6 6–2	$250,000
1991	Madison Square Garden, NY	Miss M. Seles	Miss M. Navratilova	6–4 6–0**	3–6	7–5	$250,000

*Played in the following year.   **Best of five sets.

DOUBLES

	WINNERS	RUNNERS-UP	SCORE		
1977	Miss F. Durr/Miss S. V. Wade	Mrs H. Gourlay Cawley/Miss J. Russell	6–1	4–6	6–4
1978	Mrs L. W. King/Miss M. Navratilova	Mrs G. E. Reid/Miss W. M. Turnbull	6–3	6–4	
1979*	Mrs L. W. King/Miss M. Navratilova	Miss R. Casals/Mrs J. M. Lloyd	6–4	6–3	
1980*	Miss R. Casals/Miss W. M. Turnbull	Miss C. Reynolds/Miss P. Smith	6–3	4–6	7–6
1991	Miss M. Navratilova/Miss P. H. Shriver	Miss R. Casals/Miss W. M. Turnbull	6–3	6–4	
1982	Miss M. Navratilova/Miss P. H. Shriver	Miss C. Reynolds/Miss P. Smith	6–4	7–5	
1983*	Miss M. Navratilova/Miss P. H. Shriver	Miss J. M. Durie/Miss A. Kiyomura	6–3	6–1	
1984*	Miss M. Navratilova/Miss P. H. Shriver	Miss C. Kohde-Kilsch/Miss H. Sukova	6–7	6–4	7–6
1985*	Miss H. Mandlikova/Miss W. M. Turnbull	Miss C. Kohde-Kilsch/Miss H. Sukova	6–4	6–7	6–3
1986	Miss M. Navratilova/Miss P. H. Shriver	Miss C. Kohde-Kilsch/Miss H. Sukova	7–6	6–3	
1987	Miss M. Navratilova/Miss P. H. Shriver	Miss C. Kohde-Kilsch/Miss H. Sukova	6–1	6–1	
1988	Miss M. Navratilova/Miss P. H. Shriver	Miss L. Savchenko/Miss N. Zvereva	6–3	6–4	
1989	Miss M. Navratilova/Miss P. H. Shriver	Miss L. Savchenko/Miss N. Zvereva	6–3	6–2	
1990	Miss K. Jordan/Mrs E. Smylie	Miss M. Paz/Miss A. Sanchez-Vicario	7–6	6–4	
1991	Miss M. Navratilova/Miss P. H. Shriver	Miss G. Fernandez/Miss J. Novotna	4–6	7–5	6–4

* Played in the following year.

WORLD CHAMPIONSHIP TENNIS
WCT FINALS, DALLAS

	WINNER	RUNNER-UP	SCORE				PRIZE
1971	K. R. Rosewall	R. G. Laver	6–4 1–6 7–6 7–6				$50,000
1972	K. R. Rosewall	R. G. Laver	4–6 6–0 6–3 6–7 7–6				50,000
1973	S. R. Smith	A. R. Ashe	6–3 6–3 4–6 6–4				50,000
1974	J. D. Newcombe	B. Borg	4–6 6–3 6–3 6–2				50,000
1975	A. R. Ashe	B. Borg	3–6 6–4 6–4 6–0				50,000
1976	B. Borg	G. Vilas	1–6 6–1 7–5 6–1				50,000
1977	J. S. Connors	R. D. Stockton	6–7 6–1 6–4 6–3				100,000
1978	V. Gerulaitis	E. Dibbs	6–3 6–2 6–1				100,000
1979	J. P. McEnroe	B. Borg	7–5 4–6 6–2 7–6				100,000
1980	J. S. Connors	J. P. McEnroe	2–6 7–6 6–1 6–2				100,000
1981	J. P. McEnroe	J. Kriek	7–6 6–3 4–6 0–6 6–4				100,000
1982	I. Lendl	J. P. McEnroe	6–2 3–6 6–3 6–3				150,000
1983	J. P. McEnroe	I. Lendl	6–2 4–6 6–3 6–7 7–6				150,000
1984	J. P. McEnroe	J. S. Connors	6–1 6–2 6–3				200,000
1985	I. Lendl	T. Mayotte	7–6 6–4 6–1				200,000
1986	A. Jarryd	B. Becker	6–7 6–1 6–1 6–4				200,000
1987	M. Mecir	J. P. McEnroe	6–0 3–6 6–2 6–2				200,000
1988	B. Becker	S. Edberg	6–4 1–6 7–5 6–2				200,000
1989	J. P. McEnroe	B. Gilbert	6–3 6–3 7–6				200,000

WORLD DOUBLES CHAMPIONSHIPS

	VENUE	WINNERS	RUNNERS-UP	SCORE				PRIZE
1973	Montreal	R. C. Lutz/S. R. Smith	T. S. Okker/M. C. Riessen	6–2 7–6 6–0				$40,000
1974	Montreal	R. A. J. Hewitt/F. D. McMillan	J. D. Newcombe/O. K. Davidson	6–2 6–7 6–1 6–2				40,000
1975	Mexico City	B. R. Gottfried/R. Ramirez	M. Cox/C. Drysdale	7–6 6–7 7–6 7–6				40,000
1976	Kansas City	W. Fibak/K. Meiler	R. C. Lutz/S. R. Smith	6–3 2–6 3–6 6–3 6–4				40,000
1977	Kansas City	V. Amritraj/R. D. Stockton	V. Gerulaitis/A. Panatta	7–6 7–6 4–6 6–3				80,000
1978	Kansas City	W. Fibak/T. S. Okker	R. C. Lutz/S. R. Smith	6–7 6–4 6–0 6–3				80,000
1979	Olympia, London	J. P. McEnroe/P. Fleming	I. Nastase/S. E. Stewart	3–6 6–2 6–3 6–1				80,000
1980	Olympia, London	B. E. Gottfried/R. Ramirez	W. Fibak/T. S. Okker	3–6 6–4 6–4 3–6 6–3				80,000
1981	Olympia, London	P. McNamara/P. McNamee	V. Amaya/H. Pfister	6–3 2–6 3–6 6–3 6–2				80.000
1982	Birmingham	H. Gunthardt/B. Taroczy	K. Curren/S. Denton	6–7 6–3 7–5 6–4				80,000
1983	Royal Albert Hall, London	H. Gunthardt/B. Taroczy	B. E. Gottfried/R. Ramirez	6–3 7–5 7–6				80,000
1984	Royal Albert Hall, London	P. Slozil/T. Smid	A. Jarryd/H. Simonsson	1–6 6–3 3–6 6–4 6–3				80,000
1985	Royal Albert Hall, London	K. Flach/R. Seguso	H. Gunthardt/B. Taroczy	6–3 3–6 6–3 4–6 6–0				80,000

From 1986 this event was incorporated into the Masters Doubles.

GRAND SLAMS
The Grand Slam denotes holding the four championship titles of Australia, France, Wimbledon and the United States in the same year (shown in bold below). The list also includes consecutive wins, not in the same year.

MEN'S SINGLES

J. D. Budge: Wimbledon, US 1937, **Australia, France, Wimbledon, US 1938**
R. G. Laver: **Australia, France, Wimbledon, US 1962**
R. G. Laver: **Australia, France, Wimbledon, US 1969**

WOMEN'S SINGLES

Miss M. Connolly: Wimbledon, US 1952, **Australia, France, Wimbledon, US 1953**
Mrs B. M. Court: US 1969, **Australia, France, Wimbledon, US 1970,** Australia 1971
Miss M. Navratilova: Wimbledon, US, Australia 1983, France, Wimbledon, US 1984
Miss S. Graf: **Australia, France, Wimbledon, US 1988**

MEN'S DOUBLES

F. A. Sedgman: (With J. E. Bromwich) US 1950, **(with K. McGregor) Australia, France, Wimbledon, US 1951,** Australia, France, Wimbledon 1952
K. McGregor: **(With F. A. Sedgman) Australia, France, Wimbledon, US 1951**, Australia, France, Wimbledon 1952

WOMEN'S DOUBLES

Miss A. L. Brough: (with Mrs W. du Pont) France, Wimbledon, US 1949, (with Miss D. J. Hart) Australia 1950
Miss M. E. Bueno: **(With Miss C. C. Truman) Australia 1960, (with Miss D. R. Hard)** France, Wimbledon, US 1960
Miss M. Navratilova/Miss P. H. Shriver: Wimbledon, US, Australia 1983, **France, Wimbledon, US, Australia 1984,** France 1985; *Wimbledon, US 1986, Australia, France 1987
* Miss Navratilova also won France 1986 with Miss A. Temesvari.

MIXED DOUBLES

Miss M. Smith: (With F. S. Stolle) US 1962, **(with K. N. Fletcher) Australia, France, Wimbledon, US 1963**, Australia, France 1964
K. N. Fletcher: **(With Miss M. Smith) Australia, France, Wimbledon, US 1963**, Australia, France 1964
O. K. Davidson: (With Mrs D. Fales) US 1966, **(with Miss L. R. Turner) Australia 1967, (with Mrs L. W. King) France, Wimbledon, US 1967**
Mrs L. W. King: (With O. K. Davidson) France, Wimbledon, US 1967, (with R. D. Crealy) Australia 1968

JUNIOR SINGLES

E. H. Buchholz: **Australia, France, Wimbledon, US 1958** (*Note:* the US event was not then conducted as an international event)
S. Edberg: **France, Wimbledon, US, Australia 1983**

ITF VETERAN CHAMPIONSHIPS

MEN

	VENUE	35+ SINGLES	35+ DOUBLES	45+ SINGLES	45+ DOUBLES
1981	Sao Paulo			S. Davidson	S. Davidson/H. Stewart
1982	Poertschach			I. Gulyas	J. Morton/J. Nelson
1983	Bahia			I. Gulyas	K. Fuhrmann/F. Seeman
1984	Cervia			I. Gulyas	K. Fuhrmann/F. Seeman
1985	Melbourne			I. Barclay	A. Duestler/J. Nelson
1986	Poertschach			J. Lemann	J. Lemann/I. Ribeiro
1987	Garmisch-Partenkirchen			G. Rohrich	H. Gradischnig P. Pokorny
1988	Huntington Beach, Cal.	A. Gardiner	L. Levai/R. Machan	K. Diepraam	F./G. Krauss
1989	Vina Del Mar, Chile	A. Fillol	R. Machan/L. Levai	H. Elschenbroich	B. Nitsche/G. Krauss
1990	Umag, Yugoslavia	R. Machan	R. Machan/L. Levai	H. Elschenbroich	D. Johnson/J. Parker
1991	Perth	P. Torre	Y. Tarik/A. Wijono	D. McCormick	B. Burns/J. Weaver

	VENUE	55+ SINGLES	55+ DOUBLES	60+ SINGLES	60+ DOUBLES
1981	Sao Paulo	S. Clark	S. Clark/T. Johansson		
1982	Poertschach	R. McCarthy	A. Hussmuller/L. Legenstein	T. Johansson	T. Johansson/A. Ritzenberg
1983	Bahia	R. McCarthy	A. Hussmuller/L. Legenstein	—	—
1984	Cervia	G. Merlo	J. Morton/H. Stewart	—	—
1985	Melbourne	H. Stewart	J. Morton/H. Stewart	R. Sorlein	T. Johansson/V. Zabrodsky
1986	Poertschach	L. Maine	R. Howe/R. Seymour	M. McCarthy	O. Jirkovsky/J. Karlhofer
1987	Garmisch Partenkirchen	I. Gulyas	I. Gulyas/H. Stewart	R. Howe	L. Legenstein/A. Stolpa
1988	Huntington Beach, Cal.	I. Gulyas	S. Davidson/H. Stewart	R. McCarthy	R. Howe/R. McCarthy
1989	Vina Del Mar, Chile	I. Gulyas	C. DeVoe/J. Powless	R. McCarthy	R. Howe/R. McCarthy
1990	Umag, Yugoslavia	I. Gulyas	K. Sinclair/L. Main	S. Davidson	H. Stewart/S. Davidson
1991	Perth	P. Froelich	G. Davis/H. Ahlers	L. Main	F. Sedgman/C. Wilderspin

	VENUE	65+ SINGLES	65+ DOUBLES	70+ SINGLES	70+ DOUBLES
1982	Poertschach	F. Klein	J. Becker/F. Klein	—	—
1983	Bahia	R. San Martin	F. Barboza/H. Pizani	—	—
1984	Cervia	G. Mulloy	G. Mulloy/F. Klein	—	—
1985	Melbourne	J. Gilchrist	R. Ritzenberg/F. Klein	—	—
1986	Poertschach	T. Johansson	G. Mulloy/V. Hughes	—	—
1987	Garmisch-Partenkirchen	A. Swetka	B. Kempa/W. Kessler	—	—
1988	Huntington Beach, Cal.	T. Brown	L. Hammel/B. Sherman	F. Klein	G. Hippenstiel/G. Young
1989	Vina Del Mar, Chile	A. Vieira	A. Vieira/S. Verrati	A. Ritzenberg	A. Ritzenberg/F.Klein
1990	Umag, Yugoslavia	B. McCarthy	O. Jirkovsky/J. Karlhofer	W. Parsons	A. Swetka/A. Ritzenberg
1991	Perth	B. McCarthy	B. McCarthy/B. Howe	B. Sherman	V. Hughes/M. Miller

WOMEN

	VENUE	40+ SINGLES	40+ DOUBLES	50+ SINGLES	50+ DOUBLES
1981	Sao Paulo	E. de Molina	N. Reed/M. S. Plante	A. Cury	—
1982	Poertschach	R. Drisaldi	*C. Hillebrand/N. Reed	E. Slytermann	E. Slytermann/I. Burmester
1983	Bahia	H. Masthoff	H. Masthoff/H. Orth	I. de Pla	G. Barboza/J. Borzone
1984	Cervia	H. Masthoff	H. Masthoff/H. Orth	C. Mazzoleni	H. Brabanec/P. Wearne
1985	Melbourne	H. Orth	J. Dalton/H. Orth	I. Michael	A. Fotheringham/A. Pilkinghome
1986	Poertschach ·	H. Masthoff	H. Masthoff/H. Orth	S. Brasher	S. Brasher/L. Cawthorne
1987	Garmisch-Partenkirchen	M. Pinterova	G. Lovera/M. Pinterova	S. Brasher	S. Brasher/L. Cawthorne
1988	Huntington Beach, Cal.	M. Pinterova	G. Lovera/R. Darmon	D. Matthiessen	J. Crofford/D. Matthiessen
1989	Vina Del Mar, Chile	M. Pinterova	M. Pinterova/H. Orth	I. Michael	N. Reed/B. Allendorf
1990	Umag, Yugoslavia	M. Pinterova	B. Mueller/L. Cash	M. Schultze	K. Schiavinato/J. Blackshaw
1991	Perth	C. Baily	C. Baily/B. Mueller	C. Hillebrand	J. Blackshaw/B. Whitelaw

* held as 45+ event.

	VENUE	60+ SINGLES	60+ DOUBLES
1988	Huntington Beach, Cal.	V. Glass	D. Cheney/C. Murdock
1989	Vina Del Mar, Chile	B. Pratt	D. Cheney/C. Murdock
1990	Umag, Yugoslavia	L. Owen	L. Stock/D. Young
1991	Perth	B. Pratt	R. Illingworth/A. Williams

DUBLER CUP
International Men's Team Championship for 45 year age group

FINALS

	VENUE*	WINNERS	RUNNERS-UP	SCORE
1958	Monte Carlo	Italy	West Germany	3–1
1959	Zurich	Switzerland	Italy	4–1
1960	Merano, Italy	Italy	Switzerland	5–0
1961	Bologna	Italy	Austria	4–1
1962	Merano, Italy	Italy	France	3–2
1963	Merano, Italy	Italy	Belgium	4–1
1964	Merano, Italy	Italy	West Germany	5–0
1965	Merano, Italy	Italy	Sweden	3–0
1966	Florence	Sweden	Italy	4–1
1967	Avesta, Sweden	France	Sweden	3–2
1968	Paris	USA	France	5–0
1969	St Louis	USA	Sweden	4–1
1970	Cleveland	USA	Sweden	4–1
1971	La Costa, California	USA	Sweden	3–2
1972	Le Touquet	USA	France	4–1

1973	New York	Australia	USA	3–1
1974	New York	USA	Australia	3–2
1975	New York	Australia	USA	5–0
1976	Alassio, Italy	Italy	Canada	3–2
1977	New York	USA	France	4–1
1978	New York	USA	Australia	4–1
1979	Vienna	Austria	USA	3–2
1980	Cervia, Italy	Sweden	Austria	2–1
1981	Buenos Aires	USA	Great Britain	2–1
1982	Athens	USA	Great Britain	2–1
1983	New York	USA	West Germany	2–1
1984	Bastad	West Germany	USA	3–0
1985	Perth	West Germany	Australia	2–1
1986	Berlin	West Germany	Switzerland	3–0
1987	Poertschach	Italy	Austria	2–1
1988	Huntington Beach, Cal.	USA	West Germany	3–0
1989	Montevideo	USA	West Germany	2–1
1990	Bol, Yugoslavia	Germany	USA	2–1
1991	Sydney	USA	Germany	3–0

* From 1958 to 1979 the early rounds were played zonally

AUSTRIA CUP
International Men's Team Competition for 55 year age group

	VENUE	WINNERS	RUNNERS-UP	FINAL SCORE
1977	Baden b. Wien	Great Britain	Austria	2–1
1978	Brand (Austria)	USA	Sweden	2–1
1979	Brand (Austria)	USA	Sweden	3–0
1980	Brand (Austria)	USA	Sweden	2–1
1981	Poertschach	USA	Sweden	3–0
1982	Cervia, Italy	Australia	USA	2–1
1983	New York	Australia	USA	2–1
1984	Poertschach	USA	Australia	2–1
1985	Perth	Australia	USA	3–0
1986	Poertschach	Australia	Canada	2–1
1987	Umag	Canada	Australia	3–0
1988	Huntington Beach, Cal.	Canada	West Germany	3–0
1989	Buenos Aires	Canada	USA	2–1
1990	Poertschach	Canada	USA	3–0
1991	Sydney	USA	Australia	3–0

YOUNG CUP
International Women's Team Competition for 40 year age group

	VENUE	WINNERS	RUNNERS-UP	FINAL SCORE
1977	Malmo	Argentina	Not available	
1978	Ancona	Italy	Not available	
1979	Cannes	West Germany	USA	3–0
1980	Bad Wiessee, Germany	West Germany	Italy	3–0
1981	Bad Wiessee, Germany	France	Italy	2–1
1982	Brand, Austria	France	Italy	3–0
1983	Cervia, Italy	West Germany	France	2–1
1984	Cervia, Italy	USA	France	3–0
1985	Poertschach, Austria	West Germany	France	3–0
1986	Brand	West Germany	USA	2–1
1987	Venice	France	USA	2–1
1988	Bagnoles de l'Orne, France	Great Britain	West Germany	3–0
1989	Poertschach	France	West Germany	3–0
1990	Keszthely, Hungary	France	USA	3–0
1991	Brisbane	Australia	Germany	2–1

MARIA ESTHER BUENO CUP
International Women's Team Competition for 50 year age group

	VENUE	WINNERS	RUNNERS-UP	FINAL SCORE
1983	Poertschach	Great Britain	USA	2–1
1984	Le Touquet, France	USA	France	3–0
1985	Bremen	USA	Great Britain	3–0
1986	Brand	USA	Great Britain	2–1
1987	Helsinki	USA	Great Britain	2–1
1988	Bahia	USA	Canada	2–1
1989	Bournemouth	USA	Great Britain	2–1
1990	Barcelona	Australia	Spain	2–1
1991	Perth	USA	France	3–0

ITALIA CUP
International Men's Team Competition for 35 year age group

	VENUE	WINNERS	RUNNERS-UP	FINAL SCORE
1982	Cervia, Italy	Italy	USA	2–1
1983	Cervia, Italy	West Germany	USA	2–1
1984	Brand, Austria	West Germany	France	2–1
1985	Reggio Calabria, Italy	USA	Italy	2–0
1986	Normandy, France	West Germany	USA	3–0
1987	Grado	USA	Austria	2–1
1988	Bol, Yugoslavia	West Germany	USA	3–0
1989	Mainz, W. Germany	West Germany	USA	3–0
1990	Glasgow	Spain	Australia	2–1
1991	Melbourne	Australia	Spain	3–0

BRITANNIA CUP
International Men's Team Competition for 65 year age group

	VENUE	WINNERS	RUNNERS-UP	FINAL SCORE
1979	Queen's Club, London	USA	Great Britain	3–0
1980	Frinton-on-Sea	USA	Sweden	3–0
1981	Hurlingham Club, London	USA	Sweden	3–0
1982	New York	USA	Canada	3–0
1983	Poertschach	USA	Australia	3–0
1984	Poertschach	USA	Australia	3–0
1985	Poertschach	USA	Australia	3–0
1986	Bournemouth	USA	Norway	3–0
1987	Bastad	USA	Sweden	2–1
1988	Huntington Beach, Cal.	USA	France	3–0
1989	Umag	USA	France	3–0
1990	Bournemouth	USA	Australia	2–1
1991	Canberra	Austria	Australia	2–1

THE CRAWFORD CUP
International Men's Team Competition for 75 year age group

	VENUE	WINNERS	RUNNERS-UP	FINAL SCORE
1983	Brand, Austria	USA	Sweden	3–0
1984	Helsinki, Finland	USA	Great Britain	3–0
1985	Brand, Austria	USA	Australia	3–0
1986	Seefeld, Austria	USA	France	3–0
1987	Poertschach	USA	Great Britain	3–0
1988	Keszthely, Hungary	USA	Great Britain	3–0
1989	Bol	USA	Brazil	3–0
1990	Brand, Austria	USA	Brazil	3–0
1991	Canberra	Germany	USA	2–1

ALICE MARBLE CUP
International Women's Team Competition for 60 year age group

	VENUE	WINNERS	RUNNERS-UP	FINAL SCORE
1988	Poertschach	USA	West Germany	3–0
1989	Brand	USA	West Germany	2–1
1990	Paderborn, Germany	USA	Germany	2–1
1991	Perth	USA	Great Britain	3–0

GOTTFRIED VON CRAMM CUP
International Men's Team Competition for 60 year age group

	VENUE	WINNERS	RUNNERS-UP	FINAL SCORE
1989	Kempten	Australia	New Zealand	3–0
1990	Ontario	USA	Austria	2–1
1991	Adelaide	USA	New Zealand	2–1

FRED PERRY CUP
International Men's Team Competition for 50 year age group

	VENUE	WINNERS	RUNNERS-UP	FINAL SCORE
1991	Bournemouth	Germany	Great Britain	3–0

AUSTRALIAN INTERNATIONAL JUNIOR CHAMPIONSHIPS
BOYS' SINGLES

1946	F. Sedgman	1956	R. Mark	1965	G. Goven
1947	D. Candy	1957	R. Laver	1966	K. Coombes
1948	K. McGregor	1958	M. Mulligan	1967	B. Fairlie (NZL)
1949	C. Wilderspin	1959	E. Buchholz (USA)	1968	P. Dent
1950	K. Rosewall	1960	W. Coghlan	1969	A. McDonald
1951	L. Hoad	1961	J. Newcombe	1970	J. Alexander
1952	K. Rosewall	1962	J. Newcombe	1971	C. Letcher
1953	W. Gilmour	1963	J. Newcombe	1972	P. Kronk
1954	W. Knight	1964	A. Roche	1973	P. McNamee
1955	G. Moss				

	WINNER	RUNNER-UP	SCORE		
1974	H. Brittain				
1975	B. Drewett (AUS)				
1976	R. Kelly				
1977	(Jan.) B. Drewett (AUS)				
1977	(Dec.) R. Kelly				
1978	P. Serrett (AUS)	C. Johnstone (AUS)	6–4	6–3	
1979	G. Whitecross (AUS)	C. Miller (AUS)	6–4	6–3	
1980	C. Miller (AUS)	W. Masur (AUS)	7–6	6–2	
1981	J. Windahl (SWE)	P. Cash (AUS)	6–4	6–4	
1982	M. Kratzman (AUS)	S. Youl (AUS)	6–3	7–5	
1983	S. Edberg (SWE)	S. Youl (AUS)	6–4	6–4	
1984	M. Kratzman (AUS)	P. Flyn (AUS)	6–4	6–1	
1985	S. Barr (AUS)	S. Furlong (AUS)	7–6	6–7	6–3
1986	Not held				
1987	J. Stoltenberg (AUS)	T. Woodbridge (AUS)	6–2	7–6	
1988	J. Anderson (AUS)	A. Florent (AUS)	7–5	7–6	
1989	N. Kulti (SWE)	T. Woodbridge (AUS)	6–2	6–0	
1990	D. Dier (FRG)	L. Paes (IND)	6–4	7–6	
1991	T. Enqvist (SWE)	S. Gleeson (AUS)	7–6	6–7	6–1

GIRLS' SINGLES

1946	S. Grant	1956	L. Coghlan	1965	K. Melville
1947	J. Tuckfield	1957	M. Rayson	1966	K. Krantzcke
1948	B. Penrose	1958	J. Lehane	1967	A. Kenny
1949	J. Warnock	1959	J. Lehane	1968	L. Hunt
1950	B. McIntyre	1960	L. Turner	1969	L. Hunt
1951	M. Carter	1961	R. Ebbern	1970	E. Goolagong
1952	M. Carter	1962	R. Ebbern	1971	P. Coleman
1953	J. Staley	1963	R. Ebbern	1972	P. Coleman
1954	E. Orton	1964	K. Dening	1973	C. O'Neill
1955	E. Orton				

	WINNER	RUNNER-UP	SCORE		
1974	J. Walker				
1975	S. Barker (GBR)				
1976	S. Saliba (AUS)				
1977	(Jan.) P. Bailey				
1977	(Dec.) A. Tobin (AUS)				
1978	E. Little (AUS)	S. Leo (AUS)	6–1	6–2	
1979	A. Minter (AUS)	S. Leo (AUS)	6–4	6–3	
1980	A. Minter (AUS)	E. Sayers (AUS)	6–4	6–2	
1981	A. Minter (AUS)	C. Vanier (FRA)	6–4	6–2	
1982	A. Brown (GBR)	P. Paradis (FRA)	6–3	6–4	
1983	A. Brown (GBR)	B. Randall (AUS)	7–6	6–3	
1984	A. Croft (GBR)	H. Dahlstrom (SWE)	6–0	6–1	
1985	J. Byrne (AUS)	L. Field (AUS)	6–1	6–3	
1986	*Not held*				
1987	M. Jaggard (AUS)	N. Provis (AUS)	6–2	6–4	
1988	J. Faull (AUS)	E. Derly (FRA)	6–4	6–4	
1989	K. Kessaris (USA)	A. Farley (USA)	6–1	6–2	
1990	M. Maleeva (BUL)	L. Stacey (AUS)	7–5	6–7	6–1
1991	N. Pratt (AUS)	K. Godridge (AUS)	6–4	6–3	

BOYS' DOUBLES

	WINNERS	RUNNERS-UP	SCORE		
1983	J. Harty (AUS)/D. Tyson (AUS)	A. Lane (AUS)/D. Cahill (AUS)	3–6	6–4	6–3
1984	M. Kratzman (AUS)/M. Baroch (AUS)	B. Custer (AUS)/D. Macpherson (AUS)	6–2	5–7	7–5
1985	B. Custer (AUS)/D. Macpherson (AUS)	C. Suk (TCH)/P. Korda (TCH)	7–5	6–2	
1986	*Not held*				
1987	J. Stoltenberg (AUS)/T. Woodbridge (AUS)	S. Barr (AUS)/D. Roe (AUS)	6–2	6–4	
1988	J. Stoltenberg (AUS)/T. Woodbridge (AUS)	J. Anderson (AUS)/R. Fromberg (AUS)	6–3	6–2	
1989	J. Anderson (AUS)/T. Woodbridge (AUS)	J. Morgan (AUS)/A. Kratzmann (AUS)	6–4	6–2	
1990	R. Petterson (SWE)/M. Renstroem (SWE)	R. Janecek (CAN)/E. Munoz de Cote (MEX)	4–6	7–6	6–1
1991	G. Doyle (AUS)/J. Eagle (AUS)	J. Holmes (AUS)/P. Kilderry (AUS)	7–6	6–4	

GIRLS' DOUBLES

	WINNERS	RUNNERS-UP	SCORE		
1983	B. Randall (AUS)/K. Staunton (AUS)	J. Byrne (AUS)/J. Thompson (AUS)	3–6	6–3	6–3
1984	L. Field (AUS)/L. Savchenko (URS)	M. Parun (NZL)/J. Masters (AUS)	7–6	6–2	
1985	J. Byrne (AUS)/J. Thompson (AUS)	A. Scott/S. McCann	6–0	6–3	
1986	*Not held*				
1987	N. Provis (AUS)/A. Devries (BEL)	D. Jones (AUS)/G. Dwyer (AUS)	6–3	6–1	
1988	R. McQuillan (AUS)/J. Faull (AUS)	R. Stubbs (AUS)/K. McDonald (AUS)	6–1	7–5	
1989	A. Strnadova (TCH)/E. Sviglerova (TCH)	N. Pratt (AUS)/A. Woolcock (AUS)	6–2	6–0	
1990	L. Zaltz (ISR)/R. Mayer (ISR)	J. Hodder (AUS)/N. Pratt (AUS)	6–4	6–4	
1991	K. Habsudova (TCH/B. Rittner (GER)	J. Limmer (AUS)/A. Woolcock (AUS)	6–2	6–0	

FRENCH INTERNATIONAL JUNIOR CHAMPIONSHIPS
BOYS' SINGLES

	WINNER	RUNNER-UP	SCORE		
1974	C. Casa (FRA)	U. Marten (FRG)	2–6	6–1	6–4
1975	C. Roger-Vasselin (FRA)	P. Elter (FRG)	6–1	6–2	
1976	H. Gunthardt (SUI)	J. L. Clerc (ARG)	4–6	7–6	6–4
1977	J. P. McEnroe (USA)	R. Kelly (AUS)	6–1	6–1	
1978	I. Lendl (TCH)	P. Hjertquist (SWE)	7–6	6–4	
1979	R. Krishnan (IND)	B. Testerman (USA)	2–6	6–1	6–0
1980	H. Leconte (FRA)	A. Tous (ESP)	7–6	6–3	
1981	M. Wilander (SWE)	J. Brown	7–5	6–1	
1982	T. Benhabiles (FRA)	L. Courteau (FRA)	7–6	6–2	
1983	S. Edberg (SWE)	F. Fevrier (FRA)	6–4	7–6	
1984	K. Carlsson (SWE)	M. Kratzman (AUS)	6–3	6–3	
1985	J. Yzaga (PER)	T. Muster (AUT)	2–6	6–3	6–0
1986	G. Perez Roldan (ARG)	S. Grenier (FRA)	4–6	6–3	6–2
1987	G. Perez Roldan (ARG)	J. Stoltenberg (AUS)	6–3	3–6	6–1
1988	N. Pereira (VEN)	M. Larsson (SWE)	7–6	6–3	
1989	F. Santoro (FRA)	J. Palmer (USA)	6–3	3–6	9–7
1990	A. Gaudenzi (ITA)	T. Enqvist (SWE)	2–6	7–6	6–4
1991	A. Medvedev (URS)	T. Enqvist (SWE)	6–4	7–6	

GIRLS' SINGLES

	WINNER	RUNNER-UP	SCORE		
1974	M. Simionescu (RUM)	S. Barker (GBR)	6–3	6–3	
1975	R. Marsikova (TCH)	L. Mottram (GBR)	6–3	5–7	6–2
1976	M. Tyler (GBR)	M. Zoni (ITA)	6–1	6–3	
1977	A. E. Smith (USA)	H. Strachonova (TCH)	6–3	7–6	
1978	H. Mandlikova (TCH)	M. Rothschild (FRG)	6–1	6–1	
1979	L. Sandin (SWE)	M. L. Piatek (USA)	6–3	6–1	
1980	K. Horvath (USA)	K. Henry (USA)	6–2	6–2	
1981	B. Gadusek (USA)	H. Sukova (TCH)	6–7	6–1	6–4
1982	M. Maleeva (BUL)	P. Barg (USA)	7–5	6–2	
1983	P. Paradis (FRA)	D. Spence (USA)	7–6	6–3	
1984	G. Sabatini (ARG)	K. Maleeva (BUL)	6–3	5–7	6–3
1985	L. Garrone (ITA)	D. Van Rensburg (SAF)	6–1	6–3	
1986	P. Tarabini (ARG)	N. Provis (AUS)	6–3	6–3	
1987	N. Zvereva (URS)	J. Pospisilova(TCH)	6–1	6–0	
1988	J. Halard (FRA)	A. Farley (USA)	6–2	4–6	7–5
1989	J. Capriati (USA)	E. Sviglerova (TCH)	6–4	6–0	
1990	M. Maleeva (BUL)	T. Ignatieva (URS)	6–2	6–3	
1991	A. Smashnova (ISR)	I. Gorrochategui (ARG)	2–6	7–5	6–1

BOYS' DOUBLES

	WINNERS	RUNNERS-UP	SCORE		
1983	M. Kratzman (AUS)/S. Youl (AUS)	A. Chesnokov (URS)/A. Olhovskiy (URS)	6–2	6–3	
1985	P. Korda (TCH)/C. Suk (TCH)	V. Godrichidze (URS)/V. Volkov (URS)	4–6	6–0	7–5
1986	F. Davin (ARG)/G. Perez-Roldan (ARG)	T. Carbonell (ESP)/J. Sanchez (ESP)	7–5	5–7	6–3
1987	J. Courier (USA)/J. Stark (USA)	F. Davin (ARG)/G. Perez-Roldan (ARG)	6–7	6–4	6–3
1988	J. Stoltenberg (AUS)/T. Woodbridge (AUS)	C. Coratti (ITA)/G. Ivanisevic (YUG)	7–6	7–5	
1989	J. Anderson (AUS)/T. Woodbridge (AUS)	L. Herrera (MEX)/M. Knowles (BAH)	6–3	4–6	6–2
1990	S. La Reau (CAN)/P. Le Blanc (CAN)	C. Marsh (AUS)/M. Ondruska (RSA)	7–6	6–7	9–7
1991	T. Enqvist (SWE)/M. Martinelle (SWE)	J. Knowle (AUT)/J. Unterberger (AUT)	6–1	6–3	

GIRLS' DOUBLES

	WINNERS	RUNNERS-UP	SCORE		
1983	C. Anderholm (SWE)/H. Olsson (SWE)	K./M. Maleeva (BUL)	6–4	6–1	
1985	M.U Perez Roldan (ARG)/P. Tarabini (ARG)	A. Holikova (TCH)/R. Szrubakova (TCH)	6–3	5–7	6–4
1986	L. Meskhi (URS)/N. Zvereva (URS)	J. Novotna (TCH)/R. Rajchrtova (TCH)	1–6	6–3	6–0
1987	N. Medvedeva (URS)/N. Zvereva (URS)	M. Jaggard (AUS)/N. Provis (AUS)	6–3	6–3	
1988	A. Dechaume (FRA)/E. Derly (FRA)	J. Halard (FRA)/M. Laval (FRA)	6–4	3–6	6–3
1989	N. Pratt (AUS)/S.-T. Wang (TPE)	C. Caverzasio (ITA)/S. Farina (ITA)	7–5	3–6	8–6
1990	R. Dragomir (ROM)/I. Spirlea (ROM)	T. Ignatieva (URS)/I. Soukhova (URS)	6–3	6–1	
1991	E. Bes (ESP)/I. Gorrochategui (ARG)	Z. Malkova (TCH)/E. Martincova (TCH)	6–1	6–3	

INTERNATIONAL WIMBLEDON JUNIOR CHAMPIONSHIPS

The event originated as an invitation tournament, boys' singles in 1947 and girls' singles in 1948. It became a championship event in 1975.

BOYS' SINGLES

1948	S. Stockenberg (SWE)	1957	J. I. Tattersall (GBR)	1966	V. Korotkov (URS)
1949	S. Stockenberg (SWE)	1958	E. Buchholz (USA)	1967	M. Orantes (ESP)
1950	J. A. T. Horn (GBR)	1959	T. Lejus (URS)	1968	J. G. Alexander (AUS)
1951	J. Kupferburger (RSA)	1960	A. R. Mandelstam (RSA)	1969	B. Bertram (RSA)
1952	R. K. Wilson (GBR)	1961	C. E. Graebner (USA)	1970	B. Bertram (RSA)
1953	W. A. Knight (GBR)	1962	S. Matthews (GBR)	1971	R. Kreiss (USA)
1954	R. Krishnan (IND)	1963	N. Kalogeropoulous (GRE)	1972	B. Borg (SWE)
1955	M. P. Hann (GBR)	1964	I. El Shafei (EGY)	1973	W. Martin (USA)
1956	R. Holmberg (USA)	1965	V. Korotkov (URS)	1974	W. Martin (USA)

	WINNER	RUNNER-UP	SCORE		
1975	C. J. Lewis (NZL)	R. Ycaza (ECU)	6–1	6–4	
1976	H. Gunthardt (SUI)	P. Elter (FRG)	6–4	7–5	
1977	V. Winitsky (USA)	E. Teltscher (USA)	6–1	1–6	8–6
1978	I. Lendl (TCH)	J. Turpin (USA)	6–3	6–4	
1979	R. Krishnan (IND)	D. Siegler (USA)	6–3	6–4	
1980	T. Tulasne (FRA)	H. D. Beutel (FRG)	6–4	3–6	6–4
1981	M. Anger (USA)	P. Cash (AUS)	7–6	7–5	
1982	P. Cash (AUS)	H. Sundstrom (SWE)	6–4	6–7	6–3
1983	S. Edberg (SWE)	J. Frawley (AUS)	6–3	7–6	
1984	M. Kratzman (AUS)	S. Kruger (SAF)	6–4	4–6	6–3
1985	L. Lavalle	E. Velez (MEX)	6–4	6–4	
1986	E. Velez (MEX)	J. Sanchez (ESP)	6–3	7–5	
1987	D. Nargiso (ITA)	J. Stoltenberg (AUS)	7–6	6–4	
1988	N. Pereira (VEN)	G. Raoux (FRA)	7–6	6–2	
1989	N. Kulti (SWE)	T. Woodbridge (AUS)	6–4	6–3	
1990	L. Paes (IND)	M. Ondruska (RSA)	7–6	6–2	
1991	T. Enqvist (SWE)	M. Joyce (USA)	6–4	6–3	

GIRLS' SINGLES

1948	O. Miskova (TCH)	1957	M. Arnold (USA)	1966	B. Lindstrom (FIN)
1949	C. Mercelis (BEL)	1958	S. M. Moore (USA)	1967	J. Salome (HOL)
1950	L. Cornell (GBR)	1959	J. Cross (RSA)	1968	K. Pigeon (USA)
1951	L. Cornell (GBR)	1960	K. Hantze (USA)	1969	K. Sawamatsu (JAP)
1952	ten Bosch (HOL)	1961	G. Baksheeva (URS)	1970	S. Walsh (USA)
1953	D. Kilian (RSA)	1962	G. Baksheeva (URS)	1971	M. Kroschina (URS)
1954	V. A. Pitt (GBR)	1963	D. M. Salfati (RSA)	1972	I. Kloss (RSA)
1955	S. M. Armstrong (GBR)	1964	P. Barkowicz (USA)	1973	A. Kiyomura (USA)
1956	A. S. Haydon (GBR)	1965	O. Morozova (URS)	1974	M. Jausovec (YUG)

	WINNER	RUNNER-UP	SCORE		
1975	N. Y. Chmyreva (URS)	R. Marsikova (TCH)	6–4	6–3	
1976	N. Y. Chmyreva (URS)	M. Kruger (SAF)	6–3	2–6	6–1
1977	L. Antonoplis (USA)	Mareen Louie (USA)	6–5	6–1	
1978	T. A. Austin (USA)	H. Mandlikova (TCH)	6–0	3–6	6–4
1979	M. L. Piatek (USA)	A. Moulton (USA)	6–1	6–3	
1980	D. Freeman (AUS)	S. Leo (AUS)	7–6	7–5	
1981	Z. Garrison (USA)	R. Uys (SAF)	6–4	3–6	6–0
1982	C. Tanvier (FRA)	H. Sukova (TCH)	6–2	7–5	
1983	P. Paradis (FRA)	P. Hy (HKG)	6–2	6–1	
1984	A. N. Croft (GBR)	E. Reinach (SAF)	3–6	6–3	6–2
1985	A. Holikova (TCH)	J. Byrne (AUS)	7–5	6–1	
1986	N. Zvereva (URS)	L. Meskhi (URS)	2–6	6–2	9–7
1987	N. Zvereva (URS)	J. Halard (FRA)	6–4	6–4	
1988	B. Schultz (HOL)	E. Derly (FRA)	7–6	6–1	
1989	A. Strnadova (TCH)	M. McGrath (USA)	6–2	6–3	
1990	A. Strnadova (TCH)	K. Sharpe (AUS)	6–2	6–4	
1991	B. Rittner (GER)	E. Makarova (URS)	6–7	6–2	6–3

BOYS' DOUBLES

	WINNERS	RUNNERS-UP	SCORE			
1982	P. Cash (AUS)/F. Frawley (AUS)	R. Leach (USA)/J. Ross (USA)	6–3	6–2		
1983	M. Kratzman (AUS)/S. Youl (AUS)	M. Nastase (RUM)/O. Rahnasto (FIN)	6–4	6–4		
1984	R. Brown (USA)/B. Weiss (USA)	M. Kratzman (AUS)/L. Svensson (SWE)	1–6	6–4	11–9
1985	A. Moreno (MEX)/J. Yzaga (PER)	P. Korda (TCH)/C. Suk (TCH)	7–6	6–4		
1986	T. Carbonell (ESP)/P. Korda (TCH)	S. Barr (AUS)/H. Karrasch (CAN)	6–1	6–1		
1987	J. Stoltenberg (AUS)/T. Woodbridge (AUS)	D. Nargiso (ITA)/E. Rossi (ITA)	6–3	7–6		
1988	J. Stoltenberg (AUS)/T. Woodbridge (AUS)	D. Rikl (TCH)/T. Zdrazila (TCH)	6–4	1–6	7–6
1989	J. Palmer (USA)/J. Stark (USA)	J.-L. De Jager (RSA)/W. Ferreira (RSA)	7–6	7–6		
1990	S. Lareau (CAN)/S. LeBlanc (CAN)	C. Marsh (RSA)/M. Ondruska (RSA)	7–6	4–6	6–3
1991	K. Alami (MAR)/G. Rusedski (CAN)	J-L. De Jager (RSA)/A. Medvedev (URS)	1–6	7–6	6–4

GIRLS' DOUBLES

	WINNERS	RUNNERS-UP	SCORE			
1982	B. Herr (USA)/P. Barg (USA)	B. S. Gerken (USA)/G. Rush (USA)	6–1	6–4		
1983	P. Fendick (USA)/P. Hy (HKG)	C. Anderholm (SWE)/H. Olsson (SWE)	6–1	7–5		
1984	C. Kuhlman (USA)/S. Rehe (USA)	V. Milvidskaya (URS)/L. Savchenko (URS)	6–3	5–7	6–4
1985	L. Field (AUS)/J. Thompson (AUS)	E. Reinach (SAF)/J. Richardson (NZL)	6–1	6–2	
1986	M. Jaggard (AUS)/L. O'Neill (AUS)	L. Meskhi (URS)/N. Zvereva (URS)	7–6	6–4	
1987	N. Medvedeva (URS)/N. Zvereva (URS)	I. S. Kim (KOR)/P. M. Modena (HKG)	2–6	7–5	6–0
1988	J. Faull (AUS)/R. McQuillan (AUS)	A. Dechaume (FRA)/E. Derly (FRA)	4–6	6–2	6–3
1989	J. Capriati (USA)/M. McGrath (USA)	A. Strnadova (TCH)/E. Sviglerova (TCH)	6–4	6–2	
1990	K. Habsudova (TCH)/A. Strnadova (TCH)	N. Pratt (AUS)/K. Sharpe (AUS)	6–2	6–4	
1991	C. Barclay (AUS)/L. Zaltz (ISR)	J. Limmer (AUS)/A. Woolcock (AUS)	6–4	6–4	

US INTERNATIONAL JUNIOR CHAMPIONSHIPS

BOYS' SINGLES

	WINNER	RUNNER-UP	SCORE		
1974	W. Martin (USA)	F. Taygan (USA)	6–4	6–2	
1975	H. Schonfield (USA)	C. J. Lewis (NZL)	6–4	6–3	
1976	Y. Ycaza (ECU)	J. L. Clerc (ARG)	6–4	5–7	6–0
1977	V. Winitsky (USA)	E. Teltscher (USA)	6–4	6–4	
1978	P. Hjertquist (SWE)	S. Simonsson (SWE)	7–6	1–6	7–6
1979	S. Davis (USA)	J. Gunnarsson (SWE)	6–3	6–1	
1980	M. Falberg (USA)	E. Korita (USA)	6–0	6–2	
1981	T. Hogstedt (SWE)	H. Schwaier (FRG)	7–5	6–3	
1982	P. Cash (AUS)	G. Forget (FRA)	6–3	6–3	
1983	S. Edberg (SWE)	S. Youl (AUS)	6–2	6–4	
1984	M. Kratzman (AUS)	B. Becker (FRG)	6–3	7–6	
1985	T. Trigueiro (USA)	J. Blake (USA)	6–2	6–3	
1986	J. Sanchez (ESP)	F. Davin (ARG)	6–2	6–2	
1987	D. Wheaton (USA)	A. Cherkasov (URS)	7–5	6–0	
1988	N. Pereira (VEN)	N. Kulti (SWE)	6–1	6–2	
1989	J. Stark (USA)	N. Kulti (SWE)	6–4	6–1	
1990	A. Gaudenzi (ITA)	M. Tillstroem (SWE)	6–2	4–6	7–6
1991	L. Paes (IND)	K. Alami (MAR)	6–4	6–4	

GIRLS' SINGLES

	WINNER	RUNNER-UP	SCORE		
1974	I. Kloss (SAF)	M. Jausovec (YUG)	6–4	6–3	
1975	N. T. Chmyreva (URS)	G. Stevens (SAF)	6–7	6–2	6–2
1976	M. Kruger (SAF)	L. Romanov (RUM)	6–3	7–5	
1977	C. Casabianca (ARG)	L. Antonoplis (USA)	6–3	2–6	6–2
1978	L. Siegel (USA)	I. Madruga (ARG)	6–4	6–4	
1979	A. Moulton (USA)	M. L. Piatek (USA)	7–6	7–6	
1980	S. Mascarin (USA)	K. Keil (USA)	6–3	6–4	
1981	Z. Garrison (USA)	K. Gompert (USA)	6–0	6–3	
1982	B. Herr (USA)	G. Rush (USA)	6–3	6–1	
1983	E. Minter (AUS)	M. Werdel (USA)	6–3	7–5	
1984	K. Maleeva (BUL)	N. Sodupe (USA)	6–1	6–2	

1985	L. Garrone (ITA)	A. Holikova (TCH)	6–2 7–6
1986	E. Hakami (USA)	S. Stafford (USA)	6–2 6–1
1987	N. Zvereva (URS)	S. Birch (USA)	6–0 6–3
1988	C. Cunningham (USA)	R. McQuillan (AUS)	6–3 6–1
1989	J. Capriati (USA)	R. McQuillan (AUS)	6–2 6–3
1990	M. Maleeva (BUL)	N. Van Lottum (FRA)	7–5 6–2
1991	K. Habsudova (TCH)	A. Mall (USA)	6–1 6–3

BOYS' DOUBLES

	WINNERS	RUNNERS-UP	SCORE
1982	J. Canter (USA)/M. Kures (USA)	P. Cash (AUS)/J. Frawley (AUS)	7–6 6–3
1983	M. Kratzman (AUS)/S. Youl (AUS)	P. McEnroe (USA)/B. Pearce (USA)	6–1 7–6
1984	L. Lavelle (MEX)/M. Nastase (RUM)	J. Icaza (PER)/A. Moreno (MEX)	7–6 1–6 6–1
1985	J. Blake (USA)/D. Yates (USA)	P. Flynn (USA)/D. McPherson (USA)	3–6 6–3 6–4
1986	T. Carbonell (ESP)/J. Sanchez (ESP)	J. Tarnago (USA)/D. Wheaton (USA)	6–4 1–6 6–1
1987	G. Ivanisevic (YUG)/D. Nargiso (ITA)	Z. Ali (IND)/B. Steven (NZL)	3–6 6–4 6–3
1988	J. Stark (USA)/J. Yoncey (USA)	M. Boscatta (ITA)/S. Pescosolido (ITA)	7–6 7–5
1989	W. Ferreira (RSA)/G. Stafford (RSA)	M. Damm (TCH)/J. Kodes (TCH)	6–3 6–4
1990	M. Renstroem (SWE)/M. Tillstroem (SWE)	S. LeBlanc (CAN)/G. Rusedski (CAN)	6–7 6–3 6–4
1991	K. Alami (MAR)/J-L. De Jager (RSA)	M. Joyce (USA)/V. Spadea (USA)	6–4 6–7 6–1

GIRLS' DOUBLES

	WINNERS	RUNNERS-UP	SCORE
1982	P. Barg (USA)/B. Herr (USA)	A. Hulbert (AUS)/B. Randall (AUS)	1–6 7–5 7–6
1983	A. Hulbert (AUS)/B. Randall (AUS)	N. Riva (URS)/L. Savchenko (URS)	6–4 6–2
1984	G. Sabatini (ARG)/M. Paz (MEX)	S. MacGregor (USA)/S. London (USA)	6–4 3–6 6–2
1985	R. Zrubakova (TCH)/A. Holikova (TCH)	P. Tarabini (ARG)/M. Perez Roldan (ARG)	6–4 2–6 7–5
1986	R. Zrubakova (TCH)/J. Novotna (TCH)	E. Brukhovets (URS)/L. Meskhi (URS)	6–4 6–2
1987	M. McGrath (USA)/K. Po (USA)	Il-Soon Kim (KOR)/Shi-Ting Wang (TPE)	6–4 7–5
1988	M. McGrath (USA)/K. Po (USA)	K. Caverzasio (ITA)/L. Lapi (ITA)	6–3 6–1
1989	J. Capriati (USA)/M. McGrath (USA)	J. Faull (AUS)/R. McQuillan (AUS)	6–0 6–3
1990	K. Godridge (AUS)/K. Sharpe (AUS)	E. deLone (USA)/L. Raymond (USA)	4–6 7–5 6–2
1991	K. Godridge (AUS)/N. Pratt (AUS)	A. Carlsson (SWE)/C. Cristea (ROM)	7–6 7–5

ITF JUNIOR WORLD RANKING LEADERS

BOYS' SINGLES

1978	Ivan Lendl (TCH)
1979	Raul Viver (ECU)
1980	Thierry Tulasne (FRA)
1981	Pat Cash (AUS)
1982	Guy Forget (FRA)
1983	Stefan Edberg (SWE)
1984	Mark Kratzman (AUS)
1985	Claudio Pistolesi (ITA)
1986	Javier Sanchez (ESP)
1987	Jason Stoltenberg (AUS)
1988	Nicolas Pereira (VEN)
1989	Nicklas Kulti (SWE)
1990	Andrea Gaudenzi (ITA)
1991	Thomas Enqvist (SWE)

GIRLS' SINGLES

1978	Hana Mandlikova (TCH)
1979	Mary-Lou Piatek (USA)
1980	Susan Mascarin (USA)
1981	Zina Garrison (USA)
1982	Gretchen Rush (USA)
1983	Pascale Paradis (FRA)
1984	Gabriela Sabatini (ARG)
1985	Laura Garrone (USA)
1986	Patricia Tarabini (ARG)
1987	Natalia Zvereva (URS)
1988	Cristina Tessi (ARG)
1989	Florencia Labat (ARG)
1990	Karina Habsudova (TCH)
1991	Zdenka Malkova (TCH)

BOYS' DOUBLES

1982	Fernando Perez (MEX)
1983	Mark Kratzman (AUS)
1984	Augustin Moreno (MEX)
1985	Petr Korda (TCH) and Cyril Suk (TCH)
1986	Tomas Carbonell (ESP)
1987	Jason Stoltenberg (AUS)
1988	David Rikl (TCH) and Tomas Zdrazila (TCH)
1989	Wayne Ferreira (RSA)
1990	Marten Renstroem (SWE)
1991	Karim Alami (MAR)

GIRLS' DOUBLES

1982	Beth Herr (USA)
1983	Larisa Savchenko (URS)
1984	Mercedes Paz (ARG)
1985	Mariana Perez Roldan (ARG) and Patricia Tarabini (ARG)
1986	Leila Meskhi (URS)
1987	Natalia Medvedeva (URS)
1988	JoAnne Faull (AUS)
1989	Andrea Strnadova (TCH)
1990	Karina Habsudova (TCH)
1991	Eva Martincova (TCH)

WORLD YOUTH CUP

International Team Championship for boys and girls aged 16 and under. Early rounds played zonally.

BOYS' FINALS

1985 Australia d. USA 2–1, Kobe Japan: R. Fromberg lost to F. Montana 2–6 2–6, S. Barr d. J. A. Falbo 6–4 6–4; Barr/J. Stoltenberg d. Montana/Falbo 1 0 0 7 7 6.

1986 Australia d. USA 2–1, Tokyo, Japan: J. Stoltenberg d. J. Courier 6–2 6–4; R. Fromberg lost to M. Chang 4–6 4–6; Stoltenberg/T. Woodbridge d. Courier/Kass 7–6 6–2.

1987 Australia d. Netherlands 3–0, Freiburg, West Germany: T. Woodbridge d. P. Dogger 7–5 3–6 6–2; J. Anderson d. F. Wibier 6–0 6–1; J. Morgan/Woodbridge d. Dogger/Wibier 6–3 6–2.

1988 Czechoslovakia d. USA 2–1, Perth, Australia: J. Kodes d. J. Leach 7–6 6–2; M. Damm d. B. MacPhie 6–2 6–7 6–4; Damm/L. Hovorka lost to W. Bull/Leach 4–6 4–6.

1989 West Germany d. Czechoslovakia 2–1, Asuncion, Paraguay: S. Gessner lost to L. Thomas 5–7 5–7; G. Paul d. P. Gazda 6–4 6–4; Paul/D. Prinosil d. Gazda/Thomas 7–5 6–1.

1990 USSR d. Australia 2–1, Rotterdam, Netherlands: D. Thomashevitch d. T. Vasiliadis 6–3 6–2; A. Medvedev lost to G. Doyle 6–2 4–6 5–7; E. Kafelnikov/Medvedev d. Doyle/B. Sceney 7–6 6–3.

1991 Spain d. Czechoslovakia 2–1, Barcelona, Spain: G. Corrales d. D. Skock 7–5 7–5; A. Costa lost to F. Kascak 4–6 5–7; Corrales /Costa d. Kascak/Skock 6–4 6–2.

GIRLS' FINALS

1985 Czechoslovakia d. Australia 3–0, Kobe, Japan: J. Pospisilova d. S. McCann 6–4 6–4; R. Zrubakova d. N. Provis 7–6 7–5; Pospisilova/Zrubakova d. Provis/W. Frazer 7–5 6–4.

1986 Belgium d. Czechoslovakia 2–1, Tokyo, Japan: A. Devries d. R. Zrubakova 6–3 6–4; S. Wasserman d. P. Langrova 6–4 7–5; Devries/C. Neuprez lost to Langrova/Zrubakova 4–6 2–6.

1987 Australia d. USSR 2–1, Freiburg, West Germany: J. Faull lost to N. Medvedeva 6–4 2–6 2–6; R. McQuillan d. E. Brioukhovets 3–6 6–2 6–3; Faull/McQuillan d. Brioukhovets/Medvedeva 6–3 6–1.

1988 Australia d. Argentina 2–0, Perth, Australia: K. A. Guse d. F. Haumuller 7–6 6–4; L. Guse d. C. Tessi 7–6 1–6 6–2; K. A. Guse/K. Sharpe d. I. Gorrachategui/Tessi 6–0 6–2.

1989 West Germany d. Czechoslovakia 2–1, Asuncion, Paraguay: M. Skulj-Zivec d. K. Matouskova 6–0 7–5; A. Huber d. K. Habsudova 6–0 6–3; K. Duell/Skulj-Zivec lost to Habsudova/P. Kucova 3–6 0–6.

1990 Netherlands d. USSR 2–1, Rotterdam, Netherlands: P. Kamstra d. I. Soukhova 6–1 7–6; L. Niemantsverdriet lost to T. Ignatieva 0–6 6–1 4–6; Kamstra/Niemantsverdriet d. Ignatieva/Soukhova 6–3 4–6 6–1.

1991 Germany d. Paraguay 2–1, Barcelona, Spain: H. Rusch lost to L. Schaerer 6–7 3–6; M. Kochta d. R de los Rios 6–3 6–1; K. Freye/Kochta d. de los Rios/Schaerer 5–7 6–3 6–3.

NTT WORLD JUNIOR TENNIS EVENT

International Team Championship for boys and girls aged 14 and under.

BOYS' FINALS

1991 Spain d. Italy 2–1, Yamanakako, Japan: A. Martin d. C. Zoppi 6–2 7–6; J-A. Saiz d. P. Tabini 6–2 6–1; Martin/J-M. Vincente lost to A. Ciceroni/Tabini 7–5 4–6 6–8.

GIRLS' FINALS

1991 Czechoslovakia d. Australia 3–0, Yamanakako, Japan: L. Cenkova d. A. Ellwood 7–5 6–2; A. Havrlkova d. A. Venkatesan 6–1 6–2; Cenkova/Havrlkova d. Ellwood/E. Knox 6–2 7–6.

ORANGE BOWL

International 18 and Under Championship played in Miami each December.

BOYS' SINGLES

	WINNER	RUNNER-UP	SCORE				
1974	W. Martin (USA)	T. Smid (TCH)	6–7	4–6	6–2	6–1	7–6
1975	F. Luna (ESP)	B. E. Gottfried (USA)	6–4	6–4			
1976	J. P. McEnroe (USA)	E. Teltscher (USA)	7–5	6–1			
1977	I. Lendl (TCH)	Y. Noah (FRA)	4–6	7–6	6–3		
1978	G. Urpi (ESP)	S. van der Merwe (SAF)	6–3	6–1			
1979	R. Viver (ECU)	P. Arraya (PER)	7–6	6–4			
1980	J. Nystrom (SWE)	C. Castqtellan (ARG)	7–5	7–6			
1981	R. Arguello (ARG)	R. Joaquim (BRA)	6–2	6–1			
1982	G. Forget (FRA)	J. Bardou (ESP)	7–5	2–6	6–1		
1983	K. Carlsson (SWE)	E. Sanchez (ESP)	6–2	6–4			
1984	R. Brown (USA)	J. Berger (USA)	6–3	6–3			
1985	C. Pistolesi (ITA)	B. Oresar (YUG)	6–2	6–0			
1986	J. Sanchez (ESP)	A. Parker (USA)	6–3	6–4			
1987	J. Courier (USA)	A. Cherkasov (URS)	6–3	6–2			
1988	M. Rosset (USA)	S. Pescosolido (ITA)	7–6	3–6	6–1		

1989	F. Meligeni (ARG)	G. Lopez (ESP)	7–6 7–6
1990	A. Medvedev (URS)	O. Fernandez (MEX)	6–4 2–6 6–2
1991	M. Charpentier (ARG)	K. Alami (MAR)	6–4 6–3

GIRLS' SINGLES

	WINNER	RUNNER-UP	SCORE
1974	L. Epstein (USA)	C. Penn (USA)	6–1 6–2
1975	L. Epstein (USA)	S. McInerny (USA)	6–2 6–1
1976	M. Kruger (SAF)	A. .E. Smith (USA)	2–6 6–3 6–4
1977	A. E. Smith (USA)	H. Strachonova (TCH)	7–6 7–5
1978	A. Jaeger (USA)	R. Fairbank (SAF)	6–1 6–3
1979	K. Horvath (USA)	P. Murgo (ITA)	7–5 6–0
1980	S. Mascarin (USA)	R. Sasak (YUG)	6–3 3–6 6–4
1981	P. Barg (USA)	H. Fukarkova (TCH)	6–2 6–3
1982	C. Bassett (CAN)	M. Maleeva (BUL)	6–4 ret'd
1983	D. Spence (USA)	A. Cecchini (ITA)	2–6 7–5 6–4
1984	G. Sabatini (ARG)	K. Maleeva (BUL)	6–1 6–3
1985	M. J. Fernandez (USA)	P. Tarabini (ARG)	7–5 6–1
1986	P. Tarabini (ARG)	B. Fulco (ARG)	6–2 6–2
1987	N. Zvereva (URS)	L. Lapi (ITA)	6–2 6–0
1988	C. Cunningham (USA)	L. Lapi (ITA)	6–0 6–1
1989	L. Spadea (USA)	S. Albinus (DEN)	6–0 6–3
1990	P. Perez (ESP)	S. Ramon (ESP)	6–1 7–6
1991	E. Likhovtseva (URS)	M-J. Gaidono (ARG)	7–6 6–1

GALEA CUP

International Men's Team Competition for players aged 20 and under.

FINAL ROUNDS

Played at Deauville

1950 Italy d. France 4–1: U. Bergamo d. R. L. Haillet 6–2 6–3, d. A. Lemyze 8–10 7–5 7–5; F. Gardini d. Lemyze 6–1 6–2; A. Parri lost to F. Nys 3–6 2–6; Gardini/H. Clerici d. Lemyze/Nys 6–1 6–3.

1951 France d. West Germany 5–0: A. Lemyze d. B. Pottinger 8–6 10–8; R. L. Haillet d. F. Feldbausch 6–4 6–4; G. Pilet d. C. Biederlack 1–6 6–2 6–2; P. Darmon d. J. Gulcz 6–4 1–6 6–1; Haillet/Lemyze d. Feldbausch/Pottinger 6–1 6–3 6–1.

Played at Vichy

1952 Italy d. France 4–1: N. Pietrangeli d. X. Perreau-Saussine 6–8 6–2 6–2, d. G. Pilet 7–5 6–1; A. Maggi lost to Pilet 3–6 6–2 3–6, d. Perreau-Saussine 6–4 7–5; Maggi/Pietrangeli d. J. N. Grinda/Pilet 10–8 6–3 6–3.

1953 France d. Italy 4–1: G. Pilet d. N. Pietrangeli 5–7 6–1 6–0, d. S. Jacobini 6–2 6–4; J. N. Grinda d. Jacobini 6–0 6–2, d. Pietrangeli 6–4 6–1; P. Darmon/Pilet lost to M. Pirro/Pietrangeli 3–6 5–7 7–9.

1954 Italy d. Yugoslavia 3–2: S. Jacobini d. L. Jagec 6–2 7–5, d. L. Backor 6–3 4–6 7–5; M. Pirro lost to Backor 6–3 4–6 4–6, lost to Jagec 0–6 5–7; Jacobsini/Pirro d. Backor/Jagec 10–8 4–6 6–4 6–1.

1955 Italy d. Spain 5–0: S. Jacobini d. A. Gimeno 3–6 6–3 6–4; F. Bonetti d. J. Moure 6–1 6–4; G. Morelli d. Moure 6–2 6–4; M. Drisaldi d. M. Santana 6–4 4–6; Drisaldi/Jacobini d. Arilla/Gimeno 6–3 6–4 2–6 6–1.

1956 Spain d. Italy 4–1: M. Santana d. F. Bonetti 6–3 5–7 7–5, d. G. Bonairi 4–6 6–5 7–5; A. Gimeno d. Bonetti 6–3 6–2, d. Bonairi 5–7 6–2 6–3: A. Arilla/A. Gimeno lost to M. Drisaldi/A. Maggi 6–1 4–6 3–6 3–6.

1957 Spain d. Italy 4–1: M. Santana d. G. Morelli 9–7 6–4, d. E. Casini 6–4 6–4; A. Gimeno d. F. Bonetti 6–3 6–4; J. L. Arilla lost to Morelli 3–6 6–8; A. Arilla/Gimeno d. Bonetti/A. Maggi 6–4 6–3 6–3.

1958 Spain d. West Germany 3–2: M. Santana d. W. Bungert 6–3 7–5 4–6 6–0, lost to D. Eklebe 1–6 5–7 6–1 3–6; A. Arilla d. Eklebe 6–1 9–7 4–6 7–5; J. Gisbert lost to W. Stuck 0–6 2–6 0–6; A. Arilla/Santana d. Eklebe/Stuck 7–6 6–3 6–3.

1959 West Germany d. USSR 4–1: W. Stuck d. A. Pontanin 6–3 6–0 6–1, d. T. Lejus 6–4 6–1 6–0; W. Bungert d. Lejus 6–2 6–3 6–2; L. Sanders lost to Pontanin 4–6 3–6 6–1 7–5 2–6; Bungert/Stuck d. Lejus/S. Likachev 6–4 5–7 3–6 7–5 6–4.

1960 France d. USSR 3–2: A. Bresson d. S. Likachev 6–3 6–2 6–4, d. T. Lejus 2–6 3–6 6–3 6–0 6–3; C. Duxin lost to Lejus 5–7 4–6 8–10, lost to Likachev 2–6 3–6 1–6; D. Contet/F. Jauffret d. Lejus/Likachev 8–6 6–2 4–6 6–2.

1961 France d. Spain 3–2: C. Duxin lost to J. Gisbert 1–6 3–6 2–6, d. T. Casado 6–2 6–1 6–1; F. Jauffret d. Casado 6–3 6–2 6–3, lost to Gisbert 6–1 4–6 3–6 6–4 3–6; D. Contet/Jauffret d. J. L. Arilla/Gisbert 6–2 6–0 6–2.

1962 France d. USSR 3–2: J. C. Barclay d. S. Mdzinarichvili 6–2 6–4, d. A. Metreveli 6–4 6–2 8–6; F. Jauffret lost Metreveli 6–3 2–6 3–6 4–6, d. Mdzinarichvili 8–6 6–1 0–6 6–2; C. Duxin/Jauffret lost to Mdzinarichvili/Metreveli 8–6 3–6 4–6 5–7.

1963 Czechoslovakia d. Italy 3–2: S. Koudelka lost to G. Maioli 3–6 6–4 3–6 5–7; d. G. Di Maso 6–4 6–2 6–2; M. Holecek d. Di Maso 6–4 11–9 6–4, d. Maioli 6–0 6–3 8–6; Holecek/Koudelka lost to Di Maso/Maioli 6–8 4–6 9–7 7–9.

1964 USSR d. Czechoslovakia 3–2: A. Metreveli d. J. Kodes 6–3 6–3 4–6 17–15, d. S. Koudelka 6–1 6–4 6–1; A. Ivanov lost to Koudelka 6–4 8–10 6–8 2–6, lost to Kodes 7–5 6–4 8–10 6–8 3–6; Ivanov/Metreveli d. Koudelka/F. Pala 6–4 5–7 9–7 8–6.

1965 Czechoslovakia d. USSR 3–2: J. Kodes lost to A. Ivanov 5–7 6–3 6–3 2–6 1–6, d. V. Korotkov 6–2 5–7 7–5 6–1; M. Laudin d. Korotkov 6–2 9–7 6–0, lost to Ivanov 8–10 2–6 2–6; Kodes/J. Stoces d. Ivanov/Korotkov 6–2 6–3 6–1.
1966 Czechoslovakia d. USSR 4–1: J. Kodes d. S. Kakoulia 6–3 6–1 6–1; M. Laudin d. V. Korotkov 6–2 3–6 6–1 6–4, lost to Kakoulia 1–6 0–6 7–5 3–6; Kodes/J. Medonos d. A. Egorov/Korotkov 6–4 6–3 6–1.
1967 France d. Great Britain 3–1: J. B. Chanfreau d. G. Battrick 6–4 6–3 4–6 7–5, d. D. A. Lloyd 6–2 6–3 6–8 7–5; G. Goven d. D. A. Lloyd 3–6 6–3 6–2 6–2; Goven/Chanfreau d. Battrick/Lloyd 8–10 6–3 6–4 6–2.
1968 Spain d. France 3–2: M. Orantes d. G. Goven 6–4 6–2 6–3, d. P. Proisy 6–1 10–8 6–3; A. Munoz lost to Proisy 6–4 9–11 6–8 6–3 1–6, d. Goven 6–2 3–6 6–3 4–6 7–5; Munoz/Orantes lost to Goven/P. Dominguez 1–6 6–0 1–6 1–6.
1969 Spain d. Czechoslovakia 3–2: A. Munoz d. P. Hutka 1–6 6–3 6–1 6–3; M. Orantes d. J. Hrebec 6–2 6–4 7–5; J. Gisbert lost to Hutka 2–6 6–2 3–6 4–6; A. Muntanola lost to J. Pisecki 3–6 1–6 5–7; Munoz/Orantes d. Hrebec/Hutka 5–7 6–3 6–1 6–4.
1970 Czechoslovakia d. Spain 3–2: I. Pisecki lost to A. Munoz 7–5 4–6 4–6 2–6, d. A. Riba 6–1 6–2 6–2; J. Hrebec d. Riba 6–3 6–2 6–0, lost to Munoz 3–6 3–6 8–6 1–6; Hrebec/Pisecki d. Munoz/Riba 6–3 6–2 6–0.
1971 Sweden d. France 5–0: K. Johansson d. J. Lovera 6–1 0–6 6–1 6–3, d. E. Deblicker 10–12 6–4 6–3 1–6 7–5; T. Svensson d. Deblicker 6–2 6–2 6–2, d. Lovera 5–7 7–5 8–6; K./L. Johansson d. Naegelen/J. F. Caujoulle 6–4 6–4 6–2.
1972 Great Britain d. Spain 4–1: C. J. Mottram d. J. Herrera 6–1 4–6 6–0 2–6 7–5; S. Warboys d. J. Higueras 6–2 6–2 1–6 6–3, d. Herrera 6–3 6–2 0–6 2–6 7–5; J. M. Lloyd d. Higueras 6–2 10–8; Mottram/Warboys lost to Higueras/J. Moreno 6–3 3–6 4–6 6–1 5–7.
1973 Spain d. Great Britain 4–1: J. Higueras d. J. M. Lloyd 4–6 6–2 6–2 0–6 6–4; J. Moreno d. C. J. Mottram 3–6 3–6 6–3 6–1 6–3, d. Lloyd 6–1 6–1 6–3; Higueras/Moreno lost to S. Warboys/M. J. Farrell 7–9 3–6 2–6.
1974 Czechoslovakia d. Spain 4–1: P. Slozil d. S. Cabeza 6–4 6–2 6–1; T. Smid d. J. Soler 0–6 6–4 6–0 11–9, d. J. Garcia 6–3 1–6 6–3; J. Granat lost to A. Gimenez 4–6 2–6; Slozil/Smid d. Gimenez/Soler 6–4 6–2 6–4.
1975 Czechoslovakia d. Spain 3–2: T. Smid d. A. Gimenez 6–1 4–6 3–6 6–2 6–2, d. M. Mir 3–6 8–6 6–2 7–5; P. Slozil d. Mir 8–6 3–6 6–3 6–2, lost to A. Gimenez 4–6 8–6 1–6 5–7; Slozil/Smid lost to Gimenez/Mir 8–6 6–4 3–6 2–6 1–6.
1976 West Germany d. Italy 3–2: W. Zirngibl lost to F. Merlone 2–6 2–6 7–5 4–6, d. G. Ocleppo 6–1 6–1 6–4; P. Elter lost to Ocleppo 2–6 2–6 6–2 4–6, d. Merlone 6–3 3–6 6–4 6–4; U. Marten/K. Eberhard d. V. Vattuone/G. Marchetti 3–6 6–3 6–4 6–4.
1977 Argentina d. France 3–2: F. Dalla Fontana lost to C. Roger-Vasselin 4–6 6–1 4–6 4–6, d. C. Casa 6–3 7–6 6–3; J. L. Clerc lost to Casa 4–6 5–7 6–2 4–6, d. Roger-Vasselin 3–6 6–3 6–0 6–4; Clerc/A. Gattiker d. D. Bedel/Noah 2–6 4–6 7–5 6–1 6–4.
1978 France d. Czechoslovakia 4–1: Y. Noah d. D. Kulhaj 6–1 6–4 6–4; P. Portes d. I. Lendl 8–6 4–6 6–2 6–2; G. Morreton lost to Lendl 3–6 13–15; Portes d. M. Lacek 6–2 6–1; Morreton/Noah d. Kulhaj/Lendl 9–7 6–1 5–7 3–6 6–4.
1979 France d. Czechoslovakia 3–2: Y. Noah d. M. Lacek 6–3 6–1 6–1, d. D. Pohl 6–3 6–2 6–2; P. Portes lost to I. Lendl 1–6 3–6 5–7; T. Pham lost to Lacek 3–6 1–6; Noah/Portes d. Lacek/Lendl 14–12 5–7 8–6 7–5.
1980 France d. Spain 3–2: T. Tulasne d. A. Tous 6–4 6–3 6–2, d. J. B. Avendano 6–2 6–2 6–1; J. Potier lost to Avendano 6–8 2–6 2–6, lost to Tous 4–6 3–6; H. Leconte/Potier d. Avendano/Tous 6–0 7–5 3–6 6–1.
1981 West Germany d. Australia 5–0: C. Zipf d. G. Whitecross 5–7 7–5 9–11 6–2 6–2, d. C. Miller 8–6 3–6 11–9; H. D. Beutel d. Miller 3–6 8–6 6–2 6–1, d. Whitecross 6–4 6–2; Beutel/Zipf d. P. Doohan/Miller 6–4 7–5 6–2.
1982 Australia d. Spain 3–2: P. Cash d. A. Tous 4–6 6–2 8–10 6–4 6–1, lost to S. Casal 0–6 1–6; C. Miller d. Casal 6–4 1–6 9–7 6–3, lost to Tous 5–7 1–6; Cash/Miller d. Casal/M. Jaite 6–4 6–1 6–4.
1983 France d. Spain 5–0: G. Forget d. J. Bardou 6–2 6–2 5–7 4–6 10–8, d. M. Jaite 7–6 6–3; L. Courteau d. Jaite 6–4 10–8 3–6 6–2, d. Bardou 6–3 4–6 6–1; Courteau/Forget d. Bardou/Jaite 6–2 3–6 6–4.
1984 Czechoslovakia d. Argentina 4–1: M. Mecir d. G. Garetto 3–2 6–8 6–0 6–2, d. E. Masso 7–5 6–3; M. Vajda d. Masso 6–2 8–6 6–2, lost to Garetto 9–7 6–1; Mecir/K. Novacek d. Masso/Mena 6–4 6–4 6–1.
1985 Italy d. USA 3–2: P. Cane d. L. Jensen 6–2 6–1 8–6, d. R. Reneberg 6–3 6–0 6–4; C. Pistolesi lost to Reneberg 3–6 3–6 3–6, d. B. Pearce 10–8 4–6 4–6 6–1 6–1; Cane/M. Fioroni lost to Jensen/B. Pearce 1–6 6–3 1–6 2–6.
1986 Spain d. Czechoslovakia 3–2: J. Sanchez d. M. Strelba, d. P. Korda 6–2 6–3 6–2; F. Garcia lost to Strelba 4–6 12–14 8–10, d. Korda 1–6 6–4 6–4 10–8; Garcia/Sanchez lost to Korda/ C. Suk 11–13 4–6 3–6.
1987 France d. Czechoslovakia 3–1: O. Delaitre d. P. Korda 6–3 6–0, d. C. Suk 6–1 6–1; S. Grenier lost to P. Korda 7–6 2–6 11–13, d. C. Suk 6–3 6–2.
1988 Australia d. Spain 3–2: J. Stoltenberg d. J. Sanchez 6–3 3–6 6–4, lost to T. Carbonell 4–6 3–6; R. Fromberg lost to Sanchez 2–6 3–6, d. Carbonell 6–2 6–3; Stoltenberg/T. Woodbridge d. Carbonell/Sanchez 6–2 6–3.
1989 France d. Australia 3–2: A. Boetsch d. T. Woodbridge 6–1 6–1, d. J. Anderson 6–0 6–2; F. Fontang lost to Woodbridge 4–6 1–6, lost to Anderson 3–6 2–6; Boetsch/G. Raoux d. J. Morgan/Woodbridge 6–1 6–4.
1990 Spain d. Czechoslovakia 3–2: G. Lopez d. D. Rikl 7–6 6–3; d. C. Dosedel 6–3 6–2; J. Conde lost to Dosedel 6–7 5–7; E. Alvarez lost to D. Vacek 3–6 5–7; Lopez/Alvarez d. T. Zdrazila/Rikl 6–3 6–2.
1991 Tournament no longer exists.

VASCO VALERIO CUP

International Team Championship for boys aged 18 and under. Played zonally with the final stages in Lesa, Italy.

FINALS
1970 Sweden d. France 4–1: L. Johansson d. F. Caujolle 10–8 6–3; T. Svensson d. E. Naegelen 6–4 6–0; R. Norbeg lost to E. Deblicker 4–6 0–6; M. Stig d. A. Collinot 6–3 6–1; Johansson/Stig d. Deblicker/Naegelen 6–3 6–3.
1971 Italy d. West Germany 4–0: M. Consolini d. U. Pinner 6–2 1–0 ret'd; N. Gasparini d. R. Gehring 6–1 3–6 6–0; C. Borea d. A. Hongsag 3–6 6–4 6–3; C. Barazzutti v L. Jelitto 5–1 abandoned; Barazzutti/Gasparini d. Gehring/Jelitto 6–4 6–4.

1972 *Czechoslovakia d. USSR 3–2:* I. Hora lost to V. Borisov 6–4 7–9 5–7; P. Slozil d. A. Machavez 6–2 2–6 6–4; Slozil/J. Granat d. A. Bogomolov/Borisov 6–3 7–5; T. Smid lost to K. Pugaev 3–6 8–6 4–6; Granat d. Bogomolov 6–3 6–4.

1973 *Czechoslovakia d. USSR 4–1:* A. Jankowski lost to V. Borisov 6–4 2–3 ret'd; P. Slozil d. A. Machavez 6–3 5–7 6–4; J. Granat d. K. Pugaev 3–6 6–4 6–3; T. Smid d. V. Katsnelson 6–4 6–4; Jankowski/Slozil d. Borisov/Pugaev 6–8 10–8 6–3.

1974 *Spain d. Italy 3–2:* L. Fargas d. A. Meneschincheri 6–1 6–1; A. Capitan /M. Mir lost to A. Marchetti/A. Vattuone 6–3 4–6 3–6; M. Mir lost to G. Ocleppo 4–6 2–6; A. Torralbo d. Vattuone 9–11 6–4 6–3; Capitan d. G. Marchetti 8–6 3–6 6–3.

1975 *Italy d. USSR 3–2:* G. Ocleppo d. S. Baranov 7–5 6–5 ret'd; A. Spiga d. S. Molodoikov 6–4 6–8 6–0; A. Merlone d. V. Gruzman 6–2 0–6 6–3; A. Meneschincheri lost to S. Elerdashvili 9–11 4–6; Ocleppo/Merlone lost to Baranov/Gruzman 5–7 4–6.

1976 *West Germany d. France 4–1:* P. Elter d. P. Portes 6–3 6–2; W. Popp lost to Y. Noah 3–6 0–6; J. Henn d. J. Kuentz 6–2 6–2; A. Maurer d. G. Geniau 6–4 6–3; Elter/Popp d. G. Moretton/Noah 6–3 3–6 6–3.

1977 *Italy d. Rumania 5–0:* G. Rinaldini d. E. Pana 6–1 6–1; M. Rivaroli d. L. Mancas 6–2 6–4; N. Canessa d. A. Dirzu 6–3 2–6 6–4; P. Parrini d. F. Segarceanu 6–1 6–0; Canessa/Parrini d. Dirzu/Segarceanu 7–5 6–2.

1978 *Sweden d. Italy 3–2:* M. Wennberg d. F. Moscino 6–2 6–2; P. Hjertquist/S. Simonsson d. M. Alciati/C. Panatta 6–1 6–3; Hjertquist d. M. Ferrari 6–1 6–3; Simonsson lost to Alciati 4–6 1–6; A. Jarryd lost to Panatta 0–6 1–6.

1979 *Sweden d. West Germany 4–1:* S. Simonsson d. H. D. Beutel 6–4 6–0; T. Svensson d. C. Zipf 2–6 6–4 6–4; A. Jarryd d. K. Vogel 6–2 7–5; J. Gunnarsson d. A. Schulz 7–5 6–4; Simonsson/Svensson lost to Beutel/Zipf 3–6 6–2 6–8.

1980 *Spain d. France 4–1:* J. Aguilera d. T. Pham 6–4 1–6 6–3; A. Tous/S. Casal d. J. Potier/J. M. Piacentile 6–2 3–6 6–4; Tous lost to Potier 1–6 6–7; R. Mensua d. P. Kuchna 6–4 6–1; Casal d. Miacentile 6–1 6–1.

1981 *Sweden d. Italy 3–2:* H. Sundstrom d. S. Ercoli 6–4 6–2; J. Nystrom/M. Tideman lost to L. Botazzi/F. Cancellotti 6–1 3–6 4–6; Nystrom d. Botazzi 6–3 6–2; J. Carlsson lost to Bardou 4–6 2–6; K. Carlsson d. E. Sanchez 3–6 6–0 6–1; P. Lundgren d. L. F. Garcia 6–3 6–4.

1982 *Italy d. Spain 3–2:* S. Ercoli lost to M. Jaite 2–6 6–7; M. Fiorini d. D. de Miguel 6–2 7–5; P. Cane d. E. Sanchez 6–1 3–6 6–4; M. Zampieri lost to J. Bardou 4–6 4–6; Cane/Fioroni d. Bardou/Jaite 4–6 6–3 8–6.

1983 *Sweden d. Spain 4–1:* J. Svensson d. G. R. Fernando 4–6 6–4 7–5; J./K. Carlsson d. D. de Miguel/J. Bardou 6–2 1–6 6–2; J. Carlsson lost to Bardou 4–6 2–6; K. Carlsson d. E. Sanchez 3–6 6–0 6–1; P. Lundgren d. L. F. Garcia 6–3 6–4.

1984 *Italy d. France 3–1:* F. Ricci d. G. Tournant 6–4 3–6 7–5; N. Devide d. P. Gardarein 6–3 6–4; I. Cappelloni d. O. Cayla 7–5 7–6; Gardarein/Winogradski d. Devide/Pistolesi 5–7 6–4 6–4.

1985 *Italy d. Sweden 3–2:* A. Baldoni lost to D. Engel 2–6 1–6; C. Pistolesi/S. Mezzadri d. C. Allgaardh/T. Nydahll 6–4 6–4; Pistolesi d. Allgaardh 6–3 6–4; U. Colombini d. C. Bergstrom 7–6 6–2; O. Camporese lost to U. Stenlund 0–6 3–6.

1986 *Italy d. Spain 3–2:* E. Rossi lost to J. Sanchez 6–7 4–6; O. Camporese lost to T. Carbonell 3–6 4–6; U. Pigato d. F. Anda 6–1 6–3; A. Baldoni d. F. Roig 7–5 6–4; Camporese/Rossi d. Carbonell/Sanchez 3–6 6–3 6–4.

1987 *Czechoslovakia d. West Germany 2–0:* D. Rikl d. C. Arriens 6–1 6–1; T. Zdrazila d. S. Nensel 6–1 4–6 6–2.

1988 *Sweden d. Israel 3–0:* N. Kulti d. R. Weidenfeld 7–6 6–2; L. Jonsson d. B. Merenstein 6–2 6–1; Kulti/M. Larsson d. Merenstein/O. Weinberg 6–3 3–6 6–4.

1989 *Sweden d. West Germany 3–0:* O. Kristiansson d. A. Kloodt 6–2 6–3; R. PettersAoson d. R. Leissler 6–2 6–1; D. Geivald/Kristiansson d. Kloodt/Leissler 6–7 6–1 6–2.

1990 *Sweden d. USSR 2–1:* M. Renstroem d. A. Rybalko 6–3 7–6; O. Ogorodov lost to R. Petterson 6–3 6–7 0–6; Renstroem/M. Tillstroem d. Ogordov/Rybalko 6–2 6–1

1991 *Spain d. Germany 2–0:* A. Berasategui d. S. Gessner 6–4 6–2; A. Corretja d. G. Paul 6–2 3–6 6–0.

JEAN BOROTRA CUP

International Team Championship for boys aged 16 and under; originally the Jean Becker Cup. Finals played in Le Touquet.

FINALS

1972 *Spain d. France 4–1:* M. Mir d. Ph. Gruthchet 6–3 6–2; F. Riba d. C. Freyss 6–2 1–6 6–4; A. Capitan d. R. Brunet 6–3 7–5; Masana/Mir lost to Frantz/Grutchet 6–4 6–7 3–6; Capitan/Riba d. Brunet/Freyss 7–5 3–6 9–7.

1973 *Italy d. West Germany 3–2:* M. Attolini lost to K. Eberhardt 6–1 6–6; G. Sileo d. P. Elter 7–5 6–4; M. Spiga d. U. Wellerdieck 6–2 7–5; Attolini/Sileo lost to Eberhardt/Elter 0–6 5–7; Mazzocchi/Spiga d. Liebthal/WellerAdieck 6–3 6–2.

1974 *West Germany d. Italy 4–1:* Buchbinder d. G. Rinaldi 6–2 6–2; P. Elter d. Risi 6–0 6–1; A. Maurer d. Gardi 6–7 7–5 6–1; Buchbinder/W. Popp lost to Gardi/Rinaldi 6–2 6–7 8–10; Elter/Maurer d. Risi/M. Rivarolli 6–0 6–3.

1975 *Czechoslovakia d. Italy 3–2:* M. Lacek d. G. Rinaldini 7–5 6–1; I. Lendl d. A. Ciardi 6–1 6–3; J. Kucera d. P. Parreni 6–4 6–4; Lacek/Kucera lost to Parreni/A. Rivaroli 4–6 4–6; Lendl/A. Vantuch lost to Ciardi/Rinaldini 6–1 4–6 3–6.

1976 *Sweden d. Czechoslovakia 3–2:* P. Hjertquist lost to I. Lendl 6–0 3–6 4–6; S. Simonsson d. A. Vikopa 6–3 6–0; H. Johansson d. T. Pitra 6–3 6–2; Simonsson/A. Fritzner lost to Lendl/J. Kerezek 6–4 3–6 1–6; Hjertquist/Johansson d. Pitra/J. Vikopal 6–3 6–2.

1977 *Italy d. Sweden 3–2:* A. Costa d. A. Jarryd 7–5 6–2; A. Giacomini lost to S. Simonsson 1–6 1–6; A. Moscino d. S. Svensson 6–4 6–4; Giacomini/A. Odling lost to Simonsson/Jarryd 3–6 4–6; Costa/Moscino d. Svensson/M. Wennberg 6–2 6–4.

1978 *Sweden d. France 3–2:* S. Svensson d. T. Tulasne 6–4 6–2; H. Simonsson lost to J. Potier 6–3 2–6 7–9 disqualified; J. Gunnarsson d. T. Pham 6–2 7–5 6–2; M. Wilander lost to J. L. Cotard 2–6 7–5 4–6; Svensson/Simonsson d. Cotard/J. M. Piacentile 6–3 6–1.

1979 *Sweden d. France 4–1:* J. Windahll lost to T. Tulasne 2–6 1–6; M. Wilander d. H. Leconte 6–2 1–6 6–3; T.

Hogstedt d. P. Kuchna 6–2 6–1; J. Sjogren d. J. M. Piacentile 6–1 6–1; Hogstedt/Wilander d. Leconte/Piacentile 3–6 6–3 6–4.

1980 Sweden d. Czechoslovakia 3–0: M. Wilander d. M. Mecir 3–6 6–1 6–1; A. Mansson d. K. Novacek 6–3 6–3; H. Sundstrom/Wilander d. Mecir/B. Stankovic 6–3 3–0 ret'd.

1981 France d. Sweden 3–2: T. Benhabiles d. S. Edberg 6–4 6–4; F. Hamonet d. J. B. Svensson 6–0 6–2; T. Chamsion lost to P. Svensson 3–6 6–2 0–6; O. Cayla lost to A. Henricsson 6–1 4–6 3–6; Hamonet/G. Forget d. Fdherg/P. Svensson 6–4 1–6 6–2.

1982 Sweden d. Spain 4–1: J. Svensson d. J. Maso 6–2 6–2; S. Edberg d. F. Garcia 6–4 6–4; P. Svensson d. J. Oltra 6–2 6–1; J. Carlsson lost to S. Castello 5–7 1–6; Edberg/P. Svensson d. Garcia/Oltra 6–2 6–1.

1983 Sweden d. USSR 3–2: D. Engel d. V. Gabritchidze 7–5 6–1; K. Carlsson d. A. Volkov 6–2 6–4; C. Allgaardh d. A. Tchernetsky 7–5 6–3; C. Bergstrom lost to I. Metreveli 6–0 6–7 3–6; Carlsson/Allgaardh d. Volkov/Metreveli 6–3 6–7 6–3.

1984 Italy d. Sweden 4–1: P. Chinellato lost to T. Nydhal 4–6 6–4 3–6; O. Camporese d. H. Holm 6–4 6–0; A. Baldoni d. A. Rosen 6–4 6–0; S. Sorensen d. N. Utgren 6–2 6–4; Baldoni/E. Rossi d. T. Nydal/P. Henricsson 7–6 1–6 6–3.

1985 Sweden d. France 3–2: P. Henricsson lost to A. Boetsch 3–6 2–6; P. Wennberg d. P. Ventura 6–2 6–2; N. Utgren d. S. Blanquie 6–1 6–2; M. Zeile d. C. Sebastiani 6–1 6–3; Henricsson/Utgren lost to Boetsch/R. Pedros 2–6 6–3 4–6.

1986 Italy d. Netherlands 3–2: F. Mordegan lost to P. Dogger 5–7 6–3 1–6; D. Nargiso lost to J. Eltingh 5–7 2–6; C. Caratti d. J. Siemerink 7–5 6–0; R. Furlan d. R. Heethius 7–5 5–7 7–5; Caratti/Nargiso d. Eltingh/Siemerink 4–6 7–5 6–3.

1987 Austria d. Italy 3–2: T. Buchmayer d. F. Pisilli 6–3 6–1; O. Fuchs lost to S. Pescosolido 4–6 1–6; H. Priller d. M. Ardinghi 6–3 6–4; G. Bohm lost to M. Boscatto 6–2 1–6 6–8; Buchmayer/Priller d. Boscatto/Pescosolido 1–6 6–4 6–4.

1988 Sweden d. Czechoslovakia 3–2: J. Alven d. M. Damm 6–1 6–4; R. Pettersson d. J. Kodes 2–6 7–5 6–3; J. Sunnemark lost to L. Hovorka 6–3 0–6 3–6; M. Renstroem d. P. Gazda 6–1 2–6 6–2; Alven/Pettersson lost to Damm/Horkova 0–6 6–3 6–7.

1989 Czechoslovakia d. West Germany 4–1: P. Gazda d. A. Kriebel 7–5 6–3; R. Hanak d. D. Prinosil 6–0 6–4; L. Thomas d. J. Weinzierl 6–2 6–4; B. Galik d. M. Kohlmann 6–4 6–2; Gazda/Thomas lost to M. Kuckenbecker/Prinosil 6–4 3–6 4–6.

1990 France d. Spain 3–2: N. Kischkewitz d. J. Gisbert 6–4 6–2; P. Lasserre d. A. Corretja 6–4 6–3; J. Hanquez lost to J. Martinez 7–6 5–7 2–6; O. Tauma d. G. Corrales 3–6 6–4 6–0; Kischkewitz/Tauma lost to Corretja/Gisbert 3–6 2–6.

1991 Spain d. Czechoslovakia 4–1: A. Costa d. F. Kascak 6–4 6–2; G. Corrales d. P. Pala 6–7 6–1 6–3; R. Carretero d. D. Skoch 5–7 7–6 7–5; J. Balcells lost to D. Miketa 5–7 6–1 1–6; Corrales/Costa d. Kascak/Pala 6–1 6–4.

DEL SOL CUP

International Team Championship for boys aged 14 and under. Played in zones with finals in Barcelona.

FINALS

1979 Italy d. France 3–2: M. Fioroni d. M. Cartier 6–0 6–2; G. Possani d. G. Forget 6–7 7–5 6–3; A. Paris lost to T. Benhabiles 0–6 5–7; L. Baglioni lost to F. Hamonet 0–6 0–6; Possani/Paris d. Benhabiles/Hamonet 6–1 6–4.

1980 Sweden d. Italy 4–1: P. Svensson d. R. Salemme 6–4 7–6; S. Edberg d. F. Ricci 7–5 6–3; R. Lofquist d. F. Filippi 6–3 6–4; J. Svensson lost to P. Poggioli 4–6 2–6; Edberg/P. Svensson d. Filippi/A. Vacca 6–4 6–3.

1981 Sweden d. Israel 3–2: T. Johansson lost to A. Naor 2–6 6–7; C. Allgaardh lost to G. Blom 4–6 6–2 4–6; K. Carlsson d. R. Weinberg 6–0 6–0; C. Bergstrom d. M. Osherov 2–6 7–5 7–5; Allgaardh/Carlsson d. Blom/Osherov 6–2 6–1.

1982 Sweden d. West Germany 4–1: H. Kolm d. U. Kraft 6–1 6–0; K. Carlsson d. O. Sachau 6–0 6–0; P. Ekstrand lost to I. Kroll 0–6 2–6; T. Nydahl d. C. Guhl 6–0 1–6 6–1; Carlsson/Nydahl d. Guhl/Kraft 6–1 6–4.

1983 Sweden d. West Germany 3–2: U. Persson d. H. Stang 6–2 6–2; P. Henricsson d. P. Pfleger 6–4 6–1; U. Eriksson lost to U. Kraft 7–6 3–6 2–6; P. Wennberg lost to L. Orzessek 2–6 3–6; Henricsson/M. Urgren d. Kraft/Orzessek 6–2 6–3.

1984 West Germany d. Spain 4–1: S. Scheider d. F. Alfonso 6–3 4–6 7–5; F. Loddenkemper/A. Thoms d. J. Olivert/S. Bruguera 6–3 6–2; Loddenkemper d. Olivert 7–6 7–6; D. Richter d. A. Martinez 6–1 7–5; A. Thoms lost to Bruguera 3–6 2–4 6.

1985 Austria d. Italy 5–0: G. Bohm d. F. Casa 6–4 6–2; T. Buchmayer/O. Fuchs d. S. Pescosolido/F. Pisilli 6–2 6–3; Buchmayer d. Pescosolido 6–3 4–6 6–4; Fuchs d. Pisilli 6–3 7–6; H. Prilled d. M. Ardinghi 6–2 6–1.

1986 Sweden d. Yugoslavia 4–1: J. Alven d. S. Hirszon 6–3 6–4; R. Pettersson lost to B. Trupy 2–6 3–6; M. Ekstrand d. A. Tonejc 3–6 6–4 6–3; J. Henriksson d. S. Ban 6–4 7–6; Alven/Pettersson d. Hirszon/Trupej 6–2 6–4.

1987 West Germany d. Austria 4–1: J. Weinzierl lost to R. Wawra 3–6 2–6; G. Paul d. N. Patzak 6–0 6–1; S. Petraschek d. J. Knowle 3–6 6–2 6–2; A. Kriebel d. H. Kugler 6–2 6–3; Paul/Petraschek d. Knowle/Wawra 4–6 6–2 6–2.

1988 West Germany d. Spain 3–2: M. Kohlman d. A. Corretja 6–2 6–1; T. Ruhle lost to A. Bragado 0–6 3–6; J. Schors d. J. Martinez 6–2 6–4; G. Hecht lost to J. Velasco 6–0 5–7 1–6; Kohlman/M. Nacke d. Bragado/Corretja 7–6 7–6.

1989 France d. Sweden 4–1: N. Bertsch d. T.A Johansson 7–5 7–6; A. De Cret d. K. Bergh 6–4 6–2; S. Martinez d. P. Salasca 6–2 6–3; M. Dallay d. D. Winberg 7–5 6–4; Bertsch/De Cret lost to Johansson/Salasca 6–4 3–6 1–6 7–6 7–6.

1990 France d. Spain 5–0: M. Boye d. A. Pastor 7–6 3–6 6–4; N. Maurier d. J. Diaz 7–6 6–4; J. Van Lottum d. A. Gandarias 1–6 6–2; K. Dous d. E. Xapelli 6–4 6–1; Boye/Maurier d. Diaz/Pastor 6–2 6–2.

1991 Spain d. USSR 5–0: J-A. Saiz d. I. Pridankine 7–6 6–1; F. Vincente d. J. Michejev 7–6 6–7 6–4; J. Vincente d. A. Gonopolskij 6–0 6–4; A. Martin d. A. Stoljarov 6–7 6–3 8–6; Martin/J. Vincente d. Pridankine/Stoljarov 7–6 6–3.

ANNIE SOISBAULT CUP

International Team Championship for women aged 20 and under. Played zonally with final stages in Le Touquet.

FINALS

1965 Netherlands d. France 2–1: M. Jansen lost to J. Venturino 1–6 1–6; B. Stove d. C. Spinoza 6–1 1–6 6–3; Jansen/Stove d. Spinoza/Venturino 10–8 6–4.

1966 France d. Netherlands 2–1: A. A. Seghers lost to A. Bakker 4–6 7–5 2–6; J. Venturino d. M. Jansen 6–4 6–4; Seghers/Venturino d. Bakker/Jansen 7–5 6–8 6–4.

1967 Netherlands d. France 2–1: A. Bakker lost to O. de Roubin 3–6 0–1 ret'd; A. Suurbeck d. N. Cazeaux 8–6 6–2; Bakker/Suurbeck d. Cazeaux/de Roubin 6–0 6–0.

1968 USSR d. Czechoslovakia 3–0: O. Morozova d. M. Holubova 6–2 10–8; R. Islanova d. K. Vaneckova 7–5 6–2; Morozova/A. Eremeeva d. Holubova/Vaneckova 6–3 6–2.

1969 USSR d. Hungary 3–0: O. Morozova d. J. Szorenyi 6–0 6–1; S. Yansone d. A. Graczol 4–6 6–4 6–2; Yansone/E. Izopajitis d. Szorenyi/A. Barogh 8–6 6–1.

1970 USSR d. France 3–0: E. Izopajitis d. N. Fuchs 6–3 6–1; M. Kroshina d. A. M. Cassaigne 4–6 6–1 9–7; Izopajitis/K. Zincevic d. Fuchs/M. C. Brochard 6–4 2–6 6–3.

1971 France d. Czechoslovakia 2–1: N. Fuchs d. M. Kozeluhova 6–2 6–3; F. Guedy lost to R. Tomanova 4–6 1–6; M. C. Brochard/Fuchs d. Kozeluhova/Tomanova 1–6 7–5 6–3.

1972 USSR d. Great Britain 2–1: M. Kroshina d. G. L. Coles 6–3 6–4; E. Biriukova d. V. Burton 6–2 4–6 6–3; Biriukova/E. Granatuzova lost to L. J. Charles/Coles 3–6 2–6.

1973 Great Britain d. USSR 2–1: G. L. Coles d. M. Kroshina 7–5 4–6 6–3; S. Barker d. E. Granaturova 6–4 7–5; Barker/Coles lost to Granaturova/Kroshina 4–6 6–3 3–6.

1974 Czechoslovakia d. Great Britain 2–1: M. Navratilova d. G. L. Coles 6–1 6–2; R. Tomanova lost to S. Barker 3–6 2–6; Navratilova/Tomanova d. Baker/Coles 6–2 6–8 7–5.

1975 Great Britain d. Rumania 2–1: S. Barker d. V. Ruzici 4–6 6–4 6–2; L. J. Mottram lost to M. Simionescu 4–6 9–7 1–6; Barker/Mottram d. Ruzici/Simionescu 6–4 6–0.

1976 Czechoslovakia d. Great Britain 2–1: H. Strachonova lost to M. Tyler 7–5 4–6 4–6; R. Marsikova d. L. J. Mottram 6–2 6–4; Marsikova/K. Skronska d. Mottram/B. L. Thompson 6–3 8–10 6–1.

1977 Czechoslovakia d. Switzerland 3–0: H. Strachonova d. A. M. Ruegg 6–0 6–3; R. Marsikova d. M. Simmen 6–0 4–6 6–0; Marsikova/H. Mandlikova d. Ruegg/Simmen 8–6 6–4.

1978 USSR d. Switzerland 3–0: N. Chmyreva d. A. M. Ruegg 6–4 6–4; Eliseenko d. P. Delhees 7–5 6–4; Chmyreva/Eliseenko d. Ruegg/M. Simmen 6–1 6–0.

1979 Czechoslovakia d. Great Britain 2–1: H. Mandlikova d. A. E. Hobbs 4–6 6–3 6–3; I. Budarova lost to J. M. Durie 6–8 6–4 6–8; Budarova/Mandlikova d. Durie/D. Jevans 1–6 6–2 6–3.

1980 Czechoslovakia d. Australia 2–1: I. Budarova d.S. Leo 6–4 6–4; M. Skuherska lost to D. Evers 0–6 3–6; Budarova/Skuherska d. Evers/M. Sawyer 6–3 6–3.

1981 Netherlands d. USSR 2–0: M. Van der Torre d. J. Salnikova 6–1 6–4; N. Shutte d. O. Zaitzeva 6–1 6–4.

1982 USSR d. Great Britain 2–1: O. Zaitseva d. S. Walpole 6–2 6–4; N. Reva d. A. Brown 6–1 6–3; J. Kashevarova/Zaitseva lost to Brown/J. Salmon 5–7 6–0 2–6.

1983 France d. Czechoslovakia 2–1: P. Paradis d. N. Herreman 7–5 1–6 6–2; N. Herreman d. O. Votavova 6–4 6–0; Paradis/P. Thanh lost to Fukarkova/Votavova 6–4 3–6 4–6.

1984 USA d. Czechoslovakia 3–0: G. Rush d. O. Votavova 6–3 6–1; D. Spence d. A. Holikova 6–2 7–5; Rush/N. Kuhlman d. Votavova/Holikova 6–3 6–2.

1985 Czechoslovakia d. Argentina 3–0: A. Holikova d. P. Tarabini 3–6 7–5 6–4; O. Votavova d. M. Perez-Roldan 0–6 6–3 6–2; Holikova/J. Novotna d. Tarabini/Perez-Roldan 7–5 7–5.

1986 Czechoslovakia d. West Germany 2–1: R. Zrubakova d. M. Schropp 6–2 6–2; R. Rajchrtova d. A. Betzner 6–1 6–2; Rajchrtova/Zrubakova lost to Betzner/Schropp 6–7 2–6.

1987 Australia d. Czechoslovakia 2–1: N. Provis d. R. Rajchrtova 2–6 6–2 6–1; J. Byrne lost to J. Novotna 5–7 6–3 3–6; Byrne/Provis d. Novotna/Rajchrtova 6–4 0–6 6–3.

1988 Czechoslovakia d. Spain 2–1: R. Zrubakova d. C. Martinez 6–4 6–3; P. Langrova lost to A. Segura 2–6 1–6; Langrova/Zrubakova d. Martinez/N. Souto 6–3 2–6 9–7.

1989 Czechoslovakia d. Australia 2–0: J. Pospisilova d. J. Faull 6–4 3–6 6–4; P. Langrova d. R. Stubbs 6–0 6–2.

1990 USSR d. Australia 2–1: N. Medvedeva d. K. Sharpe 6–4 6–3; E. Brioukhovets d. K. MacDonald 6–1 1–6 6–3; N. Biletskaia/S. Komleva lost to MacDonald/R. Stubbs 1–6.

1991 Tournament no longer exists.

HM QUEEN SOFIA CUP

International Team Championship for girls aged 18 and under. Played zonally with the final stages in Spain.

FINALS

1972 Rumania d. West Germany 3–2: F. Mihai d. A. Spiedel 6–4 7–5; V. Ruzici/M. Simionescu d. B. Portcheller/B. Kasler 8–6 6–1; Ruzici d. Portcheller 2–6 6–0 6–1; Simionescu lost to Kasler 4–6 3–6; M. Neuweiller lost to K. Pohmann 4–6 3–6.

1973 Great Britain d. Spain 4–1: B. L. Thompson d. G. Nogues 6–4 6–4; L. J. Mottram d. J. Mateo 6–3 12–10; S. Barker d. J. Alvarez 7–5 6–0; Barker/Mottram d. Mateo/C. Chillida 6–2 6–2; J. Potterton lost to Chillida 3–6 0–6.

1974 Czechoslovakia d. France 4–1: L. Plchova d. M. Cozaux 6–4 6–1; Y. Brzakova lost to B. Simon 6–8 6–2 4–6; H. Strachonova d. C. Gimmig 6–3 6–0; R. Marsikova d. F. Thibault 8–4 6–4; Brzakova/A. Kulankova d. Thibault/A. Duguy 9–7 4–6 6–4.

1975 *Great Britain d. Czechoslovakia 4–1:* M. Tyler d. A. Kulhankova 6–1 3–6 6–3; C. Harrison d. J. Kopekova 6–3 6–3; L. J. Mottram d. H. Strachonova 2–6 11–9 6–3; J. Cottrell lost to K. Skronska 1–6 1–6; A. Cooper/Cottrell d. Skronska/Kulhankova 1–6 6–4 6–4.

1976 *Great Britain d. Switzerland 3–1:* J. M. Durie d. C. Jolissaint 4–6 6–3 6–4; A. Cooper lost to M. Simmen 6–4 0–6 4–6; C. Harrison d. A. Ruegg 6–4 6–7 6–2; M. Tyler d. P. Delhees 6–2 6–2.

1977 *Czechoslovakia d. Sweden 5–0:* H. Mandlikova d. M. Wiedel 6–2 6–2; I. Budarova d. H. Brywe 6–1 6–1; Mandlikova/Budarova d. A. C. Mansson/A. Nilsson 6–1 6–3; M. Skuherska d. Nilsson 6–0 6–4; H. Strachonova d. Mansson 6–3 7–5.

1978 *Czechoslovakia d. Sweden 5–0:* M. Skuherska d. L. Jacobson 6–3 6–2; H. Mandlikova d. H. Brywe 6–1 6–1; I. Budarova/Mandlikova d. Jacobson/L. Sandin 6–3 6–1; I. Petru d. A. Nilsson 6–1 6–2; Budarova d. Sandin 6–3 5–7 7–5.

1979 *Czechoslovakia d. Switzerland 3–1:* I. Bendlova d. P. Frey 6–1 6–1; M. Skuherska/I. Petru lost to C. Jolissaint/I. Villiger 3–6 4–6; Skuherska d. Villiger 3–6 6–1 6–1; I. Novakova d. Jolissaint 6–7 6–3 6–3; Petru v C. Pasquale 5–7 abandoned.

1980 *Switzerland d. USSR 3–2:* K. Stampfli d. J. Kashevarova 6–3 6–3; I. Villiger/L. Drescher lost to O. Zaitseva/S. Cherneva 4–6 5–7; Villiger d. Zaitseva 6–2 7–5; C. Pasquale lost to Cherneva 4–6 7–5 7–9; Drescher d. J. Salnikova 7–6 6–4.

1981 *Sweden d. Czechoslovakia 3–2:* B. Bjort d. P. Dutkova 6–2 6–3; M. Lindstrom/C. Lindqvist d. H. Sukova/M. Pazderova 6–3 6–3; C. Jexell lost to Pazderova 6–3 2–6 0–6; Lindqvist d. N. Piskackova 6–2 6–2; Lindstrom lost to Sukova 6–7 3–6.

1982 *Italy d. Czechoslovakia 4–1:* R. Reggi d. I. Petru 6–3 6–4; N. Virgintino lost to H. Fukarkova 7–5 2–6 3–6; A. Cecchini d. P. Dutkova 7–6 7–6; F. Bonsignori d. A. Souckova 6–3 6–0; Reggi/Virgintino d. Petru/Fukarkova 7–5 4–6 6–2.

1983 *Italy d. Czechoslovakia 4–1:* L. Ferrando d. A. Souckova 6–0 6–3; B. Romano/N. Virgintino d. A. Holikova/Souckova 6–3 6–7 6–3; A. M. Cecchini d. O. Votavova 6–7 6–3 6–1; Virgintino d. P. Tesarova 6–3 6–1; S. Dalla Valle lost to Holikova 5–7 3–6.

1984 *Sweden d. Czechoslovakia 3–2:* H. Dahlstrom d. O. Votavova 6–3 6–3; A. Karlsson d. A. Holikova 6–3 6–0; A. Souckova d. M. Lundquist 7–5 7–5; K. Karlsson d. P. Tesarova 6–1 6–2; Votavova/Holikova d. Lundquist/Olsson 6–4 6–2.

1985 *Italy d.weden 4–1:* L. Lapi lost to C. Dahlman 0–6 1–6; L. Garrone/L. Golarsa d. A. K. Ollson/M. Lundquist 6–1 6–3; Garrone d. H. Dahlstrom 6–2 6–7 6–2; C. Nozzoli d. Ollson 6–4 6–4; Golarsa d. Lundquist 6–2 6–0.

1986 *Czechoslovakia d. Sweden 5–0:* R. Rajchrtova d. C. Dahlstrom 6–4 6–0; R. Zbrubakova d. J. Jonerup 6–3 6–3; J. Novotna d. M. Stradlund 6–4 6–2; D. Krajcovicova d. M. Ekstrand 6–3 7–5; Novotna/Rajchrtova d. M. Nilsson/Stradlund 6–0 6–1.

1987 *France d. Czechoslovakia 3–0:* A. Dechaume d. R. Zrubakova 6–4 6–3; E. Derly d. P. Langrova 7–5 6–1; Dechaume/S. Niox-Chateau d. Langrova/Zrubakova 6–7 6–4 6–3.

1988 *Spain d. USSR 2–1:* A. Sanchez d. N. Medvedeva 3–6 6–2 6–3; C. Martinez d. E. Brioukhovets 6–2 6–2; Martinez/Sanchez lost to Brioukhovets/Medvedeva 7–0–4 ret'd.

1989 *Spain d. Czechoslovakia 3–0:* A. Sanchez d. A. Strnadova 6–1 6–3; N. Avila d. J. Dubcova 6–3 6–0; S. Ramon/Sanchez d. K. Balnova/Strnadova 6–4 7–5.

1990 *Spain d. France 2–1:* P. Perez d. A. Zugasti 6–4 6–0; S. Ramon lost to A. Fusai 6–3 4–6 1–6; Perez/Ramon d. Fusai/Zugasti 7–5 6–2.

1991 *Spain d. Sweden 3–0:* E. Botini d. A. Carlsson 5–7 6–2 6–4; E. Bes d. M. Vallin 6–2 6–1; Botini/C. Torrens d. Vallin/Carlsson 4–6 7–6 6–2.

HELVETIE CUP

International Team Championship for girls aged 1 6 and under. Played zonally with final stages at Leysin, Switzerland.

FINALS

1977 *Italy d. Switzerland 3–2:* P. Cigognani lost to C. Jolissaint 0–6 3–6; B. Rossi d. I. Villiger 6–3 6–7 8–6; M. Calabria d. K. Stampfli 6–1 6–2; P. Murgo d. C. Pasquale 6–3 6–3; Rossi/Murgo lost to Jolissaint/Villiger 4–6 3–6.

1978 *Bulgaria d. West Germany 5–0:* M. Condova d. C. Kohde 1–6 6–3 6–1; A. Veltcheva d. Haas 6–3 5–7 6–4; I. Chichkova d. Hammig 6–3 6–0; I. Christova d. Wilmsmeyer 3–6 7–6 6–3; Condova/Veltcheva d. Kohde/Haas 3–6 6–2 6–2.

1979 *Sweden d. France 5–0:* C. Lindqvist d. I. Vernhes 6–7 6–3 6–0; B. Bjork d. C. Vanier 4–6 6–3 6–3; A. Flodin d. S. Gardette 6–0 6–1; H. Olsson/K. Marivall d. M. Callejo/Vanier 6–3 6–3; Olsson d. Calleja 6–2 6–1.

1980 *Sweden d. West Germany 3–2:* C. Anderholm d. M. Schropp 6–1 6–2; H. Olsson lost to K. Reuter 5–7 4–6; M. Schultz d. P. Keppeler 6–4 6–4; N. Nielson d. M. Reinhard 6–7 6–3 6–2; Olsson/Schultz lost to Reuter/Reinhard 6–1 4–6 5–7.

1981 *Sweden d. Italy 3–2:* A. Bjork lost to F. Sollenti 2–6 6–7; H. Olsson/C. Anderholm d. R. Reggi/F. Virgintino 0–6 6–2 6–1; Olsson d. A. M. Cecchini 6–4 7–5; Anderholm d. Reggi 6–3 3–6 6–4; I. Sjogreen lost to Virgintino 0–6 0–6.

1982 *USSR d. France 3–2:* I. Fishkina d. I. Demongeot 6–1 6–2; L. Savchenko/V. Milvidskaya lost to P. Paradis/N. Phan-Thanh 4–6 7–5 4–6; N. Bykova lost to Paradis 1–6 2–6; Savchenko d. Phan-Thanh 6–2 6–3; Mildvidskaya d. N. Herreman 6–1 6–4.

1983 *USSR d. Sweden 3–2:* A. Kuzmina d. A. K. Olsson 6–3 1–6 6–3; V. Milvidskaya d. H. Dahlmstrom 3–6 6–2 6–4; I. Fischkina lost to M. Lundquist 4–6 4–6; I. Fateeva lost to E. Helmersson 2–6 3–6; Fishkina/Mildvidskaya d. Dahlstrom/Lundquist 6–4 7–5.

1984 *Czechoslovakia d. West Germany 4–1:* R. Wlona lost to M. Gartner 7–6 3–6 4–6; J. Novotna/R. Rajchrtova d. S. Meier/R. Weiser 6–0 7–6; Novotna d. Meier 7–5 6–2; Rajchrtova d. Weiser 6–3 4–6 6–1; P. Sedkackova d. S. Hack 6–4 4–6 6–2.

1985 **West Germany d. Sweden 4–1:** M. Schurhoff d. M. Ekstrand 6–2 4–6 6–4; M. Gartner/S. Hack lost to M. Strandlund/M. Nilsson 3–6 3–6; Gartner/J. Jonerup 7–6 6–2; Hack d. Strandlund 6–1 6–1; W. Probst d. M. Nilsson 6–1 6–1.

1986 **Switzerland d. Czechoslovakia 3–1** (one rubber not played): E. Zardo d. M. Frimmelova 6–4 6–2; M. Strebel d. L. Laskova 7–5 6–1; S. Jaquet v. P. Langrova not played; M. Plocher d. E. Sviglerova 6–4 6–2; Jacquet/Plocher lost to Frimmelova/Langrova 6–0 1–6 5–7.

1987 **Netherlands d. Switzerland 3–2:** N. Van Dierendonck lost to S. Jacquet 6–7 3–6; B. Sonneveld lost to M. Plocher 6–2 3–6 4–6; Y. Grubben d. G. Villiger 7–5 7–6; E. Haslinghuis d. S. Bregnard 6–1 6–0; Sonneveld/Van Dierendonck d. Jacquet/Plocher 7–5 6–3.

1988 **West Germany d. Czechoslovakia 3–2:** V. Martinek d. K. Balnova 6–3 6–0; K. Duell lost to A. Strnadova 2–6 3–6; M. Skulj-Zivec d. H. Vildova 7–5 6–1; A. Popp lost to R. Bobkova 4–6 6–1 5–7; C. Hofmann/Martinek d. Balnova/Strnadova 7–5 7–5.

1989 **Czechoslovakia d. USSR 3–2:** R. Bobkova d. S. Komleva 6–2 6–1; K. Habsudova d. E. Makarova 7–6 6–0; K. Matouskova lost to M. Chirikova 3–6 6–3 5–7; K. Kroupova lost to T. Ignatieva 2–6 2–6; Bobkova/Matouskova d. Chirikova/Komleva 4–6 6–0 8–6.

1990 **USSR d. West Germany 3–2:** T. Ignatieva d. K. Freye 6–4 4–6 6–3; I. Soukhova d. S. Wachterhauser 7–5 6–2; V. Vitels lost to M. Babel 4–6 0–3 ret.; G. Beleni lost to P. Begerow 3–6 3–6; Ignatieva/Soukhova d. Babel/J. Dobberstein 6–4 6–4.

1991 **Czechoslovakia d. Spain 4–1:** Z. Malkova d. E. Jiminez 6–4 6–0; E. Martincova lost to M. Cruells 3–6 6–7; E. Hostacova d. A. Ortuno 6–3 7–5; M. Hautova d. A. Montolio 4–6 6–3 6–1; Malkova/Martincova d. Cruells/Jiminez 6–3 6–1.

EUROPA CUP

International Team Championship for girls aged 14 and under.

FINALS

1981 **West Germany d. France 3–2, Winterslag, Belgium:** I. Cueto d. J. Clerin 6–3 2–6 6–1; R. Wieser lost to E. Folcher 1–6 6–3 1–6; S. Graf d. M. Phan-Thanh 7–5 6–3; S. Luidinant d. E. Grousseau 6–2 6–2; Graf/Wieser lost to Folcher/Grousseau 6–4 2–6 1–6.

1982 **Sweden d. West Germany 3–2, Mons, Belgium:** C. Dahlman d. S. Meier 7–5 7–5; H. Dahlstrom d. B. Herget 6–0 6–4; E. Helmersson lost to I. Cueto 3–6 7–6 0–6; I. Mattiasson lost to E. Walliser 5–7 2–6; Dahlstrom/Helmersson d. Cueto/Walliser 6–2 6–2.

1983 **West Germany d. France 3–2, Lee-on-Solent, Hampshire:** N. Vassen d. S. N. Chateau 4–6 6–3 6–2; W. Probst d. M. C. Rolet 7–5 5–7 ret'd; S. Hack lost to C. Bourdais 6–3 2–6 0–6; M. Gartner d. A. Dechaume 6–4 4–6 7–5; Gartner/Vassen lost to Bourdais/Dechaume 3–6 1–6.

1984 **France d. Sweden 4–1:** S. Dussault lost to R. Narbe 0–6 6–4 3–6; A. Dechaume/E. Derly d. M. Ekstrand/H. Johnsson 6–3 6–3; Dechaume d. Ekstrand 7–5 6–2; Derly d. Salsgard 6–4 3–6 6–1; M. Laval d. Johnsson 6–4 6–4.

1985 **USSR d. Italy 3–2:** N. Zvereva d. A. Dell'Orso 6–2 4–6 6–4; T. Tchernysova lost to F. Romano 3–6 2–6; E. Brihovec lost to S. Favini w.o.; A. Blumberga d. G. Boscheiro 6–3 4–6 6–4; Zvereva/Tchernysova d. Boscheiro/Dell'Orso 6–4 6–3.

1986 **Netherlands d. Italy 3–2:** Y. Grubben lost to Boscheiro 5–7 4–6; N. Van Lottum d. Favini 6–2 6–1; E. Markestein d. Migliori 6–4 6–4; E. Haslinghuis lost to Bertelloni 2–6 2–6; Grubben/Van Lottum d. Boscheiro/Migliori 6–2 6–2.

1987 **Czechoslovakia d. Austria 3–2:** P. Kucova lost to U. Priller 3–6 1–6; R. Bobkova d. D. Bidmon 6–2 6–4; P. Markova lost to N. Dobrovits 4–6 1–6; K. Matouskova d. S. Suchan 1–6 6–0 10–8; Bobkova/Kucova d. Dobrovits/Priller 6–4 4–6 7–5.

1988 **Hungary d. West Germany 3–2:** A. Foeldenyi d. A. Huber 6–0 3–6 8–6; B. Bathory lost to K. Denn-Samuel 0–6 3–6; M. Zsoldos d. P. Kemper 6–1 4–6 6–4; K. Kocsis lost to M. Kochta 6–4 1–6 1–6; Foeldenyi/Zsoldos d. Denn-Samuel/Huber 4–6 7–6 6–3.

1989 **Czechoslovakia d. Italy 5–0:** E. Martiucova d. R. Grande 7–6 6–3; I. Malkova d. G. Pizzichini 6–2 7–5; O. Hostacova d. S. Pifferi 5–7 6–1 7–5; M. Hautova d. A. Serra-Zanetti 6–0 6–2; Malkova/Martiucova d. Grande/Pifferi 6–1 6–4.

1990 **Czechoslovakia d. Yugoslavia 3–2:** S. Radevicova lost to I. Majoli 2–6 6–4 1–6; Z. Rebekova lost to T. Doric 5–7 4–6; A. Havrlikova d. S. Milas 6–1 6–2; A. Gersi d. D. Karadz 7–6 6–0; Havrlikova/Redevicova d. Doric/Majoli 6–3 7–5.

1991 **Germany d. Czechoslovakia 5–0:** M. Vladulescu d. A. Havrlikova 6–0 6–3; N. Raidt d. R. Surova 7–6 6–2; S. Schmidle d. K. Bakalarova 6–0 6–4; A. Barna d. R. Pelikanova 6–2 6–4; Barna/T. Karsten d. L. Cenkova/Havrlikova 6–2 6–1.

US INTERCOLLEGIATE CHAMPIONSHIPS

MEN'S SINGLES

WINNER	WINNER
1883 *Spring:* J. S. Clark (Harvard)	1888 P. S. Sears (Harvard)
1883 *Autumn:* H. A. Taylor (Harvard)	1889 R. P. Huntington (Yale)
1884 W. P. Knapp (Yale)	1890 F. H. Hovey (Harvard)
1885 W. P. Knapp (Yale)	1891 F. H. Hovey (Harvard)
1886 G. M. Brinley (Trinity, Con.)	1892 W. A. Larned (Cornell)
1887 P. S. Sears (Harvard)	1893 M. G. Chace (Brown)

1894 M. G. Chace (Yale)	1944 F. Segura (Miami)
1895 M. G. Chace (Yale)	1945 F. Segura (Miami)
1896 M. D. Whitman (Harvard)	1946 R. Falkenburg (USC)
1897 S. G. Thompson (Princeton)	1947 G. Larned (Wm & Mary)
1898 L. E. Ware (Harvard)	1948 H. E. Likas (U of San Francisco)
1899 D. F. Davis (Harvard)	1949 J. Tuero (Tulane)
1900 R. D. Little (Princeton)	1950 H. Flam (USC)
1901 F. B. Alexander (Princeton)	1951 M. A. Trabert (U of Cincinnati)
1902 W. J. Clothier (Harvard)	1952 H. Stewart (USC)
1903 E. B. Dewhurst (U of Penn)	1953 H. Richardson (Tulane)
1904 R. LeRoy (Columbia)	1954 H. Richardson (Tulane)
1905 E. B. Dewhurst (U of Penn)	1955 J. Aguero (Tulane)
1906 R. LeRoy (Columbia)	1956 A. Olmedo (USC)
1907 G. P. Gardner (Harvard)	1957 B. McKay (U of Michigan)
1908 N. W. Niles (Harvard)	1958 A. Olmedo (USC)
1909 W. F. Johnson (U of Penn)	1959 W. Reed (San Jose State)
1910 R. A. Holden (Yale)	1960 L. Nagler (UCLA)
1911 E. H. Whitney (Harvard)	1961 A. Fox (UCLA)
1912 G. M. Church (Princeton)	1962 R. H. Osuna (USC)
1913 R. N. Williams (Harvard)	1963 R. D. Ralston (USC)
1914 G. M. Church (Princeton)	1964 R. D. Ralston (USC)
1915 R. N. Williams (Harvard)	1965 A. R. Ashe (UCLA)
1916 G. C. Caner (Harvard)	1966 C. Pasarell (UCLA)
1917–18 *Not held*	1967 R. C. Lutz (USC)
1919 C. S. Garland (Yale)	1968 S. R. Smith (USC)
1920 L. M. Banks (Yale)	1969 J. Loyo-Mayo (USC)
1921 P. Neer (Stanford)	1970 J. Borowiak (UCLA)
1922 R. N. Williams (Yale)	1971 J. S. Connors (UCLA)
1923 C. H. Fischer (Phil. Osteo.)	1972 R. L. Stockton (Trinity, Texas)
1924 W. Scott (Washington)	1973 A. A. Mayer (Stanford)
1925 E. G. Chandler (California)	1974 J. Whitlinger (Stanford)
1926 E. G. Chandler (California)	1975 W. Martin (UCLA)
1927 W. Allison (Texas)	1976 W. Scanlon (Trinity, Texas)
1928 H. Siligson (Lehigh)	1977 M. Mitchell (Stanford)
1929 B. Bell (Texas)	1978 J. P. McEnroe (Stanford)
1930 C. Sutter (Tulane)	1979 K. Curren (Texas)
1931 K. Gledhill (Stanford)	1980 R. Van't Hof (USC)
1932 C. Sutter (Tulane)	1981 T. Mayotte (Stanford)
1933 J. Tidball (UCLA)	1982 M. Leach (Michigan)
1934 G. Mako (USC)	1983 G. Holmes (Utah)
1935 W. Hess (Rice)	1984 M. Pernfors (Georgia)
1936 E. Sutter (Tulane)	1985 M. Pernfors (Georgia)
1937 E. Sutter (Tulane)	1986 D. Goldie (Stanford)
1938 F. D. Guernsey (Rice)	1987 A. Burrow (U of Miami)
1939 F. D. Guernsey (Rice)	1988 R. Weiss (Pepperdine)
1940 D. McNeill (Kenyon Coll)	1989 D. Leaycraft (LSU)
1941 J. R. Hunt (US Naval Acad)	1990 S. Bryan (Texas)
1942 F. R. Schroeder (Stanford)	1991 J. Palmer (Stanford)
1943 F. Segura (Miami)	

WOMEN'S SINGLES

WINNER	WINNER
1958 D. R. Hard (Pomona)	1975 S. Tolleson (Trinity, Texas)
1959 D. Floyd (Wm & Mary)	1976 B. Hallquist (USC)
1960 L. Vail (Oakland City)	1977 B. Hallquist (USC)
1961 T. A. Fretz (Occidental)	1978 S. Margolin (USC)
1962 R. Allison (Alabama)	1979 K. Jordan (Stanford)
1963 R. Allison (Alabama)	1980 W. White (Rollins)
1964 J. Albert (Stanford)	1981 A. M. Fernandez (Rollins)
1965 M. Henreid (UCLA)	1982 A. Moulton (Stanford)
1966 C. Martinez (San Francisco State)	1983 B. Herr (USC)
1967 O. Rippy (Odessa Jr)	1984 L. Spain (Georgia)
1968 E. Burrer (Trinity, Texas)	1985 L. Gates (Stanford)
1969 E. Burrer (Trinity, Texas)	1986 P. Fendick (Stanford)
1970 L. DuPont (N Carolina)	1987 P. Fendick (Stanford)
1971 P. Richmond (Arizona State)	1988 S. Stafford (Florida)
1972 J. Metcalf (Redlands)	1989 S. Birch (Stanford)
1973 J. Metcalf (Redlands)	1990 D. Graham (Stanford)
1974 C. Meyer (Marymount)	1991 S. Birch (Stanford)

THE INTERNATIONAL TENNIS FEDERATION

REGIONAL REPORTS
ITF JUNIOR RESULTS
ITF VETERAN TENNIS
NATIONAL RANKINGS

A winner of the junior titles in Melbourne and at Wimbledon, the 17-year-old Swede, Thomas Enqvist, was the outstanding junior of the year and headed the ITF rankings table.
(T. Henshaw)

THE INTERNATIONAL TENNIS FEDERATION

The International Tennis Federation
Palliser Road, Barons Court, London W14 9EN
Telephone: 071-381 8060. Cables: Intennis London W14. Telex: 919253 ITF G. Telefax: 071-381 3989

President: Brian Tobin.
Honorary Life President: Philippe Chatrier.
Honorary Life Vice-Presidents: Jean Borotra, Allan Heyman, Pablo Llorens, Giorgio de Stefani.
Vice-Presidents: Robert Cookson, David Markin, Heinz Grimm.
Honorary Life Counsellors: Paolo Angeli, Hunter Delatour, Lazslo Gorodi, J. Randolph Gregson, John Harrison, Gordon Jorgensen, Padma Bhushan R. K. Khanna, Stan Malless, Radmilo Nikolic, William Woods.
Trustees: Hunter Delatour, David Jude, Pablo Llorens.
Committee of Management: Brian Tobin, Olle Bergstrom, Jim Cochrane, Robert Cookson, Jean-Claude Delafosse, Heinz Grimm, Eiichi Kawatei, Juan Margets, Eduardo Moline O'Connor, Geoff Pollard, Francesco Ricci Bitti, Claus Stauder.
Honorary Treasurer: David Jude.
Auditors: Messrs Ernst & Young, Becket House, 1 Lambeth Palace Road, London SE1 7EU.
Legal Counsel: UK – Townleys;
                 UK – Wedlake Bell;
                 USA – James W. Lillie.
Sub-Committees: *Davis Cup*; *Federation Cup*; Finance; Futures; Junior Competitions; Long Range Planning; Olympic; Rules of the ITF; Rules of Tennis; Technical; Veterans.
Commissions: Media; Medical.
Secretariat: Brian Tobin – President; Mike Davies – General Manager; Thomas Hallberg – Director of *Davis Cup* Competition; Sally Holdsworth – Director of Administration and Personnel; Debbie Jevans – Director of Women's Tennis; Doug MacCurdy – Director of Development; Christopher Stokes – Director of Commercial Operations; Bill Babcock – Manager of Men's Professional Tournaments; Malcolm Bool – Finance Manager; Ian Barnes – Media Administrator; Frances Cason – Accounts Administrator; Tony Gathercole – Veterans Administrator; Johanna Kelly – Sponsorship Public Relations Administrator; David Miley – Development Administrator; Jackie Nesbitt – Junior Competitions Administrator; John Treleven – Computer Rankings Administrator.

GRAND SLAM COMMITTEE
Australian Open: Geoff Pollard; *French Open:* Philippe Chatrier; *Wimbledon:* John Curry; *US Open:* Robert Cookson.
Grand Slam Committee Administrator: Bill Babcock

WOMEN'S INTERNATIONAL PROFESSIONAL TENNIS COUNCIL
ITF Representatives: Voting Members – J. Howard Frazier, Heinz Grimm, Debbie Jevans, Brian Tobin (Alternate: Virginia Wade). *WTA Representatives: Voting Members* – Peachy Kellmeyer, Kathy Jordan, Gerry Smith, Wendy Turnbull (Alternates – Elise Burgin and Ana Leaird). *Tournament Representatives: USA: Voting Members* – Sara Fornaciari, William Goldstein (Alternate – Cliff Buchholz). *European: Voting Member* – George Hendon (Alternate – John Feaver). *Rest of World: Voting Member* – Geoff Pollard (Alternate – Shigeyuki Shindo). *Managing Director:* Anne Person.
Kraft General Foods: Non-voting Representatives: Tom Keim; Edy McGoldrick.
Virginia Slims: Non-voting Representatives: Ina Broeman; Leo McCullagh.
ITF Representatives on Satellites Joint Committee: Bill Babcock, Heinz Grimm, Eiichi Kawatei, Joan Zekala.
ITF Representatives on Challengers Joint Committee: Heinz Grimm, Eiichi Kawatei, Ms Joan Zekala.

WORLD CHAMPIONS PANEL
Fred Perry, Frank Sedgman, Tony Trabert.

AFRICAN TENNIS CONFEDERATION

President: Jean-Claude Delafosse.

1991 was an exciting year for competitive tennis in Africa. The West African Junior Championships/Air Afrique Trophy attracted over thirty teams. Morocco won the team championship with consistent performances in all categories, while Madagascar finished second by dominating the girls' events.

Success at the junior level was achieved by numerous African players in competitions around the world. Morocco's Karim Alami finished second in the Prince Junior World Ranking based on outstanding results in the Grand Slam and other Group A tournaments. Fourteen-year-old Dally Randriantefy won the Swiss Junior Open and, with a magnificent effort, paired with her sister to lead Madagascar to a third place finish in the first NTT World Junior Tennis team championship for players 14-and-under. These accomplishments represent a major breakthrough at international level. Other significant results were achieved by junior players from Mozambique and Zimbabwe.

Within the African continent there was a tremendous amount of competitive tennis, supported by the Grand Slam Development Fund. The events ranged from a 14-and-under junior circuit in Southern Africa to Satellite Circuits for both men and women in various zones of Africa. Other ITF initiatives included the operation of an ITF African Training Centre in Abidjan and the continued appointment of a full-time development officer in East Africa.

At senior level, the first ITF World Class Team of African players played in professional tournaments worldwide. The team consisted of Byron Black (Zimbabwe), Clement N'Goran (Cote d'Ivoire), Paul Wakesa (Kenya) and Karim Alami (Moroco).

Kenya won the Euro-African Group II of the *Davis Cup* and advanced to Group I for 1992.

Finally, the most encouraging occurrence during 1991 was the re-admission of South Africa to the ITF. Their participation in African tennis should have a very positive impact on the development of tennis on the African continent.

THE ASIAN TENNIS FEDERATION

President: Eiichi Kawatei, *Secretary General:* Herman Hu, *Hon. Treasurer:* Sung-Ok Cho.

Tennis activities in Asia during 1991 were very encouraging. Although upset by the Gulf War at the beginning of the year, Kuwait returned to the tennis scene very soon afterwards and were able to participate in the *Davis Cup* tie in Singapore in May.

Our university players from Japan, China and Korea surprised the tennis world in July by capturing four of the five gold medals at the World Student Games in Sheffield. In the same month the Indonesian ladies also had considerable success. After winning the consolation event for the last two years, they reached the quarter-finals of the *Federation Cup by NEC* in Nottingham. This is the best result achieved by an Asian team.

Five regional events, the Ghafar Cup (Asian Nations Cup), Salem Asian Championships, Asian Juniors, Asian University Games, and Asian Veterans were also staged successfully during the year.

The Salem Asian Championships and AGM of the Asian Tennis Federation were held in Hong Kong in November. It was the first time in the history of the ATF that we had a title sponsor for the Championships, which were also the most successful we have staged. Korea, China and Taipei dominated the event with Eui-Jong Chang (KOR) and Shi-Ting Wang (TPE) winning the Men's and Ladies' singles titles respectively.

The number of tournaments, from junior to professional level, also increased dramatically, which helped Asian players improve their rankings. There are at least one or two tournaments held every week in our calendar. The standard of our players has also increased. There are three ladies in the top fifty and several young men coming up in the ITF Junior Rankings. The Japanese players are still top amongst the Asians in the Men's, Women's and Junior rankings. All other Asian players are working hard and looking forward to achieving better results in 1992.

With the help of the ITF, seven officiating schools were held in various Asian cities. Asian officials found the schools very useful and all achieved excellent results.

A new milestone was set during the AGM. The Constitution was revised to catch up with the fast-changing environment of the tennis world. The Committee of Management was expanded and nine sub-committees were formed to look after men's and women's tennis, juniors, veterans, development, coaching, officiating, rules and regulations, general affairs and promotion/marketing. Various goals were set to improve the standard and popularity of tennis in Asia. We also aimed to help those countries in Asia that are not yet members.

It was also decided that a permanent ATF office will be established in Hong Kong with the assistance of the ITF. A co-ordinator will be employed on a full time basis to liaise with all members, the ITF and other regional associations.

EUROPEAN TENNIS ASSOCIATION

The activity of the European Tennis Association (ETA) in organising the official competitions where the titles of European Champions are at stake (for individuals and nations – professional, junior and veteran events) has been duly rewarded by a constant increase in terms of participants, spectator attendance and media coverage.

As far as the participants are concerned, the following figures clearly indicate the interest generated by the ETA competitions.

Twenty-eight nations entered in the Men's and twenty-five nations entered in the Women's Team Championships open to professional players and won respectively by Czechoslovakia and by the Netherlands.

A total of 178 national teams competed in the European Junior Team Championships and in the Winter Cups. It must be noted that Spain was successful in 4 of the Team Championships (boys 18, girls 18, boys 16 and boys 14). The individual Championships held in Berlin (boys and girls 14 and under) and Barcelona (boys and girls 18–16 and under) registered about 260 players coming from 28 different countries.

The boom of veteran tennis was again confirmed by the participation of 900 competitors at the traditional venues of the European Veteran Championships (indoor and outdoor) in Seefeld, Baden Baden and Portschach.

Also the ETA Championships reserved to the Champion Clubs of the European Nations proved to be popular and attracted an increasing number of teams in each of the three events organised in 1991 (Open, Veterans 45 age group and Veterans 55 age group).

The distinction of 'European Championship' has also been awarded in 1991 to the two prestigious Women's Tournaments held in Zurich (indoor) and Geneva (outdoor) included in the 'Kraft General Foods World Tour'.

Finally the European Tennis Association has strengthened its efforts for creating, in association with the International Tennis Federation, courses for Officials, in organising a Symposium for Coaches and Recreational Tennis and in initiating a pilot scheme for developing tennis activities in a selected European Eastern Country (Poland) with the support of the Grand Slam Fund.

Last but not least it must be mentioned that the ETA is constantly devoting energies and manpower in the coordination of the professional tournaments in Europe below the level of the world Men's and Women's Tours. For the women's events the ETA is also handling the entries in the tournaments. The total number of ETA sanctioned events in 1991 came to an impressive figure of 393 tournaments.

A review of European Tennis in 1991 cannot be considered duly completed without mentioning the outstanding results achieved by European Teams in the ITF world competitions. The triumph of Spain in the *Federation Cup* and of France in the *Davis Cup* as well as the victories of Germany (Girls) and Spain (Boys) in the World Youth Cup, combined with the successes registered in the new competition for 14 and under, the NTT World Junior Tennis, by Czechoslovakia (Girls) and Spain (Boys) are a clear indication of the European role in international competition at any level of the game. Eurocard, the Official General Sponsor of the European Tennis Association, has continued in 1991 to give their generous support to the ETA activities. Eurocard also instituted for the first time a trophy to be assigned to the European Nation who scored the best results in the ETA Official Events (team and individual Championships) open to Professional, Junior and Veteran Players.

A weighted system of the allocation of points to the various Championships has indicated that Germany is the winning nation of the 1991 Eurocard Trophy.

CONFEDERACION SUDAMERICANA DE TENIS

In 1991 COSAT maintained its busy schedule, exceeding the already successful 1990 period.

As customary the South American Junior Circuit was organised from January to March with 10 tournaments, each of which well exceeded the points established in its group.

For the first time a circuit for 14- and 16-year-old boys and girls was held in different countries and the South American National Championships for Juniors up to 18 years took place in Venezuela.

The World Junior qualifying event for the 16-year-old age group was played in Asuncion (Paraguay) and a 14-year-old age event in Brasilia (Brazil).

The COSAT-Cup for boys and girls was held in different South American countries with Ecuador, Chile, Brazil and Argentina qualifying in the girls' group and Colombia, Paraguay, Argentina, and Brazil in the boys' group.

Again, as in previous years, a girls' and a boys' team of under-18 juniors toured Europe with mixed success, the boys faring better than the girls.

Argentina, Chile and Brazil qualified for the World Youth Cup in the boys' group whilst Argentina, Brazil and Paraguay qualified in the girls' section.

Similarly two teams, one for boys and another for girls, under 14 years of age, toured Europe.

The work involved by COSAT's Secretariat became very hectic when dealing with entries for the much increased and improved women's and men's satellite tournaments which exceeded a total of 15 tournaments for ladies and 10 complete satellites for men.

The COSAT's technical team held four courses for coaches in Brazil, Paraguay, Argentina and Peru.

Ken Farrar and Stephen Winyard conducted one white badge officiating course in Brazil and three silver badge courses in Buenos Aires, Argentina, making it possible for South America now to have its own white and silver badge certified umpires and referees.

In the veteran field, COSAT arranged for the organisation of the South American Cups in all categories in the city of Porto Alegre, Brazil, and other events in Nuovo Hamburgo and Curitiba (Brazil). In 1992 these events will be held in Lima (Peru).

With all the tennis activities taking place during the year, the circulating of new rules and daily information, and the close liaison with the ITF administration, the work done by COSAT has been absorbing and varied but successful and of utmost importance for tennis in this part of the world.

THE PANAMERICAN TENNIS CONFEDERATION

During the 1990 to 1991 period, the Confederation successfully organised its two main events: the Central American and Caribbean Games, held in November 1990, in Mexico, and the Panamerican Games: held in August 1991, in Habana.

For both events the Confederation saw fit to modify the rules of play to allow professional players to compete. These modifications were made after discussing them with the organisations in charge of the general competitions, ODECABE and PASO, who agreed to the changes. In the Central American and Caribbean Games an intermediate arrangement was made allowing professionals ranked 100 or beyond in the World Ranking to participate. In the Panamerican Games, participation was open.

Tennis players from fifteen countries competed in the Central American and Caribbean Games and from twenty-four countries in the Panamerican Games, making Tennis the second most prominent sport after Track and Field.

Currently, the Confederation endeavours to have the events it organises recognised by the tennis organisations of the world.

HISTORY OF WHEELCHAIR TENNIS

Since its inception in 1976, wheelchair tennis has been the fastest growing and one of the most challenging and exciting of all wheelchair sports. It has provided opportunities for many disabled people to enjoy competitive tennis, as well as sharing experiences with family and able and disabled friends of all age groups.

Wheelchair tennis follows the same rules as able-bodied tennis except the wheelchair tennis player is allowed two bounces of the ball. An official recognition of the two bounce rule was given when The International Tennis Federation included this rule of wheelchair tennis in its official rules of tennis.

Initially, wheelchair tennis was a sport played mainly in the United States. In 1980, the National Foundation of Wheelchair Tennis (NFWT) was founded as the organizing body of the sport in the USA. By giving clinics and exhibitions the NFWT has given a lot of exposure to wheelchair tennis worldwide.

In October, 1988, The International Wheelchair Tennis Federation (IWTF) was founded as the organising body for wheelchair tennis at an international level. Representatives from organisations involved in wheelchair tennis present at this meeting came from Australia, Canada, Great Britain, France, Holland, Israel, Japan and the United States of America. With the efforts of the IWTF and its members, wheelchair tennis extended into an international realm. Many countries around the globe began to develop and organise wheelchair tennis nationally. There are currently 15 member nations and additional nations are expected to join in the near future. Today wheelchair tennis is played in approximately 40 countries.

Every year more and more tournaments are organised all over the world. In 1992 there will be over 200 tournaments worldwide. About 70 of them will count for the world rankings. Wheelchair tennis will also be an official medal sport in the Paralympics in Barcelona, Spain. The official Teams Event of the IWTF is called the World Team Cup.

An easy chair for the uncrowned King of Moscow, Andrei Cherkasov, who won his home title for the second year running — and has the trophies to prove it.   (M. Cole)

REVIEW OF THE JUNIOR GAME 1991

Jackie Nesbitt

With six circuit event titles in 1991 under his belt, Thomas Enqvist (Sweden) finished a worthy winner of the race to become the boys' singles Junior World Champion. These victories came at the South Australian and Victorian Junior Championships and, importantly, the Australian Open. In Europe Thomas won the Apple Bowl in Spain, the LTA International Junior Championships, Surbiton, and the title at Wimbledon.

Pushing him until the very end was Karim Alami (Morocco) who distinguished himself during the year. Karim struggled to adapt to grass court play but managed a semi-final placing at the French Open, where he was defeated by Enqvist, and was runner-up at both the US Open and the Orange Bowl. In third place, Kenneth Carlsen (Denmark) had good results in all the major events. In addition to reaching the quarter-finals of Wimbledon and the US Open, he won the Swedish Indoor Championships and the Canadian Open.

The leading Asian junior, Hyeong-Keun Song (Korea, Rep. of), finished the year in fourth position. The highlights for Hyeong-Keun were his successful trips to Belgium where he won both the Flanders Cup and the Astrid Bowl, and victory in the Group A Japanese event, the J.A.L. Cup. Australia's leading junior, Grant Doyle, completes the top five boys. His home' campaign was not as successful as he may have hoped, although he did reach the quarter-finals of the Australian Open. Europe brought more rewards when Grant finished runner-up at the Astrid Bowl and took the title at the Italian Open.

The girls' championship race was neck and neck for several months with Ai Sugiyama (Japan) and Zdenka Malkova (Czechoslovakia) finishing the year level on points. The title, however, goes to Zdenka Malkova by virtue of her stronger performances in the group A events throughout the year. Behind on points going into the Rolex Orange Bowl, Zdenka just managed to draw level with Ai thanks to a crucial semi-final placing which earned her an extra 40 points to add to her previous top six total. Ai had probably hoped her last effort of the year would secure the title for her with victory in the J.A.L. Cup. Despite her disappointment at losing so narrowly to Zdenka, she should look back over the year with some pride following quarter-final placings at both the Australian Open and the US Open.

Zdenka must now be thankful for her consistency which included quarter-final placings in Venezuela, the French Open, Wimbledon, and also victory at the Italian Open.

In third place, Elena Makarova (USSR), gave herself only just over two months to start and finish her Junior World Ranking campaign. Competing only in the major European events she still managed to post a very impressive set of results. In Italy she was runner-up at Alessandria, a semi-finalist in Santa Croce, and a finalist in the Italian Junior Open, losing to Malkova. She was also runner-up at Wimbledon, losing to Germany's Barbara Rittner who was competing in one of her rare Junior World Ranking events; she is already highly ranked in the senior game and a *Federation Cup* player for her nation.

There were more Europeans at 4 and 5 with Elena Likhovtseva's (USSR) victory at the Orange Bowl lifting her to fourth, and Catalina Cristea (Romania) posting victories in Italy, Czechoslovakia and USA, to take fifth place.

Although unable to catch Enqvist in the singles, Karim Alami built up an impressive lead in the doubles and finished well ahead of his nearest rivals. He took the doubles titles in Venezuela with Juan-Ignacio Garat (Argentina), Wimbledon with Greg Rusedski (Canada), and the US Open with John de Jager (South Africa). Australian players occupy the next three positions with Joshua Eagle, Grant Doyle and Paul Kilderry at 2, 3 and 4 respectively. Joshua and Grant paired together for most of the circuit and their most notable victories came in Australia and Italy. Joshua just moved ahead of Grant in the rankings by virtue of a semi-final placing at the Astrid Bowl, partnered by Swede Fredrik Giers.

Fourth-placed Paul Kilderry teamed with compatriot Jamie Holmes for many doubles events, with victory in the Suntory Japan Open and runner-up in the Australian Open followed by victory at the Orange Bowl, partnered by Enrique Abaroa (Mexico).

Fifth place went to Argentine Juan-Ignacio Garat who had victories at the Canadian Open, the Yucatan Cup, Mexico and the Eddie Herr Tournament, USA. The victory that probably brought him most satisfaction, however, was his win at the beginning of the year in the Venezuelan Group A tournament, where he partnered Karim Alami.

Czechoslovakian girls have dominated the doubles rankings over the past few years. Keeping up this tradition, Eva Martincova's strong start to the year, with victories in Colombia, Ecuador, Czechoslovakia and at the Italian Open, was enough to maintain her no. 1 ranking to the very end. A relatively quiet second half of the circuit saw only a quarter-final placing at Wimbledon and a semi-final position at the J.A.L. Cup. She also had good Group A performances when, partnered by Zdenka Malkova, she reached the finals of both the Venezuela Junior Championships and the French Open.

More Australians chased Eva to the title, with Joanne Limmer and Angie Woolcock finishing at 2 and 3 respectively. Joanne and Angie combined throughout most of the year with Joanne reaching the semi-finals at Wimbledon with compatriot Lisa McShea to ease ahead in the final listings. They finished as runners-up at the Australian Open and Wimbledon, semi-finalists at the J.A.L. Cup and quarter-finalists at both the Italian and French Opens, with victory at the Queensland and New South Wales Championships, the Astrid Bowl and at the LTA International Junior Tournament, Thames Ditton.

In fourth and fifth places are two players who teamed up for most of the circuit. Elena Likhovtseva and Julia Lutrova (USSR) won the German and Canadian Opens, were quarter-finalists at the US Open, reached the semi-final of the Eddie Herr Tournament, and were runners-up at both the J.A.L. Cup and the Orange Bowl.

1991, then, belonged very much to the European players, although Karim Alami's achievements for Africa are very encouraging.

In the Team Competitions the year will certainly be one for Spain to remember as their boys' teams in the various age group events met with almost unprecedented success. They took the 14 & Under Copa del Sol title following a 5–0 victory over USSR and, in doing so, claimed one of the Boys' European qualifying positions for the new NTT World Junior Tennis Competition held in Japan. Here, too, they proved dominant, taking the inaugural title with a 2–1 victory over Italy. Prospects look good for Czechoslovakian girls at 14 & Under. Although defeated 5–0 by Germany in the Europa Cup Final, the event now also used as the Girls' European NTT World Junior Tennis qualifying zone, in Japan they claimed the title with a 3–0 defeat of Australia.

The Jean Borotra Cup and the Helvetie Cup competitions act as the World Youth Cup European Qualifying zones, and this resulted in a record number of entries in 1991. The final of the boys' Jean Borotra Cup was to be a dress rehearsal for the World Youth Cup Final with the Spanish team emerging victors on both occasions, winning 4–1 and 2–1 over Czechoslovakia. The Czechoslovakian girls gained revenge in the Helvetie Cup where they defeated Spain 4–1. However, neither team could manage a top placing in the World Youth Cup Final, with Germany defeating Paraguay 2–1 in the deciding doubles match.

On to the 18 & Under team events where this time Spain managed a double. Their boys defeated Germany 2–0 in the final of the Vasco Valerio Cup and their girls' team proved too strong for Sweden, winning 3–0 in the final of the H.M. Queen Sofia Cup.

Teams from the rest of the world got their chance to take on the Spanish in the Sunshine and Continental Players Cup Competitions. After a disappointing campaign at the World Youth Cup Finals, the girls from the USA made the most of home advantage and took the Continental Players Cup in impressive style from the Netherlands, winning the final 2–0.

It was Spain again who won through to the final of the boys' Sunshine Cup where they faced spirited opposition from the French. Despite losing the opening rubber, the Spanish were not to be denied the perfect year and took the next two rubbers for a winning 2–1 margin. Congratulations, then, to the Real Federación Española de Tenis. Their boys' teams have set a record that at best can only ever be equalled in future.

PRINCE JUNIOR WORLD RANKING 1991

Only those players who qualified for a year-end ranking are listed. The minimum requirements for this were having played 6 Prince Junior World Ranking events, 3 of which were outside their own country and 3 of which were Group A status.

BOYS' SINGLES

1 Thomas Enqvist (SWE); **2** Karim Alami (MAR); **3** Kenneth Carlsen (DEN); **4** Hyeong-Keun Song (KOR); **5** Grant Doyle (AUS); **6** Michael Joyce (USA); **7** Juan-Ignacio Garat (ARG); **8** Paul Kilderry (AUS); **9** Marcelo Charpentier (ARG); **10** Mose Navarra (ITA); **11** Carlos Tarantino (ARG); **12** Stephen Gleeson (AUS); **13** Brian Dunn (USA); **14** Jamie Holmes (AUS); **15** Johannes Unterberger (AUT); **16** Nicolas Kischkewitz (FRA); **17** Alexandru Radulescu (ROM); **18** Joshua Eagle (AUS); **19** David Witt (USA); **20** Sule Ladipo (NGR).

GIRLS' SINGLES

1 Zdenka Malkova (TCH); **2** Ai Sugiyama (JPN); **3** Elena Makarova (URS); **4** Elena Likhovtseva (URS); **5** Catalina Cristea (ROM); **6** Mami Donoshiro (JPN); **7** Eva Martincova (TCH); **8** Anna Smashnova (ISR); **9** Maja Muric (YUG); **10** Joanne Limmer (AUS); **11** Rossana De Los Rios (PAR); **12** Eleonora Vegliante (VEN); **13** Seong-Heui Park (KOR); **14** Maria-Jose Gaidano (ARG); **15** Pam Nelson (USA); **16** Chanda Rubin (USA); **17** Caroline Hunt (GBR); **18** Lena Niemantsverdriet (HOL); **19** Suvimol Duangchan (THA); **20** Katarzyna Malec (POL).

BOYS' DOUBLES

1 Karim Alami (MAR); **2** Joshua Eagle (AUS); **3** Grant Doyle (AUS); **4** Paul Kilderry (AUS); **5** Juan-Ignacio Garat (ARG); **6** Enrique Abaroa (MEX); **7** Emmanuel Udozorh (NGR); **8** Magnus Martinelle (SWE); **9** Jamie Holmes (AUS); **10** Allan Larsen (DEN); **11** Kenneth Carlsen (DEN); **12** Sule Ladipo (NGR); **13** Thomas Enqvist (SWE); **14** Patricio Delgado (CHI); **15** Oscar Ortiz (MEX); **16** Julian Knowle (AUT); **17** Hyeong-Keun Song (KOR); **18** Mose Navarra (ITA); **19** Massimo Bertolini (ITA); **20** Andres Urencio (MEX).

GIRLS' DOUBLES

1 Eva Martincova (TCH); **2** Joanne Limmer (AUS); **3** Angie Woolcock (AUS); **4** Elena Likhovtseva (URS); **5** Julia Lutrova (URS); **6** Zdenka Malkova (TCH); **7** Mami Donoshiro (JPN); **8** Seong-Heui Park (KOR); **9** Catherine Barclay (AUS); **10** Ai Sugiyama (JPN); **11** Maja Muric (YUG); **12** Helene Kappler (VEN); **13** Eleonora Vegliante (VEN); **14** Jennifer Saret (PHI); **15** Catalina Cristea (ROM); **16** Asa Carlsson (SWE); **17=** Rossana De Los Rios (PAR); **17=** Larissa Schaerer (PAR); **19** Maria Cianfragna (ARG); **20** Karolina Bulat (POL).

PRINCE JUNIOR WORLD RANKING 1991 – POINTS EXPLANATION

The Prince Junior World Ranking is a world-wide points-linked circuit of 105 tournaments, 5 continental championships and 4 team competitions in 60 countries, under the management of the International Tennis Federation. There are ten separate points categories covering the three types of events. There is no limit to the number of tournaments in which a player may compete each year. The best six results from tournaments (Groups A and 1–5), continental championships (Groups B1–B3) and team competitions (Group C) count towards a player's ranking. To qualify for a final year-end ranking a player must have competed in at least six events, including at least three Group A tournaments and at least three outside his or her own country.

POINTS TABLE (Tournaments & Regional Championships)

SINGLES

	A	1	2	3	4	5	B1	B2	B3
Winner	250	120	80	60	40	30	180	100	80
Runner Up	180	100	65	50	30	20	120	80	50
Semi-Finalists	120	75	50	30	20	10	80	60	30
Quarter-Finalists*	80	50	30	20	10	5	60	40	15
Losers in last 16**	50	30	15	10	5	—	30	25	5
Losers in last 32***	30	20	—	—	—	—	20	10	—

* only if 16 or more players in draw (excluding withdrawals)
** only if 32 or more players in draw (excluding withdrawals)
***only if 64 or more players in draw (excluding withdrawals)

DOUBLES (Each Player)

	A	1	2	3	4	5	B1	B2	B3
Winners	180	100	65	50	30	20	120	80	50
Runners-up	120	75	50	30	20	10	80	60	30
Semi-Finalists*	80	50	30	20	10	5	60	40	15
Quarter-Finalists**	60	30	15	10	5	—	30	25	5
Losers in last 16***	30	20	—	—	—	20	10	—	

* only if 8 or more pairs in draw (excluding withdrawals)
** only if 16 or more pairs in draw (excluding withdrawals)
***only if 32 or more pairs in draw (excluding withdrawals)

POINTS TABLE (Group C – Team Competition)

	No. 1 Singles Player Win	No. 2 Singles Player Win	Doubles Win Each Player
Final	100	80	80
Semi-Final	80	60	60
Quarter-Final	60	40	40

POINTS TABLE (Group A Super Series Bonus Points)

	Singles	Doubles
Winner of 3 or more Group A events	150	150

Yahya Doumbia of Senegal, whose success in Challenger tournaments helped him to improve his world ranking by more than 300 places, despite injuries to knee and elbow. (M. Phillips)

ITF JUNIOR WORLD RANKING CIRCUIT 1991

DATE	TOURNAMENT	GROUP	BOYS' SINGLES FINAL	GIRLS' SINGLES FINAL
24–30 Dec	Casablanca Cup, Mexico	2	J. Margotto d. E. Casas 6–2 6–1	A. Gallardo d. C. Hunt 6–2 7–5
27 Dec–1 Jan	African Closed, Ivory Coast	B3	H. Arazi d. E. N'Goran 6–3 2–6 7–6	D. Randriantefy d. S. Bel Guezzar 6–1 6–2
29 Dec–2 Jan	Queensland Girls', Australia	3	—	A. Woolcock d. J. Limmer 7–5 7–6–1
29 Dec–3 Jan	South Australian Boys'	3	T. Enqvist d. J. Holmes 6–4 6–4	—
31 Dec–6 Jan	Venezuelan Champs	A	J-I. Garat d. P. Gazda 6–0 Ret.	E. Maia d. M. Muric 6–4 7–6
1–6 Jan	Salk Indoor, Sweden	3	A. Radulescu d. M. Martinelle 6–4 6–2	A. Carlsson d. M. Linusson 6–3 6–2
1–6 Jan	Coqui Bowl, Puerto Rico	3	J. Margotto d. J. De Jager 6–3 7–6	L. Pavlov d. M-A. Vento 6–4 6–4
3–9 Jan	New South Wales, Australia	1	M. Navarra d. J. Eagle 6–3 7–5	J. Limmer d. A. Woolcock 2–6 6–3 6–4
7–11 Jan	Vasteras Indoor, Sweden	1	M. Martinelle d. F. Giers 7–5 7–5	M. Vallin d. A. Carlsson 6–7 7–3 7–L
7–11 Jan	Pony Malta Cup, Colombia	1	K. Alami d. M. Hood 6–2 6–1	M. Bernard d. C. Hunt 2–6 7–6 6–4
7–13 Jan	Coffee Bowl, Costa Rica	3	J. De Jager d. J. Margotto 6–3 3–6 6–3	I. Petrov d. W. Martinez 6–3 7–6
14–19 Jan	Victoria, Australia	3	T. Enqvist d. J. Eagle 7–5 6–2	A. Sugiyama d. S-H. Park 7–6 6–2
14–20 Jan	Ecuador Cup, Quito	2	M. Leite d. C. Tarantino 3–6 7–6 6–2	Z. Malikova d. E. Martincova 6–2 2–0 Ret.
21–17 Jan	Australian Open	2	T. Enqvist d. S. Gleeson 7–6 6–7 6–1	N. Pratt d. K. Godridge 6–4 6–3
21–27 Jan	Inka Bowl, Peru	A	C. Tarantino d. C. Reano 6–3 6–3	M. Donoshiro d. K. Malec 6–4 6–1
28 Jan–3 Feb	Condor De Plata, Bolivia	3	G. Silberstein d. P. Delgado 7–5 7–5	V. Valdovinos d. S. Ugarriza 2–6 6–3 7–6
4–10 Feb	Milo Cup, Chile	3	F. Ruiz d. C. Liggett 6–4 6–3	R. De Los Rios d. C. Ampuero 7–6 6–2
4–10 Feb	Indian International, India	5	R. Reddy d. N. Kirtane 6–4 6–1	D. Merchant d. S. Jadhav 6–4 6–1
11–15 Feb	Inter-Continental Hotel, Sri Lanka	5	S. Kirtane d. R. Reddy 6–3 6–1	S. Duangchan d. A. Reddy 7–6 6–2
11–17 Feb	Argentina Cup, Cordoba	4	C. Tarantino d. G. Silberstein 6–0 5–7 6–4	R. De Los Rios d. V. Valdovinos 6–3 6–4
11–17 Feb	Start Indoor	4	Cancelled	Cancelled
18–24 Feb	Carrasco Bowl, Uruguay	2	C. Tarantino d. L. Arnold 6–3 6–1	E. Vegliante d. A. Quezada 6–0 6–2
18–24 Feb	Sri Lanka Champs	4	S. Kirtane d. S. Pospelov 6–4 2–6 6–0	S. Duangchan d. A. Reddy 0–6 7–5 6–4
19–24 Feb	Czechoslovakian Indoor	3	P. Gazda d. K. Carlsen 6–7 7–6 6–1	K. Kroupova d. C. Cristea 6–2 6–1
25 Feb–2 March	Asuncion Bowl, Paraguay	5	C. Tarantino d. M. Pastura 6–2 6–3	R. De Los Rios d. S. Ugarriza 6–3 6–2
25 Feb–2 March	Qatar Champs		Cancelled	Cancelled
26 Feb–2 March	Asian Closed, Brunei	B2	S. Kirtane d. H-K. Song 6–1 6–2	S-H. Park d. K. Summa 5–7 6–3 6–1
27 Feb–3 March	Swedish Indoor	3	K. Carlsen d. M. Martinelle 7–6 6–3	A. Carlsson d. T. Soderstrom 3–0 Ret.
5–10 March	Banana Bowl, Brazil	1	J. Unterberger d. M. Saliola 4–6 6–1 6–4	R. Burzagli d. K. Malec 6–3 7–6
11–17 March	Sun Cup, Belgium	4	J. Van Garsse-Lysens d. J. Van Herck 6–7 7–5 6–2	N. Feber d. R. Liziero 7–6 6–3
11–17 March	Malaysian Champs	4	S. Pospelov d. M. Bhupathi 6–2 6–4	J. Saret d. K-R. Chin 6–7 6–4 6–2
11–17 March	Singapore International	5	A. Adams d. F. Factura 6–1 3–6 6–2	J. Merchant d. F. La'o 1–6 6–2 6–1
12–17 March	Bavarian Indoor, Germany	4	D. Prchlik d. J. Knowle 6–4 4–6 6–2	M. Skulj-Zivec d. J. Jehs 6–3 7–6
12–18 March	South American Closed, Brazil	B2	L. Arnold d. M. Saliola 6–7 6–1 6–3	R. De Los Rios d. V. Strappa 0–6 6–2 7–5
20–24 March	British Indoor	5	L. Sabin d. N. Weal 6–3 7–5	J. Pullin d. F. Stoner 6–3 6–4
25–30 March	Dubitzky Junior, Israel	4	A. Ben David d. N. Behr 6–4 7–6	R. Mayer d. A. Smashnova 7–5 6–2
25–31 March	Thailand Int., Bangkok	3	E-Y. Suyono d. N. Ploysook 6–3 6–2	K. Summa d. D. Merchant 3–6 7–6 6–2
25 March–1 April	Florence Int.	1	C. Borroni d. R. Wawra 6–1 7–6	S. Vernier d. E. Diez 6–4 6–2
27–31 March	Pascuas Bowl, Paraguay	5	A. Salgado d. M. Wolff 6–3 5–7 6–2	S. Ugarriza d. M-J. Gaidano 6–2 7–6
1–7 April	Philippines Int., Manila	3	M. Bhupathi d. J. Greenhaigh 6–3 2–1 Ret.	F. La'o d. J. Saret 6–3 6–3

DATE	TOURNAMENT	GROUP	BOYS' SINGLES FINAL	GIRLS' SINGLES FINAL
1–7 April	Grasse Int., France	3	Cancelled	S-T. Wang d. A. Sugiyama 6–3 6–0
10–14 April	Japan Champs, Tokyo	1	P. Kilderry d. B. Wijaya 4–6 6–2 6–2	S. Duangchan d. D. Merchant 6–3 4–6 6–3
15–21 April	Hong Kong Int.	3	J. Greenhalgh d. S. Kirtane 6–2 6–0	M. Tsitsuasvili d. K. Kureguin 4–6 6–4 6–2
15–21 April	Tashkent Int., USSR	3	D. Tomachevitch d. P. Zhoromsky 6–1 6–1	A. Vanc d. B. Schett 7–5 6–3
16–20 April	Katoro Cup, Yugoslavia	3	D. Prchlik d. M. Marcelo 6–2 3–6 6–4	S. Chatsuthipan d. J. Krishnamoorthy 3–6 6–3
22–28 April	Indonesia Int., Jakarta	4	E-Y. Suyono d. D. Susetio 6–3 6–4	M. Chirikova d. K. Kureguiar 6–3 6–1
22–28 April	Sochi Int., USSR	3	S. Sargsian d. A. Bovarin 6–4 6–2	L. Pavlov d. B. Schett 6–4 3–6 6–3
24–28 April	Spring Bowl, Austria	4	A. Krell d. N. Patzak 6–3 7–5	K. Kroupova d. Z. Boogert 6–3 6–2
29 April–4 May	Panasonic Cup, Germany	4	A. Caspari d. C. Tambue 6–4 6–4	M-J. Gaidano d. I. Horvat 6–3 6–2
29 April–5 May	Salsomaggiore, Italy	2	C. Borroni d. M. Bertolini 6–1 6–3	
30 April–3 May	Zibans Cup, Algeria	5	Cancelled	
6–12 May	Alessandria, Italy	2	C. Borroni d. F. Beraldo 6–3 6–0	S. Indemini d. E. Makarova 6–4 7–6
13–18 May	Santa Croce, Italy	2	F. Messori d. G. Doyle 6–3 6–1	C. Cristea d. A. Vanc 7–6 4–5 6–3
19–25 May	Italian Junior Champs	A	G. Doyle d. K. Carlsen 1–6 6–3 9–7	Z. Malkova d. E. Makarova 6–2 6–1
27 May–1 June	Astrid Bowl, Belgium	1	H-K. Song d. G. Doyle 6–3 6–7 6–1	D. Monami d. J. Limmer 6–4 6–4
3–9 June	French Junior Open, Paris	A	A. Medvedev d. T. Enqvist 6–4 7–6	A. Smashnova d. I. Gorrochategui 2–6 7–5
10–15 June	Flanders Cup, Belgium	A	H-K. Song d. K. Goossens 6–4 7–6	N. Feber d. E. Vegliante 6–2 6–0
10–16 June	Apple Bowl, Spain	4	T. Enqvist d. J-S. Martinez 6–1 6–2	A. Ortuno d. V. Castellano 6–2 6–3
11–15 June	Danubius Cup, Hungary	2	W. Eschauer d. R. Svetlik 6–2 6–0	M. Prorokova d. Z. Rebekova 6–1 6–2
18–23 June	LTA Int., Thames Ditton, England	2	G. Rusedski d. J. Eagle 6–1 6–4	S-H. Park d. C. Barclay 7–6 6–1
24–29 June	Danish Int.	4	J. Hermansson d. J. Hede 7–6 6–4	V. Antonella d. C. Vincent 6–1 6–2
25–30 June	LTA Int., Surbiton, England	4	T. Enqvist/P. Gazda Rain suspended play	E. Martincova d. C. Rubin 6–4 6–1
1–7 July	Wimbledon Junior	A	W. Black d. R. Wassen 7–5 6–1	B. Rittner d. E. Makarova 6–7 6–2 6–3
1–8 July	Netherlands Champs	4	F. Kascak d. S. Ladipo 6–0 7–6	K. Bitter d. K. De Weille 6–3 7–5
8–14 July	German Junior Open	1	P. Motylewski d. S. Balan 4–6 6–2 6–2	M. Donoshiro d. A. Sugiyama 4–6 6–3 6–2
15–19 July	Friendship Cup, Poland	4	K. Zakharia d. N. Malcolm 3–6 7–6 6–3	K. Malec d. S. Rynarzewska 6–7 6–4 6–2
15–21 July	Jamaican Int.	5	E. Couto d. B. Jacob 6–2 7–5	K. Walter d. S. Hanna 6–1 6–0
18–20 July	Ebel Champs, Switzerland	C	Spain d. Germany 2–0	D. Randriantefy d. S. Loche 7–5 1–6 6–1
18–20 July	European Boys Team, France	C	Spain d. Sweden 3–0	
21–28 July	European Girls Team, Spain	B1	A. Berasategui d. K. Carlsen 6–3 6–1	A. Fusai d. K. Kroupova 3–6 7–5 3–0
22–27 July	Slazenger Winchester, England	5	A. Radulescu d. T. Kilbert 6–3 6–1	S. Hamplett d. A. Voina 6–2 6–3
4–11 July	European Closed, Spain	1		L. Davenport d. K. Schluker 7–5 6–1
5–10 Aug	Nigerian Int.	5	G. Adenekan d. G. Otu 6–3 4–6 6–3	N. Okonkwo d. U. Oghereno 6–2 6–3
5–10 Aug	Botswana Champs	5	C. N'Goran d. L. Ilou 6–3 6–7 6–4	L. Mulevu d. S. Fourie 4–6 6–0 6–3
5–11 Aug	Slovakia Cup, Czechoslovakia	3	F. Gardavsky d. K. Ritz 7–6 6–3	C. Cristea d. E. Krejcova 4–5 6–2 6–2
6–14 Aug	USTA Closed Boys, USA	1	M. Joyce d. I. Baron 2–6 6–2 7–5	
7–11 Aug	Alpen-Adria Z Cup, Austria	1	W. Eschauer d. S. Leiner 3–6 6–4 6–0	A. Dracz d. N. Murn 7–6 4–3 6–1
12–18 Aug	Crystal Cup, Czechoslovakia	2	D. Prchlik d. D. Miketa 3–6 6–1 6–4	C. Cristea d. M. Hautova 6–1 7–5
12–18 Aug	USTA INT. Grass, USA	3	R. Leol d. V. Goncalves 6–3 6–4	K. Schlukebir d. W. Crabtree 6–4 6–0
13–17 Aug	Nyirfa Cup, Hungary	2	B. Bosnjakovic d. Z. Fule 6–4 6–4	K. Gyorke d. M. Gargulakova 6–3 6–2
13–17 Aug	Zimbabwe Champs, Harare	5	C. N'Goran d. L. Illou 6–2 6–4	N. Joshi d. A. Vaughan 6–3 6–3
20–24 Aug	USTA Int. Hard, USA	3	I. Thomson d. V. Goncalves 7–6 6–6 3	L. Kurk d. A. Brand 7–6 6–3

DATE	TOURNAMENT	GROUP	BOYS' SINGLES FINAL	GIRLS' SINGLES FINAL
20–24 Aug	Zeralda Cup, Algeria	5	Cancelled	N. Joshi d. A. Berthe 6–3 6–4
20–25 Aug	Zambia Champs	5	L. Ilou d. D. Lebeta 6–4 1–6 6–3	P-A. Short d. M. Ah Hoy 6–4 6–4
26–31 Aug	South Pacific Closed, American Samoa	B3	H. Movriswala d. D. Roberts 6–4 7–5	A. Mall d. C. Cristea 6–2 7–5
26 Aug–1 Sept	Canadian Open, Quebec	1	K. Carlsen d. M. Navarra 6–4 5–7 7–5	N. Joshi d. L. Mulevu 6–3 6–4
27 Aug–1 Sept	Kenya Champs, Nairobi	5	D. Lebeta d. L. Ilou 4–6 6–0 6–3	K. Habsudova d. A. Mall 6–1 6–3
2–8 Sept	US Open Junior, New York	A	L. Paes d. K. Alami 6–4 6–4	M. Alexe d. L. Zirnoveanu 6–3 7–6
2–8 Sept	Romanian Champs	4	T. Georgescu d. E. Samson 4–6 7–5 6–2	G. Beleni d. M. Nakonechnaya 6–4 6–4
9–15 Sept	Aphrodite Cup, Cyprus	5	S. Baranov d. P. Moschoutis 6–3 6–4	Z. Nemsakova d. A. Kremer 6–4 6–4
11–15 Sept	Luxembourg Champs	4	P. Kudrnac d. T. Janda 6–1 6–3	L. Richterova d. M. Gargulakova 6–1 7–6
17–22 Sept	Pelikan Bowl, Bulgaria	5	R. Murashko d. S. Balan 6–1 6–3	A. Quezada d. A. Randrup 6–3 6–2
26–29 Sept	Saloman Melnick, Chile	5	G. Silberstein d. M. Fernandez 7–6 3–6 6–3	T. Tanasugarn d. P. Kansuthi 3–0 Ret.
30 Sept–5 Oct	Burnei Int.	4	Venkataraghavan d. Chotiyarnwong 1–6 7–5 6–4	
30 Sept–5 Oct	Northern Territory, Australia	5	Cancelled	
7–13 Oct	Mercu Buana, Indonesia	3	T. Tandjung d. A. Soepardi 6–7 6–3 6–4	R. Tejakusuma d. M. Chernovita 6–3 7–6
14–19 Oct	Taipei Champs	3	N. Ploysook d. S. Yongchantanaskul 6–3 6–1	J. Lee d. S. Mingmolee 6–1 6–2
22–26 Oct	JAL Cup, Japan	A	H-K. Song d. A. Belobrajdic 6–2 6–1	A. Sugiyama d. M. Donoshiro 7–5 6–0
28 Oct–3 Nov	East Asian Champs, Hong Kong	3	N. Kirtane d. A. Mierzwinski 6–4 6–1	L-Y. Tang d. Q. Huang 7–6 6–3
4–9 Nov	Gaungzhou Int., China	3	I-Y. Yoon d. J-W. Yun 6–3 6–1	L-Y. Tang d. Y. Cai 6–1 3–6 6–4
11–17 Nov	Singha Junior, Thailand	3	N. Kirtane d. A. Mierzwinski 4–6 6–2 6–4	X. Ye d. N. Joshi 6–1 6–0
18–24 Nov	Bangladesh Int.	4	A. Chotiyarnwong d. A. Shafik 7–5 6–3	S. Chatsuthipan d. T. Tanasugarn 7–5 6–3
25–30 Nov	Yucatan Cup, Mexico	4	J-I. Garat d. M. Hood	I. Petrov d. G. Devercelli 6–0 6–0
1–7 Dec	Pakistan Champs	5	M. Khaliq d. A. Shafik 6–2 6–0	
2–7 Dec	Eddie Herr Int., USA	2	B. Jacob d. M. Kohlmann 6–4 6–2	P. Bergerow d. C. Cristea 6–4 6–3
9–14 Dec	Maureen Connolly-Brinker, USA	C		USA d. Netherlands 2–0
9–14 Dec	Sunshine Cup, USA	C	Spain d. France 2–1	
16–22 Dec	Orange Bowl, USA	A	M. Charpentier d. K. Alami 6–4 6–3	E. Likhovtseva d. M-J. Gaidano 7–5 6–1
23–29 Dec	Port Washington, USA	2	K. Carlsen d. A. Savolt 6–1 6–2	C. Cristea d. T. Doric 6–2 6–3

VASCO VALERIO CUP *(Boys' 18 & Under International Team Championship)*
22 nations competed. Played in Vichy, France, 18–20 July.
Quarter-finals: Italy d. Czechoslovakia 2–1; Germany d. Sweden 3–0; France d. Poland 2–1; Spain d
Yugoslavia 3–0. *Semi-finals:* Germany d. Italy 2–1; Spain d. France 2–1. *3rd place play-off:* Italy d
France 2–0. *Final:* Spain d. Germany 2–0 (A. Berasategui d. S. Gessner 6–4 6–2; A. Corretja d. G. Pau
0–2 3–0 0–0).

HM QUEEN SOFIA CUP *(Girls' 18 & Under International Team Championship)*
15 nations competed. Played in Lerida, Spain, 18–20 July.
Quarter-finals: USSR d. Hungary 3–0; Sweden d. France 2–1; Spain d. Germany 3–0; Belgium d
Czechoslovakia 2–1. *Semi-finals:* Sweden d. USSR 2–1; Spain d. Belgium 2–1. *3rd place play-off.*
USSR d. Belgium 3–0. *Final:* Spain d. Sweden 3–0 (E. Botini d. A. Carlsson 5–7 6–2 6–4; E. Bes d. M
Vallin 6–2 6–1; Botini/C.Torrens d. Vallin/Carlsson 4–6 7–6 6–2).

COPA DEL SOL CUP *(Boys' 14 and Under Team Championship)*
18 nations competed. Semi-finals and final played in Playa de Aro, Spain, 5–7 July.
Quarter-finals: Sweden d. France 3–2; USSR d. Germany 3–2; Czechoslovakia d. Italy 3–2; Spain d.
Great Britain/Belgium round-robin. *Semi-finals:* USSR d. Italy 3–2; Spain d. Sweden 4–1. *3rd place
play-off:* Italy d. Sweden 3–2. *Final:* Spain d. USSR 5–0 (J-A. Saiz d. I. Pridankine 7–6 6–1; F. Vincente
d. J. Michejev 7–6 6–7 6–4; J. Vincente d. A. Gonopolskij 6–0 6–4; A. Martin d. A. Stoljarov 6–7 6–3 8–6;
Martin/J. Vincente d. Pridankine/Stoljarov 7–6 6–3).

EUROPA CUP *(Girls' 14 & Under International Team Championship)*
18 nations competed. Semi-finals and finals played in Alessandria, Italy, 4–7 July.
Quarter-finals: Yugoslavia d. Hungary 3–2; Italy d. France 3–1; Czechoslovakia d. Netherlands 5–0;
Germany d. Spain 3–2. *Semi-finals:* Czechoslovakia d. Yugoslavia 5–0; Germany d. Italy 3–2. *3rd place
play-off:* Yugoslavia d. Italy 5–0. *Final:* Germany d. Czechoslovakia 5–0 (M. Vladulescu d. A. Havrlikova
6–0 6–3; N. Raidt d. R. Surova 7–6 6–2; S. Schmidle d. K. Bakalarova 6–0 6–4; A. Barna d. R. Pelikanova
6–2 6–4; Barna/T. Karsten d. L. Cenkova/Havrlikova 6–2 6–1).

JEAN BOROTRA CUP *(Boys' 16 & Under International Team Championship)*
21 nations competed. Final played in Le Touquet, France, 4–6 August.
Quarter-finals: Czechoslovakia d. Switzerland 4–1; France d. Sweden 4–1; Germany d. Italy 5–0;
Spain d. Netherlands 5–0. *Semi-finals:* Czechoslovakia d. France 4–1; Spain d. Germany 3–2. *3rd place
play-off:* Germany d. France 4–1. *Final:* Spain d. Czechoslovakia 4–1 (A. Costa d. F. Kascak 6–4 6–2; G.
Corrales d. P. Pala 6–7 6–1 63; R. Carretero d. D. Skoch 5–7 7–6 7–5; J. Balcells lost to D. Miketa 5–7
6–1 1–6; Corrales/Costa d. Kascak/Pala 6–1 6–4).

HELVETIE CUP *(Girls' 16 & Under International Team Championship)*
22 nations competed. Final played in Leysin, Switzerland, 4–6 August.
Quarter-finals: USSR d. Netherlands 3–2; Czechoslovakia d. Italy 4–1. *Semi-finals:* Spain d. USSR
3–2; Czechoslovakia d. Germany 3–2. *3rd place play-off:* Germany d. USSR 3–2. *Final:* Czechoslovakia d. Spain 4–1 (Z. Malkova d. E. Jiminez 6–4 6–0; E. Martincova lost to M. Cruells 3–6 6–7; E.
Hostacova d. A. Ortuno 6–3 7–5; M. Hautova d. A. Montolio 4–6 6–3 6–1; Malkova/Martincova d.
Cruells/Jiminez 6–3 6–1).

SUNSHINE CUP *(Boys' 18 & Under International Team Championship)*
34 nations competed. Played in Weston, Florida, USA, 9–14 December.
Quarter-finals: USSR d. Argentina 2–1; France d. Israel 3–0; Chile d. USA 2–1; Spain d. South Africa
2–1. *Semi-finals:* France d. USSR 2–1; Spain d. Chile 2–1. *Final:* Spain d. France 2–1 (J. Martinez lost
to S. Matheu 4–6 6–1 3–6; A. Berasategui d. L. Roux 6–4 7–6; Martinez/Berasategui d. Matheu/Roux
6–2 7–6).

MAUREEN CONNOLLY BRINKER CONTINENTAL PLAYERS' CUP
(Girls' 18 & Under International Team Championship)
27 nations competed. Played in Plantation, Florida, USA, 9–14 December.
Quarter-finals: Spain d. Venezuela 2–0; Netherlands d. Great Britain 2–1; Italy d. Austria 3–0; USA d.
South Africa 3–0. *Semi-finals:* Netherlands d. Spain 2–0; USA d. Italy 2–1. *Final:* USA d. Netherlands
2–0 (P. Nelson d. L. Bitter 6–2 7–5; L. Davenport d. L. Niemantsverdriet 6–2 6–4).

ITF VETERAN TENNIS

THE VETERANS GO DOWN UNDER

Australia played host to all the Team Events and the Veterans Individual Championships in 1991 – a very commendable operation indeed that called for co-operation and organisational skills on a large scale. The scale extended from Brisbane in the east to Perth in the west, stopping off at Sydney, Canberra, Melbourne and Adelaide in between.

The original plan was for the Italia Cup to be played in Indonesia but unfortunately this had to be rearranged at short notice owing to circumstances in the Middle East and Melbourne came to the rescue.

At the players' Open Forum in Perth it was apparent that the ultimate goal in age categories has yet to be reached with many supporters for the five year age gaps between all ages and a fervent plea for a 75 Age Category for Men. It is only reasonable to suggest that five years at the senior level is an acceptable age difference for competition and it is the Veteran Committee's intention to fulfil that goal in due course. It is also an accepted fact that once an age category tournament is introduced, then the request for a Team Event soon follows. The intention is to evaluate the support for new categories at tournaments and then, when buoyant, to introduce Team Events.

The introduction of the Fred Perry Computer Ranking Programme for 1991 produced some interesting data much of which was contrary to what was expected. As a result the Rules for 1992 have been revised. It was expected that the first year would be a trial period before going live in 1992 and so it proved. In the light of this information it is expected that meaningful Ranking Lists for all ages will be produced on a regular basis in 1992.

1991 saw the first sponsored Team Event in the Veterans' Calendar. Fred Perry Sportswear (UK) Ltd sponsored the Fred Perry Team Trophy for Men in the 50 age category which was staged at the West Hants Tennis Club, Bournemouth and attracted 17 teams from all over the world. Malaysia competed for the first time in any Veteran Team Event. Fred Perry and his wife, Bobbie, were very much in evidence during the week and Fred must have signed almost as many autographs as he did when winning Wimbledon in the 1930s. As the self-styled Chairman of the Fred Perry Friendship Committee he did a wonderful job. Germany were the first winners of the Trophy with Great Britain the worthy runners-up.

Europe plays host to ten Team Events in 1992 with the new Maureen Connolly Team Event for Ladies 55 being hosted by the USTA in Tyler, Texas.

Veterans tennis goes from strength to strength each year.

ITALIA CUP

Men's 35 Age Group
MELBOURNE, AUSTRALIA, 7–12 APRIL
Quarter-finals: Spain d. Canada 3–0; France d. Netherlands 2–1; Italy d. Germany 2–1; Australia d. Hong Kong 3–0.
Semi-finals: Spain d. France 2–1; Australia d. Italy 3–0.
Final: Australia d. Spain 3–0 (P. McNamee d. J. Moreno 6–3 6–2; P. McNamara d. E. Vasquez 6–3 7–6; P. McNamee/P. McNamara d. E. Vasquez/J. Velasco 7–5 6–3).

DUBLER CUP

Men's 45 Age Group
SYDNEY, AUSTRALIA, 7–12 APRIL
Quarter-finals: Germany d. Indonesia 3–0; France d. Italy 2–1; Australia d. Austria 3–0; USA d. Sweden 2–1.
Semi-finals: Germany d. France 3–0; USA d. Australia 3–0.
Final: USA d. Germany 3–0 (D. Nash d. H. Plotz 6–2 7–5; C. Hoeveler d. H. Elschenbroich 7–6 (9–7 6–3; D. Nash/J. Parker d. B. Nitsche/G. Krauss 6–4 4–6 6–1).

FRED PERRY CUP

Men's 50 Age Group
BOURNEMOUTH, GREAT BRITAIN, 8–13 SEPTEMBER
Quarter-finals: Austria d. France 3–0; Germany d. Australia 2–1; Great Britain d. Sweden 2–1; USA d. Chile 3–0.
Semi-finals: Germany d. Austria 3–0; Great Britain d. USA 2–1.
Final: Germany d. Great Britain 3–0 (K. Fuhrmann d. D. Howarth 6–3 6–4; G. Prell d. D. Shears 6–2, 6–1; G. Prell/B. Reinholz d. D. Shears/B. Storr 6–3 7–5).

AUSTRIA CUP

Men's 55 Age Group
SYDNEY, AUSTRALIA, 7–12 APRIL
Quarter-finals: Australia d. Canada 2–1; Great Britain d. Japan 2–0; Germany d. Ireland 3–0; USA d. Yugoslavia 3–0.
Semi-finals: Australia d. Great Britain 2–1; USA d. Germany 3–0.
Final: USA d. Australia 3–0 (G. Davis d. P. Froelich 7–6 (7–3) 4–6 6–1; K. van Nostrand d. K. Taylor 6–3 7–6 (7–4); J. Nelson/L. Lindborg d. K. Taylor/P. Froelich 6–1 6–4).

GOTTFRIED VON CRAMM CUP

Men's 60 Age Group
ADELAIDE, AUSTRALIA, 7–12 APRIL
Quarter-finals: USA d. Canada 3–0; Australia d. Great Britain 3–0; New Zealand d. France 3–0; Sweden d. Germany 2–1.
Semi-finals: USA d. Australia 2–1; New Zealand d. Sweden 3–0.
Final: USA d. New Zealand 2–1 (W. Bonham d. P. Becroft 6–3 7–6 (7–4); C. Devoe lost to J. Barry 5–7 4–6; C. Devoe/W. Davis d. J. Barry/P. Becroft 6–3 7–5).

BRITANNIA CUP

Men's 65 Age Group
CANBERRA, AUSTRALIA, 4–9 APRIL
Quarter-finals: USA d. France 3–0; Austria d. Sweden 3–0; Great Britain d. Canada 2–1; Australia d. Germany 3–0.
Semi-finals: Austria d. USA 2–1; Australia d. Great Britain 2–1.
Final: Austria d. Australia 2–1 (O. Jirkovsky d. R. Wilson 6–4 7–5; L. Legenstein d. R. McCarthy 6–4 6–0; O. Jirklovsky/J. Karlhofer lost to D.Billings/C. McInnes 3–6 4–6).

CRAWFORD CUP

Men's 70 Age Group
CANBERRA, AUSTRALIA, 4–9 APRIL
Quarter-finals: USA d. Sweden 3–0; Great Britain d. Canada 2–1; Germany d. France 2–1; Australia d. Austria 2–1.
Semi-finals: USA d. Great Britain 3–0; Germany d. Australia 3–0.
Final: Germany d. USA 2–1 (H. Moritz lost to W. Parsons 0–6 1–6; B. Kempa d. J. McGrath 7–6 7–6; W. Kessler/B. Kempa d. V. Hughes/M. Miller 6–2 6–4).

YOUNG CUP

Women's 40 Age Group
BRISBANE, AUSTRALIA, 7–12 APRIL
Quarter-finals: USA d. Canada 2–1; Australia d. Sweden 3–0; Great Britain d. Belgium 3–0; Germany d. Netherlands 3–0.
Semi-finals: Australia d. USA 2–1; Germany d. Great Britain 2–1.
Final: Australia d. Germany 2–1 (L. Bowrey d. R. Schroder 4–6 6–3 6–4; W. Gilchrist lost to H. Eisterlehner 1–6 6–3 3–6; E. Craig/C. Campling d. H. Eisterlehner/ M. Ohlendick 6–3 7–5).

MARIA ESTHER BUENO CUP

Women's 50 Age Group
PERTH, AUSTRALIA, 7–12 APRIL
Quarter-finals: Australia d. Ireland 3–0; USA d. Japan 3–0; Canada d. Germany 2–1; France d. Great Britain 3–0.
Semi-finals: USA d. Australia 2–1; France d. Canada 3–0.
Final: USA d. France 3–0 (C. Hillebrand d. D. Bouteleux 6–2 6–4; A. Cohen lost to R. Darmon 3–6 3–6; C. Hillebrand/A. Cohen d. R. Darmon/C. Rouire 3–6 7–6 6–1).

ALICE MARBLE CUP

Women's 60 Age Group
PERTH, AUSTRALIA, 7–12 APRIL
Quarter-finals: USA d. Japan 3–0; Australia d. Canada 2–1; Great Britain d. New Zealand 3–0; Germany d. Ireland 3–0.
Semi-finals: USA d. Australia 2–1; Great Britain d. Germany 3–0.
Final: USA d. Great Britain 3–0 (B. Pratt d. A. Williams 6–3 6–0; M. Kohler d. R. Illingworth 6–3 7–5; B. Pratt/N. Neeld d. H. Cheadle/J. Walker-Smith 7–5 6–2).

ITF VETERAN CHAMPIONSHIPS

PERTH, AUSTRALIA, 17–23 APRIL
MEN'S OVER 35 SINGLES – Final: P. Torre (FRA) d. S. Sorensen (IRL) 3–7 7–5 6–2.
MEN'S OVER 35 DOUBLES – Final: Tarik/Wijono (INA) d. Wunschig (FRG)/Machan (HUN) 6–3 6–4.
MEN'S OVER 45 SINGLES – Final: D. McCormick (CAN) d. J. Cooper (AUS) 6–7 6–4 7–6.
MEN'S OVER 45 DOUBLES – Final: Burns/Weaver (AUS) d. Parker (USA)/Berges (FRA) 6–3 6–4.
MEN'S OVER 55 SINGLES – Final: P. Froelich (AUS) d. G. Davis (USA) 6–3 6–3.
MEN'S OVER 55 DOUBLES – Final: Davis/Ahlers (USA) d. Storr/Shear (GBR) 6–4 6–4.
MEN'S OVER 60 SINGLES – Final: L. Maine (CAN) d. J. Barry (NZL) 6–2 7–6.
MEN'S OVER 60 DOUBLES – Final: Sedgman/Wilderspin (AUS) d. Stewart (USA)/Davidson (SWE) w.o.
MEN'S OVER 65 SINGLES – Final: R. McCarthy (AUS) d. L. Legenstein (AUT) 6–4 7–5.
MEN'S OVER 65 DOUBLES – Final: McCarthy/Howe (AUS) d. Legenstein (AUT)/Hussmuller (FRG) 6–1 6–3.
MEN'S OVER 70 SINGLES – Final: R. Sherman (USA) d. A. Swetka (USA) 6–1 6–3.
MEN'S OVER 70 DOUBLES – Final: Hughes/Miller (USA) d. Kessler/Kempa (FRG) 6–4 6–1.
WOMEN'S OVER 40 SINGLES – Final: C. Baily (USA) d. N. Cazaux (FRA) 6–2 6–1.
WOMEN'S OVER 40 DOUBLES – Final: Baily/Mueller (USA) d. Russo/Hillebrand (USA) 6–1 6–4.
WOMEN'S OVER 50 SINGLES – Final: C. Hillebrand (USA) d. R. Darmon (FRA) 6–4 4–6 6–2.
WOMEN'S OVER 50 DOUBLES – Final: Whitelaw/Blackshaw (AUS) d. Bouteleux/Rouire (FRA) 3–6 6–1 6–4.
WOMEN'S OVER 55 SINGLES – Final: C. Wood (USA) d. N. Marsh (AUS) 6–2 3–6 7–6.
WOMEN'S OVER 55 DOUBLES – Final: Wood/Kohler (USA) d. Weber/Grieve (CAN) 6–1 6–2.
WOMEN'S OVER 60 SINGLES – Final: B. Pratt (USA) d. B. Rae (AUS) w.o.
WOMEN'S OVER 60 DOUBLES – Final: Illingworth/Williams (GBR) d. Adler/Murdock (USA) 6–2 6–4.

1991 ITF VETERANS WORLD RANKINGS

MEN

35 AGE GROUP
1 P. Torre (FRA); **2** S. Birner (TCH); **3** R. Machan (HUN); **4** L. Levai (GER). **Alphabetical:** R. Casey (AUS), S. Castillo (USA); P. French (GBR); J. Moreno (ESP); J. Pruchta (TCH); F. Rocchi (ITA); H. Seuss (GER).

45 AGE GROUP
1 C. Hoeveler (USA); **2** D. Nash (USA); **3** D. McCormick (CAN); **4** J. Cooper (AUS); **5** H. Elschenbroich (GER); **6** P. Pokorny (AUT); **7** H. Andren (SWE); **8 eq** H.-J. Plotz (GER), R. Staguhn (GER); **10** G. Rohrich (ITA).

55 AGE GROUP
1 I. Gulyas (HUN); **2** K. van Nostrand (USA); **3** F. Hainka (AUT); **4 eq** P. Froelich (AUS), K. Taylor (AUS); **6 eq** G. Davis (USA), B. Duesler (USA); **8** W. Mertins (GER); **9** J. O'Brien (AUS); **10** W. Schneiders (GER).

60 AGE GROUP
1 L. Main (CAN); **2** J. Barry (NZL); **3** C. DeVoe (USA); **4** A. Bailey (AUS); **5 eq** H. Crutchet (FRA), A. Funes (ARG); **7** S. Davidson (SWE); **8** H. Stewart (USA); **9** W. Bonham (USA); **10** C. Hassell (GBR).

65 AGE GROUP
1 L. Legenstein (AUT); **2** B. Howe (AUS); **3** T. Brown (USA); **4** B. McCarthy (AUS); **5** F. Koveleski (USA); **6** O. Jirkovsky (AUT); **7** L. Lenart (HUN); **8** A. Hussmuller (GER); **9** R. Wilson (AUS); **10** G. Ihns (GER).

70 AGE GROUP
1 B. Sherman (USA); **2** M. Miller (USA); **3** B. Kempa (GER); **4** B. Hay (AUS); **5** A. Swetka (USA); **6** J. McGrath (USA); **7** A. Ritzenberg (USA); **8 eq** G. Henley (AUS), E. Meidhof (GER); **10** T. Johannson (SWE).

WOMEN

40 AGE GROUP
1 C. Baily (USA); **2** M. Pinterova (HUN); **3** H. Eisterlehner (GER); **4** N. Cazaux (FRA); **5** W. Gilchrist (AUS); **6** M. Russo (USA); **7** R. Schroder (GER); **8** M. Wenaweser-Heeb (LIE); **9** M. Oppenheimer (GBR); **10** M. McClean (USA).

50 AGE GROUP
1 C. Hillebrand (USA); **2** R. Darmon (FRA); **3** M. Schultze (ESP); **4** D. Bouteleux (FRA); **5** J. Blackshaw (AUS); **6** M. Wayte (AUS); **7** R. Mayer-Zdralek (GER); **8** E. Jackson (CAN); **9** A. Erbe (GER); **10** C. Rouire (FRA).

55 AGE GROUP
1 C. Wood (AUS); **2** N. Marsh (AUS); **3 eq** I. Michael (GER), E. Perusch (AUT); **5** B. Jung (GER); **6 eq** A. Theyson (GER), E. Zell (GER).

60 AGE GROUP
1 B. Pratt (USA); **2** B. Rae (AUS); **3** R. Lauder (GBR); **4** M. Kohler (USA); **5** J. Pla (ARG); **6** M. Blom (HOL); **7** R. Illingworth (GBR); **8** K. Sorge (GER); **9** M. Kyburz (SUI); **10** E. Steinle (GER).

NATIONAL ASSOCIATIONS, RANKINGS AND CHAMPIONSHIPS

MEMBERS WITH VOTING RIGHTS (94)

Abbreviations: C. = Cable address; T. = Telephone number; TX. = Telex number; Fax. = Facsimile number. Number following country's name denotes year of foundation.

ALGERIA (1962)

Fédération Algérienne de Tennis, Centre des Fédérations Sportives, Cité Olympique B.P. 88 El Biar, Algers 16030.
T. (213–2) 79 0988/3939; TX. 61379 KFS DZ; *Pres.* Col Ali Tounsi; *Ex. Dir.* Mr Yahia Chettab.

ARGENTINA (1921)

Asociación Argentina de Tenis, Av. San Juan 1315/17, (1148) Capital Federal, Buenos Aires.
C. Argtennis, Buenos Aires; T. (54–1) 26 1569/27 0101/26 4696 (1148); TX. 17336 ARGTEN AR; Fax. (54–1) 3340296; *Pres.* Mr Juan Jose Vasquez; *Secs* Mr Juan Carlos Zamboni, Mr Francisco A. Turno.

AUSTRALIA (1904)

Tennis Australia, Private Bag 6060, Richmond South 3121, Victoria.
T. (61–3) 655 1277; TX. 36893 TENCRT AA; Fax. (61–3) 650 2743; *Pres.* Mr Geoff Pollard; *Admin. Man.* Mr Mike Daws; *Tennis Man.* Mr Barry F. McMillan.
MEN: **1** Wally Masur; **2** Jason Stoltenberg; **3** Todd Woodbridge; **4** Richard Fromberg; **5** Mark Woodforde; **6** Darren Cahill; **7** Pat Cash; **8** Simon Youl; **9** Johan Anderson; **10** Sandon Stolle.
WOMEN: **1** Rachel McQuillan; **2** Nicole Provis; **3** Anne Minter; **4** Kristin Godridge; **5** Elizabeth Smylie; **6** Jenny Byrne; **7** Michelle Jaggard; **8** Kristine Radford; **9** Rennae Stubbs; **10** Louise Field.

AUSTRIA (1902)

Österreichischer Tennisverband, Haekelstrasse 33, 1235 Vienna, Austria.
C. Austriatennis, Vienna; T. (43–222) 8654506/1235 (43–1) 8654506; TX. 131598 OETEN A; Fax. (43–222) 86545065/85 (43–1) 8654506/85; *Pres.* Dr Theodor Zeh; *Sec.* Mr Peter Nader.
MEN: **1** Thomas Muster; **2** Horst Skoff; **3** Alexander Antonitsch; **4** Thomas Buchmayer; **5** Gilbert Schaller; **6** Harald Mair; **7** Gerald Mandl; **8** Martin Schaffl; **9** Stefan Lochbihler; **10** Reinhard Wawra.
WOMEN: **1** Judith Wiesner; **2** Barbara Paulus; **3** Petra Ritter; **4** Marion Maruska; **5** Sandra Dopfer; **6** Beate Reinstadler; **7** Nike Dobrovits; **8** Heidi Sprung; **9** Katharina Buche; **10** Desiree Leupold.

National Closed Championships
MEN'S SINGLES – Semi-finals: T. Muster d. H. Mair 6–3 6–3; M. Schaffl d. O. Ploner 2–6 6–3 6–4. **Final:** Muster d. Schaffl 6–0 6–3 6–4.
WOMEN'S SINGLES – Semi-finals: P. Ritter d. U. Priller 6–4 6–2; N. Dobrovits d. B. Reinstadler 6–2 0–6 7–6. **Final:** Petra d. Nike 7–5 6–2.

BAHAMAS (1961)

The Bahamas Lawn Tennis Association, PO Box N-10169, Nassau.
T. (32–809) 363 3000/327 8410; TX. 20170 BRITBEACH B; Fax. (1–809) 363 3957; *Pres.* Mr J Barrie Farrington; *Sec.* Ms Linda Hield.

MEN: 1 Mark Knowles; 2 Leo Rolle; 3 Sterling Cooke; 4 Sean Cartwright; 5 Eugene Higgs; 6 Nige
Saul; 7 Dirk Saunders; 8 Jason Watson; 9 Donald Archer; 10 Vince Andrews.
WOMEN: 1 Kim Griffith; 2 Robyn Farrington; 3 Lori Feingold; 4 Theda Bethel; 5 Eldwyth Roberts; 6
Natalia Bradshaw; 7 Rosalie Austin; 8 Josephine Farrington; 9 Ann Simons; 10 Janelle Watson.

BAHRAIN (1981)

Bahrain Lawn Tennis Federation, PO Box 26985, Bahrain.
C. Tennis, Bahrain; T. (973) 687236; TX. 8738 GPIC BN; *Pres.* Shaikh Ahmed Bin Salman Al Kalifa; *Sec*
Mr Yousif Abdulla Ali.

BANGLADESH (1972)

Bangladesh Tennis Federation, Tennis Complex, Ramna Green, Dhaka 1000.
C. Tennisfed, Dhaka; T. (880–2) 506650; TX. 642401 SHER BJ (Att. Tennis); Fax. (880–2) 832975
832915; *Pres.* Mr Khondaker Asaduzzaman; *Sec.* Mr A. Morshed Khan Chowdbury.

BARBADOS (1948)

Barbados Lawn Tennis Association, PO Box 615c, Bridgetown.
T. (1–809) 436 0634/6727; Fax. (1–809) 429 4014/4854; *Pres.* Mr Peter G. Symmonds; *Sec.* Ms Donna
Symmonds.

BELGIUM (1902)

Royal Belgian Tennis Federation, Passage International Rogier 6, BTE 522, 1210 Brussels.
C. Tennisfeder, Brussels; T. (32–2) 217 2365; TX. 24023 TENFED B; Fax. (32–2) 217 6732; *Pres.* M
Henri Denis; *Secs* Mr Walter Goethals, Mr Franz Lemaire.
MEN: 1 Eduardo Masso; 2 Filip Dewulf; 3 Xavier Daufresne; 4 Guido Van Rompaey; 5 Libor Pimek; 6
Johan Van Herck; 7 Denis Langaskens; 8 Tom Vanhoudt; 9 Kris Goossens; 10 Christophe Delzenne.
WOMEN: 1 Sabine Appelmans; 2 Dominique Monami; 3 Sandra Wasserman; 4 Ann Devries; 5 Els
Callens; 6 Kathleen Schuurmans; 7 Nancy Feber; 8 Daphne Vandezande; 9 Vicky Maes; 10 Raphaella
Liziero.
National Closed Championships
MEN'S SINGLES – Semi-finals: G. Van Rompaey d. D. Langaskens 6–0 6–1; F. Dewulf d. G
Vanderveeren 7–5 6–3. **Final:** Dewulf d. Van Rompaey 6–1 6–2 1–6 6–3.
WOMEN'S SINGLES – Semi-finals: S. Appelmans d. D. Monami 6–2 6–1; S. Wasserman d. E. Callens
6–2 1–6 6–4. **Final:** Appelmans d. Wasserman 6–1 6–4.

BOLIVIA (1937)

Federación Boliviana de Tennis, Calle Mexico no. 1638, Casilla Postal No.14752, La Paz.
T. (591–2) 378769; TX. 2220 CABPULP BV; Fax. (591–2) 367625/367909; *Pres.* Vicente Calderon
Zeballos.

BRAZIL (1956)

Confederacao Brasileira de Tenis, Av. Paulista Nr. 352 - Sala 64, 6 Andar, Conjunto, 64 Cept - 01 310, Sac
Paulo.
C. Cebetenis Rio de Janeiro; T. (55–11) 251 3920; TX. 113 2733 CTEN-BR; Fax. (55–11) 289 9404; *Pres*
Mr Walter Elias; *Sec.* Marilia Silberberg.
MEN: 1 Jaime Oncins; 2 Fernando Roese; 3 Luiz Mattar; 4 Danilo Marcelino; 5 Jose Daher; 6 Fabic
Silberberg; 7 Cassio Motta; 8 Roberto Jabali; 9 Marcelo Saliola; 10 Cesar Kist.
WOMEN: 1 Luciana Corsato; 2 Claudia Chabalgoity; 3 Sabrina Giusto; 4 Andrea Vieira; 5 Sumara
Passos; 6 Roberta Burzagli; 7 Alessandra Kaul; 8 Cristina Rozwadowski; 9 Stephanie Mayorkis; 10
Eugenia Maia.
National Closed Championships
MEN'S SINGLES – Semi-finals: D. Marcelino d. M. Menezes 1–1 ret; N. Aerts d. M. Aquino 6–3 6–4
Final: Marcelino d. Aerts 6–4 5–7 7–5.
WOMEN'S SINGLES – Semi-finals: A. Vieira d. L. Corsato ret; S. Mayorkis d. S. Giusto 2–6 6–4 6–3
Final: Vieira d. Mayorkis 6–2 4–6 7–6.

BULGARIA (1930)

Bulgarian Tennis Federation, 18 Tolbouhin Blvd, Sofia.
C. Besefese Tennis, Sofia; T. (359–2) 803710 or 808651 ext. 1040/213/488; TX. 22723/22724 BSFS BG; Fax. (359–2) 879670; *Pres.* Mr Roumen Serbezov; *Sec.* Mr Tzvetan Tzvetkov.
MEN: 1 Milen Velev; **2** Krasimir Lazarov; **3** Milko Petkov; **4** Orlin Stanoichev; **5** Ivan Keskinov; **6** Ruslan Rainov; **7** Mihail Kanev; **8** Todor Bandev; **9** Radoslav Radev; **10** Georgi Kranchev.
WOMEN: 1 Katerina Maleeva; **2** Magdalena Maleeva; **3** Elena Pampulova; **4** Lubomira Bacheva; **5** Galia Angelova; **6** Tzvetelina Nikolova; **7** Svetla Krivencheva; **8** Dora Dgilianova; **9** Teodora Nedeva; **10** Maia Dimitrova.

National Closed Championships
MEN'S SINGLES – Semi-Finals: M. Petkov d. Mihail Kanev 6–3 4–6 6–2; K. Lazarov d. V. Gadgev 6–1 6–2. **Final:** Petkov d. Lazarov 6–4 6–2 2–6 6–3.
WOMEN'S SINGLES – Semi-finals: G. Angelova d. M. Dimitrova 6–2 6–4; S. Krivencheva d. T. Nikolova 6–2 6–7 7–5. **Final:** Angelova d. Krivencheva 6–1 6–3.

CAMEROON (1966)

Fédération Camerounaise de Lawn Tennis, BP 1121, Yaounde.
C. Fecatennis-MJS-Yaounde; T. (237) 233860/1310 or 224329; TX. 8568 KN/MNFA 8261 KN; *Pres.* Mr Zacharie Noah; *Sec.* Dr Noaki Mboulet.

CANADA (1890)

Tennis Canada, 3111 Steeles Avenue West, Downsview, Ontario M3J 3H2.
T. (1–416) 665 9777; TX. 02618419 CAN TENNIS TOR; Fax. (1–416) 665 9017; *Pres.* Mr. Robert H. Moffat; *Sec.* Ms Shelley Evanochko.
MEN: 1 Grant Connell; **2** Chris Pridham; **3** Andrew Sznajder; **4** Martin Laurendeau; **5** Martin Wosten-holme; **6** Daniel Nestor; **7** Glenn Michibata; **8** Albert Chang; **9** Brian Gyetko; **10** Sebastien Lareau.
WOMEN: 1 Helen Kelesi; **2** Patricia Hy; **3** Rene Alter; **4** Maureen Drake; **5** Jill Hetherington; **6** Caroline Delisle; **7** Jillian Alexander; **8** Suzanne Italiano; **9** Teresa Dobson; **10** Monica Mraz.

National Closed Championships
MEN'S SINGLES – Semi-finals: G. Connell d. S. Lareau 2–6 6–3 6–4; A. Sznajder d. C. Pridham 7–5 6–4. **Final:** Connell d. Sznajder 7–6 6–2.
WOMEN'S SINGLES – Semi-finals: H. Kelesi d. R. Alter 7–6 6–2; P. Hy d. M. Drake 6–1 6–2. **Final:** Hy d. Kelesi 6–1 2–6 6–3.

CHILE (1920)

Federación de Tenis de Chile, Almirante Simpson, No. 36 Providencia, Casilla 1149, Santiago.
T. (56–2) 2227279/342416; TX. 240976 COCH CL; Fax. (56–2) 2229291; *Pres.* Mr Rogelio U. Rojas; *Sec.* Mr Rodolfo M. Salauez.
MEN: 1 Felipe Rivera; **2** Pedro Rebolledo; **3** Jose A. Fernandez; **4** Sergio Cortes; **5** Oscar Bustos; **6** Ernesto Diaz; **7** Ruben Gajardo; **8** Marcelo Rebolledo; **9** Gerardo Vacarezza; **10** Ulises Cerda.
WOMEN: 1 Paula Cabezas; **2** Macarena Miranda; **3** Paulina Sepulveda; **4** Carolina Espinoza; **5** Pamela Gonzalez; **6** Alejandra Quezada; **7** Melissa Castro; **8** Ma. Graceila Breiding; **9** Loreto Barriga; **10** Andrea Anania.

National Closed Championships
MEN'S SINGLES – Semi-finals: S. Cortes d. F. Rivera 6–3 6–7 7–6; J.P. Queirolo d. J.A. Fernandez 6–3 6–2. **Final:** Queirolo d. Cortes 6–1 2–6 6–4.
WOMEN'S SINGLES – Semi-finals: P. Cabezas d. P. Sepulveda 6–2 2–6 6–3; M. Zuleta d. M. Miranda 6–4 2–6 6–1. **Final:** Cabezas d. Zuleta 7–6 6–7 7–6.

CHINA, PEOPLE'S REPUBLIC OF (1953)

Tennis Association of the People's Republic of China, 9 Tiyukuan Road, Beijing 100016.
C. Sportschine, Beijing; T. (86–1) 7012233; TX. 22034 ACSF CN/22323 CHOCH CN; Fax. (86–1) 7015858; *Pres.* Mr Lu Zhengcao; *Sec.* Ms Zhang Dacheng.
MEN: 1 Bing Pan; **2** Jiaping Xia; **3** Jiuhua Zhang; **4** Qianghua Meng; **5** Di Lin; **6** Tao Geng; **7** Jian Guo; **8** Shuiming Liu; **9** Liwu Zhang; **10** Meng Xu.
WOMEN: 1 Li Chen; **2** Fang Li; **3** Ying Bi; **4** Jingqian Yi; **5** Yanling Li; **6** Yujie Cai; **7** Tingjie Zhu; **8** Min Tang; **9** Ning Lin; **10** Liyao Tang.

National Closed Championships
MEN'S SINGLES – Semi-finals: X. Jiaping d. Z. Jiuhua 6–4 1–6 6–4 6–4; P. Bing d. M. Qianghua 6–4 6–4 7–6. **Final:** Bing d. Jiaping 7–5 6–3 5–7 6–2.
WOMEN'S SINGLES – Semi-finals: C. Li d. B. Ying 6–3 7–5; L. Fang d. Y. Jingqian 6–3 6–1. **Final:** Li d. Fang 6–3 7–5.

CHINESE TAIPEI (1973)

Chinese Taipei Tennis Association, 6th Floor, No. 285, Sec 4, Chung Shaio East Rd, Taipei, Taiwan ROC.
C. Sinovision, Taipei; T. (886–2) 7313026/7510051; TX. 22949 PACICON; Fax. (886–2) 7711696; Pres. Mr M. C. Chang; Sec-Gen. Mr Hu Cheng.
MEN: 1 Yu-Hui Lien; 2 Chih-Jung; 3 Cheng-Fong Chang; 4 Yuen-Hong Lee; 5 Jinn-Yen Chiang; 6 Chung-Hswg Liu; 7 Chang-Long Wu; 8 Chao-Hsy Hung; 9 Huang-Jung Hsu; 10 Shiu-Ming Lee.
WOMEN: 1 Shi-Ting Wang; 2 Ya-Yui Lin; 3 Su-Lin Lai; 4 Chiu-Mei Ho; 5 Fang-Lin Lin; 6 Mei-Chun Lin; 7 Su-Yin Lai; 8 Tzu-Ting Weng; 9 Yi-Chin Wu; 10 Su-Ping Lin.

National Closed Championships
MEN'S SINGLES – Semi-finals: Y-H. Lien d. C-F. Chang 6–1 6–0; Y-H. Lee d. S-M. Lee 6–2 6–4. **Final** Lien d. Lee 6–0 6–2.
WOMEN'S SINGLES – Semi-finals: S-T. Wang d. S-Y. Lai 6–2 6–3; Y-H. Lin d. S-L. Lai 6–4 6–3. **Final** Wang d. Lin 6–2 6–3.

CIS

'Commonwealth' Tennis Federation, Leningradski Prospekt 36, Dinamo Stadium, Petrovski Park Tennis Club, 125167 Moscow.
C. Sportkomitet, Moscow; T. (7–095) 201 08 64; TX. 411287 PRIZ SU; Fax. (7–095) 299 299 4529/248 0814; Pres. Mr Shamil Tarpishev; Gen. Sec. Mr Boris Fomenko; Exec. Dir. Mr Dmitriy Vikharev.
MEN: 1 Andrei Chesnokov; 2 Andrei Cherkasov; 3 Alexander Volkov; 4 Dmitry Polyakov; 5 Andrei Olkhovsky; 6 Vladimir Gabrichidze; 7 Andrei Medvedev; 8 Andrei Merinov; 9 Sergei Skakun; 10 Andrei Rybalko.
WOMEN: 1 Leila Meskhi; 2 Natalia Zvereva; 3 Larisa Savchenko; 4 Natalia Medvedeva; 5 Elena Bryukhovets; 6 Eugenia Manyukova; 7 Yulia Apostoli; 8 Viktoria Milvidskaya; 9 Tatyana Ignatyeva; 10 Elena Makarova.

National Closed Championships
MEN'S SINGLES – Semi-finals: D. Palyonov d. V. Bogatyryov 6–3 6–4; A. Rybalko d. E. Kafelnikov 1–6 6–2 6–3. **Final:** Palyonov d. Rybalko 6–4 6–1.
WOMEN'S SINGLES – Semi-finals: E. Manyukova d. A. Khalatyan 6–1 6–2; S. Komleva d. N Biletskaya 6–1 6–4. **Final:** Komleva d. Manyukova 6–3 6–2.

COLOMBIA (1932)

Federación Colombiana de Tenis, Apartado No. 10917, Calle 28 No. 25–18 Bogota.
C. Fedetenis, Bogota, T. (57–1) 288 3323; TX. 41275 ICJD CO; Fax. (57–1) 287 7963; Pres. Dr Ricardo Mejia P; Sec. Mr Hernando Ossa.
MEN: 1 Mauricio Hadad; 2 Miguel Tobon; 3 Alvaro C. Jordan; 4 Luis A. Gonzalez; 5 Jaime Cortes; 6 Beimar Zapata; 7 Jorge Falla; 8 Luis Lagarcha; 9 Mario Aragon; 10 Sigifredo Hidalgo.
WOMEN: 1 Cecilia Hincapie; 2 Catalina Ramirez; 3 Carolina Torres; 4 Carolina Hadau; 5 Ximena Trujillo; 6 Adriana Garcia; 7 Carmina Giraldo; 8 Giana Gutierre; 9 Catalina Jaramillo.

National Closed Championships
MEN'S SINGLES – Semi-finals: M. Hadad d. L.A. Gonzalez 6–2 7–5; J. Cortes d. A. C. Jordan 6–3 6–3 **Final:** Hadad d. Cortes 6–4 6–4.
WOMEN'S SINGLES – Semi-finals: C. Torres d. X. Trujillo 4–6 6–2 6–4; C. Hincapie d. C. Ramirez 6–7 6–3 7–6. **Final:** Hincapie d. Torres 3–6 6–2 6–4.

CONGO (1962)

Fédération Congolaise de Lawn Tennis, Stade de la Revolution BP 2061, Brazzaville.
T. (242) 833328; TX. 5237 KG BANKCGO; Fax. (242) 835502; Pres. Mr Germain Ickonga Akindou; Sec Mr Antoine Ouabonzi.

MEN: 1 Alain Bemba; 2 Christian Bemba; 3 Stanislas Dzon; 4 Crepin Ossombi; 5 Vianey Lebvova; 6 Fulgence Tsiba; 7 Thierry Tuali; 8 Noncisse Ngangou; 9 Christian Zuali; 10 Chatian Gnitou.
WOMEN: 1 Marie Josee Likibi; 2 Michaello Likibi; 3 Blandine Madena; 4 Arlette Matoko; 5 Okouya Ikiya; 6 Nadine Tamba; 7 Christine Bibingoli; 8 Rosine Kibindza; 9 Leley Doulou; 10 Arlette Reney.

Closed National Championships
MEN'S SINGLES – Semi-finals: C. Bemba d. S. Dzon 6–1 6–1 6–7 3–6 6–1; A. Bemba d. C. Ossombi 6–3 6–1 6–2. **Final:** (A) Bemba d. (C) Bemba 0–6 7–5 6–3 5–6 ret.
WOMEN'S SINGLES – Semi-finals: M. Likibi d. A. Matoko 6–0 6–0; M-J. Likibi d. B. Madena 6–4 6–2. **Final:** (M-J.) Likibi d. (M) Likibi 6–2 6–4.

COSTA RICA (1960)

Federación Costarricense de Tenis, PO Box 326-1005, Barrio Mexico, San Jose.
T. (506) 55 4793/4824; TX. 2509 CODINCO; Fax. (506) 33 5678; *Pres.* Ms Cecilia Sanchez; *Sec:* Mr Domingo Rivera.

COTE D'IVOIRE (1969)

Fédération Ivoirienne de Tennis, 01 BP V 273, Abidjan 01.
T. (225) 44 13 54; TX. 23555 or 23493 IHCHOT CI; Fax. (225) 44 71 13/44 00 50; *Pres.* Mr Jean-Claude Delafosse; *Gen. Sec.* Mr Kouame Kouadjo.

CUBA (1925)

Federación Cubana de Tenis de Campo, Calle 13 NR 601 ESQ AC, Vedado Habana 4.
C. Olimpicuba, Habana; T. (53–7) 403581; TX. 511332 INDER CU; Fax. (53–7) 407677/625604/625605/409037; *Pres.* Mr Rolando Martinez; *Sec.* Mr M. O. Rodriguez.
MEN: 1 Mario Tabares; 2 Juan Pino; 3 Armando Perez; 4 Duvier Medina; 5 Roberto Rodriguez; 6 Ivan Perez; 7 Tomas Rodriguez; 8 Alexander Tabares; 9 Pedro Leon; 10 Nelson Vale.
WOMEN: 1 Rita Pichardo; 2 Belkis Rodriguez; 3 Iluminada Concepcion; 4 Yoanis Montesino; 5 Maria Garcia; 6 Yamile Cordova; 7 Lissetty Cabrera; 8 Rosa Tito; 9 Maria Rodriguez; 10 Gretty Herrera.

National Closed Championships
MEN'S SINGLES – Semi-finals: M. Tabares d. A. Perez 6–2 7–5; J. Pino d. W. Henry 6–3 6–2. **Final:** Pino d. Tabares 7–5 4–6 6–3.
WOMEN'S SINGLES – Semi-finals: R. Pichardo d. M. Garcia 6–3 6–4; Y. Montesino d. I. Concepcion 5–7 6–1 6–4. **Final:** Pichardo d. Montesino 6–3 6–2.

CYPRUS (1951)

Cyprus Tennis Federation, 20 Ionos Str, PO Box 3931, Nicosia.
T. (357–2) 366822/450875; TX. 5300 OLYMPIC CY; Fax. (357–2) 464355; *Pres.* Mr Philios Christodoulou; *Sec.* Mr George Georgiades.

CZECHOSLOVAKIA (1906)

Ceskoslovenska Tenisova Asociace, Ostrov Stvanice 38, 170 00 Prague 7.
C. Sportsvaz, Prague; T. (42–2) 2311484/2311678; TX. 122650 CSTVC; Fax. (42–2) 2311868; *Pres.* Mr Jiri Lendl; *Sec.* Mr Michal Polak.

DENMARK (1920)

Dansk Tennis Forbund, Idraettens Hus, Broendby Stadion 20, 2605 Broendby.
C. Tennisforbund, Copenhagen; T. (45–42) 455555; TX. 33111 IDRAET DK (Att. Tennis); Fax. (45–43) 435045; *Pres.* Mr Jorn Iversen; *Vice Pres.* Mr John Ahlstrand; *Gen. Sec.* Mr Hans Kristensen.

DJIBOUTI (1978)

Fédération Djiboutienne de Tennis, rue Pierre-Pascal, BP 16, Djibouti.
C. PO Box 16, Djibouti; T. (253) 352286; TX. 5871 DJ PRESIDEN; *Pres.* Mr Houmed Houssein; *Gen. Sec.* Mr Araita Ahmed.

DOMINICAN REPUBLIC (1929)

Federación Dominicana de Tenis, Club Deportivo Naco, Calle Central, Ens. Naco, Santo Domingo.
T. (1–809) 541 3685/3488; TX. 3460418 BONELLY; Fax. (1–809) 688 0647/541 0640; *Pres.* Mr Gonzalo
Mejia; *Sec.* Mr J. Ravello.

ECUADOR (1967)

Federación Ecuatoriana de Tenis, PO Box # 716, Guayaquil.
C. Fetenis, Guayaquil; T. (593–4) 313600/304605/306800; TX. 04 3332 BANMAC ED; Fax. (593–4)
313642/313123; *Pres.* Mr Mario Canessa; *Sec.* Ms N. Guzman.
MEN: 1 Andres Gomez; 2 Raul Viver; 3 Giorgio Carneade; 4 Pablo Campana; 5 Andres Alarcon; 6 Luis
A. Morejon; 7 Ernesto Lingen; 8 Hugo Nunez; 9 Nicolas Lapentti; 10 Nelson Ramos.
WOMEN: 1 M-Dolores Campana; 2 Nuria Niemes; 3 M-Angeles Ycaza; 4 Cecilia Piedrahita; 5
Montserrat Martinez; 6 Mercedes Ramos; 7 M-Pilar Gallegos; 8 Priscilla Cordovez; 9 Monica Martinez;
10 Elisabeth Isonhood.

EGYPT (1920)

Egyptian Lawn Tennis Federation, 13 Kasr el Nil Street, Cairo.
C. Gyplawnten, Cairo; T. (20–2) 753235; TX. 93697 SAFLM UN (Att. Tennis)/21554 STC UN/93000
OLYMP UN; Fax. (20–2) 760345; *Pres.* Gen. Mohamed Tawfik; *Sec.* Prof. Hussein I. Nasr.
MEN: 1 Khaled El Salawy; 2 Amr Ghonem; 3 Hani Nasser; 4 Adly El Shafi; 5 Moustafa Naim; 6
Karim Afifi; 7 Tamer Rahmi; 8 Ismaail Sarwat; 9 Bassel Rahmi; 10 Guihad El Dib.
WOMEN: 1 Shahira Tawfik; 2 Alia Wl Shishini; 3 Mona Saleh; 4 Nahla El Sharawi; 5 Marwa El
Shourbagui; 6 Hala Abdel Wahab; 7 Cherry Kalifa; 8 Mehry Shawki; 9 Amira Assem; 10 Laila Abdel
Salam.

National Closed Championships
MEN'S SINGLES – Semi-finals: A. Ghonem d. K. Afifi 7–5 4–6 6–2 6–4; K. El Salawy d. H. El
Aroussi 6–3 6–7 6–1 6–1. **Final:** Ghonem d. El Salawy 6–3 5–7 6–1 4–6 6–1.
WOMEN'S SINGLES – Semi-finals: S. Tawfik d. H. Abdel Wahab 6–1 6–2; N. Sharawi d. M. El
Shourbagui 2–6 7–5 6–2. **Final:** Tawfik d. Sharawi 6–0 6–1.

EL SALVADOR (1949)

Federación Salvadorena de Tenis, Apartado Postal (01) 110, San Salvador.
C. Molino; T. (503) 25 6022; TX. 20542 MOLINO SR; Fax. (503) 263832/256366; *Pres.* Mr Enrique
Molins Rubio; *Sec.* Mr Roberto Sanchez Alegria.
MEN: 1 Manuel Tejada; 2 Ronald Pineda; 3 Allan Lopez; 4 Miguel Campos; 5 Jorge Mendez; 6
Nelson Salazar; 6 Inocente Quintanilla; 7 Daniel Rivera; 8 Pedro Benitez; 9 Rafael Fuentes.
WOMEN: 1 Ingrid Gonzales; 2 Annette Falkenberg; 3 Carolina Molins; 4 Claudia Harrison; 5 Renate
Larrave; 6 Rocio Bolanos; 7 Nadine Trabanino; 8 Carolina Sanabria; 9 Olga Quintanilla; 10 Celia
Vilanova.

National Closed Championships
MEN'S SINGLES – Semi-finals: M. Tejada d. M. Mendez 6–2 6–3; A. Lopez d. R. Fuentes 1–6 6–7
6–4. **Final:** Tejada d. Lopez 6–4 6–1 6–1.
WOMEN'S SINGLES – Semi-finals: A. Falkenberg d. C. Harrison 6–3 6–3; I. Gonzales d. R. Larrave
ret. **Final:** Gonzales d. Falkenberg 7–6 6–0.

FINLAND (1911)

Suomen Tennisliitto, Radiokatu 20, SF-00240 Helsinki.
C. Tennisliitto, Helsinki; T. (358–0) 158 2301; TX. 121797 SVUL SF; Fax. (358–0) 1582328; *Pres.* Mr
Raimo Taivalkoski; *Sec.* Mr Eero Kiuttu.
MEN: 1 Veli Paloheimo; 2 Aki Rahunen; 3 Olli Rahnasto; 4 Pasi Virtanen; 5 Alexander Lindholm; 6
Janne Holtari; 7 Kimmo Hurme; 8 Juha Pesola; 9 Juha Lemponen; 10 Tomi Jaakkola.
WOMEN: 1 Petra Thoren; 2 Nanne Dahlman; 3 Anne Aallonen; 4 Anu Varpula; 5 Minna Hatakka; 6
Linda Jansson; 7 Marja-Liisa Kuurne; 8 Katriina Saarinen; 9 Tina-Helen Soderstrom; 10 Katja Kokko.

National Closed Championships
MEN'S SINGLES – Semi-finals: A. Rahunen d. J. Pesola 6–2 6–4; O. Rahnasto d. J. Lemponen 1–6 6–2 6–2. *Final:* Rahunen d. Rahnasto 6–3 6–4.
WOMEN'S SINGLES – Semi-finals: P. Thoren d. A. Aallonen 6–4 6–0; N. Dahlman d. A. Varpula 6–2 6–2. *Final:* Dahlman d. Thoren 6–1 2–6 6–3.

FRANCE (1920)

Fédération Française de Tennis, Stade Roland Garros, 2 avenue Gordon Bennett, 75016 Paris.
C. Tenisfedet Paris; T. (33–1) 47 43 48 00; TX. TENFED 611871 F; Fax. (33–1) 47 43 04 94; *Pres.* Mr Philippe Chatrier; *Sec.* Mr Jean Claude Collinot.
MEN: **1** Guy Forget; **2** Fabrice Santoro; **3** Thierry Champion; **4** Olivier Delaitre; **5** Cedric Pioline; **6** Arnaud Boetsch; **7** Jean-Philippe Fleurian; **8** Frederic Fontang; **9** Henri Leconte; **10** Rodolphe Gilbert.
WOMEN: **1** Nathalie Tauziat; **2** Julie Halard; **3** Mary Pierce; **4** Karine Quentrec; **5** Alexia Dechaume; **6** Isabelle Demongeot; **7** Pascale Paradis-Mangon; **8** Nathalie Herreman; **9** Catherine Suire; **10** Sandrine Testud.

GERMANY, FEDERAL REPUBLIC OF (1902)

Deutscher Tennis Bund e.v., Hallerstrasse 89, 2000 Hamburg 13.
T. (49–40) 411780; Fax. (49–40) 4104480; *Pres.* Dr Claus Stauder; *Exec. Dir.* Mr Gunter Sanders.
MEN: **1** Boris Becker; **2** Michael Stich; **3** Carl-Uwe Steeb; **4** Eric Jelen; **5** Christian Saceanu; **6** Udo Riglewski; **7** Patrick Baur; **8** Patrick Kuhnen; **9** Alexander Mronz; **10** Markus Zoecke.
WOMEN: **1** Steffi Graf; **2** Anke Huber; **3** Claudia Porwik; **4** Karin Kschwendt; **5** Barbara Rittner; **6** Veronika Martinek; **7** Marketa Kochta; **8** Wiltrud Probst; **9** Silke Meier; **10** Katja Oeljeklaus.

National Closed Championships
MEN'S SINGLES – Semi-finals: P. Kuhnen d. K. Braasch 7–6 6–4; D. Buljevic d. M. Nacwie 6–3 5–7 7–5. *Final:* Kuhnen d. Buljevic 6–4 6–7 6–3.
WOMEN'S SINGLES – Semi-finals: S. Frankl d. S. Hack 6–1 6–4; K. Kschwendt d. M. Pawlik 6–1 2–0 (ret). *Final:* Kschwendt d. Frankl 6–3 6–1.

GHANA (1909)

Ghana Tennis Association, c/o National Sports Council, PO Box 1272, Accra.
C. Ghansport; T. (233–021) 663924/25/26/27; TX. 2519 GHANSPORT; Fax. (233–021) 223910; *Pres.* Mr Edmund Annan; *Sec.* Mr Gershon Komla Ayiih.

GREAT BRITAIN (1888)

Lawn Tennis Association, The Queens Club, West Kensington, London, W14 9EG.
C. Lawntenna, London W14; T. (44–71) 385 2366; TX. 8956036 THELTA G; Fax. (44–71) 381 5965; *Pres.* Mr. Ian King; *Exec. Dir.* Mr Ian D. Peacock; *Sec.* Mr John C. U. James.
MEN: **1** Jeremy Bates; **2** Nick Brown; **3** Danny Sapsford; **4** Andrew Castle; **5** Mark Petchey; **6** Chris Wilkinson; **7** James Turner; **8** Stephen Botfield; **9** Paul Hand; **10** Nick Fulwood.
WOMEN: **1** Jo Durie; **2** Sarah Loosemore; **3** Sara Gomer; **4** Monique Javer; **5** Samantha Smith; **6** Clare Wood; **7** Julie Salmon; **8** Kaye Hand; **9** Belinda Borneo; **10** Sarah Bentley.

National Closed Championships
MEN'S SINGLES – Semi-finals: S. Cole d. A. Foster 6–3 6–4; A. Castle d. M. Petchey 6–4 6–3. *Final:* Castle d. Cole 7–6 2–6 10–8.
WOMEN'S SINGLES – Semi-finals: J. Durie d. S. Smith 7–5 6–2; S. Gomer d. M. Javer 7–5 6–0. *Final:* Durie d. Gomer 6–2 6–2.

GREECE (1938)

Hellenic Tennis Federation, Fokionos Negri 9, 115 57 Athens.
C. Efotennis, Athens; T. (30–1) 8654365/8654314; TX. 222415 EFOA GR; Fax. (30–1) 8654365; *Pres.* Mr Dimitris Stefanides; *Sec.* Mr Dionyssis Gangas.
MEN: **1** George Kalovelonis; **2** Tasos Bavelas; **3** John Rigas; **4** Andreas Fikas; **5** John Kabakoglou; **6** Konst Efremoclou; **7** Michael Papageorgiou; **8** Theodoros Glavas; **9** Stavros Michalopoulos; **10** Kons Georgoulas.

WOMEN: 1 Angeliki Kanellopoulou; 2 Christina Papadaki; 3 Christina Zachariadou; 4 Sandra Retzoula; 5 Mariza Georgitsi; 6 Helen Kagalou; 7 Olga Tsarbopoulou; 8 Lidia Soulti; 9 Fransis Kalapoda; 10 Magda Gavriilidou.

National Closed Championships
MEN'S SINGLES – Semi-finals: T. Bavelas d. J. Rigas 6–2 6–4; A. Fikas d. G. Kalovelonis 6–1 6–2. **Final:** Bavelas d. Kalovelonis 6–3 1–6 7–6.
WOMEN'S SINGLES – Semi-finals: C. Papapdaki d. S. Retzoula 6–5 6–4; C. Zachariadou d. M. Georgitsi 7–6 4–6 6–1. **Final:** Papapdaki d. Zachariadou 6–3 6–1.

GUATEMALA (1950)

Federación Nacionale de Tenis, Palacio de Los Deportes, Zona 4, Guatemala City.
T. (502–2) 310261; TX. 6077 C0G GU; Fax. (502–2) 311152; *Pres.* Lic Enrique Gonzalez Rodriguez; *Sec.* Mr David Vargas Bettancourt.
MEN: 1 Daniel Chavez; 2 Jacobo Chavez; 3 Luis Perez; 4 Jorge Tejada; 5 Edgar Valencia; 6 Luis Valencia; 7 Walter Barahona; 8 Carlos Chavez; 9 Hector Zapeta; 10 Hugo Rojas.
WOMEN: 1 Monica Aguero; 2 Flor Urrea; 3 Saira Sanchinelli; 4 Lili Aguirre; 5 Brenda Rojas; 6 Alejandra Gomez; 7 Blanca Alvarado; 8 Heidi Markmann; 9 Carola De Leon; 10 Karla Morales.

National Closed Championships
MEN'S SINGLES – Semi-finals: D. Chavez d. E. Valencia 6–4 6–2; J. Chavez d. C. Chavez 6–4 6–4. **Final:** (D) Chavez d. (J) Chavez 6–4 4–6 6–4 3–6 6–3.
WOMEN'S SINGLES – Semi-finals: M. Aguero d. L. Aguirre 6–1 6–1; F. Urrea d. S. Sanchinelli 6–2 3–6 6–4. **Final:** Aguero d. Urrea 6–1 6–3.

HAITI (1950)

Fédération Haitienne de Tennis, PO Box 1442, Port-au-Prince.
C. Joetienne, Port-au-Prince; T. (509–4) 50703/51461/51462; Fax. (509–4) 51451/51461; *Pres.* Mr Frantz Liautaud; *Sec.* Mr Hulzer Adolphe.

HONG KONG (1909)

Hong Kong Tennis Association Ltd, Victoria Park Centre Court, Victoria Park, Hing Fat Street, Causeway Bay.
C. Tennis, Hong Kong; T. (852) 890 1132; TX. 41224 JSCEN HX (Att HKTA); Fax. (852) 894 8704; *Pres:* Dr Philip Kwok; *Sec:* Mr Herman Hu; *Exec Dir:* Dr Edward Hardisty.

HUNGARY (1907)

Magyar Tenisz Szovetseg, Dozsa Gyorgy ut 1-3, H-1143 Budapest.
C. Comsport Tennis, Budapest; T. (36–1) 252 6687; TX. 225105 AISHK H; Fax. (36–1) 157 1304; *Pres.* Mr Gyorgy Hole; *Sec.* Mr Laszlo Nyiro.
MEN: 1 Sandor Noszaly; 2 Jozsef Krocsko; 3 Rudolf Fekete; 4 Viktor Nagy; 5 Zoltan Krasznai; 6 Levente Baratosi; 7 Krisztian Keresztes; 8 Miklos Hornok; 9 Balazs Rajo; 10 Peter Makray.
WOMEN: 1 Annamaria Foldenyi; 2 Virag Csurgo; 3 Maria Zsoldos; 4 Csilla Dohn; 5 Greta Schmitt; 6 Katalin Kocsis; 7 Agnes Muzamel; 8 Zsuzsa Turi; 9 Lilla Buza; 10 Nora Koves.

National Closed Championships
MEN'S SINGLES – Semi-finals: S. Noszaly d. R. Fekete 6–3 6–2 6–4; V. Nagy d. J. Krocsko 0–6 6–2 7–6 1–6 6–2. **Final:** Noszaly d. Nagy 6–4 4–6 4–6 6–2 13–11.
WOMEN'S SINGLES – Semi-finals: A. Foldenyi d. M. Zsoldos 6–3 6–0; K. Miskolczi d. K. Kuti Kis 6–2 6–2. **Final:** Foldenyi d. Miskolczi 6–0 6–2.

INDIA (1920)

All India Tennis Association, B-7/3 Asaf Ali Road, New Delhi 110 001, India.
C. TAX ASSIST NEW DELHI; T. (91–11) 3276716/3274177/3274178; TX. 3163426 RKCO IN; *Pres.* Mr Kanwar Natwar Singh; *Gen. Sec.* Mr R. K. Khanna.

INDONESIA (1935)

Indonesian Tennis Association, Gelora Senayan Tennis Stadium, Jakarta 10270.
C. Tennis Indonesia, Jakarta; T. (62 21) 5700157; TX. 62794 PELTI IA; Fax. (62–21) 5700157; *Pres.* Mr
Cosmas Batubara; *Gen. Sec.* Mr Eddy Katimansah.
MEN: 1 Benny Wijaya; **2** Dede Suhendar; **3** Tjahjono; **4** Justedjo Tarik; **5** Aga Soemarno; **6** Bonit
Wiryawan; **7** Donny Susetyo; **8** Suharyadi; **9** Daniel Heryanto; **10** Sulistyo Wibowo.
WOMEN: 1 Yayuk Basuki; Tanti Trayono; **3** Irawati Moerid; **4** Joice Riana Sutedja; **5** Lukky Tedjamukti;
6 Tanya Soemarno; **7** Waya Walalangi; **8** Mimma Chernovita; **9** Solihati Moerid; **10** Agustina Wibisono.

IRAN (1937)

Tennis Federation of Islamic Republic of Iran, Shahid Shiroodi Stadium, Shahid Mofatteh St., Tehran.
C. Sportsiran; T. (98–21) 826999/832555; TX. 212691 VARZ IR; *Pres.* Mr M. Golsham Shirazi; *Sec.* Mr
M. Sefatti.

IRAQ (1959)

Iraqi Tennis Federation, c/o Iraqi National Olympic Committee, PO Box No 441, Baghdad.
C. Iroq, Baghdad; T. (964–1) 7748261; TX. 213409 IROC IK; Fax. (964–1) 7728424; *Pres.* Mr Suhil N.
Abdulla; *Sec.* Mr Saadoun Hasan.

IRELAND (1895)

Tennis Ireland, 54 Wellington Road, Ballsbridge, Dublin 4.
C. Irishtennis Dublin; T. (010 353–1) 681841; Fax. (010 353–1) 683411; *Pres.* Ms Anne Taylor; *Hon.*
Sec. Mrs Mavis Hogg; *Chief Exec.* Mr John Taylor.
National Closed Championships
MEN'S SINGLES – Semi-final: E. Collins d. J. Draper 6–3 6–0; O. Casey d. S. Doyle 6–0 6–2.
Final: Casey d. Collins 6–1 6–2.
WOMEN'S SINGLES – Semi-finals: S. Nicholson d. L. O'Halloran 6–1 6–4; G. Niland d. C. O'Sulli-
van 6–4 6–1. **Final:** Nicholson d. Niland 6–2 6–1.

ISRAEL

Israel Tennis Association, PO Box 51112, Tel Aviv 67 137.
C.ILTA, Tel Aviv; T. (972–3) 5603911/5660320; TX. 341118 BXTVIL; Fax. (972–3) 5660319; *Chmn*
Mr David Harnik; *Sec.* Mr Zvi Meyer.
MEN: 1 Amos Mansdorf; **2** Gilad Bloom; **3** Raviv Weidenfeld; **4** Ohad Weinberg; **5** Oren
Motevassel; **6** Michael Daniel; **7** Boaz Merenstein; **8** Ofer Sela; **9** Eyal Ran; **10** Shahar Perkiss.
WOMEN: 1 Ilana Berger; **2** Yael Segal; **3** Anna Smashnova; **4** Rona Mayer; **5** Limor Zaltz; **6** Liat
Cohen; **7** Shiri Burstein; **8** Tsipora Obziler; **9** Medi Dadochi; **10** Dahlia Coriat.

ITALY (1910)

Federazione Italiana Tennis, viale Tiziano 70, 00196 Rome.
C. Italtennis, Rome; T. (39–6) 323 3799/396 6743; TX. 626343 FIT I; Fax. (39–6) 36858166; *Pres.*
Mr Paolo Galgani; *Sec.* Mr Giuliano Annibali.
MEN: 1 Omar Comporese; **2** Cristiano Caratti; **3** Renzo Furlan; **4** Stefano Pescosolido; **5** Gianluca
Pozzi; **6** Diego Nargiso; **7** Claudio Pistolesi; **8** Paolo Cane; **9** Massimo Cierro; **10** Nicola Bruno.
WOMEN: 1 Sandra Cecchini; **2** Raffaella Reggi; **3** Federica Bonsignori; **4** Katia Piccolini; **5** Silvia
Farina; **6** Laura Garrone; **7** Linda Ferrando; **8** Cristina Salvi; **9** Natalia Baudone; **10** Francesca
Romano.
National Closed Championships
MEN'S SINGLES – Semi-finals: P. Pambianco d. C. Rigagnoli 6–7 7–6 6–1; M. Cierro d. M.
Naroucci 6–4 6–2. **Final:** Cierro d. Pambianco 6–0 6–2 ret.
WOMEN'S SINGLES – Semi-finals: S. Cecchini d. L. Ferrando 7–5 3–6 6–4; K. Piccolini d. F.
Bonsignori 1–6 6–0 6–4. **Final:** Piccolini d. Cecchini 4–6 6–4 7–5.

JAMAICA

Jamaica Lawn Tennis Association, 2A Piccadilly Road, PO Box 175, Kingston 5.
C. Lawntenna, Kingston; T. New Kingston (1–809) 9295878; TX. c/o 2441 JAMINTEL; Fax. (1–809)
9292135/9235617/9222282; *Pres.* Mr Ken Spencer; *Hon. Sec.* Mr Carmen Bell.

JAPAN (1921)

Japan Tennis Association, c/o Kishi Memorial Hall, 1-1-1 Jinnan, Shibuya-ku, Tokyo 150.
C. Niplotenis, Tokyo; T. (81–3) 3481 2321; TX. 2428222 JTENIS J; Fax. (81–3) 3467 5192; *Pres.* M
Tokusaburo Kosaka; *Sec.* Mr Shin-ichi Shimizu.
MEN: 1 Shuzo Matsuoka; 2 Bong-soo Kim; 3 Yasufumi Yamamoto; 4 Toshihisa Tsuchihashi; 5
Tsuyoshi Fukui; 6 Ignace Rotman; 7 Ryuzo Tsujino; 8 Daijiro Furusho; 9 Joseph Russel; 10 Kentaro
Masuda.
WOMEN: 1 Naoko Sawamatsu; 2 Kimiko Date; 3 Akiko Kijimuta; 4 Maya Kidowaki; 5 Rika Hiraki; 6
Nana Miyagi; 7 Mana Endo; 8 Misumi Miyauchi; 9 Tamaka Takagi; 10 Kumiko Okamoto.

National Closed Championships
MEN'S SINGLES – Semi-finals: T. Tsuchihashi d. T. Hidehiko 5–7 6–4 6–3 6–1; Y. Yamamoto d. T
Fukui 6–2 6–2 6–3. **Final:** Yamamoto d. Tsuchihashi 6–3 6–4 3–6 5–7 6–1.
WOMEN'S SINGLES – Semi-finals: K. Date d. R. Hiraki 6–3 6–3; E. Okagawa d. M. Kidowaki 6–2 6–0
Final: Date d. Okagawa 6–1 6–3.

JORDAN (1980)

Jordan Tennis Federation, PO Box 961046, Amman.
C. Tenfed, Amman; T. (962 6) 682796; TX. 24000 OLYMP; Fax. (962 6) 687950; *Chmn* Dr Daouc
Hanania; *Sec.* Dr Mohammed Sukhen.

KENYA (1922)

Kenya Lawn Tennis Association, PO Box 43184, Nairobi.
C. Tennis, Nairobi; T. (254–2) 745164; TX. 22119 MTSTRAV KE; Fax. (254–2) 729277; *Chmn* Mr W. D
Katibi; *Sec.* Mr B. Aggarwal.

National Closed Championships
MEN'S SINGLES – Semi-finals: B. Tekleab d. P. Nganga 6–4 4–6 6–4; D. Odipo d. S. Kipkoech 7–6
6–4. **Final:** Odipo d. Tekleab 6–3 6–3.
WOMEN'S SINGLES – Semi-finals: K. Perini d. V. Demello 6–3 7–5; A. Aggarwal d. J. Barralis 6–1
6–1. **Final:** Perini d. Aggarwal 6–1 6–2.

KOREA, REPUBLIC OF (1945)

Korea Tennis Association, Room 108, Olympic Gym. No. 2, 88-2, Oryun-dong, Songpa-gu, Seoul
138-678.
C. Kortennis, Seoul; T. (82–2) 420 4285/4286/3333 ext. 659/660; TLX. 24989 KOCSEL K; Fax. (82–2)
420 4284; *Pres.* Mr Choong-Kun Cho; *Sec.* Mr Yeoung-Moo Huh.

KUWAIT (1967)

Kuwait Tennis Federation, PO Box 1462, Hawalli 32015.
C. Tennis Kuwait; T. (965) 265 8148/265 8149; TX. 23192 COMITE KT (Att. Tennis Ass); Fax. (965) 539
0617. *Pres.* Mr Khalid Al-Bannai; *Sec.* Mr Abdul Ridha Ghareeb.

LEBANON (1945)

Fédération Libanaise de Tennis, PO Box 113-5591, Hamra, Beirut.
C. Tennispong, Beyrouth; T. (1–961) 1342282; TX. 21665/20680 JOEINT LE (Att. E A Yazbeck); *Pres.*
Mr Abdel Karim Matar; *Hon. Sec.* Mr Emile A. Yazbeck.
MEN: 1 Raymond Kattoura; 2 Karim Khoury; 3 Said Karam; 4 Adoni Abou Naoum; 5 Edward Nehme; 6
Ali Tawbi; 7 Bishara Abu Rahal; 8 Hussein Badreddine; 9 Toufic Zahlan; 10 Amin Khalaf.
WOMEN: 1 Tania Zaytouni; 2 Nahia Abu Khalil; 3 Maya Hajjar; 4 Sherene Rbeiz; 5 Raymonde Ayoub; 6
Dia Elzir; 7 Lena Zaytouni; 8 Rima Rabbat; 9 Sharifa Abu Ezzedin; 10 Michelene Dib.

National Closed Championships
MEN'S SINGLES – Semi-finals: E. Nehme d. H. Badreddine 6–1 6–3 6–2; R. Kattoura d. K. Khoury 1–6 2–6 7–5 6–4 6–2. *Final:* Kattoura d. Nehme 6–3 3–6 6–1 6–2.
WOMEN'S SINGLES – Semi-finals: M. Hajjar d. N. Abu Khalil 7–6 6–1; T. Zaytouni d. S. Rbeiz 6–3 (def). *Final:* Hajjar d. Zaytouni 6–2 6–2.

LIBYA (1947)

Jamahiriya Tennis Federation, Alfatah September Street, PO Box 2729, Tripoli.
C. Tennis Libya; T. (218–21) 39150/46883; TX. 20420 OLYMPIC LIBYA; *Pres.* Mr Omran Danna; *Sec.* Mr Mohamed Behelil.

LIECHTENSTEIN (1968)

Liechtensteiner Tennisverband, Bartlegroschstrasse 36, 9490 Vaduz.
T. (41–75) 56659; Fax. (41–75) 56518; *Pres.* Mr Walter Walser; *Sec.* Mr Werner Schaechle.

LUXEMBOURG (1946)

Fédération Luxembourgeoise de Tennis, Boîte Postale 38, L 9201 Diekirch, Luxembourg.
C. Fédération Luxembourgeoise de Tennis Luxembourg; T. (352) 81 75 41; Fax. (352) 81 77 25; *Pres.* Mr Michel Wolter; *Vice Pres. Gen. Sec.* Jean Goederich.
MEN: **1** Johny Goudenbour; **2** Jacques Radoux; **3** Serge Bruck; **4** Thierry Neiens; **5** Patrick Remackel.
WOMEN: **1** Anne Kremer; **2** Marie-Christine Goy; **3** Rosabel Moyen; **4** Michele Wagner.

National Closed Championships
MEN'S SINGLES – Semi-finals: P. Hoffmann d. M. Van Kauvenbergh 6–4 3–6 6–4; J. Goudenbour d. J.–M. Goy 6–0 7–5. *Final:* Hoffmann d. Goudenbour 6–2 6–2.
WOMEN'S SINGLES – Semi-finals: A. Kremer d. S. Wolff 6–2 6–2; M-C. Goy d. R. Moyen 6–3 6–0.
Final: Kremer d. Goy 7–5 6–1.

MALAYSIA (1921)

Lawn Tennis Association of Malaysia, c/o National Tennis Centre, Jalan Duta, 50480 Kuala Lumpur, Malaysia.
C. Tennis Kuala Lumpur; T. (60–3) 2938070/2938050; Fax. (60–3) 2925041; TX. NTC MA 28061; *Pres.* Mr Abdul Ghafar Baba; *Sec.* Mr Zainal Abidin Ali.

MALTA (1966)

Malta Lawn Tennis Association, PO Box 50, Sliema Post Office, Sliema.
T. (356) 512368/335728 (Sec); TX. 623 MERGRU MW; Fax. (356) 221135/242259; *Pres.* Dr L. Farrugia Sacco; *Gen. Sec.* Mr Michael J. Borg Cardona.

MEXICO (1952)

Mexican Tennis Federation, Miguel Angel de Quevedo 953, Mexico City 04330 DF.
C. Mextenis, Mexico City, T. (52–5) 689 9733; TX. 1761056 FMDTME; Fax. (52–5) 689 6307/549 1956; *Pres.* Mr Jesus Topete Enriquez; *Sec.* Mr Fernando Palafox Valadez.

MONACO (1927)

Fédération Monegasque de Lawn Tennis, 27 Boulevard de Belgique, 98000 Monaco.
C. Fédération-Tennis-Monaco; T. (33–93) 25 55 74; (Att. LTA); Fax. (33–93) 30 54 82; *Sec.* Mr Jean-Paul Samba.
MEN: **1** Bernard Balleret; **2** Christophe Boggetti; **3** Jerome Seguin; **4** Christian Collange; **5** Olivier Peyret; **6** Jacques Vincileoni.
WOMEN: **1** Emmanuelle Gagliardi; **2** Agnes Barthelemy; **3** Nadine Balleret; **4** Axel Rollin; **5** Frederique Nalbandian; **6** Jessica Giordano.

National Closed Championships
MEN'S SINGLES – Final: Jerome Seguin d. Christian Collange 6–3 6–1 6–2.
WOMEN'S SINGLES – Final: **1** Emmanuelle Gagliardi d. Nadine Balleret 6–0 6–2.

MOROCCO (1957)

Fédération Royale Marocaine de Tennis, Parc de la Ligue Arabe, BP 15794, Casablanca.
C. Tenisfede, Maroc; T. (212) 278731/262448/262855; TX. 23745 FRTENNIS; Fax. (212–2) 262652;
Pres. Mr Mohamed M'Jid; *Sec.* Mr Ahmed Mansouri.
MEN: **1** Youness El Aynaoui; **2** Karim Alami; **3** Mohamed Ridaoui; **4** Arafa Chokrouni; **5** Salahddine
Adbib; **6** Hicham Arazi; **7** Mohamed Dlimi; **8** Houcine Saber; **9** Yassine Lalaoui; **10** Amine Boustani.
WOMEN: **1** Lamia Alami; **2** Rachida Ennajmi; **3** Sanaa Belguezzar; **4** Nadia Hizazi; **5** Mouna Kharchafi; **6**
Chaabia Saber; **7** Yasmine Benziane; **8** Chamssi Filali; **9** Safaa Najdi; **10** Hind Tajeddine.

National Closed Championships
MEN'S SINGLES – Semi-finals: H. Arazi d. M. Dlimi 6–0 6–1; Y. El Aynaoui d. S. Adbib 6–4 7–5. *Final:*
El Aynaoui d. Arazi 6–3 6–0.
WOMEN'S SINGLES – Semi-final: L. Alami d. S. Belguezzar 3–6 6–4 6–1; C. Saber d. S. Islami 7–5
6–0. *Final:* Alami d. Saber 6–3 7–6.

NETHERLANDS (1899)

Koninklijke Nederlandse Lawn Tennis Bond, PO Box 107, 1200 AC Hilversum.
C. Tennisbond, Hilversum; T. (31–35) 246 941; TX. 43061 KNLTB NL; Fax. (31–35) 240 760; *Pres.* Mr
Ruurd de Boer; *Vice Pres.* Mrs H. V. Mook-Grunberg, *Sec.* Mr Martin Mallon.
MEN: **1** Jan Siemerink; **2** Richard Krajicek; **3** Paul Haarhuis; **4** Michiel Schapers; **5** Mark Koevermans; **6**
Jacco Eltingh; **7** Tom Kempers; **8** Ralph Kok; **9** Sander Groen; **10** Fernon Wibier.
WOMEN: **1** Brenda Schultz; **2** Manon Bollegraf; **3** Nicole Muns-Jagerman; **4** Miriam Oremans; **5** Petra
Kamstra; **6** Stephanie Rottier; **7** Simone Schilder; **8** Monique Kiene; **9** Heleen Van Den Berg; **10** Esmir
Hoogendoorn.

National Closed Championships
MEN'S SINGLES – Semi-finals: R. Krajicek d. T. Kempers 3–6 6–1 6–0 1–6 6–2; P. Haarhuis d. J.
Eltingh 7–6 3–6 6–1 7–6. *Final:* Krajicek d. Haarhuis 6–4 3–6 6–3 4–6 6–4.
WOMEN'S SINGLES – Semi-finals: E. Hoogendoorn d. M. Kiene 6–2 6–2; H. Van Den Berg d. S. De
Vries 6–4 6–1. *Final:* Van Den Berg d. Hoogendoorn 6–4 1–6 7–5.

NEW ZEALAND (1886)

New Zealand Lawn Tennis Association, PO Box 11541, Manners Street, Wellington.
C. Tennis, Wellington; T. (64–4) 4731115; Fax. (64–4) 4712152; *Chmn* Mr Ian D. Wells; *Admin. Sec.* Ms
Maggi Kerr-Andrew.
MEN: **1** Kelly Evernden; **2** Brett Steven; **3** Steven Guy; **4** Bruce Derlin; **5** David Lewis; **6** Glenn Wilson;
7 Alistair Hunt; **8** William Laban; **9** Troy Turnbull; **10** Justin McKenzie.
WOMEN: **1** Belinda Cordwell; **2** Claudine Toleafoa; **3** Julie Richardson; **4** Hana Adamkova; **5** Ruth
Seeman; **6** Angelique Lodewyks; **7** Amanda Trail; **8** Jacqui Gunthorp; **9** Michelle Parun; **10** Katherine
Costain.

National Closed Championships
MEN'S SINGLES – Semi-finals: K. Evernden d. J. Greenhalgh 7–6 6–4; B. Steven d. G. Wilson 6–3
6–2. *Final:* Evernden d. Steven 6–2 3–6 7–6.
WOMEN'S SINGLES – Semi-finals: C. Toleafoa d. A. Lambert 6–1 6–1; J. Richardson d. A. Trail 6–3
4–6 6–3. *Final:* Richardson d. Toleafoa 7–6 6–4.

NIGERIA (1927)

Nigeria Lawn Tennis Association, National Stadium, Surulere, PO Box 145, Lagos.
C. Tennis Natsports, Lagos, T. (234–1) 83 0649; TX. 26559 ADEFNL NG; *Life Patron* Alhaji Raheem A.
Adejumo; *Chmn* Mr Chuka Momah; *Sec.* Miss Chinedu Ezealah.

NORWAY (1909)

Norges Tennisforbund, Haslevangen 33, PO Box 2870511, Oslo 5.
C. Norsktennis, Oslo; T. (47–2) 657550; TX. 78586 NIF N (Att. Tennis); Fax. (47–2) 646409; *Pres.* Mr
Jarl H Bibow; *Sec.* Mr Jon-Erik Ross.

PAKISTAN (1947)

Pakistan Tennis Federation, 30–A Jinnah Stadium, Pakistan Sports Complex, Kashmir Highway, Islamabad.
C. Paktennis, Wah Cantt; T. (92–51) 818288/821004/825772; TX. 54288 ENMAR PK; Fax. (92–51) 212 440; *Pres.* Mr Wasim Sajjad; *Vice Pres.* Mr Saeed Hai; *Sec.* Mr Munir Pirzada.
MEN: 1 Rashid Malik; **2** Hamid-Ul Haq; **3** Inam-Ul Haq; **4** Mushaf Zia; **5** Muhammad Khalid; **6** Aman Asghar; **7** Nadir Ali Khan; **8** Muhammad Khaliq; **9** Hamayoon Pervez; **10** Arif Feroz.
WOMEN: 1 Tehmina Mohtasham; **2** Mariam N. Rahim; **3** Sadia Jan; **4** Farah Khursheed; **5** Aysha Shamshad; **6** Tasmeen Tayyap; **7** Ghazala Yasmeen; **8** Rubina Hai; **9** Razia Khan; **10** Noreen Akram.

National Closed Championships
MEN'S SINGLES – Semi-finals: R. Malik d. M. Zia 6–1 6–2; H. Ul Haq d. I. Ul Haq 7–5 6–4. **Final:** Malik d. Haq 6–3 4–6 6–3.
WOMEN'S SINGLES – Semi-finals: M. N. Rahim d. B. Leibing 7–6 6–1; S. Jan d. T. Mohtasham 7–5 6–2. **Final:** Jan d. Rahim 2–6 6–2 6–1.

PARAGUAY (1920)

Asociación Paraguaya de Tenis, Colón 1054, 1st Floor, Asunción.
T. (595–21) 497756; TX. 25005 DIESA PY; Fax. (595 21) 503721; *Pres.* Mr Miguel Carrizosa; *Exec. Dir.* Mr Daniel Lugo Llamosas.

PERU (1930)

Federación Peruana de Tenis, Cercado Campo de Marte, s/n Jesus Maria, Casilla 2243, Lima.
T. (51–14) 249979; TX. 25056 PE FPTENIS; Fax. (51–14) 420015; *Pres.* Mr Bartolome Puiggros Planas; *Sec.* Mr Peter Relton Ruddock.

PHILIPPINES (1946)

Philippine Tennis Association, Rizal Memorial Sports Complex, Vito Cruz Street, Manila.
C. Philta, Manila; T. (63–2) 583535/588248; TX. 23297 ALTIS PH/40255 ALTA PM; Fax. (63–2) 522 0229; *Pres.* Col Salvador H Andrada; *Sec.* Armando P Alcaraz.
MEN: 1 Felix Barrientos; **2** Roland So; **3** Danilo Pila; **4** Camoy Palahang; **5** Robert Angelo; **6** Joseph Lizardo; **7** Jun Alerre; **8** Ronald San Andres; **9** Manny Tolentino; **10** Pio Tolentino.
WOMEN: 1 Jennifer Saret; **2** Francesca La'o; **3** Joanna Feria; **4** Dorothy J. Suarez; **5** Carol Roqul; **6** Gladys Imperial; **7** Mia Fernandez; **8** Josephine Paguyo; **9** Giselle Sta. Maria.

National Closed Championships
MEN'S SINGLES – Semi-finals: J. Lizardo d. D. Pila 7–5 7–5; R. Angelo d. C. Palahang 3–6 7–6 6–2. **Final:** Lizardo d. Angelo 6–4 6–3.
WOMEN'S SINGLES – Semi-finals: F. La'o d. C. Roque 6–1 6–4; D. J. Suarez d. G. Imperial 6–2 6–1. **Final:** La'o d. Suarez 4–6 6–1 6–2.

POLAND (1921)

Polski Zwiazek Tenisowy, ul. Marszalkowska 2, 3rd Floor, 00 - 581 Warsaw.
C. Poltenis, Warsaw; T. (48–22) 21 80 01/29 26 21; TX. 816494 PAISP PL/812466 COS PL; *Pres.* Prof. Kazimierz Doktor; *Director* Mr Janusz Dorosiewicz
MEN: 1 W. Kowalski; **2** B. Dabrowski; **3** T. Iwanski; **4** L. Bienkowski; **5** T. Lichon; **6** L. Sidor; **7** S. Gruzman; **8** K. Ganszczyk; **9** P. Baranowski; **10** R. Major.
WOMEN: 1 K. Nowak; **2** M. Mroz; **3** K. Teodorowicz; **4** A. Werblinska; **5** A. Moll; **6** M. Starosta; **7** M. Madura; **8** S. Czopek; **9** M. Rachalewska; **10** K. Malec.

Closed National Championships
MEN'S SINGLES – Semi-finals: L. Bienkowski d. L. Sidor 6–1 6–1 6–1; B. Dabrowski d. A. Skrzypczak 6–7 6–3 6–4 2–6 6–0. **Final:** Dabrowski d. Sidor 6–2 6–4 6–3.
WOMEN'S SINGLES – Semi-finals: M. Mroz d. R. Skrzypczynska 4–6 6–2 6–0; H. Kuklinska d. K. Malec 4–6 6–3 6–4. **Final:** Mroz d. Kuklinska 6–1 6–0.

PORTUGAL (1925)

Federacao Portugesa de Tenis, Estadio Nacional, Apartado 210, 2796 Linda-a-Velha Codex, Portugal.
C. TENIS PORTUGAL; T. (351–1) 4151356/4151394; TX. 65257 TENFED P; Fax. (351–1) 419 0888; *Pres.* Mr Manuel Cordeiro dos Santos; *Sec.* Mr Antonio Sequeira.

PUERTO RICO (1959)

Puerto Rico Tennis Association, PO Box 40456, Minillas Sta, Santurce, PR 00940.
T. (1–809) 765 7711; TX 345 4212 PRTA PD; Fax. (1–809) 767 7427; *Pres.* Mr Carlos Garcia Rullan; *Sec.* Mr Jaime Ariza.
MEN: **1** Joey Rive; **2** Juan Rios; **3** Miguel Nido: **4** John O'Brien: **5** Francis Gonzalez: **6** Jaime Frontera: **7** Stephen Diaz.
WOMEN: **1** Gigi Fernandez; **2** Emily Viqueira; **3** Joanna Bauza; **4** Natalie Adsuar; **5** Beatriz Luna; **6** Gloria Gonzalez.

National Closed Championships
MEN'S SINGLES – Semi-finals: J. Rios d. J. O'Brien 6–2 6–1; J. Rive d. M. Nido 6–7 6–1 6–3. *Final:* Rive d. Rios 6–4 6–2.
WOMEN'S SINGLES – Semi-finals: E. Viqueira d. J. Bauza 6–2 6–4; G. Gernandez d. N. Adsuar 6–1 6–2. *Final:* Fernandez d. Viqueira 6–2 6–4.

QATAR (1984)

Qatar Tennis and Squash Federation, PO Box 4959, Doha.
C. QATSF DOHA; T. (974) 351629/351631/454444; TX. 4749 QATFOT DH; Fax. (974) 351626; *Pres.* Mr Ali Al Fardan; *Sec.* Mr Ali Mohammad Yousef.

ROMANIA (1929)

Federatia Romana de Tennis, Str. Vasile Conta 16, 70139 Bucharest.
C. Sportrom, Bucharest; T. (40–0) 120 160; TX. 11180 SPORT R; Fax. (40–0) 120 161; *Pres.* Mr Constantin Iurea; *Sec.* Prof. Lucian Vasiliu.

SAUDI ARABIA (1956)

Saudi Arabian Tennis Federation, PO Box 4674, Riyadh 11412.
C. Koratawla, Riyadh; T. (966–1) 4820188/4822829; TX. 404130 TENNIS SJ; Fax. (966–1) 4822829; *Pres.* Mr Soliman Aljabhan; *Sec.* Mr Saud Ali Abdulaziz.
MEN: **1** Bader Al Mogail; **2** Osman Al Anzi; **3** Fahmey Saleh; **4** Gamal Oshban; **5** Moutaz Mashour; **6** Tawfik Ibrahim; **7** Nabil Amoudy; **8** Mohamed Al Mofa; **9** Abdullah Mesned.

National Closed Championships
MEN'S SINGLES – Semi-finals: B. Mogail d. K. Fitiani 6–4 6–3; O. Al Anzi d. F. Saleh 7–5 7–6. *Final:* Mogail d. Al Anzi 6–3 6–4.

SENEGAL (1960)

Fédération Sénégalaise de Tennis, Sporting Club, 28 Avenue Roosevelt, BP 510, Dakar.
T. (221) 210239; TX. 61159 SG CTDSENE; Fax. (221) 22 93 93; *Pres.* Mr Mamadou Bary; *Sec.* Layti Ndiaye.

SINGAPORE (1928)

Singapore Lawn Tennis Association, 4 Normanton Park, # 07-115, Singapore 0511.
T. (65) 274 1774; TX. 35467 NASTAD RS; Fax. (65) 272 2704; *Pres.* Dr Ong Leong Boon; *Hon. Sec.* Maj. S. Uthrapathy.

SOUTH AFRICA (1991)

Tennis South Africa, Box 2211, Johannesburg 2000.
T. (27) 11 407 4893 (Pres.)/(27) 11 402 3580 (Chief Exec.); Fax. (27) 11 407 4662 (Pres.)/(27) 11 402 6940 (Chief Exec.); *Pres.* Mr Chris Ngcobo; *Chief Exec.* Mr Ian Laxton; *Gen. Sec.* Mr Moss Mashishi.

SPAIN (1901)

Real Federación Española de Tenis, Avda. Diagonal 618 3 D, 08021 Barcelona.
C. FEDETENIS Barcelona; T. (34–3) 2005355/2010844/2005878/2015586; Fax. (34°3) 2021279; *Pres.* Mr Agustin Pujol; *Sec.* Mr Tomas Garcia Balmaseda.

SRI LANKA (1915)

Sri Lanka Tennis Association, 45 Sir Marcus Fernando Mawatha, Colombo 7.
C. Tennis, Colombo; T. (94–1) 686174; TX. 21537 METALIX CE; Fax. (94–1) 580721; *Pres.* Mr D. L. Seneviratne; *Sec.* Mr Dhyan Peiris.

SUDAN (1956)

Sudan Lawn Tennis Association, PO Box 1553, Khartoum.
T. (249–11) 70081; TX. 22345 ARART SD/22558 DIGES SD; *Pres.* Mr Mohamed Ahmed Giha; *Sec.* Dr Fatih Hasabrasoul.

SWEDEN (1906)

The Swedish Tennis Association, Box 27915, S–11594 Stockholm.
C. Svensktennis; T. (46–8) 6679770; TX. 12235 TENNIS S; Fax. (46–8) 6646606; *Pres.* Mr Olle Bergstrom; *Gen. Sec.* Mr Rolf Levin.

SWITZERLAND (1896)

Schweizerischer Tennisverband, Talgut Zentrum 5, CH 3063, Ittigen/BE.
C. Suissetennis, Bern; T. (41–31) 587444; TX. 911391 STVCH; Fax. (41–31) 582924; *Pres.* Mrs Christine Ungricht; *Sec.* Mr Daniel Gundelfinger.
MEN: 1 Jakob Hlasek; **2** Marc Rosset; **3** Claudio Mezzadri; **4** Thierry Grin; **5** Zoltan Kuharszky; **6** Valentin Frieden; **7** Ignace Rotman; **8** Roland Stadler; **9** Reto Staubli; **10** Stefano Mezzadri.
WOMEN: 1 Manuela Maleeva-Fragnière; **2** Emanuela Zardo; **3** Christelle Fauche; **4** Cathy Caverzasio; **5** Csilla Bartos; **6** Natalie Tschan; **7** Michele Strebel; **8** Gabrielle Villiger; **9** Celine Cohen; **10** Eva Krapl.

National Closed Championships
MEN'S SINGLES – Semi-finals: M. Walder d. R. Fiorina 7–5 6–2; R. Staubli d. T. Grin 3–6 7–6 7–6.
Final: Staubli d. Walder 4–6 4–6 6–2 6–1 6–4.
WOMEN'S SINGLES – Semi-finals: E. Zardo d. C. Fauche 7–6 6–0; C. Bartos d. C. Caverzasio 6–7 6–4 6–1. **Final:** Zardo d. Bartos 2–6 6–4 6–2.

SYRIA, ARAB REPUBLIC (1953)

Syrian Arab Tennis Federation, PO Box 421, Damascus.
T. (963–11) 225026/34/52; TX. 411578 SPOFED SY; *Pres.* Mr Ahmad Al Hamed; *Sec.* Mr Mustafa Hendi.

THAILAND (1927)

The Lawn Tennis Association of Thailand, c/o Sports Authority of Thailand, Hua Mark, Bangkok 10240.
C. Thai Tennis, Bangkok; T. (66–2) 3190484/3184318; Fax. (66–2) 3195868/2214841; *Pres.* Mr Somchitr Tongpradab; *Sec.* Mr Prachitr Srichaiyan.
MEN: 1 Thanakorn Srichaphan; **2** Narathorn Srichaphan; **3** Woraphon Thongkamchou; **4** Wittaya Samrej; **5** Noppadon Srijarean; **6** Panomkorm Pladchuenil; **7** Siri Thamsiriboon; **8** Charoenchai Taitilannunt; **9** Jiravas Rakkarnpat; **10** Tomorn Chantra.
WOMEN: 1 Suvimol Duangchan; **2** Benjamas Sangaram; **3** Sudsopee Chartsurhipun; **4** Sasithon Thangthienkul; **5** Siriluk Mingmolee; **6** Pattamika Pongsuriyamas; **7** Chavisa Rareng; **8** Tamarine Tanasugarn; **9** Pimpisamai Kansuthi; **10** Apichaya Kunpitak.

National Closed Championships
MEN'S SINGLES – Semi-finals: T. Srichaphan d. W. Thongkamchou 6–4 6–4; N. Srichaphan d. W. Samrej 6–4 6–3. **Final:** Srichaphan d. Srichaphan 6–3 6–1.
WOMEN'S SINGLES – Semi-finals: B. Sangaram d. A. Kunpitak 6–2 6–3; P. Pongsuriyamas d. N. Keawborisuth 6–4 6–4. **Final:** Sangaram d. Pongsuriyamas 6–4 7–5.

TOGO (1955)

Fédération Togolaise de Tenis, BP 3601, Lome.
T. (228) 215965/210920/210920/210607; TX. 5442 GRD TG; Fax. (228) 210607; *Pres.* Mr Kwao Aquereburu; *Sec.* Mr Koffi Galokpo.

TRINIDAD AND TOBAGO (1951)

The Lawn Tennis Association of Trinidad and Tobago, 16 Scott Street, St Augustine, Trinidad.
C. Lawntenna, Port of Spain; T. (1–809) 662 5876; Fax. (1–809) 627 5278; *Pres.* Mr Emile P. Elias; *Sec.* Mr Richardson Henry.

National Closed Championships
MEN'S SINGLES – Semi-finals: O. Adams d. J. Hodge 2–6 6–2 6–3 6–1; M. Webster d. B. Khan 3–6 6–1 6–4 6–4. **Final:** Adams d. Webster 6–3 6–2 6–3.
WOMEN'S SINGLES – Semi-finals: B. Corbie d. A. Ali 6–0 6–2; J. Ayers d. R. Mark 6–2 6–1. **Final:** Corbie d. Ayers 6–1 6–2.

TUNISIA (1954)

Fédération Tunisienne de Tennis, Cité Nationale, Sportive - El Menzah, 1004 Tunis.
T. (216–1) 238 144; TX. 14637 TOPMED TN; Fax. (216–1) 786 188; *Pres.* Mr Fathi Farah; *Sec.* Mr Mohamed Ali Lazrak.
MEN: 1 Souheil Zekri; 2 Adel Karti; 3 Elies Bramly; 4 Adel Brahim; 5 Selim Ben Haj Ali; 6 Hichem Bramly; 7 Walid Celcio Caracci; 8 Karim Jelassi; 9 Bessem Zouaoui; 10 Mourad Jelassi.
WOMEN: 1 Selima Sfar; 2 Issem Essaies; 3 Bessima Mehressi; 4 Dorra Zdiri; 5 Aigha Ferjani; 6 Amina Razgallah; 7 Mouna Hedhili; 8 Selma Mouelhi; 9 Imene Ben Arbi; 10 Mouna Bey.

National Closed Championships
MEN'S SINGLES – Semi-finals: S. Zekri d. H. Bramly 4–6 6–4 6–2; A. Karti d. M. Jelassi 6–4 6–1. **Final:** Zekri d. Karti 3–6 6–1 6–3.
WOMEN'S SINGLES – Semi-finals: I. Esseiss d. I. Ben Arbi 6–1 6–2; S. Mouelhi d. M. Marrakchi 6–0 6–1. **Final:** Esseis d. Mouehi 6–0 6–0.

TURKEY (1923)

Turkiye Tenis Federasyonu, Ulus Is Hani, Ankara.
C. Tennis Sport, Ankara; T. (90–4) 310 3960/7345; TX. 44 531 BTGM TR; Fax. (90–4) 311 2554; *Pres.* Mr Gunesi Olcay; *Sec.* Mr Sadi Toker.

USA (1881)

United States Tennis Association Inc, 12th Floor, 1212 Avenue of the Americas, New York, NY 10036.
C. Ustennis, New York; T. (1–212) 302 3322; TX. 424499 ULTA UI; Fax. (1–212) 764 1838; *Pres.* Mr Robert Cookson; *First Vice Pres.* Mr J. Howard Frazer; *Exec. Dir.* Mr M. Marshall Happer III; *Sec.* Mr Harry A. Marmion.

National Closed Championships
MEN'S SINGLES – Semi-finals: S. Edberg d. I. Lendl 6–3 6–3 6–4; J. Courier d. J. Connors 6–3 6–3 6–2. **Final:** Edberg d. Courier 6–2 6–4 6–0.
WOMEN'S SINGLES – Semi-finals: M. Navratilova d. S. Graf 7–6 6–7 6–4; M. Seles d. J. Capriati 6–3 3–6 7–6. **Final:** Seles d. Navratilova 7–6 6–1.

URUGUAY (1915)

Asociación Uruguya de Tennis, Galicia 1392, CP 11.200, Montevideo.
C. Urutennis, Montevideo; T. (598–2) 91 50 20; TX. 22333 CADE UY; Fax. (598–2) 92 18 09; *Pres.* Mr Carlos Rymer Estrada; *Sec.* Enrique Dentone.
MEN: 1 Marcelo Filippini; 2 Diego Perez; 3 Victor Caldarelli; 4 Enrique Perez; 5 Philippe Pinet; 6 Nicolas Zurmendi; 7 Federico Dondo; 8 Hugo Roverano; 9 Carlos Freira; 10 Joaquin Elola.
WOMEN: 1 Patricia Miller; 2 Claudia Brause; 3 Laura Olave; 4 Natalia De Cola; 5 Silvana Casaretto; 6 Maria Martha Gallinal; 7 Guadalupe Herraiz; 8 Cecilia Juricich; 9 M. Teresa Ruiz; 10 Elena Juricich.

National Closed Championships
MEN'S SINGLES – Semi-finals: E. Perez d. N. Zurmendi 2–6 7–5 7–6; P. Pinet d. H. Roverano 2–6 6–4 6–0. **Final:** Perez d. Pinet 7–6 6–3.
WOMEN'S SINGLES – Semi-finals: C. Brause d. M. Teresa Ruiz 6–1 6–4; G. Herraiz d. C. Juricich 6–2 6–0. **Final:** Brause d. Herraiz 6–2 6–0.

VENEZUELA (1927)

Federación Venezolana de Tenis, Apartado 70539, Los Ruices, Caracas 1070 A.
C. Fevetenis, Caracas; T. (58–2) 9792421/9791487; Fax. (58–2) 9792694; *Pres.* Mr Fermin Perez; *Sec.* Mr Alfredo Lanciani.
MEN: **1** Yaser Zaatini; **2** Valerio Boccitto; **3** Ivan Bello; **4** Maxsy Jimenez; **5** Boro Colvee; **6** Rodolfo Beniter; **7** Jimy Szymanski; **8** Inigo Ojer; **9** Rodrigo Diaz; **10** Abraham Levy.
WOMEN: **1** Eleonora Vegliante; **2** Melissa Mazzotta; **3** Ninfa Marra; **4** Marvi Francesa; **5** Helene Kappler; **6** Elizabeth Nieto; **7** Erika Bove; **8** Vanessa Levy; **9** Gipsy Goldin; **10** Maria Vegliante.
National Closed Championships
MEN'S SINGLES – Semi-finals: Y. Zaatini d. U. Corda 6–4 6–2; V. Boccitto d. R. Y. Benitez 6–4 7–6.
Final: Zaatini d. Boccitto 4–6 6–4 6–4.
WOMEN'S SINGLES – Semi-finals: M. Francesa d. V. Levy 6–4 6–0; N. Marra d. E. Nieto 5–7 6–2 6–0.
Final: Marra d. Francesa 6–4 6–3.

YUGOSLAVIA (1922)

Tenis Savez Yugoslavije, Terazije 35, 11000 Belgrade.
C. Tesaj, Belgrade; T. (38–11) 33 33 36; TX. 12595 SFKJ YU; *Pres.* Mr Petar Marinkovic; *Sec.* Mr Zoran Peric.

ZAMBIA (1975)

Zambia Lawn Tennis Association, PO Box 31980, Lusaka.
T. (260–1) 224145; TX. 43400 ZA; Fax. (260–1) 221440; *Pres.* Mr Mwansa M. Mutanuka; *Sec.* Ms Beatrice Nachilombe.

ZIMBABWE (1904)

Tennis Association of Zimbabwe, PO Box No A575, Avondale, Harare.
T. (263–4) 35073 (Pres.); TX. 22386 ZW; Fax. (263–4) 61881; *Pres.* Mr Paul Chingoka; T. (263–4) 68377; *Dep. Pres.* Ms Veronica Dolman T. (263–4) 792011; Fax. (263–4) 790198; *Sec.* Ms Julie le Roux.
MEN: **1** Byron Black, **2** Wayne Black; **3** Rashid Hassan; **4** Malcolm Birch; **5** Jeremy Dutoit; **6** Gwinyai Tongoona; **7** Alan Hounsell; **8** Greg Rodger; **9** Martin Lock; **10** Zaheed Essof.
WOMEN: **1** Julia Muir; **2** Paula Iversen; **3** Sally-Ann McDonald; **4** Nikkie Wagstaff; **5** Leslie Barbour; **6** Alison Vaughan; **7** Diana Mills; **8** Adele Robertson; **9** Cara Black; **10** Ashleigh Dolman.

Associate members without voting rights (68)

AFGHANISTAN Afghan Lawn Tennis Association, c/o National Olympic Committee of Afghanistan, Ghasi Stadium, Kabul.
C. Olympic Kabul; TX. 205; *Pres.* Mr Homayun Parvanta; *Sec.* Mr Nematullah Mangal.

AMERICAN SAMOA (1985) American Samoa Tennis Association, PO Box PPB, Pago Pago, American Samoa 96799.
T. (684) 644 5251; Fax. (684) 644 5005; *Pres.* Mr Perelini Perelini; *Sec.* Dr Jerome Amoa.

ANDORRA Federacio Andorrana de Tenis, San Antoni, 5 Entresol A. Escaldes, Principaute d'Andorre.
T. (33–628) 26728; Fax. (33–628) 23182; *Pres.* Mr Alexandre Escale; *Sec.* Mr Claudi Sala.

ANGOLA Federacao Angolana de Tenis, PO Box 3677, Luanda.
T. (244–1) 361152/350961; TX. 3121 EMISSORA AN/3052 INTSER AN; Fax. (244–1) 33 02 81; *Pres.* Mr Luis Lopes; *Sec.* Mr Nelson Assis.

ANTIGUA (1982) The Antigua and Barbuda Tennis Association, PO Box 48 (Pres)/PO Box 530 (Sec), St. John's, Antigua.
T. (809) 461 0597 (Pres); T. 462 2955/0818 (Sec); *Pres.* Mr Cedric Nanton; *Sec.* Mr Patrick Labadie.

ARUBA Aruba Lawn Tennis Bond, Fergusonstraat nr 40–A, P O Box 1151, Oranjestad Aruba, Netherlands Antilles.
T. (297–8) 22485; Fax. (297–8) 34605; *Pres.* Mr Albert Pouson; *Sec.* Mr Winston Kock.

BELIZE (1910)   Belize Tennis Association, PO Box 365 (Pres), Belize City, Belize.
T. (501) 2 77070; TX. 266 BRODIE BZE; Fax. (501) 2 75593; *Pres.* Mr Edward Nabil Musa; *Sec.* Mr
Clement Usher.

BENIN   Fédération Béninoise de Lawn Tennis, BP 2709, Cotonou 1.
C. Lawn Tenkninq; T. (229) 300123/330448; TX. 5342 COTONOU; Fax. (229) 314684; *Pres.* Mr
Edgar-Yves Monnou; *Sec.* Mr M. F. Adedjouma.

BERMUDA   Bermuda Lawn Tennis Association, PO Box HM 341, Hamilton HM BX.
C. Ernstaudit, Bermuda, T. (1–809) 295 0319/295 7272; TX. 3680 ERNST BA; Fax. (1–809) 295 5193;
Pres. Mr Allan Simmons; *Sec.* Mrs Gill Butterfield.

BHUTAN (1976)   Bhutan Tennis Federation, PO Box 103, Thimphu.
C. Olympic; *Pres.* Mr T. Dorji; *Sec.* Mr L. Tsering.

BOTSWANA (1964)   Botswana Lawn Tennis Association, PO Box 1174, Gaborone.
T. (267–31) 373193; TX. 2424 BD; Fax. (267–31) 4108; *Pres.* Dr Quill Hermans; *Sec.* Mrs Jenny
Hayzelden.

BRITISH VIRGIN ISLANDS (1983)   British Virgin Islands Tennis Association, PO Box 665, Road Town,
Tortola.
C. Veritatem Tortola; T. (1–809–49) 49 45471; TX. 7918 PMMBVI VB; Fax. (1–809–49) 49 45477; *Pres.*
Dr Ken Adamson; *Sec.* Mr Noel Barton.

BRUNEI DARUSSALAM (1967)   Brunei Darussalam Lawn Tennis Association, PO Box 859, Gadong
Post Office 3108, Negara.
T. (673–2) 225344; TX. BERSATU BU 2357; Fax. (673–2) 229355; *Pres.* Mr Tom Butcher; *Sec.* Mr John
Chia.

BURKINA FASO (1970)   Fédération Burkinabe de Tennis, BP 1765, Ouagadougou 1. Fax. (226)
306116; TX. 5268 CHAMCOM; *Pres.* Mr Issoufou Zongo; *Sec.* Mr Oumdouba Ouedraogo.

CAPE VERDE (1986)   Federacao Cabo-Verdiana de Tenis, Ministerio da Informacao, Cultura e Despor-
tos, Rua 5 de Julho, Praia.
T. 613309; Tlx. 6030; *Pres.* Mr Antero Barros; *Sec.* Mr Antonio Ferreira.

CAYMAN ISLANDS (1973)   Tennis Federation of the Cayman Islands, PO Box 1813, Grand Cayman,
Cayman Islands, British West Indies.
T. (1 809 949) 7000; TX. 4310 CORPSER CP; Fax. (1–809–949) 8154; *Pres.* Mr C. D. Johnson; *Sec.* Mr
Barry Smith.

COMORES (1985)   Fédération Comorienne de Tennis, B P 701, Moroni.
T. (269) 732113/732648; TX. 219 MAE RFIC KO; Fax. (269) 733166; *Pres.* Dr Mtara Maecha; *Sec.* Mr
Kamal Abdoulwahab.

COOK ISLANDS (1947)   Cook Islands Tennis Association, PO Box 72, Rarotonga.
T. (682) 22327; TX. 62026 SSIRARO; Fax. (682) 20979; *Pres.* Mr Brian R. Baudinet; *Sec.* Mr Bret
Gibson.

DOMINICA (1960)   Dominica Lawn Tennis Association, c/o The President, PO Box 199; Canefield
Industrial Estate, Canefield, Dominica, West Indies.
C 'Durapaints' Dominica; T. (1–809) 448 3000/3011; TX. 8655 DOMLEC DO; Fax. (1–809) 449 2051;
Pres. Mr Ninian Marie; *Sec.* Mr Thomas Dorsett.

ETHIOPIA (1972)   Ethiopian Lawn Tennis Federation; c/o Sport Commission; PO Box 3241, Addis
Ababa.
C. Addis Ababa (c/o Sports Commission); T. (251 –1) 156795; TX. 21377 NESCO ET; *Pres.* Mr Hailu
Ballha; *Sec.* Mr Werekey Ferede.

FIJI (1934)   Fiji Lawn Tennis Association, PO Box 2399, Government Buildings, Suva.
T. (679) 315988/300280; TX. 2276 USP FJ; Fax. (679) 300482; *Pres.* Mr Cliff Benson; *Sec.* Mr Paras
Naidu.

GABON (1988)   Fédération Gabonaise de Tennis, BP 3623, Libreville, Gabon.
T. (241) 733218; TX. 5219 CENATEC GO; *Pres.* Mr A. Paul-Apandina; *Sec.* Mr Jean-Jacques Massima
Landji.

GAMBIA (1938)   Gambia Tennis Association, PO Box 146 or PO Box 194, Banjul, The Gambia.
C. SSHOKSECURITY; T. (220) 28688/29848; TX. 2274 SSHOFIC/2362 MASS GV (Sec); *Pres.* Mr B.O.
Semega-Janneh; *Sec.* Mr Geoffrey M. Renner.

GRENADA (1973)   Grenada Lawn Tennis Association, PO Box 221, St George's, Grenada.
T. (1–809–440) 2434; *Pres.* Mr E. Gresham; *Sec.* Mr R. L. Hughes.

GUAM   Tennis Association of Guam, PO Box 4379, Agana, Guam 96910.
C. Chelsea, Guam; T. (671) 734 2624; Fax. (671) 477 4826; *Pres.* Mr Moe Cotton; *Sec.* Miss Ginny Dancel.

GUINEE CONAKRY (1980)   Fédération Guinéenne de Tennis, Au Secrétariat d'Etat à la Jeunesse et aux Sports, BP 262.
C. FGT BP 262, Conakry Guinee; T. 441962; TX. 22302 MJ GE; *Pres.* Mr Aly Sylla; *Sec.* Mme Magass. Malado Diallo.

GUYANA (1933)   Guyana Lawn Tennis Association, PO Box 10205, Georgetown.
C. Lawntenna, Georgetown. T.(592–2) 62936/53471 (Pre.); 56701/72613 (Sec.); TX. 3054 REPBANK; Fax. (592–2) 71612; *Pres.* Mr W. A. Lee; *Sec.* Dr R. S. Surujbally.

ICELAND (1987)   Icelandic Tennis Association, Ithrotamidstoedinni i Laugardal, 104 Reykjavik.
T. (354–1) 83377; TX. 2314 ISI-IS; Fax. (354–1) 678848; *Pres.* Mr Pall Stefansson; *Sec.* Mr Sigurdur Halldorsson.

KOREA, PEOPLE'S DEMOCRATIC REPUBLIC (1945)   Tennis Association of the Democratic People's Republic of Korea, Munsin-Dong, Dongdaewon Dist. Pyongyang.
C. Tennis Pyongyang; T. (82) 62386/63998/73198/22386/23998; TX. 5472 kp; *Pres.* Mr Kim Ju Yong; *Sec.* Mr Li Won Gun.

LESOTHO (1920)   Lesotho Lawn Tennis Association, PO Box 156, Maseru 100.
C. LIPAPALI; TX. 4330 FOREIN LO; Fax. (266) 310047; *Pres.* Mr P. M. Makotoane; *Sec.* Mr Clement M. Nots'i.

LIBERIA (1987)   Liberia Lawn Tennis Association, PO Box 1742, Monrovia.
T. (231) 222877/262932; Fax. (231) 261257; *Pres.* Dr W. Taylor Neal; *Sec.* Mr Clemenceau Urey.

MADAGASCAR (1979)   Fédération Malgache de Tennis, 38 rue Ravoninahitriniarivo, Antanimena, Antananarivo.
T. (261) 2 215 19; TX. 223 50 MALAKY MG; Fax. (261) 2 260 01; *Pres.* Mr Serge Ramiandrasoa; *Sec.* Mr Josoa Rakatonindriana.

MALAWI (1966)   Lawn Tennis Association of Malawi, PO Box 1417, Blantyre.
T. (265) 670033 (Chm); TX. 44114; Fax. (265) 670808; *Chmn* Mr Duncan Gumbi; *Sec.* Mrs Ann Carter.

THE MALDIVES (1983)   Tennis Association of the Maldives, c/o Maldives Olympic Committee, Male.
T. (960) 322 443; TX. 77039 MINHOM MF; Fax. (960) 324 739/323 972 via NOC; *Chmn* Mr Ahmed Aslam; *Sec.* Mr Abdul Rasheed.

MALI (1963)   Fédération Malienne de Tennis, B P 1888, Bamako.
T. (223) 226329 (Vice Pres.); TX. 2522/2535 (Vice Pres.); *Pres.* Mr Alpha Bocar Nafo; *Sec.* Mr Charles Blonda Traore.

MAURETANIA (1989)   Fédération Mauritanienne de Tennis, B P 6234, Nouakchott.
T. (33–1) 45 43 03 98 (Vice Pres.); *Pres.* Mr M Ragel; *Sec.* Cheickh Ould Horomtala.

MAURITIUS (1910)   Mauritius Lawn Tennis Association, PO Box 46, Rose Hill.
C. Tennis, Mauritius; T. (230) 464 5311; TX. 4729 SPORTS IW (Att. MLTA); Fax. (23) 6319 442; *Pres.* Mr John Glover; *Sec.* Mr Philippe Chan Tin.

MONGOLIA (1990)   Mongolian Tennis Association, Central Post Office, PO Box 109, Ulaanbaatar 13.
T. 20311 (via operator); *Pres.* Mr Ch Ganbold; *Sec.* Mr J. Batjargal.

MONTSERRAT (1984)   Montserrat Tennis Association, PO Box 209, Plymouth, Montserrat, British West Indies.
T. (1–809–491) 2478; *Pres.* Ms Candia Williams; *Sec.* Mr George Barratt.

MOZAMBIQUE (1979)   Federacao Mocambicana de Tenis, Caixa Postal 4351, Maputo.
C. JOFIRES, MAPUTO; T. (258) 27027; TX. 6614 BMS MO; Fax. (258–1) 420349/425078; *Pres.* Mr Pedro Figueiredo; *Sec.* Mr Victorino Nhabangue.

MYANMAR (1949)   Myanmar Tennis Federation, Aung San Memorial Stadium, Mingala Taung Nyunt, P O Box 11221, Yangon.
C. Ubsped, Rangoon; T. (95–1) 0171731; *Pres.* Mr Tha Oo; *Sec.* Mr Pe Than Tun.

NAMIBIA (1930)   Namibia Tennis Association, PO Box 479, Windhoek 9000.
T. (264–61) 51718; Fax. (264–61) 51718; *Pres.* Dr Pietie Loubser; *Sec.* Mr Patrick Gardner.

NEPAL (1968)   All Nepal Tennis Association, PO Box 2090, Dasarath Stadium, Kathmandu.
T. (977) 211732/215712; TX. 2390 NSCNP/2614 INSURE NP; *Pres.* Mr Siddheshwar Singh; *Sec.* M
Sarad Lama

NETHERLANDS ANTILLES (1941)   Nederlandse Antilliaanse Tennis Ass, PO Box 3571, Emmastad
Curacao.
T. (599–9) 73192; Fax. (599) 681423; *Pres.* Mr. Maximo Rufino Paul; *Sec.* Mr Hilberto Thomas.

NIGER (1988)   Fédération Nigerienne de Tennis, BP 10 788, Niamey, République du Niger.
T. (227) 735893; TX. 5460 NI; Fax. (227) 735711; *Pres.* Mr. Ahmed Ousman Diallo; *Sec.* Mr. Boubaca
Djibo.

NORTHERN MARIANA ISLANDS   Northern Mariana Islands Tennis Association, Caller Box PPP
Saipan, MP 96950.
T. (670–234) 8438; TX. 236503484285 MCIUW; Fax. (670–234) 5545; *Pres.* Mr Jeff Race; *Sec.* M
Faye Crozat.

OMAN (1986)   Oman Tennis Association, PO Box 5226, Ruwi, Sultanate of Oman.
T. (968) 703461; Fax. (968) 798846; *Pres.* Mr Hamoud Sangoor Hashim; *Sec.* Mr Mohamad Salin
Khawwar.

PANAMA, REPUBLIC OF (1964)   Federación Panamena de Tenis, Apartado 6-4965, El Dorado.
T. (507) 27 2728/27 2960; TX. 2534 INDE PG or 3429 OLIMPAN PG; *Pres.* Dr Bey Mario Lombana; *Sec*
Dr Juan San Martin.

PAPUA-NEW GUINEA (1963)   Papua New Guinea Lawn Tennis Association, PO Box 5656, Boroko
Papua New Guinea.
T. (675) 252 889/255 803; Fax. (675) 252 889/255 803; *Pres.* Mr Robert Ainsi; *Sec.* Mr Chris Langton.

RWANDA (1984)   Federation Rwandaise de Tennis, B P 1958, Kigali.
T. (250) 7 4032; Fax. (250) 7 4031; Tx 90922517; *Pres.* Mr Gaspard Musabyimana; *Sec.* Mr Vedaste
Nkanika.

ST KITTS AND NEVIS (1962)   St Kitts Lawn Tennis Association, c/o Denise Morris, St Kitts and Nevis
Port Authority, PO Box 186, Basseterre, St Kitts.
T. (809 465) 8121; Fax. (809 465) 6661; *Pres.* Mr Nigel Rawlins; *Sec.* Ms Denise Morris.

ST LUCIA   St Lucia Lawn Tennis Association, c/o PO 308, Castries, Saint Lucia, West Indies.
T. (1 809 45) 22434; Fax. (1–809–45) 22 534; *Pres.* Mr Ornan Monplaisir.

ST VINCENT AND GRENADINES (1972)   St Vincent and the Grenadines Lawn Tennis Association,
PO Box 604, Halifax Street, St Vincent. *Pres.* Mr Michael Nanton; *Sec.* Miss Diane DaSilva.

SAN MARINO (1956)   Federazione Sammarinese Tennis, Casella Postale no 2, Dogana, 47031
Republic of San Marino.
T. (39-549) 905303; TX. 284 CONSMAR SO; Fax. (39-549) 908187; *Pres.* Mr Remo Raimondi; *Sec.*
Maria Teresa Righi.

SEYCHELLES (1955)   Seychelles Tennis Association, PO Box 602, Victoria, Mahe.
T. (248) 47414; TX. 2305 MINED SZ; Fax. (248) 24497; *Pres.* Mr Placid Andre; *Sec.* Kingsley
Pouponneau.

SIERRA LEONE (1965)   Sierra Leone Lawn Tennis Association, c/o National Sports Council, PO Box
1181, Freetown.
T. (232–22) 40562/40167/41340; TX. 3590 ENG CON; *Pres.* Mr Henry Moore; *Sec.* Mr E. T. Ngandi.

SOMALIA   Somali Amateur Tennis Association, PO Box 523, (Sec: Box 3894) Mogadishu.
T. (252–1) 28042/20589; TX. 3061 SONOC SM; *Pres.* Mr Mohamed Farah Siad; *Sec.* Mr Sa'ad Omar
Gedi.

SURINAM (1936)   Surinaamse Tennisbond, PO Box 2087, Zinniastraat 3, Paramaribo.
T. (597) 97279/76727; TX. 240 LBBANK SN; *Pres.* Mr C. Pigot; *Sec.* Mrs Shirley Relyveld.

SWAZILAND (1968)   Swaziland Tennis Union, Box 2397; Manzini.
T. (268) 4391/44011; TX. 2052; Fax. (268) 45619; *Pres.* Mr Satch Khumalo; *Sec.* Mr Bheki Nsibande.

TANZANIA   Tanzania Lawn Tennis Association, PO Box 965, Dar Es Salaam.
T. (255–51) 126010; TX. 41009 CMCDAR LZ; *Pres.* Mr Richard Rugimbana; *Sec.* Mr Godfrey Zimba.

Industry was rewarded when Karel Novacek rose from No. 34 to No. 8 in the rankings after completing the heaviest schedule (30 tournaments) of any player. *(R. Adams)*

TONGA (1959) Tonga Amateur National Tennis Association, c/o Tonga Sports Association, PO Box 1278, Nuku-Alofa.
T. (676) 21 283/21 288; TX. 66295 TASNOC TS; Fax. (676) 23572; *Acting Pres.* Fuka Kitekeiaho.

UGANDA (1948) Uganda Tennis Association, c/o National Council of Sports, PO Box 9825, Kampala Telegrams. LUGOGO; T. (256–41) 254 478; TX. 61069 OPM UGA; *Chmn* Mr Paul Bakashaharuhanga; *Sec.* Mr P. Jemba-Kaggwa.

UNITED ARAB EMIRATES (1982) United Arab Emirates Tennis Association, PO Box 87, Dubai.
T. (971–4) 690393; TX. 46347 FAGEN EM; Fax. (971–4) 521802; *Pres.* Mr Hassan Khansaheb; *Sec.* Mr Nasser Madani.

US VIRGIN ISLANDS (1973) Virgin Island Tennis Association, PO Box 11181, St Thomas, USVI 00801.
T. (1–809) 774 8547; Fax. (1–809) 776 1558; *Pres.* Mr William F. McComb; *Sec.* Joyce Wisby.

VANUATU (1990) Fédération de Tennis de Vanuatu, B P 563, Port Vila.
T. (678) 2 2698; Fax. (678) 2 2576; *Pres.* Mr Raymond Vallette; *Sec.* Mr Michel Mainguy.

WESTERN SAMOA (1955) Western Samoa Lawn Tennis Association, PO Box 1843, Apia.
T. (685) 21018/21874; TX. 245 SAMSHIP SX; Fax. (685) 24461; *Pres.* Mr Poao Ah Hoy; *Sec.* Mr Kenet Viliamu.

YEMEN (1902) Yemen Tennis Federation, PO Box 174, Sanaa.
TX. 2710 YOUTH YE; *Sec.* Mr Mohamed Ahmed Abdulgalil.

ZAIRE (1984) Fédération Zairoise de Lawn Tennis, BP 20750 Kin 15, Kinshasa.
T. (243–12) 30546/30080/78053; TX. 21160 SGA KIN ZR; Fax. (243–12) 30546; *Pres.* Mr Kanyama Mishindu; *Sec.* Mr Eleko Botuna Bo'osisa.

*The McEnroe brothers who contested the Chicago final with John **(left)** beating Patrick with their proud father looking on. By the years' end Patrick had joined John as one of the game's prize-money millionaires.* (R. Adams)

INDEX